JONES AND DOOBAY ON EXTRADITION AND MUTUAL ASSISTANCE

AUSTRALIA
Law Book Co.
Sydney

CANADA and USA
Carswell
Toronto

HONG KONG
Sweet & Maxwell Asia

NEW ZEALAND
Brookers
Auckland

SINGAPORE and MALAYSIA
Sweet & Maxwell Asia
Singapore and Kuala Lumpur

JONES AND DOOBAY
ON
EXTRADITION AND MUTUAL ASSISTANCE

Alun Jones, Q.C.
of Gray's Inn, Barrister

Anand Doobay
Peters & Peters, Solicitor

LONDON
SWEET & MAXWELL
2005

Printed in 2004
Sweet & Maxwell Limited, of
100, Avenue Road, Swiss Cottage,
London NW3 3PF
http://www.sweetandmaxwell.co.uk
Typeset by Servis Filmsetting Ltd, Manchester
and printed and bound in Great Britain by MPG Books Ltd, Bodmin, Cornwall

No natural forests were destroyed to make this product; only farmed timber was used and replanted.

A CIP catalogue record for this book is available from the British Library.

ISBN 0 421 88690 0

ISBN 0-421-88690-0

9 780421 886902

INTRODUCTION

Anand Doobay has become a valued co-author of this third edition, and Michael O'Kane, a partner at Peters & Peters, solicitors, has contributed heavily to the mutual assistance chapters, 19–21.

Since the last edition of this book was published in September 2001, the Extradition Act 2003 has brought into effect the most radical change in the subject since the Extradition Act 1870. The law of mutual legal assistance in criminal matters has also undergone drastic revision in the Crime (International Co-operation) Act 2003. In this book, these two statutes are referred to, respectively, as "the 2003 Act" and "CICA".

Twenty years ago, extradition and mutual assistance law were regarded as technical subjects, of little interest outside a small group of specialists. They have now become subjects of political as well as legal controversy. The Parliamentary debates on the Bills in 2003 reflect the sometimes intense conflict between the importance of international co-operation in the prosecution of crime and the rights of individuals. They show a degree of conviction absent from the debates preceding the Extradition Act 1989 and the Criminal Justice (International Co-operation) Act 1990.

This substantial revision in the law does not diminish the importance of the history and general principles of the subject. Concepts such as speciality, double criminality, territorial and extra-territorial jurisdiction, irregular rendition and immunities, as internationally and historically understood, remain relevant and are discussed in this book, as in the first two editions.

There have been two separate but related stimuli provoking the changes in the law. One is the increasing influence of the European Union on criminal, extradition and mutual assistance law, following the Treaty of Amsterdam of 1997 and the Tampere meeting in 1999. This has culminated in the European Arrest Warrant, the present basis of our extradition arrangements with other EU states, and the sudden development of the transnational European criminal justice institutions described in detail in Chapter 19.

The second stimulus is the combined political and legal response to the terrorist attacks upon the United States of America in September 2001, which led, among other consequences, to the signing of a new extradition treaty between the United Kingdom and the United States of America in March 2003.

The EU changes are unquestionably political as well as legal in character. The Home Office "The Law on Extradition; a Review" of March 2001 contained this large aspiration:

> "Total harmonisation of our domestic timetable and the EU agenda could be very difficult to achieve and waiting for reciprocal action by our EU partners could be an unacceptable delay. We have an opportunity to be in the European vanguard for setting the pace for changes in extradition within the EU."

The speed with which innovations have been introduced provides reason to doubt that the effects of such change have been considered properly. The timetable for implementing the European Arrest Warrant was truncated immediately after the September 2001 attacks, in spite of the fundamental character of the change to the mutual recognition of judgments and warrants. The fear of terrorism was used to justify the large number of offences in the European Framework List for which the requirements of double criminality, hitherto a central principle of extradition law, have been cast aside.

It is common among some groups of lawyers in international seminars and conferences uncritically to treat all these developments in "Euro" criminal law as necessarily benign and progressive. There has been no obvious attempt to analyse the success or shortcomings of previous legislation before fresh proposals are enthusiastically advanced. No time was available for a critical assessment of the European Arrest Warrant, instituted in January 2004, before the proposal was made for the far-reaching European Evidence Warrant, discussed in Chapter 19. Concern may legitimately be expressed as to whether institutions such as Europol and Eurojust will prove accountable to courts and will function transparently.

In the United Kingdom, three fundamental criminal law statutes (governing extradition, mutual legal assistance and criminal justice) passed at the same time through Parliament in 2003 in view of the urgency which the Government has sought change as a response to terrorism, as well as for the purpose of standing in the "vanguard" of change. In extradition law, this haste has produced a statute which is the result of various Parliamentary compromises, which has tempered the European Framework Decision, but which has produced a statute containing some obvious anomalies and lacunae.

Further evidence of the pace and political character of the change in the law is to be found in the extradition treaty agreed between the United Kingdom and the United States of America in March 2003. There was no publication of this treaty, and therefore no discussion, before it was signed. The United Kingdom has agreed that it will no longer be necessary for US authorities to produce a *prima facie* case when requesting extradition from the United Kingdom, whereas the treaty maintains the obligation on the United Kingdom to establish probable cause in the converse case. To agree to this imbalance is surely to strike a political attitude rather than to assert a coherent legal principle.

This treaty had its origin in the "war against terrorism". It is never easy to strike a balance between rights and duties in war-time, if indeed we are at "war". It is unfortunate that so much of the legislative history of statutory changes in Europe and the USA refers to the "battle" against organised crime, or the "fight" against drugs. It is an irony that the US Government has found difficulty in securing the ratification of this new treaty in its own legislature. Sections of the US Senate are concerned that the new treaty will facilitate the extradition of suspected Irish terrorists to the United Kingdom. They do not fear harsh sentences: they doubt that terrorist suspects can receive a fair trial in the United Kingdom.

Among the anomalies of the new Act is the definition of "extradition offence", discussed in Chapter 6. It is extraordinary that the draughtsman has chosen to define the concept by reference to territorial and extra-territorial crimes, and has apparently willfully ignored the detailed jurisprudence on the previous definition of extradition crime, which even in 1870 rested upon the flexible concept of "jurisdiction", rather than territory.

In the opinion of the authors, recourse to Hansard will be much more important than it is in less controversial legislation. Often the bare provisions of the 2003 Act do not reflect governmental assurances as to the scope of individual rights, inade in a spirit of compromise to ensure the passage of the bill. These assurances are particularly important in the application of the human rights protections. Many of these assurances are set out within the text in this book. There will be a powerful temptation for the legal representatives of overseas jurisdictions, and perhaps even courts, to seek to minimise the application and importance of the provisions of the Act designed to mitigate the severity of the new regime.

Perhaps the most far-reaching change introduced by the 2003 Act is the abolition of the general discretion of the Home Secretary to initiate extradition proceedings and ultimately to surrender the person sought at the end of the court process. Under the repealed law, the Secretary of State faced an increasingly obvious conflict of interest between his desire to express trust and respect for the criminal justice institutions of a state with which the United Kingdom maintains extradition arrangements on the one hand, and his duty to prevent an unfair or oppressive extradition on the other. Over the last twenty years the courts have repeatedly emphasised that they themselves possessed no general fairness or abuse of process jurisdiction in extradition cases; the courts' inherent jurisdiction had been excluded by the conferment by Parliament of this general discretion on the Home Secretary.

This approach did not, as was intended, simplify and discipline the extradition process. It often simply moved the real dispute in a case from the courts to the Home Office. This tendency developed more noticeably after the requirement to produce a *prima facie* case was abrogated for Commonwealth and Council of Europe countries by the Extradition Act 1989. The Secretary of State became in effect a forum within which the general merits and fairness of a proposed extradition was debated. This caused much additional unwelcome labour within the Home Office, which, not being a court, was ill-equipped to resolve questions of fact, yet was open to judicial review of its decisions. Occasionally, in cases in which the defendant argued that it would be oppressive to extradite him by reason of many years delay in making the application, the Home Office became enmeshed absurdly in factual disputes between the requesting state and the defendant for a further two years or more, thus aggravating the delay.

The removal of the general discretion is, rightly or wrongly, consistent with the principle of mutual recognition of warrants, the basis of Part 1 of the 2003 Act. It is therefore appropriate that the court should have the responsibility for ensuring that extradition does not take place in unjust or oppressive circumstances. In Part 2 cases, the Secretary of State has slightly greater powers (in respect of speciality, death penalty, earlier extradition to the UK) but no general discretion.

The removal of this discretion changes fundamentally the role of the UK courts in extradition proceedings. Who is, ultimately, responsible for the decision to extradite or surrender a person? One reading of the statue might suggest that each decision maker is fulfilling a limited role, and answering only certain narrowly defined questions. On such an approach, no provision of the Act, either expressly or by implication, considered by itself, could prevent an extradition even though every decision-maker in the process considered that a surrender would be unfair.

In fact, the removal of the general discretion places all the critical issues in extradition firmly within the boundaries of the lower court, before the District Judge, subject to appeal. A broad and purposive approach to the human rights provisions, consistent with the intention of Parliament as Chapter 11 of this book makes clear, can prevent abuses and make this statute fair and workable. It is the experience of the authors of this book, shared by many other practitioners, that the extradition of suspected persons even to close legal and political partners is sometimes demonstrably unfair or oppressive. Extradition requests are made by individuals, prosecutors or investigating judges, who vary in competence, integrity and professionalism. In some states, prosecutions are now brought in a heightened retributive atmosphere by politically motivated prosecutors. It cannot be assumed that every person extradited will be treated fairly. To argue to the contrary is, again, to make a political rather than legal judgment.

There are two strands of judicial dicta which, considered together, demonstrate that extradition law is a balance. Often, only one strand is cited, having regard to the factual merits of the case under consideration. Two very general statements are regularly quoted by prosecutors. In *Re Arton (No.2)*,[1] Lord Russell of Killowen said, in the course of a discussion about the interpretation of an offence listed in the UK-France extradition treaty:

> "Is extradition to be refused? . . . To do so would be to hinder the operation of the most salutary international arrangements. . . . In my judgement these treaties ought to receive a liberal interpretation, which means no more than that they should receive their true construction according to their language, object and intent."

[1] [1896] 1 Q.B. 509 at 517L.

This quotation is frequently to be found in judgments of the Divisional Court. Another less subtle expression of this general statement of policy is to be found in the speech of Lord Templeman in *Re Evans*[2]*:*

> "Extradition arrangements have been transformed as a result of the invention of the jet aeroplane and the mutual acceptance by means of extradition treaties by and between countries of the integrity of their different legal systems. A criminal can flee from country to country in order to avoid or postpone retribution. A suspect once apprehended can be returned for prosecution with equal speed. Extradition is only available in respect of serious offences and in circumstances which are not oppressive."

By contrast, some courts have expressed powerfully a recognition of the importance of safeguards applicable to particular cases. In *R. v Governor of Brixton Prison Ex p. Percival*[3] Lord Alverstone C.J. said, in the context of a statutory requirement to prove a provision of foreign law:

> "That is a very important matter, and having regard to the fact that we are dealing with the criminal law, we must apply the general principles of the criminal law, and the prosecutor must make out his case. We are also dealing with a branch of the criminal law which affects the liberty of the subject, and that condition should under ordinary circumstances be clearly fulfilled."

In *R. v Secretaty of State for the Home Department Ex p. Launder*[4] it was said:

> "He [the Secretary of State] cannot ignore representations . . . on the ground that it must be assumed that a foreign government with which this country has diplomatic relations will adhere to its treaty obligations. If issues of that kind are raised in a responsible manner, by reference to evidence and supported by reasoned argument, he [the Secretary of State] must consider them. The greater the perceived risk to life or liberty the more important it will be to give them detailed scrutiny."

It often seems that the facts of a case impel one or other of these contrasting judicial approaches. Paragraph 7 of the Explanatory Notes to the 2003 Act emphasises the balance.

> "The law should provide a quick and effective framework to extradite a person to the country where he is accused or has been convicted of a serious crime, provided this does not breach his fundamental human rights."

2 [1994] 1 W.L.R. 1006 at 1008C.
3 [1907] 1 K.B. 96.
4 [1997] 1 W.L.R. 839 at 855G, *per* Lord Hope of Craighead.

In proceedings under the 2003 Act, courts are entitled to apply a presumption, as they have done before, that the system of a foreign requesting jurisdiction, party to reciprocal arrangements, is fair. But presumptions yield to facts. The duty imposed on the courts by the removal of the general discretion of the Home Secretary is to test this presumption against evidence in any case. Factual evidence may be called before the courts in support of an argument, among others, that a defendant's extradition would be incompatible with his human rights. This evidence of course may be subject to cross-examination, and may be challenged by evidence in opposition. The 2003 Act has the potential to achieve a proper balance.

It remains to be seen how rigorously the duty to act on evidence rather than presumptions will be enforced by the higher courts.

Acknowledgements
Alun Jones wished to acknowledge his continuing debt to Michael Blanchflower S.C., of Hong Kong and Canada, for the benefit of his international knowledge of extradition law and its history; to his wife, Elizabeth Jones, and his daughter Amanda Jones, barrister; to Angela Kulemeka, barrister, for her research and encouragement; to his colleagues at 3 Raymond Buildings, Gray's Inn; and to Michael O'Kane, assisted by Ari Alibhai, barrister, for his invaluable and selfless contribution to the mutual assistance chapters of this edition.

Anand Doobay wishes to acknowledge the assistance and constant support of his parents, Buddy and Sattie Doobay, and his family; the encouragement and help of Monty Raphael, Julia Balfour-Lynn and many others at Peters & Peters; and he expresses his appreciation to Sophy Thomas, former criminal law policy advisor at the Law Society of England and Wales, for her advice and encouragement.

Both authors are grateful to their many professional colleagues who have willingly shared their expertise and experience, and for the advice and patient support of many at Sweet & Maxwell.

We have endeavoured to state the law as at September 1, 2004.

Alun Jones Q.C.
37 Great James Street
London WC1N 3HB

Anand Doobay
Peters & Peters
2 Harewood Place
Hanover Square
London W1S 1BX
adoobay@petersandpeters.co.uk

CONTENTS

CHAPTER 2
General Principles

CHAPTER 3
Irregular Rendition and Abduction

CHAPTER 4
International Crimes and Immunities

CHAPTER 7
Arrest

CHAPTER 8
Initial Hearing

CHAPTER 9
The Extradition Hearing

CHAPTER 10
Bars to Extradition

CHAPTER 11
Convention Rights

CHAPTER 12
Role of the Secretary of State

CHAPTER 15

Sundry Statutory Matters; Time Limits, Costs, Withdrawal of Claim, Competing Claims, Repatriation and Re-extradition

CHAPTER 16

Matters Arising After Extradition

TABLE OF CASES

R. v Governor of Pentonville Prison Ex p. Ecke (1981) 73 Cr. App. R. 223; [1974] Crim. L.R. 102; (1973) 118 S.J. 168, DC 2–007, 6–040
R. v Governor of Pentonville Prison Ex p. Fernandez; sub nom. Fernandez v Singapore [1971] 1 W.L.R. 987; [1971] 2 All E.R. 691; 115 S.J. 469, HL 1–034, 10–006
R. v Governor of Pentonville Prison Ex p. Kirby (Note) [1979] 1 W.L.R. 541; [1979] 2 All E.R. 1094, DC 9–031
R. v Governor of Pentonville Prison Ex p. Lee; sub nom. R. v Bow Street Metropolitan Stipendiary Magistrate Ex p. Lee [1993] 1 W.L.R. 1294; [1993] 3 All E.R. 504; [1993] C.O.D. 310; *The Times*, February 15, 1993; *Independent*, March 3, 1993, QBD 2–037, 9–007
R. v Governor of Pentonville Prison Ex p. Narang; sub nom. Union of India v Narang [1978] A.C. 247; [1977] 2 W.L.R. 862; [1977] 2 All E.R. 348; (1977) 64 Cr. App. R. 259; [1977] Crim. L.R. 352, HL 1–034, 2–037, 10–006
R. v Governor of Pentonville Prison Ex p. Osman (No.1); sub nom. Osman (No.1), Re [1990] 1 W.L.R. 277; [1989] 3 All E.R. 701; (1990) 90 Cr. App. R. 281; [1988] Crim. L.R. 611; (1990) 87(7) L.S.G. 32; (1990) 134 S.J. 458; *The Times*, April 13, 1988; *Independent*, November 26, 1991, QBD 6–003, 9–031, 9–035, 9–036, 17–004
R. v Governor of Pentonville Prison Ex p. Osman (No.2); sub nom. Osman (No.2), Re [1989] C.O.D. 446, DC 4–020
R. v Governor of Pentonville Prison Ex p. Sinclair; sub nom. Sinclair v DPP; Sinclair v USA [1991] 2 A.C. 64; [1991] 2 W.L.R. 1028; [1991] 2 All E.R. 366; (1991) 93 Cr. App. R. 329; (1991) 135 S.J.L.B. 477; *The Times*, April 16, 1991; *Independent*, April 16, 1991; *Guardian*, April 24, 1991, HL; affirming [1990] 2 Q.B. 112; [1990] 2 W.L.R. 1248; [1990] 2 All E.R. 789; [1990] Crim. L.R. 584; [1990] C.O.D. 242; (1990) 87(24) L.S.G. 43, DC 1–016, 1–018, 2–009, 2–047, 3–019, 9–048
R. v Governor of Pentonville Prison Ex p. Sotiriadis; sub nom. West Germany v Sotiriadis [1975] A.C. 1; [1974] 2 W.L.R. 253; [1974] 1 All E.R. 692; [1974] Crim. L.R. 250; 118 S.J. 148, HL; reversing [1974] 1 All E.R. 504; [1974] Crim. L.R. 44; (1973) 117 S.J. 913; *The Times*, November 8, 1973, DC 6–003, 9–035
R. v Governor of Pentonville Prison Ex p. Tarling *see* Tarling v Singapore
R. v Governor of Pentonville Prison Ex p. Teja [1971] 2 Q.B. 274; [1971] 2 W.L.R. 816; [1971] 2 All E.R. 11; 115 S.J. 305, QBD 2–012, 4–020
R. v Governor of Pentonville Prison Ex p. Voets [1986] 1 W.L.R. 470; [1986] 2 All E.R. 630; (1986) 83 L.S.G. 1058; (1986) 130 S.J. 245, DC 9–034
R. v Guildford Justices Ex p. Healy [1983] 1 W.L.R. 108; [1983] Crim. L.R. 111; (1983) 80 L.S.G. 29; 126 S.J. 746, DC 3–011, 3–012
R. v Guildhall Magistrates Court Ex p. Primlaks Holdings Co (Panama) Inc [1990] 1 Q.B. 261; [1989] 2 W.L.R. 841; (1989) 89 Cr. App. R. 215; [1989] Crim. L.R. 448; [1989] C.O.D. 359; (1989) 133 S.J. 628, DC 17–021, 17–022, 20–049
R. v Hartley [1978] N.Z.L.R. 199 .... 3–010, 3–011, 3–013, 3–016
R. v Hedworth [1997] 1 Cr. App. R. 421, CA (Crim Div) 20–018
R. v Horseferry Road Magistrates Court Ex p. Bennett (No.1); sub nom. Bennett v Horseferry Road Magistrates Court [1994] 1 A.C. 42; [1993] 3 W.L.R. 90; [1993] 3 All E.R. 138; (1994) 98 Cr. App. R. 114; [1994] C.O.D. 123; (1993) 157 J.P.N. 506; (1993) 143 N.L.J. 955; (1993) 137 S.J.L.B. 159; *The Times*, June 25, 1993; *Independent*, July 1, 1993, HL; reversing [1993] 2 All E.R. 474; (1993) 97 Cr. App. R. 29; (1993) 157 J.P. 713; [1993] C.O.D. 22; (1993) 157 J.P.N. 189; (1993) 137 S.J.L.B. 159; *The Times*, September 1, 1992; *Independent*, September 14, 1992 (C.S.), QBD 3–001, 3–013, 3–014, 3–016, 9–048, 18–011
R. v Horseferry Road Magistrates Court Ex p. Bennett (No.4) [1995] 1 Cr. App. R. 147; *The Times*, April 1, 1994; *Independent*, May 6, 1994, QBD 3–017
R. v Humphreys [1977] A.C.1 10–003
R. v Immigration Appeal Tribunal Ex p. Shah; sub nom. Secretary of State for the Home Department Ex p. Shah; Islam v Secretary of State for the Home Department [1999] 2 A.C.

TABLE OF STATUTES

2003 Extradition Act (c.41)—*contd*
- s.186(2)–(6) 15–030
  - (4) **15–030**
  - (5) **15–030**
  - (9) 15–030
- s.187 15–030
  - (1) 15–030
  - (2) 15–030
  - (3) 15–030
  - (8) 15–030
- s.188 15–030
  - (1) **15–031**
  - (2) **15–031**
  - (3) **15–031**
- s.189 15–030
  - (1) **15–032**
  - (2) **15–032**
  - (3) **15–032**
- s.190(1)–(3) 8–013
- s.191 8–014
- s.192(1)–(8) 8–015
  - (9) 8–015
- s.193 .... 4–001, 5–017
  - (2) 5–017
  - (4) 5–017
- s.194 5–004
  - (1) 5–018
  - (2) 5–018
  - (3) 5–018
  - (4)(b) 5–018
  - (5) 5–018
- s.195 11–008
- s.196 .... 6–013, 6–020, 6–026, 6–031
- s.197(1) 8–007
  - (2) 8–007
  - (6) 8–007
- s.198 8–008
  - (1)–(3) 8–008
  - (4) 8–008
  - (5) 8–008
  - (6) 8–008
  - (7)–(11) 8–008
  - (12)–(14) 8–008
  - (13) 8–008
- s.199 8–009
- s.200 8–010
- s.201 8–011
- s.202 9–006
- s.203 9–006
- s.204 9–006

2003 Extradition Act (c.41)—*contd*
- s.205 9–006
- s.206 9–006
- s.207 6–032
- s.208(2) 12–002
  - (3) 12–002
  - (4) 12–002
  - (5) 12–002
  - (6) 12–002
  - (7) 12–002
  - (8) 12–002
  - (9) 12–002
- s.209 17–009
- s.215(1) 6–008
- s.216(9) 13–005
- s.218 .... 5–001, 5–011
- s.220 5–011
- s.222 5–005
- s.223(5) 5–009, 5–012, 5–014, 6–008, 18–003
  - (6) 5–009, 5–012, 5–014, 6–008, 18–003
  - (7) 5–017
- s.226 .... 5–003, 17–011
- s.240 18–024
- s.243 18–024
  - (3) 18–024
- Sch.1 18–011
- Sch.2 .... 6–001, 6–008
- Sch.4 .... 5–001, 5–011

2003 Criminal Justice Act (c.44) 10–004, 18–024
- Pt 10 10–004
- ss.75–97 10–004
- ss.116–117 20–025
- Sch.36, para.16 20–012

Australia

1966 Extradition (Foreign States) Act
- s.4(1A) 2–022

1988 Extradition Act
- s.5 2–022
- s.19(2)(c) 2–015, 2–022

Bahamas

1994 Extradition Act 2–020

TABLE OF STATUTORY INSTRUMENTS

PART A

THE HISTORICAL AND INTERNATIONAL CONTEXT

CHAPTER 1

HISTORY

I. EXTRADITION WITH FOREIGN STATES BEFORE 1870

Few references to the subject may be found in legal treatises before the first recognisable extradition statutes of 1843. The student of the history of our criminal law will recognise the unrewarding character of the search for the sources. Such evidence as we have of earlier extradition law is sporadic, undeveloped and contradictory. 1–001

Some writers speak of a repugnance between the common law and the notion of extradition. Until recent decades the approach of Coke and, later, Dicey, neither of whom allows lawful surrender at common law, has been thought correct:

> "It is holden, and hath been so resolved, that divided kingdoms under several kings in league one with another are sanctuaries for servants or subjects flying for safety from one kingdom to another, and upon demand made by them, are not by the laws and liberties of kingdoms to be delivered: and this (some hold)

is grounded upon the law of Deuteronomy. *Non trades servum domine suo, qui ad te confugerit.*"[1]

"English courts have no jurisdiction to entertain an action: (1) for the enforcement, either directly or indirectly, of a penal, revenue or other public law of a foreign state; or (2) founded on an act of state."[2]

Sir Francis Piggott, Chief Justice of Hong Kong, writing in 1910, dedicated his book *Extradition: A Treatise on the Law relating to Fugitive Offenders* to Dicey. He spoke of:

> "... the doctrines of the common law, to which extradition is an exception: the right to liberty, and the locality of crime. The latter means that crime is local in its commission, local in its legal effect, and local in its punishment. It is of course no more than a special illustration of the larger principle that all law is territorial: that is, local to the country in which it is promulgated; and this again is the special illustration of the still larger doctrine that sovereignty is local, and its exercise circumscribed by the limits of the territory subject to the sovereign. Each phase of this doctrine is involved in the common law right to liberty upon which extradition encroaches."[3]

SURRENDER WITHOUT TREATIES

1–002 There are, however, contrary indications. The executive surrender of criminals to and by foreign jurisdictions may have been more common and less controversial in earlier times than the common lawyers acknowledged. A review of this subject is more than of merely historical interest. The extent of the practice before formal extradition treaties were concluded is relevant to the questions whether it may be lawful for the Crown to make an extradition request in the absence of, or outside the terms of, a formal extradition agreement; and whether it would be an abuse of process to try a person surrendered to the United Kingdom pursuant to such an extra-statutory request.

Modern United States law recognises that a person abducted from a foreign state by US agents may nonetheless be tried in the United States.[4] In 1997, the Department of Trade and Industry raised an argument in the English courts, which it did not eventually pursue, that a request made to the United States for an offence which was not an extradition crime was not necessarily unlawful, because the Crown might request the extradition of a person outside statute and treaty.[5]

[1] Coke's Institutes, Pt 3, p.181.
[2] Dicey and Morris, *The Conflict of Laws* (13th ed., 2000), p.89.
[3] at p.7.
[4] *United States v Alvarez-Machain* 504 U.S. 655; 119 L. Ed. 2d 441; 112 S. Ct. 2188 (1992); see Ch.3.
[5] *R. v Department of Trade and Industry Ex p. Levitt*, unreported, October 31, 1997, CO/3811/97; see Ch.18.

In earlier times, when a variety of courts or jurisdictions competed for legal supremacy in England, it is clear that extradition procedures were from time to time agreed between England and other countries as simple acts of state. In 1174, a treaty made between Henry II of England and William of Scotland provided for the exchange of criminals who fled from one country to the other, and, as an alternative, that such fugitives might be tried where arrested in the other country.

Other arrangements, such as the treaty of 1303 between Edward I and the King of the French, and the "Intercursus" between Henry VII and the Flemings of 1497, made provision for the expulsion of the enemies of the one from the territories of the other,[6] although these agreements seem to have been recognised as police measures, rather than as the first stages of criminal process.[7]

Clive Parry[8] criticises the passage cited from Coke, above, in these terms:

> "A detailed examination of the early history of the subject would probably explode the notion, which seems to be based upon the view of Coke and on the treaties of 1661–2 with Denmark and Holland for the recovery of the English regicides, that extradition, though now generally applying to all others except political offenders, originated as a device for the punishment of treason and rebellion."

Parry mentions a number of other extradition treaties concluded between England and foreign states between the fourteenth and seventeenth centuries as follows:

Portugal June 16, 1373 (*British and Foreign State Papers*, Vol.1, p.465);
France July 18, 1498 (Rymer, *Foedera*, Vol.XII, p.694);
Spain July 10, 1499, February 9, 1506, October 19, 1515, and June 16, 1522 (*Calendar of State papers, Spanish*, 1485–1509, 211, 380; *ibid.*, 1509–25, 269, 435);
France April 2, 1559, April 11, 1564, August 29, 1610 (*General Collection of Treatys etc* (1710–32) Vol.2, pp.56, 61, 175);
Spain November 15, 1630 (*ibid.*, Vol.2, p.281).

Professor I.A. Shearer pointed out that these earlier treaties did not represent a systematic international effort to co-operate in the suppression of crime. An agreement to surrender criminals was just one of a number of gestures of friendship and co-operation.[9]

However, many recorded surrenders or unsuccessful requests appear to have involved what was recognised in later legislation as "political offences" before the concept of political offences was weakened and then removed by subsequent legislation. The Earl of Suffolk was surrendered from Spain to Henry VII and executed. The King of Scotland refused the request of Henry VII to surrender the pretender

6 *Clarke on Extradition* (4th ed., 1904), p.19.
7 See *Holdsworth's History of the Criminal Law*, (5th ed.) pp.49–50.
8 *British Digest of International Law* (Stevens, London 1965), Ch.17, pp.444–5
9 *Extradition in International Law* (1971, Manchester University Press).

Perkin Warbeck. Queen Elizabeth I promised the Scots that she would either surrender Boswell or send him into exile.

1–003 Three lawyers advised James I in 1618 on the right of the Crown to demand the surrender of a Dutch captain who had arrested in Scottish waters a King's messenger and abducted him to the States of the United Provinces. They considered that such a request was justified in customary international law.

> "There are good authorities that if a subject of one state commit a heinous crime within the territory of another state (though against a private person), the subject so offending ought to be remitted to the place where the crime was committed, if it be required."

Acknowledging that there were opinions to the contrary, they advised:

> "Two very particular circumstances about this offence seem necessarily to enforce the remission of the Dutch captain to his Majesty (1) taken from the person of Brown, who was a public messenger sent by the state of Scotland on the affairs of the Prince, and ought to have been inviolable by the Laws of nations, and therefore a wrong was done to him *contra jus gentium*; (2) taken from the manner of the wrong, which was *nomine publico* - viz. by a pretended commission from the lords of the States."[10]

In 1661, after the Restoration, a treaty was signed between Charles II and Denmark, by which Denmark agreed to surrender on requisition all those who had been concerned in the execution of Charles I. Switzerland refused to return others. The States-General of Holland surrendered some alleged regicides without treaty; but a treaty for such surrender was agreed between the two countries in 1662.[11]

1–004 Two cases in English law give indications contrary to the approach of *Coke*, but the dicta are *obiter*. In *East India Co v Campbell* in 1749, the judgment of the whole court on the equity side of the Court of Exchequer, which included the Lord Chancellor and the Chief Baron, asserted, "The Government may send a prisoner to answer for a crime wherever committed, that he may not involve his country, and to prevent reprisals."[12]

In 1811, a longer dictum of Heath J. was delivered in *Mure v Kay*,[13] an action for false imprisonment, part of which was said to have been committed in Scotland. "By the comity of nations the country in which the criminal has been found has aided the police of the country against which the crime was committed in bringing the criminal to punishment." He cites an example "in Lord Loughborough's time",

[10] Brit.Mus. Lansdowne MSS, 142, fol.398, 400, cited by Fulton *The Sovereignty of the Sea* (1911) (McNair, *International Law Opinions* (1956) Vol.2, p.42).

[11] Clarke, *op. cit.*, p.20; Holdsworth, *A History of English Law*, Vol.V, p.50.

[12] (1749) 1 Ves. Sen 246.

[13] (1811) 4 Taunt 34.

untraced in the reports, of a return by English authorities of mutineers on a Dutch ship from Kent to Holland.

Sir Edward Clarke[14] cites an opinion given to the Government by Sergeant Hill in 1792, at the time of outbreak of war with revolutionary France, upon the question of the King's prerogative to expel aliens from the kingdom:

> "As to subjects of states in amity, I think the king hath no power over any, if they do not offend against his laws, but such as are charged by the states whose subjects they are with high treason, murder, or defrauding their state, or other atrocious crimes. And as to them, if the sovereign of such state applies to have them delivered up, I think his majesty is, by the constitution, invested with the power of granting or refusing the application, and, if granted, may issue a proclamation either to quit his dominions, or else may order them to be apprehended, and sent in safe custody and delivered to such persons as the sovereign of the state to which they belong may appoint; and if any of them should procure a writ of habeas corpus, the special matter might be returned, and they would not be entitled to be discharged, for this is warranted by the practice of nations, and is therefore not part of the legislative, but of the executive power, which is invested solely in the king, who, as has been observed, by a late learned judge (1 Bl. Comm. 253), with regard to foreign concerns, is representative of his people, and what is done by the royal authority with regard to foreign powers (he adds) is the act of the whole nation; and the prerogative in this respect has always been taken to be so clear that no foreigner ever contested it in the English courts of justice, and the habeas corpus appears to have been designedly so penned as not to interfere with it; for the prohibition in that Act [the Habeas Corpus Act 1679[15]] against removing persons from one prison to another, or sending them abroad, is confined to subjects of this realm, whereas all the other provisions of the Act extend to all persons and all prisoners, without once mentioning subjects of the realm, and therefore all the others are intended to extend to aliens, and this is not so."

In 1792, the Senate of Hamburg surrendered the Irish nationalist Napper Tandy to the British Government. He was tried in Dublin, and acquitted.

Relying on *East India Co v Campbell* and *Mure v Kay*, *Chitty on the Criminal Law* suggested in 1826 that "an English magistrate may also cause to be arrested, and committed for trial, an offender against the Irish law or accused of having perpetrated a crime in a foreign country" and "if a prisoner, having committed a felony in a foreign country, come into England, he may be arrested here and conveyed and given up to the magistrate of the country against the laws of which the offence was committed." The mechanics of such renditions are unexplained.

In the Australian case of *Brown v Lizars*,[16] it was asserted that the extradition of fugitive offenders had been an exercise of the executive or prerogative before 1–005

[14] *ibid.*, p.25.

[15] 31 Charles II, c.2.

[16] (1905) 2 C.L.R. 852, 859, 861.

extradition statutes. In *Barton v The Commonwealth of Australia*,[17] Mason J. agreed with the court in *Brown v Lizars*, holding:

> "Contrary to previous thinking, it seems that from the late twelfth century onwards England became a party to a large number of treaties with various European states which contained provision for the mutual non-reception, or the mutual surrender, of fugitive criminals and rebels. It was not until the seventeenth and eighteenth centuries that the number of treaties providing for extradition or surrender of fugitive offenders, to which Great Britain was a party, sharply diminished, no doubt partly as a result of the Habeas Corpus Amendment Act 1679, for one of the consequences of that statute was that statutory authority became necessary for the extradition from Great Britain of a fugitive offender who was a British subject. This was, however, for a long time a matter of debate. Indeed it seems that it was not until the nineteenth century that it was finally settled that extradition from Great Britain could not take place in the absence of statutory authority for the issue of a warrant Even then there was some judicial authority to support a contrary view (*East India Co v Campbell; Mure and Kay*)."

The question whether extradition was possible at common law was discussed in *R. v Governor of Brixton Prison Ex p. Soblen*,[18] Lord Denning M.R. quoted with approval the opinion of Lord McNair in *International Law Opinions* (1956) Vol.2, p.41:

> "For some time the law was doubtful, but later it became recognised that the Crown could not surrender an alleged criminal even if it wished to do so, unless the surrender was authorised by legislation."

EARLY TREATIES

1–006 Shearer refers to 92 treaties concluded internationally between 1718 and 1830 which provided for the surrender of criminals, mostly between neighbouring states in Europe.[19] He contrasts this co-operation with the more cumbersome procedural requirements which the common law system insisted upon until more recent times, where geographical isolation led to a more jealous protection of traditions of asylum.

The first modern British treaty is known as the Jay Treaty of 1794, providing for the mutual exchange of offenders between the United States of America and Great Britain. It appears that this arrangement must have been directed in intention, and

[17] (1974) 131 C.L.R. 477, 494 (considered further in Ch.18).

[18] [1963] 2 Q.B. 243, 300.

[19] *op. cit.*, citing the Russian scholar, de Martens, *Recueil de traites* (1801–26); *Supplements au recueil des principaux traites* (1802–42).

restricted in practice, to surrenders to and from the United States and the British North American colonies.[20] (Clarke does not mention this treaty. It has left no mark in the law reports in England.) Only a few fugitives were surrendered under the Jay Treaty. It lapsed in 1807, but, according to La Forest, Canada and the USA continued to extradite to each other. An attempt was made to regularise the matter by statute in Upper Canada, but the British Government doubted its validity.

The treaty was an instrument of "amity, commerce and navigation". Article 27 embodied a recognisably modern requirement to produce *prima facie* evidence of guilt:

> "It is further agreed that His Majesty and the United States on mutual requisitions . . . will deliver up to justice all persons who, being charged with murder or forgery, committed within the jurisdiction of either, shall seek asylum within any of the countries of the other, provided that this shall only be done on such evidence of criminality as, according to the laws of the place where the fugitive or person so charged shall be found, would justify his apprehension and commitment for trial, if the offence had there been committed. The expense of such apprehension and delivery shall be borne and defrayed by those who make the requisition and receive the fugitive."

In 1802, Great Britain and the other signatories to the Peace of Amiens, that is, France, Spain and Holland, agreed for the mutual surrender of offenders for offences of murder, forgery or fraudulent bankruptcy. The agreement lapsed with the early resumption of the Napoleonic wars, but the provision reappeared in the treaties of 1814 and 1815 with France, but only so as to apply between the British and French possessions in India.

THE BILATERAL "EXTRADITION" STATUTES OF 1843

The British law of extradition may be said to date from these statutes. Sir James Stephen,[21] having referred to the previous dicta in the reports as to common law powers of extradition as a "faint trace" which "has been entirely superseded by subsequent legislation", quoted with approval from Clarke: 1–007

> "The history of the subject in England begins with the treaties made with the United States of America in October, 1842, and with France in 1843."

An attempt had been made between 1824–28 to negotiate a new treaty between the United Kingdom and the United States, but it failed because of the unwillingness of the United Kingdom to undertake the return of runaway slaves.[22] In 1841 the

[20] G.V. La Forest, *Extradition to and From Canada*, 1961.
[21] *History of the Criminal Law of England*, Vol.2, p.66.
[22] Moore, *A Treatise on Extradition and Interstate Rendition* (1891), Vol.1, pp.90–2.

absence of extradition arrangements between Great Britain and the United States of America was exposed by the case of the *Creole*.[23] A number of slaves revolted on an American ship, murdered a slave-owner, injured the captain and crew and took the ship to the Bahamas, a British possession. The Governor refused to surrender them to the American authorities. The matter was debated in the House of Lords. *Hansard* cites Lord Brougham:

> "He thought the interests of good neighbourhood required, that in two countries bordering upon one another, as the United States and Canada, and even that in England, and in the European countries of France, Holland and Belgium, there ought to be laws on both sides giving power, under due regulation and safeguards, to each government to secure persons who have committed offences in the territory of the other."

It was the unanimous view of the House of Lords that extradition without an Act of Parliament was unlawful.

The United Kingdom signed a treaty with the United States of America in 1842, called the "Webster-Ashburton Treaty". Its "extradition" provisions remained in force, supplemented by later arrangements, until a new treaty was negotiated in 1931. It was entitled:

> "A Treaty to Settle and define the Boundaries Between the Territories of the United States and the possessions of Her Britannic Majesty in North America, for the Final Suppression of the African Slave Trade, and for the Giving Up of Criminals, Fugitive from Justice, in Certain Cases."

Another treaty was concluded with France a few months later. Effect was given to the views expressed in the House of Lords by Lord Brougham and others, when both treaties were incorporated into law by statutes in 1843, "An Act for giving effect to a Convention between Her Majesty and the King of the French for the Apprehension of Certain Offenders",[24] and "An Act for giving effect to a treaty between Her Majesty and the United States of America for the Apprehension of Certain Offenders".[25] (The Canadian and American authorities had put the new treaty into immediate effect). Eleven years after slavery was abolished in all Her Majesty's Dominions, the British Parliament considered whether to exclude slaves from the operation of the act, but upon the advice of the Attorney-General decided against such an exemption.[26]

1–008 The acts were, by modern standards, limited in scope. They were repealed by the Extradition Act of 1870, but the following features remain of interest:

[23] Clarke, p.127.
[24] 6 & 7 Vict. c.75.
[25] c.76.
[26] *Hansard*, Reg. lxxxiv.312.

(1) The acts applied only to accused persons: fugitive convicts were immune.

(2) The arrangements covered a limited number of crimes. The French treaty provided for the surrender of fugitives for offences of murder, attempt to commit murder, forgery and fraudulent bankruptcy. The American treaty was wider, and applied to murder, assault with intent to commit murder, piracy, arson, robbery, forgery and the utterance of forged paper. (This was the only significant distinction between the statutes.)

(3) It was necessary for the requesting state to show that "the Commission of the Crime be so established as that the Laws of the Country where the fugitive or Person so accused should be found would justify his Apprehension and Commitment for Trial if the Crime had been there committed". In substance this test has continued through the Extradition Act 1870 to the 2003 Act in respect of all countries with whom the United Kingdom has extradition arrangements except the signatories to the European Convention on Extradition and EU Member States, Australia, Canada, New Zealand and the USA.

(4) Upon receipt of a "Requisition", a Secretary of State would issue a warrant requiring magistrates to arrest the fugitive and examine the evidence; that evidence might be in the form of copies of authenticated depositions sent by the requesting state, but the reception of oral evidence by the magistrate who heard the case was expressly provided for.

(5) A person detained for more than two months from the magistrate's "commitment" might apply to a judge for discharge. Such discharge would be granted "unless sufficient cause be shown . . . why such Discharge ought not to be ordered."

(6) In neither Act is there a "political offence" exception, nor an express requirement for "speciality", that is, the restriction imposed upon the requesting state to confine its prosecution to the crime for which surrender was made.

The first British request for extradition under the American treaty in respect of Christiana Cochrane, a Scot, was apparently made on the ship conveying the instrument of ratification. She was extradited for poisoning her husband, and was returned in spite of evidence of her insanity.[27] The first US request, for forgery, failed when a judge discharged the fugitive on the ground that the implementation of the Act and treaty had no retrospective effect.[28]

These statutes were ineffective. According to Clarke,[29] 14 Requisitions were made by the French between 1843 and 1852, of which only one, from Jersey, was successful. The French Government made diplomatic complaint, and in 1852 a replacement convention was agreed which added to the list almost every type of offence against

[27] Parry, *op. cit.*, p.446 h.

[28] Clinton (1845) 6 L.T. (NS) 66 (Forsyth, *Cases and Opinions on Constitutional Law* (1869), p.366; Clarke, *op. cit.*, pp.131–3).

[29] p.34.

property, manslaughter, rape, child stealing and perjury. Requisitions were to be made only for serious crimes (in England, felonies punishable with death, transportation or imprisonment with hard labour). A person surrendered might not be tried for "any political offence" committed before surrender, though there was no other speciality requirement. Conviction cases were now included.

1–009 An attempt was made to enact the Convention, but the Bill failed in the House of Lords, where it was introduced. A number of technical objections were raised, but the principal opposition was aroused by the proposed abandonment of the evidence requirement, taken together with a recent law in France providing for the trial of foreigners in French courts for crimes committed outside France. Another 149 years were to pass before the first extraditions to foreign countries could take place without the production and examination of evidence, by virtue of "general" or "special" arrangements under Pt III of the Extradition Act 1989.

Parry records that after the failed attempt of 1852, seven French attempts to procure extradition between 1854–56 failed, whereas the United Kingdom secured the return from France of two of seven requested persons between 1852–59.[30]

The treaty with the United States was slightly more effective. Clarke records that seven applications were made between 1854 and 1859, of which six were successful, but all of these were cases of murder or attempted murder committed on board ships which put into Liverpool. However, there were other, unsuccessful, applications in the few years before the 1870 Act, the decisions in two of which are helpful in construing provisions of the 1870 Act.

The case of *Re Ternan*[31] concerned a request from the United States of America for the return of ships' passengers who had allegedly committed piracy. The fugitives were subjects of the Confederate States who had overwhelmed the captain and crew after the ship had left port in Mexico, bound for New York. They set the captain and crew ashore, took the ship to Belize and abandoned her, before travelling to Liverpool. The fugitives claimed to have been acting in furtherance of the Civil War in America. By a majority, the Court of Queen's Bench decided that the fugitives, being belligerents, were not pirates at all, but were in any event not guilty of piracy "committed within the jurisdiction of the United States of America", since the piracy alleged was piracy *jure gentium*, and the treaty and act applied only to crimes committed within the exclusive jurisdiction of one party. The case is important in determining the meaning that Parliament attached to the phrase "jurisdiction of the requesting state" within s.26 of the Act of 1870.

In Re Winsor[32] demonstrates the limitations on the types of crimes for which extradition was available under the Ashburton Treaty. The Court of Queen's Bench held that conduct defined as forgery in a statute in the state of New York, though not within the federal law of the United States, was not forgery in English law, though it amounted to a different English offence of fraud. (Offences of fraud generally were not within the treaty.) Extradition might be granted only for the listed

[30] *op. cit.*, p.447.
[31] (1864) 9 Cox C.C. 522; in some reports, the case is referred to as *Re Tivnan*.
[32] (1865) 10 Cox C.C. 118.

offences against the law of England and the general law of the United States, and not for offences made criminal only by the laws of a particular state in the American Union. Under the 1870 Act, comparison of offence is not permitted, and it is immaterial whether the offence is a state, rather than a federal offence.[33]

In 1862, a third extradition treaty was signed, with Denmark.[34] The provisions were very similar to those of the French and American treaties, except for more developed requirements for the authentication of written evidence, and the inclusion of convicted fugitives. The treaty was silent as to political offences. 1–010

In 1864, a treaty was signed with Prussia for extradition, but Parliament voted down the bill. It seems that foreign governments were reluctant to negotiate treaties which might then be rejected by Parliament, a contingency obviously unfamiliar to many European governments of the mid-nineteenth century.

Controversy arose in 1865 when the French Government, in accordance with the treaty, gave six months' notice of its intention to terminate the agreement, complaining of the failure rate (by now one case in 23 years had resulted in surrender) and the refusal of the British Government to surrender convicted persons. Whereas France had over 50 treaties of extradition, Great Britain had only 3. La Forest contrasts the failure of Great Britain to make workable even those limited arrangements which it had put into effect with the greater readiness of the USA and the Canadian judges to co-operate.[35] No doubt our physical insularity has a bearing upon this. However, an aversion to the surrender of political offenders or refugees was an important inhibiting factor, as debates and discussions upon the passing of the Extradition Act 1870 made clear.

An attempt was made to improve the operation of the three treaties in 1866 by "An Act for the Amendment of the Laws relating to Treaties of Extradition".[36] It made modest reforms for providing for the admission in evidence of foreign warrants and depositions if authenticated in a way that formed the model for some of the provisions of the 1870 Act.

TREATIES WITH CHINA

Very early after the transfer of Hong Kong to Great Britain, the "Treaty of Nankin" or "Treaty of the Bogue" made provision for the return from Hong Kong to China of Chinese people who had committed offences against their own government "on proof or admission of their guilt". New and replacement provisions were made by the Treaty of Tientsin of 1858. These provisions were tested in *Attorney-General for Hong Kong v Kwok-a-Sing*,[37] an appeal from the Supreme Court of Hong Kong, the only "extradition" case to reach the Privy Council in the nineteenth century. 1–011

[33] *Government of the United States of America v McCaffery* [1984] 1 W.L.R. 867, HL. See also *R. v Governor of Holloway Prison Ex p. Jennings* [1984] 1 A.C. 624, HL.

[34] This was embodied in the statute 25 & 26 Vict. c.70.

[35] *op. cit.* p.3.

[36] 29 & 30 Vict., c.121.

[37] (1873) 5 L.R.C.P. 179.

The case is illuminating in its consideration of the requirements of "double criminality"; in its approach to questions of extra-territorial jurisdiction; and for the law it declares as to second applications for habeas corpus arising out of the same cause.

A French ship set sail from Macao for Peru carrying 300 Chinese emigrants, some of whom may have been kidnapped. Kwok-a-Sing and others attacked and killed some of the crew of the French ship and returned to China. Kwok-a-Sing fled to Hong Kong. The Colonial Secretary received a requisition for rendition from China and informed a magistrate who issued a warrant. This recited the requisition and ordered the fugitive's arrest pending the receipt of orders from the Lieutenant-Governor on the ground that "there is cause to believe that the said Defendant is a subject of China, and has committed the said crimes against the laws of China by feloniously seizing the said ship at sea, and by murdering the captain and crew of the said ship . . ."

The fugitive was committed to custody, but discharged by the Chief Justice of Hong Kong. He was then re-arrested on a warrant for piracy *jure gentium*, to be tried in Hong Kong, but was again discharged from custody, on the ground that he had been committed for the second time for the same offence, contrary to s.6 of the Habeas Corpus Act 1679.

The Attorney-General of Hong Kong appealed. The Privy Council upheld the first order for discharge. It could not be assumed in the absence of evidence that Chinese law made punishable a murder by one of its subjects committed outside its territory, when English law had "up to a comparatively late period, no such laws". Further, even if there were such provision in China, the offence was committed "within French territory" and ought to be treated as an offence against French law, and not as an offence against Chinese law.

There was, however, evidence of the commission of piracy *jure gentium*, which was triable in Hong Kong by virtue of traditional principles of English law. Although it would be assumed that the acts constituted piracy according to the municipal law of China, this piracy was not within the treaty, because it was justiciable everywhere. Section 6 of the Habeas Corpus Act did not apply because the question on the second warrant raised different questions than on the first. The appeal was therefore allowed on the second warrant, it being held that Kwok-a-Sing might be tried in Hong Kong.

II. EXTRADITION LAW IN ENGLAND BETWEEN 1870 AND 1989

THE EXTRADITION ACT 1870

> "The Extradition Act stands, I think, as a monument of successful draftsmanship."[38]

[38] Preface to Sir Francis Piggott, *Treatise on the Law of Extradition* 1910. (Piggott was Chief Justice of Hong Kong.)

This statute remained in force, virtually complete, for 119 years, its operation enlarged by the Extradition Act 1873, and supplemented in minor respects by later statutes. Occasional difficulties were insufficiently serious or prolonged to justify the controversy and effort of changing the Act until 1989. Even until the end of 2003 the scheme of the 1870 Act remained the basis under the 1989 Act of our extradition arrangements with the United States and other foreign states except fellow signatories to the European Convention on Extradition, Brazil, the Hong Kong SAR, Commonwealth countries and colonies. 1–012

The new Act was the first in the United Kingdom to use the term "extradition". Shearer notes[39] that the word was of French origin, first used in a decree of 1791, and used in official US contexts from 1848. Parry cites[40] several government papers between 1868 and 1901 which appear to confine the use of the word "extradition" to surrenders effected pursuant to formal treaties; whereas the words "surrender" or "rendition" were appropriate to the return of, for example, military deserters under particular military agreements. The word "extradition" was never used to apply to the return of fugitive offenders within the British Empire.

In 1868 a Parliamentary Select Committee had reported in favour of a more comprehensive approach than had existed under the bilateral statutes. Its recommendations became the basis of the 1870 Act. The Parliamentary debates in the course of the bill's passage disclose a certain shame at Great Britain's backwardness in extradition law, compared with France. Readers of Sir James Fitzjames Stephen's writings on the criminal law in late Victorian England will recognise this interest and respect for French institutions. The Attorney-General, moving the second reading of the bill, observed that France had 53 treaties of extradition, while Great Britain had three:

> "but this was partly owing to jealousy, less they might be required to surrender political offenders, and to violate the right of asylum always afforded here to political refugees, and partly because a separate act of Parliament had been required for each treaty."

Mr Bouverie, the Chairman of the Select Committee, noting that the Bill was based almost entirely upon the Committee's proposals, took a more critical approach. The Bill:

> "would remove a defect in their criminal jurisprudence which was a disgrace to them as a civilised country; and it would place them on the same footing as the other civilised countries of Europe."

The following general features of the Act should be noted.

[39] *op. cit.*, p.12.
[40] *op. cit.*, p.444.

THE IMPORTANCE OF TREATIES

1–013 The 1870 Act provided that it should apply in any case where "an arrangement" had been made with any foreign state for extradition and where an Order in Council directed it to apply to such state. It therefore enacted a general system, which might be introduced in full or in modified form with any foreign state. The Act acknowledged that extradition was primarily a political act; the surrender by one government to another of an alleged criminal. Thus, the Secretary of State was given a discretion in every case whether to issue an order to proceed under s.7. At the end of the court process he was given by s.11 a further discretion whether to surrender.

Arrest, however, might be effected without an order from a Secretary of State, though the Secretary of State had power to cancel such a warrant and to decline to order further proceedings.

The magistrate was given the duty to determine whether the evidence produced by the foreign state would have been sufficient to justify committal for trial if the conduct had been committed in England, and in determining this question was given "the same jurisdiction and powers, as near as may be", as if he were dealing with a defendant in ordinary committal for trial proceedings. Properly authenticated written depositions were receivable as a substitute for oral evidence.

EXTRADITION CRIMES

1–014 The "double criminality" principle, discussed in Ch.2, was acknowledged by the requirement that the foreign crime alleged should be an "extradition crime", namely, "a crime which, if committed in England, would be one of the crimes described in the first schedule to this Act." These crimes were described either specifically (*e.g.* murder, rape, piracy by the law of nations) or generically (*e.g.* "fraud by a bailee, banker, agent, factor, trustee, or director, or member, or public officer, of any company made criminal by any Act for the time being in force").

The Act also required that a magistrate must inform a fugitive on committal of his right to apply for a writ of habeas corpus, and that he would not be surrendered before the expiry of at least 15 days after committal to allow for such an application.

POLITICAL OFFENCES

1–015 The restriction in relation to political offenders was the most characteristic feature of the Act. Surrender might not be made for offences of a political character, or even if it were proved that "the requisition for his surrender has in fact been made with a view to try or punish him for an offence of a political character." Nor should a "fugitive criminal" be surrendered unless provision were made by the law of the foreign state that he "shall not, until he has been restored to or had an opportunity of returning to Her Majesty's Dominions, be detained or tried for any offence committed prior to his surrender other than the extradition crime proved by the facts on which his surrender was grounded."

In this respect, the Act appears as a creature of its time. The Convention of 1852 which contemplated, and sought to prevent, the prosecution of an extradited person for a prior political offence was signed four years after the failed revolutions in various parts of Europe of 1848. 1870 was the year of the Franco-Prussian war, the culmination of many years of German military expansionism. Italy had asserted its independence from larger continental powers in the previous ten years. The English constitutional mind was offended by even the possibility that an autocratic foreign power might pursue a refugee and enlist the English courts for the purpose.[41]

The recommendations of the Select Committee included the proposal that the political crime exception should not include assassination:

> "These limits cannot however be wider in the case of treason and insurrection than they are in the case of legitimate war. If we allow to a man who by the law of his country is a rebel or a traitor, and who would be so in our own, the privileges of a belligerent, it is surely as much as he is entitled to ask for; and as assassination is not allowable in war, so neither should it be allowed in insurrection, or treason, whether open or secret."

This intended exception was not enacted by Parliament.

THE ABSENCE OF PROTECTIONS AGAINST DELAY AND OPPRESSION

In marked contrast to the fear that English courts might be used as an instrument of foreign political prosecutions, there was a striking absence in the Act of other discretionary protections against the law's delay and the insolence of office. Other abuses, such as trivial, oppressive and delayed requests, were not guarded against. 1–016

The Fugitive Offenders Act 1881 provided, on the other hand, a wide power to the High Court to discharge a defendant, committed by a magistrate, on the ground that it would be unjust or oppressive to return him. On the other hand, the 1881 Act contained no exception for political offences, listing "treason" specifically as an offence for which surrender might be made, and contained no speciality protections.

The absence of the political exception in the 1881 Act may be explained on the ground that the Act applied only to the Queen's Dominions: the absence of discretionary protections from the 1870 Act, however, and from the later statutes that amended it, is less easy to understand. Modern judges are not troubled, in the absence of statutory encouragement, by the dangers posed to "political" offenders by a request from a foreign power friendly enough to share common extradition arrangements with

[41] A detailed review of nineteenth-century attitudes to the political offence exception appears in the speech of Lord Simon of Glaisdale in *R. v Governor of Pentonville Prison Ex p. Cheng* [1973] A.C. 931, 947 *et seq.*

us.[42] They might, however, be disposed to treat with more sympathy the plight of a fugitive who the requesting state had declined through inefficiency to pursue for many years, or who had in other respects been treated oppressively.

Applications to stay criminal proceedings on the ground of abuse of process are commonplace in modern English criminal practice. The 1870 Act, as renewed in the 1989 Act, denied any such jurisdiction to the magistrate in extradition proceedings.[43] The power to control abuse of extradition procedures lay exclusively with the Secretary of State. The Royal Commission on Extradition of 1877, discussed below, considered it unnecessary to provide statutory protection against extradition for trivial crimes.

All the treaties made and applied pursuant to the Act speak of agreements and shared obligations to extradite. It is remarkable that Parliament should have conferred such discretions in relation to the fugitive exclusively upon the Secretary of State, the person charged with the duty of fulfilling those treaty obligations. This discretion was maintained by the 1989 Act, but, so great did the burden of determining in each case whether it was right to order extradition become, that the Extradition Act 2003 severely limited it.

THE EXTRADITION ACT 1873

1–017 This was a modest amending statute. It added a number of crimes to the list contained in the schedule to the 1870 Act, describing the additions by reference to English statutes. It included, for example, any indictable offence under the Malicious Damage Act, Forgery Act, Coinage Act, and Offences against the Person Act, all of 1861. It made accessories before and after the fact liable to extradition where principal offenders would be liable, and it contained the important procedural change that authenticated evidence given on "affirmation" was admissible as well as evidence given on oath in any proceedings under the 1870 Act.

The innovation lay in a provision for a magistrate to take evidence "for the purposes of any criminal matter pending in any foreign state" upon receipt of an order from a Secretary of State ". . . provided that nothing in this section shall apply in the case of any criminal cause or matter." The modern way of obtaining evidence in pursuance of letters of request is considered in Pt E of this book, but it is instructive to note that Parliament in 1873 associated the process with the subject of extradition rather than the general criminal law.

THE ROYAL COMMISSION OF 1877

1–018 The Royal Commission, established for the purpose of examining the operation of the new laws and treaties, made radical proposals. Its members included some of the

[42] See *T v Home Secretary* [1996] A.C. 742.
[43] See *R. v Governor of Pentonville Prison Ex p. Sinclair* [1991] 2 A.C. 64, discussed in Ch.9 at 9–048.

greatest nineteenth-century judges, the Lord Chief Justice (Sir Alexander Cockburn), Lord Selborne, Lord Blackburn, Lord Esher and Sir James Fitzjames Stephen, among others. Parliament did not adopt its recommendations in fresh legislation, but the Commission's report repays study. It indicates differences of attitude between Parliament and Judiciary in this new area of co-operation between states for the punishment of crime.

The most challenging of the Commission's recommendations was that:

> "even if any state should fail to concede full reciprocity, there is no principle which should make this country unwilling to surrender, and so get rid of, the fugitive subjects of other States, whose subjects have been guilty of crime, and whose surrender is asked for."

Accordingly, statutory powers should be given to the Government to surrender fugitive criminals in the absence of treaties, whose purpose was to ensure reciprocity. The Commission suggested that extradition might be permitted only to countries listed for the time being in an Order in Council.

The Commission was concerned with provisions in existing treaties which forbade the extradition of a country's own nationals to the other. In *R. v Wilson*[44] the magistrate committed an alleged fugitive, a British subject, although the relevant treaty forbade the extradition of Britons to Switzerland and Swiss to Great Britain. He took the view, purporting to follow a dictum of Blackburn J. in *Re Counhaye*[45] that non-compliance with the treaty was a matter for the Secretary of State to take into account in deciding whether to issue an Order to Proceed to the magistrate. In this the magistrate was technically correct. (In *R. v Governor of Pentonville Prison Ex p. Sinclair*[46] the House of Lords determined that the magistrate had no power to interpret the treaty.) On an application for habeas corpus, Cockburn C.J., in discharging Wilson on the ground that the treaty forbade the surrender, resolved to draw the matter to the attention of the Commission, of which he was chairman.

The Royal Commission identified the reasons for this restriction. It was said that a state fails in its duty to its subjects if it hands them over to a foreign jurisdiction; that unqualified confidence could not be placed in the capacity of foreign courts to try the subjects of other states; that the subject would have to defend himself where his language was not understood, and where he was unable to call character witnesses.

The Commission recommended that this restriction should be omitted in subsequent treaties, so far as Parliament should continue to regard treaties as necessary. Some treaties in the following years omitted the restriction entirely; others contained a modified provision allowing the requesting state a discretion whether to surrender its own subjects. However, the subsequent treaty with Switzerland retained the absolute restriction upon the surrender of Swiss nationals to Great Britain, but the corresponding restriction on British subjects became discretionary.

44 (1877) 3 Q.B.D. 42.
45 (1873) L.R. 8 Q.B. 410.
46 [1991] 2 A.C. 64, HL.

1–019 The Commissioners took a less sensitive approach than Parliament to political crimes. It was recommended that crimes which were political in themselves (presumably treason, sedition, etc.) should remain exempt from extradition, whereas other crimes, committed with a political motive, should be extraditable in the discretion of the requested state:

> "And however odious the character of the rebel who disturbs the peace of his own country and gives rise to bloodshed and disorder from interested motives, or reckless disregard of the miseries attendant upon civil discord, yet both from history and our own experience we know that there are exceptional instances in which resistance to usurpation or tyranny may be inspired by the noblest motives, and in which, though unsuccessful, it may escape condemnation, and even command sympathy."

The judges were not alone in this approach, though they differed from Parliament. The Select Committee in 1868 had also been less enthusiastic than Parliament, as we have seen, about the political exception. Clarke noted in 1904 with satisfaction that the Commissioners' recommendation "exactly corresponds with the opinion expressed in the first edition of this work."

A further recommendation of the Commissioners was the removal of a power to prevent the extradition of crimes of a political character from the judiciary and to confine it to the executive. The proposal has never been adopted in legislation.

The Commission thought it unnecessary to legislate against extradition for a trivial crime:

> "It may safely be assumed that a foreign government will not seek to obtain the surrender of an offender for a merely trivial offence."

Four years later, as already described, Parliament did indeed embody protections of this kind in the 1881 Act for cases within Her Majesty's Dominions.

1–020 The Commissioners examination of the duties of the magistrate is of interest. The evidence test should be retained, but "the English magistrate cannot be expected to know or interpret the foreign law. It is not desirable that he should be required to do more than to see that the facts proved constitute prima facie an offence which would have been within judicial cognisance if done in this country." Consequently, "the magistrate should look to the facts proved before him rather than to the form in which the case may be presented on the documents." This seems generally to have been the approach of the High Court on application for habeas corpus under the Act in the nineteenth century, though in individual cases, especially in the 1890s, the courts assumed the duty and power to examine foreign law to ensure compliance with the treaties. Examples are *Re Bellencontre*,[47] and *Re Arton (No.2)*.[48] Only in the 1980s was the practice

[47] [1891] 2 Q.B. 122.
[48] [1896] 1 Q.B. 508.

definitively disapproved in the courts and the attitude of the 1877 Royal Commissioners followed.

Modern criminal lawyers may be struck by the innovative approach of the Royal Commission, but will also note that the judiciary of the time seemed to attach greater concern to the preservation of order than to the risk of injustice. The Commissioners asserted:

> "Extradition, as a system, is based on the supposition that in the great majority of instances the person whose surrender is claimed has, in fact, violated the law of the country demanding the surrender. The instances in which the surrender of an innocent person may be demanded will be exceedingly rare. With the safeguards, which we shall advert to further on, the possibility of an innocent man being unjustly dealt with will be remote in the extreme."

The safeguards are confined to the evidence test, the speciality provision, and the duty to refuse to extradite a fugitive for an offence of a political character.

EXTRADITION IN THE COURTS UNDER THE 1870 ACT

Between 1870 and 1904, Clarke noted,[49] some 35 treaties were concluded and imple- 1–021
mented under the 1870 Act, for the most part with countries from Europe, and North and South America. It should not be deduced from this that Great Britain had become involved in a worldwide exchange of criminals. Although 32 cases of habeas corpus in the High Court, arising from proceedings under the 1870 Act, are reported, they concern only seven countries. Three of the cases arise from requests from the United States. All the others were cases from our near neighbours in Western Europe, namely, France (14), Germany (6), Belgium (5), Switzerland (2), Italy (2) and the Netherlands (1). In three of these cases the crime alleged is not identified in the reports. Two cases only alleged violence. One was a Swiss request in a murder case, *Castioni*[50] (one of only three cases under the Extradition and Fugitive Offenders Acts where the "political" defence has succeeded), and the other was *Meunier*,[51] a French request alleging that the fugitive was an anarchist who had caused explosions in Paris. The "political" defence was raised in this case too, but it failed. All the other cases involved crimes of ordinary dishonesty and fraud, many of them allegations of offences by bankrupts.

By comparison with the present day, none of the cases except *Castioni* appears to be grave or notorious. In almost all, however, the Attorney-General appeared in the High Court to justify the imprisonment on the return to the writ, frequently with the Solicitor-General and at least one other junior. The fugitive was usually represented by one junior barrister, sometimes two. As today, the same counsel tended to

[49] *op. cit.*, p.206, and its Appendix.
[50] [1891] 1 Q.B. 149.
[51] [1894] 2 Q.B. 415.

appear in cases of the same period (Clarke, Besley, Tickell) and the applications were usually, but not always, refused.

It is important to bear in mind in discussing any extradition case decided before 1960, and indeed any habeas corpus matter, that it was not until the enactment of the Administration of Justice Act 1960 that a right of appeal was created in respect of a decision of the High Court on an application for habeas corpus "in a criminal cause or matter". The construction of this phrase in s.47 of the Judicature Act 1873 was considered by the Court of Appeal in *R. v Weil*.[52] The Court did not decide the question whether it had jurisdiction to hear an appeal, but assumed it did and rejected the appeal from the Divisional Court on other grounds. In *Ex p. Alice Woodall*,[53] it was determined that an application for habeas corpus following a committal by the magistrate in proceedings under the Extradition Act was indeed a case from which no appeal from the Divisional Court lay. The House of Lords had therefore no opportunity to consider the new extradition arrangements.

Two statutes amended the Acts of 1870 and 1873. The Extradition Act 1895 allowed for a committal hearing to be held elsewhere than at Bow Street if the health of the fugitive required it. (It appears that this Act was passed because a suspected fraudster claimed to be too ill to appear at court in London. It was intended to conduct the proceedings at Bournemouth, but he died after the act was enacted.[54] There is no evidence that the Act was ever used.) The Extradition Act 1906 added "bribery" to the list of extradition crimes in the first schedule to the 1870 Act.

1–022 There are remarkably few cases or alterations in the law in this period. Extradition law and practice flourish in England only after long periods of peace.[55] Two Acts of Parliament were passed in this period which added new extradition crimes, the Extradition Act 1932, adding "offences against any enactment for the time being in force relating to dangerous drugs" and attempts to commit such offences, and the Counterfeit Currency Act 1935 adding various offences of forging and counterfeiting coin and money (probably unnecessarily, since the generic offences of forging and counterfeiting listed in the Extradition Act 1873 were very wide).

Only two cases merit attention in a historical review. *R. v Governor of Brixton Prison Ex p. Kolczynski*,[56] often known as the *Polish Seamen's* case, was the second case in which the High Court granted habeas corpus on the ground of the political exception.

R. v Governor of Brixton Prison Ex p. Minervini[57] is an important case on the meaning of the word "territory" within the meaning of the treaties. Offences were extraditable only if committed within the "territory" of the requesting state. It was held that the word was equivalent to the word "jurisdiction".

In 1957, the United Kingdom signed the European Convention on Extradition. It did not enact its provisions, however, until 1989. Nonetheless, it is remarkable

52 (1882) 9 Q.B.D. 701.

53 (1888) 20 Q.B.D. 832.

54 Biron and Chalmers, *The Law and Practice of Extradition* (1903), p.91.

55 *cf.* the unsuccessful attempt to extradite the Kaiser from the Netherlands for war crimes considered in Ch.4.

56 [1955] 1 Q.B. 540.

57 [1959] 1 Q.B. 155, DC; considered in Ch.6.

that the United Kingdom took an active part in the six years of discussions within the Council of Europe from 1951 as the terms of the multilateral scheme were formulated.

The modern body of extradition case law may be traced to the introduction of appeals in habeas corpus matters "in a criminal cause or matter" to the House of Lords. The right is conferred by ss.1 and 15(3) of the Administration of Justice Act 1960. Section 15(3) opened the door more widely by declaring that an appeal in habeas corpus lay with the leave of either the High Court or the House of Lords. It was not limited, as in the case of an appeal from a decision in relation to the prerogative orders, or an appeal from the Court of Appeal (Criminal Division), to cases in which the High Court, or Court of Appeal,[58] certified that a point of law of public importance was involved. In this way, it was easier to appeal to the House of Lords in criminal habeas corpus matters than in any other type of case. 1–023

The effect of this change on the development of extradition law can scarcely be exaggerated. Partly because the appeal route was relatively free from impediments, extradition cases came before the House of Lords out of proportion to their number, and to the benefit of the general criminal law.[59]

Substantial additions to the list of extradition crimes were made in this period, allowing the Act to apply to modern crime, and crime of an international character.

DANGEROUS DRUGS

A number of extradition crimes were added to the first schedule to the 1870 Act. Section 33 of the Misuse of Drugs Act 1971 provided that conspiring to commit any offence against any enactment for the time being in force in relation to dangerous drugs was an extradition crime. Previously, the Dangerous Drugs Act 1932 had added offences against any enactment for the time being in force in relation to dangerous drugs. Section 22 of the Criminal Justice (International Co-operation) Act 1990 provided that a drug trafficking offence within the meaning of the Drug Trafficking Offences Act 1986 was to be inserted after para.15 of Sch.1 to the Extradition Act 1989.[60] 1–024

TERRORISM

The Suppression of Terrorism Act 1978 made important amendments to both the 1870 Act and the 1967 Act. Section 3 added any offence under the Explosive Substances Act 1883 and any indictable offence under the Firearms Act to the list 1–025

[58] Criminal Appeal Act 1968, s.33(2).

[59] See Ch.13 at 13–002 for a discussion of the Extradition Act 2003 and habeas corpus.

[60] It was held by the Divisional Court in *R. v Governor of Pentonville Prison Ex p. Chinoy* [1992] 1 All E.R. 317, DC that such an offence was already within the schedule, and that the 1990 provision was made out of an abundance of caution.

of extradition crimes in the 1870 Act. It also added any attempt to commit any crime listed in the schedule, including crimes added after the 1978 Act itself, thus remedying a strange omission in the 1870 scheme. The Act also made substantial inroads into the political exception, embodying the terms of the European Convention on the Suppression of Terrorism.

Four other statutes, also enacting international conventions, provided for other extradition crimes of a terrorist and international character, and provided that the extra-territorial crimes contemplated would be deemed to be committed within the jurisdiction of the requesting state. These are the Internationally Protected Persons Act 1978, the Taking of Hostages Act 1982, the Aviation Security Act 1982 and the Nuclear Material (Offences) Act 1983.

SUNDRY ADDITIONS

1–026 Other extradition crimes added to Sch.1 to the 1870 Act included offences under the Indecency with Children Act 1960, offences under the Suicide Act 1961, assisting offenders contrary to s.4(1) of the Criminal Law Act 1967, offences contrary to the Genocide Act 1969, the Protection of Children Act 1978 (taking or publishing indecent photographs of children) and the Prohibition of Female Circumcision Act 1985.

III. THE HISTORY OF FUGITIVE OFFENDERS LEGISLATION

SURRENDER BETWEEN HER MAJESTY'S POSSESSIONS

1–027 A legal opinion of Sergeant Hill in 1792 referred to s.16 of the Habeas Corpus Act 1679. Section 16 acknowledged an existing practice and provided that:

> "If any person resiant in this Realm shall have committed any Capital offence in Scotland or Ireland, or foreign Plantations of the King . . . where he or she ought to be tried for such Offence, such Person may be sent to such Place, there to receive such Trial, in such manner as the same might have been used before the making of this Act; any Thing herein contained to the contrary notwithstanding."

The provision applied only to capital offences, of which, of course, there were many.

In 1843 an "Act for the better Apprehension of certain Offenders"[61] provided a procedure for such surrenders, and was enacted less than a month before the acts in relation to France and the United States of America. This is the first statutory procedure for extradition in English law, enacted two months before the bilateral arrangements with the United States of America and France. It introduces concepts

[61] 6 & 7 Vict. c.34.

and practices still in force today. A fugitive from Her Majesty's Dominions could be arrested in Great Britain or Ireland, provided that a warrant for his arrest had been issued where his trial was sought, and provided that warrant was endorsed by a Secretary of State. The warrant, thus endorsed, empowered a Justice of the Peace or constable in the country where the fugitive was believed to be to arrest him and bring him before a Justice of the Peace.

When the fugitive was brought before the court, if "such Evidence of Criminality as would justify his Committal if the Offence had been committed in that Part of Her Majesty's Dominions" were produced, it was lawful "to commit such supposed Offender to prison, there to remain until he can be sent back". The Secretary of State was then to be notified formally. Similar provisions were made for return to Great Britain and Ireland. Copies of the depositions "upon which the original warrant was granted, certified under the Hand of the Person or Persons issued by such warrant, and attested by the Person producing them to be true copies of the original depositions, may be received in Evidence of the Criminality of the Person so apprehended."

If the alleged offender was not returned within two months of his committal, he would, on application to a judge, be discharged "unless sufficient cause be shown to such judge why such discharge ought not to be ordered." Delay after surrender was also considered. If a person surrendered had not been indicted within six months of arrival in the part of Her Majesty's Dominions which had requested him, it would be lawful for a Secretary of State in Great Britain, or other described representatives of government in Ireland and the colonies, "if he think fit, upon the Request of the Person so Apprehended, to cause such person to be sent back, free of Cost to such Person, and with as little delay as possible, to that Part of Her Majesty's Dominions in which he shall have been so apprehended."

THE FUGITIVE OFFENDERS ACT 1881

This statute was treated as unimportant by earlier writers on extradition. Clarke scarcely referred to it, and few law reports appear in relation to the statute until after the Second World War. Stephen[62] commented: 1–028

> " It is unnecessary to notice its provisions in detail; they are merely administrative, and involve no principle of any interest."

The preamble read:

> "Whereas it is expedient to make more effectual provision for the apprehension and trial of offenders against the laws who may be in other parts of Her Majesty's Dominions than those in which their offences were committed;"

[62] *op. cit.*, Vol.2, p.74.

The Act began to assume greater significance after India and Pakistan became independent in 1947. When independence had been granted to numerous former colonies in Africa it became a controversial piece of legislation, and was finally repealed and replaced in 1967.

The 1881 Act provided for arrest by either full or provisional warrant. A full warrant might be issued by a judge of a superior court or, in England, a metropolitan magistrate at Bow Street, or, in a British possession, the governor. Any magistrate might issue a provisional warrant, which, when executed, the Secretary of State or governor might discharge "if he think fit." The next stage of the hearing required evidence of the offence to be placed before the magistrate. If "a strong and probable presumption that the fugitive committed the offence" was found, the magistrate committed to custody and had the power to send a report to the Secretary of State. The magistrate was obliged to inform the fugitive that he would not be surrendered for 15 days, and that he was entitled to apply for habeas corpus. At the end of the process, if the fugitive had not been discharged, the Secretary of State had a discretion whether to surrender.

1–029 These provisions were of course modelled on the 1870 Act. It is the differences between the two schemes, however, that command attention. Section 9 provided that "This part of the Act shall apply to the following offences, namely, to treason and piracy, and to every offence, whether called felony, misdemeanour, crime, or by any other name, which is for the time being punishable in that part of Her Majesty's dominions in which it was committed, either on indictment or on information, by imprisonment with hard labour for a term of twelve months or more, or by any greater punishment". Not only was there no express political exception; the inclusion of treason made it impossible to imply one.

Section 10 conferred on "a superior court" the discretionary power, so conspicuously absent from the 1870 Act, to refuse extradition on grounds of unfairness. A modified version of this protection became s.8(3) of the Fugitive Offenders Act 1967, and thereafter s.11(3) of the Extradition Act 1989, applying not only to Commonwealth and colonial extraditions, but also to Pt III "general arrangement" and "special arrangement" countries, in which it co-exists with the political character exception similar to that contained in the 1870 Act.

The 1881 Act contained no speciality protection.

Part II of the Act contained a detailed backing of warrants scheme[63] based on practice within the British Isles which could be applied to contiguous territories among foreign possessions.[64]

Only a few cases were reported under this act between 1881 and 1950, justifying Clarke's and Pigott's lack of interest in it. The first, *R. v Spilsbury*,[65] decided that the High Court has inherent powers to grant bail after committal by the magistrate, a principle that remains important in extradition cases generally.

[63] Applied by statutory instrument to a group of possessions in southern Africa.
[64] *cf.* Home Office Review "The Law on Extradition" of March 2001.
[65] [1898] 2 Q.B. 615.

1–030 *R. v Brixton Prison Governor Ex p. Savakar*[66] is most interesting for what the report omits. Savarkar's return was sought by the Government of India. The offences were "Waging, and abetting the waging of, war against the King; conspiring to wage war against the King; collecting arms with intent to wage war against the King; sedition; abetment of murder", all contrary to the Indian Penal Code. Application was made to the Divisional Court relying upon s.10 and was refused. Savarkar sought then to appeal to the Court of Appeal. The report deals at length with the distinction between the jurisdiction of the Court of Appeal by virtue of s.10, which confers an original jurisdiction, and the 1870 Act, where there was no escape from the provisions of the Judicature Act 1873, prohibiting an appeal "in a criminal cause or matter." The report sets out in full the judgment of three Lords Justices, all of which concluded that the Court of Appeal did have jurisdiction, but the report concludes, "The application was then heard and ultimately was dismissed."

It is suggested in Savarkar's affidavit, which is fortuitously reproduced in the report in full, that some of the offences alleged took place in 1906, and that the substance of the allegations of sedition was that he circulated pamphlets and made speeches in England in 1908 and procured the supply of arms to India for use against the Government. These allegations are very similar to those made against Mohammed Rafiq Kahan by the Government of Fiji, which requested his return from England in 1988. Kahan was discharged because his offence was held to be of a political character. Savarkar could only rely upon s.10, and was unsuccessful in both the Divisional Court and Court of Appeal, for reasons which it was not thought important to record.[67]

R. v Governor of Brixton Prison Ex p. Percival[68] established that it was necessary to prove by expert evidence that the conduct constituting the offence alleged in a colony was punishable, as the Act required, by a minimum of 12 months imprisonment. There were similarities between this provision and the definition of an extradition crime in s.2 of the 1989 Act.

R. v Governor of Brixton Prison Ex p. Bidwell[69] dealt with the "strong and probable presumption" test. It was disapproved in *Armah v Government of Ghana*.[70]

OPERATION OF THE FUGITIVE OFFENDERS ACT FROM 1950 TO 1967[71]

1–031 The first of the cases dealing with the power of a superior court to discharge under s.10 arose in 1950.[72] It was followed by a number of others, all concerning newly-

[66] [1910] 2 K.B. 1056.

[67] Although the decision of the Court of Appeal was made three months before the publication of Piggott's book, he does not mention it.

[68] [1907] 1 K.B. 696.

[69] [1937] 1 K.B. 305.

[70] [1968] A.C. 192.

[71] An interesting review of the operation of the 1881 Act in this period was written by Paul O'Higgins [1965] Crim L.R. 133.

[72] *Henderson* [1950] 1 All E.R. 283.

independent Commonwealth countries.[73] Section 11 (3) of the 1989 Act enacted a similar test for Pt III extraditions and the notoriety of the cases of *Zacharia*, *Enaharo*, and *Armah* needs to be considered historically. These cases demonstrated that an act designed to operate within the Empire was no longer appropriate in the case of independent countries, and they were important in provoking the repeal of the Act and in shaping the Fugitive Offenders Act 1967.

Zacharia's return was sought in 1961 by the Government of Cyprus, the year after Cyprus became independent, for offences of murder and other forms of violence. It was clearly accepted in both the Divisional Court and the House of Lords that there was a serious risk to the life of Zacharia and his co-defendant, and that there had been at least three attempts to assassinate him in Cyprus. Lord Parker C.J. conceded that there was a "real danger that evidence against him has been or will be fabricated." He had a clear association with the EOKA movement which had been prominent in the serious disturbances in the years before independence was granted. His application for habeas corpus and his subsequent appeal failed, however. The House of Lords disapproved a dictum of Lord Goddard C.J. in *Mubarak Ali Ahmed*[74] to the effect that, in an appropriate case, the Divisional Court would apply the political exception to a case under the Fugitive Offenders Act.

1–032 In 1962 the Government of Nigeria requested the return of Chief Enaharo for offences, among others, of treasonable felony, conspiracy to commit treason. His application under s.10 also failed. Such was the controversy engendered by the proposed surrender that the Secretary of State, having decided to exercise his discretion under the Act in favour of the Government of Nigeria, was moved to postpone the implementation of the order pending a Parliamentary debate about the justice of his decision. The concerns aroused by the case are indicated by the undertakings requested and given to the Divisional Court on the question of the fugitive's legal representation at trial. When doubts were expressed as to the form and effect of these undertakings, the matter was approached diplomatically, and the Prime Minister of Nigeria repeated the assurances in a personal letter to the Secretary of State. Enaharo was surrendered.

Armah had been a minister in the Government of Ghana under President Nkrumah. That Government was overthrown and the constitution was suspended in 1966, six years after independence. Two months later, Armah was arrested in London at the request of the new Government, which sought his return for alleged offences of corruption. Shortly before his arrest, a decree in Ghana declared that "all ministers of the Government of Kwame Nkrumah" be "kept in protective custody for such period as the National Liberation Council may determine."

[73] *Mubarak Ali Ahmed* [1952] 1 All E.R. 1060 (India); *Ex p. Naranjan Singh* [1962] 1 Q.B. 211 (India); *Zacharia* [1963] A.C. 634, HL (Cyprus); *Enahoro* [1963] 2 Q.B. 455 (Nigeria); *Armah* [1968] A.C. 192, HL (Ghana).

[74] [1952] 1 All E.R. 1060, 1063; doubted by R.Y. Jennings, "The Commonwealth and International Law" (1953) 30 B.Y.B.I.L. 320 at 326.The decision itself is explicable on the basis that the 1881 Act contained no political offence exception. See Paul O'Higgins, "Extradition within the Commonwealth" (1960) 9 I.C.L.Q. 488.

The magistrate found a "strong and probable presumption" of guilt and committed Armah to custody. As in *Enaharo*, undertakings were given to the Divisional Court, on this occasion to the effect that, if Armah were acquitted, he would be deprived of the advantages of "protective custody" and would be allowed to leave Ghana. The Divisional Court acted upon these assurances and refused the applications under s.10.

An appeal to the House of Lords succeeded, not on the s.10 argument, but upon the basis that the requesting state had not succeeded in establishing a "strong and probable presumption" of guilt, a more onerous test than the ordinary test in ordinary committal for trial proceedings and cases under the 1870 Act. The House of Lords did not resolve the s.10 argument.

The 1881 Act, together with the "strong and probable presumption" test, was repealed the following year.

THE FUGITIVE OFFENDERS ACT 1967

In an number of fundamental respects, this Act created a "stricter and more demanding scheme than its predecessor".[75] Extradition became significantly more difficult to obtain than under the 1870 Act. The Act was based upon the 1966 "Scheme for the Rendition of Fugitive Offenders within the Commonwealth" (Cmnd.3008). This Scheme, often called "the London scheme", was revised in 1983,[76] and the latest version is dated 1990. The foreword to the 1966 Scheme demonstrated the desire for reciprocity, which was not, in fact, a condition of the Act: 1–033

> "At the meeting of Commonwealth Law Ministers, held at Marlborough House, London, from 26th April to 3rd May 1966, the arrangements for the extradition of fugitive offenders within the Commonwealth were reviewed in the light of the constitutional changes which have taken place since the passing of the Fugitive Offenders Act 1881."

The following extract from the communique issued at the conclusion of the meeting explained the purpose of the Scheme:

> "The meeting considered that Commonwealth extradition arrangements should be based upon reciprocity and substantially uniform legislation incorporating certain features commonly found in extradition treaties, eg a list of returnable offences, the establishment of a prima facie case before return, and restrictions upon the return of political offenders. The meeting accordingly formulated a Scheme setting out principles which could form the basis of

[75] *per* Lord Elwyn-Jones, *Government of Canada v Aronson* [1990] 1 A.C. 579, HL.

[76] On the basis of a paper prepared by Professor Shearer at the Commonwealth Law Ministers' meeting in Sri Lanka in 1983.

legislation within the Commonwealth and recommended that effect should be given to the Scheme in each Commonwealth country."

1–034 The Act applied to Commonwealth countries designated by Orders in Council and to colonies. Its main features were as follows:

(1) *Double criminality*. Surrender might be made only for a "relevant offence". This unusual and tight application of the double criminality rule is discussed in Ch.2;
(2) *The position of the Secretary of State*. Under the 1967 Act, the Secretary of State stood in the same relation to the courts as under the 1870 Act. He had a discretion under s.5(3) as to whether to launch extradition proceedings at all, or to cancel a provisional warrant and discharge the person arrested thereunder (s.6(3)). He had a discretion whether to surrender at the end of all court proceedings (s.9(1));
(3) *The magistrate's duties*. The magistrate had the same duties in relation to warrants of arrest under s.6, and in the conduct of the committal proceedings as he would in domestic committals ("as nearly as may be") under s.7. The strong and probable presumption was replaced; the magistrate would commit if "the evidence would be sufficient to warrant his trial for that offence if it had been committed within the jurisdiction of the court.";
(4) *The "political" exception*. The list in the schedule resembled the list in Sch.1 to the 1870 Act, as amended. There were no offences of treason or sedition. Section 4 prohibited a return if it appeared to the Secretary of State, court of committal or High Court on an application for habeas corpus:

    (a) that the offence of which the person was accused or was convicted was an offence of a political character;
    (b) that the request for his return (though purporting to be made on account of a relevant offence) was in fact made for the purpose of prosecuting or punishing him on account of his race, religion, nationality or political opinions; or
    (c) that he might, if returned, be prejudiced at his trial or punished, detained or restricted in his personal liberty by reason of his race, religion, nationality or political opinions.

    Of these restrictions, the latter two were new, deriving from Art.3 of the European Convention on Extradition, 1957, which the United Kingdom ratified after the enactment of the 1989 Act. They were considered by the House of Lords in *R. v Governor of Pentonville Prison Ex p. Fernandez*.[77]

[77] [1971] 1 W.L.R. 987.

(5) *The speciality rule*. A person might not be returned unless provision was made by the law of the requesting country, or by arrangement with it, that he would only be tried for the relevant offence for which he was returned, any lesser offence proved by the facts before the court of committal, or for any other relevant offence to the trial of which the Secretary of State consented (s.4(3)). Similar protection was extended to fugitives returned to England from Commonwealth countries or possessions (s.14);

(6) *Autrefois acquit and convict*. A person might not be returned if he would be entitled to be discharged for this reason if the offence had been committed in England (s.4(2));

(7) *Habeas corpus*. As under the 1870 Act, the committing magistrate had to inform the fugitive that he had a right to apply for habeas corpus and that he would not be surrendered for 15 days to permit him to make such application. Upon such application, the court could discharge the fugitive by applying provisions only slightly, but significantly, changed from s.10 of the 1881 Act, now contained in s.8(3). Three major cases in the House of Lords in the course of which s.8(3) was considered were *R. v Governor of Pentonville Prison Ex p. Tarling*,[78] *R. v Governor of Pentonville Prison Ex p. Narang*,[79] and *Kakis v Government of Cyprus*.[80]

The Act contained the innovation that committal proceedings might, in contrast to committals under the 1870 Act, be conducted in Scotland, before "the sheriff or sheriff-substitute of the Lothian and Peebles", the legality of whose acts might be tested by an application for an order of review to the High Court of Justiciary.

From 1967 to 1989 the same additions, adding relevant offences, were made to the 1967 Act as to the 1870 Act, particularly in relation to terrorism.

IV. EXTRADITION LAW IN ENGLAND BETWEEN 1989 AND 2003

PROPOSALS FOR CHANGE; THE 1989 ACT

In the decade before the passing of the Extradition Act 1989, a number of deficiencies in the Acts of 1870 and 1873 were identified. An Interdepartmental Working Party of the Home Office made a number of recommendations in its report of May 1982. It suggested a simplified procedure for voluntary return. The Acts had not provided for a person to return otherwise than by undergoing the full statutory procedure. From time to time the rigour of this rule was mitigated informally by means of dubious devices such as allowing a fugitive bail on the understanding that he would accompany a policeman to the airport and board a plane bound for the requesting state. 1–035

[78] (1980) 70 Cr.App.R. 77, DC and HL; [1979] 1 W.L.R.1417, DC.
[79] [1978] A.C. 247.
[80] [1978] 1 W.L.R. 779.

The report also recommended the enactment of the provisions of the European Convention on Extradition, but with the retention of the requirement of prima facie evidence. The Report is a useful source of case law and statistics.

THE GREEN AND WHITE PAPERS

1–036 In February 1985, the Government published a Green Paper on Extradition (Cmnd.9421), and in March 1986 a White Paper (Cm.9658). It referred to the recent:

> "huge expansion in international crime. Terrorism, drug trafficking and international fraud have presented new challenges which our extradition arrangements with other states must meet. The basic framework of United Kingdom extradition law has not, however, changed with the expansion of international crime . . . The United Kingdom is widely regarded as one of the most difficult countries from which to secure extradition."

The central proposal was the harmonisation of the law with the laws of the other signatories to the European Convention on Extradition so as to enable the United Kingdom to become a party to it.

The most controversial recommendation was the removal of the requirement for the requesting state to establish a prima facie case in the United Kingdom courts. Further, extradition should be allowed where the minimum sentence that could be imposed for the crime was one of 12 months' imprisonment; the "list" system in the 1870 and 1967 Acts should be abolished. There should be provision for *ad hoc* arrangements for extradition, by the creation of special extradition arrangements. The speciality rule should be relaxed by providing that an offender, after return, might be tried for other extradition crimes than those for which he was returned, if the Secretary of State consented.

THE CRIMINAL JUSTICE ACT 1988

1–037 The long title to the 1988 Act begins, "An Act to make fresh provision for extradition". Part 1 of this statute enacted a detailed reform of the law of extradition in relation to foreign states, so as to allow for the application of international arrangements such as the European Convention on Extradition, but it was never brought into operation. Many of its provisions were based on the recommendations in the White Paper, and were the model for the Pt III procedures in the Act of 1989. It sought to amend, but not to repeal, the Acts of 1870 and 1873, and the Act of 1967. By virtue of s.136 (1) of, and para.4 of Sch.1 to, the 1988 Act, it was intended to extend the list of extradition crimes in the first schedule to the 1870 Act by adding the crimes of torture contrary to s.134 of the 1988 Act, crimes under the Company Securities (Insider Dealing) Act 1985 and offences under s.24 of the Drug Trafficking Offences Act

1986. Section 38(4) of the 1989 Act declared that the provision should enter into force immediately before the coming into force of the 1989 Act itself. This complicated form of drafting has the effect of making such crimes "extradition crimes", for the purposes of Sch.1 extraditions in the 1989 Act, as defined in para.20 of that Schedule.

Section 170 in Pt XII of the 1988 Act made important insertions into a number of modern statutes which have resulted from international conventions which deal with a number of serious international terrorist and drugs crimes. These insertions resulted in the terms of s.22 of the 1989 Act.

Although the 1988 Act has left slight marks on the history of extradition, its provisions may fall to be examined if provisions of the 1989 Act are difficult to construe. However, the Act uses definitions of, for example, "extradition crime" that derive from other Acts, notably, the Fugitive Offenders Act 1967, and, it may be argued, the Fugitive Offenders Act 1881.

A further short Report of the Law Commission was published in June 1989 (Cm.712) throwing light on a few of the minor changes introduced by the Bill that became the 1989 Act.

DEVELOPMENTS SINCE THE PASSING OF THE 1989 ACT

As outlined above, the Extradition Act 1989 was essentially a consolidation of Pt 1 of the Criminal Justice Act 1988, the Fugitive Offenders Act 1967 and the Extradition Act 1870 (as amended). **1–038**

The UK signed two EU Conventions in 1995 and 1996: the Convention on simplified extradition procedure between the Member States of the EU[81] and the Convention relating to extradition between the Member States of the EU.[82] This prompted a domestic review, begun in 1997, to consider what amendments were required for the UK's extradition legislation to give effect to these Conventions.[83] This process was suspended during the *Pinochet* case which started in October 1998.[84] The scope of the review was also extended following further developments at an EU level.

The Tampere European Special Council produced conclusions of October 15 and 16, 1999,[85] which outlined a programme to implement the principle agreed of mutual recognition of judicial decisions.[86] Point 35 of the conclusions also called for formal extradition procedures to be abolished among Member States for defendants who have been sentenced and for extradition procedures to be expedited for those persons suspected of having committed offences.

[81] March 10, 1995; [1995] O.J. C78/2.

[82] September 27, 1996; [1996] O.J. C313/12.

[83] Accession to these Conventions was approved by both Houses of Parliament on December 19, 2001. The Extradition Act 1989 was eventually amended to give effect to the Conventions by The European Union Extradition Regulations 2002 (SI 2002/419). The European Union Extradition (Amendment) Regulations 2002 (SI 2002/1662) corrected errors in SI 2002/419.

[84] Considered in detail in Ch.4.

[85] [2001] O.J. C12/10.

[86] Point 37.

Following this review, the Government published its proposals to reform the law on extradition in a consultation document "The Law on Extradition: A Review" in March 2001. There was then a consultation process. However, the review was again overtaken by developments at an EU level. A Framework Decision was issued on June 13, 2002 on the European Arrest Warrant and surrender procedures between Member States.[87] The Extradition Bill was published in draft on June 27, 2002 and it sought, *inter alia*, to implement the provisions of the Framework Decision. After a further consultation process the Bill was published in November 2002, and following Parliamentary scrutiny and further amendment the Extradition Act 2003 was enacted on November 20, 2003.

The significance of these developments is discussed in the context of the legislative history of the Extradition Act 2003 below. It is submitted that the previous legislation will continue to be important in construing the 2003 Act.

[87] 2002/584/JHA.

Chapter 2

GENERAL PRINCIPLES

I. INTRODUCTION

Two widely (but not universally) accepted principles of extradition law and procedure may be expressed conveniently in the following simple terms: **2–001**

(i) *double criminality*; a person may be extradited only for conduct which is criminal in both requested and requesting jurisdictions;
(ii) *speciality*; a person shall be tried or punished, after extradition, only for the criminal conduct for which his surrender has been made, unless the requested state, after surrender, gives consent to further trial or punishment.

These principles appear expressly in most extradition treaties and bilateral arrangements, and where they do not, their existence may often be presumed from other instruments or statutory provisions, or from the nature of the arrangement itself.[1] Under the Extradition Act 2003, it is unnecessary for many purposes to examine any underlying treaties, but this statute was of course enacted against the background of international agreements and conventions.

This chapter discusses the problems inherent in identifying the criminal conduct alleged by the requesting state, seeks to demonstrate the prevalence of the broad

[1] The Fugitive Offenders Act 1967, and the succeeding provisions applicable to Commonwealth countries and colonies in the Extradition Act 1989, for example, did not expressly require double criminality, but the Commonwealth scheme of 1966 on which these provisions were based assumes the existence of similar systems of law in the countries to which it applies.

conduct-based approach to extradition and points to consequential difficulties that can arise in the requested state after return.

II. DOUBLE CRIMINALITY

2–002 Before the 2003 Act, the modern United Kingdom statutory technique, employed in the body of the Extradition Act 1989, was to classify conduct according to the level of sentence which the crime can attract, subject to exceptions in the case of political or military offences, etc. An exception remained in Sch.1 to the 1989 Act, in which the old list system, deriving from statute and treaty, remained.

Whichever system is used, a recurring problem arises. How is the requesting state to identify the criminal conduct of which the fugitive is accused or has been convicted? Is that conduct to be found in the generality of the witness statements and exhibits which accompany a request for extradition, or in the particulars of the foreign offence as set out in the foreign warrant or indictment?

The question has been considered in most developed jurisdictions in recent decades, but writers were emphasising the general "conduct" basis of extradition crimes before the matter was considered definitively by the highest courts. Shearer observed[2]:

> "The basic rule observed by the enumerative and 'no list' treaties alike is the rule of double criminality. This rule requires that an act shall not be extraditable unless it constitutes a crime according to the laws of both the requesting and requested States . . . The validity of the double criminality rule has never seriously been contested, resting as it does in part on the basic principle of reciprocity, which underlies the whole structure of extradition, and in part on the maxim *nulla poena sine lege*. For the double criminality rule serves the most important role of ensuring that a person's liberty is not restricted as a consequence of offences not recognised as criminal by the requested state. The social conscience is not embarrassed by an obligation to extradite a person who would, according to its own standards, be guilty of acts deserving punishment."

Mr Justice La Forest wrote[3]:

> "An extradition crime may broadly be defined as an act of which a person is accused, or has been convicted, of having committed within the jurisdiction of one state that constitutes a crime in that state and in the state where that person is found, and that is mentioned or described in an extradition treaty between those states under a name or description by which it is known in each state.

[2] *Extraditionin International Law* (1971), p.137.
[3] *Extradition to and from Canada* (2nd ed., 1977).

This definition can be broken down into several propositions:

(1) the act charged must have been committed within the jurisdiction of the demanding state;
(2) it must be a crime in the demanding state;
(3) it must also be a crime in the requested state; and
(4) it must be listed in an extradition treaty between the two states under some name or description by which it is known in each state."

THE ENGLISH LAW APPROACH

The English courts have tackled the question, characteristically, as a matter of strict statutory construction. They reached radically different conclusions under the Extradition Act 1870 and Fugitive Offenders Act 1967. These conclusions need to be studied so that the provisions of the 2003 Act can be better understood. 2–003

"EXTRADITION CRIME" IN THE 1870 ACT AND SCH.1 TO THE EXTRADITION ACT 1989; THE RULE IN *NIELSEN* AND *MCCAFFERY*

In 1984 the House of Lords held conclusively in these two separate cases[4] that, in order to determine whether a person who was alleged to have committed an "extradition crime" in a foreign state with which a bilateral extradition arrangement had been made, it was necessary to look only at the conduct disclosed in the evidence supplied by the requesting state in, or pursuant to, its request. However, the history of the subject illuminates the problem identified above. 2–004

Section 6 of the 1870 Act declared that, where that Act applied in the case of any foreign state, every "fugitive criminal" of that state in or suspected of being in England:

> "shall be liable to be apprehended and surrendered in manner provided by this act."

A fugitive criminal was defined by s.26 as:

> "Any person accused or convicted of an extradition crime committed within the jurisdiction of any foreign state"

The definition of "extradition crime" provided by s.26 was:

> "The term 'extradition crime' means a crime which, if committed in England or within English jurisdiction, would be one of the crimes described in the first schedule to this Act."

[4] *Re Nielsen* [1984] A.C. 606; *Government of the United States of America v McCaffery* [1984] 1 W.L.R. 867.

Those crimes, as supplemented by later legislation, were described in terms of English law.

It has been noted in Ch.1 that the pre-1870 Acts, directly enacting the terms of bilateral treaties, contained short lists of crimes for which fugitives might be extradited. *Re Winsor*[5] decided that a fugitive, accused of forgery contrary to a law of the State of New York, was not liable to be extradited, since his fraudulent conduct, though criminal in English law, was not "forgery" according to the English statute. The offences had to be the same in both countries.

EARLY CASES

2–005 The early judicial attitudes to the 1870 Act clearly foreshadowed the Nielsen approach, rejecting the scheme of the old Acts. For example, Stephen J. in *R. v Jacobi and Hiller*[6] pointed out:

> " Every one of the extradition crimes, when you come to look at them, are taken from English law, and everybody who is at all familiar with such subjects must be well aware of the fact that the definitions of crimes given in the law of England are peculiar to English law . . . For instance, in some cases, the English definitions are wider, and in some other cases the English definitions are narrower, than those which prevail on the Continent . . . For instance the definition of manslaughter, which is one of the crimes for which extradition may be made, according to English law, is exceedingly wide. Suppose it be a fact, as I rather think it is, a foreign magistrate, acting according to the French or the German Penal Code, were to issue a warrant for a man's apprehension for having in some way wounded or assaulted another, which wound had been followed by death; and suppose that assaulting or wounding was not an extradition crime, if it appeared in evidence before the magistrate that death had followed upon such wounding, then, although the man might be tried, and probably would be tried, for something very much less than causing death, viz., for causing the injury which led to death, I think the magistrate, if he saw his way to commit him for manslaughter if the act had been done in England, would have to issue his warrant for extradition."

(This assumes, of course, that manslaughter is within the descriptions of extraditable offences within the treaty.)

The Royal Commission extradition of 1878, of which Stephen J. was a member, had no doubt that this was correct:

> "It is and always must be necessary that a prima facie case shall be made out before a magistrate in order to support the application for extradition. But the

[5] (1865) 10 Cox C.C. 118.
[6] L.T 46 (NS) 595, 597.

English magistrate cannot be expected to know or interpret the foreign law. It is not desirable that he should be required to do more than to see that the facts proved constitute prima facie an offence which would have been within the judicial cognizance if done within this country.

At the same time, while holding that the acts against the party whose surrender is asked for should constitute an offence by our law, we by no means intend to say that the offence under the foreign law must be the same in point of denomination, or must fall within the same class or category, or be dealt with according to the same procedure, or be subject to the same punishment as it would be under our own. Any such requirement is calculated to create unnecessary difficulty, and may cause obstruction where extradition ought undoubtedly to take place. It being once ascertained that the facts proved constitute an offence coming within the principle of extradition, the particular form and character which the offence assumes must be left to the foreign law, this being the law which is alleged to have been broken, and by which, beyond all question, if the accused is surrendered, his guilt or innocence must be determined. The magistrate, therefore, should be authorised to grant extradition upon sufficient proof before him of facts which constitute an extradition offence, although the description of the offence in the demand, or in the documents produced in support of it, or the facts as therein stated, may not be sufficient to constitute the particular offence to which that description is appropriated by British law; in other words, the magistrate should look to the facts proved before him rather than to the form in which the case may be presented on the documents."

THE "SUBSTANTIAL SIMILARITY" ERROR

From 1890 onwards, a less disciplined approach crept into the law. The courts fell into the error of holding that, as a matter of course, it was necessary for the magistrate, exercising his duties under ss.9 and 10 (paras 6 and 7 of Sch.1 to the Extradition Act 1989), to consider whether the crime alleged was a crime against the law of both requesting and requested state, and to consider the relevant treaty for this purpose. 2–006

In Re Bellencontre[7] clearly shows the "substantial similarity" error. The Government of France requisitioned for the return of Bellencontre for 19 offences of fraud. The magistrate committed him to prison, describing the offences as "fraud by a bailee and fraud by an agent", adopting the words of the extraditable offences listed both in the first schedule to the act and in the treaty. It is clear from the report[8] that the order to proceed of the Secretary of State (described as his "warrant") also described the offences as "fraud by a bailee". Cave J. recited the terms of the French warrant, which stated an offence of fraud under item 18 in the list of extraditable offences of the treaty, and noted that the Secretary of State translated this into the

[7] [1891] 2 Q.B. 122.
[8] at 136.

English version of item 18 as "fraud by a bailee, which expresses in more general terms what is expressed more specifically in the French warrant". It is submitted that this was an error. The Secretary of State was describing an extradition crime, or a group of them, listed in the schedule, which incidentally coincided with the language of the treaty. The warrant of committal alleged "fraud by a bailee".

In *Re Arton (No.2)*[9] the High Court set itself a similar task:

> "We are here dealing with a crime alleged to have been committed against the law of France; and if we find, as I hold that we do, that such a crime is a crime against the law of both countries, and is, in substance, to be found in each version of the treaty, although under different heads, we are bound to give effect to the claim for extradition."

The Court remitted the case to the magistrate to set out that the crime of "faux" had been committed.

2–007 A similar approach was taken in *R. v Dix*,[10] an American request, in which the magistrate committed for two charges. It was conceded that the first charge, "based upon a statute of the State of Washington", did not allege conduct criminal in England. But the magistrate also committed on a second "information" for an offence contrary to s.81 of the Larceny Act 1861. Darling J. held on the application for habeas corpus:

> "But the essential thing was to see whether what the evidence showed prima facie that the prisoner had done was a crime in both countries, and came within the treaty"

It seemed to him:

> "that in this case the same thing had been made a criminal offence in England and in the United States"

but it was not essential that the offence should be called by the same name in both countries. The case was remitted for the magistrate to amend his warrant of committal to delete the first charge. In *R. v Governor of Brixton Prison Ex p. Ecke*,[11] the Divisional Court, following *Arton (No.2)*, regarded its duty as satisfying itself that the crime alleged was a crime within English law and within the descriptions of both versions of the UK-Germany treaty.

In *R. v Governor of Pentonville Prison Ex p. Budlong*,[12] a request from the United States of America, it was alleged that Budlong and another had organised a burglary of government offices in which copies of documents relating to the Church of

[9] [1896] 1 Q.B. 509, 517.
[10] (1902) 18 T.L.R 231, 232.
[11] (1973) 73 Cr. App. R. 223.
[12] [1980] 1 W.L.R 1110.

Scientology, of which they were members, were stolen. After committal, their grounds of application for habeas corpus contained the argument:

> "that the American definitions of the crime ought to have been identical, since, in accordance with the principle of double criminality, the offence had to be established under both American and English law."

Rejecting the argument, Griffiths J. appreciated the theoretical risk that, unless identity of offence is required, a person might be extradited from England and be convicted where he would not be convicted here. He concluded[13]:

> ". . . double criminality in our law is satisfied if it is shown: that the crime for which extradition is demanded would be substantially similar in both countries; that there is a prima facie case that the conduct of the accused amounted to the commission of a crime according to English law."

Two reasons may be suggested why the original strict English law approach to the words "extradition crime" became obscured. First, s.10 of the Act required the magistrate to commit for sufficiency of evidence "if the foreign warrant authorising the arrest of such criminal is duly authenticated"; such a warrant will naturally draw the attention of the court to the foreign offence; secondly, thc identification of the "crime" in the Secretary of State's order to proceed under s.7 appears often, especially in the early cases, to have been expressed in the general words of the treaty rather than in terms of an English crime.

THE BROAD CONDUCT TEST

Nielsen was charged in Denmark with " breach of trust", which appeared to be a broad continuing offence of dishonesty by a person occupying a fiduciary position as a company director, and which embraced many accusations of individual acts. McCaffery was charged with committing "wire fraud" in the United States, a charge involving activity committed between, or in, more than one state. This type of charge is a common device employed by the federal prosecutors in the United States to remove a case from state jurisdiction into the federal courts. 2–008

In each case, the Secretary of State specified in his order to proceed various crimes under the Theft Act 1968, which formed the basis of several charges before the magistrate's court, upon which the magistrate committed. The magistrate declined to commit Nielsen because, referring to Divisional Court authority,[14] he considered that it was necessary that the charges in requesting and requested state should be "substantially similar in concept" and, as he put it, "aimed at the same evil."

[13] at 1120H.

[14] *Ex p. Budlong* (in which it was held that such a test was satisfied).

The Divisional Court allowed the application for judicial review brought by the requesting state,[15] holding that the Secretary of State must select the charge on the order to proceed which the magistrate is to examine "by reference to the crime of which the fugitive is accused or convicted by the foreign law", provided that that crime appears within the list of crimes appearing in the treaty with the state concerned. The judgment of Robert Goff L.J. referred repeatedly to the "conduct complained of" and proceeded upon the basis that the Secretary of State paid attention primarily to the conduct alleged by the foreign charge rather than the generality of the facts contained in the evidence supplied. It was only, of course, if the Secretary of State could determine that the fugitive criminal was accused of conduct which was a crime in the requesting state, and within the treaty, that he had jurisdiction to issue an order to proceed at all.

The House of Lords upheld the decision of the Divisional Court. Lord Diplock observed[16] that the Act did not specify that any particular documents needed to be sent by the foreign state with its "requisition", and, since the treaty between the United Kingdom and Denmark referred to the "acts charged against him", there would be no difficulty in examining the conduct alleged and specifying an appropriate English charge. He pointed out that in the Danish treaty, the agreed list of crimes for which extradition might be granted corresponded to the list in the first schedule to the 1870 Act.

2–009 The Secretary of State should identify in his order to proceed the crimes that the magistrate should consider, selecting them from the offences falling within the list, described in English law. The magistrate had then to determine simply whether the evidence presented disclosed an offence in English law upon which he would commit for trial had the offence been committed in England. The House of Lords considered that the magistrate had no power to examine the foreign law, except in cases (unlike *Nielsen's*) where a treaty required specifically that a crime had to be criminal, or extraditable, under the laws of both requesting and requested state. This *obiter dictum* was disapproved by the House of Lords seven years later: it was the function of the Secretary of State to ensure compliance with the treaty, not the magistrate.[17]

McCaffery was charged with "wire fraud" ("using wire, radio or television to transmit communications for fraudulent purposes in interstate commerce"), a federal offence, centred on Georgia, USA. There is, of course, no corresponding offence in English law. It should be noted in relation to *McCaffery's* case that the treaty with the United States contained a "Protocol of Signature", constituting an agreement that Art.III permits the extradition to the United States of persons:

> "for an offence to which the treaty relates when the United States federal jurisdiction is based on interstate transport or transportation or the use of mails or of interstate facilities, these aspects being jurisdictional only".[18]

[15] *R. v Chief Metropolitan Magistrate Ex p. Government of Denmark* (1984) 79 Cr. App. R. 1.
[16] [1984] A.C. 606, 614 *et seq.*
[17] *R. v Governor of Pentonville Prison Ex p. Sinclair* [1991] 2 A.C. 64, HL.
[18] [1984] 1 W.L.R. 867, 871F; 7.

The House of Lords applied the same rule.[19] These two cases settled the basic principle. It may be said that, as in many extradition cases in the House of Lords, there was a strong "policy" aspect in these decisions.[20] The process of obtaining extradition from the United Kingdom was normally successful, but was time-consuming, and attended by unnecessary technicalities. Undoubtedly, there was some merit in the argument presented by the defendants. If, they argued, a man had been accused of a wide offence in the requesting state, reflected before the magistrate in 18 separate charges of Theft Act offences, how was the speciality rule to be enforced? This problem is explored in the "Speciality" section of this chapter.

HOW MUCH OF THE CONDUCT IS TRANSFERRED?

The simplicity of the *Nielsen* approach left open a difficult and interesting question. 2–010
A foreign jurisdiction may allege that a person is guilty of dishonesty in his management of a company because he appropriated or falsely accounted for property by failing to observe the terms of a banking or company law regulation. The question may turn on the true interpretation of such an instrument. There are two possible approaches: (1) the magistrate does not interpret the foreign law, but asks himself simply whether the conduct, if it had occurred in England, would be dishonest, perhaps because it would breach some provision of the Companies Act or Banking Act; or (2) he transposes the foreign regulatory system into English law and decides, with the help of evidence as to its true import, whether the defendant is prima facie guilty of theft or false accounting by acting in breach of it.

The question was raised but not resolved in *R. v Secretary of State Ex p. Norgren*,[21] in which it was argued that an allegation of insider dealing committed in the United States was not an extradition crime because the United Kingdom statute applied only in relation to dealings on the London Stock Exchange, and the dealings complained of took place in relation to an overseas exchange. Does the act require simply a notional transfer of the conduct, or should the United Kingdom authorities also substitute the identity of the exchange concerned? The issue may also be likely to arise in cases involving alleged tax fraud. It is notable that the draftsman of the replacement for Art.5 of the European Convention on Extradition, effected by the Second Additional Protocol of 1978,[22] felt it necessary to deal with this issue expressly by requiring correspondence in the case of "offences in connection with taxes, duties, customs and exchange", but stating that extradition:

> "may not be refused on the ground that the law of the requested Party does not impose the same kind of tax or duty or does not contain a tax, duty, customs, or exchange regulation of the same kind as the law of the requesting Party".

[19] [1984] 1 W.L.R. 867.
[20] Often referred to as "purposive construction".
[21] [2000] 3 W.L.R. 181.
[22] Embodied in The European Convention on Extradition (Fiscal Offences) Order 1993 (SI 1993/2663) (in force from June 6, 1994).

"RELEVANT OFFENCE" IN THE FUGITIVE OFFENDERS ACT 1967; THE RULE IN *ARONSON*

2–011 A completely different and strict approach to double criminality was adopted in this statute, no doubt for the historical reasons discussed in Ch.1. This formulation has obvious similarities with the approach to "extradition offence" in the 2003 Act. Surrender might be made only for a "relevant offence". This had to be in the first instance one "within the description" of offences listed in Sch.1 to the Act and punishable by at least 12 months' imprisonment. In addition, it was necessary to show under s.3(1)(c) that the:

> "act or omission constituting the offence, or the equivalent act or omission, would constitute an offence against the law of the United Kingdom . . .".

The 1967 Act concentrated therefore upon the elements of the legal offence charged. It accordingly became necessary to show that the offence alleged in the requesting country contained all the elements necessary to establish an offence within the description of crimes listed in the schedule, particularly because s.3(2) required:

> "In determining for the purposes of this section whether an offence against the law of a designated Commonwealth country falls within a description set out in the said Schedule 1, any special intent or state of mind or special circumstances of aggravation which may be necessary to constitute that offence under the law shall be disregarded."

An example of the problems posed is provided by s.338(1) of the Criminal Code of Canada, with which the defendant had been charged in the case of *Government of Canada v Aronson*[23]:

> "Everyone who, by deceit, falsehood or other fraudulent means, whether or not it is a false pretence within the meaning of this Act, defrauds the public . . . is guilty of an indictable offence."

A person might have been guilty of this offence in Canada who would not have been guilty of any offence in England. The English offences most nearly resembling this crime were theft and obtaining property by deception, contrary to ss.1 and 15 of the Theft Act 1968. Each English offence required the additional element of an intention permanently to deprive; and s.15 required proof of a deception which operated on the minds of the victim. The Canadian offence appeared to have alleged a substantive crime of "fraud", which in England was not by itself criminal in the absence of conspiracy. A person charged under s.338(1) could therefore be convicted in Canada but acquitted in England on the same facts.

[23] [1989] 1 A.C. 579.

Attempts were made between 1967 and 1989 on the part of requesting states in three cases to argue that the words "act or omission constituting the offence" referred to the conduct alleged. Upon an allegation under s.338(1), for example, this construction would require a magistrate to commit to prison if he found that the elements of the nearest English offence alleged were *prima facie* satisfied, provided that the schedule requirement of the 1967 Act was met. The argument in the Divisional Court failed within a year of the new Act[24] and again in 1972.[25] 2–012

The matter was not tested in the House of Lords until 1989, when the 1967 scheme was about to be replaced. Aronson had allegedly committed 78 offences in Canada. His conduct was said to have been the obtaining of computer equipment from retailers, by various deceptions and the use of forged documents, without an intention to pay for them. Having been committed by the magistrate on all but one of the charges, the Divisional Court held that it was bound by the case of *Gardner* to interpret s.3 narrowly, and allowed the application for habeas corpus in relation to 69 of the 77 charges. Both judges expressed the view that, unconstrained by authority, they would have preferred the "conduct" interpretation.

The House of Lords refused the appeal by the Government of Canada by a majority of three to two and upheld the interpretation in *Gardner*,[26] holding that the 1967 Act prohibited Aronson's return from England to Canada in order to be charged with the s.338(1) offences.

This requirement, repealed by the 1989 Act, had curious consequences in the case of Aronson. The offences had allegedly been committed in different parts of Canada, and prosecutors had followed different practices in respect of the same alleged conduct. It was a matter of haphazard that the surviving eight charges, alleging contraventions of other sections of the Code, did indeed pass the test of s.3.

THE RATIONALE OF THE RULE IN *ARONSON*

However, there was clear logic behind the restriction embodied by the concept of the "relevant offence". Parliament must have intended to make it impossible for a fugitive to be returned from England to a Commonwealth country, and to be convicted upon findings of fact which would have required his acquittal in England. For this reason, it enacted, not that the legal elements of the offence in the requesting state and England be identical, but that all of the elements of the corresponding offence in English law must be present in the foreign offence. If the Canadian offence contained elements A, B and C, but the English contained A, B, C and D, the fugitive could not be returned. He could be returned, however, in the converse case. 2–013

24 *R. v Governor of Brixton Prison Ex p. Gardner* [1968] 2 Q.B. 399 (a New Zealand request).

25 *Ex p. Myers*, unreported, December 6, 1972 (Canada). See also *Ex p. Rush* [1969] 1 W.L.R. 165; and *Ex p. Teja* [1971] 2 Q.B. 274.

26 Aronson became, therefore, only the third "defendant" (after Armah and Kakis) to win his case in the House of Lords in a case under the Fugitive Offenders Acts.

THE EXTRADITION ACT 1989 APPROACH

2–014 The Extradition Act 1989 adopted a new formula (except in Sch.1 which preserved for certain foreign states the 1870 scheme). Where procedures under Pt III of that Act would be available, a person in the United Kingdom who:

> "(a) is accused in that state of the commission of an extradition crime ; or
> (b) is alleged to be unlawfully at large after conviction of an extradition crime by a court in that state,
>
> may be arrested and returned to that state in accordance with those procedures."

"Extradition crime" is described in s.2(1). The basic test is:

> "In this Act, except in Schedule 1, 'extradition crime' means;
>
> (e) conduct in the territory of a foreign state, a designated Commonwealth country or a colony which, if it occurred in the United Kingdom, would constitute an offence punishable with imprisonment for a term of twelve months, or any greater punishment, and which, however described in the law of the foreign Commonwealth country or colony, is so punishable under that law;
> (b) . . . [extraterritorial offences]"

THE TIMING POINT

2–015 It was argued for the Government of Spain in *R. v Bow Street Magistrates Court Ex p. Pinochet (No.3)*[27] that the question whether the conduct was punishable in the United Kingdom fell to be determined at the time of the extradition request, not at the time the conduct was committed; there was an abundance of protections for defendants in the Act, and to hold that the matter was to be tested at the time of the conduct was likely (a) to lead to anomalies when states ratified international conventions at different times; and (b) to frustrate the legitimate use of conspiracy charges which might span a time when the law changed in England.

The Divisional Court[28] agreed unanimously. Lord Lloyd strongly supported that approach on the first hearing of the appeal.[29] At the second full hearing, it was also argued on behalf of the requesting state[30] that the legislative history of the 1989 Act supported the holding. Sections 5 and 9 of the Fugitive Offenders Act 1881, and

[27] [2000] 1 A.C. 147.
[28] Lord Bingham of Cornhill C.J.; Collins and Richards J.J.
[29] [2000] 1 A.C 61, 88E.
[30] 181F–185A.

s.3(1) of the Fugitive Offenders Act 1967, suggested a "present tense" examination of the double criminality test, a simple logical exercise quite separate from the examination of the conduct as required by other provisions of those acts. This was to be read into the scheme of the 1989 Act. None of the Lords of Appeal commented upon this argument, deciding the matter by reference to the definition of "extradition crime" in the 1870 Act alone.

The House of Lords held[31] that the test was whether the conduct would have been punishable in this country at the time it took place. Accordingly, since the offence of torture, enacted pursuant to the United Nations Convention on Torture of 1984, became a crime in England only in December 1998,[32] offences of torture committed earlier were not extradition crimes, because, if committed outside the jurisdiction, they would not then have been punishable or criminal in the United Kingdom.[33]

A developing tendency in modern extradition statutes is to stipulate expressly that the time of the request is the point at which the criminality of the conduct is to be assessed. See, for example, s.19(2)(c) of the Australian Extradition Act 1988, cited below, and Art.2(4) of the Australia-Hong Kong extradition treaty.

"CONDUCT" IN THE 1989 ACT

The use of the word "conduct" in s.2(1)(a) suggested that the draftsman sought to reflect the *Nielsen* approach. On the other hand, the statutory reference to the foreign legal provision relating to sentence raised again the question not decisively answered by the *Nielsen* and *McCaffery* decisions, namely, did the Secretary of State identify the extradition crime by reference to the crime as particularised in the foreign warrant or indictment, or by the generality of the evidence provided in the particulars or evidential materials sent by the requesting state? The approach of the Divisional Court in *Nielsen* suggested the former: of the House of Lords in that case, the latter. 2–016

It was not essential for the House of Lords to provide such definitive guidance in the 1870 Act cases, which were concerned primarily with the powers of the magistrate who acted under a statutory scheme which did not require by express provision any reference to the foreign law.

Why, if the draftsman of the 1989 Act intended to follow the *Nielsen* approach, did he introduce this express requirement to consider the law of both states? There are two answers. First, the "list" system of defining extraditable conduct is replaced by the 1989 Act by the more flexible 12 months' imprisonment rule which does not require statutory amendment when new criminal offences are created. The sentence provision reflects, of course, the very similar provision in Art.2 of the European Convention on Extradition, and is taken from the repealed Criminal Justice Act 1988, which was designed to apply only to foreign states with which new arrangements would be made.

31 [2000] A.C. 147, 193–6.

32 s.134 of the Criminal Justice Act 1988.

33 For a further criticism, see Michael Birnbaum Q.C., "Pinochet and Double Criminality" [2000] Crim. L.R. 127.

2–017 Secondly, it is important to bear in mind that the new 1989 definition of "extradition crime" applies to designated Commonwealth countries and colonies, as well as to foreign states with which extradition arrangements under Pt III will be available. The Act does not require that there be any formal agreement with Commonwealth countries, but some form of double criminality stipulation was needed to replace the strict and rigorous requirements of the 1967 Act.

The legislative history of the 1989 Act suggested that the intention of Parliament in 1989 was to provide a broad conduct test. The Green Paper of February 1985 (Cmnd.9421) had as its third Recommendation:

> "The double criminality rule contained in the 1870 Act, as it has been interpreted by the courts (most recently in *McCaffery*), should be reproduced in new legislation."

The White Paper "Plans for Justice" of March 1986 (Cm.9658) did not support an argument that Parliament intended in 1989 to narrow the criteria for extradition. It referred (para.48) to the challenges presented by the "huge expansion in international crime"and continued:

> "It is also clear that parts of our law and practice do not fit easily with those of many of our countries with which we have or would wish to have extradition arrangements. The United Kingdom is thus widely regarded as one of the most difficult countries from which to secure extradition."

THE EUROPEAN CONVENTION ON EXTRADITION

2–018 The European Convention on Extradition contained a simple test in Art.2, which does not expressly answer the question whether extradition is offence-based or conduct-based:

> "ARTICLE 2
>
> EXTRADITABLE OFFENCES
>
> Extradition shall be granted in respect of offences punishable under the laws of the requesting Party and of the requested Party by deprivation of liberty or under a detention order for a maximum period of at least a year or by a more severe penalty"

In fact the *travaux preparatoires* of the European Convention disclose that much discussion took place about the double criminality requirement in the five years before the Convention was signed in 1957. So, for example, the substantial document "Recommendation 66", adopted by the Consultative Assembly of the Council of

Europe in 1954, contained a version of Art.1, almost identical to the final Article, headed "Extraditable Acts". The Recommendation cites Professor Brierley[34] with approval:

> "On the whole we consider that, if the States should decide to adopt a general convention on extradition the most convenient method of dealing with this particular matter would be to grant extradition for any act punishable with a certain severity, either in the two States concerned, or in the State demanding extradition, and not attempt a detailed list of crimes."

The draft of Art.2 of the Convention in Recommendation 66 (then numbered Art.1) read as follows:

> "The following persons shall be liable to extradition:
>
> (a) Persons claimed by a High Contracting Party for an act which is an offence in both the requesting and requested High Contracting Parties and is punishable in the requesting High Contracting Party by at least one year's imprisonment; and
> (b) Persons who have already been convicted of such an offence and have already been sentenced to at least three months' imprisonment in the requesting High Contracting Party."

Nothing in the substantial papers retained by the Council of Europe suggests that by 1957 the Council intended to enforce a regime requiring similarity of legal ingredients. Although a scheme requiring similar elements of offence is plausible, and indeed worked fairly well until 1990 under the Fugitive Offenders Act 1967, operating in relation to legal systems which had a common origin, and which employed the same language, it is not reasonable to assume that the draftsmen of the European Convention between 1952 and 1957 took the same approach. The negotiators included lawyers and government officials from the United Kingdom and a wide variety of continental jurisdictions. They could not have contemplated that extradition would lie only where the offences in requesting and requested countries were of a similar kind; and would not be granted where, for example, the English authorities had charged conspiracy, which might be an offence unknown to the law of a particular continental jurisdiction.

Against this background, the broad *Nielsen* "conduct" approach was affirmed in the context of the 1989 Act by the Divisional Court in *R. v Secretary of State for the Home Department Ex p. Hill.*[35] The defendant was accused on a South African indictment, with others, of forgery and uttering forged documents, common law offences in South Africa which resembled the English offences of making and using false instruments under ss.1 and 3 of the Forgery and Counterfeiting Act 1981. 2–019

[34] Report to a Committee of Experts of the League of Nations (*Publication of the League of Nations v Legal*, 1926) (Brierley wrote his first edition of *The Law of Nations* in 1928).

[35] [1999] Q.B. 886 (decided in February 1997); the first extradition request from South Africa after it became a "designated Commonwealth country" on March 18, 1996.

The authority to proceed issued by the Secretary of State specified offences of making and using false instruments, and also conspiracy to commit such offences, and conspiracy to obtain by deception. It was argued that the defendant was not "accused" of conspiracy within the meaning of s.1 of the 1989 Act, but only of substantive offences; the "conduct" of which he was accused was not the act of agreement which is the essence of a charge of conspiracy, and was not punishable by 12 months' imprisonment or more within the meaning of s.2(1)(a).

The court acknowledged that[36]:

> "It is probably simpler to find the conduct in the charges rather than the evidence or other material furnished to the Secretary of State and the committal court. It would avoid the rather unlikely situation of the requesting state requesting his return for one offence, e.g. a substantive offence and he being returned on and only on a different offence, e.g. conspiracy."

Nonetheless, the court concluded,[37] citing from Lord Diplock's speech in *Nielsen*:

> "In my judgment, the Secretary of State is entitled to include in the authority to proceed any offences under the laws of this country which are disclosed by the documents accompanying the request."

This applied even where the indictment did not include a factual allegation that there had been an agreement. The House of Lords refused leave to appeal.

Similar arguments were advanced by the defence in *R. v Bow Street Magistrates Court Ex p. Pinochet (No.3)*.[38] The second provisional warrant of October 1998, and the authority to proceed of December 1998, contained allegations of conspiracy to commit torture and other offences. The House of Lords determined that charges of hostage-taking were not justified on the facts of the request, but nonetheless upheld the provisional warrant and authority to proceed so far as the offence of conspiracy to torture was concerned, although the Spanish warrant did not accuse the defendant of the crime of conspiracy. The case of *Hill* was cited, and not disapproved, but none of the speeches analysed the question whether similarity of offence was required. By implication the House of Lords can be taken to have proceeded on the basis that *Hill* was rightly decided.

THE LAW OF COMMONWEALTH COUNTRIES

2–020 The statutes of Commonwealth countries show a variety of statutory formulations of the double criminality rule. Some (such as St. Christopher and Nevis) maintain unchanged the Extradition Act 1870 and Orders in Council in force at the time of independence. The following examples are not intended to be exhaustive, but to

[36] at 905G.
[37] at 908G.
[38] [2000] A.C. 147.

show the employment, at different times, of different techniques, which may be useful for comparative purposes.

The Privy Council considered the provisions of The Bahamas Extradition Act 1994 in *Rey v Government of Switzerland*.[39] This statute is in all essential respects identical to the Jamaican Extradition Act 1991. Each distinguishes between Commonwealth countries and foreign states, but each defines "extradition crime" as one that is punishable in the jurisdiction of the requesting state by two years imprisonment or more, and each contains the same definition set out in s.3(1)(c) of the UK Fugitive Offenders Act 1967, cited above. Neither statute, however, contains a section equivalent to s.3(2) of the 1967 Act. Lord Steyn, giving the judgment of the Board, construed the Bahamian provision in the context of other provisions of the same act, and concluded purposively that the statute in fact enacted a broad conduct approach. He held that it was not necessary that the elements of the Swiss offence should be identical or similar to those of the Bahamian offences put before the magistrate for the purposes of determining sufficiency of evidence.

It will remain important in Commonwealth jurisdictions which retain statutes similar to the Extradition Act 1870 and Fugitive Offenders Act 1967 to determine as a matter of precise statutory construction whether the *Nielsen* or *Aronson* approach is correct.

THE LONDON SCHEME

The terms of "A Scheme Relating to the Rendition of Fugitive Offenders within the Commonwealth" agreed by Ministers in 1966 (called the "London Scheme" by the Commonwealth Secretariat) are an important guide to construction of Commonwealth statutes regulating extradition between Commonwealth countries. **2–021**

Article 2 read:

> "(1) A fugitive will only be returned for a returnable offence.
>
> (2) For the purposes of this Scheme a returnable offence is an offence described in Annex 1 (whatever the name of the offence under the law of the countries and territories concerned and whether or not it is described in that law by reference to some special intent or any special circumstances of aggravation), being an offence which is punishable by a competent court in the country or territory to which return is requested by imprisonment for twelve months or a greater penalty."

Article 10 read:

> "The return of a fugitive offender will either be precluded by law or be subject to refusal by the competent executive authority if the facts on which the

[39] [1999] 1 A.C. 54.

request for his return is grounded do not constitute an offence under the law of the country or territory in which he was found."

Barbados is an example of a Commonwealth country which adopted this test almost verbatim in its Extradition Act 1980, and expressed as a statutory purpose its adoption of the principles in the London Scheme, applying it to foreign states and Commonwealth countries.

The third and latest version of the Scheme, as amended in 1990, reproduces the former Art.10 as Art.12, and contains an altered Art.2, namely:

"(1) [As before]

(2) For the purpose of this Scheme a returnable offence is an offence however described which is punishable in the part of the Commonwealth where the fugitive is located and the part of the Commonwealth to which return is requested by imprisonment for two years or a greater penalty.

(3) Offences described in paragraph (2) are returnable offences notwithstanding that any such offences are of a purely fiscal character, where such offences are returnable under the law of the requested part of the Commonwealth."

AUSTRALIA

2–022 Section 4(1A) of the Extradition (Foreign States) Act 1966 of Australia showed a different statutory approach to this problem. It was construed in *Commonwealth of Australia v Riley*[40] by the Federal Court of Australia. It read:

"An offence against the law of, or of a part of, a foreign state, is an extradition crime if, and only if, the act or omission constituting the offence, or, where the offence is constituted by more than one act or omission, any of those acts or omissions, or any equivalent act or omission, would, if it took place in, or within the jurisdiction of, the part of Australia where the persons accused . . . of the offence is found, constitute an offence against the law in force in that part of Australia that—

(a) is described in Schedule 1; or
(b) would be so described if the description concerned contained a reference to any intent or state of mind on the part of the person committing the offence, or to any circumstance of aggravation, necessary to constitute the offence."

Following and applying *McCaffery*, the court held that a person accused of the US offence of "continuing criminal enterprise" was liable to extradition because one or

[40] (1985) 57 A.L.R. 249; 87 I.L.R. 144; Deane J. expressed disapproval of the decision of the Divisional Court in the English case of *Ex p. Gardner*, above.

more of the acts constituting the composite US offence would be an offence against Australian law. However, extradition was refused for these offences, though not of others alleged in the case, because the offence of continuing criminal enterprise was not within the relevant treaty.

The Australian Extradition Act 1988 repealed this semi-*Aronson* approach, so as to define (for all practical purposes) "extradition offence" as offences attracting a minimum sentence of 12 months' imprisonment or the death penalty (s.5). The statute repeatedly uses the phrase "conduct constituting the offence". Section 19(2)(c) declares that a person is liable to extradition only if:

> "the magistrate is satisfied that, if the conduct of the person constituting the offence in relation to the extradition country or equivalent conduct, had taken place in the part of Australia where the extradition proceedings are being conducted and at the time at which the extradition request in relation to the persons was received, that conduct would have constituted an extradition offence in relation to that part of Australia."

"Continuing criminal enterprise"[41] and "RICO"[42] are crimes in the United States which have little correspondence with criminal offences in other countries. Like "wire fraud" and "mail fraud in interstate commerce", they are characteristic of the modern US tendency to create composite crimes alleging, in one count, repeated or continuing activity. English lawyers sometimes look at them with suspicion.[43] They contrast sharply with the traditional English common law approach of penalising only individual acts and omissions, as required by the procedural rule against duplicity. These US offences should not, however, be regarded less favourably by extradition courts on that account. Lord Macaulay's Indian Penal Code, in force in India from 1860, and still the basis of the criminal law of India, Bangladesh, Singapore and much of Malaysia, contains lucid examples of offences capable of penalising, in one allegation or count, continuing criminal conduct. Section 409, for example, reads:

> "Whoever, being in any manner entrusted with property, or with any dominion over property, in his capacity of a public servant, or in the way of his business as a banker, factor, broker, attorney, or agent, commits criminal breach of trust in respect of that property, shall be punished . . ."

Our own English offences of fraudulent trading, and, particularly, the regularly enlarged common law offences of conspiracy to defraud, cheating the revenue, and

41 (1988) 21 U.S.C.A 1961–8.

42 *Racketeer-Influenced and Corrupt Organisations* (1988) 21 U.S.C.A 848 (b).

43 Two judges considered in the Divisional Court in *McCaffery* that such crimes were not extradition crimes under the 1870 Act.

doing acts tending to pervert the course of justice, are also allegations of continuing crime, which break the spirit of the rule against duplicity, and promote the role of the judge as a fact-finder after a general verdict of guilty by a jury. These wide offences are much less sharply fashioned than the American examples cited above, or the breach of trust offences made criminal in continental Europe and under the Indian Penal Code.

CANADA

2-023 The Ontario Supreme Court held in *Sudar v United States*[44] that a US indictment alleging an enterprise and a pattern of racketeering, based on acts of murder, arson and extortion, was not extraditable:

> "The only real substantive components of the indictment against Sudar for the purposes of the extradition are the conspiracy (very loosely defined in United States law) and the activities of murder, threats to murder, etc. There is no doubt as to the criminality of these activities and of any conspiracy in relation thereto. They are recognised as such the world over."

In *State of Washington v Canada*[45] the Supreme Court of Canada considered, in a conviction case, the following definition of extradition crime in s.2 of the Canadian Extradition Act R.S.C 1970:

> " 'extradition crime' may mean any crime that, if committed in Canada, or within Canadian jurisdiction would be one of the crimes described in Schedule 1; and in the application of this Act to the case of any extradition arrangement, 'extradition crime' means any crime described in such arrangement, whether or not it is comprised in that schedule."

The court agreed that "the double criminality rule is conduct based", noting that in 1974 the court had decided in *Cotroni v Attorney-General*[46] that the foreign offence alleged could have been laid under two wholly separate statues had it been committed in Canada, and that "[t]he test is what is the essence of the crime charged."

However, the application of that test did not lead to a finding that the defendant had been convicted of an extradition crime. The defendant had been convicted in the United States of "theft in the second degree". He had been given an organ on terms requiring him to return it within 30 days if he was unable to sell it for the owners. Such second degree theft, unlike the Canadian offence of theft, did not require proof of a fraudulent intent. The treaty between the two countries stipulated conventionally that

[44] (1981) 25 S.C.R. (3d) 183, 187.
[45] (1988) 40 C.C.C. (3d) 546.
[46] (1974) 18 C.C.C. (2d) 513.

the offence had to be punishable by the laws of both contracting parties by a term of imprisonment exceeding more than one year.

By a majority of four to three, the Supreme Court held that the double criminality requirement could be satisfied in one of two ways: either by calling evidence that fraudulent intent was indeed required by the law of the US state concerned, though the requirement did not appear on the face of the statute; or by establishing that the particular facts underlying the US charge would have constituted a Canadian offence of dishonesty under the Criminal Code. Neither of these tests was satisfied; and dishonesty could not be inferred from the fact of non-return alone.[47]

In 1990, in *Hagerman v United States*[48] the Canadian Court of Appeal held that, in an American request for return for continuing criminal enterprise, namely, a series of incidents relating to dangerous drugs that the law that the description of offences between the two countries must be matched had changed. It was no longer required that there be a complete correspondence between the definitions of a crime in the two countries. It was now based on conduct. The underlying drug offences were common to both countries and, therefore, the principle of double criminality in the treaty was not breached because "continuing criminal enterprise" was not itself a crime in Canada.

In 1997, the Canadian Supreme Court decisively re-affirmed the importance of the broad conduct test in *United States of America v Dynar*.[49] The fugitive had been the target of a failed "sting" operation in the United States and was charged with various money-laundering offences. The problem was that the US offence was complete where the person acted on a representation that money was the proceeds of crime, whether it was or not. The Canadian offence required that the money must actually have been the proceeds of crime, and that the accused knew that to be the case. The Supreme Court held in a detailed analysis of the Canadian and English criminal laws of conspiracy and attempt that the defendants could be extradited under the Canada Extradition Act of 1985, as amended in 1992, because their conduct disclosed offences of conspiracy and attempt "if their conduct had taken place here."

Section 3 of the Canadian Extradition Act 1999 contains requirements that the offence is punishable in the requesting jurisdiction by two years imprisonment or more, that the conduct of the person, had it occurred in Canada, would have constituted an offence punishable by at least two or (in the case of a request based on "a specific agreement") at least five years' imprisonment, and:

> "(2) For greater certainty it is not relevant whether the conduct referred to in subsection 1 is named, defined or characterised by the extradition partner in the same way as it is in Canada."

[47] The case illustrates the problems that can arise in a conviction case, where the basis of a jury's verdict may not be known.
[48] 92 I.L.R. 719.
[49] 147 D.L.R. (4th) 399.

TRINIDAD AND TOBAGO

2–024 The *Nielsen* approach has been followed in 1995 by the Trinidad and Tobago Court of Appeal in *Saroop v Maharaj*,[50] a dangerous drugs case brought by the US Government under the 1931 treaty between the US and the United Kingdom, which had continued after independence in 1962. The US conduct was represented in terms of the law of Trinidad and Tobago upon which the magistrate committed to custody.

HONG KONG

2–025 The Court of Appeal of Hong Kong unhesitatingly adopted the *Nielsen* conduct approach to extradition in a US continuing criminal enterprise case in 1987; *Levy v Attorney-General*.[51]

The 1997 treaty between Australia and Hong Kong Special Administrative Region[52] uses a clear technique to preserve the *Nielsen* approach. It preserves the list system of categorising offences, but uses it in very wide terms. Article 3(3) reads:

> "For the purposes of this Article, in determining whether an offence is an offence punishable under the laws of both Parties the totality of the acts or omissions alleged against the person whose surrender is sought shall be taken into account without reference to the elements of the offence prescribed by the law of the requesting party."

THE UNITED STATES OF AMERICA

2–026 In *Collins v Loisel*[53] the defendant was wanted in India for an offence of cheating, contrary to s.420 of the Indian Penal Code. This was described in evidence presented as an allegation of obtaining valuable property by false pretences. The fugitive argued that the offence of cheating was not among the offences listed in the applicable extradition treaty. (Treaties take effect automatically in the United States as part of the law of the land, and are instruments of which all courts, federal and state, take judicial notice; *United States v Rauscher*.[54])

Justice Brandeis pointed to the different descriptions of the offence contained in the requisition and observed:

> "The law does not require that the name by which the crime is described in the two countries shall be the same; nor that the liability shall be the same in the two countries. . . . The offence charged was clearly extraditable".[55]

50 [1996] Commonwealth L.R. 1.
51 90 I.L.R. 412.
52 Brought into force on June 29, 1997.
53 259 U.S. 309 (1922).
54 119 U.S. 407; 30 L. Ed. 425; 7 S. Ct. 234 (1886).
55 See also *Wright v Henkel* 190 U.S. 40 (1903) ; *Glucksman v Henkel* 221 U.S. 508 (1911).

In *Factor v Laubenheimer*[56] the Supreme Court of the United States went further and held that the crime of receiving money knowing it to be fraudulently obtained, for which the United Kingdom sought his extradition, was extraditable because it fell within the list of offences in the Webster-Ashburton Treaty of 1842, as supplemented by a later treaty of 1889, notwithstanding that it was not a crime against the law of the State of Illinois, where the fugitive was found.

THE HARVARD RESEARCH

The Draft Convention on Extradition prepared by the Harvard Research in International Law 1933–5[57] provided for a lucid factual approach to extradition: 2–027

> "Article 2. Extraditable acts.
> Except as otherwise provided in this Convention, a requested State shall extradite a person claimed for an act:
> (a) For which the law of the requesting State, in force when the act was committed, provides a possible penalty of death or deprivation of liberty for a period of two years or more; and
> (b) For which the law, in force in that part of the territory of the requested State in which the person claimed is apprehended, provides a possible penalty of death or deprivation of liberty for a period of two years or more, which would be applicable if the act were there committed."

THE MONTEVIDEO CONVENTION

The 1933 Convention, signed by 18 states and ratified by the United States, the Dominican Republic, Chile and Colombia between 1934 and 1936, adopted a similar position; 2–028

> "Each one of the signatory States in harmony with the stipulations of the present Convention assumes the obligation of surrendering to any one of the States which make the requisition the persons who may be in their territory and who are accused or are under sentence. This right shall be claimed only in the following circumstances:
> (a) That the demanding State have the jurisdiction to try and to punish the delinquency which is attributed to the individual whom it desires to extradite.
> (b) That the act for which extradition is sought constitutes a crime and is punishable under the laws of the demanding and surrendering States with a minimum penalty of imprisonment for one year."

56 290 U.S. 276 (1933); 54 S.Ct. 191.
57 American Journal of Int'l law, Vol.29, Nos 1 and 2, Jan and April 1935.

It was held in *Re Extradition of John Demjanjuk*[58] that because the extradition of the defendant, wanted for serious war crimes committed in the Second World War, was permitted by treaty, the extradition was not prohibited on the ground that the offence of "mass murder" was not prosecutable in the US.[59]

On appeal to the United States Court of Appeals, Sixth Circuit,[60] it was held that the double criminality requirement was satisfied. It was not necessary that the law of both states should describe the crime in the same way or that the scope of the liability should be the same in both states. It was enough that the particular act for which extradition was sought should be extraditable in both countries. Since the acts of which Demjanjuk was accused would constitute murder in every State in the United States, the fact that there was no separate offence of mass murder or the murder of Jews was irrelevant.

Article III of the treaty between the USA and the United Kingdom of 1972 itself suggests in its opening words a conduct-based approach by the words "extradition shall be granted for an act or omission the facts of which disclose an offence within any of the description listed in the Schedule annexed to this treaty . . .", although the succeeding provisions of the Article tend to obscure the clarity of the conduct-based approach.

2–029 The Government of the United States of America engages in a process of regular review and renegotiation of treaties, preferring bilateral treaties to the more cumbersome multilateral arrangements. An example of a modern US treaty, and its approach to the definition of extraditable crimes, may be found in the US-Bahamas treaty of March 1990. This definition plainly seeks to deal with the difficulties caused by such decisions as *Riley* in Australia, but thc emphasis in the language on offences, conspiracy, attempt, etc. is not, perhaps, entirely harmonious with the general "conduct" rather than "offence" approach of modern English-language jurisdictions. It lacks the clarity of the Harvard draft and the Montevideo Conventions:

> "Article 2:
>
> (1) An offense shall be an extraditable offense if it is punishable under the laws in both Contracting States by deprivation of liberty for a period of more than one year or by a more severe penalty.
> (2) An offense shall also be an extraditable offense if it consists of an attempt or conspiracy to commit, aiding or abetting, counselling or procuring the commission of, or being an accessory before or after the fact to, an offense described in paragraph 1.
> (3) For the purposes of this Article, an offense shall be an extraditable offense;

58 612 F. Supp. 544, 569 (N.D. Ohio 1985).

59 For the US position in greater detail, see Bassiouni, *International Extradition, United States Law and Practice* (1996), Ch.VII.

60 (1989) 79 I.L.R. 535; 776 F.2d 571 (6th Circuit 1985).

(a) whether or not the law in the Contracting States place the offense within the same category of offenses or describe the offense by the same terminology; or;

(b) whether or not the offense is one for which United States federal law requires the showing of interstate transportation, or use of the mails or other facilities affecting interstate or foreign commerce, such matters being merely for the purpose of establishing jurisdiction in a United States federal court.

(4) An offense described in this Article shall be an extraditable offense whether or not the offense was committed within the territory of the requesting state. However, if the offense was committed outside the territory of the requesting State, extradition shall be granted if the law of the Requested State provides for punishment of an offense committed outside its territory in similar circumstances."

SWITZERLAND

The Swiss Federal Tribunal had to consider in *M v Federal Department of Justice*[61] the treaty of 1880 made between the United Kingdom and Switzerland in a request from South Africa for the extradition of a man accused of fraud. The treaty, embodied in an Order in Council made pursuant to the 1870 Act, had been extended to South Africa before independence.[62] The Court concluded: 2–030

"By reason of its universal validity, double criminality was a tacit precondition for the application of the treaty . . . Provided that the act in question was punishable according to the criminal laws of both States it was not necessary that the facts charged were the subject of identical criminal provisions in the states concerned."

THE UNITED NATIONS MODEL TREATY

The United Nations "Model Treaty on Extradition", adopted by the General Assembly in 1991, is a clear expression of the conduct-based approach. Article 2(b) stipulates that it shall not matter whether: 2–031

"Under the laws of the Parties, the constituent elements of the offence differ, it being understood that the totality of the acts or omissions as presented by the requesting State shall be taken into account."

[61] (1979) 75 I.L.R. 107.

[62] A number of treaties negotiated between Great Britain and other European states in the early decades after 1870 survive between Commonwealth countries and those states, many years after independence, and long after they have been superseded in the United Kingdom by the European Convention on Extradition.

Article 1 of this arrangement recalls the wording of the Fugitive Offenders Act 1967 by providing that "'Offence' or 'Offences' means the fact or facts which constitute a criminal offence or criminal offences under the laws of the Member States."

CONCLUSION

2–032 It can be seen from the above review that the prevailing approach in the common law world is to examine all the conduct on which the requesting state relies in its extradition request in order to discover whether the person whose return is sought is accused of extraditable conduct. However, each statute or treaty must be examined with care in order to determine which of the two historical approaches was intended by the draftsman. It will be argued below that the 2003 Act may, irrespective of its legislative history, have reverted to a narrower approach.

III. SPECIALITY

2–033 The modern approach to double criminality, though procedurally simple in proceedings in the requested state, is liable to cause difficulties in the application of the speciality rule. This rule has often been treated shortly in (particularly English) extradition textbooks, because it has not given rise to serious difficulties in the English courts in modern times. This may be explained by the fact that United Kingdom law insists in the case of extraditions to other jurisdictions only that there be an arrangement with the foreign state, or provision in its law, to enforce the rule. The courts will not look behind this arrangement or law in habeas corpus proceedings, but in recent years have started to do so in proceedings for judicial review of decisions of the Secretary of State to surrender. This problem remains under the 2003 Act.

In particular, the practice of some of the Circuits of the United States of America show developing problems in the application of the speciality rule.

UNITED KINGDOM PROVISIONS BEFORE 2003

2–034 Paragraph 1(3) of Sch.1 to the Extradition Act 1989 re-enacted s.3(2) of the Extradition Act 1870:

> "A fugitive criminal shall not be surrendered to a foreign state unless provision is made by the law of that state, or by arrangement, that the fugitive criminal shall not, until he has had an opportunity of returning to Her Majesty's dominions, be detained or tried in that foreign state for any offence committed prior to his surrender other than the extradition crime for which the surrender is grounded."

Paragraph 17 of the Schedule provided similar protection for a person surrendered to the United Kingdom "in pursuance of any arrangement with a foreign state". In neither paragraph was provision made for consent by the requested state, after extradition, to trial for other offences, in spite of the recommendation to this effect in the White Paper of 1986.[63]

Only the conduct underlying the magistrate's decision to commit, identifiable by reference to the charges upon which he has committed, could form the basis of trial in the requesting state. It is clear under this statutory technique that, the greater the difference between the English and foreign charges, the greater the difficulties that will arise after extradition.

Article XII of the treaty of 1972 between the United Kingdom and the United States of America, embodied in The United States of America (Extradition) Order[64] as the "arrangement" contemplated by para.1(3), declares:

> "(1) A person extradited shall not be detained or proceeded against in the territory of the requesting Party for any offence other than an extraditable offence established by the facts in respect of which his extradition has been granted, or on account of any other matters, nor be extradited by that party to a third state-
>
> (a) until after he has returned to the territory of the requested Party; or
> (b) until the expiration of thirty days after he has been free to return to the territory of the requested Party.
>
> (2) The provisions of paragraph 1 of this article shall not apply to offences committed, or matters arising, after the extradition."

As at August 2004, this treaty remains in force, certainly under US law, because its 2003 successor has not been ratified by Congress. This statutory instrument was made pursuant to s.2 of the Extradition Act 1870, which provided that an Order in Council embodying an arrangement with a foreign state might apply the Act to that state "subject to such conditions, exceptions, and qualifications as might be deemed expedient."

"Extradition crime", as we have seen, was defined in the 1870 Act so as to refer 2–035
to English law alone. The fact that the speciality requirement refers to the trial in the requesting state for an extradition crime was the one of the principal arguments advanced by the defence in *Nielsen*[65] in support of an argument that the offences for which extradition was requested had to be substantially the same in the requested and requesting jurisdictions. The problem was identified by Robert Goff L.J. when the case was before the Divisional Court, and he suggested that the Secretary of State might, if appropriate, draw to the attention of the requesting state the consequence that the conduct rule might expose the defendant to a greater penalty in the requested state than he would be liable to in the United Kingdom:

[63] Cm.9658.
[64] 1976 (SI 1976/144).
[65] [1984] A.C. 608H, 610C–E.

> "Whether in any particular case he is bound to do so, and whether for that purpose he should qualify his surrender of the fugitive in order to invoke the relevant provisions of the Treaty (here Article 6 of the treaty with Denmark[66]), are matters that do not arise for decision in this case, and we express no opinion upon them."[67]

The express terms of para.1(3) to Sch.1 suggested clearly that, though a person might be extradited for an extradition crime very different from the crime alleged against him in the foreign warrant, on return he could expect to be protected from trial for an offence significantly wider than that proved before the committing court.

The position was more complex in cases under Pt III of the 1989 Act. Section 6 provides:

> "(4) A person shall not be returned, or committed or kept in custody for the purposes of return, unless provision is made by the relevant law, or by an arrangement made with the relevant foreign state, Commonwealth country or colony, for securing that he will not, unless he has first had an opportunity to leave it, be dealt with there for or in respect of any offence committed before his return other than —
>
> (a) the offence for which his return is ordered; or
> (b) an offence, other than an offence excluded by subsection (5), below, which disclosed by the facts in respect of which the surrender was ordered, or
> (c) subject to subsection (6), below, any offence being an extradition crime in respect of which the Secretary of State may consent to his being dealt with.
>
> (5) The offences excluded from paragraph (b) of subsection (4) above are offences in relation to which an order for the return of the person concerned could not lawfully be made.
>
> (6) The Secretary of State may not give consent under paragraph (c) of that subsection in respect of an offence in relation to which it appears to him that an order for the return of the person concerned could not lawfully be made, or would not in fact be made.
>
> (7) Any such arrangement as is mentioned in subsection (4) above which is made with a designated Commonwealth country or a colony may be an arrangement made for the particular case or an arrangement of a more general nature; and for the purposes of that subsection a certificate issued by or under the authority of the Secretary of State confirming the existence of

[66] The speciality provision.
[67] (1984) 79 Cr. App. R. 1, 14.

an arrangement with a Commonwealth country and stating its terms shall be conclusive evidence of the matters contained in the certificate."

These provisions were mirrored in ss.18 and 19 of the 1989 Act in the case of extraditions to the United Kingdom. It was hard to reconcile the provisions of s.6(4) with the broad and pragmatic interpretation of the words "extradition crime" in s.2(1). The "offence" (not "crime") in s.6(4)(a) is obviously the English offence. It is the offence found by the magistrate under s.9(8), having been identified in English terms in the authority to proceed by the Secretary of State as required by s.7(5). Some of the alleged offences may have fallen away in the course of proceedings, as in *R. v Secretary of State for the Home Department Ex p. Hill*.[68] The magistrate may have committed only on certain charges; the Secretary of State may have deleted certain charges himself at the surrender stage in the exercise of his general discretion, as in *R. v Governor of Brixton Prison Ex p. Levin*.[69]

Subsections (4)(b) and (c), by contrast, both use "offence" in the context of the overseas offence charged, as if it is assumed that the foreign offence can be categorised as an "extradition crime", capable of being recognised by the Secretary of State in the United Kingdom. 2–036

Section 6(4) is the product, it is submitted, of poor Parliamentary drafting. Its terms were relied on unsuccessfully by the applicant in *Ex p. Hill* in support of a narrow ingredients-based approach to the definition of "extradition crime". In fact, the section has been transplanted from s.4(3) of the Fugitive Offenders Act 1967, with the simple but inadequate substitution of the words "extradition crime" for "relevant offence." The provision had meaning and substance in the 1967 Act, and was easy to apply because similarity of offence in requesting and requested state was required.

THE CONCLUSIVE EVIDENCE PROVISION

Courts were not given power by statute to question these arrangements. In *R. v Governor of Pentonville Prison Ex p. Osman (No.3)*[70] it was held that the speciality protections of the colony of Hong Kong were effective for proceedings brought in England to return a fugitive to Hong Kong, although Hong Kong would be returned to Chinese sovereignty in 1997. The court was not required by s.6(4) to challenge the speciality arrangements. 2–037

The same approach was applied in another Hong Kong case, *R. v Governor of Pentonville Prison Ex p. Lee*.[71] The change of sovereignty argument was for the Secretary of State to consider.

68 [1999] Q.B. 996.

69 [1997] A.C. 741. (In fact, an American request under Sch.1 to the 1989 Act; the Secretary of State deleted certain charges drawn under the Computer Misuse Act which had been upheld in the courts.)

70 [1992] 1 All E.R. 122, DC. The case is called "No.3" because, although it was the fifth occasion that Osman took his case to the Divisional Court, it is the third reported case.

71 [1993] 1 W.L.R. 1294.

It has even been said that the courts are not entitled to look behind the terms of the certificate of the Secretary of State for the purposes of determining whether it would be unjust and oppressive to surrender a person for the reasons set out in s.11(3) of the Act.[72]

SPECIALITY AND THE DECISION TO SURRENDER

2–038 The defendant was, however, free to argue that the Secretary of State ought to exercise his discretion under s.12(1) of the 1989 Act not to surrender at the end of the extradition process on the ground that the speciality protection in the requesting state is not strong enough; or cannot be applied because the foreign offence charged is neither an extradition crime, nor the offence for which the defendant's return had been ordered. Cases in which such arguments are advanced have become common.

The awkwardness of the statutory provision is clearly demonstrated by *Ex p. Hill*. Following the invariable practice of the United Kingdom Government in Commonwealth countries, the Attorney-General of Witwatersrand (one of more than a dozen South African attorneys-general), gave, on request, an undertaking in which he simply recited that defendant "would not after surrender be tried for any offence other than . . . [here he recited verbatim the words of s.6(4)(a)(b) and (c), without, it may be assumed, having an easy and familiar understanding of the definition of 'extradition crime' in English law.]" The Secretary of State then gave a certificate under subs.(7) confirming that this undertaking constituted an "arrangement".

The applicant, having been committed by the magistrate, applied for habeas corpus, arguing that he could not be extradited or kept in custody under s.6(4), especially when the committal charges were in different terms from the South African indictment. He also applied for judicial review of the s.6(7) certificate, arguing that no reasonable Secretary of State could have signed a certificate given the status of the Attorney-General as "independent" of the Government in South African law, and having regard to the opaque terms of the undertaking, reflecting, as it did, the difficult wording of s.6(4).

The Attorney-General concerned asserted in an affidavit that it had always been accepted in practice that an attorney-general could give such an undertaking which would be adhered to by the others by convention. Statements of other Attorneys-General were attached, saying that they also agreed to be bound.

An affidavit of the Home Office offered detailed evidence describing the process by which the undertaking had been requested and obtained, and asserting that the undertaking had come through the diplomatic route, namely the South Africa High Commission. The South African authorities had confirmed that it was proper for the undertaking to be given by the Attorney-General. The Divisional Court held that the undertaking was therefore given by the "relevant . . . Commonwealth country" as required by s.6(4), and it could not say that the Secretary of State had

[72] See the judgment of Slynn J. and the speech of Lord Keith in *R. v Governor of Pentonville Prison Ex p. Narang* [1978] A.C. 247, 251G, 297A, DC and HL.

acted in a *Wednesbury* irrational way. The High Court held that a reasonable Secretary of State was entitled to regard these undertakings as sufficient compliance with the provisions of s.6(4).

2–039 Challenge to the efficacy of the speciality rule was also made to the Secretary of State in *R. v Secretary of State for the Home Department Ex p. Launder*,[73] and thereafter by way of judicial review proceedings. In the latter case the point was confined to the general argument that Launder would not be sufficiently protected from removal from the Hong Kong Special Administrative Region to the People's Republic of China. The Hong Kong charges of corruption alleged were similar to those that would have been charged in England. The argument failed.

The Divisional Court took a similar approach in *R. v Secretary of State for the Home Department Ex p. Launder (No.2)*.[74] The applicant had been in the process of a long challenge to his proposed extradition at the time when Hong Kong reverted to the sovereignty of the People's Republic of China. The speciality undertaking, previously embodied in a s.6(7) certificate, had been given in the name of the authorities who had functioned under the Crown. A new speciality undertaking, sought and accepted by the United Kingdom Government, was made by the new Chief Executive of the Hong Kong SAR.

The Divisional Court held that the new Chief Executive of the Hong Kong SAR had the power to give an undertaking. Simon Brown L.J. held that, since the law of Hong Kong applied the English common law, any attempt to prosecute for an offence outside the undertaking would be an abuse of process.[75] In any event, on a purposive construction of the Fugitive Offenders Ordinance, the requisite protection was provided by the law of the Hong Kong SAR.

The Court rejected an argument that the giving of the undertaking was an act of a foreign state upon which the courts would not adjudicate.[76] The examination of the matter did not involve an assessment whether the Hong Kong Government would act in good faith[77]; but rather an examination into the sufficiency of the speciality protection in that law; that type of exercise had been performed in detail in *Ex p. Alice Woodall*.[78]

This approach was followed in *R. v Governor of Brixton Prison Ex p. Lodhi*.[79]

THE PROBLEMS — ESPECIALLY IN US CASES

2–040 Modern US law raises increasingly difficult questions as to the application and enforcement of the speciality law. A review of earlier UK and US law and practice is illuminating, and points to a developing problem.

73 [1997] 1 W.L.R. 839, HL.
74 [1998] Q.B. 994. *cf.* [1997] 1 W.L.R. 94.
75 Citing *R. v Bloomfield* [1997] 1 Cr. App. R 135; *Chu piu-wing v Atorney-General* [1984] H.K.L.R. 411.
76 *cf. Buttes Gas v Hammer* [1982] A.C. 888.
77 An undertaking which the House of Lords had held to be improper in *R. v Government of Greece Ex p. Kotronis* [1971] A.C. 250.
78 (1888) 20 Q.B.D. 832.
79 March 13, 2001; CO/3635/2000.

Two cases under the 1870 Act, *Ex p. Bouvier*,[80] and *Re Alice Woodhall*,[81] established that in the cases of France and the United States, respectively, speciality provision was made in the national law by virtue, at least, of the enactment in each country of the applicable treaty of 1843. The second of these demonstrates that the United Kingdom courts will readily examine the foreign law, where necessary, to investigate whether it confers the protection required by the United Kingdom statute.[82] A circular containing the restriction, issued to the law officers in France by the Minister of Justice was a "provision made by law". It was also held in *Bouvier* that the law of France had embodied the "international law" of speciality in a more general sense.

Biron and Chalmers[83] describe the case of *Lawrence* of 1875 in which the fugitive was returned to the United States for an allegation of forgery. The British Government was informed that it was intended to try him for smuggling, which was not an extraditable offence. It protested. The authors tell us:

> "Lord Derby declined to recede, and refused to give up various other American fugitives whose surrender had been asked for, in especial one Winslow, also charged with forgery, unless the United States would agree to try them only for the offences for which they were surrendered. (Citing the Case of the Lennie mutineers, Old Bailey 4th May 1876, where it was held a prisoner surrendered by France for murder could not be tried as an accessory after the fact)."

The American authorities gave way and provided an undertaking.

In *Ex p. Piot*[84] the sufficiency of a warrant of committal was considered alleging "fraud by an agent". It was held that this vague description, complying with the generic description of a category of crime listed in the first schedule to the 1870 Act, was not a description which prevented the French from applying the speciality rule. It was the facts upon which the surrender was grounded which were important; not the offence.

In *Re Bluhm*,[85] it was held that, where it was alleged that evidence to support 30 of the 31 charges had been received outside the two months allowed by Art.XII of the treaty between the United Kingdom and Germany, habeas corpus would not be granted because the fugitive was undoubtedly in custody lawfully on one charge; the fugitive might take the point in Germany under the speciality provisions of the treaty.

2–041 Clive Parry's review of cases before 1914 concerned with the speciality rule covers some 80 pages of his work.[86] He provides details of numerous cases in which

[80] (1872) Cox C.C. 303,QBD.
[81] (1878) 16 Cox C.C. 478, DC.
[82] See the discussion in *R. v Home Secretary Ex p. Launder (No.2)* [1998] Q.B. 994, 1003.
[83] at 30.
[84] (1883) 15 Cox C.C. 208, 216.
[85] [1901] 1 Q.B. 764.
[86] 6 British Digest of International Law (Stevens, London 1965), Ch.17.

the Law Officers were asked to advise upon problems arising after the extradition of persons from the United Kingdom. Many of the problems in the case of the United States of America, including that in the *Lawrence* case, arose because, although the Extradition Act 1870 had repealed the 1843 Act embodying the Webster-Ashburton Treaty, the treaty itself was still in force, still constituted the law of the USA, but contained no speciality provision.[87] In 1883 a US draft of a new treaty proposed a speciality provision in the following terms:

> "A fugitive criminal, surrendered by one to either of the Contracting Parties for trial for the crime or offence named in the extradition warrant, may be tried for any other of the crimes or offences, committed prior to his extradition, mentioned in the [treaty]",

subject to giving 60 days' notice to the requesting state.

Such a proposal would have required an amendment to the 1870 Act, of course, and it was not effected. As will be seen, however, this formulation appears to form the basis of practice in some of the Unites States Circuits today.

The case of *Rauscher*

Rauscher was extradited from England under the 1842 treaty for murder of a sailor on a ship on the high seas, in US jurisdiction. He was acquitted of murder but convicted of a prior assault upon the deceased, causing him cruel and unusual punishment by the same acts as had been alleged in the extradition proceedings. This assault was not listed in the treaty as an extraditable offence. 2–042

According to the headnote, the Supreme Court of the United States[88] held by a majority of two to one that a treaty to which the United States was party was part of the law of the land; that Rauscher could not have been tried, under the treaty, for any other offence after surrender than murder even though the treaty contained no express speciality provision; and that:

> "The treaty, the Acts of Congress, and the proceedings by which he was extradited, clothe him with the right to exemption from trial for any other offense, until he has had an opportunity to return to the country from which he was taken for the purpose alone of trial for the offense specified in the demand for his surrender. The national honor also required that good faith be kept with the country which surrendered him."

Mr Justice Miller, one of the judges in the majority, considered that the construction of the treaty was central to this issue:

[87] Parry records at p.603 that the repeated efforts to negotiate a new treaty failed because agreement on the political offence objection could not be reached. The 1842 treaty remained in force, supplemented by later agreements, until it was replaced entirely by a new treaty in 1931.

[88] 119 U.S. 407, 425 (1886).

"Prior to these treaties, and apart from them, it may be stated as the general result of the writers upon international law that there was no well-defined obligation on one country to deliver up such fugitives to another, and though such delivery was often made, it was upon the principle of comity, and within the discretion of the government whose action was invoked; and it has never been recognised as among those obligations of one government towards another which rest upon established principles of international law."

Noting that a treaty was primarily a contract between nations, that the treaty was part of the law of the land, that its provisions prescribed a rule by which the rights of the private citizen might be determined, Mr Justice Miller observed in the light of *Lawrence* and other controversies that:

"the operation of this principle of the recognition of the rights of prisoners under such circumstances by the courts before whom they are brought for trial, relieves the relations between the United States Government and the courts of a State before whom such cases may be pending, of a tension which has more than once become very delicate and troublesome."

Mr Justice Gray agreed with the conclusion of Mr Justice Miller, but only on the very narrow ground that a separate US statute suggested that a person returned could only be tried for the offences specified in the warrant of extradition. Chief Justice Waite dissented on the ground that the treaty did not prohibit trial for other offences.[89]

In 1889 an amendment to the 1842 treaty was made in terms which reflected s.3(2) of the 1870 Act:

" A fugitive criminal surrendered to either of the High Contracting Parties under the provisions of [the treaty of 1842], of this Convention, shall not, until he has had an opportunity of returning to the State by which he has been surrendered, be detained or tried for any crime committed prior to his surrender, other than the extradition crime proved by the facts upon which his surrender was grounded."[90]

Arton's case

2–043 The case of *Arton*,[91] extradited to France, dealt with a problem that now arises in modern American cases. *Arton's* case was one of the most notable reported extradition cases in England before the First World War, dealing, as we have seen, with double criminality, encouraging the "liberal" construction of treaties, and affirming

[89] The decision may not, therefore, fully justify the conclusions in the headnote, which, the law reporter notes at p.425, was written by Mr Justice Miller.

[90] Parry, p.608.

[91] Parry, pp.631–635.

the principle that the courts of one state (in the absence of a statutory power) cannot question the good faith of a requesting state.[92]

After his surrender Arton was charged not just with the offences for which he had been extradited but with other offences for which he had been convicted some years before *par contumace*. A diplomatic note from the French Government alleged that Arton had voluntarily renounced the protection against trial for other offences. The French Government informed the United Kingdom authorities of its intentions. The Law Officers invited the French authorities to ask the United Kingdom Government formally for its consent, considering that it might be possible to give such consent if the defendant had wished to be tried for the offence.

The French authorities replied with an appeal to the rules of international law; the treaty was silent on the question where a person consented to a waiver of the rule, and because international law did not object to the second trial of a person convicted *par contumace*, no breach of international law was involved in a voluntary renunciation case.

Sir John Bridge, Chief Metropolitan Magistrate, disagreed. Section 3(2), and the speciality provision in the treaty, were clear, and no recourse to international law was required. The Law Officers agreed with the magistrate, and replied to the French Government:

> "The [speciality] Article does not say that he should not be so tried 'except with his consent', but that he should not be tried. Her Majesty's Government can waive this stipulation if they are satisfied that the accused desires it. If the accused does not desire it, they cannot properly waive it, as they are morally bound to enforce it for his benefit. It seems to us quite an impossible contention that the consent of a prisoner in custody is required to authorise such a proceeding. Any such practice is obviously capable of the gravest abuse. The French Government obtained the surrender of Arton on the promise made, by the IVth Article of the Convention, to the British Government, that he should not be tried for any other offence. It is for the British Government to determine whether they will waive this stipulation, and, with a view to this, it is the British Government, not the French, that must be satisfied that Arton consents."

Parry records, uncertainly, that, "The French government appears to have proceeded with the trial in spite of remonstrances."

The modern US approach to speciality

In 1931, the Webster-Ashburton Treaty and its supplementary instruments were 2–044
replaced by a new treaty, embodied in an Order in Council under s.2 of the 1870 Act.[93] The speciality provision in Art.7 was:

[92] *Re Arton (No.1)* [1896] 1 Q.B. 108; *Re Arton (No.2)* [1896] 1 Q.B. 509.

[93] The United States of America (Extradition) Order 1935 (SI 1935/574.) This was in return replaced by the 1972 treaty, embodied in the 1976 Order in Council No.2144 supplemented by SI 1986/2020.

"A person surrendered can in no case be kept in custody or be brought to trial in the territories of the High Contracting Party to whom the surrender has been made for any other crime or offence, or on account of any other matters, than those for which the extradition shall have taken place, until he has been restored, or has had an opportunity of returning to the territories of the High Contracting Party by whom he has been surrendered. This stipulation does not apply to crimes or offences committed after extradition."

It appears that this provision was typical of extradition treaties of the time.

Recent decades have seen a very different approach to speciality from that which prevailed in *Rauscher*. In *Fioccioni v Attorney-General of the United States*[94] the Court of Appeals of the Second Circuit considered the case of two French citizens, extradited from Italy to the United States to be tried in Massachusetts for conspiracy to import heroin. Although there was an extradition treaty between Italy and the United States, it did not apply to narcotics offences. However, an agreement was made between the two Governments, recognising that the offence was a crime against the laws of both states, by which the two defendants were surrendered as an act of comity. After release on bail in Massachusetts, the defendants were taken to New York and charged there with substantive offences of receiving, selling and stealing with 37 kilograms of heroin, allegations which had not been laid before the Italian authorities before surrender.

The Court of Appeals rejected an application for habeas corpus in respect of the New York offences. It accepted the argument that under the principle in *Rauscher*, the protection of the speciality principle applied, even though there was no express speciality provision under the adhoc arrangement in Fiocconi's case; "the need for excepting the United States from a breach of faith is equally strong."

Nonetheless, the court referred to the *Lawrence* problem that had arisen before *Rauscher* and declared:

"However the *Rauscher* remedy must be applied in light of the considerations that gave it birth. Since the object of the rule was to prevent the United States from violating international obligations, it becomes essential to determine, as best one can, whether the surrendering state would regard the prosecution at issue as a breach . . . The 'principle of specialty' reflects a fundamental concern of governments that persons who are surrendered should not be subject to indiscriminate prosecution by the receiving government, especially for political crimes."

Because "it is hard to believe that Italy would have objected" to the new charges, habeas corpus would not be granted. The court referred to the terms of the Italy-US treaty of 1888:

[94] 402 F.2d 475 (1972).

> "The person delivered up for the crime enumerated shall in no case be tried for any crime, committed previously to that for which his surrender is asked."

and considered that it was less prohibitive than other speciality provisions, and:

> "could well be read as an acquiescence in trial for crimes committed before surrender, at least of the same general nature, provided only that they were not antecedent to that for which the surrender was asked."

Other Circuits have built upon this case. In *Demjanjuk v Petrovsky*,[95] doubt was expressed as to whether the individual had standing to raise the matter on the ground that "the right to insist on the application of the principle of specialty belongs to the requested state, not to the individual whose extradition is requested."

In *United States of America v Kaufman*,[96] two brothers, called Franks, were arrested in Mexico and returned to Louisiana to be tried for a drugs conspiracy. The Court of Appeals acted upon the assumption that there had been an extradition as opposed to a deportation or "just being kicked out." After a trial, at which one brother was convicted and the other acquitted, both were transferred to Texas and were tried and convicted of other drugs offences. On appeal against conviction, the defendants relied on Art.7 of the US-Mexico treaty, which was in these simple terms: 2–045

> "A person extradited under the present treaty shall not be detained, tried, or punished in the territory of the requesting party for an offense other than that for which extradition has been granted."

Relying on *Fiocconi*, the Court purported to distinguish *Rauscher* on the ground that the British Government had expressed strong feelings about the speciality matter in other cases. There was no evidence that the Mexican Government objected to the Texas trial.

> "Indeed, the Mexicans were apparently only too happy to have the Frankses off their hands."

The Court distinguished *Rauscher* on the additional ground that the drugs offences in Texas were "of the same nature and character" as the Louisiana offences, whereas the assault charge in *Rauscher* was not extraditable within the 1842 treaty. Accordingly, applying the reasoning in *Fiocconi*, it was unnecessary to decide an additional question, namely, whether the defendants had any standing at all to raise the speciality question, or whether it was simply a matter for the High Contracting parties to decide themselves.

95 Above, 776 F.2d 571, 583–4.
96 858 F.2d 994 (5th Cir. 1988).

In *United States v Andonian*,[97] the Court of Appeals of the Ninth Circuit reached a similar conclusion, rejecting an argument that a superseding indictment which contained more counts than had formed the basis of extradition from Uruguay violated the rule of speciality:

> "The superseding indictment altered neither the nature of the scheme alleged nor the particular offenses alleged . . ."[98]

In *United States of America v Lebaron*,[99] the Fifth Circuit Court of Appeals took the same position, again without deciding whether the defendant had standing to invoke the speciality rule in the treaty. The defendant had been extradited from Mexico. Citing *Fiocconi*, *Kaufman*, and *Andonian*, the court said:

> "These cases suggest that the doctrine of specialty is concerned primarily with prosecution for different substantive offenses that those for which consent has been given. The appropriate test for a violation of specialty 'is whether the extraditing country would consider the acts for which the defendant was prosecuted as independent from those for which he was extradited.' "

Applying this principle, it had been permissible to try the defendant for conspiracy to obstruct religious beliefs, where the Government of Mexico had consented to his trial for "criminal conspiracy to commit homicide", because the new offence "was not so separate from the one for which he was extradited as to be a breach of faith by the United States."

These cases are cited as evidence of a much looser attitude to speciality in the United States than is contemplated in other jurisdictions, and than appears to be permitted by the provisions of its treaties. An appeal to the "principle" of speciality by the courts of the Second and Fifth Circuits, rather than an application of the specific terms of the treaty itself, recalls the attitude of the French Government in *Arton's* case. However, treaties do not assert baldly that the rule of speciality applies: they stipulate the precise test to be applied according to the standards accepted by the parties, after negotiation, when they were signed.[1]

The debate about speciality has generated intense discussion in the United States. It is recorded[2] that the Eighth,[3] Ninth,[4] and Tenth[5] Circuits allow a defendant to raise any violation of speciality as a defence in court unless the surrendering

[97] 29 F. 3d 1432, 1435.

[98] See also *United States v Paroutian* 299 F.2d 486 (2nd Cir) 1962 n.

[99] 156 F. 3d 621 (1998).

[1] Reference may be made to Art.14 of the US-Bahamas treaty of 1990 for an example of a modern and characteristic speciality provision negotiated by the United States Government. *cf.* Art.18 of the Hong Kong-Australia Treaty of 1997.

[2] Jacques Semmelman, "The Doctrine of Specialty in the Federal Courts: Making Sense of United States v Rauscher" (1993) 34 Virginia Journal of International Law 71.

[3] *United States v Thirion* 813 F.2d 146 (1987).

[4] *United States v Najohn* 785 F.2d 1420 (1986).

[5] *United States v Levy* 905 F.2d 326 (1990).

nation consents to prosecution. It appears that all the Circuits will assume that the requested state would object to fresh charges "not of the same nature", but, in the absence of objection, will assume that, where the fresh allegations are of the same kind, no objection would be forthcoming.

United States speciality cases after extradition from the United Kingdom

In *United States of America v Herbage*,[6] it was argued on appeal against conviction that, where a defendant had been extradited after a magistrate had committed him for several offences under the Theft Act 1968, he should not have been tried for mail fraud and transporting stolen items in interstate commerce; such a trial violated the rule of speciality. Assuming without deciding that an individual might invoke the rule, the Court held that there had been no violation, because the UK courts knew from the protocol to the 1972 treaty that the use of the mails was but a jurisdictional element of mail fraud. 2–046

The Court does appear, however, to have assumed by referring to this protocol that some similarity between the charge for which the defendant was extradited and that for which he was tried should exist. The use of the protocol would not assist in a case where a defendant was tried in the US for racketeering or continuing criminal enterprise. The ratio of the decision was:

> "Herbage's argument is that misuse of the mails is a substantive crime different from ordinary fraud for extradition purposes. In the light of the treaty language and the fact of the case, it is evident that Herbage was convicted of the identical crimes for which he was extradited."

In *United States of America v Diwan*,[7] the defendant had been extradited from England and was tried in Florida for the federal offences of mail fraud and conspiracy to persuade a minor to engage in sexually explicit conduct for the purpose of producing photographs. It was alleged that she had conspired with others to induce parents to allow naked photographs of children to be taken for the purpose of sending them to theatrical agencies which might be interested in obtaining modelling assignments for the children: whereas the photographs were in fact to be used for the gratification of two male conspirators, one of whom was serving a long prison sentence for sexual offences against children.

The Secretary of State in England had specified in his order to proceed offences of obtaining by deception and indecency under the Protection of Children Act 1978. The magistrate committed on the obtaining, but not the indecency, charges, finding that the photographs were not indecent; they were photographs of naked children of the kind that parents might innocently take.

[6] 850 F.2d 1463 (11th Cir 1988).

[7] 864 F.2d 715 (11th Cir 1989).

Diwan was thereafter extradited in respect of the dishonesty charges only. Having unsuccessfully moved to quash the indictment, Diwan pleaded guilty, but appealed on the grounds, among others, that Art.XII of the treaty forbade her prosecution upon charges alleging indecency.

The US Justice Department requested the United Kingdom authorities to assert that it did not object to the prosecution of Diwan on all 19 counts in which she was named. The Home Office replied by referring to Art.XII and confirming that "the United Kingdom has no objection to the indictment of Ms Diwan as proposed."

Whereas s.4(3) of the Fugitive Offenders Act 1967[8] conferred a power on the Secretary of State in certain cases to permit the prosecution abroad of a defendant for other relevant offences than those for which he had been returned, no such express power was conferred by the Extradition Act 1870; if it had been, it is surely unlikely that it could rationally have been exercised so as to permit the trial, after extradition, for an offence upon which the magistrate, on the same material, had declined to commit.[9]

2–047 It may be assumed that, since the Secretary of State "monitors" a treaty,[10] the High Court would be prepared to imply a limited power in the Secretary of State to inform a foreign government of its own interpretation of Art.XII, where, for example, the meaning of a magistrate's committal might be open to question. As Parry's research makes clear, the Secretary of State has historically filled this role. However, the consequence in Diwan's case seems to involve a plain violation of s.3(2) of the 1870 Act, now para.1(3) of Sch.1 to the 1989 Act. The difference between categories of offence in the two jurisdictions cannot justify, it is submitted, departure from the stark requirements of Art.XII, read in the light of para.1(3) of Sch.1. The element of indecency and "sexually explicit conduct" was not the "extradition crime proved by the facts on which [her] surrender [had been] grounded."

The Florida court's reasoning was that :

> "In determining whether the prosecution of Diwan was a breach of the extradition treaty, it is essential that we determine whether Great Britain would regard the prosecution as an affront to its own sovereignty . . ."

The court concluded:

> "The extradited individual, therefore, can raise only those objections to the extradition process that the surrendering country might consider a breach of the extradition treaty."

Article XII does not assert that an extradited person may be tried for an offence for which he has not been extradited provided that the requested state, after extradition,

[8] See s.6(4)(c) of the 1989 Act.

[9] The decision of the Secretary of State in Diwan's case to approve the trial for the indecency charges would surely have been amenable to judicial review.

[10] *Re Nielsen* [1984] A.C. 606; *R. v Governor of Pentonville prison Ex p. Sinclair* [1991] 2 A.C. 64.

fails to object. However, such a construction of the speciality provision is clearly not unusual in American courts.

In *United States v Sensi*,[11] the defendant was convicted, like Herbage, of crimes of mail fraud and transport of stolen goods in interstate commerce, having been extradited from the United Kingdom after a magistrate had found various charges under the Theft Act were established. The Court of Appeals dismissed his argument that the speciality provision had been breached, but nonetheless examined the evidence presented to the Bow Street magistrate in order to determine whether it supported each of the 26 crimes in the US indictment. The undertaking of this exercise is, of course, envisaged by para.1(3) of the Extradition Act 1989.

In the case of *Vladimir Levin*,[12] the Secretary of State, following representations from the defendant at the surrender stage of the proceedings, deleted offences under the Computer Misuse Act from his warrant of surrender, returning the defendant to face charges of "wire fraud" and "bank fraud" in the United States. Nonetheless, Levin was convicted of computer offences in the United States, having entered a plea bargain with his New York federal prosecutors. This outcome is very similar to the case of *Arton* in 1897, in which the United Kingdom Government considered that such a course was permissible only if the United Kingdom satisfied itself that a defendant genuinely consented, such matters being so vulnerable to abuse.

The case of Dr Robert Gross

The case of Robert Gross, brought unsuccessfully by the Government of the United States of America for the extradition of a psychiatrist to Texas, has demonstrated the acute problems that can arise as a result of modern US indictments, sentencing procedures, and attitudes to the speciality provision. 2–048

Dr Gross was indicted for fraud in relation to the provision of publicly funded medical care to children and minors. The affidavit of the prosecuting attorney disclosed that the defendant also "was tried and convicted of criminal contempt, and still awaits sentencing for that contempt conviction." Contempt (said to have been committed by or in the act of absconding to the United Kingdom) is not an extradition crime within the meaning of para.20 of Sch.1 to the Act, nor, therefore, within the meaning of Art.III of the treaty. The US evidence contained direct admissible evidence in relation to six individual allegations of obtaining a total of $3,450 by deception, and one case of obtaining a passport by deception, set out, in US terms, in the US indictment. These were reflected before the magistrate in specific English charges.

However, the preamble to the US indictment alleged a much wider scheme of criminal conduct, including the acceptance of bribes by Dr Gross totalling over $800,000. The US prosecutor referred in this connection in his affidavit to the evidence of three individuals, whose statements alleging wider criminal conduct were

[11] 879 F.2d 888 (D.C. Cir 1989).

[12] The facts of which are reported in [1997] A.C. 741, HL.

included in the papers, and who had apparently pleaded guilty to unspecified charges which were not specifically included in the indictment. He continued, "Prosecutors intend to prove that during the period from 1988 through 1992, Gross received compensation valued at . . . specifically ($861,616)." There were suggestions that this larger sum was composed at least in part of bribes paid to the defendant.

The Texas prosecutor held discussions with Dr Gross's English lawyers while the proceedings were pending as to the conditions on which he might return to Texas voluntarily. The indictment represented the high point of the allegations, he said, in relation to which a plea bargain might take place. It was also clear that Dr Gross would inevitably face imprisonment for the contempt charge. The prosecutor set out in a letter to a defence lawyer in Dallas details of mitigating and aggravating features in the case which would contribute to a numerical "points" total under which, with a very limited area of discretion, the judge would have to sentence. The total points included the entire value of the fraud alleged.

2–049 Further indications that the US authorities were preparing to prosecute on the extended basis appeared in the Texas press. One report about the speciality arguments raised in London read:

> "The confusion stems from the fact that in an alleged scheme to defraud the prosecution does not have to prove every instance of fraud, explains a source in the US attorney's office. The total amount of the theft is an issue for the judge to determine at sentencing. The $800,000 in alleged kickbacks was not a count on which Gross was indicted, but is mentioned in the preamble to the indictment so the prosecutors can introduce it at trial."

It was represented to the Secretary of State on behalf of Dr Gross that the Texas authorities were proposing a breach of Art.XII of the treaty because the proposed trial would cover a much wider range of criminal conduct than had been proved, *prima facie*, before the committing court. The modern US speciality cases were cited. It was argued therefore that no reasonable Secretary of State could extradite Dr Gross when he knew that a breach of the Article was planned.

The Home Office submitted these representations for comment to the US Department of Justice. A letter from the Texas prosecutor to that Department was in due course submitted to the Home Office, and thence to Dr Gross' lawyers for further comment. It contained the assurance that the prosecution would not ask for Dr Gross to be dealt with on the contempt charge, nor on any charges of bribery (for which no indictment lay). However, the prosecutor did assert that he intended to pursue the defendant for the whole sum alleged in the indictment as part of a scheme to defraud, on the ground that "The British magistrate who found that Gross should be extradited to stand trial on counts 1 to 4 was fully aware of the scope of the scheme to defraud encompassed by those counts . . . Consequently, to the extent that the United States expects to present evidence of the scheme to defraud as presented in the indictment, this will include evidence of the total amount of the financial loss caused by the scheme to defraud."

The defence again argued that even this position demonstrated that the US authorities intended that the defendant would be proceeded against for offences wider than those established by the facts on which his surrender had been grounded. Surrender was only available in respect of the conduct, particularised in charges, which the magistrate has found amounts to "extradition crimes". It was simply not sufficient to argue that unproven allegations were "before" the magistrate. The extradition would not have been granted for wider, unproved facts alleged in the affidavit of a prosecutor. 2–050

After several months of inquiry and reflection, the Secretary of State announced in May 2000 that the US authorities had withdrawn their request. The US prosecutor in Texas explained to Dr Gross's lawyer that the purpose of this abandonment was to prosecute Dr Gross for all the allegations against him whenever he might be arrested, anywhere in the world.

The US authorities would not give the undertaking sought by the defence, and no doubt could not give it by reason of their own sentencing and indictment procedures.

The wide factual assertions in the indictment in the Gross case are characteristic of many US extradition requests. These often contain allegations in an affidavit tendered by the case prosecutor, and sometimes in affidavits of witnesses, which extend far beyond the allegations presented in the indictment. No doubt it is believed widely in the United States that it is sufficient if allegations of a wide criminal scheme are "before" the courts of the requested state; and that the foreign court, by committing to prison pending a decision whether to extradite, impliedly approves these wide allegations in some way. Furthermore, in the Fifth Circuit, the home of the *Kaufman* decision, it is understandable that compliance with the speciality rule as expressed in the treaty is not an important consideration for the prosecutor unless the requesting country raises it as a problem.

The English tendency, encouraged by cases such as *Nielsen* and *McCaffery*, to specify ordinary English charges should often have a limiting effect upon criminal prosecutions in the requested state after extradition, even though prosecution lawyers who draft the English charges for committal are often tempted to frame them as widely as possible in a vaguely-formulated desire to reduce speciality problems after return. A person returned for even a large number of cases of theft cannot always be tried for "wire fraud" within the framework of Art.XII.

Conclusions to be drawn from the American cases

The review in this chapter of the voluminous American law on the subject is incomplete.[13] It is intended to demonstrate that those who represent prosecution and defence in US cases, and extradition officials in both governments, should be acutely aware of these problems, of the loose attitude to speciality in certain Circuits, and of the important precedent set by Dr Gross' successful challenge to the lawfulness and rationality of his proposed extradition to the USA. 2–051

[13] For a detailed review of the law and principles, see Bassiouni, *International Extradition United States Law and Practice* (3rd ed., 1995), Ch.7.

UNITED KINGDOM PROVISIONS 2003

2–052 The 2003 Act approach to speciality is considered in detail in Chs 10 and 12.

The cases of *R. v Governor of Brixton Prison Ex p. Hill*[14] and *R. v Home Secretary of State Ex p. Launder*[15] demonstrate that the courts will examine the adequacy of undertakings by foreign authorities on applications for judicial review of the Secretary of State, even though there may be statutory "conclusive evidence" provisions.

The Courts may be hostile to the notion that overseas governments should give undertakings to courts: but they will review the question whether undertakings of overseas governments given to our government are sufficient to provide the required protection. No "conclusive evidence" provision purports to inhibit a Secretary of State from requiring undertakings as to the enforcement of the speciality rule, or deters the courts from inquiring into the adequacy of the foreign protection in proceedings in review or appellate proceedings.

[14] [1988] 3 W.L.R. 1011.
[15] [1998] Q.B. 994.

CHAPTER 3

IRREGULAR RENDITION AND ABDUCTION

I. INTRODUCTION

When a person is extradited from another country to the United Kingdom, he faces trial or punishment in the normal way, subject to the statutory protection of the speciality rule. What is the position, however, if the defendant has been abducted or enticed by deception into the United Kingdom? Until the case of *R. v Horseferry Road Magistrates Court Ex p. Bennett*,[1] the English decisions were contradictory. **3–001**

The cases, in the United Kingdom and other national jurisdictions, will be reviewed chronologically in order to demonstrate the divergent positions taken in different jurisdictions, including the European Court of Human Rights.

II. THE EARLY CASES

In *Ex p. Susannah Scott*,[2] an applicant for habeas corpus had been brought to England from Brussels by an English police constable to be tried for perjury. It was **3–002**

1 [1994] 1 A.C. 42.
2 (1829) 9 B.&C. 446.

already established that in cases of felony the court would not inquire, on such an application, into the means by which the applicant came to be detained. In civil cases, however, the court would inquire into the circumstances in which the person came to be arrested, and, if the means had been improper, would discharge the offended party. Perjury was a misdemeanour, and the issue was whether the procedure appropriate to felony or civil arrest should apply. Lord Tenterden C.J. held that the court could not inquire into the circumstances in which the applicant had been brought within the jurisdiction:

> "If the Act complained of were done against the law of the foreign country, that country might have vindicated its own law. If it gave her a right of civil action, she might sue upon it."

In *R. v Nelson Brand*[3] Cockburn C.J. summed up to the jury:

> "Suppose a man to commit a crime in this country, say murder, and that before he can be apprehended he escapes into some country with which we have not got an extradition treaty so that we could not get him delivered up to us by the authorities, and suppose that an English police officer were to pursue the malefactor and finding him in some place where he could easily reach the sea, got him on board a ship and brought him before a magistrate, the magistrate could not refuse to commit him. If he were brought here for trial, it would be not a plea to the jurisdiction of the court that he had escaped from justice, and that by some illegal means he had been brought back. It would be said; 'Nay, you are here; you are charged with having committed a crime, and you must stand your trial. We leave you to settle with the party who may have done an illegal act in bringing you into this position; settle that with him.'"

In *Ker v Illinois*[4] the Supreme Court of the United States of America considered an abduction case. A "messenger" had been given extradition papers by the United States Government to take to Peru to apply under an extradition treaty for Ker's extradition for embezzlement. On arrival in Peru the messenger abducted Ker by force without presenting his papers, probably because Lima was occupied at the time by the Chilean army, and took him by force via Honolulu and Sydney to California, and then to Illinois. Ker was tried and convicted.

It was held that Ker had failed to establish that any constitutional right had been infringed. The existence of the extradition treaty did not confer a right on the plaintiff to be removed from Peru only in accordance with the extradition treaty. He could not invoke the terms of the treaty therefore to show that he had been tried in

[3] (1867), cited by O'Higgins, "Unlawful Seizure and Irregular Extradition" [1960] B.Y.B.I.L. XXXVI.

[4] 119 U.S. 446 (1886); judgment was delivered by Mr Justice Miller on the same day as he delivered his judgment in the case of *Rauscher*, considered in Ch.2.

breach of the specialty rule. The case was distinguished from *Rauscher*[5] in that Rauscher had been extradited in accordance with the terms of a treaty, into which the court was prepared to imply a specialty agreement. *Ex p. Scott* was relied on, together with other United States authority, to hold that the abduction of Ker had no legal consequence of the kind the court could enforce.

In *Sinclair v HM Advocate*,[6] warrants for arrest were issued in Glasgow for offences of embezzlement, and an authorisation for the Sheriff-substitute of Lanarkshire "to receive Matthew Sinclair into custody from the Government of Spain". A Scottish police officer procured Sinclair's arrest in Lisbon by Portuguese officials. He was detained for more than a month, without charge or authorised detention, then removed by ship, and forbidden by the Scottish officer to leave the ship when it entered harbour in a Spanish port. The ship sailed for London, where the officer took Sinclair by force, without warrant, to Scotland by train. 3–003

There was no extradition treaty with Portugal,[7] but there was a treaty with Spain, covering embezzlement offences. The Court of Justiciary declined to order Sinclair's release from custody. Only two (civil) cases were cited in the course of the three judgments. The Lord Justice-Clerk said:

> "If the Government of Portugal or Spain has done anything illegal or irregular in arresting and delivering over the complainer his remedy is to proceed against those governments. That is not a matter for our consideration at all, and we cannot be the judges of the regularity of such proceedings. But even if the proceedings here were irregular I am of the opinion that where a Court of competent jurisdiction has a prisoner before it upon a competent complaint they must proceed to try him, no matter what happened before, even though he may have been harshly treated by a foreign Government, and irregularly dealt with by a subordinate officer."

Lord McLaren said:

> "The extradition of a fugitive is an act of sovereignty on the part of the state which surrenders him. Each country has its own ideas and its own rules in such matters. Generally it is done under treaty arrangements, but if a state refuses to bind itself by treaty, and prefers to deal with each case on its merits, we must be content to receive the fugitive on these conditions . . ."

The alleged failure of the officer to act under a warrant in London did not need to be examined, because the magistrate in Scotland had jurisdiction, and:

> ". . . is bound to exercise it without any consideration of the means which have been used to bring him into this jurisdiction. In a case of substantial

5 119 U.S. 407 (1886).
6 (1890) 17 R. (J) 38.
7 One came into force in 1892.

infringement of this right, this Court will always give redress, but the public interest in the punishment of crime is not to be prejudiced by irregularities on the part of junior officers of the law in relation to the prisoner's apprehension and detention."

The judgment left unexplained the interesting questions of what the "right" was, what the court's powers and duties would have been if there had been a "substantial infringement", and whether irregularities committed by senior officers of the law would have led to a different outcome.

3–004 Such were the few stark British authorities reported on the subject before the Second World War. Parry,[8] however, shows from his research into government papers that the subject was sometimes controversial. He reports[9] the case of 1865 of one Townsend, who allegedly robbed a bank in Connecticut and fled to England, and was then abducted from Liverpool by a United States police officer to face trial. The Law Officers advised the Government that:

> "the English police officers who aided in his capture and his abduction were guilty of a violation of the law [and presumably would] be the subject of due animadversion; it would be proper and expedient that the attention of the Government of the United States should be called to this case, in order that such instructions may be given to the police authorities as may prevent the repetition of similar proceedings."

It does not appear that the Government considered that it had, or should exercise, a right to demand the return or release of the abducted man.

The case of *Blair*[10] shows the converse case, and the application of rough expediency. Blair, a Sheffield tradesman, failed in business and fled in 1876 to Nebraska, to the prejudice of his creditors, who then sent a "detective" after him. Blair was removed under a dubious warrant to Chicago, and thence to New York by force, and placed, handcuffed, on a ship and returned to Liverpool, where he was committed for trial. A Foreign Office memorandum of 1910 recorded that Mr Justice Mellor "refused to go into any question of international law" when Blair protested.

The memorandum also records that there was no power to restore the man to the United States; that he had a remedy in damages if he wished to pursue it; but that, by reason of the outrage, Blair should be pardoned:

> "It was finally arranged that Blair should be pardoned on condition that he leave the country and not return during the currency of his eighteen month sentence. His expenses were paid to Chicago."

[8] British Digest of International Law (1964), Ch.17.

[9] Parry, p.480.

[10] Parry, p.482.

The *Savarkar*[11] case excited international controversy in 1910. After Savarkar was ordered to be returned to India for various offences of sedition and waging war against the King, the ship carrying him berthed at Marseilles, and Savarkar swam to shore. A Foreign Office memorandum[12] suggested that Savarkar was re-arrested by a combination of Indian officers from the ship and French gendarmes, and forcibly re-embarked. His trial in India was adjourned, pending a resolution of a dispute between the United Kingdom and France.

The United Kingdom Attorney-General and Lord Chancellor both considered that the action in restoring the fugitive to the ship was an act of expulsion, or deportation, but this was not accepted by the French Government. The two Governments agreed to submit the matter to arbitration, at which the French Government argued that Savarkar should be returned to French soil, because he had been extradited from France to the custody of the Indian officials without proper process. 3–005

The United Kingdom response was:

> "Sovereign states have several ways (well recognised in international law) of ridding themselves of aliens whose presence they do not desire — (1) exclusion (2) expulsion, (a) *proprio motu* without reference to any claim by any other state, (b) in response to a demand made either directly or indirectly through diplomatic channels for the removal of the refugee from the country of refuge to a place where he will come into the hands of the authorities of the State from which he has fled. . . . The surrender of fugitive criminals is no doubt usually effected by *la voie diplomatique*, but extradition *par la voie directe* is occasionally resorted to."

The Tribunal accepted the United Kingdom view; there was no rule of international law requiring the surrender of Savarkar in these circumstances to France.[13] The Court attached weight to the fact that French agents participated in the detention of Savarkar in Marseilles. The judgment turns on the fact that the Indian officers had acted in good faith, and an honest mistake had been made. By implication, therefore, it appears that, had the removal from Marseilles taken place without the consent of a French officer, the French demand for Savarkar's return would have been justified.

III. MODERN CASES

In *R. v Officer Commanding, RASC Colchester Ex p. Elliott*,[14] the Divisional Court adopted and applied the English and Scottish cases of *Scott* and *Sinclair*. An army 3–006

[11] The proceedings in England are considered in Ch.1 under the Fugitive Offenders Act 1881.

[12] Parry, p.489.

[13] Scott, Hague Court Reports, p.275.

[14] [1949] 1 All E.R. 373.

deserter had been arrested in Belgium by British and Belgian officers, and escorted to British Army quarters in Germany. Lord Goddard C.J. said:

> "... the law of both countries is exactly the same on this point and we have no power to go into the question, once a prisoner is in lawful custody in this country, of the circumstances in which he may have been brought here. The circumstances in which the applicant may have been arrested in Belgium are no concern of this court."

The court did suggest, however, that in appropriate circumstances, such matters might be relevant to the court's traditional power to grant bail on an application for habeas corpus. No other precedents or overseas authorities were cited.

In *Frisbie v Collins*[15] the United States Supreme Court applied the rule in *Ker v Illinois* to allow an appeal brought by the warden of a prison against the decision to grant an order of habeas corpus. The applicant had alleged that he had been kidnapped by officers from Michigan in Chicago, and taken to Michigan to be tried. Even if this were true, the Supreme Court held, a forcible abduction would not justify release. The Court of Appeals had been wrong to hold that a refusal of habeas corpus "would in practical effect lend encouragement to the commission of criminal acts by those sworn to enforce the law". The constitutional right to "due process" was restricted to the guarantee of a constitutionally fair trial.

In *United States v Sobell*,[16] United States agents co-operated with Mexican agents in the seizure of a United States citizen who was taken to the United Sates for trial for espionage. The Second Circuit Court of Appeals considered the case indistinguishable in principle from *Ker*.

THE EICHMAN *CASE*

3–007 The most notable authority on this subject is *Attorney-General of Israel v Eichman*.[17] The reasoning and citation of both the District Court of Jerusalem[18] and, on appeal, Supreme Court,[19] is wide-ranging and detailed. Eichman was abducted from Argentina, without the knowledge of the Argentina Government or other authorities, and brought to Israel to be tried for grave war crimes against the Jewish people of Europe. Citing the cases set out above and other authorities to the same effect in the United States, courts constituted under the Palestine mandate, and writers in continental Europe, the District Court said it had been able to discover only one case, in a court of first instance[20] in Avesnes, France, in 1933, where a tribunal had dismissed such a prosecution, holding that all proceedings were vitiated after an

[15] (1952) 342 U.S. 519.
[16] 142 F. Supp 515 (1957).
[17] (1961–2) 36 I.L.R. 5; it is cited in none of the United Kingdom authorities.
[18] at 59–79.
[19] at 304–308.
[20] In *Ke Jolis* (1933–4 Annual Digest of Public Int'l Law Cases 77).

illegal arrest by French agents had been effected in Belgium, about which Belgium had protested.

The Court referred to the draft Art.16 of the Harvard Research of 1935 which read:

> "Apprehension in Violation of International law. In exercising jurisdiction under this Convention, no State shall prosecute or punish any person who has been brought within its territory or a place subject to its authority by recourse to measures in violation of international law or international convention without first obtaining the consent of the State or States whose rights have been violated by such measures."

The District Court cited the commentary of the author of the draft, Professor Davidson:

> "It is frankly conceded that the present article is in the nature of legislation . . . In Great Britain, the United States, and perhaps elsewhere, the national law is not in accord with this article in cases in which a person has been brought within the State or a place subject to its authority by recourse to measures in violation of customary international law."

Although Argentina had protested formally against the abduction, it had abandoned its complaint by the time of the trial. The Court acted upon the basis, doubted in many quarters, that the abductors had not acted for the Israel Government. Since it concluded that only Argentina might raise the objection, and that Eichman had no *locus standi* to argue it, the defence objection failed. The Supreme Court upheld this reasoning.

DIFFERENCES IN THE UK AND US APPROACH

In *R. v Governor of Brixton Prison Ex p. Soblen*,[21] the English courts considered the relationship between extradition and deportation. Soblen was sentenced to life imprisonment in the United States for delivering defence information to the Soviet Union. He fled to Israel, where he was forcibly expelled on a flight to New York, stopping at London. He cut his wrists on the plane and was moved to hospital in London. The Home Secretary had already determined that his presence in the United Kingdom was undesirable. Among the arguments on the application for habeas corpus was the question whether the deportation was a "disguised extradition" for the non-extraditable offence of espionage. 3–008

The Court of Appeal commented on two apparently conflicting principles; that a man is not to be surrendered for punishment in a foreign state except in accordance

[21] [1963] 2 Q.B. 243; discussed by O'Higgins, "Disguised Extradition; the Soblen case" (1964) 27 M.L.R. 52; and Thornberry "Dr Soblen and the Alien Law of the United Kingdom" 12 I.C.L.Q. 414.

with the Extradition Acts; but that the Secretary of State may deport a man to his own country if he considers it conducive to the public good to take that course:

> "How are we to decide between these two principles? It seems to me that it depends on the purpose with which the act is done . . . If, therefore, the purpose of the Home Secretary in this case was to surrender the applicant as a fugitive criminal to the United States of America because they had asked for him, then it would be unlawful. But if the Home Secretary's purpose was to deport him to his own country because the Home Secretary considered his presence here not to be conducive to the public good, then the Home Secretary's action is lawful."[22]

If the deportation order were valid on its face, the court would not question its validity in the absence of evidence of bad faith.[23]

3–009 In 1971, Shearer[24] commented, "The jurisprudence of common law countries has consistently denied that the circumstances under which a person has been brought before a competent court in any way affect the jurisdiction of the court to try him." However, he continued:

> "The consequences of an abduction, by international and municipal law, have been discussed by a number of writers. Interesting though these cases may be, present purposes would not be served by a detailed discussion. For abduction is such a manifestly extra-legal act, and in practice so hazardous and uncertain, that it is unworthy of serious consideration as an alternative method to extradition in securing custody of fugitive offenders."

In *Barton v Commonwealth of Australia*[25] Barwick C.J. considered:

> "There are obvious objections to the use of immigration or expulsive powers as a substitute for extradition."

In 1974, the Second Circuit of the United States allowed an appeal against conviction in *United States of America v Toscanino*[26] where the defendant, an Italian citizen, had alleged that he had been abducted in Uruguay with the connivance of United States officials. He alleged that he had then been taken to Brazil and tortured, and then transported in a drugged state to the United States by US agents.

22 *per* Lord Denning at 302; see, further, *R. v Bow Street Magistrates Court Ex p. Van der Holst* (1986) 83 Cr.App.R 114, 127, DC.

23 Following *R. v Secretary of State Ex p. Chateau Thierry* [1917] 2 K.B. 522, 922, CA. Other cases involving expulsion in war time for the purposes of fulfilling military service aborad are *R. v Brixton Prison Governor Ex p. Sarno* [1916] 2 K.B. 742; and *Amand v Home Secretary and Minister of Defence of the Royal Netherlands Government* [1943] A.C. 147.

24 *Extradition in International Law*, pp.72–5.

25 [1974] 131 C.L.R. 477, considered in Ch.1

26 500 F.2d 267.

The court held that dicta in the *Ker* and *Frisbie* approach were inconsistent with subsequent decisions of the Supreme Court which enlarged due process rights. If the allegations of the defendant were true, the criminal process of the court would be "abused and degraded", and such "abuse" would not be tolerated. The case was remitted to the lower court for the evidence on the issue to be heard.

However, in *United States Ex rel Lujan v Gengler*,[27] the Second Circuit reaffirmed the *Ker* principle by holding that a federal court might divest itself of jurisdiction only if the conduct of a United States agent abroad which brought the defendant within the jurisdiction was "conduct of the most outrageous and reprehensible kind."

The first case outside the United States of America to take a different approach, and to imply rights in a person abducted, was the New Zealand case of *R. v Hartley*.[28] The appellant had been convicted of manslaughter, having been removed from Australia by force—in an aeroplane—to New Zealand. The Court of Appeal found that the New Zealand police had co-operated in this removal. Accepting that the court was bound by the three cases of *Ex p. Scott*, *Sinclair*, and *Elliott* to hold that the New Zealand courts had jurisdiction to try the matter, the court nonetheless considered that it had a discretion deriving from the inherent jurisdiction of a court to prevent an abuse of process. Strong reliance was placed on *Connelly v Director of Public Prosecutions*,[29] and particularly the now celebrated passage from the speech of Lord Devlin[30]: 3–010

> "Are the courts to rely on the Executive to protect their process from abuse? Have they not themselves an inescapable duty to secure fair treatment for those who come or are brought before them? To questions of this sort there is only one possible answer. The courts cannot contemplate for a moment the transference to the Executive of the responsibility for seeing that the process of law is not abused . . . the only way in which the court could act would be by refusing to allow the indictment to go for trial."

The Court gave emphasis to the specific requirements of the extradition process:

> "And in our opinion there can be no possible question here of the Court turning a blind eye to action of the New Zealand police which had deliberately ignored those imperative requirements of the statute."[31]

The Court relied on the description of Griffith C.J. in the Australian case of *Brown v Lizars*[32] of extradition as "a great prerogative power, supposed to be

[27] 510 F.2d 62.
[28] [1978] N.Z.L.R. 199. See also *Moevao v Department of Labour* [1980] 1 N.Z.L.R. 464.
[29] [1984] A.C. 1254.
[30] at 1354.
[31] [1978] N.Z.L.R. 199, 216.
[32] (1905) 2 C.L.R. 837, 852.

an incident of sovereignty", and the same judge's rejection of the notion that extradition:

> "could be put in motion by any constable who thought it desirable that a person whom he suspected of having offended against that law should be surrendered to that country to be punished."

The court declined in *Hartley* to allow an appeal against conviction on this ground alone (finding also that a statement of admission by the defendant had been wrongly admitted) on the ground that the "abuse of process" argument had not been determined by the trial judge in the exercise of a discretion.

3–011 The United Kingdom courts followed *Hartley* in *R. v Bow Street Magistrates' Court Ex p. Mackeson*.[33] Mackeson had left England for Rhodesia in 1977, and in 1979 was detained there pending deportation on account of allegations of fraud which had been made in London. Extradition arrangements between the United Kingdom and Rhodesia had lapsed. However, Mackeson was not deported to London until after "legality" had been restored to the state of Zimbabwe-Rhodesia.

The court found that the deportation was an attempt to achieve extradition "by the back door", and that the English police had taken part in that exercise. The Divisional Court granted an order of prohibition, directing that committal proceedings should not take place. It may be thought that the following observations would have been insufficient to discourage police officers from attempting the same conduct in the future:

> ". . . the Metropolitan police, no doubt due to an excess of enthusiasm, certainly not due to any conscious intent to do wrong, transgressed the line . . ."[34]

The following year, the Divisional Court applied the same principles in *R. v Guildford Magistrates Court Ex p. Healy*,[35] a case in which a United Kingdom subject, fleeing from charges of fraud, was deported, rather than extradited, from the United States. The case took the form of a judicial review of a decision of a magistrate who had quashed a committal, after hearing argument on this point. The court found that, although English police officers had given "information" to the United States judge which had to consider whether Healy was an illegal immigrant, the police had in no way encouraged the United States authorities to deport as opposed to extradite him. Certiorari was refused. The Court indicated that applications that proceedings of this kind should be stayed should be determined by the Divisional Court in the exercise of its supervisory jurisdiction before committal, as had happened in *Mackeson*. They should not be made before examining justices.

[33] (1981) 75 Cr. App. R. 199.
[34] at 33, *per* Lord Lane C.J.
[35] [1983] 1 W.L.R. 108.

In the case of *Bozano v France*[36] the European Court of Human Rights found a violation of Art.5 of the European Convention on Human Rights: 3–012

> "Everyone has a right to liberty and security of person. No-one shall be deprived of his liberty save in the following cases and in accordance with a procedure prescribed by law;
>
> (a) the lawful detention of a person after conviction by a competent court;
>
> . . .
>
> (f) the lawful arrest or detention of a person . . . against whom action is taken with a view to deportation or extradition."

An Italian request for extradition to the French authorities failed for technical reasons. The French authorities then deported him to Switzerland, who extradited him under the European Convention on Extradition to Italy. The court held that the deportation had been a disguised form of extradition, and was in breach of Art.5 as an attempted circumvention of the decision of the French court to refuse extradition. In this way it could not be treated as action "taken with a view to deportation." However, the Court declined to order France to make diplomatic approaches to Italy to secure the return of Bozano to France.

It appears that the incidence of international abduction of suspects was increasing in the 1980s. In 1985 the Court of Appeal (Criminal Division) upheld sentences of between 10 and 14 years' imprisonment on men who had sought to remove to Nigeria one Dr Dikko, who had been a minister in a former government of that country. Dikko was discovered drugged in a crate at Stansted Airport. The defendants included three Israelis, one of whom was an anaesthetist. The sentences were imposed after pleas of guilty, and were upheld on appeal.[37] Lord Justice Croom-Johnson remarked:

> "There are very many political refugees or exiles of one sort or another living in this country, refugees or exiles from countries whose governments indeed may change with some frequency or rapidity. People who come to settle in this country must be free from any threat or fear of being forcibly abducted and taken back to a place where there may be somebody who considers them to be severe and serious criminals. In the present offence there is an element of what has been called, and I can only describe as, public affront. In the view of this Court the method of trying to get Dr Dikko back was an affront to this country, and to the rule of law and our sovereignty, which cannot for a moment be allowed."

Nonetheless, the next year, the Divisional Court in *R. v Plymouth Justice Ex p. Driver*,[38] reaffirmed the old *Scott* and *Sinclair* principle that the courts of this country will not inquire into the circumstances in which a defendant is found in this

[36] (1986) 9 E.H.H.R. 297.

[37] *R. v Barak* (1985) 7 Cr. App. R. (S) 404.

[38] [1986] 1 Q.B. 95.

country. There is an obvious inconsistency here. If the *Driver* principle were right, it follows that the United Kingdom courts would have been able to punish the *Barak* defendants with the same severity even if they had succeeding in leaving Stansted Airport with Dr Dikko, but had themselves been abducted from Nigeria with the connivance of United Kingdom police officers, and been returned to England.

Driver was detained in Turkey after suspicions had arisen that he had committed murder in Devon. Having been advised that there were no extradition arrangements with Turkey, the Devon police asked the Turkish authorities to deport him to the United Kingdom, "if it was within their power to do so." Driver was given to believe in Turkey, however, that the English police had lost interest in him, and that he was to be deported to London. He did not protest against his deportation. The Divisional Court found that the United Kingdom authorities had not acted improperly, and that therefore the applications for certiorari to quash the warrant of arrest, and for prohibition to prohibit committal proceedings, would be refused.

Nonetheless, the Court proceeded to hold that the decisions of *Mackeson* and *Healy* had been decided *per incuriam*, in that *Scott* and *Sinclair* had not been cited. The courts had no power to inquire into the circumstances in a person was brought into the jurisdiction for the purpose of refusing to try him, or to try a person who had been lawfully arrested within the jurisdiction for a crime committed there. The court failed to deal with the question why the developing jurisdiction of "abuse of process" should not have mitigated the severity of the *Scott*, *Sinclair* and *Elliott* doctrine.

3–013 The following year an Israeli scientist, Mordechai Vanunu, gave information to the *Sunday Times* in London about Israel's nuclear capability. Soon after, he disappeared and re-appeared in custody in Israel. It was reported that he was tricked by a woman Mossad agent into travelling to Italy, where he was drugged and taken covertly to Israel. There is no evidence that the judicial condemnation of the conduct demonstrated in *Barak* prompted the United Kingdom Government to protest. Vanunu was convicted and sentenced to 18 years' imprisonment.

The Supreme Court of South Africa considered the issue in the case of *S v Ebrahim*[39] after a member of the African National Congress had been abducted by agents of the South African state, returned to South Africa, detained under security legislation, and then was convicted of treason and sentenced to 20 years' imprisonment. It applied Romano- Dutch law and the *Hartley* and *Toscanino* approach, holding that where the abduction had been carried out by agents of the state that wished to try or punish the defendant, the court was presented with a serious injustice and had lacked jurisdiction to try the defendant. The headnote reads:

> "The court further held that the above rules embodied several fundamental legal principles, viz those that maintained and promoted human rights, good relations between states and the sound administration of justice: the individual had to be protected against unlawful detention and against abduction, the limits of territorial jurisdiction and the sovereignty of states had to be respected, the

[39] 1991 (2) S.A. 553.

fairness of the legal process guaranteed, and the abuse thereof prevented, so as to protect and promote the dignity of the judicial system. The state was bound by these rules and had to come to court with clean hands, as it were, when it was itself party to proceedings, and this requirement was clearly not satisfied when the state was involved in the abduction of persons across the country's borders."

A similar view was taken by the Supreme Court of Zimbabwe in 1991 in *Beahan v State*.[40] The defendant had been arrested in Botswana and delivered to the Zimbabwean authorities. The Court sought to draw a distinction between an abduction which was an affront to international law and the sovereignty of the state of refuge, from the voluntary restoration in breach of extradition arrangements by a well-disposed neighbour; not a distinction that is consistent with the rule in *Bennett*.

THE CASES OF ALVAREZ-MACHAIN *AND* BENNETT

Against this complex background, the highest courts of the United States and the United Kingdom have moved in different directions. *The United States of America v Alvarez-Machain*[41] tested the *Ker-Frisbie* rule severely. An agent of the United States Drug Enforcement Administration was tortured to death in Mexico. DEA agents were then responsible for the abduction of Dr Alvarez-Machain, a Mexican citizen, from his medical office in Mexico and they arranged for his removal by private plane to Texas. It was alleged that he was party to the murder. Alvarez-Machain moved to dismiss the indictment on the ground that his abduction constituted outrageous governmental conduct in violation of the extradition treaty between Mexico and the United States. He succeeded before the federal court and the Ninth Circuit Court of Appeals, who ordered his discharge and repatriation. 3–014

The Supreme Court allowed the prosecution's appeal by a majority of six to three. Chief Justice Rehnquist, for the majority, said that the only difference between *Ker* and the instant case was that in the former there had been no governmental involvement in the abduction. It was necessary to investigate whether there was an implied term in the treaty that abduction was forbidden. If there was, then the treaty was violated, as in the case of *Rauscher*[42]; if not, the rule in *Ker* applied.[43]

Article 9 of the treaty permitted the requested party to refuse the extradition of its own nationals, providing, in common form, that, if it did so refuse, it should submit the case to its own prosecuting authority. The defence argued that each nation reserved the right to choose where its own national would be prosecuted, and that this right would be frustrated if either state were free to kidnap nationals of the other state in order to prosecute them.

[40] 103 I.L.R. 203.

[41] 504 U.S. 655 (June 1992) ; see also *United States v Verdugo-Urquidez* 494 U.S. 259.

[42] 119 U.S. 407 (1886).

[43] Although various works on international law are cited, the only case from a jurisdiction outside the United States cited in the judgments is the South African case of *Ebrahim*, referred to by the dissenting judges.

The Court disagreed:

> "Extradition treaties exist so as to impose mutual obligations to surrender individuals in certain defined sets of circumstances, following established procedures . . . The treaty thus provides a mechanism which would not otherwise exist requiring, under certain circumstances, the United States and Mexico to extradite individuals to the other country, and establishing the procedures to be followed when the treaty is invoked."

It also rejected the argument that, since the treaty was to be considered against the background of customary international law, under which abductions were plainly unlawful, there would therefore have been no need to formulate an express prohibition on abductions. The Chief Justice considered that, whereas in *Rauscher* it was a small step to imply a specialty provision into a treaty which the parties had invoked in the course of the prosecution process:

> "the general principles cited by the Respondent simply fail to persuade us that we should imply in the United States-Mexico Extradition Treaty a term prohibiting international abductions."

The respondent defendant might have been right to describe the abduction as "shocking", and it might have been a violation of international law principles. Mexico had protested the abduction diplomatically. The Supreme Court held that the rule in *Ker* applied, however, and the question whether the defendant should be returned to Mexico was outside the treaty and a matter for the executive.

3–015 The dissenting judges expressed the view that the treaty's manifest scope and object plainly implied a mutual undertaking to respect territorial integrity; and that the majority view failed critically to distinguish between abductions by private persons and those authorised by the Executive Branch of the Federal Government. Referring to *Ebrahim*, Stevens J. concluded:

> "The Court of Appeal of South Africa — indeed I suspect most courts throughout the civilised world — will be deeply disturbed by the 'monstrous' decision the Court announces today. For every nation that has an interest in preserving the Rule of Law is affected, directly or indirectly, by a decision of this character. As Thomas Paine warned 'an avidity to punish is always dangerous to liberty' because it leads a nation 'to stretch, to misinterpret, and to misapply even the best of laws'. To counter that tendency he reminds us:
>
>> 'He that would make his own liberty secure must guard even his enemy from oppression; for if he violates this duty he establishes a precedent that will reach to himself.' "[44]

[44] *The Complete Writings of Thomas Paine* p.588.

Against the background of *Alvarez-Machain*, it is not surprising that the Eleventh Circuit Court of Appeals rejected the argument of General Noriega, taken from Panama when United States forces invasion in 1990, that his treatment had been unlawful. It held that his seizure, abduction and removal to the United States was not: "so unconscionable as to constitute a violation of substantive due process"[45]

THE MODERN UK APPROACH

In *R. v Horseferry Road Magistrates Court Ex p. Bennett*[46] the applicant for habeas corpus, a New Zealander, was wanted for offences in England of dishonesty in connection with the acquisition of a helicopter. He and the helicopter were traced to South Africa. Bennett could only have been extradited from South Africa if "special extradition arrangements" had been created under s.15 of the 1989 Act for his case. No such arrangements were made. Bennett claimed that he had been kidnapped from South Africa and sought to argue that the magistrate had no jurisdiction to commit for trial. The magistrate committed him, and Bennett applied for judicial review to quash the committal. 3–016

The Divisional Court,[47] bound by *R. v Plymouth Justices Ex p. Driver*, held that there was no jurisdiction in an English court to enquire into the circumstances in which a defendant was found within the jurisdiction for the purpose of refusing to try him. Lord Woolf expressly considered that the approach of the Divisional Court in *Driver* had been, in general, correct, but:

> "Speaking for myself I am not satisfied that there could not be some form of residual discretion which in limited circumstances would enable a court to intervene, not on the basis of an abuse of process, but on some other basis which in appropriate circumstances could avail a person in a situation where he contends that the prosecution are involved in improper conduct."[48]

The Divisional Court certified the question:

> "Whether in the exercise of its supervisory jurisdiction the court has power to enquire into the circumstances in which a person has been brought within the jurisdiction and if so what remedy is available if any to prevent his trial where that person has been lawfully arrested within the jurisdiction for a crime committed within the jurisdiction."

45 See for a further detailed commentary on the US position, *International Extradition: United States Law and Practice* (3rd ed., 1996), Chs IV and V.

46 [1994] 1 A.C. 43.

47 (1993) 97 Cr. App. R. 32.

48 at 32–33.

The House of Lords reversed the decision of the Divisional Court, Lord Oliver dissenting, and overruled *Driver*. Lord Griffiths, with whom Lords Bridge, Lowry and Slynn expressly agreed in the course of concurring speeches, held after extensive citation of English, Commonwealth and American authority[49]:

> "If the court is to have the power to interfere with the prosecution in present circumstances it must be because the judiciary accept a responsibility for the maintenance of the rule law that embraces a willingness to oversee executive action and to refuse to countenance behaviour that threatens either basic human rights or the rule of law.
>
> My Lords, I have no doubt that the judiciary should accept this responsibility in the field of criminal law. The great growth of administrative law during the latter half of this century has occurred because of the recognition by the Judiciary and Parliament alike that it is the function of the High Court to ensure that executive action is exercised responsibly and as Parliament intended. So also should it be in the field of criminal law and if it comes to the attention of the court that there has been a serious abuse of power it should, in my view, express its disapproval by refusing to act on it . . .
>
> In my view Your Lordships should now declare that where process of law is available to return an accused to this country through extradition procedures our courts will refuse to try him if he has been forcibly brought within our jurisdiction in disregard of those procedures by a process to which our own police, prosecuting or other executive authorities have been a knowing party."

The ratio of the speech, as expressed in the answer to the certified question,[50] must be read in the light of the above passages, though couched in the language of discretion:

> "The High Court in the exercise of its supervisory jurisdiction has power to inquire into the circumstances by which a person has been brought into the jurisdiction and if satisfied that it was in breach of extradition procedures it may stay the prosecution and order the release of the accused."

The foundation-stone for this approach, according to Lord Griffiths, was the series of English law cases holding that a court has a discretion, or a duty,[51] to prevent an abuse of its process.[52] The present decision was an extension of that doctrine, and the *Hartley* approach was correct.

[49] at 61H.

[50] at 64E.

[51] Lord Diplock said that a court had a duty to prevent an abuse of process in *Hunter v Chief Constable of the West Midlands Police* [1982] A.C. 529, 536D ("I disavow the word 'discretion' ").

[52] *Connelly v DPP* [1964] A.C. 1254.

Lord Bridge, concurring, expressed the principle in wide terms:

> "When it is shown that the law enforcement agency responsible for bringing a prosecution has only been enabled to do so by participating in violations of international law and of the laws of another state in order to secure the presence of the accused within the territorial jurisdiction of the court, I think that the rule of law demands that the court take cognisance of that circumstance. To hold that the court may turn a blind eye to executive lawlessness beyond its frontiers of its own jurisdiction is, to my mind, an insular and unacceptable view."

He adopted the description of a trial after a foreign abduction, given by Woodhouse J. in *Hartley*, as an "abuse of the criminal jurisdiction", and that of Mansfield J. in *Toscanino* as a "degradation" of the criminal process.

Lord Lowry, concurring, and Lord Oliver, dissenting, also analysed the problem by reference to the abuse of process doctrine. Lord Oliver pointed out that, at common law, there was no discretion to refuse to admit illegally obtained evidence: and that in *R. v Sang*[53] it had been held that a judge had no power to refuse to try a man who had been enticed to commit a crime by an agent provocateur. There was no general discretion in a court to inquire into the conduct of executive officers before and leading up to criminal proceeding, the courts having ruled repeatedly that conduct obtained by illegal entry or excessive force, or by subterfuge, was admissible. Why, then, should the return by collaborating police forces of a person who had fled the jurisdiction be in a separate category? No "right" accrued in English law, by virtue of the act of flight, not to be returned informally. Lord Slynn agreed with Lords Griffiths and Lowry. 3–017

Although the majority use the framework of the abuse of process doctrine, in which the word "discretion", rightly or wrongly, is frequently employed, the trenchant words of Lord Griffiths and Lord Bridge, and to a lesser extent Lord Lowry, appear to leave little or no room for the operation of a discretion or balancing exercise, where an abduction abroad in breach of extradition procedures has been found.

Subsequently, the Divisional Court determined, after hearing live evidence and argument over two weeks, that Bennett had been brought into the United Kingdom unlawfully. They discharged him.[54]

WHAT IS THE EXTENT OF THE BENNETT *DOCTRINE?*

The extent and meaning of the *Bennett* principle has been the subject of discussion and will inevitably return to the House of Lords for further consideration. Sedley J. remarked in the Divisional Court stages of *In Re Schmidt*[55]: 3–018

[53] [1980] A.C. 402.
[54] *R. v Horseferry Raod Magistrates Court Ex p. Bennett (No.3)* [1995] 1 Cr. App. R. 147.
[55] [1995] 1 A.C. 339, 357F.

"In total, the decision of the House of Lords enlarges the concept of abuse of process to embrace serious abuses of power where it is only by the abuse of power that legal process has become possible. It articulates the supervisory obligation of the High Court to maintain the rule of law as something different from and greater than the maintenance of individual rules of law. In constitutional terms the decision, it seems to me, is of the highest importance, establishing a principle which will take time to be worked out in our jurisprudence."

A more cautious approach has been expressed in Scotland. The High Court of Justiciary considered the facts of Bennett's case in *Bennett v HM Advocate*,[56] but considered that the facts which the Divisional Court had found amounted to an abuse, may simply have revealed that the South African authorities were taking their own decisions about the method of deportation, of which the English authorities simply sought to take advantage. Lord Hope referred to the observations of Lord Bridge, cited above, and remarked:

"If we had been satisfied that that was the state of the facts and that this was indeed a case where, to use Lord Bridge's words, the law enforcement agencies in England had participated in violations of international law and of the laws of South Africa in order to secure the presence of the petitioner within the territorial jurisdiction of the English court, we would have wished the decision in *Sinclair v H.M. Advocate (*1890) 17 R. 38 to be reviewed by a larger court."[57]

This caution as to the extent of the *Bennett* principle demonstrates the importance of Lord Oliver's dissenting speech in the House of Lords. He identified the potential width of the *Bennett* principle.

THE BENNETT *PRINCIPLE IN EXTRADITIONS FROM THE UNITED KINGDOM, AND IN ENGLAND*

3–019 In *Re Schmidt*,[58] the House of Lords held that, for the reasons set out in *Atkinson v Government of the United States of America*[59] and *R. v Governor of Pentonville Prison Ex p. Sinclair*,[60] the High Court has no such general discretion in cases of extradition from the United Kingdom.[61]

In *R. v Latif*[62] a suspected drug smuggler in Pakistan was asked by an undercover agent from the Drug Enforcement Administration of the United States to import heroin to the United Kingdom. The defendant agreed and handed a package to an

[56] [1995] S.L.T. 510.
[57] The Appellate Committee hearing Bennett's case had contained no Scottish Law Lords.
[58] [1995] 1 A.C. 339, HL.
[59] [1971] A.C. 197, HL.
[60] [1991] 2 A.C. 64, HL.
[61] This subject is discussed in Ch.9 in the context of the provisions of the Extradition Act 2003.
[62] [1996] 1 W.L.R. 104; [1996] 2 Cr. Ap. R. 92.

undercover officer of the Customs and Excise, who brought it into the United Kingdom. The defendant was then encouraged by a customs officer who had procured a visa for him to come to the United Kingdom. He was arrested on arrival, and charged with the importation.

The trial judge rejected a submission that the prosecution was an abuse of the process of the court. His decision was upheld by the House of Lord, but on the basis that the trial judge had exercised his discretion upon proper principles. Lord Steyn cited *Bennett* for the following proposition:

> "The law is settled. Weighing countervailing considerations of policy and justice, it is for the judge in the exercise of his discretion to decide whether there has been an affront to the public conscience and requires the criminal proceedings to be stayed . . . The speeches in *Bennett* conclusively establish that proceedings may be stayed in the exercise of the judge's discretion not only where a fair trial is impossible but also where it would be contrary to the public interest in the integrity of the criminal justice system that a trial should take place. General guidance as to how the discretion should be exercised in particular circumstances will not be useful. But it is possible to say that in a case such as the present the judge must weigh in the balance the public interest in ensuring that those that are charged with grave crimes should be tried and the competing public interest in not conveying the impression that the court will adopt the approach that the end justifies the means."

The trial judge had concluded that there are some circumstances in which trickery and deception have to be used "otherwise the courts will not get to try this sort of offence against people who are seriously involved in it". The House of Lords, acting on the basis that the Customs officer was guilty of the criminal offence of being concerned in the importation of heroin, considered that the conduct of the customs officer was not so "unworthy or shameful that it was an affront to the public conscience." It is not easy to reconcile the approach of Lord Steyn, who emphasised the *discretion* of the courts to stay proceedings, with the *duty* to do so emphasised in *Bennett* and *Hunter*.

In *R. v Staines Magistrate Court Ex p. Westfallen*[63] the Divisional Court considered three cases in which persons wanted for trial in England had been deported to the United Kingdom (or in one case, deported from Canada to Ireland, but in a plane which, according to its normal schedule, landed first at Glasgow, where the applicant was arrested.) Magistrates refused to stay the proceedings, and judicial review was applied for. Relief was refused in all cases, on the ground that the United Kingdom authorities had not procured the deportation of the applicants as a substitute for extradition; they may have welcomed it, but the deportations were decided upon by the overseas authorities according to their normal procedures. 3–020

[63] [1998] 1 W.L.R. 652.

In *R. v Mullen*,[64] the Court of Appeal (Criminal Division) allowed an appeal against conviction where new evidence disclosed that an unlawful deportation had taken place from Zimbabwe. Mullen, a suspected terrorist, was wanted for conspiracy to cause explosions in England. It was appreciated that an application for his extradition would be supported by strong evidence, but was likely to fail on the political offence exception. It was recognised by the Foreign Office, Home Office, Security Services and police that Mullen could be tried if he were deported, but by reason of the authority of *Mackeson*, there had to appear to be no collusion. There was indeed collusion between the authorities of both states. Lord Justice Rose found:

> "The British authorities initiated and subsequently assisted in and procured the deportation of the Appellant by unlawful means in circumstances in which there were specific extradition facilities between this country and Zimbabwe. In so acting they were not only encouraging the unlawful conduct but they were also acting in breach of public international law . . . the conduct represents, in the view of this court, a blatant and extremely serious failure to adhere to the rule of law with regard to the production of a defendant for prosecution in the English courts."[65]

The Court concluded that "*Bennett*-type" abuse, where it would be offensive to try the defendant at all, was different from the type of abuse which rendered a fair trial impossible, arising as it does from the prosecutions relationship with the court. Rose L.J. referred to the dicta in *Connelly* indicating that the court "must suppress any abuses of its process and . . . defeat any attempted thwarting of its process"[66] and, "The courts cannot contemplate for a moment the transference to the Executive of the responsibility for seeing that the process of the law is not abused."[67] It did not matter, therefore, that the trial judge had not been asked to exercise a discretion. The matter was aggravated by the failure of the prosecution to disclose the illegality at the time.

3–021 Perhaps the most interesting aspect, however, of the *Mullen* judgment lies in the following *obiter dictum*:

> "In arriving at this conclusion we strongly emphasise that nothing in this judgement should be taken to suggest that there may not be cases, such as *Latif*, in which the seriousness of the crime is so great relative to the nature of the abuse of process that it would be a proper exercise of judicial discretion to permit a prosecution to proceed to allow a conviction to stand notwithstanding an abuse of process of this kind. In each case it is a matter of discretionary balance, to be approached with regard to the particular conduct complained of and the particular offence charged . . . "[68]

[64] [1999] 2 Cr. App. R. 143.
[65] at 156D–E.
[66] *per* Lord Morris [1964] A.C. 1301.
[67] *per* Lord Devlin [1964] A.C. 1354.
[68] at 158A–D.

Curiously, the prosecution did not seek leave to appeal to the House of Lords, notwithstanding that the conduct of Mullen had been so serious as to have attracted a sentence of 30 years' imprisonment. The Court of Appeal was considering Mullen's case after the appellant had been in prison for many years, and in the context of the continuing government policy of releasing for political reasons those convicted of terrorist offences connected with Northern Ireland.

If the law in *Bennett* had been recognised at the time of his trial, and if the material had been disclosed to the judge, it is interesting to speculate whether Mullen would have been tried. Under the principle in *Latif*, and the *obiter dictum* in *Mullen*, the countervailing consideration of the gravity of the offence, and the requirements of the fight against terrorism, might have led, nonetheless, to a trial, in spite of the wide principle expressed in *Bennett*.

In *R. v Gokal*[69] the Court of Appeal held that a trial judge had been entitled, in the exercise of his discretion, to refuse a defence application that the prosecution should disclose material relevant to his contention that he had been lured to Germany from Pakistan, from where he could be extradited by deceit to the United Kingdom.

Gokal was travelling to the United States to speak to prosecutors about the collapse of BCCI under a promise that he would not be prosecuted there. He alleged that an agreement was made by the Serious Fraud Office and United States prosecutors investigating the BCCI collapse, by deceiving him into the belief that he had safe conduct to the United States; alternatively that the Serious Fraud Office had deceived the United States authorities into a belief that the Serious Fraud Office respected the promise of safe passage.

The Court of Appeal held that the judge had been entitled to hold that the conduct alleged, if true, was not so outrageous as to be an affront to the public conscience. The public interest in the trial of fraud offences of the utmost gravity was of great importance. The lower court had rightly declined to order disclosure of material relevant to the defendant's allegations, because, taking the defence allegations at their highest, he would not exercise his discretion in its favour. The Court of Appeal declined to certify that a point of law of public importance was involved in this decision.

THE MODERN STRASBOURG APPROACH

After *Bozano*, reviewed above, the principal authority in this area of the law in the European Court of Human Rights has been *Ocalan v Turkey*.[70] **3–022**

Ocalan was a Turkish citizen and a Kurdish separatist leader. Numerous offences of involvement in serious and prolonged terrorism were alleged against him by authorities in Turkey, and warrants had been issued for his arrest and circulated internationally through Interpol. He was ultimately arrested in controversial circumstances in Kenya in an aeroplane in the international zone of Nairobi airport. He was then returned immediately to Turkey. No extradition treaty was in force

[69] Unreported, March 11, 1999, CA 9704132S2.
[70] (2003) 37 E.H.R.R. 10.

between Turkey and Kenya. Ocalan argued that he had been abducted by Turkish agents co-operating with Kenyan agents who were not acting on behalf of the Kenyan authorities. There had been a breach of Kenyan sovereignty and international law, and accordingly a breach of Art.5(1) of the European Convention on Human Rights, since he had been deprived of his liberty unlawfully. He had been the subject of a disguised extradition.

The Government of Turkey claimed that its responsibility was not engaged, because Art.1 of the Convention requires that the Contracting Parties "shall secure to everyone within their jurisdiction the rights and freedoms defined . . .", and these events occurred outside Turkey. It also relied on the case of *Illich Ramirez Sanchez v France*[71] in which the Commission had held that where there had been co-operation between two states, France and Sudan, in the removal to France of a terrorist suspect for the purposes of trial, and where an arrest warrant had been issued in France, even an extradition in disguise could not be regarded as being contrary to Convention rights.

3–023 The Court held that Art.1 of the Convention was indeed engaged, since the applicant was under the effective jurisdiction of Turkish security forces in Kenya. Adopting an opinion of the Commission in *Stocke v Germany*[72] the Court held further:

> ". . . the Convention does not prevent cooperation between States, within the framework of extradition treaties or in matters of deportation, for the purpose of bringing fugitive offenders to justice, provided it does not interfere with any specific rights recognised within the Convention."

The Court found as a fact that there had been a decision by the Kenyan authorities to hand over the applicant, and that therefore Kenyan sovereignty and international law had not been violated. Where one state is party to the Convention, the other is not, and no extradition treaty exists between them, the fact of co-operation between those States in the removal of the suspect for trial in the state which took him is a relevant factor in determining whether that arrest was lawful and within Art.5.

The applicant had failed to make out a case beyond reasonable doubt that the Turkish authorities had acted in a way that was inconsistent with the sovereignty of the host state and therefore contrary to international law. His arrest and detention were therefore in accordance with a "procedure prescribed by law" for the purposes of Art.5(1)(c) of the Convention.

It is submitted that the ratio of this decision, on the facts as found, is consistent with the House of Lords decision in *Bennett*, because there were no available extradition procedures in the *Ocalan* case. Dicta in the *Ramirez* and *Ocalan* decisions suggesting that a disguised extradition is not necessarily a breach of Convention rights, do not however necessarily deprive a defendant in England of the application of the possibly wider *Bennett* principle.

[71] Application No.28780/95, Commission decision of June 24, 1986; D.R. 86, 155.

[72] October 12, 1989, Series A No.199, p.24, para.169.

It seems likely that, if the case of *Bennett* were decided today, it would be held that the common law principle there identified was consistent with the rights protected by Art.5.1 of the Convention, and that a breach of Art.5(1) had occurred in that case.[73]

IV. CONCLUSION

3–024 It was argued in the first edition of this book in 1994 that *Bennett* had settled the law on the question of abduction and subsequent trial in the United Kingdom. This proposition is no longer advanced with confidence. *Latif* and *Mullen* appear to leave room for the weighing of public interest factors and the exercise of judicial discretion in such cases, so that, in the case of a really grave crime, a court may in future decide that the condemnation of executive lawlessness would be outweighed by the public interest in trying and punishing the alleged criminal. Those shocked by the abduction of Alvarez-Machain or Vanunu are probably not disturbed by the abduction of Eichman. The different reaction has nothing to do with the existence or non-existence of extradition arrangements: it arises because Eichman's crimes were so dreadful.

It must always be borne in mind also that the *Bennett* principle would not necessarily forbid the trial of a person abducted by agents of the United Kingdom abroad, where an unsuccessful attempt to negotiate special extradition arrangements had been made under s.15 of the 1989 Act; or, perhaps, if it was certain to fail if attempted.

If, however:

(a) criminals are tricked to come into the country by persons employed by the state acting as agents provocateurs and co-conspirators; or
(b) a prosecuting body flouts or ignores an agreement for the safe passage of a person assisting a prosecuting body in a friendly country, thus securing his presence in the United Kingdom;

the courts are likely to hold, following *Gokal*, if the crime is a serious one, that the end justifies the means, whatever the consequences for future cases and the reputations of the agents or prosecuting bodies concerned. The moral of the *Gokal* case is that those who fear arrest for serious crimes should not believe that promises of free passage, for the purposes of assisting law enforcement authorities, will be honoured. Bodies such as the Serious Fraud Office have judicial permission in the United Kingdom to break them with impunity.

Abroad, the principle in *Ex p. Scott* appears still to apply in most jurisdictions, subject to the rule in *Bozano* and the approach in *Ocalan* in ECHR states. The rule in *Alvarez-Machain* continues to shock, and has the capacity to embarrass the United States in international discussions on the subject of extradition and criminal law.

[73] See, for example, *R. v Governor of Brockhill Prison Ex p. Evans (No.2)* [2001] A.C. 19.

GENERAL INTERNATIONAL PRACTICE

3–025 In large parts of the world, the doctrine in *Bennett* must appear, as a matter of practice, to be a jurisprudential delicacy. At a conference in the Caribbean, the author enquired, as a matter of interest, why all the reported West Indies extradition cases appeared to originate in requests from Europe or North America. He was cheerfully told that requests for people to be returned from one Caribbean jurisdiction to another were presumably dealt with by removing the suspect, simply and conveniently, at the airport, without litigation or controversy.

It is for this reason that a practitioner in extradition law need not feel morally compromised if a fugitive enquires of him in what jurisdiction he can feel free from the fear of expulsion to a state in which he is accused or convicted of crime. The only honest answer is "nowhere", other than in pariah states in which conditions would be dangerous and life intolerable.

A NOTE ON PROCEDURE

3–026 It is clear from *Bennett* that the Divisional Court, in its supervisory jurisdiction, is the proper forum for argument of the kind under consideration. The matter is too important to be left to magistrates.

Nonetheless, the matter can obviously be raised before the trial judge. It was held in *Mullen* that it can be raised for the first time at the Court of Appeal if new material has come to light since conviction. If it is argued before the judge at trial, and does not succeed, the argument is amenable to review on appeal, notwithstanding that the single test on appeal against conviction is whether the conviction is "unsafe" (the statutory test in s.2(1)(a) of the Criminal Appeal Act, as amended by the Criminal Appeal Act 1995). In this event, the Court of Appeal will approach the matter by asking whether the judge's discretion had been exercised unreasonably or wrongly.

The effect of the 1995 amendment on the powers of the Court of Appeal has, however, been the subject of debate. In *R. v Chalkley and Jeffries*[74] the Court of Appeal had considered that the change to "unsafe" precluded any examination of matters other than the safety of the conviction itself. The Court in *Mullen* decided that this approach was inappropriate.

If the matter is argued before trial, however, the High Court will exercise a first instance, fact-finding jurisdiction on the question, in accordance with *Bennett*. Abuse of process and ECHR arguments tend, in practice, to be more attractive and successful if they are taken at the earliest opportunity.

[74] [1998] Q.B. 848.

CHAPTER 4

INTERNATIONAL CRIMES AND IMMUNITIES

I. INTRODUCTION

Sir William Blackstone propounded the classic division of law into "private wrongs", susceptible to redress at the suit of an individual by civil action, and "public wrongs", prosecuted as crimes in the name of the Crown because the whole community was injured by such wrongs.[1] **4–001**

English and international law now recognise the important and developing concept of "international crimes", crimes against the international community. The importance of trying such crimes overrides all deference to traditional notions by which criminal jurisdiction is limited to the territory in which the crime was committed, as modestly extended by the active and passive personality principles allowing for wider jurisdiction in the case of crimes committed by or against nationals of the state of trial.

Characteristically, it is required in the case of international crimes that the political offence exception (now excluded from the 2003 Act) does not apply, that a state has an obligation either to prosecute or extradite persons found within its territory who are accused of such crimes, and that states shall co-operate in their investigation and prosecution.

[1] *Commentaries on the Law of England* (1st ed., 1765–69), Vol.4, pp.1–2.

The obligation either to prosecute or extradite is a concept often referred to by international lawyers as "*aut dedere, aut judicare*".[2] Another concept associated closely with the concept of international crime is that of *jus cogens*, namely, the principle that there is a body of general rules of law (national and international), the non-observance of which may so affect the very essence of the legal system to which they belong, that the subject of law may not depart from them in particular instances. In the *Pinochet* case, a majority of the House of Lords held that torture had become an international crime against humanity and *jus cogens* before the Convention against Torture opened for signature in 1984.

The development, number and character of these crimes is analysed in this Chapter, first, to provide a greater understanding of the international agreements which are relevant to the powers of the Secretary of State under s.193 of the 2003 Act.[3] Secondly, the concept is relevant to claims of state immunity, head of state immunity, and the invocation of doctrines of "non-justiciability" (or "act of state") when extradition is sought for those who have acted in a governmental capacity; issues which arose, and which extended much more widely than simply to the position of former heads of state, in *R. v Bow Street Metropolitan Magistrate Ex p. Pinochet Ugarte*.[4]

II. THE MODERN HISTORY OF INTERNATIONAL CRIMES

4–002 The oldest such rule is that which prohibits piracy (*In Re Piracy Jure Gentium*[5]), in which the Privy Council, in holding that actual robbery was not an essential element of the offence, recognised that trial of such crimes is normally the function of national tribunals:

> "With regard to crimes as defined by international law, that law has no means of trying or punishing them. The recognition of them as constituting crimes, and the trial and punishment of the criminals are left to the municipal law of each country."

Piracy *jure gentium* was, of course, listed as an extradition crime in the first schedule to the 1870 Act.

The Privy Council emphasised that international law is not a crystallised code at any time, but is a living and expanding branch of the law, and described its sources[6]:

> ". . . the Board is permitted to consult a wider range of authority that that which it examines when the question for determination is one of municipal law only.

[2] See further Bassiouni and Wise, *Aut Dedere aut Judicare; The Duty to Prosecute or extradite in International Law* (1995, Martinus Nijhof); *Oppenheim's International Law* (1992) Vol.1, p.971; Lord Mustill *T v Home Secretary* [1996] A.C. 742, 763A–C.

[3] See Ch.5 at 5–017.

[4] *(No.1)* [2000] A.C. 61; *(No.3)* [2000] A.C. 147.

[5] [1934] A.C. 586, 589.

[6] at 588.

The sources from which international law is derived include treaties between various states, State papers, municipal Acts of Parliament and the decisions of municipal courts, and last, but not least, the opinions of jurisconsults or text-book writers."

THE FIRST WORLD WAR

In 1915 the Allied governments issued a condemnation of Turkish massacres of the Armenians as a crime against humanity: 4–003

> "In view of these new crimes of Turkey against humanity and civilisation, the Allied governments announce publicly . . . that they will hold personally responsible . . . all members of the Ottoman government and those of its agents who are implicated in such massacres."[7]

Nothing came of this when hostilities ended. In 1919, however, there was an unsuccessful attempt to put the Kaiser on trial before an international tribunal for other crimes. The Versailles conference established a Commission on the Responsibility of the Authors of the War and the Enforcement of Penalties. In March 1919 it charged Germany and her allies with extensive violations of the laws of war. It declared that all persons "without distinction of rank, including Chiefs of State, who have been guilty of offences against the laws and customs of war or the laws of humanity, are liable to criminal prosecution."

However, the United States objected that the subjection of heads of state to this degree of responsibility was unprecedented in national or international law and would be contrary to the principle of national sovereignty. A compromise led to Arts 227–230 in the Treaty of Versailles, under which the Kaiser was to be tried by an international panel of five judges for "a supreme offence against international morality and the sanctity of treaties". The Government of the Netherlands, where the Kaiser had taken refuge, declined to make him available for trial, on the ground that the offence charged was unknown to Dutch law, was mentioned in no extradition treaty to which the Netherlands was party, and appeared to be of a political rather than criminal character.

By Art.228, the German Government recognised the right of the allied powers to bring before military tribunals persons accused of crimes "in violation of the laws and customs of war". The Allied powers submitted a list of 896 persons to Germany to be extradited, including Hindenburg and Ludendorff, but accepted, after protests from Germany, that a more limited number would instead be tried at a court in Leipzig. In the end, only six persons were convicted, and sentenced to short terms of imprisonment. The Allied mission attending the trials withdrew, and the remaining trials collapsed.[8]

7 Dadrian (1989)14(2) TheYale Journal of International Law 221–34.

8 Yues Beigbeder, *Judging War criminals; The Politics of International Justice* (Palgrave, 1999).

THE SECOND WORLD WAR; THE NUREMBERG CHARTER AND TRIBUNAL AND INTERNATIONAL CONVENTIONS

4–004 The Nazi war criminals were tried at Nuremberg according to the Charter of the International Military Tribunal, which was not genuinely international, but a joint enterprise by the four major powers, the United Kingdom, the United States of America, France, and the Soviet Union.[9] According to Oppenheim's *International Criminal Law*,[10] the Big Four Powers were exercising a right which each of them could have exercised separately. The Tribunal said in its judgment:

> "... the very essence of the Charter is that individuals have international duties which transcend the national obligations of obedience imposed by the individual state. He who violates the rules of war cannot obtain immunity while acting in pursuance of the authority of the state if the state in authorising action moves outside its competence under international law . . . The principle of international law, which under certain circumstances protects the representatives of a state, cannot be applied to acts which are condemned as criminal by international law."

The jurisdiction of the Tribunal was based on a definition of the following crimes set out in Art.6 of the Charter:

> "(a) Crimes against Peace, namely planning, preparation, initiation, or waging of a war in violation of international treaties, agreements or assurances, or participation in a common plan or conspiracy for the accomplishment of any of the foregoing;
>
> (b) War crimes : namely, violations of the laws or customs of war. Such violations shall include, but not be limited to, murder, ill-treatment, or deportation to slave labour or for any other purpose of civilian population of or in occupied territory, murder or ill-treatment of prisoners of war or persons on the seas, killing of hostages, plunder of public or private property, wanton destruction of cities, towns or villages, or devastation not justified by military necessity;
>
> (c) Crimes against humanity; namely, murder, extermination, enslavement, deportation, and other inhumane acts committed against any civilian population, before or during the War, or persecutions on political, racial or religious grounds in execution of or in connection with any crime within the jurisdiction of the Tribunal, whether or not in violation of the domestic law of the country where perpetrated.
>
> Leaders, organisers, instigators and accomplices participating in the formulation or execution of a common plan or conspiracy to commit any

[9] 19 other states later associated themselves with the Charter.
[10] Hersch Lauterpacht, ed. (7th ed., 1952), Vol.II.

of the foregoing crimes are responsible for all acts performed by any person in execution of such plan."

Article 7 declared:

> "The official position of defendants, whether as heads of state or responsible officials in Government Departments, shall not be considered as freeing them from responsibility or mitigating punishment."

Article 6 of the Charter of the International Military Tribunal, Tokyo, was phrased in slightly different terms, omitting express reference to the head of state:

> "*Responsibility of Accused.* Neither the official position, at any time, of an accused, nor the fact that an accused acted pursuant to order of his government or of a superior shall, of itself, be sufficient to free such accused from responsibility for any crime with which he is charged, but such circumstances may be considered in mitigation of punishment if the Tribunal determines that justice so requires."

The Nuremberg Tribunal ruled that crimes against humanity fell within its jurisdiction only if they were committed in the execution of, or in connection, with, crimes against peace or war crimes, but this appears to have been a limitation imposed by its terms of reference, particularly Art.6. It does not appear that the Tribunal considered this to be a substantive requirement of international law.

The principles of the Charter were unanimously affirmed by Resolution 95 of the General Assembly of the United Nations in 1946. The Assembly entrusted the formulation of principles of international law recognised in the Charter to the International Law Commission. When it reported in 1950, it rejected the principle that international criminal responsibility for crimes against humanity should be limited to crimes committed in connection with war or crimes against peace. However, recognising the need to distinguish international from earlier crimes, the Commission proposed that acts would constitute international crimes only if they were committed at the instigation or toleration of state authorities. It recognised that: 4–005

> "the fact that a person who committed an act which constitutes a crime under international law acted as a head of state or responsible government official does not relieve him of responsibility under international law".[11]

In 1948, the United Nations Convention on the Prevention and Suppression of the Crime of Genocide was signed, and it declared by Art.4 that:

[11] This provision became Art.3 of the International Law Commission's Draft Code of Offences against the peace and Security of Mankind, 1954.

> "Persons committing genocide or any of the other acts enumerated in article III shall be punished, whether they are constitutionally responsible rulers, public officials, or private individuals".[12]

Article 6 did not make genocide a crime of universal jurisdiction. It required that persons charged with genocide be tried either in the territory where the offence was committed, or by "such international penal tribunal as may have jurisdiction with respect to those Contracting Parties which shall have adopted its jurisdiction." Article 7 provided:

> "Genocide and the other acts enumerated in article III shall not be considered as political crimes for the purposes of extradition. The High Contracting Parties pledge themselves in such cases to grant extradition in accordance with their laws and treaties in force."

In 1949 the four Geneva Conventions on Humanitarian Law were signed, applying specifically to war crimes, (i) for the Amelioration of the Condition of the Wounded and Sick in Armed Forces in the Field; (ii) for the Amelioration of the Condition of the Wounded, Sick and Shipwrecked Members of the Armed Forces at Sea; (iii) Relative to the Treatment of Prisoners of War; and (iv) Relative to the Protection of Civilian persons in Time of War.

4–006 These Conventions embodied the accepted obligation to prosecute or extradite. Article 31 of the first Convention stated:

> "The High Contracting Parties undertake to enact any legislation necessary to provide effective penal sanctions for person committing, or ordering to be committed, any of the grave breaches of the present Convention defined in the following Article.
>
> Each High Contracting Party shall be under an obligation to search for persons alleged to have committed, or to have ordered to be committed, such grave breaches, and shall bring such person, regardless of their own nationality, before its courts. It may also, if it prefers, and in accordance with the provisions of its own legislation, hand such persons over for trial to another High Contracting Party concerned, provided such High Contracting Party has made out a prima facie case."

Hersch Lauterpacht wrote in 1952 of war crimes, which could be punished on capture of the offenders[13]:

> "They include acts contrary to International Law perpetrated in violation of the law of the criminal's own State, such as killing or plunder for satisfying private lust and gain, as well as criminal acts contrary to the rules of war committed by

[12] This article was omitted from the United Kingdom Genocide Act 1969.

[13] Oppenheim, Vol.2, p.567.

order and on behalf of the enemy state. To that extent the notion of war crimes is based on the view that States and their organs are subject to criminal responsibility under International Law."

The Government of Israel v Eichmann[14] is a landmark case in the development of the concept of international crime. Following a detailed review of international authority, including the *Case of Lotus SS*,[15] the Supreme Court held: 4–007

(a) there was no rule of law forbidding a state from trying a foreign national for an act committed outside its borders[16];
(b) war crimes and atrocities on the scale of the Holocaust are crimes of universal jurisdiction under customary international law;
(c) the fact that an accused committed the crimes under the influence of "superior orders" in the exercise of his duties as a responsible officer of the state is no bar to the jurisdiction of a national court.

The decision was followed in the United States in *Demjanjuk v Petrovsky*[17–18] in which it was held that the crimes of which the defendant was accused were crimes of universal jurisdiction:

> "International law provides that certain offences may be punished by any state because the offenders are enemies of all mankind and all nations have an equal interest in their apprehension and punishment."

In the decades following the Nuremberg Charter, the concept of "international crimes" became detached from its association with the world wars, and became crimes against humanity. Article 5 of the Universal Declaration of Human Rights of 1948, Art.3 of the European Convention for the Protection of Human Rights of 1950,[19] and Art.7 of the International Covenant on Civil and Political Rights of 1966 all provided, in slightly varying terms, that no-one shall be subjected to torture or cruel, inhuman or degrading treatment or punishment.

In 1973 the General Assembly of the United Nations proclaimed the need for international co-operation in the detection, arrest, extradition and punishment of persons guilty of war crimes and crimes against humanity. Another resolution of the General Assembly in 1975 proclaimed the desire to make the struggle against torture more effective.

In 1979 the International Convention on the Taking of Hostages opened for signature against a background of repeated hijacks over the previous decade, and

[14] 36 I.L.R. 5, considered in Ch.3 in relation to irregular extradition and abduction.
[15] Permanent Court of International Justice, Judgment No.9 of September 1927; PCIJ, Series A, No.10.
[16] *cf.* English law principles relating to extraterritorial jurisdiction and "comity", particularly the speech of Lord Diplock in *Treacy* [1971] A.C 537, 558–562.
[17–18] USA Court of Appeals Sixth Circuit (1985) 776 F.2d 571.
[19] See now Sch.1 to the Human Rights Act 1998.

incidents in which the involvement of governments was acknowledged or suspected, for example the seizure of American hostages in Iran in 1979, and the Entebbe airport El-Al aircraft crisis in June 1976.

Article 5 of that Convention obliges the contracting parties to take such measures as may be necessary to establish its jurisdiction over any of the offences defined which are committed in its territory or on board ships or aircraft registered in that State, by any of its nationals, in order to compel that state to do or abstain from doing an act, or with respect of a hostage who is a national of that State. It also obliges each state to take such measures as may be necessary to establish its jurisdiction over the specified offences where the alleged offender is found in its territory and it does not extradite, and further provides; "This Convention does not exclude any criminal jurisdiction exercised in accordance with internal law."

4–008 In fact the United Kingdom has taken the widest possible jurisdiction in s.1 of the Taking of Hostages Act 1982:

> "(1) A person, whatever his nationality, who, in the United Kingdom or elsewhere, —
>
> (a) detains any other person ("the hostage"), and
> (b) in order to compel a State, international governmental organisation or person to do or abstain from doing any act, threatens to kill, injure or continue to detain the hostage,
>
> commits an offence."

Similar provisions appear in Art.5 of the Convention against Torture of 1975 and s.134 of the Criminal Justice Act 1988, giving effect to it in the United Kingdom. In neither of these Conventions, however, is it said expressly that heads of state have individual criminal liability.

The leading modern Conventions creating international crimes are listed in Ch.5.[20–21] The terms of the Conventions in respect to jurisdiction, extradition and procedure differ from one to another, but the concepts of obligation to prosecute or re-extradite, to co-operate in the prosecution and investigation, and the limitation of the political offence exception are characteristic of the modern international approach to these grave crimes.

THE YUGOSLAV AND RWANDA TRIBUNALS AND THE ROME STATUTE

4–009 The development of the law of international crimes has quickened with the establishment by the United Nations in 1993 of the International Tribunal for the Former Yugoslavia, for the prosecution of those responsible for serious violations of international humanitarian law committed in that territory since 1991, and in

[20–21] See 5–017.

1994 of the International Criminal Tribunal for Rwanda for the prosecution of genocide and other grave crimes committed there in 1994. Further, in 1998, 120 states voted in Rome[22] to establish a Permanent International Criminal Court. The operation of these tribunals is outside the scope of this book, but some provisions of the statutes are relevant to the concept of international crime, claims of immunity and extradition.

Power was given to the Tribunals to prosecute for grave breaches of the Geneva Conventions of 1949 (Art.2), violations of the laws or customs of war (Art.3), genocide (Art.4) and crimes against humanity, including murder, extermination, enslavement, deportation, imprisonment, torture, rape, persecution of political, racial or religious grounds, and "other inhumane acts". Article 7 declared: "The position of any accused person, whether as Head of State or Government or as a responsible government official, shall not relieve such person of criminal responsibility nor mitigate punishment."

Similar provisions appear in the Rwanda Statute.

These tribunals were established under decisions of the United Nations Security Council in the exercise of its powers under Ch.VII of the United Nations Charter. The Resolutions are binding on the United Kingdom by virtue of Art.25 of the Charter.

DELIVERY OF SUSPECTS TO THE TRIBUNALS

These obligations in these Resolutions have been implemented in the United Kingdom by The United Nations (International Tribunal) (Former Yugoslavia) Order 1996[23] and The United Nations (International Tribunal) (Rwanda) Order 1996,[24] made pursuant to s.1(1) of the United Nations Act 1946. The procedure, largely identical in each case, is modelled on the Backing of Warrants Act 1965. Paragraph 4 of each Order provides for a warrant of arrest issued by the Tribunal to be endorsed for execution in the United Kingdom. Once such a warrant has been executed, the person is brought under para.6(1) before a competent court (a District Judge). If the court is satisfied under para.6(5) that the warrant is genuine, that the person brought before it is the person sought, that the offence for which his return is sought is an International Tribunal crime, and that the person is not entitled to be discharged on any rule of law relating to a previous acquittal or conviction, it makes an order under s.6(1) for delivery to the International Tribunal in accordance with arrangements made by the Secretary of State. 4–010

Paragraph 7 of each Order makes provisions for the Statement of a Case, and para.11 provides for a period of 15 days in which an application for habeas corpus can be made.

[22] With 7 votes, including the United States of America, against, and 21 abstentions. The procedure for delivery of suspects to the Court is set out in the International Criminal Court Act 2001.

[23] SI 1996/716.

[24] SI 1996/1296.

In November 2000 Tharcisse Muvunyi was delivered to the Rwanda Tribunal charged with genocide, complicity in genocide, incitement to commit genocide and crimes against humanity committed, it was alleged, when he was a Lieutenant-Colonel in the Rwanda army. Having been made the subject of a delivery order by the magistrate, he abandoned an application for habeas corpus.

Article 5 of the Rome Statute adopted a classification of international crimes similar to those in the Yugoslavia statutes, namely, (a) the crime of genocide; (b) crimes against humanity; (c) war crimes; and (d) the crime of aggression. It defined crimes against humanity as "meaning any of the following acts when committed as part of a widespread or systematic attack directed against any civilian population, with knowledge of the attack:

(a) Murder;
(b) Extermination;
(c) Enslavement;
(d) Deportation or forcible transfer of population;
(e) Imprisonment or other severe deprivation of physical liberty in violation of fundamental rules of international law;
(f) Torture;
(g) Rape, sexual slavery, enforced prostitution, forced pregnancy, enforced sterilisation, or any other form of sexual violence of comparable gravity;
(h) Persecution against any identifiable group or collectivity on political, racial, national, ethnic, cultural, religious, gender [as defined], or other grounds that are universally recognised as impermissible under international law, in connection with any act referred to in this paragraph or any crime within the jurisdiction of the court;
(i) Enforced disappearance of persons;
(j) The crime of apartheid;
(k) Other inhumane acts of a similar character intentionally causing great suffering, or serious injury to body or to mental or physical health.

Under Art.27, heads of state or governments, and government officials are all individually liable.

III. IMMUNITIES

4–011 In potential conflict with the Conventions applying to international crimes are practices and rules of international law providing immunities. Thus, in the United Kingdom, the Diplomatic Privileges Act 1964 incorporates certain articles of the Vienna Convention on Diplomatic Relations[25] of that year. These articles confer, *inter alia*, immunity from taxation, arrest, prosecution and civil suit in the receiving

[25] Cmnd.1368.

state. Part 1 of the State Immunity Act 1978 confers an immunity on foreign states from the jurisdiction of the courts of the United Kingdom, but it does not apply, by virtue of s.16(4), to criminal proceedings.

By virtue of s.20 of the Act in Pt III, however, the provisions of the Diplomatic Privileges Act 1964 shall apply "subject to . . . any necessary modification" to a sovereign or other head of state, members of his family and household, as it applied to the head of a diplomatic mission.

It is clear that these provisions reflect established provisions of international law.

HEAD OF STATE IMMUNITY

A Head of State enjoys complete immunity *ratione personae* from arrest, prosecution or suit in another state, whatever the crime alleged, but only partial immunity after he has left office, that is, in relation to official or governmental acts (immunity *ratione materiae*). This principle is set out in Oppenheim[26] and also Satow's *Guide to Diplomatic Practice*[27]: 4–012

> "2.2 The personal status of a head of a foreign state therefore continues to be regulated by long-established rules of customary international law which can be stated in simple terms. He is entitled to immunity — probably without exception — from criminal and civil jurisdiction . . .
>
> 2.44 A head of state who has been deposed or replaced or has abdicated or resigned is of course no longer entitled to immunity as a head of state. He will be entitled to continuing immunity in regard to acts which he performed in his official capacity; in this his position is no different from that of an agent of the state. He cannot claim to be entitled to privileges as of right, although he may continue to enjoy certain privileges in other states as a matter of courtesy."

In his Hague lectures "The Legal Position in International Law of Heads of States, Heads of Governments and Foreign Ministers",[28] Sir Arthur Watts said:

> "A head of state clearly can commit a crime in his personal capacity; but it seems equally clear that he can, in the course of his public functions as head of state, engage in conduct which may be tainted by criminality or other form of wrongdoing. The critical test is whether the conduct was engaged in under colour of or in ostensible exercise of the head of state's public authority. If it was, it must be treated as official conduct, and so not a matter subject to the jurisdiction of other states, whether or not it was wrongful or illegal under the law of his own state."

[26] 1992, pp.1043–44.
[27] 5th ed., 1979, pp.9–10.
[28] (1994-III) 247 Recueil des cours 56–7.

However, later he said this[29]:

> "While generally international law does not directly involve obligations on individuals personally, that it not always appropriate particularly for acts of such seriousness that they constitute not merely international wrongs (in the broad sense of a civil wrong), but rather international crimes which offend against the public order of the international community . . . The idea that individuals who commit international crimes are *internationally* accountable for them has now become an accepted part of international law. Problems in this area — such as the non-existence of any standing international tribunal to have jurisdiction over such crimes, and the lack of agreement as to what acts are internationally criminal for this purpose — have not affected the general acceptance of the principle of individual responsibility for international criminal conduct . . . It can no longer be doubted that as a matter of general customary international law a head of state will personally be liable to be called to account if there is sufficient evidence that he authorised or perpetrated such serious international crimes."

STATE IMMUNITY

4–013 Allied to the head of state immunity doctrine is the classic international law doctrine, now much eroded, that states do not adjudicate on the conduct of other states ("*par in parem non habet imperium*"). This is the doctrine underlying Pt 1 of the State Immunity Act. Accordingly, a person may not sue a foreign state: *Al-Adsani v Government of Kuwait*[30]; *Argentine Republic v Amerada Hess Shipping Corporation*[31]; *Siderman de Blake v Republic of Argentina*,[32] all cases in which there was a statutory bar.

NON-JUSTICIABILITY ("ACT OF STATE")

Associated with the state immunity doctrine is the doctrine of non-justiciability (sometimes called, confusingly, the "act of state" doctrine), under which states refrain from examining acts of a foreign state, those acts being non-justiciable on the ground that judicial intervention may trespass on other branches of government. This doctrine in English law is explained in *Duke of Brunswick v King of Hanover*,[33] and more recently in *Buttes Gas v Hammer*.[34]

[29] pp.82–4.
[30] An English case; (1996) 107 I.L.R. 536, CA. See also *Jones v Saudi Arabia* [2004] EWCA Civ 1394.
[31] 109 S. Ct.683 (USA).
[32] 965 F.2d 699 (USA).
[33] 2 H.L. Cas 1.
[34] [1982] A.C. 888.

THE PINOCHET *CASE*[35]

4–014 The *Pinochet* case required a resolution of the question whether General Pinochet, whose extradition was sought by the Government of Spain for various grave crimes committed in Chile and elsewhere (including Spain) between 1973 and 1990, was immune for criminal proceedings brought under the Extradition Act 1989. Pinochet, who seized power in a military coup d'etat in September 1973, had been head of state of Chile at all relevant times. Spain had, like the United Kingdom, taken wide extraterritorial jurisdiction over crimes such as torture, hostage-taking and genocide.

It was alleged in great detail in the Spanish extradition request that systematic and widespread torture, murder, and forced disappearances had been committed in Chile and other states at Pinochet's instigation, for the purpose of spreading terror in Chile and among those of his political opponents who were abroad.

The central issue was whether such immunity as Pinochet had under customary law or the State Immunity Act withstood the provisions of the Torture Convention,[36] and in particular the terms of Art.1 (as reflected in s.134 of the Criminal Justice Act 1988) which defined torture as meaning any act of a defined quality "when such pain or suffering is inflicted by or at the instigation of or with the consent or acquiescence of a public official or any other person acting in an official capacity".

The Divisional Court had held on October 29, 1998 that General Pinochet was immune from criminal process in the United Kingdom. The first appellate committee of the House of Lords, sitting in November 1998, held by a majority of three to two that there was no immunity. The judgment of the House of Lords was, however, set aside by the House itself in *R. v Bow Street Magistrates Court Ex p. Pinochet Ugarte (No.2)*,[37] because one of the Lords of Appeal in the majority at the first appeal hearing had been an unpaid director of a charity associated with Amnesty International, which had appeared through counsel at that hearing. Although the first judgment is therefore not binding, the following observations of the Lords of Appeal are noteworthy.

4–015 Lord Nicholls of Birkenhead[38] distinguished between sovereign immunity, now largely codified in the State Immunity Act 1978, the non-justiciability doctrine and head of state immunity. He considered that decisions such as *Al-Adsani* did not apply because, unlike criminal proceedings, they fell within the particular provisions of Pt 1 of the 1978 Act; the doctrine of non-justiciability yielded to a contrary intention shown by Parliament. The definition of torture in s.134 of the 1988 Act made it clear that Parliament did not intend this doctrine to apply in such cases.

Section 20 of the 1978 Act, he said, conferred the same protections on the head of state as on the head of a diplomatic mission. With the "necessary modifications" required by that section, this meant that a former head of state "shall continue to

[35] [2001] 1 A.C. 61 *(No.1)*; [2000] 1 A.C. 147 *(No.3)*.
[36] Which had been ratified by the United Kingdom, Spain and Chile.
[37] [2000] 1 A.C. 119.
[38] at 104.

enjoy immunity from the criminal jurisdiction with respect to acts performed by him in the exercise of his functions as a head of state." However:

> "International law has made plain that certain types of conduct, including torture and hostage-taking are not acceptable conduct on the part of anyone. This applies as much to heads of state, or even more so, as it does to everyone else; the contrary conclusion would make a mockery of international law. This was made clear long before 1973 . . ."

Lord Nicholls also concluded that there was no residual state immunity attaching to public officials acting on behalf of their states: to accord such immunity was inconsistent with the conventions against torture and the taking of hostages.

Lord Steyn[39] emphasised that it was alleged by the Spanish authorities that the criminal acts committed were part of a systematic campaign of repression by use of state mechanisms and personnel in secret. He agreed that the immunity *ratione materiae* attaching to General Pinochet protected him "with respect to his official acts performed in the exercise of his functions as head of state." He disagreed with the Divisional Court which had held that immunity would prevail, even in respect of acts of torture, because it was impossible to draw the line between governmental and private acts:

> ". . . the development of international law since the second world war justifies the conclusion that by the time of the 1973 coup d'etat, and certainly ever since, international law condemned genocide, torture, hostage-taking, and crimes against humanity (during armed conflict or in peace time) as international crimes deserving punishment. Given this state of international law, it seems to me difficult to maintain that the commission of such high crimes may amount to acts performed in the exercise of the functions of a head of state . . . I am satisfied that . . . the charges brought by Spain against General Pinochet are properly to be classified as conduct falling beyond the scope of his functions as head of state."[40]

Lord Slynn[41] and Lord Lloyd,[42] dissenting, each attached importance to the absence of reference to "head of state" in s.134 of the Criminal Justice Act 1988 and the Torture Convention itself, and in the Taking of Hostages Act and Convention: by contrast there were specific references to heads of state and government in the Genocide Convention and other instruments such as the Rwanda, Yugoslavia and Rome statutes. This was an indication that it was not intended to remove the head of state immunity in the case of torture and hostage-taking.

4–016 Lord Slynn was not satisfied that even in 1998 there was a clear definition of "crimes against humanity". Believing that national courts must proceed with

[39] at 111.
[40] at 115G–116D.
[41] at 77–9.
[42] at 96E–97A.

caution in respect of crimes where no international tribunals had been established, he could find no clear statement in any relevant convention displacing the immunity which customary international law conferred upon a former head of state for official acts which may be criminal:

> "I conclude that the reference to public officials in the Torture Convention does not include heads of state or former heads of state, either because states did not wish to provide for the prosecution of heads of state of former heads of state or because they were unable to agree that a plea in bar to the proceedings based on immunity should be removed."[43]

Once a person was entitled to claim this immunity, the doctrine of judicial restraint would apply in respect of his official acts.

In the first appeal, it was conceded by General Pinochet's lawyers that the definition of extradition crime set out in s.2(1) of the Extradition Act 1989 fell to be determined at the date of the consideration of the issue by the United Kingdom authorities. In the second appeal, argued in January and February 1999, it was submitted by them, and it was held unanimously, that the question had to be examined at the date of the alleged conduct.[44]

Seven Lords of Appeal heard the appeal, holding by a majority of six to one that no immunity protected General Pinochet after December 8, 1988, the date when the Torture Convention took effect in the law of the United Kingdom, and that there was an allegation of a continuing conspiracy to torture after that time, and one draft substantive charge of torture. It was also held that no charges of hostage-taking in accordance with the Taking of Hostages Act 1982 were alleged in the formal requisition and supplementary particulars, furnished under Arts 12 and 13 of the European Convention on Extradition.

Lord Browne-Wilkinson reviewed the history of international crimes since the Second World War: 4–017

> ". . . in the light of the authorities to which I have referred, (and there are many others) I have no doubt that long before the Torture Convention of 1984 state torture was an international crime in the highest sense."[45]

However, before the 1984 Torture Convention:

> "I have doubts whether . . . the existence of the international crime of torture as jus cogens was enough to justify the conclusion that the organisation of state torture could not rank for immunity purposes as performance of an official function . . . At that stage there was no international tribunal to punish torture and no general jurisdiction to permit or require its punishment in domestic courts."[46]

[43] at 84A.
[44] See Ch.6.
[45] at 198G.
[46] at 204H.

He found it impossible, however, to conclude that it was intended to omit heads of state from the category of public officials in the Convention. A single act of torture was enough to displace the immunity.

Lord Hope agreed, but considered, by reference to among other sources, Articles in the Rwanda and Yugoslavia Statutes, that the immunity would only be lost if there had been widespread or systematic acts of torture, notwithstanding that the Convention had proscribed even a single act of torture. There was no settled international practice in 1989 holding that a single act of torture was an "international" crime.[47] If the matter proceeded, therefore, the magistrate should consider whether the single act of conspiracy alleged, and the conspiracy which continued after December 8, 1988, was indeed part of such widespread or systematic conduct, sufficient to overcome the immunity.

Lord Hutton considered,[48] for the same reasons as Lord Nicholls, that the *Al-Adsani* and *Siderman de Blake* line of cases did not apply, as they were covered by statutes dealing with state immunity in civil cases. Like Lord Browne-Wilkinson, he considered that the development of international crimes since the Second World War justified the view that even a single act of torture was an international crime sufficient to displace immunity. Lord Saville took a similar approach.[49]

4–018 Lord Millett took a radical position. Tracing the doubts that governmental authority could confer immunity on its agents for acts beyond its powers under international law to 1841, he considered that modern international developments, including the Eichmann trial, justified the proposition that:

> ". . . crimes prohibited under international law attract universal jurisdiction if two criteria are satisfied. First, they must be contrary to a peremptory norm of international law so as to infringe a jus cogens. Secondly they must be so serious and on such a scale that they can justly be regarded as an attack on the international public order . . . In my opinion the systematic use of torture on a large scale and as an instrument of state policy had joined piracy, war crimes and crimes against humanity as an international crime of universal jurisdiction well before 1984. I consider it had done so by 1973 . . . The Torture Convention did not create a new international crime. But it redefined it."[50]

Every state, in his view, has jurisdiction under customary international law to exercise extraterritorial jurisdiction in respect of international crimes which satisfy the relevant criteria. For these reasons, Lord Millett considered that there was already extraterritorial jurisdiction in the United Kingdom before the Torture convention, and for that reason, the crimes alleged were "extradition crimes" within the meaning

[47] at 246H–249C.
[48] at 249C.
[49] at 265C.
[50] at 275E–276F.

of s.2(1) of the 1989 Act. He noted the speed with which international law was developing and cited the observation of Glueck[51]:

> "unless we are prepared to abandon every principle of growth for international law, we cannot deny that our own day has the right to institute customs".

Lord Phillips expressed scepticism as to whether the immunity attaching to former heads of state was well established in academic writing or case law. Pointing out that the Government of Chile itself had accepted in the course of argument that torture was prohibited by international law, and that the prohibition has the character of jus cogens, he considered that the entirety of the conduct alleged constituted an international crime, displacing any claim to immunity. No immunity attached to any of the "extradition crimes" within the definition advanced by Lord Browne-Wilkinson and Lord Hope.

However, although the claim to immunity in respect of torture failed, it is striking that immunity was held to attach to another undoubted "extradition crime", namely, a specific and detailed allegation that General Pinochet had conspired to murder a political opponent in Spain (justiciable in English law according to the common law rule in *Liangsiriprasert v USA*[52]). This is the conclusion of Lord Browne-Wilkinson,[53] Lord Hope,[54] Lord Hutton,[55] and Lord Saville.[56] Lord Goff dissented altogether,[57] holding that the accession by Chile to the Torture Convention did not amount to a waiver of the immunity *ratione materiae* which was enjoyed by General Pinochet in respect of all criminal conduct alleged. Any such waiver must be express.

CONCLUSION

It is submitted that the majority decision in *Pinochet (No.3)* justifies the following propositions of English law: 4–019

(1) Former heads of state, and state officials, do not enjoy immunity *ratione materiae* in the United Kingdom in respect of participation in international crimes, that is, conduct recognised in international law as constituting crimes against the international order as recognised by multilateral conventions and international tribunals, including conduct falling under the general titles of war crimes, crimes against peace, crimes against humanity and genocide.

[51] 59 Harv.L.Rev. 396, 398.
[52] [1991] 1 A.C. 225.
[53] at 205H. (Contrary to Lord Browne-Wilkinson's implication that no separate arguments had been advanced on this point, it had been argued for the Spanish authorities that such a crime did not attract immunity for the same reason that the Lockerbie defendants would not enjoy it if, as alleged in the indictment against them, they had acted on behalf of organs of the state of Libya.)
[54] at 248G–H.
[55] at 249D–E, 265B.
[56] at 267H. (See also headnote, at 148H.)
[57] at 21G–223B.

(2) International crimes of a *jus cogens* character are no longer confined to grave criminal conduct committed in the course of armed conflict.
(3) Specifically, there is no immunity even for a single act of torture, there being no requirement of international law that the crime should have been systematic or widespread.
(4) The United Kingdom is free to take by legislation wide, even universal, jurisdiction over such international crimes in its own courts, and is obliged by the terms of Conventions to make arrangements for the extradition or prosecution of persons accused of such crimes.
(5) Former heads of states (and arguably public officials of other states) enjoy immunity (personal or state immunity) *rationae materiae* for crimes such as murder and conspiracy to murder, in England, if committed in the furtherance of governmental policy, and not committed out of some act of purely personal malice.

This last ratio of the case is startling indeed, especially in a country which attracts so many refugees from foreign tyrants, and which has a long and rich tradition of extending asylum. The *Pinochet* case raised many passions. It is doubtful whether this aspect of the House of Lords decision (unjustified by specific reasons in any of the speeches of the five Lords of Appeal who agreed with it) will survive a plea made on behalf of the employee of a tyrant, or by a former tyrant himself, who is, by general agreement, beyond the pale of civilised behaviour.

The correctness of the decision of the House of Lords was, however, doubted by the International Court of Justice in *Democratic Republic of Congo v Belgium* of February 2002.[58] It held that, where the Government of Belgium had issued an international arrest warrant against the Foreign Minister of the Democratic Republic of the Congo for, among other offences, crimes against humanity and breaches of the 1940 Geneva Conventions, immunity from criminal jurisdiction was not removed by the issue of the warrant: serving ministers had immunity from arrest, and former ministers had immunity in respect of all official acts *(rationae materiae)* committed while in office.

DIPLOMATIC IMMUNITY

4–020 As we have seen, diplomatic immunity is defined in the Vienna Convention, articles of which are attached to the Diplomatic Privileges Act 1964. Immunity is attached to diplomatic agents, their staff and families forming part of their households in the circumstances there defined. Immunity attaches only to diplomatic agents who hold that status while in the country.

Section 4 of the 1964 Act provides that if any question arises in any proceedings as to immunity, a certificate of the Secretary of State stating any fact "shall be conclusive evidence of that fact."

[58] *www.icj-cij.org.*

In *R. v Governor of Pentonville Prison Ex p. Teja*[59] an Indian citizen had fled from the USA to Costa Rica after criminal proceedings for fraud were begun against him in India. An attempt by India to extradite him from Costa Rica failed. Teja was then issued by the Government of Costa Rica with a diplomatic passport and a "letter of credence" describing him as an economic adviser to the Government. He travelled to England and was arrested. The Secretary of State issued a certificate under s.4, declaring that Teja was not accredited to the Court of St James.

The Court held that that certificate determined the matter. A unilateral action by a state appointing a diplomatic agent did not confer immunity; he had to be accepted and received as a *persona grata*. The Court also held *per curiam* that it was almost impossible to say that a man employed by a government to negotiate commercial agreements, rather than with governments, was engaged on a diplomatic mission.

A claim for diplomatic immunity was made in *R. v Governor of Pentonville Prison Ex p. Osman (No.2)*.[60] Again a certificate by the Secretary of State was decisive of the issue against the applicant, a Malay who was sought by the Government of Hong Kong in respect of very serious alleged frauds, and who produced documents showing that he had been appointed an "ambassador-at-large" by the Government of Liberia before he came to the United Kingdom. The Divisional Court, following the principle in *Teja*, rejected the claim to immunity.

It is submitted that retired diplomats enjoy only immunity *ratione materiae*, as defined in relation to their official acts, as considered above in relation to heads of state.

[59] [1971] 2 Q.B. 274, DC.
[60] Unreported, December 21, 1988, DC.

PART B

EXTRADITION TO AND FROM THE UNITED KINGDOM

Chapter 5

THE APPLICATION OF THE EXTRADITION ACT 2003 AND THE CATEGORIES OF TERRITORIES

I. RETROSPECTIVE APPLICATION

The Extradition Act 2003 ("the 2003 Act") received Royal Assent on November 20, 2003 and was brought into force on January 1, 2004.[1] The Extradition Act 1989 ("the 1989 Act") and the Backing of Warrants (Republic of Ireland) Act 1965 ("the 1965 Act") have generally ceased to have effect[2] and Sch.4 repeals these Acts. **5–001**

However, any extradition request received by the UK before January 1, 2004 will continue to be dealt with under the 1989 Act or the 1965 Act.[3] Any post-extradition requests which are made for a person extradited to or from the UK on or before the December 31, 2003 will continue to be governed by the provisions of the 1989 Act.[4]

One of the principal purposes of the 2003 Act was the implementation of the European Arrest Warrant scheme ("EAW Scheme"), contained in the European Union Council Framework Decision on the European arrest warrant, and of the surrender procedure between Member States ("the Framework Decision").[5] Article 32 of the Framework Decision allows a Member State to make a statement, at the time of its adoption of the Framework Decision, that it would continue to deal

1 Extradition Act 2003 (Commencement and Savings) Order 2003 (SI 2003/3103).
2 s.218.
3 Art.3, SI 2003/3103 as amended by the Extradition Act (Commencement and Savings) (Amendment No 2) Order 2003 (SI 2003/3312).
4 Art.4, SI 2003/3103.
5 June 13, 2002/584/JHA, App.C–006.

with requests relating to acts committed before a specified date[6] under existing extraditions arrangements.

5–002 A number of Member States have made statements[7] but the UK chose not to do so.[8] The Government of the United Kingdom has observed that extradition requests are often made which relate to conduct occurring years before the submission of the requests. It was therefore sought to avoid the continuation of parallel extradition schemes for a protracted and indefinite time.

In spite of the Government's intention, there is no express provision applying the 2003 Act to offences committed before it came into force. However, the Divisional Court considered this matter in relation to the 1989 Act, which similarly contained no provision applying it to earlier offences. It was held in *R. v Governor of Brixton Prison Ex p. Hill*[9] that the 1989 Act applied to extradition crimes committed both before and after it came into force. It can be said with confidence that, for the same reasons, the 2003 Act will apply to extradition offences[10] committed before it came into force.

Territories may have made unsuccessful extradition requests under the 1989 Act, or may have refrained from making extradition requests in the belief that a request would fail. Failed extradition requests may be renewed under the 2003 Act, and other requests may be made in the belief that defendants have fewer protections under the 2003 Act.[11] The Government expects that concerns about any requests made in these circumstances will be embodied in submissions that extradition should be barred on the ground that it would be unjust or oppressive to extradite by reason of the passage of time.[12]

II. TERRITORIAL APPLICATION OF THE 2003 ACT

ENGLAND, WALES, SCOTLAND AND NORTHERN IRELAND

5–003 The United Kingdom consists of England, Wales, Scotland and Northern Ireland.[13]

The 2003 Act applies to England subject to the exceptions in s.226.

Extradition is a reserved matter under Sch.5 to the Scotland Act 1998. However, the 2003 Act applies to Scotland subject to the exceptions in s.226. Certain provisions of the 2003 Act are modified when applied to Scotland; these are discussed in later chapters.

6 No later than August 7, 2002.

7 France, Italy and Austria [2002] O.J. L190/19.

8 This led to a concern that the application of the EAW Scheme to offences committed before the 2003 Act came into force might amount to a breach of Art.7 of the ECHR. See, for example, Justice Briefing on the Extradition Bill for Second Reading in the House of Commons December 9, 2002 *www.justice.org.uk*.

9 [1999] Q.B. 886 at 902 and 918.

10 See Ch.6.

11 As discussed in detail in subsequent chapters.

12 Mr Bob Ainsworth, Committee, 8th sitting, col.245. See Ch.10 for the passage of time bar.

13 Interpretation Act 1978, s.5 and Sch.1.

The 2003 Act applies to Wales and Northern Ireland, subject to the exceptions in s.226. The Explanatory Notes state that "The Act does not affect the powers of the National Assembly for Wales".[14] If there are different provisions or procedures for Northern Ireland, these are discussed in later chapters.

BRITISH OVERSEAS TERRITORIES

British overseas territories are listed in Sch.6 to the British Nationality Act 1981 (as amended): 5–004

- Anguilla
- Bermuda
- British Antarctic Territory
- British Indian Ocean Territory
- Cayman Islands
- Falkland Islands
- Gibraltar
- Montserrat
- Pitcairn, Henderson, Ducie and Oeno Islands
- St Helena and dependencies
- South Georgia and the South Sandwich Islands
- The Sovereign Base Areas of Akrotiri and Dhekelia (as mentioned in s. 2(1) of the Cyprus Act 1960)
- Turks and Caicos Islands
- Virgin Islands

Section 177 of the 2003 Act allows for extradition from a British overseas territory to a category 1 territory, the UK, a category 2 territory, one of the Channel Islands or the Isle of Man. An Order in Council may be made applying provisions of the 2003 Act, with modifications, to extradition requests received by a British overseas territory.[15]

Section 178 applies to extradition requests made by a British overseas territory to a category 1 territory, the UK, a category 2 territory, one of the Channel Islands or the Isle of Man. It allows an Order in Council to be made applying provisions of the 2003 Act, with modifications, to extradition requests made to a British overseas territory.[16]

At the time of writing, no Order in Council has been made under these sections. Therefore, all requests received by a British overseas territory, with the exception of Gibraltar, will continue to be dealt with under the 1989 Act.[17] This will continue

[14] Para.15, Explanatory Notes, Extradition Act 2003.

[15] This is subject to the restrictions in s.177(2) and (3).

[16] This is subject to the restrictions in s.178(2) and (3).

[17] Art.5, Extradition Act 2003 (Commencement and Savings) Order 2003 (SI 2003/3103) as amended by the Extradition Act (Commencement and Savings) (Amendment) Order 2003 (SI 2001/3258).

until the coming into force of provisions which replace the 1989 Act. These provisions may be passed by the legislature of the British overseas territory, or may be included in an Order in Council made under s.177 or 178 of the 2003 Act.

The explanatory note to the Extradition Act 2003 (Commencement and Savings) Order 2003[18] explains that the 2003 Act will apply to Gibraltar which will be designated as a category 1 territory. Article 33(2) of the Framework Decision applies it to Gibraltar. However, Gibraltar has not yet implemented the necessary domestic legislation to give effect to the EAW Scheme and so at present it is not designated as a category 1 territory.[19] As Gibraltar has also not been designated as a category 2 territory[20] it appears that any extradition request from Gibraltar would have to be dealt with under s.194.[21]

CHANNEL ISLANDS AND ISLE OF MAN

5–005 The Channel Islands are Jersey, Guernsey, Alderney and Sark.

An Order in Council may be made under s.222 of the 2003 Act extending it to any of the Channel Islands or the Isle of Man with specified modifications. At the time of writing, no Order in Council has been made under this section. Therefore, the 1989 Act will continue to apply to the Channel Islands and the Isle of Man.[22] This will continue until the coming into force of provisions which replace the 1989 Act. These provisions may be passed by the legislature of the dependency or be included in an Order in Council made under s.222 of the 2003 Act.

III. CATEGORISATION OF TERRITORIES

5–006 The 2003 Act is divided into Pts 1 and 2 which deal respectively with extradition to category 1 and 2 territories. The Secretary of State designates by order the territories in categories 1 and 2.

There are further provisions in the 2003 Act dealing with territories which are neither designated as category 1 nor 2, but are parties with the UK to international conventions, or are territories with which the UK may wish to have ad hoc extradition arrangements. The designation of territories is primarily a political decision made by the Secretary of State, although it is subject to some Parliamentary scrutiny and a prohibition on the designation of a category 1 territory which imposes the death penalty.

18 SI 2003/3103.
19 Extradition Act 2003 (Designation of Part 1 Territories) Order 2003 (SI 2003/3333).
20 Extradition Act 2003 (Designation of Part 2 Territories) Order 2003 (SI 2003/3334).
21 See 5–018.
22 Art.5, Extradition Act 2003 (Commencement and Savings) Order 2003 (SI 2003/3103) as amended by the Extradition Act (Commencement and Savings) (Amendment) Order 2003 (SI 2001/3258).

CATEGORY 1

DESIGNATED CATEGORY 1 TERRITORIES

5–007 Category 1 territories are designated by an order made by the Secretary of State (s.1(1)–(2)).

The following territories have been designated[23]:

- Austria
- Belgium
- Cyprus
- Denmark
- Finland
- France
- Hungary
- Ireland
- Latvia
- Lithuania
- Luxembourg
- Malta
- The Netherlands
- Poland
- Portugal
- Slovenia
- Spain
- Sweden

EAW SCHEME AND CATEGORY 1

5–008 The primary purpose of Pt 1 of the 2003 Act is to give effect to the EAW Scheme.[23a] The Framework Decision[24] required Member States to have implemented domestic legislation to give effect to the Framework Decision by December 31, 2003.[25] However, not all Member States complied with this timetable. As further Members States implement the necessary domestic legislation they will be re-designated as category 1 territories.

On May 1, 2004, Cyprus, the Czech Republic, Estonia, Hungary, Latvia, Lithuania, Malta, Poland, Slovakia and Slovenia joined the EU as full members. These territories were obliged to have enacted the necessary domestic legislation to give effect to the Framework Decision by May 1, 2004. However, only four

[23] Extradition Act 2003 (Designation of Part 1 Territories) Order 2003 (SI 2003/3333) as amended by Art.2 of the Extradition Act 2003 (Amendment to Designations) Order 2004 (SI 2004/1898).
[23a] See *The Office of the King's Prosecutor v Armas* [2004] EWHC 2019 (Admin).
[24] 2002/584/JHA, App.C–006.
[25] Art.34(1).

territories complied with this deadline. Again, in due course these territories will be re-designated as category 1 territories when they have implemented the EAW Scheme.

On July 14, 2004, the Under-Secretary of State for the Home Department said that Germany, Greece, Estonia and Slovakia had recently confirmed to the UK Government that they had enacted the necessary domestic legislation. Therefore, these territories will all be re-designated as category 1 in due course.[26] The only remaining Member States are the Czech Republic, which said it hoped to complete implementation shortly,[27] and Italy, which was unable to confirm when it would be ready to implement the Framework Decision.

CATEGORY 1 AND NON-EU MEMBER STATES

5–009 However, there is nothing within the 2003 Act which restricts the designation of category 1 territories to those which operate the EAW Scheme. Indeed the Government explicitly said in the course of the Parliamentary scrutiny of the Extradition Bill:

> ". . . it is possible that at some point in the future it would be desirable to add another country- perhaps a trusted Commonwealth or bilateral treaty partner- to Part 1 and the Government does not believe that we should remove the flexibility to allow for this."[28]
>
> "We intend to designate existing members of the European Union as part 1 countries, together with, in all probability, Iceland and Norway."[29]

The Government hoped that during the passage of the Extradition Bill Norway and Iceland would have agreed to and implemented the EAW Scheme by the time the 2003 Act came into force. As this had not happened by December 31, 2003, these territories are not designated as category 1.

The suggestion that non-EU Member States could be designated as category 1 territories caused some concern. The EAW Scheme was agreed as part of the broader EU policy of mutual recognition:

> "The objective set for the Union to become an area of freedom, security and justice leads to abolishing extradition between Members States and replacing it by a system of surrender between judicial authorities. Further, the introduction of a new *simplified system* of surrender of sentenced and suspected persons for the purposes of execution or prosecution of criminal sentences makes it possible to remove the complexity and potential for delay inherent in the present extradition

[26] Caroline Flint, *Hansard*, col.4 (July 14, 2004).

[27] On August 23, 2004 it was reported that the President of the Czech Republic had vetoed the proposal of the legislature to incorporate the EAW into Czech law.

[28] Government response to the Committee's First Report, February 26, 2003, HC 475.

[29] Mr Bob Ainsworth, Committee, 1st Sitting, col.22.

procedures. Traditional cooperation relations which have prevailed up till now between Member States should be replaced by a system of free movement of judicial decisions in criminal matters, covering both pre-sentenced and final decisions, within an area of freedom, security and justice."[30] [Emphasis added.]

The simplified system in the Framework Decisions involves the removal of the fundamental double criminality requirement for certain types of conduct.[31] The EAW Scheme is said to be based on the high level of confidence held by the Member States for one another,[32] and was agreed on the (doubtful) basis that a defendant would receive the same level of protection under the criminal justice system of any Member State. All Member States purport to apply the ECHR, and allegations of breaches of the ECHR by Member States can be determined by the European Court of Human Rights.

The Extradition Bill proposed that territories could be designated as category 1 simply by an order by the Secretary of State, subject to annulment by a resolution of either House of Parliament. There was concern about the designation of category 1 territories which might not have the same procedural and human rights safeguards as EU Member States. Therefore, s.223(5) and (6) of the 2003 Act now require that the draft of any order designating a category 1 territory must be approved by a resolution of both Houses of Parliament.

The other major concern expressed during consideration of the Extradition Bill 5–010
was that no territory which imposed the death penalty, such as the USA, should be included in category 1. No Member State imposes the death penalty.[33] Although the Government said that it had no intention of designating the USA as a category 1 territory[34] it did eventually agree an amendment to meet the more general concern, which became s.1(3).

This subsection prohibits the designation of a category 1 territory if a person found guilty of a criminal offence may be sentenced to death for the offence under the general criminal law of the territory.[35] The inclusion of the phrase "under the general criminal law" leaves open the question of what would happen if a territory imposed the death penalty under emergency legislation or under military law. During the course of Parliamentary debate, the Government said it believed that extradition could not take place if a category 1 territory might impose the death sentence in an individual case because this would involve a breach of a Convention Right.[36] In summary, Lord Bassam said:

"I hope also that the words that have been spoken today into the Official Report make it fairly clear that it is absolutely our intention that we would not seek to

[30] Para.5, Preamble, Framework Decision, 2002/584/JHA.
[31] See further Ch.6 at 6–008 and 6–016.
[32] Para.10, Preamble, Framework Decision 2002/584/JHA.
[33] Art.1, 6th Protocol to the ECHR; *cf.* 13th Protocol to ECHR.
[34] Mr Bob Ainsworth, Committee, 1st Sitting, cols 22–23.
[35] The Secretary of State considers the issue of the death penalty under Pt 2 cases — see Ch.12 at 12–012.
[36] Lord Bassam of Brighton, Vol.648, col.GC 161. See Ch.11 for Convention Rights.

extradite in circumstances where someone was at risk from the death penalty. That is the Government's position."[37]

REPUBLIC OF IRELAND

5–011 Extradition arrangements between the UK and the Republic of Ireland were previously governed by the 1965 Act. Although the Republic is a signatory to the European Convention of Extradition (see 5–013 below) the European Convention on Extradition Order[38] did not apply to the Republic. The 1965 Act was intended to produce an informal system of extradition between close neighbours, of the kind common among other groups of neighbouring states in Europe (the Scandinavian states, for example). The scheme under the 1965 Act was in some respects similar to the EAW Scheme, involving the recognition and enforcement by a UK court of a warrant issued in the Republic.

The 2003 Act repealed the 1965 Act.[39] The Republic, as a Member State, has implemented the Framework Decision and the Secretary of State has accordingly designated it as a category 1 territory. (The first EAW was received in the UK from the Republic of Ireland on January 16, 2004. The person arrested consented to his surrender, which took place on January 30, 2004, 14 days after the receipt of the request.)

CATEGORY 2

DESIGNATED CATEGORY 2 TERRITORIES

5–012 Category 2 territories are designated by an order made by the Secretary of State (s.69). The order must be laid in draft before Parliament and approved by a resolution of each House of Parliament (s.223(5)–(6)). All territories with which the UK has general extradition arrangements which are not designated as category 1 territories, have been designated in category 2.[40]

Those Member States which had not implemented the EAW Scheme by December 31, 2003 were initially designated as category 2 territories. However, some Member States which have now implemented the EAW Scheme have been re-designated (see 5–008 above) and this group includes most of the 10 territories which joined the EU on May 1, 2004. When the remaining territories have implemented the necessary domestic legislation, they should in due course be re-designated in category 1.

[37] Lord Bassam of Brighton, Vol.648, col.GC 163.

[38] SI 2001/962.

[39] ss.218 and 220 and Sch.4. See also 5–001 above for extradition requests received before December 31, 2003 and post-extradition matters.

[40] *Hansard*, col.6 (December 15, 2003).

The following have been designated as category 2 territories[41]:

- **Albania**
- **Andorra**
- Antigua and Barbuda
- Argentina
- **Armenia**
- **Australia**
- **Azerbaijan**
- The Bahamas
- Bangladesh
- Barbados
- Belize
- Bolivia (65 days)
- Bosnia and Herzegovina (65 days)
- Botswana
- Brazil
- Brunei
- **Bulgaria**
- **Canada**
- Chile (95 days[42])
- Colombia
- Cook Islands
- **Croatia**
- Cuba (65 days)
- **Czech Republic**
- Dominica
- Ecuador
- El Salvador
- **Estonia**
- Fiji
- The Gambia
- **Georgia**
- **Germany**
- Ghana
- **Greece**
- Grenada
- Guatemala
- Guyana
- Hong Kong Special Administrative Region
- Haiti (65 days)
- **Iceland**
- India
- Iraq (65 days)
- **Israel**
- **Italy**
- Jamaica
- Kenya
- Kiribati
- Lesotho
- Liberia (95 days)
- **Liechtenstein**
- **Macedonia FYR**
- Malawi
- Malaysia
- Maldives
- Mauritius
- Mexico
- **Moldova**
- Monaco (65 days)
- Nauru
- **New Zealand**
- Nicaragua (65 days)
- Nigeria
- **Norway**
- Panama (65 days)
- Papua New Guinea
- Paraguay (65 days)
- Peru (95 days)
- **Romania**
- **Russian Federation**
- Saint Christopher and Nevis
- Saint Lucia

[41] Art.2, Extradition Act 2003 (Designation of Part 2 Territories) Order 2003 (SI 2003/3334).

[42] Art.4(2) of the Extradition Act 2003 (Designation of Part 2 Territories) Order 2003 (SI 2003/3334) as amended by Art.3 of the Extradition Act 2003 (Amendment to Designations) Order 2004 (SI 2004/1898).

- Saint Vincent and the Grenadines
- San Marino (65 days)
- **Serbia and Montenegro**
- Seychelles
- Sierra Leone
- Singapore
- **Slovakia**
- Solomon Islands
- **South Africa**
- Sri Lanka
- Swaziland
- **Switzerland**
- Tanzania
- Thailand (65 days)
- Tonga
- Trinidad and Tobago
- **Turkey**
- Tuvalu
- Uganda
- **Ukraine**
- Uruguay
- **The United States of America (65 days)**
- Vanuatu
- Western Samoa
- Zambia
- Zimbabwe

This list highlights in bold those territories which have also been designated for the purposes of ss.71(4), 73(5), 84(7) and 86(7), considered at 5–014 below.[43]

THE EUROPEAN CONVENTION ON EXTRADITION 1957

5–013 The Council of Europe ("COE") was established in 1949 and has 45 members. It should not be confused with the EU, which is a separate body, although many territories are part of both the COE and the EU. Membership of the Council of Europe is sometimes regarded as a preliminary step towards membership of the EU. Members of the COE are not necessarily in the continent of Europe. The COE does not make law, but it does produce conventions which are open for signature by its members.

The European Convention on Extradition was opened for signature in 1957. Its aim was to simplify the process of extradition between COE Member States.

The UK signed the Convention in 1957 but did not ratify it by domestic legislation at this time. Accordingly, the European Convention Extradition Order[44] was made on July 24, 1990 and came into force on May 14, 1991 under the general terms of Pt III of the 1989 Act. The most significant change was the removal of the requirement, where a person was accused of an offence, that a requesting territory must produce admissible evidence to make out a prima facie case. Instead, "particulars" of information, normally provided in the requesting territory's domestic arrest warrant, were sufficient.[44a]

[43] Art.3, The Extradition Act 2003 (Designation of Part 2 Territories) Order 2003 (SI 2003/3334).
[44] SI 1990/1507.
[44a] See also Ch.1.

DESIGNATIONS UNDER SS.71(4), 73(5), 84(7) AND 86(7)

The 2003 Act allows category 2 territories to be further designated so that: 5–014

- a territory only has to provide information rather than evidence to satisfy the test in s.71(3) for an arrest warrant to be issued[45];
- a territory only has to provide information rather than evidence to satisfy the test in s.73(4) for a provisional arrest warrant to be issued[46];
- a judge will not apply the sufficiency of evidence test in s.84(1) if the extradition request is for a person who has not been convicted[47];
- a judge will not apply the sufficiency of evidence test in s.86(1) if the extradition request is for a person who was convicted in their absence.[48]

Categories designated are those marked in bold in the list in 5–012, above. The designated territories are made up of signatories to the 1957 European Convention on Extradition, and Australia, Canada, New Zealand and the USA. Any order designating a territory in this sub-category cannot be made unless a draft is laid before Parliament and approved by both Houses of Parliament.[49]

THE PARTICULAR CIRCUMSTANCES OF THE USA

The designation of the USA has provoked controversy.[50] In seeking to provide reassurance that any person extradited to the USA would be fairly treated, the Government referred to a statement made by the Government of the USA: 5–015

> "Every person who is extradited to stand trial in the criminal justice system within the United States is entitled to the fundamental right of due process under the United States constitution. All extraditees have the right to a fair trial, before an impartial jury, and enjoy the right to counsel, the right to confront adverse witnesses, and the right to compulsory process to call witnesses favourable to the defense. No extraditee can be convicted except on the basis of proof beyond a reasonable doubt. Every extraditee has the right to appeal a conviction."[51]

On March 31, 2003,[52] the United Kingdom and the United States of America signed an extradition treaty, intending to replace the treaty of 1972,[53] as amended

[45] s.71(4). See Ch.7 at 7–012.
[46] s.73(5). See Ch.7 at 7–014.
[47] s.84(7), see Ch.9 at 9–028.
[48] s.86(7), see Ch.9 at 9–039.
[49] s.223(5)–(6).
[50] Paul Garlick Q.C., "The mysterious case of the new US extradition scheme" [2004] N.L.J. 738.
[51] *Hansard*, col.24 (December 15, 2003).
[52] App.C–007
[53] Embodied in SI 1976/2144; App.B–001

in minor respects in 1985. This new treaty is not incorporated in the 2003 Act. It has been ratified by the United Kingdom, but not yet by the US legislature. It appears that it may not be ratified, because its provisions are controversial, particularly among the Irish-American community which fears that the treaty will make extradition of suspected Irish republican terrorists easier.

Nonetheless, the evidence requirement for extradition requests from the USA has been abrogated, as will be shown in Ch.9. Article 8.3 of the new treaty requires, but only in the case of extradition requests to the United States, that information providing a reasonable basis to believe that the person whose return is sought committed the offence. This abandonment of reciprocity by the UK Government has been much criticised.

DESIGNATIONS UNDER S.74(11)(B)

5–016 If a person is arrested under a provisional warrant with a view to extraditing him to a category 2 territory, the judge must discharge the person if he has not received a copy of the extradition request, the required certificate from the Secretary of State and a copy of any relevant Order in Council within 45 days of the arrest (s.74(10)).[54] A category 2 territory designated under s.74(11)(b) will be allowed a longer period.

Those territories which have been designated under s.74(11)(b) are shown in the list at 5–012 with the period allowed in brackets.[55]

INTERNATIONAL CONVENTIONS

5–017 The UK does not of course have general extradition arrangements with every territory. It is party to a number of international conventions which require the UK to deal with extradition requests from other parties to these conventions for specific offences. Section 193 allows the UK to comply with its obligations under international conventions for those territories with which it does not have general extradition arrangements, and for offences which would not otherwise satisfy the definition of an extradition offence in ss.137 and 138.[56]

The Secretary of State can designate by order a territory which is neither a category 1 nor a category 2 territory but which is a party to an international convention to which the UK is also a party (s.193). Procedures of this kind were previously governed by s.22 of the 1989 Act.

The UK is a party to the following conventions which may be relevant:

- The Convention on Offences and certain other Acts committed on board Aircraft, which was signed at Tokyo on September 14, 1963[57];

[54] See Ch.8.
[55] Art.4, Extradition Act 2003 (Designation of Part 2 Territories) Order 2003 (SI 2003/3334).
[56] See Ch.6.
[57] *www.unodc.org/unodc/terrorism_convention_aircraft.html.*

- The Convention for the Suppression of Unlawful Seizure of Aircraft, which was signed at the Hague on December 16, 1970[58];
- The Convention on the Prevention and Punishment of Crime against Internationally Protected Persons adopted by the United Nations General Assembly in 1973[59];
- The International Convention against the Taking of Hostages opened for signature at New York on December 18, 1979[60];
- The Convention on the Physical Protection of Nuclear Material opened for signature at Vienna and New York on March 3, 1980[61];
- The United Nations Convention against Torture and other Cruel, Inhuman or Degrading Treatment or Punishment adopted by the United Nations General Assembly on December 10, 1984[62];
- The United Nations Convention against Illicit Traffic in Narcotic Drugs and Psychotropic Substances which was signed in Vienna on December 20, 1988[63];
- The Convention for the Suppression of Unlawful Acts against the Safety of Maritime Navigation, which was signed at Rome on March 10, 1988[64];
- The Convention on the Safety of the United Nations and Associated Personnel adopted by the General Assembly of the United Nations on December 9, 1994[65];
- The Convention for the Suppression of Terrorist Bombings, which was opened for signature at New York on January 12, 1998[66];
- The Convention for the Suppression of the Financing of Terrorism, which was opened for signature at New York on January 10, 2000.[67]

Any order made is subject to annulment by a resolution of either House of Parliament (s.223(7)).

Territories which are designated under this section will be treated as category 2 territories (s.193(2)) but the following provisions of Pt 2 will not apply:

- ss.71(4), 73(5), 84(7) and 86(7)[68];
- s.74(11)(b)[69];
- ss.137 and 138 which define extradition offences.

58 *www.unodc.org/unodc/terrorism_convention_aircraft_seizure.html.*
59 *www.unodc.org/unodc/terrorism_convention_protected_persons.html.*
60 *www.unodc.org/unodc/terrorism_convention_hostages.html.* See also ss.16 and 83 which deal with hostage-taking considerations and are discussed in Ch.10.
61 *www.unodc.org/unodc/terrorism_convention_nuclear_material.html.*
62 *www.un.org/documents/ga/res/39/a39r046.htm.*
63 *www.unodc.org/pdf/convention_1988_en.pdf.*
64 *www.unodc.org/unodc/terrorism_convention_maritime_navigation.html.*
65 *www.un.org/law/cod/safety.htm.*
66 *www.unodc.org/unodc/terrorism_convention_terrorist_bombing.html.*
67 *www.un.org/law/cod/finterr.htm.*
68 See 5–014.
69 See 5–016.

The conduct that will constitute an extradition offence will be specified in the order made by the Secretary of State designating the territory. Conduct may only be specified if the convention for which the territory is designated applies to the conduct (s.193(4)–(5)).

SPECIAL EXTRADITION ARRANGEMENTS

5–018 The 2003 Act, like the 1989 Act, allows for ad hoc extradition arrangements with territories which are neither designated as category 1 nor 2. The Secretary of State may certify that he believes an arrangement has been made with a territory which is neither category 1 nor 2 for the extradition of a person to that territory (s.194(1) and (2)). His certificate is conclusive evidence of the fact that the arrangement has been made and that the territory is not a category 1 or 2 territory (s.194(5)).

If the Secretary of State issues this certificate, the 2003 Act applies to procedures for the extradition of that person to the territory as if it was a category 2 territory (s.194(3)). However, the following sections of Pt 2 will not apply:

- ss.71(4), 73(5), 84(7) and 86(7)[70];
- s.74(11)(b).[71]

Further modifications to Pt 2 may be set out in the certificate (s.194(4)(b)).

[70] See 5–014.
[71] See 5–016.

CHAPTER 6

EXTRADITION OFFENCES

I. INTRODUCTION

A person may only be extradited if he is accused or convicted of an offence which satisfies the definition for an extradition offence.[1] This concept is fundamental to the 2003 Act. **6–001**

There are similarities in the definitions of "extradition offence" in Pts 1 and 2. A significant difference is the removal of the requirement of double criminality in Pt 1 for conduct listed in Sch.2 to the 2003 Act (which is taken from Art.2(2) of the Framework Decision). This change is radical, as it allows a person to be extradited for the first time for conduct which is not made criminal under UK law. The rule of double criminality is discussed in detail in Ch.2.

TIMING

Although, as argued in Ch.5, the 2003 Act applies to conduct committed before it came into force, the Act is silent as to whether the judge must apply the law in the **6–002**

[1] In the 1989 Act the term "extradition crime" was used. There are a number of significant differences between an "extradition crime" and an "extradition offence" as defined in the 2003 Act.

UK at the time when the conduct is alleged to have taken place, or at the time when the extradition request is made, for the purpose of deciding whether the person is accused or convicted of an "extradition offence".

This question was considered by the House of Lords under the 1989 Act, which also omitted reference to the time at which the conduct was to be considered, in *R. v Bow Street Magistrates' Court Ex p. Pinochet (No.3)*.[2] It was held that the test was whether the conduct would have been punishable in the UK at the time it took place. In that case, the relevant offence of torture only became an extra-territorial crime in the UK in December 1988. Offences of torture committed outside the UK before this date could not be an extradition crime as they would not have been punishable in the UK.

CHARGES

6–003 In previous extradition statutes, the Secretary of State specified the crimes in English law terms which the magistrate should examine for the purpose of determining whether a prima facie case had been made out.[3] Thereafter those representing the requesting state framed charges with particulars of those specified crimes.

In the context of proceedings under the Fugitive Offenders Act 1967 Lord Griffiths said in *Government of Canada v Aronson*[4]:

> "It is axiomatic that a person charged with a crime is entitled to know not only the offence with which he is charged, be it a statutory or a common law crime, but also to have particulars of the conduct which it is alleged constitutes the crime."

Rule 100 of the Magistrates' Courts Rules 1981 requires that:

> "Every information, summons, warrant or other document laid, issued or made for the purposes of, or in connection with, any proceedings before a magistrates' court for an offence shall be sufficient if it describes the specific offence with which the person is charged, or of which he is convicted, in ordinary language avoiding as far as possible the use of technical terms and without necessarily stating all the elements of the offence, and give such particulars as may be necessary for giving reasonable information of the nature of the offence."

Under the 1989 Act, the representative of the requesting state formulated the charges by the start of committal hearing and provided the defence with a copy.[5]

2 [2000] 1 A.C. 147. Also considered in Ch.4.
3 *R. v Governor of Pentonville Prison Ex p. Sotiriadis* [1975] A.C. 1.
4 [1990] 1 A.C. 579, 594Df.
5 *Re Nagdhi* [1990] 1 W.L.R. 317. See also *R. v Governor of Pentonville Prison Ex p. Osman* [1990] 1 W.L.R. 277, 302.

Although it was appropriate to draft those charges in terms of an English law offence, it was not necessary that the charges should specify the enactment that they contravened in English law.[6] In *R. v Bow Street Magistrates' Court Ex p. Kline*,[7] a Sch.1 case, the Divisional Court agreed that the magistrate was free to commit on different particulars of the charges than the foreign government had laid.

In *Charron v The Government of the Unites States of America*,[8] the Privy Council held, on the hearing of an appeal from the Court of Appeal of The Bahamas, that a committal to prison, in a case brought by the United States of America, was not invalidated where Bahamian charges had not been formulated. However, it was emphasised that in the circumstances of the simple factual allegations, the details of the charges brought against the appellant were known and "therefore the appellant had suffered no procedural unfairness or prejudice." This practice of laying charges in English law terms is already continuing in extradition proceedings under the 2003 Act; the justification remains the same.

The judge is not restricted under the 2003 Act to finding whether the conduct in the Pt 1 warrant or Pt 2 request amounts to an offence in any list provided on behalf of a requesting territory. The judge must apply the definitions of an extradition offence in the 2003 Act, and can find that the conduct amounts to any UK offence, where it is necessary for him to investigate the question. In effect, the list is prepared to assist the court in applying the definition of an extradition offence to the particular Pt 1 warrant or Pt 2 request. Under the 1989 Act, the judge was not free to go beyond the crimes listed in the "order [or authority] to proceed"; a limitation that no longer applies since the concept of the "order [or authority] to proceed" has been abolished.

"ANOTHER FORM OF DETENTION" AND "HOWEVER IT IS DESCRIBED IN THAT LAW"

The phrase "another form of detention" is used repeatedly in the definitions of "extradition offence". The Government explained the reasoning for the inclusion of this phrase: 6–004

> "UK courts send young people to young offenders institutions, not to prison. Equally, in appropriate cases, people may be detained in mental institutions rather than imprisoned. One size does not fit all in the UK, and there is no reason why the situation should be any different in any other country. I do not know the different titles that different . . . countries give to their detention facilities and we cannot be over-prescriptive."[9]

6 *In Re Boutros Abdul Aziz Al-Salaam*, unreported, CO/1622/94, April 11, 1997.

7 Unreported, June 30, 1999; CO/813/99.

8 [2001] 1 W.L.R. 1793.

9 Mr Bob Ainsworth, Committee, 2nd sitting, col.57. See also Arts 2(1) and 4(1) of the Framework Decision which refer to detention orders.

The phrase "however it is described in that law" is also used repeatedly in the definition of an extradition offence. The Government has again explained the reason:

> "We believe that those words ['however it is described in that law'] are necessary. They enable us to deal with cases where our extradition partners use different language or terminology to describe the concept of imprisonment or detention. It would be most unfortunate if we ever found ourselves in a position where we were unable to extradite simply because another country, although clearly recognising and operating the notion of imprisonment, described it in a different way in its law."[10]

II. PART 1

6–005 Section 64 defines an extradition offence for a person who has not been sentenced and s.65 deals with a person who has been sentenced.

DEFINITIONS

6–006 Section 66 provides definitions for some of the terms used in ss.64 and 65.

An appropriate authority of a category 1 territory is a judicial authority which the appropriate judge[11] believes has the function of issuing arrest warrants in that territory (s.66(2)).

The law of a territory is the general criminal law (s.66(3)).

The relevant part of the UK is the part where the proceedings in which it is necessary to decide whether conduct constitutes an extradition offence are taking place (s.66(4) and (5)).

EXTRADITION OFFENCE: PERSON NOT SENTENCED FOR OFFENCE

6–007 Section 64 applies to the conduct of a person who is either:

(a) accused in a category 1 territory of the commission of an offence constituted by the conduct; or
(b) alleged to be unlawfully at large having been convicted by a court in a category 1 territory for an offence constituted by the conduct but has not been sentenced for the offence (s.64(1)).

[10] Lord Bassam, Vol.650, col.GC 224.
[11] See s.67 for definition of "appropriate judge" as discussed in Ch.8 at 8–016.

There are then definitions depending on the "territory" where the conduct took place, and there is provision for extra-territorial offences.

CONDUCT OCCURS IN CATEGORY 1 TERRITORY AND FALLS WITHIN EUROPEAN FRAMEWORK LIST

The conduct constitutes an extradition offence if: 6–008

(a) the conduct occurs in the category 1 territory and no part of it occurs in the UK; and
(b) a certificate is issued by the appropriate authority of the category 1 territory which shows that the conduct falls within the European framework list; and
(c) the certificate also shows that the conduct is punishable with imprisonment or another form of detention for a term of 3 years or a greater punishment (s.64(2)).

The European framework list is the list of conduct set out in Sch.2 (s.215(1)).

Schedule 2 lists the following 32 types of conduct:

(1) Participation in a criminal organisation.
(2) Terrorism.
(3) Trafficking in human beings.
(4) Sexual exploitation of children and child pornography.
(5) Illicit trafficking in narcotic drugs and psychotropic substances.
(6) Illicit trafficking in weapons, munitions and explosives.
(7) Corruption.
(8) Fraud, including that affecting the financial interests of the European Communities within the meaning of the Convention of July 26, 1995 on the protection of the European Communities' financial interests.
(9) Laundering of the proceeds of crime.
(10) Counterfeiting currency, including of the euro.
(11) Computer-related crime.
(12) Environmental crime, including illicit trafficking in endangered animal species and in endangered plant species and varieties.
(13) Facilitation of unauthorised entry and residence.
(14) Murder, grievous bodily injury.
(15) Illicit trade in human organs and tissue.
(16) Kidnapping, illegal restraint and hostage-taking.
(17) Racism and xenophobia.
(18) Organised or armed robbery.
(19) Illicit trafficking in cultural goods, including antiques and works of art.
(20) Swindling.
(21) Racketeering and extortion.
(22) Counterfeiting and piracy of products.

(23) Forgery of administrative documents and trafficking therein.
(24) Forgery of means of payment.
(25) Illicit trafficking in hormonal substances and other growth promoters.
(26) Illicit trafficking in nuclear or radioactive materials.
(27) Trafficking in stolen vehicles.
(28) Rape.
(29) Arson.
(30) Crimes within the jurisdiction of the International Criminal Court.
(31) Unlawful seizure of aircraft/ships.
(32) Sabotage.

This list of conduct is taken from Art.2(2) of the Framework Decision but this article refers to the list as containing offences rather than conduct. The Secretary of State is given the power to amend Sch.2 to ensure that it reflects any future changes to Art.2(2). However, a draft order to amend Sch.2 must be approved by both Houses of Parliament (s.223(5)–(6)).

6–009 It is foreseeable that the European framework list will be amended, as two recent draft Framework Decisions use an expanded version of this list including also traffic offences, smuggling, criminal damage and theft.[12] The Framework Decision allows for the amendment of the list in Art.2(2) by a unanimous decision of Member States.[13]

Section 64(2) requires only that the conduct must be certified to fall within the European framework list.[14] The list of conduct is in generic terms and it is possible that particular conduct will only arguably fall within one of the categories. It does not appear from the wording of the 2003 Act that a court will be able to question the certification.[15]

However, the Court in *The Office of the King's Prosecutor, Brussels v Armas*[16] considered the issue of certification in respect of s.65(2)[17] which is in similar terms to s.64(2). The European Arrest Warrant is in a standard form which is annexed to the Framework Decision[18] and it includes a list of the 32 offences with a tick box for each. In *Armas*, the original Warrant was in Flemish and had three boxes ticked whereas the English translation of the Warrant had no boxes ticked. The Court held that the certificate in this case was the Flemish version of the Warrant rather than the English translation.

The Court also commented: ". . . whether section 65(2)(b) applies does not depend solely on the list of tick boxes: if the certificate shows the alleged conduct

[12] Draft Framework Decision on the application of the principle of mutual recognition of financial penalties ([2001] O.J. 278/4) and Draft Framework Decision on the European Evidence Warrant for obtaining objects, documents and data for use in proceedings in criminal matters (2003/270 (CNS)).

[13] Art.2(3): Art.34(3) obliges the Commission to report on the operation of the Framework Decision by December 31, 2004 and the Council of the European Union will consider in light of this report whether the list in Art.2(2) should be extended or amended (Art.2(3)).

[14] See also s.65(2) which contains a similar requirement for a person who has been sentenced.

[15] European Scrutiny Committee, HC (2001–02) 152-xvii, para.19.

[16] [2004] EWHC 2019 (Admin).

[17] See 6–016 below.

[18] See App.C–006.

falls within the European framework list, it matters not that the applicable tick box has not been ticked." This meant that the Court believed it could look at the description of the offences in the Warrant and make its own decision as to whether these showed conduct falling in the European framework list even if the relevant box had not been ticked.

The approach in this *obiter* comment is problematic. First the European framework list is not made up of offences common to all Member States and it may be difficult to assess whether an offence under the law of another Member State falls into one of the categories in the list. Furthermore, it leaves open the question of how the court would approach any inconsistencies between the ticking of a box for a European framework list offence and the description of the conduct and/or offences in the rest of the Warrant.

CONDUCT OCCURS IN CATEGORY 1 TERRITORY AND DOES NOT FALL WITHIN EUROPEAN FRAMEWORK LIST

The conduct constitutes an extradition offence in relation to the category 1 territory if: **6–010**

- (a) the conduct occurs in the category 1 territory;
- (b) the conduct would constitute an offence under the law of the relevant part of the UK if it occurred in that part of the UK; and
- (c) the conduct is punishable under the law of the category 1 territory with imprisonment or another form of detention for a term of 12 months or a greater punishment (however it is described in that law) (s.64(3)).

There is no requirement that the offence under UK law carry a punishment above a specified level. This reflects the Framework Decision.[19]

EXTRA-TERRITORIAL: CONDUCT OCCURS OUTSIDE THE CATEGORY 1 TERRITORY AND MAY TAKE PLACE IN THE UK

The conduct constitutes an extradition offence for the category 1 territory if: **6–011**

- (a) the conduct occurs outside the category 1 territory;
- (b) the conduct is punishable under the law of the category 1 territory with imprisonment or another form of detention for a term of 12 months or a greater punishment (however it is described in that law); and
- (c) in corresponding circumstances equivalent conduct would constitute an extra-territorial offence under the law of the relevant part of the UK punishable with imprisonment or another form of detention for a term of 12 months or a greater punishment (s.64(4)).

[19] See Art.2(1) and (4), Framework Decision.

EXTRA-TERRITORIAL: CONDUCT OCCURS OUTSIDE THE CATEGORY 1 TERRITORY BUT NOT IN THE UK

6–012 The conduct constitutes an extradition offence in relation to the category 1 territory if:

- (a) the conduct occurs outside the category 1 territory and no part of it occurs in the UK;
- (b) the conduct would constitute an offence under the law of the relevant part of the UK punishable with imprisonment or another form of detention for a term of 12 months or a greater punishment if it occurred in that part of the UK; and
- (c) the conduct is so punishable under the law of the category 1 territory (however it is described in that law) (s.64(5)).

INTERNATIONAL CRIMINAL COURT OFFENCES: CONDUCT OCCURS OUTSIDE THE CATEGORY 1 TERRITORY BUT NOT IN THE UK

6–013 Under s.64(6), conduct constitutes an extradition offence in relation to the category 1 territory if:

- (a) the conduct occurs outside the category 1 territory and no part of it occurs in the UK;
- (b) the conduct is punishable under law of the category 1 territory with imprisonment or another form of detention for a term of 12 months or a greater punishment however it is described; and
- (c) the conduct constitutes, or if committed in the UK would constitute, one of the following offences under the International Criminal Court Act 2001 ("ICCA") or the International Criminal Court (Scotland) Act 2001 ("ICCSA"):
    - (i) genocide, crimes against humanity and war crimes (s.51 or 58 ICCA, s.1 ICCSA);
    - (ii) conduct ancillary to genocide, crimes against humanity and war crimes committed outside the jurisdiction (s.52 or 59 ICCA, s.2 ICCSA);
    - (iii) an ancillary offence for an offence under paras (i) or (ii) (s.55 or 62 ICCA, s.7 ICCSA) (s.64(7)).

It is not an objection to extradition that the person could not have been punished for the offence under the law in force at the time when and in the place where he committed or is alleged to have committed the conduct (s.196).

FISCAL OFFENCES

If the conduct in s.64(3), (4) or (5) relates to tax or duty, it is immaterial if the law of the relevant part of the UK does not impose the same kind of tax or duty or does not contain rules of the same kind as that of the category 1 territory (s.64(8)(a)). 6–014

If the conduct in s.64(3), (4) or (5) relates to customs or exchange, it is immaterial if the law of the relevant part of the UK does not contain rules of the same kind as those of the law of the category 1 territory (s.64(8)(b)).

EXTRADITION OFFENCE: PERSON SENTENCED FOR OFFENCE

Section 65 applies to the conduct of a person if he is alleged to be unlawfully at large having been convicted by a court in a category 1 territory of an offence constituted by the conduct, and if he has been sentenced for the offence (s.65(1)). 6–015

There are differing definitions which depend on where the conduct took place; the concept of "territory" is used, instead of the familiar concept of "jurisdiction" in the 1989 Act. These definitions include extra-territorial offences which apply if none of the conduct took place in a category 1 territory but this territory nonetheless claims jurisdiction and the right to prosecute.

CONDUCT OCCURS IN CATEGORY 1 TERRITORY AND FALLS WITHIN EUROPEAN FRAMEWORK LIST

The conduct constitutes an extradition offence if: 6–016

(a) the conduct occurs in the category 1 territory and no part of it occurs in the UK; and
(b) a certificate is issued by the appropriate authority of the category 1 territory which shows that the conduct falls within the European framework list; and
(c) the certificate also shows that a sentence of imprisonment or another form of detention for a term of 12 months or a greater punishment has been imposed in the category 1 territory in respect of the conduct (s.65(2)).

The European framework list is discussed at 6–008 above. There is no requirement for double criminality.

CONDUCT OCCURS IN CATEGORY 1 TERRITORY AND DOES NOT FALL WITHIN EUROPEAN FRAMEWORK LIST

The conduct constitutes an extradition offence in relation to the category 1 territory if: 6–017

(a) the conduct occurs in the category 1 territory;

(b) the conduct would constitute an offence under the law of the relevant part of the UK if it occurred in that part of the UK; and
(c) a sentence of imprisonment or another form of detention for a term of four months or a greater punishment has been imposed in the category 1 territory in respect of the conduct (s.65(3)).

There is no requirement that the offence under UK law carry a punishment above a specified level. This reflects the Framework Decision.[20]

EXTRA-TERRITORIAL: CONDUCT OCCURS OUTSIDE THE CATEGORY 1 TERRITORY AND MAY TAKE PLACE IN THE UK

6–018 The conduct constitutes an extradition offence for the category 1 territory if:

(a) the conduct occurs outside the category 1 territory;
(b) a sentence of imprisonment or another form of detention for a term of four months or a greater punishment has been imposed in the category 1 territory in respect of the conduct; and
(c) in corresponding circumstances equivalent conduct would constitute an extra-territorial offence under the law of the relevant part of the UK punishable with imprisonment or another form of detention for a term of 12 months or a greater punishment (s.65(4)).

EXTRA-TERRITORIAL: CONDUCT OCCURS OUTSIDE THE CATEGORY 1 TERRITORY BUT NOT IN THE UK

6–019 The conduct constitutes an extradition offence in relation to the category 1 territory if:

(a) the conduct occurs outside the category 1 territory and no part of it occurs in the UK;
(b) the conduct would constitute an offence under the law of the relevant part of the UK punishable with imprisonment or another form of detention for a term of 12 months or a greater punishment if it occurred in that part of the UK; and
(c) a sentence of imprisonment or another form of detention for a term of four months or a greater punishment has been imposed in the category 1 territory in respect of the conduct (s.65(5)).

[20] See Art.2(1) and (4), Framework Decision.

INTERNATIONAL CRIMINAL COURT OFFENCES: CONDUCT OCCURS OUTSIDE THE CATEGORY 1 TERRITORY BUT NOT IN THE UK

Under s.64(6), conduct constitutes an extradition offence in relation to the category 1 territory if: 6–020

(a) the conduct occurs outside the category 1 territory and no part of it occurs in the UK;
(b) a sentence of imprisonment or another form of detention for a term of four months or a greater punishment has been imposed in the category 1 territory in respect of the conduct; and
(c) the conduct constitutes, or if committed in the UK would constitute, one of the offences under the International Criminal Court Act 2001 or the International Criminal Court (Scotland) Act 2001 set out at 6–013 above.[21]

FISCAL OFFENCES

If the conduct in s.64(3), (4) or (5) relates to tax or duty, customs or exchange then s.65(8) has equivalent provisions to those in s.64(8) considered at 6–014 above. 6–021

III. PART 2

EXTRADITION OFFENCE: PERSON NOT SENTENCED FOR OFFENCE

Section 137 applies to the conduct of a person who is either: 6–022

(a) accused in a category 2 territory of the commission of an offence constituted by the conduct; or
(b) alleged to be unlawfully at large having been convicted by a court in a category 2 territory for an offence constituted by the conduct but has not been sentenced for the offence (s.137(1)).

There are again definitions which use the concept of "territory", rather than "jurisdiction". These include extra-territorial offences which apply if none of the conduct took place in a category 1 territory, but this territory nonetheless claims jurisdiction and the right to prosecute.

[21] It is not an objection to extradition that the person could not have been punished for the offence under the law in force at the time when and in the place where he committed or is alleged to have committed the conduct (s.196).

Double criminality is required by all the definitions. If the conduct amounts to an offence under military law of the category 2 territory but does not constitute an offence under the general criminal law of the relevant part of the UK, it will not satisfy the definition for an extradition offence (s.137(7)).

The relevant part of the UK is defined for the purposes of s.137 as being the part of the UK where:

(a) the extradition hearing took place, if the question of whether the conduct constitutes an extradition offence is to be decided by the Secretary of State; or
(b) proceedings in which it is necessary to decide that question are taking place, in any other case (s.137(8)).

CONDUCT OCCURS IN CATEGORY 2 TERRITORY

6–023 The conduct constitutes an extradition offence in relation to a category 2 territory if:

(a) the conduct occurs in the category 2 territory;
(b) the conduct would constitute an offence under the law of the relevant part of the UK punishable with imprisonment or another form of detention for a term of 12 months or a greater punishment if it occurred in that part of the UK; and
(c) the conduct is so punishable under the law of the category 2 territory (however it is described in that law) (s.137(2)).

EXTRA-TERRITORIAL: CONDUCT OCCURS OUTSIDE THE CATEGORY 2 TERRITORY AND MAY OCCUR IN THE UK

6–024 The conduct constitutes an extradition offence in relation to the category 2 territory if:

(a) the conduct occurs outside the category 2 territory;
(b) the conduct is punishable under the law of the category 2 territory with imprisonment or another form of detention for a term of 12 months or a greater punishment (however it is described in that law); and
(c) in corresponding circumstances equivalent conduct would constitute an extra-territorial offence under the law of the relevant part of the UK punishable with imprisonment or another form of detention for a term of 12 months or a greater punishment (s.137(3)).

EXTRA-TERRITORIAL: CONDUCT OCCURS OUTSIDE THE CATEGORY 2 TERRITORY BUT NOT IN THE UK

The conduct constitutes an extradition offence in relation to the category 2 territory if: 6–025

(a) the conduct occurs outside the category 2 territory and no part of it occurs in the UK;
(b) the conduct would constitute an offence under the law of the relevant part of the UK punishable with imprisonment or another form of detention for a term of 12 months or a greater punishment if it occurred in that part of the UK; and
(c) the conduct is so punishable under the law of the category 2 territory (however it is described in that law) (s.137(4)).

INTERNATIONAL CRIMINAL COURT OFFENCES: CONDUCT OCCURS OUTSIDE THE CATEGORY 2 TERRITORY BUT NOT IN THE UK

Under s.137(5), conduct constitutes an extradition offence in relation to the category 2 territory if: 6–026

(a) the conduct occurs outside the category 2 territory and no part of it occurs in the UK;
(b) the conduct is punishable under law of the category 2 territory with imprisonment or another form of detention for a term of 12 months or a greater punishment however it is described; and
(c) the conduct constitutes or if committed in the UK would constitute one of the following offences under the International Criminal Court Act 2001 ("ICCA") or the International Criminal Court (Scotland) Act 2001 ("ICCSA"):

    (i) genocide, crimes against humanity and war crimes (s.51 or 58 ICCA, s.1 ICCSA);
    (ii) conduct ancillary to genocide, crimes against humanity and war crimes committed outside the jurisdiction (ss.52 or 59 ICCA, s.2 ICCSA);
    (iii) an ancillary offence in relation to offence under paras (i) or (ii) (s.55 or 62 ICCA, s.7 ICCSA) (s.137(6)).

It is not an objection to extradition that the person could not have been punished for the offence under the law in force at the time when and in the place where he committed or is alleged to have committed the conduct (s.196).

EXTRADITION OFFENCE: PERSON SENTENCED FOR OFFENCE

6–027 Section 138 applies to the conduct of a person if he is alleged to be unlawfully at large having been convicted by a court in a category 2 territory of an offence constituted by the conduct and if he has been sentenced for the offence (s.138(1)).

The same pattern of definitions using the concept of territory follows. These include extra territorial offences which apply if none of the conduct took place in a category 1 territory but this territory nonetheless claims jurisdiction and the right to prosecute.

Double criminality is required by all of the definitions. If the conduct amounts to an offence under military law of the category 2 territory, but does not constitute an offence under the general criminal law of the relevant part of the UK, then it will not satisfy the definitions for an extradition offence (s.138(7)).

The relevant part of the UK is defined for the purposes of s.138 as being the part of the UK where:

(a) the extradition hearing took place, if the question of whether the conduct constitutes an extradition offence is to be decided by the Secretary of State; or
(b) proceedings in which it is necessary to decide that question are taking place, in any other case (s.138(8)).

CONDUCT OCCURS IN CATEGORY 2 TERRITORY

6–028 The conduct constitutes an extradition offence in relation to the category 2 territory if:

(a) the conduct occurs in the category 2 territory;
(b) the conduct would constitute an offence under the law of the relevant part of the UK punishable with imprisonment or another form of detention for a term of 12 months or a greater punishment if it occurred in that part of the UK; and
(c) a sentence of imprisonment or another form of detention for a term of four months or a greater punishment has been imposed in the category 2 territory in respect of the conduct (s.138(2)).

EXTRA-TERRITORIAL: CONDUCT OCCURS OUTSIDE THE CATEGORY 2 TERRITORY AND MAY OCCUR IN THE UK

6–029 The conduct constitutes an extradition offence in relation to the category 2 territory if:

(a) the conduct occurs outside the category 2 territory;

(b) a sentence of imprisonment or another form of detention for a term of four months or a greater punishment has been imposed in the category 2 territory in respect of the conduct; and
(c) in corresponding circumstances equivalent conduct would constitute an extra-territorial offence under the law of the relevant part of the UK punishable with imprisonment or another form of detention for a term of 12 months or a greater punishment (s.138(3)).

EXTRA-TERRITORIAL: CONDUCT OCCURS OUTSIDE THE CATEGORY 2 TERRITORY BUT NOT IN THE UK

The conduct constitutes an extradition offence in relation to the category 2 territory if: 6–030

(a) the conduct occurs outside the category 2 territory and no part of it occurs in the UK;
(b) the conduct would constitute an offence under the law of the relevant part of the UK punishable with imprisonment or another form of detention for a term of 12 months or a greater punishment if it occurred in that part of the UK; and
(c) a sentence of imprisonment or another form of detention for a term of four months or a greater punishment has been imposed in the category 2 territory in respect of the conduct (s.138(4)).

INTERNATIONAL CRIMINAL COURT OFFENCES — CONDUCT OCCURS OUTSIDE THE CATEGORY 2 TERRITORY BUT NOT IN THE UK

Under s.137(5), conduct constitutes an extradition offence in relation to the category 2 territory if: 6–031

(a) the conduct occurs outside the category 2 territory and no part of it occurs in the UK;
(b) the conduct is punishable under law of the category 2 territory with imprisonment or another form of detention for a term of 12 months or a greater punishment however it is described; and
(c) the conduct constitutes or if committed in the UK would constitute one of the offences under the International Criminal Court Act 2001 or the International Criminal Court (Scotland) Act 2001 set out at 6–026 above.[22]

[22] It is not an objection to extradition that the person could not have been punished for the offence under the law in force at the time when and in the place where he committed or is alleged to have committed the conduct (s.196).

IV. PART 1 WARRANTS AND PART 2 REQUESTS FOR MORE THAN ONE OFFENCE

6–032 Section 207 allows the Secretary of State to provide by order for the 2003 Act to have effect with specified modifications if a Pt 1 warrant or extradition request is made for more than one offence. The Extradition Act 2003 (Multiple Offences) Order 2003[23] provides for modifications to the 2003 Act for Pt 1 warrants or Pt 2 requests for more than one offence.

The general effect of these modifications is that any reference in the 2003 Act to an offence or extradition offence is to be construed as a reference to offences or extradition offences respectively. There are a large number of specific modifications set out in the Schedule to this statutory instrument. If the Pt 1 warrant or Pt 2 request deals with more than one offence, the provisions described in the following chapters should be read as subject to the modifications set out in the Schedule.

One of the reasons for the modifications is to allow for the partial execution of a Pt 1 warrant or Pt 2 request where the judge and / or the Secretary of State must consider more than one offence for which extradition is sought. By applying the modifications it is possible that extradition will be refused for only some offences allowing extradition to take place for the remaining offence/s.

V. DISCUSSION

6–033 The concept and definition of "extradition offence" in the 2003 Acts poses a number of questions. For the reasons set out in Ch.2, it is possible to define the crimes for which extradition will be sought in terms either of conduct or of the elements of the foreign offence.

It appears from the plain wording of the statute that the draftsman of the 2003 Act has chosen the narrower approach, similar to that which appeared in the Fugitive Offenders Act 1967, though the courts may be tempted to make a "purposive" construction in favour of a broad conduct test in the light of the legislative history.

Section 10(2) (for Pt 1) and s.78(4)(b) require the court to examine the foreign offence. It would have been easy for the draftsman to have required in these sections that the court be satisfied that:

> "the conduct specified in the request" is an extradition offence; or
> "the conduct described in the request" is an extradition offence,

[23] SI 2003/3150, see App.B–004.

but he did not. The court is required to make findings as to "the offence specified in the request", which must be particularised as required by ss.2(2) and (3), and 70(3) and (4).

Sections 64(1) and 137(1)(a) are important because for the first time the concept of "conduct" is introduced for Pt 1 and Pt 2. A person is accused of a foreign offence "constituted by the conduct". Accordingly, ss.64(2), 65(2), 137(2) and 138(2) (and the following subsections of each of these sections) are to be read as: "The conduct (which constitutes the foreign offence) constitutes an extradition offence in relation to the category 1 [2] territory if . . ."

As appears in Ch.2, under the Extradition Act 1870, the Fugitive Offenders Act 1967, and the Extradition Act 1989, which repealed the two earlier statutes, there were numerous authorities in the High Court and the House of Lords which grappled with the problems caused where an offence in one jurisdiction was different in scope or character from the offence or offences which would be charged had the conduct occurred in England. It was determined under the 1870 Act and the 1989 Act that it was appropriate to look at the broad conduct alleged: but under the 1967 Act, it was appropriate to look at the elements of the foreign offence charged, and to determine whether proof of those elements necessarily involved proof of an English offence or offences.

The definition of "extradition crime" in s.26 of the Extradition Act 1870, surviving in para.20 of Sch.1 to the Extradition Act 1989 until the end of 2003, was very different to the 2003 formulation:

> "The term 'extradition crime' means a crime which, if committed in England or within English jurisdiction, would be one of the crimes described in the first schedule to this Act"

These crimes, as supplemented in later statutes, were all expressed in English law terms, generally or specifically.

Accordingly, it was necessary to examine the factual allegations laid against the defendant, and to ask whether that conduct, had it occurred in England or within English jurisdiction, would have amounted to one of the listed crimes. See *In Re Nielsen.*[24]

The material parts of s.3 of the Fugitive Offenders Act 1967 are: 6–034

> "(1) For the purposes of this Act an offence of which a person is accused or has been convicted in a designated Commonwealth or United Kingdom dependency is a relevant offence if —
>
> (a) in the case an offence against the law of a designated Commonwealth country, it is an offence which, however described in that law, falls within any of the descriptions set out in Schedule 1 to this Act, and is punishable

[24] (1984) 79 Cr. App. R. 1; [1984] A.C. 606.

under that law with imprisonment for a term of twelve months or any greater punishment;

(b) in the case of an offences against a the law of a United Kingdom dependency, it is punishable under that law, on conviction by or before a superior court, with imprisonment for a term of twelve months or any greater punishment; and

(c) the act or omission constituting the offence, or the equivalent act or omission, would constitute an offence against the law of the United Kingdom if it took place within the United Kingdom or, in the case of an extra-territorial offence, in corresponding circumstances outside the United Kingdom."

(2) In determining for the purposes of this section whether an offence against the law of a designated Commonwealth country falls within the description set out in Schedule 1, any special circumstances of aggravation which may be necessary to constitute the offence under the law shall be disregarded."

The 1967 Act concentrated therefore upon the elements of the legal offence charged. It accordingly became necessary to show that the offence alleged in the requesting country contained all the elements necessary to establish an offence within the description of crimes listed in the schedule. See *Government of Canada v Aronson.*[25]

The 1989 Act contained a definition of extradition crime which favoured the "conduct" approach in the 1870 Act (see *R. v Secretary of State for the Home Department Ex p. Hill*[26]) over the 1967 Act approach:

"**2.**—(1) In this Act, except in Schedule 1, extradition crimes means —

(a) conduct in the territory of a foreign state, a designated Commonwealth country or a colony which, if it occurred in the United Kingdom, would constitute an offence punishable with imprisonment for a term of twelve months or any greater punishment and which, however described in the law of the foreign state, Commonwealth country or colony, is so punishable under that law;

(b) an extra-territorial offence against the law of a foreign state, Commonwealth country or designated Commonwealth country or colony which is punishable under that law with imprisonment for a term of twelve months or any greater punishment, and which satisfies —

(i) the condition mentioned in subsection (2) below; or
(ii) all the conditions specified in subsection (3) below.

[25] [1990] 1 A.C. 579.
[26] [1999] Q.B. 886.

(2) The condition mentioned in subsection (1)(b)(i) above is that in corresponding circumstances equivalent conduct would constitute an extra-territorial offence against the law of the United Kingdom punishable with imprisonment for a term of 12 months or any greater punishment.

(3) The conditions mentioned in subsection (1)(b)(ii) above are —

(a) that the foreign state, Commonwealth country or colony bases its jurisdiction on the nationality of the offender;
(b) that the conduct constituting the offence occurred outside the United Kingdom; and
(c) that, if it occurred in the United Kingdom, it would constitute an offence punishable for a term of 12 months or any greater punishment."

The 2003 Act appears on its face to favour the narrower approach of the kind set out in the 1967 Act. The investigation of the foreign offence is essentially the same; the separate requirement for the finding of sufficient evidence set out in s.7(5) of the 1967 Act is matched by the requirement to produce, in Pt 2 cases, sufficient evidence in s.84 (unless abrogated). Further, the words "particulars of the offence specified in the request" in s.78(2)(c) suggest particulars of an offence of the kind specified in the Indictments Rules.

It is also noteworthy that the specialty provisions of ss.17(3) and 95(4) are much more consistent with a narrow construction of the phrase "extradition offence", because a distinction is drawn between "the offence in respect of which the person is extradited" and "an extradition offence disclosed by the same facts as that offence". **6–035**

For the reasons advanced in Ch.2, the narrow approach to the definition of extraditable offences or conduct is in the case of most jurisdictions defensible and practicable. This construction will not, however, facilitate extradition to the USA for the artificial federal offences of wire fraud, mail fraud or bank fraud. Lord Diplock commented on these offences in *McCaffery*[27] holding that conduct underlying such a charge could be an "extradition crime" within the 1870 Act:

> "A device that is not uncommonly employed for the purpose of founding such Federal criminal jurisdiction is to charge the accused not with underlying fraud itself but with the use of interstate transport or interstate communication for the purpose of carrying out the fraud. Reference to this practice which upon first encountering it strikes an English or Scots lawyer as strange, not to say disingenuous is found in . . . [the 1972 extradition treaty]."

The UK-US extradition treaty agreed between the UK and the USA of March 31, 2003,[28] which has not been ratified by the United States, contains in Art.2.2(b) a

[27] [1984] 1 W.L.R. at 871D.
[28] App.C–007.

definition of "extraditable offences" which appears to allow for the extradition to the United States of persons accused of crimes denominated by such US devices. An offence shall be an extraditable offence:

> "whether or not the offense is one for which United States federal law requires the showing of such matters as interstate transportation, or use of mails or of other facilities affecting interstate commerce, such matters being jurisdictional only."

The European Framework Decision[29] contains this provision in Art.2.4:

> "For offences other than those covered by paragraph 2, surrender may be subject to the condition that the acts for which the European arrest warrant has been issued constitute an offence under the law of the executing Member State, whatever the constituent elements or however it is described."

The existence of these provisions may suggest strongly that Parliament intended to adopt a broad conduct-based test in the 2003: the question arises however why the draftsman adopted such very different language.

6–036 A second group of questions is posed by the concept of "territory" rather than "jurisdiction" in the definitions of extradition offence contained in ss.64, 65, 137 and 138. Modern approaches to territorial jurisdiction are very difficult to fit within this framework. The approach of the 1870 Act, preserved in Sch.1 to the 1989 Act, was much better suited to modern conditions.

The definition of "extradition crime" in the 1870 Act, cited above, refers to English "jurisdiction". This therefore required transposition, as discussed at length by the House of Lords in *R. (Al-Fawwaz) v Governor of Brixton Prison*.[30] That case decided that "jurisdiction" was not confined to "territory". The 1870 Act also had a number of sections which deemed various acts to have been committed within a state's "jurisdiction". See, for example, s.25 (which became para.19 of Sch.1 to the 1989 Act):

> "For the purposes of this Act, every colony, dependency, and constituent part of a foreign state, and every vessel of that state, shall (except where expressly mentioned as distinct in this Act) be deemed to be within the jurisdiction of and be part of that foreign state."

See also Sch.1 to the 1989 Act, para.15. Section 22(6) of the 1989 Act stipulated:

> "For the purposes of general extradition procedures under Part III of this Act, in their application (whether or not by virtue of such an Order in Council) as between the United Kingdom and any other state, any act or mission, wherever it takes place, which constitutes —

[29] App.C–006.
[30] [2001] UKHL 69; [2002] 1 A.C. 556.

(d) an offence under this section; and
(e) an offence against the law of that state,

shall be deemed to be an offence committed within the territory of that state."

That section was limited to the international offences mentioned in that section; but the provision illustrates that the draftsman of the 2003 Act, who referred to provisions in the 1989 Act in his drafting of "extradition offences", did not enact such deeming provisions for s.137(2). He deliberately preferred the concept of "territory" to "jurisdiction", in spite of the authority of the recent case of *Al-Fawwaz*. (He also took this approach in the definition of extradition offence in Pt 3 of the 2003 Act, governing extradition to the United Kingdom. (See ss.142 and 148.))

In using the concept of "territory" in the 2003 Act, Parliament, it can be seen at once, appears to have left a *lacuna* or made a deliberate omission. It fails to cater for cases where part of the conduct takes place in the requesting territory and part in the UK.

Taking the definitions appropriate to Pt 2 cases, s.137(2) and s.138(2) apply obviously to cases of ordinary crime which occur entirely in one territory, where there is no international element, such as robbery, assault, or theft.

Extra-territorial offences are covered by subss.(3) and (4). Examples of extradition offences within subs.(3) are cases where English law has always asserted extra-territorial jurisdiction, such as murder committed by a British national abroad (s.4 of the Offences against the Person Act 1861) and modern international crimes such as torture, hostage-taking, hijacking and crimes against internationally protected persons. Hostage-taking, for example, "would constitute an extra-territorial offence under the law of the relevant part of the United Kingdom", as required by subs.(3)(b) by reason of s.1 of the Taking of Hostages Act 1982: 6–037

"A person, whatever his nationality, who, in the United Kingdom or elsewhere,—

(f) detains any other person ("the hostage"); and
(g) in order to compel a State, international governmental organisation or person to do or abstain from doing any act, threatens to kill, injure or continue to detain the hostage,

commits an offence."

To understand the purpose of subs.(4), and the origin of the phrase "and no part of it occurs in the United Kingdom", it is necessary to appreciate that the draftsman drew the shape of this section from s.2 of the 1989 Act, but in some ways enlarged and in some ways limited its scope. The former subs.2(1)(b)(ii) and (3) permitted the UK to extradite, for example, a German accused of committing robbery or fraud outside Germany, because Germany based jurisdiction on the nationality of the offender, provided he had not committed that offence in the United Kingdom.

Subsection (4) widens this, so as to allow the extradition of a person, whatever his nationality, to a state which claims universal jurisdiction over criminal conduct, that is, jurisdiction to try people for crimes wherever committed, provided only that the conduct (i) would be punishable in England by 12 months if committed in England; and (ii) in fact occurs entirely outside the United Kingdom.

6–038 Section 137(2)(a) does not say "part of the conduct occurs in the category 2 territory"; whereas s.137(4) contemplates a case where "no part of [the conduct] occurs in the United Kingdom". Therefore it appears clear that where part of the "conduct" in s.137(2)(a) occurs in the United Kingdom, the "offence constituted by the conduct", within the meaning of s.137(1)(a) and (b) is not an extradition offence.

However, another construction is superficially plausible. In Pt 1, s.64(3)(4) and (5) and s.65(3), (4) and (5) mirror ss.137(2)(3) and (4) and 138(2)(3) and (4), respectively. However s.64(2)(a) declares that conduct constitutes an extradition offence in the case of European Framework cases if "the conduct occurs in the category 1 territory and no part of it occurs in the United Kingdom". The second part of this definition does not appear in ss.64(3)(a), 65(4)(a), 137(2)(a) and 138(2)(a). Therefore the phrase in this group of offences "the conduct occurs in the category 1 [2] territory" does not mean "all the conduct".

The phrase "and no part of it occurs in the United Kingdom" was added by the Government as an amendment to the Extradition Bill to meet concerns about the removal of double criminality for the European framework list. The Government believed that it was clear from the Bill that no one could be extradited from the UK for conduct which had taken place in the UK and did not amount to a criminal offence under UK law. The Government argued that this must be the ordinary meaning of "the conduct occurs in the category 1 territory".

However, in order to meet widespread concern about this issue, it proposed an amendment to insert the phrase "and no part of it occurs in the United Kingdom" into what is now ss.64(2)(a) and 65(2)(a). The Government described the effect of the amendments as ". . . to put beyond any possible doubt that the provisions in Part 1 of the Bill allowing for extradition without dual criminality cannot apply if any part of the conduct that forms the extradition request has occurred in the United Kingdom."[31]

6–039 The appearance of the additional words in s.64(2) does not, in any event, resolve the issue. This is because ss.64(3)(b), 65(3)(b), 137(2)(b) and 138(2)(b) all require that the "conduct" in (a) of each subsection should be transposed to the United Kingdom; that is, on the approach under consideration, that "part of the conduct" which occurs in the requesting territory is notionally transposed, for the purpose of determining whether that "conduct" is punishable in the United Kingdom. If part of the conduct has in fact occurred in the United Kingdom, no sense can be attached to the concluding words of (b) "if it occurred in that part of the United Kingdom."

[31] Baroness Scotland, *Hansard*, Vol.650, col.GC 202 (July 1, 2003).

There is in fact a clear justification in accusation cases for the construction that cases where part of the conduct occurred in the UK are not extraditable. They can be tried here. Part 1 of the Criminal Justice Act 1993 greatly enlarges the jurisdictional reach of UK law. The facility to try cases here that are within ss.64(5) and 137(4) is the obvious justification for the exclusion of cases within those subsections where part of the conduct occurs within the UK. The same principle must apply to cases within ss.64(3), 65(3), 137(2) and 138(2).

The Divisional Court has taken a different view. In *Office of the Brussels Prosecutor v Armas*,[32] the defence argued in a Pt 1 conviction case that in respect of offences which fell within the Framework Decision, since part at least of the person's conduct had taken place in the UK, he could not be extradited by virtue of the plain words of s.65(2)(a). This approach was compatible with the provisions of Art.4.7 of the Framework Decision. However, acknowledging that the construction of the Act was difficult, the Court determined that the offences were also within subss.(3)–(6). The Court properly found that conduct amounting to an offence in the European framework list might also satisfy the definitions in subss.(3)–(6). Accepting that the normal meaning of "the conduct" in s.65(3) meant "all the conduct", the Court nonetheless held that, by reason of the added words "and no part of it occurs in the United Kingdom" that appear in s.65(2), the words "the conduct" in subs.3 meant "part of the conduct". **6–040**

The Court justified this approach by relying on the oft-quoted words of the High Court in *In Re Arton (No.2)*[33] that an extradition treaty should be interpreted in such a way as would not "hinder the working and narrow the operation of most salutary international arrangements".

It is respectfully submitted that this decision is flawed. Assuming the modern European arrangements to be salutary for the sake of argument, the *Arton* approach applies to treaties, not statutes. It is intended to ensure that treaties are construed in the same way by all jurisdictions party to them, and not by reference to possibly idiosyncratic local canons of statutory construction.[34] Further, there is no recognition or discussion in the judgment of the canon of construction against doubtful penalisation. This unquestionably applies to extradition proceedings,[35] and the ambiguities in the definitions under discussion are patent.

The court also held in reaching a "workable" interpretation that it would be unfortunate if a possibly minor act committed in this country prevented a trial in the requesting territory. It did not, however, recognise the possibility that conversely a requesting state with an aggressive jurisdictional reach, such as the USA, could seek extradition where only a fraction of the conduct occurred in the USA, and where

[32] [2004] EWHC 2019 (Admin).

[33] [1896] 1 Q.B. 509, 517.

[34] See, for example, *R. v Governor of Pentonville Prison Ex p. Ecke* (1981) 73 Cr. App. R. 23; *R. v Governor of Ashford Remand Centre Ex p. Postlethwaite* [1988] 1 A.C. 924, HL; Art.31 of the Vienna Convention on the Law of Treaties.

[35] *Government of Canada v Aronson* [1990] 1 A.C. 579 at 590H, *per* Lord Elwyn-Jones, 618F–G, *per* Lord Lowry, 590F–G, *per* Lord Bridge.

the natural and obvious forum for trial would be the UK, under a statutory scheme where the Secretary of State no longer has the discretion to prevent an unfair extradition.[36]

[36] An argument is available that where the UK is the natural and obvious forum for trial, extradition to the USA in such circumstances would constitute a breach of a person's Art.8 rights under the ECHR; see Ch.11.

CHAPTER 7

ARREST

I. INTRODUCTION

Although there are similarities between the schemes in Pts 1 and 2 governing arrest procedures, there are different requirements for the contents of the documents required to effect an arrest and the procedure which should be followed. Therefore, each Part is considered separately. **7–001**

II. PART 1

There are two means by which a person can be arrested under Pt 1. The first can be used if a Pt 1 warrant has been received by the designated authority and certified. The second is a provisional arrest warrant which can be issued if there are reasonable grounds for believing that a Pt 1 warrant has been or will be issued. Part 4 of the 2003 Act deals with police powers, and this includes provisions which are relevant to arrest and detention. Part 4 is considered in Ch.17. Defence funding is dealt with at 8–002 *et seq.* in Ch.8. **7–002**

PART 1 WARRANT AND CERTIFICATE

7–003 Section 2 applies if a Pt 1 warrant is received by an authority which has been designated by the Secretary of State for the purposes of Pt 1 (s.2(1) and (9)). The Secretary of State has designated the National Criminal Intelligence Service ("NCIS") and the Crown Agent of the Crown Office in Scotland.[1]

A Pt 1 Warrant is an arrest warrant which is issued by a judicial authority of a category 1 territory (s.2(2)) and which contains either:

(a) the statement in s.2(3) and the information in s.2(4) for accusation cases; or
(b) the statement in s.2(5) and the information in s.2(6) for conviction cases.

ACCUSED OF AN OFFENCE

7–004 The statement in s.2(3) is that:

(a) the person in respect of whom the Pt 1 warrant is issued is accused in the category 1 territory of the commission of an offence specified in the warrant; and
(b) the Pt 1 warrant is issued with a view to his arrest and extradition to the category 1 territory for the purpose of being prosecuted for the offence.[2]

The meaning of "accused" was controversial under the 1989 Act. In some cases, foreign jurisdictions were suspected of asking for a person's extradition merely for the purposes of preliminary investigation or interrogation. Liability for extradition under s.1(1) of the 1989 Act lay simply where a person was "accused" (or convicted) of an extradition offence. That Act contained no such requirement and protection as now appears in s.2(3)(b) of the 2003 Act. Australian authority suggests that if it appears that the person is wanted only for the purpose of investigation, he cannot properly be termed an "accused" person.[3]

In *Re Ismail*,[4] the House of Lords, considering the meaning of the word "accused" in s.1 of the 1989 Act, made it clear that each case would have to be considered carefully because different systems of law may operate in a requesting state. The House of Lords approved of the test used by the Divisional Court in the case under consideration:

> "For my part, I am satisfied that the Divisional Court in this case posed the right test by addressing the broad question whether the competent authorities in the foreign jurisdiction had taken a step which can fairly be described as the

[1] Art.2, Extradition Act 2003 (Part 1 Designated Authorities) Order 2003 (SI 2003/3109).

[2] *cf.* Art.4(1) Framework Decision: "The European arrest warrant is a judicial decision issued by a Member State with a view to the arrest and surrender by another Member States of a requested person, *for the purposes of conducting a criminal prosecution* . . ." [emphasis added].

[3] *Kainhofer v Director of Public Prosecutions* 124 A.L.R. 665 (Australian Federal Court of Appeals); and 132 A.L.R. 483 (Australian High Court).

[4] [1999] 1 A.C. 320.

commencement of a prosecution. But in light of the diversity of cases which may come before the courts it is right to emphasise that ultimately the question whether a person is 'accused' within the meaning of section 1 of the Act of 1989 will require an intense focus on the particular facts of each case."[5]

There was some concern in Parliament that the Pt 1 warrant should not be used for evidence gathering purposes, or simply to extradite a person in order to interview him. The Government sought to allay these fears saying:

> ". . . the warrant must have been issued with a view to his [the person's] arrest and extradition to the category 1 territory for the purpose of being prosecuted for the offence. That is unambiguous language: it is not about interrogation, and it does not allow extradition for the purpose of evidence gathering or fishing expeditions; it is about putting a person on trial. No other meaning can be attached to those words."[6]

If the warrant contains the statement in s.2(3), it must also have the information listed in s.2(4):

(a) particulars of the person's identity;
(b) particulars of any other warrant issued in the category 1 territory for the person's arrest in respect of the offence;
(c) particulars of the circumstances in which the person is alleged to have committed the offence. This must include the conduct alleged to constitute the offence, the time and place at which he is alleged to have committed the offence and any provision of the law of the category 1 territory under which the conduct is said to constitute an offence;
(d) particulars of the sentence which may be imposed under the law of the category 1 territory in respect of the offence if the person is convicted of it.

Section 2(4)(c) is phrased in similar terms to Art.12(2)(b) of the European Convention on Extradition.[7] Territories making a request to the UK under this Convention did not need to provide sufficient evidence but had to provide a description of the conduct as required by Art.12(2)(b). In *Castillo v Spain and the Governor of Belmarsh*,[8] a case under the 1989 Act, it was suggested that the description of the offences in the extradition request was seriously inaccurate and incomplete in the light of the underlying evidence. The applicant submitted that if the request had accurately described the conduct, it would be impossible to say that the description constituted the UK offences which the court was considering. Thomas L.J. said: 7–005

> "It is in my view very important that a state requesting extradition from the UK fairly and properly describes the conduct alleged, as the accuracy and fairness

[5] *per* Lord Steyn at 327.
[6] Mr Bob Ainsworth, *Hansard*, Vol.647, col.165.
[7] The UK also made a reservation to this article which is found in Sch.2 to the European Convention on Extradition Order 2001 (SI 2001/962).
[8] [2004] EWHC 1676 (Admin).

> of the description plays such an important role in the decisions that have to be made by the Secretary of State and the Court in the UK. Scrutiny of the description of the conduct alleged to constitute the offence alleged, where as here a question is raised as to its accuracy, is not an enquiry into evidential sufficiency; the court is not concerned to assess the quality or sufficiency of the evidence in support of the conduct alleged, but it is concerned, if materials are put before it which call into question the accuracy and fairness of the description, to see if the description of the conduct alleged is fair and accurate."[9]

Clearly the same principle will apply to warrants under the new scheme. This further significance of this authority is considered in Ch.9 in relation to the judge's duties at the extradition hearing.

CONVICTED OF AN OFFENCE

7–006 The statement in s.2(5) is that:

(a) the person in respect of whom the Pt 1 warrant is issued is alleged to be unlawfully at large after conviction of an offence specified in the warrant by a court in the category 1 territory; and
(b) the Pt 1 warrant is issued with a view to his arrest and extradition to the category 1 territory for the purpose of being sentenced for the offence or of serving a sentence of imprisonment or another form of detention imposed in respect of the offence.

There is no definition of "unlawfully at large" in the 2003 Act. However, this term was also used in the 1989 Act and was generally taken to mean that a person was liable to immediate arrest and detention in the requesting territory with a view to his being sentenced or serving his sentence.[10] In many civil jurisdictions a defendant does not become liable to immediate arrest and detention until his appeal has been determined.[11]

If the warrant contains the statement in s.2(5), it must also have the information listed in s.2(6):

(a) particulars of the person's identity;
(b) particulars of the conviction;
(c) particulars of any other warrant issued in the category 1 territory for the person's arrest in respect of the offence;
(d) particulars of the sentence which may be imposed under the law of the category 1 territory in respect of the offence if the person has not been sentenced;

[9] *ibid.* at para.25.
[10] *Re Anderson* [1993] Crim. L.R. 954; *Slepcik v Governor of HM Prison Brixton* [2004] E.Q.H.C. 1224.
[11] *Urru v Governor of Brixton Prison and Government of Italy*, unreported, May 22, 2000, CO/4009/99.

(e) particulars of the sentence which has been imposed under the law of the category 1 territory in respect of the offence if the person has been sentenced.

CERTIFICATE

The designated authority (*i.e.* NCIS or the Crown Agent) may issue a certificate if it believes that the warrant has been issued by an authority which has the function of issuing arrest warrants in the category 1 territory (s.2(7)). This authority must be a judicial authority as in some jurisdictions non-judicial officers can issue arrest warrants.[12] **7–007**

ARREST UNDER CERTIFIED PT 1 WARRANT

If a certificate has been issued under s.2(7), the warrant may be executed in any part of the UK by a constable or customs officer (s.3(2)). The warrant can also be executed by a service policeman in certain circumstances (see s.3(3), (4) and (6)). **7–008**

There is no definition of constable included within the Act but the Government has made clear that the common law definition of constable should apply and that on appointment, every constable in a police force must "be attested as a constable by making the appropriate declaration".[13]

The Economic and Specialist Crime branch is within the Specialist Crime Directorate of the Metropolitan Police Service. Within this branch is the Extradition and International Assistance Unit. The main function of this unit is to find and arrest persons who are the subject of extradition warrants or requests.[14] The unit has a national responsibility which extends to Northern Ireland, the Channel Islands, the Isle of Man, and in certain cases, Scotland. If the Extradition and International Assistance Unit does not carry out an arrest in Scotland, any warrant will be executed by the Scottish police acting on instructions from the Crown Office.

The warrant can be executed even if the person executing it does not have the warrant or a copy of it with him at the time of arrest (s.3(5)). A copy of the warrant must be given to the arrested person as soon as practicable after his arrest (s.4(2)).

PROVISIONAL ARREST

A person may be arrested by a constable or customs officer in any part of the UK if he has reasonable grounds for believing that a Pt 1 warrant has been or will be issued in respect of the person by an authority which has the function of issuing arrest warrants in a category 1 territory (s.5(1)). A service policeman can exercise this power of arrest in certain circumstances (see s.5(1),(3),(4) and (5)). **7–009**

12 s.2(1).

13 Lord Bassam, Vol.649, col.GC 304.

14 The unit also provides advice to other police officers in the UK on the procedure for the UK to make an extradition request. See Ch.18 for extradition to the UK.

Within 48 hours of the time of arrest the person must be brought before the appropriate judge[15] and the Pt 1 warrant and certificate issued by NCIS or the Crown Agent produced to the judge (s.6(2)). The person can apply to the judge who must order his discharge if these conditions are not complied with.

The arrested person must be provided with a copy of the warrant as soon as practicable after his arrest (s.6(5)). If s.6(5) is not complied with, the person can apply to the judge who may order his discharge.

If a person is provisionally arrested but is then discharged because s.6(2) or 6(5) have not been complied with, he must not be provisionally arrested again on the basis of a belief relating to the same Pt 1 warrant (s.6(9) and (10)).

The 1989 Act and its predecessors did not allow arrest without a warrant, and the proposed introduction of this power was controversial. The Government said it believed that the power to carry out a provisional arrest would hardly ever be used and should only be used in extreme and unusual situations.[16]

III. PART 2

7–010 There are two circumstances when a person can be arrested under Pt 2. The first is where an extradition request has been received by the Secretary of State and he has issued a certificate. The second is where a provisional warrant has been issued by a justice of the peace. Part 4 of the 2003 Act deals with police powers, and this includes provisions which are relevant to arrest and detention. Part 4 is considered in Ch.17. Defence funding is dealt with at 8–002 *et seq.* in Ch.8.

EXTRADITION REQUEST AND CERTIFICATE

7–011 If the Secretary of State receives an extradition request from a category 2 territory, he will consider whether it is a valid request for a person who is in the UK and, if so, he must issue a certificate (s.70(1)).[17]

A request is valid if it contains the statement in s.70(4) and is made in the approved way. The statement in s.70(4) is one that the person:

(a) is accused[18] in the category 2 territory of the commission of an offence specified in the request; or
(b) is alleged to be unlawfully at large[19] after conviction by a court in the category 2 territory of an offence specified in the request.

[15] See s.67 for definition of "appropriate judge" as discussed in Ch.8 at 8–016.
[16] Lord Bassam, *Hansard*, Vol.649, col.GC 347.
[17] If there is a competing request made by a category 2 territory, the Secretary of State does not have to issue a certificate if he decides that this request should not proceed (s.70(2)). See Ch.12.
[18] See 7–004 for meaning of "accused".
[19] See 7–006 for meaning of "unlawfully at large".

A request from a category 2 territory is made in the approved way if it is made:

(a) by an authority which the Secretary of State believes has the function of making extradition requests in that territory; or
(b) by a person recognised by the Secretary of State as a diplomatic or consular representative of that territory (s.70(7)).

If the category 2 territory is a British overseas territory, the request is made in the approved way if it is made by or on behalf of the person administering the territory (s.70(5)). If the category 2 territory is the Hong Kong SAR, the request is made in the approved way if it is made by or on behalf of the Government of the Region (s.70(6)).

If the Secretary of State issues a certificate, it must state that the request is made in the approved way and the certificate must be sent with the request and a copy of any relevant Order in Council to the appropriate judge[20] (s.70(8) and(9)).

ISSUING OF ARREST WARRANT FOLLOWING RECEIPT OF EXTRADITION REQUEST

Once the Secretary of State has sent these documents to the appropriate judge, the judge may issue a warrant for the arrest of the person whose extradition is requested if he has reasonable grounds for believing that the offence in the request is an extradition offence[21] and there is evidence falling within s.71(3). 7–012

Section 71(3) requires the judge to have reasonable grounds for believing that there is:

(a) evidence that would justify the issue of a warrant for the arrest of a person accused of the offence within the judge's jurisdiction, if the person whose extradition is requested is accused of the commission of the offence; or
(b) evidence that would justify the issue of a warrant for the arrest of a person unlawfully at large after conviction of the offence within the judge's jurisdiction, if the person whose extradition is requested is alleged to be unlawfully at large after conviction of the offence.

This sets a low evidential threshold.[22]

If a category 2 territory has been designated by the Secretary of State under s.71(4), the judge must only be satisfied that there is sufficient information rather than evidence. A number of territories have been designated by Art.3 of the

20 See s.139 for definition of "appropriate judge" as discussed in Ch.8 at 8–016.

21 See Ch.6 for the definition of an extradition offence.

22 "There must be some evidence, but very little will do, for it is merely for the purpose of detaining the man." *per* Jessel M.R., *R. v Weil* (1882) 9 Q.B. 701 at 706; followed and applied in *R. v Governor of Pentonville Prison Ex p. Osman (No.3)* [1990] 1 W.L.R. 878. See also *Re Dokleja*, unreported, January 31, 1994, DC; CO/532/93.

Extradition Act 2003 (Designation of Part 2 Territories) Order 2003 (see Ch.5 at 5–014).[23]

ARREST AFTER RECEIPT OF EXTRADITION REQUEST AND ISSUING OF WARRANT

7–013 If the judge issues a warrant, it can be executed in any part of the UK by any person to whom it is directed, a constable or a customs officer, regardless of whether he has the warrant or a copy of it with him at the time of arrest (s.71(5)). The warrant may also be executed by a service policeman who may execute it outside the UK in certain circumstances (s.71(6) and (8)).

The arrested person must be brought before the appropriate judge[24] as soon as practicable (s.72(3)). Section 72(3) does not apply if the person has been given police bail[25] or the Secretary of State has received a competing Pt 2 extradition request and decided under s.126[26] to proceed with the competing request (s.72(4)). If s.72(3) is not complied with, the person can apply to the judge who must order his discharge (s.72(6)).

A copy of the warrant must be given to the arrested person as soon as practicable after his arrest (s.72(2)). If s.72(2) is not complied with, the person can apply to the judge who may order his discharge (s.72(5)).

ISSUING A PROVISIONAL ARREST WARRANT

7–014 Section 73 allows a provisional arrest warrant to be issued for a person who is in or on his way to the UK. Requests for the issue of a provisional arrest warrant are generally made through police channels in advance of receipt by the Secretary of State of an extradition request.

Section 73 applies if a justice of the peace receives an information,[27] in writing and on oath, that a person is or is believed to be either in the UK or on his way to the UK (s.73(1)). The justice of the peace must be satisfied that the person is accused[28] in a category 2 territory of the commission of an offence or is alleged to be unlawfully at large[29] after conviction by a court in a category 2 territory of an offence (s.73(2)).

The justice of the peace may issue a provisional arrest warrant for the person if

[23] SI 2003/3334

[24] See s.139 for definition of "appropriate judge" as discussed in Ch.8 at 8–016.

[25] In Scotland the police can not grant bail and so s.72(4) is amended to remove the words "by a constable" (s.72(10)).

[26] See Ch.15.

[27] In Northern Ireland, the justice of the peace must receive a complaint rather than an information (s.73(11)).

[28] See 7–004 for meaning of "accused".

[29] See 7–006 for meaning of "unlawfully at large".

he has reasonable grounds for believing that the offence of which the person is accused or has been convicted is an extradition offence[30] and there is written evidence falling within s.73(4) (s.73(3)).

Section 73(4) requires:

(a) evidence that would justify the issue of a warrant for the arrest of a person accused of the offence within the justice's jurisdiction, if the person in respect of whom the warrant is sought is accused of the commission of the offence; or
(b) evidence that would justify the issue of a warrant for the arrest of a person unlawfully at large after conviction of the offence within the judge's jurisdiction, if the person in respect of whom the warrant is sought is alleged to be unlawfully at large after conviction of the offence.

Again, this involves a low evidential threshold.[31–32]

Section 73(5) allows the Secretary of State to designate category 2 territories so that information rather than evidence is required by s.73(3) and (4). A number of territories have been designated by Art.3 of the Extradition Act 2003 (Designation of Part 2 Territories) Order 2003.[33] Section 73(10) makes modifications to s.73 for applications made in Scotland.

The application for a provisional arrest warrant is generally made *ex parte* and the applicant for the warrant is under a duty to make full and frank disclosure to the court of all material matters relating to the decision to be taken by the justice of the peace.[34] The reason for applying the principle in criminal proceedings has been expressed in this way: 7–015

> "Generations of justice have, or I would hope have, been brought up to recognise that the issue of a search warrant is a very serious interference with the liberty of the subject and a step which would only be taken after the most mature careful consideration of all the facts of the case."[35]

Previously, the doctrine was much more developed in civil proceedings:

> "It is perfectly well settled that a person who makes an ex parte application to the court - that is to say, in the absence of the person who will be affected by that which the court is asked to do - is under an obligation to the court to make the fullest possible disclosure of all material facts within his knowledge, and if he does not make that fullest possible disclosure, then he cannot obtain any advantage from the proceedings, and he will be deprived of any advantage he

[30] See Ch.6.
[31–32] See n.22 above.
[33] SI 2003/3334.
[34] *R. v Lewes Crown Court Ex p. Hill* (1991) 93 Cr. App. R. 60.
[35] *Williams v Summerfield* [1972] 2 Q.B. 512, 581, *per* Lord Widgery C.J.

may have already obtained by means of the order which has thus wrongly been obtained by him. That is perfectly plain and requires no authority to justify it."[36]

For an example of the importance of the duty of full and frank disclosure in an application for a search warrant in a criminal case brought in aid of a foreign government, see *R. v Crown Court at Southwark Ex p. Gross.*[37] It is submitted that the importance of the duty is even greater in international criminal proceedings than conventional civil proceedings, because requesting territories are treated with respect and trust, and it is important that these are retained.

7–016 The court has the discretion to hear representations from the person who is to be the subject of the provisional arrest warrant before issuing the warrant but this discretion will only be exercised in exceptional circumstances.[38]

The Explanatory Notes explain that a request for the provisional arrest of a person is made if the person is considered to be at risk of leaving or travelling to another jurisdiction.[39] The Government has said that "Provisional arrest is most likely to be used in urgent cases where there is good reason why it has not been possible for a full request to be made."[40] Although the issuing of a warrant is a preliminary step in the extradition process, it is an emergency procedure for taking a person into custody[41] and there is no certainty that an extradition request will ever be made. It is possible that a person arrested pursuant to a provisional warrant will be detained in custody until an extradition request has been received or until the period for providing the request has elapsed. Therefore, although the 2003 Act does not include an explicit test of urgency, it is arguable that a justice of the peace should consider this issue in the interests of justice when deciding whether to exercise his discretion under s.73(3) to issue a provisional arrest warrant.

By contrast, Art.VIII of the UK-USA 1972 extradition treaty between the UK and the USA,[42] and Art.16 of the European Convention on Extradition of 1957,[43] provided that provisional arrest was available, respectively, "In urgent cases" and "in case of urgency", a condition which limited the statutory provisions of the 1989 Act.[44]

[36] *R. v Kensington Income Tax Commissioners Ex p. Princess Edmond de Polignac* [1917] 1 K.B. 486, 509, *per* Warrington L.J.; cited with approval by Donaldson J. in *Bank Mellat v Nikpour* [1985] F.S.R. 87, 90 in the context of an application for a *Mareva* injunction. Donaldson J. added "The rule requiring full disclosure seems to me to be of fundamental importance."

[37] July 24, 1998; CO/1759/98; [1998] C.O.D. 45.

[38] *cf. R. v West London Stipendiary Magistrate Ex p. Klahn* [1979] 1 W.L.R. 933. This case considered whether a proposed defendant had the right to be heard before the issue of the summons.

[39] Para.213, Explanatory Notes, EA 2003.

[40] Bob Ainsworth, *Hansard*, Committee, 4th sitting, col.144.

[41] *R. v Governor of Pentonville Prison Ex p. Osman (No.3)* [1990] 1 All E.R. 999 at 1013.

[42] SI 1976/2144.

[43] SI 2001/962.

[44] See *R. v Government of the United States of America Ex p. Allison*, unreported, CO/1003/May 13, 1997.

EXECUTION OF A PROVISIONAL ARREST WARRANT

7–017 If the justice of the peace issues a provisional arrest warrant, it can be executed in any part of the UK by any person to whom it is directed, a constable or a customs officer even if he does not have the warrant or a copy of it with him at the time of arrest (s.73(6) and (8)). The warrant may also be executed by a service policeman who may execute it outside of the UK in certain circumstances (s.73(6), (7) and (9)).

The arrested person must be brought as soon as practicable before the appropriate judge[45] unless he has been given police bail[46] or the Secretary of State has received a competing Pt 2 extradition request and decided, under s.126, to proceed with the competing request (s.74(3) and (6)).

A copy of the warrant must be given to the arrested person as soon as practicable after his arrest (s.74(2)). If s.74(2) is not complied with, the person can apply to the judge who may order his discharge (s.72(5)).

[45] See s.139 for definition of "appropriate judge" as discussed in Ch.8 at 8–016.

[46] In Scotland the police can not grant bail and so s.74(4) is amended to remove the words "by a constable" (s.4(12)).

CHAPTER 8

INITIAL HEARING

I. INTRODUCTION

8–001 Subjects considered in this chapter are general matters relevant to the initial hearing, including the status of the court and the representation of the parties. A number of matters arise when a person first appears before the judge, including the question of identity in Pt 1 cases and setting a date for the extradition hearing. These requirements differ in Pts 1 and 2 and different considerations arise according to whether the person was or was not the subject of provisional arrest.

II. DEFENCE FUNDING

A defendant may, of course, fund his own defence. The 2003 Act amends the relevant legal aid provisions to ensure that legal aid is available for extradition proceedings under this Act. 8–002

LEGAL AID: ENGLAND AND WALES

Section 12 of the Access to Justice Act 1999 obliges the Legal Services Commission to maintain the Criminal Defence Service "for the purpose of securing that individuals involved in criminal investigations or criminal proceedings have access to such advice, assistance and representation as the interests of justice require". Section 182 of the 2003 Act amends s.12 of the 1999 Act so that proceedings under the 2003 Act are included within the definition of criminal proceedings. Therefore, the provisions in Pt 1 of the Access to Justice Act 1999 apply to extradition proceedings in the same way that they apply to domestic criminal proceedings in England and Wales. 8–003

The Legal Service Commission has issued guidance on the implications of the 2003 Act and the amendments it contains.[1] Attendance at the police station is covered under the Criminal Investigations class of the General Criminal Contract and should be claimed in the same way as attendance at the police station for domestic police investigations.

Extradition proceedings, including bail applications, are covered by the Criminal Proceedings class of the General Criminal Contract. Applications for a Representation Order should be made to the magistrates' court using Form A. Advice and assistance can also be provided for extradition proceedings under CDS 1/2 if the person whose extradition is sought is eligible.

The guidance states that extradition remains a specialist area, and a Representation Order is likely to be granted for extradition proceedings with enhanced rates payable where appropriate. A representation order for proceedings before a magistrates' court will include representation by an advocate only if the court believes that this is desirable because there are circumstances which make the proceedings unusually grave or difficult.[2]

A magistrates' court cannot grant a representation order for Queen's Counsel and junior counsel or Queen's Counsel alone for extradition proceedings in the magistrates' court.[3] Although an application can be made to the Costs Committee to

[1] "The Extradition Act 2003 — Funding Implications" Focus on CDS, Issue 14, March 2004 *www.legalservices.gov.uk*.

[2] reg.2, Criminal Defence Service (General) (No.2) 2001 (SI 2001/1437). Although this refers to the 1989 Act, it will be read as referring to the 2003 Act by virtue of s.17(2) of the Interpretation Act 1978: "Where an Act repeals and re-enacts, with or without modification, a previous enactment then, unless the contrary intention appears any reference in any other enactment to the enactment so repealed shall be construed as a reference to the provision re-enacted . . ."

[3] reg.14(14), Criminal Defence Service (General) (No.2) 2001 (SI 2001/1437).

obtain authority for certain types of expenditure, this is restricted to proceedings in the Crown Court.[4–5]

LEGAL AID: SCOTLAND

8–004 Extradition proceedings under Pts 1, 2 and 5 of the 2003 Act will be treated as summary proceedings in applying the Legal Aid (Scotland) Act 1986 (s.183).

LEGAL AID: NORTHERN IRELAND

8–005 Section 184 allows the judge to grant free legal aid for proceedings under Pts 1 or 2 if it appears that the person's means are insufficient to enable him to obtain legal aid and it is desirable in the interests of justice that he should be granted free legal aid. If there is any doubt as to whether either of these tests is satisfied, the judge should assume that the relevant test is satisfied. The judge can assign a solicitor and/or counsel.

Section 185 applies various existing legal aid rules in Northern Ireland to a grant of free legal aid under s.184. The provisions are in the Legal Aid, Advice and Assistance (Northern Ireland) Order 1981[6] and relate to:

- the person's statement of means in connection with a grant of legal aid;
- the payment of legal aid coming from money provided by Parliament;
- the Lord Chancellor's power to make rules regarding the practical arrangements for legal aid;
- the exclusion of certain solicitors from legal aid work;
- the amounts payable to solicitors and counsel for legal aid work;
- the exemption of legal aid certificates from stamp duty.

The relevant provisions are applied as if s.184 formed part of the Legal Aid, Advice and Assistance (Northern Ireland) Order 1981.[7]

III. CUSTODY AND BAIL

8–006 The 2003 Act provides that a person may be remanded in custody. It also makes significant amendments to the Bail Act 1976 so far as it applies to extradition proceedings.

[4–5] reg.19, Criminal Defence Service (General) (No.2) 2001 (SI 2001/1437).

[6] SI 1981/228 (NI 8).

[7] SI 1981/228 (NI 8).

CUSTODY

8–007 A person remanded in custody must be committed to the institution to which he would have been sent if he had been charged with a domestic offence (s.197(1)). Similarly a person who escapes from custody can be apprehended in any part of the UK as if he had escaped having been detained under a domestic warrant (s.197(2)). A person will be treated as continuing in legal custody if he is required to be moved within the UK by sea or air having been remanded in custody under the 2003 Act. A constable or any person to whom an extradition order is directed may lawfully keep a person in custody, and then transport him to the territory to which he is to be extradited (s.197(6)).

BAIL: ENGLAND AND WALES

8–008 Section 198 amends the Bail Act 1976 so that extradition proceedings under the 2003 Act are governed by the bail provisions that apply in other domestic criminal proceedings (s.198(1)–(3)).

The amendments to s.4 of the Bail Act 1976 extend the presumption in favour of bail to extradition proceedings where a person is accused of an offence (s.198(4) and (5)). Before the 2003 Act, the presumption in favour of bail did not apply expressly to extradition proceedings; these amendments remove this anomaly. The presumption in favour of bail does not apply to convicted persons.

If a person has already been granted bail, a court can vary or impose bail conditions or withhold bail if an application is made on behalf of the requesting territory (s.198(6)).

If a person has been granted bail during extradition proceedings, he can be arrested on the same grounds as if he had been granted bail in domestic criminal proceedings (s.198(7)–(11)). In the case of a failure to surrender as required, a magistrates' court has the power therefore to issue a warrant for the person's arrest. In addition, where there is reason to believe that the person is likely to break his bail conditions or fail to surrender, the person may be arrested without warrant by a constable. A constable also has this power if a person's surety gives notice in writing that the person is unlikely to surrender and the surety asks to be relieved of his obligations. A person arrested on these grounds without a warrant must be brought before a justice of the peace within 24 hours.[8] The justice of the peace will then decide whether to be grant bail again or to commit the person to custody.

Section 198(12)–(14) amends Pt 1 of Sch.1 to the Bail Act 1976. This governs the decision-making process for granting bail in criminal cases involving imprisonable offences and it is amended so that it applies to extradition proceedings.

The exceptions in Sch.1 to the Bail Act 1976 will apply when the judge is deciding whether to grant bail. The most common exceptions relevant to extradition

[8] This period will not include Sundays and some public holidays.

proceedings are that there are substantial grounds for believing that the defendant if released on bail would:

(a) fail to surrender to custody; or
(b) commit an offence on bail; or
(c) interfere with witnesses.[9]

Section 198(13) amends the Bail Act 1976 to include an additional ground for refusing bail. It inserts para.2B to Sch.1 to that Act:

> "The defendant need not be granted bail in connection with extradition proceedings if —
>
> (a) the conduct constituting the offence would, if carried out by the defendant in England and Wales, constitute an indictable offence or an offence triable either way; and
> (b) it appears to the court that the defendant was on bail on the date of the offence."

BAIL: SCOTLAND

8–009 Section 199 amends the Criminal Procedure (Scotland) Act 1995. A new s.24A is inserted into Pt 3 of that Act, modifying the Act's bail provisions in relation to extradition proceedings. The effect of the new provisions is that the existing Scottish law on bail applies to extradition proceedings.

In Scotland, unlike in England and Wales, the police have no power to grant bail. However, the Lord Advocate has the power to grant bail to any person charged with any crime or offence and he can exercise this power for a person subject to extradition proceedings.

The new s.24A also includes a power to allow Scottish Ministers to make orders to amend the bail provisions in the Criminal Procedure (Scotland) Act 1995 for extradition proceedings if they consider it necessary or expedient.

APPEAL AGAINST GRANT OF BAIL

8–010 Section 200 amends the Bail (Amendment) Act 1993 to give the requesting territory the right to appeal against a judge's decision to grant a person bail in extradition proceedings. The prosecution has a similar right of appeal in some domestic criminal proceedings.

There are conditions which must be complied with before an appeal can be brought. For example, an appeal can only be brought if representations were made against bail before it was granted. Similarly, if an appeal is intended, oral notice of

[9] para.2, Sch.1, Bail Act 1976.

this must be given at the end of the proceedings in which bail was given, and before the person has been released from custody.

Written notice of the appeal must then be given within two hours of the conclusion of the relevant proceedings, or the appeal will be treated as having been disposed of. Any appeal brought under this section must start within two working days of the date on which oral notice was given.

REMAND TO LOCAL AUTHORITY ACCOMMODATION

Section 201 amends s.23 of the Children and Young Persons Act 1969[10] to deal with the detention of a child or young person subject to extradition proceedings. If a child or young person subject to extradition proceedings is not granted bail, he will be remanded to local authority accommodation. That accommodation may be secure accommodation only if three conditions are met. 8–011

The first condition is that the person is 12 or older and is of a prescribed description. This description can be by reference to age or sex or both and will be specified in an order made by the Secretary of State. The second condition is that:

- the offence for which extradition is sought would, if committed in the United Kingdom by an adult, attract imprisonment for 14 years or more; and/or
- the person has previously absconded from proceedings connected with the offence or from the extradition proceedings in question (whether in the UK or the requesting territory).

The third condition is that the court is of the opinion, after considering all the options available, that it is necessary to remand the person to secure local authority accommodation:

- to protect the public from serious harm from him; or
- to prevent the commission by him of imprisonable offences.

IV. REQUESTING TERRITORY

Historically, the Crown Prosecution Service ("CPS") has normally acted on behalf of the requesting territory in extradition proceedings in England and Wales. Until 10 or 15 years ago, some foreign jurisdictions used to instruct private solicitors and counsel. Hong Kong, for example, adopted this course throughout the seven years between 1985 and 1992 that it took to extradite Lorrain Osman to be tried for very large and complex frauds, and in many other cases. It is surprising that more 8–012

[10] The effect of this is to also amend s.98(1) of the Crime and Disorder Act 1998.

jurisdictions have not taken advantage of this opportunity to maintain greater influence over events in difficult or controversial cases, at the cost of paying itself for the proceedings.

Curiously, there was no statutory authority for the CPS to perform this role, and considerable uncertainty about the basis on which it did so. Conscious of this, the Government decided to include in the 2003 Act provisions dealing with the role of the CPS (in England and Wales), the Lord Advocate (in Scotland) and the Director of Public Prosecutions and Crown Solicitor (in Northern Ireland). These sections impose a duty on the relevant authority to conduct the extradition proceedings unless the requesting state wishes to instruct its own lawyers privately.[11]

ENGLAND AND WALES — CROWN PROSECUTION SERVICE

8–013 The 2003 Act amends the Prosecution of Offences Act 1985 so that the Director of Public Prosecutions must conduct any extradition proceedings in England and Wales unless the requesting territory asks him not to. The Director must also give advice to the extent he considers appropriate on actual or proposed extradition proceedings to any person he considers appropriate (s.190(1)–(3)). The costs of conducting the extradition proceedings will be borne by the CPS.

The Casework Directorate at the Crown Prosecution Service acts on behalf of the requesting territory if the proceedings are in England or Wales. The Directorate also provides advice to law enforcement agencies who are considering making an extradition request to the UK.

SCOTLAND — LORD ADVOCATE

8–014 The Lord Advocate must conduct any extradition proceedings in Scotland unless the requesting territory asks him not to. He must give, as he feels appropriate, advice on actual or proposed extradition proceedings in Scotland, to any party he thinks appropriate (s.191).

NORTHERN IRELAND — DPP AND CROWN SOLICITOR

8–015 Section 192 makes amendments to the relevant legislation so that the DPP may have conduct of extradition proceedings in Northern Ireland. He may also give advice, as he feels appropriate, on actual or proposed extradition proceedings in Northern Ireland to any party he feels appropriate (s.192(1)–(8)). The Crown Solicitor is given similar powers in s.192(9). As the DPP and Crown Solicitor are not obliged to have conduct of any extradition proceedings in Northern Ireland, they can agree with a requesting territory that it will privately instruct lawyers.

[11] Baroness Scotland, *Hansard*, Vol.654, cols 396–7.

V. THE APPROPRIATE JUDGE

Extradition proceedings must be heard by an appropriate judge. The appropriate judge is the primary decision maker under Pt 1. The definition of the appropriate judge for Pt 1 (s.67) is identical to the definition for Pt 2 (s.139). 8–016

The appropriate judge is:

- in England and Wales, a District Judge (Magistrates' Court) designated by the Lord Chancellor;
- in Scotland, the Sheriff of Lothian and Borders;
- in Northern Ireland any county court judge or resident magistrate designated by the Lord Chancellor.

A designation can be made for all cases, for specific types of cases or for an individual case and more than one designation can be made.

Historically all magistrates' court extradition proceedings in England and Wales have been conducted by Bow Street Magistrates' Court. This continues to be the case, but the Government has indicated that it expects the number of extradition requests to increase. Therefore, it has indicated that it may designate District Judges based in a small number of magistrates' courts outside London in due course.[12] At the time of writing, the Chief Magistrate, the Deputy Chief Magistrate and four other District Judges at Bow Street Magistrates' Court have been designated for the purposes of Pts 1 and 2 for England and Wales.

References to a judge in the chapters dealing with the 2003 Act should be read as references to an appropriate judge.

VI. PUBLICITY

There are no statutory restrictions on publicity for extradition hearings. 8–017

Before 1996, proceedings at committal were likened to proceedings for committal for trial. There was therefore an argument, though an unconvincing one, that publicity should not be given to those proceedings before an eventual trial. Since proceedings have been likened to summary trial, as they are under the 2003 Act, it has not been doubted that publicity may be given to the Bow Street proceedings, as well as to proceedings in the higher courts. It would have been curious if the Bow Street proceedings against General Pinochet could not have been publicised.

In English criminal proceedings, courts have the power to insist that blackmail victims be referred to as, for example, "Mr X". See, for example, *R. v Socialist Worker Ex p. Attorney-General*.[13] This power is supplemented by the power conferred by s.11 of the Contempt of Court Act 1981 to make an ancillary order

[12] Lord Bassam, *Hansard*, Vol.651, col.GC 79.
[13] [1975] Q.B. 637.

forbidding the publication of names or other matter which might identify the name of the person whose identity is protected.

By virtue of s.4(2) of the Contempt of Court Act 1981, "the court may, where it appears necessary for avoiding a substantial risk of prejudice to the administration of justice in those proceedings, or in any proceedings pending or imminent, order that the publication or a report of the proceedings, or any part of the proceedings, be postponed for such period as the court thinks necessary for that purpose." There may, exceptionally, be circumstances in which this provision may be invoked in extradition proceedings if publicity appeared likely to affect adversely related English criminal proceedings.

VII. PART 1

8–018 There are a number of preliminary matters which must be dealt with on the first occasion that a person appears before the judge.

ARREST UNDER CERTIFIED PT 1 WARRANT

8–019 If a person has been arrested under a certified Pt 1 warrant, he must be brought before the appropriate judge as soon as practicable after his arrest (s.4(3)). The person can apply to the judge who must order his discharge if the condition in s.4(3) is not complied with (s.4(5)).

A copy of the warrant must be given to the arrested person as soon as practicable after his arrest (s.4(2)). Again, if this section is not complied with, the person can apply to the appropriate judge who may order his discharge (s.4(4)).

PROVISIONAL ARREST

8–020 A person provisionally arrested under s.5(1) must within 48 hours of the arrest be brought before the appropriate judge, and the Pt 1 warrant and certificate issued by NCIS or the Crown Agent[14] must be produced to the judge (s.6(2)). The person can apply to the judge who must order his discharge if these conditions have not been complied with (s.6(6)).

The arrested person must be provided with a copy of the warrant as soon as practicable after his arrest (s.6(5)). The person can apply to the judge if s.6(5) is not complied with, and the judge may order his discharge.

IDENTITY OF THE PERSON ARRESTED

8–021 When the arrested person is first brought before the court, the judge will consider the identity of person who has been provisionally arrested[15] or was arrested under

[14] See Ch.7 at 7–003 for details of the Pt 1 warrant and certificate.

[15] However, the conditions in s.6(2) must have been complied with before the judge will consider the issue of identity (s.7(1)(b)).

a certified Pt 1 warrant (s.7(1)). The judge must decide, on the balance of probabilities, whether the person who has been arrested is the same person referred to in the Pt 1 warrant (s.7(2)–(3)).

Identity is not normally an issue in extradition cases. It is the usual practice of the Extradition Squad to ask a person to confirm his name and date of birth before arresting him. Admissions or statements by a person on arrest may be sufficient evidence of identity.[16] The judge is entitled to compare a photograph, supplied by the requesting territory, with the person who has been arrested to assess whether it is the same person.[17] However, if identity is in issue the person who has been arrested is entitled to adduce evidence about this question.[18]

If the initial hearing is in England or Wales, the judge will have the same powers (as nearly as may be) as a magistrates' court would have in dealing with a summary trial of an information against the person (s.7(6)). If the initial hearing is in Scotland, the judge will have the same powers (as nearly as may be) as if the proceedings were summary proceedings for an offence alleged to have been committed by the person. However, the judge will be able to rely on evidence from a single source in deciding the identity of the person (s.7(7)). In Northern Ireland the judge has the same powers (as nearly as may be) as a magistrates' court would have if the proceedings were the hearing and determination of a complaint against the person (s.7(8)).

If the judge exercises his power to adjourn the initial hearing, he must remand the person in custody or on bail (s.7(9)). In England and Wales, the judge has the power to adjourn the hearing pursuant to s.7(6).[19] If the person is remanded in custody, the judge may later grant bail (s.7(10)).

If the judge finds that the arrested person is not the person named in the Pt 1 warrant, he must order his discharge (s.7(4)). Otherwise he will proceed to deal with the matters set out in s.8.

DATE OF EXTRADITION HEARING, CONSENT AND REMAND

DATE OF THE EXTRADITION HEARING

If the judge is satisfied about the identity of the person arrested, he must fix a date when the extradition hearing[20] is to begin (s.8(1)(a)). The date fixed must be within 21 days of the date of arrest (s.8(4)). However, at any time before the date fixed for the extradition hearing, a party may make an application for a postponement, and if the judge believes it is in the interests of justice to allow this, he may fix a later 8–022

[16] *Re Parisot* (1889) 5 T.L.R. 344; *Meunier* [1894] 2 Q.B. 415.

[17] *Re Rodriguez*, unreported, November 15, 1984, CO/952/84; *Re Mullin*, unreported, July 31, 1992. CO/0341/92; *R. v Dodson and Williams* [1984] 79 Cr. App. R. 220; *Savvas v Government of Italy* [2004] EWHC 1233 (Admin).

[18] *Re Osbourne* January 1993 CO/2628/92; Crim L.R. 694, DC; *Re Anthony*, unreported, June 27, 1995, CO/1657/94.

[19] s.10(1), Magistrates' Court Act 1980.

[20] See Ch.9.

date (s.8(5)). There is no limit on the number of applications for a postponement which can be made.

When dealing with an application made on behalf of the arrested person for a postponement, the judge must take account of his obligations to act compatibly with the ECHR.[21] Article 5(4) gives the person the right to have adequate time and facilities for the preparation of a challenge to the legality of his detention.[22] The judge should take account of this to allow sufficient time for the person to collect any evidence he might wish to adduce at the extradition hearing when considering whether a postponement is in the interests of justice.[23]

If the extradition hearing does not take place by the date which has been fixed, the person can make an application to the judge to be discharged which must be granted unless reasonable cause is shown for the delay (s.8(6) and (7)). Even if the person does not make an application, the judge must still order his discharge on the first occasion when he appears in court after the date fixed for the extradition hearing unless reasonable cause is shown for the delay (s.8(6) and (8)).

INFORMATION AND CONSENT

8–023 The judge must inform the person of the contents of the Pt 1 warrant (s.8(1)(b)) and give him the required information about consent (s.8(1)(c)); that is, that he may consent to his extradition to the category 1 territory which has issued the Pt 1 warrant. The judge must explain the effect of giving consent, and the procedure which will apply if consent is given (s.8(3)). The person must also be informed that consent must be given before the judge and that it is irrevocable (s.8(3)(c)). Consent is considered in Ch.14.

REMAND

8–024 The judge must remand the person in custody or on bail (s.8(1)(d)). If the judge remands in custody, he can grant bail later (s.8(2)).

VIII. PART 2

8–025 Where a person is arrested under a warrant issued after the receipt of an extradition request, there are a number of matters that must be dealt with on the first occasion when he appears before the appropriate judge. If a person has been arrested under a provisional warrant, there are additional matters which must be dealt with on this occasion.

[21] s.6(1), Human Rights Act 1998; see further Ch.11.
[22] *Lamy v Belgium* (1989) 11 E.H.R.R. 529; see further Ch.11.
[23] *cf. R. v Governor of Brixton Prison Ex p. Gross* [1999] Q.B. 538.

ARREST UNDER PROVISIONAL WARRANT

INITIAL HEARING

The arrested person must be brought as soon as practicable before the appropriate judge unless he has been given police bail,[24] or the Secretary of State has received a competing Pt 2 extradition request and decided, under s.126, to proceed with the competing request (s.74(3) and (6)).[25] 8–026

A copy of the warrant must be given to the arrested person as soon as practicable after arrest (s.74(2)). If s.74(2) is not complied with, the person can apply to the judge who may order his discharge (s.74(5)).

The judge must inform the arrested person that he is accused of the commission of an offence in a category 2 territory, or alleged to be unlawfully at large after conviction of an offence by a court in a category 2 territory (s.74(7)).

The judge must also give him the required information about consent (s.74 (7)(b)). The required information about consent is that the person may consent to his extradition to the category 2 territory in which he is accused of the commission of an offence, or is alleged to have been convicted of an offence. The judge must explain the effect of giving consent and the procedure which will apply if consent is given (s.74(8)). The judge has to inform him that consent must be given in writing and is irrevocable (s.8(3)(c)). Unlike Pt 1 cases, consent does not need to be given before the judge. Consent is dealt with in Ch.14.

The judge must remand the person in custody or on bail (s.74(7)(c)). If the person is remanded in custody, the judge can later grant bail (s.74(9)).

DATE OF EXTRADITION HEARING

The judge must order the person's discharge if he does not receive from the Secretary of State the extradition request, the Secretary of State's certificate and any relevant Order in Council within the required period (s.74(10)). The required period is 45 days from the date of arrest. Section 77(11)(b) allows the Secretary of State to designate category 2 territories to allow a longer period so as to apply the required period.[26] Certain category 2 territories have been designated under this section (see Ch.5 at 5–016). 8–027

If the judge receives these documents within the required period, he must fix a date no later than two months from the date he received the documents for the extradition hearing to begin (s.76(1)–(3)).

However, at any time before the date fixed for the extradition hearing a party may make an application for a postponement and if the judge believes it is in the

[24] In Scotland the police can not grant bail and so s.74(4) is amended to remove the words "by a constable" (s.74(12)).

[25] See Ch.15.

[26] A longer period may be required to reflect the extradition arrangements in a particular extradition treaty.

interests of justice to allow this, he may fix a later date (s.8(5)).[27] There is no limit on the number of applications for a postponement which can be made.

If the extradition hearing does not begin by the date which has been fixed, the person can make an application to the judge to be discharged which must be granted (s.76(5)).

ARREST UNDER WARRANT ISSUED FOLLOWING RECEIPT OF EXTRADITION REQUEST

8–028 The arrested person must be brought before the appropriate judge[28] as soon as practicable (s.72(3)). Section 72(3) does not apply if the person has been given police bail[29] or the Secretary of State has received a competing Pt 2 extradition request and decided under s.126[30] to proceed with the competing request (s.72(4)). If s.72(3) is not complied with, the person can apply to the judge who must order his discharge (s.72(6)). The judge must inform the person of the contents of the extradition request and give him the required information about consent (s.72(7)).

The required information about consent is that the person may consent to his extradition to the category 2 territory in which he is accused of the commission of an offence or is alleged to have been convicted of an offence. The judge must also explain the effect of giving consent and the procedure which will apply if consent is given (s.74(8)). The person must also be informed that consent must be given in writing and is irrevocable (s.74(8)(c)). Unlike Pt 1 cases, consent does not need to be given before the judge. Consent is dealt with in Ch.14.

When the person is first brought before the appropriate judge, the judge must fix a date, within two months of this date, for the extradition hearing to begin (s.75(1)–(2)).

However, at any time before the date fixed for the extradition hearing a party may make an application for a postponement and if the judge believes it is in the interests of justice to allow this, he may fix a later date (s.75(3)).[31] There is no limit on the number of applications for a postponement which can be made.

If the extradition hearing does not begin by the date which has been fixed, the person can make an application to the judge to be discharged which must be granted (s.75(4)).

The judge must remand the person in custody or on bail (s.72(7)(c)). If the person is remanded in custody, the judge can later grant bail (s.72(9)).

[27] See 8–022 above for ECHR submissions which may be relevant.

[28] See s.139 for definition of "appropriate judge" as discussed at 8–016, above.

[29] In Scotland the police can not grant bail and so s.72(4) is amended to remove the words "by a constable" (s.72(10)).

[30] See Ch.15.

[31] See 8–022 above for ECHR submissions which may be relevant.

CHAPTER 9

THE EXTRADITION HEARING

I. INTRODUCTION

The extradition hearing is now the central event in extradition proceedings and of far greater significance under the 2003 Act because this Act has abolished the broad discretion whether to extradite, given by previous statutes to the Secretary of State. **9–001**

In Pt 1 cases all substantive issues are dealt with at this hearing, subject to appeal. In Pt 2 cases, the judge sends the case to the Secretary of State for his decision on extradition if he has not discharged the person during the course of, or at the conclusion of, the extradition hearing. The judge has the power to adjourn the extradition hearing once it has begun. The different procedures for Pts 1 and 2 are here considered separately.

II. ISSUES AND EVIDENCE

9–002 A fundamental question is this. On which of the issues that the Judge must determine can evidence be given, by prosecution and defence? To demonstrate the importance of this question, and to seek to answer it, it is necessary to look at previous extradition legislation.

Under the scheme of the 1870 Act, preserved in Sch.1 to the 1989 Act for foreign states with which the UK had bilateral extradition treaties which were not superseded by "general extradition arrangements" within the meaning of that Act, it remained necessary for the requesting state to show a prima facie case of guilt. If there was such evidence as would justify the finding of a case to answer, if the matter had come before the court as an ordinary UK crime, the magistrate would commit for trial.

It was confirmed in *R. v Governor of Brixton Prison Ex p. Gross*[1] that a defendant could both give and call evidence in his own defence in such committal proceedings. The Divisional Court referred to this power as a "historic right". The magistrate had therefore to decide the question of sufficient evidence in the light of evidence from both prosecution and defence. This provided a real safeguard for accused persons. In the extradition proceedings brought against *Pin Chakkaphak* by the Government of Thailand under Sch.1 to the 1989 Act in 2000–01, the defence was able to produce in evidence documents referred to but not supplied by the requesting state, and to adduce expert accountancy evidence. This facility led to the defendant's partial discharge by the Judge, and his complete exoneration in the Divisional Court. It was conceded by the defence that it was of course of no avail for the defence to call evidence contradicting evidence given by the requesting state. Such a conflict simply raised a triable issue. If, however, as in that case, the defence evidence merely supplemented and explained the prosecution evidence in a case founded on circumstantial evidence, the defence evidence could make a crucial difference to the court.

It was also open to the defence, of course, to call evidence in Sch.1 cases on the question whether the crime for which the defendant's extradition was sought was a political crime. Indeed, the House or Lords recognised in *R. v Governor of Brixton Prison Ex p. Schtraks*[2] that informal evidence could be presented, because the accused might not be in a position to secure duly authenticated material from the requesting state.

9–003 In cases under Pt III of the 1989 Act, however, the position was different. Part III governed extradition requests from the Commonwealth and United Kingdom colonies, and foreign states with which "general extradition arrangements" had been made. The latter category included states party to the European Convention on Extradition 1957. In the case of appropriate general extradition arrangements, the Secretary of State could by statutory instrument declare that it was not necessary for a case to answer to be shown. In such cases, it was sufficient if the foreign court provided particulars of the conduct alleged, as envisaged in Art.12 of the 1957 Convention.

[1] [1999] Q.B. 538 at 545.
[2] [1964] A.C. 556.

The task of the lower court was therefore limited in such a case to finding that the particulars sent by the foreign state showed that the conduct of which the person was accused was punishable in both requesting and requested states by at least 12 months' imprisonment. The task of the magistrate (s.9(8) of the 1989 Act) was to make this determination "after hearing any representations made in support of the extradition request or on behalf of that [accused] person".

In *Re Evans*,[3] the defence sought to argue that, in order to decide whether the defendant was in fact accused of conduct punishable in Sweden, the evidence of a Swedish lawyer should be admitted in order to show that the documents relied on by the Swedish authorities in fact contained a provision, not made known in the foreign government's particulars supplied to the English courts, that a hiring could be terminated only if a particular notice had been served on the accused. The Swedish court documents showed that such a notice had not been served. The defence did not seek to contradict the particulars; only to show the English court that the Swedish trial papers, as a whole, did not show punishable conduct. 9–004

Leading counsel for the Government of Sweden, on behalf of the CPS, resisted this argument, submitting that the function of the magistrate was to act as "a rubber stamp". The House of Lords held that the magistrate could not hear even this documentary evidence. It could act only on the material presented in the particulars.

The narrow justification offered by Lord Templeman, giving the only reasoned speech, was that the defendant could make "representations", and the statute and European Convention prescribed the documents he could look at. The wider justification was an intensely purposive construction:

> "My Lords, extradition arrangements are designed to ensure that persons who commit crimes in one country do not escape trial of punishment. Extradition arrangements have been transformed as a result of the invention of the jet aeroplane and the mutual acceptance by means of extradition treaties of the integrity of their different legal systems. A criminal can flee from country to country with ease in order to avoid or postpone retribution. A suspect once arrested can be returned for prosecution with equal speed."[4]

No extradition scheme has ever attempted the goal expressed in the last sentence. Where, he said:

> ". . . requests for extradition allege acts of violence, theft, fraud, or the like, courts should be slow to pay heed to any representations that such acts do not constitute offences under foreign law."[5]
> (It was not clear why this exhortation did not apply to drugs crimes).

Lord Templeman also attached great significance to the role of the Secretary of State in deciding whether it was fair to extradite a suspect. He suggested that the

[3] [1994] 1 W.L.R. 1006.
[4] at 1008C.
[5] at 1014F.

Secretary of State might decline to order surrender if Evans returned the cars he was alleged to have stolen, or if he demonstrated his innocence to him, the Secretary of State. He also suggested that the defence did, however have a right to present conflicting evidence as to the effect of the foreign law in habeas corpus proceedings.

However, in spite of *Evans*, it was clear under the 1989 Act that there was power in a conviction case to call evidence to prove that the defendant was not the person sought.[6] It was permissible for the defence to call evidence on the question whether a defendant was "unlawfully at large".[7] It was also never doubted that defendants in Pt III extradition cases could give evidence on the bars to surrender contained in s.6 of the 1989 Act.[8]

9–005 In *Castillo v Spain and the Governor of Belmarsh*[9] the Divisional Court in a case under Pt III of the 1989 Act case took a radically different approach to the question of the adequacy of a foreign state's particulars. It commented that:

> ". . . given the fact there is no enquiry into evidential sufficiency, it is of the utmost importance that the description of the conduct alleged is framed with the greatest care; it is an essential protection to the person whose extradition is sought. It is to be expected that the description will be framed with very considerable care and expressed in terms in which it can be easily understood by the court in the state to which the request is addressed."[10]

This was precisely the argument put forward, but summarily rejected, in *Evans*. In *Castillo,* it was held that the particulars submitted by the Government of Spain did not reflect the contents of the dossier in Spain.

The policy reasoning behind the judgment in *Castillo* is that apparent from earlier cases such as *R. v Governor of Brixton Ex p. Percival,*[11] which reflected, unlike the decision in *Evans*, a deep concern to protect the liberty of the individual in extradition cases. The dossier in *Castillo* was ultimately made available to the court in London by the Government of Spain, but it would be curious if the defence could not provide evidence of the inadequacy of the foreign particulars itself if necessary.

It is submitted that Parliament intended that whenever a finding of fact is necessary to determine any of the questions that the Judge must consider under the 2003 Act, the defence as well as the prosecution can call relevant evidence. Plainly this does not include evidence from the defendant simply contradicting the assertions of guilt made by the requesting state, because the question of guilt or innocence is not an issue under the 2003 Act.

Further, the relaxation of the conditions of admissibility of documents and the Parliamentary concern expressed about the use of summaries, discussed below, lend

[6] *Re Osbourne* [1993] Crim L.R. 694, DC; *Re Anthony,* unreported, June 27, 2004, CO/1657/94.

[7] *Re Kiriacos*, unreported, November 7, 1996, CO/744/96; *R. v Governor of Brixton Prison Ex p. Delli*, unreported, June 11, 1999.

[8] See, for example, *Re Barone*, unreported, November 7, 1997, CO/2734/97.

[9] [2004] EWHC 1672 (Admin).

[10] *ibid.* at para.43.

[11] [1907] 1 K.B. 696.

support to the view that defence material is admissible in relation to the true meaning and effect of material provided by the requesting territory.

III. EVIDENCE AND BURDEN OF PROOF

ADMISSIBILITY OF DOCUMENTS AND EVIDENCE; ss.202–206

A serious deficiency under the 1989 Act was the rigidity and formality of the conditions of admissibility in evidence of foreign and Commonwealth affidavits, affirmations and documentary exhibits, whether produced by prosecution or defence. These artificialities have been set aside in the 2003 Act. **9–006**

Section 202 specifies those documents which can be received in evidence in extradition proceedings, including a Pt 1 warrant. A document which is "duly authenticated" can be received in evidence. It will be duly authenticated if it purports to be signed by a judge, magistrate or other judicial authority of the requesting territory, or it purports to be authenticated by the oath or affirmation of a witness. However, documents which are not duly authenticated may still be received in evidence.

Sections 203 allows a printout of a faxed document to be treated as if it was the document used to send the fax transmission. Section 204 applies if a Pt 1 warrant is issued and the information in it is transmitted electronically to NCIS or the Crown Office. The information received will be treated as if it was the Pt 1 warrant and may be received in evidence on this basis.

Section 205 applies the provisions in the Criminal Justice Act 1967 and the Criminal Justice (Miscellaneous Provisions) Act (Northern Ireland) 1968. These allow written statements to be adduced where there is no objection and formal admissions to be made in the same way as for domestic criminal proceedings.

Section 206 clarifies the burden and standard of proof to be applied in extradition proceedings. The appropriate test is to treat the extradition proceedings as if they were a domestic prosecution for the offence and use the burden or standard of proof which would apply. The person who is the subject of the extradition claim is treated as the person accused of the extradition offence and the requesting territory as the prosecution. This applies unless there is a specific provision in the 2003 Act which specifies the burden and standard of proof; for example ss.7(3)[12] and 78(5)[13] which prescribe the standard of proof needed to establish the identity of an arrested person.

DISCLOSURE

It is not clear from the authorities to what extent there is a duty on the requesting state to make disclosure of material that may be exculpatory, or relevant to any of **9–007**

[12] See Ch.8 at 8–021.
[13] See 9–025 below.

the matters arising in Pt 1 or Pt 2 cases. The relevance of the duty of disclosure is not confined, it is submitted, to evidential questions arising under some Pt 2 cases, where the requirement to produce sufficient evidence remains. The duty of disclosure is surely also relevant to the findings the Judge must make as to, for example, extraneous considerations, and most fundamentally the Convention rights. In *R. v Governor of Pentonville Prison Ex p. Lee*[14] the Divisional Court held that under the 1989 Act it was for the requesting state alone to decide what material should be put before the court. That state was not under a duty to comply with any requests for material, including unused material, which might be made on behalf of the person who was the subject of the extradition request. The court came to the bleak conclusion that there was no criterion of fairness which should be considered by the committing court.[15]

In *R. v Governor of Brixton Prison Ex p. Kashamu*,[16] the committal was quashed because of serious non-disclosure by the requesting state. In this case, it was conceded on behalf of the requesting territory that disclosure of the material should have been made to the court. Therefore, the court did not give any guidance on the general duty of disclosure in extradition proceedings. However, the Court did state that, in light of the Human Rights Act 1998 and the ECHR, the judgment in *Lee* was now not correct insofar as it had said that fairness was not a criterion relevant to the function of the committing court.

Article 5(4) of the ECHR, which applies to an extradition hearing, places a limited duty of disclosure on the requesting territory.[17] It is submitted that the requesting territory should disclose the contents of, or a description of, any material which may undermine or contradict the evidence or information it places before the court, and, if appropriate, the material itself. It should also, if requested, supply any material which may raise a statutory bar. A failure or refusal to provide this disclosure by the requesting territory may support a submission that there is a risk that the person's extradition would be incompatible with the Convention rights.[18]

The significance of this duty is much increased under the 2003 Act. Under Sch.1 to the 1989 Act, applicable to the United States and other states with which the UK had not entered into "general extradition arrangements" such as parties to the European Convention on Extradition 1957, the lower court had no power at all to question the fairness of the extradition request. That power lay exclusively in the Secretary of State. Under Pt III of that Act, the magistrate had only limited powers to investigate the question whether the request had been made for improper reasons (because they were purely military offences, or made on the grounds of the race, religion, nationality, etc. of the alleged offender.)

14 [1993] 1 W.L.R. 1294 at 1298.
15 *ibid.* at 1300C.
16 Unreported, October 6, 2000, CO/2141/2000.
17 *Lamy v Belgium* (1989) 11 E.H.R.R. 529.
18 See Ch.11 for detailed discussion of Convention rights and the relevant sections of the 2003 Act.

The lower court now has to determine whether extradition would be compatible with a person's human rights. It is entitled to expect frankness from an applicant territory. It is submitted that in appropriate cases, the court will be required to make requests under mutual assistance provisions considered in Pt E of this book.

IV. PUBLICITY

See Ch.8 at 8–017 for discussion of restrictions on publicity. 9–008

V. PART 1

The extradition hearing is the hearing at which the appropriate judge decides 9–009
whether the person for whom a Pt 1 warrant has been issued is to be extradited to the category 1 territory which issued the warrant (s.68).

JUDGE'S POWERS AND ADJOURNMENTS

In England and Wales, the judge has the same powers (as nearly as may be) at the 9–010
extradition hearing as a magistrates' court would have if it was dealing with the summary trial of an information against the person (s.9(1)). In Scotland, the judge's powers are equivalent to those he has in summary proceedings (s.9(2)) and in Northern Ireland the judge's powers are the same as those of a magistrates' court hearing and in determining a complaint (s.9(3)).

If the judge adjourns the extradition hearing, he must remand the person in custody or on bail and he can grant bail at a later stage if the person was initially remanded in custody (s.9(4) and (5)).

EXTRADITION HEARING

EXTRADITION OFFENCE

The first issue which the judge must decide is whether the offence in the Pt 1 9–011
warrant is an "extradition offence" as defined in ss.64 and 65 (s.10(1) and (2)). The definition of an extradition offence is dealt with in Ch.6. If the judge decides that it is not, he must order the person's discharge (s.10(3)). It is submitted, for the reasons discussed above, that the defence may call evidence as to the conduct which is in fact alleged against the person. If the judge decides that it is an extradition offence, he must consider whether one of the bars to extradition in s.11 applies (s.10(4)).

BARS TO EXTRADITION

9–012 The bars to extradition are set out in s.11(1). Extradition may be barred by reason of:

(a) the rule against double jeopardy;
(b) extraneous considerations;
(c) the passage of time;
(d) the person's age;
(e) hostage-taking considerations;
(f) speciality;
(g) earlier extradition to the UK from another category 1 territory;
(h) earlier extradition to the UK from a non-category 1 territory.

These bars are defined in ss.12–19 and are considered in detail in Ch.10. If the judge finds that the person's extradition to the category 1 territory is barred for one of the reasons set out in s.11, he must order the person's discharge (s.11(3)).

If the person is suffering from physical or mental ill health, s.25 may also operate as a bar to extradition (see 9–019 below).

Evidence from either party is admissible, it is submitted, in respect of any of these issues.

PERSON ALLEGED TO BE UNLAWFULLY AT LARGE AFTER CONVICTION

9–013 If the judge finds that there is no bar to extradition and the person is accused of the extradition offence, but is not alleged to be unlawfully at large after conviction, he will proceed to consider the subject of human rights (s.11(5)).

If the person is alleged to be unlawfully at large after conviction of the extradition offence and there is no bar to his extradition, the judge must consider whether the person was convicted in the person's presence (ss.11(4) and 20(1)). Evidence from prosecution and defence can, it is submitted, be called on this issue. If the judge decides the person was convicted in his presence, he will proceed to consider the question of human rights (s.20(2)).

If the judge finds that the person was convicted in his absence, he will consider whether the person deliberately absented himself from his trial (again an evidential issue). If the judge finds the person deliberately absented himself, the judge will proceed to consider human rights issues (s.20(3) and (4)).

If the judge finds that the person was convicted in his absence and did not deliberately absent himself from his trial, the judge must decide (on the evidence) whether the person would be entitled to a retrial or, on appeal, a review amounting to a retrial (s.20(5)). The judge must not decide that the person would be entitled to a retrial or a review amounting to a retrial unless the person would have the right:

(a) to defend himself in person or through legal assistance of his own choosing or, if he had not sufficient means to pay for legal assistance, to be given it free when the interests of justice so required; and
(b) to examine or have examined witnesses against him and to obtain the attendance and examination of witnesses on his behalf under the same conditions as witnesses against him (s.20(8)).[19]

Concerns were raised when the Extradition Bill was published that it failed to confer adequate rights on defendants who were to be extradited having been convicted in their absence. In many countries there are restrictions on the rights of defendants who are retried or allowed an appeal having been convicted in their absence. In some countries an appeal does not allow a defendant to produce further evidence.

Seeking to meet these concerns, the Government agreed to an amendment to set out certain fundamental and basic rights. The rights set out in s.20(8) are simply those selected by the Government and should not be taken to be a comprehensive list of the rights which a defendant should be entitled to in a retrial. This is made clear in the Explanatory Notes to the Act which refer to the fact the rights set out in subs.(8) can be found in Art.6(3) of the ECHR.[20] Therefore, additional submissions may be made to the judge about other rights which should apply in a retrial. Indeed this was the basis on which the Government argued against the proposal to amend the section to include the rights now listed at s.20(8): 9–014

> "As regards the term 'retrial', in our view a retrial must confer the same rights on an individual as a trial. If it does not, it is not a retrial. The right to a fair trial is, of course, guaranteed by Article 6 of the ECHR. Extradition would be barred under the ECHR provisions where a judge or court is of the opinion that a person would not be afforded these rights, either at trial or a retrial, on return to the requesting state . . . We have made plain that a review must have the same features as a retrial."[21]

Further clarifying statements were made by the Government during the Parliamentary passage of the Extradition Bill:

> "A retrial is differentiated from a simple appeal by the fact that the process starts again with a presumption of innocence."[22]
> "All the evidence is tested afresh and witnesses are cross-examined. The same arrangements for legal assistance and the payment of defence counsel apply."[23]

[19] *cf.* Art.5(1) of the Framework Decision which refers to the person being given the opportunity to apply for a retrial of the case and to be present at the judgment.
[20] para.65, Explanatory Notes, 2003 Act.
[21] Baroness Scotland, *Hansard*, Vol.650, col.GC 122–123.
[22] *Hansard*, Vol.396, col.44 (December 9, 2002).
[23] Mr Bob Ainsworth (Parliamentary Under-Secretary of State, Home Office), *Hansard*, Committee, 5th sitting, col.112.

In deciding whether to find that the person is entitled to a retrial or a review amounting to a retrial the judge is clearly obliged to consider whether the full range of protections under the ECHR will be afforded.

If the judge finds that the person would be entitled to a retrial or a review amounting to a retrial, he must proceed to consider the issue of human rights (s.20(6)). If the judge finds that the person is not entitled to a retrial or a review amounting to a retrial, he must order the person's discharge (s.20(7)).

Obviously, evidence from both parties is admissible on this issue.

HUMAN RIGHTS

9–015 The final issue the judge must consider is whether the person's extradition would be compatible with the Convention rights within the meaning of the Human Rights Act 1998 (s.21(1)).

The Convention Rights are considered in Ch.11. If the judge finds that the extradition would be incompatible, he must order the person's discharge (s.21(2)). If he finds that the extradition would be compatible, he must order the extradition of the person to the category 1 territory which issued the Pt 1 warrant (s.21(3)). If the judge makes an order for extradition, he can remand the person in custody or on bail to await extradition (s.21(4)). Even if the person is initially remanded in custody the judge is able to grant him bail at any later time before he is extradited (s.21(5)).

MATTERS WHICH MAY ARISE DURING THE EXTRADITION HEARING

PERSON CHARGED WITH AN OFFENCE IN THE UK

9–016 If the judge is informed at any time during the extradition hearing that the person is charged with an offence in the UK, the judge must adjourn the extradition hearing until:

(a) the charge is disposed of; or
(b) the charge is withdrawn; or
(c) proceedings in respect of the charge are discontinued; or
(d) an order is made for the charge to lie on the file or, in Scotland, the diet is deserted *pro loco et tempore* (s.22(1)–(2)).[24]

If the judge has already decided whether the person's extradition is barred because of the rule against double jeopardy before he adjourns the hearing under

[24] This means that although proceedings on the charge are discontinued there is the possibility that a fresh prosecution on the same charge could be brought in the future.

this section, he must decide this question again when the hearing is resumed (s.22(4)).

If a criminal charge in the UK leads to a sentence of imprisonment or another form of detention, the judge may adjourn the extradition hearing until the sentence has been served (s.22(3)).

PERSON SERVING A SENTENCE IN THE UK

If the judge is informed during the extradition hearing that the person is serving a sentence of imprisonment or another form of detention in the UK, he may adjourn the extradition hearing until the sentence has been served (s.23). 9–017

A DIFFERENT EXTRADITION REQUEST MADE UNDER PT 2

The judge must remand the person in custody or on bail if the judge is informed during the extradition hearing that: 9–018

- (a) the Secretary of State has issued a certificate under s.70[25] having received a valid request from a category 2 territory;
- (b) the request has not been disposed of; and
- (c) the Secretary of State has made an order under s.179(2)[26] for further proceedings on the Pt 1 warrant to be deferred until the Pt 2 request has been disposed of (s.24).

The judge has the power later to grant bail to a person remanded in custody.

PHYSICAL OR MENTAL CONDITION

If at any time during the extradition hearing it appears to the judge that it would be unjust or oppressive to extradite the person because of his mental or physical condition, the judge must either order the person's discharge or adjourn the extradition hearing. The adjourned hearing can be resumed if the person's condition improves so that it appears to the judge that extradition would no longer be unjust or oppressive (s.25). 9–019

COSTS

See Ch.15 at 15–013. 9–020

[25] See Ch.7.
[26] See Ch.15.

VI. PART 2

9–021 The extradition hearing is the hearing at which the appropriate judge deals with a request for extradition to a category 2 territory (s.140).

JUDGE'S POWERS AND ADJOURNMENTS

9–022 In England and Wales, the judge has the same powers (as nearly as may be) at the extradition hearing as a magistrates' court would have if it was dealing with the summary trial of an information against the person (s.77(1)). In Scotland, the judge's powers are equivalent to those he has in summary proceedings, but he can use evidence from only a single source to decide under s.78(4)(a) the identity of the person (s.77(2)). In Northern Ireland the judge's powers are the same as those of a magistrates' court hearing and determining a complaint (s.77(3)).

If the judge adjourns the extradition hearing, he must remand the person in custody or on bail (s.77(4)). The judge can grant bail at a later stage if he initially remands the person in custody (s.77(5)).

INITIAL STAGES OF THE EXTRADITION HEARING

9–023 Section 78 requires the judge to begin the extradition hearing by considering the adequacy of the extradition request and the supporting documentation sent to him by the Secretary of State.

DOCUMENTS SENT BY THE SECRETARY OF STATE

9–024 The judge must decide whether the documents sent to him by the Secretary of State consist of or include:

(a) the extradition request, the certificate issued by the Secretary of State and a copy of any relevant Order in Council;
(b) particulars of the person whose extradition is requested;
(c) particulars of the offence specified in the request;
(d) an arrest warrant or a reference to a judicial document authorising arrest[27] issued in the category 2 territory if the person is accused of an offence;
(e) a certificate issued in the category 2 territory of the conviction and, if the person has been sentenced, the sentence (if the person is alleged to be unlawfully at large after conviction) (s.78(2)).

[27] s.78(8).

If the judge decides that the documents sent by the Secretary of State do not include the specified documents and particulars, he must order the person's discharge (s.78(3)).

If he finds that the documents satisfy these requirements, he must decide whether copies of these documents have been served on the person (s.78(4)(c)). If they have not, he must order the person's discharge (s.78(6)).

IDENTITY

The judge must decide on the balance of probabilities[28] whether the person appearing or brought before him is the person whose extradition is requested (s.78(4)(a)). If the judge decides this question in the negative, he must order the person's discharge (s.78(6)). Evidence from either party is admissible for the purpose of determining this question (see 9–006, above). **9–025**

EXTRADITION OFFENCE

The judge must also decide whether the offence specified in the request is an extradition offence as defined in ss.137 and 138 (s.78(4)(b)). The definition of an extradition offence is considered in Ch.6. It is submitted, for the reasons discussed at 9–006, above, that the defence may call evidence as to the conduct which is in fact alleged against the person. If the judge decides that the offence in the request is not an extradition offence, he must order the person's discharge (s.78(6)). If the judge decides that the offence is an extradition offence, he must proceed to consider whether there is a bar to extradition (s.78(7)). **9–026**

BARS TO EXTRADITION

The bars to extradition are set out in s.79(1) and a person's extradition may be barred by reason of: **9–027**

(a) the rule against double jeopardy;
(b) extraneous considerations;
(c) the passage of time;
(d) hostage-taking considerations.

These bars are defined in ss.80-83 and are considered in detail in Ch.10.

If the judge finds that the person's extradition to the category 2 territory is barred for one of the reasons set out in s.11, he must order the person's discharge (s.79(3)). If the person is suffering from physical or mental ill health, s.91 may also operate as

[28] s.78(5). See further 8–021.

a bar to extradition (see 9–045 below). Evidence from either party is admissible, it is submitted, on any of these issues.

If the person is not discharged, and he is accused of the commission of the extradition offence but is not alleged to have been convicted, the judge must consider s.84, considered at 9–028, below (s.79(4)). If the person is not discharged and he is alleged to be unlawfully at large after conviction of the extradition offence, the judge must consider s.85 dealt with at 9–038 below (s.79(5)).

CASES WHERE A PERSON HAS NOT BEEN CONVICTED

SUFFICIENCY OF EVIDENCE

9–028 If the person has not been convicted, the judge must decide whether there is evidence which would be sufficient to make a case requiring an answer by the person if the proceedings were the summary trial of an information against him (s.84(1)).

In Scotland, "the summary trial of an information against him" is read instead as "summary proceedings for an offence alleged to have been committed by the person" (s.84(8)).[29] In Northern Ireland, "the summary trial of an information" is substituted by "the hearing and determination of a complaint" (s.84(9)).

Section 84(7) allows the Secretary of State to designate category 2 territories. If a category 2 territory has been designated, the judge does not consider the test in s.84(1). Instead he proceeds to consider the question of human rights (s.84(7)). A number of category 2 territories have been designated, and these are dealt with in Ch.5 at 5–014.

ADMISSIBILITY OF DOCUMENTS AND OTHER EVIDENCE

9–029 There are detailed provisions dealing with the admissibility of evidence where the judge is required to proceed under s.84.

The judge may treat a statement made by a person in a document as admissible evidence of a fact if the statement is made by the person to a police officer or another person charged with the duty of investigating offences or charging offenders and direct oral evidence by the person of the fact would be admissible (s.84(2)). A summary in a document of a statement made by a person must be treated as a statement made by the person in the document for the purpose of s.84(2) (s.84(4)).

When deciding whether to treat a statement made by a person in a document as admissible evidence of a fact, the judge must have particular regard to the following factors:

[29] Except that evidence from a single source shall be sufficient.

(a) the nature and source of the document;
(b) whether, having regard to the nature and source of the document and to any other circumstances that appear to the judge to be relevant, it is likely the document is authentic;
(c) the extent to which the statement appears to supply evidence which would not be readily available if it was not treated as being admissible evidence of a fact;
(d) the relevance of the evidence the statement appears to supply to any issue likely to have be determined by the judge in deciding whether there is sufficient evidence;
(e) the risk that the admission or exclusion of the statement will result in unfairness to the person whose extradition is sought, having regard in particular to whether it is likely to be possible to controvert the statement if the person making it does not attend to give oral evidence in the proceedings (s.84(3)).

This list is not exhaustive and the judge may take into account other factors in deciding whether to treat a statement or a summary as admissible. This section was inserted by the Government in part to take account of the concerns about the use of a summary under s.84(4). It is modelled on s.25 of the Criminal Justice Act 1988, which deals with the admissibility of documentary evidence in domestic criminal proceedings.

These provisions amount to a significant change to the previous rules on admissibility of evidence governing extradition proceedings and gave rise to considerable controversy during Parliamentary consideration of the Extradition Bill. In particular, concerns were raised when the Bill was published that it would be difficult for a judge to decide whether any summary was fair, impartial or indeed complete if the judge did not have the primary statement to consider together with the summary. However, the Government robustly defended the inclusion of this subsection stating that: 9–030

> "The judge must be satisfied that the evidence he is taking a decision to use is bona fide, authentic and appropriate. If he is not satisfied, he has an unhindered discretion not to allow it as evidence."[30]

The Government gave two examples of situations when it would be appropriate to use a summary rather than a statement. The first example was evidence of an alleged fraud which might include long and detailed accountancy statements. The Government considered that it would be unnecessary for the judge to receive these detailed statements, and that a summary would suffice for the purpose of establishing there was sufficient evidence. The second example offered was the existence of

[30] Mr Bob Ainsworth (Parliamentary Under-Secretary of State, Home Office), *Hansard*, Committee, 5th sitting, col.149.

broadly similar evidence given by a large number of witnesses, such as itemised bills produced by telephone company employees. It was argued that in many cases such summaries would be uncontested:

> "It will of course be open to the fugitive [*sic*] and his lawyers to challenge the summaries at the extradition hearing . . . We would not expect this facility [the use of summaries] to be used often. In most cases we would expect the full written witness statement to be put before the court."[31]

The Government also contended that the judge would have the discretion to call for the full statement to be provided to the court if it was unclear whether the summary should be admissible.[32] The Government also made it clear that a person would be able to challenge the admissibility of any summary which it is proposed to be used.[33] (The right of the person who is the subject of the extradition request to give evidence and call witnesses appears from this alone to form part of the policy behind the 2003 Act.)

9–031 Under the 1989 Act, it was necessary to establish by admissible evidence that the person whose return was requested was *prima facie* guilty of the offence, except where the rule had been specifically abrogated. Written evidence from the requesting country could always be given in evidence without the consent of the defendant. It is one of the characteristic features of the extradition process that written evidence is receivable, and that the defence cannot insist on the right to cross-examine. This principle has not been doubted in England since *R. v Brixton Prison Ex p. Caldough*,[34] but is sometimes attacked, unsuccessfully, in other jurisdictions in which extradition proceedings are less common.[35]

It was however necessary formally to prove translations by duly authenticated evidence. See *Kruger v Northward Prison*,[36] (Cayman Islands), *R. v Governor of Brixton Prison Ex p. Saifi*,[37] and *R. v Governor of Brixton Prison Ex p. Lodhi*[38]. It will obviously remain necessary under the 2003 Act to show that documents are properly translated.

31 Lord Filkin, Grand Committee, 8th sitting, Vol.652, col.GC 113.

32 Lord Filkin, Grand Committee, 8th sitting, Vol.652, col.GC 116.

33 Lord Filkin, Grand Committee, 8th sitting, Vol.652, col.GC 112–13.

34 [1961] 1 W.L.R. 464; even if not taken for the purpose of the proceedings; see *R. v Secretary of State for India Ex p. Ezekiel* [1941] 2 K.B. 169.

35 For a Caribbean expression of the principle, see *Saroop v Maharaj* [1996] 3 L.R.C. 1 (Trinidad and Tobago); the evidence of two conspirators was admissible by way of depositions sworn out of court and they were not required to come to court to give evidence orally, notwithstanding that the charge was one of conspiracy, since the evidence was sufficient to commit the appellant to custody to await extradition and had been sworn pursuant to the provisions of the 1870 Act (p.3b–c). This decision was applied and accepted in the extradition proceedings brought by the Government of the United States in *Re Miller, Matthew and Heath* (Neville Smith J.; High Court, St Christopher and Nevis, April 10, 1998).

36 [1996] C.I.L.R. 157, Harre C.J.

37 December 20, 2000; see below.

38 March 13, 2001; CO/3635/2001.

It was however critical under the 1989 Act to comply with the rule against hearsay. In *R. v Governor of Pentonville Prison Ex p. Kirby*[39] it was argued on behalf of the Canadian Government that a statement made by an investigator, summarising the case and drawing upon the evidence of others, was admissible by virtue of s.11 of the 1967 Act; it was immaterial if the evidence would have been inadmissible in an English trial as an infringement of the rule against hearsay. The High Court disagreed, distinguishing between admissible evidence as required by English law and statutory rules under the Extradition Act governing the admissibility of such evidence in Bow Street proceedings. It was held that the authentication provisions in the Fugitive Offenders Act 1967 could not make admissible inadmissible evidence. The rule in *Kirby* was followed and applied in *R. v Governor of Pentonville Prison Ex p. Osman (No.1)*,[40] *Re Dokleja*[41] and *R. v Governor of Brixton prison Ex p. Saifi*.[42]

The new provisions plainly render admissible hearsay evidence under the 2003 Act.

Written evidence which complies with s.9 of the Criminal Justice Act 1967, and evidence of formal admissions made in accordance with s.10 of the Criminal Justice Act 1967, are obviously admissible in proceedings under the 2003 Act,[43] as is oral evidence. At common law, statements made in foreign and Commonwealth public documents are admissible as to the truth of their contents if they satisfy the terms of the common law and they would be admissible in their country of origin. See, for example, *Lyell v Kennedy*[44] and *Phipson on Evidence*.[45]

This follows because proceedings are likened ("as nearly as may be") to summary trial.

SECTION 78(1) POLICE AND CRIMINAL EVIDENCE ACT 1984

There is, however, an exclusionary power. 9–032

The question whether s.78(1) applied to extradition proceedings under Sch.1 to the 1989 Act was considered by the House of Lords in *R. v Governor of Brixton Prison Ex p. Levin*.[46] The Government of the United States of America wished to submit evidence originating from a computer which, it was thought, had to comply with the provisions[47] of s.69 of the 1984 Act. The issue was whether extradition proceedings were "criminal proceedings" in which case s.78 would *prima facie* apply. Holding that they were, Lord Hoffman cited from the domestic committal case

39 [1979] 1 W.L.R. 541.
40 [1990] 1 W.L.R. 277, 306–9, DC.
41 Unreported, January 31,1994; CO/523/93.
42 December 21, 2000; CO/4176/1999; *The Times* January 24, 2001.
43 s.205, discussed at 9–006 above.
44 (1889) 14 App. Cas. 437, HL (E).
45 14th ed., Ch.41.
46 [1997] A.C. 741.
47 Repealed with effect from April 2000.

R. v King's Lynn Justices Ex p. Holland,[48] which held that it would be better for examining justices to leave the exercise of the discretion to the trial judge because he:

> "will be in a better position to assess the effect on the fairness of the proceedings and have greater experience of deciding such questions."

Furthermore, Lord Hoffman considered[49]:

> "In extradition proceedings there is even less scope for the exercise of the discretion because, as McCowan L.J. pointed out in *ex parte Francis* (quoting the Supreme Court of Canada in *Kindler v. Canada (Minister of Justice)*[50] extradition procedure is founded on concepts of comity and reciprocity. It would undermine the effectiveness of international treaty obligations if the courts were to superimpose discretions based on local notions of fairness on the ordinary rules of admissibility. I do not wish to exclude the possibility that the discretion may be used in extradition proceedings founded upon evidence which, though technically admissible, has been obtained in a way which outrages civilised values. But such cases are also likely to be very rare."

Plainly, this decision was influenced by the important fact that proceedings were then likened to committal for trial, rather than a summary trial.

9–033 *R. (Saifi) v Governor of Brixton Prison*[51] re-affirmed that s.78 of the Police and Criminal Evidence Act 1984 applies to extradition proceedings. The court gave guidance as to how s.78 should be applied.

> "The operative words of section 78 of PACE are:
>
> > 'In any proceedings the court may refuse to allow evidence on which the prosecution proposes to rely to be given if it appears to the court that, having regard to all the circumstances... the admission of the evidence would have such an adverse effect on the fairness of the proceedings that a court ought not to admit it.'
>
> Section 78 confers a power in terms wide enough for its exercise on the court's own motion. The power is to be exercised whenever an issue appears as to whether the court could conclude that the evidence should not be admitted. The concept of a burden of proof has no part to play in such circumstances. No doubt it is for that reason that there is no express provision as to the burden of proof, and we see no basis for implying such a burden. The prosecution desiring to adduce and the defence seeking to exclude evidence will each seek to persuade the court about impact on fairness. We regard the position as neutral

48 [1993] 1 W.L.R. 324, 328.
49 [1997] A.C. 748D-E.
50 (1991) 84 D.L.R. (4th) 438, 488.
51 [2001] 1 W.L.R. 1134.

and can see no reason why section 78 should be understood as requiring the courts to consider upon whom the burden of proof rests . . .

The ambit [of circumstances relevant to the court's decision] is not confined to what emanates from the defence. Circumstances may appear to the court other than those raised by the defendant . . .

Under section 78 any circumstance which can reasonably have a bearing on fairness should be considered. The weight to be attached to an individual circumstance may increase or decrease because of the presence of other related or unrelated circumstances. The preponderance of all of the circumstances may show that the admission of the evidence would have such an adverse effect on fairness as to require its exclusion.

The absence from section 78 of words suggesting that facts are to be established or proved to any particular standard is, in our judgement, deliberate. It leaves the matter open and untrammelled by rigid evidential considerations." [52]

Similar reasoning may be found in *Re Proulx*.[53]

Section 78(1) will allow the court, in appropriate circumstances, to exclude evidence obtained in breach of English rules of evidence, or English rules of practice. The courts held under previous extradition statutes that evidence admissible by English law would be admitted even if rules of practice in English criminal procedure would lead to its exclusion in English domestic proceedings. **9–034**

In this way, the following evidence was held admissible in extradition proceedings:

- accomplice evidence where the witnesses had not been sentenced in the requesting country (*R. v Governor of Pentonville Prison Ex p. Schneider and Newall*[54]);
- evidence obtained in a foreign state in breach of principles set out in English Judges' Rules (*Beese v Governor of Ashford Remand Centre*[55]);
- evidence from anonymous witnesses contrary to English procedures (*R. (Al-Fawwaz) v Governor of Brixton Prison*[56]);
- evidence obtained by refreshing memory from documents (*R. v Governor of Gloucester Prison Ex p. Miller*[57]);
- evidence of identity in breach of English *Turnbull* guidelines and Codes of Practice (*R. v Governor of Pentonville Prison Ex p. Voets*[58]; *R. v Governor of Brixton Prison Ex p. Bekar*[59]).

[52] *ibid.* at 1153–1155, *per* Rose L.J.
[53] [2000] 1 W.L.R. 57.
[54] (1981) 73 Cr. App. R. 200.
[55] [1973] 1 W.L.R. 1426.
[56] [2002] 1 A.C. 556.
[57] [1979] 2 All E.R. 1103.
[58] [1986] 1 W.L.R. 470.
[59] *The Times*, June 10, 1997.

There is also clear authority that courts have the power in extradition proceedings to exclude evidence of confession obtained from a defendant in breach of s.76 of the Police and Criminal Evidence Act 1984.[60]

TEST FOR SUFFICIENCY OF EVIDENCE

9–035 The test set out in the 2003 Act begs the question of what is "sufficient" evidence for committal.

Lord Reid set out the traditional test, which it is submitted continues to apply, in *R. v Governor of Brixton Prison Ex p. Schtraks*[61]:

> "... the proper test for the magistrate to apply is whether, if this evidence stood alone at trial, a reasonable jury, properly directed, could accept it and find a verdict of guilty."

In *R. v Governor of Pentonville Prison Ex p. Osman (No.1)*,[62] the nature of the test under s.7 (5) of the 1967 Act ("sufficient to warrant his trial") was discussed at length. The committing magistrate's duty was to apply the same test that he has to apply:

> "day in day out in his working life. It is to weigh the evidence to see whether that evidence is such that a reasonable directed is such that upon it a reasonable jury properly directed could convict."

The Divisional Court held that the test in *R. v Galbraith*[63] should apply, and gave reasons:

> " It would be illogical if the approach of examining magistrates in a domestic committal were more favourable to the accused than the approach of the judge at the end of the prosecution case; and there is no reason why the approach of the chief magistrate in an extradition case, or a case under the Fugitive Offenders Act 1967, should be more favourable to the accused than in the case of a domestic committal."

Lloyd L.J. noted[64] that the word "weigh" had been used in a number of authorities, including the House of Lords cases of *Ex p. Tarling*,[65] and *Ex p. Sotiriadis*.[66] He observed that the word "weigh" was ambiguous. It could mean "weigh against other evidence"; or, on the other hand, it could mean "weigh up".

[60] *R. v Bow Street Magistrates Court Ex p. Proulx* [2001] 1 All E.R. 57.
[61] [1964] A.C. 556, 580, HL.
[62] [1990] 1 W.L.R. 277, DC.
[63] (1981) 73 Cr. App. R. 124, CA. The test is cited below.
[64] at p.299D.
[65] (1980) 70 Cr. App. R. 77, 114, DC and HL.
[66] [1975] A.C. 1, 30.

The second approach was to be preferred. It was not the duty of the magistrate to compare one witness with another. That was the function of the jury at trial. The magistrate was therefore not concerned with inconsistencies in the evidence of the accomplice on whom the Government of Hong Kong relied; his evidence would only have been disregarded if the inconsistencies and contradiction had made his evidence worthless.

The Court approved the magistrate's formulation of the test, cited above, subject to substituting "consider" for "weigh". Words used by the Divisional Court in *Tarling* capable of being interpreted as a different approach to "weighing", were explicable by the extreme paucity of the reasons that had been given by the magistrate on committal.

In *R. v Governor of Pentonville Prison Ex p. Alves*,[67] it was held that the applicable test under the 1870 Act was that set out in *R. v Galbraith*. The Government of Sweden relied upon the duly authenticated evidence of an accomplice who, after serving his sentence, gave evidence for the fugitive at Bow Street, repudiating his earlier deposition on the ground that it had been procured by threats. Lord Goff cited the words of Lord Lane C.J. in *Galbraith*: 9–036

> "How then should the judge approach a submission of 'no case'? (1) If there is no evidence that the crime alleged has been committed, there is no difficulty. The judge will of course stop the case. (2) The difficulty arises where there is some evidence but it is of a tenuous character, for example, because of inherent weakness or vagueness or because it is inconsistent with other evidence. (a) Where the judge comes to the conclusion that the evidence, taken at its highest, is such that a jury properly directed could not properly convict upon it, it is his duty, upon a submission being made, to stop the case. (b) Where however the prosecution evidence is such that its strength or weakness depends on the view to be taken of a witness's reliability, or other matters which are generally speaking within the province of the jury and where on one possible view of the facts there is evidence upon which a jury could properly come to the conclusion that the defendant is guilty, then the judge should allow the matter to be tried by the jury . . . There will of course, as always in this branch of the law, be borderline cases. They can safely be left to the discretion of judge."

The House of Lords held that the magistrate had been entitled to commit.

In *Galbraith* the Court of Appeal had sought to reconcile conflicting approaches in the Court of Appeal as to the judge's duty at the end of the prosecution case on trial on indictment. Two authorities only are cited in the judgment. The headnote to the report in the Criminal Appeal Reports correctly describes the above passage as "guidelines". Nonetheless, the rule in *Galbraith* is now binding in extradition proceedings.

67 [1992] 3 W.L.R. 844, 848–850, HL.

The House of Lords referred in *Alves* without disapproval to *Osman (No.1)*.

9–037 There is an apparent difference between the approaches of Lord Reid in *Schtraks* and Lord Goff in *Alves*. Lord Goff made this observation, omitting the word "reasonable":

> "If the magistrate concludes, on the evidence before him, that the previous evidence is such that a jury, properly directed could not properly convict upon it, then, on the principle stated by Lord Lane CJ in [*Galbraith*] he should not commit."[68]

The "previous" evidence was the authenticated deposition on which the requesting government relied. One can be confident that the omission of the word "reasonable" was not intended to be significant, because Lord Goff referred with approval to the words of Lord Reid in *Schtraks*, cited above.

It is submitted, nonetheless, that the *Galbraith* guidelines encourage the attitude that a *prima facie* case is established if there is evidence of each element of the offence in the evidence, whether or not that evidence appears credible to the court. No doubt the fact that modern committal proceedings in England were conducted without live evidence at least partly explains this attitude: in the days of *Schtraks* a magistrate was obliged to hear oral evidence before committing for trial.

It should be remembered that the House of Lords in *Alves* did not decide that the evidence of a witness, later retracted on oath, did amount to a prima facie case; only that the magistrate, in that case, where the authenticated deposition had contained a wealth of detail, was entitled to commit. The cases are rare in which the High Court on an appeal will interfere with a judge's assessment of the evidence.

It is submitted that the task of the judge in judging the sufficiency of evidence continues to require not just the mechanical task of identifying the necessary elements of an offence; that might be achieved behind closed doors on the basis of written material alone; it also requires an assessment of whether a "reasonable" jury could convict. It is for this purpose, of course, that a judge must hear any evidence that the defendant wishes to give or to call.

If the judge decides that there is not sufficient evidence, he must order the person's discharge (s.84(5)). If he finds that there is sufficient evidence, he must go onto consider the issue of human rights dealt with at 9–040 below (s.84(6)).

CASES WHERE A PERSON HAS BEEN CONVICTED

9–038 Section 85(1) requires the judge to consider whether the person was convicted in their own presence. This is a factual question on which either party can give evidence. If the judge decides the person was convicted in his presence, he will proceed to consider the subject of human rights (s.85(2)).

[68] at 850F.

If the judge finds that the person was convicted in his absence, the judge will consider whether the person deliberately absented himself from his trial and, if so, the judge will proceed to consider the issue of human rights (s.85(3) and (4)).

If the judge finds that the person was convicted in his absence and did not deliberately absent himself from his trial, the judge must decide whether the person would be entitled to a retrial or, on appeal, a review amounting to a retrial (s.85(5)). The judge must not decide that the person would be entitled to a retrial or a review amounting to a retrial unless the person would have the right to:

(a) to defend himself in person or through legal assistance of his own choosing or, if he had not sufficient means to pay for legal assistance, to be given it free when the interests of justice so required; and
(b) to examine or have examined witnesses against him and to obtain the attendance and examination of witnesses on his behalf under the same conditions as witnesses against him (s.85(8)).

See 9–013 for a detailed discussion of retrial and review amounting to a retrial.

If the judge finds that the person would be entitled to a retrial or on appeal a review amounting to a retrial, he must proceed under s.86 (s.85(6)). If the judge finds that the person is not entitled to a retrial or on appeal a review amounting to a retrial, he must order the person's discharge (s.85(7)).

CONVICTION IN A PERSON'S ABSENCE (S.86)

The judge must decide under s.86 whether there is evidence which would be sufficient to make a case requiring an answer by the person if the proceedings were the summary trial of an information against him[69] (s.86(1)). This is exactly the same test as in s.84(1) and the provisions of s.86 are almost identical to s.84. Therefore, reference should be made to 9–028 *et seq.* for details of admissibility of evidence and the test for sufficiency of evidence which should be applied. 9–039

Section 86(7) allows the Secretary of State to designate category 2 territories and if a category 2 territory has been designated, the judge does not consider this test in s.86(1) but instead continues to consider the question of human rights (s.84(7)). A number of category 2 territories have been designated and are dealt with in Ch.5 at 5–014.

If the judge decides that there is not sufficient evidence, he must order the person's discharge (s.86(5)). If he finds that there is sufficient evidence, he must proceed to consider the matter of human rights (s.86(6)).

[69] This is subject to modification in Scotland and Northern Ireland in the same terms as s.84(1) discussed at 9–028.

HUMAN RIGHTS

9–040 As the final stage in the extradition hearing the judge must consider whether the person's extradition would be compatible with the Convention rights within the meaning of the Human Rights Act 1998 (s.87(1)). Evidence from either party is obviously admissible on this question.

This section refers to "the extradition". Reassurance was sought from the Government that this phrase was intended to apply both to the extradition proceedings and the person's treatment after his extradition. This assurance was given by Lord Filkin on behalf of the Government.[70]

The Convention rights are considered in Ch.11. If the judge finds that the extradition would be incompatible, he must order the person's discharge (s.87(2)). If he finds that the extradition would be compatible, he must send the case to the Secretary of State for his decision whether the person is to be extradited (s.87(3)).

CASE SENT TO SECRETARY OF STATE

9–041 If the judge sends the case to the Secretary of State, he can remand the person in custody or on bail to await the Secretary of State's decision and his eventual extradition if the Secretary of State orders that this should happen (s.92(4)). The matters which must be dealt with by the Secretary of State when making his decision are considered in Ch.12. Even if the person is initially remanded in custody the judge is able to grant him bail at any later stage before he is extradited (s.92(5)).

Unless the person has consented to his extradition under s.127,[71] the judge must inform the person "in ordinary language" that he has a right of appeal to the High Court and that an appeal will not be heard until the Secretary of State has made his decision (s.92(2)–(3)).

MATTERS WHICH MAY ARISE DURING THE EXTRADITION HEARING

PERSON CHARGED WITH AN OFFENCE IN THE UK

9–042 If the judge is informed at any time in the extradition hearing that the person is charged with an offence in the UK, the judge must adjourn the extradition hearing until:

(a) the charge is disposed of; or
(b) the charge is withdrawn; or
(c) proceedings in respect of the charge are discontinued; or

[70] Lord Filkin, Vol.650, cols GC 138–9.
[71] See Ch.14.

(d) an order is made for the charge to lie on the file or, in Scotland, the diet is deserted *pro loco et tempore* (s.88(1) and (2)).[72]

If the judge has already decided whether the person's extradition is barred because of the rule against double jeopardy before he adjourns the hearing under this section, he must decide this question again when the hearing is resumed (s.88(4)). If the charge in the UK leads to a sentence of imprisonment or another form of detention, the judge may adjourn the extradition hearing until the sentence has been served (s.88(3)).

PERSON SERVING A SENTENCE IN THE UK

If the judge is informed during the extradition hearing that the person is serving a sentence of imprisonment or another form of detention in the UK, he may adjourn the extradition hearing until the sentence has been served (s.89). **9–043**

COMPETING PT 1 WARRANT OR PT 2 REQUEST

The judge must remand the person in custody or on bail if the judge is informed during the extradition hearing that the conditions in s.90(2) or s.90(3) are met. **9–044**

The conditions in s.90(2) are that:

(a) the Secretary of State has received another valid request for the person's extradition to a category 2 territory;
(b) the request has not been disposed of; and
(c) the Secretary of State has made an order under s.126(2)[73] for further proceedings to be deferred until the competing request has been disposed of.

The conditions in section 90(3) are that:

(a) a certificate has been issued under s.2 in respect of a Pt 1 warrant for the person; and
(b) the warrant has not been disposed of;
(c) the Secretary of State has made an order under s.179(2)[74] for further proceedings on the request to be deferred until the warrant has been disposed of.

If the person is remanded in custody, the judge is able to grant him bail later.

[72] This means that although proceedings on the charge are discontinued there is the possibility that a fresh prosecution on the same charge could be brought in the future.
[73] See Ch.15.
[74] See Ch.15.

PHYSICAL OR MENTAL CONDITION

9–045 If at any time during the extradition hearing it appears to the judge that it would be unjust or oppressive to extradite the person because of his mental or physical condition, the judge must either order his discharge or adjourn the extradition hearing (s.91). The adjourned hearing can be resumed if the person's condition improves so that it appears to the judge that extradition would no longer be unjust or oppressive.

COSTS

9–046 See Ch.15 at 15–015.

VII. DISCUSSION — ABUSE OF PROCESS

9–047 Can the Judge dismiss proceedings brought by a territory on the grounds that they are an abuse of process?

It is submitted that as a matter of first principle the court hearing extradition proceedings has an inherent power to prevent abuse of its own procedures and processes, and that this power has not been excluded by the 2003 Act. This power did not exist under the Extradition Act 1870, the Backing of Warrants Act 1965, the Fugitive Offenders Act 1967, or the Extradition Act 1989.

The leading case under the 1870 Act was *Atkinson v United States Government*.[75] It was argued for the defence that the conduct of the US authorities in Louisiana in obtaining an indictment was so unfair that extradition would be an abuse of process. Reliance was placed upon the observations of the House of Lords in *Connelly v DPP*.[76] Lord Reid, for example, had said:

> "... there must always be a residual discretion to prevent anything that savours of abuse of process." [77]

The House of Lords held in *Atkinson* that this principle did not apply to proceedings under the 1870 Act, ruling that the magistrate had no power to decide whether it would be unfair to try the defendant, where he had no such power in English committal for trial proceedings. Further, the Secretary of State had the power to decline to surrender "whenever in his view it would be unjust or oppressive to surrender the man".[78]

[75] [[1971] A.C. 197; see also *R. v Governor of Brixton Prison Ex p. Kotronis* [1971] A.C. 250, HL.
[76] [1964] A.C. 1254.
[77] At 1296.
[78] See 232C–233B.

The Secretary of State was answerable to Parliament:

> "... In my judgment Parliament by providing this safeguard has excluded the jurisdiction of the courts".

As the abuse of process jurisdiction became established in relation to proceedings for ordinary committals for trial in magistrates' courts,[79] it was assumed in a number of Divisional Court cases that the jurisdiction did apply in extradition committal proceedings, where the unfairness to a defendant was said to lie in a misuse of court procedures in England, as opposed to the extradition request in itself.[80]

In *R. v Governor of Brixton Prison Ex p. Sinclair*,[81] the House of Lords held, 9–048
however, in a case in which the complaint was of delay in bringing the proceedings in a conviction case, that the rule in *Atkinson* continued to apply. This decision was followed in *Re Schmidt*,[82] in which it was contended by the defendant that he had been tricked to come from Ireland by an officer of the Metropolitan Police Extradition Squad, in order that he could be arrested and brought to court in England in respect of extradition proceedings brought by the Federal Republic of Germany.

This allegation unquestionably involved arguments that the processes and procedures of the court had been misused. It was contended that, since the House of Lords had held in *R. v Horseferry Road Ex p. Bennett*[83] that it would be an abuse of process to abduct a person and bring him to the United Kingdom to be tried, it was similarly an abuse of process to induce a person by deception to enter the United Kingdom for the purposes of bringing extradition proceedings against him.

The House of Lords rejected the argument on the basis that it could be assumed that other states had *Bennett*-type jurisdiction,[84] and the Secretary of State had the power to prevent an extradition:

> "The Secretary of State's general discretion under section 12 [of the 1989 Act] is the principal safeguard for the subject of extradition proceedings."

Other House of Lords case where the same principle was applied are *R. v Governor of Pentonville Prison Ex p. Alves*,[85] and *R. v Secretary of State for the Home Department Ex p. Launder*.[86]

In spite of the rigour of this doctrine, the Divisional Court did hold that the subject of an extradition request could abuse the process of the Divisional Court,[87] and that an application for habeas corpus might be dismissed on this ground.

[79] See, for example, *R. v Derby Crown Court, Ex p. Brooks* (1985) 80 Cr. App. R 164.
[80] *R. v Bow Street Magistrates Court Ex p. Van Der Holst* (1986) 83 Cr. App. R. 114; *In Re Rees* [1986] 1 A.C. 937.
[81] [1991] 2 A.C. 64.
[82] [1995] 1 A.C. 339.
[83] [1994] 1 A.C. 42.
[84] A misapprehension in the case of the USA; see Ch.4.
[85] [1993] A.C. 284.
[86] [1997] 1 W.L.R. 839.
[87] *R. v Governor of Brixton Prison Ex p. Osman (No.4)* [1992] 1 All E.R. 579, 595.

9–049 In *R. v Governor of Belmarsh Prison Ex p. Gilligan; R. v Governor of Exeter Prison Ex p. Ellis*,[88] the House of Lords considered whether courts could exercise an abuse of process jurisdiction in proceedings brought under the 1965 Act, where the Secretary of State had no discretion in the matter of surrender. It held, by reference to the scheme of the Act, that there was no such power:

> "The United Kingdom and the Republic of Ireland are neighbours with close ties. Thus there are no immigration controls between Ireland and the United Kingdom. . . . The special position of Ireland in each part of the law of the United Kingdom is the explanation for the system for the rendition of persons in accordance with a reciprocal system for backing and enforcing warrants between the two countries."

The 2003 Act has now abolished the general discretion of the Secretary of State. The inevitable consequence of the approach of the courts from the case of *Atkinson* onwards was not to simplify extradition proceedings, something that the courts repeatedly stressed was desirable, but to move the resolution of facts relevant to the question of the fairness of the extradition from the courts to the Secretary of State, whose discretion could of course be the subject of judicial review.

It became common for the Secretary of State to investigate these facts for over a year, sometimes more than two years. It was the sheer burden of this work, not legal principle, that led to the exclusion of the general discretion from the 2003 Act.

It is submitted that the abolition of this discretion removes the implication that Parliament has prevented a court from staying a case on the ground that the requesting territory has abused the court's processes, where it has done so in a way which is outside the protections contained in the bars to surrender and the human rights provisions, set out in Chs 10 and 11.

It is not possible to enumerate all the possible circumstances, but the deliberate manipulation of procedures governing warrants, alleged in *Van Der Holst*, manipulation of provisions relating to time limits, as alleged in *Rees*, the procurement of the proceedings by deception, as alleged in *Schmidt*, or delay in bringing proceedings until the 2003 Act came into force, all seem to be matters which, as a matter of general principle, courts are entitled to consider and act upon in the exercise of their inherent powers.

[88] [2001] A.C. 84.

CHAPTER 10

BARS TO EXTRADITION

I. INTRODUCTION

The appropriate judge[1] must determine as part of the extradition hearing in both Pts 1 and 2 whether any of the bars to extradition applies.[2] Procedure governing the extradition hearing is dealt with in Ch.9. The bars applicable to Pt 1 cases are listed in s.11(1) and the definitions are in ss.12–19. The bars applicable to Pt 2 cases are listed in s.79(1) and ss.80–83 provide the definitions. **10–001**

The table below shows which factors will operate as a bar to extradition, and the appropriate fact-finding person. This chapter considers those bars which may fall for consideration at the extradition hearing. The matters which may fall for the Secretary of State's consideration in Pt 2 cases are dealt with in Ch.12. There is no specific bar in Pt 2 dealing with the age of the person who is the subject of the extradition request.

[1] See 8–016.

[2] Pt 1, see Ch.9 at 9–012; Pt 2, see Ch.9 at 9–027.

Bar	Part 1	Part 2
Rule against double jeopardy	Judge	Judge
Extraneous considerations	Judge	Judge
The passage of time	Judge	Judge
Hostage-taking considerations	Judge	Judge
The person's age	Judge	
Speciality	Judge	Secretary of State[3]
Earlier extradition from another category 1 territory	Judge	Secretary of State[4]
Earlier extradition from a non-category 1 territory	Judge	Secretary of State[5]

II. RULE AGAINST DOUBLE JEOPARDY

RULE AGAINST DOUBLE JEOPARDY

10–002 The rule against double jeopardy is made applicable by s.12 for Pt 1 cases and s.80 for Pt 2 cases.

A person's extradition is barred if it appears that the person would be entitled to be discharged under any rule of law relating to previous acquittal or conviction if he was charged with the extradition offence in the part of the UK where the judge hearing the extradition hearing exercises his jurisdiction.[6]

In Pt 1 cases, the judge is entitled to assume that the conduct constituting the extradition offence constituted an offence in the part of the UK where the judge exercises his jurisdiction (s.12). This provision is included to ensure that the protection against double jeopardy applies to conduct which satisfies the definition of an extradition offence in Pt 1, but does not constitute an offence in the UK. Conduct which does not amount to an offence in the UK may satisfy the definition of an extradition offence in Pt 1 if it is included in the European framework list.[7]

3 See ss.93 and 95, Ch.12 at 12–013.
4 See ss.93 and 96, Ch.12 at 12–014.
5 See ss.93 and 96, Ch.12 at 12–014.
6 Art.3(2) of the Framework Decision refers to the requested person having been finally judged by a Member State in respect of the same acts.
7 See Ch.6 at 6–008 and 6–016.

RULES OF LAW RELATING TO PREVIOUS ACQUITTAL OR CONVICTION

There is no description or definition in the 2003 Act of rules of law relating to a previous acquittal or conviction which would allow a defendant to be discharged in the UK. 10–003

In domestic proceedings, a defendant may raise a *plea in bar*, before arraignment, of *autrefois acquit* or *autrefois convict* and submit that he should not be tried on indictment because he has either been convicted or acquitted[8] of the same or substantially the same offence alleged.[9] The *plea in bar* operates for any offence for which the defendant could properly have been convicted when convicted of the first offence.[10] "The facts which constitute the one must be sufficient to justify a conviction for the other."[11] It also operates if the offence for which a person has been acquitted has the same essential ingredients as an offence with which he is later charged. In *Connelly v Director of Public Prosecutions*, the authorities and principles governing the application of a plea in bar were extensively considered by the House of Lords.[12]

The House of Lords, finding that there was no such plea available on the facts of that case, nevertheless held there is a wider discretionary power to stay proceedings as an abuse of process if it appears that the general rule against double jeopardy is infringed[13]:

> "The court has, I think, a power to apply, in the exercise of its judicial discretion, the broader principles to cases that do not fit the actual pleas and a duty to stop a prosecution which on the facts offends against those principles and creates abuse and injustice."[14]

In *Beedie,*[15] the Court of Appeal held that *autrefois acquit* is only available where the same offence is charged in the second indictment, but that the judge has an inherent discretion to stay the proceedings where the second offence arises out of the same or substantially the same set of facts as the first offence.[16] This discretion should be exercised in favour of the defendant unless there are special circumstances for not doing so.[17] This discretion would seem to be a relevant rule of law relating to previous acquittal or conviction (ss.12 and 80).[18] This approach is

[8] These are also known as the doctrines of *autrefois convict* and *autrefois acquit*.

[9] *Connelly v DPP* [1964] A.C. 1254; *DPP v Nasrulla* [1967] 2 A.C. 238.

[10] *Barron's case* [1914] 2 K.B. 570 at 574.

[11] *R. v Kupferberg* (1918) 34 T.L.R. 587.

[12] *per* Lord Morris, *ibid.* at 1305–1306.

[13] The application of this wider doctrine is considered in Ch.9.

[14] *ibid.* at 1365. See also 1296 and *R. v Humphreys* [1977] A.C. 1 at 40–1 and 54, HL.

[15] [1997] 2 Cr. App. R. 167.

[16] See also *R. v Humphreys* [1977] A.C. 1 at 41.

[17] The Court considered the issue of special circumstances at 176 referring also to the speech of Lord Devlin in *Connelly.*

[18] It is suggested that the judgment of the court *In Re Andre Caddoux and Andre Caddoux v Bow Street Magistrates Court* [2004] EWHC 642, can be distinguished. The court found that the narrow bar of

supported by the wording of the Framework Decision which refers to "acts" rather than offences.[19]

The Government considered that the position in domestic UK proceedings is that a previous conviction or acquittal which takes place following proceedings outside the UK may operate as a bar.[20] This would accord with the wording used in Art.3(2) of the Framework Decision which says that a Member State must refuse to execute an EAW "if the executing judicial authority is informed that the requested person has been finally judged *by a Member State* in respect of the same acts . . ." [emphasis added].[21]

It was held that a person who was discharged under the Extradition Act 1870 because of insufficient of evidence could not plead *autrefois acquit* if another extradition request was made for the same offence at a later date.[22]

CRIMINAL JUSTICE ACT 2003

10–004 Parliament considered the then Extradition and Criminal Justice Bills at the same time. Part 10 of the now Criminal Justice Act 2003 provides for the retrial of serious offences but is not in force at the time of writing.[23] When it is brought into force, Pt 10 will radically alter the longstanding protection against double jeopardy.

In summary, Pt 10 will allow the prosecution to apply to the Court of Appeal for an order quashing a person's previous acquittal and ordering his retrial. An application can also be made, if a person has been acquitted following a trial outside the UK, for an order from the Court of Appeal that the acquittal is not a bar to the person being tried in the UK. The Court of Appeal will allow an application if it is satisfied that there is both new and compelling evidence and that it is in the interests of justice to make the order requested.

The Government was asked during the passage of the Bill what effect Pt 10 of the Criminal Justice Act 2003 would have on the definitions of the rule against double jeopardy in the 2003 Act. For example, where an extradition request is made for a person who has already been tried for an extradition offence in another territory, but whose acquittal had been quashed by a court in that territory applying similar provisions to Pt 10 of the Criminal Justice Act 2003, it is not clear whether the rule against double jeopardy will apply. The Government considered that the drafting of ss.12 and 80 of the 2003 Act, which define the scope of the rule against double jeopardy, would cause the judge to apply the domestic law on double jeopardy, as modified by Pt 10 of the Criminal Justice Act, 2003 when it comes into force.

autrefois convict was not made out in this case. It then considered whether the court had a freestanding abuse of process jurisdiction. It is suggested that the correct approach is to assess whether the exercise of the abuse of process jurisdiction is a "relevant rule of law" for the purposes of ss.12 and 80.

[19] Art.3(2).

[20] Lord Bassam, Vol.649, cols 401 and 402.

[21] See also *R. v Roche* (1775) 1 Leach 134; *R. v Aughet* (1918) 13 Cr. App. R. 101.

[22] *Re Rees* [1986] A.C. 936 at 944, HL.

[23] ss.75–97, Criminal Justice Act 2003.

Lord Bassam indicated how he thought the position would be dealt with by a judge in these circumstances:

> "If the person's acquittal had not been quashed, we would have to refuse the request, even if the requesting state told us that it intended to quash it. Similarly, we would have to refuse the request if the acquittal had been quashed in a manner which did not command confidence. Indeed, the ECHR would prevent extradition in those circumstances."[24]

III. EXTRANEOUS CONSIDERATIONS[25]

Extradition may be barred by reason of extraneous considerations if (and only if) it appears that: 10–005

(a) a Pt 1 warrant or Pt 2 extradition request (though purporting to be made on account of an extradition offence) is in fact made for the purpose of prosecuting or punishing a person on account of his race, religion, nationality, gender, sexual orientation, or political opinions; or
(b) if extradited he might be prejudiced at his trial or punished, detained or restricted in his personal liberty by reason of his race, religion, nationality, gender, sexual orientation or political opinions.
(Pt 1 — s.13; Pt 2 — s.81)

A similar bar was included in Art.3 of the European Convention on Extradition 1957, and in both the 1989 Act and the preceding Fugitive Offenders Act 1967. The previous High Court and House of Lords authorities remain relevant.

The 2003 Act represents the demise in the United Kingdom of the historic principle that persons were not to be extradited for a "political offence" or "an offence of a political character".[26] The authorities were reviewed in full in the first two editions of this work. The exception was eroded by statute, most notably the Suppression of Terrorism Act 1978, which, *inter alia*, removed the protection for designated states in the case of serious offences.

There are few who regret the passing of this exception in an age of international terrorism. The advantage to the more modern formulations, embodied now in the 2003 Act, is that they focus attention on the alleged offender, and the requesting territory's attitude to him, rather on the alleged offence.

The person who is the subject of the warrant or request must prove that this bar applies. He must also show that the making of the extradition request or the

[24] Lord Bassam, Vol.649, col. GC 402.
[25] *cf.* para.12, Preamble, Framework Decision.
[26] The authorities were reviewed comprehensively in *T v Secretary of State for the Home Department* [1996] A.C. 742.

potential prejudice set out in (b) is causally linked to one of the extraneous considerations.[27] The state of mind of the requesting territory at the time of the making of the extradition claim must be considered in assessing whether (a) applies.[28]

10–006 The House of Lords considered the burden of proof which was appropriate under s.4(1)(c) of the 1967 Act (which is in similar terms to (b)). It held that although the defendant bears the burden of showing that this bar is made out he only has to show there is "a reasonable chance" or "serious possibility" of prejudice.[29]

One of the grounds for claiming refugee status in the UK is "a well-founded fear of being persecuted for reasons of race, religion, nationality, membership of a particular social group or political opinion". This is based on the obligations of the Government under the Convention relating to the Status of Refugees.[30] The authorities relevant to the meaning of persecution on these grounds are therefore relevant to submissions under ss.13 and 81. For refugee and asylum purposes, submissions about persecution on the basis of gender or sexual orientation will be considered under the ground of membership of a particular social group.[31] Some of the principles which are applied when interpreting these grounds are set out below[32]:

(a) a broad definition of race which includes membership of ethnic groups should be adopted[33];
(b) nationality should be interpreted broadly to include a specific cultural or linguistic minority identifying itself as such[34];
(c) political opinion covers any opinion perceived to challenge governmental authority[35]; and
(d) political opinion may be express, implied or imputed.[36]

When considering this bar, Art.18 of the ECHR should also be considered as this prohibits the use of the restrictions on the rights in the ECHR for any purpose other than those for which they have been prescribed. This subject is considered in Ch.11.

27 *Lodhi v Governor of Brixton Prison* [2001] EWHC 178.
28 *Jaroslave Slepcik v Governor of HM Prison Brixton and Government of Czech Republic* [2004] EWHC 1224 (Admin) at para.23.
29 *Fernandez v Government of Singapore* [1971] 1 W.L.R. 987 at 994; *Kenan Ozen v Republic of Germany* [2003] EWHC Admin 2851.
30 Art.1A(2) (1951) as amended by the 1967 Protocol.
31 *R. v Immigration Appeal Tribunal and Secretary of State for the Home Department Ex p. Shah*; *Islam v Immigration Appeal Tribunal* [1999] 2 A.C. 629.
32 Reference should be made to immigration and asylum textbooks for more detailed analysis and a full review of the case law. See for example, Macdonald Q.C. and Webber, eds, *Immigration Law and Practice in the United Kingdom*; Symes and Jorro, *Asylum Law and Practice*.
33 *Sewa Singh Mandla v Dowell Lee* [1983] 2 A.C. 548 at 563–4.
34 EU Joint Position (96/196/JHA), March 4, 1996 at para.7.3.
35 *Gomez* [2000] I.N.L.R. 549.
36 *Adan and Lazarevic v Secretary of State for the Home Department* [1997] Imm. A.R. 251.

IV. PASSAGE OF TIME

Extradition will be barred if it appears that it would be unjust or oppressive to extradite the person because of the passage of time since he is alleged to have committed the extradition offence or become unlawfully at large (Pt 1 — s.14; Pt 2 — s.82). 10–007

This definition is almost identical to s.11(3)(b) of the 1989 Act, which in turn derived from s.8(3) of the Fugitive Offenders Act 1967 and s.10 of the Fugitive Offenders Act 1881.[37] These powers were reserved to the High Court in previous legislation, but are now conferred on the lower court. This transfer has the considerable advantage that the evidence on the matter can be given live, and subject to cross-examination. The Divisional Court has traditionally been reluctant to receive evidence other than on affidavit.

It is no longer possible, subject to human rights arguments, to find that it would be unjust or oppressive to extradite a person on the ground that the accusation against the person is not made in good faith, or because the offence is trivial, grounds contained in previous legislation. (Hence the words "(and only if)" in ss.14 and 82.) However, as discussed in Chs 9, 11 and 13, the abuse of process, habeas corpus and human rights protections may be wide enough to embrace these grounds. It would indeed be curious if it appeared to a Judge that the request was made in bad faith and for a trivial offence, but that he could do nothing about it.

The words unjust and oppressive are not defined in the 2003 Act but the meaning of these terms was considered in *Kakis v Government of the Republic of Cyprus* by Lord Diplock[38]:

> "'Unjust' I regard as directed primarily to the risk of prejudice to the accused in the conduct of the trial itself, 'oppressive' as directed to hardship to the accused resulting from changes in his circumstances that have occurred during the period to be taken into consideration; but there is room for overlapping, and between them they would cover all cases where to return him would not be fair."

The speeches of all the Lords of Appeal in this case are relevant to the test.

The period of time to be is considered is taken from the date of the alleged offence.[39] However, it is not necessarily only the length of time which may be relevant. "It is not merely a question whether the length of time passed would make it unjust or oppressive to return the fugitive. Regard must be had to all circumstances . . . They include circumstances taking place during the passage of time which may . . . give the particular passage of time a quality or significance leading to a conclusion that return would be unjust or oppressive."[40]

37 See *Union of India v Narang* [1978] A.C. 247.
38 [1978] 1 W.L.R. 779 at 782.
39 *Kakis v Republic of Cyprus* [1978] 1 W.L.R. 779 at 782.
40 *per* Lord Russell, *Kakis v Republic of Cyprus* [1978] 1 W.L.R. 779 at 785.

Delay which is caused by the person who is the subject of the extradition request cannot generally be relied on. This includes delay caused by the person fleeing, concealing his whereabouts or evading arrest.[41] However, culpable delay on the part of the requesting territory may be sufficient to show that it would be unjust or oppressive to extradite.[42] If the passage of time might affect the fairness of a trial in the requesting territory, this is a relevant consideration when assessing whether extradition would be unjust.[43] A defendant who argues that this bar applies may have difficulty in demonstrating that it would be unjust to surrender him if he declines to disclose his defence.[44]

10–008 The court in *Woodcock v Government of New Zealand*[45] explained the reasoning process it considered was involved in assessing whether it would be unfair to return the person to undergo a trial. The court assesses what safeguards exist in the law of the requesting territory to ensure that the person would not have an unjust trial there. If after making this assessment the court concludes that a court in the requesting territory would be bound to hold that a fair trial of the person is impossible, it would be unjust or oppressive, or both, to order extradition. If the court in the requesting territory does not have satisfactory procedures equivalent to the abuse of process jurisdiction in the UK, the court will have to reach its own conclusion on whether a fair trial is possible in the requesting territory. It is submitted that the words of the statutory test do not make this type of assessment obligatory or decisive of the issue.

In domestic proceedings the court has an abuse of process jurisdiction to stay proceedings if a defendant can show he will be prejudiced in the conduct or preparation of his defence at his trial by reason of delay since the commission of the alleged offence.[46] The bar in the 2003 Act is wider than this domestic principle. The court may still find it would be "oppressive" to extradite by reason of the passage of time. The gravity of the offence is relevant to the question of oppression.[47]

In considering whether the passage of time is such that it would be oppressive to extradite, the court in *Kakis* took account of a belief fostered by the actions of the requesting territory that no extradition request would be made.[48] There are a number of cases which suggest that delay by itself may be sufficient in a particular case to make extradition unjust or oppressive.[49]

41 *R. v Secretary of State for the Home Department Ex p. Launder* [1997] 1 W.L.R. 839.

42 *Kakis v Republic of Cyprus* [1978] 1 W.L.R. 779 at 783.

43 *Kakis v Republic of Cyprus* [1978] 1 W.L.R. 779 at 788.

44 *R. v Secretary of State for the Home Department Ex p. Launder* [1997] 1 W.L.R. 839.

45 [2003] EWHC 2668 Admin at para.21.

46 *R. v Derby Crown Court Ex p. Brooks* (1985) 80 Cr. App. R. 164.

47 *Kakis v Republic of Cyprus* [1978] 1 W.L.R. 779 at 784.

48 *Kakis v Republic of Cyprus* [1978] 1 W.L.R. 779 at 790.

49 *R. v Secretary of State Ex p. Patel* (1995) 7 Admin. L.R. 56; *Sagnam v Government of Turkey* [2001] EWHC Admin 474; *Re Oncel* [2001] EWHC Admin 1142.

V. HOSTAGE-TAKING CONSIDERATIONS

The UK is a state party to the International Convention against the Taking of Hostages[50] (the "Hostage-taking Convention"), and enacted the Taking of Hostages Act 1982 to give effect to it in national law. Article 9 of this Convention states that: 10–009

> "(1) A request for the extradition of an alleged offender, pursuant to this Convention, shall not be granted if the requested State Party has substantial grounds for believing:
>
> . . .
>
> (b) that the person's position may be prejudiced:
>
> . . .
>
> (ii) for the reason that communication with him by the appropriate authorities of the State entitled to exercise rights of protection cannot be effected.
>
> (2) With respect to the offences as defined in this Convention, the provisions of all extradition treaties and arrangements applicable between States Parties are modified as between States Parties to the extent that they are incompatible with this Convention."

In order to comply with its obligations under Art.9(2) of the Convention, the UK has included s.16 for Pt 1 and s.83 for Pt 2 to introduce a bar to extradition on the basis of hostage-taking considerations.

In order for the bar to apply, the category 1 territory issuing the Pt 1 warrant, or the category 2 territory making the extradition request, must be a party to the Hostage-taking Convention. A certificate issued by the Secretary of State is conclusive evidence that a territory is a party to the Hostage-taking Convention.[51]

The conduct constituting the extradition offence must also constitute an offence or an attempt to commit an offence under s.1 of the Taking of Hostages Act 1982:

> "(1) A person, whatever his nationality, who, in the United Kingdom or elsewhere,
>
> (a) detains any other person ('the hostage'),
> (b) in order to compel a State, international governmental organisation or person to do or abstain from doing any act, threatens to kill, injure or continue to detain the hostage,
>
> commits an offence."

[50] Opened for signature in New York on December 18, 1979. *www.unodc.org/unodc/terrorism_convention_hostages.html.*

[51] ss.16(3) and 83(3).

If these two conditions are met, the judge must also consider whether it appears that the person might be prejudiced at his trial because communications would not be possible between him and the appropriate authorities. The appropriate authorities are the authorities of the territory which are entitled to exercise rights of protection in relation to him. The Explanatory Notes to the 2003 Act explain that these are consular authorities.[52]

VI. AGE[53]

10–010 Extradition is barred if it would be presumed conclusively that by reason of his age the defendant could not be guilty of the extradition offence (s.15). In making this assessment, the judge must assume that the conduct constituting the extradition offence constituted an offence in the part of the UK where the judge exercises jurisdiction and that the conduct was carried out by the person in the same part of the UK at the time as the alleged conduct amounting to the extradition offence.

In England, Wales and Northern Ireland it is conclusively presumed that a child under 10 years old can not be guilty of an offence.[54] In Scotland it is presumed that a child under eight can not be guilty of an offence.[55]

VII. SPECIALITY[56]

HISTORY OF SPECIALITY PROTECTION

10–011 This is considered in its international context in Ch.2. The Parliamentary draftsman has preferred the French term "speciality" to the solecism, hallowed by long use, "specialty".

SPECIALITY AND PT 1

10–012 If there are no speciality arrangements with the category 1 territory issuing the Pt 1 warrant, the person's extradition will be barred (s.17).

Speciality arrangements can either be contained in the domestic law of the category 1 territory or in arrangements made between the territory and the UK

[52] Paras 51 and 242, Explanatory Notes, EA 2003.
[53] See Art.3(3) of the Framework Decision.
[54] England and Wales — s.50 Children and Young Persons Act 1933 as amended by s.16(1), Children and Young Persons Act 1963; Northern Ireland — art.3, Criminal Justice (Children) (Northern Ireland) Order 1998.
[55] s.41, Criminal Procedure (Scotland) Act 1995.
[56] This is an issue which is considered by the Secretary of State for Pt 2 cases — see Ch.12.

(s.17(2)). Arrangements with a Commonwealth country or a British overseas territory[57] can be made for a particular case or more generally (s.17(6)). A certificate issued by the Secretary of State confirming the existence of the arrangements with the Commonwealth country or British overseas territory and stating the terms is conclusive evidence of these matters (s.17(7)). For other territories, any certificate issued by the Secretary of State is not conclusive and the judge can, therefore, consider whether the arrangements are sufficient to satisfy s.17.

The law of the requesting category 1 territory or the arrangements between the territory and the UK must only allow a person extradited from the UK to be dealt with in the category 1 territory for an offence committed before his extradition if the offence falls within s.17(3) or the condition in s.17(4) is satisfied.[58]

Section 17(3) contains the following offences:

(a) the offence for which the person is extradited;
(b) an extradition offence disclosed by the same facts as that offence;
(c) an extradition offence for which the judge gives consent under s.55[59];
(d) an offence which is not punishable with imprisonment or another form of detention;
(e) an offence for which the person will not be detained in connection with his trial, sentence or appeal;
(f) an offence which does not otherwise fall in s.17(3) but which the person's waives his right not to be dealt with for.

The condition in s.17(4) is that the person is given an opportunity to leave the category 1 territory after he has been extradited; and he does not leave within 45 days of arriving in the territory, or he returns to the territory after he has left within this period (s.17(4) and (5)).

VIII. EARLIER EXTRADITION TO THE UK FROM A CATEGORY 1 TERRITORY[60]

This bar may apply if there has been an earlier extradition of the person to the UK from another category 1 territory ("the extraditing territory") (s.18). If the arrangements between the UK and the extraditing territory require that territory's consent for the person's extradition to a different category 1 territory for the 10–013

[57] See Ch.5 for list of British overseas territories.

[58] Art.27(1) of the Framework Decision allows Member States to provide notification that consent will be presumed for all offences prior to extradition to be dealt with. The UK has made no notification under this Article and so Art.27(2)–(4) which set out the exceptions to the speciality rule will apply.

[59] The 2003 Act provides a procedure for the judge to give consent for a person who has been extradited to a category 1 territory to be dealt with for other offences — see Ch.14.

[60] This is an issue considered by the Secretary of State in Pt 2 cases — see Ch.12.

extradition offence under consideration,[61] and the required consent has not been given, the extradition is barred.

IX. EARLIER EXTRADITION TO THE UK FROM A NON-CATEGORY 1 TERRITORY[62]

10–014 This bar may apply if there has been an earlier extradition of the person from a non-category 1 territory ("the extraditing territory") (s.19). If under the arrangements between the UK and the extraditing territory that territory's consent is required for the person's extradition to a category 1 territory for the extradition offence under consideration,[63] and the required consent has not been given, the extradition is barred.

Speciality in Pt 2 cases is considered in Ch.12 because it is a responsibility of the Secretary of State.

[61] See, for example, Art.28 of the Framework Decision which deals with surrender or subsequent extradition.

[62] This is an issue considered by the Secretary of State in pt 2 cases — see Ch.12.

[63] For example, Art.18(2) of the Extradition Treaty between the UK and the USA (Cm. 5821) prohibits onward extradition or surrender for any offence committed prior to extradition unless the state which has initially extradited the person consents.

CHAPTER 11

CONVENTION RIGHTS

I. INTRODUCTION

As the Explanatory Notes to the 2003 Act emphasise, there is a balance to be struck in the extradition process: "The law should provide a quick and effective framework to extradite a person to the country where he is accused or has been 11–001 convicted of a serious crime, provided this does not breach his fundamental human rights."[1]

FRAMEWORK DECISION

11–002 The EAW Scheme recognises the need for respect for human rights:

> "This Framework Decision respects fundamental rights and observes the principle is recognised by Article 6 of the Treaty on European Union and reflected in the Charter of Fundamental Rights of the European Union[2], in particular Chapter VI thereof."[3]

This approach is reinforced by Art.1(3):

> "This Framework Decision shall not have the effect of modifying the obligation to respect fundamental rights and fundamental legal principles as enshrined in Article 6 of the Treaty on European Union."

The purpose of the Framework Decision is to continue the mutual recognition programme of the European Union in respect of criminal law decisions. One of the fundamental precepts underlying this programme is the trust and confidence that the EU Member States are said to have in one another's criminal justice systems.

All Member States must have criminal justice systems which meet the obligations under Arts 5 and 6 of the ECHR. However, there are no EU common standards in respect of minimum procedural safeguards for criminal proceedings. The ECHR case law amply demonstrates that Member States do not always act in compliance with the ECHR, and the ECtHR does not have the resources to deal with its ever increasing case load.[4]

Therefore, a proposal has been published for a Framework Decision to set common minimum standards for certain procedural rights applying to criminal proceedings in the EU.[5] It is noteworthy that these minimum standards have not been set in advance of the programme of mutual recognition measures but the proposal is to be welcomed although it is limited in scope.

[1] para.7, Explanatory Notes — Extradition Act 2003. The Joint Committee on Human Rights considered the Extradition Bill in its Twentieth Report and reference will be made to the report where relevant.

[2] [2000] O.J. C364/1.

[3] Para.12 of the Preamble to the Framework Decision.

[4] See Protocol 14 to the ECHR amending the control system of the ECHR (CETS 194) *www.echr.coe.int/Library/annexes/194E.pdf.* The preamble considers the urgent need to amend provisions of the ECHR to maintain and improve the efficiency of the control system for the long term in light of the continuing increase in the workload of the ECHR and the Committee of Ministers of the Council of Europe. This has been opened for signature but is not yet in force.

[5] COM (2004) 328/F April 28, 2004.

A Green Paper on this issue was presented in February 2003[6] and the responses to it indicated significant opposition. However, the proposal for a framework decision proposes five initial areas for common standards which are:

- access to legal advice (both before the trial and at trial);
- access to interpretation and translation;
- protecting defendants who cannot understand or follow the proceedings;
- communication and consular assistance for foreign detainees;
- provision of a short standard written statement of basic rights.

It remains to be seen whether the text for a framework decision can be agreed which overcomes the concerns of individual Member States.

HUMAN RIGHTS AND UK EXTRADITION LAW

THE 1989 ACT

Since the Human Rights Act 1998 ("HRA 1998") came into force on October 2, 2000 the courts have been obliged to act compatibly with the Convention rights of a person subject to extradition proceedings.[7] The Government recognised in the course of parliamentary debate that even under the 1989 Act the UK was obliged to consider how a person was likely to be treated after extradition in deciding whether to order extradition.[8] 11–003

It was firmly established under 1989 Act and its predecessors that (except for some specific statutory protections in Pt III cases under the 1989 Act) it was not for a court to consider any suggestion that a person would not be treated fairly after extradition.[9] As this approach was repeatedly re-emphasised in the face of the developing domestic "abuse of process" doctrine, it became common for fairness issues to be argued in detail in written form before the Secretary of State.[10] The House of Lords approached the matter in this way. "If issues of that kind are raised in a responsible manner, by reference to evidence and supported by reasoned argument, he [the Secretary of State] must consider them. The greater the perceived risk to life or liberty the more important it will be to give them detailed scrutiny."[11]

The case of *R. (Ramda) v Secretary of State for the Home Department* established that the ability to bring proceedings after extradition before the ECtHR to complain of a breach of Art.6(1), or by extension any other article of the ECHR, cannot be

[6] COM (2003) 75 final, February 19, 2003.
[7] s.6(1), HRA 1998.
[8] *Hansard*, col.8 (December 15, 2003).
[9] *Atkinson v Government of the USA* [1971] A.C. 197; *R. v Governor of Brixton Prison Ex p. Kotronis* [1971] A.C. 250 at 278–9; *In Re Schmidt* [1995] 1 A.C. 399.
[10] For example, *R. (St John) v Governor of Brixton Prison* [2002] Q.B. 613 at 624.
[11] *R. v Secretary of State for the Home Department Ex p. Launder* [1997] 1 W.L.R. 839 at para.48.

used to overcome any objection to extradition due to the risk of a breach of the ECHR.[12]

THE 2003 ACT

11–004 The Secretary of State is no longer responsible for whether to extradite a person under Pt 1. Although he is responsible finally for ordering order an extradition in Pt 2 cases, the 2003 Act removes his overall role in ensuring that it is fair to extradite a person, and the role of the appropriate judge is therefore increased greatly in both Pt 1 and Pt 2 cases.

As the principal arbiter in the extradition hearing in Pt 1 cases, the judge must consider whether the extradition would be compatible with the Convention rights (s.21(1)). If the judge finds that the extradition would be incompatible, he must order the person's discharge (s.21(2)).

Similarly in Pt 2 cases, the judge must consider whether the extradition would be compatible with the Convention rights within the meaning of the HRA 1998 and if not, the person must be discharged (s.87(1)). This section refers to "the extradition" and reassurance was sought from the Government that this phrase was intended to apply both to the extradition proceedings and the person's treatment after his extradition. This assurance was given on behalf of the Government by Lord Filkin.[13]

When considering the Extradition Bill and the provisions requiring the judge to consider whether extradition would be compatible with Convention rights, the Joint Committee on Human Rights commented: "One can at least say that the treatment awaiting the person in the requested territory would have to be considered by the court if there were any doubt on the matter."[14] The Home Office Minister, Bob Ainsworth, said in a press statement commenting on the Extradition Bill that "Extradition will not take place where there is *a real risk* it would breach a fugitive's rights to a fair trial as set out in the European Convention on Human Rights . . ."[15] [emphasis added].

This chapter seeks to summarise the main provisions of the HRA 1998 which affect the extradition process.[16] It also sets out Convention rights and case law which may be relevant for extradition proceedings. However, a detailed and comprehensive review of the ECHR and its case law is outside of the scope of this work.[17]

[12] [2002] EWHC 1278 at para.27.

[13] Lord Filkin, Vol.650, cols GC 138–9.

[14] Para.18 of Joint Committee on Human Rights, Twentieth Report on the Extradition Bill.

[15] Home Office Press Release "Delivering Swifter Justice for the Victims of Crime", November 14, 2002.

[16] For a detailed commentary on the HRA 1998 see Keir Starmer, *European Human Rights Law*; Lord Lester of Herne Hill Q.C. and David Pannick Q.C., eds, *Human Rights Law and Practice*.

[17] For a detailed review of the ECHR and case law see Keir Starmer, *European Human Rights Law*; Lord Lester of Herne Hill Q.C. and David Pannick Q.C., eds, *Human Rights Law and Practice*; Richard Clayton and Hugh Tomlinson; *The Law of Human Rights*.

II. HUMAN RIGHTS ACT 1998

CONVENTION RIGHTS

Section 1(1) defines Convention rights as the rights and fundamental freedoms in: 11–005

(a) Arts 2–12 and 14 of the ECHR;
(b) Arts 1–3 of the First Protocol; and
(c) Art.1 of the Thirteenth Protocol[18]

as read with Arts 16–18 of the ECHR.

When a court in the UK considers any issue in connection with a Convention Right it must take into account any relevant:

(a) judgment, decision, declaration or advisory opinion of the European Court of Human Rights ("ECtHR");
(b) opinion of the Commission given in a report adopted under Art.31 of the ECHR;
(c) decision of the Commission in connection with Art.26 or 27(2) of the ECHR;
(d) decision of the Committee of Ministers taken under Art.46 of the ECHR.

The ECtHR's comments in *Tyrer v UK* are relevant in considering ECHR case law. In this case the Court made it clear that the ECHR "is a living instrument . . . which must be interpreted in the light of present-day conditions".[19]

LEGISLATION

Legislation must be read and given effect to, in so far as it is possible to do so, in a way which is compatible with the Convention rights (s.3(1) HRA 1998).[20] 11–006

EXTRADITION PROCEEDINGS

It is unlawful for a public authority, which includes a court or the Secretary of State, to act in any way which is incompatible with a Convention Right (s.6(1) and (3) HRA 1998). However, this does not apply if provisions in primary legislation mean that it is impossible to act differently or it is impossible to read or give effect to any legislative provisions in a way which is compatible with Convention rights (s.6(2) HRA 1998). 11–007

[18] As amended by The Human Rights Act (Amendment) Order 2004 (SI 2004/1574).
[19] (1978) 2 E.H.R.R. 1 at 10.
[20] s.4 of the HRA 1998 allows a court to make a declaration of incompatibility if it is satisfied that a legislative provision is incompatible with a Convention right.

APPROPRIATE TRIBUNAL

11–008 Section 7(1) of the HRA 1998 allows a person who claims that a public authority has acted or proposes to act in a way that is unlawful under s.6(1) to bring proceedings in the appropriate tribunal *or* rely on the Convention right or rights concerned in any legal proceedings.

Section 195 of the 2003 Act appoints the appropriate judge as the only appropriate tribunal for proceedings brought under s.7(1)(a) of the HRA 1998 if the proceedings relate to extradition under Pt 1 or Pt 2 of the 2003 Act.

However, it appears that this does not prohibit the making of submissions about a breach of Convention rights to the Court of Appeal or the House of Lords under s.7(1)(b) of the HRA 1998. Indeed, s.9(1) requires any proceedings under s.7(1)(a) in respect of judicial acts to be brought by exercising a right of appeal.

III. ARTICLE 2 ECHR — RIGHT TO LIFE

11–009

> "1. Everyone's right to life shall be protected by law. No one shall be deprived of his life intentionally save in the execution of a sentence of a court following his conviction of a crime for which this penalty is provided by law.
>
> 2. Deprivation of life shall not be regarded as inflicted in contravention of this Article when it results from the use of force which is no more than absolutely necessary:
>
> (a) in defence of any person from unlawful violence;
> (b) in order to effect a lawful arrest or to prevent the escape of a person lawfully detained;
> (c) in action lawfully taken for the purpose of quelling a riot or insurrection."

Extradition cases in which there is a risk that the death penalty may be imposed or carried out may engage Art.2. Such cases are considered at 11–030 below as they may also engage Art.1 of the Thirteenth Protocol.

If there is a risk that the life of the person whose extradition is sought may be in jeopardy after being extradited, Art.2 will be breached.[21] Article 2 imposes a positive obligation on the UK to take action to safeguard the lives of those in its jurisdiction.[22] The House of Lords has said that "The positive obligation on member states to provide individuals with suitable protection against immediate threats to their lives from non-state actors abroad may be relevant, in exceptional circumstances, to an immigration decision."[23]

[21] *Chahal v UK* (1997) 23 E.H.R.R. 413; *Lynas v Switzerland* (1976) 6 D.R. 141.
[22] *Osman v UK* Case No.87/1997/871/1083 at para.115.
[23] *R. v Special Adjudicator Ex p. Ullah* [2004] UKHL 26 at para.40.

There must be a "near certainty" that the person will be killed to establish a violation of Art.2.[24] However, if there is a "real risk" of loss of life, this may amount to inhuman treatment under Art.3 (as discussed below).[25] The House of Lords has held that "there are principled grounds for not drawing a bright-line between articles 2 and 3."[26]

IV. ARTICLE 3 ECHR — PROHIBITION OF TORTURE

> "No one shall be subjected to torture or to inhuman or degrading treatment or punishment." 11–010

The prohibition in Art.3 is absolute and is not limited by exceptions, regardless of reprehensible conduct on the part of the victim, the aims of a state, or the difficulties faced by states in investigating organised crime or terrorism.[27] There is no balancing exercise to be performed.

Not all mistreatment will be sufficient to fall under Art.3.[28] The assessment of the required level is relative and dependent on matters including the duration of the treatment and its physical or mental effects. It is also depends on the age, sex, vulnerability and state of health of the victim.[29]

In *Soering v UK*,[30] the ECtHR held that it would be a breach of Art.3 to extradite the applicant to the USA on charges of capital murder having regard to the long detention on "death row" to which he would be subject before execution. The Court held that the decision by "a Contracting State to extradite a fugitive may give rise to an issue under Article 3, and hence engage the responsibility of the State under the Convention where *substantial grounds* have been shown for believing that the person concerned, if extradited, faces *a real risk* of being subjected to torture or degrading treatment or punishment in the requesting country."[31] [emphasis added]. The ECtHR has also said that if physical force is used which is not strictly necessary by reason of the applicant's own conduct, there is in principle a breach of Art.3.[32] The standards of treatment in detention may also give rise to a breach of Art.3.[33]

24 *Launder v UK* Application No.27279/95. This is the same approach adopted by the ECtHR for expulsion cases.

25 *R. v Special Adjudicator Ex p. Ullah* [2004] UKHL 26 at para.15; *Dehwari v Netherlands* (2000) 29 E.H.R.R. CD74 at para.61.

26 *R. v Special Adjudicator Ex p. Ullah* [2004] UKHL 26 at para.40.

27 *Chahal v UK* (1996) 23 E.H.R.R. 413 at paras 79–80; *Aksoy v Turkey* (1997) 23 E.H.R.R. 553 at para.62; *Selçuk and Asker v Turkey* (1998) 26 E.H.R.R 477 at para.75.

28 *Thampibillai v The Netherlands* Application No.61350/00 at para.60.

29 *Ireland v UK* (1978) 2 E.H.R.R. 25 at para.162.

30 (1989) 11 E.H.R.R. 439. It may also be possible to argue that life imprisonment without any possibility of release will be a breach of Art.3. *Einhorn v France* Application No.71555/01 at para.27.

31 *Soering v UK* (1989) 11 E.H.R.R. 439 at para.91; *cf. Vilvarajah v UK* Case No.45/1990/236/302–306 at para.107.

32 *Ribitsch v Austria* (1995) 21 E.H.R.R. 573 at para.38.

33 *Peers v Greece* April 19, 2001, Application No.28524/95; *Keenan v UK* April 3, 2001, Application No.27229/95; *Price v UK* July 10, 2001, Application No.33394/96; *Lorse v Netherlands* February 4,

In *D v UK* the ECtHR found that the proposed expulsion to St Kitts and Nevis of a person suffering from AIDS gave rise to a breach.[34]

The ECtHR has discussed the distinction between torture, inhuman or degrading treatment and inhuman or degrading punishment.

TORTURE

11–011 Torture is defined in Art.1 of the Convention against Torture and Other Cruel Inhuman or Degrading Treatment or Punishment 1984 as:

> "any act by which severe pain or suffering, whether physical or mental , is intentionally inflicted on a person for such purposes as obtaining from him or a third person information or a confession, punishing him for an act he or a third person has committed or is suspected of having committed, or intimidating or coercing him or a third person, or for any reasons based on discrimination of any kind, when such pain or suffering is inflicted by or at the instigation of or with the consent or acquiescence of a public official or other person acting in a public capacity. It does not include pain or suffering arising any from, inherent in, or incidental to lawful sanction."

In *Ireland v UK* the ECtHR distinguished torture from other ill-treatment covered by Art.3 by reference to the intensity of the suffering inflicted. It considered that torture attached a special stigma to deliberate inhuman treatment causing very serious and cruel suffering.[35]

INHUMAN OR DEGRADING TREATMENT

11–012 In *Ireland v UK*, the ECtHR considered five techniques:

> "applied in combination, with premeditation and for hours at a stretch; they caused, if not actual bodily injury, at least intense physical and mental suffering to the persons subjected thereto and also led to acute psychiatric disturbances during interrogation. They accordingly fell into the category of inhuman treatment within the meaning of Article 3. The techniques were also degrading since they were such as to arouse in their victim's feelings of fear, anguish and inferiority capable of humiliating and debasing them and possibly breaking their physical or moral resistance."[36]

2003, Application No.52750/99; *McGlinchey v UK* April 29, 2003, Application No.50390/99; *Kalashnikov v Russia* (2002) 36 E.H.R.R. 587.

[34] (1997) 24 E.H.R.R. 423. The House of Lords in *Ullah* said that it was clear that the applicant would have succeeded under Art.2 if the ECtHR had not found a breach of Art.3. *R. v Special Adjudicator Ex p. Ullah* [2004] UKHL 26 at para.40.

[35] *ibid.* at para.167.

[36] *ibid.* at para.167.

If there is a "real risk" of loss of life, rather than the "near certainty" required for a breach of Art.2, this may amount to inhuman treatment under Art.3.[37]

V. ARTICLE 5 ECHR — RIGHT TO LIBERTY AND SECURITY

"1. Everyone has the right to liberty and security of person. No one shall be deprived of his liberty save in the following cases and in accordance with a procedure prescribed by law: 11–013

. . .

(c) the lawful arrest or detention of a person effected for the purpose of bringing him before the competent legal authority on reasonable suspicion of having committed an offence or when it is reasonably considered necessary to prevent his committing an offence or fleeing after having done so;

. . .

(f) the lawful arrest or detention of a person to prevent his effecting an unauthorised entry into the country or of a person against whom action is being taken with a view to deportation or extradition.

2. Everyone who is arrested shall be informed promptly, in a language which he understands, of the reasons for his arrest and of any charge against him.

3. Everyone arrested or detained in accordance with the provisions of paragraph 1(c) of this Article shall be brought promptly before a judge or other officer authorised by law to exercise judicial power and shall be entitled to trial within a reasonable time or to release pending trial. Release may be conditioned by guarantees to appear for trial.

4. Everyone who is deprived of his liberty by arrest or detention shall be entitled to take proceedings by which the lawfulness of his detention shall be decided speedily by a court and his release ordered if the detention is not lawful.

5. Everyone who has been the victim of arrest or detention in contravention of the provisions of this Article shall have an enforceable right to compensation."

ARTICLE 5(1)(F)

Article 5(1)(f) allows the detention of a person against whom action is being taken with a view to extradition. The term "lawful" means that the arrest under domestic law must be lawful and not arbitrary (as discussed in 11–016 below).[38] The 11–014

[37] *R. v Special Adjudicator Ex p. Ullah* [2004] UKHL 26 at para.15; *Dehwari v Netherlands* (2000) 29 E.H.R.R. CD74 at para.61.

[38] *De Jong, Baljet and Van den Brink v Netherlands* (1986) 8 E.H.R.R. 20 (para.44); *Kemmache v France (No.3)* (1994) 19 E.H.R.R. 349 (para.42); *Chahal v UK* (1996) 23 E.H.R.R. 413 (para.118).

ECtHR in *Quinn v France* held that, "It is clear from the wording of both the French and the English versions of Article 5 para.1 (f) (art. 5-1-f) that deprivation of liberty under this sub-paragraph will be justified only for as long as extradition proceedings are being conducted. It follows that if such proceedings are not being prosecuted with due diligence, the detention will cease to be justified under Article 5 para.1 (f)".[39] The court found that the delays in the case had been excessive leading to a breach of Art.5(1).

ARTICLE 5(3)

11–015 Any person detained under Art.5(1)(c) must be eligible for bail. However, this has been extended to extradition proceedings by the Commission's remarks in *Osman v United Kingdom*:

> "Nevertheless, given the primordial importance of the right to liberty ensured by Article 5 para.1 (Art. 5-1) of the Convention, the Commission may examine whether the refusal of bail to an individual, even if his detention falls within Article 5 para.1 (f) (Art. 5-1-f) of the Convention, could be said to be unreasonable or arbitrary, thus affecting the general notion of lawfulness, which is a common thread throughout the provisions of Article 5 para.1 (Art. 5-1) of the Convention."[40]

ARTICLE 5(4)

11–016 Even before 2003 Act it was accepted that Art.5(4) rights applied to extradition proceedings.[41] The Administrative Court held that in order to comply with Art.5(4) of the ECHR, the Magistrates' Court dealing with the committal proceedings[42] has the jurisdiction to determine whether a person's detention is lawful as required by the ECHR.[43] This involves answering three questions[44]:

(a) Is the detention lawful under domestic law?
(b) Does the detention comply with the general requirements of the ECHR? These include the requirements that the domestic law must be sufficiently accessible to the individual and sufficiently precise to enable the individual to foresee the consequence of the restriction.[45]

[39] March 22, 1995 at para.48. See also *Lynas v Switzerland* Application No.7317/75; *Kolompar v Belgium* (1992) 16 E.H.R.R. 197; *Farmakopoulos v Belgium* Application No.00011683/85.
[40] Para.2, Application No.15933/89.
[41] *R. v Kashamu* [2001] EWHC Admin 980. See 13–002 for discussion of habeas corpus.
[42] Committal proceedings under the 1989 Act were broadly equivalent to the extradition hearing in the 2003 Act.
[43] *R. (Kashamu) v Governor of Brixton Prison* [2002] Q.B. 887.
[44] *R. v Governor of Brockhill Prison Ex p. Evans* [2001] 2 A.C. 19 at 38B–E.
[45] *Sunday Times v UK* [1979] 2 E.H.R.R. 245; *Zamir v UK* [1983] 40 D.R. 42 at 55 (paras 90–1).

(c) Is the detention open to criticism on the grounds that it is arbitrary because, for example, it was resorted to in bad faith or was not proportionate?[46]

It held that detention arising from bad faith or an abuse of power would make detention unlawful and arbitrary in the Convention sense.

The tribunal determining the issue must be impartial and independent.[47] Article 5(4) requires that the proceedings must be truly adversarial[48] and there must be "equality of arms" (see 11–018 below).[49] The person who has been detained must be given disclosure of relevant material held by the authorities[50] and must have adequate time to prepare an application for release.[51] Legal advice should be provided if this is necessary for an effective application to be made[52] and legal aid should be provided if the person has insufficient means to instruct lawyers privately.

VI. ARTICLE 6 ECHR — RIGHT TO A FAIR TRIAL

"1. In the determination of his civil rights and obligations or of any criminal charge against him, everyone is entitled to a fair and public hearing within a reasonable time by an independent and impartial tribunal established by law. Judgment shall be pronounced publicly but the press and public may be excluded from all or part of the trial in the interest of morals, public order or national security in a democratic society, where the interests of juveniles or the protection of the private life of the parties so require, or to the extent strictly necessary in the opinion of the court in special circumstances where publicity would prejudice the interests of justice. 11–017

2. Everyone charged with a criminal offence shall be presumed innocent until proved guilty according to law.

3. Everyone charged with a criminal offence has the following minimum rights:

(a) to be informed promptly, in a language which he understands and in detail, of the nature and cause of the accusation against him;

(b) to have adequate time and facilities for the preparation of his defence;

46 *Engel v Netherlands (No.1)* [1976] 1 E.H.R.R. 647 (para.58); *Tsirlis and Koulompas v Greece* Case No.54/1996/673/859–860 at para.56.

47 *K v Austria* (1993) Series A/255-B.

48 Para.51, *Sanchez-Reisse v Switzerland* (1986) 9 E.H.R.R. 71. The Court in this case also considers the question of how speedily the decision must be taken to comply with Art.5(4).

49 *Toth v Austria* (1991) 14 E.H.R.R. 551 at para.84; *Lamy v Belgium* (1989) 11 E.H.R.R. 529 at para.29; *Sanchez-Reisse v Switzerland* (1986) 9 E.H.R.R. 71 at para.52; *Frommelt v Lichtenstein* Application No.49158/99 at para.29.

50 *Frommelt v Lichtenstein* Application No.49158/99 at para.33.

51 *Farmakopoulos v Belgium* (1992) 16 E.H.R.R. 197.

52 *Winterwerp v Netherlands* (1979) 2 E.H.R.R. 387 at para.60.

(c) to defend himself in person or through legal assistance of his own choosing or, if he has not sufficient means to pay for legal assistance, to be given it free when the interests of justice so require;

(d) to examine or have examined witnesses against him and to obtain the attendance and examination of witnesses on his behalf under the same conditions as witnesses against him;

(e) to have the free assistance of an interpreter if he cannot understand or speak the language used in court."

RIGHTS UNDER ART.6

11–018 Article 6 enshrines the fundamental principle of the rule of law; it must therefore be given a broad and purposive interpretation.[53] When deciding whether there has been a breach of the right to a fair hearing the ECtHR may consider the trial as a whole in addition to specific inadequacies in the process.[54]

The ECtHR has made it clear that a defendant should normally be present at his trial.[55] A fair hearing requires that the defendant is notified of the proceedings against him.[56] A defendant in a criminal trial should have the opportunity to present his arguments adequately and participate effectively.[57] He should be entitled to be represented at trial and on appeal irrespective of whether he is present or has previously absconded.[58]

The right to a fair hearing requires that a person must have a reasonable opportunity of presenting his case under conditions which do not place him at a material disadvantage to the prosecution. This is known as the "equality of arms" principle.[59] To some extent this principle overlaps with the specific guarantees in Art.6(3) for criminal proceedings but it is not constrained by these.[60] In *Jespers v Belgium* the Commission held that the "equality of arms" principle imposes on prosecuting and investigating authorities an obligation to disclose material they hold or might gain access to which might assist the defendant in proving his innocence or reducing any sentence. This includes material which might undermine the credibility of a prosecution witness.[61] If a defence expert is not given the

[53] *Salabiaku v France* (1988) 13 E.H.R.R. 379 (para.28); *Delcourt v Belgium* (1970) 1 E.H.R.R. 355; *Moreira de Azevedo v Portugal* (1990) 13 E.H.R.R. 721 (para.66).

[54] *Barberà, Messegué and Jabardo v Spain* (1988) 11 E.H.R.R. 360 at para.68.

[55] *Poitrimol v France* (1993) 18 E.H.R.R. 130 at 146 (para.35); *Pelladoah v The Netherlands* (1994) 19 E.H.R.R. 81 at 94 (para.40); *Lala v The Netherlands* (1994) 18 E.H.R.R. 586 at 597 (para.33).

[56] *Colozza v Italy* (1985) 7 E.H.R.R. 516 at 523–524 (para.28); *Brozicek v Italy* (1989) 12 E.H.R.R. 371.

[57] *Ensslin, Baader and Raspe v Germany* (1978) 14 D.R. 64 at 115; *Stanford v UK* Case No.50/1992/395/473.

[58] *Delcourt v Belgium* (1970) 1 E.H.R.R. 355 at 366–367 (para.25); *Poitrimol v France* (1993) 18 E.H.R.R. 130 at 146–7 (paras 34 and 38); *Pelladoah v The Netherlands* (1994) 19 E.H.R.R. 81 at 94 (para.40); *Lala v The Netherlands* (1994) 18 E.H.R.R. 586 at 597–8 (paras 33–34); *Omar v France* (1998) 29 E.H.R.R. 210 at 233 (paras 41–42).

[59] *Neumister v Austria* (1968) 1 E.H.R.R. 91 at para.22; *Delcourt v Belgium* (1970) 1 E.H.R.R. 355 at para.28; *De haes and Gijsels v Belgium* (1997) 25 E.H.R.R. 1 at para.53.

[60] *Jespers v Belgium* (1981) 27 D.R. 61 at para.54.

[61] *ibid.* at para.58.

same facilities as a prosecution or court expert, this will also offend against the principle.[62]

The failure to exclude illegally obtained evidence does not necessarily breach Art.6 but can give rise to unfairness in a particular case.[63] The right to a fair trial in criminal cases also includes "the right of anyone charged with a criminal offence . . . to remain silent and not to contribute to incriminating himself."[64] The conviction of a defendant based on evidence obtained from him as a result of torture will breach Art.6 although the breach of Art.6(1) is not the use of torture, which is a separate breach of Art.3. Instead the breach derives from the permission of the court of the use of this evidence.[65]

Article 6(1) requires that there should be a hearing within a reasonable time. In a criminal case this period starts from the time of charge, which is normally the time when a person is "substantially affected" by the proceedings taken against him.[66] This is normally the date of charge by the police but it may in certain circumstances be earlier.[67] The particular facts of each case will affect what is a "reasonable time". For example, the complexity of the case and the conduct of the defendant, the prosecution authorities and the courts may be relevant.[68] 11–019

In *Attorney-General's Reference (No.2 of 2001)*[69] the House of Lords held, in a domestic criminal case, that a breach of the right to trial within a reasonable time should result in a stay of the indictment only if (a) a fair trial is no longer possible, or (ii) it would for some other compelling reason be unfair to the defendant; cases where it might be unfair to try a person would include cases of bad faith, executive manipulation and abuse of process, and also cases where the delay was of such an order, or where the prosecutor's breach of duty was such as to make it unfair that the proceedings should continue, but such cases would be exceptional, and a stay would never be an appropriate remedy if any lesser remedy would adequately vindicate the defendant's Convention rights.

The rights set out in Arts 6(3)(a)–(e) are not exhaustive.[70] Article 6(3)(b) guarantees a defendant the right to have adequate time and facilities for the preparation of his defence. The complexity of the case will be relevant when assessing what is an adequate period of time.[71]

[62] *Bonisch v Austria* (1985) 9 E.H.R.R. 191.

[63] *Schenk v Switzerland* (1988) 13 E.H.R.R. 242 at paras 46-48; *X v Federal Republic of Germany* (1989) 11 E.H.R.R. 84.

[64] *Funke v France* (1993) 16 E.H.R.R. 297; *Saunders v UK* (1996) 23 E.H.R.R. 313. See *Murray v UK* (1996) 22 E.H.R.R. 29 for consideration of adverse inferences.

[65] *Austria v Italy* (1963) 6 Y.B. 740; *R. (Ramda) v Secretary of State for the Home Department* [2002] EWHC 1278 (Admin) at para.9; *Montgomery v HM Advocate* [2001] 2 W.L.R. 779 at 785.

[66] *Deweer v Belgium* (1980) 2 E.H.R.R. at para.46.

[67] *Ewing v UK* (1986) 10 E.H.R.R. 141; *X v UK* (1978) 14 D.R. 26.

[68] *Zimmerman and Steiner v Swtizerland* (1983) 6 E.H.R.R. 17 at paras 27–32.

[69] [2004] 2 W.L.R. 1.

[70] *Edwards v UK* (1992) 15 E.H.R.R. 417 at para.33.

[71] *Albert and LeCompte v Belgium* (1983) 5 E.H.R.R. 533 at para.41.

APPLICATION OF ART.6 RIGHTS — "DETERMINATION OF A CRIMINAL CHARGE"

11–020 Even before the 2003 Act it had been accepted in principle that an assessment of a likely breach of Art.6 might be relevant to a decision on extradition.[72] It is now clear that the judge must take account of the potential treatment of a person after extradition in assessing whether his trial, conviction and sentencing will accord with the rights in Art.6.[73] Extradition will involve a breach of Art.6 if there is a real risk that the defendant will suffer a flagrant denial of justice in the requesting territory.[74]

It is less clear to what extent a person subject to extradition proceedings in the UK is entitled to the rights in Art.6 during these proceedings.

EXTRADITION/SURRENDER

11–021 The Framework Decision is intended to give effect to the process of mutual recognition of criminal judicial decisions.[75] The aim of the Framework Decision appears to be to abolish the system of extradition between Member States and to replace this instead with a system of surrender between judicial authorities.[76] Article 1 of the Framework Decision states that the EAW is a judicial decision issued with "a view to the arrest and *surrender*" [emphasis added] of the requested person. Extradition is an arrangement between countries and is not a process whereby an arrest warrant issued by one country is recognised by a court in another country and then executed. This distinction may be more than merely academic as the Art.6 rights may apply to a hearing in the UK which is effectively the enforcement of an arrest warrant issued in another territory pursuant to a scheme of mutual recognition.

The references to the system of surrender in the Framework Decision were highlighted when an amendment was proposed in the Grand Committee stage in the House of Lords to refer to the Framework Decision and in particular the "surrender procedures" set out in this. Lord Filkin, on behalf of the Government, made it plain that it is the Government's view that the EAW did not abolish the process of extradition between Member States and that the Act therefore still left in place extradition procedures between Member States.[77] However, this view is obviously not determinative of the issue. If the Framework Decision, and the domestic legislation implementing it, does substantively change the process from extradition to mutual recognition of an arrest warrant, this would further support

[72] *Soering v UK* (1989) 11 EHRR 439 at para.114.

[73] ss.21 and 87 of the 2003 Act.

[74] *R. (Ramda) v Secretary of State for the Home Department* [2002] EWHC 1278 (Admin) at para.10; *Drozd v France and Spain*(1992) 14 E.H.R.R. 745 at 793; *Soering v UK* (1989) 11 E.H.R.R. 439 at para.113. This does not mean that other legal systems should necessarily be judged by reference to the UK (*R. (Abdullah) v Home Secretary* [2001] EWHC Admin 263 at paras 42–3).

[75] For example, paras 2 and 6, Preamble, Framework Decision.

[76] Para.5, Preamble, Framework Decision.

[77] Vol.648, cols GC 117–123.

an argument that the full range of Art.6 rights should apply to the extradition proceedings in the UK.[78]

EVIDENTIAL SUFFICIENCY

In those Pt 2 cases where the requesting territory must satisfy the sufficiency of evidence test, it is again strongly arguable that a person subject to extradition proceedings should be entitled to the protections in Art.6 during the proceedings.[79] Applying the reasoning in *Osman* discussed at 11–015 above the general notion of lawfulness required by Art.5 may extend to some of the rights guaranteed by Art.6. In addition, Art.5(4) provides many of the same procedural protections that are also found in Art.6. 11–022

"BAD FAITH"

Under s.11(3) of the 1989 Act, extradition would be prohibited if the accusation was not made in good faith in the interests of justice.[80] This restriction has not been explicitly included in the 2003 Act but it should be noted that when an amendment was proposed to include this as a restriction for Pt 2 cases, the Government argued that any argument as to bad faith could either be made under the bar for extraneous considerations or as part of a submission that extradition would breach the person's Convention rights: 11–023

> "If a judge in a requesting state had a personal animus against a person and sought to use the extradition process to take him back, there would be significant doubt as to whether that person, if extradited, would experience a fair trial. That again, would be caught by the ECHR provision."[81]

This statement is a demonstration of the importance and scope that Parliament attached to the human rights provisions in the 2003 Act.

VII. ARTICLE 7 ECHR — NO PUNISHMENT WITHOUT LAW

> "1. No one shall be held guilty of any criminal offence on account of any act or omission which did not constitute a criminal offence under national or international law at the time when it was committed. Nor shall a heavier penalty be imposed than the one that was applicable at the time the criminal offence was committed. 11–024

[78] See discussion at pp.19–20 in Alegre and Leaf, *European Arrest Warrant: A solution ahead of its time?* (Justice).

[79] See Ch.9 at for sufficiency of evidence cases.

[80] s.11(3)(c), 1989 Act.

[81] Lord Filkin, Vol.651, col.GC 108. See also discussion on bad faith at 11–016.

> 2. This Article shall not prejudice the trial and punishment of any person for any act or omission which, at the time when it was committed, was criminal according to the general principles of law recognised by civilised nations."

Although extradition is not a penalty for the purposes of Art.7,[82] the penalty in the requesting state, whether imposed before or after extradition, may be. Therefore, if extradition would lead to a real risk that a person would face a prosecution in the requesting territory for a retrospectively applied offence, the extradition may be incompatible with Art.7.

If the extradition request is made under Pt 1 and the conduct is certified to fall within the European Framework, then the conduct may not constitute a criminal offence in the UK. If the EAW is applied retrospectively to offences which occurred prior to the coming into force of the EAW, the principle of certainty under Art.7 could be threatened. In practical terms, retrospective application of the EAW could lead to the receipt of requests which apply to people who may have been involved in conduct which was not criminal in the UK. These people may have been settled in the UK with this knowledge or precisely because the UK does not criminalise this type of conduct. This could affect the principle of proportionality.[83]

VIII. ARTICLE 8 ECHR — RIGHT TO RESPECT FOR PRIVATE AND FAMILY LIFE

11–025 "1. Everyone has the right to respect for his private and family life, his home and his correspondence.

> 2. There shall be no interference by a public authority with the exercise of this right except such as is in accordance with the law and is necessary in a democratic society in the interests of national security, public safety or the economic well-being of the country, for the prevention of disorder or crime, for the protection of health or morals, or for the protection of the rights and freedoms of others."

CONCEPT OF PRIVATE LIFE

11–026 Article 8 provides a broad protection which extends to more than just a right to privacy.[84] The ECtHR has given a broad and non-exhaustive definition of "private life" saying:

[82] *X v Netherlands* (1976) 6 D.R. 184.

[83] See discussion at pp.22–23, 40 in Alegre and Leaf, *European Arrest Warrant: A solution ahead of its time?* (Justice).

[84] *cf.* Art.17 International Covenant on Civil and Political Rights 1966: "1. No one shall be subject to arbitrary or unlawful interference with his privacy, family, home or correspondence, nor to unlawful attacks on his honour and reputation. 2. Everyone has the right to the protection of the law against such interference or such attacks." The rights in Art.17 and Art.8 ECHR often overlap.

"The Court does not consider it possible or necessary to attempt an exhaustive definition of the notion of 'private life'. However, it would be too restrictive to limit the notion to an 'inner circle' in which the individual may live his own personal life as he chooses and to exclude therefrom entirely the outside world not encompassed within that circle. Respect for private life must also comprise to a certain degree the right to establish and develop relationships with other human beings.

There appears, furthermore, to be no reason of principle why this understanding of the notion of 'private life' should be taken to exclude activities of a professional or business nature since it is, after all, in the course of their working lives that the majority of people have a significant, if not the greatest, opportunity of developing relationships with the outside world.

This view is supported by the fact that, as was rightly pointed out by the Commission, it is not always possible to distinguish clearly which of an individual's activities form part of his professional or business life and which do not. Thus, especially in the case of a person exercising a liberal profession, his work in that context may form part and parcel of his life to such a degree that it becomes impossible to know in what capacity he is acting at a given moment of time."

INTERFERENCE WITH RIGHTS UNDER ART.8(1)

The following are examples of interference with the rights under Art.8(1): **11–027**

- intrusive surveillance[85];
- enforced fingerprinting or photographing as part of a criminal investigation[86];
- telephone tapping.[87]

JUSTIFICATION FOR INTERFERENCE UNDER ART.8(2)

Any interference with the rights under Art.8(1) by a public authority must be in **11–028**
accordance with the law[88] and necessary in a democratic society[89] in the interests of, *inter alia*, national security,[90] public safety or the economic well-being of the

[85] *Klass v Federal Republic of Germany* (1978) 2 E.H.R.R. 214 at para.41.

[86] *Murray v UK* (1994) 19 E.H.R.R. 193 at para.86.

[87] *Malone v UK* (1984) 7 E.H.R.R. 14 at para.64; *Klass v Federal Republic of Germany* (1978) 2 E.H.R.R. 214 at para.49.

[88] *Klass v Federal Republic of Germany* (1978) 2 E.H.R.R. 214; *Malone v UK* (1984) 7 E.H.R.R. 14.

[89] In examining whether this ground is made out the court must assess "whether the interference complained of corresponded to a pressing social need, whether it was proportionate to the legitimate aim pursued, whether the reasons given by the national authorities are relevant and sufficient . . ." *Sunday Times v UK* (1979) 2 E.H.R.R. 245 at para.62.

[90] *Leander v Sweden* (1987) 9 E.H.R.R. 433 at para.49.

country[91] or for the prevention of disorder or crime.[92] Extradition may obviously breach a person's rights under Art.8(1) and it is then necessary to examine, in the context of the particular facts, whether the justification under Art.8(2) is made out.[93] The Commission has said that "... it is only in exceptional circumstances that the extradition of a person to face trial on charges of serious offences committed in the requesting State would be held to be an unjustified and disproportionate interference with the right to respect for family life."[94]

Some foreign states, particularly the USA, have criminal justice systems with a long jurisdictional reach. It is increasingly common for such jurisdictions to seek extradition to the USA to prosecute for cases which have only a minor or incidental link with the requesting territory.

It is understood that there was an established but unpublished policy in operation between the United States of America and the United Kingdom under previous extradition statutes to negotiate and agree the appropriate forum for trial in such transnational cases, including fraud and terrorism. Such a policy may not survive the reduction of the role of the Secretary of State in extradition cases under the 2003 Act.

It is submitted that Art.8 provides a remedy for those accused of crimes abroad which would naturally be tried in this jurisdiction.[95] If the obvious or natural forum for the trial of such issues would be the United Kingdom, it would surely be proper in the case of a UK citizen for a court to find that there was no justification within Art.8(2). The principles relating to "forum non conveniens" will, it is submitted, be relevant.[96]

IX. ARTICLE 18 ECHR — LIMITATION ON RESTRICTIONS ON RIGHTS

11–029 "The restrictions permitted under this Convention to the said rights and freedoms shall not be applied for any purpose other than those for which they have been prescribed."

In*Gusinskiy v Russia*[97] the ECtHR found for the first time that there had been a violation of Art.18 of the ECHR. The Russian Federation claimed that it had procured the detention of Mr Gusinskiy in connection with allegations of fraud. However, it was submitted on behalf of Mr Gusinskiy that his detention had in fact been

[91] *Funke v France* (1993) 16 E.H.R.R. 297 at paras 52–59. A search by French customs officers of the applicant's home was in the interests of the economic well-being of the country but the scope of the search and seizure powers was too wide to be proportionate to this legitimate aim.
[92] *Campbell and Fell v UK* (1984) 7 E.H.R.R. 165.
[93] *Launder v UK* Application No.27279/95; *cf. Moustaquim v Belgium*, February 18, 1991.
[94] *Launder v UK* Application No.27279/95.
[95] See the discussion of the definition of "extraction offence" in Ch.6.
[96] See for example, *Schalk Willem Burger Lubbe v Cape PLC* [2001] 1 W.L.R. 1545.
[97] Application No.70276/01 *www.echr.coe.int/Eng/Judgments.htm*.

procured for the purpose of stifling the media organisations controlled by Mr Gusinskiy which had criticised the Russian leadership. The Court found on the facts that Mr Gusinskiy's liberty was restricted "for the purpose of bringing him before a competent legal authority on reasonable suspicion of having committed an offence" as allowed by Art.5(1)(c) of the ECHR. However, the Court found that his prosecution had also been used to intimidate him. The Court commented that "it is not the purpose of the such public-law matters as criminal proceedings and detention on remand to be used as part of commercial bargaining strategies." Therefore, the Court found that the restriction on Mr Gusinskiy's liberty permitted by Art.5(1)(c) had been applied not only for the purpose of bringing him before competent legal authorities on reasonable suspicion of having committed an offence but also for "alien reasons", and there had therefore been a breach of Art.18. It is important to note that even if a restriction in the ECHR has been applied for the purpose prescribed, there may still be a breach of Art.18 if there is another purpose which is not prescribed.

X. ARTICLE 1, THIRTEENTH PROTOCOL TO ECHR — ABOLITION OF THE DEATH PENALTY

> "The death penalty shall be abolished. No one shall be condemned to such penalty or executed." 11–030

The UK has now signed the Thirteenth Protocol to the ECHR[98] which it ratified on October 10, 2003. This abolishes the death penalty in all circumstances without exception.[99] Arts 2 and 3 prohibit any derogation or reservation to this protocol.

The UK Government has said it will apply this protocol to Great Britain, Northern Ireland, the Isle of Man, the Bailiwick of Guernsey and the Bailiwick of Jersey and the Sovereign Base Areas of Akrotiri and Dhekelia in Cyprus. Therefore, the HRA 1998 has been amended to replace the now superseded Arts 1 and 2 of the Sixth Protocol, which also dealt with the abolition of the death penalty, with Art.1 of the Thirteenth Protocol.[1]

Article 2 of the Sixth Protocol allowed a state to impose the death penalty for acts committed in wartime or with the imminent threat of war.[2] This exception is removed in the Thirteenth Protocol.

98 CET 187 *www.echr.coe.int/Library/annexes/187E.pdf.*

99 Art.1.

1 ss.1(1)(c) and 21(1) and Pt 3 of Sch.1 were amended by the Human Rights Act 1998 (Amendment) Order 2004 (SI 2004/1574) which came into force on June 22, 2004.

2 However, the UK had already abolished the death penalty for offences committed in wartime, s.21(5) HRA 1998. *cf.* s.36 Crime and Disorder Act 1998.

It has been held to be a breach of the Sixth Protocol to extradite a person to a territory if there is a real risk that the death penalty will be imposed.[3] This must mean that it will similarly be a breach of the Thirteenth Protocol to extradite a person to a territory if there is a real risk that the death penalty will be imposed or carried out.

The Secretary of State must receive a satisfactory assurance that the death penalty will not be carried out if the person subject to an extradition request could be, will be or has been sentenced to death before he can order extradition.[4] Section 94 of the 2003 Act allows the Secretary of State to order extradition under Pt 2[5] if he receives a written assurance which he considers adequate that a sentence of death:

(a) will not be imposed; or
(b) will not be carried out (if imposed).

However, (b) would seem to involve a breach of Protocol 13 which states in terms that no one should be sentenced to the death penalty. Therefore, it is submitted that the Secretary of State would not be acting compatibly with a person's Convention rights if he accepted an assurance which allowed a real possibility that the death penalty might be imposed after extradition.

11–031 Whether an adequate assurance can be provided may be difficult to assess. In most territories it will be the function of the court, rather than the executive, to impose the sentence after conviction. However, a court will not normally give an assurance about sentence. It may not have the power to do so in advance of a hearing. Although the executive may instead provide an assurance, it may not bind a court under the doctrine of the separation of powers.[6] Therefore, it is submitted that the Secretary of State must ensure fastidiously that any assurance he receives provides the necessary certainty.

The position is even more complicated in the case of extradition requests made by the USA. Any assurance will be given by the Department of Justice on behalf of the Federal Government. However, in almost all cases the death penalty is imposed by a state court on the application of the local state prosecutor. (Since almost all murder cases are tried in state courts, the death penalty is rarely imposed by federal courts.) US Federal authorities have been unable to prevent states from carrying out executions in the past in spite of an agreement to stay an execution given by the Federal authorities.[7] In *Soering v UK*, the state prosecutor said that he would in fact

[3] *Riadl v Austria Application* No.25342/94; *Aylor-Davis v France* Application No.22742/93.

[4] s.94 2003 Act and *St John v Governor of Brixton Prison and the Government of the USA* [2002] 2 W.L.R. 221 at para.49.

[5] A territory can not be designated as a category 1 territory if a person found guilty of a criminal offence may be sentenced to death under the general criminal law of the territory. s.1(3) 2003 Act is discussed in Ch.5.

[6] If the contrary is true then this may constitute a breach of Art.6(1).

[7] *Paraguay v US www.icj-cij.org/icjwww/idocket/ipaus/ipausframe.htm; Germany v US www.icj-cij.org/icjwww/idocket/igus/igusframe.htm.*

ask the court to impose the death penalty but would inform the sentencing judge that "it is the wish of the UK that the death penalty should not be imposed or carried out."[8] In light of this past practice the Secretary of State must be satisfied that any assurance given by the Federal authorities will take effect at a state level before accepting that the assurance is adequate.[9]

8 (1989) 11 E.H.R.R. 439 at para.97.

9 See similar concerns of the Joint Committee on Human Rights at para.28 of the Twentieth Report.

CHAPTER 12

ROLE OF THE SECRETARY OF STATE

I. INTRODUCTION

12–001 The Secretary of State has a very limited involvement in a Pt 1 extradition. He can intervene on the grounds of national security to stop proceedings under Pt 1 at any time. If a competing extradition request is made by a category 2 territory, he will decide whether the Pt 1 warrant or Pt 2 request will be dealt with first. If an asylum claim is made by a person who is the subject of a Pt 1 warrant, the Secretary of State will have to decide whether to grant asylum. Finally, the Secretary of State will deal with any request for re-extradition to a category 2 territory which is made after extradition to a category 1 territory.

For Pt 2 cases, the Secretary of State has a role both at the start of the extradition process and at the end when he must decide whether to order extradition. He has no general discretion and must apply the specific grounds in the 2003 Act when taking the decision. The Secretary of State can again intervene on the grounds of national security to stop proceedings under Pt 2. If a competing Pt 2 request or Pt 1 warrant is issued then the Secretary of State will decide which should be dealt with first. Again, the Secretary of State will have to decide whether to grant asylum if a claim is made by a person subject to a Pt 2 extradition request. There are various other provisions which deal with requests for consent for a person to be dealt with for an offence alleged to have been committed prior to extradition for which he was not extradited.

The provisions of the 2003 Act dealing with competing extradition requests are considered together in Ch.15.

The significance of the reduction of the role of the Secretary of State has been discussed in Chs 9 and 11.

II. NATIONAL SECURITY

Section 208 allows the Secretary of State to prevent a person's extradition under either Pt 1 or 2 if it would be against the interests of national security. 12–002

The Secretary of State must believe that a person's extradition is sought or will be sought under Pt 1 or 2 in respect of an offence (s.208(2)). The Secretary of State must also be satisfied that:

(a) the person was acting for the purpose of assisting in the exercise of a statutory power of the UK in engaging in the conduct amounting to or alleged to amount to the offence; or
(b) the person is not liable under the criminal law of any part of the UK for the conduct amounting to or alleged to amount to the offence as a result of authorisation given by the Secretary of State (s.208(3)).

If both of these conditions are satisfied, the Secretary of State must also believe that the person's extradition in respect of the offence would be against the interests of national security (s.208(4)).

The Secretary of State can then certify that the three conditions are satisfied in relation to the person and may direct that a Pt 1 warrant or Pt 2 request for his extradition for the offence is not to be proceeded with (s.208(5)–(6)). As well as or instead of making this direction, the Secretary of State may order the person's discharge (s.208(7)).

If the Secretary of State issues a direction under s.208(6) that extradition proceedings should not continue, the provisions in s.208(8) will apply for Pt 1 proceedings and the provisions in s.208(9) will apply for Pt 2 proceedings. The effect of these provisions is to bring the extradition proceedings to an end. A certificate under s.108(5), a direction under s.108(6) or an order under s.108(7) must be made under the hand of the Secretary of State (s.108(10)).

This section is modified so that references to the Secretary of State will be read as Scottish Ministers when applying the provisions to Scotland (s.108(11)).

III. PART 1

COMPETING EXTRADITION REQUEST FROM A CATEGORY 2 TERRITORY

12–003 See Ch.15 at 15–025.

CONSENT TO FURTHER EXTRADITION TO CATEGORY 2 TERRITORY (S.58)

12–004 Section 58 will apply if:

(a) a person is extradited to a category 1 territory ("the requesting territory") under Pt 1;
(b) the Secretary of State receives a request from the requesting territory for consent to the person's extradition to a category 2 territory for an offence; and
(c) the request is certified by the designated authority[1] once it is satisfied that the authority making the request is a judicial authority of the requesting territory *and* the authority has the function of making requests for this type of consent.

The Secretary of State must serve notice on the person that he has received the request for consent unless he is satisfied that it would not be practicable to do so (s.58(4)).

The Secretary of State must first decide whether the offence is an extradition offence, as defined in s.137,[2] for the category 2 territory. If the Secretary of State finds it is not an extradition offence, he must refuse consent (s.58(6)). Otherwise he must go on to decide whether a judge would send the case to him for his decision on whether to order extradition. When carrying out this assessment he must proceed as if the person was in the UK and the judge was required to proceed under s.79 to consider ss.79–91 for the offence for which the Secretary of State's consent is requested.[3]

If the Secretary of State decides that the judge would not send the case to him, he must refuse consent (s.58(8)). Otherwise, the Secretary of State must consider whether, if the person was in the UK, his extradition would be prohibited under s.94, 95 or 96 (see 12–012—12–014 below). If the extradition would be prohibited under any of these sections then the Secretary of State muse refuse consent (s.58(11)). Otherwise the Secretary of State *may* give consent (s.58(10)).

[1] NCIS and the Crown Agent of the Crown Office in Scotland are designated authorities. See 7–003.
[2] The definition of an extradition offence in s.137 is considered in Ch.6.
[3] ss.79–91 are considered in Ch.9.

If any function under this section falls to be exercised in relation to Scotland only, references to the Secretary of State should be read as references to Scottish Ministers.

ASYLUM CLAIM

GENERAL

It is not uncommon for a person who is the subject of an extradition request to make an asylum claim. Often it will be submitted that the making of an extradition request is another method of persecuting the person on the grounds which allow them to claim asylum under the Refugee Convention. These grounds are similar to the bar on extradition for extraneous considerations.[4] The 2003 Act includes provisions which regulate the interaction of an asylum claim and extradition proceedings. 12–005

ASYLUM CLAIM AND PT 1

Section 39 applies if: 12–006

(a) a person in respect of whom a Pt 1 warrant is issued makes an asylum claim after a certificate has been issued under s.2[5] and before he is extradited pursuant to the warrant; and
(b) an order is made under Pt 1 for the person to be extradited in pursuance of the warrant.

The person must not be extradited until the asylum claim is finally determined unless the Secretary of State has certified that the conditions in s.40(2) or (3) are satisfied[6] (s.39(3)–(4)). Sections 35, 36, 47 and 49, which provide time limits for extradition, have effect subject to this requirement.[7]

The claim is finally determined when the Secretary of State makes his decision if he decides to allow the claim (s.39(5)). If the Secretary of State rejects the asylum claim, it is finally determined:

(a) when the Secretary of State makes his decision if there is no right of appeal against his decision;
(b) when the period permitted for appealing against the Secretary of State's decision ends if no appeal is brought;
(c) when any appeal which is made is finally determined or is withdrawn or abandoned (s.39(6)).

[4] See ss.13 (Pt 1) and 81 (Pt 2) discussed in Ch.10.
[5] See Ch.7.
[6] See 12–007 below.
[7] ss.35 and 36 are considered in Ch.15. Sections 47 and 49 are considered in Ch.14.

An appeal against the Secretary of State's decision on an asylum claim is not finally determined for the purpose of s.39(6) at any time when a further appeal or application for leave to bring a further appeal:

(a) has been instituted and has not been finally determined[8] or withdrawn or abandoned; or
(b) may be brought. (s.39(7))

The possibility of an appeal out of time with leave must be ignored for the purposes of ss.39(6) and (7).

CERTIFICATE IN RESPECT OF ASYLUM CLAIMANT

12–007 Section 40 allows the Secretary of State to certify that the conditions in subs.(2) or (3) are satisfied. The effect of this section is that a pending asylum claim will not stop extradition taking place if the requesting territory has responsibility for the person's for the asylum claim or will only send the person to another country in accordance with the Refugee Convention.[9]

The conditions in s.40(2) are that:

(a) the category 1 territory to which the person's extradition has been ordered has accepted that, under standing arrangements, it is the responsible State for the person's asylum claim; and
(b) in the opinion of the Secretary of State the person is not a national or citizen of that territory.

Standing arrangements are the arrangements in force between the UK and the category 1 territory for determining which state is responsible for considering applications for asylum (s.40(4)).

The conditions in s.40(3) are that, in the opinion of the Secretary of State:

(a) the person is not a national or citizen of the category 1 territory to which his extradition has been ordered;
(b) the person's life and liberty would not be threatened in that territory by reason of his race, religion, nationality, political opinion or membership of a particular social group; and
(c) the government of the territory would not send the person to another country otherwise than in accordance with the Refugee Convention.

8 The remittal of an appeal is not a final determination (s.39(8)).

9 The Government has said that this section reflects the overall approach in asylum and immigration legislation as exemplified by ss.11 and 12 of the Immigration and Asylum Act 1999 as amended by s.80 of the Nationality and Immigration Act 2002. Baroness Scotland, *Hansard*, Vol.654, col.54.

The Refugee Convention is defined in s.167(1) of the Immigration and Asylum Act 1999 (s.40(4)).

ASYLUM CLAIM MADE BEFORE A CERTIFICATE HAS BEEN ISSUED UNDER S.2

The 2003 Act does not explicitly determine whether extradition should take place if an asylum claim which has been made before a certificate has been issued under s.2 has not been finally determined. However, it would seem manifestly unfair if a person who has made an application prior to the issue of a certificate should be extradited before his asylum claim has been finally determined. 12–008

The Government explained that the reason for the inclusion of the provisions dealing with asylum claims in the 2003 Act was to avoid the making of asylum claims in the course of extradition proceedings to delay and frustrate them.[10] It is of course much more difficult to suggest that an asylum claim made before an extradition request has been received is made with an intention to delay or frustrate extradition proceedings. It is the Government's position that "a person who genuinely fears persecution should not be prevented from having the opportunity to seek refuge . . . Any asylum application made after the extradition request was received would be considered in the normal way, but as a matter of priority."[11] Applying this reasoning, it would appear that a person should not be extradited until and unless any asylum claim made prior to a certificate being issued under s.2 has been finally determined.

IV. PART 2

SCOTLAND

Any function of the Secretary of State in Pt 2 which is exercised only in relation to Scotland will generally be carried out by Scottish Ministers (s.141(1)). However, this does not apply to: 12–009

(a) the issuing of a certificate that a territory is party to the Hostage-taking Convention (s.83(3))[12];
(b) amending the list in s.101(4) of the senior officials who are allowed to sign an order for extradition or discharge (s.101(5))[13];
(c) deciding an asylum claim (s.121)[14] (s.141(2)).

[10] Baroness Scotland, Vol.654, col.54.
[11] Baroness Scotland, Vol.650, col.GC 169.
[12] See Ch.10.
[13] See 12–020 below.
[14] See 12–021 below.

RECEIVING THE EXTRADITION REQUEST AND ISSUING A CERTIFICATE UNDER S.70

12–010 The Extradition Team at the Judicial Co-operation Unit of the Home Office deal with requests received by the UK to be considered under Pt 2 of the 2003 Act.

For Pt 2 cases, the Secretary of State is involved at the start of the extradition process. The Secretary of State must receive the extradition request and will issue a certificate under s.70 if the conditions in this section are met. If the Secretary of State issues a certificate, he must send the request, the certificate and a copy of any relevant Order in Council to the appropriate judge. This process is considered in detail in Ch.8.

SECRETARY OF STATE'S DECISION

12–011 If the judge does not discharge the person during the extradition hearing, he will send the case to the Secretary of State.[15] The Secretary of State will decide whether the person is to be extradited (s.87(3)).

The Secretary of State must decide whether he is prohibited from ordering extradition because of s.94 (death penalty), s.95 (speciality), or s.96 (earlier extradition to the UK from another territory) (s.93(2)). These three issues are discussed below.

The Secretary of State must consider any representations received by him within six weeks of the appropriate day[16] when deciding the questions in s.93(2). The Secretary of State can accept representations after the six week period has elapsed although he is not obliged to consider them. If the Secretary of State decides extradition is prohibited under any of the grounds in ss.94–96, he must order the person's discharge (s.93(3)).

If the Secretary of State decides that extradition is not prohibited, he must order the person's extradition unless:

- (a) he is informed the request has been withdrawn; or
- (b) he makes an order under s.126(2) or 179(2) for further proceedings to be deferred having received a competing extradition request or Pt 1 warrant and the person is discharged under s.180[17]; or
- (c) he orders the person's discharge under s.208 on the grounds of national security (see above) (s.93(4)).

DEATH PENALTY

12–012 The Secretary of State must not order a person's extradition to a category 2 territory if he could be, will be or has been sentenced to death for the extradition offence

[15] Ch.9 deals with the matters the judge must consider during the extradition hearing.

[16] See 12–019 below for the definition of the appropriate day.

[17] Ch.15 considers competing Pt 1 warrants and extradition requests.

in this territory (s.94(1)). However, this bar does not apply if the Secretary of State receives a written assurance, which he considers adequate, that a sentence of death will not be imposed or, if imposed, will not be carried out (s.94(2)). There is further consideration of this prohibition in Ch.11.

SPECIALITY (S.95)

The speciality protection is discussed generally in Ch.2, and in Ch.10. The Secretary of State must not order a person's extradition to a category 2 territory if there are no speciality arrangements with that territory (s.95(1)). This restriction does not apply if the person has consented to his extradition under s.127[18] before his case was sent to the Secretary of State (s.95(2)). 12–013

Speciality arrangements may be in the domestic law of the category 2 territory or in arrangements made between the territory and the UK (s.95(3)). Arrangements with a Commonwealth country or a British overseas territory[19] can be made for a particular case or more generally (s.95(5)). A certificate issued by or under the authority of the Secretary of State confirming the existence of the arrangements with the Commonwealth country or British overseas territory and stating the terms is conclusive evidence of these matters (s.95(6)). For other territories, any certificate issued by or under the authority of the Secretary of State is not conclusive.

The law of the requesting category 2 territory or the arrangements between the territory and the UK must allow a person extradited from the UK to be dealt with in the territory for an offence committed before his extradition only if the offence falls within s.95(4) or he is first given an opportunity to leave the territory.

The categories of offences in s.95(4) are:

(a) the offence for which the person is extradited;
(b) an extradition offence disclosed by the same facts as that offence unless the death sentence could be imposed;
(c) an extradition offence in respect of which the Secretary of State consents to the person being dealt with (see 12–024 below);
(d) an offence which does not otherwise fall in s.95(4) but which the person's waives his right not to be dealt with for.

The significance of these provisions in construing the definition of the term "extradition offence" is discussed in Ch.6.

The Secretary of State may have particular problems in relation to these provisions in respect of the United States of America, for the reasons set out in Ch.2 and by reason of the wide-ranging provisions of the US Federal Sentencing Guidelines.

[18] Consent is considered in Ch.14.
[19] See Ch.5 for list of British overseas territories.

EARLIER EXTRADITION TO THE UK FROM OTHER TERRITORY

12–014 Section 96 prohibits the Secretary of State from ordering a person's extradition to a category 2 territory if:

(a) the person was extradited to the UK from another territory ("the extraditing territory");
(b) the arrangements between the UK and the extraditing territory require the extraditing territory's consent for the person's extradition to another territory for the extradition offence under consideration; and
(c) consent has not been given on behalf of the extraditing territory.

DEFERRAL OF THE SECRETARY OF STATE'S DECISION

12–015 The Secretary of State can defer making a decision if the person has been charged with an offence or is serving a sentence in the UK.

PERSON SERVING A SENTENCE IN THE UK

12–016 Section 97 applies if the case has been sent by the judge to the Secretary of State for his decision on extradition and the person has been charged with an offence in the UK. In these circumstances, the Secretary of State must not make a decision until either:

(a) the charge is disposed of; or
(b) the charge is withdrawn; or
(c) proceedings in respect of the charge are discontinued; or
(d) an order is made for the charge to lie on the file or in Scotland the diet is deserted *pro loco tempore.* This means that although proceedings on the charge are discontinued there is the possibility that a fresh prosecution on the same charge could be brought in the future (s.97(2)).

If a sentence of imprisonment or another form of detention is imposed for the UK offence, the Secretary of State may defer making a decision until the sentence has been served.

PERSON SERVING A SENTENCE IN THE UK

12–017 Section 98 applies if the case has been sent by the judge to the Secretary of State for his decision on extradition and the person is serving a sentence of imprisonment or another form of detention in the UK. If these conditions are met, the Secretary of State may defer making a decision until the sentence has been served (s.98(2)).

TIME LIMIT FOR THE SECRETARY OF STATE'S ORDER FOR EXTRADITION OR DISCHARGE

Section 99 applies if the judge sends the case to the Secretary of State for his decision on extradition and the Secretary of State does not make a decision within the required period. The required period is two months starting on the appropriate day (s.99(3)). The appropriate day is defined in s.102 (see 12–019 below). The Secretary of State can apply before the end of the required period, on more than one occasion, to the High Court for it to be extended. However, if the Secretary of State does not make his decision before the end of the initial two month period or any extended period allowed by the High Court, the person may make an application to the High Court which must order his discharge (s.99(2)). 12–018

THE APPROPRIATE DAY

Section 102 defines the appropriate day for the purposes of ss.93 and 99. 12–019

Unless the conditions in subss.(2)–(5) are met, the appropriate day is the day on which the judge sends the case to the Secretary of State for his decision on extradition (s.102(7)).

If the person is charged with an offence in the UK, the appropriate day is the day on which either:

(a) the charge is disposed of; or
(b) the charge is withdrawn; or
(c) proceedings in respect of the charge are discontinued; or
(d) an order is made for the charge to lie on the file or, in Scotland, the diet is deserted *pro loco tempore.* This means that although proceedings on the charge are discontinued there is the possibility that a fresh prosecution on the same charge could be brought in the future (s.102(2)).

If the Secretary of State defers making a decision under s.97(3) or 98(2) until the person has served a sentence in the UK, the appropriate day is the day on which the person finishes serving the sentence (s.102(3)).

If the Secretary of State receives a competing request from a category 2 territory and s.126 applies,[20] the appropriate day is either:

(a) the day on which the Secretary of State makes an order under that section if he orders the proceedings on the other request to be deferred; or
(b) the day on which an order under s.180 is made, if the order under s.126 is for proceedings on the request which has been sent to the Secretary of State to be deferred and the order under s.180 is for the proceedings to be resumed (s.102(4)).

[20] Ch.15 deals with competing extradition requests.

If the Secretary of State receives a competing Pt 1 warrant and s.179 applies, the appropriate day is either:

(a) the day on which the Secretary of State makes an order under that section if he orders the proceedings on the Pt 1 warrant to be deferred; or
(b) the day on which an order under s.180 is made, if the order under s.179 is for proceedings on the request to be deferred and the order under s.180 is for the proceedings to be resumed (s.102(5)).

If more than one of the subss.(2)–(5) apply, the appropriate day is the latest of the days which result from applying the relevant subsections (s.102(6)).

ORDER FOR EXTRADITION

12–020 If the Secretary of State orders a person's extradition, he must:

(a) inform him of the order providing a copy of any assurance about the death penalty envisaged by s.94(2)[21–22] (s.100(2));
(b) inform him in ordinary language that he has a right of appeal to the High Court unless the person has already consented to his extradition under s.127[23] (s.100(2)); and
(c) inform a person acting on behalf of the category 2 territory of the order (s.100(1)).

Section 101 specifies who is entitled to sign an order under s.93 for a person's extradition or an order under s.93 or 123 for a person's discharge.

Subsections (1)–(4) explain that an order for a person's extradition or discharge under s.93 or 123 must be made under the hand of the Secretary of State, a Minister of State, a Parliamentary Under-Secretary of State or a senior official. A senior official is defined to be a member of the Senior Civil Service or a member of the Senior Management Structure of Her Majesty's Diplomatic Service (s.101(4)).

In Scotland, an order under s.93 or 123 must be made under the hand of a member of the Scottish Executive, a junior Scottish Minister or a senior official who is a member of the staff of the Scottish Administration.

Subsection (5) allows the Secretary of State to amend, by order, the definition of a senior official in s.101(4) to take account of any future changes to structure or grading in the civil service.

[21–22] See 12–012 above.
[23] Consent is dealt with in Ch.10.

ASYLUM CLAIM[24]

Section 121 applies if: 12–021

(a) a person whose extradition is requested makes an asylum claim after a certificate has been issued under s.70[25] and before he is extradited pursuant to the request; and
(b) an order is made under Pt 2 for the person to be extradited in pursuance of the request.

The person must not be extradited until the asylum claim is finally determined (s.121(3)). Sections 117 and 118, which provide time limits for extradition, have effect subject to this requirement.[26]

The claim is finally determined when the Secretary of State makes his decision if he decides to allow the claim (s.121(4)). If the Secretary of State rejects the asylum claim then it is finally determined:

(a) when the Secretary of State makes his decision if there is no right of appeal against his decision;
(b) when the period permitted for appealing against the Secretary of State's decision ends if no appeal is brought;
(c) when any appeal which is made is finally determined or is withdrawn or abandoned (s.121(5)).

An appeal against the Secretary of State's decision on an asylum claim is not finally determined for the purpose of s.121(5) at any time when a further appeal or application for leave to bring a further appeal:

(a) has been instituted and has not been finally determined[27] or withdrawn or abandoned; or
(b) may be brought (s.121(6)).

The possibility of an appeal out of time with leave must be ignored for the purposes of s.121(5) and (6).

The 2003 Act does not explicitly determine whether extradition can take place if an asylum claim which has been made before a certificate has been issued under s.70 has not been finally determined. The issue of asylum claims made before extradition proceedings have started is considered at 12–008 above.

[24] See 12–005 above which deals with asylum claims generally.
[25] See Ch.7.
[26] ss.117 and 118 are considered in Ch.15.
[27] The remittal of an appeal is not a final determination (s.121(7)).

COMPETING PT 2 REQUEST OR PT 1 WARRANT

COMPETING PT 2 EXTRADITION REQUEST

12–022 Under s.126, the Secretary of State will decide which extradition request is dealt with first if competing Pt 2 requests are received. This is dealt with in detail in Ch.15 at 15–024.

COMPETING PT 1 WARRANT

12–023 Under s.179, the Secretary of State will decide which is dealt with first if a competing Pt 2 extradition request and Pt 1 warrant are received. This section is considered in Ch.15 at 15–025.

MATTERS ARISING AFTER EXTRADITION

CONSENT TO OTHER OFFENCE BEING DEALT WITH

12–024 Section 129 applies if a person has already been extradited to a category 2 territory and the Secretary of State then receives a valid request for his consent to the person being dealt with in the territory for an offence other than the offence for which he was extradited.

A request for consent is valid if it is made by an authority of the territory and the Secretary of State believes it has the function of making requests for this type of consent (s.129(2)). The Secretary of State must serve notice on the person of receipt of the request for consent unless he is satisfied that it would not be practicable to do so (s.129(3)).

If s.129 applies, the Secretary of State must first decide whether the offence is an extradition offence.[28] If he finds it is not an extradition offence then he must refuse consent (s.129(7)). Otherwise he must proceed to decide whether a judge would send the case to him for his decision as to whether to order extradition if the person was in the UK and the judge was required under s.79 to consider ss.79–91 for the offence for which the Secretary of State's consent is requested.[29]

If the Secretary of State decides that the judge would not send the case to him then he must refuse consent (s.129(7)). Otherwise, the Secretary of State must consider whether if the person was in the UK his extradition would be prohibited under s.94, 95 or 96 (see above). If the extradition would be prohibited under any of these sections then the Secretary of State must refuse consent (s.129(9)). Otherwise the Secretary of State may give consent (s.129(10)).

[28] Extradition offences are defined in ss.137 and 138 and are considered in Ch.6.
[29] ss.79–91 are considered in Ch.9.

The requirement of service on the person and the discretion conferred upon the Secretary of State imply that the Secretary of State must take into account conflicting arguments and factors in deciding whether to give consent, though what should guide the Secretary of State is not clear. There was no Parliamentary discussion about these proposals. It is not easy to understand why notice should be served on the person unless it is "impracticable" to do so; it is surely always practicable to find a person subject to legal process in a foreign state, either in prison or on bail.

This problem is likely to arise particularly in the case of the USA. It is common for superseding indictments to be preferred in the USA, involving more detailed as well as different allegations of criminal conduct.

There is no provision for legal aid for a person to make representations to the Secretary of State.

CONSENT TO FURTHER EXTRADITION TO CATEGORY 2 TERRITORY

Section 130 applies if a person is extradited to a category 2 territory ("the requesting territory") in accordance with Pt 2 and the Secretary of State then receives a valid request for his consent to the person's extradition to another category 2 territory for an offence other than the offence for which the person was extradited. 12–025

A request for consent is valid if it is made by an authority of the territory and the Secretary of State believes it has the function of making requests for this type of consent (s.130(2)). The Secretary of State must serve notice on the person of receipt of the request for consent unless he is satisfied that it would not be practicable to do so (s.130(3)).

If s.130 applies the Secretary of State must first decide whether the offence is an extradition offence in relation to the category 2 territory to which the requesting territory wants to extradite the person.[30] If he finds it is not an extradition offence, he must refuse consent (s.130(5)). If the Secretary of State finds it is an extradition offence, he must go on to decide whether a judge would send the case to him for his decision on extradition if the person was in the UK and the judge was required to proceed under s.79 to consider ss.79–91 for the offence for which the Secretary of State's consent is requested.[31]

If the Secretary of State decides that the judge would not send the case to him, he must refuse consent (s.130(7)). Otherwise, the Secretary of State must consider whether if the person was in the UK his extradition would be prohibited under s.94, 95 or 96 (see above). If the extradition would be prohibited under any of these sections, the Secretary of State must refuse consent (s.130(9)). Otherwise the Secretary of State may give consent (s.130(10)).

The observations as to notice and the discretion given to the Secretary of State considered at 12–024 apply also here.

[30] Extradition offences are defined in ss.137 and 138 and are discussed in Ch.6.

[31] ss.79–91 are considered in Ch.9.

CONSENT TO FURTHER EXTRADITION TO CATEGORY 1 TERRITORY

12–026 Section 131 applies if a person is extradited to a category 2 territory ("the requesting territory") in accordance with Pt 2 and the Secretary of State then receives a valid request from the requesting territory for consent to the person's extradition to a category 1 territory for an offence other than the offence for which he was extradited.

A request for consent is valid if it is made by an authority of the territory and the Secretary of State believes it has the function of making requests for this type of consent (s.131(2)). The Secretary of State must serve notice on the person of receipt of the request for consent unless he is satisfied that it would not be practicable to do so (s.131(3)).

If s.131 applies, the Secretary of State must first decide whether the offence is an extradition offence as defined by s.64 in relation to the category 1 territory.[32]If he finds it is not an extradition offence within the definition of s.64, he must refuse consent (s.131(5)). Otherwise he must go on to decide whether the appropriate judge would order extradition under ss.11–25 if the person was in the UK and the judge was required to proceed under s.11 for the offence for which the Secretary of State's consent is requested.[33]

If the Secretary of State decides that the judge would not order extradition, he must refuse consent (s.131(8)). Otherwise, the Secretary of State must give consent (s.131(7)).

[32] See Ch.6.

[33] ss.11–25 are considered in Ch.9.

CHAPTER 13

APPEALS AND THE HIGHER COURTS

I. INTRODUCTION

One of the primary aims of the 2003 Act is to simplify the appeals procedure. Under the scheme of previous statutes, challenges at different stages of the extradition process were possible. In theory, challenges to the High Court could be made to the issue of a provisional warrant, the issue of an order or authority to proceed, the committal order and the ultimate decision whether to surrender. A "case stated" procedure was available to the requested state under Pt III of the 1989 Act, for the purpose of challenging the decision of the lower court to discharge a defendant. It became common practice to seek to review decisions taken by the court and the Secretary of State both by way of judicial review and the right to an application for 13–001 habeas corpus, which latter remedy the Acts of 1870, 1967 and 1989 contemplated would be the basis for High Court challenges to committal by the lower court.

The aim of the new appeals procedure in the 2003 Act is to provide a single simplified appeal for an extradition case.[1] There is a right of appeal to the High Court which in Pt 2 cases will hear an appeal against the decisions of the court and the Secretary of State together. There is then a further restricted right of appeal to the House of Lords, with leave, on a point of law of general public importance. There are different procedures and considerations for Pts 1 and 2; it is convenient to deal with the appeals procedure for each part separately.

It appears from the substitution of appeal for habeas corpus and judicial review, and the powers conferred on the appellate courts, set out below, that it was the intention of Parliament to give the Administrative Court full power to correct error. Under previous extradition statutes, the approach of the High Court on applications for habeas corpus had become assimilated in practice to the relief available by way of judicial review,[2] so that, in the formulation of Lord Diplock in the House of Lords in *Council of Civil Service Unions v Minister of State for the Civil Service*,[3] relief would lie, in the discretion of the court, for error of law, procedural propriety or *Wednesbury* irrationality.

No doubt the higher courts will continue to give particular respect to findings of fact made by a judge who has received live evidence, but otherwise the powers now available to the Administrative Court appear to be exercisable on less constrained grounds than formerly, on matters of fact as well as law.

II. HABEAS CORPUS, ARBITRARY DETENTION AND BAD FAITH

13–002 The Home Office has said that the 2003 Act will have no effect on the common law right to make an application for habeas corpus. The writ of habeas corpus is a prerogative process which allows an effective means of securing immediate release from unlawful or unjustifiable custody. By means of the writ the High Court can compel the production before it of a person who is in custody and inquire into the cause of his detention. Although the right has been confirmed and regulated by statute, it exists independently at common law.

The aim of the 2003 Act is to remove the statutory acknowledgment of the right to make an application for habeas corpus under the 1989 Act, and to replace it with a right of appeal to the High Court. Section 11 and paras 8(1) and (2) of Sch.1 to the 1989 Act provided a statutory right to apply for habeas corpus. Section 11(3) set out certain grounds, specific to Pt III extradition proceedings, on which the High Court should order a person's discharge:

[1] para.14, Explanatory Notes, 2003 Act.

[2] The subject was discussed extensively in Ch.14 of the second edition of this book, written in 2001. Relevant authorities are *R. v Governor of Brixton Prison Ex p. Armah* [1968] A.C. 192; *R. v Secretary of State for the Home Department Ex p. Muboyayi* [1992] 1 Q.B. 244; *R. v Home Secretary Ex p. Cheblak* [1991] 1 W.L.R. 890; *R. v Oldham Justices Ex p. Cawley* [1997] Q.B. 1.

[3] [1985] A.C. 374.

"11.—(3) Without prejudice to any jurisdiction of the High Court apart from this section, the court shall order the applicant's discharge if it appears to the court in relation to the offence, or each of the offences, in respect of which the applicant's return is sought, that —

(a) by reason of the trivial nature of the offence; or
(b) by reason of the passage of time since he is alleged to have committed it or become unlawfully at large, as the case may be;[4] or
(c) because the accusation made against him is not made in good faith in the interests of justice,[5]

it would, having regard to all the circumstances, be unjust or oppressive to return him."

However, in addition to these specific grounds the High Court retained its ordinary jurisdiction in respect of a common law application for habeas corpus.

The Government has said that "The common law right of *habeas corpus* goes back many centuries and there is nothing in the [Extradition] Bill that affects it . . . It is always open to a fugitive to raise *habeas corpus* issues. At every stage, the district judge is required to consider whether remanding in custody or granting bail is appropriate and to ensure that custody issues are properly taken into account."[6] This implies an intention that a common law application for habeas corpus can continue to be made in respect of proceedings under the 2003 Act if it is contended that the detention of the person is not lawful, or that, for example, the person enjoys immunity from prosecution or other legal process.[7] The right exists even if a person is on bail as for the purposes of a habeas corpus application he will be treated as if he was in custody.[8]

Sections 34 and 116 deal with the means by which a decision of the judge or the Secretary of State (in Pt 2 cases) can be challenged. Section 34 states that a decision of a judge under Pt 1 may be questioned in legal proceedings only by means of an appeal using the procedure in Pt 1. Similarly, s.116 states that a decision of a judge or the Secretary of State under Pt 2 may be questioned in legal proceedings only by means of an appeal using the procedure in Pt 2.[8a] These sections appear to seek to remove the ability of a person to make a common law application to the 13–003

4 A similar bar is included in the 2003 Act in ss.14 and 82 considered in Ch.10.

5 There is no exact equivalent to this bar in the 2003 Act. However, if the accusation has not been made in good faith then the bar against extraneous considerations in ss.13 and 81 may be relevant. These sections are considered in Ch.10. In these circumstances it may also be possible to submit that a person's extradition would not be compatible with the Convention rights (ss.21 and 87). This is considered in detail in Ch.11. It may also be possible to argue that an accusation not made in good faith renders detention unlawful and in breach of Art.5 of the ECHR as discussed below.

6 Bob Ainsworth, *Hansard Committee*, 4th sitting, col.119.

7 See *R. v Bow Street Stipendiary Magistrate Ex p. Pinochet Ugarte (No.3)* [2000] 1 AC. 247.

8 *R. v Secretary of State Ex p. Launder (No.2)* (1998) 3 W.L.R. 221; *Re Amand* [1941] 2 K.B. 239 at 249.

8a However, permission has been granted at an oral hearing to judicially review the decision of the Secretary of State to issue a certificate pursuant to s.70 (*Bleta v Secretary of State* [2004] EWHC 2034). The challenge was successful but it is not clear whether the restriction in s.116 was specifically considered. It remains to be seen whether the courts will allow any further applications for judicial review in spite of this section.

High Court for habeas corpus in advance of the time when an appeal under Pt 1 or 2 can be brought before the High Court. However, it is questionable whether these provisions effectively exclude this right, since the writ may not in general be refused merely because an alternative remedy exists which can be used to question the validity of the detention.[9] The ability to bring an appeal under the 2003 Act may mean that the High Court will not grant an application for habeas corpus. However, for Pt 2 cases there may be a substantial delay between any decision made by the appropriate judge and an appeal against this decision as an appeal must be heard after the Secretary of State's decision on extradition (see further below).

An application can be made to the High Court when making an appeal under the provisions in the 2003 Act. Given the width of the matters which the High Court can consider on appeal, it is difficult to see what grounds could be argued on an application for habeas corpus which could not also be argued on an ordinary appeal under the 2003 Act.

Article 5(4) of the ECHR is also relevant when considering a challenge to the legality of a person's detention:

> "Everyone who is deprived of his liberty by arrest or detention shall be entitled to take proceedings by which the lawfulness of his detention shall be decided speedily by a court and his release shall be ordered if his detention is not lawful."

The Administrative Court held that in order to comply with Art.5(4) of the ECHR, the Magistrates' Court dealing with the committal proceedings[10] must have the jurisdiction to determine whether a person's detention was lawful as required by the ECHR.[11] It held that detention arising from bad faith or an abuse of power would make detention unlawful and arbitrary in the Convention sense.

Therefore, it appears that the ability to make an application that detention is unlawful because an extradition claim is made in bad faith exists both before the appropriate judge and before the High Court as part of an appeal.[12] However, it remains to be seen how a court will consider this issue under the 2003 Act.

III. RULES OF COURT

13–004 The provisions in the 2003 Act dealing with appeals refer to rules of court. The relevant rules of court are in Pt 52 of the Civil Procedure Rules and Practice Direction 52 (Appeals) as amended.[13]

[9] See *R. v Governor of Pentonville prison Ex p. Azam* [1973] 2 All E.R. 741 at 751.

[10] Committal proceedings under the 1989 Act were broadly equivalent to the extradition hearing in the 2003 Act.

[11] *R. (Kashamu) v Governor of Brixton Prison* [2002] Q.B. 887.

[12] See n.5 above.

[13] *www.dca.gov.uk/civil/procrules_fin/contents/practice_directions/pd_part52.htm.*

IV. HIGH COURT AND HOUSE OF LORDS

All appeals to the High Court under the 2003 Act must be brought in the Administrative Court of the Queen's Bench Division.[14] 13–005

For Scotland, references to the High Court will be read as the High Court of Justiciary (s.216(9)). The High Court of Justiciary is the final court of appeal for criminal matters in Scotland. The 2003 Act, therefore, removes the right of appeal to the House of Lords for Scottish extradition proceedings.

V. DEFENCE FUNDING

A person may fund his own defence. Legal aid is discussed generally in Ch.8 at 8–003.[15] 13–006

ENGLAND AND WALES

High Court proceedings will be classed as criminal proceedings under the General Criminal Contract. Applications for a Representation Order for an appeal to the High Court should be made to the High Court and not the Magistrates' Court. 13–007

Representation on appeal to the House of Lords will be funded separately by an application to the relevant court in accordance with reg.10 of the Criminal Defence Service (General) (No.2) Regulations 2001.[16] The effect of reg.10 is that the House of Lords is not permitted to grant a Representation Order and so an application must be made orally or in writing to the Court of Appeal or the registrar of the Court of Appeal.

The criteria for assessing whether representation by Queen's Counsel or more than one advocate is necessary are set out in reg.14.[17]

SCOTLAND

The provisions of the Legal Aid (Scotland) Act 1986 will be applied to an appeal to the High Court which will be treated as an appeal in summary proceedings (s.183). 13–008

[14] Para.22.6A(2), Practice Direction 52.

[15] See "The Extradition Act 2003 — Funding Implications" Focus on CDS, Issue March 14, 2004 *www.legalservices.gov.uk*.

[16] SI 2001/1437 as amended by the Criminal Defence Service (General) (No.2) (Amendment) Regulations 2002 (SI 2002/712).

[17] Criminal Defence Service (General) (No.2) Regulations 2001 (SI 2001/1437) as amended by the Criminal Defence Service (General) (No.2) (Amendment) Regulations 2002 (SI 2002/712).

NORTHERN IRELAND

13–009 The judge or the High Court can grant free legal aid for an appeal before the High Court (s.184). If the judge refuses to grant free legal aid, there is a right of appeal to the High Court which can then itself grant free legal aid.

The judge or the High Court can grant free legal aid only if it appears that the person's means are insufficient to enable him to obtain legal aid and it is desirable in the interests of justice that the person should be granted free legal aid (s.184(5)). If there is any doubt as to whether either of these conditions is satisfied, it must be assumed, in the person's favour, that the relevant condition is satisfied (s.184(9)). A solicitor and/or counsel may be assigned to represent the person on appeal to the High Court (s.184(10)).

The High Court can grant free legal aid for an appeal to the House of Lords. It must apply the same criteria when making its decision and must again resolve any doubt in favour of the person making the application. It can also assign solicitor or counsel or both for the appeal.

Section 185 applies various articles of the Legal Aid, Advice and Assistance (Northern Ireland) Order 1981[18] to proceedings before the judge or the High Court. This section also sets out assumptions which must be made when applying these articles. Fees for an appeal before the House of Lords must be paid by the Lord Chancellor and must not exceed the amount allowed by the House of Lords.

VI. PART 1

APPEAL BY PERSON AGAINST ORDER FOR HIS EXTRADITION

13–010 If a judge orders a person's extradition under Pt 1, the person has a right of appeal on a question of fact or law to the High Court against the order (s.26(1) and (3)). The right of appeal does not apply if the order is made under s.46 or 48 after the person has consented to his extradition (s.26(2)). Notice of the appeal must be given in accordance with the rules of court within seven days of the making of the order.[19] The notice must be endorsed with the date of the person's arrest[20] and must be served by the appellant on the Crown Prosecution Service if it is not a party to the appeal.[21] Unless the High Court orders otherwise, the notice must also be served on each respondent to the appeal as soon as practicable and, in any event, within seven days of the filing of the notice.[22]

18 SI 1981/228 (NI 8).
19 See also para.22.6A(3)(a), Practice Direction 52.
20 para.22.6A(3)(b), Practice Direction 52.
21 para.22.6A(3)(d), Practice Direction 52.
22 r.52.4(3), Civil Procedure Rules.

The High Court may allow or dismiss the appeal (s.27(1)). It may allow the appeal only if the conditions in s.27(3) or s.27(4) are satisfied (s.27(2)). The conditions in s.27(3) are that:

(a) the appropriate judge ought to have decided a question before him at the extradition hearing differently; and
(b) if he had decided the question in the way he ought to have done, he would have been required to order the person's discharge.

The conditions in s.27(4) are that:

(a) an issue is raised that was not raised at the extradition hearing or evidence is available that was not available at the extradition hearing;
(b) the issue or evidence would have resulted in the appropriate judge deciding a question before him at the extradition hearing differently; and
(c) if he had decided the question in that way, he would have been required to order the person's discharge.

If the court allows the appeal, it must order the person's discharge and quash the order for his extradition (s.27(5)).

APPEAL BY CATEGORY 1 TERRITORY AGAINST ORDER FOR DISCHARGE

RIGHT OF APPEAL AND NOTICE OF APPEAL

If the judge orders a person's discharge at the extradition hearing, the authority which issued the Pt 1 warrant may appeal on a question of law or fact to the High Court against the decision which resulted in the order for discharge (s.28). No appeal can be brought if the discharge was ordered under s.41 because of the withdrawal of the Pt 1 warrant (s.28(2)).[23] Notice of an appeal under this section must be given in accordance with the rules of court within seven days of the order being made for the person's discharge. The requirements in the rules of court are dealt with at 13–010 above. 13–011

DETENTION PENDING CONCLUSION OF APPEAL UNDER S.28

If the judge is informed immediately after he orders the person's discharge that the authority which issued the Pt 1 warrant intends to appeal under s.28, he must remand the person in custody or on bail while the appeal is pending (s.30). The judge can later grant bail if he initially remands the person in custody. 13–012

[23] See Ch.15 which deals with withdrawal of a Pt 1 warrant.

The appeal ceases to be "pending" on the earliest of the following dates:

(a) when the proceedings on the appeal are discontinued;
(b) when the High Court dismisses the appeal *if the authority does not immediately inform the court that it intends to apply for leave to appeal to the House of Lords*;
(c) twenty eight days after leave to appeal to the House of Lords is granted;
(d) when there is no further step which can be taken by the authority which issued the Pt 1 warrant in relation to the appeal, ignoring any power a court has to grant leave for a step to be taken out of time. (s.30(4); italics added)

In Scotland, this subsection is modified to omit the words in italics in (b) and to omit (c) to reflect the fact that there is no right of appeal to the House of Lords in Scotland.[24]

HIGH COURT'S POWERS ON APPEAL UNDER S.29

13–013 The High Court may allow or dismiss the appeal (s.29(1)). It may allow the appeal only if the conditions in s.29(3) or (4) are satisfied (s.29(2)).

For this section a question is the relevant question if the judge's decision on it resulted in an order for the person's discharge (s.29(6)). The conditions in s.29(3) are that:

(a) the judge ought to have decided the relevant question differently; and
(b) if he had decided the question in the way he ought to have done, he would not have been required to order the person's discharge.

The conditions in s.29(4) are that:

(a) an issue is raised that was not raised at the extradition hearing or evidence is available that was not available at the extradition hearing;
(b) the issue or evidence would have resulted in the judge deciding the relevant question differently; and
(c) if he had decided the question in that way, he would not have been required to order the person's discharge.

If the court allows the appeal, it must quash the order discharging the person and remit the case to the judge directing him to proceed as he would have been required to do if he had decided the relevant question differently at the extradition hearing (s.29(5)).

[24] See 13–005 above.

APPEAL TO THE HIGH COURT: TIME LIMIT FOR START OF HEARING

Rules of court must prescribe the period ("the relevant period") within which the High Court must begin to hear an appeal under s.26 or 28 (s.31(1)). The relevant period is calculated from the date of arrest, regardless as to whether the person was provisionally arrested under s.5 (s.31(2)).[25] The relevant period is 40 days and the High Court must begin to hear the substantive appeal within 40 days of the person's arrest.[26] 13–014

The High Court can extend the relevant period, on more than one occasion and after the initial 40 day period has expired, if it believes it is in the interests of justice to do so (s.31(4)–(5)).[27] If the High Court has not begun to hear the appeal before the end of the initial relevant period, or any extended period allowed under s.31(4)), the appeal is treated as being automatically determined under s.31(6) or (7).

If the appeal is brought by the person under s.26 and it has not started within the relevant period:

(a) the appeal must be taken to have been allowed by a decision of the High Court;
(b) the person whose extradition has been ordered must be taken to have been discharged by the High Court;
(c) the order for the person's extradition must be taken to have been quashed by the High Court (s.31(6)).

If the appeal is brought by the authority which issued the Pt 1 warrant under s.28 and it has not started in the relevant period, the appeal must be taken to have been dismissed by a decision of the High Court (s.31(7)).

APPEAL TO THE HOUSE OF LORDS

LEAVE TO APPEAL AND TIME LIMITS

It is possible to appeal the decision of the High Court under s.26 or 28 to the House of Lords (s.32(1)), as it has been in extradition proceedings since the Administration of Justice Act 1960. An appeal can be brought by the person who is the subject of the Pt 1 warrant or the authority which issued the Pt 1 warrant (s.32(2)). 13–015

An appeal to the House of Lords can only be made with the leave of the High Court or the House of Lords (s.32(3)). However, leave to appeal must not be granted unless the High Court has certified that there is a point of law of general public importance involved in the decision and it appears to the court granting

[25] See Ch.7 for arrest under Pt 1 generally.
[26] para.22.6a(3)(c), Practice Direction 52.
[27] See also para.22.6A(4), Practice Direction 52.

leave that the point is one which ought to be considered by the House of Lords (s.32(4)).

An application to the High Court for leave to appeal must be made within 14 days starting with the day on which the High Court making its decision on the appeal to it. If the High Court refuses leave to appeal, an application must be made to the House of Lords for leave within 14 days starting on the day on which the High Court refuses leave to appeal.

If leave to appeal is granted, the appeal must be brought within 28 days starting with the day on which leave is granted. If the appeal is not brought within this period then the appeal will be taken to have been brought and dismissed by the House of Lords immediately after the end of the 28 day period (s.32(8)). The power of a court to extend the period for bringing the appeal or to grant leave to take a step out of time must be ignored for the purposes of s.32(8)(b) (s.32(9)).

The High Court has the power to grant bail to a person appealing to the House of Lords or applying for leave to appeal (s.32(10)).

Subsections (11) and (12) apply provisions of the Appellate Jurisdiction Act 1876 which concern the composition of the House of Lords for the hearing and determination of appeals.

Section 32 does not apply to Scotland (see above).

POWERS OF THE HOUSE OF LORDS

13–016 The House of Lords has the power to either allow or dismiss the appeal (s.33(1)). The House is obliged to take different actions on allowing an appeal, dependent on the decisions reached by the judge and the High Court on appeal.

If the appeal to the House of Lords is brought by the person whose extradition is sought and the House of Lords upholds the appeal, it must order the person's discharge. If the person had been ordered to be extradited by the judge following the extradition hearing and the High Court rejected the person's appeal, the House of Lords must also quash the order for extradition (s.33(2)–(3)).

If the judge makes an extradition order and the person successfully appeals this to the High Court, and the authority which issued the Pt 1 warrant then successfully appeals the High Court's decision to the House of Lords, the House of Lords must quash the order of the High Court discharging the person and order that the person is extradited (s.33(4)–(5)).

If the judge orders that the person is discharged and the authority which issued the Pt 1 warrant unsuccessfully appeals this to the High Court and the House of Lords finds in favour of the authority, s.33(7) and (8) apply (s.33(6)). A question is the relevant question for ss.33(7) and (8) if the judge's decision on it resulted in the order for the person's discharge (s.33(9)).

If the judge would have been required to order extradition if he had decided the relevant question differently, the House of Lords must quash the order of the judge discharging the person and order his extradition (s.33(7)). In any other case, the

House of Lords must quash the order of the judge discharging the person, remit the case to the judge and direct the judge to proceed as he would have been required to do if he had decided the relevant question differently at the extradition hearing (s.33(8)).

COSTS

See Ch.15 at 15–013. 13–017

VII. PART 2

APPEAL WHERE CASE SENT TO SECRETARY OF STATE

If the judge sends a case to the Secretary of State under Pt 2 for his decision as to 13–018
whether a person is to be extradited, the person may appeal to the High Court against the relevant decision (s.103(1)). The relevant decision is the decision that resulted in the case being sent to the Secretary of State (s.103(3)). There is no right of appeal if the person has consented to his extradition under s.127 before his case was sent to the Secretary of State (s.103(2)).[28]

The appeal may be brought on a question of fact or law and must not be heard until after the Secretary of State makes his decision (s.103(5)). If the Secretary of State decides not to order extradition, an appeal must not be brought or proceeded with. However, this does not apply if the category 2 territory has given notice of an appeal under s.110 against the decision which resulted in the discharge unless the High Court has already made its decision on appeal (s.103(8)).

Notice of an appeal under s.103 must be given in accordance with the rules of court within 14 days of the day on which the Secretary of State informs the person under s.100 that he has either ordered his extradition or discharge.[29] The requirements in the rules of court are dealt with in 13–010 above.

The High Court may:

(a) allow the appeal;
(b) direct the judge to answer again a question (or questions) which he decided at the extradition hearing; or
(c) dismiss the appeal (s.104(1)).

It may allow the appeal only if the conditions in s.104(3) or s.104(4) are satisfied (s.104(2)).

[28] Consent is dealt with in Ch.14.
[29] See also para.22.6A(5), Practice Direction 52.

The conditions in s.104(3) are that:

(a) the judge ought to have decided a question before him at the extradition hearing differently; and
(b) if he had decided the question in the way he ought to have done, he would have been required to order the person's discharge.

The conditions in s.104(4) are that:

(a) an issue is raised that was not raised at the extradition hearing or evidence is available that was not available at the extradition hearing;
(b) the issue or evidence would have resulted in the judge deciding a question before him at the extradition hearing differently; and
(c) if he had decided the question in that way, he would have been required to order the person's discharge.

If the court allows the appeal it must order the person's discharge and quash any order for his extradition (s.104(5)).

If the High Court directs the judge to decide a question (or questions) again under s.104(1)(b), and the judge comes to a different decision on any of these questions, the judge must order the person's discharge (s.104(6)). If the judge comes to the same decision having been directed to decide again a question (or questions), the appeal is taken to have been dismissed by a decision of the High Court (s.104(7)).

APPEAL AGAINST DISCHARGE AT EXTRADITION HEARING

RIGHT OF APPEAL AND NOTICE OF APPEAL

13–019 If the judge orders a person's discharge at the extradition hearing, an appeal on a question of law or fact can be brought on behalf of the category 2 territory against the relevant decision (s.105(1)). The relevant decision is the decision which resulted in the order for the person's discharge (s.105(3)). An appeal cannot be brought if the order for discharge was made under s.122 because of the withdrawal of the request.[30] Notice of the appeal must be given in accordance with the rules of court within 14 days of the day on which the order for discharge is made (s.105(5)).[31–32] The requirements for the notice in the rules of court are dealt with in 13–010 above.

DETENTION PENDING CONCLUSION OF APPEAL UNDER S.105

13–020 If immediately after the judge orders the person's discharge he is informed on behalf of the category 2 territory of an intention to appeal under s.105, he must

[30] See Ch.15 which considers withdrawal of an extradition request.
[31–32] See also para.22.6A(6), Practice Direction 52.

remand the person in custody or on bail while the appeal is pending (s.107). The judge can later grant bail if he initially remands the person in custody.

The appeal ceases to be "pending" on the earliest of the following dates:

(a) when the proceedings on the appeal are discontinued;
(b) when the High Court dismisses the appeal *if the court is not immediately informed on behalf of the category 2 territory of an intention to apply for leave to appeal to the House of Lords*;
(c) twenty eight days after leave to appeal to the House of Lords is granted;
(d) when there is no further step which can be taken on behalf of the category 2 territory in relation to the appeal, ignoring any power a court has to grant leave for a step to be taken out of time. (s.107(4); italics added)

In Scotland, this subsection is modified to omit the words in italics in (b) and to omit (c) to reflect the fact that there is no right of appeal to the House of Lords in Scotland.

HIGH COURT'S POWERS ON APPEAL UNDER S.105

The High Court may: 13–021

(a) allow the appeal;
(b) direct the judge to decide the relevant question again; or
(c) dismiss the appeal (s.106(1)).

A question is the relevant question if the judge's decision on it resulted in the order for the person's discharge (s.106(2)). The court can only allow the appeal on two grounds.

It may allow the appeal only if the conditions in s.106(4) or s.106(5) are satisfied (s.106(3)). The conditions in s.106(4) are that:

(a) the judge ought to have decided the relevant question differently; and
(b) if he had decided the question in the way he ought to have done, he would not have been required to order the person's discharge.

The conditions in s.106(5) are that:

(a) an issue is raised that was not raised at the extradition hearing or evidence is available that was not available at the extradition hearing;
(b) the issue or evidence would have resulted in the judge deciding the relevant question differently; and
(c) if he had decided the question in that way, he would not have been required to order the person's discharge.

If the court allows the appeal, it must quash the order discharging the person, remit the case to the judge and direct him to proceed as he would have been required to do if he had decided the relevant question differently at the extradition hearing (s.106(6)).

If the High Court directs the judge to decide the relevant question again under s.106(1)(b), and the judge decides the relevant question differently, he must proceed as he would have been required to do if he had decided the question differently at the extradition hearing (s.106(7)). If the judge does not decide the relevant question differently having been directed to decide it again, the appeal is taken to have been dismissed by a decision of the High Court (s.106(8)).

APPEAL AGAINST EXTRADITION ORDER

13–022 If the Secretary of State orders a person's extradition under Pt 2, the person may appeal to the High Court on a question of law or fact against this order (s.108(1)). The right of appeal does not apply if the person has consented to his extradition under s.127.[33] Notice of the appeal must be given in accordance with the rules of court within 14 days of the Secretary of State informing the person under s.100(1) of his order to extradite.[34] The requirements in the rules of court are dealt with in 13–010 above.

The High Court may allow the appeal or dismiss the appeal (s.109(1)). It may allow the appeal only if the conditions in s.109(3) *or* s.109(4) are satisfied (s.109(2)). Section 109(3) requires that the High Court finds that:

(a) the Secretary of State ought to have decided a question before him differently; and
(b) if he had decided the question in the way he ought to have done, he would not have ordered the person's extradition.

Section 109(4) requires that the High Court finds that:

(a) an issue is raised that was not raised when the case was being considered by the Secretary of State or information is available that was not available at that time;
(b) the issue or information would have resulted in the Secretary of State deciding a question before him differently; and
(c) if he had decided the question in that way, he would not have ordered the person's extradition.

If the court allows the appeal, it must order the person's discharge and quash the order for his extradition (s.109(5)).

[33] Consent is dealt with in Ch.14.
[34] See also para.22.6A(7), Practice Direction 52.

APPEAL AGAINST DISCHARGE BY THE SECRETARY OF STATE

RIGHT OF APPEAL AND NOTICE OF APPEAL

If the Secretary of State makes an order for a person's discharge under Pt 2, an appeal on a question of law or fact can be brought on behalf of the category 2 territory against the relevant decision (s.110(1)). The relevant decision is the decision which resulted in the order for the person's discharge (s.110(3)). An appeal is not possible if the order for discharge was under s.123 because of the withdrawal of the request.[35] Notice of the appeal must be given in accordance with the rules of court within 14 days of the day on which the Secretary of State under s.100(4) informs a person acting on behalf of the category 2 territory of the order (s.110(5)).[36] The requirements in the rules of court are dealt with in 13–010 above. 13–023

DETENTION PENDING CONCLUSION OF APPEAL UNDER S.110

Section 112 applies if immediately after the Secretary of State orders the person's discharge under Pt 2 he is informed on behalf of the category 2 territory of an intention to appeal under s.110. The judge must remand the person in custody or on bail while the appeal is pending. The definition of when an appeal ceases to be pending is identical to that in s.107 dealt with at 13–020 above. The judge can later grant bail if he initially remands the person in custody. 13–024

HIGH COURT'S POWERS ON APPEAL UNDER S.110

The High Court may allow the appeal or dismiss the appeal (s.111(1)). It may allow the appeal only if the conditions in s.111(3) or s.111(4) are satisfied (s.111(2)). The conditions in s.111(3) are that: 13–025

(a) the Secretary of State ought to have decided a question before him differently; and
(b) if he had decided the question in the way he ought to have done, he would have ordered the person's extradition.

The conditions in s.111(4) are that:

(a) an issue is raised that was not raised when the case was being considered by the Secretary of State or information is available that was not available at that time;

[35] See Ch.15 which considers withdrawal of an extradition request.
[36] See also para.22.6A(6), Practice Direction 52.

(b) the issue or information would have resulted in the Secretary of State deciding a question before him differently; and
(c) if he had decided the question in that way, he would have ordered the person's extradition.

If the court allows the appeal, it must quash the order discharging the person and order the person's extradition (s.111(5)).

APPEAL TO THE HIGH COURT: TIME LIMIT FOR START OF HEARING

13–026 Rules of court must prescribe the period ("the relevant period") within which the High Court must begin to hear an appeal under s.103, 105, 108 or 110. The High Court must begin to hear the substantive appeal within 76 days of the filing of the appellant's notice (the relevant period).[37] However, if an appeal is brought under s.103 before the Secretary of State has decided whether to order extradition then the period of 76 days does not start until the day on which the Secretary of State informs the person of his decision.[38] The Secretary of State must also inform the High Court of his decision and the date on which he informed the person of his decision as soon as practicable after informing the person.[39]

The High Court can extend the relevant period on more than one occasion if it believes it is in the interests of justice to do so (s.113(3)).[40] The High Court can exercise the power in s.113(3) even after the end of the relevant period. This allows it to grant an initial extension before the end of the required period and then to grant further extensions even after the end of the initial required period of 76 days. If the High Court has not begun to hear the appeal before the end of the relevant period, as extended by s.113(3), the appeal is treated as being automatically determined under s.113(5) or (6).

If the appeal is brought by the person subject to the extradition request under s.103 or 108, and it has not started within the relevant period:

(a) the appeal must be taken to have been allowed by a decision of the High Court;
(b) the person whose extradition has been ordered must be taken to have been discharged by the High Court;
(c) the order for the person's extradition must be taken to have been quashed by the High Court (s.113(5)).

[37] para.22.6A(9), Practice Direction 52.
[38] para.22.6A(10)(a), Practice Direction 52.
[39] para.22.6A(10)(b), Practice Direction 52.
[40] See also para.22.6A(11), Practice Direction 52.

If the appeal is brought on behalf of the category 2 territory under s.105 or 110, and it has not started within the relevant period, it must be taken to have been dismissed by a decision of the High Court (s.113(6)).

APPEAL TO THE HOUSE OF LORDS

LEAVE TO APPEAL AND TIME LIMITS

It is possible to appeal a decision of the High Court under s.114 to the House of Lords when the appeal by the High Court has been heard under s.103, 105, 108 or 110. Section 114 is in similar terms to s.32 dealt with at 13–015 above. **13–027**

POWERS OF HOUSE OF LORDS

The House of Lords has the power either to allow or to dismiss the appeal (s.115(1)). **13–028**

If the House of Lords allows an appeal by the person whose extradition is requested, it must order his discharge and quash any order for extradition which has been made (s.115(2)–(3)).

Section 115(5) applies if the person subject to the extradition request has been ordered to be discharged by either the Secretary of State or the High Court and this order has been successfully appealed to the House of Lords on behalf of the category 2 territory. If s.115(5) applies, the House of Lords must quash the order discharging the person and order him to be extradited (s.115(5)).

Section 115(7) applies if the judge has made an order discharging the person and an unsuccessful appeal has been made to the High Court on behalf of the category 2 territory but the House of Lords has allowed a further appeal brought on behalf of the category 2 territory. If s.115(7) applies, the House of Lords must quash the order discharging the person and remit the case to the judge directing him to proceed as he would have been required to do if he had decided the relevant question differently at the extradition hearing.

A question is the relevant question if the judge's decision on it resulted in the order for the person's discharge (s.115(8)).

COSTS

See Ch.15 at 15–015. **13–029**

CHAPTER 14

CONSENT

I. INTRODUCTION

14–001 An important aim of the 2003 Act is to allow for a faster and more efficient process for those people who wish to consent to extradition. Under the 1989 Act, which introduced for the first time the possibility of voluntary return, it was not clear whether a person who waived his rights, either before of after the committal proceedings, also waived speciality protection.[1]

The appropriate judge is required to give a person who has been arrested information about the consent procedure on the first occasion that the person appears before the court. This initial hearing is dealt with in Ch.9.

It is important that a person fully appreciates the consequences before he consents to be extradited as consent is irrevocable once given. Consent will also entail a waiver by the person of the important speciality protection.

[1] See for example, *R. v Governor of Brixton Prison Ex p. Syed Akbar*, unreported, DC, CO/1707/96; and *R. v Secretary of State for the Home Department Ex p. Johnson* [1999] Q.B. 1174.

II. PART 1

CONSENT TO EXTRADITION

A person who is provisionally arrested under s.5 or arrested under a Pt 1 warrant can consent to be extradited to the category 1 territory in which the warrant was issued (s.45(1)–(2)). However, if a person consents to be extradited, he is taken to have waived any right he would have (apart from the consent) not to be dealt for an offence committed before his extradition (s.45(2)). Therefore, by consenting to his extradition, the person loses the speciality protection when he is extradited to the category 1 territory.[2] 14–002

Consent under s.45 must be given before the appropriate judge, must be recorded in writing and is irrevocable (s.45(4)). A person may not give his consent under s.45 unless he is legally represented[3] before the appropriate judge at the time he gives his consent unless s.45(6) applies to him (s.45(5)).

Section 45(6) applies to a person if:

(a) he has been informed of his right to apply for legal aid and has had the opportunity to apply for legal aid but he has either refused or failed to apply; or
(b) he has applied for legal aid but his application has been refused; or
(c) he was granted legal aid but the legal aid was withdrawn.

Legal aid is defined in s.45(7) and legal aid is discussed more generally in Ch.8. The Explanatory Notes to the 2003 Act interpret s.45(5)–(6) as having "the effect that no person can consent to his extradition without having received, or having had the opportunity to receive, legal advice".[4] However, this is not strictly true for (b) and (c). There are a number of reasons why it is important for the person to receive legal advice prior to consenting to extradition. The first is the serious and irrevocable effect of consent as discussed above. The second is a possibility that a person given the information about consent by the judge on his first appearance in court may well misunderstand and believe that he is being given an instruction by the judge to consent. This is especially true in the case of a person whose first language is not English. These factors should be taken into account when a decision is made on an application for legal aid or consideration is being given to withdrawing legal aid.

2 The speciality rule is considered in Ch.10 for Pt 1 cases.

3 A person is treated as legally represented before the appropriate judge if (and only if) he has the assistance of counsel or a solicitor to represent him in the proceedings before the appropriate judge (s.45(8)).

4 Para.133, Explanatory Notes — Extradition Act 2003.

EXTRADITION ORDER FOLLOWING CONSENT

14–003 If the person consents to his extradition under s.45, the judge must remand him in custody or on bail (s.46). If the judge remands the person in custody he can later grant bail. If the judge has not fixed a date under s.8 for the extradition hearing to begin he is not required to do so. If the extradition hearing has begun the judge is not required to continue with it. The judge must order the extradition of the person to the category 1 territory within 10 days of consent (s.46(6)). However, s.46(6) has effect subject to ss.48 and 51, discussed below, which deal with a competing Pt 1 warrant or Pt 2 request. If the judge fails to order extradition within this 10 day period, the person can apply to the judge who must order his discharge (s.46(8)).

EXTRADITION TO CATEGORY 1 TERRITORY FOLLOWING CONSENT

14–004 Section 47 applies if the judge makes an order under s.46(6) for a person's extradition to a category 1 territory. If s.47 applies the person must be extradited to the category 1 territory before the end of the required period (s.47(2)). The required period is either:

(a) 10 days starting on the day on which the order is made; or
(b) 10 days starting on a later date agreed between the judge and authority which issued the Pt 1 warrant.

If the person is not extradited within the required period, he can apply to the judge who must order his discharge unless reasonable cause[5] is shown for the delay (s.47(4)). If the judge is informed by a designated authority (NCIS or the Crown Agent of the Crown Office[6]) that the Pt 1 warrant has been withdrawn before the person is extradited to the category 1 territory, s.47(2) does not apply and the judge must order the person's discharge.

ANOTHER PT 1 WARRANT ISSUED FOLLOWING CONSENT

COMPETING PT 1 WARRANT

14–005 Section 48 applies if:

(a) a person consents under s.45 to his extradition to a category 1 territory; and
(b) before the judge orders his extradition under s.46(6):

  (i) the judge is informed that another Pt 1 warrant has been issued in respect of the person;

[5] See Ch.15 at 15–002 which considers the meaning of "reasonable cause".
[6] See Ch.7 for designated authorities.

(ii) the warrant falls to be dealt with by the judge or by a judge who is the appropriate judge in another part of the UK; and
(iii) the warrant has not been disposed of.

In these circumstances, s.46(6) does not apply but the judge may:

(a) order the person's extradition in pursuance of his consent; or
(b) order further proceedings on the warrant under consideration to be deferred until the other warrant has been disposed of (s.48(3)).

However, this is subject to s.51 which deals with competing Pt 2 extradition requests and is discussed below (s.48(4)).

The judge must take account of the following when deciding which order to make under s.48(3):

(a) the relative seriousness of the offences concerned;
(b) the place where each offence was committed or was alleged to have been committed;
(c) the date on which each warrant was issued;
(d) whether for each offence the person is accused or is alleged to have been convicted.

This list is not exhaustive and there is no indication what weight should be attached to each matter. It is also not clear what effect (b) and (d) would have on the judge's decision.[7]

EXTRADITION TO A CATEGORY 1 TERRITORY

If the judge makes an order under s.48(3)(a) for the person's extradition to a category 1 territory, s.49 will apply. If s.49 applies the person must be extradited to the category 1 territory before the end of the required period (s.49(2)). The required period is either: 14–006

(a) 10 days starting on the day on which the order is made; or
(b) 10 days starting on a later date agreed between the judge and authority which issued the Pt 1 warrant.

If the person is not extradited within the required period, he can apply to the judge who must order his discharge unless reasonable cause[8] is shown for the delay (s.49(4)). If the judge is informed by a designated authority (NCIS or the Crown Agent of the Crown Office[9]) that the Pt 1 warrant has been withdrawn before the

[7] *cf.* Art.16, Framework Decision— discussed in Ch.11.
[8] See Ch.15 at 15–002 which considers the meaning of "reasonable cause".
[9] See Ch.7 for designated authorities.

person is extradited to the category 1 territory, s.49(2) does not apply and the judge must order the person's discharge.

PROCEEDINGS DEFERRED

14–007 If the judge makes an order under s.48(3)(b) for proceedings on the Pt 1 warrant to be deferred, he must remand the person in custody or on bail (s.50). The judge can grant bail later if he initially remands the person in custody. If an order is made under s.180[10] for proceedings to be resumed, the period within which an extradition order must be made under s.46(6) is 10 days starting with the day on which the order under s.180 is made.

EXTRADITION REQUEST FOLLOWING CONSENT

14–008 Section 51 applies if:

(a) a person in respect of whom a Pt 1 warrant is issued consents under s.45 to his extradition to the category 1 territory issuing the warrant; and
(b) before the judge orders his extradition under s.46(6) or 48(3)(a):

    (i) the judge is informed that a certificate has been issued by the Secretary of State in respect of a request for the person's extradition; and
    (ii) the request has not been disposed of.

The judge must not order extradition under s.46(6) or 48(3) until the Secretary of State has made an order under s.179(2). If there is a competing Pt 1 warrant and Pt 2 extradition request, s.179 allows the Secretary of State to determine which should be dealt with first.[11]

If the Secretary of State makes an order under s.179(2) that further proceedings on the warrant should be deferred until the request is disposed of, the judge must remand the person in custody or on bail (s.51(4)). The judge can later grant bail if he initially remands the person in custody. If at a later stage an order is made under s.180 for proceedings on the warrant to be resumed then the period in s.46(6) must be taken to be 10 days starting with the day on which the order under s.180 is made (s.51(6)).

If the Secretary of State makes an order under s.179(2) for further proceedings on the request to be deferred until the warrant has been disposed of, the period in s.46(6) must be taken to be 10 days starting with the day on which the order under s.180 is made (s.180(7)).

[10] s.180 is discussed in Ch.15.
[11] s.179 is considered in Ch.15.

UNDERTAKING IN RELATION TO A PERSON SERVING A SENTENCE

If the judge makes an order for extradition under s.46(6) or 48(3)(a) but the person is serving a sentence of imprisonment or another form of detention in the UK, the judge may make an order for extradition on the condition that extradition will not take place until the category 1 territory gives an undertaking in terms specified by the judge. 14–009

If the person is accused of an offence in the Pt 1 warrant the judge may request an undertaking including the terms:

(a) that the person be kept in custody until the proceedings against him for the offence and any other offence which he is permitted to be dealt with for are concluded;
(b) that the person be returned to the UK to serve the remainder of his sentence on the conclusion of those proceedings (s.52(3)).

If the person is alleged in the Pt 1 warrant to be unlawfully at large after conviction of an offence, the judge may ask for an undertaking including the term that the person will be returned to the UK to serve the remainder of his sentence after serving any sentence imposed on him in the category 1 territory for the offence and any other offence which he is permitted to be dealt with for in the category 1 territory (s.52(4)).

If the judge makes an order subject to receiving an undertaking, the required period for the purposes of ss.47(2) and 49(2) within which the person must be extradited is 10 days starting on the day the judge receives the undertaking (s.52(5)).

EXTRADITION FOLLOWING DEFERRAL FOR COMPETING CLAIM

Section 53 applies if an order is made for deferral of the proceedings on the warrant[12] because of a competing claim after the judge has ordered extradition under s.46(6) or 48(3). The appropriate judge can then make an order under s.181(2) for the person's extradition in pursuance of the warrant to cease to be deferred. In these circumstances, the required period for the purposes of ss.47(2) and 49(2), within which the person must be extradited, is 10 days starting on the day the judge makes an order under s.181(2) (s.53(2)). 14–010

III. PART 2

CONSENT TO EXTRADITION

A person who is arrested under a warrant issued under s.71 may consent to his extradition to the category 2 territory to which his extradition is requested (s.127(1)). 14–011

[12] Under s.44(4)(b) or 179(2)(b).

A person who is arrested under a provisional warrant may consent to his extradition to the category 2 territory in which he is accused of the commission of an offence or alleged to have been convicted of an offence (s.127(2)). Consent under this section must be given in writing and is irrevocable (s.127(3)).

Consent under s.127 which is given by a person before his case is sent to the Secretary of State must be given before the appropriate judge (s.127(4)). There are similar provisions to those in s.45 discussed at 14–001 above to try and ensure that the person has had access to legal advice.

If consent has been given to the appropriate judge under s.127, s.128 applies. The judge is not required to fix a date for the extradition hearing under s.75 or 76 if he has not already done so (s.128(2)). If the extradition hearing has already begun the judge is not required to proceed with the hearing (s.128(3)). The judge must send the case to the Secretary of State for his decision whether the person should be extradited. The person is taken to have waived any right he would have (apart from consent) not to be dealt with in the category 2 territory for an offence committed before his extradition. This means that if a person consents prior to his case being sent to the Secretary of State he will lose the speciality protection.[13]

If the case has already been sent to the Secretary of State, consent must be given to the Secretary of State (s.127(5)). The Secretary of State cannot normally order extradition if there are no speciality arrangements with the category 2 territory (s.93(2)(b)). However, s.95(2) removes this prohibition if the person has consented to his extradition under s.127 before his case was sent to the Secretary of State. There appears to be no loss of the speciality protection if a person consents to his extradition under s.127 after his case has been sent to the Secretary of State.

[13] The speciality rule is considered in Ch.12 for Pt 2.

CHAPTER 15

SUNDRY STATUTORY MATTERS; TIME LIMITS, COSTS, WITHDRAWAL OF CLAIM, COMPETING CLAIMS, REPATRIATION AND RE-EXTRADITION

I. INTRODUCTION

This chapter deals with a number of other matters which may arise in the extradition process. **15–001**

The 2003 Act was designed to create a more efficient process. It imposes time limits for the extradition of a person. There are also provisions for costs and these allow, for the first time, an award of costs against a person whose extradition has been ordered.

There are procedures which apply if the requesting territory withdraws its extradition claim after extradition proceedings have begun. The Act includes provisions relating to competing extradition claims to allow a decision to be made as to which claim will be dealt with first.

If a person has been sentenced in one territory, but was serving his sentence in a different territory and absconds, an extradition request may be made by either territory.

The 2003 Act refers to such cases as repatriation cases and the statutory provisions are modified according to which territory makes a request.

An extradition request may be received for a person who is serving a sentence in the UK. If the request alleges that he has committed an offence, he may be extradited to the territory making the request to be tried for the offence. On conviction, the person may be returned to the UK to complete the remainder of his pre-existing sentence in the UK. On completion of his UK sentence, and before he can be sent to the territory to serve the sentence imposed after extradition, a re-extradition hearing must be held.

II. TIME LIMITS

PART 1

EXTRADITION WHERE NO APPEAL

15–002 If the judge orders a person's extradition to a category 1 territory under Part 1, and no notice of appeal is given under s.26 within the permitted period,[1] the person must be extradited within the required period (s.35(1) and (3)). This section does not apply if the order for extradition is made under s.46 or 48, which apply if the person has consented to his extradition.[2]

The required period is either:

(a) 10 days starting on the day on which the judge makes the order; or
(b) 10 days starting on a later date agreed between the judge and authority which issued the Part 1 warrant.

If the person is not extradited within the required period, he can apply to the judge who must order his discharge unless reasonable cause is shown for the delay (s.35(5)).

Section 16 and para.10 of Sch.1 to the 1989 Act contained similar provisions imposing a time limit for extradition which, if breached, would lead to the discharge of a person unless "sufficient cause" was shown for the delay. Cases determined under those or preceding provisions[3] may be useful in interpreting "reasonable cause" in s.35.

[1] See Ch.13 at 13–010 for the period permitted for notice of appeal under s.26 to be given. Any power of a court to extend the period permitted for giving notice of appeal or to grant leave to take a step out of time must be ignored for the purpose of s.35(1) (s.35(6)).

[2] See Ch.14, which considers consent in Pt 1 cases.

[3] *Re Shuter* [1960] 1 Q.B. 142 (DC); *R. v Governor of Brixton Prison Ex p. Enahoro* [1963] 2 Q.B. 455 (DC); *Re Shrian Oskar* unreported, February 29, 1988, CO/190/88 (DC); *R. v Governor of Brixton Prison Ex p. Syed Akbar* unreported, July 31, 1996, CO/1707/96, 1142/96 (DC).

EXTRADITION FOLLOWING APPEAL

Section 36 applies where there is an appeal to the High Court under s.26 against an order for a person's extradition to a category 1 territory and the effect of the decision of the relevant court on appeal is that the person is to be extradited.[4] 15–003

The relevant court is the High Court if there is no appeal against the decision of the High Court to the House of Lords or the House of Lords if an appeal is made (s.36(4)).

If s.36 applies, the person must be extradited to the category 1 territory within the required period. The required period is either:

(a) 10 days starting with the day on which the decision of the relevant court on the appeal becomes final or proceedings on the appeal are discontinued; or
(b) 10 days starting on a later date agreed between the relevant court and authority which issued the Pt 1 warrant (s.36(3)).

The decision of the High Court on the appeal becomes final:

(a) when the period permitted for applying to the High Court for leave to appeal to the House of Lords ends if there is no application;
(b) when the period permitted for applying to the House of Lords for leave to appeal ends if the High Court refuses leave and there is no application to the House of Lords for leave;
(c) when the House of Lords refuses leave to appeal to it;
(d) at the end of the permitted period, which is 28 days starting on the day on which leave to appeal to the House of Lords is granted, if no appeal is brought before the end of that period (s.36(5)).[5]

The decision of the House of Lords on appeal becomes final when it is made (s.36(7)).

If the person is not extradited within the required period, he can apply to the judge who must order his discharge unless reasonable cause[6] is shown for the delay (s.36(8)).

As there is no right of appeal to the House of Lords in Scotland,[7] this section is modified accordingly for Scotland (s.36(9)).

UNDERTAKING IN RELATION TO PERSON SERVING SENTENCE IN THE UK

If the judge makes an order for extradition to a category 1 territory under Pt 1 but the person is serving a sentence of imprisonment or another form of detention in the 15–004

[4] See Ch.13 for appeals in Pt 1 cases.
[5] Any power of a court to extend the period permitted for applying for leave to appeal or to grant leave to take a step out of time must be ignored for the purpose of s.36(5) (s.36(6)).
[6] See 15–002 for meaning of "reasonable cause".
[7] See Ch.13 at 13–005.

UK, the judge may make the order conditional on receiving an undertaking given on behalf of the category 1 territory in terms specified by the judge (s.37(1) and (3)).

Section 37 does not apply if the order for extradition is made under s.46 or 48 after the person has consented to his extradition.[8]

If the person is accused of an offence in the Part 1 warrant, the judge may request an undertaking including the terms:

(a) that the person be kept in custody until the proceedings against him for the offence and any other offence which he is permitted to be dealt with for in the category 1 territory are concluded;
(b) that the person be returned to the UK to serve the remainder of his sentence on the conclusion of those proceedings (s.37(4)).

If the person is alleged in the Pt 1 warrant to be unlawfully at large after conviction of an offence, the judge may ask for an undertaking including the term that the person will be returned to the UK to serve the remainder of his sentence after serving any sentence imposed on him in the category 1 territory for the offence, and any other offence which he is permitted to be dealt with for in the category 1 territory (s.37(5)).

If the judge makes an order subject to receiving an undertaking and the judge does not receive an undertaking within 21 days starting on the day on which he makes the order, the person can apply to the judge who must order his discharge (s.37(7)).

If the judge receives the undertaking within the 21 day period, and there are no appeal proceedings, the required period for s.35(3)[9] is 10 days, starting with the day on which the judge receives the undertaking. If there are appeal proceedings, the required period for the purposes of s.36(2)[10] is 10 days, starting with the day on which the decision of the relevant court on appeal becomes final (as defined in s.36) or, if later, the day on which the judge receives the undertaking (s.37(8)).

EXTRADITION FOLLOWING DEFERRAL FOR COMPETING CLAIM

15–005 Section 38 applies if:

(a) an order is made under Pt 1 for a person to be extradited to a category 1 territory in pursuance of a Pt 1 warrant;
(b) before the person is extradited to the territory an order is made under s.44(4)(b) or s.179(2)(b) for the person's extradition in pursuance of the warrant to be deferred;
(c) the appropriate judge makes an order under s.181(2) for the person's extradition in pursuance of the warrant to cease to be deferred.

[8] See Ch.14 which considers consent in Pt 1 cases.
[9] See 15–002 above.
[10] See 15–003 above.

Sections 44 and 179 allow a decision to be taken if a competing Pt 1 warrant or Pt 2 extradition request are received as to which extradition claim will be deferred. These provisions are discussed at 15–023 and 15–025 below. Section 38 does not apply if the order for extradition is made under s.46 or 48 after the person has consented to his extradition.[11]

If an order under s.181(2) is made and there are no appeal proceedings, the required period for s.35(3)[12] is ten days, starting with the day on which the order under s.181(2) is made (s.38(3)). If there are appeal proceedings, the required period for the purposes of s.36(2)[13] is 10 days, starting with the day on which the decision of the relevant court on appeal becomes final (as defined in s.36) or, if later, the day on which the order under s.181(2) is made (s.38(4)).

ASYLUM CLAIM

Sections 39 and 40 will determine the circumstances when a person who is subject to a Pt 1 warrant and has made an asylum claim can be extradited. The Secretary of State will consider the asylum claim; these sections are considered at 12–006. 15–006

PART 2

EXTRADITION WHERE NO APPEAL

Section 117 applies if the Secretary of State orders a person's extradition to a category 2 territory under Pt 2, and no notice of appeal under s.103 or 108 is given within 14 days starting with the day on which the Secretary of State informs the person under s.100(1) that he has ordered extradition.[14] 15–007

If s.117 applies, the person must be extradited within the required period of 28 days of the Secretary of State making the order (s.117(2)). If the person is not extradited within the required period, he can apply to the judge who must order his discharge unless reasonable cause[15] is shown for the delay (s.117(3)).

EXTRADITION FOLLOWING APPEAL

Section 118 applies if there is an appeal to the High Court under s.103, 108 or 110 against an order for a person's extradition to a category 2 territory, and the effect of the decision of the relevant court on appeal is that the person is to be extradited there.[16] 15–008

[11] See Ch.14 which considers consent in Pt 1 cases.

[12] See 15–002 above.

[13] See 15–003 above.

[14] For the purposes of defining the permitted period, any power of a court to extend the period permitted for applying for leave to appeal or to grant leave to take a step out of time must be ignored (s.117(4)).

[15] See 15–002 for meaning of "reasonable cause".

[16] See 13–008 *et seq.* appeals in Pt 2 cases.

The relevant court is the High Court if there is no appeal against the decision of the High Court to the House of Lords, or the House of Lords if an appeal is made (s.118(3)).

If s.118 applies the person must be extradited to the category 2 territory before the end of the required period. The required period is 28 days starting with:

(a) the day on which the decision of the relevant court on the appeal becomes final; or
(b) the day on which proceedings on the appeal are discontinued (s.118(2)).

The decision of the High Court on the appeal becomes final:

(a) when the period permitted for applying to the High Court for leave to appeal to the House of Lords ends if there is no application;
(b) when the period permitted for applying to the House of Lords for leave to appeal ends if the High Court refuses leave and there is no application to the House of Lords for leave;
(c) when the House of Lords refuses leave to appeal to it;
(d) at the end of the permitted period, which is 28 days starting on the day on which leave to appeal to the House of Lords is granted, if no appeal is brought before the end of that period (s.118(4)).[17]

The decision of the House of Lords on appeal becomes final when it is made (s.118(6)).

If the person is not extradited within the required period, he can apply to the judge who must order his discharge unless reasonable cause[18] is shown for the delay (s.118(7)).

As there is no right of appeal to the House of Lords in Scotland,[19] this section is modified accordingly for Scotland (s.118(8)).

Undertaking in relation to person serving sentence in the UK

15–009 If the Secretary of State makes an order for extradition to a category 2 territory under Pt 2, but the person is serving a sentence of imprisonment or another form of detention in the UK, the Secretary of State may make the order conditional on receiving an undertaking given on behalf of the category 2 territory in terms specified by him (s.119(1)–(2)).

[17] Any power of a court to extend the period permitted for applying for leave to appeal or to grant leave to take a step out of time must be ignored for the purpose of s.118(4) (s.118(5)).
[18] See 15–002 for "reasonable cause".
[19] See Ch.13 at 13–005.

If the person is accused of an offence, the Secretary of State may request an undertaking including the terms:

(a) that the person be kept in custody until the proceedings against him for the offence and any other offence which he is permitted to be dealt with for in the category 2 territory are concluded;
(b) that the person be returned to the UK to serve the remainder of his sentence on the conclusion of those proceedings (s.119(3)).

If the person is alleged in the request to be unlawfully at large after conviction of an offence by a court in a category 2 territory, the judge may ask for an undertaking including the term that the person will be returned to the UK to serve the remainder of his sentence after serving any sentence imposed on him in the category 2 territory for the offence and any other offence which he is permitted to be dealt with for in the category 2 territory (s.119(4)).

If the Secretary of State makes an order subject to receiving an undertaking, and he does not receive the undertaking within 21 days starting on the day on which he makes the order, the person can apply to the High Court, which must order his discharge (s.119(6)).

If the Secretary of State receives the undertaking within the 21 day period and there are no appeal proceedings, the required period for s.117(2)[20] is 28 days, starting with the day on which the Secretary of State receives the undertaking. If there are appeal proceedings, the required period for the purposes of s.118(2)[21] is 28 days, starting with the day on which the decision of the relevant court on appeal becomes final (as defined in s.118) or, if later, the day on which the Secretary of State receives the undertaking (s.119(7)).

Extradition following deferral for competing claim

Section 120 applies if: 15–010

(a) an order is made under Part 2 for a person to be extradited to a category 2 territory in pursuance of an extradition request;
(b) before the person is extradited to the territory an order is made under s.126(2) or s.179(2) for the person's extradition in pursuance of the request to be deferred;
(c) the appropriate judge makes an order under s.181(2) for the person's extradition in pursuance of the request to cease to be deferred.

Sections 126 and 179 allow a decision to be taken on which extradition claim will be deferred if a competing Pt 2 extradition request or Pt 1 warrant is received. These provisions are discussed at 15–024 and 15–025 below.

[20] See 15–007 above.
[21] See 15–008 above.

If an order under s.181(2) is made and there are no appeal proceedings, the required period for s.117(2)[22] is 28 days starting with the day on which the order under s.181(2) is made (s.120(2)). If there are appeal proceedings, the required period for the purposes of s.118(2)[23] is:

- 28 days, starting with the day on which the decision of the relevant court on appeal becomes final (as defined in s.118); or,
- if later, the day on which the order under s.181(2) is made (s.120(3)).

Asylum claim

15–011 If a person who is subject to a Pt 2 extradition request has also made an asylum claim, s.121 will determine when they can be extradited. The Secretary of State will consider the asylum claim; this section is considered at 12–021.

III. COSTS

15–012 General guidance is provided by the Practice Direction on Costs in Criminal Proceedings which took effect on May 18, 2004.[24]

PART 1

Costs where extradition ordered (s.60)

15–013 Section 60 allows for an order for costs to be made against a person who is the subject of extradition proceedings under Pt 1.[25]

Section 60 applies if any of the following occurs in relation to any person in respect of whom a Pt 1 warrant is issued:

(a) an order for the person's extradition is made under Pt 1;
(b) the High Court dismisses an appeal under s.26;
(c) the High Court or the House of Lords dismisses an application made by the person for leave to appeal to the House of Lords under s.32;
(d) the House of Lords dismisses an appeal brought by the person under s.32.

In a case falling within (a), the appropriate judge may make such order as he considers just and reasonable with regard to the costs to be paid by the person (s.60(2)).

22 See 15–007 above.
23 See 15–008 above.
24 *www.courtservice.gov.uk/cms/media/costs_pd_180504.pdf.*
25 "This is based on section 18 of the Prosecution of Offences Act 1985, which allows a court in a criminal case to make an award of costs against the accused." para.178, Explanatory Notes — 2003 Act.

In a case falling within (b), (c) or (d), the court which dismisses the appeal or application may make such order as it considers just and reasonable in respect of the costs to be paid by the person (s.60(3)).

An order for costs under s.60 must specify the amount and may name the person to whom the costs are to be paid (s.60(4)).

COSTS WHERE DISCHARGE ORDERED

If the person is ordered to be discharged under Pt 1 or taken to be discharged owing to the operation of this part, an order for costs can be made in favour of the person by the judge, High Court or House of Lords. 15–014

Section 61 applies if any of the following occurs in relation to any person in respect of whom a Pt 1 warrant is issued:

(a) an order for the person's discharge is made under Pt 1;
(b) the person is taken to be discharged under Pt 1;
(c) the High Court dismisses an appeal under s.28;
(d) the High Court or the House of Lords dismisses an application made by the authority which issued the warrant for leave to appeal to the House of Lords under s.32;
(e) the House of Lords dismisses an appeal brought by the authority which issued the warrant under s.32.

In a case falling within (a), an order for costs in favour of the person may be made by the appropriate judge, the High Court or the House of Lords, whichever made the order for discharge. In a case falling within (b), the appropriate judge may make an order for costs in favour of the person. In a case falling within (c), (d) or (e), the court which dismisses the application or appeal may make an order for costs in favour of the person.

An order under this section in favour of the person is an order for payment of the appropriate amount to be paid out of money provided by Parliament (s.61(5)).

The appropriate amount is the amount that is reasonably sufficient to compensate the person for any expenses properly incurred by him in the proceedings under Pt 1 (s.61(6)). These expenses are not necessarily restricted only to his legal costs.

However, if the judge or court making the order believes that there are circumstances which make it inappropriate for the person to receive the appropriate amount, the judge or court must assess what amount would be just and reasonable and make an order for this amount (s.61(7)).

Unless s.61(7) applies, the appropriate amount:

(a) must be specified in the order, if the court considers this appropriate and the person agrees the amount; or

(b) if the amount is not specified in the order, it must be determined in accordance with regulations issued by the Lord Chancellor for the purposes of this section (s.61(8)).

Sections 20(1) and (3) of the Prosecution of Offences Act 1985 are applied to s.61 in the same way as they would apply in relation to Pt 2 of that Act (s.62(1)–(2)). In Northern Ireland, the relevant provision is s.7 of the Costs in Criminal Case Act (Northern Ireland) 1968 which applies to s.61 as it would to ss.2 to 5 of that Act (s.62(3)).

PART 2

Costs where extradition ordered

15–015 There are powers given in s.133 to allow a court to make an order for costs to be paid by a person subject to a Pt 2 extradition request if he is ordered to be extradited. These provisions are similar to those in s.60 for Pt 1 cases which is discussed at 15–013 above.

Additionally, for Pt 2 cases the High Court on an appeal under s.103 has the power to direct the judge to decide again a question/s which he decided at the extradition hearing (s.104(1)(b)). If the judge reaches the same decision, the appeal will be taken to be dismissed by a decision of the High Court (s.104(7) discussed in Ch.13 at 13–018). In these circumstances the judge will decide whether to make an order for costs against the person (s.133(3)).

Costs where discharge ordered

15–015A The court has the power under s.134 to make an order for costs in favour of the person who is the subject of the extradition request if he is ordered to be discharged. This is in similar terms to s.61 for Pt 1 cases, discussed at 15–014 above. Section 135 applies certain statutory provisions to s.134, and this is similar to s.62 for Pt 1 cases, considered at 15–014 above.

IV. WITHDRAWAL OF WARRANT OR REQUEST

PART 1

Withdrawal of Pt 1 warrant

15–015B Section 41 applies if at any time in the relevant period the appropriate judge is informed by the designated authority[26] that a Pt 1 warrant issued in respect of a person has been withdrawn (s.41(1)).

[26] NCIS or the Crown Agent of the Crown Office, see 7–003.

The relevant period starts when the person is first brought before the judge following his arrest and ends when the person is extradited in pursuance of the warrant or discharged (s.41(2)).

If s.41 applies the judge must order the person's discharge. If the person is not before the judge when the judge orders his discharge, the judge must inform him of the order as soon as practicable.

WITHDRAWAL OF WARRANT WHILE APPEAL TO HIGH COURT PENDING

Section 41 applies if at any time in the relevant period the High Court is informed by the designated authority[27] that a Pt 1 warrant issued in respect of a person has been withdrawn (s.42(1)). **15–016**

The relevant period starts when notice of an appeal is given by the person or the authority which issued the warrant, and ends when the court makes a decision about the appeal or the appeal proceedings are discontinued (s.42(2)).

If s.42 applies, the court must order the person's discharge and quash the order for his extradition if the appeal is under s.26, or dismiss the appeal if it is under s.28. If the person is not before the court when his discharge is ordered, the court must inform him of the order as soon as practicable.

WITHDRAWAL OF THE WARRANT WHILE APPEAL TO THE HOUSE OF LORDS IS PENDING

Section 43 applies if at any time in the relevant period the House of Lords is informed by the designated authority[28] that a Pt 1 warrant issued in respect of a person has been withdrawn (s.43(1)). **15–017**

The relevant period starts when leave to appeal to the House of Lords is granted to the person or the authority which issued the warrant, and ends when the House of Lords decides the appeal or the appeal proceedings are discontinued (s.43(2)).

If the appeal is brought by the person subject to the warrant, the House of Lords must order his discharge and quash any order for his extradition which may have been made (s.43(3)). If the appeal is brought by the authority which issued the warrant, the House of Lords must dismiss the appeal (s.43(4)). The House of Lords must inform the person of the order for his discharge as soon as practicable if he is not before the House of Lords when the order is made.

[27] NCIS or the Crown Agent of the Crown Office, see 7–003.

[28] NCIS or the Crown Agent of the Crown Office, see 7–003.

PART 2

WITHDRAWAL OF REQUEST BEFORE END OF EXTRADITION HEARING

15–018 Section 122 applies if at any time in the relevant period the appropriate judge is informed by the Secretary of State that a request for a person's extradition has been withdrawn (s.122(1)).

The relevant period starts when the person is first brought before the judge following his arrest, and ends when the person is discharged by the judge or the judge sends the case to the Secretary of State for his decision on extradition (s.122(2)).

If s.122 applies, the judge must order the person's discharge. If the person is not before the judge when the judge orders his discharge, the judge must inform him of the order as soon as practicable.

WITHDRAWAL OF REQUEST AFTER CASE SENT TO SECRETARY OF STATE

15–019 Section 123 applies if at any time in the relevant period the Secretary of State is informed that a request for a person's extradition has been withdrawn (s.123(1)).

The relevant period starts when the judge sends the case to the Secretary of State for his decision whether the person is to be extradited, and ends when the person is discharged or the person is extradited in pursuance of the request (s.123(2)).

If s.123 applies the Secretary of State must order the person's discharge.[29]

WITHDRAWAL OF WARRANT WHILE APPEAL TO HIGH COURT PENDING

15–020 Section 124 applies if at any time in the relevant period the High Court is informed by the Secretary of State that a request for a person's extradition has been withdrawn (s.124(1)).

The relevant period starts when notice of an appeal to the court is given by the person or on behalf of the category 2 territory, and ends when the appeal is decided or appeal proceedings are discontinued (s.124(2)).

If s.124 applies and the appeal is under s.103 or 108, the court must order the person's discharge and quash the order for extradition if the Secretary of State has made one (s.124(3)). If the appeal is under s.105 or 110 the court must dismiss the appeal (s.124(4)).

If the person is not before the court when the court orders his discharge, it must inform him of the order as soon as practicable.

[29] s.101 lists those people who can sign an order for discharge: see 12–020.

WITHDRAWAL OF THE WARRANT WHILE APPEAL TO THE HOUSE OF LORDS PENDING

Section 125 applies if at any time in the relevant period the House of Lords is informed by the Secretary of State that a request for a person's extradition has been withdrawn (s.125(1)). 15–021

The relevant period starts when leave to appeal to the House of Lords is granted to the person or to a person acting on behalf of the category 2 territory, and ends when the appeal is decided or appeal proceedings are discontinued (s.125(2)).

If s.125 applies and the appeal is brought by the person whose extradition is requested, the House of Lords must order the person's discharge and quash any order for extradition (s.125(3)). If the appeal is brought by a person acting on behalf of the category 2 territory, the House of Lords must dismiss the appeal (s.125(4)).

If the person is not before the House of Lords when it orders his discharge, it must inform him of the order as soon as practicable.

V. COMPETING EXTRADITION CLAIMS

These provisions deal with competing extradition claims. 15–022

COMPETING PT 1 WARRANTS

Section 44 applies if in the relevant period the following conditions are met in relation to a person in respect of whom a Pt 1 warrant has been issued: 15–023

(a) the judge is informed that another Pt 1 warrant has been issued in respect of the person; and
(b) the warrant falls to be dealt with by the judge or by a judge who is the appropriate judge in another part of the UK; and
(c) the other warrant has not been disposed of.

The relevant period begins when the person is brought before the judge after arrest, and ends when the person is discharged or extradited in pursuance of the warrant (s.44(2)).

If s.44 applies, the judge may:

(a) order further proceedings on the warrant under consideration to be deferred until the other warrant has been disposed of (if the warrant under consideration has not been disposed of); or
(b) order the person's extradition in pursuance of the warrant under consideration to be deferred until the other warrant has been disposed of (if an

order for extradition has been made in pursuance of the warrant under consideration) (s.44(4)).

The judge must take account of the following when deciding whether to make an order under s.44(4):

(a) the relative seriousness of the offences concerned;
(b) the place where each offence was committed or was alleged to have been committed;
(c) the date on which each warrant was issued;
(d) whether for each offence the person is accused or is alleged to have been convicted.

This list is not exhaustive and there is no indication what weight should be attached to each factor. It is also not clear what effect (b) and (d) would have on the judge's decision. The criteria in s.44(4) are derived from Art.16 of the Framework Decision which deals with competing European Arrest Warrants. Art.16(2) gives the judge the option of seeking advice from Eurojust[30] when deciding which of two competing European Arrest Warrants should be dealt with first.

If the judge makes an order under s.44(4) and the person is not already remanded in custody or on bail then he must remand the person in custody or on bail. If the judge remands the person in custody he may later grant bail.

COMPETING EXTRADITION REQUESTS

15–024 Section 126 applies if:

(a) the Secretary of State receives a valid request for a person's extradition to a category 2 territory; and
(b) the person is in the UK; and
(c) before the person is extradited in pursuance of the request or discharged, the Secretary of State receives another valid request for the person's extradition.

In these circumstances there will be two Pt 2 requests made by different category 2 territories for the same person.

The Secretary of State may:

(a) order proceedings (or further proceedings) on one of the requests to be deferred until the other one has been disposed of; or

[30] See Council Decision 2002/187/JHA of February 28, 2002 setting up Eurojust with a view to reinforcing action against serious crime [2002] O.J. L63/1.

(b) order the person's extradition in pursuance of the request under consideration to be deferred until the other request has been disposed of (if an order for extradition has been made for the request under consideration) (s.126(2)).

The Secretary of State must take account of the following when applying s.126(2):

(a) the relative seriousness of the offences concerned;
(b) the place where each offence was committed or alleged to have been committed;
(c) the date on which each request was received;
(d) whether the person is alleged to have been convicted of each offence.

There is nothing in the 2003 Act which indicates how the Secretary of State should balance the factors he must take into account. The Government was asked to make clear in the Act how the Secretary of State should consider these issues. The Government did not feel that this was appropriate, saying instead that, "It is up to the Secretary of State's discretion to weigh them [the matters set out in s.126(3)] up in the particular circumstances of each case."[31] However, the Government has made it clear that the list of criteria is not exhaustive, and the Secretary of State can consider any matter in making his decision.[32]

COMPETING PT 1 WARRANT AND PT 2 EXTRADITION REQUEST

Section 179 considers competing extradition claims under Pts 1 and 2. It applies if at the same time: 15–025

(a) there is a Pt 1 warrant in respect of a person, a certificate has been issued under s.2 for the warrant and the person has not been extradited under the warrant or discharged; and
(b) there is a request for the same person's extradition, a certificate has been issued under s.70 for the request and the person has not been extradited under the request or discharged (s.179(1)).

The Secretary of State may:

(a) order proceedings (or further proceedings) on either the warrant or the request to be deferred until the other one has been disposed of (if neither has been disposed of); or

[31] Mr Bob Ainsworth, *Hansard* Committee, 7th Sitting, col.189.
[32] Lord Filkin, Vol.652, col.GC 16.

(b) order the person's extradition in pursuance of the warrant to be deferred until the request has been disposed of (if an order for extradition pursuant to the warrant has been made); or
(c) order the person's extradition in pursuance of the request to be deferred until the warrant has been disposed of (if an order for extradition pursuant to the request has been made) (s.179(2)).

The Secretary of State must take account in particular of these matters when applying s.179(2):

(a) the relative seriousness of the offences concerned;
(b) the place where each offence was committed or was alleged to have been committed;
(c) the date when the warrant was issued and the date when the request was received;
(d) whether the person is alleged to have been convicted of each offence (s.179(3)).

This list is not exhaustive and although the Secretary of State must consider in particular these factors, he can consider any other matters he considers are relevant.[33]

If both the request and the warrant were certified in Scotland, it will be a Scottish Minister rather than the Secretary of State who will make an order under this section (s.179(4)).

PROCEEDINGS ON DEFERRED WARRANT OR REQUEST

15–026 Section 180 provides for the resumption of deferred extradition proceedings once a competing extradition claim has been disposed of. It applies if:

(a) an order is made under the 2003 Act deferring proceedings on an extradition claim in respect of a person (the deferred claim) until another extradition claim in respect of the person has been disposed of; and
(b) the other extradition claim is disposed of.

An extradition claim is made in respect of a person either if a Pt 1 warrant is issued for him or a request for his extradition is made (s.180(9)).

In these circumstances, the judge may make an order for proceedings on the deferred claim to be resumed within 21 days of the day on which the other extradition claim is disposed of ("the required period") (s.180(2),(3) and (6)).

[33] See further at 15–024 above.

If the person applies to the appropriate judge[34] to be discharged, the judge must order his discharge if the required period has ended, and the judge has not made an order under s.180(2) or ordered the person's discharge (s.180(5)). If the person applies to the appropriate judge before the required period has ended, the judge may order his discharge (s.180(4)).

PROCEEDINGS WHERE EXTRADITION IS DEFERRED

Section 181 allows an extradition order to be given effect to if it had been deferred to allow a competing claim to be disposed of, and this claim has been disposed of. 15–027

It applies if:

(a) an order is made under the 2003 Act, deferring a person's extradition in pursuance of an extradition claim (the deferred claim) until another extradition claim in respect of him has been disposed of; and
(b) the other extradition claim is disposed of.

An extradition claim is made in respect of a person either if a Pt 1 warrant is issued for him or a request for his extradition is made (s.181(9)).

In these circumstances, the judge may make an order for the person's extradition in pursuance of the deferred claim to be deferred within 21 days of the day on which the other extradition claim is disposed of ("the required period") (s.181(2), (3) and (6)).[35]

If the person applies to the appropriate judge[36] to be discharged, the judge must order his discharge if the required period has ended, and the judge has not made an order under s.181(2) or ordered the person's discharge (s.181(5)). If the person applies to the appropriate judge in any other circumstances, the judge may order his discharge (s.181(4)).

VI. REPATRIATION CASES (PERSONS SERVING SENTENCES OUTSIDE TERRITORY WHERE CONVICTED)

The provisions of Pts 1 and 2 have effect with specified modifications if the person who is the subject of the Pt 1 warrant or Pt 2 request is alleged to be unlawfully at large, having been convicted of an offence in one territory ("the convicting territory"); but after absconding from a prison in another territory ("the imprisoning 15–028

[34] If the proceedings on the deferred claim were under Pt 1 then s.67 applies for determining the appropriate judge (s.180(7)). If the proceedings on the deferred claim were under Pt 2 then s.139 applies for determining the appropriate judge (s.180(8)). See further Ch.8 at 8–016.

[35] The time limit for extradition for a deferred Pt 1 case is in s.38 considered at 15–005 above. The time limit for extradition for a deferred Pt 2 case is in s.120 considered at 15–010 above.

[36] If the proceedings on the deferred claim were under Pt 1 then s.67 applies for determining the appropriate judge (s.181(7)). If the proceedings on the deferred claim were under Pt 2 then s.139 applies for determining the appropriate judge (s.181(8)). See further Ch.8 at 8–016.

territory"), where he was serving his sentence under international arrangements for the repatriation of prisoners to serve their sentences. The modifications differ according to whether the warrant or request is issued by the convicting or imprisoning territory.

Section 63 lists the modifications for Pt 1 cases and s.136 provides the modifications for Pt 2 cases.

VII. RE-EXTRADITION

15–029 The 2003 Act includes novel provisions to cater for the following situation. A person who was serving a sentence in the UK may be extradited to be tried in another territory. He may then be returned to the UK, after conviction and sentence in the requesting territory, to serve the remainder of the UK sentence. The 2003 Act provides that there must then be a re-extradition hearing when the person has finished serving the UK sentence before the person can be extradited to serve the sentence imposed in the other territory to which he has already been extradited.

Section 187 applies if the conditions in s.186(2)–(6), shown below, are satisfied.

The first condition is that the person was extradited to a territory in accordance with Pt 1 or 2.

The second condition is that the person was serving a sentence of imprisonment or another form of detention in the UK (the UK sentence) before he was extradited.

The third condition is that:

(a) if the person was extradited under Pt 1 then the Pt 1 warrant contained a statement that it was issued with a view to his extradition for the purpose of being prosecuted for an offence; or
(b) if the person was extradited under Pt 2 then the request contained a statement that the person was accused of the commission of an offence.

15–030 The fourth condition is that a certificate issued by the judicial authority of the territory shows that:

(a) a sentence of imprisonment or another form of detention for a term of four months or greater punishment (the overseas sentence) was imposed on the person in the territory; and
(b) the overseas sentence was imposed on him in respect of:
    (i) the offence specified in the warrant or request; or
    (ii) any other offence committed before his extradition for which he was permitted to be dealt with in the territory.

The fifth condition is that before serving the overseas sentence the person was returned to the UK to serve the remainder of the UK sentence.

If s.187 applies to a person, as soon as practicable after the relevant time he must be brought before the appropriate judge[37] for a decision as to whether the person is to be extradited to the territory in which the overseas sentence was imposed (s.187(1)). The relevant time is the time when the person would otherwise be released from detention pursuant to a UK sentence (whether or not on licence) (s.187(2)). If s.187(1) is not complied with, the person can apply to the judge who must order his discharge (s.187(3)). The person must be treated as continuing in legal custody until he is brought before the appropriate judge under subs.(1) or discharged under subs.(3).

The judge must decide whether the territory which imposed the overseas sentence is a category 1 or 2 territory. If it is a category 1 territory s.188 applies. If it is a category 2 territory, s.189 applies. If it is neither category 1 nor 2 the judge must order the person's discharge (s.187(8)).

A person's discharge under s.187, 188 or 189 does not affect any conditions on which he is released from detention pursuant to the UK sentence (s.186(9)).

RE-EXTRADITION TO CATEGORY 1 TERRITORIES

If s.188 applies, the 2003 Act applies as it would if: 15–031

(a) a Pt 1 warrant had been issued in respect of the person;
(b) the warrant had contained a statement that:
    (i) the person was alleged to be unlawfully at large after conviction of the relevant offence; and
    (ii) the warrant was issued with a view to the person's arrest and extradition to the territory for the purpose of serving a sentence imposed in respect of the relevant offence;
(c) the warrant were issued by the authority of territory which issued the certificate referred to in s.186(5);
(d) the relevant offence were specified in the warrant;
(e) the judge were the appropriate judge for the purposes of Pt 1;
(f) the hearing at which the judge is to make the decision referred to in s.187(1) were the extradition hearing;
(g) the proceedings before the judge were under Pt 1.

The relevant offence is the offence in respect of which the overseas sentence is imposed (s.188(3)).

The 2003 Act will be applied by s.188(1) subject to the modifications in Pt 1 of Sch.1 (s.188(2)).

[37] s.139 applies for determining the appropriate judge. See 8–016.

RE-EXTRADITION TO CATEGORY 2 TERRITORIES

15–032 If s.189 applies, the 2003 Act applies as it would if:

(a) a valid request for the person's extradition to the territory had been made;
(b) the request had contained a statement that the person was alleged to be unlawfully at large after conviction of the relevant offence;
(c) the relevant offence were specified in the request;
(d) the hearing at which the appropriate judge is to make the decision referred to in s.187(1) were the extradition hearing;
(e) the proceedings before the judge were under Pt 2.

The relevant offence is the offence in respect of which the overseas sentence is imposed (s.189(3)).

The 2003 Act will be applied by s.189(1), subject to the modifications in Pt 2 of Sch.1 (s.189(2)).

CHAPTER 16

MATTERS ARISING AFTER EXTRADITION

I. INTRODUCTION

16–001 Most extradition arrangements between the UK and other territories have included speciality protection. They often also prohibit re-extradition without the consent of the UK. Therefore, requests for consent by the UK to allow a person to be dealt with for another offence, or to re-extradite him to another territory, may be received after he has been extradited from the UK. In addition, the 2003 Act makes provision for a person who is extradited whilst serving a sentence in the UK and is then returned to the UK to complete his sentence.

II. PART 1

REQUEST FOR CONSENT TO ANOTHER OFFENCE BEING DEALT WITH

16–002 Section 54 applies if:

(a) a person is extradited to a category 1 territory in respect of an offence; and

(b) the appropriate judge[1] receives a request for consent to the person being dealt with in the territory for another offence; and
(c) the request is certified under this section by the designated authority—NCIS and the Crown Agent of the Crown Office are designated authorities.[2]

The designated authority may certify a request for consent under this section if it believes the authority making the request is a judicial authority of the territory and it has the function of making requests for this type of consent (s.54(2)).[3]

The judge must serve notice on the person that he has received the request for consent unless he is satisfied that it would not be practicable to do so (s.54(4)). The consent hearing[4] must begin within the required period, that is within 21 days of the receipt of the request for consent by the designated authority. The judge may extend the required period, on more than one occasion and after the end of the 21 day period, if he believes that it is in the interests of justice to do so (s.54(6) and (7)). Section 54(8) requires that the judge must refuse consent if the hearing does not begin within the required period and no extension has been allowed by the judge under s.54(6). The judge may at any time adjourn the consent hearing.

The judge must first decide whether consent is required for the person to be dealt with in the territory for the offence for which consent is requested (s.55(1)). Consent is not required if the person has been given an opportunity to leave the territory and has not done so within the permitted period, or if he leaves before the end of the permitted period and then returns to the territory (s.55(8)). The permitted period is 45 days, starting with the day on which the person arrived in the territory following his extradition there in accordance with Pt 1 (s.55(9)). Subject to s.55(8), the judge must decide whether consent is required by reference to what he believes to be the law of the territory or the extradition arrangements between the territory and the UK (s.55(9)).

If consent is not required, the judge will inform the authority making the request (s.55(2)). If consent is required, the judge must decide whether the offence is an extradition offence (s.55(3)).[5] If he finds it is not an extradition offence, the judge must refuse consent (s.55(4)). If the judge finds it is an extradition offence, he must decide whether he would order the person's extradition under ss.11–25 if the person were in the UK and the judge was required to proceed under s.11 for the offence for which consent is requested (s.55(5)).[6] If the judge finds that he would have ordered extradition, he must give consent (s.55(6)). If he finds that he would not have ordered extradition, he must refuse consent (s.55(7)).

1 See 8–016 for definition of the appropriate judge.
2 See Ch.7 at 7–003 for designated authorities.
3 The certificate must certify that the authority making the request is a judicial authority of the territory *and* that it has the function of making this type of request for consent (s.54(3)).
4 The consent hearing is the hearing at which the judge is to consider the request for consent (s.54(10)).
5 See Ch.6 for definition of extradition offence for Pt 1.
6 ss.11–25 are considered in Ch.9.

REQUEST FOR CONSENT TO FURTHER EXTRADITION TO A CATEGORY 1 TERRITORY

Section 56 applies if: 16–003

(a) a person is extradited to a category 1 territory ("the requesting territory") in accordance with Pt 1; and
(b) the appropriate judge receives a request for consent to the person's extradition to another category 1 territory for an offence;
(c) the request is certified under s.56 by the designated authority.[7]

The designated authority may certify a request for consent under this section if it believes the authority making the request is a judicial authority of the territory and it has the function of making requests for this type of consent (s.56(2)).[8]

The judge must serve notice on the person of receipt of the request for consent unless he is satisfied that it would not be practicable to do so (s.56(4)). The consent hearing must begin before the end of the required period. The provisions about the required period are almost identical to those in s.54 discussed at 16–002 above.

Section 57 deals with the questions which must be decided by the judge at the consent hearing and these are equivalent to those in s.55 which will be decided on a request for consent to another offence being dealt with. Section 55 is considered at 16–002 above.

CONSENT TO FURTHER EXTRADITION TO A CATEGORY 2 TERRITORY

If a person has been extradited to a category 1 territory and the Secretary of State receives a request from the category 1 territory for consent to the person's extradition to a category 2 territory for an offence, the Secretary of State will decide whether to give consent under s.58. This is considered in Ch.12 at 12–004. 16–004

RETURN OF PERSON TO SERVE REMAINDER OF SENTENCE

Section 59 applies if a person who is serving a sentence of imprisonment or another form of detention in the UK is extradited to a category 1 territory in accordance with Pt 1, and is then returned to the UK to serve the remainder of his sentence. The person is liable to be detained in pursuance of his sentence on his return (s.59(2)). If he is at large, he must be treated as being unlawfully at large (s.59(3)). The period of time when the person was not in the UK as a result of his extradi- 16–005

7 NCIS and the Crown Agent of the Crown Office are designated authorities, see Ch.7 at 7–003.

8 The certificate must certify that the authority making the request is a judicial authority of the territory *and* that it has the function of making this type of request for consent (s.56(3)).

tion does not count as time served by him as part of his sentence (s.59(4)). However, s.59(4) does not apply if:

(a) the person was extradited for the purpose of being prosecuted for an offence; and
(b) the person has not been convicted of the offence or any other offence in respect of which he was permitted to be dealt with in the category 1 territory (s.59(5)).

If s.59(5) applies, time during which the person was not in the UK as a result of his extradition counts as time served as part of his sentence if (and only if) it was time spent in custody in connection with the offence or any other offence in respect of which he was permitted to be dealt with in the territory (s.59(6)).

III. PART 2

CONSENT TO OTHER OFFENCE BEING DEALT WITH

16–006 If a person has been extradited to a category 2 territory and the Secretary of State receives a request for consent to the person being dealt with for an offence other than the offence in respect of which he was extradited, this will be dealt with under s.129. This is part of the Secretary of State's role and is considered in Ch.12 at 12–024.

CONSENT TO FURTHER EXTRADITION TO CATEGORY 2 TERRITORY

16–007 The Secretary of State will consider any request for re-extradition to another category 2 territory if a person has already been extradited to a category 2 territory. This is considered in Ch.12 at 12–025.

CONSENT TO FURTHER EXTRADITION TO CATEGORY 1 TERRITORY

16–008 Similarly the Secretary of State will consider any request for re-extradition to a category 1 territory if a person has already been extradited to a category 2 territory. This is considered in Ch.12 at 12–026.

RETURN OF PERSON TO SERVE REMAINDER OF SENTENCE

16–009 Section 132 applies if a person who is serving a sentence of imprisonment or another form of detention in the UK is extradited to a category 2 territory in accordance with Pt 2, and is then returned to the UK to serve the remainder of his sentence. The provisions in s.132 dealing with the person's liability to detention and any reduction of his sentence by virtue of time spent in custody in the category 2 territory are equivalent to those in s.59, considered at 16–005 above.

PART C

POLICE POWERS

CHAPTER 17

POLICE POWERS

I. INTRODUCTION

FRAMEWORK DIRECTIVE AND UK / US EXTRADITION TREATY 2003

17–001 The UK may have obligations to other territories to search for and, if found, transmit property connected to the alleged extradition offence. These obligations will be contained in the relevant extradition treaty or, in the case of EU Member States, in the Framework Decision.

Article 29 of the Framework Decision provides for the seizure and transmission of property.

> "(1) At the request of the issuing judicial authority or on its own initiative, the executing judicial authority shall, in accordance with its national law, seize and hand over property which
>
> (a) may be required as evidence; or
> (b) has been acquired by the requested person as a result of the offence.
>
> (2) The property referred to in paragraph 1 shall be handed over even if the European arrest warrant cannot be carried out owing to the death or escape of the requested person.
>
> (3) If the property referred to in paragraph 1 is liable to seizure or confiscation in the territory of the executing Member State, the latter may, if the property is needed in connection with pending criminal proceedings, temporarily retain it or hand it over to the issuing Member State on the condition that it is returned.
>
> (4) Any rights which the executing Member State or third parties may have acquired in the property referred to in paragraph 1 shall be preserved. Where such rights exist, the issuing Member State shall return the property without charge to the executing Member State as soon as the criminal proceedings have been terminated."

Article 16 of the UK/US Extradition Treaty 2003[1] contains similar provisions to Art.29 of the Framework Decision:

> "(1) To the extent permitted under its law, the Requested State may seize and surrender to the Requesting State all items in whatever form, and assets, including proceeds, that are connected with the offence in respect of which extradition is granted. The items and assets mentioned in this Article may be surrendered even when the extradition can not be effected due to the death, disappearance or escape of the person sought.

[1] Cm.5821; App.C–007.

(2) The Requested State may condition the surrender of the items upon satisfactory assurances from the Requesting State that the property will be returned to the Requested State as soon as practicable. The Requested State may also defer the surrender of such items if they are needed as evidence in the Requested State."

Both provisions oblige the UK to seize and surrender items only to the extent permitted by UK domestic law. There may be similar obligations contained in extradition arrangements between the UK and other territories.

THE 1989 ACT

Section 8(6) of the 1989 Act contained the only provision in that Act for issuing a search warrant in extradition proceedings.[2] However, it was limited in its application and a search warrant could only be issued by a justice of the peace in the UK[3] if the extradition offence was alleged to be stealing or receiving stolen property in designated Commonwealth countries and colonies. In these circumstances, the justice of the peace had the same power to issue a search warrant for the property as would have existed if the offence had been committed in the UK. **17–002**

POLICE AND CRIMINAL EVIDENCE ACT 1984

The Police and Criminal Evidence Act 1984 ("the 1984 Act") provided powers for domestic criminal investigations. It is divided into a number of Parts which include: **17–003**

Pt II Powers of entry, search and seizure;
Pt III Arrest;
Pt IV Detention; and
Pt V Questioning and treatment of persons by police.

The provisions in this Act codified many pre-existing powers and also provided new powers.

ARREST WARRANT ISSUED UNDER THE 1989 ACT

If an arrest warrant issued under the 1989 Act did not fulfil the criteria in s.8(6) of that Act, problems arose. It was unclear what powers, either common law or statutory, the police had to search for and seize property when affecting an arrest. **17–004**

[2] This section replicated powers found in the previous extradition legislation; for example, s.6(5) of the Fugitive Offenders Act 1967.

[3] In Scotland, a sheriff had an equivalent power to the justice of the peace.

This issue was considered by the House of Lords in *R. (on the application of Rottman) v Commissioner of Police for the Metropolis.*[4] In that case, it was submitted that Rottman's rights under Art.8 of the ECHR had been infringed because his house was searched following his arrest in the driveway of this property. The German government had made a request for extradition and a provisional warrant for Rottman's arrest had been issued under the 1989 Act. The police had entered his house after arresting him and searched the property before seizing a number of items.

The police submitted that there was a common law power which entitled them to carry out this search, and that the common law power had survived the enactment of the 1984 Act; secondly, and in the alternative, that the powers in ss.18, 19 and 32 of that Act extended to cases where the offence in question was not alleged to have been committed in the UK.

The court held that s.18 did not apply because the arrestable offence referred to in s.18 was defined in s.24; this definition would not encompass the extradition crime alleged against the defendant in Germany.[5]

The House of Lords followed and approved the decision in *R. v Southwark Crown Court and HM Customs and Excise Ex p. Sorsky Defries*,[6] in which the Divisional Court held that the words in s.19(3)(a) of the 1984 Act "any other offence", were confined to domestic offences; in the absence of an express provision to the contrary the word "offence" in a statute meant a domestic offence.[7] Therefore, ss.19 and 32 of the 1984 Act did not apply to an offence in another territory.[8]

The House then considered whether a common law power of search existed and, if it did, whether it had survived the enactment of the 1984 Act. This issue was considered in *R. v Governor of Pentonville Prison Ex p. Osman.*[9] The court considered that for domestic offences a police officer had a power when lawfully arresting a person to take any goods or documents which he reasonably believed to be material evidence in relation to the crime for which the defendant was being arrested.[10] In *Osman*, the court held that there was no difference between the common law search and seizure powers available to the police in the execution of a domestic arrest warrant and those available in respect of a provisional extradition arrest warrant. In *Rottman*, Lord Hope considered *Osman* and concluded: "Therefore before PACE came into operation I am of the opinion that the police had power under common law, after arresting a person in his house or in the grounds of his house pursuant to section 8(1)(b) of [the 1989 Act], to search the house and seize articles which they

4 [2002] 2 All E.R. 865.
5 *ibid.* at 887.
6 [1996] Crim. L.R. 195.
7 *R. v Cox* [1961]3 All E.R. 1194 and [1963] A.C. 48; *Air India v Wiggins* [1980] 2 All E.R. 593; *Macleod v A-G for New South Wales* [1891] A.C. 455.
8 Lord Hutton, *ibid.* at 887–8.
9 [1990] 1 W.L.R. 277.
10 *ibid.* at 311. See *Ghani v Jones* [1969] 3 All E.R. 1700 at 1703. Although this case concerned a search without warrant, Lord Denning M.R. considered the position where a search had been carried out after a lawful arrest.

reasonably believed to be material evidence in relation to the crime for which they had arrested that person."[11]

Lord Hope considered that the correct question was not whether the 1984 Act saved this common law power, but whether it extinguished it. "It is a well-established principle that a rule of the common law is not extinguished by a statute unless the statute makes this clear by express provision or clear implication."[12] Therefore, the court found that this common law power survived the enactment of the 1984 Act; the search and seizure of the property did not constitute a violation of the defendant's Art.8 right. It was in accordance with the law, and the power was proportionate in that it could only be exercised after an arrest warrant has been issued for an extradition crime, which itself could only take place if evidence had been produced which would justify the issuing of a domestic arrest warrant if a person had been accused of a similar domestic offence.[13]

The scope of the surviving common law power was considered in *Hewitson v Chief Constable of Dorset Police*.[14] It was accepted, on behalf of the Chief Constable, that the common law authorities were not wide enough to cover the circumstances of the search in that case. The relevant features were:

(a) the physical separation of the location of arrest and the premises which were searched;
(b) the lapse of time between the arrest and the search; and
(c) the tenuous nature of the link between the person arrested and the premises searched.

It was submitted on behalf of the Chief Constable that there should be an extension of the common powers to cover these circumstances. The court considered that to allow this extension would involve a substantial leap rather than an incremental development of the common law. The police had acted unlawfully in carrying out the search.

PART 4 OF THE 2003 ACT

Part 4 now provides a statutory basis for search and seizure and, together with any additional common law powers, it will limit the ability of the UK to comply with any obligations it has to other territories as part of its extradition arrangements (see 17–001 above). Part 4 also deals with the treatment of a person following his arrest under Pt 1 or 2 of the 2003 Act. Before this Act, it was unclear whether the Codes of Practice issued under the 1984 Act for domestic arrests would apply to a person arrested and detained pursuant to a warrant issued under extradition legislation. **17–005**

[11] *ibid.* at 885.
[12] *per* Lord Hope, *ibid.* at 890.
[13] *per* Lord Hope, *ibid.* at 891.
[14] [2003] EWHC 3296 (Admin).

Part 4 contains:

(a) ss.156-160, which allow for the issuing of warrants and production orders;
(b) ss.161-165, which provide powers of search and seizure which are exercisable without a warrant; and
(c) ss.166-171, which deal with treatment of a person after arrest.

Section 172 provides for the delivery of seized property to the requesting territory and s.174 defines a number of terms used in Pt 4.

Many of these provisions are modelled on the equivalent powers for domestic offences which are found in the 1984 Act.

CODES OF PRACTICE

17–006 Section 173 requires the Secretary of State to issue codes of practice which deal with:

(a) the exercise of the powers in Pt 4;
(b) the retention, use and return of anything seized or produced under Pt 4;
(c) access to, photographing or copying of material seized or produced; and
(d) the retention, use, disclosure and destruction of fingerprints, samples or photographs taken under Pt 4.

The Secretary of State issued codes of practice in draft to allow a consultation process, and the codes were then amended in light of responses received.[15] The "Extradition Act 2003: Codes of Practice"[16] ("the 2003 Codes") came into operation on January 1, 2004.[17] Paragraph 1.5 of the Introduction to the 2003 Codes makes clear that, where they are silent, police officers should refer to the relevant domestic provisions in the 1984 Act Codes of Practice ("1984 Act Codes").[18] The 2003 Codes cross-refer to the 1984 Act Codes where the procedures in extradition cases are identical to those for domestic cases. There are no powers under the 2003 Act to stop and search, or to conduct interviews, and so the 2003 Codes contain no equivalent to the 1984 Act Codes A and E.

The 2003 Codes apply to police officers operating in England, Wales and Northern Ireland and customs officers operating throughout the UK (para.1.12, Introduction, 2003 Codes).

A failure of a constable to comply with a provision of the 2003 Codes does not of itself make him liable to criminal or civil proceedings (s.173(6)). The 2003 Codes are

[15] This is required by s.173(2).

[16] *www.homeoffice.gov.uk/docs2.extradition.html.*

[17] art.2, the Extradition Act 2003 (Police Powers: Codes of Practice) Order 2003 (SI 2003/3336). Section 173 gives the Secretary of State power to amend the whole or any part of the Codes.

[18] The revised edition of the 1984 Act Codes of Practice is effective as of July 31, 2003. Further revisions to these Codes are proposed following a joint review by the Home Office and Cabinet Office. *www.homeoffice.gov.uk/crimpol/police/system/pacecodes.html.*

admissible in evidence in proceedings under the 2003 Act and must be taken into account by a court if the court believes it is relevant to a question the court is deciding (s.173(7)).

ARREST

On arrest a person will hear the caution: "You do not have to say anything, but anything you do say may be given in evidence."[19] The officer must take all reasonable steps to ensure that the person understands that he is being arrested and why. The custody officer will assess the need for an interpreter on arrival at the police station[20] and, if necessary, the process of arrest can be repeated with an interpreter present.[21] **17–007**

SEARCHES

Paragraph 1.3 of 2003, Code B sets out a very important limitation on the exercise of the powers of search under the 2003 Act: **17–008**

> "Searches conducted under powers in the Extradition Act 2003 (the Act) may only be undertaken for the purpose of obtaining evidence of the extradition offence for use in the prosecution of the person accused of the extradition offence. Officers may not investigate crimes on behalf of the requesting authority or territory, other than to speak to persons for the purpose of assisting establishing ownership or connection to property. Items relating to a person's identity and offences other than the extradition offence may, if found, be seized in accordance with the provisions of the Act and this Code. Police powers in respect of offences committed in the UK are not limited by this paragraph."

REASONABLE FORCE

Section 209 allows a person to use reasonable force, if necessary, in exercising a power under Pt 4. Paragraph 1.5 of the 2003 Code B also provides that reasonable force should only be used when it is proportionate to the circumstances. **17–009**

HUMAN RIGHTS ACT 1998

Paragraph 1.4 of 2003 Code B refers to the right to privacy and personal property as key principles of the Human Rights Act 1998. "Powers of entry, search and seizure should be fully and clearly justified before use, because they may significantly inter- **17–010**

[19] para.2.1, 2003 Code C. However, minor variations in the wording will not constitute a breach of the 2003 Codes providing the sense is preserved (para.2.2).

[20] para.4.3, 2003, Code C.

[21] para.2.6, 2003, Code C.

fere with an individual's privacy. Officers should consider whether the necessary objectives can be met by less intrusive means."[22]

EXTENT

17–011 Section 226 restricts the application of various sections in Pt 4 to different parts of the UK.

CUSTOMS OFFICERS AND SERVICE POLICEMEN

17–012 Section 174 allows the Treasury to make an order authorising customs officers to perform the function of police officers given in Pt 4 with any necessary modifications specified in the order.

Section 175 allows the Secretary of State to make an order authorising members of the services' police forces to perform the functions of police officers given in this Pt 4 with any necessary modifications specified in the order.

II. DEFINITIONS

17–013 Section 174 provides definitions for terms used in Pt 4. These definitions refer to the following legislation:

- Police and Criminal Evidence Act 1984 ("the 1984 Act");
- Police and Criminal Evidence (Northern Ireland) Order 1989[23] ("the 1989 Order"); and
- Proceeds of Crime Act 2002 ("the 2002 Act").

EXTRADITION ARREST POWER

17–013A Section 174(2) explains that an "extradition arrest power" is the power of arrest or provisional arrest given in Pts 1 and 2 of the 2003 Act.

EXCLUDED MATERIAL

17–014 In England and Wales "excluded material" has the same meaning given by s.11 of the 1984 Act (s.174(3)).

Section 11 provides that "excluded material" consists of three categories of material held in confidence:

[22] See further Ch.11.
[23] SI 1989/1341 (NI 12).

(a) personal records (as defined in s.12 of the 1984 Act);
(b) samples of human tissue or tissue fluid taken for the purpose of diagnosis or medical treatment; and
(c) journalistic material (as defined in s.13 of the 1984 Act).

Section 11(2) and (3) defines when these three classes of material are held in confidence.

In Northern Ireland "excluded material" has the meaning given by Art.13 of the 1989 Order which is in similar terms to s.11 of the 1984 Act.

ITEMS SUBJECT TO LEGAL PRIVILEGE

"Items subject to legal privilege" has the meaning given by s.10 of the 1984 Act in England and Wales. This encompasses: **17–015**

(a) communications between a professional legal adviser and his client or any person representing his client made in the connection with the giving of legal advice to the client;
(b) communications between a professional legal adviser and his client or any person representing his client or between the adviser, client, any person representing the client and any other person made in connection with or in contemplation of legal proceedings and for the purposes of such proceedings; and
(c) items enclosed with or referred to in such communications and made
    (i) in connection with the giving of legal advice; or
    (ii) in connection with or in contemplation of legal proceedings and for the purposes of such proceedings, when they are in the possession of a person who is entitled to possession of them (s.10(1)).[24]

Items held with the intention of furthering a criminal purpose are not items subject to legal privilege by virtue of s.10(2) of the 1984 Act.[25] This section has been held to be capable of referring to the intention not of a legal advisor, nor even of the client, but of the third party who provided the funds to the client, with the result that the documents held innocently by the solicitor remained outside the protection of privilege if that third party's intention was criminal or fraudulent.[26]

[24] For case law considering the ambit of legal professional privilege see *R. v Derby Magistrates Court Ex p. B* [1996] A.C. 487; *Balabel v Air India* [1988] Ch.317; *Nederlandse Reassurantie Groep Holding NV Bacon & Woodrow* [1995] 1 All E.R. 976; *Three Rivers District Council v The Governor and Company of the Bank of England* [2003] EWCA Civ 474 and [2004] EWCA Civ 218 (subject to appeal to the House of Lords at the time of writing); *USA v Philip Morris Inc* [2004] EWCA Civ 330.

[25] Se *R. v Cox & Railton* (1884) 14 Q.B.D. 153; *R. v Central Criminal Court Ex p. Francis & Francis (the firm)* [1989] A.C. 346; *Bullivant v Attorney General for Victoria* [1901] A.C. 196; *Finers v Miro* [1991] 1 W.L.R. 35.

[26] *R. v Central Criminal Court Ex p. Francis & Francis (the firm)* [1989] A.C. 346.

In Scotland this phrase has the meaning given by s.412 of the 2002 Act:

> "'legal privilege' means protection in legal proceedings from disclosure, by virtue of any rule of law relating to confidentiality of communications; and 'items subject to legal privilege' are —
>
> (a) communications between a professional legal adviser and his client, or
> (b) communications made in connection with or in contemplation of legal proceedings and for the purposes of those proceedings,
>
> which would be so protected."

In Northern Ireland it has the meaning given by art.12 of the 1989 Order which is in identical terms to s.10 of the 1984 Act.

Paragraph 2.3 of the 2003 Code B makes it clear that the principle of legal privilege applies equally to material that has originated or been sent from abroad. The definition of "items subject to legal privilege" in the Glossary to the 2003 Codes is wholly unhelpful and inaccurate: "Communications between a professional legal adviser and the client that is concerned with the proceedings. Anything held with the intention of furthering a criminal cause is not covered." It is not even clear from this what proceedings are being referred to; it is possible that an officer will interpret this as meaning the extradition proceedings in the UK. Since the 2003 Codes provide guidance for officers who will be carrying out searches, it is to be hoped that the Codes are amended as soon as possible to give an accurate and helpful definition. This will avoid the disturbing prospect that legally privileged material will be seized and retained owing to a misunderstanding of the definition of "items subject to legal privilege".

PREMISES

17–016 Section 174(5) gives "premises" the meaning in s.23 of the 1984 Act in England and Wales. This covers any place, including any vehicle, vessel, aircraft, hovercraft, offshore installation,[27] tent or movable structure.

In Scotland, this term has the meaning given by s.412 of the 2002 Act, which is in identical terms to s.23.

In Northern Ireland, it is as defined in art.25 of the 1989 Order, which is identical to s.23.

SPECIAL PROCEDURE MATERIAL

17–017 "Special procedure material" has the meaning given in s.14 of the 1984 Act in England and Wales (s.174(6)). This is material which is neither "excluded materials" nor "items subject to legal privilege", but which is held in a professional or

[27] As defined by s.1 of the Mineral Working (Offshore Installations) Act 1971.

official capacity. Section 14 of the 1984 Act contains detailed provisions dealing with employees and associated companies. The material must also be held subject to an implied[28] or express undertaking to hold it in confidence or subject to an obligation of secrecy.

In Northern Ireland this term has the meaning given by art.16 of the 1989 Order.

OTHER TERMS

Other terms used in Pt 4 have the meanings given by s.65 of the 1984 Act in England and Wales (s.174(7)–(8)).[29] 17–018

"Appropriate consent" is:

- the person's own consent (if he has reached the age of 17 years);
- the person's consent and his parent or guardian's consent (if he has reached 14 but is not yet 17);
- the consent of the person's parent or guardian (if he is not yet 14).

The term "fingerprints" includes palm prints.

An "intimate search" is a search consisting of the physical examination of a person's body orifices other than the mouth.

A "non-intimate sample" means a sample of hair other than pubic hair, a sample taken from a nail or under a nail, a swab taken from the body (but not an orifice), a footprint or other such impression (but not of the hand).

III. WARRANTS AND ORDERS

2003 CODE B

Before making an application for a search and seizure warrant or a production order, 17–019
an officer must take reasonable steps to check that the information given by the requesting authority or territory is accurate, recent and not provided maliciously or irresponsibly.[30] Applications must be supported by a signed written authority from an officer of at least inspector rank or, if the case is urgent, the next most senior officer on duty.[31]

[28] See *Gilbert v Star Newspapers Ltd* (1984) 11 T.L.R. 4; *Talbot v General Television Corp Pty Ltd* [1981] RPC 1; *Fraser v Thames Television Ltd* [1984] Q.B. 44; *Coco v AN Clark (Engineers) Ltd* [1969] R.P.C. 41 at 47.

[29] In Northern Ireland these terms have the meanings given by art.53 of the 1989 Order which is in similar terms to s.65 of the 1984 Act.

[30] para.3.1, 2003 Code B

[31] para.3.4, 2003 Code B

Paragraph 7.7 refers to an officer's statutory obligation to retain an original document or other article only when a photograph or copy would not be sufficient.[32] Material seized in relation to an extradition offence should only be retained until:

(a) the person is ordered to be extradited and the extradition proceedings are completed; or
(b) the person is discharged; or
(c) the extradition request is refused or withdrawn; or
(d) it is determined that the material is no longer required for the prosecution of the extradition offence.[33]

ISSUING AND EXECUTION OF SEARCH WARRANTS: SS.15 AND 16 OF THE 1984 ACT

17–020 Sections 15 and 16 contain general safeguards governing the issue and execution of search warrants. Section 15(1) makes clear that this section and s.16 "have effect in relation to the issue to constables under any enactment contained in any Act passed after this Act, of warrants to enter and search premises, and an entry on or search of premises under a warrant is unlawful unless it complies with" these sections. Therefore, these provisions apply to and govern the execution of a warrant to enter and search premises under the 2003 Act and non-compliance with these sections render entry and search unlawful.

Under s.15, a constable on applying for a warrant is under a duty:

(a) to state the ground on which the application is made and the enactment under which the warrant would be issued;
(b) to specify the premises[34] to be entered and searched;
(c) to identify, as far as practicable, the articles or the persons to be sought.

The application should be made *ex parte* and be supported by an information in writing. The constable must answer on oath any question put by the justice of the peace hearing the application.

The warrant must only authorise entry on one occasion and shall:

(a) specify the name of the person applying for it, the date it was issued, the enactment under which it was issued and the premises to be searched; and
(b) shall identify, as far as practicable, the article or the person to be sought.[35]

Two copies, clearly certified as copies, must be made of the warrant.

[32] s.22(4) of the 1984 Act.
[33] para.7.16, 2003 Code B.
[34] A search warrant must relate to premises and it can never authorise a search for material wherever it may be found: *R. v Chief Constable of Warwickshire Constabulary Ex p. Fitzpatrick*[1998] 1 All E.R. 65 at 71.
[35] The court does not necessarily require great precision. See *IRC v Rossminster* [1980] A.C. 952, HL.

Section 16 of the 1984 Act governs the execution of a warrant. The warrant may be executed by any constable and may authorise persons to accompany a constable executing the warrant. The warrant must be executed within one month from the date of issue at a reasonable hour unless the purposes of the search would, in the opinion of the constable, be frustrated by entry at a reasonable hour. If the occupier of the premises, or some other person who appears to the constable to be in charge of the premises, is present when the warrant is executed, the constable must:

(a) identify himself and, if not in uniform, produce documentary evidence he is a constable; and
(b) produce and supply a copy of the warrant.

If there is no person present who appears to the constable to be in charge of the premises, he must leave a copy of the warrant in a prominent place in the premises.

Any search must only be to the extent that it is required for the purpose for which the warrant was issued. A constable executing a warrant must endorse it, stating whether the articles or persons sought were found and whether any articles were seized other than the articles which were sought.

A warrant which has been executed or has not been executed within the time allowed for execution must be returned to:

(a) the chief executive of the petty sessions area of the justice of the peace who issued it; or
(b) if it was issued by a judge, to the appropriate officer of the court from which it was issued.

The returned warrant must be retained for 12 months from its return, and if the occupier of the premises asks to inspect it during this period, he must be allowed to do so.

SEARCH AND SEIZURE WARRANTS

Section 156 of the 2003 Act sets out the procedure for the application for and issue of a search and seizure warrant in an extradition case. **17–021**

A justice of the peace has the power to issue a search and seizure warrant, on the application of a constable, if he is satisfied that the requirements in s.156 are met (s.156(1)).

The application for a search and seizure warrant must state that the warrant is sought in connection with the extradition of a person under Pt 1 or 2. It must also specify the premises, the material (or a description of the material) for which the warrant is sought, and that the specified material is believed to be on the premises (s.156(2)).

The application must also state that the person is accused of a specified extradition offence[36] in a specified category 1 or 2 territory (s.156(3)–(4)).

A search and seizure warrant authorises a constable[37] to enter and search the specified premises and to seize and retain any material falling in s.156(6) found there. Material may be seized if it would be likely to be admissible evidence at a trial in the UK for the specified offence assuming that the offence would constitute an offence in the UK (s.156(6)). However, the material must not include anything that is subject to legal privilege, excluded material or special procedure material (see 17–013 *et seq.* above).

Before a search and seizure warrant is issued there must be reasonable grounds to believe that:

- (a) the specified offence has been committed by the person named;
- (b) that person is in or on his way to the UK;
- (c) the offence in question is an extradition offence, in accordance with the definition given either in s.64, for Pt 1, or s.137, for Pt 2, as appropriate; and
- (d) there is material within s.156(6) on the premises (s.156(8)).

In addition, there must be reasonable grounds for believing that one of the conditions in s.156(9) applies. The conditions are:

- (a) that it is not practicable to communicate with someone who is entitled to allow entry to the premises;
- (b) that it is not practicable to communicate with a person entitled to give access to the material in question;
- (c) that permission to enter the premises will not be given without a warrant; or
- (d) that the purpose of a search may be frustrated or seriously prejudiced unless immediate entry to the premises can be secured.

It does not have to be shown that other methods of obtaining the material have been tried unsuccessfully.[38] The justice considering the application must himself be satisfied that there are reasonable grounds for believing that all the necessary conditions are met and can not simply rely on the assertions of the police officer applying for the warrant.[39]

Section 156(10) makes the necessary modifications for this section to apply in Scotland.

PRODUCTION ORDERS

17–022 Section 157 outlines the procedure for applying for a production order in an extradition case.

[36] See Ch.6.

[37] para.3.7(g) of the 2003 Code B envisages that the application for the warrant may include a provision for the constable executing it to be accompanied by other persons. See also paras 3.13–3.14.

[38] See the reasoning of the court considering an application under s.8 of the 1984 Act in *R. v Billericay Justices and Dobbyn Ex p. Frank Harris (Coaches) Ltd* [1991] Crim. L.R. 472.

[39] *cf. R. v Guildhall Magistrates' Court Ex p. Primlaks Holdings Co (Panama) Inc* [1989] 2 W.L.R. 841.

A judge may make a production order, on the application of a constable, if he is satisfied that the requirements in this section and s.158 are met. In England and Wales this power is given to a circuit judge and in Northern Ireland to a Crown Court Judge (s.157(8)).

The application must state that the production order is sought in connection with the extradition of a person under Pt 1 or 2 of the 2003 Act. It must also specify the premises and the material for which the order is sought. It must state that this material is special procedure material or excluded material (see 17–013 *et seq.* above). It must also state that the person specified in the application appears to be in possession or control of the material (s.157(2)).

In addition, the application must state that the person is accused of a specified extradition offence in a specified category 1 or 2 territory (s.157(3)–(4)).

Section 158 specifies the conditions to be met for a production order to be made.

There must be reasonable grounds to believe that:

(a) the offence in question has been committed by the person named;
(b) that person is in or on his way to the UK;
(c) the offence in question is an extradition offence as defined in s.64 (for Pt 1) or s.137 (for Pt 2);
(d) there is material which is special procedure material or excluded material on the premises involved; and
(e) the material would be likely to be admissible evidence at a trial in the UK for the specified offence assuming that the offence would constitute an offence in the UK (s.158(2)).[40]

Considering Sch.1 of the 1984 Act, which provides a similar power for domestic offences, the Divisional Court made it clear that there must be reasonable grounds for belief, not merely suspicion, and that the material sought must not merely be general information which might be helpful to police enquiries but evidence which would be "relevant and admissible" at a trial.[41]

In addition, it must appear to the judge that other ways of obtaining the material have already failed or other ways of obtaining the material have not been tried because they were bound to fail (s.158(4)).

Finally, an overarching test is that it must be in the public interest that the material should be produced, or that access to it should be given (s.158(5)).

If all of the requirements for the application are met, and the judge is satisfied that the conditions in s.158 are fulfilled, he may make a production order.

A production order requires the person named in the application to hand over the

[40] The judge must be personally satisfied that reasonable grounds exist for believing that these conditions are met. *Cf. R. v Guildhall Magistrates' Court Ex p. Primlaks Holdings Co (Panama) Inc* [1989] 2 W.L.R. 841.

[41] *R. v Central Criminal Court Ex p. Bright* [2001] 2 All E.R. 244 at 260.

material described in the order for a police constable[42] to take away, or requiring this person to allow the constable access to the material, within a specified period (s.157(5)). This period must be seven days unless the judge making the order considers that a longer period is appropriate (s.157(6)). Production orders have effect as court orders and so it is a contempt of court to fail to comply with an order (s.157(7)).

If material specified in an application for a production order is held in electronic form, the material must be produced (or a constable given access to it) in a form in which it is visible and legible[43] (s.159).

The following principles should also apply to applications for a production order under the 2003 Act; they are derived from the authorities considering the equivalent provisions for domestic offences in the 1984 Act.

A person making an application must observe the basic principle that me must disclose to the court all the material it needs to make a decision including anything which might suggest that an order should not be made.[44] This is especially important as such applications are usually made without notice. However, it is always preferable for applications which concern special procedure material to be made *inter partes*. The courts have frequently emphasised that this procedure is a serious inroad into the liberty of the subject and it is the responsibility of the court to ensure that the procedure is not abused.[45]

WARRANTS: SPECIAL PROCEDURE MATERIAL AND EXCLUDED MATERIAL

17–023 Section 160 sets out the procedure governing the application for and issue of a search and seizure warrant relating to special procedure material or excluded material in an extradition case.

A judge[46] may, on the application of a police constable, issue a warrant if he is satisfied that the requirements for issuing a production order are fulfilled[47] and one of the following additional conditions in s.160(8) is met:

(a) it is not practicable to communicate with a person entitled to grant entry to the premises;
(b) it is not practicable to communicate with a person entitled to give access to the material in question; or

42 para.3.9(i) of the 2003 Code B envisages that the application for the order may include a provision for the constable executing it to be accompanied by other persons. See also paras 3.13–3.14.
43 The phrase "visible and legible" is also used in s.20 of the 1984 Act which deals with information stored in an electronic form. See also para.7.6 of Code B of the 1984 Act Codes.
44 *R. v Lewes Crown Court Ex p. Hill* (1990) 93 Cr. App. R. 60.
45 *R. v Southampton Crown Court Ex p. J and P* [1993] Crim. L.R. 962; *R. v Lewes Crown Court Ex p. Hill* (1990) 93 Cr. App. R. 60; *R. v Central Criminal Court Ex p. Bright* [2001] 2 All E.R. 244.
46 A circuit judge in England and Wales and a Crown Court judge in Northern Ireland (s.160(9)).
47 See 17–022 above.

(c) the material includes information classified as restricted or secret by statute and that it is likely to be disclosed in breach of that classification.

The application must state that the warrant is sought in connection with extradition of a person under Pt 1 or 2 of the 2003 Act. It must also specify the premises and the special procedure material or excluded material for which the warrant is sought (s.160(2)). In addition, the application must state that the person is accused of a specified extradition offence in a specified category 1 or 2 territory (s.160(3)–(4)).

A warrant under s.160 authorises a constable[48] to enter and search the specified premises. He may seize and retain any special procedure material and/or excluded material, subject to subs.(6), if the application states that the warrant is sought in relation to such material (s.160(5)). Material can only be seized and retained if it would be likely to be admissible evidence at a trial in the UK for the specified offence assuming that the offence would constitute an offence in the UK (s.160(6)).

ENTRY AND SEARCH OF PREMISES FOR PURPOSES OF ARREST

Section 161 gives a police constable the power to enter and search premises to effect arrest. **17–024**

If a police constable has the power to arrest a person under an extradition arrest power,[49] he may enter and search any premises to exercise this power (s.161(1)–(2)). However, he must have reasonable grounds for believing that the person is on the premises and the power to search is allowed only insofar as it is reasonably necessary to effect arrest (s.161(2)–(3)).

A constable may then seize and retain anything which is on the premises where he has reasonable grounds to believe:

(a) that is has been obtained as the result of an offence or is evidence of an offence (including offences committed outside the UK); and
(b) that it is necessary to seize it to avoid it being concealed, lost, damaged, altered or destroyed (s.161(4)–(5)).

If the premises include multiple dwellings (for example, a block of flats), s.161(6) restricts the power of entry and search. A constable is only allowed to enter and search the communal areas of the premises and any dwelling where he has reasonable grounds to believe the person sought might be.

[48] para.3.11(h) of the 2003 Code B envisages that the application for the warrant may include a provision for the constable executing it to be accompanied by other persons. See also paras 3.13.–3.14.

[49] See 17–013 above for the definition of an extradition arrest power.

ENTRY AND SEARCH OF PREMISES ON ARREST

17–025 Section 162 applies if a person has been arrested under an extradition arrest power at any place other than a police station.

A police constable may enter and search any premises where the person was at the time of arrest or immediately before arrest if he has reasonable grounds to believe that there is evidence on the premises of the relevant offence (in accusation cases) or of the person's identity (in all cases) (s.162(2)). "Evidence" in this context does not include items subject to legal privilege.

The relevant offence is one on the basis of which a Pt 1 warrant has been or will be issued, or on the basis of which extradition has been or will be formally requested under Pt 2 (s.162(3)).

A police constable may search premises only for evidence (which does not include items subject to legal privilege) relating to the relevant offence, in accusation cases, and the person's identity (s.162(4)). This power may be exercised only to the extent that it is reasonably necessary to find such evidence and s.162(6) allows the seizure and retention of any evidence satisfying the description in s.162(4).

After entering premises in exercise of this power, a constable may also seize and retain anything he finds there if he has reasonable grounds to believe:

(a) that it has been obtained as the result of an offence or is evidence of an offence (including offences committed outside the UK); and
(b) that it is necessary to seize it to prevent it being concealed, lost, damaged, altered or destroyed (s.162(7)–(8)).

If the premises in question include multiple dwellings, a constable is allowed to enter and search only the communal areas of the premises and any dwelling where the arrest took place, or in which the person was immediately before arrest (s.162(9)).

SEARCH OF PERSON ON ARREST

17–026 S.163 gives a police constable power to search a person on arrest under an extradition arrest power unless the arrest takes place at a police station.

A police constable is allowed to search the person if he reasonably believes that the person could be a danger to himself or anyone else (s.163(2)). The constable may also seize and retain anything he finds as a result of this search if he reasonably believes that the person might use it to cause physical injury to himself or another person (s.163(6)).

A police constable is also allowed to search the person if he reasonably believes that the person may have something concealed on him that:

(a) might be used to assist him to escape from custody; or
(b) might be evidence relating to an offence or the person's identity (s.163(3)).

A police constable may use the power to search a person under subs. (3) only for anything described in that subsection and only so far as is reasonably necessary to find any such thing (s.163(4)). The police constable has power to seize and retain anything found during such a search if he has reasonable grounds for believing that the person might use the item to assist in an escape from custody, that the item is evidence of an offence or of the person's identity, or that it has been obtained as the result of an offence (s.163(7)).

The search powers under s.163(2) and (3) are not unlimited. The constable may not require a person to remove in public any clothes other than an outer coat, jacket or gloves (s.163(5)). However, the constable is allowed to conduct a search of the person's mouth.

The provisions of this s. do not affect the powers of a police constable to search a person suspected of terrorist offences under s.43 of the Terrorism Act 2000 (s.163(9)).

Guidance on the application of this search power is provided by paras 4.3–4.11 of 2003 Code B.

ENTRY AND SEARCH OF PREMISES AFTER ARREST

Section 164 applies if a person has been arrested under an extradition arrest power. 17–027

A constable may enter and search premises occupied or controlled by the arrested person if he has reasonable grounds for suspecting that there is evidence on the premises of the relevant offence (in accusation cases) or of the person's identity (in any case) (s.164(2)). This does not include any items subject to legal privilege. The relevant offence is one on the basis of which a Pt 1 warrant has been or will be issued, or on the basis of which extradition has been or will be formally requested under Pt 2 (s.164(3)).

A police constable may use the power to search premises only for evidence relating to the relevant offence (for accusation cases) and the person's identity other than items subject to legal privilege (s.164(4)). This power is exercisable only so far as is reasonably necessary to find such evidence and the constable can seize and retain anything for which he is entitled to search (s.164(5)–(6)).

The powers to search premises and seize and retain evidence given in ss.164(2) and (6) may only be used with the written authorisation of a police officer of the rank of inspector or above (s.164(9)). However, the power to search in subs.(2) may be carried out without this authorisation before the arrested person is taken to a police station if the holding of the person somewhere other than a police station is necessary for an effective search to occur (s.164(10)). Lord Filkin was asked about the use of the power without authorisation. He explained that it was modelled on s.18(5) of the 1984 Act and gave an example of when it might be appropriate to use this power.

> "One can envisage the circumstance in which the police find a person who is wanted for, say, a bank robbery in Portugal, at address A and the person

indicates that he is willing to co-operate with the police and that there is further evidence or money at another address — just further down the road, for example. In those circumstances, as a consequence of having to obtain prior authorisation, one would significantly reduce the likelihood of being able to seize the evidence or proceeds of crime."[50]

Lord Filkin also believed that the provisions in the 2003 Codes would provide further safeguards against abuse of these powers. Paragraph 4.13, 2003 Code B requires the authorisation of the most senior officer available (below the rank of inspector) if the case is urgent and an inspector is not readily available. Paragraph 4.14 states that the authorising officer should record the authority on the Notice of Powers and Rights and sign the Notice and that the grounds for the search and the nature of the evidence sought should be recorded in the custody record.[51]

The powers of subss.(2) and (6), to enter and search premises and to retain any evidence found as a result, may be exercised in Scotland without this written authority (s.164(11)). The Government believed that there was no need for the additional safeguard of written authorisation in Scotland. In Scotland all powers of search are exercised by Scottish police officers under the guidance of the Procurator Fiscal and/or the Crown Office and no search can take place without their instruction.[52]

A police constable may, having entered premises in exercise of the power in subs.(2), seize and retain anything he finds there if he has reasonable grounds to believe:

(a) that is has been obtained as the result of an offence (including an offence committed outside of the UK) or is evidence of an offence; and
(b) that it is necessary to seize it to avoid the evidence being concealed, lost, damaged, altered or destroyed (s.164(7)–(8)).

ADDITIONAL SEIZURE POWERS

17–028 Section 165 amends the Criminal Justice and Police Act 2001 so that the additional powers given in ss.50 and 51 of that Act will be available in extradition cases.[53] These powers supplement other seizure powers in cases where it is not reasonably practicable to determine whether something found on premises or on a person can be seized in exercise of the other seizure power, or it is not reasonably practicable to separate something which a constable has power to seize from something which he does not have power to seize.[54]

[50] Lord Filkin, 9th sitting, Vol.652, col.GC 2.

[51] If there is no custody records then this information should be recorded in the officer's pocket book or the search record.

[52] Baroness Scotland, 30/10/03, Vol.654, col.391.

[53] These provisions were introduced after the judgement in *R. v Chesterfield Justices Ex p. Bramley* [2000] 1 All E.R. 411. The effect of this judgment was that if items were seized unlawfully then this did not make the search itself unlawful. However, the items which had been improperly seized had to be returned immediately and damages might have to be paid.

[54] See also paras 7.9–7.12 of 2003 Code B and 1984 Act Code B, paras 7.7–7.13.

ACCESS, COPYING AND RETURN OF SEIZED PROPERTY

Section 21 of the 1984 Act requires a constable who has seized anything in the exercise of a power conferred by an Act passed after that Act (including the 2003 Act) to provide a record of items seized if a request is made by a person who shows himself to be either the occupier of the premises from which the material has been seized or the person who had custody or control of the items immediately before seizure. The record must be provided within a reasonable time once the request has been made.[55] 17–029

Sections 21(3)–(8) govern any requests made by a person for access to items seized and retained by the police for the purpose of investigating an offence.

There are specific provisions for providing copies or photographs of items which have been seized. Generally, if a request is made by or on behalf of a person who had custody or control of a seized item immediately before seizure for:

(a) access to the seized items, this will be allowed under the supervision of a constable;
(b) copies or photographs of seized items, this will be allowed under the supervision of a constable or the police will copy/photograph the items and provide these to the person making the request.

However, a request may be refused if the officer in charge of the investigation has reasonable grounds for believing that to grant the request might prejudice the investigation for which the item was seized or any other investigation of an offence or any criminal proceedings which may be brought as a result of his investigation or any other investigation.[56] A challenge to an allegedly wrongful refusal of access under this section should be by way of judicial review.[57]

Section 1 of the Police Property Act 1897 gives power, on an application by the police or a claimant of the property, to a court to make orders relating to property in the possession of the police.

Section 59 of the Criminal Justice and Police Act 2001 applies when anything has been seized in exercise or purported exercise of a relevant power of seizure. By subs.(10) a relevant power of seizure will include a power conferred by the 2003 Act. This section allows for a person with a relevant interest in seized property to make an application to the appropriate judicial authority for the return of some or all of the seized property on one or more of the grounds in subs.(3). These grounds include the absence of a power to make the seizure, and that items subject to legal professional privilege or excluded material or special procedure material was included in the seized material, contrary to the relevant statutory provisions.

[55] para.7.19, 2003 Code B.
[56] See para.7.20 of 2003 Code B which applies para.7.17 of 1984 Act Code B.
[57] *Allen v Chief Constable of Cheshire*, *The Times*, July 16, 1988, CA.

IV. TREATMENT FOLLOWING ARREST

FINGERPRINTS AND SAMPLES

17–030 Section 166 applies if a person is arrested under an extradition arrest power and detained at a police station.

A constable has the power to take fingerprints and non-intimate samples only if the person has given his written consent or if authorisation has been given by a police officer of at least the rank of inspector. See 17–018 for the definition of fingerprints and non-intimate samples.

Paragraph 3.3. of 2003 Code D states that fingerprints or non-intimate samples may be taken for five specified reasons and under para.3.8(a) the person should be informed of the reason for taking the fingerprints or the sample. If the person is subsequently discharged, the fingerprints and samples must be destroyed after they have fulfilled the purpose for which they were taken unless the person has given consent for them to be retained.[58]

For these reasons, a legal adviser attending a police station should ensure that the reason for the taking of fingerprints and samples is given by the police officer. If the arrested person gives written consent for the taking of fingerprints and/or a non-intimate sample, this consent should be restricted to the retention of fingerprints and samples only for the purpose specified. This will allow an application to be made for the destruction of these records if the person is subsequently discharged and the purpose for which they were taken has been fulfilled.

SEARCHES AND EXAMINATION

17–031 If a person is arrested under an extradition arrest power and detained at a police station, s.167 applies. The person may be searched or examined for the purpose of ascertaining his identity with the authorisation of a police officer of the rank of inspector or above (s.167(2)). This purpose includes establishing that he is not a particular person (s.167(7)).

If, during the course of a search or examination, an identifying mark[59] is found, it may be photographed[60] with the person's consent. The identifying mark may still be photographed if consent if withheld or it is not practicable to obtain consent (s.167(3)). The only people allowed to conduct a search or examination or take a photograph under this section are police constables or persons given this responsibility by the appropriate police officer (s.167(4)). The appropriate officer is the chief police officer for the area where the police station is for England and Wales or for

[58] paras 3.17 and 3.18, 2003 Code D.

[59] A mark includes a feature or injury and a mark is an identifying mark if its existence facilitates the ascertaining of a person's identity (s.167(9)).

[60] Taking a photograph includes any process by which a visual image may be produced (s.167(8)).

Northern Ireland the Chief Constable of the Police Service of Northern Ireland (s.167(10)).

No one is allowed to conduct a search or examination or photograph any part (other than the face) of a person of the opposite sex (s.167(5)). This section does not allow an intimate search to be conducted (s.167(6)).

PHOTOGRAPHS

Section 168 applies if a person is arrested under an extradition arrest power and detained at a police station. The person may be photographed[61] with the appropriate consent but he may still be photographed if he withholds consent or it is impractical to obtain consent (s.168(2)). Paragraph 4.12 of the 2003 Code D clarifies that a photograph (without consent) may be taken by making of a copy of an image taken from any camera system installed in the police station. **17–032**

A person proposing to take photograph under this section can require the arrested person to remove anything worn on the head or face and if the person refuses, the person taking the photograph is allowed to remove such item or substance from the head or face (s.168(3)).

The only people allowed to take a photograph under this section are police constables or persons given this responsibility by the appropriate police officer.[62]

EVIDENCE OF IDENTITY

Section 169 amends the 1984 Act. The 1984 Act provisions that cover the identity issues outlined in ss.166 to 168 of the 2003 Act will no longer apply to a person arrested under an "extradition arrest power" as in future the provisions in the 2003 Act will apply. This relates to England and Wales only. **17–033**

Section 170 makes similar amendments to the 1989 Order for Northern Ireland.

OTHER TREATMENT AND RIGHTS

Section 171 applies if a person has been arrested at a police station, taken to a police station after arrest or detained after arrest in an extradition case. In these cases the Secretary of State can apply by order the specified sections of the 1984 Act or the 1989 Order for Northern Ireland with specified modifications (s.171(3)). **17–034**
The specified provisions of the 1984 Act are:

(a) s.54 (searches of detained persons);
(b) s.55 (intimate searches);

[61] Taking a photograph includes any process by which a visual image may be produced (s.168(5)).
[62] The definition of the appropriate police officer is identical to that in s.167 discussed at 17–031 above.

(c) s.56 (right to have someone informed when arrested);
(d) s.58 (access to legal advice).

The Secretary of State has applied ss.54, 55, 56 and 58 of the 1984 Act with modifications.[63] The modifications have the effect of substituting "an offence" or "a serious arrestable offence" in the earlier Act with "a relevant offence (within the meaning of section 164(3) of the Extradition Act 2003)".[64] Provisions in the 1984 Act relating to the proceeds of crime have been omitted.[65]

The Secretary of State has applied arts 55, 56, 57 and 59 of the 1989 Order with similar modifications.[66]

V. DELIVERY OF SEIZED PROPERTY

17–035 Section 172 relates to the handing of seized property to an authority of a category 1 or category 2 territory. This section applies to anything seized or produced under Pt 4 or anything seized under s.50 or 51 of the Criminal Justice and Police Act 2001 in reliance of a power of seizure conferred by Pt 4 (s.172(1)).

A police constable may deliver such items to a person acting on behalf of an authority if he has reasonable grounds for believing that it is an authority of the relevant territory and it has functions that make it appropriate to hand the items over to it (s.172(2)).

If the material was seized under a warrant issued under Pt 4 or was produced pursuant to an order under Pt 4, the relevant territory is the category 1 or 2 territory in the warrant or order (s.172(3)).

Where anything is seized without a specific search warrant,[67] s.172(4)–(6) apply to determine the relevant territory.

For Pt 1, the relevant territory is the one in which the Pt 1 warrant was issued, or in a provisional arrest case, the one in which a constable has reasonable grounds to believe such a warrant has been or will be issued.

For Pt 2, the relevant territory is the one which has requested the person's extradition, or in a provisional arrest case, the one in which the person is accused or has been convicted of an offence.

Sections 172(7)–(9) set out the necessary modifications in the application of this section to Scotland.

Paragraph 8.3 of 2003 Code B prohibits officers from delivering evidence (including copies) relating to the extradition offence to the requesting territory until extradition has been ordered and the extradition proceedings are concluded.

[63] The Extradition Act 2003 (Police Powers) Order 2003 (SI 2003/3106).
[64] *i.e.* the offence for which extradition is sought, s.164(3) is discussed above.
[65] Article 4: ss.56(5A), 56(5B), 58(8A) and 58(8B) of 1984 Act are omitted.
[66] The Extradition Act 2003 (Police Powers) Northern Ireland Order 2003 (SI 2003/3107).
[67] s.161(4), 162(6) or (7), 163(6) or (7) or 164(6) or (7).

However, the requesting territory can send an appropriate representative to view this material before extradition takes place.[68]

Material which is seized under the 2003 Act which is required for use in other proceedings abroad can only be delivered if a successful mutual legal assistance request is made.[69]

68 para.8.4, 2003 Code B.

69 See paras 8.11–8.14, 2003 Code B. See further Pt E of this book.

PART D

EXTRADITION TO THE UNITED KINGDOM

CHAPTER 18

EXTRADITION TO THE UNITED KINGDOM

I. INTRODUCTION

Before the passing of the 2003 Act, there was no statutory basis for a UK request to another territory for extradition. Instead, the UK made a request by the exercise of a prerogative power.[1] **18–001**

Part 3 of the 2003 Act sets out the statutory procedure to apply for a Pt 3 warrant for extradition from a category 1 territory to the UK. A Pt 3 warrant will comply with the terms of the Framework Decision and therefore allow a request to be made

[1] See the historical review in *Barton v Commonwealth of Australia* (1974) 131 C.L.R. 477.

to a category 1 territory which operates the European Arrest Warrant scheme. However, although category 1 territories are presently restricted to those operating the European Arrest Warrant, other territories which do not operate this scheme may be designated as category 1 territories in the future.[2] The extradition arrangements with territories which have not implemented the Framework Directive may include requirements for an extradition request which may not necessarily be fulfilled by a Pt 3 warrant.

There appears to be no restriction in the 2003 Act on the ability of UK authorities to make extradition requests to category 1 territories using the prerogative power rather than the statutory procedure for the issue of a Pt 3 warrant. In the case of a Pt 3 warrant the offence for which extradition is to be requested must satisfy the definition of an extradition offence in the 2003 Act.[3] If UK authorities wish to make an extradition request to a category 1 territory for an offence which does not fall within this definition, it would be necessary to use the prerogative power, invoking if possible the extradition treaty or other extradition arrangements existing between the UK and the relevant category 1 territory.

All extradition requests to category 2 territories will continue to be made using the prerogative power.

II. EXTRADITION FROM CATEGORY 1 TERRITORIES

18–002 The 2003 Act sets out the procedure and requirements governing the issue of a Pt 3 warrant and other provisions dealing with subsequent extradition from a category 1 territory.

APPLICATION TO ISSUE A PT 3 WARRANT

18–003 Section 142 allows an application to be made to an appropriate judge to issue a Pt 3 warrant. An appropriate judge is defined in s.149 as:

(a) in England and Wales — a District Judge (Magistrates' Courts), a justice of the peace or a judge entitled to exercise the jurisdiction of the Crown Court;
(b) in Scotland — a sheriff;
(c) in Northern Ireland — a justice of the peace, a resident magistrate or a Crown Court judge.

This definition applies to ss.142–147.

2 See Ch.5 at 5–009.
3 s.148, see below. The definition of "extradition of offences" is considered in Ch.6.

The application must be made by a constable or an appropriate person except in Scotland where it can only be made by a procurator fiscal. The Secretary of State has the power under s.142(9) to define an appropriate person.[4]

The Secretary of State has exercised this power, and the following are appropriate persons:

- any Inland Revenue officer of grade B1 or above attached to the Inland Revenue Extradition Group;
- any member of the Serious Fraud Office designated by the Director of the Serious Fraud Office under s.1(7) of the Criminal Justice Act 1987;
- the Director of Public Prosecutions, any Crown Prosecutor and any counsel or solicitor instructed by the Crown Prosecution Service for the purposes of the case concerned;
- the Commissioners of Customs & Excise.[5]

The wording of the designation suggests that a Commissioner of Customs & Excise will have to apply personally. This exhaustive list precludes the making of an application by an individual who might, for example, wish to request extradition in order to bring a private prosecution. 18–004

Before he issues a Pt 3 warrant, the judge must be satisfied that a domestic warrant has been issued. A domestic warrant is defined in s.142(8) as a warrant for the arrest or apprehension of a person issued under:

(a) s.72 of the Criminal Justice Act 1967; or
(b) s.7 of the Bail Act 1976; or
(c) s.51 of the Judicature (Northern Ireland) Act 1978; or
(d) s.51 of the Magistrates' Courts Act 1980; or
(e) art.20 or 25 of the Magistrates' Courts (Northern Ireland) Order 1981; or
(f) the Criminal Procedure (Scotland) Act 1995.

Before granting the application the judge must also find there are reasonable grounds for believing either:

(a) that the person has committed an extradition offence; or
(b) that the person is unlawfully at large after conviction of an extradition offence by a court in the UK.

It is submitted that there is no reason why the lawyers representing the person who would be the subject of the Pt 3 warrant should not attend court, at the discretion of the judge, to cross-examine and even call evidence, although there is no right to do so.[6]

4 The order must be laid in draft before Parliament and approved by both Houses (s.223(5) and (6)).
5 The Extradition Act (Part 3 Designation) Order 2003 (SI 2003/3335).
6 *R. v West London Stipendiary Magistrate Ex p. Klahn* [1979] 1 W.L.R. 933.

EXTRADITION OFFENCES

18–005 Section 148 defines an extradition offence for the purposes of ss.142–147.

The definitions in s.148(1) and (2) apply only if the person is not alleged to be unlawfully at large having been convicted by a court in the UK and sentenced.

Conduct constitutes an extradition offence if the conduct occurs in the UK and is punishable under the law of the relevant part of the UK with imprisonment or another form of detention for 12 months or a greater punishment (s.148(1)).

Conduct also constitutes an extradition offence if the conduct occurs outside of the UK and constitutes an extra-territorial offence punishable under the law of the relevant part of the UK with imprisonment or another form of detention for twelve months or a greater punishment (s.148(2)).

The relevant part of the UK is the part of the UK where the proceedings in which it is necessary to decide whether conduct constitutes an extradition offence are taking place (s.148(6) and (7)). Most obviously this will be the hearing where an application is made to issue a Pt 3 warrant under s.142 (see above).

Sections 148(3) and (4) may apply if a person is alleged to be unlawfully at large having been convicted by a court in the UK and sentenced.

Conduct constitutes an extradition offence if it occurs in the UK and a sentence of imprisonment or another form of detention for a term of four months or a greater punishment has been imposed in the UK in respect of the conduct (s.148(4)).

Conduct also constitutes an extradition offence if it occurs outside the UK, constitutes an extra-territorial offence and a sentence of imprisonment or another form of detention for a term of four months or a greater punishment has been imposed in the UK (s.148(5))[7].

CONTENTS OF THE PT 3 ARREST WARRANT

18–006 Section 142 sets out the information which a Pt 3 warrant must include. It must contain a statement that either:

(a) the person in respect of whom the warrant is issued is accused in the UK of the commission of an extradition offence specified in the warrant and the warrant is issued with a view to his arrest and extradition to the UK for the purpose of being prosecuted for the offence (s.142(4)); or
(b) the person in respect of whom the warrant is issued is alleged to be unlawfully at large after conviction by a court in the UK of the extradition offence specified in the warrant and the warrant is issued with a view to his arrest and extradition to the UK for the purpose of being sentenced for the offence or of serving a sentence of imprisonment or another form of detention imposed in respect of the offence (s.142(5)).

[7] See the discussion in Ch.6.

The Pt 3 warrant must also contain a certificate certifying:

(a) whether the conduct constituting the extradition offence specified in the warrant falls within the European framework list;[8]
(b) whether the offence is an extra-territorial offence;
(c) the maximum sentence which can be imposed on conviction for the offence or, if the person has already been sentenced, the sentence imposed (s.142(6)).

Conduct which constitutes an attempt, conspiracy or incitement to carry out conduct falling within the European Framework list will be treated for the purposes of s.142(6) as if it was within the list. In addition, conduct which constitutes aiding, abetting, counselling or procuring the carrying out of conduct falling within the list will also be treated for the purposes of s.142(6) as if it was within the list (s.142(7)).

EXTRADITION OF PERSON SERVING SENTENCE TO THE UK

If a Pt 3 warrant is issued for a person serving a sentence of imprisonment or another form of detention in a category 1 territory, his extradition to the UK may be conditional upon an undertaking about the person's treatment in the UK and /or his return to the category 1 territory. **18–007**

Section 143 allows the Secretary of State, in these circumstances, to give an undertaking dealing with both of these matters.

If the person is accused of an offence in the UK the undertaking may include terms:

(a) that the person be kept in custody until the conclusion of the proceedings against him for the offence and any other offence for which he is permitted to be dealt with in the UK;
(b) that the person be returned to the category 1 territory to serve the remainder of his sentence on the conclusion of those proceedings (s.143(3)).

If the person is alleged to be unlawfully at large after conviction of an offence by a UK court, the Secretary of State can give an undertaking that the person will be returned to the category 1 territory to serve the remainder of his sentence once he has completed any sentence imposed in the UK.

If the Pt 3 warrant is issued by a sheriff in Scotland then the undertaking will be given by a Scottish Minister rather than the Secretary of State (s.143(5)).

8 See Ch.6 at 6–008.

RETURN TO CATEGORY 1 TERRITORY TO SERVE SENTENCE IMPOSED IN THE UK

18–008 The 2003 Act makes provision for extradition to the UK which is conditional on the person extradited serving any sentence imposed by a UK court in the category 1 territory from which he was extradited.

Section 144 applies if the following conditions are met:

(a) a Pt 3 warrant is issued for the extradition of a person;
(b) the warrant states it is issued with a view to secure extradition to prosecute him for an offence;
(c) he is extradited to the UK in pursuance of the warrant;
(d) he is extradited on the condition that if he is convicted of the offence and receives a sentence of imprisonment or another form of detention then he must be returned to the category 1 territory to serve the sentence;
(e) he is convicted of the offence and a sentence of imprisonment or another form of detention is imposed in respect of it.

If all these conditions are met, the person must be returned to the category 1 territory to serve the sentence as soon as reasonably practicable after it is imposed. If the person is returned, the punishment must be treated as remitted but the conviction will be treated as a conviction for all other purposes. If the person is not returned to the category 1 territory as soon as reasonably practicable, he can apply to the judge who must order his discharge unless reasonable cause[9] is shown for the delay.

SERVICE OF SENTENCE IMPOSED BY UK COURT IN CATEGORY 1 TERRITORY

18–009 The 2003 Act envisages circumstances in which a sentence imposed in the UK is served in a category 1 territory, removing the need for extradition.

Section 145 applies if:

(a) a Pt 3 warrant is issued;
(b) the warrant certifies that a sentence has already been imposed on the person who is the subject of the warrant;
(c) the category 1 territory gives an undertaking that the person will be required to serve the sentence in the territory;
(d) on the basis of this undertaking the person is not extradited to the UK from the category 1 territory.

[9] See 15–002 for meaning of reasonable cause.

In these circumstances, the punishment for the offence must be treated as remitted but the conviction must be treated as a conviction for all other purposes (s.145(2)).

SPECIALITY

S.146 contains the speciality protection[10] for a person who is extradited to the UK from a category 1 territory pursuant to a Pt 3 warrant. This limits the offences for which a person can be prosecuted on his return to the UK. **18–010**

If a person is extradited to the UK from a category 1 territory in pursuance of a Pt 3 warrant he can only be dealt with in the UK for an offence committed before his extradition if the offence falls within s.146(3) or the condition in s.146(4) is satisfied.

The offences in s.146(3) are:

- (a) the offence for which the person is extradited;
- (b) an offence disclosed by the information provided to the category 1 territory in respect of that offence;
- (c) an extradition offence in respect of which consent to the person being dealt with is given on behalf of the category 1 territory;
- (d) an offence which is not punishable with imprisonment or another form of detention;
- (e) an offence for which the person will not be detained in connection with his trial, sentence or appeal;
- (f) an offence for which the person waives the right that he would have had but for s.146(3) not to be dealt with for the offence — *i.e.* an offence for which the person waives his speciality protection.

The condition in s.146(4) is that the person is given an opportunity to leave the UK after he has been extradited and he does not leave within 45 days of arriving in the UK or he returns to the UK after he has left within the 45 day period.

If a person consents to his extradition to the UK from a category 1 territory pursuant to a Pt 3 warrant he may lose the benefit of the speciality protection in s.146(2). Consent must be given in accordance with the law of the category 1 territory (s.147(1)).

There are alternative circumstances in which the person loses the speciality protection.

The first is where the effect of the person's consent, under the law of the category 1 territory, is automatically to waive his right to the speciality protection in s.146(2), and he has not subsequently validly revoked his consent if revocation is allowed under the law of the category 1 territory (s.147(3)).

The second situation is where the effect of the person's consent, under the law of the category 1 territory, is not to waive his right to the speciality protection in

[10] See Chs 2, 10 and 12 for speciality generally.

s.146(2) but he does in fact expressly waive his right to the speciality protection in s.146(2) in accordance with the law of the category 1 territory. Provided that the person has not subsequently revoked the giving of consent or the waiver of the speciality protection in s.146(2) (if either revocation is permissible under the law of the category 1 territory), he will lose the speciality protection in s.146(2) (s.147(4)).

The case law relevant to the speciality protection in UK domestic proceedings is dealt with below at 18–022.

III. EXTRADITION FROM CATEGORY 2 TERRITORIES

EXTRADITION REQUEST

18–011 The content of an extradition request to a category 2 territory will be governed by the treaty provisions between the UK and the category 2 territory. A request will be made as an exercise of the prerogative power.

In *R. v Department of Trade and Industry Ex p. Levitt*,[1] in 1997, a request was made by the Department of Trade and Industry through the normal diplomatic channel, in accordance with the procedures set out in the treaty between the UK and the US, for the extradition of Roger Levitt for crimes under the Companies Act. As a result, the person sought was remanded in custody for a week in New York, until released on bail when it was appreciated after an intervention by the defendant's London lawyers that those alleged crimes were not extradition crimes under Sch.1 to the 1989 Act.

Leave was granted to move for judicial review, but the Department of Trade and Industry gave notice that it intended to argue that:

(a) the request for extradition was an exercise of a prerogative power, not dependent on treaty or statute, and of that class of prerogative decision that was not amenable to judicial review,[2] and was "non-justiciable";
(b) until the person sought was returned to the UK, all matters relating to the return were solely for the foreign state[3];
(c) it appeared that the offences for which extradition was sought were regarded by US government lawyers as falling within the treaty;
(d) neither the 1989 Act nor its predecessors sought to limit the Crown's power to request surrender from other states;
(e) that if Levitt were returned he could not rely on the statutory specialty protections, only those in the treaty, but could present an argument that he had been unlawfully returned and that proceedings against him should be

[1] Unreported, October 31, 1997, CO/3811/97.

[2] See *Council for the Civil Service Unions v Minister for the Civil Service* [1985] A.C. 374, 410 *per* Lord Diplock.

[3] Relying on *Re Osman* [1988] 2 H.K.L.R. 378.

stayed in accordance with *R. v Horseferry Road Magistrates Court Ex p. Bennett*.[4]

Reliance was placed on the decision of the High Court of Australia of *Barton v Commonwealth of Australia*.[5] Although there was no extradition treaty between Australia and Brazil, the Australian government had made a request to the Brazilian authorities for the detention of the fugitive pending his extradition. Barton was accused of crimes which were within the Australian definition of extraditable offences and it appeared that Brazil had powers in its own legislation to effect the surrender. In an extensive review of extradition history the court held that a request could lawfully be made. Mason J. was particularly influenced by the number of extradition requests that had been made by the English government before the first extradition statute were passed.[6] Barwick C.J. considered that after the enactment of the 1870 Act: 18–012

> "the Crown retained a prerogative to seek and accept from a non-treaty state the surrender of a fugitive, subject only to the limitation of specialty imposed by section.19 of the Extradition Act 1870".[7]

McTiernan and Menzies J.J. held:[8]

> "Accordingly, we are satisfied that unless statute either expressly or by necessary implication had deprived the executive of part of its inherent power, it may make such requests as it considers proper for the assistance of other states in bringing fugitive offenders to justice."

However, the DTI abandoned the argument before the substantive hearing, perhaps because it was obvious that the Department had indeed, as it conceded, misunderstood the law, and had not intended to make an extra-treaty request, and for this reason realised that it would not survive a *Wednesbury* challenge. The general point remains open.

It should be noted, however, that on at least two occasions, the British government has adopted the position that the extradition of a British subject by a foreign government to a third state in the absence of a treaty was contrary to international law. In the case of *Thornley*,[9] the Law Officers of the British government protested to France against the proposed surrender to Russia of Thornley:[10] 18–013

[4] [1994] 1 A.C. 42, discussed in Ch.3.
[5] (1974) 131 C.L.R. 477.
[6] See further Ch.1.
[7] at 485.
[8] at 491.
[9] Parry, "British Digest of International Law" (Stevens, London 1965) Ch.17, pp.463–5.
[10] Until it became clear that Thornley had Russian as well as British nationality.

> "... there is not so much even as an imperfect obligation, by international law, for one nation to execute or assist in executing any part of the criminal law of another nation, in the absence of any treaty to that effect."

Similarly, the UK protested to Hungary in 1962 when the British businessman Greville Wynne was surrendered to the Soviet Union for espionage on two grounds, that the surrender was made without a treaty and was made for offences of a political character.

In the case of *Walker v Governor of HM Prison, Nottingham*,[11] a request had been made by the Customs and Excise for extradition from the US by HM Customs and Excise. The Customs authorities wrongly informed the US court that the VAT offences for which Walker's extradition was sought were extraditable in English law.

The Divisional Court held that, because he had consented to his return before a formal extradition request had been made, it could not be said that he had been extradited. Specialty protection did not therefore apply.[12]

SPECIALITY

18–014 Most extradition treaties require speciality protection for any person extradited to the UK; ss.150 and 151 provide this speciality protection. The case law governing claims to the speciality protection in UK domestic proceedings is considered below at 18–022.

SPECIALITY — EXTRADITION FROM COMMONWEALTH COUNTRIES, BRITISH OVERSEAS TERRITORIES AND THE HONG KONG SPECIAL ADMINISTRATIVE REGION ("SAR")

18–015 Section 150 deals with the speciality protection for a person extradited from a category 2 territory under the law of the territory corresponding to Pt 2 of the 2003 Act if the territory is a Commonwealth country, a British overseas territory or the Hong Kong SAR.

A person can only be dealt with in the UK for an offence committed before his extradition if it falls within the list of offences in s.150(3) or satisfies the condition in s.150(6).

A person is dealt with in the UK for an offence if he is tried for it in the UK or detained with a view to trial for the offence in the UK (s.150(8)).

[11] [2002] EWHC 39 (Admin).

[12] See also the Canadian case of *R. v Gagnon* (1956) 117 C.C.C. 61.

The categories of offences specified in s.150(3) are:

(a) the offence for which the person is extradited;
(b) a lesser offence disclosed by the information given to the category 2 territory in respect of that offence;
(c) an offence for which consent to the person being dealt with is given by or on behalf of the relevant authority.

A lesser offence is one carrying a less severe maximum punishment than the maximum punishment for the offence for which the person is extradited (s.150(4)).

The relevant authority is the government of a Commonwealth country, the person administering a British overseas territory or the Hong Kong SAR government (s.150(5)).

The condition in s.150(6) is that 45 days have elapsed from the date when the person is given an opportunity to leave the UK.

SPECIALITY — EXTRADITION FROM CATEGORY 2 TERRITORIES OTHER THAN COMMONWEALTH COUNTRIES, BRITISH OVERSEAS TERRITORIES AND THE HONG KONG SAR

Section 151 provides speciality protection for a person extradited from a category 2 territory not dealt with under s.150. 18–016

A person may only be dealt with in the UK for an offence committed before his extradition if it falls into one of the categories of offences set out in s.151(3) or the condition in s.151(4) is satisfied.

A person is dealt with in the UK for an offence if he is tried in the UK for it, or detained with a view to trial for the offence in the UK (s.151(5)).

The categories of offences in s.151(4) are:

(a) the offence for which the person is extradited;
(b) an offence disclosed by the information provided to the category 2 territory in respect of that offence;
(c) an offence for which consent is given by or on behalf of the territory for the person to be dealt with.

The condition in s.151(4) is that either:

(a) the person has returned to the category 2 territory from which he was extradited; or
(b) the person has been given an opportunity to leave the UK.

IV. GENERAL PROVISIONS

18–017 Sections 152–155 set out general provisions which apply to persons extradited from both category 1 and category 2 territories.

CONVICTIONS FOR UK OFFENCES NOT PART OF EXTRADITION REQUEST

18–018 If a person is extradited to the UK from either a category 1 or category 2 territory and before his extradition he was convicted of an offence in the UK for which he was not extradited, the punishment for this other offence must be treated as remitted (s.152). This section gives effect to the speciality rule which would mean that the UK would normally be unable to continue proceedings for any offence which was not part of the extradition request. However, the conviction will be treated as a conviction for all other purposes (s.152(2)). This would include, for example, the recording of the fact of the conviction in the relevant criminal records.

RETURN OF PERSON ACQUITTED OR NOT TRIED

18–019 If a person is extradited to the UK from a category 1 or category 2 territory but is not tried within a specified time or is acquitted then s.153 allows him to apply for his return to this territory.

Section 153 applies if the person is accused in the UK of the commission of an offence and he is extradited from a category 1 territory[13] or a category 2 territory[14] and the condition in either s.153(2) or (3) is satisfied.

If proceedings are not begun within six months of the day when the person arrives in the UK after his extradition, he can ask the Secretary of State within three months of the expiry of the six month period to return him to the territory from which he was extradited (s.153(2)).

If the person is acquitted or discharged under a specified list of provisions he can ask the Secretary of State, within three months starting immediately after the date of his acquittal or discharge, to return him to the territory from which he was extradited (s.153(3)).

Section 153(4) lists the specified provisions:

(a) s.12(1) of the Powers of Criminal Courts (Sentencing) Act 2000;
(b) s.246(1), (2) or (3) of the Criminal Procedure (Scotland) Act 1995;
(c) art.4(1) of the Criminal Justice (Northern Ireland) Order 1996.

[13] The extradition must take place under the law of the category 1 territory corresponding to Pt 1 of the Act.

[14] The extradition must take place under the law of the category 2 territory corresponding to Pt 2 of the Act.

If this section applies the Secretary of State must arrange for him to be sent back free of charge with as little delay as possible to the territory from which he was extradited to the UK in respect of the offence (s.152(5)).

In the case of a person accused of committing an offence in Scotland, references to the Secretary of State in s.153 should be treated as if they were references to Scottish Ministers (s.152(6)).

RESTRICTIONS ON BAIL WHERE UNDERTAKING GIVEN BY SECRETARY OF STATE

Extradition to the UK may be granted following undertakings given by the Secretary of State.[15] Section 154 applies if the Secretary of State has given an undertaking in connection with a person's extradition which includes a term that he will be kept in custody until the conclusion of any proceedings against him in the UK for an offence. In these circumstances, a court, judge or justice of the peace may grant bail to the person in the proceedings only if he considers that there are exceptional circumstances to justify it (s.154(2)). This section should allow the court to ensure that there is no breach of Art.5(3) and (4) of the ECHR and should be interpreted accordingly.[16] **18–020**

SERVICE PERSONNEL

The Secretary of State can provide by order for Pt 3 to have effect with specified modifications if the person whose extradition is sought or ordered is subject to military law, air-force law or the Naval Discipline Act 1957 (s.155). **18–021**

V. ASSERTING SPECIALITY PROTECTION IN DOMESTIC UK PROCEEDINGS

There are a number of cases which give guidance on the application of the speciality protection to domestic proceedings in the UK which take place following extradition. **18–022**

The burden of proof is on the defendant to show that his trial or sentence breaches the speciality rule.[17] However, in order to determine this question, the court can examine material used in the extradition proceedings.[18]

A UK court will only have to apply the speciality rule as set out in the 2003 Act, and will not consider any additional restriction which may be in an extradition treaty pursuant to which extradition has taken place.[19]

The speciality rule does not prohibit civil proceedings. However, it will be an

[15] See, *e.g.* s.143.
[16] See Ch.11.
[17] *R. v Corrigan* [1931] 1 K.B. 527 at 533.
[18] *R. v Aubrey-Fletcher Ex p. Ross-Munro* [1968] 1 Q.B. 620.
[19] *R. v Davidson* (1977) 64 Cr. App. R. 209 at 212.

abuse of process if it can be shown that an extradition request has been made not for the *bona fide* purpose of punishing a person for a crime but instead with the indirect aim of allowing civil proceedings to be brought.[20]

VI. ENGLAND AND WALES: CREDITING PERIOD OF REMAND IN CUSTODY

CRIMINAL JUSTICE ACT 1967

18–023 Section 67 of the Criminal Justice Act 1967 currently deals with the computation of sentences of imprisonment passed in England and Wales. It specifies that the length of any sentence of imprisonment will be treated as reduced by any "relevant period" previously spent in custody. Section 47 of the Criminal Justice Act 1991 gives a court the discretion to specify the "relevant period" which will be used for s.67 of the 1967 Act for an "extradited prisoner".

> "(1) A short-term or long-term prisoner is an extradited prisoner for the purposes of this section if —
>
> (a) he was tried for the offence in respect of which his sentence was imposed —
>
> (i) after having been extradited to the United Kingdom; and
> (ii) without first having been restored and had an opportunity of leaving the United Kingdom; and
>
> (b) he was for any period kept in custody while awaiting his extradition to the United Kingdom as mentioned in paragraph (a) above."[21]

This section refers to the 1989 Act and the Backing of Warrants (Republic of Ireland) Act 1965, but this will be read as a reference to the 2003 Act by virtue of s.17(2) of the Interpretation Act 1978.[22] Section 47 gives a court the discretion as to what period to specify, if any, as a "relevant period" for the purpose of s.67 of the 1967 Act. Previous authority suggests that an person who has deliberately prolonged the period in custody while awaiting extradition should not have the full period spent in custody credited as the relevant period.[23]

[20] *Pooley v Whetham* [1880] 15 Ch.D. 435.

[21] s.47(1) Criminal Justice Act 1991.

[22] "Where an Act repeals and re-enacts, with or without modification, a previous enactment then, unless the contrary intention appears any reference in any other enactment to the enactment so repealed shall be construed as a reference to the provision re-enacted . . ."

[23] For application of s.47 of Criminal Justice Act 1991 see *R. v Scalise and Rachel* 7 Cr. App. R. (S) 395, CA; *R. v Stone* 10 Cr. App. R. (S) 332, CA; *R. v Peffer* 13 Cr. App. R. (S) 150, CA; *R. v Vincent* [1996] 2 Cr. App. R. (S) 6, CA; *R. v Andre and Burton* [2002] 2 Cr. App. R. (S) 24, CA; *R. v M* [2004] EWCA Crim 2085.

The definition of an "extradited prisoner" in s.47 does not apply to a person who is extradited having already been convicted. However, the Court of Appeal has reduced a sentence to allow for time spent in custody before being extradited to serve a sentence which has already been imposed. The principles which the court will apply when deciding how much time should be allowed are discussed in the context of specific cases.[24]

CRIMINAL JUSTICE ACT 2003

Section 67 of the Criminal Justice Act 1967 will be repealed when Ch.6 of the Criminal Justice Act 2003 is brought into force and Ch.6 contains similar provisions. The Home Office expect this to take place at the end of 2004. **18–024**

Section 240 of the 2003 Act will apply when a court sentences an offender to imprisonment for an offence committed after the commencement of this section and the person has been remanded in custody for the offence or a related offence. An offence is related if the charge is founded on the same facts or evidence.

The court must generally direct that the period of time spent in custody for the offence or a related offence will count as time served as part of the sentence imposed. However, the court does not have to make a direction in respect of the full time spent in custody if it believes it is just to make a direction for a lesser amount or not at all.

Section 243 of the 2003 Act defines an "extradited prisoner" as a person who was kept in custody while awaiting extradition and who, having been extradited to the UK,[25] was tried for the offence for which his sentence was imposed without having first been restored or had an opportunity to leave the UK. The definition of an "extradited prisoner" in s.243 does not apply to a person who is extradited having already been convicted.

The court will then treat the time spent in custody while awaiting extradition as if it was time spent in custody in the UK when applying s.240 to make a direction. It is likely that the court will apply the principles in the cases referred to at 18–023 in deciding what direction it would be just to give. The court would also still have the ability, apart from the statutory scheme, to reduce a sentence to allow for time spent in custody before being extradited to serve a sentence which has already been imposed.[26]

If the person has been extradited under the EAW scheme then the Member State from which the person was extradited should have provided information about the period of time spent in custody awaiting extradition at the time of surrender to the UK.[27]

[24] *R. v De Simone* [2000] 2 Cr. App. R. (S) 332; *R. v Lodde and Lodde*, *The Times*, March 8, 2000.

[25] s.243(3) defined "extradited to the UK" by reference to the extradition legislation preceding the 2003 Act. This section has been repealed by art.3 of the Extradition Act 2003 (Repeals) Order 200 (SI 2004/1897). The Government said in the Explanatory Memorandum accompanying the draft SI that the meaning of the phrase is sufficiently clear without the need for definitions.

[26] See 18–023 above.

[27] Art.26(2), Framework Decision; App.C–006.

PART E

MUTUAL LEGAL ASSISTANCE

CHAPTER 19

MUTUAL LEGAL ASSISTANCE IN CRIMINAL MATTERS; GENERAL PRINCIPLES AND INSTITUTIONS

(by Alun Jones and Michael O'Kane)

I. HISTORICAL PERSPECTIVE

INTRODUCTION

19–001 The legislative changes to the field of mutual legal assistance made in 2003 were impelled by powerful policy, even political, considerations. In introducing the Bill in the House of Commons, the Home Secretary, David Blunkett, stated:

> "We live in an increasingly global and mobile world, where serious and organised criminals operate across national borders. We need to keep one step ahead of the game in tackling the criminals whose business is terror, or trafficking people, drugs and arms across the world."[1–3]

States increasingly recognise the international nature of serious criminal activity. Co-operation began at state and law enforcement level. It has taken the form of provisions intended to improve the detection, investigation and effective trial of crime, as well as closer co-operation in extradition. Many of these provisions fall under the general description of "mutual legal assistance". This description covers a range of activities relating to transnational provision of information or material for use in the investigation or prosecution of alleged criminal activity.

Most criminal justice systems recognise that the most pressing transnational concerns are organised crime and terrorism. UK law enforcement authorities began to consider these threats seriously about twenty years ago[4] and now seek to promote assistance principally through UK membership of the European Union and the Commonwealth as well by means of the close relationship between the UK and the United States of America. The UK has become party to numerous treaties, conventions, protocols, and Framework Decisions designed to give effect to a political will to improve cooperation in such matters. It is important to note that nothing in these agreements or statutes prevents the UK from assisting countries with which it has no such formal arrangements.

Many of these international instruments have been amended, supplemented and replaced. The basic legal commitments and obligations imposed on the UK are of course set out in the domestic legislation that applies to this subject.[5] However, before a comprehensive examination of the current domestic legislation is attempted, it is important to consider aspects of the international and national history, and to take note of a number of international institutions that are intended to play an important part in mutual legal assistance.

[1–3] Home Office Press Release October 30, 2003.

[4] See Harare Scheme at App. C–004.

[5] Mainly the Crime (International Co-operation) Act 2003, App.A–002.

MUTUAL LEGAL ASSISTANCE IN THE UK

Historically the law in the UK as to mutual legal assistance was limited. The Extradition Act 1873 allowed the Secretary of State to require a magistrate or justice of the peace to require the production of documents or to take evidence for any pending criminal matter in a foreign court as if he were taking a deposition in committal proceedings for an indictable offence.[6] Under this Act a witness could be compelled to testify and produce documents if such evidence would similarly be compellable in domestic proceedings. The law of perjury applied to false evidence, but there was an exemption from all of these requirements if the alleged offence was of a political character. Some of these themes are repeated in much later legislation and instruments.[7–8] 19–002

The 1873 Act provisions remained in force until 1975 when the criminal law provisions of the Evidence (Proceedings in Other Jurisdictions) Act 1975 repealed but substantially re-enacted them. From 1975, there was provision for a foreign state to request evidence to be produced in documentary form by a witness or suspect and/or for that individual to provide oral or written testimony. There was no power allowing UK law enforcement authorities to search and seize material at the request of the foreign state, nor to serve process.

The 1873 Act and the criminal law provisions of the 1975 Act were repealed by the Criminal Justice (International Co-Operation) Act 1990 ("the 1990 Act"). The 1990 Act gave effect to the 1959 European Convention on Mutual Assistance in Criminal Matters, the 1978 Additional Protocol to the European Convention, and the 1986 Commonwealth Scheme.

THE EUROPEAN CONVENTION ON MUTUAL ASSISTANCE IN CRIMINAL MATTERS 1959

The 1959 European Convention is the foundation upon which most of the further EU mutual legal assistance measures have been built. Its origins lay in a desire by leading states of the Council of Europe to promote greater co-operation in extradition arrangements, which had culminated in the European Convention on Extradition, 1957. In the course of drafting this instrument of extradition law, it was realised that mutual legal assistance was also an important aspect of effective judicial co-operation and provisions were included accordingly. 19–003

The mutual assistance Convention was signed in 1959 by Austria, Belgium, Denmark, Germany, Greece, Italy, Luxembourg and Sweden, and almost all of the Council of Europe states have signed subsequently. 19–004

The Convention Articles contain the following guiding provisions that have also been influential in the drafting of many subsequent measures:

[6] s.5 Extradition Act 1873.

[7–8] Art.2 of the 1959 European Convention (App.C–002) and para.7 of the Harare Scheme (App.C–003).

- Signatory states will provide as wide assistance as possible to requesting states in criminal matters.[9]
- Assistance can be refused in relation to offences which the requested state considers to be political or fiscal in nature or where refusal is made for the purpose of protecting sovereignty, security or public order.[10]
- Assistance is to be sought by a requesting state through a "letter rogatory" outlining the nature of the request, and which would be transmitted to the home affairs ministry of the requested state.[11]
- Before coercive powers (search and seizure) can be exercised by the requested state, the offence must be extraditable in the requested state, the execution must be consistent with the law of the requested state, and the alleged offence must be a criminal offence in both states.
- A uniform format and process is prescribed in respect of letters rogatory and the service of process.[12]

The UK incorporated the major provisions of the 1959 European Convention in domestic legislation in the 1990 Act. The 1990 Act has largely been repealed by the Crime (International Co-operation) Act 2003 ("CICA"), considered in detail in Chs 20 and 21.

THE 1978 FIRST ADDITIONAL PROTOCOL TO THE CONVENTION

19–005 The European Convention was supplemented in 1978 by an Additional Protocol, signed in Strasbourg. The main element of this Protocol was the inclusion of fiscal offences, which had been specifically excluded in the 1959 European Convention.[13] Art.1 removes the right of a state to refuse assistance on the ground that a matter is a fiscal one. There is no definition within the Protocol of "fiscal offence"; however, Art.2.2 states that:

> "the request may be refused on the ground that the law of the requested party does not impose the same kind of tax or duty or does not contain a tax, duty, customs and exchange regulation of the same kind as the law of the requesting party."

THE COMMONWEALTH SCHEME RELATING TO MUTUAL ASSISTANCE IN CRIMINAL MATTERS ("THE HARARE SCHEME")

19–006 In 1983 the Commonwealth Law Ministers initiated the creation of a mutual legal assistance convention that would enable Commonwealth countries to cooperate

[9] Art.1.
[10] Art.2.
[11] Arts 3–6.
[12] Arts 7–20.
[13] Art.2.

more effectively. In 1986 the Commonwealth Law Ministers adopted such a scheme in Zimbabwe ("the Harare Scheme") which was not binding upon member states until they had enacted domestic legislation enabling them to provide and seek assistance. The UK enacted the Scheme by means of the 1990 Act.

The Harare Scheme (which has been subsequently amended[14]) contained many provisions similar to those in the 1959 European Convention. However it provided wider grounds upon which a request could be refused. It laid down that assistance may not be provided in a number of circumstances, for example, where the criminal conduct alleged was not criminal in both states, where the offence alleged was political in nature, and where the principle against double jeopardy would be infringed. It extended the scope of mutual legal assistance to cover the tracing, seizing and confiscation of assets.[15] This part of the Scheme became a source for similar EU initiatives.

The Commonwealth Secretariat is a unit created to facilitate the terms of the Scheme and to enhance co-operation between Commonwealth nations.[16]

THE MAASTRICHT TREATY

On February 7, 1992 the Maastricht Treaty was signed, introducing a new level of 19–007
European state integration. Maastricht created the concept of the European Union, led to the creation of the Euro, and introduced the "three pillar" structure applicable to EU policy. Separate pillars for the "community", for "Common Foreign and Security Policy" and for "Justice and Home Affairs" were built, with the third pillar supporting close co-operation between member states. This "third pillar" underpins nine areas of common interest, including international fraud, police and customs and judicial co-operation in both civil and criminal matters. Maastricht provided the framework for more co-operative European security policy, including, in 1995, the implementation of the Schengen agreement and Schengen Information System (SIS).

THE SCHENGEN AGREEMENT AND CONVENTION

On June 14, 1985 this agreement was signed in Schengen, Luxembourg by France, 19–008
Germany, Belgium, Luxembourg and the Netherlands. Its object was the eventual abolition of checks at common borders between signatory states. The Agreement was implemented by the Schengen Convention of June 19, 1990, which entered into force on September 1, 1993. As the abolition of cross-border controls had security implications this Agreement dealt with measures to enhance cross-border judicial and policing co-operation. From May 1, 1999 this Agreement has been incorporated into the framework of the EU.

14 May 1999 amendments to paras 27 and 28 of the Scheme.

15 para.7 of the Harare Scheme.

16 See 19–029.

Most other EU states have signed protocols and accession agreements to the June 1990 Convention,[17] and the combination of Schengen agreements, the Convention and the Protocols together constitute what has become known as the "Schengen Acquis". The concept of the Acquis has been used to refer to an evolving concept, as states add their decisions and agreements to it. On December 1, 2000 the European Council adopted the Decision on the application of the Schengen Acquis in Denmark, Finland, Sweden, Norway and Iceland (the Nordic Passport Union countries), and decided that, from March 21, 2001, the Schengen Agreement would apply to these Nordic states. Denmark, although a signatory to the Convention, retained the right to choose whether to apply any new decision taken on the basis of the Schengen Acquis.

A secondary objective of the Schengen Agreement was to strengthen borders with non-signatory states. Police from Schengen states were permitted to conduct pursuit of suspects across the borders of their Schengen neighbours ("hot pursuit"). Co-operation was further enhanced by the creation of the Schengen Information System, a database within which states can share information concerning individuals and lost or stolen objects.[18]

Art.51 of the Schengen Convention amended the 1959 Convention to limit the ability of States to refuse a request for search and seizure. The following conditions were to apply :

- that the offence under investigation is punishable under the law of both States by a sentence of a maximum of at least six months; or
- that the offence is punishable under the law of one of the two States by an equivalent penalty, and under the law of the other as an infringement which is prosecuted by administrative authorities where the decision may give rise to proceedings before a criminal court; and
- that the execution is otherwise consistent with the law of the requested State.

THE SCHENGEN INFORMATION SYSTEM ("SIS")

19–009 SIS began its operations in March 1995, and by March 2003 it was subscribed to by 13 of the (then) 15 EU Member States,[19] as well as Norway and Iceland.[20] EU officials claim that there are 125,000 access terminals allowing authorities to share intelligence across the Schengen area. Member States provide information to SIS through their national networks (N-SIS), which connect to a central system

[17] A term denoting the 1985 Agreement, 1990 Protocol and subsequent Agreements by Italy November 27, 1990, Spain and Portugal June 25, 1991, Greece November 6, 1992, Austria April 28, 1985 and Denmark, Finland and Sweden December 19, 1996.

[18] See 19–009.

[19] The UK and Ireland were not signatories, although may join at a later date.

[20] Iceland and Norway signed an agreement with the EU on May 18, 1999 expanding their previous association with the Schengen Acquis.

(C-SIS) and in turn is supplemented by a further system, SIRENE.[21] SIRENE's contract ended on August 23, 2001, and a new system, SISNET will replace it, and eventually become a "European Information System".

The main categories of data contained in the SIS relate to:

- persons wanted for arrest for extradition and from January 1, 2004, for transfer in the context of the European Arrest Warrant (Art.95);
- third country nationals refused entry into Schengen territory (Art.96);
- missing persons (Art.97);
- witnesses and persons required to appear before the judicial authorities to locate their whereabouts (Art.98);
- persons or vehicles to be put under surveillance or for specific checks (Art.99);
- certain categories of objects (vehicles, identity documents, bank notes etc.) which have been stolen, misappropriated or lost (Art.100).

The SIS may be used by police and customs officers, and parts of the databases by authorities responsible for delivering visas and residence permits. Because technology changes, and in an effort to improve the integration of the computer network, the Council has mandated the Commission to design and introduce a new generation of Schengen Information System ("SIS II").

SIS II will allow the UK and Ireland as well as the 10 2004 accession states to have access to this system.[22] SIS II is designed for the expanded membership of the EU, and will reflect developments in technology since SIS was introduced. It will also introduce new functions to the system, including the storing of biometric data, new search categories of "terrorist suspects" and "violent troublemakers", and will be supported by a second database, the Visa Information System (VIS).

THE UK AND THE SCHENGEN ACQUIS

The UK opted out of the full Agreement. The most important section which the 19–010
UK did not adopt is the commitment to a relaxation of border controls between signatory states. The UK does take part in provisions relating to police and legal co-operation. The European Commission made a recommendation that the Council of Ministers should regard the UK's request for partial participation in Schengen favourably, whilst emphasising that the ultimate aim was for the UK to participate fully. Art.4 of the Protocol to the Schengen Convention allows for the UK to request participation in some or all of Schengen, requiring that all 13 Schengen states be in agreement through the Council of Ministers as to the request.

In March 1999 the UK made a request to take part in certain aspects of Schengen activity, including cooperation in police and judicial matters as well as SIS. This

[21] Supplementary Information Request at the National Entry.

[22] Council Decision December 6, 2001 on the development of the second generation SIS.

request was approved in relation to the UK's participation in police and legal co-operation in criminal matters, enforcement in relation to dangerous drugs and SIS on May 29, 2000.[23] This date was later than anticipated following Spain's objection to the UK arising from the dispute between the two countries over Gibraltar.

THE TREATY OF AMSTERDAM

19–011 On October 2, 1997 the Amsterdam Treaty was signed, following the intergovernmental conference at the Turin European Council on March 29, 1996. With effect from May 1, 1999 the Treaty of Amsterdam incorporated the Schengen Convention into the framework of the EU. The Treaty expressly amended the Treaty of European Union, strengthening the EU's competence in police and judicial co-operation in criminal matters.

The Treaty sought to concentrate EU "third pillar" co-operation on the subjects of organised crime, xenophobia, and police and judicial activity within a new Title VI of the Treaty of the European Union. Organised crime was regarded as an essential focus of "third pillar" activity because it was by its nature a cross-border activity and therefore of immediate relevance to the EU. The "third pillar" outlined the approach intended to achieve the aims of the Amsterdam Treaty. Investigative and prosecuting authorities were expected to collaborate through institutions such as Europol[24] in areas including training, the prevention of crime, and the exchange of information.

THE TAMPERE MEETING

19–012 On October 15 and 16, 1999 the European Council held an "extraordinary meeting" at Tampere, Finland, on the subjects of freedom, security and justice, and again emphasised the importance of co-operation, particularly in the investigation and prosecution of money laundering. At the meeting the British proposal[25] that the foundation of policy in this area should be the principle of mutual recognition was endorsed. The Council asserted that:

> "enhanced mutual recognition of judicial decisions and judgements and the necessary approximation of legislation would facilitate co-operation between authorities . . . The principle should apply to both judgements and to other decisions of judicial authorities[26]".

This principle of mutual recognition has subsequently been invoked by the EU to enhance co-operation in further Decisions.[27] The conclusions of the meeting

[23] Decision 2000/365/EC.

[24] See 19–023.

[25] See statement to Parliament by the Prime Minister on October 19, 1999.

[26] Point 33 Tampere European Council.

[27] Introductory para.(1) Council Framework Decision 2003/577/JHA of July 22, 2003.

included a proposal for the establishment of Eurojust to co-ordinate member states' prosecuting authorities, the development of a European police college, and the development of a European Police Chiefs' operational task force.[28] As well as strengthening Europol by extending its mandate to deal with matters such as money laundering,[29] the Tampere meeting also proposed the creation of "Joint Investigative Teams" ("JITS")[30] to investigate drug and human trafficking as well as terrorism.

Later in 2004 the EU Commission will issue an evaluation of the Tampere programme, in an attempt to judge whether the proposals and ideas discussed at Tampere have been implemented properly.

EUROPEAN CONVENTION ON MUTUAL LEGAL ASSISTANCE IN CRIMINAL MATTERS[31] *("MLAC 2000")*

On May 29, 2000, after five years of negotiations, the Council of Ministers adopted the Convention on Mutual Assistance designed to make mutual assistance more efficient and effective.[32] The importance of these measures was emphasised at a European Council meeting in Nice on December 7, 2000. The first Council Framework on money laundering followed these meetings on June 26, 2001, and outlined procedures intended to identify, track, freeze and confiscate the proceeds of crime. 19–013

The 2000 Convention was also adopted by the Council of Europe and signed by all member states. The Convention spans 30 Articles and is divided into five "Titles":

- Title 1, Arts 1–7, deals with mutual assistance;
- Title 2, Arts 8–16, is principally concerned with letters of request and the types of available assistance;
- Title 3, Arts 17–22, deals with the interception of communications;
- Title 4, Art.23, deals with data protection questions;
- Title 5, Arts 24–30, deals with the enforcement of the Convention.

Unlike previous meetings and Treaties, MLAC 2000 was an attempt to offer EU states practical guidance about mutual assistance, and to lay the foundation for more efficient co-operation. Title 5 concentrates entirely on the implementation of the Convention, including the requirement that member states should name their relevant prosecuting and investigative authorities, as well as the central authority responsible for processing requests.[33] MLAC 2000 has been 19–014

[28] Paras 44, 46, 47 Presidency Conclusions, Tampere.
[29] Point 52.
[30] see Ch.20.
[31] [2000] O.J. C197/01; App.C–004.
[32] Arts 3–9 of the Convention.
[33] Art.24.

implemented in the UK by the Crime (International Co-operation) Act 2003 ("CICA"), and it is therefore necessary to look at the more important provisions of this Convention as follows:

Article 3:- This extended the type of proceedings in which mutual legal assistance could be sought to include certain administrative proceedings. These are defined within the body of the Convention as proceedings which relate to "offences punishable under the national law of the requesting or the requested Member State, or both, as infringements of legal rules where the decision may result in proceedings before a court having jurisdiction in particular criminal matters". It appears that an important element in determining whether proceedings are "administrative" in nature is whether they can at some stage be brought before a court which has jurisdiction over the matter, particularly over criminal cases.

Article 4:- This alters the balance of mutual legal assistance requests which had been established under the 1959 Convention, where a request had to be executed in a manner provided for by the law of the requested state.[34] Under MLAC the requested state must provide, where possible, that assistance be supplied in a manner stipulated by the requesting member state. Accordingly, a UK authority can request assistance from a signatory state to this Convention in a format that may not be allowed in that particular country, for example, an interview under caution using protections prescribed by the Police and Criminal Evidence Act 1984.

The requested state can refuse such a request only if it is contrary to a fundamental principle of law.

This Article also recognises the significance of the power to specify certain time limits for complying with a request, and commits states to recognise such deadlines.

19–015 **Article 5:-** This establishes the general rule that procedural documents that are required to be sent by a Member State to a person in the territory of another Member State should be sent directly to that person by post, together with accompanying explanatory documents.

Article 6:- This Article also shifts the emphasis established under the 1959 Convention in relation to the transmission of requests. Under that Convention the requests were transmitted through the medium of central authorities in most cases. This Article now requires that such requests should as a general rule be transmitted directly between judicial

[34] Art.3 of the 1959 Convention.

authorities. Recognising that the role of judicial authorities in the UK is different to that in the civil law jurisdictions of most signatory states, the UK has a discretion to declare that such request should still be transmitted via the central authority.

Article 7:- This Article formalises the previously informal mutual legal assistance arrangements in existence for many years between law enforcement agencies within the EU[35] It allows the police to engage in the spontaneous communication of information to and from their counterparts in other Member States.[36]

Article 10:- This Article permits evidence to be given remotely by video link by a witness or expert in proceedings in another Member State. It must be shown that attendance in person would be undesirable, for example on the grounds of ill health or age, or that it would not be possible or practical, for the witness to attend the proceedings in person if he would be in danger.

Article 11:- Similarly to Article 10, this allows for evidence to be given by telephone in certain circumstances. 19–016

Article 13:- This Article allows for the establishment of "Joint Investigative Teams" for a particular criminal investigation and for a particular period of time, as envisaged at Tampere

Article 14:- Under this Article covert investigations conducted by law enforcement officers from one Member State may in certain circumstances be conducted on the territory of another Member State. Drafted with considerable flexibility, this Article recognises the need for tight controls over such activity, and wide discretion is left to each state as to how these arrangements should operate in practice.

Article 16:- This allows for a Member state to request the interception of a telecommunication and the transmission of that material to the requesting state. Again, in the light of the potential breach of privacy, this provision allows states some flexibility in implementation. This is particularly important in the case of the UK where under the Regulation of Investigative Powers Act 2000 ("RIPA") it is a criminal offence to disclose intercept product.[37] Although this is a coercive power, there is no requirement of double criminality as there is in relation to powers of search and seizure.

[35] For example Kent Constabulary established a European Liaison Unit in the 1960s to handle transnational enquiries.

[36] Such arrangements also formalised in the UK for the FSA under s.354 Financial Services and Markets Act 2000 placing a duty on the FSA to take such steps as it considers appropriate to co-operate with other persons in the UK *or elsewhere* who have functions similar to the FSA in relation to the prevention or detection of crime.

[37] See RIPA Ch.23 s.1.

FIRST PROTOCOL TO THE 2000 MLAC CONVENTION

19–017 On October 16, 2001 a Protocol to MLAC 2000 was signed, dealing primarily with assistance in respect of banking information and confidentiality in relation to serious fraud and money-laundering in particular. The protocol is designed to be read with the Convention, and expands on the range of assistance which may be provided. The Protocol allows, in certain circumstances, member states to exchange details of the bank accounts of suspects. Sections 32–36 of CICA form the UK's domestic legislative response to the 2001 Protocol, applying to the use of banking information. However, these sections of the Act are not yet in force.

EFFECT OF THE TERRORIST ATTACKS OF SEPTEMBER 11, 2001

19–018 The above developments demonstrate that, in the investigation and prosecution of crimes, drug trafficking, serious fraud and money laundering offences were usually the stimulus for closer international legal co-operation. The stimulus changed to terrorism after the attacks on New York and Washington DC in September 2001.

On September 19, 2001 the European Commission published its proposed Framework Decision on terrorism. On September 21, 2001 the EU announced an "Action Plan", consolidating its position in relation to US assistance, security and terrorism. The September 2001 attacks undoubtedly brought world-wide attention to transnational crime, creating an atmosphere in which greater co-operation was attempted as a matter of urgency. The effect of such co-operation is evident not only from the subsequent adoption of new extradition arrangements, but from the EU-US mutual assistance and extradition agreement signed on the June 28, 2003.

EU/US CONVENTION ON MUTUAL LEGAL ASSISTANCE 2003[37a]

19–019 Before the signing of the 2003 Convention only bilateral arrangements existed between EU Member States and the USA in mutual assistance matters.[38]

This 2003 Convention is the first comprehensive treaty between the EU as a whole and any non-EU state on criminal law. Under the Treaty of Amsterdam the EU has the power under Art.38 to negotiate and agree such treaties.[39] The Convention builds on existing bilateral treaties in force between most EU countries and the US in relation to extradition and mutual assistance procedures. In the UK the relevant instrument was the 1994 Treaty which came into force on December 2, 1996 and covered assistance in respect of:

[37a] See App.C–008.

[38] Other instruments such as the US and 123 countries signed the UN Convention against Transnational Organised Crime in Palermo in December 15, 2000. This Convention was particularly important in relation to countries where the US does not have a mutual assistance treaty.

[39] Art.38, in conjunction with Art.24, enables international agreements in third pillar matters to be concluded by the Council on a recommendation by the Presidency.

"identifying, tracing, freezing, seizing and forfeiting the proceeds and instrumentalities of crime".[40]

Although modelled on MLAC 2000 and the subsequent Protocol to that Convention, the EU/US Convention is in some respects more developed. The main provisions are as follows: 19–020

- — The Convention gives US authorities access to information from banking and non-banking financial institutions (especially bureaux de change)[41] in investigations into criminal offences. Assistance may not be refused on the grounds of bank secrecy.[42]
- — The Convention establishes that "Joint Investigative Teams" can be set up for the purpose of facilitating investigations or prosecutions involving the US and one or more Member States.[43] Unlike the MLAC provisions, there is no clear guidance here as to how these teams will operate in practice and who will be responsible for them.
- — The Convention allows for the video transmission of evidence of a witness or expert in proceedings in or from the US.[44]
- — The Convention extends the categories of authorities that can seek assistance to "administrative" authorities, provided that that authority is investigating conduct with a view to a criminal prosecution.[45]

States retain the right to refuse a request from the USA under any grounds that existed under any bilateral treaty, or if no such treaty existed, to refuse on grounds of security, sovereignty or other essential interest. There is no express provision allowing the EU requested State to refuse a request on the ground that it relates to an investigation or prosecution where the death penalty might be applied.[46] It would appear that each case will be considered by the relevant authority on its merits,[47] even though all EU states have signed Protocol 13 to the European Convention on Human Rights, which prohibits the death penalty absolutely.

THE FRAMEWORK DECISION ON THE FREEZING OF PROPERTY AND EVIDENCE[48]

The Council adopted this Framework Decision on July 22, 2003, following principles first discussed at Tampere in 1999. The objective set out at Art.1 is to establish 19–021

[40] Art.1(2).
[41] para.32 House of Lords Select Committee on the European Union 38th Report.
[42] Art.4.
[43] Art.5.
[44] Art.6.
[45] Art.8.
[46] Art.13 of the extradition agreement provides such a safeguard.
[47] para.30 House Lords Select Committee on the European Union 38th Report.
[48] July 22, 2003, 2003/577/JHA; App.C–010.

rules and procedures, such as the requirement that the requesting state issues a certificate of request, under which Member States may recognise and implement a freezing order. This Decision requires the mutual recognition of orders issued for the purpose of freezing evidence with a view to its eventual transfer to the issuing State, or for the purpose of freezing property with a view to its eventual confiscation. It is limited to provisional measures to prevent the destruction or disposal of evidence or property. These measures, including coercive measures, are a matter for the law of the executing State and the transfer of any evidence obtained is still governed by the well established rules of mutual legal assistance.

Title 2, encompassing Arts 4–12, outlines the procedure for freezing evidence, and retaining any property so held. Arts 5 and 6 emphasise the need for member states to recognise freezing orders issued by other EU states without further procedure than that contained in the Decision itself.[49] Article 7 provides grounds which allow a state to refuse to recognise or execute such an order:[50]

- The certificate of request has not been produced, is incomplete or manifestly does not correspond to the freezing order;
- There is immunity or privilege under the law of the executing state making it impossible to execute the order;
- It is immediately clear from the information provided in the certificate that to render assistance would infringe the *ne bis in idem* principle (double jeopardy);
- The act on which the order is based does not constitute an offence under the law of the executing State. This exception does not however apply to orders involving taxes or duties where the executing state does not impose the same type of tax or duty.

19–022 The language of Art.7 emphasises that refusal to recognise a request will be exercised exceptionally, so that the vast majority of requests will be processed, recognised and implemented as efficiently as practicable.

This Decision is implemented in the UK by CICA.[51]

II. MUTUAL LEGAL ASSISTANCE BODIES

EUROPOL

19–023 Europol is an EU organisation responsible for European criminal intelligence matters, proposed at the Maastricht Treaty and established by the Europol

[49] Art.5(1) Framework Decision.
[50] Art.7(1) (a)–(d) Framework Decision.
[51] Ch.20.

Convention which came into force on October 1, 1998. On July 1, 1999 this organisation commenced operations from its base at The Hague.

Europol was given a greater involvement in EU policing matters than its predecessor, the European Drugs Unit, which had begun operations in January 1994. Initially the organisation's function was limited to certain EU-specific offences, including illegal immigration, drug trafficking, money laundering and people smuggling.[52] From 2002 the remit has been broadened to include all serious international crime Europol's main functions are as follows:

- Facilitating the exchange of information, in accordance with national law, between Europol Liaison Officers (ELOs). ELOs are seconded to Europol by the Member States as representatives of their national law enforcement agencies.
- Providing operational analysis in support of member states' operations.
- Generating strategic reports (*e.g.* threat assessments) and crime analysis on the basis of information and intelligence supplied by member states, generated by Europol or gathered from other sources.
- Providing expertise and technical support for investigations and operations carried out within the EU, under the supervision and the legal responsibility of the member states concerned.

In addition to the above functions, Europol is obliged under its Convention to maintain a computer system (TECS) which encompasses: 19–024

- an information system;
- an analysis system;
- an index system.

The analysis and index systems are already established. A provisional version of the information system became operational on January 1, 2002, whereas the establishment of the final version that will connect all member states is under development.

The system will combine technical data from the European Central Bank with personal data provided by member states. Europol's annual report 2002 cited unexpected technical problems as the reason for the delay in launching EIS. The system is now described as fully functional, although no information is available concerning the number of available terminals or whether the system is actually "online".

The EU Accession States[53] must adopt the Europol Convention and send notification of their intention to join Europol before membership can be considered. An applicant state can only become a member of Europol three months after notification is received by Europol.

[52] Annexe to the Europol Convention for full list of relevant crimes.

[53] Cyprus, Czech Republic, Estonia, Hungary, Latvia, Lithuania, Malta, Poland, Slovakia and Slovenia. All joined on May 1, 2004.

NATIONAL CRIMINAL INTELLIGENCE SERVICE ("NCIS")

19–025 The International Division of NCIS is composed of the National Central Bureau (otherwise known as Interpol UK or Interpol London); this is the UK Division of Europol and the International Liaison Office. The International Liaison Office supports the Crime and Drug Liaison Officer network in Europe and the US.

NCIS provides a centre within the UK for the provision of informal mutual assistance to foreign law enforcement bodies as well as outward requests from regional law enforcement bodies within the UK.

THE EUROPEAN JUDICIAL NETWORK IN CRIMINAL MATTERS ("EJN")

19–026 This body was created as a result of a joint action by the European Council on June 29, 1998[54] and was launched on December 1, 2002. It is based in the Hague, in the headquarters of Eurojust. This body was established to facilitate mutual legal assistance throughout the EU. The EJN is made up of:

- the central authorities responsible for judicial co-operation;
- a series of contact points in each member state;
- Liaison Magistrates located within each state to provide assistance.[55]

EUROJUST

19–027 Eurojust was planned at Tampere and was established on the February 28, 2002. Its asserted purpose is to reinforce measures taken against serious organised crime, by improving assistance between criminal justice agencies, facilitating more effective cross-border criminal investigations and prosecutions, including assistance in respect of extradition as well as mutual legal assistance.

The College of Eurojust was originally composed of members from Germany, France, Portugal, Sweden and Belgium, was expanded later, and now includes the recently acceded states. It is based in The Hague and has a representative from each state, normally a prosecutor, judge or police officer of similar competence, and an elected President whose term of office is three years.

It is intended that Eurojust will work closely with Europol. Eurojust is not intended to be an organisation by which established mutual legal assistance procedures can be avoided: rather it is intended to be used by prosecutors to ensure that requests for assistance are dealt with expeditiously. Experience has shown that many requests for assistance have presented problems which established routes of communication been inadequate to remedy. One of the more important functions of

[54] Council Joint Action 98/428/JHA.
[55] Joint Action 98/277/JHA.

Eurojust will be to provide expeditious assistance. Eurojust's work in this area is claimed to have increased by 50 per cent in the 12 months from 2002–2003 to 300 cases in 2003.[56–57]

Eurojust also is also designed to provide a forum for prosecutors and investigators involved in transnational cases to meet and discuss those cases.

It is also intended that Eurojust will also play an active role in assisting Joint Investigative Teams. There have always been informal arrangements between cross-border investigative agencies but formal regulation of JITs was established by Art.13 of MLAC 2000. These teams will deal with criminal investigations that have a wider European dimension. A team will be based in the State most involved in the investigation and will have team members seconded from other States where criminal conduct is being or is to be investigated. Eurojust will provide legal assistance to these teams, and it can request that a member State set up such a team in respect of a particular investigation.

THE FINANCIAL ACTION TASK FORCE ("FATF").

In the late 1980s the G7 (now G8) group decided to initiate an international approach to the organised international laundering of the proceeds of crime. FATF was established. A number of other nations were invited to join and FATF has expanded considerably. FATF produced forty recommendations (largely drawn from the 1988 UN Convention Against Illicit Traffic in Narcotic drugs and Psychotropic Substances and the Statement of Principles of the Basel Committee on Banking Regulations) setting out what it regarded as global best practice. These recommendations were subsequently supplemented following the terrorist attacks of September 2001 by a further eight special recommendations to counter terrorist financing. A number of regional task forces have been created following FATF initiatives (Asia-Pacific Group against money laundering, The Caribbean Financial Action Task Force). 19–028

THE COMMONWEALTH SECRETARIAT

The Secretariat. established in 1965, is the main intergovernmental agency of the Commonwealth, providing for co-operation between member states. It has a Criminal Law Section, based in London, with a responsibility in the mutual legal assistance field to build contacts and provide advice and assistance to member states in respect of these matters. The Secretariat is particularly associated with the Harare Scheme. 19–029

[56–57] Eurojust 2003 Annual Report.

III. FUTURE DEVELOPMENTS

19–030 UK legislative provisions have hitherto been based on the concept of mutual legal assistance. Within the European Union, the principle of mutual recognition of judicial decisions is intended to become the basis for judicial co-operation in both civil and criminal matters, so that when a decision has been made by a judicial/prosecutorial figure at the appropriate level within a State, that decision should automatically be accepted in other States.

This principle lies behind the European Arrest Warrant. The European Commission has proposed the introduction of a similar type of warrant (the European Evidence Warrant ("EEW")) for the obtaining of objects, data or documents that could have been obtained under procedural law measures such as production orders and search and seizure orders.[58] In broad principle this means that certain categories of evidence will, subject to compliance with certain procedures, be provided by authorities within states to other authorities without having to pass through a filtering governmental body, such as the Home Office in the UK.

This proposal at present excludes statements from witnesses or suspects and does not deal with interception of communications or bank monitoring orders. It its present form the Commission Green Paper suggests the repeal of the current safeguard conditions requiring double criminality and consistency with the law of the requested state before coercive powers can be exercised.[59] At present the only mandatory grounds for refusal contemplated are where the investigation or proceedings in the requested state contravenes the double jeopardy principle, or the privilege against self-incrimination.[60]

19–031 It should be noted that there is no requirement for member states to establish legal remedies before the use of coercive powers or after the use of non-coercive powers.[61] Any challenge in relation to the lawfulness of the EEW must be taken in the jurisdiction of the requesting state. Accordingly, if the subject of the EEW is in the UK, and the warrant is executed at the request of an Italian Investigating Magistrate, that person can challenge the execution of the warrant only in Italy.[62]

The Commission considers this proposal to be the first step towards a single mutual recognition instrument that would in due course replace all of the existing mutual assistance regimes.[63] The consultation process in the UK in respect of this proposal has been completed and is being assessed,[64] and it is clear that the UK Government is broadly supportive. Accordingly to the Parliamentary Under-Secretary of State at the Home Office (Caroline Flint):

58 An initiative under Art.34, para.2 Treaty of the European Union.

59 Art.2(b) 1959 Convention and Art.51 Schengen Agreement.

60 Art.12 para.1 Commission Proposal.

61 Art.19 Commission Proposal.

62 Art.19 para.2 Commission Proposal.

63 Explanatory Note to the Council Framework Decision COM (2003) 688 Final.

64 See *www.homeoffice.gov.uk*.

> "The Government supports the principle of mutual recognition, and welcomes measures which may lead to more effective an efficient judicial co-operation. The concept of the EEW is a reasonable development of the mutual recognition programme of 2001 because the EEW would provide greater legal certainty that evidence within the scope of the decision can be obtained from other Member States."[65]

The current estimate is that this proposal will be implemented by domestic legislation in early 2007.

IV. CRIME (INTERNATIONAL CO-OPERATION) ACT 2003 ("CICA")

INTRODUCTION

In introducing this new Act, considered in detail in Chs 20 and 21, the Home Secretary, David Blunkett, asserted: 19–032

> "The Crime (International Co-operation) Act 2003 will significantly improve our ability to take effective and prompt action. We have already been setting the EU agenda in police and judicial co-operation and this Act has given us the opportunity to turn words into action".[66]

CICA implements measures contained in seven separate European Union agreements.[67] It repeals the following sections and schedules of the Criminal Justice (International Co-operation)1990 Act[68]:

- s.1: — service of overseas process in the UK.
- s.2: — service of UK process overseas.
- s.3: — provision of evidence from overseas for use in UK proceedings.
- s.4: — provision of evidence in the UK for use overseas.
- s.7: — search and seizure in England and Wales of material for use in overseas investigation.
- s.8: — search and seizure in Scotland of material for use in overseas investigation.
- s.11: — service of UK process as applied to courts-martial, etc.
- Sch.1: — supports s.4 above in relation to the provision of UK evidence for use overseas.
- Sch.4, paras 6(2) and 8: — supplemental.

65 4th Report of the Select committee on European Scrutiny.

66 Home Office Press Release October 30, 2003.

67 Schengen 1990/MLAC/1959 Convention/Protocol to that Convention 2001/Framework Decision on freezing assets and evidence/Framework Decision on combating terrorism/ Convention on driving disqualifications & Framework Decision on non-cash means of payment agreed in 2001 (applies to all member states of the EU plus Norway and Iceland).

68 Referred to as the 1990 Act.

The other sections and schedules of the 1990 Act remain in force and, where relevant, are referred to below. The principal remaining provisions of the 1990 Act deal with the transfer of prisoners[69] and these procedures, although not repealed, have been supplemented by CICA.[70]

19–033 Sections 1–9, 13–19, 26–31 and 47–51 of Part One of CICA came into force on April 26, 2004.[71] Sections 32–46 implement the Protocol to the Convention on Mutual Assistance in Criminal Matters. Sections 10–12 and 20–25 implement the Framework Decision on the recognition in the EU of orders freezing property and evidence.

Although many of the provisions of CICA emanate from the EU, CICA covers all overseas assistance and is not restricted to EU countries. It extends to the whole of the UK, with the following exceptions:[72]

- ss.32 to 36 (which relate to requests for information about banking transactions in England, Wales and Northern Ireland for use abroad) extend only to England, Wales and Northern Ireland;
- ss.37 to 41 (which relate to requests for information about banking transactions in Scotland for use abroad) extend only to Scotland.

The Act is in five parts; these chapters concentrate primarily on Pt 1, the section of the Act that contains the main provisions dealing with mutual legal assistance.[73]

Mutual legal assistance in this context covers the following activities both in the UK and on behalf of the UK:

- the service of process (summonses, judgements and other procedural documents);
- the freezing, obtaining and transmission of evidence (including witness statements on oath, documentary and banking evidence);
- the exercise of search and seizure powers;
- the temporary transfer of prisoners, with their consent, to assist with criminal investigations and proceedings.
- television and telephone links for court hearings.

19–034 In general terms the UK is now required to provide assistance that falls under the above headings to any requesting State or territory. It is not a condition that the requesting State must also be in a position to provide a reciprocal level of assistance to the UK. The principle of "double criminality" no longer applies.[74] The exception is where the assistance is sought in the absence of agreement in relation to fiscal

69 ss.5 & 6.
70 ss.47 & 48 CICA.
71 Home Office MLA Circular; App.C–013.
72 Neither of these provisions is in force yet.
73 Other miscellaneous provisions deal with police co-operation and recognition of driving disqualifications.
74 See Chs 2 and 6 in respect of extradition law.

offences[75] and where the assistance sought requires the use of search and seizure powers.[76]

Assistance in the restraint and confiscation of the proceeds of crime is dependent on a bilateral agreement or other international agreements. Those applicable which have been ratified by the UK are:

- 1959 European Convention and the 1978 Protocol;
- the 1990 European Convention on Laundering, Search, Seizure and Confiscation of the Proceeds from Crime;
- the 1988 UN Convention against Illicit Traffic in Narcotic Drugs and Psychotrophic Substances (The Vienna Convention);
- the Harare Scheme.[77]

UK CENTRAL AUTHORITIES

There are three central authorities principally responsible for dealing with requests in respect of mutual legal assistance:[78] 19–035

a) England and Wales:- the United Kingdom Central Authority ("UKCA"), located within the Judicial Co-operation Unit of the Home Office. This authority represents the Secretary of State;
b) Scotland:- the Scottish Crown Office, which represents the Lord Advocate;
c) Northern Ireland:- the Northern Ireland Office, which represents the Secretary of State.

In CICA reference is made to "central authorities" and "territorial authorities". Subject to certain exceptions, such references are to the Secretary of State to the Home Department.[79] Where assistance is sought by, from or through the Secretary of State, such assistance is given effect by the UK Central Authority, located within the Judicial Co-operation Unit of the Home Office.[80–81] The UKCA is the initial point of contact for general inquiries in respect of mutual legal assistance, and it has the task of ensuring that incoming and outgoing requests are submitted and forwarded correctly. The UKCA is not responsible for dealing with judicial co-operation with the Channel Islands, the Isle of Man or the UK Overseas Territories. Requests between Gibraltar and EU/ Schengen States must be routed through the Foreign & Commonwealth Office "post-box".[82]

[75] CICA 2003 s.14.
[76] CICA 2003 s.16.
[77] See para.1.5.
[78] Customs & Excise can deal with letters of request when the power has been delegated by the Treasury s.27(1)
[79] Home Secretary.
[80–81] Or the other bodies in NI and Scotland (UKCA used for clarity).
[82] See App.C–012.

19–036 The responsibilities of the UKCA include:[83]

- ensuring that requests for legal assistance conform with the requirements of law in the relevant part of the UK and the UK's international obligations;
- ensuring that execution of requests is not inappropriate on public policy grounds, (requests which, for example, breach the principle of double jeopardy will not be executed);
- deciding on the best way to execute a request;
- maintaining the confidentiality of a request where necessary;
- ensuring that assistance is provided in a timely manner;
- drawing the attention of the courts, police and other agencies to requests that evidence be obtained in the presence of foreign law officers prosecutors or defence lawyers;
- seeking requesting authorities' agreement to meet extra-ordinary costs of executing requests and for services such as interpreters or stenographers or for duplication of documents;
- transmitting evidence received to the requesting authorities when it is not returned directly.

In the case of incoming requests, the UKCA will determine the appropriate law enforcement body to execute the request (local police, SFO, NCIS). In the case of outgoing requests that are also routed through the UKCA, it will establish and ensure that the correct recipient is identified. The UKCA now has established close links with Eurojust[84] as well as EJN[85] to ensure more effective co-operation.

INFORMAL MUTUAL ASSISTANCE

19–037 Although the Secretary of State deals with a large number of requests for legal assistance, many requests are dealt with on an informal basis between law enforcement agencies. In the UK such requests will normally be routed through the UK National Bureau of Interpol at NCIS[86] without the requirement to go through the central authority. Such requests include:[87]

- interviewing witnesses or suspects in criminal investigations where the person to be interviewed is willing to co-operate, without appearing or needing to appear before a judicial authority in the UK;

[83] Home Office Guidelines, App.C–012.
[84] See 19–027.
[85] See 19–026.
[86] See 19–025.
[87] Home Office Guidelines, App.C–012.

- sharing of information and intelligence concerning investigations into offences which have been committed in the UK (provided that the information or intelligence is not being requested for use in proceedings);
- asset tracing enquiries;
- providing details of previous convictions;
- providing, for investigative purposes details of UK telephone subscribers;
- providing details of keepers of motor vehicles registered in the UK and of driving licences issued in the UK;
- obtaining medical or dental statements or records where the patient has given written consent.

Such requests should only be made through the Secretary of State if to do so is a requirement of the authority making the request. Requests that have mixed legal assistance and investigative assistance elements may be sent to both the central authority and the UK NCB of Interpol and should be clearly marked as such.[88]

Such informal assistance can also be exercised by other law enforcement agencies such as the FSA, DTI, OFT, normally by the use of a Memorandum of Understanding.

[88] See appendix to the former Home Office Guidelines to the 1990 Act.

CHAPTER 20

MUTUAL LEGAL ASSISTANCE IN THE UNITED KINGDOM; THE 2003 STATUTORY SCHEME

(by Alun Jones and Michael O'Kane)

I. SERVICE OF OVERSEAS PROCESS IN THE UK

Sections 1 and 2 of the Crime International Co-operation Act 2003 ("CICA") replace s.1 of the 1990 Act. The categories of proceedings in respect of which process can be served have been extended,[1] but there is otherwise little change of substance. 20–001

Section 1 deals with the service of process, that is, process from overseas authorities to persons in the UK, which must be sent through the Secretary of State;[2] it will mostly relate to countries outside the EU.[3]

> "1.—(1) The power conferred by subsection (3) is exercisable where the Secretary of State receives any process or other document to which this section applies from the government of, or other authority in, a country outside the United Kingdom, together with a request for the process or document to be served on a person in the United Kingdom.
>
> (2) This section applies —
>
> (a) to any process issued or made in that country for the purposes of criminal proceedings,
>
> (b) to any document issued or made by an administrative authority in that country in administrative proceedings,
>
> (c) to any process issued or made for the purposes of any proceedings on an appeal before a court in that country against a decision in administrative proceedings,
>
> (d) to any document issued or made by an authority in that country for the purposes of clemency proceedings.
>
> (3) The Secretary of State may cause the process or document to be served by post or, if the request is for personal service, direct the chief officer of police for the area in which that person appears to be to cause it to be personally served on him.
>
> (4) In relation to any process or document to be served in Scotland, references in this section to the Secretary of State are to be read as references to the Lord Advocate."

1 See 20–003.
2 Also known as the central authority.
3 The Schengen Agreement and MLAC 2000 allow EU Member States to serve most of their procedural documents directly by post without having to send them through a central authority.

WHAT IS "PROCESS"?

20–002 The term "process" is used for the purposes of England, Wales and Northern Ireland to denote any summons or order made by a court. In the case of Scotland it refers to any citation by a court or prosecuting authority as well as any court order. In Scotland the term "citation" is used rather than "process" to describe the procedure under which a person is called to court to answer an action or give evidence as a witness. In both cases it includes:

- any document issued or made by a court for service on parties or witnesses;
- any document issued by a prosecuting authority outside the UK for the purpose of criminal proceedings, for administrative proceedings that have the right of appeal to a court with a criminal jurisdiction, and clemency proceedings.

The 1990 Act was narrower, and applied only to a summons or other process requiring a person to appear as a defendant or as a witness in criminal proceedings.

PROCEEDINGS TO WHICH CICA APPLIES

20–003 CICA implements the Schengen Agreement[4] and the EU European Convention on Mutual Legal Assistance in Criminal Matters 2000 ("MLAC 2000")[5] by extending the categories of proceedings over which assistance can now be sought to include "administrative proceedings" and "clemency proceedings", as well as "criminal proceedings".[6] It appears from the drafting that a document may belong to more than one class.

The categories of proceedings are as follows:

ADMINISTRATIVE PROCEEDINGS

20–004 These are defined in s.51(1) as:

> "proceedings outside the United Kingdom to which Article 3(1) of the Mutual Legal Assistance Convention applies (proceedings brought by administrative authorities in respect of administrative offences where a decision in the proceedings may be the subject of an appeal before a court."

This category exists in a number of states, particularly within the EU. Under the provisions of the Schengen Convention and MLAC 2000, the UK is obliged to

4 Art.49(c).
5 App. C–004, Art.3(1).
6 s.1(2).

provide requested assistance in these such proceedings, and CICA extends that obligation to all overseas states.

In some EU states such as Holland, Germany, Austria and Belgium,[7] administrative proceedings include some driving offences which would constitute minor criminal offences in this country. In Scandinavian states, certain environmental actions or claims are classified as administrative, not criminal. "Administrative offences" are included in this section of CICA to enable these EU states to request assistance in circumstances in which the UK would be able to request assistance itself.

The definition requires the availability of appeal to a criminal court. The example given in the explanatory report to MLAC 2000 is a German offence, not classified as a criminal offence, punishable by way of a fine imposed by an administrative authority, where there is a right to appeal to the ordinary criminal courts.[8]

CLEMENCY PROCEEDINGS

These are defined in s.51(1) as: 20–005

> "... proceedings in a country outside the United Kingdom, not being proceedings before a court exercising criminal jurisdiction, for the removal or reduction of a penalty imposed on conviction of an offence."

Clemency and certain other civil proceedings are obviously associated with criminal proceedings. It is not clear how a court can consider the removal of a penalty imposed on conviction if it is not "a court exercising criminal jurisdiction". The relationship between these proceedings and administrative proceedings is unclear. During the Parliamentary debates upon this section the Attorney General, Lord Goldsmith QC, struggled with this alien judicial concept:

> "The basic case will be that where there has been a conviction of an offence and there is a procedure called a clemency proceeding that goes before a body that is not exercising criminal jurisdiction that considers whether the penalty should be removed or reduced. If that is wrong, someone will write to correct me".[9]

CIVIL PROCEEDINGS JOINED TO CRIMINAL PROCEEDINGS

Art.49(d) of the Schengen Acquis requires assistance to be given in this extended 20–006
category, in which proceedings are attached to criminal proceedings, and a final

7 *Hansard* Lord Goldsmith, 25/2/03 at col.145.
8 See Explanatory Notes to Art.3 of MLAC 2000.
9 *Hansard* Text January 23, 2003.

decision has yet to be reached in those criminal proceedings. For this purpose criminal proceedings are defined as including

> "… criminal proceedings outside the United Kingdom in which a civil order may be made".[10]

THE SERVICE OF PROCESS IN THE UK

20–007 Section 1(3) is not an obligatory provision. It confers a discretion on the Secretary of State in relation to such requests for the service of process.[11]

Sections 1 and 2, above, deal with the service of process by an overseas state[12] which it is not sent directly, and must therefore be transmitted through the central authority in the requested state. Direct service between the state and the recipient, by-passing the central authority, gives effect to the Council of Europe's second additional Protocol to MLAC 2000.[13] The Secretary of State has a discretion to expand this provision to "any other country designated by an order".[14] This allows the Secretary of State to designate non-EU countries at different times for different provisions of the Act.[15]

When such process is received by the Secretary of State, he has two options. He may forward the process to the ultimate recipient using the postal system, or he may direct the Chief Officer of police in the relevant area to serve it personally, if the requesting state has asked for personal service.[16] A simple onward postal service requires the recipient to sign and return a receipt. Should the recipient fail to comply with this request, the Secretary of State will advise the requesting state that process has not been served and the requesting state may then request that the process be served by personal service. If the process is served by the police, the police must inform the central authority whether and how it was served, and obtain a receipt signed by the recipient, if possible. Accordingly, it appears that if there is no signed receipt, but the police confirm that the process was served, the central authority will advise the requesting state that the process has been served. The law of the country in question, not that of the UK, will determine whether the document has been served sufficiently.

20–008 There is no requirement that the recipient of the process in the UK be resident in the UK; simply that he is "in the territory"[17] at the relevant time. When the

[10] s.51(1).

[11] See *R. v Secretary of State for the Home Department Ex p. Fininvest Spa* [1997] 1 W.L.R. 743 consideration of the exercise of such a discretion.

[12] Normally a non-EU/Schengen country although EU & Schengen countries may also serve process via the central authority in the requested state if that is required by their domestic law for that type of process serving

[13] The Council has 44 members (25 EU member states and 19 non-EU states).

[14] s.51(2).

[15] By way of statutory instrument.

[16] s.1(3).

[17] Art.5 of MLAC 2000.

process has been served by post from the central authority, a notice will be included with the process that:

- informs the recipient that this overseas process requiring a person to appear as a party or attend as a witness does not impose any obligation under UK law to comply with it;
- advises the recipient that he may wish to seek legal advice on the consequences of non-compliance under the law of the issuing state;
- advises the recipient that he might not have the same rights and privileges in the overseas proceedings as in proceedings in the UK.[18]

This notice replicates s.1(3) to (6) of the 1990 Act. It is apparently drafted with Art.6 of the ECHR in contemplation.

Although co-operation between states (particularly within the EU) has developed quickly, there is no indication at present that witnesses resident in one state will be compelled to attend proceedings in another jurisdiction.

The recipient of such a notice is under no obligation in UK law to comply with it.[19] There may however be adverse consequences for him if he were to travel to the requesting State where he could be compelled to comply.[20] If the person is a witness in proceedings in an EU state, he should be granted immunity from arrest or prosecution for a period of 15 days after the date when he or she could have left the jurisdiction of the requesting country.[21] Although a person is advised within the notice to seek legal advice, there is currently no provision to allow an individual facing such a request to obtain legal advice under the legal aid scheme. If process has been received from any overseas state (non-EU/Schengen) by any agency within the UK, that agency must forward the process to the appropriate central authority.

II. THE SERVICE OF UK PROCESS OVERSEAS

Sections 3 and 4 of CICA apply to the service of UK process, for the purposes of criminal proceedings, on persons overseas. These sections replace s.2 of the 1990 Act and enable service of all documents issued or made for the purposes of criminal proceedings, ensuring consistency with the interpretation of "procedural documents" envisaged in the Schengen Convention and MLAC 2000.[22] There is no provision for the service of documents relating to administrative or clemency proceedings, because the UK does not have proceedings of this kind. 20–009

[18] Home Office Circular para.20, App. C–013.

[19] *Re Durkin*,unreported 16/03/01 (CO/1378/1999).

[20] *ibid*.

[21] Art.12 of the European Convention on Mutual Assistance 1959, App. C–001.

[22] Art.5.

"**3.**—(1) This section applies to any process issued or made for the purposes of criminal proceedings by a court in England and Wales or Northern Ireland.

(2) The process may be issued or made in spite of the fact that the person on whom it is to be served is outside the United Kingdom.

(3) Where the process is to be served outside the United Kingdom and the person at whose request it is issued or made believes that the person on whom it is to be served does not understand English, he must—

(a) inform the court of that fact, and
(b) provide the court with a copy of the process, or of so much of it as is material, translated into an appropriate language.

(4) Process served outside the United Kingdom requiring a person to appear as a party or attend as a witness—

(a) must not include notice of a penalty,
(b) must be accompanied by a notice giving any information required to be given by rules of court.

(5) If process requiring a person to appear as a party or attend as a witness is served outside the United Kingdom, no obligation to comply with the process under the law of the part of the United Kingdom in which the process is issued or made is imposed by virtue of the service.

(6) Accordingly, failure to comply with the process does not constitute contempt of court and is not ground for issuing a warrant to secure the attendance of the person in question.

(7) But the process may subsequently be served on the person in question in the United Kingdom (with the usual consequences for non-compliance).

4.—(1) Process to which section 3 applies may, instead of being served by post, be served on a person outside the United Kingdom in accordance with arrangements made by the Secretary of State.

(2) But where the person is in a participating country, the process may be served in accordance with those arrangements only if one of the following conditions is met.

(3) The conditions are—

(a) that the correct address of the person is unknown,
(b) that it has not been possible to serve the process by post,
(c) that there are good reasons for thinking that service by post will not be effective or is inappropriate."

METHODS OF SERVICE OF PROCESS

As in the case of service in the UK of overseas process, the process can be served either directly by post or through the Secretary of State. 20–010

Where the recipient is in a Schengen state, the process should be submitted by post unless one of the following conditions applies:

- the person's address is unknown;
- it has not been possible to serve the process by post;
- there are good reasons for thinking that service by post will not be effective or is inappropriate.

Where the recipient is not in a Schengen state, the process may still be submitted directly or through the Secretary of State.[23]

If the process is sent through the Secretary of State, that authority may:

- transmit the process directly by post to the recipient if it should have been sent directly to them by the issuing authority;
- transmit the process to the central or other competent authority in the country where the recipient is present with a request for postal service;
- transmit the process to the central authority in the country where the recipient is present with a request for personal service.

Where the process is sent through the overseas central authority, the Secretary of State may seek proof of service from that authority and will forward this to the court upon request.[24] 20–011

The serving process imposes no obligation on the recipient under UK law to comply; therefore failure to comply does not constitute contempt of court. However, if the process is later served on the person in the UK, the usual consequences for non-compliance will apply.[25] If the recipient of the process is a witness summoned from overseas to give evidence in the UK, that person[26] can seek immunity from prosecution or arrest for a period of fifteen days after the date when he or she could have left the UK jurisdiction.[27] Such an assurance should be given by the UK unless it is not in the public interest to do so.

The Home Office Codes of Practice stipulate that the Home Office will arrange for the execution of all requests for service of summonses within 10 working days of receipt.

[23] From June 1, 2003 the US Department of Justice has delegated process serving to a private contractor, Process Forwarding International of Seattle Washington.

[24] Home Office Circular April 2004 para.26.

[25] Subs.3(4) to (7) of the 2003 Act replaces s.2(3) and (4) of the 1990 Act but does not change the existing practice.

[26] Or the authority in the requested state.

[27] Art.12 of the European Convention on Mutual Assistance 1959 and Harare Scheme.

REQUIREMENTS FOR SERVICE OF PROCESS

20–012 The following must be adhered to by UK parties serving process overseas:[28–29]

- the process must not contain reference to any penalty for non-compliance;
- if the requesting authority has reason to believe that the recipient does not understand English, it must inform the court and the court must then provide a translation of the document into an appropriate language;[30–31]
- a notice containing details of the authority able to provide information about the recipient's rights and obligations under UK law must accompany the process.[32] The person on whose behalf the process is written is responsible for preparing and translating this process;

Process should be sent direct by post to a recipient in a Schengen state unless the address of the recipient is unknown, or postal service is not possible, or there are good reasons for thinking that postal service will not be effective or appropriate.[33–34]

PROOF OF SERVICE

20–013 Where service has been effected otherwise other than by post, the Secretary of State may seek proof of service from the overseas authority.[35] When such proof has been provided and the Secretary of State is satisfied, such proof, if requested, should be forwarded to the court by way of a certificate. The effect of the issue of such a certificate confirming that process has been served, together with the manner and date as that certificate, it is admissible as evidence of any facts so stated.[36]

III. OBTAINING EVIDENCE FROM OVERSEAS

MUTUAL ASSISTANCE IN OBTAINING EVIDENCE FROM OVERSEAS

20–014 Sections 7 and 8 of CICA allow authorities in the UK to request assistance in obtaining evidence from abroad.

[28–29] Home Office MLA Circular, App. C–013.

[30–31] The Magistrates' Courts (Crime (International Co-operation)) Rules 2004 s.3(5); implements Art.5.3 of MLAC 2000.

[32] The Magistrates' Courts (Crime (International Co-operation)) Rules 2004 s.3(2) & (4); Home Office Circular.

[33–34] s.4 of CICA 2003 will be amended by Sch.36 (para.16) of the Criminal Justice Act 2003 when it comes into force.

[35] Home Office Circular to Crime (International Co-operation) Act 2003 para.28.

[36] The Magistrates' Courts (Crime (International Co-operation)) Rules 2004 s.4.

MAKING THE REQUEST

Sections 7 to 9 deal with requests to obtain evidence from abroad in relation to a prosecution or investigation taking place in the UK. The only countries from which the UK cannot effectively request assistance will be those that require a treaty before they can provide assistance.[37] Ss.7 to 9 expand on s.3 of the 1990 Act, which they replace. 20–015

Section 7 of CICA states:

"7.—(1) If it appears to a judicial authority in the United Kingdom on an application made by a person mentioned in subsection (3) —

(a) that an offence has been committed or that there are reasonable grounds for suspecting that an offence has been committed, and

(b) that proceedings in respect of the offence have been instituted or that the offence is being investigated,

the judicial authority may request assistance under this section.

(2) The assistance that may be requested under this section is assistance in obtaining outside the United Kingdom any evidence specified in the request for use in the proceedings or investigation.

(3) The application may be made —

(a) in relation to England and Wales and Northern Ireland, by a prosecuting authority,

(b) in relation to Scotland, by the Lord Advocate or a procurator fiscal,

(c) where proceedings have been instituted, by the person charged in those proceedings.

(4) The judicial authorities are —

(a) in relation to England and Wales, any judge or justice of the peace,

(b) in relation to Scotland, any judge of the High Court or sheriff,

(c) in relation to Northern Ireland, any judge or resident magistrate.

(5) In relation to England and Wales or Northern Ireland, a designated prosecuting authority may itself request assistance under this section if –

(a) it appears to the authority that an offence has been committed or that there are reasonable grounds for suspecting that an offence has been committed, and

(b) the authority has instituted proceedings in respect of the offence in question or it is being investigated.

"Designated" means designated by an order made by the Secretary of State.

[37] Only three members of the Council of Europe have not signed MLAC 2000 (Andorra, Bosnia & Herzegovina and San Marino). There are bilateral treaties with many countries including the Hong Kong SAR and the US and a mutual understanding with Commonwealth countries (the Harare Scheme).

(6) In relation to Scotland, the Lord Advocate or a procurator fiscal may himself request assistance under this section if it appears to him —

(a) that an offence has been committed or that there are reasonable grounds for suspecting that an offence has been committed, and
(b) that proceedings in respect of the offence have been instituted or that the offence is being investigated.

(7) If a request for assistance under this section is made in reliance on Article 2 of the 2001 Protocol in connection with the investigation of an offence, the request must state the grounds on which the person making the request considers the evidence specified in it to be relevant for the purposes of an investigation."

Section 7 sets out the ways in which the prosecution and the defence are entitled to seek assistance in obtaining evidence abroad.

REQUESTS BY THE PROSECUTION[38]

20–016 A designated prosecuting authority may make a direct request for assistance.[39] Such prosecuting authorities are designated by the Secretary of State by statutory instrument. The current list of designated prosecuting authorities is as follows:[40]

- The Attorney-General for England and Wales;
- The Director of Public Prosecutions and any Crown Prosecutor;
- The Director of the Serious Fraud Office;
- The Secretary of State for Trade and Industry;
- The Commissioners of Customs and Excise;
- The Attorney-General for Northern Ireland;
- The Director of Public Prosecutions for Northern Ireland;
- The Lord Advocate for Scotland;
- The Procurator Fiscal for Scotland;
- The Financial Services Authority.

Most requests for mutual legal assistance from the UK are made by designated prosecuting authorities. Before assistance can be sought from abroad, it must appear to the designated prosecuting authority making the application that:

- an offence has been committed or that there are reasonable grounds for suspecting that an offence has been committed; and

[38] Requests for information on banking transactions.
[39] s.7(5).
[40] Annexe C Home Office Circular, App. C–013.

- proceedings in respect of the offence have been instituted by the designated prosecuting authority or that the offence is being investigated.[41]

The request must relate to the obtaining of "evidence . . . for use in the proceedings or investigation."[42] In the context of a criminal case the permissible area of search for evidence will normally be wider during the investigative stage then it would be when the investigation has concluded and the prosecution has commenced.[43]

The request from the designated prosecuting authority can be routed directly to a court exercising jurisdiction in the place where the evidence is situated, or to any authority recognised by the government of the country in question as the appropriate authority for receiving requests of that kind.[44–45] 20–017

This arrangement is new. Designated prosecuting authorities under the 1990 Act had not only to comply with theses conditions outlined above, but the requests had to be sent through the Secretary of State. A prosecuting authority that has not been designated cannot directly make a request for assistance, but must go the court and seek a judicial request.[46]

Assistance may be sought by a UK judicial authority[47] only if it appears that:

- an offence has been committed or that there are reasonable grounds for suspecting that an offence has been committed; and
- proceedings in respect of the offence have been instituted or that the offence is being investigated.

REQUESTS BY THE DEFENCE

When proceedings have been instituted, a person charged in those proceedings is entitled to make an application to the judicial authority for that judicial authority to request assistance on his behalf.[48–49] 20–018

The provisions in respect of seeking such judicial assistance are set out above. A clear distinction is made between the designated prosecuting authority, entitled to make requests itself and to transmit them directly to the requested state, and the defendant, who must apply to the judge to make a request which, if granted, is transmitted through the Secretary of State.

[41] s.7(5).
[42] s.7(2).
[43] *per* Brown L.J. in *R. v Secretary of State Ex p. Fininvest Spa* [1997] 1 W.L.R. 743.
[44–45] s.8(1).
[46] s.7(3)(a).
[47] The "judicial authority" is in England or Wales, any Judge or Justice of the Peace, in Scotland any High Court judge or sheriff and in Northern Ireland any judge or resident magistrate, s.7(4). It applies to the Court of Appeal also see *Atlan v United Kingdom*, T.L.R. July 3, 2001.
[48–49] s.7(1)(b) when read in conjunction with s.7(3)(c).

A defendant remains able to make an application for such judicial assistance only after the institution of the proceedings.[50] Proceedings are "instituted" when a person is either charged or an information is laid against him.[51] The prosecuting authority, however, whether designated or not, is entitled to apply at any time after the commencement of an investigation.[52–56] This may put the defendant at a serious disadvantage. A suspect involved in a serious fraud investigation lasting many years is unable to seek exculpatory evidence that might prevent proceedings being brought against him. In such a circumstance he must waiting until proceedings have commenced, or seek the assistance of the prosecution. The latter option would in practice require the defendant to set out in detail his answer to the allegations, and the prosecuting authority might well decline to help him.

The most likely forum for a defence request will be the Crown Court. Before such a request is made it will be important to identify the exact nature of the evidence to be sought and to examine whether an informal route would be appropriate. The defence may wish to seek the assistance of a witness overseas by way of statement or live evidence. The defence will normally be entitled to make contact with this witness in order to establish if he is willing to assist in the way requested. The Home Office advises that such contact should normally be made on behalf of the defendant by his solicitor or even counsel.[57] If a defendant is unable to secure the voluntary assistance of the witness, he may formally request judicial assistance.[58]

If such judicial assistance is requested, the court should exercise its discretion in favour of the defence application unless there is good reason for refusing.[59] The remedy for a defendant after a refusal is to seek judicial review of this refusal,[60] or plead the refusal as a ground of appeal against conviction.[61]

Irrespective of the identity of the requesting authority, it may be that the offence in question must be one that is under investigation or the subject of proceedings in the UK although this is not expressly stated in CICA. A judge held in *Cuoghi v Governor of Brixton Prison*,[62] that "offence" in s.3(1) of the 1990 Act was limited to domestic offences. On the other hand, in *R. v Governor of Brixton Prison Ex p.*

[50] s.7(3)(c).
[51] s.1 Magistrates Courts Act 1980.
[52–56] s.7(1)(b) and (5)(b).
[57] See Home Office Guidlines, App. C–012.
[58] In the USA this would be pursuant to Title 28, s.1782, of the United States Code, which is available for use in connection with both civil and criminal proceedings in foreign jurisdictions. (See Home Office Guidelines to the 2003 Act for outlined US procedure).
[59] *R. v Forsyth* [1997] 2 Cr. App. R. 299 at 311.
[60] Judicial Review may be available only before arraignment, by virtue of s.28 of the Supreme Court Act 1981. An interlocutory appeal under s.9(11) of the Criminal Justice Act 1987 is unlikely to be available; see *R. v Hedworth* [1997] 1 Cr. App. R. 421.
[61] Only if the refusal is at the preparatory stage (normally used in cases of serious and complex fraud); by virtue of s.9(11) of the Criminal Justrtice Act 1987, an interlocutory appeal to the Court of Appeal is unlikely to be available; see *R. v Hedworth* [1997] 1 Cr. App. R. 421.
[62] [1997] 1 W.L.R. 1346.

Saifi[63] evidence was obtained by the use of RSC Ord.39, r.1. from India, relevant to the question whether, for the purposes of s.11(3) of the Extradition Act 1989, a request for extradition was unjust or oppressive on the ground that the accusation had not been made in good faith. Section 14 of CICA makes it clear that incoming requests from foreign jurisdictions should be in relation to "an offence under the law of the country in question";[64] it is unclear whether the offence for which assistance by way of a request to an overseas jurisdictions is sought must always be an offence against the law of the UK.

FORMAT AND CONTENT OF REQUEST

Letters of request are the means by which the UK and all other common law jurisdictions communicate and explain what is required of the authority from which assistance is sought. Civil Code jurisdictions such as France use a "Commission Rogatoire" for the same purpose. The correct form must be used for any request, in order to ensure recognition.[65] It is important in relation to a Commission Rogatoire that "International" is included in the title as Magistrates within the same state send each other Commissions Rogatoire for evidence in domestic proceedings.[66] **20–019**

There is no official format for letters of request to overseas authorities,[67] but the following should be included:[68]

- The name of the UK judicial or prosecuting authority, and contact details of the individual responsible for the proceedings.
- The full name(s) and addresses of the subject(s) of the investigation or proceedings (if known).
- A description of the nature of the investigation and a summary of the facts of the allegation. It should be made clear from the information provided in relation to the offence(s) that there are reasonable grounds for suspecting that the offence(s) has been committed, and that either proceedings have been instituted or the offence is being investigated. The request should be drafted in sufficient detail to satisfy the above.
- The date of the trial of hearing or any relevant dates in the investigation.
- A description of the evidence or other assistance sought, and any format the evidence is required to be in.[69] This should be as detailed as possible,

63 *The Times*, January 14, 2001.
64 s.14(2)(a).
65 Home Office Guidelines, App. C–012.
66 ibid.
67 Prescribed format does exist in Scotland.
68 Home Office Circular, App. C–013.
69 It should be remembered that for the majority of EU states with judicial systems based on the Civil Code the concept of a witness statement could be alien to them and so guidance on drafting should be supplied. It is also best to avoid using words such as "affidavit" which may not have the same meaning in foreign jurisdictions.

particularly where financial/banking evidence is being sought.[70] The statement should illustrate the existence of evidence in the requested country to a reasonable degree of certainty.

- The purpose and relevance of the evidence requested. It is critical to establish a direct link between the facts of the case as outlined and the evidence sought. The courts have criticised the use of such request for the purposes of "fishing expeditions".[71] Where possible a request should specify dates between which information is sought (for example telephone billing).
- The identity, date of birth and location of any person from whom evidence is required.
- A precise description of any place to be searched.
- A description of any procedures to be followed, the manner in which testimony is to be taken, and any questions which should be asked. The request should state whether and why the presence of officers of the requesting State is required during the execution of the request. The names of such persons should be supplied.
- Details, including telephone number/e-mail address of a British law enforcement officer who is familiar with the investigation.
- Any other relevant information including any request for confidentiality.
- Annexes of Law. Where the offence has been stipulated within the body of the request, the actual legal provision should be annexed. This allows the requested authority the opportunity to determine properly whether the double criminality test (if relevant) has been satisfied.

20–020 It is important to remember that, if the implementation of the request requires a court order, a comprehensive justification within the body of the letter will be required to satisfy any judicial authority. In the USA, there are two standards that apply. In relation to a search warrant it is necessary to show "probable cause" whilst a court order will requires showing "specific and articulable facts showing reasonable grounds to believe the contents . . . or the records or information sought are relevant and material to an ongoing criminal investigation".

If a requested authority agrees to accept a request by the medium of e-mail or fax the formal original document should be sent within seven days.[72] The Code of Practice attached to the Home Office Guidelines states that the central authorities aim to ensure that requests for legal assistance are executed promptly.[73] These authorities have, in the nature of things, only limited influence after the request has been transmitted to the requested authority.

[70] In the case of banking evidence the request must provide the name and number of the account, the other account details and the address of the relevant bank.

[71] *R. v Secretary of State Ex p. Fininvest SpA* [1997] 1 W.L.R. 743.

[72] Home Office Guidelines, App. C–012.

[73] The Code of Practice to the Home Office Guidelines, App. C–012.

Normally the letter should be written in English. It should be accompanied by a letter translated into the language of the state from which assistance is sought.

There is nothing in CICA to prevent the seeking of evidence from a child.[74–75] In fact there is legislative provision which specifically contemplates a request for such evidence.[76–77] In reality any authority seeking such evidence will need to consider the appropriateness of such a request with great care. It is likely that many states will have their own rules for the taking such evidence, and that compliance with these rules will be a requirement of providing any such assistance.

BANKING TRANSACTIONS

Subsection (7) is new: the rest of s.7 essentially re-enacts the 1990 provisions. It requires that any outgoing request for information about banking transactions made to participating countries under Art.2 of the 2001 Protocol must clearly state the relevance of the evidence to the investigation. In the case of other requests the guiding principle is that set out in Art.14 of the 1959 Convention, which requires that mutual assistance requests shall indicate "the object of and reason for the request". 20–021

In the case of banking information, it was recognised during the negotiations of the Protocol that owing to the potential complexity of international financial transactions, additional requirements should apply to ensure that finite resources were not utilised on "fishing expeditions".[78]

SENDING THE REQUEST

Section 8 states that: 20–022

> "8.—(1) A request for assistance under section 7 may be sent —
>
> (a) to a court exercising jurisdiction in the place where the evidence is situated, or
>
> (b) to any authority recognised by the government of the country in question as the appropriate authority for receiving request of that kind.
>
> (2) Alternatively, if it is a request by a judicial authority or a designated prosecuting authority it may be sent to the Secretary of State[79] for forwarding to the court or authority mentioned in subsection (1).

[74–75] A person under the age of 16.
[76–77] s.7 Sex Offenders Act 1997.
[78] *Hansard*, January 13, 2003, col.GC39.
[79] In Scotland, the Lord Advocate.

(3) In cases of urgency, a request for assistance may be sent to —

(a) the International Criminal Police Organisation
(b) any body or person competent to receive it under any provisions adopted under the Treaty on European Union,

for forwarding to any court or authority mentioned in subsection (1)"

This section sets out a new procedure for sending a request for assistance. It enables requests made under s.7 to be sent directly from the requesting authority in the UK to the relevant overseas authority, rather than through the central authorities of the two countries. Under the 1990 Act it was possible to do this only in "urgent" cases. However this Act incorporates an important element of MLAC 2000. If direct transmission is employed, a copy of the letter of request must be emailed to the Secretary of State to allow the process to be logged.[80]

20–023 Where direct transmission as described is not possible because the particular authority in the overseas country is not known, the country is outside the EU, or such transmission is not permitted under MLAC 2000, the option of indirect transmission through the Secretary of State is retained.[81]

Subsection (3) implements Art.6(4) of MLAC 2000, and permits urgent requests to be submitted through either

- Interpol, or
- any other body able to receive it under any provisions adopted under the Treaty on European Union. This provision should allow in due course for requests to be provided directly to the representative of the requesting state at Eurojust in Brussels who can then deal with it directly with his counterpart.

There is no statutory definition within the Act of what constitutes "urgency"; it is therefore a matter to be considered on a request-by-request basis.

USE OF THE EVIDENCE OBTAINED

20–024 Section 9 of CICA governs the use of evidence obtained following a UK request.

"**9.**—(1) This section applies to evidence obtained pursuant to a request for assistance under section 7.

(2) The evidence may not without the consent of the appropriate overseas authority be used for any purpose other than that specified in the request.

80 Home Office Circular, App. C–013.
81 s.8(2).

(3) When the evidence is no longer required for that purpose (or for any other purpose for which such consent has been obtained), it must be returned to the appropriate overseas authority, unless that authority indicates that it need not be returned.

(4) In exercising the discretion conferred by section 25 of the Criminal Justice Act 1988 (c.33) or Article 5 of the Criminal Justice (Evidence, Etc.) (Northern Ireland) Order 1988 (S.I.1988/1847 (N.I.17)[82] in relation to a statement contained in the evidence, the court must have regard –

(a) to whether it was possible to challenge the statement by questioning the person who made it, and
(b) if proceedings have been instituted, to whether the local law allowed the parties to the proceedings to be legally represented when the evidence was being obtained.

(5) In Scotland, the evidence may be received in evidence in evidence without being sworn to by witnesses, so far as that may be done without unfairness to either party.

(6) In this section, the appropriate overseas authority means the authority recognised by the government of the country in question as the appropriate authority for receiving requests of the kind in question."

This section ensures that evidence obtained from an overseas authority may be used only for the purpose for which it was requested (unless the consent of the requested overseas authority has been obtained), and is subject to the same provisions on the admissibility of evidence as evidence obtained under normal domestic arrangements. This section replicates s.3(7) and (9) of the 1990 Act. When the proceedings or investigation for which the evidence was requested have been exhausted, the evidence must be returned to the providing authority unless it indicates that it need not be. It is clear that the requesting party must not use the material obtained for any purpose other than that specified in the request. Therefore, for example, evidence obtained for the purpose of use in trial could not be admitted to support subsequent confiscation proceedings if no consent from the requested state had been sought.[83] 20–025

Under MLAC 2000, signatory countries will be under a general obligation to comply with requests for necessary formalities and procedures to be followed, provided that they do not contradict fundamental principles of their law. The domestic court has a discretion when ruling on the admissibility of any evidence obtained from abroad and sought to be introduced.[84] The central principle remains that evidence must be admissible under the law of the UK. A statement cannot be read unless it has been agreed between the parties or the conditions in the domestic legislation have been met.[85] The source of such a statement or document should be

[82] Exclusion of evidence otherwise admissible.
[83] *R. v Gooch* [1999] 1 Cr. App. R. (S) 283.
[84] s.9(4) adopting the provision in s.25 Criminal Justice Act 1988.
[85] ss.23–26 Criminal Justice Act 1988 as amended by ss.116 and 117 Criminal Justice 2003.

sufficiently identified,[86] although in the case of business documents the court may draw an inference from the documents themselves and the way in which they are placed before the court.[87]

When admissibility has been established the judge has a discretion to exclude the evidence if to do so would be in the interests of justice.[88] In the context of evidence from overseas, the factors to be considered will be whether the defence had an opportunity to be represented during the taking of the evidence, and whether it is possible to challenge the statement by questioning the maker.[89] The latter condition is now more likely to be satisfied given the introduction of the new provisions in respect of evidence given by video link.[90] In respect of the earlier condition, if the prosecution suspects that a witness will not attend, it should seek the evidence by way of letter of request and, in appropriate circumstances, afford an opportunity to the defence to attend.[91] Important evidence obtained from a person that the accused has had no opportunity to cross examine which is decisive is the case is likely to be ruled inadmissible as incompatible with Art.6 ECHR,[92] or to be excluded under s.78(1) of the Police and Criminal Evidence Act 1984.

If a witness fails to appear through fear caused by the defendant, the evidence is unlikely to be excluded.[93]

CONFIDENTIALITY

20–026 There is no express provision in this Act for handling confidential information. The Guidelines provide that confidentiality should only be requested if it is strictly necessary.[94–95] It may be necessary to provide sensitive information in a request. In such circumstances, and because the mutual legal assistance process in not inherently confidential, consideration may have to be given as to whether there is sufficient information in the request for the requested authority to comply. In certain circumstances it may be possible to make the request conditional on the sensitive information being provided orally. In such circumstances the assistance of Eurojust may prove essential.

It should also be remembered that letters of request may well be disclosable in domestic proceedings. In addition, should the defence ask successfully to have a representative present when the evidence is taken the contents of the request may be made known.

[86] *Director of Public Prosecutions v Boo* unreported CO/2538/97.
[87] *Foxley* [1995] 2 Cr. App. R. 523.
[88] s.25 Criminal Justice Act 1988.
[89] s.9(4) and see *Kostovski v Netherlands* (1990) 12 E.H.R.R. 434.
[90] See Ch.21.
[91] *R. v Radak* [1999] 1 Cr. App. R.187.
[92] *Luca v Italy* [2001] Crim.L.R.747.
[93] *Montgomery* [2002] EWCA Crim 1655.
[94–95] Home Office Guidelines, App. C–012. The 2003 EU/US Agreement, MLAC 2000 and the Harare Scheme make just such a provision.

TELEPHONE INTERCEPTS

Section 5(1)(c) of RIPA allows the Secretary of State to issue a warrant authorising an intercept in response to a request for mutual legal assistance. Normally, any intercept product must be destroyed as soon as grounds for retaining it for one of the "authorised purposes" cease. Section 5(3)(d) makes the giving of effect to any international mutual assistance agreement an "authorised purpose" within the meaning of the Act. 20–027

It is incumbent on the Secretary of State to satisfy himself that restrictions are in force which would prevent, to such an extent as he sees fit, conduct in connection with proceedings outside the UK which would result in such a disclosure as could not be made in the UK.[96] The Secretary of State has a discretion to refuse to comply with a request if it would result in the disclosure of information pertaining to the intercept that could not be disclosed in the UK.

SHIPS AT SEA

If the police in the UK or a foreign jurisdiction wish to obtain evidence from a ship, much will depend on where the ship is registered. All ships must be registered in a state, and that state exercises exclusive criminal jurisdiction over the ship when it is on the high seas (Art.6 Geneva Convention on the High Seas and Art.92 of the UN Convention on the Law of the Sea 1982). 20–028

If therefore a ship is registered in the UK, UK police may carry out enquiries on that ship if it is on the high seas or in UK waters. If the ship is not registered in the UK but is in UK territorial waters (within 12 miles of the coast) a letter of request is necessary unless:

- the consequences of the alleged crime extend to the UK;
- the master of the ship, a diplomatic agent or consular officer of the flag state has requested assistance from the UK authorities;
- the measures are necessary to suppress the traffic in illicit drugs or psychotropic substances: s.2 of the Territorial Waters Jurisdiction Act 1878; article 19(1) of the Geneva Convention on the Territorial Sea and Contiguous Zone 1958; and Art.C27(1) of the Law of the Sea Convention;
- the ship has just left UK internal waters: Art.19(2) of the Territorial Sea Convention and Art.27(2) of the Law of the Sea Convention.

In all other circumstances a letter of request must be sent to the 'flag' state, where investigations are required on a registered ship in UK territorial waters, registered outside the UK.

[96] s.15(2) & (3).

IV. MUTUAL ASSISTANCE IN FREEZING EVIDENCE OVERSEAS

20–029 Section 10 of the 2003 Act deals with the issuing of orders from the UK to overseas authorities for the purpose of freezing evidence rather than assets. It gives effect to the 2003 Council Framework Decision,[97] and is designed to ensure that evidence which might be important in a UK investigation or prosecution and which is located in the territory of a participating country is protected before it is transferred to the UK. Unlike most of the other provisions this section has yet to come into force.

Section 10 states:

"**10.**—(1) If it appears to be a judicial authority in the United Kingdom, on an application made by a person mentioned in subsection (4):

(a) that proceedings in respect of a listed offence have been instituted or such an offence is being investigated,
(b) that there are reasonable grounds to believe that there is evidence in a participating country which satisfied the requirements of subsection (3), and
(c) that a request has been made, or will be made, under section 6 for the evidence to be sent to the authority making the request,

the judicial authority may make a domestic freezing order in respect of the evidence.

(2) A domestic freezing order is an order for protecting evidence which is in the participating country pending its transfer to the United Kingdom.

(3) The requirements are that the evidence:

(a) is on premises specified in the application in the participating country,
(b) is likely to be of substantial value (whether by itself or together with other evidence) to the proceedings or investigation,
(c) is likely to be admissible in evidence at a trial for the offence, and
(d) does not consist of or include items subject to legal privilege.

(4) The application may be made:

(a) in relation to England and Wales and Northern Ireland, by a constable,
(b) in relation to Scotland, by the Lord Advocate or procurator fiscal.

(5) The judicial authorities are:

(a) in relation to England and Wales, any judge or justice of the peace,
(b) in relation to Scotland, any judge of the High Court or sheriff,
(c) in relation to Northern Ireland, any judge or resident magistrate.

[97] Decision 2003/577/JHA, App. C–010.

(6) This section does not prejudice the generality of the power to make a request for assistance under section 7."

The application for such an order should be made by a police officer[99–99] before a judge or justice of the peace.[1] The applicant must be able to satisfy the court that there are proceedings in a participating country in respect of an offence covered by the 2003 Framework Decision,[2] or that such an offence is being investigated and that there are reasonable grounds to believe that there is such evidence in a participating country that: 20–030

- is on the premises specified in the application;
- is likely to be of substantial value;
- is likely to be admissible in evidence at trial; and
- does not consist of or include items subject to legal privilege.

In contrast to the provisions in respect of the transmission of requests for evidence,[3] such an order, once obtained, must be sent within fourteen days to the Secretary of State[4] for onward transmission, either to a court exercising jurisdiction in the place where the evidence is situated, or to any appropriate authority.[5] A time limit has been included for the sending of the order to the Secretary of State, but there is no time limit on the sending of evidence obtained pursuant to ss.7 and 8 of CICA. The purpose of the order is to protect evidence that may be removed in the near future: it was therefore thought appropriate to include such a time limit to reduce delay. No time limit is imposed on the Secretary of State for the onward transmission of such an order.[6]

Such freezing orders are a new concept in the field of mutual legal assistance; the requirement of transmitting them through the Secretary of State is designed to allow him to monitor compliance with the terms of the 2003 Framework Decision.[7]

There is no authority under this provision for the defendant in any proceedings to make such an application. A defendant can only request the material through the prosecution. The compatibility of this provision with Art.6 of the ECHR will no doubt be the subject of challenge. 20–031

The request should be accompanied by a certificate providing certain specified information.[8] There is provision for the order to be varied or revoked[9] and such an application can be made to the judicial authority that made the original order.

98–99 Procurator fiscal in Scotland.

1 High Court/Sheriff in Scotland, any judge/resident magistrate in Northern Ireland.

2 Art.3(2) of the Framework Decision see App. C–010.

3 s.8.

4 Lord Advocate in Scotland.

5 s.11.

6 Home Office Guidlines, C–012.

7 See Explanatory Notes to the Act.

8 See Annex to the 2003 Framework Decision, App. C–010.

9 s.12.

This provision would allow any person affected by the order, whether the subject of the investigation or a third party, to seek the variation or revocation of the order.

Many requests seek evidence from telecommunications providers or internet service providers. In many cases the company in possession of the information will have internal time periods for the retention of such records (often six months); such requests will often need to be dealt with expeditiously. These are the types of request most likely to be the subject of the freezing provisions before transmission.

V. THE PROVISION OF EVIDENCE TO OVERSEAS AUTHORITIES

20–032 CICA replicates many of the provisions of the 1990 Act in respect of obtaining evidence in the UK at the request of overseas authorities. However, unlike the 1990 Act, it allows evidence to be frozen in the UK at the request of an overseas authority before its transmission.[10]

Sections 13 to 15 deal with incoming requests for assistance in obtaining evidence located in the UK. These provisions build on and replace existing arrangements by setting out how the requests can be dealt with, and by specifying which authorities can make the requests. These sections replace s.4 of the 1990 Act, but the types of assistance that may be obtained are the same.

Section 13 states:

> "**13.**—(1) Where a request for assistance in obtaining overseas evidence in a part of the United Kingdom is received by the territorial authority for that part, the authority may —
>
> (a) if the conditions in section 14 are met, arrange for the evidence to be obtained under section 15, or
> (b) direct that a search warrant be applied for under or by virtue of section 16 or 17 or, in relation to evidence in Scotland, 18.
>
> (2) The request for assistance may be made only by —
>
> (a) a court exercising criminal jurisdiction, or a prosecuting authority, in a country outside the United Kingdom,
> (b) any other authority in such a country which appears to the territorial authority to have the function of making such requests for assistance,
> (c) any international authority mentioned in subsection (3).
>
> (3) The international authorities are —
>
> (a) the International Criminal Police Organisation,
> (b) any other body or person competent to make a request of the kind to which this section applies under any provisions adopted under the Treaty on European Union."

[10] See 20–058.

14.—(1) The territorial authority may arrange for evidence to be obtained under section 15 if the request for assistance in obtaining the evidence is made in connection with —

(a) criminal proceedings or a criminal investigation, being carried on outside the United Kingdom,
(b) administrative proceedings, or an investigation into an act punishable, being carried on there,
(c) clemency proceedings, or proceedings on an appeal before a court against a decision in administrative proceedings, being carried on, or intended to be carried on, there.

(2) In a case within subsection (1)(a) or (b), the authority may arrange for the evidence to be so obtained only if the authority is satisfied —

(a) that an offence under the law of the country in question has been committed or that there are reasonable grounds for suspecting that such an offence has been committed, and
(b) that proceedings in respect of the offence have been instituted in that country or that an investigation into the offence is being carried on there.

An offence includes an act punishable in administrative proceedings.

(3) The territorial authority is to regard as conclusive a certificate as to the matters mentioned in subsection (2)(a) and (b) issued by any authority in the country in question which appears to him to be the appropriate authority to do so.

(4) If it appears to the territorial authority that the request for assistance relates to a fiscal offence in respect of which proceedings have not yet been instituted, the authority may not arrange for the evidence to be so obtained unless —

(a) the request is from a country which is a member of the Commonwealth or is made pursuant to a treaty to which the United Kingdom is a party, or
(b) the authority is satisfied that if the conduct constituting the offence were to occur in a part of the United Kingdom, it would constitute an offence in that part.

15.—(1) Where the evidence is in England and Wales or Northern Ireland, the Secretary of State may by a notice nominate a court to receive any evidence to which the request relates which appears to the court to be appropriate for the purpose of giving effect to the request.

(2) But if it appears to the Secretary of State that the request relates to an offence involving serious or complex fraud, he may refer the request (or any part of it) to the Director of the Serious fraud Office for the Director to obtain

any evidence to which the request or part relates which appears to him to be appropriate for the purpose of giving effect to the request or part.

(3) Where the evidence is in Scotland, the Lord Advocate may by a notice nominate a court to receive any evidence to which the request relates which appears to the court to be appropriate for 4 the purpose of giving effect to the request.

(4) But if it appears to the Lord Advocate that the request relates to an offence involving serious or complex fraud, he may give a direction under section 27 of the Criminal Law (Consolidation)(Scotland) Act 1995 (c.39)(directions applying investigatory provisions).

(5) Schedule 1 is to have effect in relation too proceedings before a court nominated under this section."

20–033 It is clear from the above sections that, subject to the conditions set out in s.14, various overseas authorities are entitled to request certain types of assistance from the UK territorial authority. The UK "territorial authority" entitled to receive overseas requests under this section is the Secretary of State.[11] In certain circumstances references to the "territorial authority" apply equally to HM Customs and Excise.[12–14] It is intended that this provision will assist in ensuring greater direct transmission in the future. The request should be by way of a formal letter of request.

These categories of assistance are set out in ss.15–18. The authorities that may make such a request are the courts, prosecuting authorities and other authorities which have the function of making such requests, such as examining magistrates.[15] In an expansion of the 1990 Act, the overseas authorities permitted to request assistance now include Interpol[16] and any other body or person competent to make a request of the kind to which this section applies, such as Eurojust.

It was envisaged under Art.6 of MLAC 2000 that many such requests from overseas would be sent directly to the appropriate competent authority in the UK. However by reason of the complex and overlapping responsibilities of various different investigating and prosecuting authorities in the UK in the investigation and prosecution of similar matters,[17–18] the UK has special provision enabling it to opt out of the direct transmission requirement envisaged by Art.6 of MLAC 2000.

POWERS TO ARRANGE FOR THE OBTAINING OF EVIDENCE

20–034 These powers are set out in s.14 of the Act, which stipulates the conditions to be met before a court may be nominated to receive evidence under s.15. In language

[11] In relation to evidence in England and Wales or Northern Ireland, and Lord Advocate in Scotland.
[12] Except in Scotland; s.27(2).
[15] s.13(2).
[16] s.13(3)(a).
[17–18] For example, the SFO, Customs & Excise, and CPS all prosecute money laundering offences.

taken from Art.3 of MLAC 2000 and Art.49 (c) of the Schengen Convention, assistance to obtain evidence can be sought by the overseas country in respect of:

- criminal investigations or proceedings;
- administrative investigations or proceedings;
- clemency proceedings or an appeal before the court against a decision made in administrative proceedings.[19]

This section allows for the requesting state to request assistance in relation to an offence that has not been committed in the territory of a country, but within its jurisdiction.[20]

It is not a condition that the alleged offence in the requesting state would also constitute an offence in the UK. This mutual recognition provision reflects the terms of the 1990 Act and the provisions applicable to UK requests for assistance in obtaining evidence overseas under CICA. The UK authority will therefore need to consider "double criminality" only if the request is from a state that is neither part of the Commonwealth nor a party to any mutual assistance treaty to which the UK is also a signatory.

THE PROCESS TO BE FOLLOWED

Requests from overseas to the UK should be sent to the Secretary of State,[21] unless the requesting state knows that the evidence is located in Scotland or Northern Ireland or it is a matter that the Customs and Excise is competent to execute, in which case it can be sent directly to those authorities.[22] They cannot be sent directly to courts or prosecuting authorities in the UK.[23] The request should always be in writing, addressed to the relevant central authority or to the UK National Central Bureau of Interpol, according to the nature of the assistance required. They may be sent by fax or e-mail but an undertaking should be given to send the original request within a reasonable period (normally seven days).[24] **20–035**

The content of the incoming letter of request should be as that set out above[25] in respect of letters of request from the UK to overseas countries. The UK can execute the request where the subject of the investigation is unknown at the time the request has been made, but the requesting authority must inform the Secretary of State of the identity of any person(s) it later suspects of involvement.

[19] See 20–004 and 20–005 above for an explanation of the meaning of "administrative proceedings" and "clemency proceedings".
[20] s.14(2)(a).
[21] For England Wales and Northern Ireland this will in practice be the UKCA.
[22] Home Office Guidelines, App. C–012.
[23] Home Office Guidelines, App. C–012.
[24] Home Office Guidelines, App. C–012.
[25] See 20–019.

If more than one authority is engaged by any request, the request may either be sent to one of the central authorities which may then transmit it to other relevant parties, or to each central authority involved, in which case it must be made clear which other central authorities have been contacted. Contact with central authorities may be made through diplomatic channels if the requesting state so requires. In order to prevent problems as to the admissibility of any evidence transmitted, central authorities are expected as far as possible to take account of procedural requirements by the requesting state.

20–036 The Secretary of State is obliged to consider certain factors before arranging for the evidence to be obtained.[26] He must be satisfied:

- that an offence under the law of the requesting state has been committed, or
- that there are reasonable grounds for believing that such an offence (including acts punishable in administrative proceedings) has been committed and that proceedings have been instituted in that country or an investigation is being carried on there.

A certificate from an overseas authority confirming that these conditions have been satisfied is to be regarded as conclusive.[27] [28] In reality the content of the letter of request will provide sufficient information to satisfy the authority that the conditions have been met. Accordingly, a certificate is unlikely to be required, except in cases of complexity, or for the purpose of discouraging any potential objection by the receiving authority in carrying out the request.

In addition, the Secretary of State has a general discretion[29–30] to delay requests which may prejudice UK investigations or proceedings, and to refuse requests which affect national security or any other essential interest.[31] Requests will also be refused where a trial in the requesting state would result in the infringement of the "double jeopardy" principle. In respect of requests from the US, or any other country in relation to an investigation or prosecution in which the death penalty might be applied it would appear that the Secretary of State will consider each request on its merits,[32] although all EU states have signed Protocol 13 to the ECHR which prohibits the death penalty absolutely. If the offence under investigation is determined by the Secretary of State to be a political

[26] s.14(2).

[27–28] s.14(3). See *Zardari v Secretary of State* [2001] EWHC Admin 275 for discussion on the discretion to be applied when considering such certificates.

[29–30] See *Fininvest* [1997] 1 W.L.R. 743; and *per* Laws J. in *R. v Central Criminal Court Ex p. Propend Finance Property Ltd* [1996] 2 Cr. App. R. 26 see also para.7 (2) of the Harare Scheme.

[31] Home Office Guidelines, App. C–012.

[32] House of Lords European Union Select Committee 38th Report, para.30.

[33] Art.2(a) of the 1959 Convention. Also see discussion of this issue in *Fininvest* as *per* Simon Brown L.J. See also para.7(b) of the Harare Scheme.

offence, connected to a political offence,[34] or a military offence,[35] he can exercise his discretion to refuse.

If the request relates to a fiscal offence, and proceedings have not yet been instituted, the Secretary of State may not arrange for the evidence to be obtained unless the request comes from a Commonwealth country, a country with which the UK has a bilateral treaty, or the same conduct would constitute an offence in the UK if it occurred in a part of the UK.[36] This section reflects a continuing concern about banking confidentiality in relation to fiscal offences. The meaning of a fiscal offence varies from country to country; although it is not defined in the Act, Art.5 of the 1959 European Convention on Extradition described fiscal offences as "offences in connection with taxes, duties, customs and exchange". This is consistent with the 1990 Act.[37] 20–037

The Secretary of State is unable to accede to requests for interception of communications where such information is intended for use as evidence.[38]

There is an obligation on the Secretary of State to provide the requesting state with a written or oral report explaining any difficulties preventing the execution of the request in whole or in part. An opportunity must be given to the requesting state to modify its request.[39]

The request considered by the Secretary of State must be for "evidence" in accordance with the wording of s.14(1). The material sought need not be admissible,[40] and much will depend on whether the request relates to the early stages of an investigation, or proceedings that have already commenced, at which time the trial issues are more likely to be more clearly defined. It is clear that that the request cannot be a "fishing expedition", undertaken to obtain material that may possibly be of relevance.

Having considered the request, and decided to transmit it, the Secretary of State has then to determine which body should receive the request. It can be sent either to a nominated court for the court to receive any evidence to which the request relates[41] or it could be sent to the SFO if the request appears to relate to a serious or complex fraud.[42] A person who is affected by decision to grant assistance may seek a judicial review of that decision. The Divisional Court can order a stay in the execution of the request pending a full hearing.[43]

[34] Art.2(a) of the 1959 Convention. Also see discussion of this issue in *Fininvest*, *per* Simon Brown L.J. See also para.7 (b) of the Harare Scheme.

[35] Para.7(c) Harare Scheme.

[36] s.14(4).

[37] s.4(3).

[38] Such an action is prohibited by s.17 of the Regulatory of Investigatory Powers Act 2000; Home Office Guidelines, App. C–012.

[39] Art.3(d) to the 1998 Joint Action on good practice in mutual legal assistance in criminal matters.

[40] As *per* Brown L.J. in *Fininvest* [1997] 1 W.L.R. 743, 754–755.

[41] s.15(1).

[42] s.15(2)

[43] *Abacha v Secretary of State for the Home Department* [2001] EWHC Admin 424.

OBTAINING EVIDENCE AT A COURT

20–038 The overseas request may ask for evidence to be obtained on oath, or it may specify certified authenticated documentary evidence, such as banking evidence, telecommunications information and third party material.

The Secretary of State may nominate a court to receive such evidence as may appear to the court to be appropriate.[44] The court will then consider the terms of the request and making a determine the extent of evidence that should be provided. This discretion should be distinguished from that exercisable by the Secretary of State. The court does not have a discretion to enquire into the merits or otherwise of the request. Such arguments should be addressed to the Secretary of State.[45] However the court may decline, for example, to execute the request if to do so would require the production of very large quantities of documents.[46] The court may decide who may appear and take part in the proceedings, and whether a party to the proceedings should be legally represented. The court can also direct that the public be excluded if it thinks it is necessary to do so in the interests of justice.[47]

The procedural rules governing the function of the court are set out in Sch.1 to the Act.[48] The court has powers to secure the attendance of witnesses named in the request.[49] These are the same powers that it would have for securing the attendance of a witness in any other proceedings before the court.[50] When the court has been nominated it will arrange with the local police to contact the witness and establish whether that witness is willing to assist.[51] If the witness is unwilling, the court can issue a summons requiring attendance in the usual way.[52] The evidence can either be given in the form of a witness statement or an oath.[53]

20–039 There is no power to compel a person to give evidence before the nominated court if he or she could not be compelled to give the evidence in criminal proceedings in the UK or in criminal proceedings in the requesting country. This means that a defendant cannot be compelled to give evidence,[54] and the spouse of a defendant is compellable only in certain circumstances.[55]

[44] If a magistrates' court is required in most cases Bow Street Magistrates' Court will be used. For a Crown Court the normal practice is to use the Central Criminal Court.

[45] See Latham J. in *R. v Bow Street Magistrates' Court Ex p. Zardari* unreported April 29, 1998.

[46] *R. v Bow Street Magistrates' Court Ex p. King* unreported October 8, 1997.

[47] The Crown Court (Amendment) Rules 2004 and the Magistrates' Courts Crime (International Co-operation)) Rules 2004.

[48] Supplemented by the Crown Court (Amendment) Rules 2004 and the Magistrates' Courts (Crime (International Co-operation)) Rules 2004.

[49] Except in Scotland.

[50] See relevant domestic legislation on this point.

[51] This will normally be facilitated by the police liaison officer based at the court.

[52] s.97 Magistrates' Courts Act 1980 or s.2 Criminal Procedure (Attendance of Witnesses) Act 1965 as amended by s.66 Criminal Procedure and Investigations Act 1996, for the Crown Court.

[53] Sch.1 para.3.

[54] s.1 Criminal Evidence Act 1898 forbids a defendant to be compelled in his or her own prosecution.

[55] s.80 of the Police and Criminal Evidence Act 1984 as amended by s.67 and Sch.6 of the Youth Justice and Criminal Evidence Act 1999.

A witness is entitled to invoke the privilege against self incrimination, and accordingly may refuse to answer questions or provide documents that might expose him or her to proceedings for a criminal offence.[56] This claim of privilege may be made under UK law or under the law of the requesting country.[57] If the latter the Secretary of State may refer the matter to the requesting country and, if the claim is conceded by the requesting country, the evidence will not be taken. If the requesting country does not concede the claim, the correct procedure is to take the evidence but to delay transmission to the requesting country until a court in that ccountry has ruled on the matter.[58]

An appropriate officer of the court is required to keep a record of information in respect of the proceedings, such as details of witnesses, legal representatives and whether an opportunity to cross examine any witness was refused.[59] The witness will be asked questions either by a lawyer representing the requesting state or the clerk to the justices, District Judge or Crown Court Judge. Cross examination of a witness is allowed.

Often, evidence on oath is sought for the simple purpose of confirming that a document(s) is authentic, and has been created in the ordinary course of business or has come from a third party. In such circumstances, the territorial authority may nominate a court to receive such of the documentary evidence as may appear to the court to be appropriate. This evidence is normally provided by a nominated officer or custodian of the document(s) making a statement on oath at the nominated court. 20–040

In the case of banking evidence, the court will not normally notify the account holder, even if the account holder is on the face of the evidence an innocent third party. The power to notify the account holder is entirely at the discretion of the court, and there is no obligation on the bank to make this notification .[60] If an account holder is to be notified, the Secretary of State will revert to the requesting authority to ensure that to do so will not breach any existing confidentiality requirements.

In Scotland the normal procedure is for the central authority to obtain a warrant from court, which is then served on the holder of the documentary evidence. Police officers then attend and obtain this evidence as soon as possible, together with statements and documents. If the requesting state has specifically requested evidence to be given on oath in relation to such documents, or there is no double criminality, the procedure as in England and Wales is adopted.[61]

When the evidence has been obtained by the nominated court it can transmit it directly to the requesting authority or back through the Secretary of State.[62] The Justices' Clerk will send a copy of the extract of so much of the overseas record as

[56] *Rio Tinto Zinc Corpn v Westinghouse Electric Corp.* [1978] A.C. 547; *Blunt v Park Lane Hotel* [1942] 2 K.B. 253.

[57] To determine it is necessary should look at the position under UK law (*R. v Bow Street Magistrates' Court Ex p. King* unreported CO/3489/97 October 8, 1997 QBD).

[58] Home Office Guidelines, App. C–012.

[59] The Crown Court (Amendment) Rules 2004.

[60] Home Office Guidelines, App. C–012.

[61] Home Office Guidelines, App. C–012.

[62] s.6(1).

relates to the proceedings in respect of that request.[63] If the evidence consists of a document, the original or a copy should be provided. If an object is sought, a photograph or other representation may suffice for the purposes of the request.[64]

EVIDENCE OBTAINED THROUGH THE SERIOUS FRAUD OFFICE

20–041 Section 15(2) allows the Secretary of State to refer requests for assistance by use of coercive powers in serious or complex fraud cases to the SFO, for the purpose of obtaining such evidence as may appear to the Director to be appropriate. The Director of the SFO may exercise some discretion over the extent of the material sought.

Whether a fraud is "serious or complex" is largely a question of fact. One test applied by the SFO is whether the sum lost or at risk is more than £1 million.[65–67]

In executing such a request the SFO will consider the different ways in which it can obtain evidence. In common with other law enforcement bodies the office can use the following methods:

- Voluntary Interview; the witness signs a statement confirming formally the truth of its contents.
- Evidence Under Oath; the witness is summoned to the nominated Magistrates Court and gives evidence under oath, recorded in writing, signed and certified by the magistrate. Alternatively the witness may make an affidavit.
- Interview under caution; if a suspect or defendant agrees to be interviewed in this way, the SFO may allow this interview to be conducted by an appropriate representative of the requesting country. Under these circumstances the defendant may be given the caution appropriate in the requesting country. This must include details of the suspected offence and notification of this entitlement to free access to legal advice.

20–042 The SFO however has compulsory powers provided by section 2 of the Criminal Justice Act 1987. The SFO can:

- require any person or body to answer any relevant questions;[68]
- require any person or body to produce relevant documents;[69]
- obtain a warrant to search premises and seize documents; this power is exercisable in limited circumstances.[70]

[63] s.7(3) The Magistrates' Courts (Crime (International Co-operation)) Rules 2004.
[64] Sch.1 para.6.2.
[65–67] See website *www.sfo.gov.uk*.
[68] s.2(2) of the Criminal Justice Act 1987.
[69] s.2(3) of the Criminal Justice Act 1987.
[70] s.2(3) & (4) of the Criminal Justice Act 1987.

These powers are often used in the execution of letters of request. One of the most common methods is the statutory interview under compulsion. A person is subject to criminal sanctions if he refuses.[71] Similarly although there is protection against self incrimination for a witness in the proceedings described above[72] a suspect questioned using these s.2 powers has no such protection and must answer the questions.[73] If evidence is sought from a suspect under the s.2 powers, the requesting authority must provide the territorial authority with a written undertaking in the following terms:

> "If the United Kingdom secretary of State for the Home Department decides to refer this Letter of request to the Serious Fraud Office, I undertake that:-
>
> (i) No document or other information obtained will be used other than in criminal prosecutions arising from the investigation set out in this Letter of Request, without the prior consent of the Secretary of State for the Home department; and
> (ii) No statement made by any person to the Serious Fraud Office on foot of their coercive powers will be used against that person in a prosecution. Unless evidence relating to it is adduced, or a question relating to it is asked, in the proceedings, by or on behalf of that person."

If the person is a witness rather than a suspect, such an assurance does not prevent the use of the statement in the requesting country against the accused person named in the request.[74]

If an undertaking in respect of a suspect is not given by the requesting country, he may have a "reasonable excuse" for declining to answer questions put by the SFO. If an undertaking is given, but there is evidence to show that there is a real risk that the undertaken will not be honoured, the Secretary of State or the SFO has a discretion to refuse to execute the request.[75–76] 20–043

The interview is normally tape-recorded and the questions will be put by SFO investigators. The Director of the SFO may authorise an English-speaking prosecutor from the requesting country to participate actively in such an interview.

The SFO can request that a person produce certain specified documents. These powers are wide and can be used to obtain any documents that relate to any matter relevant to the investigation.[77] The recipient will receive a notice setting out the documents or the category of documents sought. The authors of the notice will rely heavily on the content of the original request. If either is deficient, it may be the subject of an application for judicial review.[78]

[71] s.2(13).
[72] See 30–039.
[73] *Saunders v United Kingdom* (1996) 23 E.H.R.R. 313.
[74] See *www.sfo.gov.uk*.
[75–76] *R. v Secretary of State for the Home Department Ex p. Launder (No.2)* [1998] Q.B. 994.
[77] s.2(3) to the CJA 1987.
[78] *Ex p. Fininvest* above.

The power to request production of documents is often used when the requesting authority seeks documents in the possession of lawyers, accountants or other professional advisers.

The subject of the s.2 notice is not entitled to receive a copy of the letter of request when justice can be done by providing him with information as to the nature of the case.[79] The SFO is entitled to seek explanations or clarifications of the content of the document for the purpose of understanding the possible significance of the document in the investigation.[80] A subject cannot resist compliance with such a notice on the ground that the documents sought have already been produced in proceedings in the UK.[81–84] A failure to respond to such an enquiry is an offence.

SFO SEARCH POWERS

20–044 CICA sets out the standard search powers that can be exercised under Pt 2 of the Police and Criminal Evidence Act 1984 ("in the 1984 Act") by the SFO as well as the police.[85] The SFO can also exercise search powers under s.2 of the Criminal Justice Act 1987 if a notice[86] to produce material:

- has not been complied with;
- has not been served because itr was impracticable to do so;
- might seriously prejudice the investigation and there are reasonable grounds for believing that there are such documents on the premises specified.

The justice of the peace is required to give reasons for the issue of the warrant.

VI. USE OF SEARCH/PRODUCTION ORDER POWERS AT OVERSEAS REQUEST

20–045 Sections 16(1) and 17 replicate s.7(1) and (2) of the 1990 Act respectively, which they also replace. These sections allow the appropriate authorities in England, Wales and Northern Ireland to apply for and execute a search warrant[87] or a production order[88] in response to an overseas request, in the same circumstances as would be appropriate in a domestic case. Section 18 applies to Scotland.

[79] *Evans v Serious Fraud Office* [2002] EWHC 2304.
[80] *Attorney General's Reference (No.2 of 1998)* [2000] Q.B. 412.
[81–84] *Marlwood Commerical Inc v Minaret Group Ltd and the Director of the Serious Fraud Office* [2004] EWCA Civ 798.
[85] see Pt II and Sch.1 of the 1984 Act.
[86] Under s.2(3).
[87] s.8 of PACE or Sch.1 of the 1984 Act.
[88] Sch.1 of the 1984 Act.

Sections 16 and 17 state that:

"**16.**—(1) Part 2 of the Police and Criminal Evidence Act 1984 (c.6) (powers of entry, search and seizure) is to have effect as if references to serious arrestable offences in section 8 of, and Schedule 1 to, that Act included any conduct which —

(a) constitutes an offence under the law of the country outside the United Kingdom, and
(b) would, if it occurred in England and Wales, constitute a serious arrestable offence.

(2) But an application for a warrant or order by virtue of subsection (1) may be made only —

(a) in pursuance of a direction given under section 13, or
(b) if it is an application for a warrant or order under section 8 of, or Schedule 1 to, that Act by a constable for the purposes of an investigation by an international joint investigation team of which he is a member.

(3) Part 3 of the Police and Criminal Evidence (Northern Ireland) Order 1989 (S.I. 1989/1341 (N.I.12))(powers of entry, search and seizure) is to have effect as if references to serious arrestable offences in Article 10 of, and Schedule 1 to, that order included any conduct which —

(a) constitutes an offence under the law of the country outside the United Kingdom, and
(b) would, if it occurred in England and Wales, constitute a serious arrestable offence.

(4) But an application for a warrant or order by virtue of subsection (3) may be made only —

(a) in pursuance of a direction given under section 13, or
(b) if it is an application for a warrant or order under section 8 of, or Schedule 1 to, that Act by a constable for the purposes of an investigation by an international joint investigation team of which he is a member.

(5) In this section, 'international joint investigative team' has the meaning given by section 88(7) of the Police Act 1996(c.16)

17.—(1) A justice of the peace may issue a warrant under this section if he is satisfied, on an application made by a constable, that the following conditions are met.

(2) But an application for a warrant under subsection (1) may be made only in pursuance of a direction given under section 13.

(3) the conditions are that —

(a) criminal proceedings have been instituted against a person in a country outside the United Kingdom or a person has been arrested in the course of a criminal investigation carried on there,
(b) the conduct constituting the offence, which is the subject of the proceedings or investigation would, if it occurred in England and Wales or (as the case may be) Northern Ireland, constitute an arrestable offence, and
(c) there are reaspnable grounds for suspecting that there is on the premises in England and Wales or (as the case may be) northern Ireland occupied or controlled by that person evidence relating to the offence.

"Arrestable offence" has the same meaning as in the Police and Criminal Evidence Act 1984 (c.60) or (as the case may be) the Police and Criminal Evidence (Northern Ireland) Order 1989 (S.I. 1989/1341 (N.I.12)).

(4) A warrant under this section may authorise a constable —

(a) enter the premises in question and search the premises to the extent reasonable required for the purpose of discovering any evidence relating to the offence,
(b) to seize and retain any evidence for which he is authorised to search."

20–046 Following a request from an overseas country, therefore, the Secretary of State may direct a police officer[89] to apply to a court for:

(a) a search warrant or a production order in circumstances where the offence(s) under investigation or the subject of proceedings overseas is an offence in that jurisdiction and would, if committed in the UK, be classified as a serious arrestable offence,[90] or
(b) a search warrant in circumstances where the subject has been arrested in the course of a criminal investigation, or he is the subject of proceedings overseas and the conduct alleged if committed in the UK would constitute an arrestable offence.[91]

The Secretary of State should stipulate which type of warrant or order should be obtained.[92]

[89] Or an officer of Customs & Excise, the SFO or a Joint Investigative Team.
[90] Defined in s.116 and Sch.5, Pts I and II the 1984 Act and Proceeds of Crime Act 2002, Sch.2, para.1 and ss.327 to 329 of that Act.
[91] Defined in s.116 and Sch.5, Pts I and II the 1984 Act and Proceeds of Crime Act 2002, Sch.2, para.1 and ss.327 to 329 of that Act.
[92] See *per* Laws J. in *R. v Central Criminal Court Ex p. Propend Finance Property Ltd.*

This part of CICA expands the powers in the 1990 Act by also allowing applications as in (a) above to be made by members of Joint Investigative Teams ("JITS").[93] This provision implements Art.13(7) of MLAC 2000 in allowing an application for a search warrant or production order to be applied for and executed without an overseas request if the constable making the application is a member of an international joint investigative team. An international joint investigative team is defined in s.88(7) of the Police Act 1996 as:

> "any investigation team formed in accordance with
>
> a. any framework decision on joint investigative teams adopted under Article 34 of the Treaty on European Union;
> b. the Convention on Mutual Legal Assistance in Criminal Matters between the Member States of the European Union, and the Protocol to that Convention established in accordance with that Article of that Treaty; or
> c. any international agreement to which the UK is a party and which is specified for the purposes of this section in an order made by the Secretary of State"

A framework for the establishment of JITS was provided by Art.13 of MLAC 2000, **20–047**
which envisaged that teams would be set up by two or more signatory states for the purpose of a specific investigation, and that officers from these teams would be able to carry out investigations in any of the states that are party to the setting up of the teams. The JITS may consist of examining magistrates, prosecutors and other legal advisers as well as police and customs officers.[94]

The team would be supervised by a "team leader" who would be appointed by the competent authorities of the participating state where the investigation is taking place at that time. If the investigation moves on to another participating state, the identity of the team leader would change. In this way, if the investigation were to move to the UK, the team leader appointed would be a UK officer. Section 16(2)(b) allows for any UK officer who is a member of such a team to apply in the unusual way under the Police and Criminal Evidence Act 1984 for a search warrant or other order.

Further, the UK officer would be able to make such an application under this subsection without a formal request for the evidence from abroad. It would suffice that the officer was part of the JIT, and that the application for a warrant or order in the UK related to an overseas investigation. No formal request from overseas would be necessary, as the officer would be acting on his own personal knowledge of the investigation.[95]

93 s.16(2)(b).
94 *Hansard* 23/01/03 (230123-23) Lord Goldsmith.
95 *Hansard supra*.

THE CONTENT OF THE REQUEST FOR SEARCH AND SEIZURE

20–048 In addition to the material required in a letter of request, it is important that when search and seizure of evidence is sought the request includes the following:[96]

- the full address or a precise description of the location to be searched;
- a comprehensive and precise description of the material sought; the request should specify so far as practicable, the items to be sought;[97]
- justification as to why it is considered that this material will be located on the identified premises;
- appropriate undertakings concerning the safekeeping and return of any seized material.

If for some reason the request provides inadequate information for such an application to the UK court, the Secretary of State will inform the requesting authority without delay. If the application is for a production order, a legal obligation[98] is imposed on the UK authorities to notify any interested parties, so that they may be represented in court when the application is being made. The Secretary of State would in these circumstances consult with the requesting authority to ensure that in making such a notification it was not going to breach any confidentiality rules or otherwise jeopardise the investigation.

CONDITIONS TO BE SATISFIED BEFORE A SEARCH WARRANT IS EXECUTED

20–049 Section 17 replicates and replaces s.7(2) of the 1990 Act. It allows for the issue of search warrants for the search of premises occupied or controlled by the suspects only, provided the conditions in subs.(3) are satisfied, namely that:

(a) criminal proceedings have been instituted against a person in a country outside the United Kingdom or a person has been arrested in the course of a criminal investigation carried on there,
(b) the conduct constituting the offence, which is the subject of the proceedings or investigation would, if it occurred in England and Wales or (as the case may be) Northern Ireland, constitute an arrestable offence, and
(c) there are reasonable grounds for suspecting that there is on the premises in England and Wales or (as the case may be) Northern Ireland occupied or controlled by that person evidence relating to the offence.

Double criminality applies because coercive powers are to be exercised.

[96] Home Office Guidelines, App. C–012.
[97] *R. v Central Criminal Court Ex p. AJD Holdings Ltd* [1992] Crim. L.R. 669.
[98] Sch.1 of the 1984 Act.

The nominated court, or the SFO, has a responsibility to ensure that terms of the resulting warrant are sufficiently narrowed so as not to result in a fishing "expedition".[99] The court must be satisfied that there are reasonable grounds for believing the various assertions set out in the application. The fact that a police officer, who has been investigating the matter states in the information that he considers that there are reasonable grounds is not enough.[1] This is particularly important as the application is most likely to be made *ex parte.* There is a heavy duty on the party making the application to make the fullest possible disclosure of all material facts within his knowledge.[2]

There are conditions such as precision in relation to the address, persons and documents identified.[3] In addition the procedural requirements in relation to the execution of the warrant[4] include the requirement that the warrant should be executed at a reasonable hour,[5] that the warrant stays remains valid for a month and that the persons executing it be identified.[6] It is imperative that, if a representative of the requesting state wishes to attend, the request should say so, so that the permission can be included in the warrant. A failure to do so could render the search unlawful, particularly if the foreign representative plays an active part in the search.[7] A person who has diplomatic status, such as an embassy attaché, is not entitled to be present. 20–050

The court or the justice of the peace may not issue the warrant[8–9] unless he or she has reasonable grounds for believing that it does not request items subject to legal professional privilege, excluded material,[10] or special procedure material.[11] If there is a doubt as to whether the documentation is subject to legal professional privilege, the normal practice is to deal with such a question during the search, unless the quantity of documentation involved, on paper or on computer, makes such an analysis impracticable. In such circumstances, material that might contain such material should be identified, sealed and taken away for consideration by independent counsel.[12]

[99] *per* Brown L.J. in *Fininvest* above.

[1] As *per* Parker L.J. in *R. v Guildhall Magistrates Court Ex p. Primlak Holdings (Panama) Ltd* [1990] 1 Q.B. 261, 272-3.

[2] *R. v Crown Court at Lewes Ex p. Hill* [1991] 93 Cr.App.R. 60.

[3] s.15 of the 1984 Act.

[4] s.16 of the 1984 Act.

[5] Undefined but normally 6 – 8 am.

[6] s.16(2) of the 1984 Act.

[7] *R. v Crown Court at Southwark Ex p. Gross* [1998] C.O.D. 45; *R. v Bow Street Magistrates Court Ex p. M* (Unreported CO/4287.97) DC April 27, 1998.

[8–9] Or freezing order see later para.7.

[10] Definition in s.11 of the 1984 Act.

[11] Definition in s.14 of the 1984 Act.

[12] *R. v Customs & Excise Commissioners Ex p. Popely* [1999] S.T.C. 1016.

PRODUCTION ORDERS

20–051 The seeking of a production order will be appropriate in circumstances where:[13]

- the offence committed is a serious arrestable offence; and
- there is material which consists of special procedure material that does not include excluded material on the premises specified in the application, and
- the material is relevant and is likely to be of substantial value to the investigation.

The application should be made to a Crown Court judge and should be heard *inter partes*. Adopting such a route should be a last resort[14–15] and so it is advised that the Secretary of State should first consider using the powers under ss.13–15 to obtain material from a witness using a nominated court.

SEARCH WARRANT IN SCOTLAND

20–052 This section is the Scottish equivalent of ss.16 and 17 and it serves the same purpose as those sections in England, Wales and Northern Ireland. It replaces and largely replicates s.8(1) and (2) of the 1990 Act.

In Scotland a procurator fiscal may be directed to obtain a search warrant. Neither the police nor Customs and Excise can apply for a search warrant in Scotland, and interested parties are not notified.

TREATMENT OF THE SEIZED EVIDENCE

20–053 Section 19 deals with the treatment of any evidence seized under the procedures set out in ss.16–18. This provision seeks to implement Art.6 of MLAC, which allows for the material obtained to be passed directly either to the court or authority that has requested assistance.

> "**19.**—(1) Any evidence seized by a constable under or by virtue of section 16, 17 or 18 is to be sent to the court or authority which made the request for assistance or to the territorial authority for forwarding to that court or authority
>
> (2) So far as may be necessary in order to comply with the request for assistance —
>
> (a) where the evidence consists of a document, the original or a copy is to be sent, and

[13] Sch.1 of the 1984 Act, para.9(1).
[14–15] As *per* Bingham L.J., in *R. v Crown Court at Lewes Ex p. Hill* [1991] 93 Cr. App. R. 60.

(b) where the evidence consists of any other article, the article itself or a description, photograph or other representation of it is to be sent

(3) This section does not apply to evidence seized under or by virtue of section 16(2)(b) or (4)(b) or 18(2)(b)"

This section is intended to expedite the provision of material for use in proceedings overseas, by by-passing the Secretary of State. Under this provision the evidence obtained under ss.16–18 by virtue of a search warrant or court order may be sent directly to the requesting authority. Previously material had to be sent to the Secretary of State for onward transmission to the requesting authority; this was often the cause of delay. Evidence obtained on behalf of a Schengen state should be returned directly to the requesting authority either by being given to a representative of that authority, or by other secure method. **20–054**

There will be some circumstances in which evidence will not be returned directly as described, as, for example, when a non-MLAC country requires that the evidence be returned through the Secretary of State. It is also clear from subs.(3) that evidence obtained by a constable acting for an international JIT does not need to comply with the requirements of this section.

The material may belong to a person who wishes to raise some challenge as to its seizure, let alone transmission. A rapid transmission process may limit impede such a challenge.

No time limit has been placed on the transmission of seized evidence to the requesting authority, although best practice since 1990 appears to imply that it should be returned as soon as possible. The Home Office Codes of Practice[16] stipulate that the central authority will in a request marked "urgent" provide the assistance sought within 20 days, or provide the requesting authority with information.

COSTS

The expense incurred in executing a request is normally met by the requesting state. In rare cases where the costs are likely to be exceptionally high the UK authority involved should institute consultation with the requesting state in relation to payment.[17] **20–055**

USE OF THE EVIDENCE BY THE REQUESTING AUTHORITY

Apart from the undertaking required in respect of the use of evidence obtained by the SFO by the use of coercive s.2 powers, there is no express limitation on the **20–056**

[16] Applies to all UK Central authorities and HMC&E.

[17] Home Office Guidelines, App. C–012.

use by a requesting state of the evidence obtained by the execution of a warrant or court order.

This is consistent with the provisions in respect of mutual legal assistance provided to the USA.[18–19] However the guidance provide by the UKCA to overseas requesting authorities contains no such similar requirement.

The territorial authority should initially send an acknowledgement to the requesting authority to confirm receipt. CICA allows for any evidence requested to be collected by a representative of the requesting authority, providing such a competent representative is available in the UK.

CONFIDENTIALITY

20–057 Established international practice dictates that such requests should be kept confidential, and that central authorities should not disclose the existence or content of letters of request outside government departments or enforcement agencies.[20] Letters of request are prima facie not disclosable at the investigatory stage.[21] Requests are therefore not shown or copied to any witness or other person, nor is a witness informed of the identity of any other witness who is a subject in the request.

VII. THE FREEZING OF EVIDENCE IN THE UK PRIOR TO TRANSMISSION

20–058 Sections 20 and 21 implement an important measure set out in the 2003 Framework Decision[22] requiring the UK to execute an order from a participating country to freeze evidence in the UK prior to its transmission to the participating country. This provision is not yet in force.

> "**20.**—(1) Section 21 applies where an overseas freezing order made by a court or authority in a participating country is received from the court or authority which made of confirmed the order by the territorial authority for the part of the United Kingdom in which the evidence to which the order relates is situated.
>
> (2) An overseas freezing order is an order:
>
> (a) for protecting, pending its transfer to the participating country, evidence which is in the United Kingdom and may be used in any proceedings or investigation in the participating country, and

[18–19] Art.7(2) of the UK/US Mutual Legal Assistance Treaty provides that any information or evidence obtained under that treaty shall not be used or disclosed without the prior consent of the requested party.

[20] Art.25 MLAC 2000, App.C–006, Article 10 Agreement between EU & US on Mutual legal Assistance, App. C–009.

[21] *Evans v Serious Fraud Office* [2002] EWHC 2304.

[22] App. C–010.

(b) in respect of which the following requirements of this section are met.

(3) The order must have been made by:

(a) a court exercising criminal jurisdiction in the country,
(b) a prosecuting authority in the country,
(c) any other authority in the country which appears to the territorial authority to have the function of making such orders.

(4) The order must relate to:

(a) criminal proceedings instituted in the participating country in respect of a listed offence, or
(b) a criminal investigation being carried on there into such an offence.

(5) The order must be accompanied by a certificate which gives the specified information; but a certificate may be treated as giving any specified information which is not given in it if the territorial authority has the information in question.

(6) The certificate must:

(a) be signed by or on behalf of the court or authority which made or confirmed the order
(b) include a statement as to the accuracy of the information given in it,
(c) if it is not in English, include a translation of it into English (or, if appropriate, Welsh).

The signature may be an electronic signature.

(7) The order must be accompanied by a request for the evidence to be sent to a court or authority mentioned in section 13(2), unless the certificate indicates when such a request is expected to be made.

(8) References below in this Chapter to an overseas freezing order include its accompanying certificate."

This section is based on the principle of mutual recognition, and allows the judicial order made in the participating country to be recognised as such in the UK jurisdiction. There is consequently no provision for non-participating countries to make such a request. 20–059

For such mutual recognition to take effect, the order must have been made by a criminal court, prosecuting authority or any other authority in the participating country that is recognised by the UK authority as having the function of making such orders.[23] Further, the order must relate to criminal proceedings that have

[23] s.20(3).

been instigated in the participating country in respect of an offence listed in the 2003 Framework Decision,[24] or to an active criminal investigation into such an offence.[25]

The order must be accompanied by a certificate giving the specified information required under the Framework Decision, and it must be translated into English, be signed, contain a statement as to its accuracy,[26] and be accompanied by a request for the evidence that is the subject of the order to be sent to the court or authority, unless there is an indication as to when such a request will be made.[27]

On receipt of such an order, the Secretary of State must nominate a court[28] and send a copy of the order to this court and the chief officer of police (procurator fiscal in Scotland) in the area where the evidence is located, informing that officer which court has been nominated.[29]

The nominated court must then consider giving effect to the order on its on initiative within a period prescribed by the rules of court,[30] but in doing so must give the police (procurator) an opportunity to be heard.[31]

20–060 The nominated court can only refuse to give effect to such an order if it concludes that:

- the certificate is not provided, is incomplete, or does not correspond with the freezing order;[32]
- the person who is the subject of investigation would be entitled to be discharged under any law relating to a previous acquittal or conviction if he were to be charged in the UK or in the participating country (s.21(6));
- giving effect to the order would be incompatible with any of the rights recognised by the ECHR.

In practice, if the nominated court gives effect to the order, a warrant is issued, authorising a police constable to:

- enter the premises to which the warrant relates and search the premises to the extent reasonably required for the purpose of discovering any evidence to which the order relates, and
- seize and retain any evidence for which he is authorised to search.

[24] These offences are listed in Art.3 to the Framework Decision, App. C–010.
[25] s.20 (4).
[26] s.20(6).
[27] s.20(7).
[28] Sheriff in Scotland.
[29] s.21(1).
[30] s.21(3).
[31] s.21(4).
[32] Art.7(2) of the Framework Decision allows the Court to specify a deadline for presentation of a corrected/completed certificate.

Although bearing a similarity, such warrants are not issued under the Police and Criminal Evidence Act 1984 ("the 1984 Act"), but under the terms of CICA in conformity with the terms of the 2003 Framework Decision.

The court may not issue a warrant in respect of any evidence unless it has reasonable grounds to believe that it does not consist or include items subject to legal professional privilege, excluded material or special procedure material.[33]

If any of the material sought in the order is excluded material or special procedure material, the nominated court should issue a production order rather than a warrant.[34] The consequence of such a production order is that the person who appears to the court to be in possession of the material is then ordered to produce it to a police constable within seven days of the date of the order, unless the order specifies a longer period.[35] Such material produced under a production order is then treated as if it were material taken away under s.21 of the 1984 Act. If the person in possession of the material fails to comply with such a production order, the court may then issue a warrant and may deal with the person for contempt of court.[36] 20–061

Finally, the nominated court has a discretion to postpone giving effect to such an overseas freezing order in two circumstances:

- in order to avoid prejudicing a criminal investigation which is taking place in the UK, or
- where, under an order made by a court in criminal proceedings in the UK, the evidence may not be removed from the UK.[37]

Evidence seized following the execution of a warrant or production order should be retained by the police constable until he receives instruction from the territorial authority to send the evidence to the overseas authority or to release it.[38]

Any person affected by such an order (including the police) may make an application to the nominated court to release any of the evidence held by the police. Such an applicant will have to persuade the court that:

- the double jeopardy rules applies,[39] and/or
- giving effect to the order would be incompatible with ECHR, or
- the order has ceased to have effect in the participating country.[40]

[33] As defined in the 1984 Act, s.28(3).
[34] s.22(2).
[35] s.22(3).
[36] s.22(5).
[37] s.23.
[38] s.24.
[39] s.21(6).
[40] s.25.

VIII. INFORMATION ABOUT BANKING TRANSACTIONS

20–062 Sections 32–46 of CICA implement the 2001 Protocol,[41] which was directed at serious crime, in particular economic crime and money laundering. Signatory countries to this Protocol are now required to assist in the identification and monitoring of certain bank accounts at the request of other participating countries, subject to certain conditions and controls. CICA distinguishes between requests to identify bank accounts and requests to monitor activity on such accounts. These sections are not yet in force.

Sections 32 and 33 implement Art.1 of the 2001 Protocol in relation to incoming requests to provide information about bank accounts in the UK relating to a person who is the subject of an investigation in a participating country.

The main provision is s.32.

> "**32.**—(1) This section applies where the Secretary of State receives a request from an authority mentioned in subsection (2) for customer information to be obtained in relation to a person who appears to him to be subject to an investigation in a participating country into serious criminal conduct.
>
> (2) The authority referred to in subsection (1) is the authority in that country which appears to the Secretary of State to have the function of making requests of the kind to which this section applies.
>
> (3) The Secretary of State may —
>
> (a) direct a senior police officer to apply, or arrange for a constable to apply, for a customer information order,
>
> (b) direct a senior customs officer to apply, or arrange for a customs officer to apply, for such an order.
>
> (4) A customer information order is an order made by a judge that a financial institution specified in the application for the order must, on being required to do so by notice in writing given by the applicant for the order, provide any such customer information as it has relating to the person specified in such an application.
>
> (5) A financial institution which is required to produce information under a customer information order must provide the information to the applicant for the order in such manner, and at or by such time, as the applicant requires.
>
> (6) Section 364 of the Proceeds of Crime Act 2002 (c.29)(meaning of customer information), except subsections (2)(f) and (3)(i), has effect for the purposes of this section as if this section were included in Chapter 2 of Part 8 of that Act.
>
> (7) A customer information order has effect in spite of any restriction on the disclosure of information (however imposed).
>
> (8) Customer information obtained in pursuance of a customer information

[41] [2002] O.J. C257/01.

order is to be given to the Secretary of State and sent by him to the authority which made the request."

A customer information order requires a financial institution specified in the application to provide details of any accounts held by a person who is the subject of an investigation into serious criminal conduct. There is no requirement on the requesting authority to specify which accounts and it is likely that this provision will be used where there is little information as to the nature and number of accounts that a particular individual or body has at a particular financial institution. **20–063**

Serious criminal conduct is defined in s.46(3) as:

"(a) an offence to which paragraph 3 of Article 1 (request for information on bank accounts) of the 2001 Protocol applies, or
(b) an offence specified in an order made by the Secretary of State or, in relation to Scotland, the Scottish ministers for the purpose of giving effect to any decision of the Council of the European Union under paragraph 6 of that Article."

Art.1(3) of the 2001 Protocol lists the circumstances in which countries obliged to provide assistance in tracing bank accounts. The list limits the general obligation to assist to particular circumstances: when the offence is punishable by a four year custodial penalty in the requesting state and two years in the requested state, or where the offence is one referred to in the Europol Convention or the Convention on the Protection of the European Communities' Financial Interests.

The second part of the definition in subs.(3)(b) enables it to be extended by order to cover new offences if the scope of Art.1(3) is amended by the Council of the EU at a future date.

The Secretary of State has a wide discretion to add by order other countries to the list of participating countries under these provisions.[42] In contrast therefore to the provisions in respect of the freezing of evidence, it is possible that these provisions could be extended to countries beyond the EU. This might be appropriate in the case of countries such as Norway and Iceland that, although not signatories to the Protocol or MLAC, are members of Schengen. The purpose of providing the Secretary of State with this discretion is to restrict the list to those countries that are under an equal obligation to provide a particular type of assistance. Therefore these provisions in respect of Customer Information Orders differ from many others in CICA in that they require reciprocal arrangements in participating countries before the UK will assist. **20–064**

The definition of customer information is derived from s.364 of the Proceeds of Crime Act 2002 ("the 2002 Act") which states that:

[42] s.32(2).

"**364.**—(1) Customer information", in relation to a person and a financial institution, is information whether the person holds, or has held, an account or accounts at the financial institution (whether solely or jointly with another) and (if so) information as to:

(a) the matters specified in subsection (2) if the person is an individual;
(b) the matters specified in subsection (3) if the person is a company or limited liability partnership or a similar body incorporated or otherwise established outside the United Kingdom.

(2) The matters referred to in subsection (1)(a) are:

(a) the account number or numbers;
(b) the person's full name;
(c) his date of birth;
(d) his most recent address and any previous addresses;
(e) the date or dates on which he began to hold the account or account and, if he has ceased to hold the account or any of the accounts, the date or dates on which he did so;
(f) such evidence of his identity as was obtained by the financial institution under or for the purposes of any legislation relating to money laundering;
(g) the full name, date of birth and most recent address, and any previous addresses, of any person who holds, or has held, an account at the financial institution jointly with him;
(h) the account number or numbers of any other account or accounts held at the financial institution to which he is a signatory and details of the person holding the other account or accounts.

(3) The matters referred to in subsection (1)(b) are:

(a) the account number or numbers;
(b) the person's full name;
(c) a description of any business which the person carries on;
(d) the country or territory in which it is incorporated or otherwise established and any number allocated to it under the Companies Act 1985 (c.6) or the Companies (Northern Ireland) Order 1986 (S.I. 1986/1032 (N.I. 6)) or corresponding legislation of any country or territory outside the United Kingdom;
(e) any number assigned to it for the purposes of value added tax in the United Kingdom;
(f) its registered office, and any previous registered offices, under the Companies Act 1985 or the Companies (Northern Ireland) Order 1986 (S.I. 1986/1032 (N.I. 6)) or anything similar under corresponding legislation of any country or territory outside the United Kingdom;

(g) its registered office, and any previous registered offices, under the Limited Liability Partnerships Act 2000 (c.12) or anything similar under corresponding legislation of any country or territory outside Great Britain;

(h) the date or dates on which it began to hold the account or accounts and, if it has ceased to hold the account or any of the accounts, the date or dates on which it did so;

(i) such evidence of its identity as was obtained by the financial institution under or for the purposes of any legislation relating to money laundering;

(j) the full name, date of birth and most recent address and any previous addresses of any person who is a signatory to the account or any of the accounts."

The scope of the 2001 Protocol is different from the 2002 Act, which is restricted to money laundering and confiscation. In practice, this power will be used in relation to investigations of this type, but it may also be exercised in relation to other investigations into serious criminal conduct as described above. **20–065**

The information obtained should be returned to the Secretary of State for forwarding to the overseas authority which made the request.[43] This is different from the procedure in respect of evidential requests which provides that, in general, evidence should be returned by direct channels.[44]

Section 33 sets out the conditions that must be satisfied before a judge makes a customer information order. They are that:

"(a) the person specified in the application is subject to an investigation in the country in question,

(b) the investigation concerns conduct which is serious criminal conduct.

(c) the conduct constitutes an offence in England and Wales or (as the case may be) Northern Ireland, or would do were it to occur there, and

(d) the order is sought for the purpose of the investigation."

An application may be made *ex parte* to a judge in chambers[45] and may subsequently be discharged or varied on application.[46]

The Act sets out various criminal offences connected with failure to comply with customer information orders. The penalties, which are financial only, are directed at non-compliant institutions, rather than at individuals.[47]

[43] s.32 (8).

[44] s.19.

[45] s.32(2).

[46] s.32(4).

[47] s.34 replicates s.366 of the 2002 Act.

ACCOUNT INFORMATION

20–066 Sections 35 and 36 implement Art.3 of the 2001 Protocol in relation to incoming requests. Art.3 provides for requests to be made for a specified account to be monitored during a particular period.

It is not necessary that a customer information order has been issued. This measure reflects a similar measure about the monitoring of accounts introduced under the 2002 Act. Separate provision is set out in this Act to ensure that the UK can respond to all requests that meet the requirements of the 2001 Protocol, which has a wider scope than the 2002 Act.

Section 35 states that:

> "**35.**—(1) This section applies where the Secretary of State receives a request from an authority mentioned in subsection (2) for account information to be obtained in relation to an investigation in a participating country into criminal conduct.
>
> (2) The authority referred to in subsection (1) is the authority in that country which appears to the Secretary of State to have the function of making requests of the kind to which this section applies.
>
> (3) The Secretary of State may —
>
> (a) direct a senior police officer to apply, or arrange for a constable to apply, for an account monitoring order,
> (b) direct a senior customs officer to apply, or arrange for a customs officer to apply, for such an order.
>
> (4) An account monitoring order is an order made by a judge that a financial institution specified in the application for the order must, for the period stated in the order, provide account information of the description specified in the order to the applicant in the manner, and at or by the time or times, state din the order.
>
> (5) Account information is information relating to an account or accounts held at the financial institution specified in the application by the person so specified (whether solely or jointly with another).
>
> (6) An account monitoring order has effect in spite of any restriction on the disclosure of information (however imposed).
>
> (7) Account information obtained in pursuance of an account monitoring order is to be given to the Secretary of State and sent by him to the authority which made the request."

20–067 Art.3(3) of the 2001 Protocol provides that the order shall be made with due regard for the national law of the requested member state. Under the 2002 Act, account monitoring orders may be made for a period of up to ninety days and the same restriction will apply to requests under the 2001 Protocol. No limit is stated because the arrangements will be made between the relevant authorities on a case by case basis, as provided for in Art.3(4) of the 2001 Protocol.

The conditions which must be satisfied before a judge may make an account monitoring order are that there must be an investigation in the country in question into criminal conduct, and the order must be sought for the purpose of the investigation.[48–49] The conditions are different from those needed for a customer information order in that there is no requirement for double criminality, nor that the offence under investigation be a serious criminal offence. All that is required is that there is an investigation into "criminal conduct". It would appear that the rationale for the distinction arose from the negotiations between the member states when agreeing to the protocol. It was agreed that CIOs are likely to impose significant demands on jurisdictions that do not have central banking registers, and therefore some degree of proportionality was required between the crime under investigation and the measure sought. Art.1 of the Protocol states that the obligation to assist is limited to cases involving "serious criminal conduct".

As in the case of customer information requests, the application can be made without notice and the information should relate to a particular account, or some or all of the accounts held by the person specified.

CICA creates an offence for which a financial institution or employee of that institution can be held criminally liable for the disclosure of information pertaining to a customer information order or an account monitoring order.[50] The financial institution needs to have been specifically named in the order. 20–068

> "**42.**—(2) If the institution or an employee of the institution, discloses any of the following information, the institution or (as the case may be) the employee is guilty of an offence.
>
> (3) That information is —
>
> (a) that the request to obtain customer information or account information or the request mentioned in subsection 1(b), has been received,
> (b) that the investigation to which the request relates is being carried out, or
> (c) that, in pursuance of the request, information has been given to the authority, which made the request.
>
> (4) An institution guilty of an offence under this section is liable —
>
> (a) on summary conviction, to a fine not exceeding the statutory maximum,
> (b) on conviction on indictment, to a fine.
>
> (5) Any other person guilty of an offence under this section is liable —

[48–49] s.36. See also *Hansard* Lord Filkin 230225-21.

[50] s.42.

(a) on summary conviction, to imprisonment to a term no exceeding six months or to a fine not exceeding the statutory maximum, or to both,

(b) on conviction on indictment, to imprisonment for a term not exceeding five years or to a fine, or to both."

This section states that the offence is committed if the disclosure is made, but it does not specify to whom the disclosure may be made.

REQUESTS FOR INFORMATION ABOUT BANKING TRANSACTIONS FOR USE IN THE UK

20–069 Section 43 makes provision for the UK to request assistance from other participating countries in obtaining details of any accounts held by a person subject to an investigation into serious criminal conduct in accordance with Art.1 of the 2001 Protocol. Whilst the general provisions in relation to the provision of material by an overseas authority as set out in s.7 are relevant, other requirements are set out.

"**43.**—(1) If it appears to a judicial authority in the United Kingdom, on an application made by a prosecuting authority, that —

(a) a person is subject to an investigation in the United Kingdom into serious criminal conduct,

(b) the person holds, or may hold, an account at a bank which is situated in a participating country, and

(c) the information which the applicant seeks to obtain is likely to be of substantial value for the purposes of the investigation.

(5) The assistance that may be requested under this section is any assistance in obtaining from a participating country one or more of the following —

(a) information as to whether the person in question holds any accounts at any banks situated in the participating country,

(b) details of any such accounts,

(c) details of transactions carried out in any period specified in the request in respect of any such accounts.

(6) A request for assistance under this section must —

(a) state the grounds on which the authority making the request thinks that the person in question may hold any account at a bank which is situated in a participating country and (if possible) specify the bank or banks in question,

(b) state the grounds on which the authority making the request considers that the information sought to be obtained is likely to be of substantial value for the purposes of the investigation, and

(c) include any information which may facilitate compliance with the request.

(7) For the purposes of this section, a person holds an account if —

(a) the account is in his name or is held for his benefit, or
(b) he has a power of attorney in respect of the account."

This provision implements Art.3 of the 2001 Protocol for the purpose of outgoing requests from the UK to other participating countries to monitor transactions conducted on a specified account or accounts.

In general, requests for assistance under s.43 or 44 must be transmitted through the Secretary of State, in contrast to the direct transmission provision introduced by s.8.[51] This is for the purpose of enabling the Secretary of State to monitor these requests, to ensure that the detailed requirements of the 2001 Protocol are met, and to assess how extensively the new powers are used. In cases of urgency, the request can be sent directly to a court in the area where the information is to be obtained.

[51] S.45.

CHAPTER 21

MISCELLANEOUS PROVISIONS OF CICA

(by Alun Jones and Michael O'Kane)

I. HEARING WITNESSES ABROAD IN UK PROCEEDINGS THROUGH VIDEO LINK

21–001 There are statutory provisions that allow witnesses to give evidence from abroad In criminal proceedings in the UK by video link in certain limited circumstances.[1] Section 29[2] does not alter these provisions but allows the Secretary of State[3] to extend the current provision to include other types of criminal proceedings in the future.

[1] s.32 Criminal Justice Act 1988 allows evidence to be given by a witness from outside the UK in cases involving murder, manslaughter and "serious and complex" frauds. See also s.273 of the Criminal Procedure (Scotland Act) 1995)

[2] Not yet in force.

[3] Or in Scotland, Scottish Ministers.

II. HEARING WITNESSES PRESENT IN THE UK IN OVERSEAS PROCEEDINGS THROUGH TELEVISION/TELEPHONE LINKS

This new provision[4] allows a witness present in the UK to give evidence in overseas[5] proceedings by way of television link. It applies to the taking of testimony from witnesses but not suspects or defendants. 21–002

The procedure governing video evidence is set out in s.30 to the 2003 Act:

> "**30.**—(1) This section applies where the Secretary of State receives a request, from an authority mentioned in subsection (2)("the external authority"), for a person in the United Kingdom to give evidence through a live television link in criminal proceedings before a court in a country outside the United Kingdom.
>
> (2) The authority referred to in subsection (1) is the authority in that country which appears to the Secretary of State to have the function of making requests of the kind to which this section applies.
>
> (3) Unless he considers it inappropriate to do so, the Secretary of State must by notice in writing nominate a court in the United Kingdom where the witness may be heard in the proceedings in question through a live television link.
>
> (4) Anything done by the witness in the presence of the nominated court which if it were done in the proceedings before the court, would constitute contempt of court is to be treated for that purpose as done in proceedings before the court.
>
> (5) Any statement made on oath by a witness giving evidence in pursuance of this section is to be treated for the purposes of —
>
> (a) section 1 of the Perjury Act 1911(c.6)
> (b) Article 3 of the Perjury (Northern Ireland) Order 1979 (S.I. 1979/1714 (N.I.19)),
> (c) Sections 44 to 46 of the Criminal Law (Consolidation)(Scotland) Act 1995(c.39) or, in relation to Scotland, any matter pertaining to the common law crime of perjury,
>
> As made in proceedings before the nominated court.
>
> (6) Part 1 of Schedule 2 (evidence given by television link) is to have effect.
>
> (7) Subject to subsections (4) and (5) and the provisions of that Schedule, evidence given pursuant to this section is not to be treated for any purpose as evidence given in proceedings in the United Kingdom.
>
> (8) In relation to Scotland, references in this section and Part 1of Schedule 2 to the Secretary of State are to be read as references to the Lord Advocate."

[4] s.30

[5] Although giving effect to MLAC 2000 it allows the UK to assist all countries, though the UN Convention against Transnational Crime, the 2nd Additional protocol to the European Convention on Mutual Assistance 2001 and the Agreement between the EU and the US on Mutual Assistance in Criminal Matters.

21–003 The request to the Secretary of State must come from an "external" authority. This is not defined in the Act but it should be taken that such authorities are those that generally make requests for mutual legal assistance, including courts, prosecutors, central authorities, examining magistrates, official persons and bodies with investigative and prosecuting functions in accordance with the definition of judicial authorities provided in Art.24 of the 1959 Convention.[6]

As well as setting out the main information normally sought in a Letter of Request, a request in respect of video link evidence should include the following information:[7]

- sufficient information to enable the Secretary of State to identify and contact the witness(es);[8]
- a list of questions to be asked if possible;
- details of the procedure to be followed in taking the evidence, including any rules on privilege which a witness or suspect may be entitled to claim;
- any caution or formal notification of rights which should be given to the witness or suspect under the law of the requesting State;
- details (if known at the time) of the technical requirements for establishing the link to ensure compatibility.

The UK may require the requesting State to reimburse all or part of the costs associated with such requests.

21–004 The Secretary of State has a general discretion to nominate a court to hear the evidence unless he considers it inappropriate to do so.[9] It is not clear in what circumstances the Secretary of State would make such a determination. It is possible that that he may refuse a request where execution would clearly contravene current UK law, or where contained insufficient information, (for example, a failure in a EU request to specify why it was impossible or undesirable for a witness to travel).

Art.10 of MLAC 2000 requires that the request should specify the reason why it is not desirable or possible for the witness or expert to attend in person, and it should state the name of the judicial authority and the persons who will conduct the hearing. Accordingly such requirements will only be placed on countries that are signatories to MLAC 2000. Consideration was given at the time of drafting CICA to expand these requirements to cover requests from all other countries, but it was decided that to do so might affect future agreements containing provisions not expressed in exactly the same terms as in MLAC, which might result in the exclusion of assistance under other agreements.[10] A request from a non-EU country will for practical reasons always have to include details of the authority conducting the hearing, and set out the reasons for requesting a video hearing.

The procedural requirements are set out in Sch.2, Pt 1 of the Act. This provides that the court shall have the same powers to secure the attendance of witnesses as it

[6] *Hansard per* Lord Bassam 230123-31.
[7] Home Office Guidelines, App. C–012.
[8] The UK will not assist with requests to hear evidence from suspects via TV/video link.
[9] s.30(3).
[10] *Hansard per* Lord Bassam 230123-31.

has for the purpose of proceedings before the court. In other words the nominated court can summons the witness to attend in accordance with s.97 of the Magistrates' Court Act 1980.[11] Such a summons would set out where and when the witness is to appear together with an explanation to the witness of the consequences of a failure to comply with the summons.

The nominated court is placed under a duty to intervene where it considers such an intervention is necessary to protect the rights of the witness.[12] Furthermore the witness cannot be compelled to give any evidence that he or she could not be compelled to give in the UK.[13–14] However the corollary is that the witness can be compelled to give evidence from the UK when under the laws of the requesting country he would not be compellable. Where, therefore, a witness is unable to travel through illness to the requesting country, it is possible that he could be compelled to give evidence even though he would not be so compellable if he was in the requesting country. It would appear that no provision preventing such a situation was included in the Act because a burden would be placed on the nominated court or Secretary of State to investigate the law relating to compellability in the requesting state.[15] However such a difficulty could be overcome by requiring the requesting state to make a declaration as to its law within the body of the request. 21–005

Although there is an explicit protection against self incrimination,[16] a practical difficulty is that the judge will be unlikely to know the detail of the case and be in a position to give the witness the appropriate warning.

In practice a witness will probably be present in the UK nominated court before a Circuit or District Judge. The questions asked on behalf of the overseas jurisdiction may but put in a foreign language. There is provision for the use of interpreters[17–18] so that the court can comply with the duties set out in Sch.2.

These proceedings will be subject to the normal rules in relation to perjury and contempt of court. This measure implements Art.10(8) of MLAC 2000 which stipulates that states must be able to deal with witnesses who refuse to testify or do not testify according to the truth under their domestic law.

There is no provision for access to legal advice for a witness in these circumstances. Under the Criminal Defence Service Regulations 2001, legal advice can be provided to a person who is a witness in criminal proceedings if that person requires advice on the subject of self-incrimination, and it is possible that legal representation for a witness could be applied for under that provision. 21–006

In the last few years there have been an increasing number of televised hearings in Magistrates' and Crown Courts, primarily for the purpose of dealing with prisoners

[11] See The Crown Court (Amendment) Rules 2004 & The Magistrates' Courts (Crime (International Co-operation)) Rules 2004.

[12] Sch.2, Pt 1 para.5.

[13–14] Sch.2, Pt 1 para.9.

[15] *Hansard* 230123-33 Lord Bassam.

[16] Sch.2 para.9 (1).

[17–18] Including sign language (*Hansard* Lord Bassam 230123–33).

on remand so that they do not have to be brought to court for preliminary hearings. The technology is available to allow the same facilities to be used for the transmission of testimony by means of a video link to an overseas hearing.

In Scotland this facility extends to the power to issue a warrant to officers of law to cite the witness for the purpose of securing his or her attendance to give evidence by way of the link.

III. HEARING A WITNESS IN THE UK BY TELEPHONE

21–007 The main provision is s.31 of CICA.

> "**31.**—(1) This section applies where the Secretary of State receives a request, from an authority mentioned in subsection (2)("the external authority") in a participating country, for a person in the United Kingdom to give evidence by telephone in criminal proceedings before a court in that country.
>
> Criminal Proceedings include any proceedings on an appeal before a court against a decision in administrative proceedings.
>
> (2) The authority referred to in subsection (1) is the authority in that country which appears to the Secretary of State to have the function of making requests of the kind to which this section applies.
>
> (3) A request under subsection (1) must —
>
> (a) specify the court in the participating country,
> (b) give the name and address of the witness,
> (c) state that the witness is willing to give evidence by telephone in the proceedings before that court.
>
> (4) Unless he considers it inappropriate to do so, the Secretary of State must by notice in writing nominate a court in the United Kingdom where the witness may be heard in the proceedings in question by telephone.
>
> (5) Anything done by the witness in the presence of the nominated court which, if it were done in proceedings before the court, would constitute contempt of court is to be treated for that purpose as done in proceedings before the court.
>
> (6) Any statement made on oath by a witness giving evidence in pursuance of this section is to be treated for the purposes of —
>
> (a) section 1 of the Perjury Act 1911 (c.6)
> (b) Article 3 of the Perjury (Northern Ireland) Order 1979 (S.I. 1979/1714 (N.I.19)),
> (c) Sections 44 to 46 of the Criminal Law (Consolidation)(Scotland) Act 1995 (c.39) or, in relation to Scotland, any matter pertaining to the common law crime of perjury,

As made in proceedings before a nominated court.

(7) Part 2 of Schedule 2 (evidence given by telephone link) is to have effect.

(8) Subject to subsections (5) and (6) and the provisions of that Schedule, evidence given in pursuance of this section is not to be treated for any purpose as evidence given in proceedings in the United Kingdom.

(9) In relation to Scotland, references in this section to the Secretary of State are to be read as references to the Lord Advocate.

This new provision reflects Art.11 of MLAC 2000 which allows courts to hear witnesses by telephone within the scope of national law. It also recognises that in certain overseas jurisdictions (notably Sweden) such a procedure is a common way of taking evidence. There is no provision in CICA or any other statute for the reception of evidence by telephone in domestic UK proceedings. 21–008

As in the case of television evidence to an overseas state, the request must be sent to the Secretary of State who must then nominate a court where the hearing will take place.

Unlike the procedure relating to television evidence, the witness in this instance must consent, and the request must state that the witness is willing to give evidence. This accords with the provision in Art.11(2) of MLAC 2000.

The same rules in relation to perjury and contempt of court apply, and except for these limited purposes the evidence given is not to be treated as evidence in UK proceedings. This fulfils a UK obligation under MLAC 2000 to ensure that perjury and contempt of court are subject to domestic sanction, as the overseas court conducting the hearing will be unable to take any direct action itself.

IV. TRANSFER OF PRISONERS

TRANSFER OF UK PRISONERS TO ASSIST INVESTIGATIONS ABROAD

Section 47 implements Art.9 of MLAC 2000 by providing for prisoners from the UK to be transferred to another participating country to assist with an investigation. 21-009

Section 47 states that:

(1) The Secretary of State may pursuant to an agreement with the competent authority of a participating country issue a warrant providing for any person to whom this section applies ("a prisoner") to be transferred to that country for the purpose of assisting there in the investigation of an offence.

The offence must be one which was or may have been committed in the United Kingdom.

(2) This section applies to a person:

(a) serving a sentence in a prison,
(b) in custody awaiting trial or sentence, or
(c) committed to prison for default in paying a fine.

(3) But, in relation to transfer from Scotland:

(a) this sections applies to any person detained in custody,
(b) references in this section to the Secretary of State are to be read as references to the Scottish Ministers.

(4) A warrant may be issued in respect of a prisoner under subsection (1) only if:

(a) the prisoner, or
(b) in the circumstances mentioned in subsection (5), a person appearing to the Secretary of State to be an appropriate person to act on the prisoner's behalf,

has made a written statement consenting to his being transferred for the purpose mentioned in subsection (1).

(5) The circumstances are those in which it appears to be the Secretary of State to be inappropriate for the prisoner to act for himself, by reason of his physical or mental condition or his youth.

(6) Such consent cannot be withdrawn after the issue of the warrant.

(7) A warrant under this section authorises:

(a) the taking of the prisoner to a place in the United Kingdom and his delivery at a place of departure from the United Kingdom into the custody of a person representing the appropriate authority of the participating country to which the prisoner is to be transferred, and
(b) the bringing of the prisoner back to the United Kingdom and his transfer in custody to the place where he is liable to be detained under the sentence or order to which he is subject.

(8) References to a prison in this section include any other institution to which the Prison Act 1952 (c.52), the Prison Act (Northern Ireland) 1953 (c.18 (N.I)) or Article 45(1) of the Criminal Justice (Children) (Northern Ireland) Order 1998 (S.I. 1998/1504 (N.I.9)) applies.

(9) Subsections (3A) to (8) of section 5 of the 1990 Act (transfer of UK prisoner to give evidence or assist investigation overseas) have effect in relation to a warrant issued under this section as they have effect in relation to a warrant issued under that section.

21–010 This section differs from the old provisions in s.5 of the 1990 Act, which deals with the transfer of UK prisoners to other countries to assist in their investigations.

This new power might be used, for example, where a prisoner assisting a UK investigation was able to identify a site or participate in an identification parade in another country. the power is unlikely to be used frequently[19] and, as under the 1990 Act, the prisoner must give his consent.

The Home Office recommends that when the request is made for the temporary transfer of a UK prisoner to give evidence, or otherwise to assist in criminal investigations or proceedings outside the UK, it should include:

- dates on which the presence abroad of the prisoner is required, including the dates on which the court or other proceedings for which the prisoner is required will commence and are likely to be concluded;
- information for the purpose of obtaining the prisoner's consent to the transfer and satisfying the UK authorities that arrangements will be made to keep the prisoner in secure custody, such as:
  - whether the prisoner will have immunity from prosecution for previous offences;
  - details of proposed arrangements for collecting the prisoner from and returning the prisoner to the UK;
  - details of the type of secure accommodation in which the prisoner will be held in the requesting State;
  - details of the type of escort available abroad to and from the secure accommodation.

If it appears to the Secretary of State that it is inappropriate for the prisoner to act for himself through physical or mental inability, or because he is young, an appropriate person can give consent on behalf of the prisoner. A young person is considered to be under the age of 18. 21–011

It is not clear how such a physical or mental state is to be established, or who is an appropriate person in these circumstances. Even should such consent be forthcoming it is very unlikely that the Secretary of State would seek the transfer of a prisoner who was unable to travel as a result of physical or mental impairment.[20]

It would appear from the absence of any provision that the giving of consent by a prisoner is an irrevocable act. It was apparently considered that a withdrawal of consent by a prisoner might make the original warrant invalid and the detention unlawful. A prisoner who consented would not be transferred if a doctor formed the view that he was not well enough. In this way the provisions reflect the wording of the 1990 Act which has not given rise to difficulties in this respect.[21]

The prisoner in question must either be serving a sentence, or on remand awaiting trial or sentence, or have been committed to prison for default in paying a fine.[22]

[19] There have been on average thirty such transfers per year under the 1990 Act (*Hansard* 230127-21 col.GC157, Lord Bessam).

[20] *Hansard* Lord Bassam 230127-20.

[21] *ibid.*

[22] Does not apply to a prisoner held without trial as a result of anti–terror legislation.

It is intended that these new provisions will make the transfer of the UK prisoner more straightforward as the request will come to the prison service from a UK authority rather than an overseas authority.

21–012 Prisoners are free to seek legal advice as to their transfer, as they were entitled to do under the 1990 Act, but such advice is not automatically available; it was considered that to provide it would impose an unnecessary burden on the prison system.[23]

It is the responsibility of the Secretary of State to arrange the:

- taking of the prisoner to a departure point in the UK and the delivery of the prisoner to a person representing the requesting authority;
- escort of the prisoner back to the UK by the requesting authority (appropriate officials from the UK should accompany the prisoner[24]); and
- transfer of the prisoner from the arrival point to his or her place of detention.[25]

The Secretary of State will not normally agree to a temporary transfer if as a consequence:

- the prisoner would not be able to participate in criminal investigations or proceedings in the UK;
- the period of the prisoner's detention would be prolonged.[26]

TRANSFER OF EU PRISONERS TO ASSIST AN INVESTIGATION

21–013 Section 48 provides for the transfer of a prisoner from a participating country to the UK in order to assist with that country's investigation. This is consistent with the old provision in s.6 of the 1990 Act. Again the consent of the prisoner is necessary.

Section 48 states that:

> (1) The Secretary of State may pursuant to an agreement with the competent authority of a participating country issue a warrant providing for any person to whom this section applies ("the overseas prisoner") to be transferred to the United Kingdom for the purpose of assisting in the investigation of an offence.
>
> The offence must be one which was or may have been committed in the participating country.
>
> (2) This section applies to a person who is detained in custody in a participating country:

[23] *Hansard* Lord Bassam 230127-19.
[24] Home Office Circular April 2004 para.91; App.C–013.
[25] Home Office Guidelines, App.C–012.
[26] Home Office Circular April 2004 para.92; App.C–013.

(a) by virtue of a sentence or order of a court exercising criminal jurisdiction there, or
(b) in consequence of having been transferred there from the United Kingdom under the Repatriation of Prisoners Act 1984 (c.47) or under any similar provision or arrangement from any other country.

(3) But, in relation to transfer to Scotland:

(a) this section applies to any person who is detained in custody in a participating country,
(b) the reference in subsection (1) to the Secretary of State is to be read as a reference to the Scottish Ministers.

(4) A warrant may be issued in respect of an overseas prisoner under subsection (1) only if the competent authority provides a written statement made by the prisoner consenting to his being transferred for the purpose mentioned in that subsection.

(5) Such consent cannot be withdrawn after the issue of the warrant.

(6) A warrant under this section authorises:

(a) the bringing of the prisoner to the United Kingdom,
(b) the taking of the prisoner to, and his detention in custody at, any place or places in the United Kingdom specified in the warrant,
(c) the returning of the prisoner to the country from which he has come.

(7) Subsections (4) and (8) of section 5 of the 1990 Act have effect in relation to a warrant issued under this section as they have effect in relation to a warrant issued under that section.

(8) A person is not subject to the Immigration Act 1971 (c.77) in respect of his entry into or presence in the United Kingdom pursuant to a warrant under this section; but if the warrant ceases to have effect while he is still in the United Kingdom:

(a) he is to be treated for the purposes of that Act as if he has then illegally entered the United Kingdom, and
(b) the provisions of Schedule 2 to that Act have effect accordingly except that paragraph 20(1) (liability of carrier for expenses of custody etc of illegal entrant) does not have effect in relation to directions for his removal given by virtue of this subsection.

The request for such a prisoner transfer will normally come from the police and be made through the Crown Prosecution Service or Customs and Excise. Where such a request is made, immunity from prosecution cannot be granted automatically.[27]

[27] Art.12 of the 1959 Convention and para.25 of Harare Scheme.

The Secretary of State must ensure that the prisoner has consented, that the period of detention in the UK would not extend beyond the earliest release date, and that the prisoner's presence in the UK would not be contrary to the public interest.[28]

V. FOREIGN SURVEILLANCE OPERATIONS IN THE UK

21–014 CICA now permits foreign law enforcement officers, in certain controlled conditions, to carry out surveillance in the UK.[29] This is a new provision and should be distinguished from provisions governing "hot pursuit" where law enforcement officers are pursuing a suspect with a view to arrest, rather than to conduct surveillance. Hot Pursuit is a part of the Schengen Acquis to which the UK has not acceded, and it only applies over land borders. As the Republic of Ireland has also declined to accede, this is a matter of marginal significance to the UK authorities. It does not apply to Gibraltar, Jersey or Guernsey, which also do not participate in these parts of Schengen.[30]

> **83.**—After section 76 of the Regulation of investigatory Powers Act 2000 (c.23) there is inserted —
>
> (1) This section applies where —
>
> (a) a foreign police or customs officers is carrying out relevant surveillance outside the United Kingdom which is lawful under the law of the country or territory where it is being carried out;
> (b) circumstances arise by virtue of which the surveillance can for the time being be carried out only in the United Kingdom; and
> (c) it is not reasonably practicable in those circumstances for a United Kingdom officer to carry out the surveillance in the United Kingdom in accordance with the authorisation under Part 2 or the Regulation of Investigatory Powers (Scotland) Act.
>
> (2) "Relevant surveillance" means surveillance which —
>
> (a) is carried out in relation to a person who is suspected of having committed a relevant crime; and
> (b) is for the purposes of Part 2, directed surveillance or intrusive surveillance.

[28] Home Office Circular April 2004 para.97.
[29] s.83.
[30] *Hansard* Commons Select Committee part 5 col.290.

(3) "Relevant crime"means crime which —

(a) falls within Article 40(7) of the Schengen Convention; or
(b) is crime for the purposes of any other international agreement to which the United Kingdom is a party and which is specified for the purposes of this section in an order made by the Secretary of State with the consent of the Scottish Ministers.

This section reflects Art.40 of the Schengen Agreement which states that:

> "Officers of one of the contracting Parties who, as part of a criminal investigation re keeping under surveillance in their country a person who is presumed to have participated in an extraditable criminal offence shall be authorised to continue their surveillance in the territory of another Contracting Party . . . "

All the Schengen signatories have adopted these provisions except Ireland. UK officers are entitled to conduct surveillance operation abroad in participating states in the same way as foreign officers as a result of s.83. Conduct is governed also by a Code of Practice known as the "Schengen Handbook". 21–015

In the great majority of cases such assistance will be requested and granted in advance. This will be achieved in practice by the foreign officers notifying NCIS[31] as soon as it seems probable that their "target" is travelling to the UK. NCIS will then notify the NCS or the local force who will then identify officers to work with the foreign officers. The UK officers will then[32] take responsibility, having sought and been granted the necessary authorisations under RIPA.

Because Great Britain is an island, foreign surveillance agents will normally have time to seek and obtain the necessary authorisations. Accordingly these provisions may be used sparingly.

However, there will no doubt be occasions when it will not be reasonably practicable for one state to provide advance notice of the surveillance to the UK in time for UK authorities to take over the operation effectively. Accordingly, this section, implementing Art.40(2) of the Schengen Convention, makes provision for a foreign police or customs officer involved in carrying out lawful surveillance in his own jurisdiction, to continue lawfully to keep a suspect under surveillance in the UK for a period of up to five hours.

The target of the surveillance must be suspected of having committed a relevant crime.[33] In such circumstances the foreign officer must notify NCIS immediately upon arrival in the UK and must request an application to be made for authorisation under RIPA to conduct surveillance.[34] The five-hour period will not commence 21–016

[31] In Scotland the Operational and Intelligence Groups of the Scottish Drug Enforcement Agency ("OIG") or Scottish Crime Squad ("SCS").

[32] *Hansard* Lord Filkin 230129-21.

[33] Offences constituting relevant crimes are set out in Art.40(7) of the Schengen Convention.

[34] s.83(6).

until the officer has entered the UK.[35] It is not always clear what constitutes "entry into the UK" for the purposes of this section, as no mention is made of territorial waters or airspace. It would appear that the intention is to include the time when the officer arrives at a port or airport, or crosses into the UK part of the Eurotunnel.[36] The officer is entitled to seek such an authorisation prior to arriving in the UK.[37]

The surveillance included in these circumstances is both directed surveillance and intrusive surveillance. It does not apply where an officer infiltrates a criminal gang and is accordingly acting as a covert human intelligence source.[38] The main conditions are that:

- the foreign officers submit a formal request to the UK authorities immediately upon entry, and
- the foreign officers do not enter any private homes or places.
- the foreign officers do not stop or question the target of their operation.

Foreign officers are also not entitled to carry firearms,[39–40] although this is not expressly stated within the body of the Act.

In addition the Secretary of State can impose by order other conditions governing the foreign operation while it is conducted in the UK.[41] A failure by the foreign investigators to comply with any of these conditions would render the operation unlawful. The consequences of this for the investigation/prosecution of any targets would depend largely on the reliance to be placed by the foreign prosecuting authority on evidence obtained in this way and the rules of admissibility should such evidence be challenged by the defence.

21–017 Foreign surveillance agents are also free of any civil liabilities (such as trespass) for conduct that is inextricably associated with the surveillance. There is a similar provision within RIPA for the protection of UK officers.[42]

During the five-hour period the UK should establish its own surveillance team, at which time a joint operation should be established in which the UK officers will take responsibility for the surveillance and the foreign officers will observe. If for whatever reason the UK has been unable to mobilise a surveillance team, the foreign officers will no longer be acting under lawful authority and will be expected to cease their operation.[43]

The Secretary of State has the power to terminate such a foreign surveillance operation within the five hour period;[44] there is no power to extend this period.

[35] s.83(7).
[36] *Hansard* 010104 part 7.
[37] subs.6(b).
[38] s.26 RIPA.
[39–40] Schengen handbook.
[41] subs.4(b).
[42] s.27(2).
[43] subs.7.
[44] subs.8.

Foreign officers engaged in such surveillance are considered to be public authorities and as such are subject to the provisions of the ECHR which will apply when the UK authorities are notified of their presence. Accordingly the powers of the Investigatory Powers Tribunal that deals with complaints about the conduct of surveillance have been extended to deal with the conduct of foreign officers acting under the auspices of this section.[45]

Section 83 also provides complementary provisions to allow UK police officers to travel to a participating country to keep a suspect under surveillance as part of a UK investigation. Previously UK police officers were not allowed to follow suspects overseas to continue surveillance. They were expected to contact the police authorities in the country that they intended to visit to request them to take over the surveillance operation.

For the purposes of establishing an offence of assaulting a police constable[46] the **21–018**
foreign officer conducting lawful surveillance in furtherance of these sections is to be treated as if he were a constable acting in the execution of his duty.[47–48] This section implements Art.42 of the Schengen Convention which states that when acting lawfully under the provisions of the Convention foreign officers are entitled to be protected by the law of the State in which they are operating. Section 104 of the Police Reform Act 2002 already provides the same rights for foreign officers who are part of Joint Investigative Teams. The protection is only afforded to the foreign officers for the period until the operation is taken over by UK officers. Should the foreign operation go beyond the five-hour period, it appears that the operation would no longer be lawful and the officers would no longer be able to claim the protection of this section.

VI. ROAD TRAFFIC PROVISIONS

CONVENTION ON DRIVING DISQUALIFICATIONS — DUTY TO GIVE NOTICE TO FOREIGN AUTHORITIES OF DRIVING DISQUALIFICATION OF NON-UK RESIDENT.

This part of CICA enacts in UK law the obligations imposed by the 1998 **21–019**
Convention on Driving Disqualifications which intended that a driver who is disqualified from driving in a Member State other than that in which he normally resides should not escape his disqualification at home.[49]

Sections 54 and 55 set out the terms upon which a duty is imposed on the relevant UK Minister[50] to notify a central authority of the EU member state where the

[45] Sch.5 para.79 amending RIPA ss.65 & 78.
[46] s.89 of the Police Act 1996.
[47–48] s.84.
[49] Art.2 of the Convention.
[50] The Secretary of State in Great Britain or the Department of Environment in Northern Ireland.

offender is normally resident about a driving disqualification. The person who is the subject of the driving disqualification imposed in the UK should be normally resident in a member state other than the UK, and must have been convicted of one or more of the offences set out in Sch.2, Pt 3.

The notice supplied by the Minister must include information required by the Convention to allow the central authority to locate the offender, together with details of the offence and the penalty.[51] If the offender did not attend the UK proceedings when he was disqualified, the Minister must also supply confirmation that the offender was notified of the proceedings.[52]

The state of residence can refuse to give effect to the driving disqualification in certain circumstances, including where the state considers that the offender was not given an adequate opportunity to defend himself.[53] If the period of disqualification is reduced or removed by a court subsequent to the appropriate Minister sending his notification, he must inform the central authority.

21–020 The circumstances in which a disqualification imposed in another Member State on a person normally resident in the UK, will be enforced in the UK are set out in s.56. Similar provisions apply here as apply to the above sections, in that the offence which gives rise to the disqualification must constitute one of the categories of conduct specified in the Convention. Importantly a disqualification will not be imposed in the UK if the relevant proceedings in the state where the offence was committed, were brought later than the time provided in the UK for the commencement of summary proceedings for a corresponding offence.[54]

The appropriate Minister in the UK must be provided by the state where the offence was committed with the information required to enforce the disqualification. The Minister then has a discretion as to whether to enforce a disqualification where the unexpired period is less than a month. Where the disqualification is effective until a condition is satisfied, the UK disqualification takes effect 21 days after notification to the offender. However, the appropriate Minister has power to substitute a longer period. The intention is that the period at the end of which the disqualification takes effect should be the same as the period for appealing under s.59.

The Convention requires that any part of the disqualification already served in the state where the offence is committed is to be taken into account in recognising the disqualification in the offender's state of residence. Section 57 grants the appropriate minister power to make regulations to prescribe how the unexpired period of disqualification is to be determined. Although the normal appeals process will have been exhausted before the disqualification is notified to the UK, if the state where the offence is committed removes the disqualification at any time during the unexpired period, the disqualification will also cease to have effect in the UK at that time.

21–021 The appeal process in relation to disqualifications imposed under s.57, on a person normally resident in the UK, is set out in ss.59 to 62. An appellant has 21

[51] Art.8 of the Convention.

[52] Art.8(2) of the Convention.

[53] Art.6(1)(d) of the Convention.

[54] Art.6(1)(d) of the Convention.

days from the date of service of the notice by the relevant Minister to lodge such an appeal, although the Minister has the power to extend this time limit. The appropriate court in England and Wales is the Magistrates' Court.[55] When the notice of appeal has been lodged the court may, if it thinks fit, suspend the disqualification until the matter is determined. This suspension can also be continued if the appellant then further appeals against the decision of the court to the High Court.

The appellant's only grounds of appeal are that s.57 is not applicable to him, and he must satisfy the court that at least one of the conditions set out in s.56 does not apply. If the appeal is allowed, the court must send a notice of this to the appropriate Minister.

Provisions relating to the production of driving licences and endorsement are set out in ss.63 to 65.

[55] Sheriff in Scotland and Court of summary jurisdiction within that petty sessional division in Northern Ireland.

APPENDICES

APPENDIX A

STATUTES

Extradition Act 2003 A–001

2003 CHAPTER 41

An Act to make provision about extradition. [20TH NOVEMBER 2003]

Be it enacted by the Queen's most Excellent Majesty, by and with the advice and consent of the Lords Spiritual and Temporal, and Commons, in this present Parliament assembled, and by the authority of the same, as follows: —

PART 1

EXTRADITION TO CATEGORY 1 TERRITORIES

Introduction

1 Extradition to category 1 territories

(1) This Part deals with extradition from the United Kingdom to the territories designated for the purposes of this Part by order made by the Secretary of State.

(2) In this Act references to category 1 territories are to the territories designated for the purposes of this Part.

(3) A territory may not be designated for the purposes of this Part if a person found guilty in the territory of a criminal offence may be sentenced to death for the offence under the general criminal law of the territory.

2 Part 1 warrant and certificate

(1) This section applies if the designated authority receives a Part 1 warrant in respect of a person.

(2) A Part 1 warrant is an arrest warrant which is issued by a judicial authority of a category 1 territory and which contains —

(a) the statement referred to in subsection (3) and the information referred to in subsection (4), or
(b) the statement referred to in subsection (5) and the information referred to in subsection (6).

(3) The statement is one that—

(a) the person in respect of whom the Part 1 warrant is issued is accused in the category 1 territory of the commission of an offence specified in the warrant, and
(b) the Part 1 warrant is issued with a view to his arrest and extradition to the category 1 territory for the purpose of being prosecuted for the offence.

(4) The information is—

(a) particulars of the person's identity;
(b) particulars of any other warrant issued in the category 1 territory for the person's arrest in respect of the offence;
(c) particulars of the circumstances in which the person is alleged to have committed the offence, including the conduct alleged to constitute the offence, the time and place at which he is alleged to have committed the offence and any provision of the law of the category 1 territory under which the conduct is alleged to constitute an offence;
(d) particulars of the sentence which may be imposed under the law of the category 1 territory in respect of the offence if the person is convicted of it.

(5) The statement is one that—

(a) the person in respect of whom the Part 1 warrant is issued is alleged to be unlawfully at large after conviction of an offence specified in the warrant by a court in the category 1 territory, and
(b) the Part 1 warrant is issued with a view to his arrest and extradition to the category 1 territory for the purpose of being sentenced for the offence or of serving a sentence of imprisonment or another form of detention imposed in respect of the offence.

(6) The information is—

(a) particulars of the person's identity;
(b) particulars of the conviction;
(c) particulars of any other warrant issued in the category 1 territory for the person's arrest in respect of the offence;
(d) particulars of the sentence which may be imposed under the law of the category 1 territory in respect of the offence, if the person has not been sentenced for the offence;
(e) particulars of the sentence which has been imposed under the law of the category 1 territory in respect of the offence, if the person has been sentenced for the offence.

(7) The designated authority may issue a certificate under this section if it believes that the authority which issued the Part 1 warrant has the function of issuing arrest warrants in the category 1 territory.

(8) A certificate under this section must certify that the authority which issued the Part 1 warrant has the function of issuing arrest warrants in the category 1 territory.

(9) The designated authority is the authority designated for the purposes of this Part by order made by the Secretary of State.

(10) An order made under subsection (9) may —

- (a) designate more than one authority;
- (b) designate different authorities for different parts of the United Kingdom.

Arrest

3 Arrest under certified Part 1 warrant

(1) This section applies if a certificate is issued under section 2 in respect of a Part 1 warrant issued in respect of a person.

(2) The warrant may be executed by a constable or a customs officer in any part of the United Kingdom.

(3) The warrant may be executed by a service policeman, but only if the service policeman would have power to arrest the person under the appropriate service law if the person had committed an offence under that law.

(4) If a service policeman has power to execute the warrant under subsection (3), he may execute the warrant in any place where he would have power to arrest the person under the appropriate service law if the person had committed an offence under that law.

(5) The warrant may be executed even if neither the warrant nor a copy of it is in the possession of the person executing it at the time of the arrest.

(6) The appropriate service law is —

- (a) the Army Act 1955 (3 & 4 Eliz. 2 c. 18), if the person in respect of whom the warrant is issued is subject to military law;
- (b) the Air Force Act 1955 (3 & 4 Eliz. 2 c. 19), if that person is subject to air-force law;
- (c) the Naval Discipline Act 1957 (c. 53), if that person is subject to that Act.

4 Person arrested under Part 1 warrant

(1) This section applies if a person is arrested under a Part 1 warrant.

(2) A copy of the warrant must be given to the person as soon as practicable after his arrest.

(3) The person must be brought as soon as practicable before the appropriate judge.

(4) If subsection (2) is not complied with and the person applies to the judge to be discharged, the judge may order his discharge.

(5) If subsection (3) is not complied with and the person applies to the judge to be discharged, the judge must order his discharge.

(6) A person arrested under the warrant must be treated as continuing in legal custody until he is brought before the appropriate judge under subsection (3) or he is discharged under subsection (4) or (5).

5 Provisional arrest

(1) A constable, a customs officer or a service policeman may arrest a person without a warrant if he has reasonable grounds for believing —

- (a) that a Part 1 warrant has been or will be issued in respect of the person by an authority of a category 1 territory, and
- (b) that the authority has the function of issuing arrest warrants in the category 1 territory.

(2) A constable or a customs officer may arrest a person under subsection (1) in any part of the United Kingdom.

(3) A service policeman may arrest a person under subsection (1) only if the service policeman would have power to arrest the person under the appropriate service law if the person had committed an offence under that law.

(4) If a service policeman has power to arrest a person under subsection (1), the service policeman may exercise the power in any place where he would have power to arrest the person for an offence under the appropriate service law if the person had committed an offence under that law.

(5) The appropriate service law is—

(a) the Army Act 1955 (3 & 4 Eliz. 2 c. 18), if the person to be arrested is subject to military law;
(b) the Air Force Act 1955 (3 & 4 Eliz. 2 c. 19), if that person is subject to air-force law;
(c) the Naval Discipline Act 1957 (c. 53), if that person is subject to that Act.

6 Person arrested under section 5

(1) This section applies if a person is arrested under section 5.

(2) The following must occur within the required period—

(a) the person must be brought before the appropriate judge;
(b) the documents specified in subsection (4) must be produced to the judge.

(3) The required period is 48 hours starting with the time when the person is arrested.

(4) The documents are—

(a) a Part 1 warrant in respect of the person;
(b) a certificate under section 2 in respect of the warrant.

(5) A copy of the warrant must be given to the person as soon as practicable after his arrest.

(6) If subsection (2) is not complied with and the person applies to the judge to be discharged, the judge must order his discharge.

(7) If subsection (5) is not complied with and the person applies to the judge to be discharged, the judge may order his discharge.

(8) The person must be treated as continuing in legal custody until he is brought before the appropriate judge under subsection (2) or he is discharged under subsection (6) or (7).

(9) Subsection (10) applies if—

(a) a person is arrested under section 5 on the basis of a belief that a Part 1 warrant has been or will be issued in respect of him;
(b) the person is discharged under subsection (6) or (7).

(10) The person must not be arrested again under section 5 on the basis of a belief relating to the same Part 1 warrant.

The initial hearing

7 Identity of person arrested

(1) This section applies if—

(a) a person arrested under a Part 1 warrant is brought before the appropriate judge under section 4(3), or

(b) a person is arrested under section 5 and section 6(2) is complied with in relation to him.

(2) The judge must decide whether the person brought before him is the person in respect of whom —

(a) the warrant referred to in subsection (1)(a) was issued, or
(b) the warrant referred to in section 6(4) was issued.

(3) The judge must decide the question in subsection (2) on a balance of probabilities.
(4) If the judge decides the question in subsection (2) in the negative he must order the person's discharge.
(5) If the judge decides that question in the affirmative he must proceed under section 8.
(6) In England and Wales, the judge has the same powers (as nearly as may be) as a magistrates' court would have if the proceedings were the summary trial of an information against the person.
(7) In Scotland —

(a) the judge has the same powers (as nearly as may be) as if the proceedings were summary proceedings in respect of an offence alleged to have been committed by the person; but
(b) in his making any decision under subsection (2) evidence from a single source shall be sufficient.

(8) In Northern Ireland, the judge has the same powers (as nearly as may be) as a magistrates' court would have if the proceedings were the hearing and determination of a complaint against the person.
(9) If the judge exercises his power to adjourn the proceedings he must remand the person in custody or on bail.
(10) If the judge remands the person in custody he may later grant bail.

8 Remand etc.

(1) If the judge is required to proceed under this section he must —

(a) fix a date on which the extradition hearing is to begin;
(b) inform the person of the contents of the Part 1 warrant;
(c) give the person the required information about consent;
(d) remand the person in custody or on bail.

(2) If the judge remands the person in custody he may later grant bail.
(3) The required information about consent is —

(a) that the person may consent to his extradition to the category 1 territory in which the Part 1 warrant was issued;
(b) an explanation of the effect of consent and the procedure that will apply if he gives consent;
(c) that consent must be given before the judge and is irrevocable.

(4) The date fixed under subsection (1) must not be later than the end of the permitted period, which is 21 days starting with the date of the arrest referred to in section 7(1)(a) or (b).
(5) If before the date fixed under subsection (1) (or this subsection) a party to the proceedings applies to the judge for a later date to be fixed and the judge believes it to be in

the interests of justice to do so, he may fix a later date; and this subsection may apply more than once.

(6) Subsections (7) and (8) apply if the extradition hearing does not begin on or before the date fixed under this section.

(7) If the person applies to the judge to be discharged the judge must order his discharge, unless reasonable cause is shown for the delay.

(8) If no application is made under subsection (7) the judge must order the person's discharge on the first occasion after the date fixed under this section when the person appears or is brought before the judge, unless reasonable cause is shown for the delay.

The extradition hearing

9 Judge's powers at extradition hearing

(1) In England and Wales, at the extradition hearing the appropriate judge has the same powers (as nearly as may be) as a magistrates' court would have if the proceedings were the summary trial of an information against the person in respect of whom the Part 1 warrant was issued.

(2) In Scotland, at the extradition hearing the appropriate judge has the same powers (as nearly as may be) as if the proceedings were summary proceedings in respect of an offence alleged to have been committed by the person in respect of whom the Part 1 warrant was issued.

(3) In Northern Ireland, at the extradition hearing the appropriate judge has the same powers (as nearly as may be) as a magistrates' court would have if the proceedings were the hearing and determination of a complaint against the person in respect of whom the Part 1 warrant was issued.

(4) If the judge adjourns the extradition hearing he must remand the person in custody or on bail.

(5) If the judge remands the person in custody he may later grant bail.

10 Initial stage of extradition hearing

(1) This section applies if a person in respect of whom a Part 1 warrant is issued appears or is brought before the appropriate judge for the extradition hearing.

(2) The judge must decide whether the offence specified in the Part 1 warrant is an extradition offence.

(3) If the judge decides the question in subsection (2) in the negative he must order the person's discharge.

(4) If the judge decides that question in the affirmative he must proceed under section 11.

11 Bars to extradition

(1) If the judge is required to proceed under this section he must decide whether the person's extradition to the category 1 territory is barred by reason of —

- (a) the rule against double jeopardy;
- (b) extraneous considerations;
- (c) the passage of time;
- (d) the person's age;
- (e) hostage-taking considerations;
- (f) speciality;
- (g) the person's earlier extradition to the United Kingdom from another category 1 territory;

(h) the person's earlier extradition to the United Kingdom from a non-category 1 territory.

(2) Sections 12 to 19 apply for the interpretation of subsection (1).

(3) If the judge decides any of the questions in subsection (1) in the affirmative he must order the person's discharge.

(4) If the judge decides those questions in the negative and the person is alleged to be unlawfully at large after conviction of the extradition offence, the judge must proceed under section 20.

(5) If the judge decides those questions in the negative and the person is accused of the commission of the extradition offence but is not alleged to be unlawfully at large after conviction of it, the judge must proceed under section 21.

12 Rule against double jeopardy

A person's extradition to a category 1 territory is barred by reason of the rule against double jeopardy if (and only if) it appears that he would be entitled to be discharged under any rule of law relating to previous acquittal or conviction on the assumption —

(a) that the conduct constituting the extradition offence constituted an offence in the part of the United Kingdom where the judge exercises jurisdiction;
(b) that the person were charged with the extradition offence in that part of the United Kingdom.

13 Extraneous considerations

A person's extradition to a category 1 territory is barred by reason of extraneous considerations if (and only if) it appears that —

(a) the Part 1 warrant issued in respect of him (though purporting to be issued on account of the extradition offence) is in fact issued for the purpose of prosecuting or punishing him on account of his race, religion, nationality, gender, sexual orientation or political opinions, or
(b) if extradited he might be prejudiced at his trial or punished, detained or restricted in his personal liberty by reason of his race, religion, nationality, gender, sexual orientation or political opinions.

14 Passage of time

A person's extradition to a category 1 territory is barred by reason of the passage of time if (and only if) it appears that it would be unjust or oppressive to extradite him by reason of the passage of time since he is alleged to have committed the extradition offence or since he is alleged to have become unlawfully at large (as the case may be).

15 Age

A person's extradition to a category 1 territory is barred by reason of his age if (and only if) it would be conclusively presumed because of his age that he could not be guilty of the extradition offence on the assumption —

(a) that the conduct constituting the extradition offence constituted an offence in the part of the United Kingdom where the judge exercises jurisdiction;
(b) that the person carried out the conduct when the extradition offence was committed (or alleged to be committed);
(c) that the person carried out the conduct in the part of the United Kingdom where the judge exercises jurisdiction.

16 Hostage-taking considerations

(1) A person's extradition to a category 1 territory is barred by reason of hostage-taking considerations if (and only if) the territory is a party to the Hostage-taking Convention and it appears that —

(a) if extradited he might be prejudiced at his trial because communication between him and the appropriate authorities would not be possible, and
(b) the act or omission constituting the extradition offence also constitutes an offence under section 1 of the Taking of Hostages Act 1982 (c. 28) or an attempt to commit such an offence.

(2) The appropriate authorities are the authorities of the territory which are entitled to exercise rights of protection in relation to him.

(3) A certificate issued by the Secretary of State that a territory is a party to the Hostage-taking Convention is conclusive evidence of that fact for the purposes of subsection (1).

(4) The Hostage-taking Convention is the International Convention against the Taking of Hostages opened for signature at New York on 18 December 1979.

17 Speciality

(1) A person's extradition to a category 1 territory is barred by reason of speciality if (and only if) there are no speciality arrangements with the category 1 territory.

(2) There are speciality arrangements with a category 1 territory if, under the law of that territory or arrangements made between it and the United Kingdom, a person who is extradited to the territory from the United Kingdom may be dealt with in the territory for an offence committed before his extradition only if —

(a) the offence is one falling within subsection (3), or
(b) the condition in subsection (4) is satisfied.

(3) The offences are —

(a) the offence in respect of which the person is extradited;
(b) an extradition offence disclosed by the same facts as that offence;
(c) an extradition offence in respect of which the appropriate judge gives his consent under section 55 to the person being dealt with;
(d) an offence which is not punishable with imprisonment or another form of detention;
(e) an offence in respect of which the person will not be detained in connection with his trial, sentence or appeal;
(f) an offence in respect of which the person waives the right that he would have (but for this paragraph) not to be dealt with for the offence.

(4) The condition is that the person is given an opportunity to leave the category 1 territory and —

(a) he does not do so before the end of the permitted period, or
(b) if he does so before the end of the permitted period, he returns there.

(5) The permitted period is 45 days starting with the day on which the person arrives in the category 1 territory.

(6) Arrangements made with a category 1 territory which is a Commonwealth country or a British overseas territory may be made for a particular case or more generally.

(7) A certificate issued by or under the authority of the Secretary of State confirming the existence of arrangements with a category 1 territory which is a Commonwealth country or a British overseas territory and stating the terms of the arrangements is conclusive evidence of those matters.

18 Earlier extradition to United Kingdom from category 1 territory

A person's extradition to a category 1 territory is barred by reason of his earlier extradition to the United Kingdom from another category 1 territory if (and only if) —

(a) the person was extradited to the United Kingdom from another category 1 territory (the extraditing territory);
(b) under arrangements between the United Kingdom and the extraditing territory, that territory's consent is required to the person's extradition from the United Kingdom to the category 1 territory in respect of the extradition offence under consideration;
(c) that consent has not been given on behalf of the extraditing territory.

19 Earlier extradition to United Kingdom from non-category 1 territory

A person's extradition to a category 1 territory is barred by reason of his earlier extradition to the United Kingdom from a non-category 1 territory if (and only if) —

(a) the person was extradited to the United Kingdom from a territory that is not a category 1 territory (the extraditing territory);
(b) under arrangements between the United Kingdom and the extraditing territory, that territory's consent is required to the person's being dealt with in the United Kingdom in respect of the extradition offence under consideration;
(c) consent has not been given on behalf of the extraditing territory to the person's extradition from the United Kingdom to the category 1 territory in respect of the extradition offence under consideration.

20 Case where person has been convicted

(1) If the judge is required to proceed under this section (by virtue of section 11) he must decide whether the person was convicted in his presence.

(2) If the judge decides the question in subsection (1) in the affirmative he must proceed under section 21.

(3) If the judge decides that question in the negative he must decide whether the person deliberately absented himself from his trial.

(4) If the judge decides the question in subsection (3) in the affirmative he must proceed under section 21.

(5) If the judge decides that question in the negative he must decide whether the person would be entitled to a retrial or (on appeal) to a review amounting to a retrial.

(6) If the judge decides the question in subsection (5) in the affirmative he must proceed under section 21.

(7) If the judge decides that question in the negative he must order the person's discharge.

(8) The judge must not decide the question in subsection (5) in the affirmative unless, in any proceedings that it is alleged would constitute a retrial or a review amounting to a retrial, the person would have these rights —

(a) the right to defend himself in person or through legal assistance of his own choosing or, if he had not sufficient means to pay for legal assistance, to be given it free when the interests of justice so required;

(b) the right to examine or have examined witnesses against him and to obtain the attendance and examination of witnesses on his behalf under the same conditions as witnesses against him.

21 Human rights

(1) If the judge is required to proceed under this section (by virtue of section 11 or 20) he must decide whether the person's extradition would be compatible with the Convention rights within the meaning of the Human Rights Act 1998 (c. 42).

(2) If the judge decides the question in subsection (1) in the negative he must order the person's discharge.

(3) If the judge decides that question in the affirmative he must order the person to be extradited to the category 1 territory in which the warrant was issued.

(4) If the judge makes an order under subsection (3) he must remand the person in custody or on bail to wait for his extradition to the category 1 territory.

(5) If the judge remands the person in custody he may later grant bail.

Matters arising before end of extradition hearing

22 Person charged with offence in United Kingdom

(1) This section applies if at any time in the extradition hearing the judge is informed that the person in respect of whom the Part 1 warrant is issued is charged with an offence in the United Kingdom.

(2) The judge must adjourn the extradition hearing until one of these occurs —

(a) the charge is disposed of;
(b) the charge is withdrawn;
(c) proceedings in respect of the charge are discontinued;
(d) an order is made for the charge to lie on the file, or in relation to Scotland, the diet is deserted *pro loco et tempore*.

(3) If a sentence of imprisonment or another form of detention is imposed in respect of the offence charged, the judge may adjourn the extradition hearing until the sentence has been served.

(4) If before he adjourns the extradition hearing under subsection (2) the judge has decided under section 11 whether the person's extradition is barred by reason of the rule against double jeopardy, the judge must decide that question again after the resumption of the hearing.

23 Person serving sentence in United Kingdom

(1) This section applies if at any time in the extradition hearing the judge is informed that the person in respect of whom the Part 1 warrant is issued is serving a sentence of imprisonment or another form of detention in the United Kingdom.

(2) The judge may adjourn the extradition hearing until the sentence has been served.

24 Extradition request

(1) This section applies if at any time in the extradition hearing the judge is informed that —

(a) a certificate has been issued under section 70 in respect of a request for the person's extradition;

(b) the request has not been disposed of;
(c) an order has been made under section 179(2) for further proceedings on the warrant to be deferred until the request has been disposed of.

(2) The judge must remand the person in custody or on bail.
(3) If the judge remands the person in custody he may later grant bail.

25 Physical or mental condition

(1) This section applies if at any time in the extradition hearing it appears to the judge that the condition in subsection (2) is satisfied.
(2) The condition is that the physical or mental condition of the person in respect of whom the Part 1 warrant is issued is such that it would be unjust or oppressive to extradite him.
(3) The judge must—

(a) order the person's discharge, or
(b) adjourn the extradition hearing until it appears to him that the condition in subsection (2) is no longer satisfied.

Appeals

26 Appeal against extradition order

(1) If the appropriate judge orders a person's extradition under this Part, the person may appeal to the High Court against the order.
(2) But subsection (1) does not apply if the order is made under section 46 or 48.
(3) An appeal under this section may be brought on a question of law or fact.
(4) Notice of an appeal under this section must be given in accordance with rules of court before the end of the permitted period, which is 7 days starting with the day on which the order is made.

27 Court's powers on appeal under section 26

(1) On an appeal under section 26 the High Court may—

(a) allow the appeal;
(b) dismiss the appeal.

(2) The court may allow the appeal only if the conditions in subsection (3) or the conditions in subsection (4) are satisfied.
(3) The conditions are that—

(a) the appropriate judge ought to have decided a question before him at the extradition hearing differently;
(b) if he had decided the question in the way he ought to have done, he would have been required to order the person's discharge.

(4) The conditions are that—

(a) an issue is raised that was not raised at the extradition hearing or evidence is available that was not available at the extradition hearing;

(b) the issue or evidence would have resulted in the appropriate judge deciding a question before him at the extradition hearing differently;
(c) if he had decided the question in that way, he would have been required to order the person's discharge.

(5) If the court allows the appeal it must—

(a) order the person's discharge;
(b) quash the order for his extradition.

28 Appeal against discharge at extradition hearing

(1) If the judge orders a person's discharge at the extradition hearing the authority which issued the Part 1 warrant may appeal to the High Court against the relevant decision.

(2) But subsection (1) does not apply if the order for the person's discharge was under section 41.

(3) The relevant decision is the decision which resulted in the order for the person's discharge.

(4) An appeal under this section may be brought on a question of law or fact.

(5) Notice of an appeal under this section must be given in accordance with rules of court before the end of the permitted period, which is 7 days starting with the day on which the order for the person's discharge is made.

29 Court's powers on appeal under section 28

(1) On an appeal under section 28 the High Court may—

(a) allow the appeal;
(b) dismiss the appeal.

(2) The court may allow the appeal only if the conditions in subsection (3) or the conditions in subsection (4) are satisfied.

(3) The conditions are that—

(a) the judge ought to have decided the relevant question differently;
(b) if he had decided the question in the way he ought to have done, he would not have been required to order the person's discharge.

(4) The conditions are that—

(a) an issue is raised that was not raised at the extradition hearing or evidence is available that was not available at the extradition hearing;
(b) the issue or evidence would have resulted in the judge deciding the relevant question differently;
(c) if he had decided the question in that way, he would not have been required to order the person's discharge.

(5) If the court allows the appeal it must—

(a) quash the order discharging the person;
(b) remit the case to the judge;
(c) direct him to proceed as he would have been required to do if he had decided the relevant question differently at the extradition hearing.

(6) A question is the relevant question if the judge's decision on it resulted in the order for the person's discharge.

30 Detention pending conclusion of appeal under section 28

(1) This section applies if immediately after the judge orders the person's discharge the judge is informed by the authority which issued the Part 1 warrant that it intends to appeal under section 28.

(2) The judge must remand the person in custody or on bail while the appeal is pending.

(3) If the judge remands the person in custody he may later grant bail.

(4) An appeal under section 28 ceases to be pending at the earliest of these times —

(a) when the proceedings on the appeal are discontinued;
(b) when the High Court dismisses the appeal, if the authority does not immediately inform the court that it intends to apply for leave to appeal to the House of Lords;
(c) at the end of the permitted period, which is 28 days starting with the day on which leave to appeal to the House of Lords against the decision of the High Court on the appeal is granted;
(d) when there is no further step that can be taken by the authority which issued the Part 1 warrant in relation to the appeal (ignoring any power of a court to grant leave to take a step out of time).

(5) The preceding provisions of this section apply to Scotland with these modifications —

(a) in subsection (4)(b) omit the words from "if" to the end;
(b) omit subsection (4)(c).

31 Appeal to High Court: time limit for start of hearing

(1) Rules of court must prescribe the period (the relevant period) within which the High Court must begin to hear an appeal under section 26 or 28.

(2) Rules of court must provide for the relevant period to start with the date on which the person in respect of whom a Part 1 warrant is issued —

(a) was arrested under section 5, if he was arrested under that section;
(b) was arrested under the Part 1 warrant, if he was not arrested under section 5.

(3) The High Court must begin to hear the appeal before the end of the relevant period.

(4) The High Court may extend the relevant period if it believes it to be in the interests of justice to do so; and this subsection may apply more than once.

(5) The power in subsection (4) may be exercised even after the end of the relevant period.

(6) If subsection (3) is not complied with and the appeal is under section 26 —

(a) the appeal must be taken to have been allowed by a decision of the High Court;
(b) the person whose extradition has been ordered must be taken to have been discharged by the High Court;
(c) the order for the person's extradition must be taken to have been quashed by the High Court.

(7) If subsection (3) is not complied with and the appeal is under section 28 the appeal must be taken to have been dismissed by a decision of the High Court.

32 Appeal to House of Lords

(1) An appeal lies to the House of Lords from a decision of the High Court on an appeal under section 26 or 28.

(2) An appeal under this section lies at the instance of —

(a) the person in respect of whom the Part 1 warrant was issued;
(b) the authority which issued the Part 1 warrant.

(3) An appeal under this section lies only with the leave of the High Court or the House of Lords.

(4) Leave to appeal under this section must not be granted unless —

(a) the High Court has certified that there is a point of law of general public importance involved in the decision, and
(b) it appears to the court granting leave that the point is one which ought to be considered by the House of Lords.

(5) An application to the High Court for leave to appeal under this section must be made before the end of the permitted period, which is 14 days starting with the day on which the court makes its decision on the appeal to it.

(6) An application to the House of Lords for leave to appeal under this section must be made before the end of the permitted period, which is 14 days starting with the day on which the High Court refuses leave to appeal.

(7) If leave to appeal under this section is granted, the appeal must be brought before the end of the permitted period, which is 28 days starting with the day on which leave is granted.

(8) If subsection (7) is not complied with —

(a) the appeal must be taken to have been brought;
(b) the appeal must be taken to have been dismissed by the House of Lords immediately after the end of the period permitted under that subsection.

(9) These must be ignored for the purposes of subsection (8)(b) —

(a) any power of a court to extend the period permitted for bringing the appeal;
(b) any power of a court to grant leave to take a step out of time.

(10) The High Court may grant bail to a person appealing under this section or applying for leave to appeal under this section.

(11) Section 5 of the Appellate Jurisdiction Act 1876 (c. 59) (composition of House of Lords for hearing and determination of appeals) applies in relation to an appeal under this section or an application for leave to appeal under this section as it applies in relation to an appeal under that Act.

(12) An order of the House of Lords which provides for an application for leave to appeal under this section to be determined by a committee constituted in accordance with section 5 of the Appellate Jurisdiction Act 1876 may direct that the decision of the committee is taken on behalf of the House.

(13) The preceding provisions of this section do not apply to Scotland.

33 Powers of House of Lords on appeal under section 32

(1) On an appeal under section 32 the House of Lords may —

(a) allow the appeal;
(b) dismiss the appeal.

(2) Subsection (3) applies if —

(a) the person in respect of whom the Part 1 warrant was issued brings an appeal under section 32, and
(b) the House of Lords allows the appeal.

(3) The House of Lords must —

(a) order the person's discharge;
(b) quash the order for his extradition, if the appeal was against a decision of the High Court to dismiss an appeal under section 26.

(4) Subsection (5) applies if —

(a) the High Court allows an appeal under section 26 by the person in respect of whom the Part 1 warrant was issued,
(b) the authority which issued the warrant brings an appeal under section 32 against the decision of the High Court, and
(c) the House of Lords allows the appeal.

(5) The House of Lords must —

(a) quash the order of the High Court under section 27(5) discharging the person;
(b) order the person to be extradited to the category 1 territory in which the warrant was issued.

(6) Subsections (7) and (8) apply if —

(a) the High Court dismisses an appeal under section 28 against a decision made by the judge at the extradition hearing,
(b) the authority which issued the Part 1 warrant brings an appeal under section 32 against the decision of the High Court, and
(c) the House of Lords allows the appeal.

(7) If the judge would have been required to order the person in respect of whom the warrant was issued to be extradited had he decided the relevant question differently, the House of Lords must —

(a) quash the order of the judge discharging the person;
(b) order the person to be extradited to the category 1 territory in which the warrant was issued.

(8) In any other case, the House of Lords must —

(a) quash the order of the judge discharging the person in respect of whom the warrant was issued;
(b) remit the case to the judge;
(c) direct him to proceed as he would have been required to do if he had decided the relevant question differently at the extradition hearing.

(9) A question is the relevant question if the judge's decision on it resulted in the order for the person's discharge.

34 Appeals: general

A decision of the judge under this Part may be questioned in legal proceedings only by means of an appeal under this Part.

Time for extradition

35 Extradition where no appeal

(1) This section applies if —

(a) the appropriate judge orders a person's extradition to a category 1 territory under this Part, and
(b) no notice of an appeal under section 26 is given before the end of the period permitted under that section.

(2) But this section does not apply if the order is made under section 46 or 48.
(3) The person must be extradited to the category 1 territory before the end of the required period.
(4) The required period is —

(a) 10 days starting with the day on which the judge makes the order, or
(b) if the judge and the authority which issued the Part 1 warrant agree a later date, 10 days starting with the later date.

(5) If subsection (3) is not complied with and the person applies to the appropriate judge to be discharged the judge must order his discharge, unless reasonable cause is shown for the delay.
(6) These must be ignored for the purposes of subsection (1)(b) —

(a) any power of a court to extend the period permitted for giving notice of appeal;
(b) any power of a court to grant leave to take a step out of time.

36 Extradition following appeal

(1) This section applies if —

(a) there is an appeal to the High Court under section 26 against an order for a person's extradition to a category 1 territory, and
(b) the effect of the decision of the relevant court on the appeal is that the person is to be extradited there.

(2) The person must be extradited to the category 1 territory before the end of the required period.
(3) The required period is —

(a) 10 days starting with the day on which the decision of the relevant court on the appeal becomes final or proceedings on the appeal are discontinued, or
(b) if the relevant court and the authority which issued the Part 1 warrant agree a later date, 10 days starting with the later date.

(4) The relevant court is —

(a) the High Court, if there is no appeal to the House of Lords against the decision of the High Court on the appeal;

(b) the House of Lords, if there is such an appeal.

(5) The decision of the High Court on the appeal becomes final —

(a) when the period permitted for applying to the High Court for leave to appeal to the House of Lords ends, if there is no such application;
(b) when the period permitted for applying to the House of Lords for leave to appeal to it ends, if the High Court refuses leave to appeal and there is no application to the House of Lords for leave to appeal;
(c) when the House of Lords refuses leave to appeal to it;
(d) at the end of the permitted period, which is 28 days starting with the day on which leave to appeal to the House of Lords is granted, if no such appeal is brought before the end of that period.

(6) These must be ignored for the purposes of subsection (5) —

(a) any power of a court to extend the period permitted for applying for leave to appeal;
(b) any power of a court to grant leave to take a step out of time.

(7) The decision of the House of Lords on the appeal becomes final when it is made.
(8) If subsection (2) is not complied with and the person applies to the appropriate judge to be discharged the judge must order his discharge, unless reasonable cause is shown for the delay.
(9) The preceding provisions of this section apply to Scotland with these modifications —

(a) in subsections (1) and (3) for "relevant court" substitute "High Court";
(b) omit subsections (4) to (7).

37 Undertaking in relation to person serving sentence in United Kingdom

(1) This section applies if —

(a) the appropriate judge orders a person's extradition to a category 1 territory under this Part;
(b) the person is serving a sentence of imprisonment or another form of detention in the United Kingdom.

(2) But this section does not apply if the order is made under section 46 or 48.
(3) The judge may make the order for extradition subject to the condition that extradition is not to take place before he receives an undertaking given on behalf of the category 1 territory in terms specified by him.
(4) The terms which may be specified by the judge in relation to a person accused in a category 1 territory of the commission of an offence include terms —

(a) that the person be kept in custody until the conclusion of the proceedings against him for the offence and any other offence in respect of which he is permitted to be dealt with in the category 1 territory;
(b) that the person be returned to the United Kingdom to serve the remainder of his sentence on the conclusion of those proceedings.

(5) The terms which may be specified by the judge in relation to a person alleged to be unlawfully at large after conviction of an offence by a court in a category 1 territory include

terms that the person be returned to the United Kingdom to serve the remainder of his sentence after serving any sentence imposed on him in the category 1 territory for —

(a) the offence, and
(b) any other offence in respect of which he is permitted to be dealt with in the category 1 territory.

(6) Subsections (7) and (8) apply if the judge makes an order for extradition subject to a condition under subsection (3).

(7) If the judge does not receive the undertaking before the end of the period of 21 days starting with the day on which he makes the order and the person applies to the appropriate judge to be discharged, the judge must order his discharge.

(8) If the judge receives the undertaking before the end of that period —

(a) in a case where section 35 applies, the required period for the purposes of section 35(3) is 10 days starting with the day on which the judge receives the undertaking;
(b) in a case where section 36 applies, the required period for the purposes of section 36(2) is 10 days starting with the day on which the decision of the relevant court on the appeal becomes final (within the meaning of that section) or (if later) the day on which the judge receives the undertaking.

38 Extradition following deferral for competing claim

(1) This section applies if —

(a) an order is made under this Part for a person to be extradited to a category 1 territory in pursuance of a Part 1 warrant;
(b) before the person is extradited to the territory an order is made under section 44(4)(b) or 179(2)(b) for the person's extradition in pursuance of the warrant to be deferred;
(c) the appropriate judge makes an order under section 181(2) for the person's extradition in pursuance of the warrant to cease to be deferred.

(2) But this section does not apply if the order for the person's extradition is made under section 46 or 48.

(3) In a case where section 35 applies, the required period for the purposes of section 35(3) is 10 days starting with the day on which the order under section 181(2) is made.

(4) In a case where section 36 applies, the required period for the purposes of section 36(2) is 10 days starting with the day on which the decision of the relevant court on the appeal becomes final (within the meaning of that section) or (if later) the day on which the order under section 181(2) is made.

39 Asylum claim

(1) This section applies if —

(a) a person in respect of whom a Part 1 warrant is issued makes an asylum claim at any time in the relevant period;
(b) an order is made under this Part for the person to be extradited in pursuance of the warrant.

(2) The relevant period is the period —

(a) starting when a certificate is issued under section 2 in respect of the warrant;
(b) ending when the person is extradited in pursuance of the warrant.

(3) The person must not be extradited in pursuance of the warrant before the asylum claim is finally determined; and sections 35, 36, 47 and 49 have effect subject to this.

(4) Subsection (3) is subject to section 40.

(5) If the Secretary of State allows the asylum claim, the claim is finally determined when he makes his decision on the claim.

(6) If the Secretary of State rejects the asylum claim, the claim is finally determined —

(a) when the Secretary of State makes his decision on the claim, if there is no right to appeal against the Secretary of State's decision on the claim;
(b) when the period permitted for appealing against the Secretary of State's decision on the claim ends, if there is such a right but there is no such appeal;
(c) when the appeal against that decision is finally determined or is withdrawn or abandoned, if there is such an appeal.

(7) An appeal against the Secretary of State's decision on an asylum claim is not finally determined for the purposes of subsection (6) at any time when a further appeal or an application for leave to bring a further appeal —

(a) has been instituted and has not been finally determined or withdrawn or abandoned, or
(b) may be brought.

(8) The remittal of an appeal is not a final determination for the purposes of subsection (7).

(9) The possibility of an appeal out of time with leave must be ignored for the purposes of subsections (6) and (7).

40 Certificate in respect of asylum claimant

(1) Section 39(3) does not apply in relation to a person if the Secretary of State has certified that the conditions in subsection (2) or the conditions in subsection (3) are satisfied in relation to him.

(2) The conditions are that —

(a) the category 1 territory to which the person's extradition has been ordered has accepted that, under standing arrangements, it is the responsible State in relation to the person's asylum claim;
(b) in the opinion of the Secretary of State, the person is not a national or citizen of the territory.

(3) The conditions are that, in the opinion of the Secretary of State —

(a) the person is not a national or citizen of the category 1 territory to which his extradition has been ordered;
(b) the person's life and liberty would not be threatened in that territory by reason of his race, religion, nationality, political opinion or membership of a particular social group;
(c) the government of the territory would not send the person to another country otherwise than in accordance with the Refugee Convention.

(4) In this section —

"the Refugee Convention" has the meaning given by section 167(1) of the Immigration and Asylum Act 1999 (c. 33);

"standing arrangements" means arrangements in force between the United Kingdom and the category 1 territory for determining which State is responsible for considering applications for asylum.

Withdrawal of Part 1 warrant

41 Withdrawal of warrant before extradition

(1) This section applies if at any time in the relevant period the appropriate judge is informed by the designated authority that a Part 1 warrant issued in respect of a person has been withdrawn.

(2) The relevant period is the period —

(a) starting when the person is first brought before the appropriate judge following his arrest under this Part;
(b) ending when the person is extradited in pursuance of the warrant or discharged.

(3) The judge must order the person's discharge.

(4) If the person is not before the judge at the time the judge orders his discharge, the judge must inform him of the order as soon as practicable.

42 Withdrawal of warrant while appeal to High Court pending

(1) This section applies if at any time in the relevant period the High Court is informed by the designated authority that a Part 1 warrant issued in respect of a person has been withdrawn.

(2) The relevant period is the period —

(a) starting when notice of an appeal to the court is given by the person or the authority which issued the warrant;
(b) ending when proceedings on the appeal are discontinued or the court makes its decision on the appeal.

(3) The court must —

(a) if the appeal is under section 26, order the person's discharge and quash the order for his extradition;
(b) if the appeal is under section 28, dismiss the appeal.

(4) If the person is not before the court at the time the court orders his discharge, the court must inform him of the order as soon as practicable.

43 Withdrawal of warrant while appeal to House of Lords pending

(1) This section applies if at any time in the relevant period the House of Lords is informed by the designated authority that a Part 1 warrant issued in respect of a person has been withdrawn.

(2) The relevant period is the period —

(a) starting when leave to appeal to the House of Lords is granted to the person or the authority which issued the warrant;
(b) ending when proceedings on the appeal are discontinued or the House of Lords makes its decision on the appeal.

(3) If the appeal is brought by the person in respect of whom the warrant was issued the House of Lords must —

(a) order the person's discharge;
(b) quash the order for his extradition, in a case where the appeal was against a decision of the High Court to dismiss an appeal under section 26.

(4) If the appeal is brought by the authority which issued the warrant the House of Lords must dismiss the appeal.

(5) If the person is not before the House of Lords at the time it orders his discharge, the House of Lords must inform him of the order as soon as practicable.

Competing Part 1 warrants

44 Competing Part 1 warrants

(1) This section applies if at any time in the relevant period the conditions in subsection (3) are satisfied in relation to a person in respect of whom a Part 1 warrant has been issued.

(2) The relevant period is the period —

(a) starting when the person is first brought before the appropriate judge following his arrest under this Part;
(b) ending when the person is extradited in pursuance of the warrant or discharged.

(3) The conditions are that —

(a) the judge is informed that another Part 1 warrant has been issued in respect of the person;
(b) the other warrant falls to be dealt with by the judge or by a judge who is the appropriate judge in another part of the United Kingdom;
(c) the other warrant has not been disposed of.

(4) The judge may —

(a) order further proceedings on the warrant under consideration to be deferred until the other warrant has been disposed of, if the warrant under consideration has not been disposed of;
(b) order the person's extradition in pursuance of the warrant under consideration to be deferred until the other warrant has been disposed of, if an order for his extradition in pursuance of the warrant under consideration has been made.

(5) If the judge makes an order under subsection (4) and the person is not already remanded in custody or on bail, the judge must remand the person in custody or on bail.

(6) If the judge remands the person in custody he may later grant bail.

(7) In applying subsection (4) the judge must take account in particular of these matters —

(a) the relative seriousness of the offences concerned;
(b) the place where each offence was committed (or was alleged to have been committed);
(c) the date on which each warrant was issued;
(d) whether, in the case of each offence, the person is accused of its commission (but not alleged to have been convicted) or is alleged to be unlawfully at large after conviction.

Consent to extradition

45 Consent to extradition

(1) A person arrested under a Part 1 warrant may consent to his extradition to the category 1 territory in which the warrant was issued.

(2) A person arrested under section 5 may consent to his extradition to the category 1 territory referred to in subsection (1) of that section.

(3) If a person consents to his extradition under this section he must be taken to have waived any right he would have (apart from the consent) not to be dealt with in the category 1 territory for an offence committed before his extradition.

(4) Consent under this section —

(a) must be given before the appropriate judge;
(b) must be recorded in writing;
(c) is irrevocable.

(5) A person may not give his consent under this section unless —

(a) he is legally represented before the appropriate judge at the time he gives consent, or
(b) he is a person to whom subsection (6) applies.

(6) This subsection applies to a person if —

(a) he has been informed of his right to apply for legal aid and has had the opportunity to apply for legal aid, but he has refused or failed to apply;
(b) he has applied for legal aid but his application has been refused;
(c) he was granted legal aid but the legal aid was withdrawn.

(7) In subsection (6) "legal aid" means —

(a) in England and Wales, a right to representation funded by the Legal Services Commission as part of the Criminal Defence Service;
(b) in Scotland, such legal aid as is available by virtue of section 183(a) of this Act;
(c) in Northern Ireland, such free legal aid as is available by virtue of sections 184 and 185 of this Act.

(8) For the purposes of subsection (5) a person is to be treated as legally represented before the appropriate judge if (and only if) he has the assistance of counsel or a solicitor to represent him in the proceedings before the appropriate judge.

46 Extradition order following consent

(1) This section applies if a person consents to his extradition under section 45.

(2) The judge must remand the person in custody or on bail.

(3) If the judge remands the person in custody he may later grant bail.

(4) If the judge has not fixed a date under section 8 on which the extradition hearing is to begin he is not required to do so.

(5) If the extradition hearing has begun the judge is no longer required to proceed or continue proceeding under sections 10 to 25.

(6) The judge must within the period of 10 days starting with the day on which consent is given order the person's extradition to the category 1 territory.

(7) Subsection (6) has effect subject to sections 48 and 51.

(8) If subsection (6) is not complied with and the person applies to the judge to be discharged the judge must order his discharge.

47 Extradition to category 1 territory following consent

(1) This section applies if the appropriate judge makes an order under section 46(6) for a person's extradition to a category 1 territory.

(2) The person must be extradited to the category 1 territory before the end of the required period.

(3) The required period is —

(a) 10 days starting with the day on which the order is made, or
(b) if the judge and the authority which issued the Part 1 warrant agree a later date, 10 days starting with the later date.

(4) If subsection (2) is not complied with and the person applies to the judge to be discharged the judge must order his discharge, unless reasonable cause is shown for the delay.

(5) If before the person is extradited to the category 1 territory the judge is informed by the designated authority that the Part 1 warrant has been withdrawn —

(a) subsection (2) does not apply, and
(b) the judge must order the person's discharge.

48 Other warrant issued following consent

(1) This section applies if —

(a) a person consents under section 45 to his extradition to a category 1 territory, and
(b) the conditions in subsection (2) are satisfied before the judge orders his extradition under section 46(6).

(2) The conditions are that —

(a) the judge is informed that another Part 1 warrant has been issued in respect of the person;
(b) the warrant falls to be dealt with by the judge or by a judge who is the appropriate judge in another part of the United Kingdom;
(c) the warrant has not been disposed of.

(3) Section 46(6) does not apply but the judge may —

(a) order the person's extradition in pursuance of his consent, or
(b) order further proceedings on the warrant under consideration to be deferred until the other warrant has been disposed of.

(4) Subsection (3) is subject to section 51.

(5) In applying subsection (3) the judge must take account in particular of these matters —

(a) the relative seriousness of the offences concerned;
(b) the place where each offence was committed (or was alleged to have been committed);
(c) the date on which each warrant was issued;
(d) whether, in the case of each offence, the person is accused of its commission (but not alleged to have been convicted) or is alleged to be unlawfully at large after conviction.

49 Other warrant issued: extradition to category 1 territory

(1) This section applies if the appropriate judge makes an order under section 48(3)(a) for a person's extradition to a category 1 territory.

(2) The person must be extradited to the category 1 territory before the end of the required period.

(3) The required period is —

(a) 10 days starting with the day on which the order is made, or
(b) if the judge and the authority which issued the Part 1 warrant agree a later date, 10 days starting with the later date.

(4) If subsection (2) is not complied with and the person applies to the judge to be discharged the judge must order his discharge, unless reasonable cause is shown for the delay.

(5) If before the person is extradited to the category 1 territory the judge is informed by the designated authority that the Part 1 warrant has been withdrawn —

(a) subsection (2) does not apply, and
(b) the judge must order the person's discharge.

50 Other warrant issued: proceedings deferred

(1) This section applies if the appropriate judge makes an order under section 48(3)(b) for further proceedings on a Part 1 warrant to be deferred.

(2) The judge must remand the person in respect of whom the warrant was issued in custody or on bail.

(3) If the judge remands the person in custody he may later grant bail.

(4) If an order is made under section 180 for proceedings on the warrant to be resumed, the period specified in section 46(6) must be taken to be 10 days starting with the day on which the order under section 180 is made.

51 Extradition request following consent

(1) This section applies if —

(a) a person in respect of whom a Part 1 warrant is issued consents under section 45 to his extradition to the category 1 territory in which the warrant was issued, and
(b) the condition in subsection (2) is satisfied before the judge orders his extradition under section 46(6) or 48(3)(a).

(2) The condition is that the judge is informed that —

(a) a certificate has been issued under section 70 in respect of a request for the person's extradition;
(b) the request has not been disposed of.

(3) The judge must not make an order under section 46(6) or 48(3) until he is informed what order has been made under section 179(2).

(4) If the order under section 179(2) is for further proceedings on the warrant to be deferred until the request has been disposed of, the judge must remand the person in custody or on bail.

(5) If the judge remands the person in custody he may later grant bail.

(6) If —

(a) the order under section 179(2) is for further proceedings on the warrant to be deferred until the request has been disposed of, and
(b) an order is made under section 180 for proceedings on the warrant to be resumed,

the period specified in section 46(6) must be taken to be 10 days starting with the day on which the order under section 180 is made.

(7) If the order under section 179(2) is for further proceedings on the request to be deferred until the warrant has been disposed of, the period specified in section 46(6) must be taken to be 10 days starting with the day on which the judge is informed of the order.

52 Undertaking in relation to person serving sentence

(1) This section applies if—

(a) the appropriate judge makes an order under section 46(6) or 48(3)(a) for a person's extradition to a category 1 territory;
(b) the person is serving a sentence of imprisonment or another form of detention in the United Kingdom.

(2) The judge may make the order for extradition subject to the condition that extradition is not to take place before he receives an undertaking given on behalf of the category 1 territory in terms specified by him.

(3) The terms which may be specified by the judge in relation to a person accused in a category 1 territory of the commission of an offence include terms—

(a) that the person be kept in custody until the conclusion of the proceedings against him for the offence and any other offence in respect of which he is permitted to be dealt with in the category 1 territory;
(b) that the person be returned to the United Kingdom to serve the remainder of his sentence on the conclusion of those proceedings.

(4) The terms which may be specified by the judge in relation to a person alleged to be unlawfully at large after conviction of an offence by a court in a category 1 territory include terms that the person be returned to the United Kingdom to serve the remainder of his sentence after serving any sentence imposed on him in the category 1 territory for—

(a) the offence, and
(b) any other offence in respect of which he is permitted to be dealt with in the category 1 territory.

(5) If the judge makes an order for extradition subject to a condition under subsection (2) the required period for the purposes of sections 47(2) and 49(2) is 10 days starting with the day on which the judge receives the undertaking.

53 Extradition following deferral for competing claim

(1) This section applies if—

(a) an order is made under section 46(6) or 48(3)(a) for a person to be extradited to a category 1 territory in pursuance of a Part 1 warrant;
(b) before the person is extradited to the territory an order is made under section 44(4)(b) or 179(2)(b) for the person's extradition in pursuance of the warrant to be deferred;
(c) the appropriate judge makes an order under section 181(2) for the person's extradition in pursuance of the warrant to cease to be deferred.

(2) The required period for the purposes of sections 47(2) and 49(2) is 10 days starting with the day on which the order under section 181(2) is made.

Post-extradition matters

54 Request for consent to other offence being dealt with

(1) This section applies if —

(a) a person is extradited to a category 1 territory in respect of an offence in accordance with this Part;
(b) the appropriate judge receives a request for consent to the person being dealt with in the territory for another offence;
(c) the request is certified under this section by the designated authority.

(2) The designated authority may certify a request for consent under this section if it believes that the authority making the request —

(a) is a judicial authority of the territory, and
(b) has the function of making requests for the consent referred to in subsection (1)(b) in that territory.

(3) A certificate under subsection (2) must certify that the authority making the request falls within paragraphs (a) and (b) of that subsection.

(4) The judge must serve notice on the person that he has received the request for consent, unless he is satisfied that it would not be practicable to do so.

(5) The consent hearing must begin before the end of the required period, which is 21 days starting with the day on which the request for consent is received by the designated authority.

(6) The judge may extend the required period if he believes it to be in the interests of justice to do so; and this subsection may apply more than once.

(7) The power in subsection (6) may be exercised even after the end of the required period.

(8) If the consent hearing does not begin before the end of the required period and the judge does not exercise the power in subsection (6) to extend the period, he must refuse consent.

(9) The judge may at any time adjourn the consent hearing.

(10) The consent hearing is the hearing at which the judge is to consider the request for consent.

55 Questions for decision at consent hearing

(1) At the consent hearing under section 54 the judge must decide whether consent is required to the person being dealt with in the territory for the offence for which consent is requested.

(2) If the judge decides the question in subsection (1) in the negative he must inform the authority making the request of his decision.

(3) If the judge decides that question in the affirmative he must decide whether the offence for which consent is requested is an extradition offence.

(4) If the judge decides the question in subsection (3) in the negative he must refuse consent.

(5) If the judge decides that question in the affirmative he must decide whether he would order the person's extradition under sections 11 to 25 if —

(a) the person were in the United Kingdom, and
(b) the judge were required to proceed under section 11 in respect of the offence for which consent is requested.

(6) If the judge decides the question in subsection (5) in the affirmative he must give consent.

(7) If the judge decides that question in the negative he must refuse consent.

(8) Consent is not required to the person being dealt with in the territory for the offence if the person has been given an opportunity to leave the territory and —

(a) he has not done so before the end of the permitted period, or
(b) if he did so before the end of the permitted period, he has returned there.

(9) The permitted period is 45 days starting with the day on which the person arrived in the territory following his extradition there in accordance with this Part.

(10) Subject to subsection (8), the judge must decide whether consent is required to the person being dealt with in the territory for the offence by reference to what appears to him to be the law of the territory or arrangements made between the territory and the United Kingdom.

56 Request for consent to further extradition to category 1 territory

(1) This section applies if —

(a) a person is extradited to a category 1 territory (the requesting territory) in accordance with this Part;
(b) the appropriate judge receives a request for consent to the person's extradition to another category 1 territory for an offence;
(c) the request is certified under this section by the designated authority.

(2) The designated authority may certify a request for consent under this section if it believes that the authority making the request —

(a) is a judicial authority of the requesting territory, and
(b) has the function of making requests for the consent referred to in subsection (1)(b) in that territory.

(3) A certificate under subsection (2) must certify that the authority making the request falls within paragraphs (a) and (b) of that subsection.

(4) The judge must serve notice on the person that he has received the request for consent, unless he is satisfied that it would not be practicable to do so.

(5) The consent hearing must begin before the end of the required period, which is 21 days starting with the day on which the request for consent is received by the designated authority.

(6) The judge may extend the required period if he believes it to be in the interests of justice to do so; and this subsection may apply more than once.

(7) The power in subsection (6) may be exercised even after the end of the required period.

(8) If the consent hearing does not begin before the end of the required period and the judge does not exercise the power in subsection (6) to extend the period, he must refuse consent.

(9) The judge may at any time adjourn the consent hearing.

(10) The consent hearing is the hearing at which the judge is to consider the request for consent.

57 Questions for decision at consent hearing

(1) At the consent hearing under section 56 the judge must decide whether consent is required to the person's extradition to the other category 1 territory for the offence.

(2) If the judge decides the question in subsection (1) in the negative he must inform the authority making the request of his decision.

(3) If the judge decides that question in the affirmative he must decide whether the offence is an extradition offence in relation to the category 1 territory referred to in section 56(1)(b).

(4) If the judge decides the question in subsection (3) in the negative he must refuse consent.

(5) If the judge decides that question in the affirmative he must decide whether he would order the person's extradition under sections 11 to 25 if —

(a) the person were in the United Kingdom, and
(b) the judge were required to proceed under section 11 in respect of the offence for which consent is requested.

(6) If the judge decides the question in subsection (5) in the affirmative he must give consent.

(7) If the judge decides that question in the negative he must refuse consent.

(8) Consent is not required to the person's extradition to the other territory for the offence if the person has been given an opportunity to leave the requesting territory and —

(a) he has not done so before the end of the permitted period, or
(b) if he did so before the end of the permitted period, he has returned there.

(9) The permitted period is 45 days starting with the day on which the person arrived in the requesting territory following his extradition there in accordance with this Part.

(10) Subject to subsection (8), the judge must decide whether consent is required to the person's extradition to the other territory for the offence by reference to what appears to him to be the arrangements made between the requesting territory and the United Kingdom.

58 Consent to further extradition to category 2 territory

(1) This section applies if —

(a) a person is extradited to a category 1 territory (the requesting territory) in accordance with this Part;
(b) the Secretary of State receives a request for consent to the person's extradition to a category 2 territory for an offence;
(c) the request is certified under this section by the designated authority.

(2) The designated authority may certify a request for consent under this section if it believes that the authority making the request —

(a) is a judicial authority of the requesting territory, and
(b) has the function of making requests for the consent referred to in subsection (1)(b) in that territory.

(3) A certificate under subsection (2) must certify that the authority making the request falls within paragraphs (a) and (b) of that subsection.

(4) The Secretary of State must serve notice on the person that he has received the request for consent, unless he is satisfied that it would not be practicable to do so.

(5) The Secretary of State must decide whether the offence is an extradition offence within the meaning given by section 137 in relation to the category 2 territory.

(6) If the Secretary of State decides the question in subsection (5) in the negative he must refuse consent.

(7) If the Secretary of State decides that question in the affirmative he must decide whether the appropriate judge would send the case to him (for his decision whether the person was to be extradited) under sections 79 to 91 if —

(a) the person were in the United Kingdom, and
(b) the judge were required to proceed under section 79 in respect of the offence for which the Secretary of State's consent is requested.

(8) If the Secretary of State decides the question in subsection (7) in the negative he must refuse his consent.

(9) If the Secretary of State decides that question in the affirmative he must decide whether, if the person were in the United Kingdom, his extradition to the category 2 territory in respect of the offence would be prohibited under section 94, 95 or 96.

(10) If the Secretary of State decides the question in subsection (9) in the negative he may give consent.

(11) If the Secretary of State decides that question in the affirmative he must refuse consent.

(12) This section applies in relation to any function which falls under this section to be exercised in relation to Scotland only as if the references in this section to the Secretary of State were to the Scottish Ministers.

59 Return of person to serve remainder of sentence

(1) This section applies if —

(a) a person who is serving a sentence of imprisonment or another form of detention in the United Kingdom is extradited to a category 1 territory in accordance with this Part;
(b) the person is returned to the United Kingdom to serve the remainder of his sentence.

(2) The person is liable to be detained in pursuance of his sentence.

(3) If he is at large he must be treated as being unlawfully at large.

(4) Time during which the person was not in the United Kingdom as a result of his extradition does not count as time served by him as part of his sentence.

(5) But subsection (4) does not apply if —

(a) the person was extradited for the purpose of being prosecuted for an offence, and
(b) the person has not been convicted of the offence or of any other offence in respect of which he was permitted to be dealt with in the category 1 territory.

(6) In a case falling within subsection (5), time during which the person was not in the United Kingdom as a result of his extradition counts as time served by him as part of his sentence if (and only if) it was spent in custody in connection with the offence or any other offence in respect of which he was permitted to be dealt with in the territory.

Costs

60 Costs where extradition ordered

(1) This section applies if any of the following occurs in relation to a person in respect of whom a Part 1 warrant is issued —

(a) an order for the person's extradition is made under this Part;
(b) the High Court dismisses an appeal under section 26;
(c) the High Court or the House of Lords dismisses an application for leave to appeal to the House of Lords under section 32, if the application is made by the person;
(d) the House of Lords dismisses an appeal under section 32, if the appeal is brought by the person.

(2) In a case falling within subsection (1)(a), the appropriate judge may make such order as he considers just and reasonable with regard to the costs to be paid by the person.

(3) In a case falling within subsection (1)(b), (c) or (d), the court by which the application or appeal is dismissed may make such order as it considers just and reasonable with regard to the costs to be paid by the person.

(4) An order for costs under this section —

(a) must specify their amount;
(b) may name the person to whom they are to be paid.

61 Costs where discharge ordered

(1) This section applies if any of the following occurs in relation to a person in respect of whom a Part 1 warrant is issued —

(a) an order for the person's discharge is made under this Part;
(b) the person is taken to be discharged under this Part;
(c) the High Court dismisses an appeal under section 28;
(d) the High Court or the House of Lords dismisses an application for leave to appeal to the House of Lords under section 32, if the application is made by the authority which issued the warrant;
(e) the House of Lords dismisses an appeal under section 32, if the appeal is brought by the authority which issued the warrant.

(2) In a case falling within subsection (1)(a), an order under subsection (5) in favour of the person may be made by —

(a) the appropriate judge, if the order for the person's discharge is made by him;
(b) the High Court, if the order for the person's discharge is made by it;
(c) the House of Lords, if the order for the person's discharge is made by it.

(3) In a case falling within subsection (1)(b), the appropriate judge may make an order under subsection (5) in favour of the person.

(4) In a case falling within subsection (1)(c), (d) or (e), the court by which the application or appeal is dismissed may make an order under subsection (5) in favour of the person.

(5) An order under this subsection in favour of a person is an order for a payment of the appropriate amount to be made to the person out of money provided by Parliament.

(6) The appropriate amount is such amount as the judge or court making the order under subsection (5) considers reasonably sufficient to compensate the person in whose favour the order is made for any expenses properly incurred by him in the proceedings under this Part.

(7) But if the judge or court making an order under subsection (5) is of the opinion that there are circumstances which make it inappropriate that the person in whose favour the order is made should recover the full amount mentioned in subsection (6), the judge or court must —

(a) assess what amount would in his or its opinion be just and reasonable;
(b) specify that amount in the order as the appropriate amount.

(8) Unless subsection (7) applies, the appropriate amount —

(a) must be specified in the order, if the court considers it appropriate for it to be so specified and the person in whose favour the order is made agrees the amount;
(b) must be determined in accordance with regulations made by the Lord Chancellor for the purposes of this section, in any other case.

62 Costs where discharge ordered: supplementary

(1) In England and Wales, subsections (1) and (3) of section 20 of the Prosecution of Offences Act 1985 (c. 23) (regulations for carrying Part 2 of that Act into effect) apply in relation to section 61 as those subsections apply in relation to Part 2 of that Act.

(2) As so applied those subsections have effect as if an order under section 61(5) were an order under Part 2 of that Act for a payment to be made out of central funds.

(3) In Northern Ireland, section 7 of the Costs in Criminal Cases Act (Northern Ireland) 1968 (c.10) (rules relating to costs) applies in relation to section 61 as that section applies in relation to sections 2 to 5 of that Act.

Repatriation cases

63 Persons serving sentences outside territory where convicted

(1) This section applies if an arrest warrant is issued in respect of a person by an authority of a category 1 territory and the warrant contains the statement referred to in subsection (2).

(2) The statement is one that—

(a) the person is alleged to be unlawfully at large from a prison in one territory (the imprisoning territory) in which he was serving a sentence after conviction of an offence specified in the warrant by a court in another territory (the convicting territory), and
(b) the person was serving the sentence in pursuance of international arrangements for prisoners sentenced in one territory to be repatriated to another territory in order to serve their sentence, and
(c) the warrant is issued with a view to his arrest and extradition to the category 1 territory for the purpose of serving a sentence or another form of detention imposed in respect of the offence.

(3) If the category 1 territory is either the imprisoning territory or the convicting territory, section 2(2)(b) has effect as if the reference to the statement referred to in subsection (5) of that section were a reference to the statement referred to in subsection (2) of this section.

(4) If the category 1 territory is the imprisoning territory—

(a) section 2(6)(e) has effect as if "the category 1 territory" read "the convicting territory";
(b) section 10(2) has effect as if "an extradition offence" read "an extradition offence in relation to the convicting territory";
(c) section 20(5) has effect as if after "entitled" there were inserted "in the convicting territory";
(d) section 37(5) has effect as if "a category 1 territory" read "the convicting territory" and as if "the category 1 territory" in both places read "the convicting territory";
(e) section 52(4) has effect as if "a category 1 territory" read "the convicting territory" and as if "the category 1 territory" in both places read "the convicting territory";
(f) section 65(1) has effect as if "a category 1 territory" read "the convicting territory";
(g) section 65(2) has effect as if "the category 1 territory" in the opening words and paragraphs (a) and (c) read "the convicting territory" and as if "the category 1 territory" in paragraph (b) read "the imprisoning territory";
(h) in section 65, subsections (3), (4), (5), (6) and (8) have effect as if "the category 1 territory" in each place read "the convicting territory".

Interpretation

64 Extradition offences: person not sentenced for offence

(1) This section applies in relation to conduct of a person if —

(a) he is accused in a category 1 territory of the commission of an offence constituted by the conduct, or
(b) he is alleged to be unlawfully at large after conviction by a court in a category 1 territory of an offence constituted by the conduct and he has not been sentenced for the offence.

(2) The conduct constitutes an extradition offence in relation to the category 1 territory if these conditions are satisfied —

(a) the conduct occurs in the category 1 territory and no part of it occurs in the United Kingdom;
(b) a certificate issued by an appropriate authority of the category 1 territory shows that the conduct falls within the European framework list;
(c) the certificate shows that the conduct is punishable under the law of the category 1 territory with imprisonment or another form of detention for a term of 3 years or a greater punishment.

(3) The conduct also constitutes an extradition offence in relation to the category 1 territory if these conditions are satisfied —

(a) the conduct occurs in the category 1 territory;
(b) the conduct would constitute an offence under the law of the relevant part of the United Kingdom if it occurred in that part of the United Kingdom;
(c) the conduct is punishable under the law of the category 1 territory with imprisonment or another form of detention for a term of 12 months or a greater punishment (however it is described in that law).

(4) The conduct also constitutes an extradition offence in relation to the category 1 territory if these conditions are satisfied —

(a) the conduct occurs outside the category 1 territory;
(b) the conduct is punishable under the law of the category 1 territory with imprisonment or another form of detention for a term of 12 months or a greater punishment (however it is described in that law);
(c) in corresponding circumstances equivalent conduct would constitute an extra-territorial offence under the law of the relevant part of the United Kingdom punishable with imprisonment or another form of detention for a term of 12 months or a greater punishment.

(5) The conduct also constitutes an extradition offence in relation to the category 1 territory if these conditions are satisfied —

(a) the conduct occurs outside the category 1 territory and no part of it occurs in the United Kingdom;
(b) the conduct would constitute an offence under the law of the relevant part of the United Kingdom punishable with imprisonment or another form of detention for a

term of 12 months or a greater punishment if it occurred in that part of the United Kingdom;
(c) the conduct is so punishable under the law of the category 1 territory (however it is described in that law).

(6) The conduct also constitutes an extradition offence in relation to the category 1 territory if these conditions are satisfied —

(a) the conduct occurs outside the category 1 territory and no part of it occurs in the United Kingdom;
(b) the conduct is punishable under the law of the category 1 territory with imprisonment or another form of detention for a term of 12 months or a greater punishment (however it is described in that law);
(c) the conduct constitutes or if committed in the United Kingdom would constitute an offence mentioned in subsection (7).

(7) The offences are —

(a) an offence under section 51 or 58 of the International Criminal Court Act 2001 (c. 17) (genocide, crimes against humanity and war crimes);
(b) an offence under section 52 or 59 of that Act (conduct ancillary to genocide etc. committed outside the jurisdiction);
(c) an ancillary offence, as defined in section 55 or 62 of that Act, in relation to an offence falling within paragraph (a) or (b);
(d) an offence under section 1 of the International Criminal Court (Scotland) Act 2001 (asp 13) (genocide, crimes against humanity and war crimes);
(e) an offence under section 2 of that Act (conduct ancillary to genocide etc. committed outside the jurisdiction);
(f) an ancillary offence, as defined in section 7 of that Act, in relation to an offence falling within paragraph (d) or (e).

(8) For the purposes of subsections (3)(b), (4)(c) and (5)(b) —

(a) if the conduct relates to a tax or duty, it is immaterial that the law of the relevant part of the United Kingdom does not impose the same kind of tax or duty or does not contain rules of the same kind as those of the law of the category 1 territory;
(b) if the conduct relates to customs or exchange, it is immaterial that the law of the relevant part of the United Kingdom does not contain rules of the same kind as those of the law of the category 1 territory.

(9) This section applies for the purposes of this Part.

65 Extradition offences: person sentenced for offence

(1) This section applies in relation to conduct of a person if —

(a) he is alleged to be unlawfully at large after conviction by a court in a category 1 territory of an offence constituted by the conduct, and
(b) he has been sentenced for the offence.

(2) The conduct constitutes an extradition offence in relation to the category 1 territory if these conditions are satisfied —

(a) the conduct occurs in the category 1 territory and no part of it occurs in the United Kingdom;
(b) a certificate issued by an appropriate authority of the category 1 territory shows that the conduct falls within the European framework list;
(c) the certificate shows that a sentence of imprisonment or another form of detention for a term of 12 months or a greater punishment has been imposed in the category 1 territory in respect of the conduct.

(3) The conduct also constitutes an extradition offence in relation to the category 1 territory if these conditions are satisfied —

(a) the conduct occurs in the category 1 territory;
(b) the conduct would constitute an offence under the law of the relevant part of the United Kingdom if it occurred in that part of the United Kingdom;
(c) a sentence of imprisonment or another form of detention for a term of 4 months or a greater punishment has been imposed in the category 1 territory in respect of the conduct.

(4) The conduct also constitutes an extradition offence in relation to the category 1 territory if these conditions are satisfied —

(a) the conduct occurs outside the category 1 territory;
(b) a sentence of imprisonment or another form of detention for a term of 4 months or a greater punishment has been imposed in the category 1 territory in respect of the conduct;
(c) in corresponding circumstances equivalent conduct would constitute an extra-territorial offence under the law of the relevant part of the United Kingdom punishable with imprisonment or another form of detention for a term of 12 months or a greater punishment.

(5) The conduct also constitutes an extradition offence in relation to the category 1 territory if these conditions are satisfied —

(a) the conduct occurs outside the category 1 territory and no part of it occurs in the United Kingdom;
(b) the conduct would constitute an offence under the law of the relevant part of the United Kingdom punishable with imprisonment or another form of detention for a term of 12 months or a greater punishment if it occurred in that part of the United Kingdom;
(c) a sentence of imprisonment or another form of detention for a term of 4 months or a greater punishment has been imposed in the category 1 territory in respect of the conduct.

(6) The conduct also constitutes an extradition offence in relation to the category 1 territory if these conditions are satisfied —

(a) the conduct occurs outside the category 1 territory and no part of it occurs in the United Kingdom;
(b) a sentence of imprisonment or another form of detention for a term of 4 months or a greater punishment has been imposed in the category 1 territory in respect of the conduct;
(c) the conduct constitutes or if committed in the United Kingdom would constitute an offence mentioned in subsection (7).

(7) The offences are —

(a) an offence under section 51 or 58 of the International Criminal Court Act 2001 (c. 17) (genocide, crimes against humanity and war crimes);
(b) an offence under section 52 or 59 of that Act (conduct ancillary to genocide etc. committed outside the jurisdiction);
(c) an ancillary offence, as defined in section 55 or 62 of that Act, in relation to an offence falling within paragraph (a) or (b);
(d) an offence under section 1 of the International Criminal Court (Scotland) Act 2001 (asp 13) (genocide, crimes against humanity and war crimes);
(e) an offence under section 2 of that Act (conduct ancillary to genocide etc. committed outside the jurisdiction);
(f) an ancillary offence, as defined in section 7 of that Act, in relation to an offence falling within paragraph (d) or (e).

(8) For the purposes of subsections (3)(b), (4)(c) and (5)(b) —

(a) if the conduct relates to a tax or duty, it is immaterial that the law of the relevant part of the United Kingdom does not impose the same kind of tax or duty or does not contain rules of the same kind as those of the law of the category 1 territory;
(b) if the conduct relates to customs or exchange, it is immaterial that the law of the relevant part of the United Kingdom does not contain rules of the same kind as those of the law of the category 1 territory.

(9) This section applies for the purposes of this Part.

66 Extradition offences: supplementary

(1) Subsections (2) to (4) apply for the purposes of sections 64 and 65.

(2) An appropriate authority of a category 1 territory is a judicial authority of the territory which the appropriate judge believes has the function of issuing arrest warrants in that territory.

(3) The law of a territory is the general criminal law of the territory.

(4) The relevant part of the United Kingdom is the part of the United Kingdom in which the relevant proceedings are taking place.

(5) The relevant proceedings are the proceedings in which it is necessary to decide whether conduct constitutes an extradition offence.

67 The appropriate judge

(1) The appropriate judge is —

(a) in England and Wales, a District Judge (Magistrates' Courts) designated for the purposes of this Part by the Lord Chancellor;
(b) in Scotland, the sheriff of Lothian and Borders;
(c) in Northern Ireland, such county court judge or resident magistrate as is designated for the purposes of this Part by the Lord Chancellor.

(2) A designation under subsection (1) may be made for all cases or for such cases (or cases of such description) as the designation stipulates.

(3) More than one designation may be made under subsection (1).

(4) This section applies for the purposes of this Part.

68 The extradition hearing

(1) The extradition hearing is the hearing at which the appropriate judge is to decide whether a person in respect of whom a Part 1 warrant was issued is to be extradited to the category 1 territory in which it was issued.

(2) This section applies for the purposes of this Part.

PART 2

EXTRADITION TO CATEGORY 2 TERRITORIES

Introduction

69 Extradition to category 2 territories

(1) This Part deals with extradition from the United Kingdom to the territories designated for the purposes of this Part by order made by the Secretary of State.

(2) In this Act references to category 2 territories are to the territories designated for the purposes of this Part.

70 Extradition request and certificate

(1) The Secretary of State must issue a certificate under this section if he receives a valid request for the extradition to a category 2 territory of a person who is in the United Kingdom.

(2) But subsection (1) does not apply if the Secretary of State decides under section 126 that the request is not to be proceeded with.

(3) A request for a person's extradition is valid if—

(a) it contains the statement referred to in subsection (4), and
(b) it is made in the approved way.

(4) The statement is one that the person—

(a) is accused in the category 2 territory of the commission of an offence specified in the request, or
(b) is alleged to be unlawfully at large after conviction by a court in the category 2 territory of an offence specified in the request.

(5) A request for extradition to a category 2 territory which is a British overseas territory is made in the approved way if it is made by or on behalf of the person administering the territory.

(6) A request for extradition to a category 2 territory which is the Hong Kong Special Administrative Region of the People's Republic of China is made in the approved way if it is made by or on behalf of the government of the Region.

(7) A request for extradition to any other category 2 territory is made in the approved way if it is made—

(a) by an authority of the territory which the Secretary of State believes has the function of making requests for extradition in that territory, or

(b) by a person recognised by the Secretary of State as a diplomatic or consular representative of the territory.

(8) A certificate under this section must certify that the request is made in the approved way.

(9) If a certificate is issued under this section the Secretary of State must send these documents to the appropriate judge —

(a) the request;
(b) the certificate;
(c) a copy of any relevant Order in Council.

Arrest

71 Arrest warrant following extradition request

(1) This section applies if the Secretary of State sends documents to the appropriate judge under section 70.

(2) The judge may issue a warrant for the arrest of the person whose extradition is requested if the judge has reasonable grounds for believing that —

(a) the offence in respect of which extradition is requested is an extradition offence, and
(b) there is evidence falling within subsection (3).

(3) The evidence is —

(a) evidence that would justify the issue of a warrant for the arrest of a person accused of the offence within the judge's jurisdiction, if the person whose extradition is requested is accused of the commission of the offence;
(b) evidence that would justify the issue of a warrant for the arrest of a person unlawfully at large after conviction of the offence within the judge's jurisdiction, if the person whose extradition is requested is alleged to be unlawfully at large after conviction of the offence.

(4) But if the category 2 territory to which extradition is requested is designated for the purposes of this section by order made by the Secretary of State, subsections (2) and (3) have effect as if "evidence" read "information".

(5) A warrant issued under this section may —

(a) be executed by any person to whom it is directed or by any constable or customs officer;
(b) be executed even if neither the warrant nor a copy of it is in the possession of the person executing it at the time of the arrest.

(6) If a warrant issued under this section in respect of a person is directed to a service policeman, it may be executed in any place where the service policeman would have power to arrest the person under the appropriate service law if the person had committed an offence under that law.

(7) In any other case, a warrant issued under this section may be executed in any part of the United Kingdom.

(8) The appropriate service law is —

(a) the Army Act 1955 (3 & 4 Eliz. 2 c. 18), if the person in respect of whom the warrant is issued is subject to military law;
(b) the Air Force Act 1955 (3 & 4 Eliz. 2 c. 19), if that person is subject to air-force law;
(c) the Naval Discipline Act 1957 (c. 53), if that person is subject to that Act.

72 Person arrested under section 71

(1) This section applies if a person is arrested under a warrant issued under section 71.

(2) A copy of the warrant must be given to the person as soon as practicable after his arrest.

(3) The person must be brought as soon as practicable before the appropriate judge.

(4) But subsection (3) does not apply if —

(a) the person is granted bail by a constable following his arrest, or
(b) the Secretary of State decides under section 126 that the request for the person's extradition is not to be proceeded with.

(5) If subsection (2) is not complied with and the person applies to the judge to be discharged, the judge may order his discharge.

(6) If subsection (3) is not complied with and the person applies to the judge to be discharged, the judge must order his discharge.

(7) When the person first appears or is brought before the appropriate judge, the judge must —

(a) inform him of the contents of the request for his extradition;
(b) give him the required information about consent;
(c) remand him in custody or on bail.

(8) The required information about consent is —

(a) that the person may consent to his extradition to the category 2 territory to which his extradition is requested;
(b) an explanation of the effect of consent and the procedure that will apply if he gives consent;
(c) that consent must be given in writing and is irrevocable.

(9) If the judge remands the person in custody he may later grant bail.

(10) Subsection (4)(a) applies to Scotland with the omission of the words "by a constable".

73 Provisional warrant

(1) This section applies if a justice of the peace is satisfied on information in writing and on oath that a person within subsection (2) —

(a) is or is believed to be in the United Kingdom, or
(b) is or is believed to be on his way to the United Kingdom.

(2) A person is within this subsection if —

(a) he is accused in a category 2 territory of the commission of an offence, or
(b) he is alleged to be unlawfully at large after conviction of an offence by a court in a category 2 territory.

(3) The justice may issue a warrant for the arrest of the person (a provisional warrant) if he has reasonable grounds for believing that —

(a) the offence of which the person is accused or has been convicted is an extradition offence, and
(b) there is written evidence falling within subsection (4).

(4) The evidence is —

(a) evidence that would justify the issue of a warrant for the arrest of a person accused of the offence within the justice's jurisdiction, if the person in respect of whom the warrant is sought is accused of the commission of the offence;
(b) evidence that would justify the issue of a warrant for the arrest of a person unlawfully at large after conviction of the offence within the justice's jurisdiction, if the person in respect of whom the warrant is sought is alleged to be unlawfully at large after conviction of the offence.

(5) But if the category 2 territory is designated for the purposes of this section by order made by the Secretary of State, subsections (3) and (4) have effect as if "evidence" read "information".

(6) A provisional warrant may —

(a) be executed by any person to whom it is directed or by any constable or customs officer;
(b) be executed even if neither the warrant nor a copy of it is in the possession of the person executing it at the time of the arrest.

(7) If a warrant issued under this section in respect of a person is directed to a service policeman, it may be executed in any place where the service policeman would have power to arrest the person under the appropriate service law if the person had committed an offence under that law.

(8) In any other case, a warrant issued under this section may be executed in any part of the United Kingdom.

(9) The appropriate service law is —

(a) the Army Act 1955 (3 & 4 Eliz. 2 c. 18), if the person in respect of whom the warrant is issued is subject to military law;
(b) the Air Force Act 1955 (3 & 4 Eliz. 2 c. 19), if that person is subject to air-force law;
(c) the Naval Discipline Act 1957 (c. 53), if that person is subject to that Act.

(10) The preceding provisions of this section apply to Scotland with these modifications —

(a) in subsection (1) for "justice of the peace is satisfied on information in writing and on oath" substitute "sheriff is satisfied, on an application by a procurator fiscal,";
(b) in subsection (3) for "justice" substitute "sheriff";
(c) in subsection (4) for "justice's", in paragraphs (a) and (b), substitute "sheriff's".

(11) Subsection (1) applies to Northern Ireland with the substitution of "a complaint" for "information".

74 Person arrested under provisional warrant

(1) This section applies if a person is arrested under a provisional warrant.

(2) A copy of the warrant must be given to the person as soon as practicable after his arrest.

(3) The person must be brought as soon as practicable before the appropriate judge.

(4) But subsection (3) does not apply if—

(a) the person is granted bail by a constable following his arrest, or
(b) in a case where the Secretary of State has received a valid request for the person's extradition, the Secretary of State decides under section 126 that the request is not to be proceeded with.

(5) If subsection (2) is not complied with and the person applies to the judge to be discharged, the judge may order his discharge.

(6) If subsection (3) is not complied with and the person applies to the judge to be discharged, the judge must order his discharge.

(7) When the person first appears or is brought before the appropriate judge, the judge must—

(a) inform him that he is accused of the commission of an offence in a category 2 territory or that he is alleged to be unlawfully at large after conviction of an offence by a court in a category 2 territory;
(b) give him the required information about consent;
(c) remand him in custody or on bail.

(8) The required information about consent is—

(a) that the person may consent to his extradition to the category 2 territory in which he is accused of the commission of an offence or is alleged to have been convicted of an offence;
(b) an explanation of the effect of consent and the procedure that will apply if he gives consent;
(c) that consent must be given in writing and is irrevocable.

(9) If the judge remands the person in custody he may later grant bail.

(10) The judge must order the person's discharge if the documents referred to in section 70(9) are not received by the judge within the required period.

(11) The required period is—

(a) 45 days starting with the day on which the person was arrested, or
(b) if the category 2 territory is designated by order made by the Secretary of State for the purposes of this section, any longer period permitted by the order.

(12) Subsection (4)(a) applies to Scotland with the omission of the words "by a constable".

The extradition hearing

75 Date of extradition hearing: arrest under section 71

(1) When a person arrested under a warrant issued under section 71 first appears or is brought before the appropriate judge, the judge must fix a date on which the extradition hearing is to begin.

(2) The date fixed under subsection (1) must not be later than the end of the permitted period, which is 2 months starting with the date on which the person first appears or is brought before the judge.

(3) If before the date fixed under subsection (1) (or this subsection) a party to the proceedings applies to the judge for a later date to be fixed and the judge believes it to be in the

interests of justice to do so, he may fix a later date; and this subsection may apply more than once.

(4) If the extradition hearing does not begin on or before the date fixed under this section and the person applies to the judge to be discharged, the judge must order his discharge.

76 Date of extradition hearing: arrest under provisional warrant

(1) Subsection (2) applies if—

(a) a person is arrested under a provisional warrant, and
(b) the documents referred to in section 70(9) are received by the appropriate judge within the period required under section 74(10).

(2) The judge must fix a date on which the extradition hearing is to begin.

(3) The date fixed under subsection (2) must not be later than the end of the permitted period, which is 2 months starting with the date on which the judge receives the documents.

(4) If before the date fixed under subsection (2) (or this subsection) a party to the proceedings applies to the judge for a later date to be fixed and the judge believes it to be in the interests of justice to do so, he may fix a later date; and this subsection may apply more than once.

(5) If the extradition hearing does not begin on or before the date fixed under this section and the person applies to the judge to be discharged, the judge must order his discharge.

77 Judge's powers at extradition hearing

(1) In England and Wales, at the extradition hearing the appropriate judge has the same powers (as nearly as may be) as a magistrates' court would have if the proceedings were the summary trial of an information against the person whose extradition is requested.

(2) In Scotland—

(a) at the extradition hearing the appropriate judge has the same powers (as nearly as may be) as if the proceedings were summary proceedings in respect of an offence alleged to have been committed by the person whose extradition is requested; but
(b) in his making any decision under section 78(4)(a) evidence from a single source shall be sufficient.

(3) In Northern Ireland, at the extradition hearing the appropriate judge has the same powers (as nearly as may be) as a magistrates' court would have if the proceedings were the hearing and determination of a complaint against the person whose extradition is requested.

(4) If the judge adjourns the extradition hearing he must remand the person in custody or on bail.

(5) If the judge remands the person in custody he may later grant bail.

78 Initial stages of extradition hearing

(1) This section applies if a person alleged to be the person whose extradition is requested appears or is brought before the appropriate judge for the extradition hearing.

(2) The judge must decide whether the documents sent to him by the Secretary of State consist of (or include)—

(a) the documents referred to in section 70(9);
(b) particulars of the person whose extradition is requested;
(c) particulars of the offence specified in the request;
(d) in the case of a person accused of an offence, a warrant for his arrest issued in the category 2 territory;

(e) in the case of a person alleged to be unlawfully at large after conviction of an offence, a certificate issued in the category 2 territory of the conviction and (if he has been sentenced) of the sentence.

(3) If the judge decides the question in subsection (2) in the negative he must order the person's discharge.

(4) If the judge decides that question in the affirmative he must decide whether—

(a) the person appearing or brought before him is the person whose extradition is requested;
(b) the offence specified in the request is an extradition offence;
(c) copies of the documents sent to the judge by the Secretary of State have been served on the person.

(5) The judge must decide the question in subsection (4)(a) on a balance of probabilities.

(6) If the judge decides any of the questions in subsection (4) in the negative he must order the person's discharge.

(7) If the judge decides those questions in the affirmative he must proceed under section 79.

(8) The reference in subsection (2)(d) to a warrant for a person's arrest includes a reference to a judicial document authorising his arrest.

79 Bars to extradition

(1) If the judge is required to proceed under this section he must decide whether the person's extradition to the category 2 territory is barred by reason of—

(a) the rule against double jeopardy;
(b) extraneous considerations;
(c) the passage of time;
(d) hostage-taking considerations.

(2) Sections 80 to 83 apply for the interpretation of subsection (1).

(3) If the judge decides any of the questions in subsection (1) in the affirmative he must order the person's discharge.

(4) If the judge decides those questions in the negative and the person is accused of the commission of the extradition offence but is not alleged to be unlawfully at large after conviction of it, the judge must proceed under section 84.

(5) If the judge decides those questions in the negative and the person is alleged to be unlawfully at large after conviction of the extradition offence, the judge must proceed under section 85.

80 Rule against double jeopardy

A person's extradition to a category 2 territory is barred by reason of the rule against double jeopardy if (and only if) it appears that he would be entitled to be discharged under any rule of law relating to previous acquittal or conviction if he were charged with the extradition offence in the part of the United Kingdom where the judge exercises his jurisdiction.

81 Extraneous considerations

A person's extradition to a category 2 territory is barred by reason of extraneous considerations if (and only if) it appears that—

(a) the request for his extradition (though purporting to be made on account of the extradition offence) is in fact made for the purpose of prosecuting or punishing him on account of his race, religion, nationality, gender, sexual orientation or political opinions, or

(b) if extradited he might be prejudiced at his trial or punished, detained or restricted in his personal liberty by reason of his race, religion, nationality, gender, sexual orientation or political opinions.

82 Passage of time

A person's extradition to a category 2 territory is barred by reason of the passage of time if (and only if) it appears that it would be unjust or oppressive to extradite him by reason of the passage of time since he is alleged to have committed the extradition offence or since he is alleged to have become unlawfully at large (as the case may be).

83 Hostage-taking considerations

(1) A person's extradition to a category 2 territory is barred by reason of hostage-taking considerations if (and only if) the territory is a party to the Hostage-taking Convention and it appears that —

(a) if extradited he might be prejudiced at his trial because communication between him and the appropriate authorities would not be possible, and
(b) the act or omission constituting the extradition offence also constitutes an offence under section 1 of the Taking of Hostages Act 1982 (c. 28) or an attempt to commit such an offence.

(2) The appropriate authorities are the authorities of the territory which are entitled to exercise rights of protection in relation to him.

(3) A certificate issued by the Secretary of State that a territory is a party to the Hostage-taking Convention is conclusive evidence of that fact for the purposes of subsection (1).

(4) The Hostage-taking Convention is the International Convention against the Taking of Hostages opened for signature at New York on 18 December 1979.

84 Case where person has not been convicted

(1) If the judge is required to proceed under this section he must decide whether there is evidence which would be sufficient to make a case requiring an answer by the person if the proceedings were the summary trial of an information against him.

(2) In deciding the question in subsection (1) the judge may treat a statement made by a person in a document as admissible evidence of a fact if —

(a) the statement is made by the person to a police officer or another person charged with the duty of investigating offences or charging offenders, and
(b) direct oral evidence by the person of the fact would be admissible.

(3) In deciding whether to treat a statement made by a person in a document as admissible evidence of a fact, the judge must in particular have regard —

(a) to the nature and source of the document;
(b) to whether or not, having regard to the nature and source of the document and to any other circumstances that appear to the judge to be relevant, it is likely that the document is authentic;
(c) to the extent to which the statement appears to supply evidence which would not be readily available if the statement were not treated as being admissible evidence of the fact;

(d) to the relevance of the evidence that the statement appears to supply to any issue likely to have to be determined by the judge in deciding the question in subsection (1);
(e) to any risk that the admission or exclusion of the statement will result in unfairness to the person whose extradition is sought, having regard in particular to whether it is likely to be possible to controvert the statement if the person making it does not attend to give oral evidence in the proceedings.

(4) A summary in a document of a statement made by a person must be treated as a statement made by the person in the document for the purposes of subsection (2).

(5) If the judge decides the question in subsection (1) in the negative he must order the person's discharge.

(6) If the judge decides that question in the affirmative he must proceed under section 87.

(7) If the judge is required to proceed under this section and the category 2 territory to which extradition is requested is designated for the purposes of this section by order made by the Secretary of State—

(a) the judge must not decide under subsection (1), and
(b) he must proceed under section 87.

(8) Subsection (1) applies to Scotland with the substitution of "summary proceedings in respect of an offence alleged to have been committed by the person (except that for this purpose evidence from a single source shall be sufficient)" for "the summary trial of an information against him".

(9) Subsection (1) applies to Northern Ireland with the substitution of "the hearing and determination of a complaint" for "the summary trial of an information".

85 Case where person has been convicted

(1) If the judge is required to proceed under this section he must decide whether the person was convicted in his presence.

(2) If the judge decides the question in subsection (1) in the affirmative he must proceed under section 87.

(3) If the judge decides that question in the negative he must decide whether the person deliberately absented himself from his trial.

(4) If the judge decides the question in subsection (3) in the affirmative he must proceed under section 87.

(5) If the judge decides that question in the negative he must decide whether the person would be entitled to a retrial or (on appeal) to a review amounting to a retrial.

(6) If the judge decides the question in subsection (5) in the affirmative he must proceed under section 86.

(7) If the judge decides that question in the negative he must order the person's discharge.

(8) The judge must not decide the question in subsection (5) in the affirmative unless, in any proceedings that it is alleged would constitute a retrial or a review amounting to a retrial, the person would have these rights—

(a) the right to defend himself in person or through legal assistance of his own choosing or, if he had not sufficient means to pay for legal assistance, to be given it free when the interests of justice so required;
(b) the right to examine or have examined witnesses against him and to obtain the attendance and examination of witnesses on his behalf under the same conditions as witnesses against him.

86 Conviction in person's absence

(1) If the judge is required to proceed under this section he must decide whether there is evidence which would be sufficient to make a case requiring an answer by the person if the proceedings were the summary trial of an information against him.

(2) In deciding the question in subsection (1) the judge may treat a statement made by a person in a document as admissible evidence of a fact if —

(a) the statement is made by the person to a police officer or another person charged with the duty of investigating offences or charging offenders, and
(b) direct oral evidence by the person of the fact would be admissible.

(3) In deciding whether to treat a statement made by a person in a document as admissible evidence of a fact, the judge must in particular have regard —

(a) to the nature and source of the document;
(b) to whether or not, having regard to the nature and source of the document and to any other circumstances that appear to the judge to be relevant, it is likely that the document is authentic;
(c) to the extent to which the statement appears to supply evidence which would not be readily available if the statement were not treated as being admissible evidence of the fact;
(d) to the relevance of the evidence that the statement appears to supply to any issue likely to have to be determined by the judge in deciding the question in subsection (1);
(e) to any risk that the admission or exclusion of the statement will result in unfairness to the person whose extradition is sought, having regard in particular to whether it is likely to be possible to controvert the statement if the person making it does not attend to give oral evidence in the proceedings.

(4) A summary in a document of a statement made by a person must be treated as a statement made by the person in the document for the purposes of subsection (2).

(5) If the judge decides the question in subsection (1) in the negative he must order the person's discharge.

(6) If the judge decides that question in the affirmative he must proceed under section 87.

(7) If the judge is required to proceed under this section and the category 2 territory to which extradition is requested is designated for the purposes of this section by order made by the Secretary of State —

(a) the judge must not decide under subsection (1), and
(b) he must proceed under section 87.

(8) Subsection (1) applies to Scotland with the substitution of "summary proceedings in respect of an offence alleged to have been committed by the person (except that for this purpose evidence from a single source shall be sufficient)" for "the summary trial of an information against him".

(9) Subsection (1) applies to Northern Ireland with the substitution of "the hearing and determination of a complaint" for "the summary trial of an information".

87 Human rights

(1) If the judge is required to proceed under this section (by virtue of section 84, 85 or 86) he must decide whether the person's extradition would be compatible with the Convention rights within the meaning of the Human Rights Act 1998 (c. 42).

(2) If the judge decides the question in subsection (1) in the negative he must order the person's discharge.

(3) If the judge decides that question in the affirmative he must send the case to the Secretary of State for his decision whether the person is to be extradited.

88 Person charged with offence in United Kingdom

(1) This section applies if at any time in the extradition hearing the judge is informed that the person is charged with an offence in the United Kingdom.

(2) The judge must adjourn the extradition hearing until one of these occurs —

(a) the charge is disposed of;
(b) the charge is withdrawn;
(c) proceedings in respect of the charge are discontinued;
(d) an order is made for the charge to lie on the file, or in relation to Scotland, the diet is deserted *pro loco et tempore*.

(3) If a sentence of imprisonment or another form of detention is imposed in respect of the offence charged, the judge may adjourn the extradition hearing until the sentence has been served.

(4) If before he adjourns the extradition hearing under subsection (2) the judge has decided under section 79 whether the person's extradition is barred by reason of the rule against double jeopardy, the judge must decide that question again after the resumption of the hearing.

89 Person serving sentence in United Kingdom

(1) This section applies if at any time in the extradition hearing the judge is informed that the person is serving a sentence of imprisonment or another form of detention in the United Kingdom.

(2) The judge may adjourn the extradition hearing until the sentence has been served.

90 Competing extradition claim

(1) This section applies if at any time in the extradition hearing the judge is informed that the conditions in subsection (2) or (3) are met.

(2) The conditions are that —

(a) the Secretary of State has received another valid request for the person's extradition to a category 2 territory;
(b) the other request has not been disposed of;
(c) the Secretary of State has made an order under section 126(2) for further proceedings on the request under consideration to be deferred until the other request has been disposed of.

(3) The conditions are that —

(a) a certificate has been issued under section 2 in respect of a Part 1 warrant issued in respect of the person;
(b) the warrant has not been disposed of;
(c) the Secretary of State has made an order under section 179(2) for further proceedings on the request to be deferred until the warrant has been disposed of.

(4) The judge must remand the person in custody or on bail.

(5) If the judge remands the person in custody he may later grant bail.

91 Physical or mental condition

(1) This section applies if at any time in the extradition hearing it appears to the judge that the condition in subsection (2) is satisfied.

(2) The condition is that the physical or mental condition of the person is such that it would be unjust or oppressive to extradite him.

(3) The judge must —

(a) order the person's discharge, or
(b) adjourn the extradition hearing until it appears to him that the condition in subsection (2) is no longer satisfied.

92 Case sent to Secretary of State

(1) This section applies if the appropriate judge sends a case to the Secretary of State under this Part for his decision whether a person is to be extradited.

(2) The judge must inform the person in ordinary language that —

(a) he has a right to appeal to the High Court;
(b) if he exercises the right the appeal will not be heard until the Secretary of State has made his decision.

(3) But subsection (2) does not apply if the person has consented to his extradition under section 127.

(4) The judge must remand the person in custody or on bail —

(a) to wait for the Secretary of State's decision, and
(b) to wait for his extradition to the territory to which extradition is requested (if the Secretary of State orders him to be extradited).

(5) If the judge remands the person in custody he may later grant bail.

Secretary of State's functions

93 Secretary of State's consideration of case

(1) This section applies if the appropriate judge sends a case to the Secretary of State under this Part for his decision whether a person is to be extradited.

(2) The Secretary of State must decide whether he is prohibited from ordering the person's extradition under any of these sections —

(a) section 94 (death penalty);
(b) section 95 (speciality);
(c) section 96 (earlier extradition to United Kingdom from other territory).

(3) If the Secretary of State decides any of the questions in subsection (2) in the affirmative he must order the person's discharge.

(4) If the Secretary of State decides those questions in the negative he must order the person to be extradited to the territory to which his extradition is requested unless —

(a) he is informed that the request has been withdrawn,
(b) he makes an order under section 126(2) or 179(2) for further proceedings on the request to be deferred and the person is discharged under section 180, or
(c) he orders the person's discharge under section 208.

(5) In deciding the questions in subsection (2), the Secretary of State is not required to consider any representations received by him after the end of the permitted period.

(6) The permitted period is the period of 6 weeks starting with the appropriate day.

94 Death penalty

(1) The Secretary of State must not order a person's extradition to a category 2 territory if he could be, will be or has been sentenced to death for the offence concerned in the category 2 territory.

(2) Subsection (1) does not apply if the Secretary of State receives a written assurance which he considers adequate that a sentence of death —

(a) will not be imposed, or
(b) will not be carried out (if imposed).

95 Speciality

(1) The Secretary of State must not order a person's extradition to a category 2 territory if there are no speciality arrangements with the category 2 territory.

(2) But subsection (1) does not apply if the person consented to his extradition under section 127 before his case was sent to the Secretary of State.

(3) There are speciality arrangements with a category 2 territory if (and only if) under the law of that territory or arrangements made between it and the United Kingdom a person who is extradited to the territory from the United Kingdom may be dealt with in the territory for an offence committed before his extradition only if —

(a) the offence is one falling within subsection (4), or
(b) he is first given an opportunity to leave the territory.

(4) The offences are —

(a) the offence in respect of which the person is extradited;
(b) an extradition offence disclosed by the same facts as that offence, other than one in respect of which a sentence of death could be imposed;
(c) an extradition offence in respect of which the Secretary of State consents to the person being dealt with;
(d) an offence in respect of which the person waives the right that he would have (but for this paragraph) not to be dealt with for the offence.

(5) Arrangements made with a category 2 territory which is a Commonwealth country or a British overseas territory may be made for a particular case or more generally.

(6) A certificate issued by or under the authority of the Secretary of State confirming the existence of arrangements with a category 2 territory which is a Commonwealth country or a British overseas territory and stating the terms of the arrangements is conclusive evidence of those matters.

96 Earlier extradition to United Kingdom from other territory

The Secretary of State must not order a person's extradition to a category 2 territory if —

(a) the person was extradited to the United Kingdom from another territory (the extraditing territory);
(b) under arrangements between the United Kingdom and the extraditing territory, that territory's consent is required to the person's extradition from the

United Kingdom to the category 2 territory in respect of the extradition offence under consideration;
(c) that consent has not been given on behalf of the extraditing territory.

97 Deferral: person charged with offence in United Kingdom

(1) This section applies if —

(a) the appropriate judge sends a case to the Secretary of State under this Part for his decision whether a person is to be extradited;
(b) the person is charged with an offence in the United Kingdom.

(2) The Secretary of State must not make a decision with regard to the person's extradition until one of these occurs —

(a) the charge is disposed of;
(b) the charge is withdrawn;
(c) proceedings in respect of the charge are discontinued;
(d) an order is made for the charge to lie on the file or, in relation to Scotland, the diet is deserted *pro loco et tempore*.

(3) If a sentence of imprisonment or another form of detention is imposed in respect of the offence charged, the Secretary of State may defer making a decision with regard to the person's extradition until the sentence has been served.

98 Deferral: person serving sentence in United Kingdom

(1) This section applies if —

(a) the appropriate judge sends a case to the Secretary of State under this Part for his decision whether a person is to be extradited;
(b) the person is serving a sentence of imprisonment or another form of detention in the United Kingdom.

(2) The Secretary of State may defer making a decision with regard to the person's extradition until the sentence has been served.

99 Time limit for order for extradition or discharge

(1) This section applies if —

(a) the appropriate judge sends a case to the Secretary of State under this Part for his decision whether a person is to be extradited;
(b) within the required period the Secretary of State does not make an order for the person's extradition or discharge.

(2) If the person applies to the High Court to be discharged, the court must order his discharge.

(3) The required period is the period of 2 months starting with the appropriate day.

(4) If before the required period ends the Secretary of State applies to the High Court for it to be extended the High Court may make an order accordingly; and this subsection may apply more than once.

100 Information

(1) If the Secretary of State orders a person's extradition under this Part he must —

(a) inform the person of the order;
(b) inform him in ordinary language that he has a right of appeal to the High Court;
(c) inform a person acting on behalf of the category 2 territory of the order.

(2) But subsection (1)(b) does not apply if the person has consented to his extradition under section 127.

(3) If the Secretary of State orders a person's extradition under this Part and he has received an assurance such as is mentioned in section 94(2), he must give the person a copy of the assurance when he informs him under subsection (1) of the order.

(4) If the Secretary of State orders a person's discharge under this Part he must —

(a) inform him of the order;
(b) inform a person acting on behalf of the category 2 territory of the order.

101 Making of order for extradition or discharge

(1) An order to which this section applies must be made under the hand of one of these —

(a) the Secretary of State;
(b) a Minister of State;
(c) a Parliamentary Under-Secretary of State;
(d) a senior official.

(2) But, in relation to Scotland, an order to which this section applies must be made under the hand of one of these —

(a) a member of the Scottish Executive or a junior Scottish Minister;
(b) a senior official who is a member of the staff of the Scottish Administration.

(3) This section applies to —

(a) an order under section 93 for a person's extradition;
(b) an order under section 93 or 123 for a person's discharge.

(4) A senior official is —

(a) a member of the Senior Civil Service;
(b) a member of the Senior Management Structure of Her Majesty's Diplomatic Service.

(5) If it appears to the Secretary of State that it is necessary to do so in consequence of any changes to the structure or grading of the home civil service or diplomatic service, he may by order make such amendments to subsection (4) as appear to him appropriate to preserve (so far as practicable) the effect of that subsection.

102 The appropriate day

(1) This section applies for the purposes of sections 93 and 99 if the appropriate judge sends a case to the Secretary of State under this Part for his decision whether a person is to be extradited.

(2) If the person is charged with an offence in the United Kingdom, the appropriate day is the day on which one of these occurs —

(a) the charge is disposed of;
(b) the charge is withdrawn;
(c) proceedings in respect of the charge are discontinued;
(d) an order is made for the charge to lie on the file, or in relation to Scotland, the diet is deserted *pro loco et tempore*.

(3) If under section 97(3) or 98(2) the Secretary of State defers making a decision until the person has served a sentence, the appropriate day is the day on which the person finishes serving the sentence.

(4) If section 126 applies in relation to the request for the person's extradition (the request concerned) the appropriate day is —

(a) the day on which the Secretary of State makes an order under that section, if the order is for proceedings on the other request to be deferred;
(b) the day on which an order under section 180 is made, if the order under section 126 is for proceedings on the request concerned to be deferred and the order under section 180 is for the proceedings to be resumed.

(5) If section 179 applies in relation to the request for the person's extradition, the appropriate day is —

(a) the day on which the Secretary of State makes an order under that section, if the order is for proceedings on the warrant to be deferred;
(b) the day on which an order under section 180 is made, if the order under section 179 is for proceedings on the request to be deferred and the order under section 180 is for the proceedings to be resumed.

(6) If more than one of subsections (2) to (5) applies, the appropriate day is the latest of the days found under the subsections which apply.

(7) In any other case, the appropriate day is the day on which the judge sends the case to the Secretary of State for his decision whether the person is to be extradited.

Appeals

103 Appeal where case sent to Secretary of State

(1) If the judge sends a case to the Secretary of State under this Part for his decision whether a person is to be extradited, the person may appeal to the High Court against the relevant decision.

(2) But subsection (1) does not apply if the person consented to his extradition under section 127 before his case was sent to the Secretary of State.

(3) The relevant decision is the decision that resulted in the case being sent to the Secretary of State.

(4) An appeal under this section may be brought on a question of law or fact.

(5) If an appeal is brought under this section before the Secretary of State has decided whether the person is to be extradited the appeal must not be heard until after the Secretary of State has made his decision.

(6) If the Secretary of State orders the person's discharge the appeal must not be proceeded with.

(7) No appeal may be brought under this section if the Secretary of State has ordered the person's discharge.

(8) If notice of an appeal under section 110 against the decision which resulted in the order for the person's discharge is given in accordance with subsection (5) of that section —

(a) subsections (6) and (7) do not apply;
(b) no appeal may be brought under this section if the High Court has made its decision on the appeal.

(9) Notice of an appeal under this section must be given in accordance with rules of court before the end of the permitted period, which is 14 days starting with the day on which the Secretary of State informs the person under section 100(1) or (4) of the order he has made in respect of the person.

104 Court's powers on appeal under section 103

(1) On an appeal under section 103 the High Court may —

(a) allow the appeal;
(b) direct the judge to decide again a question (or questions) which he decided at the extradition hearing;
(c) dismiss the appeal.

(2) The court may allow the appeal only if the conditions in subsection (3) or the conditions in subsection (4) are satisfied.

(3) The conditions are that —

(a) the judge ought to have decided a question before him at the extradition hearing differently;
(b) if he had decided the question in the way he ought to have done, he would have been required to order the person's discharge.

(4) The conditions are that —

(a) an issue is raised that was not raised at the extradition hearing or evidence is available that was not available at the extradition hearing;
(b) the issue or evidence would have resulted in the judge deciding a question before him at the extradition hearing differently;
(c) if he had decided the question in that way, he would have been required to order the person's discharge.

(5) If the court allows the appeal it must —

(a) order the person's discharge;
(b) quash the order for his extradition.

(6) If the judge comes to a different decision on any question that is the subject of a direction under subsection (1)(b) he must order the person's discharge.

(7) If the judge comes to the same decision as he did at the extradition hearing on the question that is (or all the questions that are) the subject of a direction under subsection (1)(b) the appeal must be taken to have been dismissed by a decision of the High Court.

105 Appeal against discharge at extradition hearing

(1) If at the extradition hearing the judge orders a person's discharge, an appeal to the High Court may be brought on behalf of the category 2 territory against the relevant decision.

(2) But subsection (1) does not apply if the order for the person's discharge was under section 122.

(3) The relevant decision is the decision which resulted in the order for the person's discharge.

(4) An appeal under this section may be brought on a question of law or fact.

(5) Notice of an appeal under this section must be given in accordance with rules of court before the end of the permitted period, which is 14 days starting with the day on which the order for the person's discharge is made.

106 Court's powers on appeal under section 105

(1) On an appeal under section 105 the High Court may —

(a) allow the appeal;
(b) direct the judge to decide the relevant question again;
(c) dismiss the appeal.

(2) A question is the relevant question if the judge's decision on it resulted in the order for the person's discharge.

(3) The court may allow the appeal only if the conditions in subsection (4) or the conditions in subsection (5) are satisfied.

(4) The conditions are that —

(a) the judge ought to have decided the relevant question differently;
(b) if he had decided the question in the way he ought to have done, he would not have been required to order the person's discharge.

(5) The conditions are that —

(a) an issue is raised that was not raised at the extradition hearing or evidence is available that was not available at the extradition hearing;
(b) the issue or evidence would have resulted in the judge deciding the relevant question differently;
(c) if he had decided the question in that way, he would not have been required to order the person's discharge.

(6) If the court allows the appeal it must —

(a) quash the order discharging the person;
(b) remit the case to the judge;
(c) direct him to proceed as he would have been required to do if he had decided the relevant question differently at the extradition hearing.

(7) If the court makes a direction under subsection (1)(b) and the judge decides the relevant question differently he must proceed as he would have been required to do if he had decided that question differently at the extradition hearing.

(8) If the court makes a direction under subsection (1)(b) and the judge does not decide the relevant question differently the appeal must be taken to have been dismissed by a decision of the High Court.

107 Detention pending conclusion of appeal under section 105

(1) This section applies if immediately after the judge orders the person's discharge the judge is informed on behalf of the category 2 territory of an intention to appeal under section 105.

(2) The judge must remand the person in custody or on bail while the appeal is pending.

(3) If the judge remands the person in custody he may later grant bail.

(4) An appeal under section 105 ceases to be pending at the earliest of these times —

(a) when the proceedings on the appeal are discontinued;
(b) when the High Court dismisses the appeal, if the court is not immediately informed on behalf of the category 2 territory of an intention to apply for leave to appeal to the House of Lords;
(c) at the end of the permitted period, which is 28 days starting with the day on which leave to appeal to the House of Lords against the decision of the High Court on the appeal is granted;
(d) when there is no further step that can be taken on behalf of the category 2 territory in relation to the appeal (ignoring any power of a court to grant leave to take a step out of time).

(5) The preceding provisions of this section apply to Scotland with these modifications —

(a) in subsection (4)(b) omit the words from "if" to the end;
(b) omit subsection (4)(c).

108 Appeal against extradition order

(1) If the Secretary of State orders a person's extradition under this Part, the person may appeal to the High Court against the order.

(2) But subsection (1) does not apply if the person has consented to his extradition under section 127.

(3) An appeal under this section may be brought on a question of law or fact.

(4) Notice of an appeal under this section must be given in accordance with rules of court before the end of the permitted period, which is 14 days starting with the day on which the Secretary of State informs the person of the order under section 100(1).

109 Court's powers on appeal under section 108

(1) On an appeal under section 108 the High Court may —

(a) allow the appeal;
(b) dismiss the appeal.

(2) The court may allow the appeal only if the conditions in subsection (3) or the conditions in subsection (4) are satisfied.

(3) The conditions are that —

(a) the Secretary of State ought to have decided a question before him differently;
(b) if he had decided the question in the way he ought to have done, he would not have ordered the person's extradition.

(4) The conditions are that —

(a) an issue is raised that was not raised when the case was being considered by the Secretary of State or information is available that was not available at that time;

(b) the issue or information would have resulted in the Secretary of State deciding a question before him differently;
(c) if he had decided the question in that way, he would not have ordered the person's extradition.

(5) If the court allows the appeal it must—

(a) order the person's discharge;
(b) quash the order for his extradition.

110 Appeal against discharge by Secretary of State

(1) If the Secretary of State makes an order for a person's discharge under this Part, an appeal to the High Court may be brought on behalf of the category 2 territory against the relevant decision.

(2) But subsection (1) does not apply if the order for the person's discharge was under section 123.

(3) The relevant decision is the decision which resulted in the order for the person's discharge.

(4) An appeal under this section may be brought on a question of law or fact.

(5) Notice of an appeal under this section must be given in accordance with rules of court before the end of the permitted period, which is 14 days starting with the day on which (under section 100(4)) the Secretary of State informs a person acting on behalf of the category 2 territory of the order.

111 Court's powers on appeal under section 110

(1) On an appeal under section 110 the High Court may—

(a) allow the appeal;
(b) dismiss the appeal.

(2) The court may allow the appeal only if the conditions in subsection (3) or the conditions in subsection (4) are satisfied.

(3) The conditions are that—

(a) the Secretary of State ought to have decided a question before him differently;
(b) if he had decided the question in the way he ought to have done, he would have ordered the person's extradition.

(4) The conditions are that—

(a) an issue is raised that was not raised when the case was being considered by the Secretary of State or information is available that was not available at that time;
(b) the issue or information would have resulted in the Secretary of State deciding a question before him differently;
(c) if he had decided the question in that way, he would have ordered the person's extradition.

(5) If the court allows the appeal it must—

(a) quash the order discharging the person;
(b) order the person's extradition.

112 Detention pending conclusion of appeal under section 110

(1) This section applies if immediately after the Secretary of State orders the person's discharge under this Part the Secretary of State is informed on behalf of the category 2 territory of an intention to appeal under section 110.

(2) The judge must remand the person in custody or on bail while the appeal is pending.

(3) If the judge remands the person in custody he may later grant bail.

(4) An appeal under section 110 ceases to be pending at the earliest of these times —

(a) when the proceedings on the appeal are discontinued;
(b) when the High Court dismisses the appeal, if the court is not immediately informed on behalf of the category 2 territory of an intention to apply for leave to appeal to the House of Lords;
(c) at the end of the permitted period, which is 28 days starting with the day on which leave to appeal to the House of Lords against the decision of the High Court on the appeal is granted;
(d) when there is no further step that can be taken on behalf of the category 2 territory in relation to the appeal (ignoring any power of a court to grant leave to take a step out of time).

(5) The preceding provisions of this section apply to Scotland with these modifications —

(a) in subsection (4)(b) omit the words from "if" to the end;
(b) omit subsection (4)(c).

113 Appeal to High Court: time limit for start of hearing

(1) Rules of court must prescribe the period (the relevant period) within which the High Court must begin to hear an appeal under section 103, 105, 108 or 110.

(2) The High Court must begin to hear the appeal before the end of the relevant period.

(3) The High Court may extend the relevant period if it believes it to be in the interests of justice to do so; and this subsection may apply more than once.

(4) The power in subsection (3) may be exercised even after the end of the relevant period.

(5) If subsection (2) is not complied with and the appeal is under section 103 or 108 —

(a) the appeal must be taken to have been allowed by a decision of the High Court;
(b) the person whose extradition has been ordered must be taken to have been discharged by the High Court;
(c) the order for the person's extradition must be taken to have been quashed by the High Court.

(6) If subsection (2) is not complied with and the appeal is under section 105 or 110 the appeal must be taken to have been dismissed by a decision of the High Court.

114 Appeal to House of Lords

(1) An appeal lies to the House of Lords from a decision of the High Court on an appeal under section 103, 105, 108 or 110.

(2) An appeal under this section lies at the instance of —

(a) the person whose extradition is requested;
(b) a person acting on behalf of the category 2 territory.

(3) An appeal under this section lies only with the leave of the High Court or the House of Lords.

(4) Leave to appeal under this section must not be granted unless —

- (a) the High Court has certified that there is a point of law of general public importance involved in the decision, and
- (b) it appears to the court granting leave that the point is one which ought to be considered by the House of Lords.

(5) An application to the High Court for leave to appeal under this section must be made before the end of the permitted period, which is 14 days starting with the day on which the court makes its decision on the appeal to it.

(6) An application to the House of Lords for leave to appeal under this section must be made before the end of the permitted period, which is 14 days starting with the day on which the High Court refuses leave to appeal.

(7) If leave to appeal under this section is granted, the appeal must be brought before the end of the permitted period, which is 28 days starting with the day on which leave is granted.

(8) If subsection (7) is not complied with —

- (a) the appeal must be taken to have been brought;
- (b) the appeal must be taken to have been dismissed by the House of Lords immediately after the end of the period permitted under that subsection.

(9) These must be ignored for the purposes of subsection (8)(b) —

- (a) any power of a court to extend the period permitted for bringing the appeal;
- (b) any power of a court to grant leave to take a step out of time.

(10) The High Court may grant bail to a person appealing under this section or applying for leave to appeal under this section.

(11) Section 5 of the Appellate Jurisdiction Act 1876 (c. 59) (composition of House of Lords for hearing and determination of appeals) applies in relation to an appeal under this section or an application for leave to appeal under this section as it applies in relation to an appeal under that Act.

(12) An order of the House of Lords which provides for an application for leave to appeal under this section to be determined by a committee constituted in accordance with section 5 of the Appellate Jurisdiction Act 1876 may direct that the decision of the committee is taken on behalf of the House.

(13) The preceding provisions of this section do not apply to Scotland.

115 Powers of House of Lords on appeal under section 114

(1) On an appeal under section 114 the House of Lords may —

- (a) allow the appeal;
- (b) dismiss the appeal.

(2) Subsection (3) applies if —

- (a) the person whose extradition is requested brings an appeal under section 114, and
- (b) the House of Lords allows the appeal.

(3) The House of Lords must —

- (a) order the person's discharge;

(b) quash the order for his extradition, if the appeal was against a decision of the High Court to dismiss an appeal under section 103 or 108 or to allow an appeal under section 110.

(4) Subsection (5) applies if —

(a) the High Court allows an appeal under section 103 or 108 by the person whose extradition is requested or dismisses an appeal under section 110 by a person acting on behalf of the category 2 territory,
(b) a person acting on behalf of the category 2 territory brings an appeal under section 114 against the decision of the High Court, and
(c) the House of Lords allows the appeal.

(5) The House of Lords must —

(a) quash the order discharging the person made by the High Court under section 104(5) or 109(5) or by the Secretary of State under this Part;
(b) order the person to be extradited to the category 2 territory.

(6) Subsection (7) applies if —

(a) the High Court dismisses an appeal under section 105 against a decision made by the judge at the extradition hearing,
(b) a person acting on behalf of the category 2 territory brings an appeal under section 114 against the decision of the High Court, and
(c) the House of Lords allows the appeal.

(7) The House of Lords must —

(a) quash the order of the judge discharging the person whose extradition is requested;
(b) remit the case to the judge;
(c) direct him to proceed as he would have been required to do if he had decided the relevant question differently at the extradition hearing.

(8) A question is the relevant question if the judge's decision on it resulted in the order for the person's discharge.

116 Appeals: general

A decision under this Part of the judge or the Secretary of State may be questioned in legal proceedings only by means of an appeal under this Part.

Time for extradition

117 Extradition where no appeal

(1) This section applies if —

(a) the Secretary of State orders a person's extradition to a category 2 territory under this Part, and
(b) no notice of an appeal under section 103 or 108 is given before the end of the permitted period, which is 14 days starting with the day on which the Secretary of State informs the person under section 100(1) that he has ordered his extradition.

(2) The person must be extradited to the category 2 territory before the end of the required period, which is 28 days starting with the day on which the Secretary of State makes the order.

(3) If subsection (2) is not complied with and the person applies to the appropriate judge to be discharged the judge must order his discharge, unless reasonable cause is shown for the delay.

(4) These must be ignored for the purposes of subsection (1)(b) —

(a) any power of a court to extend the period permitted for giving notice of appeal;
(b) any power of a court to grant leave to take a step out of time.

118 Extradition following appeal

(1) This section applies if —

(a) there is an appeal to the High Court under section 103, 108 or 110 against a decision or order relating to a person's extradition to a category 2 territory, and
(b) the effect of the decision of the relevant court on the appeal is that the person is to be extradited there.

(2) The person must be extradited to the category 2 territory before the end of the required period, which is 28 days starting with —

(a) the day on which the decision of the relevant court on the appeal becomes final, or
(b) the day on which proceedings on the appeal are discontinued.

(3) The relevant court is —

(a) the High Court, if there is no appeal to the House of Lords against the decision of the High Court on the appeal;
(b) the House of Lords, if there is such an appeal.

(4) The decision of the High Court on the appeal becomes final —

(a) when the period permitted for applying to the High Court for leave to appeal to the House of Lords ends, if there is no such application;
(b) when the period permitted for applying to the House of Lords for leave to appeal to it ends, if the High Court refuses leave to appeal and there is no application to the House of Lords for leave to appeal;
(c) when the House of Lords refuses leave to appeal to it;
(d) at the end of the permitted period, which is 28 days starting with the day on which leave to appeal to the House of Lords is granted, if no such appeal is brought before the end of that period.

(5) These must be ignored for the purposes of subsection (4) —

(a) any power of a court to extend the period permitted for applying for leave to appeal;
(b) any power of a court to grant leave to take a step out of time.

(6) The decision of the House of Lords on the appeal becomes final when it is made.

(7) If subsection (2) is not complied with and the person applies to the appropriate judge to be discharged the judge must order his discharge, unless reasonable cause is shown for the delay.

(8) The preceding provisions of this section apply to Scotland with these modifications —

(a) in subsections (1) and (2) for "relevant court" substitute "High Court";
(b) omit subsections (3) to (6).

119 Undertaking in relation to person serving sentence in United Kingdom

(1) This section applies if —

(a) the Secretary of State orders a person's extradition to a category 2 territory under this Part;
(b) the person is serving a sentence of imprisonment or another form of detention in the United Kingdom.

(2) The Secretary of State may make the order for extradition subject to the condition that extradition is not to take place before he receives an undertaking given on behalf of the category 2 territory in terms specified by him.

(3) The terms which may be specified by the Secretary of State in relation to a person accused in a category 2 territory of the commission of an offence include terms —

(a) that the person be kept in custody until the conclusion of the proceedings against him for the offence and any other offence in respect of which he is permitted to be dealt with in the category 2 territory;
(b) that the person be returned to the United Kingdom to serve the remainder of his sentence on the conclusion of those proceedings.

(4) The terms which may be specified by the Secretary of State in relation to a person alleged to be unlawfully at large after conviction of an offence by a court in a category 2 territory include terms that the person be returned to the United Kingdom to serve the remainder of his sentence after serving any sentence imposed on him in the category 2 territory for —

(a) the offence, and
(b) any other offence in respect of which he is permitted to be dealt with in the category 2 territory.

(5) Subsections (6) and (7) apply if the Secretary of State makes an order for extradition subject to a condition under subsection (2).

(6) If the Secretary of State does not receive the undertaking before the end of the period of 21 days starting with the day on which he makes the order and the person applies to the High Court to be discharged, the court must order his discharge.

(7) If the Secretary of State receives the undertaking before the end of that period —

(a) in a case where section 117 applies, the required period for the purposes of section 117(2) is 28 days starting with the day on which the Secretary of State receives the undertaking;
(b) in a case where section 118 applies, the required period for the purposes of section 118(2) is 28 days starting with the day on which the decision of the relevant court on the appeal becomes final (within the meaning of that section) or (if later) the day on which the Secretary of State receives the undertaking.

120 Extradition following deferral for competing claim

(1) This section applies if —

(a) an order is made under this Part for a person to be extradited to a category 2 territory in pursuance of a request for his extradition;

(b) before the person is extradited to the territory an order is made under section 126(2) or 179(2) for the person's extradition in pursuance of the request to be deferred;
(c) the appropriate judge makes an order under section 181(2) for the person's extradition in pursuance of the request to cease to be deferred.

(2) In a case where section 117 applies, the required period for the purposes of section 117(2) is 28 days starting with the day on which the order under section 181(2) is made.

(3) In a case where section 118 applies, the required period for the purposes of section 118(2) is 28 days starting with the day on which the decision of the relevant court on the appeal becomes final (within the meaning of that section) or (if later) the day on which the order under section 181(2) is made.

121 Asylum claim

(1) This section applies if —

(a) a person whose extradition is requested makes an asylum claim at any time in the relevant period;
(b) an order is made under this Part for the person to be extradited in pursuance of the request.

(2) The relevant period is the period —

(a) starting when a certificate is issued under section 70 in respect of the request;
(b) ending when the person is extradited in pursuance of the request.

(3) The person must not be extradited in pursuance of the request before the asylum claim is finally determined; and sections 117 and 118 have effect subject to this.

(4) If the Secretary of State allows the asylum claim, the claim is finally determined when he makes his decision on the claim.

(5) If the Secretary of State rejects the asylum claim, the claim is finally determined —

(a) when the Secretary of State makes his decision on the claim, if there is no right to appeal against the Secretary of State's decision on the claim;
(b) when the period permitted for appealing against the Secretary of State's decision on the claim ends, if there is such a right but there is no such appeal;
(c) when the appeal against that decision is finally determined or is withdrawn or abandoned, if there is such an appeal.

(6) An appeal against the Secretary of State's decision on an asylum claim is not finally determined for the purposes of subsection (5) at any time when a further appeal or an application for leave to bring a further appeal —

(a) has been instituted and has not been finally determined or withdrawn or abandoned, or
(b) may be brought.

(7) The remittal of an appeal is not a final determination for the purposes of subsection (6).

(8) The possibility of an appeal out of time with leave must be ignored for the purposes of subsections (5) and (6).

Withdrawal of extradition request

122 Withdrawal of request before end of extradition hearing

(1) This section applies if at any time in the relevant period the appropriate judge is informed by the Secretary of State that a request for a person's extradition has been withdrawn.

(2) The relevant period is the period —

(a) starting when the person first appears or is brought before the appropriate judge following his arrest under this Part;
(b) ending when the judge orders the person's discharge or sends the case to the Secretary of State for his decision whether the person is to be extradited.

(3) The judge must order the person's discharge.

(4) If the person is not before the judge at the time the judge orders his discharge, the judge must inform him of the order as soon as practicable.

123 Withdrawal of request after case sent to Secretary of State

(1) This section applies if at any time in the relevant period the Secretary of State is informed that a request for a person's extradition has been withdrawn.

(2) The relevant period is the period —

(a) starting when the judge sends the case to the Secretary of State for his decision whether the person is to be extradited;
(b) ending when the person is extradited in pursuance of the request or discharged.

(3) The Secretary of State must order the person's discharge.

124 Withdrawal of request while appeal to High Court pending

(1) This section applies if at any time in the relevant period the High Court is informed by the Secretary of State that a request for a person's extradition has been withdrawn.

(2) The relevant period is the period —

(a) starting when notice of an appeal to the court is given by the person whose extradition is requested or by a person acting on behalf of the category 2 territory to which his extradition is requested;
(b) ending when proceedings on the appeal are discontinued or the court makes its decision on the appeal.

(3) If the appeal is under section 103 or 108, the court must —

(a) order the person's discharge;
(b) quash the order for his extradition, if the Secretary of State has ordered his extradition.

(4) If the appeal is under section 105 or 110, the court must dismiss the appeal.

(5) If the person is not before the court at the time the court orders his discharge, the court must inform him of the order as soon as practicable.

125 Withdrawal of request while appeal to House of Lords pending

(1) This section applies if at any time in the relevant period the House of Lords is informed by the Secretary of State that a request for a person's extradition has been withdrawn.

(2) The relevant period is the period —

(a) starting when leave to appeal to the House of Lords is granted to the person whose extradition is requested or a person acting on behalf of the category 2 territory to which his extradition is requested;
(b) ending when proceedings on the appeal are discontinued or the House of Lords makes its decision on the appeal.

(3) If the appeal is brought by the person whose extradition is requested the House of Lords must —

(a) order the person's discharge;
(b) quash the order for his extradition, in a case where the appeal was against a decision of the High Court to dismiss an appeal under section 103 or 108.

(4) If the appeal is brought by a person acting on behalf of the category 2 territory the House of Lords must dismiss the appeal.

(5) If the person whose extradition is requested is not before the House of Lords at the time it orders his discharge, the House of Lords must inform him of the order as soon as practicable.

Competing extradition requests

126 Competing extradition requests

(1) This section applies if —

(a) the Secretary of State receives a valid request for a person's extradition to a category 2 territory;
(b) the person is in the United Kingdom;
(c) before the person is extradited in pursuance of the request or discharged, the Secretary of State receives another valid request for the person's extradition.

(2) The Secretary of State may —

(a) order proceedings (or further proceedings) on one of the requests to be deferred until the other one has been disposed of, if neither of the requests has been disposed of;
(b) order the person's extradition in pursuance of the request under consideration to be deferred until the other request has been disposed of, if an order for his extradition in pursuance of the request under consideration has been made.

(3) In applying subsection (2) the Secretary of State must take account in particular of these matters —

(a) the relative seriousness of the offences concerned;
(b) the place where each offence was committed (or was alleged to have been committed);
(c) the date when each request was received;
(d) whether, in the case of each offence, the person is accused of its commission (but not alleged to have been convicted) or is alleged to be unlawfully at large after conviction.

Consent to extradition

127 Consent to extradition: general

(1) A person arrested under a warrant issued under section 71 may consent to his extradition to the category 2 territory to which his extradition is requested.

(2) A person arrested under a provisional warrant may consent to his extradition to the category 2 territory in which he is accused of the commission of an offence or is alleged to have been convicted of an offence.

(3) Consent under this section —

(a) must be given in writing;
(b) is irrevocable.

(4) Consent under this section which is given by a person before his case is sent to the Secretary of State for the Secretary of State's decision whether he is to be extradited must be given before the appropriate judge.

(5) Consent under this section which is given in any other case must be given to the Secretary of State.

(6) A person may not give his consent under this section before the appropriate judge unless —

(a) he is legally represented before the appropriate judge at the time he gives consent, or
(b) he is a person to whom subsection (7) applies.

(7) This subsection applies to a person if —

(a) he has been informed of his right to apply for legal aid and has had the opportunity to apply for legal aid, but he has refused or failed to apply;
(b) he has applied for legal aid but his application has been refused;
(c) he was granted legal aid but the legal aid was withdrawn.

(8) In subsection (7) "legal aid" means —

(a) in England and Wales, a right to representation funded by the Legal Services Commission as part of the Criminal Defence Service;
(b) in Scotland, such legal aid as is available by virtue of section 183(a) of this Act;
(c) in Northern Ireland, such free legal aid as is available by virtue of sections 184 and 185 of this Act.

(9) For the purposes of subsection (6) a person is to be treated as legally represented before the appropriate judge if (and only if) he has the assistance of counsel or a solicitor to represent him in the proceedings before the appropriate judge.

128 Consent to extradition before case sent to Secretary of State

(1) This section applies if a person gives his consent under section 127 to the appropriate judge.

(2) If the judge has not fixed a date under section 75 or 76 on which the extradition hearing is to begin he is not required to do so.

(3) If the extradition hearing has begun the judge is no longer required to proceed or continue proceeding under sections 78 to 91.

(4) The judge must send the case to the Secretary of State for his decision whether the person is to be extradited.

(5) The person must be taken to have waived any right he would have (apart from the consent) not to be dealt with in the category 2 territory for an offence committed before his extradition.

Post-extradition matters

129 Consent to other offence being dealt with

(1) This section applies if —

(a) a person is extradited to a category 2 territory in accordance with this Part;
(b) the Secretary of State receives a valid request for his consent to the person being dealt with in the territory for an offence other than the offence in respect of which he was extradited.

(2) A request for consent is valid if it is made by an authority which is an authority of the territory and which the Secretary of State believes has the function of making requests for the consent referred to in subsection (1)(b) in that territory.

(3) The Secretary of State must serve notice on the person that he has received the request for consent, unless he is satisfied that it would not be practicable to do so.

(4) The Secretary of State must decide whether the offence is an extradition offence.

(5) If the Secretary of State decides the question in subsection (4) in the negative he must refuse his consent.

(6) If the Secretary of State decides that question in the affirmative he must decide whether the appropriate judge would send the case to him (for his decision whether the person was to be extradited) under sections 79 to 91 if —

(a) the person were in the United Kingdom, and
(b) the judge were required to proceed under section 79 in respect of the offence for which the Secretary of State's consent is requested.

(7) If the Secretary of State decides the question in subsection (6) in the negative he must refuse his consent.

(8) If the Secretary of State decides that question in the affirmative he must decide whether, if the person were in the United Kingdom, his extradition in respect of the offence would be prohibited under section 94, 95 or 96.

(9) If the Secretary of State decides the question in subsection (8) in the affirmative he must refuse his consent.

(10) If the Secretary of State decides that question in the negative he may give his consent.

130 Consent to further extradition to category 2 territory

(1) This section applies if —

(a) a person is extradited to a category 2 territory (the requesting territory) in accordance with this Part;
(b) the Secretary of State receives a valid request for his consent to the person's extradition to another category 2 territory for an offence other than the offence in respect of which he was extradited.

(2) A request for consent is valid if it is made by an authority which is an authority of the requesting territory and which the Secretary of State believes has the function of making requests for the consent referred to in subsection (1)(b) in that territory.

(3) The Secretary of State must serve notice on the person that he has received the request for consent, unless he is satisfied that it would not be practicable to do so.

(4) The Secretary of State must decide whether the offence is an extradition offence in relation to the category 2 territory referred to in subsection (1)(b).

(5) If the Secretary of State decides the question in subsection (4) in the negative he must refuse his consent.

(6) If the Secretary of State decides that question in the affirmative he must decide whether the appropriate judge would send the case to him (for his decision whether the person was to be extradited) under sections 79 to 91 if—

(a) the person were in the United Kingdom, and
(b) the judge were required to proceed under section 79 in respect of the offence for which the Secretary of State's consent is requested.

(7) If the Secretary of State decides the question in subsection (6) in the negative he must refuse his consent.

(8) If the Secretary of State decides that question in the affirmative he must decide whether, if the person were in the United Kingdom, his extradition in respect of the offence would be prohibited under section 94, 95 or 96.

(9) If the Secretary of State decides the question in subsection (8) in the affirmative he must refuse his consent.

(10) If the Secretary of State decides that question in the negative he may give his consent.

131 Consent to further extradition to category 1 territory

(1) This section applies if—

(a) a person is extradited to a category 2 territory (the requesting territory) in accordance with this Part;
(b) the Secretary of State receives a valid request for his consent to the person's extradition to a category 1 territory for an offence other than the offence in respect of which he was extradited.

(2) A request for consent is valid if it is made by an authority which is an authority of the requesting territory and which the Secretary of State believes has the function of making requests for the consent referred to in subsection (1)(b) in that territory.

(3) The Secretary of State must serve notice on the person that he has received the request for consent, unless he is satisfied that it would not be practicable to do so.

(4) The Secretary of State must decide whether the offence is an extradition offence within the meaning given by section 64 in relation to the category 1 territory.

(5) If the Secretary of State decides the question in subsection (4) in the negative he must refuse his consent.

(6) If the Secretary of State decides that question in the affirmative he must decide whether the appropriate judge would order the person's extradition under sections 11 to 25 if—

(a) the person were in the United Kingdom, and
(b) the judge were required to proceed under section 11 in respect of the offence for which the Secretary of State's consent is requested.

(7) If the Secretary of State decides the question in subsection (6) in the affirmative he must give his consent.

(8) If the Secretary of State decides that question in the negative he must refuse his consent.

132 Return of person to serve remainder of sentence

(1) This section applies if —

(a) a person who is serving a sentence of imprisonment or another form of detention in the United Kingdom is extradited to a category 2 territory in accordance with this Part;
(b) the person is returned to the United Kingdom to serve the remainder of his sentence.

(2) The person is liable to be detained in pursuance of his sentence.
(3) If he is at large he must be treated as being unlawfully at large.
(4) Time during which the person was not in the United Kingdom as a result of his extradition does not count as time served by him as part of his sentence.
(5) But subsection (4) does not apply if —

(a) the person was extradited for the purpose of being prosecuted for an offence, and
(b) the person has not been convicted of the offence or of any other offence in respect of which he was permitted to be dealt with in the category 2 territory.

(6) In a case falling within subsection (5), time during which the person was not in the United Kingdom as a result of his extradition counts as time served by him as part of his sentence if (and only if) it was spent in custody in connection with the offence or any other offence in respect of which he was permitted to be dealt with in the territory.

Costs

133 Costs where extradition ordered

(1) This section applies if any of the following occurs in relation to a person whose extradition is requested under this Part —

(a) an order for the person's extradition is made under this Part;
(b) the High Court dismisses an appeal under section 103 or 108;
(c) the High Court or the House of Lords dismisses an application for leave to appeal to the House of Lords under section 114, if the application is made by the person;
(d) the House of Lords dismisses an appeal under section 114, if the appeal is brought by the person.

(2) In a case falling within subsection (1)(a), the appropriate judge may make such order as he considers just and reasonable with regard to the costs to be paid by the person.
(3) In a case falling within subsection (1)(b) by virtue of section 104(7), the judge who decides the question that is (or all the questions that are) the subject of a direction under section 104(1)(b) may make such order as he considers just and reasonable with regard to the costs to be paid by the person.
(4) In any other case falling within subsection (1)(b), the High Court may make such order as it considers just and reasonable with regard to the costs to be paid by the person.
(5) In a case falling within subsection (1)(c) or (d), the court by which the application or appeal is dismissed may make such order as it considers just and reasonable with regard to the costs to be paid by the person.

(6) An order for costs under this section —

(a) must specify their amount;
(b) may name the person to whom they are to be paid.

134 Costs where discharge ordered

(1) This section applies if any of the following occurs in relation to a person whose extradition to a category 2 territory is requested under this Part —

(a) an order for the person's discharge is made under this Part;
(b) the person is taken to be discharged under this Part;
(c) the High Court dismisses an appeal under section 105 or 110;
(d) the High Court or the House of Lords dismisses an application for leave to appeal to the House of Lords under section 114, if the application is made on behalf of the category 2 territory;
(e) the House of Lords dismisses an appeal under section 114, if the appeal is brought on behalf of the category 2 territory.

(2) In a case falling within subsection (1)(a), an order under subsection (5) in favour of the person may be made by —

(a) the appropriate judge, if the order for the person's discharge is made by him or by the Secretary of State;
(b) the High Court, if the order for the person's discharge is made by it;
(c) the House of Lords, if the order for the person's discharge is made by it.

(3) In a case falling within subsection (1)(b), the appropriate judge may make an order under subsection (5) in favour of the person.

(4) In a case falling within subsection (1)(c), (d) or (e), the court by which the application or appeal is dismissed may make an order under subsection (5) in favour of the person.

(5) An order under this subsection in favour of a person is an order for a payment of the appropriate amount to be made to the person out of money provided by Parliament.

(6) The appropriate amount is such amount as the judge or court making the order under subsection (5) considers reasonably sufficient to compensate the person in whose favour the order is made for any expenses properly incurred by him in the proceedings under this Part.

(7) But if the judge or court making an order under subsection (5) is of the opinion that there are circumstances which make it inappropriate that the person in whose favour the order is made should recover the full amount mentioned in subsection (6), the judge or court must —

(a) assess what amount would in his or its opinion be just and reasonable;
(b) specify that amount in the order as the appropriate amount.

(8) Unless subsection (7) applies, the appropriate amount —

(a) must be specified in the order, if the court considers it appropriate for it to be so specified and the person in whose favour the order is made agrees the amount;
(b) must be determined in accordance with regulations made by the Lord Chancellor for the purposes of this section, in any other case.

135 Costs where discharge ordered: supplementary

(1) In England and Wales, subsections (1) and (3) of section 20 of the Prosecution of Offences Act 1985 (c. 23) (regulations for carrying Part 2 of that Act into effect) apply in relation to section 134 as those subsections apply in relation to Part 2 of that Act.

(2) As so applied those subsections have effect as if an order under section 134(5) were an order under Part 2 of that Act for a payment to be made out of central funds.

(3) In Northern Ireland, section 7 of the Costs in Criminal Cases Act (Northern Ireland) 1968 (c.10) (rules relating to costs) applies in relation to section 134 as that section applies in relation to sections 2 to 5 of that Act.

Repatriation cases

136 Persons serving sentences outside territory where convicted

(1) This section applies if —

(a) a request is made for a person's extradition to a category 2 territory and the request contains the statement referred to in subsection (2), or
(b) a provisional warrant for a person's arrest is sought on behalf of a category 2 territory and the information laid before the justice contains the statement referred to in subsection (2).

(2) The statement is one that the person —

(a) is alleged to be unlawfully at large from a prison in one territory (the imprisoning territory) in which he was serving a sentence after conviction of an offence specified in the request by a court in another territory (the convicting territory), and
(b) was serving the sentence in pursuance of international arrangements for prisoners sentenced in one territory to be repatriated to another territory in order to serve their sentence.

(3) If the category 2 territory is either the imprisoning territory or the convicting territory —

(a) section 70(3) has effect as if the reference to the statement referred to in subsection (4) of that section were a reference to the statement referred to in subsection (2) of this section;
(b) section 73(1) has effect as if the reference to a person within subsection (2) of that section were a reference to the person referred to in subsection (1)(b) of this section.

(4) If the category 2 territory is the imprisoning territory —

(a) sections 71(2)(a), 73(3)(a) and 78(4)(b) have effect as if "an extradition offence" read "an extradition offence in relation to the convicting territory";
(b) sections 74(8)(a) and 127(2) have effect as if "the category 2 territory in which he is accused of the commission of an offence or is alleged to have been convicted of an offence" read "the imprisoning territory";
(c) section 74(11)(b) has effect as if "the category 2 territory" read "the imprisoning territory";
(d) section 78(2)(e) has effect as if "the category 2 territory" read "the convicting territory";
(e) section 85(5) has effect as if after "entitled" there were inserted "in the convicting territory";
(f) section 119(4) has effect as if "a category 2 territory" read "the convicting territory" and as if "the category 2 territory" in both places read "the convicting territory";

(g) section 138(1) has effect as if "a category 2 territory" read "the convicting territory";
(h) in section 138, subsections (2), (3), (4), (5) and (7) have effect as if "the category 2 territory" read "the convicting territory".

(5) Subsection (1)(b) applies to Scotland with the substitution of "application by the procurator fiscal sets out the matters referred to in paragraphs (a) and (b) of subsection (2)" for "information laid by the justice contains the statement referred to in subsection (2)".

(6) Subsection (1)(b) applies to Northern Ireland with the substitution of "the complaint made to" for "the information laid before".

Interpretation

137 Extradition offences: person not sentenced for offence

(1) This section applies in relation to conduct of a person if—

(a) he is accused in a category 2 territory of the commission of an offence constituted by the conduct, or
(b) he is alleged to be unlawfully at large after conviction by a court in a category 2 territory of an offence constituted by the conduct and he has not been sentenced for the offence.

(2) The conduct constitutes an extradition offence in relation to the category 2 territory if these conditions are satisfied—

(a) the conduct occurs in the category 2 territory;
(b) the conduct would constitute an offence under the law of the relevant part of the United Kingdom punishable with imprisonment or another form of detention for a term of 12 months or a greater punishment if it occurred in that part of the United Kingdom;
(c) the conduct is so punishable under the law of the category 2 territory (however it is described in that law).

(3) The conduct also constitutes an extradition offence in relation to the category 2 territory if these conditions are satisfied—

(a) the conduct occurs outside the category 2 territory;
(b) the conduct is punishable under the law of the category 2 territory with imprisonment or another form of detention for a term of 12 months or a greater punishment (however it is described in that law);
(c) in corresponding circumstances equivalent conduct would constitute an extra-territorial offence under the law of the relevant part of the United Kingdom punishable with imprisonment or another form of detention for a term of 12 months or a greater punishment.

(4) The conduct also constitutes an extradition offence in relation to the category 2 territory if these conditions are satisfied—

(a) the conduct occurs outside the category 2 territory and no part of it occurs in the United Kingdom;
(b) the conduct would constitute an offence under the law of the relevant part of the United Kingdom punishable with imprisonment or another form of detention for a

term of 12 months or a greater punishment if it occurred in that part of the United Kingdom;

(c) the conduct is so punishable under the law of the category 2 territory (however it is described in that law).

(5) The conduct also constitutes an extradition offence in relation to the category 2 territory if these conditions are satisfied—

(a) the conduct occurs outside the category 2 territory and no part of it occurs in the United Kingdom;

(b) the conduct is punishable under the law of the category 2 territory with imprisonment for a term of 12 months or another form of detention or a greater punishment (however it is described in that law);

(c) the conduct constitutes or if committed in the United Kingdom would constitute an offence mentioned in subsection (6).

(6) The offences are—

(a) an offence under section 51 or 58 of the International Criminal Court Act 2001 (c. 17) (genocide, crimes against humanity and war crimes);

(b) an offence under section 52 or 59 of that Act (conduct ancillary to genocide etc. committed outside the jurisdiction);

(c) an ancillary offence, as defined in section 55 or 62 of that Act, in relation to an offence falling within paragraph (a) or (b);

(d) an offence under section 1 of the International Criminal Court (Scotland) Act 2001 (asp 13) (genocide, crimes against humanity and war crimes);

(e) an offence under section 2 of that Act (conduct ancillary to genocide etc. committed outside the jurisdiction);

(f) an ancillary offence, as defined in section 7 of that Act, in relation to an offence falling within paragraph (d) or (e).

(7) If the conduct constitutes an offence under the military law of the category 2 territory but does not constitute an offence under the general criminal law of the relevant part of the United Kingdom it does not constitute an extradition offence; and subsections (1) to (6) have effect subject to this.

(8) The relevant part of the United Kingdom is the part of the United Kingdom in which—

(a) the extradition hearing took place, if the question of whether conduct constitutes an extradition offence is to be decided by the Secretary of State;

(b) proceedings in which it is necessary to decide that question are taking place, in any other case.

(9) Subsections (1) to (7) apply for the purposes of this Part.

138 Extradition offences: person sentenced for offence

(1) This section applies in relation to conduct of a person if—

(a) he is alleged to be unlawfully at large after conviction by a court in a category 2 territory of an offence constituted by the conduct, and

(b) he has been sentenced for the offence.

(2) The conduct constitutes an extradition offence in relation to the category 2 territory if these conditions are satisfied —

(a) the conduct occurs in the category 2 territory;
(b) the conduct would constitute an offence under the law of the relevant part of the United Kingdom punishable with imprisonment or another form of detention for a term of 12 months or a greater punishment if it occurred in that part of the United Kingdom;
(c) a sentence of imprisonment or another form of detention for a term of 4 months or a greater punishment has been imposed in the category 2 territory in respect of the conduct.

(3) The conduct also constitutes an extradition offence in relation to the category 2 territory if these conditions are satisfied —

(a) the conduct occurs outside the category 2 territory;
(b) a sentence of imprisonment or another form of detention for a term of 4 months or a greater punishment has been imposed in the category 2 territory in respect of the conduct;
(c) in corresponding circumstances equivalent conduct would constitute an extra-territorial offence under the law of the relevant part of the United Kingdom punishable with imprisonment or another form of detention for a term of 12 months or a greater punishment.

(4) The conduct also constitutes an extradition offence in relation to the category 2 territory if these conditions are satisfied —

(a) the conduct occurs outside the category 2 territory and no part of it occurs in the United Kingdom;
(b) the conduct would constitute an offence under the law of the relevant part of the United Kingdom punishable with imprisonment or another form of detention for a term of 12 months or a greater punishment if it occurred in that part of the United Kingdom;
(c) a sentence of imprisonment or another form of detention for a term of 4 months or a greater punishment has been imposed in the category 2 territory in respect of the conduct.

(5) The conduct also constitutes an extradition offence in relation to the category 2 territory if these conditions are satisfied —

(a) the conduct occurs outside the category 2 territory and no part of it occurs in the United Kingdom;
(b) a sentence of imprisonment or another form of detention for a term of 4 months or a greater punishment has been imposed in the category 2 territory in respect of the conduct;
(c) the conduct constitutes or if committed in the United Kingdom would constitute an offence mentioned in subsection (6).

(6) The offences are —

(a) an offence under section 51 or 58 of the International Criminal Court Act 2001 (c. 17) (genocide, crimes against humanity and war crimes);
(b) an offence under section 52 or 59 of that Act (conduct ancillary to genocide etc. committed outside the jurisdiction);

(c) an ancillary offence, as defined in section 55 or 62 of that Act, in relation to an offence falling within paragraph (a) or (b);
(d) an offence under section 1 of the International Criminal Court (Scotland) Act 2001 (asp 13) (genocide, crimes against humanity and war crimes);
(e) an offence under section 2 of that Act (conduct ancillary to genocide etc. committed outside the jurisdiction);
(f) an ancillary offence, as defined in section 7 of that Act, in relation to an offence falling within paragraph (d) or (e).

(7) If the conduct constitutes an offence under the military law of the category 2 territory but does not constitute an offence under the general criminal law of the relevant part of the United Kingdom it does not constitute an extradition offence; and subsections (1) to (6) have effect subject to this.

(8) The relevant part of the United Kingdom is the part of the United Kingdom in which —

(a) the extradition hearing took place, if the question of whether conduct constitutes an extradition offence is to be decided by the Secretary of State;
(b) proceedings in which it is necessary to decide that question are taking place, in any other case.

(9) Subsections (1) to (7) apply for the purposes of this Part.

139 The appropriate judge

(1) The appropriate judge is —

(a) in England and Wales, a District Judge (Magistrates' Courts) designated for the purposes of this Part by the Lord Chancellor;
(b) in Scotland, the sheriff of Lothian and Borders;
(c) in Northern Ireland, such county court judge or resident magistrate as is designated for the purposes of this Part by the Lord Chancellor.

(2) A designation under subsection (1) may be made for all cases or for such cases (or cases of such description) as the designation stipulates.

(3) More than one designation may be made under subsection (1).

(4) This section applies for the purposes of this Part.

140 The extradition hearing

(1) The extradition hearing is the hearing at which the appropriate judge is to deal with a request for extradition to a category 2 territory.

(2) This section applies for the purposes of this Part.

141 Scotland: references to Secretary of State

(1) This Part applies in relation to any function which falls under this Part to be exercised in relation to scotland only as if references in this Part to the Secretary of State were to the Scottish Ministers.

(2) Subsection (1) does not apply to the references to the Secretary of State in sections 83(3), 101(5) and 121.

PART 3

EXTRADITION TO THE UNITED KINGDOM

Extradition from category 1 territories

142 Issue of Part 3 warrant

(1) The appropriate judge may issue a Part 3 warrant in respect of a person if —

(a) a constable or an appropriate person applies to the judge for a Part 3 warrant, and
(b) the condition in subsection (2) is satisfied.

(2) The condition is that a domestic warrant has been issued in respect of the person and there are reasonable grounds for believing —

(a) that the person has committed an extradition offence, or
(b) that the person is unlawfully at large after conviction of an extradition offence by a court in the United Kingdom.

(3) A Part 3 warrant is an arrest warrant which contains —

(a) the statement referred to in subsection (4) or the statement referred to in subsection (5), and
(b) the certificate referred to in subsection (6).

(4) The statement is one that —

(a) the person in respect of whom the warrant is issued is accused in the United Kingdom of the commission of an extradition offence specified in the warrant, and
(b) the warrant is issued with a view to his arrest and extradition to the United Kingdom for the purpose of being prosecuted for the offence.

(5) The statement is one that —

(a) the person in respect of whom the warrant is issued is alleged to be unlawfully at large after conviction of an extradition offence specified in the warrant by a court in the United Kingdom, and
(b) the warrant is issued with a view to his arrest and extradition to the United Kingdom for the purpose of being sentenced for the offence or of serving a sentence of imprisonment or another form of detention imposed in respect of the offence.

(6) The certificate is one certifying —

(a) whether the conduct constituting the extradition offence specified in the warrant falls within the European framework list;
(b) whether the offence is an extra-territorial offence;
(c) what is the maximum punishment that may be imposed on conviction of the offence or (if the person has been sentenced for the offence) what sentence has been imposed.

(7) The conduct which falls within the European framework list must be taken for the purposes of subsection (6)(a) to include conduct which constitutes —

(a) an attempt, conspiracy or incitement to carry out conduct falling within the list, or
(b) aiding, abetting, counselling or procuring the carrying out of conduct falling within the list.

(8) A domestic warrant is a warrant for the arrest or apprehension of a person which is issued under any of these —

(a) section 72 of the Criminal Justice Act 1967 (c.80);
(b) section 7 of the Bail Act 1976 (c.63);
(c) section 51 of the Judicature (Northern Ireland) Act 1978 (c. 23);
(d) section 1 of the Magistrates' Courts Act 1980 (c. 43);
(e) Article 20 or 25 of the Magistrates' Courts (Northern Ireland) Order 1981 (S.I. 1981/1675 (N.I. 26));
(f) the Criminal Procedure (Scotland) Act 1995 (c. 46).

(9) An appropriate person is a person of a description specified in an order made by the Secretary of State for the purposes of this section.

(10) Subsection (1)(a) applies to Scotland with the substitution of "a procurator fiscal" for "a constable or an appropriate person".

143 Undertaking in relation to person serving sentence

(1) This section applies if —

(a) a Part 3 warrant is issued in respect of a person;
(b) the person is serving a sentence of imprisonment or another form of detention in a category 1 territory;
(c) the person's extradition to the United Kingdom from the category 1 territory in pursuance of the warrant is made subject to a condition that an undertaking is given on behalf of the United Kingdom with regard to his treatment in the United Kingdom or his return to the category 1 territory (or both).

(2) The Secretary of State may give an undertaking to a person acting on behalf of the category 1 territory with regard to either or both of these things —

(a) the treatment in the United Kingdom of the person in respect of whom the warrant is issued;
(b) the return of that person to the category 1 territory.

(3) The terms which may be included by the Secretary of State in an undertaking given under subsection (2) in relation to a person accused in the United Kingdom of the commission of an offence include terms —

(a) that the person be kept in custody until the conclusion of the proceedings against him for the offence and any other offence in respect of which he is permitted to be dealt with in the United Kingdom;
(b) that the person be returned to the category 1 territory to serve the remainder of his sentence on the conclusion of those proceedings.

(4) The terms which may be included by the Secretary of State in an undertaking given under subsection (2) in relation to a person alleged to be unlawfully at large after conviction

of an offence by a court in the United Kingdom include terms that the person be returned to the category 1 territory to serve the remainder of his sentence after serving any sentence imposed on him in the United Kingdom.

(5) If the Part 3 warrant was issued by a sheriff, the preceding provisions of this section apply as if the references to the Secretary of State were to the Scottish Ministers.

144 Return to extraditing territory to serve sentence

(1) This section applies if —

(a) a Part 3 warrant is issued in respect of a person;
(b) the warrant states that it is issued with a view to his extradition to the United Kingdom for the purpose of being prosecuted for an offence;
(c) he is extradited to the United Kingdom from a category 1 territory in pursuance of the warrant;
(d) he is extradited on the condition that, if he is convicted of the offence and a sentence of imprisonment or another form of detention is imposed in respect of it, he must be returned to the category 1 territory to serve the sentence;
(e) he is convicted of the offence and a sentence of imprisonment or another form of detention is imposed in respect of it.

(2) The person must be returned to the category 1 territory to serve the sentence as soon as is reasonably practicable after the sentence is imposed.

(3) If subsection (2) is complied with the punishment for the offence must be treated as remitted but the person's conviction for the offence must be treated as a conviction for all other purposes.

(4) If subsection (2) is not complied with and the person applies to the appropriate judge to be discharged the judge must order his discharge, unless reasonable cause is shown for the delay.

145 Service of sentence in territory executing Part 3 warrant

(1) This section applies if —

(a) a Part 3 warrant is issued in respect of a person;
(b) the certificate contained in the warrant certifies that a sentence has been imposed;
(c) an undertaking is given on behalf of a category 1 territory that the person will be required to serve the sentence in the territory;
(d) on the basis of the undertaking the person is not extradited to the United Kingdom from the category 1 territory.

(2) The punishment for the offence must be treated as remitted but the person's conviction for the offence must be treated as a conviction for all other purposes.

146 Dealing with person for other offences

(1) This section applies if a person is extradited to the United Kingdom from a category 1 territory in pursuance of a Part 3 warrant.

(2) The person may be dealt with in the United Kingdom for an offence committed before his extradition only if —

(a) the offence is one falling within subsection (3), or
(b) the condition in subsection (4) is satisfied.

(3) The offences are —

(a) the offence in respect of which the person is extradited;
(b) an offence disclosed by the information provided to the category 1 territory in respect of that offence;
(c) an extradition offence in respect of which consent to the person being dealt with is given on behalf of the territory;
(d) an offence which is not punishable with imprisonment or another form of detention;
(e) an offence in respect of which the person will not be detained in connection with his trial, sentence or appeal;
(f) an offence in respect of which the person waives the right that he would have (but for this paragraph) not to be dealt with for the offence.

(4) The condition is that the person has been given an opportunity to leave the United Kingdom and —

(a) he has not done so before the end of the permitted period, or
(b) he has done so before the end of the permitted period and has returned to the United Kingdom.

(5) The permitted period is 45 days starting with the day on which the person arrives in the United Kingdom.

147 Effect of consent to extradition to the United Kingdom

(1) This section applies if —

(a) a person is extradited to the United Kingdom from a category 1 territory in pursuance of a Part 3 warrant;
(b) the person consented to his extradition to the United Kingdom in accordance with the law of the category 1 territory.

(2) Section 146(2) does not apply if the conditions in subsection (3) or the conditions in subsection (4) are satisfied.

(3) The conditions are that —

(a) under the law of the category 1 territory, the effect of the person's consent is to waive his right under section 146(2);
(b) the person has not revoked his consent in accordance with that law, if he is permitted to do so under that law.

(4) The conditions are that —

(a) under the law of the category 1 territory, the effect of the person's consent is not to waive his right under section 146(2);
(b) the person has expressly waived his right under section 146(2) in accordance with that law;
(c) the person has not revoked his consent in accordance with that law, if he is permitted to do so under that law;
(d) the person has not revoked the waiver of his right under section 146(2) in accordance with that law, if he is permitted to do so under that law.

148 Extradition offences

(1) Conduct constitutes an extradition offence in relation to the United Kingdom if these conditions are satisfied —

(a) the conduct occurs in the United Kingdom;
(b) the conduct is punishable under the law of the relevant part of the United Kingdom with imprisonment or another form of detention for a term of 12 months or a greater punishment.

(2) Conduct also constitutes an extradition offence in relation to the United Kingdom if these conditions are satisfied —

(a) the conduct occurs outside the United Kingdom;
(b) the conduct constitutes an extra-territorial offence punishable under the law of the relevant part of the United Kingdom with imprisonment or another form of detention for a term of 12 months or a greater punishment.

(3) But subsections (1) and (2) do not apply in relation to conduct of a person if —

(a) he is alleged to be unlawfully at large after conviction by a court in the United Kingdom of the offence constituted by the conduct, and
(b) he has been sentenced for the offence.

(4) Conduct also constitutes an extradition offence in relation to the United Kingdom if these conditions are satisfied —

(a) the conduct occurs in the United Kingdom;
(b) a sentence of imprisonment or another form of detention for a term of 4 months or a greater punishment has been imposed in the United Kingdom in respect of the conduct.

(5) Conduct also constitutes an extradition offence in relation to the United Kingdom if these conditions are satisfied —

(a) the conduct occurs outside the United Kingdom;
(b) the conduct constitutes an extra-territorial offence;
(c) a sentence of imprisonment or another form of detention for a term of 4 months or a greater punishment has been imposed in the United Kingdom in respect of the conduct.

(6) The relevant part of the United Kingdom is the part of the United Kingdom in which the relevant proceedings are taking place.
(7) The relevant proceedings are the proceedings in which it is necessary to decide whether conduct constitutes an extradition offence.
(8) Subsections (1) to (5) apply for the purposes of sections 142 to 147.

149 The appropriate judge

(1) The appropriate judge is —

(a) in England and Wales, a District Judge (Magistrates' Courts), a justice of the peace or a judge entitled to exercise the jurisdiction of the Crown Court;

(b) in Scotland, a sheriff;
(c) in Northern Ireland, a justice of the peace, a resident magistrate or a Crown Court judge.

(2) This section applies for the purposes of sections 142 to 147.

Extradition from category 2 territories

150 Dealing with person for other offences: Commonwealth countries etc.

(1) This section applies if —

(a) a person is extradited to the United Kingdom from a category 2 territory under law of the territory corresponding to Part 2 of this Act, and
(b) the territory is a Commonwealth country, a British overseas territory or the Hong Kong Special Administrative Region of the People's Republic of China.

(2) The person may be dealt with in the United Kingdom for an offence committed before his extradition only if —

(a) the offence is one falling within subsection (3), or
(b) the condition in subsection (6) is satisfied.

(3) The offences are —

(a) the offence in respect of which the person is extradited;
(b) a lesser offence disclosed by the information provided to the category 2 territory in respect of that offence;
(c) an offence in respect of which consent to the person being dealt with is given by or on behalf of the relevant authority.

(4) An offence is a lesser offence in relation to another offence if the maximum punishment for it is less severe than the maximum punishment for the other offence.

(5) The relevant authority is —

(a) if the person has been extradited from a Commonwealth country, the government of the country;
(b) if the person has been extradited from a British overseas territory, the person administering the territory;
(c) if the person has been extradited from the Hong Kong Special Administrative Region of the People's Republic of China, the government of the Region.

(6) The condition is that the protected period has ended.

(7) The protected period is 45 days starting with the first day after his extradition to the United Kingdom on which the person is given an opportunity to leave the United Kingdom.

(8) A person is dealt with in the United Kingdom for an offence if —

(a) he is tried there for it;
(b) he is detained with a view to trial there for it.

151 Dealing with person for other offences: other category 2 territories

(1) This section applies if —

(a) a person is extradited to the United Kingdom from a category 2 territory under law of the territory corresponding to Part 2 of this Act, and
(b) the territory is not one falling within section 150(1)(b).

(2) The person may be dealt with in the United Kingdom for an offence committed before his extradition only if —

(a) the offence is one falling within subsection (3), or
(b) the condition in subsection (4) is satisfied.

(3) The offences are —

(a) the offence in respect of which the person is extradited;
(b) an offence disclosed by the information provided to the category 2 territory in respect of that offence;
(c) an offence in respect of which consent to the person being dealt with is given on behalf of the territory.

(4) The condition is that —

(a) the person has returned to the territory from which he was extradited, or
(b) the person has been given an opportunity to leave the United Kingdom.

(5) A person is dealt with in the United Kingdom for an offence if —

(a) he is tried there for it;
(b) he is detained with a view to trial there for it.

General

152 Remission of punishment for other offences

(1) This section applies if —

(a) a person is extradited to the United Kingdom from —
    (i) a category 1 territory under law of the territory corresponding to Part 1 of this Act, or
    (ii) a category 2 territory under law of the territory corresponding to Part 2 of this Act;
(b) before his extradition he has been convicted of an offence in the United Kingdom;
(c) he has not been extradited in respect of that offence.

(2) The punishment for the offence must be treated as remitted but the person's conviction for the offence must be treated as a conviction for all other purposes.

153 Return of person acquitted or not tried

(1) This section applies if —

(a) person is accused in the United Kingdom of the commission of an offence;
(b) the person is extradited to the United Kingdom in respect of the offence from —

(i) a category 1 territory under law of the territory corresponding to Part 1 of this Act, or
(ii) a category 2 territory under law of the territory corresponding to Part 2 of this Act;

(c) the condition in subsection (2) or the condition in subsection (3) is satisfied.

(2) The condition is that —

(a) proceedings against the person for the offence are not begun before the end of the required period, which is 6 months starting with the day on which the person arrives in the United Kingdom on his extradition, and
(b) before the end of the period of 3 months starting immediately after the end of the required period the person asks the Secretary of State to return him to the territory from which he was extradited.

(3) The condition is that —

(a) at his trial for the offence the person is acquitted or is discharged under any of the provisions specified in subsection (4), and
(b) before the end of the period of 3 months starting immediately after the date of his acquittal or discharge the person asks the Secretary of State to return him to the territory from which he was extradited.

(4) The provisions are —

(a) section 12(1) of the Powers of Criminal Courts (Sentencing) Act 2000 (c. 6);
(b) section 246(1), (2) or (3) of the Criminal Procedure (Scotland) Act 1995 (c. 46);
(c) Article 4(1) of the Criminal Justice (Northern Ireland) Order 1996 (S.I. 1996/3160 (N.I. 24)).

(5) The Secretary of State must arrange for him to be sent back, free of charge and with as little delay as possible, to the territory from which he was extradited to the United Kingdom in respect of the offence.

(6) If the accusation in subsection (1)(a) relates to the commission of an offence in Scotland, subsections (2)(b), (3)(b) and (5) apply as if the references to the Secretary of State were references to the Scottish Ministers.

154 Restriction on bail where undertaking given by Secretary of State

(1) This section applies in relation to a person if —

(a) the Secretary of State has given an undertaking in connection with the person's extradition to the United Kingdom, and
(b) the undertaking includes terms that the person be kept in custody until the conclusion of any proceedings against him in the United Kingdom for an offence.

(2) A court, judge or justice of the peace may grant bail to the person in the proceedings only if the court, judge or justice of the peace considers that there are exceptional circumstances which justify it.

155 Service personnel

The Secretary of State may by order provide for the preceding provisions of this Part to have effect with specified modifications in relation to a case where the person whose extradition is sought or ordered is subject to military law, air-force law or the Naval Discipline Act 1957 (c. 53).

PART 4

POLICE POWERS

Warrants and orders

156 Search and seizure warrants

(1) A justice of the peace may, on an application made to him by a constable, issue a search and seizure warrant if he is satisfied that the requirements for the issue of a search and seizure warrant are fulfilled.

(2) The application for a search and seizure warrant must state that—

(a) the extradition of a person specified in the application is sought under Part 1 or Part 2;
(b) the warrant is sought in relation to premises specified in the application;
(c) the warrant is sought in relation to material, or material of a description, specified in the application;
(d) that material, or material of that description, is believed to be on the premises.

(3) If the application states that the extradition of the person is sought under Part 1, the application must also state that the person is accused in a category 1 territory specified in the application of the commission of an offence—

(a) which is specified in the application, and
(b) which is an extradition offence within the meaning given by section 64.

(4) If the application states that the extradition of the person is sought under Part 2, the application must also state that the person is accused in a category 2 territory specified in the application of the commission of an offence—

(a) which is specified in the application, and
(b) which is an extradition offence within the meaning given by section 137.

(5) A search and seizure warrant is a warrant authorising a constable—

(a) to enter and search the premises specified in the application for the warrant, and
(b) to seize and retain any material found there which falls within subsection (6).

(6) Material falls within this subsection if—

(a) it would be likely to be admissible evidence at a trial in the relevant part of the United Kingdom for the offence specified in the application for the warrant (on

the assumption that conduct constituting that offence would constitute an offence in that part of the United Kingdom), and
(b) it does not consist of or include items subject to legal privilege, excluded material or special procedure material.

(7) The relevant part of the United Kingdom is the part of the United Kingdom where the justice of the peace exercises jurisdiction.

(8) The requirements for the issue of a search and seizure warrant are that there are reasonable grounds for believing that —

(a) the offence specified in the application has been committed by the person so specified;
(b) the person is in the United Kingdom or is on his way to the United Kingdom;
(c) the offence is an extradition offence within the meaning given by section 64 (if subsection (3) applies) or section 137 (if subsection (4) applies);
(d) there is material on premises specified in the application which falls within subsection (6);
(e) any of the conditions referred to in subsection (9) is satisfied.

(9) The conditions are —

(a) that it is not practicable to communicate with a person entitled to grant entry to the premises;
(b) that it is practicable to communicate with a person entitled to grant entry to the premises but it is not practicable to communicate with a person entitled to grant access to the material referred to in subsection (8)(d);
(c) that entry to the premises will not be granted unless a warrant is produced;
(d) that the purpose of a search may be frustrated or seriously prejudiced unless a constable arriving at the premises can secure immediate entry to them.

(10) The preceding provisions of this section apply to Scotland with these modifications —

(a) in subsections (1) and (7) for "justice of the peace" substitute "sheriff";
(b) in subsection (1) for "constable" substitute "procurator fiscal";
(c) for "search and seizure warrant" substitute "warrant to search";
(d) in subsection (6)(b) omit the words ", excluded material or special procedure material";
(e) subsections (8)(e) and (9) are omitted.

157 Production orders

(1) A judge may, on an application made to him by a constable, make a production order if he is satisfied that the requirements for the making of a production order are fulfilled.

(2) The application for a production order must state that —

(a) the extradition of a person specified in the application is sought under Part 1 or Part 2;
(b) the order is sought in relation to premises specified in the application;
(c) the order is sought in relation to material, or material of a description, specified in the application;
(d) the material is special procedure material or excluded material;
(e) a person specified in the application appears to be in possession or control of the material.

(3) If the application states that the extradition of the person is sought under Part 1, the application must also state that the person is accused in a category 1 territory specified in the application of the commission of an offence —

(a) which is specified in the application, and
(b) which is an extradition offence within the meaning given by section 64.

(4) If the application states that the extradition of the person is sought under Part 2, the application must also state that the person is accused in a category 2 territory specified in the application of the commission of an offence —

(a) which is specified in the application, and
(b) which is an extradition offence within the meaning given by section 137.

(5) A production order is an order either —

(a) requiring the person the application for the order specifies as appearing to be in possession or control of special procedure material or excluded material to produce it to a constable (within the period stated in the order) for him to take away, or
(b) requiring that person to give a constable access to the special procedure material or excluded material within the period stated in the order.

(6) The period stated in a production order must be a period of 7 days starting with the day on which the order is made, unless it appears to the judge by whom the order is made that a longer period would be appropriate.

(7) Production orders have effect as if they were orders of the court.

(8) In this section "judge" —

(a) in England and Wales, means a circuit judge;
(b) in Northern Ireland, means a Crown Court judge.

158 Requirements for making of production order

(1) These are the requirements for the making of a production order.

(2) There must be reasonable grounds for believing that —

(a) the offence specified in the application has been committed by the person so specified;
(b) the person is in the United Kingdom or is on his way to the United Kingdom;
(c) the offence is an extradition offence within the meaning given by section 64 (if section 157(3) applies) or section 137 (if section 157(4) applies);
(d) there is material which consists of or includes special procedure material or excluded material on premises specified in the application;
(e) the material would be likely to be admissible evidence at a trial in the relevant part of the United Kingdom for the offence specified in the application (on the assumption that conduct constituting that offence would constitute an offence in that part of the United Kingdom).

(3) The relevant part of the United Kingdom is the part of the United Kingdom where the judge exercises jurisdiction.

(4) It must appear that other methods of obtaining the material —

(a) have been tried without success, or
(b) have not been tried because they were bound to fail.

(5) It must be in the public interest that the material should be produced or that access to it should be given.

159 Computer information

(1) This section applies if any of the special procedure material or excluded material specified in an application for a production order consists of information stored in any electronic form.

(2) If the order is an order requiring a person to produce the material to a constable for him to take away, it has effect as an order to produce the material in a form —

(a) in which it can be taken away by him;
(b) in which it is visible and legible or from which it can readily be produced in a visible and legible form.

(3) If the order is an order requiring a person to give a constable access to the material, it has effect as an order to give him access to the material in a form —

(a) in which it is visible and legible, or
(b) from which it can readily be produced in a visible and legible form.

160 Warrants: special procedure material and excluded material

(1) A judge may, on an application made to him by a constable, issue a warrant under this section if he is satisfied that —

(a) the requirements for the making of a production order are fulfilled, and
(b) the further requirement for the issue of a warrant under this section is fulfilled.

(2) The application for a warrant under this section must state that —

(a) the extradition of a person specified in the application is sought under Part 1 or Part 2;
(b) the warrant is sought in relation to premises specified in the application;
(c) the warrant is sought in relation to material, or material of a description, specified in the application;
(d) the material is special procedure material or excluded material.

(3) If the application states that the extradition of the person is sought under Part 1, the application must also state that the person is accused in a category 1 territory specified in the application of the commission of an offence —

(a) which is specified in the application, and
(b) which is an extradition offence within the meaning given by section 64.

(4) If the application states that the extradition of the person is sought under Part 2, the application must also state that the person is accused in a category 2 territory specified in the application of the commission of an offence —

(a) which is specified in the application, and
(b) which is an extradition offence within the meaning given by section 137.

(5) A warrant under this section authorises a constable to enter and search the premises specified in the application for the warrant and —

(a) to seize and retain any material found there which falls within subsection (6) and which is special procedure material, if the application for the warrant states that the warrant is sought in relation to special procedure material;
(b) to seize and retain any material found there which falls within subsection (6) and which is excluded material, if the application for the warrant states that the warrant is sought in relation to excluded material.

(6) Material falls within this subsection if it would be likely to be admissible evidence at a trial in the relevant part of the United Kingdom for the offence specified in the application for the warrant (on the assumption that conduct constituting that offence would constitute an offence in that part of the United Kingdom).

(7) The relevant part of the United Kingdom is the part of the United Kingdom where the judge exercises jurisdiction.

(8) The further requirement for the issue of a warrant under this section is that any of these conditions is satisfied —

(a) it is not practicable to communicate with a person entitled to grant entry to the premises;
(b) it is practicable to communicate with a person entitled to grant entry to the premises but it is not practicable to communicate with a person entitled to grant access to the material referred to in section 158(2)(d);
(c) the material contains information which is subject to a restriction on disclosure or an obligation of secrecy contained in an enactment (including one passed after this Act) and is likely to be disclosed in breach of the restriction or obligation if a warrant is not issued.

(9) In this section "judge" —

(a) in England and Wales, means a circuit judge;
(b) in Northern Ireland, means a Crown Court judge.

Search and seizure without warrant

161 Entry and search of premises for purposes of arrest

(1) This section applies if a constable has power to arrest a person under an extradition arrest power.

(2) A constable may enter and search any premises for the purpose of exercising the power of arrest if he has reasonable grounds for believing that the person is on the premises.

(3) The power to search conferred by subsection (2) is exercisable only to the extent that is reasonably required for the purpose of exercising the power of arrest.

(4) A constable who has entered premises in exercise of the power conferred by subsection (2) may seize and retain anything which is on the premises if he has reasonable grounds for believing —

(a) that it has been obtained in consequence of the commission of an offence or it is evidence in relation to an offence, and
(b) that it is necessary to seize it in order to prevent it being concealed, lost, damaged, altered or destroyed.

(5) An offence includes an offence committed outside the United Kingdom.

(6) If the premises contain 2 or more separate dwellings, the power conferred by subsection (2) is a power to enter and search only —

(a) any parts of the premises which the occupiers of any dwelling comprised in the premises use in common with the occupiers of any other dwelling comprised in the premises, and

(b) any dwelling comprised in the premises in which the constable has reasonable grounds for believing that the person may be.

162 Entry and search of premises on arrest

(1) This section applies if a person has been arrested under an extradition arrest power at a place other than a police station.

(2) A constable may enter and search any premises in which the person was at the time of his arrest or immediately before his arrest if he has reasonable grounds for believing —

(a) if the person has not been convicted of the relevant offence, that there is on the premises evidence (other than items subject to legal privilege) relating to the relevant offence;

(b) in any case, that there is on the premises evidence (other than items subject to legal privilege) relating to the identity of the person.

(3) The relevant offence is the offence —

(a) referred to in the Part 1 warrant, if the arrest was under a Part 1 warrant;

(b) in respect of which the constable has reasonable grounds for believing that a Part 1 warrant has been or will be issued, if the arrest was under section 5;

(c) in respect of which extradition is requested, if the arrest was under a warrant issued under section 71;

(d) of which the person is accused, if the arrest was under a provisional warrant.

(4) The power to search conferred by subsection (2) —

(a) if the person has not been convicted of the relevant offence, is a power to search for evidence (other than items subject to legal privilege) relating to the relevant offence;

(b) in any case, is a power to search for evidence (other than items subject to legal privilege) relating to the identity of the person.

(5) The power to search conferred by subsection (2) is exercisable only to the extent that it is reasonably required for the purpose of discovering evidence in respect of which the power is available by virtue of subsection (4).

(6) A constable may seize and retain anything for which he may search by virtue of subsections (4) and (5).

(7) A constable who has entered premises in exercise of the power conferred by subsection (2) may seize and retain anything which is on the premises if he has reasonable grounds for believing —

(a) that it has been obtained in consequence of the commission of an offence or it is evidence in relation to an offence, and

(b) that it is necessary to seize it in order to prevent it being concealed, lost, damaged, altered or destroyed.

(8) An offence includes an offence committed outside the United Kingdom.

(9) If the premises contain 2 or more separate dwellings, the power conferred by subsection (2) is a power to enter and search only —

(a) any dwelling in which the arrest took place or in which the person was immediately before his arrest, and
(b) any parts of the premises which the occupier of any such dwelling uses in common with the occupiers of any other dwelling comprised in the premises.

163 Search of person on arrest

(1) This section applies if a person has been arrested under an extradition arrest power at a place other than a police station.

(2) A constable may search the person if he has reasonable grounds for believing that the person may present a danger to himself or others.

(3) A constable may search the person if he has reasonable grounds for believing that the person may have concealed on him anything —

(a) which he might use to assist him to escape from lawful custody;
(b) which might be evidence relating to an offence or to the identity of the person.

(4) The power to search conferred by subsection (3) —

(a) is a power to search for anything falling within paragraph(a) or (b) of that subsection;
(b) is exercisable only to the extent that is reasonably required for the purpose of discovering such a thing.

(5) The powers conferred by subsections (2) and (3) —

(a) do not authorise a constable to require a person to remove any of his clothing in public, other than an outer coat, jacket or gloves;
(b) authorise a search of a person's mouth.

(6) A constable searching a person in exercise of the power conferred by subsection (2) may seize and retain anything he finds, if he has reasonable grounds for believing that the person searched might use it to cause physical injury to himself or to any other person.

(7) A constable searching a person in exercise of the power conferred by subsection (3) may seize and retain anything he finds if he has reasonable grounds for believing —

(a) that the person might use it to assist him to escape from lawful custody;
(b) that it is evidence of an offence or of the identity of the person or has been obtained in consequence of the commission of an offence.

(8) An offence includes an offence committed outside the United Kingdom.

(9) Nothing in this section affects the power conferred by section 43 of the Terrorism Act 2000 (c. 11).

164 Entry and search of premises after arrest

(1) This section applies if a person has been arrested under an extradition arrest power.

(2) A constable may enter and search any premises occupied or controlled by the person if the constable has reasonable grounds for suspecting —

(a) if the person has not been convicted of the relevant offence, that there is on the premises evidence (other than items subject to legal privilege) relating to the relevant offence;

(b) in any case, that there is on the premises evidence (other than items subject to legal privilege) relating to the identity of the person.

(3) The relevant offence is the offence —

(a) referred to in the Part 1 warrant, if the arrest was under a Part 1 warrant;
(b) in respect of which the constable has reasonable grounds for believing that a Part 1 warrant has been or will be issued, if the arrest was under section 5;
(c) in respect of which extradition is requested, if the arrest was under a warrant issued under section 71;
(d) of which the person is accused, if the arrest was under a provisional warrant.

(4) The power to search conferred by subsection (2) —

(a) if the person has not been convicted of the relevant offence, is a power to search for evidence (other than items subject to legal privilege) relating to the relevant offence;
(b) in any case, is a power to search for evidence (other than items subject to legal privilege) relating to the identity of the person.

(5) The power to search conferred by subsection (2) is exercisable only to the extent that it is reasonably required for the purpose of discovering evidence in respect of which the power is available by virtue of subsection (4).

(6) A constable may seize and retain anything for which he may search by virtue of subsections (4) and (5).

(7) A constable who has entered premises in exercise of the power conferred by subsection (2) may seize and retain anything which is on the premises if he has reasonable grounds for believing —

(a) that it has been obtained in consequence of the commission of an offence or it is evidence in relation to an offence, and
(b) that it is necessary to seize it in order to prevent it being concealed, lost, damaged, altered or destroyed.

(8) An offence includes an offence committed outside the United Kingdom.

(9) The powers conferred by subsections (2) and (6) may be exercised only if a police officer of the rank of inspector or above has given written authorisation for their exercise.

(10) But the power conferred by subsection (2) may be exercised without authorisation under subsection (9) if —

(a) it is exercised before the person arrested is taken to a police station, and
(b) the presence of the person at a place other than a police station is necessary for the effective exercise of the power to search.

(11) Subsections (9) and (10) do not apply to Scotland.

165 Additional seizure powers

(1) The Criminal Justice and Police Act 2001 (c. 16) is amended as follows.

(2) In Part 1 of Schedule 1 (powers of seizure to which section 50 of that Act applies) at the end add —

"Extradition Act 2003 (c. 41)

73D The powers of seizure conferred by sections 156(5), 160(5), 161(4), 162(6) and (7) and 164(6) and (7) of the Extradition Act 2003 (seizure in connection with extradition)."

(3) In Part 2 of Schedule 1 (powers of seizure to which section 51 of that Act applies) at the end add —

"Extradition Act 2003 (c. 41)

83A The powers of seizure conferred by section 163(6) and (7) of the Extradition Act 2003 (seizure in connection with extradition)."

Treatment following arrest

166 Fingerprints and samples

(1) This section applies if a person has been arrested under an extradition arrest power and is detained at a police station.

(2) Fingerprints may be taken from the person only if they are taken by a constable —

(a) with the appropriate consent given in writing, or
(b) without that consent, under subsection (4).

(3) A non-intimate sample may be taken from the person only if it is taken by a constable —

(a) with the appropriate consent given in writing, or
(b) without that consent, under subsection (4).

(4) Fingerprints or a non-intimate sample may be taken from the person without the appropriate consent only if a police officer of at least the rank of inspector authorises the fingerprints or sample to be taken.

167 Searches and examination

(1) This section applies if a person has been arrested under an extradition arrest power and is detained at a police station.

(2) If a police officer of at least the rank of inspector authorises it, the person may be searched or examined, or both, for the purpose of facilitating the ascertainment of his identity.

(3) An identifying mark found on a search or examination under this section may be photographed —

(a) with the appropriate consent, or
(b) without the appropriate consent, if that consent is withheld or it is not practicable to obtain it.

(4) The only persons entitled to carry out a search or examination, or take a photograph, under this section are —

(a) constables;
(b) persons designated for the purposes of this section by the appropriate police officer.

(5) A person may not under this section —

(a) carry out a search or examination of a person of the opposite sex;
(b) take a photograph of any part of the body (other than the face) of a person of the opposite sex.

(6) An intimate search may not be carried out under this section.

(7) Ascertaining a person's identity includes showing that he is not a particular person.

(8) Taking a photograph includes using a process by means of which a visual image may be produced; and photographing a person must be construed accordingly.

(9) Mark includes features and injuries and a mark is an identifying mark if its existence in a person's case facilitates the ascertainment of his identity.

(10) The appropriate police officer is —

(a) in England and Wales, the chief officer of police for the police area in which the police station in question is situated;
(b) in Northern Ireland, the Chief Constable of the Police Service of Northern Ireland.

168 Photographs

(1) This section applies if a person has been arrested under an extradition arrest power and is detained at a police station.

(2) The person may be photographed —

(a) with the appropriate consent, or
(b) without the appropriate consent, if that consent is withheld or it is not practicable to obtain it.

(3) A person proposing to take a photograph of a person under this section —

(a) may for the purpose of doing so require the removal of any item or substance worn on or over the whole or any part of the head or face of the person to be photographed, and
(b) if the requirement is not complied with may remove the item or substance himself.

(4) The only persons entitled to take a photograph under this section are —

(a) constables;
(b) persons designated for the purposes of this section by the appropriate police officer.

(5) Taking a photograph includes using a process by means of which a visual image may be produced; and photographing a person must be construed accordingly.

(6) The appropriate police officer is —

(a) in England and Wales, the chief officer of police for the police area in which the police station in question is situated;
(b) in Northern Ireland, the Chief Constable of the Police Service of Northern Ireland.

169 Evidence of identity: England and Wales

(1) The Police and Criminal Evidence Act 1984 (c. 60) is amended as follows.

(2) In section 54A (searches and examination to ascertain identity) at the end insert —

"(13) Nothing in this section applies to a person arrested under an extradition arrest power."

(3) In section 61 (fingerprinting) at the end insert —

"(10) Nothing in this section applies to a person arrested under an extradition arrest power."

(4) In section 63 (non-intimate samples) at the end insert —

> "(11) Nothing in this section applies to a person arrested under an extradition arrest power."

(5) In section 64A (photographing of suspects etc.) at the end insert —

> "(7) Nothing in this section applies to a person arrested under an extradition arrest power."

(6) In section 65 (interpretation of Part 5) after the definition of "drug trafficking" and "drug trafficking offence" insert —

> "'extradition arrest power' means any of the following —
> (a) a Part 1 warrant (within the meaning given by the Extradition Act 2003) in respect of which a certificate under section 2 of that Act has been issued;
> (b) section 5 of that Act;
> (c) a warrant issued under section 71 of that Act;
> (d) a provisional warrant (within the meaning given by that Act)."

170 Evidence of identity: Northern Ireland

(1) The Police and Criminal Evidence (Northern Ireland) Order 1989 (S.I. 1989/1341 (N.I. 12)) is amended as follows.

(2) In Article 55A (searches and examination to ascertain identity) at the end insert —

> "(13) Nothing in this Article applies to a person arrested under an extradition arrest power."

(3) In Article 61 (fingerprinting) at the end insert —

> "(10) Nothing in this Article applies to a person arrested under an extradition arrest power."

(4) In Article 63 (non-intimate samples) at the end insert —

> "(12) Nothing in this Article applies to a person arrested under an extradition arrest power."

(5) In Article 64A (photographing of suspects etc.) at the end insert —

> "(7) Nothing in this Article applies to a person arrested under an extradition arrest power."

(6) In Article 53 (interpretation) after the definition of "drug trafficking" and "drug trafficking offence" insert —

> "'extradition arrest power' means any of the following —
> (a) a Part 1 warrant (within the meaning given by the Extradition Act 2003) in respect of which a certificate under section 2 of that Act has been issued;
> (b) section 5 of that Act;
> (c) a warrant issued under section 71 of that Act;
> (d) a provisional warrant (within the meaning given by that Act)."

171 Other treatment and rights

(1) This section applies in relation to cases where a person —

(a) is arrested under an extradition arrest power at a police station;
(b) is taken to a police station after being arrested elsewhere under an extradition arrest power;
(c) is detained at a police station after being arrested under an extradition arrest power.

(2) In relation to those cases the Secretary of State may by order apply the provisions mentioned in subsections (3) and (4) with specified modifications.

(3) The provisions are these provisions of the Police and Criminal Evidence Act 1984 (c. 60) —

(a) section 54 (searches of detained persons);
(b) section 55 (intimate searches);
(c) section 56 (right to have someone informed when arrested);
(d) section 58(access to legal advice).

(4) The provisions are these provisions of the Police and Criminal Evidence (Northern Ireland) Order 1989 (S.I. 1989/1341 (N.I. 12)) —

(a) Article 55 (searches of detained persons);
(b) Article 56 (intimate searches);
(c) Article 57 (right to have someone informed when arrested);
(d) Article 59 (access to legal advice).

Delivery of seized property

172 Delivery of seized property

(1) This section applies to —

(a) anything which has been seized or produced under this Part, or
(b) anything which has been seized under section 50 or 51 of the Criminal Justice and Police Act 2001 (c. 16) in reliance on a power of seizure conferred by this Part.

(2) A constable may deliver any such thing to a person who is or is acting on behalf of an authority if the constable has reasonable grounds for believing that the authority —

(a) is an authority of the relevant territory, and
(b) has functions such that it is appropriate for the thing to be delivered to it.

(3) If the relevant seizure power was a warrant issued under this Part, or the thing was produced under an order made under this Part, the relevant territory is the category 1 or category 2 territory specified in the application for the warrant or order.

(4) If the relevant seizure power was section 161(4), 162(6) or (7), 163(6) or (7) or 164(6) or (7), the relevant territory is —

(a) the territory in which the Part 1 warrant was issued, in a case where the applicable extradition arrest power is a Part 1 warrant in respect of which a certificate under section 2 has been issued;

(b) the territory in which a constable has reasonable grounds for believing that a Part 1 warrant has been or will be issued, in a case where the applicable extradition arrest power is section 5;
(c) the territory to which a person's extradition is requested, in a case where the applicable extradition arrest power is a warrant issued under section 71;
(d) the territory in which a person is accused of the commission of an offence or has been convicted of an offence, in a case where the applicable extradition arrest power is a provisional warrant.

(5) The applicable extradition arrest power is—

(a) the extradition arrest power under which a constable had a power of arrest, if the relevant seizure power was section 161(4);
(b) the extradition arrest power under which a person was arrested, if the relevant seizure power was section 162(6) or (7), 163(6) or (7) or 164(6) or (7).

(6) The relevant seizure power is—

(a) the power under which the thing was seized, or
(b) the power in reliance on which the thing was seized under section 50 or 51 of the Criminal Justice and Police Act 2001 (c. 16).

(7) Subsection (1)(a) applies to Scotland with the insertion after "Part" of "(so far as it applies to Scotland) or for the purposes of this Act (as it so applies) by virtue of any enactment or rule of law".

(8) Subsection (2) applies to Scotland with the substitution of "procurator fiscal" for "constable".

(9) In subsection (7) "enactment" includes an enactment comprised in, or in an instrument made under, an Act of the Scottish Parliament.

Codes of practice

173 Codes of practice

(1) The Secretary of State must issue codes of practice in connection with—

(a) the exercise of the powers conferred by this Part;
(b) the retention, use and return of anything seized or produced under this Part;
(c) access to and the taking of photographs and copies of anything so seized or produced;
(d) the retention, use, disclosure and destruction of fingerprints, a sample or a photograph taken under this Part.

(2) If the Secretary of State proposes to issue a code of practice under this section he must—

(a) publish a draft of the code;
(b) consider any representations made to him about the draft;
(c) if he thinks it appropriate, modify the draft in the light of any such representations.

(3) The Secretary of State must lay the code before Parliament.

(4) When he has done so he may bring the code into operation by order.

(5) The Secretary of State may revise the whole or any part of a code issued under this section and issue the code as revised; and subsections (2) to (4) apply to such a revised code as they apply to the original code.

(6) A failure by a constable to comply with a provision of a code issued under this section does not of itself make him liable to criminal or civil proceedings.

(7) A code issued under this section is admissible in evidence in proceedings under this Act and must be taken into account by a judge or court in determining any question to which it appears to the judge or the court to be relevant.

(8) If the Secretary of State publishes a draft code of practice in connection with a matter specified in subsection (1) before the date on which this section comes into force—

(a) the draft is as effective as one published under subsection (2) on or after that date;
(b) representations made to the Secretary of State about the draft before that date are as effective as representations made to him about it after that date;
(c) modifications made by the Secretary of State to the draft in the light of any such representations before that date are as effective as any such modifications made by him on or after that date.

General

174 Interpretation

(1) Subsections (2) to (8) apply for the purposes of this Part.

(2) Each of these is an extradition arrest power—

(a) a Part 1 warrant in respect of which a certificate under section 2 has been issued;
(b) section 5;
(c) a warrant issued under section 71;
(d) a provisional warrant.

(3) "Excluded material"—

(a) in England and Wales, has the meaning given by section 11 of the 1984 Act;
(b) in Northern Ireland, has the meaning given by Article 13 of the 1989 Order.

(4) "Items subject to legal privilege"—

(a) in England and Wales, has the meaning given by section 10 of the 1984 Act;
(b) in Scotland, has the meaning given by section 412 of the 2002 Act;
(c) in Northern Ireland, has the meaning given by Article 12 of the 1989 Order.

(5) "Premises"—

(a) in England and Wales, has the meaning given by section 23 of the 1984 Act;
(b) in Scotland, has the meaning given by section 412 of the 2002 Act;
(c) in Northern Ireland, has the meaning given by Article 25 of the 1989 Order.

(6) "Special procedure material"—

(a) in England and Wales, has the meaning given by section 14 of the 1984 Act;
(b) in Northern Ireland, has the meaning given by Article 16 of the 1989 Order.

(7) The expressions in subsection (8) have the meanings given —

(a) in England and Wales, by section 65 of the 1984 Act;
(b) in Northern Ireland, by Article 53 of the 1989 Order.

(8) The expressions are —

(a) appropriate consent;
(b) fingerprints;
(c) intimate search;
(d) non-intimate sample.

(9) The 1984 Act is the Police and Criminal Evidence Act 1984 (c. 60).

(10) The 1989 Order is the Police and Criminal Evidence (Northern Ireland) Order 1989 (S.I. 1989/1341 (N.I. 12)).

(11) The 2002 Act is the Proceeds of Crime Act 2002 (c. 29).

175 Customs officers

The Treasury may by order provide for any provision of this Part which applies in relation to police officers or persons arrested by police officers to apply with specified modifications in relation to customs officers or persons arrested by customs officers.

176 Service policemen

The Secretary of State may by order provide for any provision of this Part which applies in relation to police officers or persons arrested by police officers to apply with specified modifications in relation to service policemen or persons arrested by service policemen.

PART 5

MISCELLANEOUS AND GENERAL

British overseas territories

177 Extradition from British overseas territories

(1) This section applies in relation to extradition —

(a) from a British overseas territory to a category 1 territory;
(b) from a British overseas territory to the United Kingdom;
(c) from a British overseas territory to a category 2 territory;
(d) from a British overseas territory to any of the Channel Islands or the Isle of Man.

(2) An Order in Council may provide for any provision of this Act applicable to extradition from the United Kingdom to apply to extradition in a case falling within subsection (1)(a) or (b).

(3) An Order in Council may provide for any provision of this Act applicable to extradition from the United Kingdom to a category 2 territory to apply to extradition in a case falling within subsection (1)(c) or (d).

(4) An Order in Council under this section may provide that the provision applied has effect with specified modifications.

178 Extradition to British overseas territories

(1) This section applies in relation to extradition —

(a) to a British overseas territory from a category 1 territory;
(b) to a British overseas territory from the United Kingdom;
(c) to a British overseas territory from a category 2 territory;
(d) to a British overseas territory from any of the Channel Islands or the Isle of Man.

(2) An Order in Council may provide for any provision of this Act applicable to extradition to the United Kingdom to apply to extradition in a case falling within subsection (1)(a) or (b).

(3) An Order in Council may provide for any provision of this Act applicable to extradition to the United Kingdom from a category 2 territory to apply to extradition in a case falling within subsection (1)(c) or (d).

(4) An Order in Council under this section may provide that the provision applied has effect with specified modifications.

Competing extradition claims

179 Competing claims to extradition

(1) This section applies if at the same time —

(a) there is a Part 1 warrant in respect of a person, a certificate has been issued under section 2 in respect of the warrant, and the person has not been extradited in pursuance of the warrant or discharged, and
(b) there is a request for the same person's extradition, a certificate has been issued under section 70 in respect of the request, and the person has not been extradited in pursuance of the request or discharged.

(2) The Secretary of State may —

(a) order proceedings (or further proceedings) on one of them (the warrant or the request) to be deferred until the other one has been disposed of, if neither the warrant nor the request has been disposed of;
(b) order the person's extradition in pursuance of the warrant to be deferred until the request has been disposed of, if an order for his extradition in pursuance of the warrant has been made;
(c) order the person's extradition in pursuance of the request to be deferred until the warrant has been disposed of, if an order for his extradition in pursuance of the request has been made.

(3) In applying subsection (2) the Secretary of State must take account in particular of these matters —

(a) the relative seriousness of the offences concerned;
(b) the place where each offence was committed (or was alleged to have been committed);

(c) the date when the warrant was issued and the date when the request was received;
(d) whether, in the case of each offence, the person is accused of its commission (but not alleged to have been convicted) or is alleged to be unlawfully at large after conviction.

(4) If both the certificates referred to in subsection (1) are issued in Scotland, the preceding provisions of this section apply as if the references to the Secretary of State were to the Scottish Ministers.

180 Proceedings on deferred warrant or request

(1) This section applies if —

(a) an order is made under this Act deferring proceedings on an extradition claim in respect of a person (the deferred claim) until another extradition claim in respect of the person has been disposed of, and
(b) the other extradition claim is disposed of.

(2) The judge may make an order for proceedings on the deferred claim to be resumed.

(3) No order under subsection (2) may be made after the end of the required period.

(4) If the person applies to the appropriate judge to be discharged, the judge may order his discharge.

(5) If the person applies to the appropriate judge to be discharged, the judge must order his discharge if —

(a) the required period has ended, and
(b) the judge has not made an order under subsection (2) or ordered the person's discharge.

(6) The required period is 21 days starting with the day on which the other extradition claim is disposed of.

(7) If the proceedings on the deferred claim were under Part 1, section 67 applies for determining the appropriate judge.

(8) If the proceedings on the deferred claim were under Part 2, section 139 applies for determining the appropriate judge.

(9) An extradition claim is made in respect of a person if —

(a) a Part 1 warrant is issued in respect of him;
(b) a request for his extradition is made.

181 Proceedings where extradition deferred

(1) This section applies if —

(a) an order is made under this Act deferring a person's extradition in pursuance of an extradition claim (the deferred claim) until another extradition claim in respect of him has been disposed of;
(b) the other extradition claim is disposed of.

(2) The judge may make an order for the person's extradition in pursuance of the deferred claim to cease to be deferred.

(3) No order under subsection (2) may be made after the end of the required period.

(4) If the person applies to the appropriate judge to be discharged, the judge may order his discharge.

(5) If the person applies to the appropriate judge to be discharged, the judge must order his discharge if —

(a) the required period has ended, and
(b) the judge has not made an order under subsection (2) or ordered the person's discharge.

(6) The required period is 21 days starting with the day on which the other extradition claim is disposed of.

(7) If the person's extradition in pursuance of the deferred claim was ordered under Part 1, section 67 applies for determining the appropriate judge.

(8) If the person's extradition in pursuance of the deferred claim was ordered under Part 2, section 139 applies for determining the appropriate judge.

(9) An extradition claim is made in respect of a person if —

(a) a Part 1 warrant is issued in respect of him;
(b) a request for his extradition is made.

Legal aid

182 Legal advice, assistance and representation: England and Wales

In section 12(2) of the Access to Justice Act 1999 (c. 22) (meaning of "criminal proceedings") for paragraph (c) substitute —

"(c) proceedings for dealing with an individual under the Extradition Act 2003,".

183 Legal aid: Scotland

The provisions of the Legal Aid (Scotland) Act 1986 (c. 47) apply —

(a) in relation to proceedings in Scotland before the appropriate judge under Part 1, 2 or 5 of this Act as those provisions apply in relation to summary proceedings;
(b) in relation to any proceedings on appeal arising out of such proceedings before the appropriate judge as those provisions apply in relation to appeals in summary proceedings.

184 Grant of free legal aid: Northern Ireland

(1) The appropriate judge may grant free legal aid to a person in connection with proceedings under Part 1 or Part 2 before the judge or the High Court.

(2) A judge of the High Court may grant free legal aid to a person in connection with proceedings under Part 1 or Part 2 before the High Court or the House of Lords.

(3) If the appropriate judge refuses to grant free legal aid under subsection (1) in connection with proceedings before the High Court the person may appeal to the High Court against the judge's decision.

(4) A judge of the High Court may grant free legal aid to a person in connection with proceedings on an appeal under subsection (3).

(5) Free legal aid may be granted to a person under subsection (1), (2) or (4) only if it appears to the judge that —

(a) the person's means are insufficient to enable him to obtain legal aid, and
(b) it is desirable in the interests of justice that the person should be granted free legal aid.

(6) On an appeal under subsection (3) the High Court may —

(a) allow the appeal;
(b) dismiss the appeal.

(7) The High Court may allow an appeal under subsection (3) only if it appears to the High Court that —

(a) the person's means are insufficient to enable him to obtain legal aid, and
(b) it is desirable in the interests of justice that the person should be granted free legal aid.

(8) If the High Court allows an appeal under subsection (3) it must grant free legal aid to the person in connection with the proceedings under Part 1 or Part 2 before it.

(9) If on a question of granting free legal aid under this section or of allowing an appeal under subsection (3) there is a doubt as to whether —

(a) the person's means are insufficient to enable him to obtain legal aid, or
(b) it is desirable in the interests of justice that the person should be granted free legal aid,

the doubt must be resolved in favour of granting him free legal aid.

(10) References in this section to granting free legal aid to a person are to assigning to him —

(a) a solicitor and counsel, or
(b) a solicitor only, or
(c) counsel only.

185 Free legal aid: supplementary

(1) The provisions of the Legal Aid, Advice and Assistance (Northern Ireland) Order 1981 (S.I. 1981/228 (N.I. 8)) listed in subsection (2) apply in relation to free legal aid under section 184 in connection with proceedings before the appropriate judge or the High Court as they apply in relation to free legal aid under Part III of the Order.

(2) The provisions are —

(a) Article 32 (statements of means);
(b) Article 36(1) (payment of legal aid);
(c) Article 36(3) and (4) (rules);
(d) Article 36A (solicitors excluded from legal aid work);
(e) Article 37 (remuneration of solicitors and counsel);
(f) Article 40 (stamp duty exemption).

(3) As so applied those Articles have effect as if —

(a) a person granted free legal aid under section 184 had been granted a criminal aid certificate under Part III of the Order;
(b) section 184 were contained in Part III of the Order.

(4) The fees of any counsel, and the expenses and fees of any solicitor, assigned to a person under section 184 in connection with proceedings before the House of Lords must be paid by the Lord Chancellor.

(5) The fees and expenses paid under subsection (4) must not exceed the amount allowed by —

(a) the House of Lords, or
(b) such officer or officers of the House of Lords as may be prescribed by order of the House of Lords.

(6) For the purposes of section 184 and this section the appropriate judge is —

(a) such county court judge or resident magistrate as is designated for the purposes of Part 1 by the Lord Chancellor, if the proceedings are under Part 1;
(b) such county court judge or resident magistrate as is designated for the purposes of Part 2 by the Lord Chancellor, if the proceedings are under Part 2.

Re-extradition

186 Re-extradition: preliminary

(1) Section 187 applies in relation to a person if the conditions in subsections (2) to (6) are satisfied.

(2) The first condition is that the person was extradited to a territory in accordance with Part 1 or Part 2.

(3) The second condition is that the person was serving a sentence of imprisonment or another form of detention in the United Kingdom (the UK sentence) before he was extradited.

(4) The third condition is that —

(a) if the person was extradited in accordance with Part 1, the Part 1 warrant in pursuance of which he was extradited contained a statement that it was issued with a view to his extradition for the purpose of being prosecuted for an offence;
(b) if the person was extradited in accordance with Part 2, the request in pursuance of which the person was extradited contained a statement that the person was accused of the commission of an offence.

(5) The fourth condition is that a certificate issued by a judicial authority of the territory shows that —

(a) a sentence of imprisonment or another form of detention for a term of 4 months or a greater punishment (the overseas sentence) was imposed on the person in the territory;
(b) the overseas sentence was imposed on him in respect of —
    (i) the offence specified in the warrant or request, or
    (ii) any other offence committed before his extradition in respect of which he was permitted to be dealt with in the territory.

(6) The fifth condition is that before serving the overseas sentence the person was returned to the United Kingdom to serve the remainder of the UK sentence.

187 Re-extradition hearing

(1) If this section applies in relation to a person, as soon as practicable after the relevant time the person must be brought before the appropriate judge for the judge to decide whether the person is to be extradited again to the territory in which the overseas sentence was imposed.

(2) The relevant time is the time at which the person would otherwise be released from detention pursuant to the UK sentence (whether or not on licence).

(3) If subsection (1) is not complied with and the person applies to the judge to be discharged, the judge must order his discharge.

(4) The person must be treated as continuing in legal custody until he is brought before the appropriate judge under subsection (1) or he is discharged under subsection (3).

(5) If the person is brought before the appropriate judge under subsection (1) the judge must decide whether the territory in which the overseas sentence was imposed is —

(a) a category 1 territory;
(b) a category 2 territory;
(c) neither a category 1 territory nor a category 2 territory.

(6) If the judge decides that the territory is a category 1 territory, section 188 applies.

(7) If the judge decides that the territory is a category 2 territory, section 189 applies.

(8) If the judge decides that the territory is neither a category 1 territory nor a category 2 territory, he must order the person's discharge.

(9) A person's discharge as a result of this section or section 188 or 189 does not affect any conditions on which he is released from detention pursuant to the UK sentence.

(10) Section 139 applies for determining the appropriate judge for the purposes of this section.

188 Re-extradition to category 1 territories

(1) If this section applies, this Act applies as it would if —

(a) a Part 1 warrant had been issued in respect of the person;
(b) the warrant contained a statement that —
    (i) the person was alleged to be unlawfully at large after conviction of the relevant offence, and
    (ii) the warrant was issued with a view to the person's arrest and extradition to the territory for the purpose of serving a sentence imposed in respect of the relevant offence;
(c) the warrant were issued by the authority of the territory which issued the certificate referred to in section 186(5);
(d) the relevant offence were specified in the warrant;
(e) the judge were the appropriate judge for the purposes of Part 1;
(f) the hearing at which the judge is to make the decision referred to in section 187(1) were the extradition hearing;
(g) the proceedings before the judge were under Part 1.

(2) As applied by subsection (1) this Act has effect with the modifications set out in Part 1 of Schedule 1.

(3) The relevant offence is the offence in respect of which the overseas sentence is imposed.

189 Re-extradition to category 2 territories

(1) If this section applies, this Act applies as it would if —

(a) a valid request for the person's extradition to the territory had been made;
(b) the request contained a statement that the person was alleged to be unlawfully at large after conviction of the relevant offence;
(c) the relevant offence were specified in the request;

(d) the hearing at which the appropriate judge is to make the decision referred to in section 187(1) were the extradition hearing;
(e) the proceedings before the judge were under Part 2.

(2) As applied by subsection (1) this Act has effect with the modifications set out in Part 2 of Schedule 1.
(3) The relevant offence is the offence in respect of which the overseas sentence is imposed.

Conduct of extradition proceedings

190 Crown Prosecution Service: role in extradition proceedings

(1) The Prosecution of Offences Act 1985 (c. 23) is amended as follows.
(2) In section 3 (functions of the Director) in subsection (2) after paragraph (e) insert —

"(ea) to have the conduct of any extradition proceedings;
(eb) to give, to such extent as he considers appropriate, and to such persons as he considers appropriate, advice on any matters relating to extradition proceedings or proposed extradition proceedings;".

(3) In section 3 after subsection (2) insert —

"(2A) Subsection (2)(ea) above does not require the Director to have the conduct of any extradition proceedings in respect of a person if he has received a request not to do so and —

(a) in a case where the proceedings are under Part 1 of the Extradition Act 2003, the request is made by the authority which issued the Part 1 warrant in respect of the person;
(b) in a case where the proceedings are under Part 2 of that Act, the request is made on behalf of the territory to which the person's extradition has been requested."

(4) In section 5(1) (conduct of prosecutions on behalf of Crown Prosecution Service) after "criminal proceedings" insert "or extradition proceedings".
(5) In section 14 (control of fees and expenses etc paid by the Service) in subsection (1)(a) after "criminal proceedings" insert "or extradition proceedings".
(6) In section 15(1) (interpretation of Part 1) in the appropriate place insert —

" 'extradition proceedings' " means proceedings under the Extradition Act 2003;".

191 Lord Advocate: role in extradition proceedings

(1) The Lord Advocate must —

(a) conduct any extradition proceedings in Scotland;
(b) give, to such extent as he considers appropriate, and to such persons as he considers appropriate, advice on any matters relating to extradition proceedings or proposed extradition proceedings, in Scotland.

(2) Subsection (1)(a) does not require the Lord Advocate to conduct any extradition proceedings in respect of a person if he has received a request not to do so and —

(a) in a case where the proceedings are under Part 1, the request is made by the authority which issued the Part 1 warrant in respect of the person;

(b) in a case where the proceedings are under Part 2, the request is made on behalf of the territory to which the person's extradition has been requested.

192 Northern Ireland DPP and Crown Solicitor: role in extradition proceedings

(1) The Prosecution of Offences (Northern Ireland) Order 1972 (S.I. 1972/538 (N.I. 1)) is amended as set out in subsections (2) to (4).

(2) In article 2(2) (interpretation) in the appropriate place insert —

"'extradition proceedings'" means proceedings under the Extradition Act 2003;".

(3) In article 4(7) (conduct of prosecutions on behalf of DPP) after "prosecution" insert "or extradition proceedings".

(4) In article 5 (functions of DPP) after paragraph (1) insert —

"(1A) The Director may —

(a) have the conduct of any extradition proceedings in Northern Ireland;
(b) give to such persons as appear to him appropriate such advice as appears to him appropriate on matters relating to extradition proceedings, or proposed extradition proceedings, in Northern Ireland."

(5) The Justice (Northern Ireland) Act 2002 (c. 26) is amended as set out in subsections (6) to (8).

(6) After section 31 insert —

"31A Conduct of extradition proceedings

(1) The Director may have the conduct of any extradition proceedings in Northern Ireland.
(2) The Director may give to such persons as appear to him appropriate such advice as appears to him appropriate on matters relating to extradition proceedings, or proposed extradition proceedings, in Northern Ireland."

(7) In section 36(2) (conduct of criminal proceedings on behalf of DPP) after "criminal proceedings" insert "or extradition proceedings".

(8) In section 44 (interpretation) after subsection (6) insert —

"(7) For the purposes of this Part 'extradition proceedings' means proceedings under the Extradition Act 2003."

(9) The Crown Solicitor for Northern Ireland may —

(a) have the conduct of any proceedings under this Act in Northern Ireland;
(b) give to such persons as appear to him appropriate such advice as appears to him appropriate on matters relating to proceedings under this Act, or proposed proceedings under this Act, in Northern Ireland.

Parties to international Conventions

193 Parties to international Conventions

(1) A territory may be designated by order made by the Secretary of State if —

(a) it is not a category 1 territory or a category 2 territory, and
(b) it is a party to an international Convention to which the United Kingdom is a party.

(2) This Act applies in relation to a territory designated by order under subsection (1) as if the territory were a category 2 territory.

(3) As applied to a territory by subsection (2), this Act has effect as if —

- (a) sections 71(4), 73(5), 74(11)(b), 84(7), 86(7), 137 and 138 were omitted;
- (b) the conduct that constituted an extradition offence for the purposes of Part 2 were the conduct specified in relation to the territory in the order under subsection (1) designating the territory.

(4) Conduct may be specified in relation to a territory in an order under subsection (1) designating the territory only if it is conduct to which the relevant Convention applies.

(5) The relevant Convention is the Convention referred to in subsection (1)(b) which is specified in relation to the territory in the order under subsection (1) designating it.

Special extradition arrangements

194 Special extradition arrangements

(1) This section applies if the Secretary of State believes that —

- (a) arrangements have been made between the United Kingdom and another territory for the extradition of a person to the territory, and
- (b) the territory is not a category 1 territory or a category 2 territory.

(2) The Secretary of State may certify that the conditions in paragraphs (a) and (b) of subsection (1) are satisfied in relation to the extradition of the person.

(3) If the Secretary of State issues a certificate under subsection (2) this Act applies in respect of the person's extradition to the territory as if the territory were a category 2 territory.

(4) As applied by subsection (3), this Act has effect —

- (a) as if sections 71(4), 73(5), 74(11)(b), 84(7) and 86(7) were omitted;
- (b) with any other modifications specified in the certificate.

(5) A certificate under subsection (2) in relation to a person is conclusive evidence that the conditions in paragraphs (a) and (b) of subsection (1) are satisfied in relation to the person's extradition.

Human rights

195 Human rights: appropriate tribunal

(1) The appropriate judge is the only appropriate tribunal in relation to proceedings under section 7(1)(a) of the Human Rights Act 1998 (c. 42) (proceedings for acts incompatible with Convention rights) if the proceedings relate to extradition under Part 1 or Part 2 of this Act.

(2) If the proceedings relate to extradition under Part 1, section 67 applies for determining the appropriate judge.

(3) If the proceedings relate to extradition under Part 2, section 139 applies for determining the appropriate judge.

Genocide etc

196 Genocide, crimes against humanity and war crimes

(1) This section applies if —

(a) a Part 1 warrant in respect of a person is issued in respect of an offence mentioned in subsection (2), or
(b) a valid request for a person's extradition is made in respect of an offence mentioned in subsection (2).

(2) The offences are —

(a) an offence that if committed in the United Kingdom would be punishable as an offence under section 51 or 58 of the International Criminal Court Act 2001 (c. 17) (genocide, crimes against humanity and war crimes);
(b) an offence that if committed in the United Kingdom would be punishable as an offence under section 52 or 59 of that Act (conduct ancillary to genocide, etc. committed outside the jurisdiction);
(c) an offence that if committed in the United Kingdom would be punishable as an ancillary offence, as defined in section 55 or 62 of that Act, in relation to an offence falling within paragraph (a) or (b);
(d) an offence that if committed in the United Kingdom would be punishable as an offence under section 1 of the International Criminal Court (Scotland) Act 2001 (asp 13) (genocide, crimes against humanity and war crimes);
(e) an offence that if committed in the United Kingdom would be punishable as an offence under section 2 of that Act (conduct ancillary to genocide etc. committed outside the jurisdiction);
(f) an offence that if committed in the United Kingdom would be punishable as an ancillary offence, as defined in section 7 of that Act, in relation to an offence falling within paragraph (d) or (e);
(g) any offence punishable in the United Kingdom under section 1 of the Geneva Conventions Act 1957 (c. 52) (grave breach of scheduled conventions).

(3) It is not an objection to extradition under this Act that the person could not have been punished for the offence under the law in force at the time when and in the place where he is alleged to have committed the act of which he is accused or of which he has been convicted.

Custody and bail

197 Custody

(1) If a judge remands a person in custody under this Act, the person must be committed to the institution to which he would have been committed if charged with an offence before the judge.

(2) If a person in custody following his arrest under Part 1 or Part 2 escapes from custody, he may be retaken in any part of the United Kingdom in the same way as he could have been if he had been in custody following his arrest or apprehension under a relevant domestic warrant.

(3) A relevant domestic warrant is a warrant for his arrest or apprehension issued in the part of the United Kingdom in question in respect of an offence committed there.

(4) Subsection (5) applies if—

(a) a person is in custody in one part of the United Kingdom (whether under this Act or otherwise);
(b) he is required to be removed to another part of the United Kingdom after being remanded in custody under this Act;
(c) he is so removed by sea or air.

(5) The person must be treated as continuing in legal custody until he reaches the place to which he is required to be removed.

(6) An order for a person's extradition under this Act is sufficient authority for an appropriate person—

(a) to receive him;
(b) to keep him in custody until he is extradited under this Act;
(c) to convey him to the territory to which he is to be extradited under this Act.

(7) An appropriate person is—

(a) a person to whom the order is directed;
(b) a constable.

198 Bail: England and Wales

(1) The Bail Act 1976 (c. 63) is amended as follows.

(2) In section 1(1) (meaning of "bail in criminal proceedings") after paragraph (b) insert—

", or

(c) bail grantable in connection with extradition proceedings in respect of an offence."

(3) In section 2(2) (other definitions) omit the definition of "proceedings against a fugitive offender" and in the appropriate places insert—

"'extradition proceedings' means proceedings under the Extradition Act 2003;";
"'prosecutor', in relation to extradition proceedings, means the person acting on behalf of the territory to which extradition is sought;".

(4) In section 4 (general right to bail) in subsection (2) omit the words "or proceedings against a fugitive offender for the offence".

(5) In section 4 after subsection (2) insert—

"(2A) This section also applies to a person whose extradition is sought in respect of an offence, when—

(a) he appears or is brought before a court in the course of or in connection with extradition proceedings in respect of the offence, or
(b) he applies to a court for bail or for a variation of the conditions of bail in connection with the proceedings.

(2B) But subsection (2A) above does not apply if the person is alleged to be unlawfully at large after conviction of the offence."

(6) In section 5B (reconsideration of decisions granting bail) for subsection (1) substitute —

"(A1) This section applies in any of these cases —

(a) a magistrates' court has granted bail in criminal proceedings in connection with an offence to which this section applies or proceedings for such an offence;
(b) a constable has granted bail in criminal proceedings in connection with proceedings for such an offence;
(c) a magistrates' court or a constable has granted bail in connection with extradition proceedings.

(1) The court or the appropriate court in relation to the constable may, on application by the prosecutor for the decision to be reconsidered —

(a) vary the conditions of bail,
(b) impose conditions in respect of bail which has been granted unconditionally, or
(c) withhold bail."

(7) In section 7 (liability to arrest for absconding or breaking conditions of bail) after subsection (1) insert —

"(1A) Subsection (1B) applies if —

(a) a person has been released on bail in connection with extradition proceedings,
(b) the person is under a duty to surrender into the custody of a constable, and
(c) the person fails to surrender to custody at the time appointed for him to do so.

(1B) A magistrates' court may issue a warrant for the person's arrest."

(8) In section 7(4) omit the words from "In reckoning" to "Sunday".
(9) In section 7 after subsection (4) insert —

"(4A) A person who has been released on bail in connection with extradition proceedings and is under a duty to surrender into the custody of a constable may be arrested without warrant by a constable on any of the grounds set out in paragraphs (a) to (c) of subsection (3).

(4B) A person arrested in pursuance of subsection (4A) above shall be brought as soon as practicable and in any event within 24 hours after his arrest before a justice of the peace for the petty seFssions area in which he was arrested."

(10) In section 7(5) after "subsection (4)" insert "or (4B)".
(11) In section 7 after subsection (6) insert —

"(7) In reckoning for the purposes of this section any period of 24 hours, no account shall be taken of Christmas Day, Good Friday or any Sunday."

(12) In Part 1 of Schedule 1 (defendants accused or convicted of imprisonable offences) for paragraph 1 substitute —

"1 The following provisions of this Part of this Schedule apply to the defendant if —

(a) the offence or one of the offences of which he is accused or convicted in the proceedings is punishable with imprisonment, or
(b) his extradition is sought in respect of an offence."

(13) In Part 1 of Schedule 1 after paragraph 2A insert —

"2B The defendant need not be granted bail in connection with extradition proceedings if —

(a) the conduct constituting the offence would, if carried out by the defendant in England and Wales, constitute an indictable offence or an offence triable either way; and
(b) it appears to the court that the defendant was on bail on the date of the offence."

(14) In Part 1 of Schedule 1 in paragraph 6 after "the offence" insert "or the extradition proceedings".

199 Bail: Scotland

After section 24 of the Criminal Procedure (Scotland) Act 1995 (c. 46) (bail and bail conditions) insert —

"24A Bail: extradition proceedings

(1) In the application of the provisions of this Part by virtue of section 9(2) or 77(2) of the Extradition Act 2003 (judge's powers at extradition hearing), those provisions apply with the modifications that —

(a) references to the prosecutor are to be read as references to a person acting on behalf of the territory to which extradition is sought;
(b) the right of the Lord Advocate mentioned in section 24(2) of this Act applies to a person subject to extradition proceedings as it applies to a person charged with any crime or offence;
(c) the following do not apply —
  (i) paragraph (b) of section 24(3); and
  (ii) subsection (3) of section 30; and
(d) sections 28(1) and 33 apply to a person subject to extradition proceedings as they apply to an accused.

(2) Section 32 of this Act applies in relation to a refusal of bail, the amount of bail or a decision to allow bail or ordain appearance in proceedings under this Part as the Part applies by virtue of the sections of that Act of 2003 mentioned in subsection (1) above.

(3) The Scottish Ministers may, by order, for the purposes of section 9(2) or 77(2) of the Extradition Act 2003 make such amendments to this Part as they consider necessary or expedient.

(4) The order making power in subsection (3) above shall be exercisable by statutory instrument subject to annulment in pursuance of a resolution of the Scottish Parliament."

200 Appeal against grant of bail

(1) Section 1 of the Bail (Amendment) Act 1993 (c. 26) (prosecution right of appeal against grant of bail) is amended as follows.

(2) After subsection (1) insert —

"(1A) Where a magistrates' court grants bail to a person in connection with extradition proceedings, the prosecution may appeal to a judge of the Crown Court against the granting of bail."

(3) In subsection (3) for "Such an appeal" substitute "An appeal under subsection (1) or (1A)".

(4) In subsection (4) —

(a) after subsection (1) insert "or (1A)";
(b) for "magistrates' court" substitute "court which has granted bail";
(c) omit "such".

(5) In subsection (5) for "magistrates' court" substitute "court which has granted bail".
(6) In subsection (6) for "magistrates' court" substitute "court which has granted bail".
(7) In subsection (8) —

(a) after "subsection (1)" insert "or (1A)";
(b) omit "magistrates".

(8) In subsection (10)(b) for "reference in subsection (5) above to remand in custody is" substitute "references in subsections (6) and (9) above to remand in custody are".
(9) After subsection (11) insert —

"(12) In this section —
'extradition proceedings' means proceedings under the Extradition Act 2003;
'magistrates' court' and 'court' in relation to extradition proceedings means a District Judge (Magistrates' Courts) designated for the purposes of Part 1 or Part 2 of the Extradition Act 2003 by the Lord Chancellor;
'prosecution' in relation to extradition proceedings means the person acting on behalf of the territory to which extradition is sought."

201 Remand to local authority accommodation

(1) Section 23 of the Children and Young Persons Act 1969 (c. 54) (remand to local authority accommodation) is amended as set out in subsections (2) to (11).
(2) In subsection (1) after "following provisions of this section" insert "(except subsection (1A))".
(3) After subsection (1) insert —

"(1A) Where a court remands a child or young person in connection with extradition proceedings and he is not released on bail the remand shall be to local authority accommodation."

(4) In subsection (4) after "subsections (5)" insert ," (5ZA)".
(5) In subsection (5) after "security requirement" insert "in relation to a person remanded in accordance with subsection (1) above".
(6) After subsection (5) insert —

"(5ZA) A court shall not impose a security requirement in relation to a person remanded in accordance with subsection (1A) above unless —

(a) he has attained the age of twelve and is of a prescribed description;
(b) one or both of the conditions set out in subsection (5ZB) below is satisfied; and
(c) the condition set out in subsection (5AA) below is satisfied.

(5ZB) The conditions mentioned in subsection (5ZA)(b) above are —

(a) that the conduct constituting the offence to which the extradition proceedings relate would if committed in the United Kingdom constitute an offence punishable in the case of an adult with imprisonment for a term of fourteen years or more;

(b) that the person has previously absconded from the extradition proceedings or from proceedings in the United Kingdom or the requesting territory which relate to the conduct constituting the offence to which the extradition proceedings relate.

(5ZC) For the purposes of subsection (5ZB) above a person has absconded from proceedings if in relation to those proceedings —

(a) he has been released subject to a requirement to surrender to custody at a particular time and he has failed to surrender to custody at that time, or
(b) he has surrendered into the custody of a court and he has at any time absented himself from the court without its leave."

(7) In subsection (5AA) for "subsection (5)" substitute "subsections (5) and (5ZA)".
(8) In subsection (12) for the definition of "relevant court"substitute —

" 'relevant court' —

(a) in relation to a person remanded to local authority accommodation under subsection (1) above, means the court by which he was so remanded, or any magistrates'court having jurisdiction in the place where he is for the time being;
(b) in relation to a person remanded to local authority accommodation under subsection (1A) above, means the court by which he was so remanded."

(9) In subsection (12) in the appropriate places insert —

" 'extradition proceedings' means proceedings under the Extradition Act 2003;";
" 'requesting territory' means the territory to which a person's extradition is sought in extradition proceedings;".

(10) In section 98(1)of the Crime and Disorder Act 1998 (c. 37) (modifications of section 23 of the Children and Young Persons Act 1969 (c. 54) in relation to 15 and 16 year old boys) after paragraph (b) insert "; and

(c) is not remanded in connection with proceedings under the Extradition Act 2003."

Evidence

202 Receivable documents

(1) A Part 1 warrant may be received in evidence in proceedings under this Act.
(2) Any other document issued in a category 1 territory may be received in evidence in proceedings under this Act if it is duly authenticated.
(3) A document issued in a category 2 territory may be received in evidence in proceedings under this Act if it is duly authenticated.
(4) A document issued in a category 1 or category 2 territory is duly authenticated if (and only if) one of these applies —

(a) it purports to be signed by a judge, magistrate or other judicial authority of the territory;
(b) it purports to be authenticated by the oath or affirmation of a witness.

(5) Subsections (2) and (3) do not prevent a document that is not duly authenticated from being received in evidence in proceedings under this Act.

203 Documents sent by facsimile

(1) This section applies if a document to be sent in connection with proceedings under this Act is sent by facsimile transmission.

(2) This Act has effect as if the document received by facsimile transmission were the document used to make the transmission.

204 Part 1 warrant: transmission by other electronic means

(1) This section applies if a Part 1 warrant is issued and the information contained in the warrant —

(a) is transmitted to the designated authority by electronic means (other than by facsimile transmission), and
(b) is received by the designated authority in a form in which it is intelligible and which is capable of being used for subsequent reference.

(2) This Act has effect as if the information received by the designated authority were the Part 1 warrant.

(3) A copy of the information received by the designated authority may be received in evidence as if it were the Part 1 warrant.

205 Written statements and admissions

(1) The provisions mentioned in subsection (2) apply in relation to proceedings under this Act as they apply in relation to proceedings for an offence.

(2) The provisions are —

(a) section 9 of the Criminal Justice Act 1967 (c. 80) (proof by written statement in criminal proceedings);
(b) section 10 of the Criminal Justice Act 1967 (proof by formal admission in criminal proceedings);
(c) section 1 of the Criminal Justice (Miscellaneous Provisions) Act (Northern Ireland) 1968 (c. 28) (proof by written statement in criminal proceedings);
(d) section 2 of the Criminal Justice (Miscellaneous Provisions) Act (Northern Ireland) 1968 (proof by formal admission in criminal proceedings).

(3) As applied by subsection (1) in relation to proceedings under this Act, section 10 of the Criminal Justice Act 1967 and section 2 of the Criminal Justice (Miscellaneous Provisions) Act (Northern Ireland) 1968 have effect as if —

(a) references to the defendant were to the person whose extradition is sought (or who has been extradited);
(b) references to the prosecutor were to the category 1 or category 2 territory concerned;
(c) references to the trial were to the proceedings under this Act for the purposes of which the admission is made;
(d) references to subsequent criminal proceedings were to subsequent proceedings under this Act.

206 Burden and standard of proof

(1) This section applies if, in proceedings under this Act, a question arises as to burden or standard of proof.

(2) The question must be decided by applying any enactment or rule of law that would apply if the proceedings were proceedings for an offence.

(3) Any enactment or rule of law applied under subsection (2) to proceedings under this Act must be applied as if—

(a) the person whose extradition is sought (or who has been extradited) were accused of an offence;
(b) the category 1 or category 2 territory concerned were the prosecution.

(4) Subsections (2) and (3) are subject to any express provision of this Act.
(5) In this section "enactment" includes an enactment comprised in, or in an instrument made under, an Act of the Scottish Parliament.

Other miscellaneous provisions

207 Extradition for more than one offence

The Secretary of State may by order provide for this Act to have effect with specified modifications in relation to a case where—

(a) a Part 1 warrant is issued in respect of more than one offence;
(b) a request for extradition is made in respect of more than one offence.

208 National security

(1) This section applies if the Secretary of State believes that the conditions in subsections (2) to (4) are satisfied in relation to a person.
(2) The first condition is that the person's extradition is sought or will be sought under Part 1 or Part 2 in respect of an offence.
(3) The second condition is that—

(a) in engaging in the conduct constituting (or alleged to constitute) the offence the person was acting for the purpose of assisting in the exercise of a function conferred or imposed by or under an enactment, or
(b) as a result of an authorisation given by the Secretary of State the person is not liable under the criminal law of any part of the United Kingdom for the conduct constituting (or alleged to constitute) the offence.

(4) The third condition is that the person's extradition in respect of the offence would be against the interests of national security.
(5) The Secretary of State may certify that the conditions in subsections (2) to (4) are satisfied in relation to the person.
(6) If the Secretary of State issues a certificate under subsection (5) he may—

(a) direct that a Part 1 warrant issued in respect of the person and in respect of the offence is not to be proceeded with, or
(b) direct that a request for the person's extradition in respect of the offence is not to be proceeded with.

(7) If the Secretary of State issues a certificate under subsection (5) he may order the person's discharge (instead of or in addition to giving a direction under subsection (6)).
(8) These rules apply if the Secretary of State gives a direction under subsection (6)(a) in respect of a warrant—

(a) if the designated authority has not issued a certificate under section 2 in respect of the warrant it must not do so;

(b) if the person is arrested under the warrant or under section 5 there is no requirement for him to be brought before the appropriate judge and he must be discharged;
(c) if the person is brought before the appropriate judge under section 4 or 6 the judge is no longer required to proceed or continue proceeding under sections 7 and 8;
(d) if the extradition hearing has begun the judge is no longer required to proceed or continue proceeding under sections 10 to 25;
(e) if the person has consented to his extradition, the judge is no longer required to order his extradition;
(f) if an appeal to the High Court or House of Lords has been brought, the court is no longer required to hear or continue hearing the appeal;
(g) if the person's extradition has been ordered there is no requirement for him to be extradited.

(9) These rules apply if the Secretary of State gives a direction under subsection (6)(b) in respect of a request —

(a) if he has not issued a certificate under section 70 in respect of the request he is no longer required to do so;
(b) if the person is arrested under a warrant issued under section 71 or under a provisional warrant there is no requirement for him to appear or be brought before the appropriate judge and he must be discharged;
(c) if the person appears or is brought before the appropriate judge the judge is no longer required to proceed or continue proceeding under sections 72, 74, 75 and 76;
(d) if the extradition hearing has begun the judge is no longer required to proceed or continue proceeding under sections 78 to 91;
(e) if the person has given his consent to his extradition to the appropriate judge, the judge is no longer required to send the case to the Secretary of State for his decision whether the person is to be extradited;
(f) if an appeal to the High Court or House of Lords has been brought, the court is no longer required to hear or continue hearing the appeal;
(g) if the person's extradition has been ordered there is no requirement for him to be extradited.

(10) These must be made under the hand of the Secretary of State —

(a) a certificate under subsection (5);
(b) a direction under subsection (6);
(c) an order under subsection (7).

(11) The preceding provisions of this section apply to Scotland with these modifications —

(a) in subsection (9)(a) for "he has" substitute "the Scottish Ministers have" and for "he is" substitute "they are";
(b) in subsection (9)(e) for "Secretary of State for his" substitute "Scottish Ministers for their".

(12) In subsection (3) the reference to an enactment includes an enactment comprised in, or in an instrument made under, an Act of the Scottish Parliament.

209 Reasonable force

A person may use reasonable force, if necessary, in the exercise of a power conferred by this Act.

210 Rules of court

(1) Rules of court may make provision as to the practice and procedure to be followed in connection with proceedings under this Act.

(2) In Scotland any rules of court under this Act are to be made by Act of Adjournal.

211 Service of notices

Service of a notice on a person under section 54, 56, 58, 129, 130 or 131 may be effected in any of these ways —

(a) by delivering the notice to the person;
(b) by leaving it for him with another person at his last known or usual place of abode;
(c) by sending it by post in a letter addressed to him at his last known or usual place of abode.

212 Article 95 alerts: transitional provision

(1) This section applies in a case where an article 95 alert is issued before 1 January 2004 by an authority of a category 1 territory.

(2) In such a case, this Act applies as if —

(a) the alert were a Part 1 warrant issued by the authority;
(b) any information sent with the alert relating to the case were included in the warrant.

(3) As applied by subsection (2), this Act has effect with these modifications —

(a) in sections 2(7) and (8), 28(1), 30(1) and (4)(d), 32(2)(b), 33(6)(b), 35(4)(b), 36(3)(b), 47(3)(b), 49(3)(b), 190(3) and 191(2)(a) for "authority which issued the Part 1 warrant" substitute "authority at the request of which the alert was issued";
(b) omit section 5;
(c) in sections 33(4)(b), 42(2)(a), 43(2)(a) and (4) and 61(1)(d) and (e), for "authority which issued the warrant" substitute "authority at the request of which the alert was issued";
(d) in section 66(2), for the words from "believes" to the end substitute "believes is the authority at the request of which the alert was issued".

(4) An article 95 alert is an alert issued pursuant to article 95 of the Convention implementing the Schengen agreement of 14th June 1985.

Interpretation

213 Disposal of Part 1 warrant and extradition request

(1) A Part 1 warrant issued in respect of a person is disposed of —

(a) when an order is made for the person's discharge in respect of the warrant and there is no further possibility of an appeal;
(b) when the person is taken to be discharged in respect of the warrant;
(c) when an order is made for the person's extradition in pursuance of the warrant and there is no further possibility of an appeal.

(2) A request for a person's extradition is disposed of —

(a) when an order is made for the person's discharge in respect of the request and there is no further possibility of an appeal;
(b) when the person is taken to be discharged in respect of the request;
(c) when an order is made for the person's extradition in pursuance of the request and there is no further possibility of an appeal.

(3) There is no further possibility of an appeal against an order for a person's discharge or extradition —

(a) when the period permitted for giving notice of an appeal to the High Court ends, if notice is not given before the end of that period;
(b) when the decision of the High Court on an appeal becomes final, if there is no appeal to the House of Lords against that decision;
(c) when the decision of the House of Lords on an appeal is made, if there is such an appeal.

(4) The decision of the High Court on an appeal becomes final —

(a) when the period permitted for applying to the High Court for leave to appeal to the House of Lords ends, if there is no such application;
(b) when the period permitted for applying to the House of Lords for leave to appeal to it ends, if the High Court refuses leave to appeal and there is no application to the House of Lords for leave to appeal;
(c) when the House of Lords refuses leave to appeal to it;
(d) at the end of the permitted period, which is 28 days starting with the day on which leave to appeal to the House of Lords is granted, if no such appeal is brought before the end of that period.

(5) These must be ignored for the purposes of subsections (3) and (4) —

(a) any power of a court to extend the period permitted for giving notice of appeal or for applying for leave to appeal;
(b) any power of a court to grant leave to take a step out of time.

(6) Subsections (3) to (5) do not apply to Scotland.

214 Disposal of charge

(1) A charge against a person is disposed of —

(a) if the person is acquitted in respect of it, when he is acquitted;
(b) if the person is convicted in respect of it, when there is no further possibility of an appeal against the conviction.

(2) There is no further possibility of an appeal against a conviction —

(a) when the period permitted for giving notice of application for leave to appeal to the Court of Appeal against the conviction ends, if the leave of the Court of Appeal is required and no such notice is given before the end of that period;
(b) when the Court of Appeal refuses leave to appeal against the conviction, if the leave of the Court of Appeal is required and notice of application for leave is given before the end of that period;

(c) when the period permitted for giving notice of appeal to the Court of Appeal against the conviction ends, if notice is not given before the end of that period;
(d) when the decision of the Court of Appeal on an appeal becomes final, if there is no appeal to the House of Lords against that decision;
(e) when the decision of the House of Lords on an appeal is made, if there is such an appeal.

(3) The decision of the Court of Appeal on an appeal becomes final —

(a) when the period permitted for applying to the Court of Appeal for leave to appeal to the House of Lords ends, if there is no such application;
(b) when the period permitted for applying to the House of Lords for leave to appeal to it ends, if the Court of Appeal refuses leave to appeal and there is no application to the House of Lords for leave to appeal;
(c) when the House of Lords refuses leave to appeal to it;
(d) at the end of the permitted period, which is 28 days starting with the day on which leave to appeal to the House of Lords is granted, if no such appeal is brought before the end of that period.

(4) These must be ignored for the purposes of subsections (2) and (3) —

(a) any power of a court to extend the period permitted for giving notice of appeal or of application for leave to appeal or for applying for leave to appeal;
(b) any power of a court to grant leave to take a step out of time.

(5) Subsections (2) to (4) do not apply to Scotland.

215 European framework list

(1) The European framework list is the list of conduct set out in Schedule 2.

(2) The Secretary of State may by order amend Schedule 2 for the purpose of ensuring that the list of conduct set out in the Schedule corresponds to the list of conduct set out in article 2.2 of the European framework decision.

(3) The European framework decision is the framework decision of the Council of the European Union made on 13 June 2002 on the European arrest warrant and the surrender procedures between member states (2002/584/JHA).

216 Other interpretative provisions

(1) References to a category 1 territory must be read in accordance with section 1.

(2) References to a category 2 territory must be read in accordance with section 69.

(3) References to the designated authority must be read in accordance with section 2(9).

(4) References to a Part 1 warrant must be read in accordance with section 2.

(5) References to a Part 3 warrant must be read in accordance with section 142.

(6) References to a valid request for a person's extradition must be read in accordance with section 70.

(7) "Asylum claim" has the meaning given by section 113(1) of the Nationality, Immigration and Asylum Act 2002 (c. 41).

(8) A customs officer is a person commissioned by the Commissioners of Customs and Excise under section 6(3) of the Customs and Excise Management Act 1979 (c. 2).

(9) "High Court" in relation to Scotland means the High Court of Justiciary.

(10) In relation to Scotland, references to an appeal being discontinued are to be construed as references to its being abandoned.

(11) "Police officer" in relation to Northern Ireland has the same meaning as in the Police (Northern Ireland) Act 2000 (c. 32).

(12) A provisional warrant is a warrant issued under section 73(3).

(13) A service policeman is a member of the Royal Navy Regulating Branch, the Royal Marines Police, the Royal Military Police or the Royal Air Force Police.

(14) The Provost Marshal of the Royal Air Force and any officer appointed to exercise the functions conferred on provost officers by the Air Force Act 1955 (3 & 4 Eliz. 2 c. 19) are to be taken to be members of the Royal Air Force Police for the purposes of subsection (13).

(15) This section and sections 213 to 215 apply for the purposes of this Act.

General

217 Form of documents

The Secretary of State may by regulations prescribe the form of any document required for the purposes of this Act.

218 Existing legislation on extradition

These Acts shall cease to have effect —

(a) the Backing of Warrants (Republic of Ireland) Act 1965 (c. 45);
(b) the Extradition Act 1989 (c. 33).

219 Amendments

(1) Schedule 3 contains miscellaneous and consequential amendments.

(2) The Secretary of State may by order make —

(a) any supplementary, incidental or consequential provision, and
(b) any transitory, transitional or saving provision,

which he considers necessary or expedient for the purposes of, in consequence of, or for giving full effect to any provision of this Act.

(3) An order under subsection (2) may, in particular —

(a) provide for any provision of this Act which comes into force before another such provision has come into force to have effect, until that other provision has come into force, with such modifications as are specified in the order, and
(b) amend, repeal or revoke any enactment other than one contained in an Act passed in a Session after that in which this Act is passed.

(4) The amendments that may be made under subsection (3)(b) are in addition to those made by or under any other provision of this Act.

220 Repeals

Schedule 4 contains repeals.

221 Commencement

The preceding provisions of this Act come into force in accordance with provision made by the Secretary of State by order.

222 Channel Islands and Isle of Man

An Order in Council may provide for this Act to extend to any of the Channel Islands or the Isle of Man with the modifications (if any) specified in the Order.

223 Orders and regulations

(1) References in this section to subordinate legislation are to —

(a) an order of the Secretary of State under this Act (other than an order within subsection (2));
(b) an order of the Treasury under this Act;
(c) regulations under this Act.

(2) The orders referred to in subsection (1)(a) are —

(a) an order for a person's extradition or discharge;
(b) an order deferring proceedings on a warrant or request;
(c) an order deferring a person's extradition in pursuance of a warrant or request.

(3) Subordinate legislation —

(a) may make different provision for different purposes;
(b) may include supplementary, incidental, saving or transitional provisions.

(4) A power to make subordinate legislation is exercisable by statutory instrument.
(5) No order mentioned in subsection (6) may be made unless a draft of the order has been laid before Parliament and approved by a resolution of each House.
(6) The orders are —

(a) an order under any of these provisions —

section 1(1);
section 69(1);
section 71(4);
section 73(5);
section 74(11)(b);
section 84(7);
section 86(7);
section 142(9);
section 173(4);
section 215(2);

(b) an order under section 219(2) which contains any provision (whether alone or with other provisions) amending or repealing any Act or provision of an Act.

(7) A statutory instrument is subject to annulment in pursuance of a resolution of either House of Parliament if it contains subordinate legislation other than an order mentioned in subsection (6) or an order under section 221.
(8) A territory may be designated by being named in an order made by the Secretary of State under this Act or by falling within a description set out in such an order.
(9) An order made by the Secretary of State under section 1(1) or 69(1) may provide that this Act has effect in relation to a territory designated by the order with specified modifications.

224 Orders in Council

(1) An Order in Council under section 177 or 178 is subject to annulment in pursuance of a resolution of either House of Parliament.

(2) An Order in Council under this Act —

(a) may make different provision for different purposes;
(b) may include supplementary, incidental, saving or transitional provisions.

225 Finance

The following are to be paid out of money provided by Parliament —

(a) any expenditure incurred by the Lord Chancellor under this Act;
(b) any increase attributable to this Act in the sums payable out of money provided by Parliament under any other enactment.

226 Extent

(1) Sections 157 to 160, 166 to 168, 171, 173 and 205 do not extend to Scotland.

(2) Sections 154, 198, 200 and 201 extend to England and Wales only.

(3) Sections 183 and 199 extend to Scotland only.

(4) Sections 184 and 185 extend to Northern Ireland only.

227 Short title

This Act may be cited as the Extradition Act 2003.

SCHEDULE 1

Section 188 and 189

RE -EXTRADIATION: MODIFICATIONS

PART 1

CATEGORY 1 TERRITORIES

1. In section 11(1), omit paragraphs (c), (g) and (h).
2. Omit sections 14, 18 and 19.
3. In section 21(3), for "must" substitute "may".
4. In section 31(2), for paragraphs (a) and (b) substitute "would (apart from section 187(1)) be released from detention pursuant to the UK sentence (whether or not on licence)".
5. In section 39(2)(a), for "a certificate is issued under section 2 in respect of the warrant" substitute "the person would (apart from section 187(1)) be released from detention pursuant to the UK sentence (whether or not on licence)".
6. In section 44(2)(a), for "following his arrest under this Part" substitute "under section 187(1)".
7. In section 45(1), for the words from "arrested" to "issued" substitute "brought before the appropriate judge under section 187(1) may consent to his extradition to the territory in which the overseas sentence was imposed".

PART 2

CATEGORY 2 TERRITORIES

8. In section 78, omit subsections (2), (3), (5) and (8).
9. In section 78, for subsection (4) substitute —

"(4) The judge must decide whether the offence specified in the request is an extradition offence."

10. In section 78(6), for "any of the questions" substitute "the question".
11. In section 78(7), for "those questions" substitute "that question".
12. In section 79(1), omit paragraph (c).
13. Omit section 82.
14. In section 87(3), for the words from "must send the case" to "extradited" substitute "may order the person to be extradited to the category 2 territory".
15. In section 87, after subsection (3) insert—

"(4) If the judge makes an order under subsection (3) he must remand the person in custody or on bail to wait for his extradition to the territory.
(5) If the judge remands the person in custody he may later grant bail."

16. In section 103(1)—

(a) for the words from "sends a case" to "extradited" substitute "orders a person's extradition under this Part"; and

(b) for "the relevant decision" substitute "the order".

17. In section 103(2), for the words from "the person" to "the Secretary of State" substitute "the order is made under section 128".
18. In section 103, omit subsections (3), (5), (6), (7) and (8).
19. In section 103(9), for the words from "the Secretary of State" to "person" substitute "the order is made".
20. In section 104, omit subsections (1)(b), (6) and (7).
21. In section 106, omit subsections (1)(b), (7) and (8).
22. In section 117(1)(a), for "the Secretary of State" substitute "the appropriate judge".
23. In section 117(1)(b), for the words from "permitted period" to "extradition" substitute "period permitted under that section".
24. In section 117, after subsection (1) insert—

"(1A) But this section does not apply if the order is made under section 128."

25. In section 117(2), for "the Secretary of State" substitute "the judge".
26. In section 119(1)(a), for "the Secretary of State" substitute "the appropriate judge".
27. In section 119, in subsections (2) to (6) and in each place in subsection (7), for "the Secretary of State" substitute "the judge".
28. In section 120, after subsection (1) insert—

"(1A) But this section does not apply if the order for the person's extradition is made under section 128."

29. In section 121(2)(a), for "a certificate is issued under section 70 in respect of the request" substitute "the person would (apart from section 187(1)) be released from detention pursuant to the UK sentence (whether or not on licence)".
30. In section 127(1), for the words from "arrested" to "requested" substitute "brought before the appropriate judge under section 187(1) may consent to his extradition to the territory in which the overseas sentence was imposed".
31. In section 127(3), before paragraph (a) insert—

"(aa) must be given before the appropriate judge;".

32. In section 127, omit subsections (4) and (5).
33. In section 128, after subsection (1) insert—

"(1A) The judge must remand the person in custody or on bail.
(1B) If the judge remands the person in custody he may later grant bail."

34. In section 128(4), for the words from "send the case" to "extradited" substitute "within the period of 10 days starting with the day on which consent is given order the person's extradition to the category 2 territory".

35. In section 128, after subsection (5) insert —

"(6) Subsection (4) has effect subject to section 128B.

(7) If subsection (4) is not complied with and the person applies to the judge to be discharged the judge must order his discharge."

36. After section 128 insert —

"128A Extradition to category 2 territory following consent

(1) This section applies if the appropriate judge makes an order under section 128(4) for a person's extradition to a category 2 territory.

(2) The person must be extradited to the category 2 territory before the end of the required period, which is 28 days starting with the day on which the order is made.

(3) If subsection (2) is not complied with and the person applies to the judge to be discharged the judge must order his discharge, unless reasonable cause is shown for the delay.

128B Extradition claim following consent

(1) This section applies if —

(a) a person consents under section 127 to his extradition to a category 2 territory, and

(b) before the judge orders his extradition under section 128(4), the judge is informed that the conditions in subsection (2) or (3) are met.

(2) The conditions are that —

(a) the Secretary of State has received another valid request for the person's extradition to a category 2 territory;

(b) the other request has not been disposed of.

(3) The conditions are that —

(a) a certificate has been issued under section 2 in respect of a Part 1 warrant issued in respect of the person;

(b) the warrant has not been disposed of.

(4) The judge must not make an order under section 128(4) until he is informed what order has been made under section 126(2) or 179(2).

(5) If the order under section 126(2) or 179(2) is for further proceedings on the request under consideration to be deferred until the other request, or the warrant, has been disposed of, the judge must remand the person in custody or on bail.

(6) If the judge remands the person in custody he may later grant bail.

(7) If —

(a) the order under section 126(2) or 179(2) is for further proceedings on the request under consideration to be deferred until the other request, or the warrant, has been disposed of, and

(b) an order is made under section 180 for proceedings on the request under consideration to be resumed,

the period specified in section 128(4) must be taken to be 10 days starting with the day on which the order under section 180 is made.

(8) If the order under section 126(2) or 179(2) is for further proceedings on the other request, or the warrant, to be deferred until the request under consideration has been disposed of, the period specified in section 128(4) must be taken to be 10 days starting with the day on which the judge is informed of the order.

128C Extradition following deferral for competing claim

(1) This section applies if —

(a) an order is made under section 128(4) for a person to be extradited to a category 2 territory in pursuance of a request for his extradition;

(b) before the person is extradited to the territory an order is made under section 126(2) or 179(2) for the person's extradition in pursuance of the request to be deferred;
(c) the appropriate judge makes an order under section 181(2) for the person's extradition in pursuance of the request to cease to be deferred.

(2) The required period for the purposes of section 128A(2) is 28 days starting with the day on which the order under section 181(2) is made."

SCHEDULE 2

Section 215

EUROPEAN FRAMEWORK LIST

1. Participation in a criminal organisation.
2. Terrorism.
3. Trafficking in human beings.
4. Sexual exploitation of children and child pornography.
5. Illicit trafficking in narcotic drugs and psychotropic substances.
6. Illicit trafficking in weapons, munitions and explosives.
7. Corruption.
8. Fraud, including that affecting the financial interests of the European Communities within the meaning of the Convention of 26 July 1995 on the protection of the European Communities' financial interests.
9. Laundering of the proceeds of crime.
10. Counterfeiting currency, including of the euro.
11. Computer-related crime.
12. Environmental crime, including illicit trafficking in endangered animal species and in endangered plant species and varieties.
13. Facilitation of unauthorised entry and residence.
14. Murder, grievous bodily injury.
15. Illicit trade in human organs and tissue.
16. Kidnapping, illegal restraint and hostage-taking.
17. Racism and xenophobia.
18. Organised or armed robbery.
19. Illicit trafficking in cultural goods, including antiques and works of art.
20. Swindling.
21. Racketeering and extortion.
22. Counterfeiting and piracy of products.
23. Forgery of administrative documents and trafficking therein.
24. Forgery of means of payment.
25. Illicit trafficking in hormonal substances and other growth promoters.
26. Illicit trafficking in nuclear or radioactive materials.
27. Trafficking in stolen vehicles.
28. Rape.
29. Arson.
30. Crimes within the jurisdiction of the International Criminal Court.
31. Unlawful seizure of aircraft/ships.
32. Sabotage.

SCHEDULE 3

Section 219

AMENDMENTS

Introduction

1. The amendments specified in this Schedule shall have effect.

Parliamentary Commissioner Act 1967 (c. 13)

2. In Schedule 3 to the Parliamentary Commissioner Act 1967 (c. 13) (matters not subject to investigation) for paragraph 4 substitute —

"4 Action taken by the Secretary of State under the Extradition Act 2003."

Criminal Justice Act 1967 (c. 80)

3. Section 34 of the Criminal Justice Act 1967 (c. 80) (committal of persons under twenty-one accused of extradition crimes) shall cease to have effect.

Suppression of Terrorism Act 1978 (c. 26)

4. Sections 1 (offences not to be regarded as of a political character) and 2 (restrictions on return of criminal under Extradition Act 1870 or to Republic of Ireland) of the Suppression of Terrorism Act 1978 (c. 26) shall cease to have effect.

5. For section 5 of the Suppression of Terrorism Act 1978 substitute —

"5 Power to apply section 4 to non-convention countries

(1) The Secretary of State may by order direct that section 4 above shall apply in relation to a country falling within subsection (2) below as it applies in relation to a convention country, subject to the exceptions (if any) specified in the order.

(2) A country falls within this subsection if —

(a) it is not a convention country; and
(b) it is a category 1 territory or a category 2 territory within the meaning of the Extradition Act 2003."

Criminal Justice (International Co-operation) Act 1990 (c. 5)

6. Section 22(1) of the Criminal Justice (International Co-operation) Act 1990 (c. 5) (offences to which an Order in Council under the Extradition Act 1870 can apply) shall cease to have effect.

Computer Misuse Act 1990 (c. 18)

7. Section 15 of the Computer Misuse Act 1990 (c. 18) (extradition where Schedule 1 to the Extradition Act 1989 applies) shall cease to have effect.

Aviation and Maritime Security Act 1990 (c. 31)

8. Section 49 of the Aviation and Maritime Security Act 1990 (c. 31) (extradition by virtue of Orders in Council under Extradition Act 1870) shall cease to have effect.

Criminal Justice Act 1991 (c. 53)

9. In section 47 of the Criminal Justice Act 1991 (c. 53) (persons extradited to the United Kingdom) subsection (4) shall cease to have effect.

United Nations Personnel Act 1997 (c. 13)

10. Section 6(1) of the United Nations Personnel Act 1997 (c. 13) (offences to which an Order in Council under section 2 of the Extradition Act 1870 can apply) shall cease to have effect.

Terrorism Act 2000 (c. 11)

11. Section 64(5) of the Terrorism Act 2000 (c. 11) (offences to which an Order in Council under section 2 of the Extradition Act 1870 can apply) shall cease to have effect.

International Criminal Court Act 2001 (c. 17)

12. Section 71 of the International Criminal Court Act 2001 (c. 17) (extradition: Orders in Council under the Extradition Act 1870) shall cease to have effect.

13. (1) Part 2 of Schedule 2 to the International Criminal Court Act 2001 (delivery up to International Criminal Court of persons subject to extradition proceedings) is amended as follows.

(2) For paragraph 7 (meaning of "extradition proceedings") substitute —

"7 In this Part of this Schedule "extradition proceedings" means proceedings before a court or judge in the United Kingdom under the Extradition Act 2003."

(3) In paragraph 8 (extradition proceedings in England and Wales or Northern Ireland) after sub-paragraph (5) add —

"(6) References in this paragraph to a court include references to a judge."

(4) In paragraph 9 (extradition proceedings in Scotland) after sub-paragraph (3) add —

"(4) References in this paragraph to a court include references to a judge."

(5) In paragraph 10 (power to suspend or revoke warrant or order) for sub-paragraph (1) substitute —

"(1) Where a court makes a delivery order in respect of a person whose extradition has been ordered under the Extradition Act 2003, it may make any such order as is necessary to enable the delivery order to be executed."

(6) In paragraph 10(2) omit the words "by a court or judicial officer".

Enterprise Act 2002 (c. 40)

14. Section 191 of the Enterprise Act 2002 (c. 40) (offences to which an Order in Council under the Extradition Act 1870 can apply) shall cease to have effect.

SCHEDULE 4

Section 220

REPEALS

Short title and chapter	*Extent of repeal*
Backing of Warrants (Republic of Ireland) Act 1965 (c. 45)	The whole Act.
Criminal Justice Act 1967 (c. 80)	Section 34.
Criminal Jurisdiction Act 1975 (c. 59)	In Schedule 3, paragraph 1.
Bail Act 1976 (c. 63)	In section 2(2) the definition of "proceedings against a fugitive offender".
	In section 4(2) the words "or proceedings against a fugitive offender for the offence".
	In section 7(4) the words from "In reckoning" to "Sunday".
	In Schedule 2, paragraph 33.
Criminal Law Act 1977 (c. 45)	In Schedule 12, in the entry for the Bail Act 1976, paragraph 4.

Short title and chapter	*Extent of repeal*
Suppression of Terrorism Act 1978 (c. 26)	Sections 1 and 2. In section 8 — (a) subsection (5)(a); (b) in subsection (6) the words from "an order made under section 1(4)" to "or".
Extradition Act 1989 (c. 33)	The whole Act.
Criminal Justice (International Co-operation) Act 1990 (c. 5)	Section 22.
Computer Misuse Act 1990 (c. 18)	Section 15.
Aviation and Maritime Security Act 1990 (c. 31)	Section 49.
Criminal Justice Act 1991 (c. 53)	Section 47(4).
Bail (Amendment) Act 1993 (c. 26)	In section 1 — (a) in subsection (4), the word "such"; (b) in subsection (8), the word "magistrates' ".
Criminal Justice Act 1993 (c. 36)	Section 72. Section 79(7).
Criminal Justice and Public Order Act 1994 (c. 33)	Sections 158 and 159.
United Nations Personnel Act 1997 (c. 13)	Section 6.
Justices of the Peace Act 1997 (c. 25)	In Schedule 5, paragraph 9.
Access to Justice Act 1999 (c. 22)	In Schedule 11, paragraphs 18 and 31 to 36.
Powers of Criminal Courts (Sentencing) Act 2000 (c. 6)	In Schedule 9, paragraph 124.
Terrorism Act 2000 (c. 11)	Section 64.
International Criminal Court Act 2001 (c. 17)	Sections 71 to 73. In paragraph 10(2) of Schedule 2, the words "by a court or judicial officer".
Proceeds of Crime Act 2002 (c. 29)	In Schedule 11, paragraph 18.
Enterprise Act 2002 (c. 40)	Section 191.

Crime (International Co-operation) Act 2003 A–002

2003 CHAPTER 32

PART 1

MUTUAL ASSISTANCE IN CRIMINAL MATTERS

CHAPTER 1

MUTUAL SERVICE OF PROCESS ETC.

Service of overseas process in the UK

1 Service of overseas process

(1) The power conferred by subsection (3) is exercisable where the Secretary of State receives any process or other document to which this section applies from the government of, or other authority in, a country outside the United Kingdom, together with a request for the process or document to be served on a person in the United Kingdom.

(2) This section applies —

(a) to any process issued or made in that country for the purposes of criminal proceedings,
(b) to any document issued or made by an administrative authority in that country in administrative proceedings,
(c) to any process issued or made for the purposes of any proceedings on an appeal before a court in that country against a decision in administrative proceedings,
(d) to any document issued or made by an authority in that country for the purposes of clemency proceedings.

(3) The Secretary of State may cause the process or document to be served by post or, if the request is for personal service, direct the chief officer of police for the area in which that person appears to be to cause it to be personally served on him.

(4) In relation to any process or document to be served in Scotland, references in this section to the Secretary of State are to be read as references to the Lord Advocate.

2 Service of overseas process: supplementary

(1) Subsections (2) and (3) apply to any process served in a part of the United Kingdom by virtue of section 1 requiring a person to appear as a party or attend as a witness.

(2) No obligation under the law of that part to comply with the process is imposed by virtue of its service.

(3) The process must be accompanied by a notice —

(a) stating the effect of subsection (2),
(b) indicating that the person on whom it is served may wish to seek advice as to the possible consequences of his failing to comply with the process under the law of the country where it was issued or made, and
(c) indicating that under that law he may not be accorded the same rights and privileges as a party or as a witness as would be accorded to him in proceedings in the part of the United Kingdom in which the process is served.

(4) Where a chief officer of police causes any process or document to be served under section 1, he must at once —

(a) tell the Secretary of State (or, as the case may be, the Lord Advocate) when and how it was served, and
(b) (if possible) provide him with a receipt signed by the person on whom it was served.

(5) Where the chief officer of police is unable to cause any process or document to be served as directed, he must at once inform the Secretary of State (or, as the case may be, the Lord Advocate) of that fact and of the reason.

Service of UK process abroad

3 General requirements for service of process

(1) This section applies to any process issued or made for the purposes of criminal proceedings by a court in England and Wales or Northern Ireland.

(2) The process may be issued or made in spite of the fact that the person on whom it is to be served is outside the United Kingdom.

(3) Where the process is to be served outside the United Kingdom and the person at whose request it is issued or made believes that the person on whom it is to be served does not understand English, he must —

(a) inform the court of that fact, and
(b) provide the court with a copy of the process, or of so much of it as is material, translated into an appropriate language.

(4) Process served outside the United Kingdom requiring a person to appear as a party or attend as a witness —

(a) must not include notice of a penalty,
(b) must be accompanied by a notice giving any information required to be given by rules of court.

(5) If process requiring a person to appear as a party or attend as a witness is served outside the United Kingdom, no obligation to comply with the process under the law of the part of the United Kingdom in which the process is issued or made is imposed by virtue of the service.

(6) Accordingly, failure to comply with the process does not constitute contempt of court and is not a ground for issuing a warrant to secure the attendance of the person in question.

(7) But the process may subsequently be served on the person in question in the United Kingdom (with the usual consequences for non-compliance).

4 Service of process otherwise than by post

(1) Process to which section 3 applies may, instead of being served by post, be served on a person outside the United Kingdom in accordance with arrangements made by the Secretary of State.

(2) But where the person is in a participating country, the process may be served in accordance with those arrangements only if one of the following conditions is met.

(3) The conditions are —

(a) that the correct address of the person is unknown,
(b) that it has not been possible to serve the process by post,
(c) that there are good reasons for thinking that service by post will not be effective or is inappropriate.

5 General requirements for effecting Scottish citation etc.

(1) This section applies to any citation for the purposes of criminal proceedings in Scotland and to any document issued there for such purposes by the prosecutor or by the court.

(2) The citation may proceed or document be issued in spite of the fact that the person against whom it is to be effected or on whom it is to be served is outside the United Kingdom.

(3) Where —

(a) citation or issue is by the prosecutor,
(b) the citation is to be effected or the document issued is to be served outside the United Kingdom, and
(c) the prosecutor believes that the person against whom it is to be effected or on whom it is to be served does not understand English,

the citation or document must be accompanied by a translation of it (or, in the case of a document, by a translation of so much of it as is material) in an appropriate language.

(4) Where —

(a) citation or issue is by the court,
(b) the citation is to be effected or the document issued is to be served outside the United Kingdom, and
(c) the person at whose request that is to happen believes that the person against whom it is to be effected or on whom it is to be served does not understand English,

he must inform the court of that fact, and provide the court with a copy of the citation or document (or, in the case of a document, so much of it as is material) translated into an appropriate language.

(5) A citation effected outside the United Kingdom —

(a) must not include notice of a penalty,
(b) must be accompanied by a notice giving any information required to be given by rules of court.

(6) If a citation is effected outside the United Kingdom, no obligation under the law of Scotland to comply with the citation is imposed by virtue of its being so effected.

(7) Accordingly, failure to comply with the citation does not constitute contempt of court

and is not a ground for issuing a warrant to secure the attendance of the person in question or for imposing any penalty.

(8) But the citation may subsequently be effected against the person in question in the United Kingdom (with the usual consequences for non-compliance).

6 Effecting Scottish citation etc. otherwise than by post

(1) A citation or document to which section 5 applies may, instead of being effected or served by post, be effected against or served on a person outside the United Kingdom in accordance with arrangements made by the Lord Advocate.

(2) But where the person is in a participating country, the citation may be effected or document served in accordance with those arrangements only if one of the following conditions is met.

(3) The conditions are —

(a) that the correct address of the person is unknown,
(b) that it has not been possible to effect the citation or serve the document by post,
(c) that there are good reasons for thinking that citation or (as the case may be) service by post will not be effective or is inappropriate.

CHAPTER 2

MUTUAL PROVISION OF EVIDENCE

Assistance in obtaining evidence abroad

7 Requests for assistance in obtaining evidence abroad

(1) If it appears to a judicial authority in the United Kingdom on an application made by a person mentioned in subsection (3) —

(a) that an offence has been committed or that there are reasonable grounds for suspecting that an offence has been committed, and
(b) that proceedings in respect of the offence have been instituted or that the offence is being investigated,

the judicial authority may request assistance under this section.

(2) The assistance that may be requested under this section is assistance in obtaining outside the United Kingdom any evidence specified in the request for use in the proceedings or investigation.

(3) The application may be made —

(a) in relation to England and Wales and Northern Ireland, by a prosecuting authority,
(b) in relation to Scotland, by the Lord Advocate or a procurator fiscal,
(c) where proceedings have been instituted, by the person charged in those proceedings.

(4) The judicial authorities are —

(a) in relation to England and Wales, any judge or justice of the peace,
(b) in relation to Scotland, any judge of the High Court or sheriff,
(c) in relation to Northern Ireland, any judge or resident magistrate.

(5) In relation to England and Wales or Northern Ireland, a designated prosecuting authority may itself request assistance under this section if —

(a) it appears to the authority that an offence has been committed or that there are reasonable grounds for suspecting that an offence has been committed, and
(b) the authority has instituted proceedings in respect of the offence in question or it is being investigated.

"Designated" means designated by an order made by the Secretary of State.

(6) In relation to Scotland, the Lord Advocate or a procurator fiscal may himself request assistance under this section if it appears to him —

(a) that an offence has been committed or that there are reasonable grounds for suspecting that an offence has been committed, and
(b) that proceedings in respect of the offence have been instituted or that the offence is being investigated.

(7) If a request for assistance under this section is made in reliance on Article 2 of the 2001 Protocol (requests for information on banking transactions) in connection with the investigation of an offence, the request must state the grounds on which the person making the request considers the evidence specified in it to be relevant for the purposes of the investigation.

8 Sending requests for assistance

(1) A request for assistance under section 7 may be sent —

(a) to a court exercising jurisdiction in the place where the evidence is situated, or
(b) to any authority recognised by the government of the country in question as the appropriate authority for receiving requests of that kind.

(2) Alternatively, if it is a request by a judicial authority or a designated prosecuting authority it may be sent to the Secretary of State (in Scotland, the Lord Advocate) for forwarding to a court or authority mentioned in subsection (1).

(3) In cases of urgency, a request for assistance may be sent to —

(a) the International Criminal Police Organisation, or
(b) any body or person competent to receive it under any provisions adopted under the Treaty on European Union,

for forwarding to any court or authority mentioned in subsection (1).

9 Use of evidence obtained

(1) This section applies to evidence obtained pursuant to a request for assistance under section 7.

(2) The evidence may not without the consent of the appropriate overseas authority be used for any purpose other than that specified in the request.

(3) When the evidence is no longer required for that purpose (or for any other purpose for which such consent has been obtained), it must be returned to the appropriate overseas authority, unless that authority indicates that it need not be returned.

(4) In exercising the discretion conferred by section 25 of the Criminal Justice Act 1988 (c. 33) or Article 5 of the Criminal Justice (Evidence, Etc.) (Northern Ireland) Order 1988

(S.I. 1988/ 1847 (N.I. 17)) (exclusion of evidence otherwise admissible) in relation to a statement contained in the evidence, the court must have regard —

(a) to whether it was possible to challenge the statement by questioning the person who made it, and
(b) if proceedings have been instituted, to whether the local law allowed the parties to the proceedings to be legally represented when the evidence was being obtained.

(5) In Scotland, the evidence may be received in evidence without being sworn to by witnesses, so far as that may be done without unfairness to either party.

(6) In this section, the appropriate overseas authority means the authority recognised by the government of the country in question as the appropriate authority for receiving requests of the kind in question.

10 Domestic freezing orders

(1) If it appears to a judicial authority in the United Kingdom, on an application made by a person mentioned in subsection (4) —

(a) that proceedings in respect of a listed offence have been instituted or such an offence is being investigated,
(b) that there are reasonable grounds to believe that there is evidence in a participating country which satisfies the requirements of subsection (3), and
(c) that a request has been made, or will be made, under section 7 for the evidence to be sent to the authority making the request,

the judicial authority may make a domestic freezing order in respect of the evidence.

(2) A domestic freezing order is an order for protecting evidence which is in the participating country pending its transfer to the United Kingdom.

(3) The requirements are that the evidence —

(a) is on premises specified in the application in the participating country,
(b) is likely to be of substantial value (whether by itself or together with other evidence) to the proceedings or investigation,
(c) is likely to be admissible in evidence at a trial for the offence, and
(d) does not consist of or include items subject to legal privilege.

(4) The application may be made —

(a) in relation to England and Wales and Northern Ireland, by a constable,
(b) in relation to Scotland, by the Lord Advocate or a procurator fiscal.

(5) The judicial authorities are —

(a) in relation to England and Wales, any judge or justice of the peace,
(b) in relation to Scotland, any judge of the High Court or sheriff,
(c) in relation to Northern Ireland, any judge or resident magistrate.

(6) This section does not prejudice the generality of the power to make a request for assistance under section 7.

11 Sending freezing orders

(1) A domestic freezing order made in England and Wales or Northern Ireland is to be sent to the Secretary of State for forwarding to —

(a) a court exercising jurisdiction in the place where the evidence is situated, or
(b) any authority recognised by the government of the country in question as the appropriate authority for receiving orders of that kind.

(2) A domestic freezing order made in Scotland is to be sent to the Lord Advocate for forwarding to such a court or authority.

(3) The judicial authority is to send the order to the Secretary of State or the Lord Advocate before the end of the period of 14 days beginning with its being made.

(4) The order must be accompanied by a certificate giving the specified information and, unless the certificate indicates when the judicial authority expects such a request to be made, by a request under section 7 for the evidence to be sent to the authority making the request.

(5) The certificate must include a translation of it into an appropriate language of the participating country (if that language is not English).

(6) The certificate must be signed by or on behalf of the judicial authority who made the order and must include a statement as to the accuracy of the information given in it.

The signature may be an electronic signature.

12 Variation or revocation of freezing orders

(1) The judicial authority that made a domestic freezing order may vary or revoke it on an application by a person mentioned below.

(2) The persons are —

(a) the person who applied for the order,
(b) in relation to England and Wales and Northern Ireland, a prosecuting authority,
(c) in relation to Scotland, the Lord Advocate,
(d) any other person affected by the order.

Assisting overseas authorities to obtain evidence in the UK

13 Requests for assistance from overseas authorities

(1) Where a request for assistance in obtaining evidence in a part of the United Kingdom is received by the territorial authority for that part, the authority may —

(a) if the conditions in section 14 are met, arrange for the evidence to be obtained under section 15, or
(b) direct that a search warrant be applied for under or by virtue of section 16 or 17 or, in relation to evidence in Scotland, 18.

(2) The request for assistance may be made only by —

(a) a court exercising criminal jurisdiction, or a prosecuting authority, in a country outside the United Kingdom,
(b) any other authority in such a country which appears to the territorial authority to have the function of making such requests for assistance,
(c) any international authority mentioned in subsection (3).

(3) The international authorities are —

(a) the International Criminal Police Organisation,
(b) any other body or person competent to make a request of the kind to which this section applies under any provisions adopted under the Treaty on European Union.

14 Powers to arrange for evidence to be obtained

(1) The territorial authority may arrange for evidence to be obtained under section 15 if the request for assistance in obtaining the evidence is made in connection with —

(a) criminal proceedings or a criminal investigation, being carried on outside the United Kingdom,
(b) administrative proceedings, or an investigation into an act punishable in such proceedings, being carried on there,
(c) clemency proceedings, or proceedings on an appeal before a court against a decision in administrative proceedings, being carried on, or intended to be carried on, there.

(2) In a case within subsection (1)(a) or (b), the authority may arrange for the evidence to be so obtained only if the authority is satisfied —

(a) that an offence under the law of the country in question has been committed or that there are reasonable grounds for suspecting that such an offence has been committed, and
(b) that proceedings in respect of the offence have been instituted in that country or that an investigation into the offence is being carried on there.

An offence includes an act punishable in administrative proceedings.

(3) The territorial authority is to regard as conclusive a certificate as to the matters mentioned in subsection (2)(a) and (b) issued by any authority in the country in question which appears to him to be the appropriate authority to do so.

(4) If it appears to the territorial authority that the request for assistance relates to a fiscal offence in respect of which proceedings have not yet been instituted, the authority may not arrange for the evidence to be so obtained unless —

(a) the request is from a country which is a member of the Commonwealth or is made pursuant to a treaty to which the United Kingdom is a party, or
(b) the authority is satisfied that if the conduct constituting the offence were to occur in a part of the United Kingdom, it would constitute an offence in that part.

15 Nominating a court etc. to receive evidence

(1) Where the evidence is in England and Wales or Northern Ireland, the Secretary of State may by a notice nominate a court to receive any evidence to which the request relates which appears to the court to be appropriate for the purpose of giving effect to the request.

(2) But if it appears to the Secretary of State that the request relates to an offence involving serious or complex fraud, he may refer the request (or any part of it) to the Director of the Serious Fraud Office for the Director to obtain any evidence to which the request or part relates which appears to him to be appropriate for the purpose of giving effect to the request or part.

(3) Where the evidence is in Scotland, the Lord Advocate may by a notice nominate a court to receive any evidence to which the request relates which appears to the court to be appropriate for the purpose of giving effect to the request.

(4) But if it appears to the Lord Advocate that the request relates to an offence involving serious or complex fraud, he may give a direction under section 27 of the Criminal Law (Consolidation) (Scotland) Act 1995 (c. 39) (directions applying investigatory provisions).

(5) Schedule 1 is to have effect in relation to proceedings before a court nominated under this section.

16 Extension of statutory search powers in England and Wales and Northern Ireland

(1) Part 2 of the Police and Criminal Evidence Act 1984 (c. 60) (powers of entry, search and seizure) is to have effect as if references to serious arrestable offences in section 8 of, and Schedule 1 to, that Act included any conduct which —

(a) constitutes an offence under the law of a country outside the United Kingdom, and
(b) would, if it occurred in England and Wales, constitute a serious arrestable offence.

(2) But an application for a warrant or order by virtue of subsection (1) may be made only —

(a) in pursuance of a direction given under section 13, or
(b) if it is an application for a warrant or order under section 8 of, or Schedule 1 to, that Act by a constable for the purposes of an investigation by an international joint investigation team of which he is a member.

(3) Part 3 of the Police and Criminal Evidence (Northern Ireland) Order 1989 (S.I. 1989/1341 (N.I. 12)) (powers of entry, search and seizure) is to have effect as if references to serious arrestable offences in Article 10 of, and Schedule 1 to, that Order included any conduct which —

(a) constitutes an offence under the law of a country outside the United Kingdom, and
(b) would, if it occurred in Northern Ireland, constitute a serious arrestable offence.

(4) But an application for a warrant or order by virtue of subsection (3) may be made only —

(a) in pursuance of a direction given under section 13, or
(b) if it is an application for a warrant or order under Article 10 of, or Schedule 1 to, that Order, by a constable for the purposes of an investigation by an international joint investigation team of which he is a member.

(5) In this section, "international joint investigation team" has the meaning given by section 88(7) of the Police Act 1996 (c. 16).

17 Warrants in England and Wales or Northern Ireland

(1) A justice of the peace may issue a warrant under this section if he is satisfied, on an application made by a constable, that the following conditions are met.

(2) But an application for a warrant under subsection (1) may be made only in pursuance of a direction given under section 13.

(3) The conditions are that —

(a) criminal proceedings have been instituted against a person in a country outside the United Kingdom or a person has been arrested in the course of a criminal investigation carried on there,
(b) the conduct constituting the offence which is the subject of the proceedings or investigation would, if it occurred in England and Wales or (as the case may be) Northern Ireland, constitute an arrestable offence, and

(c) there are reasonable grounds for suspecting that there is on premises in England and Wales or (as the case may be) Northern Ireland occupied or controlled by that person evidence relating to the offence.

"Arrestable offence" has the same meaning as in the Police and Criminal Evidence Act 1984 (c. 60) or (as the case may be) the Police and Criminal Evidence (Northern Ireland) Order 1989 (S.I. 1989/ 1341 (N.I.12)).

(4) A warrant under this section may authorise a constable —

(a) to enter the premises in question and search the premises to the extent reasonably required for the purpose of discovering any evidence relating to the offence,
(b) to seize and retain any evidence for which he is authorised to search.

18 Warrants in Scotland

(1) If, on an application made by the procurator fiscal, it appears to the sheriff —

(a) that there are reasonable grounds for suspecting that an offence under the law of a country outside the United Kingdom has been committed, and
(b) that the conduct constituting the offence would, if it occurred in Scotland, constitute an offence punishable by imprisonment,

the sheriff has the like power to grant warrant authorising entry, search and seizure by any constable or customs officer as he has under section 134 of the Criminal Procedure (Scotland) Act 1995 (c. 46) in respect of any offence punishable at common law in Scotland.

(2) But an application for a warrant by virtue of subsection (1) may be made only —

(a) in pursuance of a direction given under section 13, or
(b) if it is an application made at the request of an international joint investigation team for the purposes of their investigation.

"International joint investigation team" has the meaning given by section 39(6) of the Police (Scotland) Act 1967 (c. 77).

19 Seized evidence

(1) Any evidence seized by a constable under or by virtue of section 16, 17 or 18 is to be sent to the court or authority which made the request for assistance or to the territorial authority for forwarding to that court or authority.

(2) So far as may be necessary in order to comply with the request for assistance —

(a) where the evidence consists of a document, the original or a copy is to be sent, and
(b) where the evidence consists of any other article, the article itself or a description, photograph or other representation of it is to be sent.

(3) This section does not apply to evidence seized under or by virtue of section 16(2)(b) or (4)(b) or 18(2)(b).

Overseas freezing orders

20 Overseas freezing orders

(1) Section 21 applies where an overseas freezing order made by a court or authority in a participating country is received from the court or authority which made or confirmed the order by the territorial authority for the part of the United Kingdom in which the evidence to which the order relates is situated.

(2) An overseas freezing order is an order —

(a) for protecting, pending its transfer to the participating country, evidence which is in the United Kingdom and may be used in any proceedings or investigation in the participating country, and
(b) in respect of which the following requirements of this section are met.

(3) The order must have been made by —

(a) a court exercising criminal jurisdiction in the country,
(b) a prosecuting authority in the country,
(c) any other authority in the country which appears to the territorial authority to have the function of making such orders.

(4) The order must relate to —

(a) criminal proceedings instituted in the participating country in respect of a listed offence, or
(b) a criminal investigation being carried on there into such an offence.

(5) The order must be accompanied by a certificate which gives the specified information; but a certificate may be treated as giving any specified information which is not given in it if the territorial authority has the information in question.

(6) The certificate must —

(a) be signed by or on behalf of the court or authority which made or confirmed the order,
(b) include a statement as to the accuracy of the information given in it,
(c) if it is not in English, include a translation of it into English (or, if appropriate, Welsh).

The signature may be an electronic signature.

(7) The order must be accompanied by a request for the evidence to be sent to a court or authority mentioned in section 13(2), unless the certificate indicates when such a request is expected to be made.

(8) References below in this Chapter to an overseas freezing order include its accompanying certificate.

21 Considering the order

(1) In relation to England and Wales and Northern Ireland, where this section applies the Secretary of State must —

(a) by a notice nominate a court in England and Wales or (as the case may be) Northern Ireland to give effect to the overseas freezing order,
(b) send a copy of the overseas freezing order to the nominated court and to the chief officer of police for the area in which the evidence is situated,
(c) tell the chief officer which court has been nominated.

(2) In relation to Scotland, where this section applies the Lord Advocate must —

(a) by a notice nominate a sheriff to give effect to the overseas freezing order,
(b) send a copy of the overseas freezing order to the sheriff and to the procurator fiscal.

In relation to Scotland, references below in this section and in sections 22 to 25 to the nominated court are to be read as references to the nominated sheriff.

(3) The nominated court is to consider the overseas freezing order on its own initiative within a period prescribed by rules of court.

(4) Before giving effect to the overseas freezing order, the nominated court must give the chief officer of police or (as the case may be) the procurator fiscal an opportunity to be heard.

(5) The court may decide not to give effect to the overseas freezing order only if, in its opinion, one of the following conditions is met.

(6) The first condition is that, if the person whose conduct is in question were charged in the participating country with the offence to which the overseas freezing order relates or in the United Kingdom with a corresponding offence, he would be entitled to be discharged under any rule of law relating to previous acquittal or conviction.

(7) The second condition is that giving effect to the overseas freezing order would be incompatible with any of the Convention rights (within the meaning of the Human Rights Act 1998 (c. 42)).

22 Giving effect to the order

(1) The nominated court is to give effect to the overseas freezing order by issuing a warrant authorising a constable —

(a) to enter the premises to which the overseas freezing order relates and search the premises to the extent reasonably required for the purpose of discovering any evidence to which the order relates, and
(b) to seize and retain any evidence for which he is authorised to search.

(2) But, in relation to England and Wales and Northern Ireland, so far as the overseas freezing order relates to excluded material or special procedure material the court is to give effect to the order by making a production order.

(3) A production order is an order for the person who appears to the court to be in possession of the material to produce it to a constable before the end of the period of seven days beginning with the date of the production order or such longer period as the production order may specify.

(4) The constable may take away any material produced to him under a production order; and the material is to be treated for the purposes of section 21 of the Police and Criminal Evidence Act 1984 (c. 60) or (as the case may be) Article 23 of the Police and Criminal Evidence (Northern Ireland) Order 1989 (S.I. 1989/1341 (N.I.12)) (access and copying) as if it had been seized by the constable.

(5) If a person fails to comply with a production order, the court may (whether or not it deals with the matter as a contempt of court) issue a warrant under subsection (1) in respect of the material to which the production order relates.

(6) Section 409 of the Proceeds of Crime Act 2002 (c. 29) (jurisdiction of sheriff) has effect for the purposes of subsection (1) as if that subsection were included in Chapter 3 of Part 8 of that Act.

23 Postponed effect

The nominated court may postpone giving effect to an overseas freezing order in respect of any evidence —

(a) in order to avoid prejudicing a criminal investigation which is taking place in the United Kingdom, or
(b) if, under an order made by a court in criminal proceedings in the United Kingdom, the evidence may not be removed from the United Kingdom.

24 Evidence seized under the order

(1) Any evidence seized by or produced to the constable under section 22 is to be retained by him until he is given a notice under subsection (2) or authorised to release it under section 25.

(2) If —

(a) the overseas freezing order was accompanied by a request for the evidence to be sent to a court or authority mentioned in section 13(2), or
(b) the territorial authority subsequently receives such a request,

the territorial authority may by notice require the constable to send the evidence to the court or authority that made the request.

25 Release of evidence held under the order

(1) On an application made by a person mentioned below, the nominated court may authorise the release of any evidence retained by a constable under section 24 if, in its opinion —

(a) the condition in section 21(6) or (7) is met, or
(b) the overseas freezing order has ceased to have effect in the participating country.

(2) In relation to England and Wales and Northern Ireland, the persons are —

(a) the chief officer of police to whom a copy of the order was sent,
(b) the constable,
(c) any other person affected by the order.

(3) In relation to Scotland, the persons are —

(a) the procurator fiscal to whom a copy of the order was sent,
(b) any other person affected by the order.

(4) If the territorial authority decides not to give a notice under section 24(2) in respect of any evidence retained by a constable under that section, the authority must give the constable a notice authorising him to release the evidence.

General

26 Powers under warrants

(1) A court in England and Wales or Northern Ireland, or a justice of the peace, may not issue a warrant under section 17 or 22 in respect of any evidence unless the court or justice has reasonable grounds for believing that it does not consist of or include items subject to legal privilege, excluded material or special procedure material.

(2) Subsection (1) does not prevent a warrant being issued by virtue of section 22(5) in respect of excluded material or special procedure material.

(3) In Schedule 1 to the Criminal Justice and Police Act 2001 (c. 16) (powers of seizure), in Part 1 (powers to which the additional powers in section 50 apply) —

(a) paragraph 49 is omitted,
(b) after paragraph 73B there is inserted —

"73C. Crime (International Co-operation) Act 2003
The power of seizure conferred by sections 17 and 22 of the Crime (International Co-operation) Act 2003 (seizure of evidence relevant to overseas investigation or offence)."

(4) References in this Chapter to evidence seized by a person by virtue of or under any provision of this Chapter include evidence seized by a person by virtue of section 50 of the

Criminal Justice and Police Act 2001 (additional powers of seizure), if it is seized in the course of a search authorised by a warrant issued by virtue of or under the provision in question.

(5) Subsection (4) does not require any evidence to be sent to the territorial authority or to any court or authority —

(a) before it has been found, on the completion of any examination required to be made by arrangements under section 53(2) of the Criminal Justice and Police Act 2001, to be property within subsection (3) of that section (property which may be retained after examination), or

(b) at a time when it constitutes property in respect of which a person is required to ensure that arrangements such as are mentioned in section 61(1) of that Act (duty to secure) are in force.

27 Exercise of powers by others

(1) The Treasury may by order provide, in relation to England and Wales or Northern Ireland —

(a) for any function conferred on the Secretary of State (whether or not in terms) under sections 10, 11 and 13 to 26 to be exercisable instead in prescribed circumstances by the Commissioners of Customs and Excise,

(b) for any function conferred on a constable under those sections to be exercisable instead in prescribed circumstances by a customs officer or a person acting under the direction of such an officer.

"Prescribed" means prescribed by the order.

(2) The Secretary of State may by order provide, in relation to England and Wales or Northern Ireland —

(a) for any function conferred on him under sections 13 to 26 to be exercisable instead in prescribed circumstances by a prescribed person,

(b) for any function conferred on a constable under those sections to be exercisable instead in prescribed circumstances by a prescribed person.

"Prescribed" means prescribed by the order.

(3) Subsection (2)(b) does not apply to any powers exercisable by virtue of section 16(2)(b) or (4)(b).

28 Interpretation of Chapter 2

(1) In this Chapter —

"domestic freezing order" has the meaning given by section 10 (2),
"notice" means a notice in writing,
"overseas freezing order" has the meaning given by section 20,
"premises" has the same meaning as in the Police and Criminal Evidence Act 1984 (c. 60), Chapter 3 of Part 8 of the Proceeds of Crime Act 2002 (c. 29) or the Police and Criminal Evidence (Northern Ireland) Order 1989 (S.I. 1989/1341 (N.I.12)) (as the case may be),
"the relevant Framework Decision" means the Framework Decision on the execution in the European Union of orders freezing property or evidence adopted by the Council of the European Union on 22nd July 2003.

(2) The following provisions have effect for the purposes of this Chapter.

(3) In relation to England and Wales and Northern Ireland, "items subject to legal privilege", "excluded material" and "special procedure material" have the same meaning as in the

Police and Criminal Evidence Act 1984 or (as the case may be) the Police and Criminal Evidence (Northern Ireland) Order 1989.

(4) In relation to Scotland, "items subject to legal privilege" has the same meaning as in Chapter 3 of Part 8 of the Proceeds of Crime Act 2002.

(5) A listed offence means —

(a) an offence described in Article 3(2) of the relevant Framework Decision, or
(b) an offence prescribed or of a description prescribed by an order made by the Secretary of State.

(6) An order prescribing an offence or a description of offences under subsection (5)(b) may require, in the case of an overseas freezing order, that the conduct which constitutes the offence or offences would, if it occurred in a part of the United Kingdom, constitute an offence in that part.

(7) Specified information, in relation to a certificate required by section 11(4) or 20(5), means —

(a) any information required to be given by the form of certificate annexed to the relevant Framework Decision, or
(b) any information prescribed by an order made by the Secretary of State.

(8) In relation to Scotland, references above in this section to the Secretary of State are to be read as references to the Scottish Ministers.

(9) The territorial authority —

(a) in relation to evidence in England and Wales or Northern Ireland, is the Secretary of State,
(b) in relation to evidence in Scotland, is the Lord Advocate.

CHAPTER 3

HEARING EVIDENCE THROUGH TELEVISION LINKS OR BY TELEPHONE

29 Hearing witnesses abroad through television links

(1) The Secretary of State may by order provide for section 32 (1A) of the Criminal Justice Act 1988 (c. 33) or Article 81(1A) of the Police and Criminal Evidence (Northern Ireland) Order 1989 (S.I. 1989/1341 (N.I.12)) (proceedings in which evidence may be given through television link) to apply to any further description of criminal proceedings, or to all criminal proceedings.

(2) The Scottish Ministers may by order provide for section 273 (1) of the Criminal Procedure (Scotland) Act 1995 (c. 46) (proceedings in which evidence may be given through television link) to apply to any further description of criminal proceedings, or to all criminal proceedings.

30 Hearing witnesses in the UK through television links

(1) This section applies where the Secretary of State receives a request, from an authority mentioned in subsection (2) ("the external authority"), for a person in the United Kingdom to give evidence through a live television link in criminal proceedings before a court in a country outside the United Kingdom.

Criminal proceedings include any proceedings on an appeal before a court against a decision in administrative proceedings.

(2) The authority referred to in subsection (1) is the authority in that country which appears to the Secretary of State to have the function of making requests of the kind to which this section applies.

(3) Unless he considers it inappropriate to do so, the Secretary of State must by notice in writing nominate a court in the United Kingdom where the witness may be heard in the proceedings in question through a live television link.

(4) Anything done by the witness in the presence of the nominated court which, if it were done in proceedings before the court, would constitute contempt of court is to be treated for that purpose as done in proceedings before the court.

(5) Any statement made on oath by a witness giving evidence in pursuance of this section is to be treated for the purposes of —

(a) section 1 of the Perjury Act 1911 (c. 6),
(b) Article 3 of the Perjury (Northern Ireland) Order 1979 (S.I. 1979/1714 (N.I. 19)),
(c) sections 44 to 46 of the Criminal Law (Consolidation) (Scotland) Act 1995 (c. 39) or, in relation to Scotland, any matter pertaining to the common law crime of perjury,

as made in proceedings before the nominated court.

(6) Part 1 of Schedule 2 (evidence given by television link) is to have effect.

(7) Subject to subsections (4) and (5) and the provisions of that Schedule, evidence given pursuant to this section is not to be treated for any purpose as evidence given in proceedings in the United Kingdom.

(8) In relation to Scotland, references in this section and Part 1 of Schedule 2 to the Secretary of State are to be read as references to the Lord Advocate.

31 Hearing witnesses in the UK by telephone

(1) This section applies where the Secretary of State receives a request, from an authority mentioned in subsection (2) ("the external authority") in a participating country, for a person in the United Kingdom to give evidence by telephone in criminal proceedings before a court in that country.

Criminal proceedings include any proceedings on an appeal before a court against a decision in administrative proceedings.

(2) The authority referred to in subsection (1) is the authority in that country which appears to the Secretary of State to have the function of making requests of the kind to which this section applies.

(3) A request under subsection (1) must —

(a) specify the court in the participating country,
(b) give the name and address of the witness,
(c) state that the witness is willing to give evidence by telephone in the proceedings before that court.

(4) Unless he considers it inappropriate to do so, the Secretary of State must by notice in writing nominate a court in the United Kingdom where the witness may be heard in the proceedings in question by telephone.

(5) Anything done by the witness in the presence of the nominated court which, if it were done in proceedings before the court, would constitute contempt of court is to be treated for that purpose as done in proceedings before the court.

(6) Any statement made on oath by a witness giving evidence in pursuance of this section is to be treated for the purposes of —

(a) section 1 of the Perjury Act 1911 (c. 6),
(b) Article 3 of the Perjury (Northern Ireland) Order 1979 (S.I. 1979/1714 (N.I. 19)),

(c) sections 44 to 46 of the Criminal Law (Consolidation) (Scotland) Act 1995 (c. 39) or, in relation to Scotland, any matter pertaining to the common law crime of perjury,

as made in proceedings before the nominated court.

(7) Part 2 of Schedule 2 (evidence given by telephone link) is to have effect.

(8) Subject to subsections (5) and (6) and the provisions of that Schedule, evidence given in pursuance of this section is not to be treated for any purpose as evidence given in proceedings in the United Kingdom.

(9) In relation to Scotland, references in this section to the Secretary of State are to be read as references to the Lord Advocate.

CHAPTER 4

INFORMATION ABOUT BANKING TRANSACTIONS

Requests for information about banking transactions in England and Wales and Northern Ireland for use abroad

32 Customer information

(1) This section applies where the Secretary of State receives a request from an authority mentioned in subsection (2) for customer information to be obtained in relation to a person who appears to him to be subject to an investigation in a participating country into serious criminal conduct.

(2) The authority referred to in subsection (1) is the authority in that country which appears to the Secretary of State to have the function of making requests of the kind to which this section applies.

(3) The Secretary of State may —

(a) direct a senior police officer to apply, or arrange for a constable to apply, for a customer information order,

(b) direct a senior customs officer to apply, or arrange for a customs officer to apply, for such an order.

(4) A customer information order is an order made by a judge that a financial institution specified in the application for the order must, on being required to do so by notice in writing given by the applicant for the order, provide any such customer information as it has relating to the person specified in the application.

(5) A financial institution which is required to provide information under a customer information order must provide the information to the applicant for the order in such manner, and at or by such time, as the applicant requires.

(6) Section 364 of the Proceeds of Crime Act 2002 (c. 29) (meaning of customer information), except subsections (2)(f) and (3) (i), has effect for the purposes of this section as if this section were included in Chapter 2 of Part 8 of that Act.

(7) A customer information order has effect in spite of any restriction on the disclosure of information (however imposed).

(8) Customer information obtained in pursuance of a customer information order is to be given to the Secretary of State and sent by him to the authority which made the request.

33 Making, varying or discharging customer information orders

(1) A judge may make a customer information order, on an application made to him pursuant to a direction under section 32(3), if he is satisfied that —

(a) the person specified in the application is subject to an investigation in the country in question,
(b) the investigation concerns conduct which is serious criminal conduct,
(c) the conduct constitutes an offence in England and Wales or (as the case may be) Northern Ireland, or would do were it to occur there, and
(d) the order is sought for the purposes of the investigation.

(2) The application may be made ex parte to a judge in chambers.
(3) The application may specify —

(a) all financial institutions,
(b) a particular description, or particular descriptions, of financial institutions, or
(c) a particular financial institution or particular financial institutions.

(4) The court may discharge or vary a customer information order on an application made by —

(a) the person who applied for the order,
(b) a senior police officer,
(c) a constable authorised by a senior police officer to make the application,
(d) a senior customs officer,
(e) a customs officer authorised by a senior customs officer to make the application.

34 Offences

(1) A financial institution is guilty of an offence if without reasonable excuse it fails to comply with a requirement imposed on it under a customer information order.
(2) A financial institution guilty of an offence under subsection (1) is liable on summary conviction to a fine not exceeding level 5 on the standard scale.
(3) A financial institution is guilty of an offence if, in purported compliance with a customer information order, it —

(a) makes a statement which it knows to be false or misleading in a material particular, or
(b) recklessly makes a statement which is false or misleading in a material particular.

(4) A financial institution guilty of an offence under subsection (3) is liable —

(a) on summary conviction, to a fine not exceeding the statutory maximum, or
(b) on conviction on indictment, to a fine.

35 Account information

(1) This section applies where the Secretary of State receives a request from an authority mentioned in subsection (2) for account information to be obtained in relation to an investigation in a participating country into criminal conduct.
(2) The authority referred to in subsection (1) is the authority in that country which appears to the Secretary of State to have the function of making requests of the kind to which this section applies.
(3) The Secretary of State may —

(a) direct a senior police officer to apply, or arrange for a constable to apply, for an account monitoring order,
(b) direct a senior customs officer to apply, or arrange for a customs officer to apply, for such an order.

(4) An account monitoring order is an order made by a judge that a financial institution specified in the application for the order must, for the period stated in the order, provide account information of the description specified in the order to the applicant in the manner, and at or by the time or times, stated in the order.

(5) Account information is information relating to an account or accounts held at the financial institution specified in the application by the person so specified (whether solely or jointly with another).

(6) An account monitoring order has effect in spite of any restriction on the disclosure of information (however imposed).

(7) Account information obtained in pursuance of an account monitoring order is to be given to the Secretary of State and sent by him to the authority which made the request.

36 Making, varying or discharging account monitoring orders

(1) A judge may make an account monitoring order, on an application made to him in pursuance of a direction under section 35 (3), if he is satisfied that —

(a) there is an investigation in the country in question into criminal conduct, and
(b) the order is sought for the purposes of the investigation.

(2) The application may be made ex parte to a judge in chambers.

(3) The application may specify information relating to —

(a) all accounts held by the person specified in the application for the order at the financial institution so specified,
(b) a particular description, or particular descriptions, of accounts so held, or
(c) a particular account, or particular accounts, so held.

(4) The court may discharge or vary an account monitoring order on an application made by —

(a) the person who applied for the order,
(b) a senior police officer,
(c) a constable authorised by a senior police officer to make the application,
(d) a senior customs officer,
(e) a customs officer authorised by a senior customs officer to make the application.

(5) Account monitoring orders have effect as if they were orders of the court.

Requests for information about banking transactions in Scotland for use abroad

37 Customer information

(1) This section applies where the Lord Advocate receives a request from an authority mentioned in subsection (2) for customer information to be obtained in relation to a person who appears to him to be subject to an investigation in a participating country into serious criminal conduct.

(2) The authority referred to in subsection (1) is the authority in that country which appears to the Lord Advocate to have the function of making requests of the kind to which this section applies.

(3) The Lord Advocate may direct a procurator fiscal to apply for a customer information order.

(4) A customer information order is an order made by a sheriff that a financial institution specified in the application for the order must, on being required to do so by notice in writing

given by the applicant for the order, provide any such customer information as it has relating to the person specified in the application.

(5) A financial institution which is required to provide information under a customer information order must provide the information to the applicant for the order in such manner, and at or by such time, as the applicant requires.

(6) Section 398 of the Proceeds of Crime Act 2002 (c. 29) (meaning of customer information), except subsections (2)(f) and (3)(i), has effect for the purposes of this section as if this section were included in Chapter 3 of Part 8 of that Act.

(7) A customer information order has effect in spite of any restriction on the disclosure of information (however imposed).

(8) Customer information obtained in pursuance of a customer information order is to be given to the Lord Advocate and sent by him to the authority which made the request.

38 Making, varying or discharging customer information orders

(1) A sheriff may make a customer information order, on an application made to him pursuant to a direction under section 37(3), if he is satisfied that —

(a) the person specified in the application is subject to an investigation in the country in question,
(b) the investigation concerns conduct which is serious criminal conduct,
(c) the conduct constitutes an offence in Scotland, or would do were it to occur in Scotland, and
(d) the order is sought for the purposes of the investigation.

(2) The application may be made ex parte to a sheriff in chambers.

(3) The application may specify —

(a) all financial institutions,
(b) a particular description, or particular descriptions, of financial institutions, or
(c) a particular financial institution or particular financial institutions.

(4) The court may discharge or vary a customer information order on an application made by the procurator fiscal.

(5) Section 409 of the Proceeds of Crime Act 2002 (jurisdiction of sheriff) has effect for the purposes of this section as if this section were included in Chapter 3 of Part 8 of that Act.

39 Offences

(1) A financial institution is guilty of an offence if without reasonable excuse it fails to comply with a requirement imposed on it under a customer information order.

(2) A financial institution guilty of an offence under subsection (1) is liable on summary conviction to a fine not exceeding level 5 on the standard scale.

(3) A financial institution is guilty of an offence if, in purported compliance with a customer information order, it —

(a) makes a statement which it knows to be false or misleading in a material particular, or
(b) recklessly makes a statement which is false or misleading in a material particular.

(4) A financial institution guilty of an offence under subsection (3) is liable —

(a) on summary conviction, to a fine not exceeding the statutory maximum, or
(b) on conviction on indictment, to a fine.

40 Account information

(1) This section applies where the Lord Advocate receives a request from an authority mentioned in subsection (2) for account information to be obtained in relation to an investigation in a participating country into criminal conduct.

(2) The authority referred to in subsection (1) is the authority in that country which appears to the Lord Advocate to have the function of making requests of the kind to which this section applies.

(3) The Lord Advocate may direct a procurator fiscal to apply for an account monitoring order.

(4) An account monitoring order is an order made by a sheriff that a financial institution specified in the application for the order must, for the period stated in the order, provide account information of the description specified in the order to the applicant in the manner, and at or by the time or times, stated in the order.

(5) Account information is information relating to an account or accounts held at the financial institution specified in the application by the person so specified (whether solely or jointly with another).

(6) An account monitoring order has effect in spite of any restriction on the disclosure of information (however imposed).

(7) Account information obtained in pursuance of an account monitoring order is to be given to the Lord Advocate and sent by him to the authority which made the request.

41 Making, varying or discharging account monitoring orders

(1) A sheriff may make an account monitoring order, on an application made to him in pursuance of a direction under section 40 (3), if he is satisfied that —

(a) there is an investigation in the country in question into criminal conduct, and
(b) the order is sought for the purposes of the investigation.

(2) The application may be made ex parte to a sheriff in chambers.

(3) The application may specify information relating to —

(a) all accounts held by the person specified in the application for the order at the financial institution so specified,
(b) a particular description, or particular descriptions, of accounts so held, or
(c) a particular account, or particular accounts, so held.

(4) The court may discharge or vary an account monitoring order on an application made by the procurator fiscal.

(5) Section 409 of the Proceeds of Crime Act 2002 (c. 29) (jurisdiction of sheriff) has effect for the purposes of this section as if this section were included in Chapter 3 of Part 8 of that Act.

Disclosure of information

42 Offence of disclosure

(1) This section applies where —

(a) a financial institution is specified in a customer information order or account monitoring order made in any part of the United Kingdom, or
(b) the Secretary of State or the Lord Advocate receives a request under section 13 for evidence to be obtained from a financial institution in connection with the investi-

gation of an offence in reliance on Article 2 (requests for information on banking transactions) of the 2001 Protocol.

(2) If the institution, or an employee of the institution, discloses any of the following information, the institution or (as the case may be) the employee is guilty of an offence.

(3) That information is —

(a) that the request to obtain customer information or account information, or the request mentioned in subsection (1)(b), has been received,
(b) that the investigation to which the request relates is being carried out, or
(c) that, in pursuance of the request, information has been given to the authority which made the request.

(4) An institution guilty of an offence under this section is liable —

(a) on summary conviction, to a fine not exceeding the statutory maximum,
(b) on conviction on indictment, to a fine.

(5) Any other person guilty of an offence under this section is liable —

(a) on summary conviction, to imprisonment for a term not exceeding six months or to a fine not exceeding the statutory maximum, or to both,
(b) on conviction on indictment, to imprisonment for a term not exceeding five years or to a fine, or to both.

Requests for information about banking transactions for use in UK

43 Information about a person's bank account

(1) If it appears to a judicial authority in the United Kingdom, on an application made by a prosecuting authority, that —

(a) a person is subject to an investigation in the United Kingdom into serious criminal conduct,
(b) the person holds, or may hold, an account at a bank which is situated in a participating country, and
(c) the information which the applicant seeks to obtain is likely to be of substantial value for the purposes of the investigation,

the judicial authority may request assistance under this section.

(2) The judicial authorities are —

(a) in relation to England and Wales, any judge or justice of the peace,
(b) in relation to Scotland, any sheriff,
(c) in relation to Northern Ireland, any judge or resident magistrate.

(3) If it appears to a prosecuting authority mentioned in subsection (4) that paragraphs (a) to (c) of subsection (1) are met, the authority may itself request assistance under this section.

(4) The prosecuting authorities are —

(a) in relation to England and Wales and Northern Ireland, a prosecuting authority designated by an order made by the Secretary of State,
(b) in relation to Scotland, the Lord Advocate or a procurator fiscal.

(5) The assistance that may be requested under this section is any assistance in obtaining from a participating country one or more of the following —

(a) information as to whether the person in question holds any accounts at any banks situated in the participating country,
(b) details of any such accounts,
(c) details of transactions carried out in any period specified in the request in respect of any such accounts.

(6) A request for assistance under this section must —

(a) state the grounds on which the authority making the request thinks that the person in question may hold any account at a bank which is situated in a participating country and (if possible) specify the bank or banks in question,
(b) state the grounds on which the authority making the request considers that the information sought to be obtained is likely to be of substantial value for the purposes of the investigation, and
(c) include any information which may facilitate compliance with the request.

(7) For the purposes of this section, a person holds an account if —

(a) the account is in his name or is held for his benefit, or
(b) he has a power of attorney in respect of the account.

In relation to Scotland, a power of attorney includes a factory and commission.

44 Monitoring banking transactions

(1) If it appears to a judicial authority in the United Kingdom, on an application made by a prosecuting authority, that the information which the applicant seeks to obtain is relevant to an investigation in the United Kingdom into criminal conduct, the judicial authority may request assistance under this section.

(2) The judicial authorities are —

(a) in relation to England and Wales, any judge or justice of the peace,
(b) in relation to Scotland, any sheriff,
(c) in relation to Northern Ireland, any judge or resident magistrate.

(3) If it appears to a prosecuting authority mentioned in subsection (4) that the information which it seeks to obtain is relevant to an investigation into criminal conduct, the authority may itself request assistance under this section.

(4) The prosecuting authorities are —

(a) in relation to England and Wales and Northern Ireland, a prosecuting authority designated by an order made by the Secretary of State,
(b) in relation to Scotland, the Lord Advocate or a procurator fiscal.

(5) The assistance that may be requested under this section is any assistance in obtaining from a participating country details of transactions to be carried out in any period specified in the request in respect of any accounts at banks situated in that country.

45 Sending requests for assistance

(1) A request for assistance under section 43 or 44, other than one to which subsection (3) or (4) applies, is to be sent to the Secretary of State for forwarding —

(a) to a court specified in the request and exercising jurisdiction in the place where the information is to be obtained, or

(b) to any authority recognised by the participating country in question as the appropriate authority for receiving requests for assistance of the kind to which this section applies.

(2) But in cases of urgency the request may be sent to a court referred to in subsection (1)(a).

(3) Such a request for assistance by the Lord Advocate is to be sent to a court or authority mentioned in subsection (1)(a) or (b).

(4) Such a request for assistance by a sheriff or a procurator fiscal is to be sent to such a court or authority, or to the Lord Advocate for forwarding to such a court or authority.

General

46 Interpretation of Chapter 4

(1) In this Chapter —

"the court" means the Crown Court or, in Scotland, the sheriff,
"senior police officer" means a police officer who is not below the rank of superintendent and "senior customs officer" means a customs officer who is not below the grade designated by the Commissioners of Customs and Excise as equivalent to that rank.

(2) The following provisions apply for the purposes of this Chapter.

(3) Serious criminal conduct means conduct which constitutes —

(a) an offence to which paragraph 3 of Article 1 (request for information on bank accounts) of the 2001 Protocol applies, or
(b) an offence specified in an order made by the Secretary of State or, in relation to Scotland, the Scottish Ministers for the purpose of giving effect to any decision of the Council of the European Union under paragraph 6 of that Article.

(4) A financial institution —

(a) means a person who is carrying on business in the regulated sector, and
(b) in relation to a customer information order or an account monitoring order, includes a person who was carrying on business in the regulated sector at a time which is the time to which any requirement for him to provide information under the order is to relate.

"Business in the regulated sector" is to be interpreted in accordance with Schedule 9 to the Proceeds of Crime Act 2002 (c. 29).

(5) A judge means —

(a) in relation to England and Wales, a judge entitled to exercise the jurisdiction of the Crown Court,
(b) in relation to Northern Ireland, a Crown Court judge.

CHAPTER 5

TRANSFER OF PRISONERS

47 Transfer of UK prisoner to assist investigation abroad

(1) The Secretary of State may pursuant to an agreement with the competent authority of a participating country issue a warrant providing for any person to whom this section applies ("a prisoner") to be transferred to that country for the purpose of assisting there in the investigation of an offence.

The offence must be one which was or may have been committed in the United Kingdom.

(2) This section applies to a person —

(a) serving a sentence in a prison,
(b) in custody awaiting trial or sentence, or
(c) committed to prison for default in paying a fine.

(3) But, in relation to transfer from Scotland —

(a) this section applies to any person detained in custody,
(b) references in this section to the Secretary of State are to be read as references to the Scottish Ministers.

(4) A warrant may be issued in respect of a prisoner under subsection (1) only if —

(a) the prisoner, or
(b) in the circumstances mentioned in subsection (5), a person appearing to the Secretary of State to be an appropriate person to act on the prisoner's behalf,

has made a written statement consenting to his being transferred for the purpose mentioned in subsection (1).

(5) The circumstances are those in which it appears to the Secretary of State to be inappropriate for the prisoner to act for himself, by reason of his physical or mental condition or his youth.

(6) Such consent cannot be withdrawn after the issue of the warrant.

(7) A warrant under this section authorises —

(a) the taking of the prisoner to a place in the United Kingdom and his delivery at a place of departure from the United Kingdom into the custody of a person representing the appropriate authority of the participating country to which the prisoner is to be transferred, and
(b) the bringing of the prisoner back to the United Kingdom and his transfer in custody to the place where he is liable to be detained under the sentence or order to which he is subject.

(8) References to a prison in this section include any other institution to which the Prison Act 1952 (c. 52), the Prison Act (Northern Ireland) 1953 (c. 18 (N.I.)) or Article 45(1) of the Criminal Justice (Children) (Northern Ireland) Order 1998 (S.I. 1998/1504 (N.I.9)) applies.

(9) Subsections (3A) to (8) of section 5 of the 1990 Act (transfer of UK prisoner to give evidence or assist investigation overseas) have effect in relation to a warrant issued under this section as they have effect in relation to a warrant issued under that section.

48 Transfer of EU etc. prisoner to assist UK investigation

(1) The Secretary of State may pursuant to an agreement with the competent authority of a participating country issue a warrant providing for any person to whom this section applies ("the overseas prisoner") to be transferred to the United Kingdom for the purpose of assisting in the investigation of an offence.

The offence must be one which was or may have been committed in the participating country.

(2) This section applies to a person who is detained in custody in a participating country —

(a) by virtue of a sentence or order of a court exercising criminal jurisdiction there, or
(b) in consequence of having been transferred there from the United Kingdom under the Repatriation of Prisoners Act 1984 (c. 47) or under any similar provision or arrangement from any other country.

(3) But, in relation to transfer to Scotland —

(a) this section applies to any person who is detained in custody in a participating country,
(b) the reference in subsection (1) to the Secretary of State is to be read as a reference to the Scottish Ministers.

(4) A warrant may be issued in respect of an overseas prisoner under subsection (1) only if the competent authority provides a written statement made by the prisoner consenting to his being transferred for the purpose mentioned in that subsection.

(5) Such consent cannot be withdrawn after the issue of the warrant.

(6) A warrant under this section authorises —

(a) the bringing of the prisoner to the United Kingdom,
(b) the taking of the prisoner to, and his detention in custody at, any place or places in the United Kingdom specified in the warrant,
(c) the returning of the prisoner to the country from which he has come.

(7) Subsections (4) to (8) of section 5 of the 1990 Act have effect in relation to a warrant issued under this section as they have effect in relation to a warrant issued under that section.

(8) A person is not subject to the Immigration Act 1971 (c. 77) in respect of his entry into or presence in the United Kingdom pursuant to a warrant under this section; but if the warrant ceases to have effect while he is still in the United Kingdom —

(a) he is to be treated for the purposes of that Act as if he has then illegally entered the United Kingdom, and
(b) the provisions of Schedule 2 to that Act have effect accordingly except that paragraph 20(1) (liability of carrier for expenses of custody etc. of illegal entrant) does not have effect in relation to directions for his removal given by virtue of this subsection.

CHAPTER 6

SUPPLEMENTARY

49 Rules of court

(1) Provision may be made by rules of court as to the practice and procedure to be followed in connection with proceedings under this Part.

(2) Rules of court made under this section by the High Court in Scotland are to be made by Act of Adjournal.

(3) The power to make rules of court under this section does not prejudice any existing power to make rules.

50 Subordinate legislation

(1) Any power to make an order conferred by this Part on the Secretary of State, the Treasury or the Scottish Ministers is exercisable by statutory instrument.

(2) Such an order may make different provision for different purposes.

(3) A statutory instrument (other than an instrument to which subsection (5) applies) containing an order made by the Secretary of State or the Treasury is to be subject to annulment in pursuance of a resolution of either House of Parliament.

(4) A statutory instrument (other than an instrument to which subsection (5) applies) containing an order made by the Scottish Ministers is to be subject to annulment in pursuance of a resolution of the Scottish Parliament.

(5) A statutory instrument containing an order under section 51(2) (b) designating a country other than a member State is not to be made unless —

- (a) in the case of an order to be made by the Secretary of State, a draft of the instrument has been laid before, and approved by resolution of, each House of Parliament,
- (b) in the case of an order to be made by the Scottish Ministers, a draft of the instrument has been laid before, and approved by resolution of, the Scottish Parliament.

51 General interpretation

(1) In this Part —

"the 1990 Act" means the Criminal Justice (International Co-operation) Act 1990 (c. 5),

"the 2001 Protocol" means the Protocol to the Mutual Legal Assistance Convention, established by Council Act of 16th October 2001 (2001/C326/01),

"administrative proceedings" means proceedings outside the United Kingdom to which Article 3(1) of the Mutual Legal Assistance Convention applies (proceedings brought by administrative authorities in respect of administrative offences where a decision in the proceedings may be the subject of an appeal before a court),

"chief officer of police" —

- (a) in relation to any area in Scotland, means the chief constable for the police force maintained for that area,
- (b) in relation to any area in Northern Ireland, means the Chief Constable of the Police Service of Northern Ireland,

"clemency proceedings" means proceedings in a country outside the United Kingdom, not being proceedings before a court exercising criminal jurisdiction, for the removal or reduction of a penalty imposed on conviction of an offence,

"country" includes territory,

"court" includes a tribunal,

"criminal proceedings" include criminal proceedings outside the United Kingdom in which a civil order may be made,

"customs officer" means an officer commissioned by the Commissioners of Customs and Excise under section 6(3) of the Customs and Excise Management Act 1979 (c. 2),

"evidence" includes information in any form and articles, and giving evidence includes answering a question or producing any information or article,

"the Mutual Legal Assistance Convention" means the Convention on Mutual Assistance in Criminal Matters established by Council Act of 29th May 2000 (2000/C197/01),

"the Schengen Convention" means the Convention implementing the Schengen Agreement of 14th June 1985.

(2) A participating country, in relation to any provision of this Part, means —

(a) a country other than the United Kingdom which is a member State on a day appointed for the commencement of that provision, and
(b) any other country designated by an order made by the Secretary of State or, in relation to Scotland, the Scottish Ministers.

(3) In this Part, "process", in relation to England and Wales and Northern Ireland, means any summons or order issued or made by a court and includes —

(a) any other document issued or made by a court for service on parties or witnesses,
(b) any document issued by a prosecuting authority outside the United Kingdom for the purposes of criminal proceedings.

(4) In this Part, "process", in relation to service in Scotland, means a citation by a court or by a prosecuting authority, or an order made by a court, and includes any other document issued or made as mentioned in subsection (3)(a) or (b).

PART 2

TERRORIST ACTS AND THREATS: JURISDICTION

52 Jurisdiction for terrorist offences

After section 63 of the Terrorism Act 2000 (c. 11) there is inserted —

"Extra-territorial jurisdiction for other terrorist offences etc.

63A Other terrorist offences under this Act: jurisdiction

(1) If —

(a) a United Kingdom national or a United Kingdom resident does anything outside the United Kingdom, and

(b) his action, if done in any part of the United Kingdom, would have constituted an offence under section 54 or any of sections 56 to 61,

he shall be guilty in that part of the United Kingdom of the offence.

(2) For the purposes of this section and sections 63B and 63C a "United Kingdom national" means an individual who is —

(a) a British citizen, a British overseas territories citizen, a British National (Overseas) or a British Overseas citizen,
(b) a person who under the British Nationality Act 1981 is a British subject, or
(c) a British protected person within the meaning of that Act.

(3) For the purposes of this section and sections 63B and 63C a "United Kingdom resident" means an individual who is resident in the United Kingdom.

63B Terrorist attacks abroad by UK nationals or residents: jurisdiction

(1) If —

(a) a United Kingdom national or a United Kingdom resident does anything outside the United Kingdom as an act of terrorism or for the purposes of terrorism, and
(b) his action, if done in any part of the United Kingdom, would have constituted an offence listed in subsection (2),

he shall be guilty in that part of the United Kingdom of the offence.

(2) These are the offences —

(a) murder, manslaughter, culpable homicide, rape, assault causing injury, assault to injury, kidnapping, abduction or false imprisonment,
(b) an offence under section 4, 16, 18, 20, 21, 22, 23, 24, 28, 29, 30 or 64 of the Offences against the Person Act 1861,
(c) an offence under any of sections 1 to 5 of the Forgery and Counterfeiting Act 1981,
(d) the uttering of a forged document or an offence under section 46A of the Criminal Law (Consolidation) (Scotland) Act 1995,
(e) an offence under section 1 or 2 of the Criminal Damage Act 1971,
(f) an offence under Article 3 or 4 of the Criminal Damage (Northern Ireland) Order 1977,
(g) malicious mischief,
(h) wilful fire-raising.

63C Terrorist attacks abroad on UK nationals, residents and diplomatic staff etc: jurisdiction

(1) If —

(a) a person does anything outside the United Kingdom as an act of terrorism or for the purposes of terrorism,
(b) his action is done to, or in relation to, a United Kingdom national, a United Kingdom resident or a protected person, and
(c) his action, if done in any part of the United Kingdom, would have constituted an offence listed in subsection (2),

he shall be guilty in that part of the United Kingdom of the offence.

(2) These are the offences —

(a) murder, manslaughter, culpable homicide, rape, assault causing injury, assault to injury, kidnapping, abduction or false imprisonment,

(b) an offence under section 4, 16, 18, 20, 21, 22, 23, 24, 28, 29, 30 or 64 of the Offences against the Person Act 1861,
(c) an offence under section 1, 2, 3, 4 or 5(1) or (3) of the Forgery and Counterfeiting Act 1981,
(d) the uttering of a forged document or an offence under section 46A(1) of the Criminal Law (Consolidation) (Scotland) Act 1995.

(3) For the purposes of this section and section 63D a person is a protected person if—

(a) he is a member of a United Kingdom diplomatic mission within the meaning of Article 1(b) of the Vienna Convention on Diplomatic Relations signed in 1961 (as that Article has effect in the United Kingdom by virtue of section 2 of and Schedule 1 to the Diplomatic Privileges Act 1964),
(b) he is a member of a United Kingdom consular post within the meaning of Article 1(g) of the Vienna Convention on Consular Relations signed in 1963 (as that Article has effect in the United Kingdom by virtue of section 1 of and Schedule 1 to the Consular Relations Act 1968),
(c) he carries out any functions for the purposes of the European Agency for the Evaluation of Medicinal Products, or
(d) he carries out any functions for the purposes of a body specified in an order made by the Secretary of State.

(4) The Secretary of State may specify a body under subsection (3)(d) only if—

(a) it is established by or under the Treaty establishing the European Community or the Treaty on European Union, and
(b) the principal place in which its functions are carried out is a place in the United Kingdom.

(5) If in any proceedings a question arises as to whether a person is or was a protected person, a certificate—

(a) issued by or under the authority of the Secretary of State, and
(b) stating any fact relating to the question,

is to be conclusive evidence of that fact.

63D Terrorist attacks or threats abroad in connection with UK diplomatic premises etc: jurisdiction

(1) If—

(a) a person does anything outside the United Kingdom as an act of terrorism or for the purposes of terrorism,
(b) his action is done in connection with an attack on relevant premises or on a vehicle ordinarily used by a protected person,
(c) the attack is made when a protected person is on or in the premises or vehicle, and
(d) his action, if done in any part of the United Kingdom, would have constituted an offence listed in subsection (2),

he shall be guilty in that part of the United Kingdom of the offence.

(2) These are the offences—

(a) an offence under section 1 of the Criminal Damage Act 1971,
(b) an offence under Article 3 of the Criminal Damage (Northern Ireland) Order 1977,

(c) malicious mischief,
(d) wilful fire-raising.

(3) If —

(a) a person does anything outside the United Kingdom as an act of terrorism or for the purposes of terrorism,
(b) his action consists of a threat of an attack on relevant premises or on a vehicle ordinarily used by a protected person,
(c) the attack is threatened to be made when a protected person is, or is likely to be, on or in the premises or vehicle, and
(d) his action, if done in any part of the United Kingdom, would have constituted an offence listed in subsection (4),

he shall be guilty in that part of the United Kingdom of the offence.

(4) These are the offences —

(a) an offence under section 2 of the Criminal Damage Act 1971,
(b) an offence under Article 4 of the Criminal Damage (Northern Ireland) Order 1977,
(c) breach of the peace (in relation to Scotland only).

(5) "Relevant premises" means —

(a) premises at which a protected person resides or is staying, or
(b) premises which a protected person uses for the purpose of carrying out his functions as such a person.

63E Sections 63B to 63D: supplementary

(1) Proceedings for an offence which (disregarding the Acts listed in subsection (2)) would not be an offence apart from section 63B, 63C or 63D are not to be started —

(a) in England and Wales, except by or with the consent of the Attorney General,
(b) in Northern Ireland, except by or with the consent of the Advocate General for Northern Ireland.

(2) These are the Acts —

(a) the Internationally Protected Persons Act 1978,
(b) the Suppression of Terrorism Act 1978,
(c) the Nuclear Material (Offences) Act 1983,
(d) the United Nations Personnel Act 1997.

(3) For the purposes of sections 63C and 63D it is immaterial whether a person knows that another person is a United Kingdom national, a United Kingdom resident or a protected person.

(4) In relation to any time before the coming into force of section 27(1) of the Justice (Northern Ireland) Act 2002, the reference in subsection (1)(b) to the Advocate General for Northern Ireland is to be read as a reference to the Attorney General for Northern Ireland."

53 Jurisdiction for offence under section 113 of the Anti-terrorism, Crime and Security Act 2001

After section 113 of the Anti-terrorism, Crime and Security Act 2001 (c. 24) (use of noxious substances or things to cause harm and intimidate) there is inserted —

"113A Application of section 113

(1) Section 113 applies to conduct done —

(a) in the United Kingdom; or
(b) outside the United Kingdom which satisfies the following two conditions.

(2) The first condition is that the conduct is done for the purpose of advancing a political, religious or ideological cause.

(3) The second condition is that the conduct is —

(a) by a United Kingdom national or a United Kingdom resident;
(b) by any person done to, or in relation to, a United Kingdom national, a United Kingdom resident or a protected person; or
(c) by any person done in circumstances which fall within section 63D(1)(b) and (c) or (3)(b) and (c) of the Terrorism Act 2000.

(4) The following expressions have the same meaning as they have for the purposes of sections 63C and 63D of that Act —

(a) "United Kingdom national";
(b) "United Kingdom resident";
(c) "protected person".

(5) For the purposes of this section it is immaterial whether a person knows that another is a United Kingdom national, a United Kingdom resident or a protected person.

113B Consent to prosecution for offence under section 113

(1) Proceedings for an offence committed under section 113 outside the United Kingdom are not to be started —

(a) in England and Wales, except by or with the consent of the Attorney General;
(b) in Northern Ireland, except by or with the consent of the Advocate General for Northern Ireland.

(2) Proceedings for an offence committed under section 113 outside the United Kingdom may be taken, and the offence may for incidental purposes be treated as having been committed, in any part of the United Kingdom.

(3) In relation to any time before the coming into force of section 27(1) of the Justice (Northern Ireland) Act 2002, the reference in subsection (1)(b) to the Advocate General for Northern Ireland is to be read as a reference to the Attorney General for Northern Ireland."

PART 3

ROAD TRAFFIC

CHAPTER 1

CONVENTION ON DRIVING DISQUALIFICATIONS

Road traffic offences in UK

54 Application of section 55

(1) Section 55 applies where —

(a) an individual ("the offender") who is normally resident in a member State other than the United Kingdom is convicted of an offence mentioned in Schedule 3,
(b) no appeal is outstanding in relation to the offence, and
(c) the driving disqualification condition is met in relation to the offence.

(2) The driving disqualification condition is met —

(a) in relation to an offence mentioned in Part 1 of Schedule 3, if an order of disqualification is made in respect of the offence,
(b) in relation to an offence mentioned in Part 2 of that Schedule, if an order of disqualification for a period not less than the minimum period is made in respect of the offence.

(3) The minimum period is —

(a) a period of six months, or
(b) where the State in which the offender normally resides is a prescribed State, a shorter period equal to the period prescribed in relation to the State.

(4) Section 55 does not apply in prescribed circumstances.

(5) For the purposes of this section no appeal is outstanding in relation to an offence if —

(a) no appeal is brought against an offender's conviction of the offence, or any order made on his conviction, within the time allowed for making such appeals, or
(b) such an appeal is brought and the proceedings on appeal are finally concluded.

55 Duty to give notice to foreign authorities of driving disqualification of a non-UK resident

(1) Where this section applies, the appropriate Minister must give the central authority of the State in which the offender is normally resident a notice under this section.

(2) A notice under this section must —

(a) give the name, address and date of birth of the offender,
(b) give particulars of the offence,
(c) state that no appeal is outstanding in relation to it,
(d) give particulars of the disqualification,
(e) state whether or not the offender took part in the proceedings in which the disqualification was imposed,

(f) state that the offender has been informed that any decision made for the purposes of the convention on driving disqualifications will have no effect on the disqualification.

(3) A notice under this section may contain such other information as the appropriate Minister considers appropriate.

(4) A notice under this section must be accompanied by the original or a certified copy of the order of disqualification.

(5) Where the offender did not take part in the proceedings mentioned in subsection (2)(e), a notice under this section must also be accompanied by evidence that the offender was duly notified of those proceedings.

(6) Where the offender is the holder of a Community licence, a notice under this section must also be accompanied by the licence unless it has been returned to the driver —

(a) under section 91A(7)(b)(ii) of the Road Traffic Offenders Act 1988 (c. 53), or
(b) under Article 92A(7)(b)(ii) of the Road Traffic Offenders (Northern Ireland) Order 1996 (S.I. 1996/1320 (N.I.10)).

(7) Where the period of disqualification is reduced by virtue of section 34A of that Act or Article 36 of that Order, the appropriate Minister must give the central authority particulars of the reduction.

(8) Where the disqualification is removed by an order under section 42 of that Act or Article 47 of that Order, the appropriate Minister must give the central authority particulars of the removal.

(9) The appropriate Minister must provide —

(a) the central authority, or
(b) the competent authority of the State mentioned in subsection (1),

with any further information which it requires for the purposes of the convention on driving disqualifications.

Disqualification in respect of road traffic offences outside UK

56 Application of section 57

(1) Section 57 applies where —

(a) an individual ("the offender") who is normally resident in the United Kingdom is convicted in another member State of an offence falling within subsection (5),
(b) no appeal is outstanding in relation to the offence,
(c) the driving disqualification condition is met in relation to the offence, and
(d) the offender was duly notified of the proceedings ("the relevant proceedings") in which the disqualification was imposed and was entitled to take part in them.

(2) The driving disqualification condition is met —

(a) in relation to an offence falling within subsection (5)(a), if, as a result of the offence, the offender is disqualified in the State in which the conviction is made,
(b) in relation to an offence falling within subsection (5)(b), if, as a result of the offence, the offender is disqualified in that State for a period not less than the minimum period.

(3) For the purposes of this section an offender is disqualified in a State if he is disqualified in that State for holding or obtaining a licence to drive a motor vehicle granted under the law of that State (however the disqualification is described under that law).

(4) The minimum period is —

(a) a period of six months, or
(b) where the State in which the conviction is made is a prescribed State, a shorter period equal to the period prescribed in relation to that State.

(5) An offence falls within this subsection if it is constituted by —

(a) conduct falling within any of paragraphs 1 to 5 of the Annex to the convention on driving disqualifications, or
(b) other conduct which constitutes a road traffic offence for the purposes of that convention.

(6) Section 57 does not apply if the relevant proceedings were brought later than the time at which summary proceedings for any corresponding offence under the law of the part of the United Kingdom in which the offender is normally resident could have been brought.

(7) An offence is a corresponding offence if —

(a) the conduct constituting the offence outside the United Kingdom took place in any part of the United Kingdom, and
(b) that conduct is, or corresponds to, conduct which would constitute an offence under the law of that part.

(8) The appropriate Minister may make regulations treating offences under the law of a part of the United Kingdom as corresponding to offences under the law of a member State other than the United Kingdom.

(9) For the purposes of this section no appeal is outstanding in relation to an offence if —

(a) no appeal is brought against an offender's conviction of the offence, or any decision made as a result of his conviction, within the time allowed for making such appeals, or
(b) such an appeal is brought and the proceedings on appeal are finally concluded.

57 Recognition in United Kingdom of foreign driving disqualification

(1) Where this section applies, the appropriate Minister —

(a) must give the offender a notice under this section if the unexpired period of the foreign disqualification is not less than one month, and
(b) may give him a notice under this section if that period is less than one month.

(2) The unexpired period of the foreign disqualification is —

(a) the period of the foreign disqualification, less
(b) any period of that disqualification which is treated by regulations made by the appropriate Minister as having been served in the State in which the offender was convicted.

(3) The provision which may be made by regulations under subsection (2)(b) includes provision for treating any period during which a central authority or competent authority of a State has seized a licence without returning it as a period which has been served in that State.

(4) If the appropriate Minister gives the offender a notice under this section, the offender is disqualified in each part of the United Kingdom —

(a) for the relevant period, and
(b) if the foreign disqualification is also effective until a condition is satisfied, until the condition or a corresponding prescribed condition is satisfied.

(5) The relevant period is the period which —

(a) begins at the end of the period of 21 days beginning with the day on which the notice is given, and
(b) is equal to the unexpired period of the foreign disqualification.

(6) But if the foreign disqualification is at any time removed otherwise than in prescribed circumstances, the offender ceases to be disqualified in each part of the United Kingdom from that time.

(7) The appropriate Minister may make regulations substituting a longer period for the period for the time being mentioned in subsection (5)(a).

(8) Where the foreign disqualification is for life —

(a) the condition in subsection (1)(a) is to be treated as satisfied, and
(b) the other references in this section and section 58 to the unexpired period of the foreign disqualification are to be read as references to a disqualification for life.

58 Notice under section 57

(1) A notice under section 57 must —

(a) give particulars of the offence in respect of which the foreign disqualification was imposed and the period of that disqualification,
(b) state that the offender is disqualified in each part of the United Kingdom for a period equal to the unexpired period of the foreign disqualification,
(c) state the date from which, and period for which, he is disqualified,
(d) give particulars of any relevant condition mentioned in section 57(4)(b),
(e) give details of his right to appeal under section 59.

(2) A notice under section 57 must be in writing.

(3) A notice under section 57 may contain such other information as the appropriate Minister considers appropriate.

Appeals

59 Appeal against disqualification

(1) A person who is disqualified by virtue of section 57 may, after giving notice to the appropriate Minister of his intention to do so, appeal to the appropriate court against the disqualification.

(2) The appropriate court is —

(a) in relation to England and Wales, a magistrates' court acting for the petty sessions area in which the applicant resides,
(b) in relation to Scotland, the sheriff within whose jurisdiction the applicant resides,
(c) in relation to Northern Ireland, a court of summary jurisdiction acting for the petty sessions district in which the applicant resides.

(3) The appeal must be made before the end of the period of 21 days beginning with the day on which the notice under section 57 is given to the applicant.

(4) But the appropriate Minister may make regulations substituting a longer period for the period for the time being mentioned in subsection (3).

(5) If the appropriate court is satisfied that section 57 does not apply to the applicant's case, it must allow the appeal.

(6) Otherwise it must dismiss the appeal.

(7) Where on an appeal against the disqualification the appeal is allowed, the court by which the appeal is allowed must send notice of that fact to the appropriate Minister.

(8) The notice must—

(a) be sent in such manner and to such address, and
(b) contain such particulars,

as the appropriate Minister may determine.

60 Power of appellate courts in England and Wales to suspend disqualification

(1) This section applies where a person is disqualified by virtue of section 57.

(2) Where the person appeals to a magistrates' court against the disqualification, the court may, if it thinks fit, suspend the disqualification.

(3) Where the person makes an application in respect of the decision of the court under section 111 of the Magistrates' Courts Act 1980 (c. 43) (statement of case), the High Court may, if it thinks fit, suspend the disqualification.

(4) Where the person has appealed, or applied for leave to appeal, to the House of Lords under section 1 of the Administration of Justice Act 1960 (c. 65) from any decision of the High Court which is material to the disqualification, the High Court may, if it thinks fit, suspend the disqualification.

(5) Any power of a court under this section to suspend the disqualification is a power to do so on such terms as the court thinks fit.

(6) Where, by virtue of this section, a court suspends the disqualification, it must send notice of the suspension to the Secretary of State.

(7) The notice must—

(a) be sent in such manner and to such address, and
(b) contain such particulars,

as the Secretary of State may determine.

61 Power of appellate courts in Scotland to suspend disqualification

(1) This section applies where a person is disqualified by virtue of section 57.

(2) Where the person appeals to the sheriff against the disqualification, the sheriff may, if he thinks fit, suspend the disqualification on such terms as he thinks fit.

(3) Where the person appeals to the High Court of Justiciary from any decision of the sheriff, the court may, if it thinks fit, suspend the disqualification on such terms as it thinks fit.

The power conferred by this subsection may be exercised by a single judge of the court.

(4) Where, by virtue of this section, a court suspends the disqualification, it must send notice of the suspension to the Secretary of State.

(5) The notice must—

(a) be sent in such manner and to such address, and
(b) contain such particulars,

as the Secretary of State may determine.

62 Power of appellate courts in Northern Ireland to suspend disqualification

(1) This section applies where a person is disqualified by virtue of section 57.

(2) Where the person appeals to a court of summary jurisdiction against the disqualification, the court may, if it thinks fit, suspend the disqualification.

(3) Where the person makes an application in respect of the decision of the court under Article 146 of the Magistrates' Courts (Northern Ireland) Order 1981 (S.I. 1981/ 1675 (N.I. 26)) (statement of case), the Court of Appeal may, if it thinks fit, suspend the disqualification.

(4) Where the person has appealed, or applied for leave to appeal, to the House of Lords under section 41 of the Judicature (Northern Ireland) Act 1978 (c. 23) from any decision of the Court of Appeal which is material to the disqualification, the Court of Appeal may, if it thinks fit, suspend the disqualification.

(5) Any power of a court under this section to suspend the disqualification is a power to do so on such terms as the court thinks fit.

(6) Where, by virtue of this section, a court suspends the disqualification, it must send notice of the suspension to the Department.

(7) The notice must —

(a) be sent in such manner and to such address, and
(b) contain such particulars,

as the Department may determine.

Production of licence

63 Production of licence: Great Britain

(1) A person who —

(a) is given a notice under section 57 by the Secretary of State, and
(b) is the holder of a licence,

must deliver his licence and its counterpart to the Secretary of State before the end of the period of 21 days beginning with the day on which the notice is given.

(2) The Secretary of State may make regulations substituting a longer period for the period for the time being mentioned in subsection (1).

(3) If —

(a) a person delivers a current receipt for his licence and its counterpart to the Secretary of State within the period for the time being mentioned in subsection (1), and
(b) on the return of his licence and its counterpart immediately delivers them to the Secretary of State,

the duty under subsection (1) is to be taken as satisfied.

"Receipt" means a receipt issued under section 56 of the Road Traffic Offenders Act 1988 (c. 53).

(4) Subsection (1) does not apply if the competent authority of the relevant State —

(a) has the licence and its counterpart, or
(b) has delivered them to the Secretary of State.

(5) The relevant State is the State in which the offence in relation to which the notice was given was committed.

(6) If the holder of a licence does not deliver his licence and its counterpart to the Secretary of State as required by subsection (1), he is guilty of an offence.

(7) A person is not guilty of an offence under subsection (6) if he satisfies the court that he has applied for a new licence and has not received it.

In relation to the holder of a Northern Ireland licence or Community licence, a new licence includes the counterpart of such a licence.

(8) A person guilty of an offence under subsection (6) is liable on summary conviction to a fine not exceeding level 3 on the standard scale.

(9) "Licence" means a Great Britain licence, a Northern Ireland licence or a Community licence.

64 Production of licence: Northern Ireland

(1) A person who —

(a) is given a notice under section 57 by the Department, and
(b) is the holder of a licence,

must deliver his licence and its counterpart to the Department before the end of the period of 21 days beginning with the day on which the notice is given.

(2) The Department may make regulations substituting a longer period for the period for the time being mentioned in subsection (1).

(3) If —

(a) a person delivers a current receipt for his licence and its counterpart to the Department within the period for the time being mentioned in subsection (1), and
(b) on the return of his licence and its counterpart immediately delivers them to the Department,

the duty under subsection (1) is to be taken as satisfied.

"Receipt" means a receipt issued under Article 62 of the Road Traffic Offenders (Northern Ireland) Order 1996 (S.I. 1996/1320 (N.I.10)).

(4) Subsection (1) does not apply if the competent authority of the relevant State —

(a) has the licence and its counterpart, or
(b) has delivered them to the Department.

(5) The relevant State is the State in which the offence in relation to which the notice was given was committed.

(6) If the holder of a licence does not deliver his licence and its counterpart to the Department as required by subsection (1), he is guilty of an offence.

(7) A person is not guilty of an offence under subsection (6) if he satisfies the court that he has applied for a new licence and has not received it.

In relation to the holder of a Great Britain licence or Community licence, a new licence includes the counterpart of such a licence.

(8) A person guilty of an offence under subsection (6) is liable on summary conviction to a fine not exceeding level 3 on the standard scale.

(9) "Licence" means a Northern Ireland licence, a Great Britain licence or a Community licence.

65 Production of licence: Community licence holders

(1) This section applies where —

(a) the holder of a Community licence is disqualified by virtue of section 57, and
(b) the licence is sent to the Secretary of State or the Department under section 63 or 64.

(2) The Secretary of State or (as the case may be) the Department must send —

(a) the holder's name and address, and
(b) particulars of the disqualification,

to the licensing authority in the EEA State in respect of which the licence was issued.

(3) But subsection (2) does not apply if the EEA State is the same as the State in which the offence in relation to which the holder is disqualified was committed.

(4) The Secretary of State or (as the case may be) the Department must return the licence to the holder —

(a) on the expiry of the relevant period of the disqualification (within the meaning of section 57), or
(b) if earlier, on being satisfied that the holder has left Great Britain or (as the case may be) Northern Ireland and is no longer normally resident there.

(5) But subsection (4) does not apply at any time where —

(a) the Secretary of State or the Department would otherwise be under a duty under paragraph (a) of that subsection to return the licence, and
(b) the holder would not at that time be authorised by virtue of section 99A(1) of the Road Traffic Act 1988 (c. 52) or Article 15A(1) of the Road Traffic (Northern Ireland) Order 1981 (S.I. 1981/154 (N.I.1)) to drive in Great Britain or Northern Ireland a motor vehicle of any class.

(6) In that case the Secretary of State or (as the case may be) the Department must —

(a) send the licence to the licensing authority in the EEA State in respect of which it was issued, and
(b) explain to that authority the reasons for so doing.

(7) "EEA State" has the same meaning as in Part 3 of the Road Traffic Act 1988.

Disqualification

66 Effect of disqualification by virtue of section 57

Where the holder of a Great Britain licence or Northern Ireland licence is disqualified by virtue of section 57, the licence is to be treated as revoked with effect from the beginning of the period of disqualification.

67 Rule for determining end of period of disqualification

In determining the expiration of the period for which a person is disqualified by virtue of section 57, any time during which —

(a) the disqualification is suspended, or
(b) he is not disqualified,

is to be disregarded.

Endorsement

68 Endorsement of licence: Great Britain

(1) This section applies where a person who is normally resident in Great Britain is disqualified by virtue of section 57.

(2) The Secretary of State must secure that particulars of the disqualification are endorsed on the counterpart of any Great Britain licence or of any Northern Ireland licence or Community licence which the person —

(a) may then hold, or
(b) may subsequently obtain,

until he becomes entitled under subsection (4) or (5) to have a Great Britain licence and its counterpart, or a counterpart of his Northern Ireland licence or Community licence, issued to him free from those particulars.

(3) On the issue to the person of —

(a) a new Great Britain licence, or
(b) a new counterpart of a Northern Ireland licence or Community licence,

those particulars must be entered on the counterpart of the new licence or the new counterpart unless he has become so entitled.

(4) The person is entitled to have issued to him with effect from the end of the period for which the endorsement remains effective a new Great Britain licence with a counterpart free from the endorsement if he —

(a) applies for a new licence under section 97(1) of the Road Traffic Act 1988 (c. 52),
(b) surrenders any subsisting licence and its counterpart,
(c) pays the fee prescribed by regulations under Part 3 of that Act, and
(d) satisfies the other requirements of section 97(1).

(5) The person is entitled to have issued to him with effect from the end of that period a new counterpart of any Northern Ireland licence or Community licence then held by him free from the endorsement if he makes an application to the Secretary of State for that purpose in such manner as the Secretary of State may determine.

(6) The endorsement remains effective until four years have elapsed since he was convicted of the offence in relation to which he is disqualified by virtue of section 57.

(7) Where the person ceases to be disqualified by virtue of section 57(6), the Secretary of State must secure that the relevant particulars are endorsed on the counterpart of the Great Britain licence or of any Northern Ireland licence or Community licence previously held by him.

69 Endorsement of elicence: Northern Ireland

(1) This section applies where a person who is normally resident in Northern Ireland is disqualified by virtue of section 57.

(2) The Department must secure that particulars of the disqualification are endorsed on the counterpart of any Northern Ireland licence or the counterpart of any Great Britain licence or Community licence which the person —

(a) may then hold, or
(b) may subsequently obtain,

until he becomes entitled under subsection (4) or (5) to have a Northern Ireland licence and its counterpart, or a counterpart of his Great Britain licence or Community licence, issued to him free from those particulars.

(3) On the issue to the person of —

(a) a new Northern Ireland licence, or
(b) a new counterpart of a Great Britain licence or Community licence,

those particulars must be entered on the counterpart of the new licence or the new counterpart unless he has become so entitled.

(4) The person is entitled to have issued to him with effect from the end of the period for which the endorsement remains effective a new Northern Ireland licence with a counterpart free from the endorsement if he —

(a) applies for a new licence under Article 13(1) of the Road Traffic (Northern Ireland) Order 1981 (S.I. 1981/154 (N.I.1)),
(b) surrenders any subsisting licence and its counterpart,
(c) pays the fee prescribed by regulations under Part 2 of that Order, and
(d) satisfies the other requirements of Article 13(1).

(5) The person is entitled to have issued to him with effect from the end of that period a new counterpart of any Great Britain licence or Community licence then held by him free from the endorsement if he makes an application to the Department for that purpose in such manner as it may determine.

(6) The endorsement remains effective until four years have elapsed since he was convicted of the offence in relation to which he is disqualified by virtue of section 57.

(7) Where the person ceases to be disqualified by virtue of section 57(6), the Department must secure that the relevant particulars are endorsed on the counterpart of the Northern Ireland licence or the counterpart of any Great Britain licence or Community licence previously held by him.

General

70 Duty of appropriate Minister to inform competent authority

(1) This section applies where a competent authority of any State gives the appropriate Minister a notice under the convention on driving disqualifications in respect of any person.

(2) If the appropriate Minister gives a notice under section 57 to that person, he must give the competent authority particulars of the disqualification which arises by virtue of that section.

(3) If the appropriate Minister does not give such a notice, he must give his reasons to the competent authority.

71 Notices

(1) A notice authorised or required under this Chapter to be given by the appropriate Minister to an individual, or a Community licence required to be returned to its holder by section 65, may be given or returned to him by —

(a) delivering it to him,
(b) leaving it at his proper address, or
(c) sending it to him by post.

(2) For the purposes of —

(a) subsection (1), and
(b) section 7 of the Interpretation Act 1978 (c. 30) in its application to that subsection,

the proper address of any individual is his latest address as known to the appropriate Minister.

72 Regulations: Great Britain

(1) Any power to make regulations conferred by this Chapter on the Secretary of State is exercisable by statutory instrument.

(2) A statutory instrument containing any such regulations is subject to annulment in pursuance of a resolution of either House of Parliament.

(3) The regulations may make different provision for different purposes.

73 Regulations: Northern Ireland

(1) Any power to make regulations conferred by this Chapter on the Department is exercisable by statutory rule for the purposes of the Statutory Rules (Northern Ireland) Order 1979 (S.I. 1979/ 1573 (N.I. 12)).

(2) Any such regulations are subject to negative resolution (within the meaning of the Interpretation Act (Northern Ireland) 1954 (c. 33 (N.I.)).

(3) The regulations may make different provision for different purposes.

74 Interpretation

(1) In this Chapter —

"appropriate Minister" means —

(a) in relation to Great Britain, the Secretary of State,
(b) in relation to Northern Ireland, the Department,

"central authority", in relation to a State, means an authority designated by the State as a central authority for the purposes of the convention on driving disqualifications,
"Community licence" —

(a) in relation to Great Britain, has the same meaning as in Part 3 of the Road Traffic Act 1988 (c. 52),
(b) in relation to Northern Ireland, has the same meaning as in Part 2 of the Road Traffic (Northern Ireland) Order 1981 (S.I. 1981/154 (N.I.1)),

"competent authority", in relation to a State, means an authority which is a competent authority in relation to the State for the purposes of the convention on driving disqualifications,
"the convention on driving disqualifications" means the Convention drawn up on the basis of Article K.3 of the Treaty on European Union on Driving Disqualifications signed on 17th June 1998,
"counterpart" —

(a) in relation to Great Britain, has the same meaning as in Part 3 of the Road Traffic Act 1988 (c. 52),
(b) in relation to Northern Ireland, has the same meaning as in Part 2 of the Road Traffic (Northern Ireland) Order 1981 (S.I. 1981/154 (N.I.1)),

"the Department" means the Department of the Environment,
"disqualified", except in section 56, means —

(a) in relation to Great Britain, disqualified for holding or obtaining a Great Britain licence,
(b) in relation to Northern Ireland, disqualified for holding or obtaining a Northern Ireland licence,

and "disqualification" is to be interpreted accordingly,
"foreign disqualification" means the disqualification mentioned in section 56,

"Great Britain licence" means a licence to drive a motor vehicle granted under Part 3 of the Road Traffic Act 1988,
"motor vehicle" —

(a) in relation to Great Britain, has the same meaning as in the Road Traffic Act 1988,
(b) in relation to Northern Ireland, has the same meaning as in the Road Traffic (Northern Ireland) Order 1995 (S.I. 1995/ 2994 (N.I.18)),

"Northern Ireland licence" means a licence to drive a motor vehicle granted under Part 2 of the Road Traffic (Northern Ireland) Order 1981,
"prescribed" means prescribed by regulations made by the appropriate Minister.

(2) In this Chapter a disqualification, or foreign disqualification, for life is to be treated as being for a period of not less than six months.

75 Application to Crown

This Chapter applies to vehicles and persons in the public service of the Crown.

Chapter 2

Mutual Recognition within the United Kingdom etc.

76 Recognition in Great Britain of disqualifications in Northern Ireland etc.

After section 102 of the Road Traffic Act 1988 there is inserted —

"Disqualification if disqualified in Northern Ireland etc.

102A Disqualification while disqualified in Northern Ireland, Isle of Man, Channel Islands or Gibraltar

(1) A person is disqualified for holding or obtaining a licence to drive a motor vehicle of any class so long as he is subject to a relevant disqualification imposed outside Great Britain.

(2) For the purposes of this section a person is subject to a relevant disqualification imposed outside Great Britain if, in respect of any offence —

(a) a court in Northern Ireland disqualifies him for holding or obtaining a Northern Ireland licence,
(b) a court in the Isle of Man or any of the Channel Islands disqualifies him for holding or obtaining a British external licence, or
(c) a court in Gibraltar disqualifies him for holding or obtaining a licence to drive a motor vehicle granted under the law of Gibraltar.

(3) A certificate signed by the Secretary of State which states, in respect of a person, any matter relating to the question whether he is subject to a relevant disqualification imposed outside Great Britain shall be evidence (in Scotland, sufficient evidence) of the matter so stated.

(4) A certificate stating that matter and purporting to be so signed shall be deemed to be so signed unless the contrary is proved."

77 Endorsement of counterparts issued to Northern Ireland licence holders

(1) After section 109 of the Road Traffic Act 1988 (c. 52) there is inserted —

"109A Counterparts issued to Northern Ireland licence holders

(1) The Secretary of State may issue to any Northern Ireland licence holder who —

(a) has delivered his Northern Ireland licence to the Secretary of State, and
(b) has provided him with the information specified in, or required under, subsection (3) below (whether or not in pursuance of this section),

a document (referred to in this Part of this Act in relation to a Northern Ireland licence as a "counterpart").

(2) The counterpart must —

(a) be in such form, and
(b) contain such information,

designed for the endorsement of particulars relating to the Northern Ireland licence as the Secretary of State may determine.

(3) The information referred to in subsection (1) above is —

(a) the name and address (whether in Great Britain or Northern Ireland) of the Northern Ireland licence holder;
(b) his date of birth;
(c) the classes of vehicle which he is authorised by his Northern Ireland licence to drive;
(d) the period of validity of the licence;
(e) whether it was granted in exchange for a licence issued by a state other than an EEA State; and
(f) such other information as the Secretary of State may require for the purposes of the proper exercise of any of his functions under this Part or Part 4 of this Act.

(4) The Secretary of State —

(a) may endorse a Northern Ireland licence delivered to him (whether or not in pursuance of this section) in such manner as he may determine —
 (i) with any part of the information specified in, or required under, subsection (3) above; or
 (ii) with information providing a means of ascertaining that information or any part of it; and

(b) must return the Northern Ireland licence to the holder.

(5) Subsections (6) to (9), (11) (with the omission of paragraph (a)) and (12) of section 99B of this Act apply for the purposes of this section as if the references to a Community licence were references to a Northern Ireland licence."

(2) After section 91 of the Road Traffic Offenders Act 1988 (c. 53) there is inserted —

"91ZA Application to Northern Ireland licence holders

(1) The references to a licence in the following provisions of this Act include references to a Northern Ireland licence —

(a) section 7,
(b) section 26(7) and (8) and (9)(b),
(c) section 27,
(d) section 29(1),
(e) section 30,
(f) section 31(1),
(g) section 32,
(h) section 42(5),
(i) section 44(1),
(j) section 46(2),
(k) section 47(2) and (3),
(l) section 48(1) and (2).

(2) Accordingly, the reference in section 27(3)(b) of this Act to the suspension of a licence is to be construed in relation to a Northern Ireland licence holder as a reference to his ceasing to be authorised by virtue of section 109(1) of the Road Traffic Act 1988 to drive in Great Britain a motor vehicle of any class.

(3) The references in sections 26(9)(a) and 27(3) of this Act to a new licence include references to a counterpart of a Northern Ireland licence.

(4) In relation to a Northern Ireland licence holder to whom a counterpart is issued under section 109A of the Road Traffic Act 1988, the references in Part 3 of this Act (except sections 75(12), 76(8) and 77(9)) to a licence include references to a Northern Ireland licence.

(5) Where a court orders the endorsement of the counterpart of any Northern Ireland licence held by a person, it must send notice of the endorsement to the Secretary of State.

(6) The notice must —

(a) be sent in such manner and to such address, and
(b) contain such particulars,

as the Secretary of State may determine.

(7) Where a court orders the holder of a Northern Ireland licence to be disqualified, it must send the Northern Ireland licence and its counterpart (if any), on their being produced to the court, to the Secretary of State.

(8) The licence and its counterpart must be sent to such address as the Secretary of State may determine.

(9) Where —

(a) a notice is sent to the Secretary of State under subsection (5) above, and
(b) the particulars contained in the notice include —

(i) particulars of an offence in respect of which the holder of a Northern Ireland licence is disqualified by an order of a court, and
(ii) particulars of the disqualification,

the Secretary of State must send a notice containing the particulars mentioned in paragraph (b)(i) and (ii) to the licensing authority in Northern Ireland.

91ZB Effect of endorsement on Northern Ireland licence holders

Section 91B applies in relation to Northern Ireland licences as it applies in relation to Community licences."

78 Prohibition on holding or obtaining Great Britain and Northern Ireland licences

(1) The Road Traffic Act 1988 (c. 52) is amended as follows.

(2) In section 97 (grant of licences) —

(a) in subsection (1)(c), after sub-paragraph (i) there is inserted —

"(ia) any Northern Ireland licence held by him together with its Northern Ireland counterpart and its counterpart (if any) issued to him under this Part of this Act,",

(b) after subsection (1A) there is inserted —

"(1AA) Where a licence under this Part of this Act is granted to a person who surrenders under sub-paragraph (ia) of subsection (1)(c) above his Northern Ireland licence together with the counterparts mentioned in that sub-paragraph to the Secretary of State —

(a) that person ceases to be authorised by virtue of section 109(1) of this Act to drive in Great Britain a motor vehicle of any class, and
(b) the Secretary of State must send the Northern Ireland licence and its Northern Ireland counterpart to the licensing authority in Northern Ireland together with particulars of the class of motor vehicles to which the licence granted under this Part of this Act relates."

(3) In section 99 (duration of licences), after subsection (3) there is inserted —

"(3A) Where —

(a) the Secretary of State is sent under a provision of Northern Ireland law corresponding to section 97 (1AA) of this Act a licence granted under this Part of this Act to a person to drive a motor vehicle of any class, and
(b) the Secretary of State is satisfied that a Northern Ireland licence to drive a motor vehicle of that or a corresponding class has been granted to that person,

the Secretary of State must serve notice in writing on that person revoking the licence granted under this Part of this Act."

(4) In section 102 (disqualification to prevent duplication of licences), at the end there is inserted —

"(2) A person is also disqualified for holding or obtaining a licence authorising him to drive a motor vehicle of any class so long as he is authorised by virtue of section 109(1) of this Act to drive a motor vehicle of that or a corresponding class."

79 Disability and prospective disability

(1) The Road Traffic Act 1988 (c. 52) is amended as follows.
(2) After section 109A (as inserted by section 77 of this Act) there is inserted —

"109B Revocation of authorisation conferred by Northern Ireland licence because of disability or prospective disability

(1) If the Secretary of State is at any time satisfied on inquiry —

(a) that a Northern Ireland licence holder is suffering from a relevant disability, and
(b) that he would be required by virtue of section 92 (3) of this Act to refuse an application made by the holder at that time for a licence authorising him to drive a vehicle of the class in respect of which his Northern Ireland licence was issued or a class corresponding to that class,

he may serve notice in writing requiring the licence holder to deliver immediately to the Secretary of State his Northern Ireland licence together with its Northern Ireland counterpart and its counterpart (if any) issued to him under this Part of this Act ("the relevant counterparts").

(2) If the Secretary of State is satisfied on inquiry that a Northern Ireland licence holder is suffering from a prospective disability, he may —

(a) serve notice in writing on the Northern Ireland licence holder requiring him to deliver immediately to the Secretary of State his Northern Ireland licence together with the relevant counterparts, and
(b) on receipt of the Northern Ireland licence and those counterparts and of an application made for the purposes of this subsection, grant to the Northern Ireland licence holder, free of charge, a licence for a period determined by the Secretary of State under section 99(1)(b) of this Act.

(3) The Secretary of State may require a person to provide —

(a) evidence of his name, address, sex and date and place of birth, and
(b) a photograph which is a current likeness of him,

before granting a licence to him on an application for the purposes of subsection (2) above.

(4) A person who —

(a) is required under, or by virtue of, this section to deliver to the Secretary of State his Northern Ireland licence and the relevant counterparts, but
(b) without reasonable excuse, fails to do so, is guilty of an offence.

(5) Where a Northern Ireland licence holder to whom a counterpart is issued under section 109A of this Act —

(a) is required under, or by virtue of, this section to deliver his Northern Ireland licence and that counterpart to the Secretary of State, and
(b) is not in possession of them in consequence of the fact that he has surrendered them to a constable or authorised person (within the meaning of Part 3 of the Road Traffic Offenders Act 1988) on receiving a fixed penalty notice given to him under section 54 of that Act,

he does not fail to comply with any such requirement if he delivers them to the Secretary of State immediately on their return.

(6) Where a Northern Ireland licence holder is served with a notice in pursuance of this section, he shall cease to be authorised by virtue of section 109(1) of this Act to drive in Great Britain a motor vehicle of any class from such date as may be specified in the notice, not being earlier than the date of service of the notice.

(7)Where a Northern Ireland licence is delivered to the Secretary of State in pursuance of this section, he must —

(a) send the licence and its Northern Ireland counterpart to the licensing authority in Northern Ireland, and
(b) explain to them his reasons for so doing.

109C Information relating to disabilities etc

Section 94 of this Act shall apply to a Northern Ireland licence holder who is normally resident in Great Britain as if —

(a) in subsection (1), for the words from the beginning to "aware" there were substituted "If a Northern Ireland licence holder who is authorised by virtue of section 109(1) of this Act to drive in Great Britain a motor vehicle of any class, is aware immediately before the relevant date, or becomes aware on or after that date",

(b) after that subsection there were inserted —

"(1A) For the purposes of subsection (1) "relevant date" means —

(a) in the case where the licence holder first became normally resident in Great Britain on or before the date on which section 79 of the Crime (International Co-operation) Act 2003 comes into force, that date; and
(b) in any other case, the date on which he first became so resident.",
(c) for subsection (3A) there were substituted —

"(3A) A person who —

(a) is authorised by virtue of section 109(1) of this Act to drive in Great Britain a motor vehicle of any class, and
(b) drives on a road a motor vehicle of that class,

is guilty of an offence if at any earlier time while he was so authorised he was required by subsection (1) above to notify the Secretary of State but has failed without reasonable excuse to do so.",

(d) in subsection (4), the words "an applicant for, or" (in both places) were omitted,
(e) in subsection (5), the words "applicant or" and the words from the beginning of paragraph (c) to "provisional licence" were omitted,
(f) in subsection (6)(b), the words "applicant or" (in both places) were omitted,
(g) in subsection (7), the words "applicant or" were omitted, and
(h) in subsection (8) —

(i) for "93" there were substituted "109B", and
(ii) the words "applicant or" (in both places) were omitted."

(3) In section 93 (revocation of licence because of disability or prospective disability) —

(a) in subsection (2A), at the end there is inserted "or subsection (6) below",
(b) at the end there is inserted —

"(5) Where the Secretary of State —

(a) is at any time sent by the licensing authority in Northern Ireland a licence under a provision of Northern Ireland law corresponding to section 109B of this Act, and
(b) by virtue of the reasons given by that authority for sending the licence is at that time satisfied as mentioned in subsection (1)(a) and (b) above or that the licence holder is suffering from a prospective disability,

the Secretary of State may serve notice in writing on the licence holder revoking the licence with effect from such date as may be specified in the notice, not being earlier than the date of service of the notice.

(6) Where the reasons given by the licensing authority in Northern Ireland for sending the licence relate to a prospective disability of the holder, the Secretary of State may, on an application made for the purposes of this subsection, grant to the holder, free of charge, a new licence for a period determined by the Secretary of State under section 99(1)(b) of this Act."

PART 4

MISCELLANEOUS

Information

80 Disclosure of information by SFO

In section 3 of the Criminal Justice Act 1987 (c. 38) (disclosure of information) —

(a) in subsection (5), for paragraph (c) there is substituted —

"(c) for the purposes of any criminal investigation or criminal proceedings, whether in the United Kingdom or elsewhere",

(b) at the end of subsection (6) there is inserted —

"(n) any person or body having, under the Treaty on European Union or any other treaty to which the United Kingdom is a party, the function of receiving information of the kind in question,

(o) any person or body having, under the law of any country or territory outside the United Kingdom, the function of receiving information relating to the proceeds of crime",

and the "and" preceding paragraph (m) is omitted.

81 Inspection of overseas information systems

After section 54 of the Data Protection Act 1998 (c. 29) there is inserted —

"54A Inspection of overseas information systems

(1) The Commissioner may inspect any personal data recorded in —

(a) the Schengen information system,
(b) the Europol information system,
(c) the Customs information system.

(2) The power conferred by subsection (1) is exercisable only for the purpose of assessing whether or not any processing of the data has been or is being carried out in compliance with this Act.

(3) The power includes power to inspect, operate and test equipment which is used for the processing of personal data.

(4) Before exercising the power, the Commissioner must give notice in writing of his intention to do so to the data controller.

(5) But subsection (4) does not apply if the Commissioner considers that the case is one of urgency.

(6) Any person who —

(a) intentionally obstructs a person exercising the power conferred by subsection (1), or
(b) fails without reasonable excuse to give any person exercising the power any assistance he may reasonably require,

is guilty of an offence.

(7) In this section —

"the Customs information system" means the information system established under Chapter II of the Convention on the Use of Information Technology for Customs Purposes,

"the Europol information system" means the information system established under Title II of the Convention on the Establishment of a European Police Office,

"the Schengen information system" means the information system established under Title IV of the Convention implementing the Schengen Agreement of 14th June 1985, or any system established in its place in pursuance of any Community obligation."

82 Driver licensing information

Information held in any form —

(a) by the Secretary of State under Part 3 of the Road Traffic Act 1988 (c. 52), or
(b) by the Department of the Environment under Part 2 of the Road Traffic (Northern Ireland) Order 1981 (S.I. 1981/154 (N.I.1)),

(licensing of drivers of vehicles) may be disclosed for the purposes of the Schengen information system (within the meaning of section 81).

83 Foreign surveillance operations

After section 76 of the Regulation of Investigatory Powers Act 2000 (c. 23) there is inserted —

"76A Foreign surveillance operations

(1) This section applies where —

(a) a foreign police or customs officer is carrying out relevant surveillance outside the United Kingdom which is lawful under the law of the country or territory in which it is being carried out;
(b) circumstances arise by virtue of which the surveillance can for the time being be carried out only in the United Kingdom; and
(c) it is not reasonably practicable in those circumstances for a United Kingdom officer to carry out the surveillance in the United Kingdom in accordance with an authorisation under Part 2 or the Regulation of Investigatory Powers (Scotland) Act 2000.

(2) "Relevant surveillance" means surveillance which —

(a) is carried out in relation to a person who is suspected of having committed a relevant crime; and
(b) is, for the purposes of Part 2, directed surveillance or intrusive surveillance.

(3) "Relevant crime" means crime which —

(a) falls within Article 40(7) of the Schengen Convention; or
(b) is crime for the purposes of any other international agreement to which the United Kingdom is a party and which is specified for the purposes of this section in an order made by the Secretary of State with the consent of the Scottish Ministers.

(4) Relevant surveillance carried out by the foreign police or customs officer in the United Kingdom during the permitted period is to be lawful for all purposes if —

(a) the condition mentioned in subsection (6) is satisfied;
(b) the officer carries out the surveillance only in places to which members of the public have or are permitted to have access, whether on payment or otherwise; and
(c) conditions specified in any order made by the Secretary of State with the consent of the Scottish

Ministers are satisfied in relation to its carrying out; but no surveillance is lawful by virtue of this subsection if the officer subsequently seeks to stop and question the person in the United Kingdom in relation to the relevant crime.

(5) The officer is not to be subject to any civil liability in respect of any conduct of his which is incidental to any surveillance that is lawful by virtue of subsection (4).

(6) The condition in this subsection is satisfied if, immediately after the officer enters the United Kingdom —

(a) he notifies a person designated by the Director General of the National Criminal Intelligence Service of that fact; and
(b) (if the officer has not done so before) he requests an application to be made for an authorisation under Part 2, or the Regulation of Investigatory Powers (Scotland) Act 2000, for the carrying out of the surveillance.

(7) "The permitted period" means the period of five hours beginning with the time when the officer enters the United Kingdom.

(8) But a person designated by an order made by the Secretary of State may notify the officer that the surveillance is to cease being lawful by virtue of subsection (4) when he gives the notification.

(9) The Secretary of State is not to make an order under subsection (4) unless a draft of the order has been laid before Parliament and approved by a resolution of each House.

(10) In this section references to a foreign police or customs officer are to a police or customs officer who, in relation to a country or territory other than the United Kingdom, is an officer for the purposes of —

(a) Article 40 of the Schengen Convention; or
(b) any other international agreement to which the United Kingdom is a party and which is specified for the purposes of this section in an order made by the Secretary of State with the consent of the Scottish Ministers.

(11) In this section —

"the Schengen Convention" means the Convention implementing the Schengen Agreement of 14th June 1985;
"United Kingdom officer" means —

(a) a member of a police force;
(b) a member of the National Criminal Intelligence Service;
(c) a member of the National Crime Squad or of the Scottish Crime Squad (within the meaning of the Regulation of Investigatory Powers (Scotland) Act 2000);
(d) a customs officer."

84 Assaults on foreign officers

(1) For the purposes of section 89 of the Police Act 1996 (c. 16) (assaults on constables) any person who is carrying out surveillance in England and Wales under section 76A of the Regulation of Investigatory Powers Act 2000 (c. 23) is to be treated as if he were acting as a constable in the execution of his duty.

(2) For the purposes of section 41 of the Police (Scotland) Act 1967 (c. 77) (assaults on constables) any person who is carrying out surveillance in Scotland under section 76A of that Act of 2000 is to be so treated.

(3) For the purposes of section 66 of the Police (Northern Ireland) Act 1998 (c. 32) (assaults on constables) any person who is carrying out surveillance in Northern Ireland under section 76A of that Act of 2000 is to be so treated.

85 Liability in respect of foreign officers

(1) Section 42 of the Police Act 1997 (liability of Director General of NCIS for wrongful acts of constables etc.) is amended as follows.

(2) After subsection (5A) there is inserted —

"(5AA) This section shall have effect where a person is carrying out surveillance under section 76A of the Regulation of Investigatory Powers Act 2000 (foreign surveillance operations) as if —

(a) any unlawful conduct by that person in the course of carrying out the surveillance were unlawful conduct of a constable in the performance of his functions under the direction and control of the Director General of NCIS; and
(b) subsection (4) applied to the person carrying out the surveillance."

(3) Where —

(a) a sum is paid by virtue of this section out of the NCIS service fund, and
(b) the Secretary of State receives under any international agreement a sum by way of reimbursement (in whole or in part) of the sum paid out of that fund,

he must pay into that fund the sum received by him by way of reimbursement.

Extradition

86 Schengen-building provisions of the 1996 Extradition Convention

(1) This section applies where a state is a party to the 1996 Extradition Convention, but only in respect of particular provisions ("the relevant provisions").

(2) The 1996 Extradition Convention is the Convention drawn up on the basis of Article K.3 of the Treaty on European Union relating to Extradition between the Member States of the European Union and opened for signature on 27th September 1996.

(3) Her Majesty may by Order in Council provide that the Extradition Act 1989 (c. 33) is to apply, subject to specified modifications, between —

(a) the United Kingdom, and
(b) the state,

as if the relevant provisions were general extradition arrangements (within the meaning of that Act) made between the United Kingdom and the state.

(4) "Specified" means specified in the Order in Council.

(5) A statutory instrument containing the Order in Council is subject to annulment in pursuance of a resolution of either House of Parliament.

(6) The Order in Council may include supplementary, incidental, saving or transitional provisions.

87 States in relation to which 1995 and 1996 Extradition Conventions not in force

(1) Her Majesty may by Order in Council provide that Schedule 1A to the Extradition Act 1989 is to apply in relation to a specified state as if —

(a) the state were a party to the 1995 Convention and a party to the 1996 Convention (within the meaning of that Act), and
(b) the state had made a declaration under a specified provision of either Convention.

(2) "Specified" means specified in the Order in Council.
(3) A statutory instrument containing the Order in Council is subject to annulment in pursuance of a resolution of either House of Parliament.
(4) The Order in Council may include supplementary, incidental, saving or transitional provisions.

False monetary instruments

88 False monetary instruments: England and Wales and Northern Ireland

(1) Section 5 of the Forgery and Counterfeiting Act 1981 (c. 45) (offences relating to money orders, share certificates, passports, etc.) is amended as follows.
(2) In subsection (5) —

(a) in paragraph (g), at the end there is inserted "and other bills of exchange",
(b) after paragraph (h) there is inserted —

"(ha) bankers' drafts;
(hb) promissory notes;",

(c) after paragraph (j) there is inserted —

"(ja) debit cards;".

(3) After subsection (6) there is inserted —

"(7) An instrument is also an instrument to which this section applies if it is a monetary instrument specified for the purposes of this section by an order made by the Secretary of State.
(8) The power under subsection (7) above is exercisable by statutory instrument subject to annulment in pursuance of a resolution of either House of Parliament."

89 False monetary instruments: Scotland

After section 46 of the Criminal Law (Consolidation) (Scotland) Act 1995 (c. 39) there is inserted —

"*False monetary instruments*

46A False monetary instruments

(1) A person who counterfeits or falsifies a specified monetary instrument with the intention that it be uttered as genuine is guilty of an offence.
(2) A person who has in his custody or under his control, without lawful authority or excuse —

(a) anything which is, and which he knows or believes to be, a counterfeited or falsified specified monetary instrument; or

(b) any machine, implement or computer programme, or any paper or other material, which to his knowledge is specially designed or adapted for the making of a specified monetary instrument,

is guilty of an offence.

(3) For the purposes of subsections (1) and (2)(a) above, it is immaterial that the specified monetary instrument (or purported specified monetary instrument) is not in a fit state to be uttered or that the counterfeiting or falsifying of it has not been finished or perfected.

(4) A person guilty of an offence under this section is liable on summary conviction —

(a) to a fine not exceeding the statutory maximum;
(b) to imprisonment for a term not exceeding six months; or
(c) both to a fine and to such imprisonment.

(5) A person guilty of an offence —

(a) under subsection (1) above is liable on conviction on indictment —

(i) to a fine;
(ii) to imprisonment for a term not exceeding ten years; or
(iii) both to a fine and to such imprisonment;

(b) under subsection (2) above is liable on conviction on indictment —

(i) to a fine;
(ii) if it is proved that the offence was committed with the intention that the specified monetary instrument in question be uttered (or as the case may be that a specified monetary instrument be uttered), to imprisonment for a term not exceeding ten years and if it is not so proved, to imprisonment for a term not exceeding two years; or
(iii) both to a fine and to imprisonment for a term not exceeding ten years, if it is proved as mentioned in sub-paragraph (ii) above, or both to a fine and to imprisonment for a term not exceeding two years if it is not so proved.

(6) Where an offence under this section which has been committed —

(a) by a body corporate is proved to have been committed with the consent or connivance of, or to be attributable to any neglect on the part of, a director, manager, secretary or other similar officer of that body; or
(b) by a Scottish partnership is proved to have been committed with the consent or connivance of, or to be attributable to any neglect on the part of, a member of that partnership,

or by any person who was purporting to act in any such capacity, he as well as the body corporate, or as the case may be the partnership, is guilty of that offence and is liable to be proceeded against and punished accordingly.

(7) Where the affairs of a body corporate are managed by its members, subsection (6) above applies in relation to the actings and defaults of a member in connection with his functions of management as if he were a director of the body corporate.

(8) In subsections (1) to (5) above, "specified" means for the time being specified for the purposes of this section, by order made by the Scottish Ministers.

(9) The power to make an order under subsection (8) above —

(a) includes power to make such incidental, supplemental, transitional or transitory provision as the Scottish Ministers think necessary or expedient; and
(b) is exercisable by statutory instrument.

(10) A statutory instrument containing such an order is subject to annulment in pursuance of a resolution of the Scottish Parliament."

Freezing of terrorist property

90 Freezing of terrorist property

Schedule 4 is to have effect.

PART 5

FINAL PROVISIONS

CHAPTER 1

AMENDMENTS AND REPEALS

91 Amendments and repeals

(1) Schedule 5 (minor and consequential amendments) is to have effect.

(2) The enactments set out in Schedule 6 are repealed to the extent specified.

CHAPTER 2

MISCELLANEOUS

92 Northern Ireland

An Order in Council under paragraph 1(1) of the Schedule to the Northern Ireland Act 2000 (c. 1) (legislation for Northern Ireland during suspension of devolved government) which contains a statement that it is made only for purposes corresponding to those of Chapter 2 of Part 3 of this Act —

(a) is not to be subject to paragraph 2 of that Schedule (affirmative resolution of both Houses of Parliament), but
(b) is to be subject to annulment in pursuance of a resolution of either House of Parliament.

93 Supplementary and consequential provision

(1) The appropriate Minister may by order made by statutory instrument make —

(a) any supplementary, incidental or consequential provision,
(b) any transitory, transitional or saving provision,

which he considers necessary or expedient for the purposes of, in consequence of or for giving full effect to any provision of this Act.

(2) The appropriate Minister means —

(a) in relation to any provision that would, if included in an Act of the Scottish Parliament, be within the legislative competence of that Parliament, the Scottish Ministers,
(b) in relation to any other provision, the Secretary of State.

(3) The provision which may be made under subsection (1) includes provision amending or repealing any enactment or instrument.

(4) An order under this section may make different provision for different purposes.

(5) A statutory instrument (other than an instrument to which subsection (6) applies) containing an order under this section made by the Secretary of State is subject to annulment in pursuance of a resolution of either House of Parliament.

(6) A statutory instrument containing such an order which adds to, replaces or omits any part of the text of an Act is not to be made unless a draft of the instrument has been laid before, and approved by a resolution of, each House of Parliament.

(7) A statutory instrument (other than an instrument to which subsection (8) applies) containing an order under this section made by the Scottish Ministers is subject to annulment in pursuance of a resolution of the Scottish Parliament.

(8) A statutory instrument containing such an order which adds to, replaces or omits any part of the text of an Act or of an Act of the Scottish Parliament is not to be made unless a draft of the instrument has been laid before, and approved by a resolution of, the Scottish Parliament.

94 Commencement

(1) This Act (except this Chapter and the provisions mentioned in subsection (3)) is to come into force on such day as the Secretary of State may by order made by statutory instrument appoint.

(2) Any day appointed for the purposes of Part 1 (other than sections 32 to 41), and the related amendments and repeals, is to be one decided by the Secretary of State and the Scottish Ministers.

(3) The following are to come into force on such day as the Scottish Ministers may by order made by statutory instrument appoint —

(a) sections 37 to 41,
(b) section 89.

(4) An order under this section may make different provision for different purposes.

95 Extent

(1) Sections 32 to 36 extend only to England and Wales and Northern Ireland.

(2) Sections 37 to 41 extend only to Scotland.

96 Short title

This Act may be cited as the Crime (International Co-operation) Act 2003.

Appendix A

SCHEDULES

Section 15 SCHEDULE 1

Proceedings of a Nominated Court Under Section 15

Securing attendance of witnesses

1. The court has the like powers for securing the attendance of a witness as it has for the purposes of other proceedings before the court.

2. In Scotland the court has power to issue a warrant to officers of law to cite witnesses, and section 156 of the Criminal Procedure (Scotland) Act 1995 (c. 46) applies in relation to a witness so cited.

Power to administer oaths

3. The court may take evidence on oath.

Proceedings

4. Rules of court under section 49 may, in particular, make provision in respect of the persons entitled to appear or take part in the proceedings and for excluding the public from the proceedings.

Privilege of witnesses

5.—(1) A person cannot be compelled to give any evidence which he could not be compelled to give —

(a) in criminal proceedings in the part of the United Kingdom in which the nominated court exercises jurisdiction, or
(b) subject to sub-paragraph (2), in criminal proceedings in the country from which the request for the evidence has come.

(2) Sub-paragraph (1)(b) does not apply unless the claim of the person questioned to be exempt from giving the evidence is conceded by the court or authority which made the request.

(3) Where the person's claim is not conceded, he may be required to give the evidence to which the claim relates (subject to the other provisions of this paragraph); but the evidence may not be forwarded to the court or authority which requested it if a court in the country in question, on the matter being referred to it, upholds the claim.

(4) A person cannot be compelled to give any evidence if his doing so would be prejudicial to the security of the United Kingdom.

(5) A certificate signed by or on behalf of the Secretary of State or, where the court is in Scotland, the Lord Advocate to the effect that it would be so prejudicial for that person to do so is conclusive evidence of that fact.

(6) A person cannot be compelled to give any evidence in his capacity as an officer or servant of the Crown.

(7) Sub-paragraphs (4) and (6) are without prejudice to the generality of sub-paragraph (1).

Forwarding evidence

6.—(1) The evidence received by the court is to be given to the court or authority that made the request or to the territorial authority for forwarding to the court or authority that made the request.

(2) So far as may be necessary in order to comply with the request —

(a) where the evidence consists of a document, the original or a copy is to be provided,
(b) where it consists of any other article, the article itself, or a description, photograph or other representation of it, is to be provided.

Supplementary

7. The Bankers' Books Evidence Act 1879 (c. 11) applies to the proceedings as it applies to other proceedings before the court.

8. No order for costs may be made.

Sections 30 and 31 SCHEDULE 2

EVIDENCE GIVEN BY TELEVISION LINK OR TELEPHONE

PART 1

EVIDENCE GIVEN BY TELEVISION LINK

Securing attendance of witnesses

1. The nominated court has the like powers for securing the attendance of the witness to give evidence through the link as it has for the purpose of proceedings before the court.

2. In Scotland the nominated court has power to issue a warrant to officers of law to cite the witness for the purpose of securing his attendance to give evidence through the link, and section 156 of the Criminal Procedure (Scotland) Act 1995 (c. 46) applies in relation to the witness if so cited.

Conduct of hearing

3. The witness is to give evidence in the presence of the nominated court.

4. The nominated court is to establish the identity of the witness.

5. The nominated court is to intervene where it considers it necessary to do so to safeguard the rights of the witness.

6. The evidence is to be given under the supervision of the court of the country concerned.

7. The evidence is to be given in accordance with the laws of that country and with any measures for the protection of the witness agreed between the Secretary of State and the authority in that country which appears to him to have the function of entering into agreements of that kind.

8. Rules of court under section 49 must make provision for the use of interpreters.

Privilege of witness

9.—(1) The witness cannot be compelled to give any evidence which he could not be compelled to give in criminal proceedings in the part of the United Kingdom in which the nominated court exercises jurisdiction.

(2) The witness cannot be compelled to give any evidence if his doing so would be prejudicial to the security of the United Kingdom.

(3) A certificate signed by or on behalf of the Secretary of State or, where the court is in Scotland, the Lord Advocate to the effect that it would be so prejudicial for that person to do so is to be conclusive evidence of that fact.

(4) The witness cannot be compelled to give any evidence in his capacity as an officer or servant of the Crown.

(5) Sub-paragraphs (2) and (4) are without prejudice to the generality of sub-paragraph (1).

Record of hearing

10. Rules of court under section 49 must make provision —

(a) for the drawing up of a record of the hearing,
(b) for sending the record to the external authority.

PART 2

EVIDENCE GIVEN BY TELEPHONE

Notification of witness

11. The nominated court must notify the witness of the time when and the place at which he is to give evidence by telephone.

Conduct of hearing

12. The nominated court must be satisfied that the witness is willingly giving evidence by telephone.

13. The witness is to give evidence in the presence of the nominated court.

14. The nominated court is to establish the identity of the witness.

15. The evidence is to be given under the supervision of the court of the participating country.

16. The evidence is to be given in accordance with the laws of that country.

17. Rules of court under section 49 must make provision for the use of interpreters.

Section 54 SCHEDULE 3

OFFENCES FOR THE PURPOSES OF SECTION 54

PART 1

OFFENCES WHERE ORDER OF DISQUALIFICATION FOR A MINIMUM PERIOD UNNECESSARY

1.—(1) Manslaughter or culpable homicide by the driver of a motor vehicle.

(2) "Driver" —

(a) in relation to Great Britain, has the same meaning as in the Road Traffic Act 1988 (c. 52),
(b) in relation to Northern Ireland, has the same meaning as in Article 2(2) of the Road Traffic (Northern Ireland) Order 1995 (S.I. 1995/2994 (N.I.18)).

2. An offence under section 89(1) of the Road Traffic Regulation Act 1984 (c. 27) or Article 43(1) of the Road Traffic Regulation (Northern Ireland) Order 1997 (S.I. 1997/276 (N.I.2)) (exceeding speed limit).

3. An offence under any of the following sections of the Road Traffic Act 1988 or Articles of the Road Traffic (Northern Ireland) Order 1995 —

(a) section 1 or Article 9 (causing death by dangerous driving),
(b) section 2 or Article 10 (dangerous driving),
(c) section 3 or Article 12 (careless, and inconsiderate, driving),
(d) section 3A or Article 14 (causing death by careless driving when under influence of drink or drugs),
(e) section 4 or Article 15 (driving, or being in charge, when under influence of drink or drugs),
(f) section 5 or Article 16 (driving, or being in charge, of a motor vehicle with alcohol concentration above prescribed limit),
(g) section 6 or Article 17 (failing to provide a specimen of breath for a breath test),
(h) section 7 or Article 18 (failing to provide specimen for analysis or laboratory test).

4. An offence under section 12 of the Road Traffic Act 1988 (motor racing and speed trials on public ways).

5. An offence under section 103(1)(b) of the Road Traffic Act 1988 or Article 167(1) of the Road Traffic (Northern Ireland) Order 1981 (S.I. 1981/ 154 (N.I.1)) (driving while disqualified).

6. An offence under section 170(4) of the Road Traffic Act 1988 or Article 175(2) of the Road Traffic (Northern Ireland) Order 1981 (failing to stop after accident and give particulars or report of accident).

PART 2

OFFENCES WHERE ORDER OF DISQUALIFICATION FOR MINIMUM PERIOD NECESSARY

7. An offence which —

(a) is mentioned in Part 1 of Schedule 2 to the Road Traffic Offenders Act 1988 (c. 53) or Part 1 of Schedule 1 to the Road Traffic Offenders (Northern Ireland) Order 1996 (S.I. 1996/1320 (N.I.10)), but
(b) is not an offence mentioned in Part 1 of this Schedule.

Section 90 SCHEDULE 4

TERRORIST PROPERTY: FREEZING ORDERS

1. The Terrorism Act 2000 (c. 11) is amended as follows.

2. In section 123 (orders and regulations), in subsection (2)(i), for "paragraph" there is substituted "paragraphs 11A, 25A, 41A and".

3. In Part 1 of Schedule 4 (forfeiture orders: England and Wales), after paragraph 11 there is inserted —

"Domestic and overseas freezing orders

11A.—(1) This paragraph has effect for the purposes of paragraphs 11B to 11G.

(2) The relevant Framework Decision means the Framework Decision on the execution in the European Union of orders freezing property or evidence adopted by the Council of the European Union on 22nd July 2003.

(3) A listed offence means —

(a) an offence described in Article 3(2) of the relevant Framework Decision, or
(b) a prescribed offence or an offence of a prescribed description.

(4) An order under sub-paragraph (3)(b) which, for the purposes of paragraph 11D, prescribes an offence or a description of offences may require that the conduct which constitutes the offence or offences would, if it occurred in a part of the United Kingdom, constitute an offence in that part.

(5) Specified information, in relation to a certificate under paragraph 11B or 11D, means —

(a) any information required to be given by the form of certificate annexed to the relevant Framework Decision, or
(b) any prescribed information.

(6) In this paragraph, "prescribed" means prescribed by an order made by the Secretary of State.

(7) A participating country means —

(a) a country other than the United Kingdom which is a member State on a day appointed for the commencement of Schedule 4 to the Crime (International Co-operation) Act 2003, and
(b) any other member State designated by an order made by the Secretary of State.

(8) "Country" includes territory.

(9) Section 14(2)(a) applies for the purposes of determining what are the proceeds of the commission of an offence.

Domestic freezing orders: certification

11B.—(1) If any of the property to which an application for a restraint order relates is property in a participating country, the applicant may ask the High Court to make a certificate under this paragraph.

(2) The High Court may make a certificate under this paragraph if —

(a) it makes a restraint order in relation to property in the participating country, and
(b) it is satisfied that there is a good arguable case that the property is likely to be used for the purposes of a listed offence or is the proceeds of the commission of a listed offence.

(3) A certificate under this paragraph is a certificate which —

(a) is made for the purposes of the relevant Framework Decision, and
(b) gives the specified information.

(4) If the High Court makes a certificate under this paragraph —

(a) the restraint order must provide for notice of the certificate to be given to the person affected by it, and
(b) paragraph 6(2) to (4) applies to the certificate as it applies to the restraint order.

Sending domestic freezing orders

11C.—(1)If a certificate is made under paragraph 11B, the restraint order and the certificate are to be sent to the Secretary of State for forwarding to —

(a) a court exercising jurisdiction in the place where the property is situated, or
(b) any authority recognised by the government of the participating country as the appropriate authority for receiving orders of that kind.

(2) The restraint order and the certificate must be accompanied by a forfeiture order, unless the certificate indicates when the court expects a forfeiture order to be sent.

(3) The certificate must include a translation of it into an appropriate language of the participating country (if that language is not English).

(4) The certificate must be signed by or on behalf of the court and must include a statement as to the accuracy of the information given in it.

The signature may be an electronic signature.

(5) If the restraint order and the certificate are not accompanied by a forfeiture order, but a forfeiture order is subsequently made, it is to be sent to the Secretary of State for forwarding as mentioned in sub-paragraph (1).

Overseas freezing orders

11D.—(1) Paragraph 11E applies where an overseas freezing order made by an appropriate court or authority in a participating country is received by the Secretary of State from the court or authority which made or confirmed the order.

(2) An overseas freezing order is an order prohibiting dealing with property —

(a) which is in the United Kingdom,
(b) which the appropriate court or authority considers is likely to be used for the purposes of a listed offence or is the proceeds of the commission of such an offence, and
(c) in respect of which an order has been or may be made by a court exercising criminal jurisdiction in the participating country for the forfeiture of the property,

and in respect of which the following requirements of this paragraph are met.

(3) The action which the appropriate court or authority considered would constitute or, as the case may be, constituted the listed offence is action done as an act of terrorism or for the purposes of terrorism.

(4) The order must relate to —

(a) criminal proceedings instituted in the participating country, or
(b) a criminal investigation being carried on there.

(5) The order must be accompanied by a certificate which gives the specified information; but a certificate may be treated as giving any specified information which is not given in it if the Secretary of State has the information in question.

(6) The certificate must —

(a) be signed by or on behalf of the court or authority which made or confirmed the order,
(b) include a statement as to the accuracy of the information given in it,
(c) if it is not in English, include a translation of it into English (or, if appropriate, Welsh).

The signature may be an electronic signature.

(7) The order must be accompanied by an order made by a court exercising criminal jurisdiction in that country for the forfeiture of the property, unless the certificate indicates when such an order is expected to be sent.

(8) An appropriate court or authority in a participating country in relation to an overseas freezing order is —

(a) a court exercising criminal jurisdiction in the country,
(b) a prosecuting authority in the country,
(c) any other authority in the country which appears to the Secretary of State to have the function of making such orders.

(9) References in paragraphs 11E to 11G to an overseas freezing order include its accompanying certificate.

Enforcement of overseas freezing orders

11E.—(1) Where this paragraph applies the Secretary of State must send a copy of the overseas freezing order to the High Court and to the Director of Public Prosecutions.

(2) The court is to consider the overseas freezing order on its own initiative within a period prescribed by rules of court.

(3) Before giving effect to the overseas freezing order, the court must give the Director an opportunity to be heard.

(4) The court may decide not to give effect to the overseas freezing order only if, in its opinion, giving effect to it would be incompatible with any of the Convention rights (within the meaning of the Human Rights Act 1998).

11F The High Court may postpone giving effect to an overseas freezing order in respect of any property —

(a) in order to avoid prejudicing a criminal investigation which is taking place in the United Kingdom, or
(b) if, under an order made by a court in criminal proceedings in the United Kingdom, the property may not be dealt with.

11G.—(1) Where the High Court decides to give effect to an overseas freezing order, it must —

(a) register the order in that court,
(b) provide for notice of the registration to be given to any person affected by it.

(2) For the purpose of enforcing an overseas freezing order registered in the High Court, the order is to have effect as if it were an order made by that court.

(3) Paragraph 7 applies to an overseas freezing order registered in the High Court as it applies to a restraint order under paragraph 5.

(4) The High Court may cancel the registration of the order, or vary the property to which the order applies, on an application by the Director of Public Prosecutions or any other person affected by it, if or to the extent that —

(a) the court is of the opinion mentioned in paragraph 11E(4), or
(b) the court is of the opinion that the order has ceased to have effect in the participating country.

(5) Her Majesty may by Order in Council make further provision for the enforcement in England and Wales of registered overseas freezing orders.

(6) An Order in Council under this paragraph —

(a) may make different provision for different cases,
(b) is not to be made unless a draft of it has been laid before and approved by resolution of each House of Parliament."

(4) In paragraph 14 of that Schedule (enforcement of orders made in designated countries), in sub-paragraph (2), after the second "order" there is inserted "(other than an overseas freezing order within the meaning of paragraph 11D)".

(5) In Part 2 of that Schedule (forfeiture orders: Scotland), after paragraph 25 there is inserted —

"Domestic and overseas freezing orders

25A.—(1) This paragraph has effect for the purposes of paragraphs 25B to 25G.

(2) The relevant Framework Decision means the Framework Decision on the execution in the European Union of orders freezing property or evidence adopted by the Council of the European Union on 22nd July 2003.

(3) A listed offence means —

(a) an offence described in Article 3(2) of the relevant Framework Decision, or
(b) a prescribed offence or an offence of a prescribed description.

(4) An order under sub-paragraph (3)(b) which, for the purposes of paragraph 25D, prescribes an offence or a description of offences may require that the conduct which constitutes the offence or offences would, if it occurred in a part of the United Kingdom, constitute an offence in that part.

(5) Specified information, in relation to a certificate under paragraph 25B or 25D, means —

(a) any information required to be given by the form of certificate annexed to the relevant Framework Decision, or
(b) any prescribed information.

(6) In this paragraph, "prescribed" means prescribed by an order made by the Secretary of State.

(7) A participating country means —

(a) a country other than the United Kingdom which is a member State on a day appointed for the commencement of Schedule 4 to the Crime (International Co-operation) Act 2003, and
(b) any other member State designated by an order made by the Secretary of State.

(8) "Country" includes territory.

(9) Section 14(2)(a) applies for the purposes of determining what are the proceeds of the commission of an offence.

Domestic freezing orders: certification

25B.—(1) If any of the property to which an application for a restraint order relates is property in a participating country, the applicant may ask the Court of Session to make a certificate under this paragraph.

(2) The Court of Session may make a certificate under this paragraph if —

(a) it makes a restraint order in relation to property in the participating country, and
(b) it is satisfied that there is a good arguable case that the property is likely to be used for the purposes of a listed offence or is the proceeds of the commission of a listed offence.

(3) A certificate under this paragraph is a certificate which —

(a) is made for the purposes of the relevant Framework Decision, and
(b) gives the specified information.

(4) If the Court of Session makes a certificate under this paragraph —

(a) the restraint order must provide for notice of the certificate to be given to the person affected by it, and
(b) paragraph 19(2) to (4) applies to the certificate as it applies to the restraint order.

Sending domestic freezing orders

25C.—(1) If a certificate is made under paragraph 25B, the restraint order and the certificate are to be sent to the Lord Advocate for forwarding to —

(a) a court exercising jurisdiction in the place where the property is situated, or

(b) any authority recognised by the government of the participating country as the appropriate authority for receiving orders of that kind.

(2) The restraint order and the certificate must be accompanied by a forfeiture order, unless the certificate indicates when the court expects a forfeiture order to be sent.

(3) The certificate must include a translation of it into an appropriate language of the participating country (if that language is not English).

(4) The certificate must be signed by or on behalf of the court and must include a statement as to the accuracy of the information given in it.

The signature may be an electronic signature.

(5) If the restraint order and the certificate are not accompanied by a forfeiture order, but a forfeiture order is subsequently made, it is to be sent to the Lord Advocate for forwarding as mentioned in sub-paragraph (1).

Overseas freezing orders

25D.—(1) Paragraph 25E applies where an overseas freezing order made by an appropriate court or authority in a participating country is received by the Secretary of State from the court or authority which made or confirmed the order.

(2) An overseas freezing order is an order prohibiting dealing with property —

(a) which is in the United Kingdom,
(b) which the appropriate court or authority considers is likely to be used for the purposes of a listed offence or is the proceeds of the commission of such an offence, and
(c) in respect of which an order has been or may be made by a court exercising criminal jurisdiction in the participating country for the forfeiture of the property,

and in respect of which the following requirements of this paragraph are met.

(3) The action which the appropriate court or authority considered would constitute or, as the case may be, constituted the listed offence is action done as an act of terrorism or for the purposes of terrorism.

(4) The order must relate to —

(a) criminal proceedings instituted in the participating country, or
(b) a criminal investigation being carried on there.

(5) The order must be accompanied by a certificate which gives the specified information; but a certificate may be treated as giving any specified information which is not given in it if the Secretary of State has the information in question.

(6) The certificate must —

(a) be signed by or on behalf of the court or authority which made or confirmed the order,
(b) include a statement as to the accuracy of the information given in it,
(c) if it is not in English, include a translation of it into English.

The signature may be an electronic signature.

(7) The order must be accompanied by an order made by a court exercising criminal jurisdiction in that country for the forfeiture of the property, unless the certificate indicates when such an order is expected to be sent.

(8) An appropriate court or authority in a participating country in relation to an overseas freezing order is —

(a) a court exercising criminal jurisdiction in the country,
(b) a prosecuting authority in the country,
(c) any other authority in the country which appears to the Secretary of State to have the function of making such orders.

(9) References in paragraphs 25E to 25G to an overseas freezing order include its accompanying certificate.

Enforcement of overseas freezing orders

25E.—(1) Where this paragraph applies the Secretary of State must send a copy of the overseas freezing order to the Court of Session and to the Lord Advocate.

(2) The court is to consider the overseas freezing order on its own initiative within a period prescribed by rules of court.

(3) Before giving effect to the overseas freezing order, the court must give the Lord Advocate an opportunity to be heard.

(4) The court may decide not to give effect to the overseas freezing order only if, in its opinion, giving effect to it would be incompatible with any of the Convention rights (within the meaning of the Human Rights Act 1998).

25F. The Court of Session may postpone giving effect to an overseas freezing order in respect of any property —

(a) in order to avoid prejudicing a criminal investigation which is taking place in the United Kingdom, or
(b) if, under an order made by a court in criminal proceedings in the United Kingdom, the property may not be dealt with.

25G.—(1) Where the Court of Session decides to give effect to an overseas freezing order, the Deputy Principal Clerk of Session must —

(a) register the order in the Books of Council and Session,
(b) provide for notice of the registration to be given to any person affected by it.

(2) For the purpose of enforcing an overseas freezing order registered in the Books of Council and Session, the order is to have effect as if it were an order made by the Court of Session.

(3) Paragraphs 20 and 21 apply to an overseas freezing order registered in the Books of Council and Session as they apply to a restraint order under paragraph 18.

(4) The Court of Session may cancel the registration of the order, or vary the property to which the order applies, on an application by the Lord Advocate or any other person affected by it, if or to the extent that —

(a) the court is of the opinion mentioned in paragraph 25E(4), or
b) the court is of the opinion that the order has ceased to have effect in the participating country.

(5) Her Majesty may by Order in Council make further provision for the enforcement in Scotland of registered overseas freezing orders.

(6) An Order in Council under this paragraph —

(a) may make different provision for different cases,
(b) is not to be made unless a draft of it has been laid before and approved by resolution of each House of Parliament."

6. In paragraph 28 of that Schedule (enforcement of orders made in designated countries), in sub-paragraph (2), after the second "order" there is inserted "(other than an overseas freezing order within the meaning of paragraph 25D)".

7. In Part 3 of that Schedule (forfeiture orders: Northern Ireland), after paragraph 41 there is inserted —

"Domestic and overseas freezing orders

41A.—(1) This paragraph has effect for the purposes of paragraphs 41B to 41G.

(2) The relevant Framework Decision means the Framework Decision on the execution in the European Union of orders freezing property or evidence adopted by the Council of the European Union on 22nd July 2003.

(3) A listed offence means —

(a) an offence described in Article 3(2) of the relevant Framework Decision, or
(b) a prescribed offence or an offence of a prescribed description.

(4) An order under sub-paragraph (3)(b) which, for the purposes of paragraph 41D, prescribes an offence or a description of offences may require that the conduct which constitutes the offence or offences would, if it occurred in a part of the United Kingdom, constitute an offence in that part.

(5) Specified information, in relation to a certificate under paragraph 41B or 41D, means —

(a) any information required to be given by the form of certificate annexed to the relevant Framework Decision, or
(b) any prescribed information.

(6) In this paragraph, 'prescribed' means prescribed by an order made by the Secretary of State.

(7) A participating country means —

(a) a country other than the United Kingdom which is a member State on a day appointed for the commencement of Schedule 4 to the Crime (International Co-operation) Act 2003, and
(b) any other member State designated by an order made by the Secretary of State.

(8) 'Country' includes territory.

(9) Section 14(2)(a) applies for the purposes of determining what are the proceeds of the commission of an offence.

Domestic freezing orders: certification

41B.—(1) If any of the property to which an application for a restraint order relates is property in a participating country, the applicant may ask the High Court to make a certificate under this paragraph.

(2) The High Court may make a certificate under this paragraph if —

(a) it makes a restraint order in relation to property in the participating country, and
(b) it is satisfied that there is a good arguable case that the property is likely to be used for the purposes of a listed offence or is the proceeds of the commission of a listed offence.

(3) A certificate under this paragraph is a certificate which —

(a) is made for the purposes of the relevant Framework Decision, and
(b) gives the specified information.

(4) If the High Court makes a certificate under this paragraph —

(a) the restraint order must provide for notice of the certificate to be given to the person affected by it, and
(b) paragraph 34(2) to (4) applies to the certificate as it applies to the restraint order.

Sending domestic freezing orders

41C.—(1) If a certificate is made under paragraph 41B, the restraint order and the certificate are to be sent to the Secretary of State for forwarding to —

(a) a court exercising jurisdiction in the place where the property is situated, or
(b) any authority recognised by the government of the participating country as the appropriate authority for receiving orders of that kind.

(2) The restraint order and the certificate must be accompanied by a forfeiture order, unless the certificate indicates when the court expects a forfeiture order to be sent.

(3) The certificate must include a translation of it into an appropriate language of the participating country (if that language is not English).

(4) The certificate must be signed by or on behalf of the court and must include a statement as to the accuracy of the information given in it.

The signature may be an electronic signature.

(5) If the restraint order and the certificate are not accompanied by a forfeiture order, but a forfeiture order is subsequently made, it is to be sent to the Secretary of State for forwarding as mentioned in sub-paragraph (1).

Overseas freezing orders

41D.—(1) Paragraph 41E applies where an overseas freezing order made by an appropriate court or authority in a participating country is received by the Secretary of State from the court or authority which made or confirmed the order.

(2) An overseas freezing order is an order prohibiting dealing with property —

(a) which is in the United Kingdom,
(b) which the appropriate court or authority considers is likely to be used for the purposes of a listed offence or is the proceeds of the commission of such an offence, and
(c) in respect of which an order has been or may be made by a court exercising criminal jurisdiction in the participating country for the forfeiture of the property,

and in respect of which the following requirements of this paragraph are met.

(3) The action which the appropriate court or authority considered would constitute or, as the case may be, constituted the listed offence is action done as an act of terrorism or for the purposes of terrorism.

(4) The order must relate to —

(a) criminal proceedings instituted in the participating country, or
(b) a criminal investigation being carried on there.

(5) The order must be accompanied by a certificate which gives the specified information; but a certificate may be treated as giving any specified information which is not given in it if the Secretary of State has the information in question.

(6) The certificate must —

(a) be signed by or on behalf of the court or authority which made or confirmed the order,
(b) include a statement as to the accuracy of the information given in it,
(c) if it is not in English, include a translation of it into English.

The signature may be an electronic signature.

(7) The order must be accompanied by an order made by a court exercising criminal jurisdiction in that country for the forfeiture of the property, unless the certificate indicates when such an order is expected to be sent.

(8) An appropriate court or authority in a participating country in relation to an overseas freezing order is —

(a) a court exercising criminal jurisdiction in the country,
(b) a prosecuting authority in the country,
(c) any other authority in the country which appears to the Secretary of State to have the function of making such orders.

(9) References in paragraphs 41E to 41G to an overseas freezing order include its accompanying certificate.

Enforcement of overseas freezing orders

41E.—(1) Where this paragraph applies the Secretary of State must send a copy of the overseas freezing order to the High Court and to the Director of Public Prosecutions for Northern Ireland.

(2) The court is to consider the overseas freezing order on its own initiative within a period prescribed by rules of court.

(3) Before giving effect to the overseas freezing order, the court must give the Director an opportunity to be heard.

(4) The court may decide not to give effect to the overseas freezing order only if, in its opinion, giving effect to it would be incompatible with any of the Convention rights (within the meaning of the Human Rights Act 1998).

41F. The High Court may postpone giving effect to an overseas freezing order in respect of any property —

(a) in order to avoid prejudicing a criminal investigation which is taking place in the United Kingdom, or
(b) if, under an order made by a court in criminal proceedings in the United Kingdom, the property may not be dealt with.

41G.—(1) Where the High Court decides to give effect to an overseas freezing order, it must —

(a) register the order in that court,
(b) provide for notice of the registration to be given to any person affected by it.

(2) For the purpose of enforcing an overseas freezing order registered in the High Court, the order is to have effect as if it were an order made by that court.

(3) Paragraph 35 applies to an overseas freezing order registered in the High Court as it applies to a restraint order under paragraph 33.

(4) The High Court may cancel the registration of the order, or vary the property to which the order applies, on an application by the Director of Public Prosecutions for Northern Ireland or any other person affected by it, if or to the extent that —

(a) the court is of the opinion mentioned in paragraph 41E(4), or
(b) the court is of the opinion that the order has ceased to have effect in the participating country.

(5) Her Majesty may by Order in Council make further provision for the enforcement in Northern Ireland of registered overseas freezing orders.

(6) An Order in Council under this paragraph —

(a) may make different provision for different cases,
(b) is not to be made unless a draft of it has been laid before and approved by resolution of each House of Parliament."

8. In paragraph 44 of that Schedule (enforcement of orders made in designated countries), in sub-paragraph (2), after the second "order" there is inserted "(other than an overseas freezing order within the meaning of paragraph 41D)".

9. In Part 4 of that Schedule (insolvency), in paragraph 45, at the end of paragraph (c) of the definition of "restraint order" there is inserted "or an order which is enforceable in England and Wales, Scotland or Northern Ireland by virtue of paragraph 11G, 25G or 41G".

Section 91 SCHEDULE 5

MINOR AND CONSEQUENTIAL AMENDMENTS

The Internationally Protected Persons Act 1978 (c. 17)

1. The Internationally Protected Persons Act 1978 is amended as follows.

2. In section 2 (supplementary provisions), in subsections (1) and (2), for "and the United Nations Personnel Act 1997" there is substituted, "the United Nations Personnel Act 1997 and the Terrorism Act 2000".

The Suppression of Terrorism Act 1978 (c. 26)

3. The Suppression of Terrorism Act 1978 is amended as follows.

4. In section 4 (jurisdiction in respect of offences committed outside United Kingdom), in subsections (4) and (5), for "and the United Nations Personnel Act 1997" there is substituted, "the United Nations Personnel Act 1997 and the Terrorism Act 2000".

The Road Traffic (Northern Ireland) Order 1981 (S.I. 1981/154 (N.I. 1))

5. The Road Traffic (Northern Ireland) Order 1981 is amended as follows.

6. In Article 4 (exceptions to offence under Article 3), in paragraph (3) (a), after "Road Traffic Orders" there is inserted "or Chapter 1 of Part 3 of the Crime (International Co-operation) Act 2003".

The Nuclear Material (Offences) Act 1983 (c. 18)

7. The Nuclear Material (Offences) Act 1983 is amended as follows.

8. In section 3 (supplemental), in subsections (1) and (2), for "and the United Nations Personnel Act 1997" there is substituted, "the United Nations Personnel Act 1997 and the Terrorism Act 2000".

The Child Abduction Act 1984 (c. 37)

9. The Child Abduction Act 1984 is amended as follows.

10. In section 11 (consequential amendments and repeals), in subsection (3), after "the Internationally Protected Persons Act 1978" there is inserted "and sections 63B(2) and 63C(2) of the Terrorism Act 2000".

The Criminal Justice Act 1987 (c. 38)

11. The Criminal Justice Act 1987 is amended as follows.

12. In section 2 (investigation powers of Director of Serious Fraud Office)—

(a) in subsection (1A), for paragraph (b) there is substituted—

"(b) the Secretary of State acting under section 15(2) of the Crime (International Co-operation) Act 2003, in response to a request received by him from a person mentioned in section 13(2) of that Act (an 'overseas authority').",

(b) in subsection (8A), for the words from "furnished" to the end there is substituted "given to the overseas authority which requested it or given to the Secretary of State for forwarding to that overseas authority)",
(c) subsection (8B) is omitted,
(d) in subsection (8C), for "transmitted" (in both places) there is substituted "forwarded",
(e) in subsection (18), "(8B)" is omitted.

The Criminal Justice Act 1988 (c. 33)

13. The Criminal Justice Act 1988 is amended as follows.

14. In section 24 (business etc. documents), in subsection (4), for "section 3 of the Criminal Justice (International Co-operation) Act 1990" there is substituted "section 7 of the Crime (International Co-operation) Act 2003".

15. In section 26 (statements in documents that appear to have been prepared for the purposes of criminal proceedings or investigations), for "section 3 of the Criminal Justice (International Co-operation) Act 1990" there is substituted "section 7 of the Crime (International Co-operation) Act 2003".

16. In paragraph 6 of Schedule 13 (evidence before courts-martial etc.)—

(a) in sub-paragraph (1)—

(i) for "section 3 of the Criminal Justice (International Co-operation) Act 1990" there is substituted "section 7 of the Crime (International Co-operation) Act 2003", and
(ii) for "letters of request or corresponding documents" there is substituted "requests for assistance in obtaining outside the United Kingdom evidence", and

(b) in sub-paragraph (4), for "letters of request or corresponding documents" there is substituted "requests for assistance in obtaining evidence".

The Road Traffic Act 1988 (c. 52)

17. The Road Traffic Act 1988 is amended as follows.

18. In section 88 (exceptions to offence under section 87) —

(a) in subsection (1A)(b)(ii), for "section 4(1) of or paragraph 6(1) or 9(1)" there is substituted "section 4 of or paragraph 6 or 9",
(b) in subsection (1B)(a), after "Road Traffic Acts" there is inserted "or Chapter 1 of Part 3 of the Crime (International Co-operation) Act 2003".

19. In section 92 (requirements as to physical fitness of drivers), in subsection (7D), after "99D" there is inserted "or 109C".

20. In section 94A (driving after refusal or revocation of licence), in subsection (1) —

(a) in paragraph (a)(ii), for "section 93(1) or (2)" there is substituted "section 93",
(b) in paragraph (a)(iii) —

(i) after "section 99C(1) or (2)" there is inserted "or 109B",
(ii) after "Community licence" there is inserted "or Northern Ireland licence",

(c) in paragraph (b)(ii), at the end there is inserted "or Northern Ireland licence".

21. In section 97 (grant of licences), in subsection (1)(d), for "section 4 (1) of or paragraph 6(1) or 9(1)" there is substituted "section 4 of or paragraph 6 or 9".

22. In section 100 (appeals relating to licences), in subsection (1) —

(a) in paragraph (c), after "99(3)" there is inserted "or (3A)",
(b) for "or 99C" there is substituted, "99C or 109B".

23. In section 105 (regulations) —

(a) in subsection (2) —

(i) in paragraph (a), after "this Act," there is inserted "Northern Ireland licences,"
(ii) in paragraph (b)(iii), after "this Act" there is inserted, "of Northern Ireland licences",
(iii) in paragraph (ea), after "counterparts" (in the first place) there is inserted "of Northern Ireland licences or" and after "counterparts" (in the second place) there is inserted "of Northern Ireland licences or (as the case may be)",
(iv) in paragraph (f), before "Community licences" there is inserted "Northern Ireland licences or",

(b) in subsection (5), for ", 91A and" there is substituted "and 91ZA to".

24. In section 107 (service of notices), for "99B or 99E" there is substituted "99B, 99E or 109A".

25. In section 108 (interpretation), in subsection (1) —

(a) in the definition of "counterpart", the "and" at the end of paragraph (a) is omitted and after that paragraph there is inserted —

"(aa) in relation to a Northern Ireland licence, has the meaning given by section 109A of this Act (except in the definition of "Northern Ireland counterpart" below), and",

(b) in the definition of "Northern Ireland driving licence" and "Northern Ireland licence", at the end there is inserted "and 'Northern Ireland counterpart' means the document issued with the Northern Ireland licence as a counterpart under the law of Northern Ireland".

26. In section 109 (provisions as to Northern Ireland drivers' licences) —

(a) in subsection (1), after "Great Britain," there is inserted "in accordance with that licence,",
(b) in subsection (2), paragraph (b) and the "and" preceding it are omitted,
(c) subsections (3) to (5) are omitted.

27. In section 164 (power of constables to require production of driving licence etc.) —

(a) in subsection (3) —

(i) in paragraph (a), before "the Secretary of State" there is inserted "a person is required to deliver his licence and its counterpart to the Secretary of State under section 63 of the Crime (International Co-operation) Act 2003 or",
(ii) in paragraph (a)(iii), after "99C" there is inserted ", 109B",
(iii) in paragraph (b), after "99C" there is inserted ", 109B" and after "or 118" there is inserted "or section 63 of the Crime (International Co-operation) Act 2003",

(b) in subsection (11) —

(i) in the definition of "licence", after "this Act" there is inserted, "a Northern Ireland licence",
(ii) after ""counterpart"," there is inserted ""Northern Ireland licence",".

28. In section 167 (power of arrest for constable in Scotland), before "Community licence" there is inserted "Northern Ireland licence or".

29. In section 173 (forgery of documents, etc.) —

(a) in subsection (2)(aa), after "counterpart of a" there is inserted "Northern Ireland licence or",
(b) in subsection (4), for "and 'Community licence'" there is substituted, "'Community licence' and 'Northern Ireland licence'".

30. In section 176 (power to seize certain articles) —

(a) in subsection (1A), before "Community licence" (in both places) there is inserted "Northern Ireland licence or",
(b) in subsection (3A), after "such licence or" there is inserted "of a Northern Ireland licence or",
(c) in subsection (8), for "and 'Community licence'" there is substituted, "'Community licence' and 'Northern Ireland licence'".

31. In section 193A (tramcars and trolley vehicles), in subsection (2)(b), for "91A," there is substituted "91ZA to".

The Road Traffic Offenders Act 1988 (c. 53)

32. The Road Traffic Offenders Act 1988 is amended as follows.

33. In section 3 (restriction on institution of proceedings for certain offences), in subsection (2A), after "99D" there is inserted "or 109C".

34. In section 26 (interim disqualification), in subsection (10), for the words from "and 91A(5)" to "licences)" there is substituted ", 91ZA (7) and 91A(5) of this Act".

35. In section 98 (general interpretation), in subsection (1) —

(a) in the definition of "the provisions connected with the licensing of drivers", for "91A," there is substituted "91ZA to",
(b) for "and 'EEA State' 'there is substituted', 'EEA State' and 'Northern Ireland licence'".

36. In Schedule 1 (offences to which sections 1, 6, 11 and 12(1) of the Act apply) —

(a) in the entry for section 94(3) of the Road Traffic Act 1988, in column 1, at the end there is inserted "or 109C",
(b) in the entry for section 94(3A) of that Act, in column 1, at the end there is inserted "or 109C(c)",
(c) in the entry for section 94A of that Act, in column 2, at the end there is inserted "or 109B",
(d) in the entry for section 99B(11) of that Act —

(i) in column 1, at the end there is inserted "and that subsection as applied by RTA section 109A(5)",
(ii) in column 2, at the end there is inserted "or a requirement under section 99B(6) or (7) as applied by section 109A(5)".

37. In Schedule 2 (prosecution and punishment of offences) —

(a) in the entry for section 94(3) of the Road Traffic Act 1988, in column 2, at the end there is inserted "or 109C",
(b) in the entry for section 94(3A) of that Act, in column 2, at the end there is inserted "or 109C(c)",
(c) in the entry for section 94A of that Act, in column 2, at the end there is inserted "or 109B",
(d) in the entry for section 99B(11) of that Act —

(i) in column 1, at the end there is inserted "and that subsection as applied by RTA section 109A(5)",
(ii) in column 2, at the end there is inserted "or a requirement under section 99B(6) or (7) as applied by section 109A(5)",

(e) the entry for section 109 of that Act is omitted,
(f) before the entry for section 114 of that Act there is inserted —

"RTA 109B(4)	Failure to deliver section Northern Ireland licence to Secretary of State when required by notice under section 109B.	Summarily.	Level 3 on the standard scale.			"

The Criminal Justice (Evidence, Etc.) (Northern Ireland) Order 1988 (S.I. 1988/1847 (N.I. 17))

38. The Criminal Justice (Evidence, Etc.) (Northern Ireland) Order 1988 is amended as follows.

39. In Article 4 (business etc. documents), in paragraph (4), for "section 3 of the Criminal Justice (International Co-operation) Act 1990" there is substituted "section 7 of the Crime (International Co-operation) Act 2003".

40. In Article 6 (statements in documents that appear to have been prepared for the purposes of criminal proceedings or investigations), for "section 3 of the Criminal Justice (International Co-operation) Act 1990" there is substituted "section 7 of the Crime (International Co-operation) Act 2003".

The Criminal Justice (International Co-operation) Act 1990 (c. 5)

41. The Criminal Justice (International Co-operation) Act 1990 is amended as follows.

42. Sections 1 to 4, 7, 8 and 11 (mutual service of process and provision of evidence) are omitted.

43. In section 5 (transfer of UK prisoner to give evidence or assist investigation overseas), after subsection (3) there is inserted —

"(3A) A warrant under this section has effect in spite of section 127(1) of the Army Act 1955, section 127(1) of the Air Force Act 1955 or section 82A(1) of the Naval Discipline Act 1957 (restriction on removing persons out of the United Kingdom who are serving military sentences)."

44. Schedule 1 (proceedings of nominated court) is omitted.

The Road Traffic (New Drivers) Act 1995 (c. 13)

45. The Road Traffic (New Drivers) Act 1995 is amended as follows.

46. In section 2 (surrender of licences), at the end there is inserted —

"(6) In this section and section 3 'licence' includes a Northern Ireland licence."

47. In section 3 (revocation of licences) —

(a) after subsection (1) there is inserted —

"(1A) Where the Secretary of State serves on the holder of a Northern Ireland licence a notice under subsection (1), the Secretary of State must send to the licensing authority in Northern Ireland —

(a) particulars of the notice; and
(b) the Northern Ireland licence.

(1B) Where the Secretary of State is sent by that licensing authority particulars of a notice served on the holder of a licence under a provision of Northern Ireland law corresponding to subsection (1), he must by notice served on the holder revoke the licence.",

(b) in subsection (2), after "subsection (1)" there is inserted "or (1B)",
(c) at the end, there is inserted —

"(3) In this section references to the revocation of a person's Northern Ireland licence are references to its revocation as respects Great Britain; and, accordingly, the person ceases to be authorised by virtue of section 109(1) of the Road Traffic Act 1988 to drive in Great Britain a motor vehicle of any class."

48. In section 4 (re-testing) —

(a) in subsection (1) —

(i) for "section 3(1)" there is substituted "section 3",
(ii) after "full licence" (in the second place it occurs) there is inserted "or (as the case may be) full Northern Ireland licence",

(b) after subsection (1) there is inserted —

"(1A) Subject to subsection (5), the Secretary of State may not under that Part grant a person whose Northern Ireland licence has been revoked under a provision of Northern Ireland law corresponding to section 3(1) a full licence to drive any class of vehicles in relation to which the revoked licence was issued as a full Northern Ireland licence unless he satisfies the Secretary of State as mentioned in subsection (1).",

(c) in subsections (2) and (3), at the end there is inserted "or (as the case may be) full Northern Ireland licence",

(d) in subsection (5) —

(i) for "Subsection (1) does" there is substituted "Subsections (1) and (1A) do", and

(ii) for "section 3(1)" there is substituted "section 3 or whose Northern Ireland licence has been revoked under a provision of Northern Ireland law corresponding to section 3(1)".

49. In section 5 (restoration of licence without re-testing in certain cases) —

(a) in subsections (1), (4) and (6), for "section 3(1)" there is substituted "section 3",

(b) in subsections (3)(a) and (4)(c), after "section 2" there is inserted "or (as the case may be) the provision of Northern Ireland law corresponding to that section",

(c) at the end there is inserted —

"(11) Nothing in this section applies in relation to a person whose Northern Ireland licence has been revoked under section 3(1)."

50. In section 7 (early termination of probationary period) —

(a) in paragraph (b), for "section 3(1)" there is substituted "section 3",

(b) in paragraph (c) —

(i) for "paragraph 5(1)" there is substituted "paragraph 5",

(ii) for "paragraph 8(1)" there is substituted "paragraph 8".

51. In section 9 (interpretation), after subsection (2) there is inserted —

"(2A) In this Act —

"full Northern Ireland licence" means a Northern Ireland licence other than a Northern Ireland provisional licence,

"Northern Ireland provisional licence" means a Northern Ireland licence which corresponds to a provisional licence."

52. Schedule 1 (newly qualified drivers holding test certificates) is amended as follows.

53. In paragraph 1, at the end there is inserted —

"(3) In this Schedule "licence" includes a Northern Ireland licence, "full licence" includes a full Northern Ireland licence and "provisional licence" includes a Northern Ireland provisional licence.

(4) In relation to the holder of a Northern Ireland licence, the following sub-paragraphs have effect for the purposes of this Schedule.

(5) References to a test certificate are references to a certificate or other document (in this Schedule referred to as a "Northern Ireland test certificate") which is evidence that he has not more than two years previously passed a Northern Ireland test of competence to drive corresponding to the test mentioned in sub-paragraph (1).

(6) References to prescribed conditions are references to conditions subject to which the Northern Ireland provisional licence was granted."

54. In paragraph 2, after sub-paragraph (4) there is inserted —

"(4A) In relation to the holder of a Northern Ireland licence, the reference in sub-paragraph (4)(b) to section 98 (2) of the Road Traffic Act 1988 is a reference to the corresponding provision under the law of Northern Ireland."

55. In paragraph 5 —

(a) after sub-paragraph (1) there is inserted —

"(1A) Where the Secretary of State serves on the holder of a Northern Ireland licence a notice under sub-paragraph (1), the Secretary of State must send to the licensing authority in Northern Ireland particulars of the notice together with the Northern Ireland test certificate.

(1B) Where the Secretary of State is sent by that licensing authority particulars of a notice served on the holder of a licence under a provision of Northern Ireland law corresponding to sub-paragraph (1), he must by notice served on that person revoke his test certificate.",

(b) in sub-paragraph (2), after "sub-paragraph (1)" there is inserted "or (1B)",
(c) at the end there is inserted —

"(4) In this paragraph and paragraph 8 references to the revocation of a person's Northern Ireland test certificate are references to its revocation as respects Great Britain.

(5) The effect of the revocation of a person's Northern Ireland test certificate as respects Great Britain is that any prescribed conditions to which his Northern Ireland provisional licence ceased to be subject when he became a qualified driver shall again apply for the purposes of section 109(1) of the Road Traffic Act 1988."

56. In paragraph 6, in sub-paragraph (1), for "paragraph 5(1)" there is substituted "paragraph 5, or whose Northern Ireland test certificate has been revoked under a provision of Northern Ireland law corresponding to paragraph 5(1),".

57. In paragraph 8 —

(a) after sub-paragraph (1) there is inserted —

"(1A) Where the Secretary of State serves on the holder of a Northern Ireland licence a notice under sub-paragraph (1), the Secretary of State must send to the licensing authority in Northern Ireland particulars of the notice together with the Northern Ireland licence and the Northern Ireland test certificate.

(1B) Where the Secretary of State is sent by that licensing authority particulars of a notice served on the holder of a licence under a provision of Northern Ireland law corresponding to sub-paragraph (1), he must by notice served on that person revoke his licence and test certificate.",

(b) in sub-paragraph (2), after "sub-paragraph (1)" there is inserted "or (1B)",
(c) at the end there is inserted —

"(3) In this paragraph references to the revocation of a person's Northern Ireland licence are references to its revocation as respects Great Britain; and, accordingly, the person ceases to be authorised by virtue of section 109(1) of the Road Traffic Act 1988 to drive in Great Britain a motor vehicle of any class."

58. In paragraph 9 —

(a) in sub-paragraph (1), for "paragraph 8(1)" there is substituted "paragraph 8, or whose Northern Ireland licence and Northern Ireland test certificate have been revoked under a provision of Northern Ireland law corresponding to paragraph 8(1),",
(b) in sub-paragraph (4)(b)(i), after "1988" there is inserted, "or under a provision of Northern Ireland law corresponding to that section,".

59. In paragraph 10(a) —

(a) for "paragraph 5(1)" there is substituted "paragraph 5 (or a person's Northern Ireland test certificate has been revoked under a provision of Northern Ireland law corresponding to paragraph 5(1))",
(b) for "paragraph 8(1)" there is substituted "paragraph 8 (or a person's Northern Ireland licence and Northern Ireland test certificate have been revoked under a provision of Northern Ireland law corresponding to paragraph 8(1))".

60. `In paragraph 11 —

(a) in sub-paragraphs (1) and (2)(c), for "paragraph 5(1)" and "paragraph 8(1)" there is substituted "paragraph 5" and "paragraph 8" respectively,
(b) in sub-paragraph (1)(d), after "section 2" there is inserted "or (as the case may be) the provision of Northern Ireland law corresponding to that section".

The Criminal Law (Consolidation) (Scotland) Act 1995 (c. 39)

61. The Criminal Law (Consolidation) (Scotland) Act 1995 is amended as follows.

62. In section 27 (Lord Advocate's direction), in subsection (2), for "section 4(2B) of the Criminal Justice (International Co-operation) Act 1990" there is substituted "section 15(4) of the Crime (International Co-operation) Act 2003".

63. In section 28 (powers of investigation) —

(a) in subsection (8), for the words from "by the" to the end there is substituted "by virtue of section 27(2) of this Act shall be given to the overseas authority which requested it or to the Lord Advocate for forwarding to that authority",
(b) subsection (9) is omitted,
(c) in subsection (10), for "transmitted" (in both places) there is substituted "forwarded".

The Criminal Procedure (Scotland) Act 1995 (c. 46)

64. The Criminal Procedure (Scotland) Act 1995 is amended as follows.

65. In section 210(1)(c) (consideration, in passing sentence of imprisonment or detention, of time spent in custody), at the end there is inserted "so however that a period of time spent both in custody on remand and, by virtue of section 47(1) of the Crime (International Co-operation) Act 2003, abroad is not for any reason to be discounted in a determination under paragraph (a) above or specification under paragraph (b) above".

The United Nations Personnel Act 1997 (c. 13)

66. The United Nations Personnel Act 1997 is amended as follows.

67. In section 5 (supplementary provisions), in subsections (1) and (2), for "and the Nuclear Material (Offences) Act 1983" there is substituted, "the Nuclear Material (Offences) Act 1983 and the Terrorism Act 2000".

The Data Protection Act 1998 (c. 29)

68. The Data Protection Act 1998 is amended as follows.

69. In section 28(1) (national security), for "section" there is substituted "sections 54A and".

70. In section 60(2) and (3) (prosecutions and penalties), before "paragraph 12" there is inserted "section 54A and".

71. In section 63(5) (application to the Crown), for "section" there is substituted "sections 54A and".

The Powers of Criminal Courts (Sentencing) Act 2000 (c. 6)

72. The Powers of Criminal Courts (Sentencing) Act 2000 is amended as follows.

73. In section 146 (driving disqualification for any offence) —

(a) in subsection (4), the "or" at the end of paragraph (a) is omitted and after that paragraph there is inserted —

"(aa) in the case where he holds a Northern Ireland licence (within the meaning of Part 3 of the Road Traffic Act 1988), his Northern Ireland licence and its counterpart (if any); or",

(b) in subsection (5), in the definition of "counterpart", the "and" at the end of paragraph (a) is omitted and after that paragraph there is inserted —

"(aa) in relation to a Northern Ireland licence, has the meaning given by section 109A of that Act; and".

74. In section 147 (driving disqualification where vehicle used for purposes of crime), in subsection (5), the "or" at the end of paragraph (a) is omitted and after that paragraph there is inserted —

"(aa) in the case where he holds a Northern Ireland licence (within the meaning of Part 3 of the Road Traffic Act 1988), his Northern Ireland licence and its counterpart (if any); or".

The Terrorism Act 2000 (c. 11)

75. The Terrorism Act 2000 is amended as follows.

76. In section 121 (interpretation), in the definition of "premises", before "includes" (in the first place) there is inserted, "except in section 63D,".

77. In section 123 (orders and regulations), in subsection (2), after paragraph (b) there is inserted —

"(ba) section 63C(3)(d);".

The Regulation of Investigatory Powers Act 2000 (c. 23)

78. The Regulation of Investigatory Powers Act 2000 is amended as follows.

79. In section 65 (investigatory powers tribunal) —

(a) in subsection (5) —

(i) after paragraph (c) there is inserted —

"(ca) the carrying out of surveillance by a foreign police or customs officer (within the meaning of section 76A);",

(ii) in paragraph (d), at the beginning there is inserted "other",

(b) after subsection (7), there is inserted —

"(7A) For the purposes of this section conduct also takes place in challengeable circumstances if it takes place, or purports to take place, under section 76A."

80. In section 78 (orders, regulations and rules), in subsection (3)(a), for "or 71(9)" there is substituted, "71(9) or 76A(9)".

The Armed Forces Act 2001 (c. 19)

81. In section 31 of the Armed Forces Act 2001 (power to make provision in consequence of enactments relating to criminal justice), in subsection (7) —

(a) after "section" there is inserted "section 5 of the Criminal Justice (International Co-operation) Act 1990 and",
(b) for "is" there is substituted "are".

The Proceeds of Crime Act 2002 (c. 29)

82. The Proceeds of Crime Act 2002 is amended as follows.

83. In section 376 (evidence overseas) —

(a) subsection (5) is omitted,
(b) in subsection (6), for the words preceding paragraph (a) there is substituted "The person issuing a letter of request may send it",
(c) for subsection (7) there is substituted —

"(7) Alternatively, the person issuing the letter of request may send it to the Secretary of State for forwarding to the court, tribunal or authority mentioned in subsection (6).

(7A) In a case of urgency, the person issuing the letter of request may send it to —

(a) the International Criminal Police Organisation, or
(b) any body or person competent to receive it under any provisions adopted under the Treaty on European Union,

for forwarding to the court, tribunal or authority mentioned in subsection (6)."

Section 91 SCHEDULE 6

REPEALS

Short title and chapter	*Extent of repeal*
Criminal Justice Act 1987 (c. 38)	In section 2 — subsection (8B), in subsection (18), the word "(8B)". In section 3(6), the "and" preceding paragraph (m).
Road Traffic Act 1988 (c. 52)	In section 108(1), in the definition of "counterpart", the "and" at the end of paragraph (a). In section 109 — in subsection (2), paragraph (b) and the "and" preceding it, subsections (3) to (5).
Road Traffic Offenders Act 1988 (c. 53)	In Schedule 2, the entry for section 109 of the Road Traffic Act 1988.
Criminal Justice (International Co-operation) Act 1990 (c. 5)	Sections 1 to 4, 7, 8 and 11. Schedule 1. In Schedule 4, paragraphs 6(2) and 8.

Short title and chapter	*Extent of repeal*
Criminal Justice and Public Order Act 1994 (c. 33)	Section 164(1).
Criminal Law (Consolidation) (Scotland) Act 1995 (c. 39)	Section 28(9).
Powers of Criminal Courts (Sentencing) Act 2000 (c. 6)	In section 146 — in subsection (4), the "or" at the end of paragraph (a), in subsection (5), in the definition of "counterpart", the "and" at the end of paragraph (a). In section 147(5), the "or" at the end of paragraph (a).
Criminal Justice and Police Act 2001 (c. 16)	In Schedule 1, paragraph 49.
Proceeds of Crime Act 2002 (c. 29)	Section 376(5).

APPENDIX B

STATUTORY INSTRUMENTS

United States of America (Extradition) Order 1976/2144 B–001

Notes

Made: December 15, 1976

Laid before Parliament: December 23, 1976

Coming into Operation: January 21, 1977

At the Court at Buckingham Place, December 15, 1976 Present, The Queen's Most Excellent Majesty in Council.

Whereas a Treaty with Protocol of Signature was concluded on June 8, 1972 between the Government of the United Kingdom of Great Britain and Northern Ireland and the Government of the United States of America for the reciprocal extradition of offenders, the terms of which are set out in Schedule 1 to this Order: And whereas the said Treaty and Protocol were ratified on October 21, 1976: And whereas in accordance with Article II(1)(a) of the said Treaty it has been agreed by Notes exchanged on October 21, 1976 that the Treaty shall apply to those territories for the international relations of which the United Kingdom is responsible and which are specified in Schedule 2 to this Order: And whereas on the entry into force of the said Treaty the provisions of the earlier Extradition Treaty which was concluded on December 22, 1931 shall cease to have effect between the United Kingdom and the United States of America: Now, therefore, Her Majesty, in exercise of the powers conferred on Her by sections 2, 17 and 21 of the Extradition Act, 1870 or otherwise in Her Majesty vested, is pleased, by and which the advice of Her Privy Council, to order, and it is hereby ordered, as follows:—

This Order may be cited as the United States of America (Extradition) Order 1976 and shall come into operation on January 21, 1977.

The Interpretation Act 1889 shall apply to the interpretation of this Order as it applies to the interpretation of an Act of Parliament.

The Extradition Acts 1870 to 1935, as amended or extended by any subsequent enactment, shall apply in the case of the United States of America in accordance with the said Treaty of the 8th June 1972.

The operation of this Order is limited to the United Kingdom of Great Britain and Northern Ireland, the Channel Islands, the Isle of Man, and the other territories (including their dependencies) specified in Schedule 2 to this Order.

The United States of America (Extradition) Order in Council 1935 is hereby revoked.

Signatures

N.E. Leigh,
Clerk of the Privy Council.

SCHEDULE 1

1.—EXTRADITION TREATY BETWEEN THE GOVERNMENT OF THE UNITED KINGDOM OF GREAT BRITAIN AND NORTHERN IRELAND AND THE GOVERNMENT OF THE UNITED STATES OF AMERICA

The Government of the United Kingdom of Great Britain and Northern Ireland and the Government of the United States of America;

Desiring to make provision for the reciprocal extradition of offenders;

Have agreed as follows:

ARTICLE I

Each Contracting Party undertakes to extradite to the other, in the circumstances and subject to the conditions specified in this Treaty, any person found in its territory who has been accused or convicted of any offence within Article III, committed within the jurisdiction of the other Party.

ARTICLE II

(1) This Treaty shall apply:

(a) in relation to the United Kingdom: to Great Britain and Northern Ireland, the Channel Islands, the Isle of Man, and any territory for the international relations of which the United Kingdom is responsible and to which the Treaty shall have been extended by agreement between the Contracting Parties embodied in an Exchange of Notes; and

(b) to the United States of America;

and references to the territory of a Contracting Party shall be construed accordingly.

(2) The application of this Treaty to any territory in respect of which extension has been made in accordance with paragraph (1) of this Article may be terminated by either Contracting Party giving six months written notice to the other through the diplomatic channel.

ARTICLE III

(1) Extradition shall be granted for an act or omission the facts of which disclose an offence within any of the descriptions listed in the Schedule annexed to this Treaty, which is an integral part of the Treaty, or any other offence, if:

(a) the offence is punishable under the laws of both Parties by imprisonment or other form of detention for more than one year or by the death penalty;

(b) the offence is extraditable under the relevant law, being the law of the United Kingdom or other territory to which this Treaty applies by virtue of sub-paragraph (1)(a) of Article II; and

(c) the offence constitutes a felony under the law of the United States of America.

(2) Extradition shall also be granted for any attempt or conspiracy to commit an offence within paragraph (1) of this Article if such attempt or conspiracy is one for which extradition may be granted under the laws of both Parties and is punishable under the laws of both Parties by imprisonment or other form of detention for more than one year or by the death penalty.

(3) Extradition shall also be granted for the offence of impeding the arrest or prosecution of a person who has committed an offence for which extradition may be granted under this Article and which is punishable under the laws of both Parties by imprisonment or other form of detention for a period of five years or more.

(4) A person convicted of and sentenced for an offence shall not be extradited therefore unless he was sentenced to imprisonment or other form of detention for a period of four months or more or, subject to the provisions of Article IV, to the death penalty.

ARTICLE IV

If the offence for which extradition is requested is punishable by death under the relevant law of the requesting Party, but the relevant law of the requested Party does not provide for the death penalty in a similar case, extradition may be refused unless the requesting Party gives assurances satisfactory to the requested Party that the death penalty will not be carried out.

ARTICLE V

(1) Extradition shall not be granted if:

(a) the person sought would, if proceeded against in the territory of the requested Party for the offence for which his extradition is requested, be entitled to be discharged on the grounds of a previous acquittal or conviction in the territory of the requesting or requested Party or of a third State; or

(b) the prosecution for the offence for which extradition is requested has become barred by lapse of time according to the law of the requesting or requested Party; or

(c) (i) the offence for which extradition is requested is regarded by the requested Party as one of a political character; or
(ii) the person sought proves that the request for his extradition has in fact been made with a view to try or punish him for an offence of a political character.

(2) Extradition may be refused on any other ground which is specified by the law of the requested Party.

ARTICLE VI

If the person sought should be under examination or under punishment in the territory of the requested Party for any other offence, his extradition shall be deferred until the conclusion of the trial and the full execution of any punishment awarded to him.

ARTICLE VII

(1) The request for extradition shall be made through the diplomatic channel, except as otherwise provided in Article XV.

(2) The request shall be accompanied by:

(a) a description of the person sought, his nationality, if known, and any other information which would help to establish his identity;

(b) a statement of the facts of the offence for which extradition is requested;

(c) the text, if any, of the law

(i) defining that offence;
(ii) prescribing the maximum punishment for that offence; and
(iii) imposing any time limit on the institution of proceedings for that offence;

and

(d) (i) where the requesting Party is the United Kingdom, a statement of the legal provisions which establish the extraditable character of the offence for which extradition is requested under the relevant law, being the law of the United Kingdom or other territory to which this Treaty applies by virtue of sub-paragraph (1) (a) of Article II;

(ii) where the requesting Party is the United States of America, a statement that the offence for which extradition is requested, constitutes a felony under the law of the United States of America.

(3) If the request relates to an accused person, it must also be accompanied by a warrant of arrest issued by a judge, magistrate or other competent authority in the territory of the requesting Party and by such evidence as, according to the law of the requested Party, would justify his committal for trial if the offence had been committed in the territory of the requested Party, including evidence that the person requested is the person to whom the warrant of arrest refers.

(4) If the request relates to a convicted person, it must be accompanied by a certificate or the judgement of conviction imposed in the territory of the requesting Party, and by evidence that the person requested is the person to whom the conviction refers and, if the person was sentenced, by evidence of the sentence imposed and a statement showing to what extent the sentence has not been carried out.

(5) The warrant of arrest, or the judicial document establishing the existence of the conviction, and any deposition or statement or other evidence given on oath or affirmed, or any certified copy thereof shall be received in evidence in any proceedings for extradition:

(a) if it is authenticated in the case of a warrant by being signed, or in the case of any other original document by being certified, by a judge, magistrate or other competent authority of the requesting Party, or in the case of a copy by being so certified to be a true copy of the original; and

(b) where the requesting Party is the United Kingdom, by being sealed with the official seal of the appropriate Minister and certified by the principal diplomatic or consular officer of the United States of America in the United Kingdom; and where the requesting Party is the United States of America, by being sealed with the official seal of the Department of State for the Secretary of State; or

(c) if it is authenticated in such other manner as may be permitted by the law of the requested Party.

ARTICLE VIII

(1) In urgent cases the person sought may, in accordance with the law of the requested Party, be provisionally arrested on application through the diplomatic channel by the competent authorities of the requesting Party. The application shall contain an indication of intention to request the extradition of the person sought and a statement of the existence of a warrant of arrest or a conviction against that person, and, if available, a description of the person sought, and such further information, if any, as would be necessary to justify the issue of a warrant of arrest had the offence been committed, or the person sought been convicted, in the territory of the requested Party.

(2) A person arrested upon such an application shall be set at liberty upon the expiration of [sixty][1] days from the date of his arrest if a request for his extradition shall not have been received. This provision shall not prevent the institution of further proceedings for the extradition of the person sought if a request is subsequently received.

ARTICLE IX

(1) Extradition shall be granted only if the evidence be found sufficient according to the law of the requested Party either to justify the committal for trial of the person sought if the offence of which he is accused had been committed in the territory of the requested. Party or to prove that he is the identical person convicted by the courts of the requesting Party.

(2) If the requested Party requires additional evidence or information to enable a decision to be taken on the request for extradition, such evidence or information shall be submitted within such time as that Party shall require.

ARTICLE X

If the extradition of a person is requested concurrently by one of the Contracting Parties and by another State or State, either for the same offence or for different offences, the requested Party shall make its

[1] As amended by 1986/2020, sched. 1, art. 4, *post*.

decision, in so far as its law allows, having regard to all the circumstances, including the provisions in this regard in any Agreements in force between the requested Party and the requesting States, the relative seriousness and place of commission of the offences, the respective dates of the requests, the nationality of the person sought and the possibility of subsequent extradition to another State.

ARTICLE XI

(1) The requested Party shall promptly communicate to the requesting Party through the diplomatic channel the decision on the request for extradition.

(2) If a warrant or order for the extradition of a person sought has been issued by the competent authority and he is not removed from the territory of the requested Party within such time as may be required under the law of that Party, he may be set at liberty and the requested Party may subsequently refuse to extradite him for the same offence.

ARTICLE XII

(1) A person extradited shall not be detained or proceeded against in the territory of the requesting Party for any offence other than an extraditable offence established by the facts in respect of which his extradition has been granted, or on account of any other matters, nor be extradited by that Party to a third State—

(a) until after he has returned to the territory of the requested Party; or

(b) until the expiration of thirty days after he has been free to return to the territory of the requested Party.

(2) The provisions of paragraph (1) of this Article shall not apply to offences committed, or matters arising, after the extradition.

ARTICLE XIII

When a request for extradition is granted, the requested Party shall, so far as its law allows and subject to such conditions as it may impose having regard to the rights of other claimants, furnish the requesting Party with all sums of money and other articles—

(a) which may serve as proof of the offence to which the request relates; or

(b) which may have been acquired by the person sought as a result of the offence and are in his possession.

ARTICLE XIV

(1) The requested Party shall make all necessary arrangements for and meet the cost of the representation of the requesting Party is any proceedings arising out of a request for extradition.

(2) Expenses relating to the transportation of a person sought shall be paid by the requesting Party. No pecuniary claim arising out of the arrest, detention, examination and surrender of a person sought under the provisions of this Treaty shall be made by the requested Party against the requesting Party.

ARTICLE XV

A request on the part of the Government of the United States of America for the extradition of an offender who is found in any of the territories to which this Treaty has been extended in accordance with paragraph (1) of Article II may be made to the Governor or other competent authority of that territory, who may take the decision himself or refer the matter to the Government of the United Kingdom for their decision.

ARTICLE XVI

(1) This Treaty shall be ratified, and the instruments of ratification shall be exchanged at Washington as soon as possible. It shall come into force three months after the date of the exchange of instruments of ratification.

(2) This Treaty shall apply to any offence listed in the annexed Schedule committed before or after this Treaty enters into force, provided that extradition shall not be granted for an offence committed before this Treaty enters into force which was not an offence under the laws of both Contracting Parties at the time of its commission.

(3) On the entry into force of this Treaty the provisions of the Extradition Treaty of December 22, 1931 shall cease to have effect as between the United Kingdom and the United States of America.

(4) Either of the Contracting Parties may terminate this Treaty at any time by giving notice to the other through the diplomatic channel. In that event the Treaty shall cease to have effect six months after the receipt of the notice.

In witness whereof the undersigned, being duly authorised thereto by their respective Governments, have signed this Treaty.

Done in duplicate at London in the English language June 8, 1972.

For the Government of the United Kingdom of Great Britain and Northern Ireland: ANTHONY KERSHAW

For the Government of the United States of America: WALTER ANNENBERG

SCHEDULE List of offences referred to in Article III

1. Murder; attempt to murder, including assault with intent to murder.
2. Manslaughter.
3. Maliciously wounding or inflicting grievous bodily harm.
4. Unlawful throwing or application of any corrosive or injurious substance upon the person or another.
5. Rape; unlawful sexual intercourse with a female; indecent assault.
6. Gross indecency or unlawful sexual acts with a child under the age of fourteen years.
7. Procuring a woman or young person for immoral purposes: living on the earnings of prostitution.
8. Unlawfully administering drugs or using instruments with intent to procure the miscarriage of a woman.
9. Bigamy.
10. Kidnapping, abduction, false imprisonment.
11. Neglecting ill-treating, abandoning, exposing or stealing a child.
12. An offence against the law relating to narcotic drugs, cannabis sativa L, hallucinogenic drugs, cocaine and its derivatives, and other dangerous drugs.
13. Theft; larcency; embezzlement.
14. Robbery; assault with intent to rob.
15. Burglary or housebreaking or shopbreaking.
16. Receiving or otherwise handling any goods, money, valuable securities or other property, knowing the same to have been stolen or unlawfully obtained.
17. Obtaining property, money or valuable securities by false pretences or other form of deception.
18. Blackmail or extortion.
19. False accounting.
20. Fraud or false statements by company directors and other officers.
21. An offence against the bankruptcy laws.
22. An offence relating to counterfeiting or forgery.
23. Bribery, including soliciting, offering or accepting bribes.
24. Perjury; subornation of perjury.
25. Arson.
26. Malicious damage to property.
27. Any malicious act done with intent to endanger the safety of persons travelling or being upon a railway.

28. Piracy, involving ships or aircraft, according to international law.

29. Unlawful seizure of an aircraft.

PROTOCOL OF SIGNATURE

At the time of signing this day the Extradition Treaty between the Government of the United Kingdom of Great Britain and Northern Ireland and the Government of the United States of America (hereinafter referred to as "the Treaty"), the undersigned have agreed as follows:

(1) Article III of the Treaty shall permit the Government of the United States of America to obtain the extradition of a person for an offence to which the Treaty relates when United States Federal jurisdiction is based upon interstate transport or transportation or the use of the mails or of interstate facilities, these aspects being jurisdictional only.

(2) This Protocol of Signature shall form an integral part of the Treaty.

In witness whereof the undersigned, being duly authorised thereto by their respective Governments, have signed this Protocol.

Done in duplicate at London in the English language this 8th day of June, 1972.

For the Government of the United Kingdom of Great Britain and Northern Ireland: ANTHONY KERSHAW. For the Government of the United States of America: WALTER ANNENBERG.

SCHEDULE 2

Antigua
Belize
Bermuda
British Indian Ocean Territory
British Virgin Islands
Cayman Islands
Dominica
Falkland Islands and Dependencies
Gibraltar
Gilbert Islands
Hong Kong
Montserrat
Pitcairn, Henderson, Ducie and Oeno Islands
St. Christopher, Nevis and Anguilla
St. Helena and Dependencies
St. Lucia
St. Vincent
Sovereign Base Areas of Akrotiri and Dhekelia in the Island of Cyprus
Turks and Caicos Islands
Tuvalu

EXPLANATORY NOTE

This Order applies the Extradition Acts 1870 to 1935, as amended, in the case of the United States of America in accordance with the Treaty and Protocol between Her Majesty's Government and the Government of the United States of America which was concluded on June 8, 1972 (Cmnd. 5040) and extended by Notes exchanged on 21st October 1976 to the Overseas territories listed. This Treaty replaces as earlier Treaty which was concluded on December 22, 1931.

B–002 **United States of America (Extradition) (Amendment) Order 1986/2020**

Notes

Made: November 25, 1986

Laid before Parliament: November 26, 1986

Coming into operation on a date to be notified in the London, Edinburgh and Belfast Gazettes:

At the Court at Buckingham Palace, November 25, 1986 Present, The Queen's Most Excellent Majesty in Council Whereas a Treaty with Protocol of Signature[1] ("the Treaty") was concluded on June 8, 1972 between the Government of the United Kingdom of Great Britain and Northern Ireland and the Government of the United Kingdom of Great Britain and Northern Ireland and the Government of the United States of America for the reciprocal extradition of offenders, the terms of which are set out in Schedule 1 to the United States of America (Extradition) Order 1976: And whereas a Supplementary Treaty[2] ("the Supplementary Treaty") between the said Governments was signed on June 25, 1985 with the intent to make the Treaty more effective: And whereas the Supplementary Treaty was amended by an Exchange of Notes[3] between the said Governments on August 19 and 20, 1986: And whereas the terms of the Supplementary Treaty as so amended are set out in Schedule 1 to this Order: Now, therefore, Her Majesty, in exercise of the powers conferred on Her by sections 2, 17 and 21 of the Extradition Act 1870, or otherwise in Her Majesty vested, is pleased, by and with the advice of Her Privy Council, to order, and it is hereby ordered, as follows:—

This Order may be cited as the United States of America (Extradition) (Amendment) Order 1986. It shall come into operation on the date, to be notified in the London, Edinburgh and Belfast Gazettes, on which the Supplementary Treaty, as amended by the said Exchange of Notes, enters into force.

The Extradition Acts 1870 to 1895, as amended or extended by any subsequent enactment, shall apply in the case of the United States of America in accordance with the Treaty, as amended by the Supplementary Treaty, as amended by the said Exchange of Notes.

The operation of this Order is limited to the United Kingdom of Great Britain and Northern Ireland, the Channel Islands, the Isle of Man, and the other territories specified in Schedule 2 to this Order.

Signatures

G.I. de Deney,
Clerk of the Privy Council.

SCHEDULE 1

1.—SUPPLEMENTARY TREATY CONCERNING THE EXTRADITION TREATY BETWEEN THE GOVERNMENT OF THE UNITED KINGDOM OF GREAT BRITAIN AND NORTHERN IRELAND AND THE GOVERNMENT OF THE UNITED STATES OF AMERICA, SIGNED AT LONDON ON 8 JUNE 1972, AS AMENDED BY AN EXCHANGE OF NOTES ON 19 AND 20 AUGUST 1986

The Government of the United States of America and the Government of the United Kingdom of Great Britain and Northern Ireland;

[1] Cmnd. 6723.
[2] Cmnd. 9565.
[3] Cmnd. 9915.

Desiring to make more effective the Extradition Treaty between the Contracting Parties, signed at London on June 8, 1972 (hereinafter referred to as "the Extradition Treaty");

Have resolved to conclude a Supplementary Treaty and have agreed as follows:

ARTICLE 1

For the purposes of the Extradition Treaty, none of the following shall be regarded as an offense of a political character:

(a) an offense for which both Contracting Parties have the obligation pursuant to a multilateral international agreement to extradite the person sought or to submit his case to their competent authorities for decision as to prosecution;

(b) murder, voluntary manslaughter, and assault causing grievous bodily harm;

(c) kidnapping, abduction, or serious unlawful detention, including taking a hostage;

(d) an offense involving the use of a bomb, grenade, rocket, firearm, letter or parcel bomb, or any incendiary device if this use endangers any person; and

(e) an attempt to commit any of the foregoing offenses or participation as an accomplice of a person who commits or attempts to commit such an offense.

ARTICLE 2

Nothing in this Supplementary Treaty shall be interpreted as imposing the obligation to extradite if the judicial authority of the requested Party determines that the evidence of criminality presented is not sufficient to sustain the charge under the provisions of the treaty. The evidence of criminality must be such as, according to the law of the requested Party, would justify committal for trial if the offense had been committed in the territory of the requested Party.

In determining whether an individual is extraditable from the United States, the judicial authority of the United States shall permit the individual sought to present evidence on the questions of whether:

(1) there is probable cause;

(2) a defense to extradition specified in the Extradition Treaty or this Supplementary Treaty, and within the jurisdiction of the courts, exists; and

(3) the act upon which the request for extradition is based would constitute an offense punishable under the laws of the United States.

Probable cause means whether there is sufficient evidence to warrant a man of reasonable caution in the belief that:

(1) the person arrested or summoned to appear is the person sought;

(2) in the case of a person accused of having committed a crime, an offense has been committed by the accused; and

(3) in the case of a person alleged to have been convicted of an offense, a certificate of conviction or other evidence of conviction or criminality exists.

ARTICLE 3

(a) Notwithstanding any other provision of this Supplementary Treaty, extradition shall not occur if the person sought establishes to the satisfaction of the competent judicial authority by a preponderance of the evidence that the request for extradition has in fact been made with a view to try or punish him on account of his race, religion, nationality, or political opinions, or that he would, if surrendered, be prejudiced at his trial or punished, detained or restricted in his personal liberty by reason of his race, religion, nationality or political opinions.

(b) In the United States, the competent judicial authority shall only consider the defense to extradition set forth in paragraph (a) for offenses listed in Article 1 of this Supplementary Treaty. A finding under paragraph (a) shall be immediately appealable by either party to the United States district court, or court of appeals, as appropriate. The appeal shall receive expedited consideration at every state. The time for filing a notice of appeal shall be 30 days from the date of the filing of the decision. In all other respects, the applicable provisions of the Federal Rules of Appellate Procedure or Civil Procedure, as appropriate, shall govern the appeals process.

ARTICLE 4
Article VIII, paragraph (2) of the Extradition Treaty is amended to read as follows:

"(2) A person arrested upon such an application shall be set at liberty upon the expiration of sixty days from the date of his arrest if a request for his extradition shall not have been received. This provision shall not prevent the institution of further proceedings for the extradition of the person sought if a request for extradition is subsequently received."

ARTICLE 5
This Supplementary Treaty shall apply to any offense committed before or after this Supplementary Treaty enters into force, provided that this Supplementary Treaty shall not apply to an offense committed before this Supplementary Treaty enters into force which was not an offense under the laws of both Contracting Parties at the time of its commission.

ARTICLE 6
This Supplementary Treaty shall form an integral part of the Extradition Treaty and shall apply:

(a) in relation to the United Kingdom: to Great Britain and Northern Ireland, the Channel Islands, the Isle of Man and the territories for whose international relations the United Kingdom is responsible which are listed in the Annex to this Supplementary Treaty;

(b) to the United States of America; and references to the territory of a Contracting Party shall be construed accordingly.

ARTICLE 7
This Supplementary Treaty shall be subject to ratification and the instruments of ratification shall be exchanged at London as soon as possible. It shall enter into force upon the exchange of instruments of ratification. It shall be subject to termination in the same manner as the Extradition Treaty.

EXPLANATORY NOTE

This Order applies the Extradition Acts 1870 to 1895 in the case of the United States of America in accordance with the Extradition Treaty between the United Kingdom and the United States of America, signed at London on June 8, 1972, as amended by the Supplementary Treaty signed at Washington on June 25, 1985, as amended by an Exchange of Notes on August 19 and 20, 1986.

SCHEDULE 2

Anguilla
Bermuda
British Indian Ocean Territory
British Virgin Islands
Cayman Islands
Falkland Islands
Falkland Islands Dependencies
Gibraltar
Hong Kong
Montserrat
Pitcairn, Henderson, Ducie and Oeno Islands
St Helena
St Helena Dependencies
The Sovereign Base Areas of Akrotiri and Dhekelia in the Island of Cyprus
Turks and Caicos Island

Suppression of Terrorism Act 1978 (Application of Provisions) (United States of America) Order 1986/2146

B–003

Notes

Made: December 8, 1986

Coming into Operation on the date, to be notified in the London, Edinburgh and Belfast Gazettes, on which the Supplementary Treaty comes into force.:

Whereas a Treaty with Protocol of Signature ("the Treaty") was signed on June 8, 1972 between the Government of the United Kingdom of Great Britain and Northern Ireland and the Government of the United States of America for the reciprocal extradition of offenders, the terms of which are set out in Schedule 1 to the United States of America (Extradition) Order 1976: And whereas a Supplementary Treaty ("the Supplementary Treaty") between the said Governments was signed on June 25, 1985[1] with the intent to make the Treaty more effective: And whereas in an exchange of Notes dated August 19 and 20,[2] the said Governments indicated acceptance of certain amendments to the Supplementary Treaty, the provisions of the Supplementary Treaty as so amended being set out in Schedule 1 to this Order: And whereas a draft of this Order has been approved by resolution of each House of Parliament. Now, therefore, in exercise of the powers conferred upon me by section 5(1)(i) of the Suppression of Terrorism Act 1978, I hereby make the following Order:—

This Order may be cited as the Suppression of Terrorism Act 1978 (Application of Provisions) (United States of America) Order 1986.

This Order shall come into operation on the date, to be notified in the London, Edinburgh and Belfast Gazettes, on which the Supplementary Treaty comes into force.

The provisions of the Suppression of Terrorism Act 1978 specified in Schedule 2 to this Order (being provisions which, apart from section 5 thereof, would apply only in relation to convention countries) shall to the extent there mentioned apply in relation to the United States of America as they apply in relation to a convention country.

Signatures

Douglas Hurd,
One of Her Majesty's Principal Secretaries of State.
Home Office.
December 8, 1986.

SCHEDULE 1

TREATY PROVISIONS

1. — SUPPLEMENTARY TREATY CONCERNING THE EXTRADITION TREATY BETWEEN THE GOVERNMENT OF THE UNITED STATES OF AMERICA AND THE GOVERNMENT OF THE UNITED KINGDOM OF GREAT BRITAIN AND NORTHERN IRELAND SIGNED AT LONDON ON JUNE 8, 1972

ARTICLE 1

For the purposes of the Extradition Treaty, none of the following shall be regarded as an offense of a political character:

(a) an offense for which both Contracting Parties have the obligation pursuant to a multilateral international agreement to extradite the person sought or to submit his case to their competent authorities for decision as to prosecution;

(b) murder, voluntary manslaughter, and assault causing grievous bodily harm;

[1] Cmnd. 9565.

[2] Cmnd. 9915.

(c) kidnapping, abduction, or serious unlawful detention, including taking a hostage;

(d) an offense involving the use of a bomb, grenade, rocket, firearm, letter or parcel bomb, or any incendiary device if this use endangers any person; and

(e) an attempt to commit any of the foregoing offenses or participation as an accomplice of a person who commits or attempts to commit such an offense.

ARTICLE 2

Nothing in this Supplementary Treaty shall be interpreted as imposing the obligation to extradite if the judicial authority of the requested Party determines that the evidence of criminality presented is not sufficient to sustain the charge under the provisions of the treaty. The evidence of criminality must be such as, according to the law of the requested Party, would justify committal for trial if the offense had been committed in the territory of the requested Party.

In determining whether an individual is extraditable from the United States, the judicial authority of the United States shall permit the individual sought to present evidence on the questions of whether:

(1) there is probable cause;

(2) a defense to extradition specified in the Extradition Treaty or this Supplementary Treaty, and within the jurisdiction of the courts, exists; and

(3) the act upon which the request for extradition is based would constitute an offense punishable under the laws of the United States.

Probable cause means whether there is sufficient evidence to warrant a man of reasonable caution in the belief that:

(1) the person arrested or summoned to appear is the person sought;

(2) in the case of a person accused of having committed a crime, an offense has been committed by the accused; and

(3) in the case of a person alleged to have been convicted of an offense, a certificate of conviction or other evidence of conviction or criminality exists.

ARTICLE 3

(a) Notwithstanding any other provision of this Supplementary Treaty, extradition shall not occur if the person sought establishes to the satisfaction of the competent judicial authority by a preponderance of the evidence that the request for extradition has in fact been made with a view to try or punish him on account of his race, religion, nationality, or political opinions, or that he would, if surrendered, be prejudiced at his trial or punished, detained or restricted in his personal liberty by reason of his race, religion, nationality or political opinions.

(b) In the United States, the competent judicial authority shall only consider the defense to extradition set forth in paragraph (a) for offenses listed in Article 1 of this Supplementary Treaty. A finding under paragraph (a) shall be immediately appealable by either party to the United States district court, or court of appeals, as appropriate. The appeal shall receive expedited consideration at every stage. The time for filing a notice of appeal shall be 30 days from the date of the filing of the decision. In all other respects, the applicable provisions of the Federal Rules of Appellate Procedure or Civil Procedure, as appropriate, shall govern the appeals process.

ARTICLE 4

Article VIII, paragraph (2) of the Extradition Treaty is amended to read as follows:

"(2) A person arrested upon such an application shall be set at liberty upon the expiration of sixty days from the date of his arrest if a request for his extradition shall not have been received. This provision shall not prevent the institution of further proceedings for the extradition of the person sought if a request for extradition is subsequently received."

ARTICLE 5

This Supplementary Treaty shall apply to any offense committed before or after this Supplementary Treaty enters into force, provided that this Supplementary Treaty shall not apply to an offense committed before this Supplementary Treaty enters into force which was not an offense under the laws of both Contracting Parties at the time of its commission.

ARTICLE 6
This Supplementary Treaty shall form an integral part of the Extradition Treaty and shall apply:

(a) in relation to the United Kingdom: to Great Britain and Northern Ireland, the Channel Islands, the Isle of Man and the territories for whose international relations the United Kingdom is responsible which are listed in the Annex to this Supplementary Treaty;

(b) to the United States of America;

and references to the territory of a Contracting Party shall be construed accordingly.

ARTICLE 7
This Supplementary Treaty shall be subject to ratification and the instruments of ratification shall be exchanged at London as soon as possible. It shall enter into force upon the exchange of instruments of ratification. It shall be subject to termination in the same manner as the Extradition Treaty.

ANNEX
Anguilla; Bermuda; British Indian Ocean Territory; British Virgin Islands; Cayman Islands; Falkland Islands; Falkland Island Dependencies; Gibraltar; Hong Kong; Montserrat; Pitcairn, Henderson, Ducie and Oeno Islands; St. Helena; St. Helena Dependencies; The Sovereign Base Areas of Akrotiri and Dhekelia in the Island of Cyprus; and Turks and Caicos Islands.

SCHEDULE 2

APPLICABLE PROVISIONS OF SUPPERSSION OF TERRORISM ACT 1978

1.—Subsection (1), (2) and (3)(a) and (d) of section 1 (cases in which certain offences are not to be regarded as of a political character) in so far as they relate to those offences listed in Schedule 1 to the Act of 1978 which are specified in paragraph 5 below.

2.—Section 2(1) (which imposes restrictions on the return of a criminal in certain cases).

3.—Section 7 (extension to Channel Islands, Isle of Man and other countries).

4.—Section 8 (provisions as to interpretation and orders).

5.—The following paragraphs of Schedule 1 (list of offences):—

1. (murder).

2. (manslaughter or culpable homicide).

4. (kidnapping, abduction or plagium).

5. (false imprisonment).

7. (wilful fire-raising).

8. (a) and (b) (malicious wounding and causing grievous bodily harm under the Offences against the Person Act 1861).

10, 11. (offences of abduction under the Offences against the Person Act 1861).

11A. (taking of hostages)[3]

12. (a), (b) and (c) (explosives offences under the Offences against the Person Act 1861).

13. (offences under sections 2 and 3 of the Explosives Substances Act 1883).

14, 15. (firearms offences).

16, 17. (offences against property intending to endanger life or being reckless as to danger to life).

[3] Inserted by the Taking of Hostages Act 1982 (c.28), *section 3(2)*.

18, 19. (offences in relation to aircraft).

20. (attempts to commit any of the above).

EXPLANATORY NOTE

This Order, which in accordance with Article 2 comes into operation on the date, to be notified in the London, Edinburgh and Belfast Gazettes, on which the Supplementary Treaty comes into force, applies certain provisions of the Suppression of Terrorism Act 1978 to the extradition of offenders to the United States of America in pursuance of the Supplementary Treaty between the Government of the United Kingdom and the United States of America, signed on June 25, 1985 and amended as recorded in an exchange of Notes between the said Governments of August 19 and 20, 1986. The terms of the Supplementary Treaty as so amended are set out in Schedule 1.

By virtue of paragraph 1 of Schedule 2, the offences listed in paragraph 5 are not to be regarded as offences of a political character (extradition for which is precluded by section 3 of the Extradition Act 1870 (c.52)) in relation to a request for the extradition of a person to the United States of America made after the Order comes into operation, or for the purposes of a request from the United States for assistance in obtaining evidence for use in their criminal proceedings.

Paragraph 2 of Schedule 2 applies section 2(1) of the 1978 Act, which precludes surrender if the person sought proves that the requisition for his surrender was made with a view to try or punish him on account of his race, religion, nationality or political opinions or that he might, if surrendered, be prejudiced at his trial or punished, detained or restricted in his personal liberty by reason of any of those matters.

Paragraphs 3 and 4 provide for the extension of the Order to the Channel Islands, the Isle of Man and other countries and for supplementary matters.

The Extradition Act 2003 (Multiple Offences) Order 2003/3150

B–004

Made: 4th December 2003

Laid before Parliament: 11th December 2003

Coming into force: 1st January 2004

The Secretary of State, in exercise of the powers conferred on him by sections 207 and 223(3) of the Extradition Act 2003, hereby makes the following Order:

1. This Order may be cited as the Extradition Act 2003 (Multiple Offences) Order 2003 and shall come into force on 1st January 2004.

2. — (1) In this Order "the Act" means the Extradition Act 2003.

(2) The Act is to have effect with the modifications specified in the Schedule to this Order in relation to a case where —

(a) a Part 1 warrant is issued for more than one offence;
(b) a request for extradition is made in respect of more than one offence.

Signatures

Caroline Flint
Parliamentary Under-Secretary of State
Home Office
4th December 2003

Article 2(2)

SCHEDULE

MODIFICATIONS TO THE ACT

General modification

1. — (1) Unless the context otherwise requires, any reference in the Act to an offence (including a reference to an extradition offence) is to be construed as a reference to offences (or extradition offences).

(2) Sub-paragraph (1) does not apply to any reference to an offence —

(a) in a modification made by this Schedule; or

(b) in a provision of the Act which is relevant to such a modification.

Initial stage of extradition hearing

2. — (1) Section 10 is modified as follows.

(2) In subsection (2) for "the offence" substitute "any of the offences".

(3) For subsection (3) substitute —

" (3) If the judge decides the question in subsection (2) in the negative in relation to an offence, he must order the person's discharge in relation to that offence only."

(4) For subsection (4) substitute —

" (4) If the judge decides that question in the affirmative in relation to one or more offences he must proceed under section 11."

Bars to extradition

3.—(1) Section 11 is modified as follows.

(2) For subsection (3) substitute—

" (3) If the judge decides any of the questions in subsection (1) in the affirmative in relation to an offence, he must order the person's discharge in relation to that offence only."

(3) For subsection (4) substitute—

" (4) If the judge decides those questions in the negative in relation to an offence and the person is alleged to be unlawfully at large after conviction of the extradition offence, the judge must proceed under section 20."

(4) For subsection (5) substitute—

" (5) If the judge decides those questions in the negative in relation to an offence and the person is accused of the commission of the extradition offence but is not alleged to be unlawfully at large after conviction of it, the judge must proceed under section 21."

Case where person has been convicted

4.—(1) Section 20 is modified as follows.

(2) In subsection (1) after "decide" insert "in relation to each offence".

(3) In subsection (2) after "section 21" insert "in relation to the offence in question".

(4) In subsection (3) after "decide" insert "in relation to each offence".

(5) In subsection (4) after "section 21" insert "in relation to the offence in question".

Human rights

5.—(1) Section 21 is modified as follows.

(2) In subsection (1) after "decide" insert "in relation to each offence".

(3) In subsection (2) after "discharge" insert "in relation to the offence in question".

(4) In subsection (3) after "extradited" insert "for the offence in question".

Appeal against extradition order

6.—(1) Section 26 is modified as follows.

(2) In subsection (1) after "extradition" insert "in relation to an offence".

Court's powers on appeal under section 26

7.—(1) Section 27 is modified as follows.

(2) In subsection (5) after "it must" insert "in relation to the relevant offence only".

Appeal against discharge at extradition hearing

8.—(1) Section 28 is modified as follows.

(2) In subsection (1) after "discharge" insert "in relation to an offence".

Court's powers on appeal under section 28

9.—(1) Section 29 is modified as follows.

(2) In subsection (5) after "it must" insert "in relation to the relevant offence only".

Detention pending conclusion of appeal under section 28

10.—(1) Section 30 is modified as follows.

(2) In subsection (1) after "discharge" insert "in relation to an offence".

Appeal to House of Lords

11.—(1) Section 32 is modified as follows.

(2) In subsection (1) after "appeal" insert "in relation to each offence".

Powers of House of Lords on appeal under section 32

12.—(1) Section 33 is modified as follows.

(2) In subsection (3) after "must" insert "in relation to the relevant offence only".

(3) In subsection (5) after "must" insert "in relation to the relevant offence only".

(4) In subsection (7) after "must" insert "in relation to the relevant offence only".

(5) In subsection (8) after "must" insert "in relation to the relevant offence only".

Extradition where no appeal

13. — (1) Section 35 is modified as follows.

(2) In subsection (1)(a) after "extradition" insert "in relation to an offence".

(3) In subsection (4)(b) after the second "date" insert

", or

(c) if proceedings are continuing in relation to other offences contained in the same Part 1 warrant, 10 days starting with the day on which the judge, the High Court or the House of Lords make the final order in relation to the last of the offences in respect of which the same Part 1 warrant was issued."

Extradition following an appeal

14. — (1) Section 36 is modified as follows.

(2) In subsection (1)(a) after "territory" insert "in relation to an offence".

(3) In subsection (1)(b) after "there" insert "in relation to that offence".

(4) In subsection (3)(a) —

(a) for "the decision of the relevant court on the appeal becomes" substitute "all decisions of the relevant court on any appeal in relation to any offence in respect of which the same Part 1 warrant was issued become";

(b) for "the appeal are discontinued" insert "any appeal in relation to any offence in respect of which the same Part 1 warrant was issued are discontinued".

Withdrawal of warrant before extradition

15. — (1) Section 41 is modified as follows.

(2) In subsection (1) for the words from "a Part 1 warrant" to the end substitute "they do not wish to proceed with their request for extradition in relation to an offence in respect of which the Part 1 warrant was issued".

(3) In subsection (3) after "discharge" insert "in relation to that offence".

Withdrawal of warrant while appeal to High Court pending

16. — (1) Section 42 is modified as follows.

(2) In subsection (1) for the words from "a Part 1 warrant" to the end substitute "they do not wish to proceed with their request for extradition in relation to an offence in respect of which the Part 1 warrant was issued".

(3) In subsection (3)(a) after "extradition" insert "in relation to that offence".

(4) In subsection (3)(b) after "appeal" insert "in relation to that offence".

Withdrawal of warrant while appeal to House of Lords pending

17. — (1) Section 43 is modified as follows.

(2) In subsection (1) for the words from "a Part 1 warrant" to the end substitute "they do not wish to proceed with their request for extradition in relation to an offence in respect of which the Part 1 warrant was issued".

(3) In subsection (3)(a) after "discharge" insert "in relation to that offence".

(4) In subsection (3)(b) after "extradition" insert "in relation to that offence".

(5) In subsection (4) after "appeal" insert "in relation to that offence".

Consent to extradition

18. — (1) Section 45 is modified as follows.

(2) In subsection (1) after "issued" insert "in relation to any offence contained in the Part 1 warrant".

(3) In subsection (2) after the second "section" insert "in relation to any offence contained in the Part 1 warrant".

(4) In subsection (3) after "section" insert "to every offence contained in the Part 1 warrant".

Extradition to category 1 territory following consent

19. — (1) Section 47 is modified as follows.

(2) In subsection (3)(b) after the second "date" insert

", or

c) if proceedings are continuing in relation to other offences contained in the same Part 1 warrant, 10 days starting with the day on which the judge, the High Court or the House of

Lords make the final order in relation to the last of the offences in respect of which the same Part 1 warrant was issued."

(3) In subsection (5) for the words from "the Part 1 warrant" to the end substitute "they do not wish to proceed with their request for extradition in relation to an offence in respect of which the Part 1 warrant was issued".

(4) In subsection (5)(b) after "discharge" insert "in relation to that offence".

Other warrant issued: extradition to category 1 territory

20. — (1) Section 49 is modified as follows.

(2) In subsection (3)(b) after "date" insert

" , or

(c) if proceedings are continuing in relation to other offences contained in the same Part 1 warrant, 10 days starting with the day on which the judge, the High Court or the House of Lords make the final order in relation to the last of the offences in respect of which the same Part 1 warrant was issued."

(3) In subsection (5) for the words from "the Part 1 warrant" to the end substitute "they do not wish to proceed with their request for extradition in relation to an offence in respect of which the Part 1 warrant was issued".

(4) In subsection (5)(b) after "discharge" insert "in relation to that offence".

Arrest warrant following extradition request

21. — (1) Section 71 is modified as follows.

(2) For subsection (2)(a) substitute "any of the offences in respect of which extradition is requested are extradition offences".

(3) In subsection (2)(b) after "evidence" insert "in relation to that offence".

Provisional warrant

22. — (1) Section 73 is modified as follows.

(2) For subsection (3)(a) substitute —

" (a) any of the offences in respect of which extradition is requested are extradition offences."

(3) In subsection (3)(b) after "evidence" insert "in relation to that offence".

Initial stages of extradition hearing

23. — (1) Section 78 is modified as follows.

(2) In subsection (2) after "(or include)" insert "in relation to each offence".

(3) In subsection (3) after "discharge" insert "in relation to the relevant offence only".

(4) In subsection (4)(b) for "the offence" substitute "each offence".

(5) In subsection (6) after "discharge" insert "in relation to that offence".

(6) For subsection (7) substitute —

" (7) If the judge decides those questions in the affirmative in relation to one or more offences he must proceed under section 79."

Bars to extradition

24. — (1) Section 79 is modified as follows.

(2) For subsection (3) substitute —

" (3) If the judge decides any of the questions in subsection (1) in the affirmative in relation to any offence, he must order the person's discharge in relation to that offence only."

(3) For subsection (4) substitute —

" (4) If the judge decides those questions in the negative in relation to any offence and the person is accused of the commission of the extradition offences but is not alleged to be unlawfully at large after conviction of it, the judge must proceed under section 84 in relation to that offence."

(4) For subsection (5) substitute —

" (5) If the judge decides any of those questions in the negative in relation to any offence and the person is alleged to be unlawfully at large after conviction of it, the judge must proceed under section 85 in relation to that offence."

Case where person has not been convicted

25. — (1) Section 84 is modified as follows.

(2) In subsection (1) after "evidence" insert "in relation to each offence".

(3) In subsection (5) after "discharge" insert "in relation to that offence".

(4) In subsections (6) and (7) after "section 87" insert "in relation to that offence".

Case where person has been convicted

26. — (1) Section 85 is modified as follows.

(2) In subsection (1) after "decide" insert "in relation to each offence".

(3) In subsection (2) after "section 87" insert "in relation to the offence".

(4) In subsection (4) after "section 87" insert "in relation to the offence".

(5) In subsection (6) after "section 86" insert "in relation to the offence".

(6) In subsection (7) after "discharge" insert "in relation to the offence".

Conviction in person's absence

27. — (1) Section 86 is modified as follows.

(2) In subsection (1) after "decide" insert "in relation to each offence".

(3) In subsection (5) after "discharge" insert "in relation to the offence".

(4) In subsection (6) after "section 87" insert "in relation to the offence".

(5) In subsection (7)(b) after "section 87" insert "in relation to the offence".

Human rights

28. — (1) Section 87 is modified as follows.

(2) In subsection (1) after "decide" insert "in relation to each offence".

(3) In subsection (2) after "discharge" insert "in relation to the offence".

(4) In subsection (3) after "extradited" insert "for the offence in question".

Case sent to the Secretary of State

29. — (1) Section 92 is modified as follows.

(2) In subsection (2)(a) after "High Court" insert "in relation to each relevant offence".

Secretary of State's consideration of case

30. — (1) Section 93 is modified as follows.

(2) In subsection (2) after "decide" insert "in relation to each offence".

(3) In subsection (3) after "discharge" insert "in relation to the offence".

(4) In subsection (4) —

(a) after "negative" insert "in relation to the offence in question" and

(b) after "requested" insert "for that offence".

Death penalty

31. — (1) Section 94 is modified as follows.

(2) In subsection (1) after the first "territory" insert "in relation to an offence".

(3) In subsection (2) after "assurance" insert "in relation to the relevant offence".

Speciality

32. — (1) Section 95 is modified as follows.

(2) In subsection (2) after "section 127" insert "in relation to all offences contained in the extradition request".

Information

33. — (1) Section 100 is modified as follows.

(2) In subsection (1)(b) after "High Court" insert "in relation to each relevant offence".

(3) In subsection (2) after "extradition" insert "in relation to the offence".

(4) In subsection (4) after "discharge" insert "in relation to an offence".

Appeal where case sent to Secretary of State
34. — (1) Section 103 is modified as follows.

(2) In subsection (1) after "relevant decision" insert "in relation to each offence.

(3) In subsection (2) after "section 127" insert "in relation to the offence".

(4) In subsection (6) after "discharge" insert "in relation to the offence".

(5) In subsection (7) after "discharge" insert "in relation to the offence".

Court's powers on appeal under section 103
35. — (1) Section 104 is modified as follows.

(2) In subsection (5) after "it must" insert "in relation to the relevant offence only".

Appeal against discharge at extradition hearing
36. — (1) Section 105 is modified as follows.

(2) In subsection (1) after "discharge" insert "in relation to an offence".

Court's powers on appeal under section 105
37. — (1) Section 106 is modified as follows.

(2) In subsection (6) after "it must" insert "in relation to the relevant offence only".

Detention pending conclusion of appeal under section 105
38. — (1) Section 107 is modified as follows.

(2) In subsection (1) after "section 105" insert "in relation to at least one offence".

(3) In subsection (4) after "times" insert "taking all offences contained in the extradition request together".

Appeal against extradition order
39. — (1) Section 108 is modified as follows.

(2) In subsection (1) after "extradition" insert "in relation to an offence".

(3) In subsection (2) after "extradition" insert "in relation to the offence".

Court's powers on appeal under section 108
40. — (1) Section 109 is modified as follows.

(2) In subsection (5) after "it must" insert "in relation to the relevant offence only".

Appeal against discharge by Secretary of State
41. — (1) Section 110 is modified as follows.

(2) In subsection (1) after "discharge" insert "in relation to an offence".

Court's powers on appeal under section 110
42. — (1) Section 111 is modified as follows.

(2) In subsection (5) after "it must" insert "in relation to the relevant offence only".

Detention pending conclusion of appeal under section 110
43. — (1) Section 112 is modified as follows.

(2) In subsection (2) for "the appeal" substitute "any appeal".

Appeal to House of Lords
44. — (1) Section 114 is modified as follows.

(2) In subsection (1) after "High Court" insert "in relation to each offence".

Powers of House of Lords on appeal under section 114
45. — (1) Section 115 is modified as follows.

(2) In subsection (3) after "must" insert "in relation to the relevant offence only".

(3) In subsection (5) after "must" insert "in relation to the relevant offence only".

(4) In subsection (7) after "must" insert "in relation to the relevant offence only".

Extradition where no appeal
46. — (1) Section 117 is modified as follows.

(2) In subsection (1)(a) after "extradition" insert "in relation to an offence".

(3) In subsection (2) after "order" insert "or if proceedings are continuing in relation to other offences contained in the extradition request, 10 days starting with the day on which the Secretary of State makes the final order in relation to the last of the offences in respect of which the same extradition request was made".

Extradition following appeal
47. — (1) Section 118 is modified as follows.
(2) In subsection (2)(b) after "discontinued" insert

", or
(c) if there is more than one appeal outstanding in relation to offences contained in the same extradition request, the day on which the last decision of the relevant court becomes final or on which the last proceedings on the appeal are discontinued."

Withdrawal of request before end of extradition hearing
48. — (1) Section 122 is modified as follows.
(2) In subsection (1) after "extradition" insert "in relation to an offence".
(3) In subsection (3) after "discharge" insert "in relation to the offence".

Withdrawal of request after case sent to Secretary of State
49. — (1) Section 123 is modified as follows.
(2) In subsection (1) after "extradition" insert "in relation to an offence".
(3) In subsection (3) after "discharge" insert "in relation to the offence".

Withdrawal of request while appeal to High Court pending
50. — (1) Section 124 is modified as follows.
(2) In subsection (1) after "extradition" insert "in relation to an offence".
(3) In subsection (3) after "must" insert "in relation to the offence".
(4) In subsection (4) after "appeal" insert "in relation to the offence".

Withdrawal of request while appeal to House of Lords pending
51. — (1) Section 125 is modified as follows.
(2) In subsection (1) after "extradition" insert "in relation to an offence".
(3) In subsection (3) after "must" insert "in relation to the offence".
(4) In subsection (4) after "appeal" insert "in relation to the offence".

Consent to extradition: general
52. — (1) Section 127 is modified as follows.
(2) In subsection (1) after "requested" insert "in relation to one or more offences contained within the extradition request".
(3) In subsection (2) after "extradition" insert "in relation to one or more offences contained within the extradition request".

Consent to extradition before case sent to Secretary of State
53. — (1) Section 128 is modified as follows.
(2) In subsection (2) after "so" insert "unless there are other offences contained within the extradition request in relation to which the person has not consented to his extradition".
(3) In subsection (3) after "91" insert "unless there are other offences contained within the extradition request in relation to which the person has not consented to his extradition".
(4) In subsection (5) after "extradition" insert "if he has consented to his extradition in relation to every offence contained within the extradition request".

National security
54. — (1) Section 208 is modified as follows.
(2) In subsection (2) for "an offence" substitute "more than one offence".
(3) In subsection (3)(a) for "the offence" substitute "any of the offences".
(4) In subsection (3)(b) for "the offence" substitute "the offence in question".
(5) In subsection (4) after "the offence" insert "in question".
(6) For subsection (6)(a) substitute —

" (a) direct that proceedings in relation to an offence contained in the Part 1 warrant are not to be proceeded with".

(7) In subsection (6)(b) after "the offence" insert "in question only".
(8) In subsection (7) after "discharge" insert "in relation to the offence".

B–005 **The Extradition Act 2003 (Designation of Part 1 Territories) Order 2003/3333**

Made: 18th December 2003

Coming into force: 1st January 2004

Whereas a draft of this Order has been approved by each House of Parliament;

Now, therefore, the Secretary of State, in exercise of the powers conferred on him by section 1 of the Extradition Act 2003, hereby makes the following Order:

1. This Order may be cited as the Extradition Act 2003 (Designation of Part 1 Territories) Order 2003 and shall come into force on 1st January 2004.

2. — (1) The territories set out in paragraph (2) are hereby designated for the purposes of Part 1 of the Extradition Act 2003.

(2) Those territories are —

Belgium,
Denmark,
Finland,
Ireland,
Portugal,
Spain,
Sweden.

Signatures

Caroline Flint
Parliamentary Under-Secretary of State
Home Office
18th December 2003

The Extradition Act 2003 (Designation of Part 2 Territories) Order 2003/3334

B–006

Made: 18th December 2003

Coming into force: 1st January 2004

Whereas a draft of this Order has been approved by each House of Parliament;

Now, therefore, the Secretary of State, in exercise of the powers conferred on him by sections 69(1), 71(4), 73(5), 74(11)(b), 84(7) and 86(7) of the Extradition Act 2003, hereby makes the following Order:

1.—(1) This Order may be cited as the Extradition Act 2003 (Designation of Part 2 Territories) Order 2003 and shall come into force on 1st January 2004.

(2) In this Order "the Act" means the Extradition Act 2003.

2.—(1) The territories set out in paragraph (2) are hereby designated for the purposes of Part 2 of the Act.

(2) Those territories are —

Albania,
Andorra,
Antigua and Barbuda,
Argentina,
Armenia,
Australia,
Austria,
Azerbaijan,
The Bahamas,
Bangladesh,
Barbados,
Belize,
Bolivia,
Bosnia and Herzegovina,
Botswana,
Brazil,
Brunei,
Bulgaria,
Canada,
Chile,
Colombia,
Cook Islands,
Croatia,
Cuba,
Cyprus,
Czech Republic,
Dominica,
Ecuador,
El Salvador,
Estonia,
Fiji,
France,
The Gambia,
Georgia,
Germany,
Ghana,
Greece,

Grenada,
Guatemala,
Guyana,
Hong Kong Special Administrative Region,
Haiti,
Hungary,
Iceland,
India,
Iraq,
Israel,
Italy,
Jamaica,
Kenya,
Kiribati,
Latvia,
Lesotho,
Liberia,
Liechtenstein,
Lithuania,
Luxembourg,
Macedonia, FYR,
Malawi,
Malaysia,
Maldives,
Malta,
Mauritius,
Mexico,
Moldova,
Monaco,
Nauru,
The Netherlands,
New Zealand,
Nicaragua,
Nigeria,
Norway,
Panama,
Papua New Guinea,
Paraguay,
Peru,
Poland,
Romania,
Russian Federation,
Saint Christopher and Nevis,
Saint Lucia,
Saint Vincent and the Grenadines,
San Marino,
Serbia and Montenegro,
Seychelles,
Sierra Leone,
Singapore,
Slovakia,
Slovenia,
Solomon Islands,

South Africa,
Sri Lanka,
Swaziland,
Switzerland,
Tanzania,
Thailand,
Tonga,
Trinidad and Tobago,
Turkey,
Tuvalu,
Uganda,
Ukraine,
Uruguay,
The United States of America,
Vanuatu,
Western Samoa,
Zambia,
Zimbabwe.

3.—(1) The territories set out in paragraph (2) are hereby designated for the purposes of section 71(4), 73(5), 84(7) and 86(7) of the Act.

(2) Those territories are —

Albania,
Andorra,
Armenia,
Australia,
Austria,
Azerbaijan,
Bulgaria,
Canada,
Croatia,
Cyprus,
Czech Republic,
Estonia,
France,
Georgia,
Germany,
Greece,
Hungary,
Iceland,
Israel,
Italy,
Latvia,
Liechtenstein,
Lithuania,
Luxembourg,
Macedonia, FYR,
Malta,
Moldova,
The Netherlands,
New Zealand,
Norway,
Poland,
Romania,

Russian Federation,
Serbia and Montenegro,
Slovakia,
Slovenia,
South Africa,
Switzerland,
Turkey,
Ukraine,
The United States of America.

4.—(1) The territories set out in paragraph (2) are hereby designated for the purposes of section 74(11)(b) with the relevant longer period for each territory following in brackets.

(2) Those territories and relevant periods are —

Bolivia (65 days)
Bosnia and Herzegovina (65 days)
Chile (90 days)
Cuba (65 days)
Haiti (65 days)
Iraq (65 days)
Liberia (95 days)
Monaco (65 days)
Nicaragua (65 days)
Panama (65 days)
Paraguay (65 days)
Peru (95 days)
San Marino (65 days)
Thailand (65 days)
The United States of America (65 days).

Signatures

Caroline Flint
Parliamentary Under-Secretary of State
Home Office
18th December 2003

The Extradition Act 2003 (Amendment to Designations) Order 2004/1898

B–007

Made: 20th July 2004
Coming into force: 27th July 2004

Whereas a draft of this Order has been approved by each House of Parliament:

Now, therefore, the Secretary of State, in exercise of the powers conferred upon him by sections 1, 69(1), 71(4), 73(5), 74(11)(b), 84(7) and 86(7) of the Extradition Act 2003 hereby makes the following Order:

1. This Order may be cited as the Extradition Act 2003 (Amendment to Designations) Order 2004 and shall come into force on the expiry of one week beginning with the day on which it was made.

2.—(1) Articles 2(2) and 3(2) of the Extradition Act 2003 (Designation of Part 2 Territories) Order 2003[2] are amended by omitting the territories listed in paragraph (3).

(2) Article 2(2) of the Extradition Act 2003 (Designation of Part 1 Territories) Order 2003[3] is amended by inserting (in the appropriate place) the territories listed in paragraph (3).

(3) Those territories are:

Austria;
Cyprus;
France;
Hungary;
Latvia;
Lithuania;
Luxembourg;
Malta;
The Netherlands;
Poland;
Slovenia.

3. The entry in respect of Chile in article 4(2) of the Extradition Act 2003 (Designation of Part 2 Territories) Order 2003 is amended by substituting the words "(95 days)" for " (90 days) ".

Signatures

Caroline Flint
Parliamentary Under-Secretary of State
Home Office
20th July 2004

Appendix C

OTHER INSTRUMENTS

European Convention on Mutual Assistance in Criminal Matters C–001

Strasbourg, 20.IV.1959

Preamble

The governments signatory hereto, being members of the Council of Europe,

Considering that the aim of the Council of Europe is to achieve greater unity among its members;

Believing that the adoption of common rules in the field of mutual assistance in criminal matters will contribute to the attainment of this aim;

Considering that such mutual assistance is related to the question of extradition, which has already formed the subject of a Convention signed on 13th December 1957,

Have agreed as follows:

CHAPTER 1 — GENERAL PROVISIONS

Article 1

[1. The Parties undertake promptly to afford each other, in accordance with the provisions of this Convention, the widest measure of mutual assistance in proceedings in respect of offences the punishment of which, at the time of the request for assistance, falls within the jurisdiction of the judicial authorities of the requesting Party.

2. This Convention does not apply to arrests, the enforcement of verdicts or offences under military law which are not offences under ordinary criminal law.

3. Mutual assistance may also be afforded in proceedings brought by the administrative authorities in respect of acts which are punishable under the national law of the requesting or the requested Party by virtue of being infringements of the rules of law, where the decision may give rise to proceedings before a court having jurisdiction in particular in criminal matters.

4. Mutual assistance shall not be refused solely on the grounds that it relates to acts for which a legal person may be held liable in the requesting Party.][1]

Article 2

Assistance may be refused:

if the request concerns an offence which the requested Party considers a political offence, an offence connected with a political offence, or a fiscal offence;

if the requested Party considers that execution of the request is likely to prejudice the sovereignty, security, *ordre public* or other essential interests of its country.

CHAPTER II — LETTERS ROGATORY

Article 3

The requested Party shall execute in the manner provided for by its law any letters rogatory relating to a criminal matter and addressed to it by the judicial authorities of the requesting Party for the purpose of procuring evidence or transmitting articles to be produced in evidence, records or documents.

If the requesting Party desires witnesses or experts to give evidence on oath, it shall expressly so request, and the requested Party shall comply with the request if the law of its country does not prohibit it.

[1] Substituted by the Second Additional Protocol 2001, Chap. I, art. 1.

The requested Party may transmit certified copies or certified photostat copies of records or documents requested, unless the requesting Party expressly requests the transmission of originals, in which case the requested Party shall make every effort to comply with the request.

Article 4

1. On the express request of the requesting Party the requested Party shall state the date and place of execution of the letters rogatory. Officials and interested persons may be present if the requested Party consents.

[2. Requests for the presence of such officials or interested persons should not be refused where that presence is likely to render the execution of the request for assistance more responsive to the needs of the requesting Party and, therefore, likely to avoid the need for supplementary requests for assistance.][2]

Article 5

Any Contracting Party may, by a declaration addressed to the Secretary General of the Council of Europe, when signing this Convention or depositing its instrument of ratification or accession, reserve the right to make the execution of letters rogatory for search or seizure of property dependent on one or more of the following conditions:

that the offence motivating the letters rogatory is punishable under both the law of the requesting Party and the law of the requested Party;

that the offence motivating the letters rogatory is an extraditable offence in the requested country;

that execution of the letters rogatory is consistent with the law of the requested Party.

Where a Contracting Party makes a declaration in accordance with paragraph 1 of this article, any other Party may apply reciprocity.

Article 6

The requested Party may delay the handing over of any property, records or documents requested, if it requires the said property, records or documents in connection with pending criminal proceedings.

Any property, as well as original records or documents, handed over in execution of letters rogatory shall be returned by the requesting Party to the requested Party as soon as possible unless the latter Party waives the return thereof.

CHAPTER III — SERVICE OF WRITS AND RECORDS OF JUDICAL VERDICTS — APPEARANCE OF WITNESSES, EXPERTS AND PROSECUTED PERSONS

Article 7

The requested Party shall effect service of writs and records of judicial verdicts which are transmitted to it for this purpose by the requesting Party.

[2] Inserted by the Second Additional Protocol 2001, Chap. I, art. 2.

Service may be effected by simple transmission of the writ or record to the person to be served. If the requesting Party expressly so requests, service shall be effected by the requested Party in the manner provided for the service of analogous documents under its own law or in a special manner consistent with such law.

Proof of service shall be given by means of a receipt dated and signed by the person served or by means of a declaration made by the requested Party that service has been effected and stating the form and date of such service. One or other of these documents shall be sent immediately to the requesting Party. The requested Party shall, if the requesting Party so requests, state whether service has been effected in accordance with the law of the requested Party. If service cannot be effected, the reasons shall be communicated immediately by the requested Party to the requesting Party.

Any Contracting Party may, by a declaration addressed to the Secretary General of the Council of Europe, when signing this Convention or depositing its instrument of ratification or accession, request that service of a summons on an accused person who is in its territory be transmitted to its authorities by a certain time before the date set for appearance. This time shall be specified in the aforesaid declaration and shall not exceed 50 days.

This time shall be taken into account when the date of appearance is being fixed and when the summons is being transmitted.

Article 8

A witness or expert who has failed to answer a summons to appear, service of which has been requested, shall not, even if the summons contains a notice of penalty, be subjected to any punishment or measure of restraint, unless subsequently he voluntarily enters the territory of the requesting Party and is there again duly summoned.

Article 9

The allowances, including subsistence, to be paid and the travelling expenses to be refunded to a witness or expert by the requesting Party shall be calculated as from his place of residence and shall be at rates at least equal to those provided for in the scales and rules in force in the country where the hearing is intended to take place.

Article 10

If the requesting Party considers the personal appearance of a witness or expert before its judicial authorities especially necessary, it shall so mention in its request for service of the summons and the requested Party shall invite the witness or expert to appear.

The requested Party shall inform the requesting Party of the reply of the witness or expert.

In the case provided for under paragraph 1 of this article the request or the summons shall indicate the approximate allowances payable and the travelling and subsistence expenses refundable.

If a specific request is made, the requested Party may grant the witness or expert an advance. The amount of the advance shall be endorsed on the summons and shall be refunded by the requesting Party.

Article 11

[1. A person in custody whose personal appearance for evidentiary purposes other than for standing trial is applied for by the requesting Party shall be temporarily transferred to its territory, provided that he or she shall be sent back within the period stipulated by the requested Party and subject to the provisions of Article 12 of this Convention, in so far as these are applicable.

Transfer may be refused if:

(a) the person in custody does not consent;
(b) his or her presence is necessary at criminal proceedings pending in the territory of the requested Party;
(c) transfer is liable to prolong his or her detention, or
(d) there are other overriding grounds for not transferring him or her to the territory of the requesting Party.

2. Subject to the provisions of Article 2 of this Convention, in a case coming within paragraph 1, transit of the person in custody through the territory of a third Party, shall be granted on application, accompanied by all necessary documents, addressed by the Ministry of Justice of the requesting Party to the Ministry of Justice of the Party through whose territory transit is requested. A Party may refuse to grant transit to its own nationals.

3. The transferred person shall remain in custody in the territory of the requesting Party and, where applicable, in the territory of the Party through which transit is requested, unless the Party from whom transfer is requested applies for his or her release.][3]

Article 12

A witness or expert, whatever his nationality, appearing on a summons before the judicial authorities of the requesting Party shall not be prosecuted or detained or subjected to any other restriction of his personal liberty in the territory of that Party in respect of acts or convictions anterior to his departure from the territory of the requested Party.

A person, whatever his nationality, summoned before the judicial authorities of the requesting Party to answer for acts forming the subject of proceedings against him, shall not be prosecuted or detained or subjected to any other restriction of his personal liberty for acts or convictions anterior to his departure from the territory of the requested Party and not specified in the summons.

The immunity provided for in this article shall cease when the witness or expert or prosecuted person, having had for a period of fifteen consecutive days from the date when his presence is no longer required by the judicial authorities an opportunity of leaving, has nevertheless remained in the territory, or having left it, has returned.

CHAPTER IV — JUDICAL RECORDS

Article 13

A requested Party shall communicate extracts from and information relating to judicial records, requested from it by the judicial authorities of a Contracting Party and needed in a

3 Substituted by the Second Additional Protocol 2001, Ch. I, art. 3.

criminal matter, to the same extent that these may be made available to its own judicial authorities in like case.

In any case other than that provided for in paragraph 1 of this article the request shall be complied with in accordance with the conditions provided for by the law, regulations or practice of the requested Party.

CHAPTER V — PROCEDURE

Article 14

Requests for mutual assistance shall indicate as follows:

the authority making the request,
the object of and the reason for the request,
where possible, the identity and the nationality of the person concerned, and
where necessary, the name and address of the person to be served.

Letters rogatory referred to in Articles 3, 4 and 5 shall, in addition, state the offence and contain a summary of the facts.

Article 15

[1. Requests for mutual assistance, as well as spontaneous information, shall be addressed in writing by the Ministry of Justice of the requesting Party to the Ministry of Justice of the requested Party and shall be returned through the same channels. However, they may be forwarded directly by the judicial authorities of the requesting Party to the judicial authorities of the requested Party and returned through the same channels.

2. Applications as referred to in Article 11 of this Convention and Article 13 of the Second Additional Protocol to this Convention shall in all cases be addressed by the Ministry of Justice of the requesting Party to the Ministry of Justice of the requested Party and shall be returned through the same channels.

3. Requests for mutual assistance concerning proceedings as mentioned in paragraph 3 of Article 1 of this Convention may also be forwarded directly by the administrative or judicial authorities of the requesting Party to the administrative or judicial authorities of the requested Party, as the case may be, and returned through the same channels.

4. Requests for mutual assistance made under Articles 18 and 19 of the Second Additional Protocol to this Convention may also be forwarded directly by the competent authorities of the requesting Party to the competent authorities of the requested Party.

5. Requests provided for in paragraph 1 of Article 13 of this Convention may be addressed directly by the judicial authorities concerned to the appropriate authorities of the requested Party, and the replies may be returned directly by those authorities. Requests provided for in paragraph 2 of Article 13 of this Convention shall be addressed by the Ministry of Justice of the requesting Party to the Ministry of Justice of the requested Party.

6. Requests for copies of convictions and measures as referred to in Article 4 of the Additional Protocol to the Convention may be made directly to the competent authorities. Any Contracting State may, at any time, by a declaration addressed to the Secretary General of the Council of Europe, define what authorities it will, for the purpose of this paragraph, deem competent authorities.

7. In urgent cases, where direct transmission is permitted under this Convention, it may take place through the International Criminal Police Organisation (Interpol).

8. Any Party may, at any time, by a declaration addressed to the Secretary General of the Council of Europe, reserve the right to make the execution of requests, or specified requests, for mutual assistance dependent on one or more of the following conditions:

(a) that a copy of the request be forwarded to the central authority designated in that declaration;
(b) that requests, except urgent requests, be forwarded to the central authority designated in that declaration;
(c) that, in case of direct transmission for reasons of urgency, a copy shall be transmitted at the same time to its Ministry of Justice;
(d) that some or all requests for assistance shall be sent to it through channels other than those provided for in this article.

9. Requests for mutual assistance and any other communications under this Convention or its Protocols may be forwarded through any electronic or other means of telecommunication provided that the requesting Party is prepared, upon request, to produce at any time a written record of it and the original. However, any Contracting State, may by a declaration addressed at any time to the Secretary General of the Council of Europe, establish the conditions under which it shall be willing to accept and execute requests received by electronic or other means of telecommunication.

10. The provisions of this article are without prejudice to those of bilateral agreements or arrangements in force between Parties which provide for the direct transmission of requests for assistance between their respective authorities.][4]

Article 16

Subject to paragraph 2 of this article, translations of requests and annexed documents shall not be required.

Each Contracting Party may, when signing or depositing its instrument of ratification or accession, by means of a declaration addressed to the Secretary General of the Council of Europe, reserve the right to stipulate that requests and annexed documents shall be addressed to it accompanied by a translation into its own language or into either of the official languages of the Council of Europe or into one of the latter languages, specified by it. The other Contracting Parties may apply reciprocity.

This article is without prejudice to the provisions concerning the translation of requests or annexed documents contained in the agreements or arrangements in force or to be made between two or more Contracting Parties.

Article 17

Evidence or documents transmitted pursuant to this Convention shall not require any form of authentication.

[4] Substituted by the Second Additional Protocol, Ch.I, art. 4.

Article 18

Where the authority which receives a request for mutual assistance has no jurisdiction to comply therewith, it shall, *ex officio*, transmit the request to the competent authority of its country and shall so inform the requesting Party through the direct channels, if the request has been addressed through such channels.

Article 19

Reasons shall be given for any refusal of mutual assistance.

Article 20

[1. Parties shall not claim from each other the refund of any costs resulting from the application of this Convention or its Protocols, except:

(a) costs incurred by the attendance of experts in the territory of the requested Party;
(b) costs incurred by the transfer of a person in custody carried out under Articles 13 or 14 of the Second Additional Protocol to this Convention, or Article 11 of this Convention;
(c) costs of a substantial or extraordinary nature.

2. However, the cost of establishing a video or telephone link, costs related to the servicing of a video or telephone link in the requested Party, the remuneration of interpreters provided by it and allowances to witnesses and their travelling expenses in the requested Party shall be refunded by the requesting Party to the requested Party, unless the Parties agree otherwise.

3. Parties shall consult with each other with a view to making arrangements for the payment of costs claimable under paragraph 1.c above.

4. The provisions of this article shall apply without prejudice to the provisions of Article 10, paragraph 3, of this Convention.][5]

CHAPTER VI — LAYING OF INFORMATION IN CONNECTION WITH PROCEEDINGS

Article 21

Information laid by one Contracting Party with a view to proceedings in the courts of another Party shall be transmitted between the Ministries of Justice concerned unless a Contracting Party avails itself of the option provided for in paragraph 6 of Article 15.

The requested Party shall notify the requesting Party of any action taken on such information and shall forward a copy of the record of any verdict pronounced.

5 Substituted by the Second Additional Protocol, Chap. I, art. 5.

The provisions of Article 16 shall apply to information laid under paragraph 1 of this article.

CHAPTER VII — EXCHANGE OF INFORMATION FROM JUDICAL RECORDS

Article 22

1. Each Contracting Party shall inform any other Party of all criminal convictions and subsequent measures in respect of nationals of the latter Party, entered in the judicial records. Ministries of Justice shall communicate such information to one another at least once a year. Where the person concerned is considered a national of two or more other Contracting Parties, the information shall be given to each of these Parties, unless the person is a national of the Party in the territory of which he was convicted.

[2. Furthermore, any Contracting Party which has supplied the above-mentioned information shall communicate to the Party concerned, on the latter's request in individual cases, a copy of the convictions and measures in question as well as any other information relevant thereto in order to enable it to consider whether they necessitate any measures at national level. This communication shall take place between the Ministries of Justice concerned.][6]

CHAPTER VIII — FINAL PROVISIONS

Article 23

Any Contracting Party may, when signing this Convention or when depositing its instrument of ratification or accession, make a reservation in respect of any provision or provisions of the Convention.

Any Contracting Party which has made a reservation shall withdraw it as soon as circumstances permit. Such withdrawal shall be made by notification to the Secretary General of the Council of Europe.

A Contracting Party which has made a reservation in respect of a provision of the Convention may not claim application of the said provision by another Party save in so far as it has itself accepted the provision.

Article 24

[Any State shall at the time of signature or when depositing their instrument of ratification, acceptance, approval or accession, by means of a declaration addressed to the Secretary General of the Council of Europe, define what authorities it will, for the purpose of the Convention, deem judicial authorities. It subsequently may, at any time and in the same manner, change the terms of its declaration.][7]

6 Inserted by the Additional Protocol, Chap. III, Art.4.

7 Substituted by the Second Additional Protocol 2001, Chap. I, art. 6.

Article 25

This Convention shall apply to the metropolitan territories of the Contracting Parties.

In respect of France, it shall also apply to Algeria and to the overseas Departments, and, in respect of Italy, it shall also apply to the territory of Somaliland under Italian administration.

The Federal Republic of Germany may extend the application of this Convention to the *Land* of Berlin by notice addressed to the Secretary General of the Council of Europe.

In respect of the Kingdom of the Netherlands, the Convention shall apply to its European territory. The Netherlands may extend the application of this Convention to the Netherlands Antilles, Surinam and Netherlands New Guinea by notice addressed to the Secretary General of the Council of Europe.

By direct arrangement between two or more Contracting Parties and subject to the conditions laid down in the arrangement, the application of this Convention may be extended to any territory, other than the territories mentioned in paragraphs 1, 2, 3 and 4 of this article, of one of these Parties, for the international relations of which any such Party is responsible.

Article 26

Subject to the provisions of Article 15, paragraph 7, and Article 16, paragraph 3, this Convention shall, in respect of those countries to which it applies, supersede the provisions of any treaties, conventions or bilateral agreements governing mutual assistance in criminal matters between any two Contracting Parties.

This Convention shall not affect obligations incurred under the terms of any other bilateral or multilateral international convention which contains or may contain clauses governing specific aspects of mutual assistance in a given field.

The Contracting Parties may conclude between themselves bilateral or multilateral agreements on mutual assistance in criminal matters only in order to supplement the provisions of this Convention or to facilitate the application of the principles contained therein.

Where, as between two or more Contracting Parties, mutual assistance in criminal matters is practised on the basis of uniform legislation or of a special system providing for the reciprocal application in their respective territories of measures of mutual assistance, these Parties shall, notwithstanding the provisions of this Convention, be free to regulate their mutual relations in this field exclusively in accordance with such legislation or system. Contracting Parties which, in accordance with this paragraph, exclude as between themselves the application of this Convention shall notify the Secretary General of the Council of Europe accordingly.

Article 27

This Convention shall be open to signature by the members of the Council of Europe. It shall be ratified. The instruments of ratification shall be deposited with the Secretary General of the Council.

The Convention shall come into force 90 days after the date of deposit of the third instrument of ratification.

As regards any signatory ratifying subsequently the Convention shall come into force 90 days after the date of the deposit of its instrument of ratification.

Article 28

The Committee of Ministers of the Council of Europe may invite any State not a member of the Council to accede to this Convention, provided that the resolution containing such invitation obtains the unanimous agreement of the members of the Council who have ratified the Convention.

Accession shall be by deposit with the Secretary General of the Council of an instrument of accession which shall take effect 90 days after the date of its deposit.

Article 29

Any Contracting Party may denounce this Convention in so far as it is concerned by giving notice to the Secretary General of the Council of Europe. Denunciation shall take effect six months after the date when the Secretary General of the Council received such notification.

Article 30

The Secretary General of the Council of Europe shall notify the members of the Council and the government of any State which has acceded to this Convention of; the names of the signatories and the deposit of any instrument of ratification or accession;

the date of entry into force of this Convention;

any notification received in accordance with the provisions of Article 5 — paragraph 1, Article 7 — paragraph 3, Article 15 — paragraph 6, Article 16 — paragraph 2, Article 24, Article 25 — paragraphs 3 and 4, Article 26 — paragraph 4;

any reservation made in accordance with Article 23, paragraph 1;

the withdrawal of any reservation in accordance with Article 23, paragraph 2;

any notification of denunciation received in accordance with the provisions of Article 29 and the date on which such denunciation will take effect.

In witness whereof the undersigned, being duly authorised thereto, have signed this Convention.

Done at Strasbourg, this 20th day of April 1959, in English and French, both texts being equally authoritative, in a single copy which shall remain deposited in the archives of the Council of Europe. The Secretary General of the Council of Europe shall transmit certified copies to the signatory and acceding governments.

C–002 # Additional Protocol to the European Convention on Mutual Assistance in Criminal Matters

STRASBOURG, 17.III.1978

PREAMBLE

The member States of the Council of Europe, signatory to this Protocol, Desirous of facilitating the application of the European Convention on Mutual Assistance in Criminal Matters opened for signature in Strasbourg on 20th April 1959 (hereinafter referred to as "the Convention") in the field of fiscal offences;

Considering it also desirable to supplement the Convention in certain other respects, Have agreed as follows:

CHAPTER 1

Article 1

The Contracting Parties shall not exercise the right provided for in Article 2.a of the Convention to refuse assistance solely on the ground that the request concerns an offence which the requested Party considers a fiscal offence.

Article 2

In the case where a Contracting Party has made the execution of letters rogatory for search or seizure of property dependent on the condition that the offence motivating the letters rogatory is punishable under both the law of the requesting Party and the law of the requested Party, this condition shall be fulfilled, as regards fiscal offences, if the offence is punishable under the law of the requesting Party and corresponds to an offence of the same nature under the law of the requested Party.

The request may not be refused on the ground that the law of the requested Party does not impose the same kind of tax or duty or does not contain a tax, duty, customs and exchange regulation of the same kind as the law of the requesting Party.

CHAPTER II

Article 3

The Convention shall also apply to:

the service of documents concerning the enforcement of a sentence, the recovery of a fine or the payment of costs of proceedings;

measures relating to the suspension of pronouncement of a sentence or of its enforcement, to conditional release, to deferment of the commencement of the enforcement of a sentence or to the interruption of such enforcement.

CHAPTER III

Article 4[8]

. . .

CHAPTER IV

Article 5

This Protocol shall be open to signature by the member States of the Council of Europe which have signed the Convention. It shall be subject to ratification, acceptance or approval. Instruments of ratification, acceptance or approval shall be deposited with the Secretary General of the Council of Europe.

The Protocol shall enter into force 90 days after the date of the deposit of the third instrument of ratification, acceptance or approval.

In respect of a signatory State ratifying, accepting or approving subsequently, the Protocol shall enter into force 90 days after the date of the deposit of its instrument of ratification, acceptance or approval.

A member State of the Council of Europe may not ratify, accept or approve this Protocol without having, simultaneously or previously, ratified the Convention.

Article 6

Any State which has acceded to the Convention may accede to this Protocol after the Protocol has entered into force.

Such accession shall be effected by depositing with the Secretary General of the Council of Europe an instrument of accession which shall take effect 90 days after the date of its deposit.

Article 7

Any State may, at the time of signature or when depositing its instrument of ratification, acceptance, approval or accession, specify the territory or territories to which this Protocol shall apply.

Any State may, when depositing its instrument of ratification, acceptance, approval or accession or at any later date, by declaration addressed to the Secretary General of the

[8] Amends the original convention — see above.

Council of Europe, extend this Protocol to any other territory or territories specified in the declaration and for whose international relations it is responsible or on whose behalf it is authorised to give undertakings.

Any declaration made in pursuance of the preceding paragraph may, in respect of any territory mentioned in such declaration, be withdrawn by means of a notification addressed to the Secretary General of the Council of Europe. Such withdrawal shall take effect six months after the date of receipt by the Secretary General of the Council of Europe of the notification.

Article 8

Reservations made by a Contracting Party to a provision of the Convention shall be applicable also to this Protocol, unless that Party otherwise declares at the time of signature or when depositing its instrument of ratification, acceptance, approval or accession. The same shall apply to the declarations made by virtue of Article 24 of the Convention.

Any State may, at the time of signature or when depositing its instrument of ratification, acceptance, approval or accession, declare that it reserves the right:

not to accept Chapter I, or to accept it only in respect of certain offences or certain categories of the offences referred to in Article I, or not to comply with letters rogatory for search or seizure of property in respect of fiscal offences;

not to accept Chapter II;

not to accept Chapter III.

Any Contracting Party may withdraw a declaration it has made in accordance with the foregoing paragraph by means of a declaration addressed to the Secretary General of the Council of Europe which shall become effective as from the date of its receipt.

A Contracting Party which has applied to this Protocol a reservation made in respect of a provision of the Convention or which has made a reservation in respect of a provision of this Protocol may not claim the application of that provision by another Contracting Party; it may, however, if its reservation is partial or conditional claim the application of that provision in so far as it has itself accepted it.

No other reservation may be made to the provisions of this Protocol.

Article 9

The provisions of this Protocol are without prejudice to more extensive regulations in bilateral or multilateral agreements concluded between Contracting Parties in application of Article 26, paragraph 3, of the Convention.

Article 10

The European Committee on Crime Problems of the Council of Europe shall be kept informed regarding the application of this Protocol and shall do whatever is needful to facilitate a friendly settlement of any difficulty which may arise out of its execution.

Article 11

Any Contracting Party may, in so far as it is concerned, denounce this Protocol by means of a notification addressed to the Secretary General of the Council of Europe.

Such denunciation shall take effect six months after the date of receipt by the Secretary General of such notification.

Denunciation of the Convention entails automatically denunciation of this Protocol.

Article 12

The Secretary General of the Council of Europe shall notify the member States of the Council and any State which has acceded to the Convention of:

any signature of this Protocol;

any deposit of an instrument of ratification, acceptance, approval or accession;

any date of entry into force of this Protocol in accordance with Articles 5 and 6;

any declaration received in pursuance of the provisions of paragraphs 2 and 3 of Article 7;

any declaration received in pursuance of the provisions of paragraph 1 of Article 8;

any reservation made in pursuance of the provisions of paragraph 2 of Article 8;

the withdrawal of any reservation carried out in pursuance of the provisions of paragraph 3 of Article 8;

any notification received in pursuance of the provisions of Article 11 and the date on which denunciation takes effect.

In witness whereof the undersigned, being duly authorised thereto, have signed this Protocol.

Done at Strasbourg, this 17th day of March 1978, in English and in French, both texts being equally authoritative, in a single copy which shall remain deposited in the archives of the Council of Europe. The Secretary General of the Council of Europe shall transmit certified copies to each of the signatory and acceding States.

C–003 **Scheme Relating to Mutual Assistance in Criminal Matters, 1986 (The Harare Scheme)**

(AS AMENDED IN 1999)

PURPOSE AND SCOPE

1. (1) The purpose of this Scheme is to increase the level and scope of assistance rendered between Commonwealth Governments in criminal matters. It augments, and in no way derogates from existing forms of co-operation, both formal and informal; nor does it preclude the development of enhanced arrangements in other fora.
(2) This Scheme provides for the giving of assistance by the competent authorities of one country (the requested country) in respect of criminal matters arising in another country (the requesting country).
(3) Assistance in criminal matters under this Scheme includes assistance in

(a) identifying and locating persons;
(b) serving documents;
(c) examining witnesses;
(d) search and seizure;
(e) obtaining evidence;
(f) facilitating the personal appearance of witnesses;
(g) effecting a temporary transfer of persons in custody to appear as a witness;
(h) obtaining production of judicial or other official records; and
(i) tracing, seizing and confiscating the proceeds or instrumentalities of crime.

MEANING OF COUNTRY

2. For the purposes of this Scheme, each of the following is a separate country, that is to say

(a) each sovereign and independent country within the Commonwealth together with any dependent territories which that country designates; and
(b) each country within the Commonwealth which, though not sovereign and independent, is not designated for the purposes of the preceding sub-paragraph.

CRIMINAL MATTER

3. (1) For the purposes of this Scheme, a criminal matter arises in a country if the Central Authority in that country certifies that a criminal or forfeiture proceedings have been instituted in a court exercising jurisdiction in that country or that there is a reasonable cause to believe that an offence has been committed in respect of which such criminal proceedings could be so instituted.
(2) "Offence", in the case of a federal country or country having more than one legal system, includes an offence under the law of the country or any part thereof.
(3) "Forfeiture proceedings" means proceedings, whether civil or criminal, for an order

(a) restraining dealings with any property in respect of which there is reasonable cause to believe that it has been

(i) derived or obtained, whether directly or indirectly, from; or
(ii) used in, or in connection with, the commission of an offence;

(b) confiscating any property derived or obtained as provided in paragraph (a)(i) or used as provided in paragraph (a)(ii); or
(c) imposing a pecuniary penalty calculated by reference to the value of any property derived or obtained as provided in paragraph (a)(i) or used as provide in paragraph (a)(ii).

CENTRAL AUTHORITIES

4. Each country shall designate a Central Authority to transmit and receive requests for assistance under this Scheme.

ACTION IN THE REQUESTING COUNTRY

5. (1) A request for assistance under this Scheme may be initiated by any law enforcement agency or public prosecution of judicial authority competent to under the law of the requesting country.
(2) The Central Authority of the requesting country shall, if it is satisfied that the request can be properly made under this Scheme, transmit the request to the Central Authority of the requested country and shall ensure that the request contains all the information required by the provisions of this Scheme.
(3) the Central Authority of the requesting country shall provide as far as practicable additional information sought by the Central Authority of the requested country.

ACTION IN THE REQUESTED COUNTRY

6. (1) Subject to the provisions of this Scheme, the requested country shall grant the assistance requested as expeditiously as practicable.
(2) The Central Authority of the requested country shall, subject to the following provisions of this paragraph, take the necessary steps to ensure that the competent authorities of that country comply with the request.
(3) If the Central Authority of the requested country considers

(a) that the request does not comply with the provisions of this Scheme, or
(b) that in accordance with the provisions of this Scheme the request for assistance is to be refused in whole or in part, or
(c) that the request cannot be complied with, in whole or in part, or
(d) that there are circumstances which are likely to cause a significant delay in complying with the request,

it shall promptly inform the Central Authority of the requesting country, giving reasons.

REFUSAL OF ATTENDANCE

7. (1) The requested country may refuse to comply in whole or in part with a request for assistance under this Scheme if the criminal matter appears to the Central Authority of that country to concern

(a) conduct which would not constitute an offence under the law of that country; or
(b) an offence or proceedings of a political character; or
(c) conduct which in the requesting country is an offence only under military law or a law relating to military obligations; or
(d) conduct in relation to which the person accused or suspected of having committed an offence has been acquitted or convicted by a court in the requested country.

(2) The requested country may refuse to comply in whole or in part with a request for assistance under this Scheme

(a) to the extent that it appears to the Central Authority of that country that compliance would be contrary to the Constitution of that country, or would prejudice the security, international relations or other essential public interests of that country; or
(b) where there are substantial grounds leading the Central Authority of that country to believe that compliance would facilitate the prosecution or punishment of any person on account of his race, religion, nationality or political opinions or would cause prejudice for any person affected by the request.

(3) The requested country may refuse to comply in whole or in part with a request for assistance to the extent that the steps required to be taken in order to comply with the request cannot under the law of that country be taken in respect of criminal matters arising in that country.

(4) An offence shall not be an offence of a political character for the purposes of this paragraph if it is an offence within the scope of any international convention to which both the requesting and the requested countries are parties and which imposes on the parties thereto an obligation either to extradite or prosecute a person accused of the commission of the offence.

MEASURES OF COMPULSION

8. (1) The competent authorities of the requested country shall in complying with a request under this Scheme use only such measures of compulsion as are available under the law if that country in respect of criminal matters arising in that country.

(2) Where under the law of the requested country measures of compulsion cannot be applied to any person to take the steps necessary to secure compliance with a request under this Scheme but the person concerned is willing to act voluntarily in compliance or partial compliance with the terms of the request, the competent authorities of the requested country shall make available the necessary facilities.

SCHEME NOT TO COVER ARREST OR EXTRADITION

9. Nothing in this Scheme is to be construed as authorising the extradition, or the arrest or detention with a view to extradition, of any person.

CONFIDENTIALITY

10. The Central Authorities and the competent authorities of the requesting and the requested countries shall use their best efforts to keep confidential a request and its contents and the information and materials supplied in compliance with a request except for disclosure in criminal proceedings and where otherwise authorised by the Central Authority of the other country.

LIMITATION OF USE OF INFORMATION OR EVIDENCE

11. The requesting country shall not use any information or evidence obtained in response to a request for assistance under this Scheme in connection with any matter other than the criminal matter specified in the request without the prior consent of the Central Authority of the requested country.

EXPENSES OF COMPLIANCE

12. (1) Except as provided in the following provisions of this paragraph, compliance with a request under this Scheme shall not give rise to any claim against the requesting country for expenses incurred by the Central Authority or any other competent authorities of the requested country.

(2) The requesting country shall be responsible for the travel and incidental expenses of witnesses travelling to the requesting country, including those of accompanying officials, for fees of experts, and for the costs of any translation required by the requesting country.

(3) If in the opinion of the requested country, the expenses required in order to comply with the request are of an extraordinary nature, the Central Authority of the requested country shall consult with the Central Authority of the requesting country as to the terms and conditions under which the compliance with the request may continue, and in the absence of agreement the requested country may refuse to comply further with the request.

CONTENTS REQUEST FOR ASSISTANCE

13. (1) A request under the Scheme shall:

- (a) specify the nature of the assistance requested:
- (b) contain the information appropriate to the assistance sought as specified in the following provisions of this Scheme;
- (c) indicate any time-limit within which compliance with the request is desired, stating reasons;
- (d) contain the following information:
  - (i) the identity of the agency or authority initiating the request;
  - (ii) the nature of the criminal matter; and
  - (iii) whether or not criminal proceedings have been instituted.

(e) where criminal proceedings have been instituted, contain the following information:

(i) the court exercising jurisdiction in the proceedings;
(ii) the identity of the accused person;
(iii) the offences of which he stands accused, and a summary of the facts;
(iv) the stage reached in the proceedings; and
(v) any date fixed for further stages in the proceedings.

(f) where criminal proceedings have not been instituted, state the offence which the Central Authority of the requesting country has reasonable cause to believe to have been committed, with a summary of known facts.

(2) A request shall normally be in writing, and if made orally in the case of urgency, shall be confirmed in writing forthwith.

Identifying and locating persons

14. (1) A request under this Scheme may seek assistance in identifying or locating persons believed to be within the requested country.
(2) The request shall indicate the purpose for which the information is requested and shall contain such information as is available to the Central Authority of the requesting country as to the whereabouts of the person concerned and such other information as it possesses as may facilitate the identification of that person.

Service of documents

15. (1) A request under this Scheme may seek assistance in the service of documents relevant to a criminal matter arising in the requesting country.
(2) The request shall be accompanied by the documents to be served and, where those documents relate to attendance in the requesting country, such notice as the Central Authority of that country is reasonably able to provide of outstanding warrants or other judicial orders in criminal matters against the person to be served.
(3) The Central Authority of the requested country shall endeavour to have the documents served:

(a) by any particular method stated in the request unless such method is incompatible with the law of that country; or
(b) by any method prescribed by the law of that country for the service of documents in criminal proceedings.

(4) The requested country shall transmit to the Central Authority of the requesting country a certificate as to the service of the documents or, if they have not been served, as to the reasons which have prevented service.
(5) A person served in compliance with a request with a summons to appear as a witness in the requesting country and who fails to comply with the summons shall not by reason thereof be liable to any penalty or measure of compulsion in with the requesting or the requested country notwithstanding any contrary statement in the summons.

EXAMINATION OF WITNESSES

16. (1) A request under this Scheme may seek assistance in the examination of witnesses in the requested country.
(2) The request shall specify, as appropriate and so far as the circumstances permit:

(a) the names and addresses or the official designations of the witnesses to be examined;
(b) the questions to be put to the witnesses or the subject matter about which they are to be examined;
(c) whether it is desired that the witness be examined orally or in writing;
(d) whether it is desired that the oath be administered to the witnesses (or, as the law of the requested country allows, that they be required to make their solemn affirmation);
(e) any provisions of the law of the requesting country as to privilege or exemption from giving evidence which appear especially relevant to the request; and
(f) any special requirements of the law of the requesting country as to the manner of taking evidence relevant to its admissibility in that country.

(3) The request may ask that, so far as the law of the requested country permits, the accused person or his legal representative may attend the examination of the witness and ask questions of the witness.

SEARCH AND SEIZURE

17. (1) A request under this Scheme may seek assistance in the search for, and seizure of property in the requested country.
(2) The request shall specify the property to be searched for and seized and shall contain, as far as reasonably practicable, all information available to the Central Authority of the requesting country which may be required to be adduced in an application under the law of the requested country for any necessary warrant or authorisation to effect the search and seizure.
(3) The requested country shall provide such certification as may be required by the requesting country concerning the result of any search, the place and circumstances of seizure, and subsequent custody of the property seized.

OTHER ASSISTANCE IN OBTAINING EVIDENCE

18. (1) A request under this Scheme may seek other assistance in obtaining evidence.
(2) The request shall specify, as appropriate and so far as the circumstance of the case permit:

(a) the documents, records or property to be inspected, preserved, photographed, copied or transmitted;
(b) the samples of any property to be taken, examined or transmitted; and
(c) the site to be viewed or photographed.

Privilege

19. (1) No person shall be compelled in response to a request under this Scheme to give any evidence in the requested country which he can not be compelled to give:

    (a) in criminal proceedings in that country; or
    (b) in criminal proceedings in the requested country.

    (2) For the purposes of this paragraph any reference to giving evidence includes references to answering any question and to producing any document.

Production of judicial or official records

20. (1) A request under this Scheme may seek the production of judicial or official records relevant to a criminal matter arising in the requesting country.
    (2) For the purposes of this paragraph "judicial records" means judgements, orders and decisions of courts and other documents held by government departments or agencies or prosecution authorities.
    (3) The requested country shall provide copies of judicial or official records not publicly available, to the same extent and under the same conditions as apply to the provision of such records to its own law enforcement agencies or prosecution or judicial authorities.

Transmission and return of material

21. (1) Where compliance with a request under this Scheme would involve the transmission to the requesting country of any document, record or property, the requested country

    (a) may postpone the transmission of the material if it is required in connection with proceedings in that country, and in such a case shall provide certified copies of a document or record pending transmission of the original;
    (b) may require the requesting country to agree to terms and conditions to protect third party interests in the material to be transmitted and may refuse to effect such transmission pending such agreement.

    (2) Where any document, record or property is transmitted to the requesting country in compliance with a request under this Scheme, it shall be returned to the requested country when it is no longer required in connection with the criminal matter specified in the request unless that country has indicated that its return is not desired.
    (3) The requested country shall authenticate material that is to be transmitted by that country.

Authentication

22. A document or other material transmitted for the purposes of or in response to a request under this Scheme shall be deemed to be duly authenticated if it:

(a) purports to be signed or certified by a judge or Magistrate, or to bear the stamp or seal of a Minister, government department or Central Authority; or
(b) is verified by the oath of a witness or of a public officer of the Commonwealth country from which the document or material emanates.

PERSONAL APPERANCE OF WITNESSES IN THE REQUESTING COUNTRY

23. (1) A request under this Scheme may seek assistance in facilitating the personal appearance of the witnesses before a court exercising jurisdiction in the requesting country.
(2) The request shall specify

(a) the subject matter upon which it is desired to examine the witnesses;
(b) the reasons for which the personal appearance of the witnesses is required; and
(c) details of the travelling, subsistence and other expenses payable by the requesting country in respect of the personal appearance of the witnesses.

(3) The competent authorities of the requested country shall invite the persons whose appearance as witnesses in the requesting country is desired; and

(a) ask whether they agree to appear;
(b) inform the Central Authority of the requesting country of their answer; and
(c) if they are willing to appear, make appropriate arrangements to facilitate the personal appearance of the witnesses.

(4) A person whose appearance as a witness is the subject of a request and who does not agree to appear shall not by reason thereof be liable to any penalty or measure of compulsion in either the requesting or requested country.

PERSONAL APPEARANCE OF PERSONS IN CUSTODY

24. (1) A request under this Scheme may seek the temporary transfer of persons in custody in the requested country to appear as witnesses before a court exercising jurisdiction in the requesting country.
(2) The request shall specify:

(a) the subject matter upon which it is desired to examine the witnesses;
(b) the reasons for which the personal appearance of the witnesses is desired.

(3) The requested country shall refuse to comply with a request for the transfer of persons in custody if the persons concerned do not consent to the transfer.
(4) The requested country may refuse to comply with a request for the transfer of persons in custody and shall be under no obligation to inform the requesting country of the reasons for such refusal.
(5) A person in custody whose transfer is the subject of a request and who does not consent to the transfer shall not by reason thereof be liable to any penalty or measure of compulsion in either the requesting or requested country.
(6) Where persons in custody are transferred, the requested country shall notify the requesting country of:

(a) the dates upon which the persons are due under the law of the requested country to be released from custody; and
(b) the dates by which the requested country requires the return of the persons and shall notify any variations in such dates.

(7) The requesting country shall keep the persons transferred in custody, and shall return the persons to the requested country when their presence as witnesses in the requesting country is no longer required, and in any case by the earlier of the dates notified under sub-paragraph (6).

(8) The obligation to return the persons transferred shall subsist notwithstanding the fact that they are nationals of the requesting country.

(9) The period during which the persons transferred are in custody in the requesting country shall be deemed to be in service in the requested country of an equivalent period of custody in that country for all purposes.

(10) Nothing in this paragraph shall preclude the release in the requesting country without return to the requested country of any person transferred where the two countries and the person concerned agreed.

IMMUNITY OF PERSONS APPEARING

25. (1) Subject to the provisions of paragraph 24, witnesses appearing in the requesting country in response to a request made under paragraph 23 or persons transferred to that country in response to a request made under paragraph 24 shall be immune in that country from prosecution, detention or any other restriction of personal liberty in respect of criminal acts, omissions or convictions before the time of their departure from the requested country.

(2) The immunity provided for in that paragraph shall cease:

(a) in the case of witnesses appearing in response to a request under paragraph 23, when the witnesses having had, for a period of 15 consecutive days from the dates when they were notified by the competent authority of the requesting country that their presence was no longer required by the court exercising jurisdiction in the criminal matter, an opportunity of leaving have nevertheless remained in the requesting country, or having left that country have returned to it;

(b) in the case of persons transferred in response to a request under paragraph 24 and remaining in custody when they have been returned to the requested country.

TRACING THE PROCEEDS OR INSTRUMENTALITIES OF CRIME

26. (1) A request under this Scheme may seek assistance in identifying, locating and assessing the value of property believed to have been derived or obtained, directly or indirectly, from, or to have been used in, or in connection with, the commission of an offence and believed to be within the requested country.

(2) The request shall contain such information as is available to the Central Authority of the requesting country as to the nature and location of the property and as to any person in whose possession or control the property is believed to be.

SEIZING AND CONFISCATING THE PROCEEDS AND INSTRUMENTALITIES OF CRIME

27. (1) A request under this Scheme may seek assistance in securing:

(a) the making in the requested country of an order relating to the proceeds of instrumentalities of crime; or

(b) the recognition or enforcement in that country of such an order made in the requesting country.

(2) For the purpose of this paragraph, "an order relating to the proceeds of instrumentalities of crime" means:

(a) an order restraining the dealings with any property in respect of which there is reasonable cause to believe that is has been derived or obtained, directly or indirectly, from, or used in, or in connection with, the commission of an offence;
(b) an order confiscating property derived or obtained, directly or indirectly, from, or used in or in connection with, the commission of an offence; and
(c) an order imposing a pecuniary penalty calculated by reference to the value of any property so derived, obtained or used.

(3) Where the requested country cannot enforce an order made in the requesting country, the requesting country may request the making of any similar order available under the law of the requested country.
(4) The request shall be accompanied by a copy of the order made in the requesting country and shall contain as far as reasonably practicable, all information available to the Central Authority of the requesting country which may be required in connection with the procedures to be followed in the requested country.
(5) The law of the requested country shall apply to determine the circumstances and manner in which an order may be made, recognised or enforced in response to the request.
(6) The law of the requested country may provide for the protection of the interests of bona fide third parties in property restrained or confiscated as a result of a request made pursuant to this Scheme, by providing:

(a) for the giving of notice of the making of orders restraining or confiscating property; and
(b) that any third party claiming an interest in property so restrained or confiscated may make an application to a court of competent jurisdiction for an order

(i) declaring that the interest of the applicant in the property or part thereof was acquired bona fide; and
(ii) restoring such property or the value of the interest therein to the applicant.

DISPOSAL OR RELEASE OF PROPERTY

28. (1) The law of the requested country shall apply to determine the disposal of any property

(a) forfeited; or
(b) obtained as a result of the enforcement of a pecuniary penalty order as a result of a request under this Scheme.

(2) The law of the requested country shall apply to determine the circumstances in which property made the subject of interim seizure as a result of a request under this Scheme may be released from the effects of such seizure.
(3) The law of the requested country may provide that the proceeds of an order of the type referred to in sub-paragraphs 27(2)(b) and (c), or the value thereof, may be

(a) returned to the requesting country; or
(b) shared with the requesting country in such proportion as the requested country in its discretion deems appropriate in all the circumstances.

CONSULTATION

29. The Central Authorities of the requested and requesting countries shall consult promptly, at the request of either, concerning matters arising under this Scheme.

OTHER ASSISTANCE

30. After consultation between the requesting and the requested countries assistance not within the scope of this Scheme may be given in respect of a criminal matter on such terms and conditions as may be agreed by those countries.

NOTIFICATION OF DESIGNATIONS

31. Designations of dependent territories under paragraph 2 and of Central Authorities under paragraph 4 shall be notified to the Commonwealth Secretary-General.

(Acts adopted pursuant to Title VI of the Treaty on European Union)

COUNCIL ACT OF 29 MAY 2000

ESTABLISHING IN ACCORDANCE WITH ARTICLE 34 OF THE TREATY ON EUROPEAN UNION

The Convention on Mutual Assistance in Criminal Matters between the Member States of the European Union C–004

(2000/C 197/01)

THE COUNCIL OF THE EUROPEAN UNION,

Having regard to the Treaty on European Union, and in particular Articles 31(a) and 34(2)(d) thereof,

Having regard to the initiative of the Member States,

Having regard to the opinion of the European Parliament[1],

Whereas:

(1) For the purposes of achieving the objectives of the Union the rules on mutual assitance in criminal matters between the Member States of the European Union should be improved and a Convention, as set out in the Annex hereto, should be established to that end.

(2) Some of the provisions of the Convention fall within the scope of Article 1 of Council Decision 1999/437/EC of 17 May 1999 on certain arrangements for the application of the Agreement concluded by the Council of the European Union and the Republic of Iceland and the Kingdom of Norway concerning the association of those two States with the implementation, application and development of the Schengen *acquis*[2].

(3) This is the case with Articles 3, 5, 6, 7, 12 and 23, and, to the extent relevant to Article 12, with Articles 15 and 16, and, to the extent relevant to the Articles referred to, with Article 1.

(4) The procedures set out in the Agreement concluded by the Council of the European Union with the Republic of Iceland and the Kingdom of Norway concerning the latters' association with the implementation, application and development of the Schengen *acquis*[3] have been observed in respect of these provisions.

(5) When the adoption of this Act is notified to the Republic of Iceland and the Kingdom of Norway in accordance with Article 8(2)(a) of the aforementioned Agreement, those two States will be informed in particular of the contents of Article 29 on entry into force for Iceland and Norway and will be invited to submit, at the time they inform the Council and the Commission of the fulfilment of their constitutional requirements, the relevant statements under Article 24 of the Convention.

HAS DECIDED that the Convention, the text of which is given in the Annex and which has been signed today by the Representatives of the Governments of the Member States of the Union, is hereby established,

[1] Opinion delivered on 17 February 2000 (not yet published in the Official Journal).

[2] OJ L 176, 10.7.1999, p. 31.

[3] OJ L 176, 10.7.1999, p. 36.

RECOMMENDS that it be adopted by the Member States in accordance with their respective constitutional requirements,

Done at Brussels, 29 May 2000.

INVITES the Member States to begin the procedures applicable for that purpose before 1 January 2001.

For the Council
The President
A. COSTA

ANNEX

CONVENTION established by the Council in accordance with Article 34 of the Treaty on European Union, on Mutual Assistance in Criminal Matters between the Member States of the European Union

THE HIGH CONTRACTING PARTIES to this Convention, Member States of the European Union,

REFERRING to the Council Act establishing the Convention on Mutual Assistance in Criminal Matters between the Member States of the European Union,

WISHING to improve judicial cooperation in criminal matters between the Member States of the Union, without prejudice to the rules protecting individual freedom,

POINTING OUT the Member States' common interest in ensuring that mutual assistance between the Member States is provided in a fast and efficient manner compatible with the basic principles of their national law, and in compliance with the individual rights and principles of the European Convention for the Protection of Human Rights and Fundamental Freedoms, signed in Rome on 4 November 1950,

EXPRESSING their confidence in the structure and functioning of their legal systems and in the ability of all Member States to guarantee a fair trial,

RESOLVED to supplement the European Convention on Mutual Assistance in Criminal Matters of 20 April 1959 and other Conventions in force in this area, by a Convention of the European Union,

RECOGNISING that the provisions of those Conventions remain applicable for all matters not covered by this Convention,

CONSIDERING that the Member States attach importance to strengthening judicial cooperation, while continuing to apply the principle of proportionality,

RECALLING that this Convention regulates mutual assistance in criminal matters, based on the principles of the Convention of 20 April 1959,

WHEREAS, however, Article 20 of this Convention covers certain specific situations concerning interception of telecommunications, without having any implications with regard to other such situations outside the scope of the Convention,

WHEREAS the general principles of international law apply in situations which are not covered by this Convention,

RECOGNISING that this Convention does not affect the exercise of the responsibilities incumbent upon Member States with regard do the maintenance of law and order and the safeguarding of internal security, and that it is a matter for each Member States to determine, in accordance with Article 33 of the Treaty on European Union, under which conditions it will maintain law and order and safeguard internal security,

HAVE AGREED ON THE FOLLOWING PROVISIONS:

OTHER INSTRUMENTS

TITLE I

GENERAL PROVISIONS

Article 1

Relationship to other conventions on mutual assistance

1. The purpose of this Convention is to supplement the provisions and facilitate the application between the Member States of the European Union, of:

(a) the European Convention on Mutual Assistance in Criminal Matters of 20 April 1959, hereinafter referred to as the 'European Mutual Assistance Convention';
(b) the Additional Protocol of 17 March 1978 to the European Mutual Assistance Convention;
(c) the provisions on mutual assistance in criminal matters of the Convention of 19 June 1990 implementing the Schengen Agreement of 14 June 1985 on the gradual abolition of checks at common borders (hereinafter referred to as the 'Schengen Implementation Convention') which are not repealed pursuant to Article 2(2);
(d) Chapter 2 of the Treaty on Extradition and Mutual Assistance in Criminal Matters between the Kingdom of Belgium, the Grand Duchy of Luxembourg and the Kingdom of the Netherlands of 27 June 1962, as amended by the Protocol of 11 May 1974, (hereinafter referred to as the 'Benelux Treaty'), in the context of relations between the Member States of the Benelux Economic Union.

2. This Convention shall not affect the application of more favourable provisions in bilateral or multilateral agreements between Member States or, as provided for in Article 26(4) of the European Mutual Assistance Convention, arrangements in the field of mutual assistance in criminal matters agreed on the basis of uniform legislation or of a special system providing for the reciprocal application of measures of mutual assistance in their respective territories.

Article 2

Provisions relating to the Schengen acquis

1. The provisions of Articles 3, 5, 6, 7, 12 and 23 and, to the extent relevant to Article 12, of Articles 15 and 16, to the extent relevant to the Articles referred to, of Article 1 constitute measures amending or building upon the provisions referred to in Annex A to the Agreement concluded by the Council of the European Union and the Republic of Iceland and the Kingdom of Norway concerning the latters' association with the implementation, application and development of the Schengen *acquis*[1].

2. The provisions of Articles 49(a), 52, 53 and 73 of the Schengen Implementation Convention are hereby repealed.

[1] OJ L 176, 10.7.1999, p. 36.

Article 3

Proceedings in connection with which mutual assistance is also to be afforded

1. Mutual assistance shall also be afforded in proceedings brought by the administrative authorities in respect of acts which are punishable under the national law of the requesting or the requested Member State, or both, by virtue of being infringements of the rules of law, and where the decision may give rise to proceedings before a court having jurisdiction in particular in criminal matters.

2. Mutual assistance shall also be afforded in connection with criminal proceedings and proceedings as referred to in paragraph 1 which relate to offences or infringements for which a legal person may be held liable in the requesting Member State.

Article 4

Formalities and procedures in the execution of requests for mutual assistance

1. Where mutual assistance is afforded, the requested Member State shall comply with the formalities and procedures expressly indicated by the requesting Member State, unless otherwise provided in this Convention and provided that such formalities and procedures are not contrary to the fundamental principles of law in the requested Member State.

2. The requested Member State shall execute the request for assistance as soon as possible, taking as full account as possible of the procedural deadlines and other deadlines indicated by the requesting Member State. The requesting Member State shall explain the reasons for the deadline.

3. If the request cannot, or cannot fully, be executed in accordance with the requirements set by the requesting Member State, the authorities of the requested Member State shall promptly inform the authorities of the requesting Member State and indicate the conditions under which it might be possible to execute the request. The authorities of the requesting and the requested Member State may subsequently agree on further action to be taken concerning the request, where necessary by making such action subject to the fulfilment of those conditions.

4. If it is foreseeable that the deadline set by the requesting Member State for executing its request cannot be met, and if the reasons referred to in paragraph 2, second sentence, indicate explicitly that any delay will lead to substantial impairment of the proceedings being conducted in the requesting Member State, the authorities of the requested Member State shall promptly indicate the estimated time needed for execution of the request. The authorities of the requesting Member State shall promptly indicate whether the request is to be upheld nonetheless. The authorities of the requesting and requested Member States may subsequently agree on further action to be taken concerning the request.

Article 5

Sending and service of procedural documents

1. Each Member State shall send procedural documents intended for persons who are in the territory of another Member State to them directly by post.

2. Procedural documents may be sent via the competent authorities of the requested Member State only if:

(a) the address of the person for whom the document is intended is unknown or uncertain; or
(b) the relevant procedural law of the requesting Member State requires proof of service of the document on the addressee, other than proof that can be obtained by post; or
(c) it has not been possible to serve the document by post; or
(d) the requesting Member State has justified reasons for considering that dispatch by post will be ineffective or is inappropriate.

3. Where there is reason to believe that the addressee does not understand the language in which the document is drawn up, the document, or at least the important passages thereof, must be translated into (one of) the language(s) of the Member State in the territory of which the addressee is staying. If the authority by which the procedural document was issued knows that the addressee understands only some other language, the document, or at least the important passages thereof, must be translated into that other language.

4. All procedural documents shall be accompanied by a report stating that the addressee may obtain information from the authority by which the document was issued or from other authorities in that Member State regarding his or her rights and obligations concerning the document. Paragraph 3 shall also apply to that report.

5. This Article shall not affect the application of Articles 8, 9 and 12 of the European Mutual Assistance Convention and Articles 32, 34 and 35 of the Benelux Treaty.

Article 6

Transmission of requests for mutual assistance

1. Requests for mutual assistance and spontaneous exchanges of information referred to in Article 7 shall be made in writing, or by any means capable of producing a written record under conditions allowing the receiving Member State to establish authenticity. Such requests shall be made directly between judicial authorities with territorial competence for initiating and executing them, and shall be returned through the same channels unless otherwise specified in this Article.

Any information laid by a Member State with a view to proceedings before the courts of another Member State within the meaning of Article 21 of the European Mutual Assistance Convention and Article 42 of the Benelux Treaty may be the subject of direct communications between the competent judicial authorities.

2. Paragraph 1 shall not prejudice the possibility of requests being sent or returned in specific cases:

(a) between a central authority of a Member State and a central authority of another Member State; or
(b) between a judicial authority of one Member State and a central authority of another Member State.

3. Notwithstanding paragraph 1, the United Kingdom and Ireland, respectively, may, when giving the notification provided for in Article 27(2), declare that requests and communications to it, as specified in the declaration, must be sent via its central authority. These

Member States may at any time by a further declaration limit the scope of such a declaration for the purpose of giving greater effect to paragraph 1. They shall do so when the provisions on mutual assistance of the Schengen Implementation Convention are put into effect for them.

Any Member State may apply the principle of reciprocity in relation to the declarations referred to above.

4. Any request for mutual assistance may, in case of urgency, be made via the International Criminal Police Organisation (Interpol) or any body competent under provisions adopted pursuant to the Treaty on European Union.

5. Where, in respect of requests pursuant to Articles 12, 13 or 14, the competent authority is a judicial authority or a central authority in one Member State and a police or customs authority in the other Member State, requests may be made and answered directly between these authorities. Paragraph 4 shall apply to these contacts.

6. Where, in respect of requests for mutual assistance in relation to proceedings as envisaged in Article 3(1), the competent authority is a judicial authority or a central authority in one Member State and an administrative authority in the other Member State, requests may be made and answered directly between these authorities.

7. Any Member State may declare, when giving the notification provided for in Article 27(2), that it is not bound by the first sentence of paragraph 5 or by paragraph 6 of this Article, or both or that it will apply those provisions only under certain conditions which it shall specify. Such a declaration may be withdrawn or amended at any time.

8. The following requests or communications shall be made through the central authorities of the Member States:

(a) requests for temporary transfer or transit of persons held in custody as referred to in Article 9 of this Convention, in Article 11 of the European Mutual Assistance Convention and in Article 33 of the Benelux Treaty;

(b) notices of information from judicial records as referred to in Article 22 of the European Mutual Assistance Convention and Article 43 of the Benelux Treaty. However, requests for copies of convictions and measures as referred to in Article 4 of the Additional Protocol to the European Mutual Assistance Convention may be made directly to the competent authorities.

Article 7

Spontaneous exchange of information

1. Within the limits of their national law, the competent authorities of the Member States may exchange information, without a request to that effect, relating to criminal offences and the infringements of rules of law referred to in Article 3(1), the punishment or handling of which falls within the competence of the receiving authority at the time the information is provided.

2. The providing authority may, pursuant to its national law, impose conditions on the use of such information by the receiving authority.

3. The receiving authority shall be bound by those conditions.

TITLE II

REQUEST FOR CERTAIN SPECIFIC FORMS OF MUTUAL ASSISTANCE

Article 8

Restitution

1. At the request of the requesting Member State and without prejudice to the rights of *bona fide* third parties, the requested Member State may place articles obtained by criminal means at the disposal of the requesting State with a view to their return to their rightful owners.

2. In applying Articles 3 and 6 of the European Mutual Assistance Convention and Articles 24(2) and 29 of the Benelux Treaty, the requested Member State may waive the return of articles either before or after handling them over to the requesting Member State if the restitution of such articles to the rightful owner may be facilitated thereby. The rights of *bona fide* third parties shall not be affected.

3. In the event of a waiver before handing over the articles to the requesting Member State, the requested Member State shall exercise no security right or other right of recourse under tax or customs legislation in respect of these articles.

A waiver as referred to in paragraph 2 shall be without prejudice to the right of the requested Member State to collect taxes or duties from the rightful owner.

Article 9

Temporary transfer of persons held in custody for purpose of investigation

1. Where there is agreement between the competent authorities of the Member States concerned, a Member State which has requested an investigation for which the presence of the person held in custody on its own territory is required may temporarily transfer that person to the territory of the Member State in which the investigation is to take place.

2. The agreement shall cover the arrangements for the temporary transfer of the person and the date by which he or she must be returned to the territory of the requesting Member State.

3. Where consent to the transfer is required from the person concerned, a statement of consent or a copy thereof shall be provided promptly to the requested Member State.

4. The period of custody in the territory of the requested Member State shall be deducted from the period of detention which the person concerned is or will be obliged to undergo in the territory of the requesting Member State.

5. The provisions of Articles 11(2) and (3), 12 and 20 of the European Mutual Assistance Convention shall apply *mutatis mutandis* to this Article.

6. When giving the notification provided for in Article 27(2), each Member State may declare that, before an agreement is reached under paragraph 1 of this Article, the consent referred to in paragraph 3 of this Article will be required or will be required under certain conditions indicated in the declaration.

Article 10

Hearing by videoconference

1. If a person is in one Member State's territory and has to be heard as a witness or expert by the judicial authorities of another Member State, the latter may, where it is not desirable or possible for the person to be heard to appear in its territory in person, request that the hearing take place by videoconference, as provided for in paragraphs 2 to 8.

2. The requested Member State shall agree to the hearing by videoconference provided that the use of the videoconference is not contrary to fundamental principles of its law and on condition that it has the technical means to carry out the hearing. If the requested Member State has no access to the technical means for videoconferencing, such means may be made available to it by the requesting Member State by mutual agreement.

3. Requests for a hearing by videoconference shall contain, in addition to the information referred to in Article 14 of the European Mutual Assistance Convention and Article 37 of the Benelux Treaty, the reason why it is not desirable or possible for the witness or expert to attend in person, the name of the judicial authority and of the persons who will be conducting the hearing.

4. The judicial authority of the requested Member State shall summon the person concerned to appear in accordance with the forms laid down by its law.

5. With reference to hearing by videoconference, the following rules shall apply:

(a) a judicial authority of the requested Member State shall be present during the hearing, where necessary assisted by an interpreter, and shall also be responsible for ensuring both the identification of the person to be heard and respect for the fundamental principles of the law of the requested Member State. If the judicial authority of the requested Member State is of the view that during the hearing the fundamental principles of the law of the requested Member State are being infringed, it shall immediately take the necessary measures to ensure that the hearing continues in accordance with the said principles;

(b) measures for the protection of the person to be heard shall be agreed, where necessary, between the competent authorities of the requesting and the requested Member States;

(c) the hearing shall be conducted directly by, or under the direction of, the judicial authority of the requesting Member State in accordance with its own laws;

(d) at the request of the requesting Member State or the person to be heard the requested Member State shall ensure that the person to be heard is assisted by an interpreter, if necessary;

(e) the person to be heard may claim the right not to testify which would accrue to him or her under the law of either the requested or the requesting Member State.

6. Without prejudice to any measures agreed for the protection of the persons, the judicial authority of the requested Member State shall on the conclusion of the hearing draw up minutes indicating the date and place of the hearing, the identity of the person heard, the identities and functions of all other persons in the requested Member State participating in the hearing, any oaths taken and the technical conditions under which the hearing took place. The document shall be forwarded by the competent authority of the requested Member State to the competent authority of the requesting Member State.

7. The cost of establishing the video link, costs related to the servicing of the video link in the requested Member State, the remuneration of interpreters provided by it and allowances to witnesses and experts and their travelling expenses in the requested Member State shall

be refunded by the requesting Member State to the requested Member State, unless the latter waives the refunding of all or some of these expenses.

8. Each Member State shall take the necessary measures to ensure that, where witnesses or experts are being heard within its territory in accordance with this Article and refuse to testify when under an obligation to testify or do not testify according to the truth, its national law applies in the same way as if the hearing took place in a national procedure.

9. Member States may at their discretion also apply the provisions of this Article, where appropriate and with the agreement of their competent judicial authorities, to hearings by videoconference involving an accused person. In this case, the decision to hold the videoconference, and the manner in which the videoconference shall be carried out, shall be subject to agreement between the Member States concerned, in accordance with their national law and relevant international instruments, including the 1950 European Convention for the Protection of Human Rights and Fundamental Freedoms.

Any Member State may, when giving its notification pursuant to Article 27(2), declare that it will not apply the first subparagraph. Such a declaration may be withdrawn at any time.

Hearings shall only be carried out with the consent of the accused person. Such rules as may prove to be necessary, with a view to the protection of the rights of accused persons, shall be adopted by the Council in a legally binding instrument.

Article 11

Hearing of witnesses and experts by telephone conference

1. If a person is one Member State's territory and has to be heard as a witness or expert by judicial authorities of another Member State, the latter may, where its national law so provides, request assistance of the former Member State to enable the hearing to take place by telephone conference, as provided for in paragraphs 2 to 5.

2. A hearing may be conducted by telephone conference only if the witness or expert agrees that the hearing take place by that method.

3. The requested Member State shall agree to the hearing by telephone conference where this is not contrary to fundamental principles of its law.

4. A request for a hearing by telephone conference shall contain, in addition to the information referred to in Article 14 of the European Mutual Assistance Convention and Article 37 of the Benelux Treaty, the name of the judicial authority and of the persons who will be conducting the hearing and an indication that the witness or expert is willing to take part in a hearing by telephone conference.

5. The practical arrangements regarding the hearing shall be agreed between the Member States concerned. When agreeing such arrangements, the requested Member State shall undertake to:

(a) notify the witness or expert concerned of the time and the venue of the hearing;
(b) ensure the identification of the witness or expert;
(c) verify that the witness or expert agrees to the hearing by telephone conference.

The requested Member State may make its agreement subject, fully or in part, to the relevant provisions of Article 10(5) and (8). Unless otherwise agreed, the provisions of Article 10(7) shall apply *mutatis mutandis*.

Article 12

Controlled deliveries

1. Each Member State shall undertake to ensure that, at the request of another Member State, controlled deliveries may be permitted on its territory in the framework of criminal investigations into extraditable offences.

2. The decision to carry out controlled deliveries shall be taken in each individual case by the competent authorities of the requested Member State, with due regard for the national law of that Member State.

3. Controlled deliveries shall take place in accordance with the procedures of the requested Member State. The right to act and to direct and control operations shall lie with the competent authorities of that Member State.

Article 13

Joint investigation teams

1. By mutual agreement, the competent authorities of two or more Member States may set up a joint investigation team for a specific purpose and a limited period, which may be extended by mutual consent, to carry out criminal investigations in one or more of the Member States setting up the team. The composition of the team shall be set out in the agreement.

A joint investigation team may, in particular, be set up where:

(a) a Member State's investigations into criminal offences require difficult and demanding investigations having links with other Member States;

(b) a number of Member States are conducting investigations into criminal offences in which the circumstances of the case necessitate coordinated, concerted action in the Member States involved.

A request for the setting up of a joint investigation team may be made by any of the Member States concerned. The team shall be set up in one of the Member States in which the investigations are expected to be carried out.

2. In addition to the information referred to in the relevant provisions of Article 14 of the European Mutual Assistance Convention and Article 37 of the Benelux Treaty, requests for the setting up of a joint investigation team shall include proposals for the composition of the team.

3. A joint investigation team shall operate in the territory of the Member States setting up the team under the following general conditions:

(a) the leader of the team shall be a representative of the competent authority participating in criminal investigations from the Member State in which the team operates. The leader of the team shall act within the limits of his or her competence under national law;

(b) the team shall carry out its operations in accordance with the law of the Member State in which it operates. The members of the team shall carry out their tasks under the leadership of the person referred to in subparagraph (a), taking into account the conditions set by their own authorities in the agreement on setting up the team;

(c) the Member State in which the team operates shall make the necessary organisational arrangements for it to do so.

4. In this Article, members of the joint investigation team from Member States other than the Member State in which the team operates are referred to as being 'seconded' to the team.

5. Seconded members of the joint investigation team shall be entitled to be present when investigative measures are taken in the Member State of operation. However, the leader of the team may, for particular reasons, in accordance with the law of the Member State where the team operates, decide otherwise.

6. Seconded members of the joint investigation team may, in accordance with the law of the Member State where the team operates, be entrusted by the leader of the team with the task of taking certain investigative measures where this has been approved by the competent authorities of the Member State of operation and the seconding Member State.

7. Where the joint investigation team needs investigative measures to be taken in one of the Member States setting up the team, members seconded to the team by that Member State may request their own competent authorities to take those measures. Those measures shall be considered in that Member State under the conditions which would apply if they were requested in a national investigation.

8. Where the joint investigation team needs assistance from a Member State other than those which have set up the team, or from a third State, the request for assistance may be made by the competent authorities of the State of operations to the competent authorities of the other State concerned in accordance with the relevant instruments or arrangements.

9. A member of the joint investigation team may, in accordance with his or her national law and within the limits of his or her competence, provide the team with information available in the Member State which has seconded him or her for the purpose of the criminal investigations conducted by the team.

10. Information lawfully obtained by a member or seconded member while part of a joint investigation team which is not otherwise available to the competent authorities of the Member States concerned may be used for the following purposes:

(a) for the purposes for which the team has been set up;
(b) subject to the prior consent of the Member State where the information became available, for detecting, investigation and prosecuting other criminal offences. Such consent may be withheld only in cases where such use would endanger criminal investigations in the Member State concerned or in respect of which that Member State could refuse mutual assistance;
(c) for preventing an immediate and serious threat to public security, and without prejudice to subparagraph (b) if subsequently a criminal investigation is opened;
(d) for other purposes to the extent that this is agreed between Member States setting up the team.

11. This Article shall be without prejudice to any other existing provisions or arrangements on the setting up or operation of joint investigation teams.

12. To the extent that the laws of the Member States concerned or the provisions of any legal instrument applicable between them permit, arrangements may be agreed for persons other than representatives of the competent authorities of the Member States setting up the joint investigation team to take part in the activities of the team. Such persons may, for example, include officials of bodies set up pursuant to the Treaty on European Union. The rights conferred upon the members or seconded members of the team by virtue of this Article shall not apply to these persons unless the agreement expressly states otherwise.

Article 14

Covert investigations

1. The requesting and the requested Member State may agree to assist one another in the conduct of investigations into crime by officers acting under covert or false identity (covert investigations).

2. The decision on the request is taken in each individual case by the competent authorities of the requested Member State with due regard to its national law and procedures. The duration of the covert investigation, the detailed conditions, and the legal status of the officers concerned during covert investigations shall be agreed between the Member States with due regard to their national law and procedures.

3. Covert investigations shall take place in accordance with the national law and procedures of the Member States on the territory of which the covert investigation takes place. The Member States involved shall cooperate to ensure that the covert investigation is prepared and supervised and to make arrangements for the security of the officers acting under covert or false identity.

4. When giving the notification provided for in Article 27(2), any Member State may declare that it is not bound by this Article. Such a declaration may be withdrawn at any time.

Article 15

Criminal liability regarding officials

During the operations referred to in Articles 12, 13 and 14, officials from a Member State other than the Member State of operation shall be regarded as officials of the Member State of operation with respect of offences committed against them or by them.

Article 16

Civil liability regarding officials

1. Where, in accordance with Articles 12, 13 and 14, officials of a Member State are operating in another Member State, the first Member State shall be liable for any damage caused by them during their operations, in accordance with the law of the Member State in whose territory they are operating.

2. The Member State in whose territory the damage referred to in paragraph 1 was caused shall make good such damage under the conditions applicable to damage caused by its own officials.

3. The Member State whose officials have caused damage to any person in the territory of another Member State shall reimburse the latter in full any sums it has paid to the victims or persons entitled on their behalf.

4. Without prejudice to the exercise of its rights vis-à-vis third parties and with the exception of paragraph 3, each Member State shall refrain in the case provided for in paragraph 1 from requesting reimbursement of damages it has sustained from another Member State.

TITLE III

INTERCEPTION OF TELECOMMUNICATIONS

Article 17

Authorities competent to order interception of telecommunications

For the purpose of the application of the provisions of Articles 18, 19 and 20, 'competent authority' shall mean a judicial authority, or, where judicial authorities have no competence in the area covered by those provisions, an equivalent competent authority, specified pursuant to Article 24(1)(e) and acting for the purpose of a criminal investigation.

Article 18

Requests for interception of telecommunications

1. For the purpose of a criminal investigation, a competent authority in the requesting Member State may, in accordance with the requirements of its national law, make a request to a competent authority in the requested Member State for:

(a) the interception and immediate transmission to the requesting Member State of telecommunications; or
(b) the interception, recording and subsequent transmission to the requesting Member State of the recording of telecommunications.

2. Requests under paragraph 1 may be made in relation to the use of means of telecommunications by the subject of the interception, if this subject is present in:

(a) the requesting Member State and the requesting Member State needs the technical assistance of the requested Member State to intercept his or her communications;
(b) the requesting Member State and his or her communications can be intercepted in that Member State;
(c) a third Member State which has been informed pursuant to Article 20(2)(a) and the requesting Member State needs the technical assistance of the requested Member State to intercept his or her communications.

3. By way of derogation from Article 14 of the European Mutual Assistance Convention and Article 37 of the Benelux Treaty, requests under this Article shall include the following:

(a) an indication of the authority making the request;
(b) confirmation that a lawful interception order or warrant has been issued in connection with a criminal investigation;
(c) information for the purpose of identifying the subject of this interception:
(d) an indication of the criminal conduct under investigation;
(e) the desired duration of the interception; and

(f) if possible, the provision of sufficient technical data, in particular the relevant network connection number, to ensure that the request can be met.

4. In the case of a request pursuant to paragraph 2(b), a request shall also include a summary of the facts. The requested Member State may require any further information to enable it to decide whether the requested measure would be taken by it in a similar national case.

5. The requested Member State shall undertake to comply with requests under paragraph 1(a):

(a) in the case of a request pursuant to paragraph 2(a) and 2(c), on being provided with the information in paragraph 3. The requested Member State may allow the interception to proceed without further formality;
(b) in the case of a request pursuant to paragraph 2(b), on being provided with the information in paragraphs 3 and 4 and where the requested measure would be taken by it in a similar national case. The requested Member State may make its consent subject to any conditions which would have to be observed in a similar national case.

6. Where immediate transmission is not possible, the requested Member State shall undertake to comply with requests under paragraph 1(b) on being provided with the information in paragraphs 3 and 4 and where the requested measure would be taken by it in a similar national case. The requested Member State may make its consent subject to any condition which would have to be observed in a similar national case.

7. When giving the notification provided for in Article 27(2), any Member State may declare that it is bound by paragraph 6 only when it is unable to provide immediate transmission. In this case the other Member State may apply the principle of reciprocity.

8. When making a request under paragraph 1(b), the requesting Member State may, where it has a particular reason to do so, also request a transcription of the recording. The requested Member State shall consider such requests in accordance with its national law and procedures.

9. The Member State receiving the information provided under paragraphs 3 and 4 shall keep that information confidential in accordance with its national law.

Article 19

Interceptions of telecommunications on national territory by the use of service providers

1. Member States shall ensure that systems of telecommunications services operated via a gateway on their territory, which for the lawful interception of the communications of a subject present in another Member State are not directly accessible on the territory of the latter, may be made directly accessible for the lawful interception by that Member State through the intermediary of a designated service provider present on its territory.

2. In the case referred to in paragraph 1, the competent authorities of a Member State shall be entitled, for the purposes of a criminal investigation and in accordance with applicable national law and provided that the subject of the interception is present in that Member State, to carry out the interception through the intermediary of a designated service provider present on its territory without involving the Member State on whose territory the gateway is located.

3. Paragraph 2 shall also apply where the interception is carried out upon a request made pursuant to Article 18(2)(b).

4. Nothing in this Article shall prevent a Member State from making a request to the Member State on whose territory the gateway is located for the lawful interception of

telecommunications in accordance with Article 18, in particular where there is no intermediary in the requesting Member State.

Article 20

Interception of telecommunications without the technical assistance of another Member State

1. Without prejudice to the general principles of international law as well as to the provisions of Article 18(2)(c), the obligations under this Article shall apply to interception orders made or authorised by the competent authority of one Member State in the course of criminal investigations which present the characteristics of being an investigation following the commission of a specific criminal offence, including attempts in so far as they are criminalised under national law, in order to identify and arrest, charge, prosecute or deliver judgment on those responsible.

2. Where for the purpose of a criminal investigation, the interception of telecommunications is authorised by the competent authority of one Member State (the 'intercepting Member State'), and the telecommunication address of the subject specified in the interception order is being used on the territory of another Member State (the 'notified Member State') from which no technical assistance is needed to carry out the interception, the intercepting Member State shall inform the notified Member State of the interception:

(a) prior to the interception in cases where it knows when ordering the interception that the subject is on the territory of the notified Member State;
(b) in other cases, immediately after it becomes aware that the subject of the interception is on the territory of the notified Member State.

3. The information to be notified by the intercepting Member State shall include:

(a) an indication of the authority ordering the interception;
(b) confirmation that a lawful interception order has been issued in connection with a criminal investigation;
(c) information for the purpose of identifying the subject of the interception;
(d) an indication of the criminal conduct under investigation; and
(e) the expected duration of the interception.

4. The following shall apply where a Member State is notified pursuant to paragraphs 2 and 3:

(a) Upon receipt of the information provided under paragraph 3 the competent authority of the notified Member State shall, without delay, and at the latest within 96 hours, reply to the intercepting Member State, with a view to:

  (i) allowing the interception to be carried out or to be continued. The notified Member State may make its consent subject to any conditions which would have to be observed in a similar national case;
  (ii) requiring the interception not to be carried out or to be terminated where the interception would not be permissible pursuant to the national law of the notified Member State, or for the reasons specified in Article 2 of the European Mutual Assistance Convention. Where the notified Member State imposes such a requirement, it shall give reasons for its decision in writing;

(iii) in cases referred to in point (ii), requiring that any material already intercepted while the subject was on its territory may not be used, or may only be used under conditions which it shall specify. The notified Member State shall inform the intercepting Member State of the reasons justifying the said conditions;

(iv) requiring a short extension, of up to a maximum period of eight days, to the original 96-hour deadline, to be agreed with the intercepting Member State, in order to carry out internal procedures under its national law. The notified Member State shall communicate, in writing, to the intercepting Member State, the conditions which, pursuant to its national law, justify the requested extension of the deadline.

(b) Until a decision has been taken by the notified Member State pursuant to points (i) or (ii) of subparagraph (a), the intercepting Member State:

(i) may continue the interception; and

(ii) may not use the material already intercepted, except:

— if otherwise agreed between the Member States concerned; or

— for taking urgent measures to prevent an immediate and serious threat to public security. The notified Member State shall be informed of any such use and the reasons justifying it.

(c) The notified Member State may request a summary of the facts of the case and any further information necessary to enable it to decide whether interception would be authorised in a similar national case. Such a request does not affect the application of subparagraph (b), unless otherwise agreed between the notified Member State and the intercepting Member State.

(d) The Member States shall take the necessary measures to ensure that a reply can be given within the 96-hour period. To this end they shall designate contact points, on duty twenty-four hours a day, and include them in their statements under Article 24(1)(e).

5. The notified Member State shall keep the information provided under paragraph 3 confidential in accordance with its national law.

6. Where the intercepting Member State is of the opinion that the information to be provided under paragraph 3 is of a particularly sensitive nature, it may be transmitted to the competent authority through a specific authority where that has been agreed on a bilateral basis between the Member States concerned.

7. When giving its notification under Article 27(2), or at any time thereafter, any Member State may declare that it will not be necessary to provide it with information on interceptions as envisaged in this Article.

Article 21

Responsibility for charges made by telecommunications operators

Costs which are incurred by telecommunications operators or service providers in executing requests pursuant to Article 18 shall be borne by the requesting Member State.

Article 22

Bilateral arrangements

Nothing in this Title shall preclude any bilateral or multilateral arrangements between Member States for the purpose of facilitating the exploitation of present and future technical possibilities regarding the lawful interception of telecommunications.

TITLE IV

Article 23

Personal data protection

1. Personal data communicated under this Convention may be used by the Member State to which they have been transferred:

(a) for the purpose of proceedings to which this Convention applies;
(b) for other judicial and administrative proceedings directly related to proceedings referred to under point (a);
(c) for preventing an immediate and serious threat to public security;
(d) for any other purpose, only with the prior consent of the communicating Member State, unless the Member State concerned has obtained the consent of the data subject.

2. This Article shall also apply to personal data not communicated but obtained otherwise under this Convention.

3. In the circumstances of the particular case, the communicating Member State may require the Member State to which the personal data have been transferred to give information on the use made of the data.

4. Where conditions on the use of personal data have been imposed pursuant to Articles 7(2), 18(5)(b), 18(6) or 20(4), these conditions shall prevail. Where no such conditions have been imposed, this Article shall apply.

5. The provisions of Article 13(10) shall take precedence over this Article regarding information obtained under Article 13.

6. This Article does not apply to personal data obtained by a Member State under this Convention and originating from that Member State.

7. Luxembourg may, when signing the Convention, declare that where personal data are communicated by Luxembourg under this Convention to another Member State, the following applies:

> Luxembourg may, subject to paragraph 1(c), in the circumstances of a particular case require that unless that Member State concerned has obtained the consent of the data subject, the personal data may only be used for the purposes referred to in paragraph 1(a) and (b) with the prior consent of Luxembourg in respect of proceedings for which Luxembourg could have refused or limited the transmission or use of the personal data in accordance with the provisions of this Convention or the instruments referred to in Article 1.

If, in a particular case, Luxembourg refuses to give its consent to a request from a Member State pursuant to the provisions of paragraph 1, it must give reasons for its decision in writing.

TITLE V

FINAL PROVISIONS

Article 24

Statements

1. When giving the notification referred to in Article 27(2), each Member State shall make a statement naming the authorities which, in addition to those already indicated in the European Mutual Assistance Convention and the Benelux Treaty, are competent for the application of this Convention and the application between the Member States of the provisions on mutual assistance in criminal matters of the instruments referred to in Article 1(1), including in particular:

(a) the competent administrative authorities within the meaning of Article 3(1), if any:
(b) one or more central authorities for the purposes of applying Article 6 as well as the authorities competent to deal with the requests referred to in Article 6(8);
(c) the police or customs authorities competent for the purpose of Article 6(5), if any;
(d) the administrative authorities competent for the purposes of Article 6(6), if any; and
(e) the authority or authorities competent for the purposes of the application of Articles 18 and 19 and Article 20(1) to (5).

2. Statements made in accordance with paragraph 1 may be amended in whole or in part at any time by the same procedure.

Article 25

Reservations

No reservations may be entered in respect of this Convention, other than those for which it makes express provision.

Article 26

Territorial application

The application of this Convention to Gibraltar will take effect upon extension of the European Mutual Assistance Convention to Gibraltar.

The United Kingdom shall notify in writing the President of the Council when it wishes to apply the Convention to the Channel Islands and the Isle of Man following extension of the European Mutual Assistance Convention to those territories. A decision on this request shall be taken by the Council acting with the unanimity of its members.

Article 27

Entry into force

1. This Convention shall be subject to adoption by the Member States in accordance with their respective constitutional requirements.

2. Member States shall notify the Secretary-General of the Council of the European Union of the completion of the constitutional procedures for the adoption of this Convention.

3. This Convention shall, 90 days after the notification referred to in paragraph 2 by the State, member of the European Union at the time of adoption by the Council of the Act establishing this Convention, which is the eighth to complete this formality, enter into force for the eight Member States concerned.

4. Any notification by a Member State subsequent to the receipt of the eighth notification referred to in paragraph 2 shall have the effect that, 90 days after the subsequent notification, this Convention shall enter into force as between this Member State and those Member States for which the Convention has already entered into force.

5. Before the Convention has entered into force pursuant to paragraph 3, any Member State may, when giving the notification referred to in paragraph 2 or at any time thereafter, declare that it will apply this Convention in its relations with Member States which have made the same declaration. Such declarations shall take effect 90 days after the date of deposit thereof.

6. This Convention shall apply to mutual assistance initiated after the date on which it has entered into force, or is applied pursuant to paragraph 5, between the Member States concerned.

Article 28

Accession of new Member States

1. This Convention shall be open to accession by any State which becomes a member of the European Union.

2. The text of this Convention in the language of the acceding State, drawn up by the Council of the European Union, shall be authentic.

3. The instruments of accession shall be deposited with the depositary.

4. This Convention shall enter into force with respect to any State which accedes to it 90 days after the deposit of its instrument of accession or on the date of entry into force of this Convention if it has not already entered into force at the time of expiry of the said period of 90 days.

5. Where this Convention is not yet in force at the time of the deposit of their instrument of accession, Article 27(5) shall apply to acceding Member States.

Article 29

Entry into force for Iceland and Norway

1. Without prejudice to Article 8 of the Agreement concluded by the Council of the European Union and the Republic of Iceland and the Kingdom of Norway concerning the latters' association with the implementation, application and development of the Schengen *acquis* (the 'Association Agreement'), the provisions referred to in Article 2(1) shall enter into force for Iceland and Norway 90 days after the receipt by the Council and the Commission of the information pursuant to Article 8(2) of the Association Agreement upon fulfilment of their constitutional requirements, in their mutual relations with any Member State for which this Convention has already entered into force pursuant to Article 27(3) or (4).

2. Any entry into force of this Convention for a Member State after the date of entry into force of the provisions referred to in Article 2(1) for Iceland and Norway, shall render these provisions also applicable in the mutual relations between that Member State and Iceland and Norway.

3. The provisions referred to in Article 2(1) shall in any event not become binding on Iceland and Norway before the date to be fixed pursuant to Article 15(4) of the Association Agreement.

4. Without prejudice to paragraphs 1, 2 and 3 above, the provisions referred to in Article 2(1) shall enter into force for Iceland and Norway not later than on the date of entry into force of this Convention for the fifteenth State, being a member of the European Union at the time of the adoption by the Council of the Act establishing this Convention.

Article 30

Depositary

1. The Secretary-General of the Council of the European Union shall act as depositary of this Convention.

2. The depositary shall publish in the *Official Journal of the European Communities* information on the progress of adoptions and accessions, statements and reservations and also any other notification concerning this Convention.

COUNCIL DECLARATION ON ARTICLE 10(9)

When considering the adoption of an instrument as referred to in Article 10(9), the Council shall respect Member States' obligations under the European Convention on Human Rights.

DECLARATION BY THE UNITED KINGDOM ON ARTICLE 20

This Declaration shall form an agreed, integral part of the Convention

In the United Kingdom, Article 20 will apply in respect of interception warrants issued by the Secretary of State to the police service or HM Customs & Excise where, in accordance with national law on the interception of communications, the stated purpose of the warrant is the detection of serious crime. It will also apply to such warrants issued to the Security Service where, in accordance with national law, it is acting in support of an investigation presenting the characteristics described in Article 20(1).

C–005 **Second Additional Protocol to the European Convention on Mutual Assistance in Criminal Matters**

STRASBOURG, 8.XI.2001

PREAMBLE

The member States of the Council of Europe, signatory to this Protocol, Having regard to their undertakings under the Statute of the Council of Europe;

Desirous of further contributing to safeguard human rights, uphold the rule of law and support the democratic fabric of society;

Considering it desirable to that effect to strengthen their individual and collective ability to respond to crime;

Decided to improve on and supplement in certain aspects the European Convention on Mutual Assistance in Criminal Matters done at Strasbourg on 20 April 1959 (hereinafter referred to as "the Convention"), as well as the Additional Protocol thereto, done at Strasbourg on 17 March 1978;

Taking into consideration the Convention for the Protection of Human Rights and Fundamental Freedoms, done at Rome on 4 November 1950, as well as the Convention for the Protection of Individuals with regard to Automatic Processing of Personal Data, done at Strasbourg on 28 January 1981,

Have agreed as follows:

CHAPTER I

Article 1 — Scope[9]

. . .

Article 2 — Presence of officials of the requesting Party

. . .

Article 3 — Temporary transfer of detained persons to the territory of the requesting Party

. . .

Article 4 — Channels of communication

. . .

[9] This article, and articles 2–6, amend the original Convention: see above.

Article 5 — Costs

...

Article 6 — Judicial authorities

...

CHAPTER II

Article 7 — Postponed execution of requests

1. The requested Party may postpone action on a request if such action would prejudice investigations, prosecutions or related proceedings by its authorities.

2. Before refusing or postponing assistance, the requested Party shall, where appropriate after having consulted with the requesting Party, consider whether the request may be granted partially or subject to such conditions as it deems necessary.

3. If the request is postponed, reasons shall be given for the postponement. The requested Party shall also inform the requesting Party of any reasons that render impossible the execution of the request or are likely to delay it significantly.

Article 8 — Procedure

Notwithstanding the provisions of Article 3 of the Convention, where requests specify formalities or procedures which are necessary under the law of the requesting Party, even if unfamiliar to the requested Party, the latter shall comply with such requests to the extent that the action sought is not contrary to fundamental principles of its law, unless otherwise provided for in this Protocol.

Article 9 — Hearing by video conference

1. If a person is in one Party's territory and has to be heard as a witness or expert by the judicial authorities of another Party, the latter may, where it is not desirable or possible for the person to be heard to appear in its territory in person, request that the hearing take place by video conference, as provided for in paragraphs 2 to 7.

2. The requested Party shall agree to the hearing by video conference provided that the use of the video conference is not contrary to fundamental principles of its law and on condition that it has the technical means to carry out the hearing. If the requested Party has no access to the technical means for video conferencing, such means may be made available to it by the requesting Party by mutual agreement.

3. Requests for a hearing by video conference shall contain, in addition to the information referred to in Article 14 of the Convention, the reason why it is not desirable or possible for the witness or expert to attend in person, the name of the judicial authority and of the persons who will be conducting the hearing.

4. The judicial authority of the requested Party shall summon the person concerned to appear in accordance with the forms laid down by its law.

5. With reference to hearing by video conference, the following rules shall apply:

(a) a judicial authority of the requested Party shall be present during the hearing, where necessary assisted by an interpreter, and shall also be responsible for ensuring both the identification of the person to be heard and respect for the fundamental principles of the law of the requested Party. If the judicial authority of the requested Party is of the view that during the hearing the fundamental principles of the law of the requested Party are being infringed, it shall immediately take the necessary measures to ensure that the hearing continues in accordance with the said principles;
(b) measures for the protection of the person to be heard shall be agreed, where necessary, between the competent authorities of the requesting and the requested Parties;
(c) the hearing shall be conducted directly by, or under the direction of, the judicial authority of the requesting Party in accordance with its own laws;
(d) at the request of the requesting Party or the person to be heard, the requested Party shall ensure that the person to be heard is assisted by an interpreter, if necessary;
(e) the person to be heard may claim the right not to testify which would accrue to him or her under the law of either the requested or the requesting Party.

6. Without prejudice to any measures agreed for the protection of persons, the judicial authority of the requested Party shall on the conclusion of the hearing draw up minutes indicating the date and place of the hearing, the identity of the person heard, the identities and functions of all other persons in the requested Party participating in the hearing, any oaths taken and the technical conditions under which the hearing took place. The document shall be forwarded by the competent authority of the requested Party to the competent authority of the requesting Party.

7. Each Party shall take the necessary measures to ensure that, where witnesses or experts are being heard within its territory, in accordance with this article, and refuse to testify when under an obligation to testify or do not testify according to the truth, its national law applies in the same way as if the hearing took place in a national procedure.

8. Parties may at their discretion also apply the provisions of this article, where appropriate and with the agreement of their competent judicial authorities, to hearings by video conference involving the accused person or the suspect. In this case, the decision to hold the video conference, and the manner in which the video conference shall be carried out, shall be subject to agreement between the Parties concerned, in accordance with their national law and relevant international instruments. Hearings involving the accused person or the suspect shall only be carried out with his or her consent.

9. Any Contracting State may, at any time, by means of a declaration addressed to the Secretary General of the Council of Europe, declare that it will not avail itself of the possibility provided in paragraph 8 above of also applying the provisions of this article to hearings by video conference involving the accused person or the suspect.

Article 10 — Hearing by telephone conference

1. If a person is in one Party's territory and has to be heard as a witness or expert by judicial authorities of another Party, the latter may, where its national law so provides, request the assistance of the former Party to enable the hearing to take place by telephone conference, as provided for in paragraphs 2 to 6.

2. A hearing may be conducted by telephone conference only if the witness or expert agrees that the hearing take place by that method.

3. The requested Party shall agree to the hearing by telephone conference where this is not contrary to fundamental principles of its law.

4. A request for a hearing by telephone conference shall contain, in addition to the information referred to in Article 14 of the Convention, the name of the judicial authority and of the persons who will be conducting the hearing and an indication that the witness or expert is willing to take part in a hearing by telephone conference.

5. The practical arrangements regarding the hearing shall be agreed between the Parties concerned. When agreeing such arrangements, the requested Party shall undertake to:

(a) notify the witness or expert concerned of the time and the venue of the hearing;
(b) ensure the identification of the witness or expert;
(c) verify that the witness or expert agrees to the hearing by telephone conference.

6. The requested Party may make its agreement subject, fully or in part, to the relevant provisions of Article 9, paragraphs 5 and 7.

Article 11 — Spontaneous information

1. Without prejudice to their own investigations or proceedings, the competent authorities of a Party may, without prior request, forward to the competent authorities of another Party information obtained within the framework of their own investigations, when they consider that the disclosure of such information might assist the receiving Party in initiating or carrying out investigations or proceedings, or might lead to a request by that Party under the Convention or its Protocols.

2. The providing Party may, pursuant to its national law, impose conditions on the use of such information by the receiving Party.

3. The receiving Party shall be bound by those conditions.

4. However, any Contracting State may, at any time, by means of a declaration addressed to the Secretary General of the Council of Europe, declare that it reserves the right not to be bound by the conditions imposed by the providing Party under paragraph 2 above, unless it receives prior notice of the nature of the information to be provided and agrees to its transmission.

Article 12 — Restitution

1. At the request of the requesting Party and without prejudice to the rights of bona fide third parties, the requested Party may place articles obtained by criminal means at the disposal of the requesting Party with a view to their return to their rightful owners.

2. In applying Articles 3 and 6 of the Convention, the requested Party may waive the return of articles either before or after handing them over to the requesting Party if the restitution of such articles to the rightful owner may be facilitated thereby. The rights of bona fide third parties shall not be affected.

3. In the event of a waiver before handing over the articles to the requesting Party, the requested Party shall exercise no security right or other right of recourse under tax or customs legislation in respect of these articles.

4. A waiver as referred to in paragraph 2 shall be without prejudice to the right of the requested Party to collect taxes or duties from the rightful owner.

Article 13 — Temporary transfer of detained persons to the requested Party

1. Where there is agreement between the competent authorities of the Parties concerned; a Party which has requested an investigation for which the presence of a person held in custody on its own territory is required may temporarily transfer that person to the territory of the Party in which the investigation is to take place.

2. The agreement shall cover the arrangements for the temporary transfer of the person and the date by which the person must be returned to the territory of the requesting Party.

3. Where consent to the transfer is required from the person concerned, a statement of consent or a copy thereof shall be provided promptly to the requested Party.

4. The transferred person shall remain in custody in the territory of the requested Party and, where applicable, in the territory of the Party through which transit is requested, unless the Party from which the person was transferred applies for his or her release.

5. The period of custody in the territory of the requested Party shall be deducted from the period of detention which the person concerned is or will be obliged to undergo in the territory of the requesting Party.

6. The provisions of Article 11, paragraph 2, and Article 12 of the Convention shall apply *mutatis mutatis.*

7. Any Contracting State may at any time, by means of a declaration addressed to the Secretary General of the Council of Europe, declare that before an agreement is reached under paragraph 1 of this article, the consent referred to in paragraph 3 of this article will be required, or will be required under certain conditions indicated in the declaration.

Article 14 — Personal appearance of transferred sentenced persons

The provisions of Articles 11 and 12 of the Convention shall apply mutatis mutandis also to persons who are in custody in the requested Party, pursuant to having been transferred in order to serve a sentence passed in the requesting Party, where their personal appearance for purposes of review of the judgement is applied for by the requesting Party.

Article 15 — Language of procedural documents and judicial decisions to be served

1. The provisions of this article shall apply to any request for service under Article 7 of the Convention or Article 3 of the Additional Protocol thereto.

2. Procedural documents and judicial decisions shall in all cases be transmitted in the language, or the languages, in which they were issued.

3. Notwithstanding the provisions of Article 16 of the Convention, if the authority that issued the papers knows or has reasons to believe that the addressee understands only some other language, the papers, or at least the most important passages thereof, shall be accompanied by a translation into that other language.

4. Notwithstanding the provisions of Article 16 of the Convention, procedural documents and judicial decisions shall, for the benefit of the authorities of the requested Party, be accompanied by a short summary of their contents translated into the language, or one of the languages, of that Party.

Article 16 — Service by post

1. The competent judicial authorities of any Party may directly address, by post, procedural documents and judicial decisions, to persons who are in the territory of any other Party.

2. Procedural documents and judicial decisions shall be accompanied by a report stating that the addressee may obtain information from the authority identified in the report, regarding his or her rights and obligations concerning the service of the papers. The provisions of paragraph 3 of Article 15 above shall apply to that report.

3. The provisions of Articles 8, 9 and 12 of the Convention shall apply *mutatis mutandis* to service by post.

4. The provisions of paragraphs 1, 2 and 3 of Article 15 above shall also apply to service by post.

Article 17 — Cross-border observations

1. Police officers of one of the Parties who, within the framework of a criminal investigation, are keeping under observation in their country a person who is presumed to have taken part in a criminal offence to which extradition may apply, or a person who it is strongly believed will lead to the identification or location of the above-mentioned person, shall be authorised to continue their observation in the territory of another Party where the latter has authorised crossborder observation in response to a request for assistance which has previously been submitted. Conditions may be attached to the authorisation.

On request, the observation will be entrusted to officers of the Party in whose territory it is carried out.

The request for assistance referred to in the first sub-paragraph must be sent to an authority designated by each Party and having jurisdiction to grant or to forward the requested authorisation.

2. Where, for particularly urgent reasons, prior authorisation of the other Party cannot be requested, the officers conducting the observation within the framework of a criminal investigation shall be authorised to continue beyond the border the observation of a person presumed to have committed offences listed in paragraph 6, provided that the following conditions are met:

(a) the authorities of the Party designated under paragraph 4, in whose territory the observation is to be continued, must be notified immediately, during the observation, that the border has been crossed;
(b) a request for assistance submitted in accordance with paragraph 1 and outlining the grounds for crossing the border without prior authorisation shall be submitted without delay.

Observation shall cease as soon as the Party in whose territory it is taking place so requests, following the notification referred to in a. or the request referred to in b. or where authorisation has not been obtained within five hours of the border being crossed.

3. The observation referred to in paragraphs 1 and 2 shall be carried out only under the following general conditions:

(a) The officers conducting the observation must comply with the provisions of this article and with the law of the Party in whose territory they are operating; they must obey the instructions of the local responsible authorities.

(b) Except in the situations provided for in paragraph 2, the officers shall, during the observation, carry a document certifying that authorisation has been granted.
(c) The officers conducting the observation must be able at all times to provide proof that they are acting in an official capacity.
(d) The officers conducting the observation may carry their service weapons during the observation, save where specifically otherwise decided by the requested Party; their use shall be prohibited save in cases of legitimate self-defence.
(e) Entry into private homes and places not accessible to the public shall be prohibited.
(f) The officers conducting the observation may neither stop and question, nor arrest, the person under observation.
(g) All operations shall be the subject of a report to the authorities of the Party in whose territory they took place; the officers conducting the observation may be required to appear in person.
(h) The authorities of the Party from which the observing officers have come shall, when requested by the authorities of the Party in whose territory the observation took place, assist the enquiry subsequent to the operation in which they took part, including legal proceedings.

4. Parties shall at the time of signature or when depositing their instrument of ratification, acceptance, approval or accession, by means of a declaration addressed to the Secretary General of the Council of Europe, indicate both the officers and authorities that they designate for the purposes of paragraphs 1 and 2 of this article. They subsequently may, at any time and in the same manner, change the terms of their declaration.

5. The Parties may, at bilateral level, extend the scope of this article and adopt additional measures in implementation thereof.

6. The observation referred to in paragraph 2 may take place only for one of the following criminal offences:

- assassination;
- murder;
- rape;
- arson;
- counterfeiting;
- armed robbery and receiving of stolen goods;
- extortion;
- kidnapping and hostage taking;
- traffic in human beings;
- illicit traffic in narcotic drugs and psychotropic substances;
- breach of the laws on arms and explosives;
- use of explosives;
- illicit carriage of toxic and dangerous waste;
- smuggling of aliens;
- sexual abuse of children.

Article 18 — Controlled delivery

1. Each Party undertakes to ensure that, at the request of another Party, controlled deliveries may be permitted on its territory in the framework of criminal investigations into extraditable offences.

2. The decision to carry out controlled deliveries shall be taken in each individual case by the competent authorities of the requested Party, with due regard to the national law of that Party.

3. Controlled deliveries shall take place in accordance with the procedures of the requested Party. Competence to act, direct and control operations shall lie with the competent authorities of that Party.

4. Parties shall at the time of signature or when depositing their instrument of ratification, acceptance, approval or accession, by means of a declaration addressed to the Secretary General of the Council of Europe, indicate the authorities that are competent for the purposes of this article. They subsequently may, at any time and in the same manner, change the terms of their declaration.

Article 19 — Covert investigations

1. The requesting and the requested Parties may agree to assist one another in the conduct of investigations into crime by officers acting under covert or false identity (covert investigations).

2. The decision on the request is taken in each individual case by the competent authorities of the requested Party with due regard to its national law and procedures. The duration of the covert investigation, the detailed conditions, and the legal status of the officers concerned during covert investigations shall be agreed between the Parties with due regard to their national law and procedures.

3. Covert investigations shall take place in accordance with the national law and procedures of the Party on the territory of which the covert investigation takes place. The Parties involved shall co-operate to ensure that the covert investigation is prepared and supervised and to make arrangements for the security of the officers acting under covert or false identity.

4. Parties shall at the time of signature or when depositing their instrument of ratification, acceptance, approval or accession, by means of a declaration addressed to the Secretary General of the Council of Europe, indicate the authorities that are competent for the purposes of paragraph 2 of this article. They subsequently may, at any time and in the same manner, change the terms of their declaration.

Article 20 — Joint investigation teams

1. By mutual agreement, the competent authorities of two or more Parties may set up a joint investigation team for a specific purpose and a limited period, which may be extended by mutual consent, to carry out criminal investigations in one or more of the Parties setting up the team. The composition of the team shall be set out in the agreement.

A joint investigation team may, in particular, be set up where:

(a) a Party's investigations into criminal offences require difficult and demanding investigations having links with other Parties;

(b) a number of Parties are conducting investigations into criminal offences in which the circumstances of the case necessitate co-ordinated, concerted action in the Parties involved.

A request for the setting up of a joint investigation team may be made by any of the Parties concerned. The team shall be set up in one of the Parties in which the investigations are expected to be carried out.

2. In addition to the information referred to in the relevant provisions of Article 14 of the Convention, requests for the setting up of a joint investigation team shall include proposals for the composition of the team.

3. A joint investigation team shall operate in the territory of the Parties setting up the team under the following general conditions:

(a) the leader of the team shall be a representative of the competent authority participating in criminal investigations from the Party in which the team operates. The leader of the team shall act within the limits of his or her competence under national law;
(b) the team shall carry out its operations in accordance with the law of the Party in which it operates. The members and seconded members of the team shall carry out their tasks under the leadership of the person referred to in sub-paragraph a, taking into account the conditions set by their own authorities in the agreement on setting up the team;
(c) the Party in which the team operates shall make the necessary organisational arrangements for it to do so.

4. In this article, members of the joint investigation team from the Party in which the team operates are referred to as "members", while members from Parties other than the Party in which the team operates are referred to as "seconded members".

5. Seconded members of the joint investigation team shall be entitled to be present when investigative measures are taken in the Party of operation. However, the leader of the team may, for particular reasons, in accordance with the law of the Party where the team operates, decide otherwise.

6. Seconded members of the joint investigation team may, in accordance with the law of the Party where the team operates, be entrusted by the leader of the team with the task of taking certain investigative measures where this has been approved by the competent authorities of the Party of operation and the seconding Party.

7. Where the joint investigation team needs investigative measures to be taken in one of the Parties setting up the team, members seconded to the team by that Party may request their own competent authorities to take those measures. Those measures shall be considered in that Party under the conditions which would apply if they were requested in a national investigation.

8. Where the joint investigation team needs assistance from a Party other than those which have set up the team, or from a third State, the request for assistance may be made by the competent authorities of the State of operation to the competent authorities of the other State concerned in accordance with the relevant instruments or arrangements.

9. A seconded member of the joint investigation team may, in accordance with his or her national law and within the limits of his or her competence, provide the team with information available in the Party which has seconded him or her for the purpose of the criminal investigations conducted by the team.

10. Information lawfully obtained by a member or seconded member while part of a joint investigation team which is not otherwise available to the competent authorities of the Parties concerned may be used for the following purposes:

(a) for the purposes for which the team has been set up;
(b) subject to the prior consent of the Party where the information became available, for detecting, investigating and prosecuting other criminal offences. Such consent may be withheld only in cases where such use would endanger criminal investigations in the Party concerned or in respect of which that Party could refuse mutual assistance;
(c) for preventing an immediate and serious threat to public security, and without prejudice to sub-paragraph b. if subsequently a criminal investigation is opened;
(d) for other purposes to the extent that this is agreed between Parties setting up the team.

11. This article shall be without prejudice to any other existing provisions or arrangements on the setting up or operation of joint investigation teams.

12. To the extent that the laws of the Parties concerned or the provisions of any legal instrument applicable between them permit, arrangements may be agreed for persons other than representatives of the competent authorities of the Parties setting up the joint investigation team to take part in the activities of the team. The rights conferred upon the members or seconded members of the team by virtue of this article shall not apply to these persons unless the agreement expressly states otherwise.

Article 21 — Criminal liability regarding officials

During the operations referred to in Articles 17, 18, 19 or 20, unless otherwise agreed upon by the Parties concerned, officials from a Party other than the Party of operation shall be regarded as officials of the Party of operation with respect to offences committed against them or by them.

Article 22 — Civil liability regarding officials

1. Where, in accordance with Articles 17, 18, 19 or 20, officials of a Party are operating in another Party, the first Party shall be liable for any damage caused by them during their operations, in accordance with the law of the Party in whose territory they are operating.

2. The Party in whose territory the damage referred to in paragraph 1 was caused shall make good such damage under the conditions applicable to damage caused by its own officials.

3. The Party whose officials have caused damage to any person in the territory of another Party shall reimburse the latter in full any sums it has paid to the victims or persons entitled on their behalf.

4. Without prejudice to the exercise of its rights vis-à-vis third parties and with the exception of paragraph 3, each Party shall refrain in the case provided for in paragraph 1 from requesting reimbursement of damages it has sustained from another Party.

5. The provisions of this article shall apply subject to the proviso that the Parties did not agree otherwise.

Article 23 — Protection of witnesses

Where a Party requests assistance under the Convention or one of its Protocols in respect of a witness at risk of intimidation or in need of protection, the competent authorities of the requesting and requested Parties shall endeavour to agree on measures for the protection of the person concerned, in accordance with their national law.

Article 24 — Provisional measures

1. At the request of the requesting Party, the requested Party, in accordance with its national law, may take provisional measures for the purpose of preserving evidence, maintaining an existing situation or protecting endangered legal interests.

2. The requested Party may grant the request partially or subject to conditions, in particular time limitation.

Article 25 — Confidentiality

The requesting Party may require that the requested Party keep confidential the fact and substance of the request, except to the extent necessary to execute the request. If the requested Party cannot comply with the requirement of confidentiality, it shall promptly inform the requesting Party.

Article 26 — Data protection

1. Personal data transferred from one Party to another as a result of the execution of a request made under the Convention or any of its Protocols, may be used by the Party to which such data have been transferred, only:

(a) for the purpose of proceedings to which the Convention or any of its Protocols apply;
(b) for other judicial and administrative proceedings directly related to the proceedings mentioned under (a);
(c) for preventing an immediate and serious threat to public security.

2. Such data may however be used for any other purpose if prior consent to that effect is given by either the Party from which the data had been transferred, or the data subject.
3. Any Party may refuse to transfer personal data obtained as a result of the execution of a request made under the Convention or any of its Protocols where

- such data is protected under its national legislation, and
- the Party to which the data should be transferred is not bound by the Convention for the Protection of Individuals with regard to Automatic Processing of Personal Data, done at Strasbourg on 28 January 1981, unless the latter Party undertakes to afford such protection to the data as is required by the former Party.

4. Any Party that transfers personal data obtained as a result of the execution of a request made under the Convention or any of its Protocols may require the Party to which the data have been transferred to give information on the use made with such data.
5. Any Party may, by a declaration addressed to the Secretary General of the Council of Europe, require that, within the framework of procedures for which it could have refused or limited the transmission or the use of personal data in accordance with the provisions of the Convention or one of its Protocols, personal data transmitted to another Party not be used by the latter for the purposes of paragraph 1 unless with its previous consent.

Article 27 — Administrative authorities

Parties may at any time, by means of a declaration addressed to the Secretary General of the Council of Europe, define what authorities they will deem administrative authorities for the purposes of Article 1, paragraph 3, of the Convention.

Article 28 — Relations with other treaties

The provisions of this Protocol are without prejudice to more extensive regulations in bilateral or multilateral agreements concluded between Parties in application of Article 26, paragraph 3, of the Convention.

Article 29 — Friendly settlement

The European Committee on Crime Problems shall be kept informed regarding the interpretation and application of the Convention and its Protocols, and shall do whatever is necessary to facilitate a friendly settlement of any difficulty which may arise out of their application.

CHAPTER III

Article 30 — Signature and entry into force

1. This Protocol shall be open for signature by the member States of the Council of Europe which are a Party to or have signed the Convention. It shall be subject to ratification, acceptance or approval. A signatory may not ratify, accept or approve this Protocol unless it has previously or simultaneously ratified, accepted or approved the Convention. Instruments of ratification, acceptance or approval shall be deposited with the Secretary General of the Council of Europe.

2. This Protocol shall enter into force on the first day of the month following the expiration of a period of three months after the deposit of the third instrument of ratification, acceptance or approval.

3. In respect of any signatory State which subsequently deposits its instrument of ratification, acceptance or approval, the Protocol shall enter into force on the first day of the month following the expiration of a period of three months after the date of deposit.

Article 31 — Accession

1. Any non-member State, which has acceded to the Convention, may accede to this Protocol after it has entered into force.

2. Such accession shall be effected by depositing with the Secretary General of the Council of Europe an instrument of accession.

3. In respect of any acceding, State, the Protocol shall enter into force on the first day of the month following the expiration of a period of three months after the date of the deposit of the instrument of accession.

Article 32 — Territorial application

1. Any State may at the time of signature or when depositing its instrument of ratification, acceptance, approval or accession, specify the territory or territories to which this Protocol shall apply.

2. Any State may, at any later date, by declaration addressed to the Secretary General of the Council of Europe, extend the application of this Protocol to any other territory specified in the declaration. In respect of such territory the Protocol shall enter into force on the first day of the month following the expiration of a period of three months after the date of receipt of such declaration by the Secretary General.

3. Any declaration made under the two preceding paragraphs may, in respect of any territory specified in such declaration, be withdrawn by a notification addressed to the Secretary General. The withdrawal shall become effective on the first day of the month following the expiration of a period of three months after the date or receipt of such notification by the Secretary General.

Article 33 — Reservations

1. Reservations made by a Party to any provision of the Convention or its Protocol shall be applicable also to this Protocol, unless that Party otherwise declares at the time of signature or when depositing its instrument of ratification, acceptance, approval or accession. The same shall apply to any declaration made in respect or by virtue of any provision of the Convention or its Protocol.

2. Any State may, at the time of signature or when depositing its instrument of ratification, acceptance, approval or accession, declare that it avails itself of the right not to accept wholly or in part any one or more of Articles 16, 17, 18, 19 and 20. No other reservation may be made.

3. Any State may wholly or partially withdraw a reservation it has made in accordance with the foregoing paragraphs, by means of a declaration addressed to the Secretary General of the Council of Europe, which shall become effective as from the date of its receipt.

4. Any Party which has made a reservation in respect of any of the articles of this Protocol mentioned in paragraph 2 above, may not claim the application of that article by another Party. It may, however, if its reservation is partial or conditional, claim the application of that provision in so far as it has itself accepted it.

Article 34 — Denunciation

1. Any Party may, in so far as it is concerned, denounce this Protocol by means of a notification addressed to the Secretary General of the Council of Europe.

2. Such denunciation shall become effective on the first day of the month following the expiration of a period of three months after the date of receipt of the notification by the Secretary General.

3. Denunciation of the Convention entails automatically denunciation of this Protocol.

Article 35 — Notifications

The Secretary General of the Council of Europe shall notify the member States of the Council of Europe and any State which has acceded to this Protocol of:

(a) any signature;
(b) the deposit of any instrument of ratification, acceptance, approval or accession;
(c) any date of entry into force of this Protocol in accordance with Articles 30 and 31;
(d) any other act, declaration, notification or communication relating to this Protocol.

In witness whereof the undersigned, being duly authorised thereto, have signed this Protocol.

Done at Strasbourg, this 8th day of November 2001, in English and in French, both texts being equally authentic, in a single copy which shall be deposited in the archives of the Council of Europe. The Secretary General of the Council of Europe shall transmit certified copies to each member State of the Council of Europe and to the non-member States which have acceded to the Convention.

C–006 Council Framework Decision of 13 June 2002 on the European arrest warrant and the surrender procedures between Member States

(2002/584/JHA)

THE COUNCIL OF THE EUROPEAN UNION,

Having regard to the Treaty on European Union, and in particular Article 31 (a) and (b) and Article 34(2)(b) thereof,

Having regard to the proposal from the Commission[1],

Having regard to the opinion of the European Parliament[2],

Whereas:

(1) According to the Conclusions of the Tampere European Council of 15 and 16 October 1999, and in particular point 35 thereof, the formal extradition procedure should be abolished among the Member States in respect of persons who are fleeing from justice after having been finally sentenced and extradition procedures should be speeded up in respect of persons suspected of having committed an offence.

(2) The programme of measures to implement the principle of mutual recognition of criminal decisions envisaged in point 37 of the Tampere European Council Conclusions and adopted by the Council on 30 November 2000[3], addresses the matter of mutual enforcement of arrest warrants.

(3) All or some Member States are parties to a number of conventions in the field of extradition, including the European Convention on extradition of 13 December 1957 and the European Convention on the suppression of terrorism of 27 January 1977. The Nordic States have extradition laws with identical wording.

(4) In addition, the following three Conventions dealing in whole or in part with extradition have been agreed upon among Member States and form part of the Union *acquis*: the Convention of 19 June 1990 implementing the Schengen Agreement of 14 June 1985 on the gradual abolition of checks at their common borders[4] (regarding relations between the Member States which are parties to that Convention), the Convention of 10 March 1995 on simplified extradition procedure between the Member States of the European Union[5] and the Convention of 27 September 1996 relating to extradition between the Member States of the European Union[6].

(5) The objective set for the Union to become an area of freedom, security and justice leads to abolishing extradition between Member States and replacing it by a system of surrender between judicial authorities. Further, the introduction of a new simplified system of surrender of sentenced or suspected persons for the purposes of execution or prosecution of criminal sentences makes it possible to remove the complexity and potential for delay inherent in the present extradition procedures. Traditional cooperation relations which have prevailed up till now between Member States should be replaced by a system of free movement of judicial decisions in criminal matters, covering both pre-sentence and final decisions, within an area of freedom, security and justice.

(6) The European arrest warrant provided for in this Framework Decision is the first

[1] OJ C 332 E, 27.11.2001, p.305.
[2] Opinion delivered on 9 January 2002 (not yet published in the Official Journal).
[3] OJ C 12 E, 15.1.2001, p.10.
[4] OJ L 239, 22.9.2000, p.19.
[5] OJC 78, 30.3.1995, p.2.
[6] OJC 313, 13.10.1996, p.12.

concrete measure in the field of criminal law implementing the principle of mutual recognition which the European Council referred to as the 'cornerstone' of judicial cooperation.

(7) Since the aim of replacing the system of multilateral extradition built upon the European Convention on Extradition of 13 December 1957 cannot be sufficiently achieved by the Member States acting unilaterally and can therefore, by reason of its scale and effects, be better achieved at Union level, the Council may adopt measures in accordance with the principle of subsidiarity as referred to in Article 2 of the Treaty on European Union and Article 5 of the Treaty establishing the European Community. In accordance with the principle of proportionality, as set out in the latter Article, this Framework Decision does not go beyond what is necessary in order to achieve that objective.

(8) Decisions on the execution of the European arrest warrant must be subject to sufficient controls, which means that a judicial authority of the Member State where the requested person has been arrested will have to take the decision on his or her surrender.

(9) The role of central authorities in the execution of a European arrest warrant must be limited to practical and administrative assistance.

(10) The mechanism of the European arrest warrant is based on a high level of confidence between Member States. Its implementation may be suspended only in the event of a serious and persistent breach by one of the Member States of the principles set out in Article 6(1) of the Treaty on European Union, determined by the Council pursuant to Article 7(1) of the said Treaty with the consequences set out in Article 7(2) thereof.

(11) In relations between Member States, the European arrest warrant should replace all the previous instruments concerning extradition, including the provisions of Title III of the Convention implementing the Schengen Agreement which concern extradition.

(12) This Framework Decision respects fundamental rights and observes the principles recognised by Article 6 of the Treaty on European Union and reflected in the Charter of Fundamental Rights of the European Union[7], in particular Chapter VI thereof. Nothing in this Framework Decision may be interpreted as prohibiting refusal to surrender a person for whom a European arrest warrant has been issued when there are reasons to believe, on the basis of objective elements, that the said arrest warrant has been issued for the purpose of prosecuting or punishing a person on the grounds of his or her sex, race, religion, ethnic origin, nationality, language, political opinions or sexual orientation, or that that person's position may be prejudiced for any of these reasons.

This Framework Decision does not prevent a Member State from applying its constitutional rules relating to due process, freedom of association, freedom of the press and freedom of expression in other media.

(13) No person should be removed, expelled or extradited to a State where there is a serious risk that he or she would be subjected to the death penalty, torture or other inhuman or degrading treatment or punishment.

(14) Since all Member States have ratified the Council of Europe Convention of 28 January 1981 for the protection of individuals with regard to automatic processing of personal data, the personal data processed in the context of the implementation of this Framework Decision should be protected in accordance with the principles of the said Convention,

HAS ADOPTED THIS FRAMEWORK DECISION:

[7] OJC 364, 18.12.2000, p. 1.

APPENDIX C

CHAPTER 1

GENERAL PRINCIPLES

Article 1

Definition of the European arrest warrant and obligation to execute it

1. The European arrest warrant is a judicial decision issued by a Member State with a view to the arrest and surrender by another Member State of a requested person, for the purposes of conducting a criminal prosecution or executing a custodial sentence or detention order.

2. Member States shall execute any European arrest warrant on the basis of the principle of mutual recognition and in accordance with the provisions of this Framework Decision.

3. This Framework Decision shall not have the effect of modifying the obligation to respect fundamental rights and fundamental legal principles as enshrined in Article 6 of the Treaty on European Union.

Article 2

Scope of the European arrest warrant

1. A European arrest warrant may be issued for acts punishable by the law of the issuing Member State by a custodial sentence or a detention order for a maximum period of at least 12 months or, where a sentence has been passed or a detention order has been made, for sentences of at least four months.

2. The following offences, if they are punishable in the issuing Member State by a custodial sentence or a detention order for a maximum period of at least three years and as they are defined by the law of the issuing Member State, shall, under the terms of this Framework Decision and without verification of the double criminality of the act, give rise to surrender pursuant to a European arrest warrant:

- — participation in a criminal organisation,
- — terrorism,
- — trafficking in human beings,
- — sexual exploitation of children and child pornography,
- — illicit trafficking in narcotic drugs and psychotropic substances,
- — illicit trafficking in weapons, munitions and explosives,
- — corruption,
- — fraud, including that affecting the financial interests of the European Communities within the meaning of the Convention of 26 July 1995 on the protection of the European Communities' financial interests,
- — laundering of the proceeds of crime,
- — counterfeiting currency, including of the euro,
- — computer-related crime,
- — environmental crime, including illicit trafficking in endangered animal species and in endangered plant species and varieties,

— facilitation of unauthorised entry and residence,
— murder, grievous bodily injury,
— illicit trade in human organs and tissue,
— kidnapping, illegal restraint and hostage-taking,
— racism and xenophobia,
— organised or armed robbery,
— illicit trafficking in cultural goods, including antiques and works of art,
— swindling,
— racketeering and extortion,
— counterfeiting and piracy of products,
— forgery of administrative documents and trafficking therein,
— forgery of means of payment,
— illicit trafficking in hormonal substances and other growth promoters,
— illicit trafficking in nuclear or radioactive materials,
— trafficking in stolen vehicles,
— rape,
— arson,
— crimes within the jurisdiction of the International Criminal Court,
— unlawful seizure of aircraft/ships,
— sabotage.

3. The Council may decide at any time, acting unanimously after consultation of the European Parliament under the conditions laid down in Article 39(1) of the Treaty on European Union (TEU), to add other categories of offence to the list contained in paragraph 2. The Council shall examine, in the light of the report submitted by the Commission pursuant to Article 34(3), whether the list should be extended or amended.

4. For offences other than those covered by paragraph 2, surrender may be subject to the condition that the acts for which the European arrest warrant has been issued constitute an offence under the law of the executing Member State, whatever the constituent elements or however it is described.

Article 3

Grounds for mandatory non-execution of the European arrest warrant

The judicial authority of the Member State of execution (hereinafter 'executing judicial authority') shall refuse to execute the European arrest warrant in the following cases:

1. if the offence on which the arrest warrant is based is covered by amnesty in the executing Member State, where that State had jurisdiction to prosecute the offence under its own criminal law;

2. if the executing judicial authority is informed that the requested person has been finally judged by a Member State in respect of the same acts provided that, where there has been sentence, the sentence has been served or is currently being served or may no longer be executed under the law of the sentencing Member State;

3. if the person who is the subject of the European arrest warrant may not, owing to his age, be held criminally responsible for the acts on which the arrest warrant is based under the law of the executing State.

Article 4

Grounds for optional non-execution of the European arrest warrant

The executing judicial authority may refuse to execute the European arrest warrant:

1. if, in one of the cases referred to in Article 2(4), the act on which the European arrest warrant is based does not constitute an offence under the law of the executing Member State; however, in relation to taxes or duties, customs and exchange, execution of the European arrest warrant shall not be refused on the ground that the law of the executing Member State does not impose the same kind of tax or duty or does not contain the same type of rules as regards taxes, duties and customs and exchange regulations as the law of the issuing Member State;
2. where the person who is the subject of the European arrest warrant is being prosecuted in the executing Member State for the same act as that on which the European arrest warrant is based;
3. where the judicial authorities of the executing Member State have decided either not to prosecute for the offence on which the European arrest warrant is based or to halt proceedings, or where a final judgment has been passed upon the requested person in a Member State, in respect of the same acts, which prevents further proceedings;
4. where the criminal prosecution or punishment of the requested person is statute-barred according to the law of the executing Member State and the acts fall within the jurisdiction of that Member State under its own criminal law;
5. if the executing judicial authority is informed that the requested person has been finally judged by a third State in respect of the same acts provided that, where there has been sentence, the sentence has been served or is currently being served or may no longer be executed under the law of the sentencing country;
6. if the European arrest warrant has been issued for the purposes of execution of a custodial sentence or detention order, where the requested person is staying in, or is a national or a resident of the executing Member State and that State undertakes to execute the sentence or detention order in accordance with its domestic law;
7. where the European arrest warrant relates to offences which:

   (a) are regarded by the law of the executing Member State as having been committed in whole or in part in the territory of the executing Member State or in a place treated as such; or

   (b) have been committed outside the territory of the issuing Member State and the law of the executing Member State does not allow prosecution for the same offences when committed outside its territory.

Article 5

Guarantees to be given by the issuing Member State in particular cases

The execution of the European arrest warrant by the executing judicial authority may, by the law of the executing Member State, be subject to the following conditions:

1. where the European arrest warrant has been issued for the purposes of executing a sentence or a detention order imposed by a decision rendered *in absentia* and if the person

concerned has not been summoned in person or otherwise informed of the date and place of the hearing which led to the decision rendered *in absentia*, surrender may be subject to the condition that the issuing judicial authority gives an assurance deemed adequate to guarantee the person who is the subject of the European arrest warrant that he or she will have an opportunity to apply for a retrial of the case in the issuing Member State and to be present at the judgment;

2. if the offence on the basis of which the European arrest warrant has been issued is punishable by custodial life sentence or life-time detention order, the execution of the said arrest warrant may be subject to the condition that the issuing Member State has provisions in its legal system for a review of the penalty or measure imposed, on request or at the latest after 20 years, or for the application of measures of clemency to which the person is entitled to apply for under the law or practice of the issuing Member State, aiming at a non-execution of such penalty or measure;

3. where a person who is the subject of a European arrest warrant for the purposes of prosecution is a national or resident of the executing Member State, surrender may be subject to the condition that the person, after being heard, is returned to the executing Member State in order to serve there the custodial sentence or detention order passed against him in the issuing Member State.

Article 6

Determination of the competent judicial authorities

1. The issuing judicial authority shall be the judicial authority of the issuing Member State which is competent to issue a European arrest warrant by virtue of the law of that State.

2. The executing judicial authority shall be the judicial authority of the executing Member State which is competent to execute the European arrest warrant by virtue of the law of that State.

3. Each Member State shall inform the General Secretariat of the Council of the competent judicial authority under its law.

Article 7

Recourse to the central authority

1. Each Member State may designate a central authority or, when its legal system so provides, more than one central authority to assist the competent judicial authorities.

2. A Member State may, if it is necessary as a result of the organisation of its internal judicial system, make its central authority(ies) responsible for the administrative transmission and reception of European arrest warrants as well as for all other official correspondence relating thereto.

Member State wishing to make use of the possibilities referred to in this Article shall communicate to the General Secretariat of the Council information relating to the designated central authority or central authorities. These indications shall be binding upon all the authorities of the issuing Member State.

Article 8

Content and form of the European arrest warrant

1. The European arrest warrant shall contain the following information set out in accordance with the form contained in the Annex:

(a) the identity and nationality of the requested person;
(b) the name, address, telephone and fax numbers and e-mail address of the issuing judicial authority;
(c) evidence of an enforceable judgment, an arrest warrant or any other enforceable judicial decision having the same effect, coming within the scope of Articles 1 and 2;
(d) the nature and legal classification of the offence, particularly in respect of Article 2;
(e) a description of the circumstances in which the offence was committed, including the time, place and degree of participation in the offence by the requested person;
(f) the penalty imposed, if there is a final judgment, or the prescribed scale of penalties for the offence under the law of the issuing Member State;
(g) if possible, other consequences of the offence.

2. The European arrest warrant must be translated into the official language or one of the official languages of the executing Member State. Any Member State may, when this Framework Decision is adopted or at a later date, state in a declaration deposited with the General Secretariat of the Council that it will accept a translation in one or more other official languages of the Institutions of the European Communities.

Chapter 2

Surrender Procedure

Article 9

Transmission of a European arrest warrant

1. When the location of the requested person is known, the issuing judicial authority may transmit the European arrest warrant directly to the executing judicial authority.

2. The issuing judicial authority may, in any event, decide to issue an alert for the requested person in the Schengen Information System (SIS).

3. Such an alert shall be effected in accordance with the provisions of Article 95 of the Convention of 19 June 1990 implementing the Schengen Agreement of 14 June 1985 on the gradual abolition of controls at common borders. An alert in the Schengen Information System shall be equivalent to a European arrest warrant accompanied by the information set out in Article 8(1).

For a transitional period, until the SIS is capable of transmitting all the information described in Article 8, the alert shall be equivalent to a European arrest warrant pending the receipt of the original in due and proper form by the executing judicial authority.

Article 10

Detailed procedures for transmitting a European arrest warrant

1. If the issuing judicial authority does not know the competent executing judicial authority, it shall make the requisite enquiries, including through the contact points of the European Judicial Network[1], in order to obtain that information from the executing Member State.

2. If the issuing judicial authority so wishes, transmission may be effected via the secure telecommunications system of the European Judicial Network.

3. If it is not possible to call on the services of the SIS, the issuing judicial authority may call on Interpol to transmit a European arrest warrant.

4. The issuing judicial authority may forward the European arrest warrant by any secure means capable of producing written records under conditions allowing the executing Member State to establish its authenticity.

5. All difficulties concerning the transmission or the authenticity of any document needed for the execution of the European arrest warrant shall be dealt with by direct contacts between the judicial authorities involved, or, where appropriate, with the involvement of the central authorities of the Member States.

6. If the authority which receives a European arrest warrant is not competent to act upon it, it shall automatically forward the European arrest warrant to the competent authority in its Member State and shall inform the issuing judicial authority accordingly.

Article 11

Rights of a requested person

1. When a requested person is arrested, the executing competent judicial authority shall, in accordance with its national law, inform that person of the European arrest warrant and of its contents, and also of the possibility of consenting to surrender to the issuing judicial authority.

2. A requested person who is arrested for the purpose of the execution of a European arrest warrant shall have a right to be assisted by a legal counsel and by an interpreter in accordance with the national law of the executing Member State.

Article 12

Keeping the person in detention

When a person is arrested on the basis of a European arrest warrant, the executing judicial authority shall take a decision on whether the requested person should remain in detention, in accordance with the law of the executing Member State. The person may be released provisionally at any time in conformity with the domestic law of the executing Member State,

[1] Council Joint Action 98/428/JHA of 29 June 1998 on the creation of a European Judicial Network (OJ L 191, 7.7.1998, p. 4).

provided that the competent authority of the said Member State takes all the measures it deems necessary to prevent the person absconding.

Article 13

Consent to surrender

1. If the arrested person indicates that he or she consents to surrender, that consent and, if appropriate, express renunciation of entitlement to the "speciality rule", referred to in Article 27(2), shall be given before the executing judicial authority, in accordance with the domestic law of the executing Member State.

2. Each Member State shall adopt the measures necessary to ensure that consent and, where appropriate, renunciation, as referred to in paragraph 1, are established in such a way as to show that the person concerned has expressed them voluntarily and in full awareness of the consequences. To that end, the requested person shall have the right to legal counsel.

3. The consent and, where appropriate, renunciation, as referred to in paragraph 1, shall be formally recorded in accordance with the procedure laid down by the domestic law of the executing Member State.

4. In principle, consent may not be revoked. Each Member State may provide that consent and, if appropriate, renunciation may be revoked, in accordance with the rules applicable under its domestic law. In this case, the period between the date of consent and that of its revocation shall not be taken into consideration in establishing the time limits laid down in Article 17. A Member State which wishes to have recourse to this possibility shall inform the General Secretariat of the Council accordingly when this Framework Decision is adopted and shall specify the procedures whereby revocation of consent shall be possible and any amendment to them.

Article 14

Hearing of the requested person

Where the arrested person does not consent to his or her surrender as referred to in Article 13, he or she shall be entitled to be heard by the executing judicial authority, in accordance with the law of the executing Member State.

Article 15

Surrender decision

1. The executing judicial authority shall decide, within the time-limits and under the conditions defined in this Framework Decision, whether the person is to be surrendered.

2. If the executing judicial authority finds the information communicated by the issuing Member State to be insufficient to allow it to decide on surrender, it shall request that the

necessary supplementary information, in particular with respect to Articles 3 to 5 and Article 8, be furnished as a matter of urgency and may fix a time limit for the receipt thereof, taking into account the need to observe the time limits set in Article 17.

3. The issuing judicial authority may at any time forward any additional useful information to the executing judicial authority.

Article 16

Decision in the event of multiple requests

1. If two or more Member States have issued European arrest warrants for the same person, the decision on which of the European arrest warrants shall be executed shall be taken by the executing judicial authority with due consideration of all the circumstances and especially the relative seriousness and place of the offences, the respective dates of the European arrest warrants and whether the warrant has been issued for the purposes of prosecution or for execution of a custodial sentence or detention order.

2. The executing judicial authority may seek the advice of Eurojust[1] when making the choice referred to in paragraph 1.

3. In the event of a conflict between a European arrest warrant and a request for extradition presented by a third country, the decision on whether the European arrest warrant or the extradition request takes precedence shall be taken by the competent authority of the executing Member State with due consideration of all the circumstances, in particular those referred to in paragraph 1 and those mentioned in the applicable convention.

4. This Article shall be without prejudice to Member States' obligations under the Statute of the International Criminal Court.

Article 17

Time limits and procedures for the decision to execute the European arrest warrant

1. A European arrest warrant shall be dealt with and executed as a matter of urgency.

2. In cases where the requested person consents to his surrender, the final decision on the execution of the European arrest warrant should be taken within a period of 10 days after consent has been given.

3. In other cases, the final decision on the execution of the European arrest warrant should be taken within a period of 60 days after the arrest of the requested person.

4. Where in specific cases the European arrest warrant cannot be executed within the time limits laid down in paragraphs 2 or 3, the executing judicial authority shall immediately inform the issuing judicial authority thereof, giving the reasons for the delay. In such case, the time limits may be extended by a further 30 days.

5. As long as the executing judicial authority has not taken a final decision on the European arrest warrant, it shall ensure that the material conditions necessary for effective surrender of the person remain fulfilled.

6. Reasons must be given for any refusal to execute a European arrest warrant.

[1] Council Decision 2002/187/JHA of 28 February 2002 setting up Eurojust with a view to reinforcing the fight against serious crime (OJ L 63, 6.3.2002, p. 1).

7. Where in exceptional circumstances a Member State cannot observe the time limits provided for in this Article, it shall inform Eurojust, giving the reasons for the delay. In addition, a Member State which has experienced repeated delays on the part of another Member State in the execution of European arrest warrants shall inform the Council with a view to evaluating the implementation of this Framework Decision at Member State level.

Article 18

Situation pending the decision

1. Where the European arrest warrant has been issued for the purpose of conducting a criminal prosecution, the executing judicial authority must:

(a) either agree that the requested person should be heard according to Article 19;
(b) or agree to the temporary transfer of the requested person.

2. The conditions and the duration of the temporary transfer shall be determined by mutual agreement between the issuing and executing judicial authorities.

3. In the case of temporary transfer, the person must be able to return to the executing Member State to attend hearings concerning him or her as part of the surrender procedure.

Article 19

Hearing the person pending the decision

1. The requested person shall be heard by a judicial authority, assisted by another person designated in accordance with the law of the Member State of the requesting court.

2. The requested person shall be heard in accordance with the law of the executing Member State and with the conditions determined by mutual agreement between the issuing and executing judicial authorities.

3. The competent executing judicial authority may assign another judicial authority of its Member State to take part in the hearing of the requested person in order to ensure the proper application of this Article and of the conditions laid down.

Article 20

Privileges and immunities

1. Where the requested person enjoys a privilege or immunity regarding jurisdiction or execution in the executing Member State, the time limits referred to in Article 17 shall not start running unless, and counting from the day when, the executing judicial authority is informed of the fact that the privilege or immunity has been waived.

The executing Member State shall ensure that the material conditions necessary for effective surrender are fulfilled when the person no longer enjoys such privilege or immunity.

2. Where power to waive the privilege or immunity lies with an authority of the executing Member State, the executing judicial authority shall request it to exercise that power forthwith. Where power to waive the privilege or immunity lies with an authority of another State or international organisation, it shall be for the issuing judicial authority to request it to exercise that power.

Article 21

Competing international obligations

This Framework Decision shall not prejudice the obligations of the executing Member State where the requested person has been extradited to that Member State from a third State and where that person is protected by provisions of the arrangement under which he or she was extradited concerning speciality. The executing Member State shall take all necessary measures for requesting forthwith the consent of the State from which the requested person was extradited so that he or she can be surrendered to the Member State which issued the European arrest warrant. The time limits referred to in Article 17 shall not start running until the day on which these speciality rules cease to apply. Pending the decision of the State from which the requested person was extradited, the executing Member State will ensure that the material conditions necessary for effective surrender remain fulfilled.

Article 22

Notification of the decision

The executing judicial authority shall notify the issuing judicial authority immediately of the decision on the action to be taken on the European arrest warrant.

Article 23

Time limits for surrender of the person

1. The person requested shall be surrendered as soon as possible on a date agreed between the authorities concerned.

2. He or she shall be surrendered no later than 10 days after the final decision on the execution of the European arrest warrant.

3. If the surrender of the requested person within the period laid down in paragraph 2 is prevented by circumstances beyond the control of any of the Member States, the executing and issuing judicial authorities shall immediately contact each other and agree on a new surrender date. In that event, the surrender shall take place within 10 days of the new date thus agreed.

4. The surrender may exceptionally be temporarily postponed for serious humanitarian reasons, for example if there are substantial grounds for believing that it would manifestly endanger the requested person's life or health. The execution of the European arrest warrant shall take place as soon as these grounds have ceased to exist. The executing judicial

authority shall immediately inform the issuing judicial authority and agree on a new surrender date. In that event, the surrender shall take place within 10 days of the new date thus agreed.

5. Upon expiry of the time limits referred to in paragraphs 2 to 4, if the person is still being held in custody he shall be released.

Article 24

Postponed or conditional surrender

1. The executing judicial authority may, after deciding to execute the European arrest warrant, postpone the surrender of the requested person so that he or she may be prosecuted in the executing Member State or, if he or she has already been sentenced, so that he or she may serve, in its territory, a sentence passed for an act other than that referred to in the European arrest warrant.

2. Instead of postponing the surrender, the executing judicial authority may temporarily surrender the requested person to the issuing Member State under conditions to be determined by mutual agreement between the executing and the issuing judicial authorities. The agreement shall be made in writing and the conditions shall be binding on all the authorities in the issuing Member State.

Article 25

Transit

1. Each Member State shall, except when it avails itself of the possibility of refusal when the transit of a national or a resident is requested for the purpose of the execution of a custodial sentence or detention order, permit the transit through its territory of a requested person who is being surrendered provided that it has been given information on:

(a) the identity and nationality of the person subject to the European arrest warrant;
(b) the existence of a European arrest warrant;
(c) the nature and legal classification of the offence;
(d) the description of the circumstances of the offence, including the date and place.

Where a person who is the subject of a European arrest warrant for the purposes of prosecution is a national or resident of the Member State of transit, transit may be subject to the condition that the person, after being heard, is returned to the transit Member State to serve the custodial sentence or detention order passed against him in the issuing Member State.

2. Each Member State shall designate an authority responsible for receiving transit requests and the necessary documents, as well as any other official correspondence relating to transit requests. Member States shall communicate this designation to the General Secretariat of the Council.

3. The transit request and the information set out in paragraph 1 may be addressed to the authority designated pursuant to paragraph 2 by any means capable of producing a written record. The Member State of transit shall notify its decision by the same procedure.

4. This Framework Decision does not apply in the case of transport by air without a scheduled stopover. However, if an unscheduled landing occurs, the issuing Member State shall provide the authority designated pursuant to paragraph 2 with the information provided for in paragraph 1.

5. Where a transit concerns a person who is to be extradited from a third State to a Member State this Article will apply *mutatis mutandis.* In particular the expression "European arrest warrant" shall be deemed to be replaced by "extradition request".

CHAPTER 3

EFFECTS OF THE SURRENDER

Article 26

Deduction of the period of detention served in the executing Member State

1. The issuing Member State shall deduct all periods of detention arising from the execution of a European arrest warrant from the total period of detention to be served in the issuing Member State as a result of a custodial sentence or detention order being passed.

2. To that end, all information concerning the duration of the detention of the requested person on the basis of the European arrest warrant shall be transmitted by the executing judicial authority or the central authority designated under Article 7 to the issuing judicial authority at the time of the surrender.

Article 27

Possible prosecution for other offences

1. Each Member State may notify the General Secretariat of the Council that, in its relations with other Member States that have given the same notification, consent is presumed to have been given for the prosecution, sentencing or detention with a view to the carrying out of a custodial sentence or detention order for an offence committed prior to his or her surrender, other than that for which he or she was surrendered, unless in a particular case the executing judicial authority states otherwise in its decision on surrender.

2. Except in the cases referred to in paragraphs 1 and 3, a person surrendered may not be prosecuted, sentenced or otherwise deprived of his or her liberty for an offence committed prior to his or her surrender other than that for which he or she was surrendered.

3. Paragraph 2 does not apply in the following cases:

(a) when the person having had an opportunity to leave the territory of the Member State to which he or she has been surrendered has not done so within 45 days of his or her final discharge, or has returned to that territory after leaving it;
(b) the offence is not punishable by a custodial sentence or detention order;
(c) the criminal proceedings do not give rise to the application of a measure restricting personal liberty;

(d) when the person could be liable to a penalty or a measure not involving the deprivation of liberty, in particular a financial penalty or a measure in lieu thereof, even if the penalty or measure may give rise to a restriction of his or her personal liberty;
(e) when the person consented to be surrendered, where appropriate at the same time as he or she renounced the speciality rule, in accordance with Article 13;
(f) when the person, after his/her surrender, has expressly renounced entitlement to the speciality rule with regard to specific offences preceding his/her surrender. Renunciation shall be given before the competent judicial authorities of the issuing Member State and shall be recorded in accordance with that State's domestic law. The renunciation shall be drawn up in such a way as to make clear that the person has given it voluntarily and in full awareness of the consequences. To that end, the person shall have the right to legal counsel;
(g) where the executing judicial authority which surrendered the person gives its consent in accordance with paragraph 4.

4. A request for consent shall be submitted to the executing judicial authority, accompanied by the information mentioned in Article 8(1) and a translation as referred to in Article 8(2). Consent shall be given when the offence for which it is requested is itself subject to surrender in accordance with the provisions of this Framework Decision. Consent shall be refused on the grounds referred to in Article 3 and otherwise may be refused only on the grounds referred to in Article 4. The decision shall be taken no later than 30 days after receipt of the request.

For the situations mentioned in Article 5 the issuing Member State must give the guarantees provided for therein.

Article 28

Surrender or subsequent extradition

1. Each Member State may notify the General Secretariat of the Council that, in its relations with other Member States which have given the same notification, the consent for the surrender of a person to a Member State other than the executing Member State pursuant to a European arrest warrant issued for an offence committed prior to his or her surrender is presumed to have been given, unless in a particular case the executing judicial authority states otherwise in its decision on surrender.

2. In any case, a person who has been surrendered to the issuing Member State pursuant to a European arrest warrant may, without the consent of the executing Member State, be surrendered to a Member State other than the executing Member State pursuant to a European arrest warrant issued for any offence committed prior to his or her surrender in the following cases:

(a) where the requested person, having had an opportunity to leave the territory of the Member State to which he or she has been surrendered, has not done so within 45 days of his final discharge, or has returned to that territory after leaving it;
(b) where the requested person consents to be surrendered to a Member State other than the executing Member State pursuant to a European arrest warrant. Consent shall be given before the competent judicial authorities of the issuing Member State and shall be recorded in accordance with that State's national law. It shall be drawn up in such a way as to make clear that the person concerned has given it voluntarily and in full awareness of the consequences. To that end, the requested person shall have the right to legal counsel;

(c) where the requested person is not subject to the speciality rule, in accordance with Article 27(3)(a), (e), (f) and (g).

3. The executing judicial authority consents to the surrender to another Member State according to the following rules:

(a) the request for consent shall be submitted in accordance with Article 9, accompanied by the information mentioned in Article 8(1) and a translation as stated in Article 8(2);
(b) consent shall be given when the offence for which it is requested is itself subject to surrender in accordance with the provisions of this Framework Decision;
(c) the decision shall be taken no later than 30 days after receipt of the request;
(d) consent shall be refused on the grounds referred to in Article 3 and otherwise may be refused only on the grounds referred to in Article 4.

For the situations referred to in Article 5, the issuing Member State must give the guarantees provided for therein.

4. Notwithstanding paragraph 1, a person who has been surrendered pursuant to a European arrest warrant shall not be extradited to a third State without the consent of the competent authority of the Member State which surrendered the person. Such consent shall be given in accordance with the Conventions by which that Member State is bound, as well as with its domestic law.

Article 29

Handing over of property

1. At the request of the issuing judicial authority or on its own initiative, the executing judicial authority shall, in accordance with its national law, seize and hand over property which:

(a) may be required as evidence, or
(b) has been acquired by the requested person as a result of the offence.

2. The property referred to in paragraph 1 shall be handed over even if the European arrest warrant cannot be carried out owing to the death or escape of the requested person.

3. If the property referred to in paragraph 1 is liable to seizure or confiscation in the territory of the executing Member State, the latter may, if the property is needed in connection with pending criminal proceedings, temporarily retain it or hand it over to the issuing Member State, on condition that it is returned.

4. Any rights which the executing Member State or third parties may have acquired in the property referred to in paragraph 1 shall be preserved. Where such rights exist, the issuing Member State shall return the property without charge to the executing Member State as soon as the criminal proceedings have been terminated.

Article 30

Expenses

1.Expenses incurred in the territory of the executing Member State for the execution of a European arrest warrant shall be borne by that Member State.

2. All other expenses shall be borne by the issuing Member State.

Chapter 4

General and Final Provisions

Article 31

Relation to other legal instruments

1. Without prejudice to their application in relations between Member States and third States, this Framework Decision shall, from 1 January 2004, replace the corresponding provisions of the following conventions applicable in the field of extradition in relations between the Member States:

(a) the European Convention on Extradition of 13 December 1957, its additional protocol of 15 October 1975, its second additional protocol of 17 March 1978, and the European Convention on the suppression of terrorism of 27 January 1977 as far as extradition is concerned;
(b) the Agreement between the 12 Member States of the European Communities on the simplification and modernisation of methods of transmitting extradition requests of 26 May 1989;
(c) the Convention of 10 March 1995 on simplified extradition procedure between the Member States of the European Union;
(d) the Convention of 27 September 1996 relating to extradition between the Member States of the European Union;
(e) Title III, Chapter 4 of the Convention of 19 June 1990 implementing the Schengen Agreement of 14 June 1985 on the gradual abolition of checks at common borders.

2. Member States may continue to apply bilateral or multilateral agreements or arrangements in force when this Framework Decision is adopted in so far as such agreements or arrangements allow the objectives of this Framework Decision to be extended or enlarged and help to simplify or facilitate further the procedures for surrender of persons who are the subject of European arrest warrants.

Member States may conclude bilateral or multilateral agreements or arrangements after this Framework Decision has come into force in so far as such agreements or arrangements allow the prescriptions of this Framework Decision to be extended or enlarged and help to simplify or facilitate further the procedures for surrender of persons who are the subject of European arrest warrants, in particular by fixing time limits shorter than those fixed in Article 17, by extending the list of offences laid down in Article 2(2), by further limiting the grounds for refusal set out in Articles 3 and 4, or by lowering the threshold provided for in Article 2(1) or (2).

The agreements and arrangements referred to in the second subparagraph may in no case affect relations with Member States which are not parties to them.

Member States shall, within three months from the entry into force of this Framework Decision, notify the Council and the Commission of the existing agreements and arrangements referred to in the first subparagraph which they wish to continue applying.

Member States shall also notify the Council and the Commission of any new agreement or arrangement as referred to in the second subparagraph, within three months of signing it.

3. Where the conventions or agreements referred to in paragraph 1 apply to the territories of Member States or to territories for whose external relations a Member State is responsible to which this Framework Decision does not apply, these instruments shall continue to govern the relations existing between those territories and the other Members States.

Article 32

Transitional provision

1. Extradition requests received before 1 January 2004 will continue to be governed by existing instruments relating to extradition. Requests received after that date will be governed by the rules adopted by Member States pursuant to this Framework Decision. However, any Member State may, at the time of the adoption of this Framework Decision by the Council, make a statement indicating that as executing Member State it will continue to deal with requests relating to acts committed before a date which it specifies in accordance with the extradition system applicable before 1 January 2004. The date in question may not be later than 7 August 2002. The said statement will be published in the *Official Journal of the European Communities.* It may be withdrawn at any time.

Article 33

Provisions concerning Austria and Gibraltar

1. As long as Austria has not modified Article 12(1) of the 'Auslieferungs- und Rechtshilfegesetz' and, at the latest, until 31 December 2008, it may allow its executing judicial authorities to refuse the enforcement of a European arrest warrant if the requested person is an Austrian citizen and if the act for which the European arrest warrant has been issued is not punishable under Austrian law.

2. This Framework Decision shall apply to Gibraltar.

Article 34

Implementation

1. Member States shall take the necessary measures to comply with the provisions of this Framework Decision by 31 December 2003.

2. Member States shall transmit to the General Secretariat of the Council and to the Commission the text of the provisions transposing into their national law the obligations imposed on them under this Framework Decision. When doing so, each Member State may indicate that it will apply immediately this Framework Decision in its relations with those Member States which have given the same notification.

The General Secretariat of the Council shall communicate to the Member States and to the Commission the information received pursuant to Article 7(2), Article 8(2), Article 13(4) and Article 25(2). It shall also have the information published in the *Official journal of the European Communities.*

3. On the basis of the information communicated by the General Secretariat of the Council, the Commission shall, by 31 December 2004 at the latest, submit a report to the European Parliament and to the Council on the operation of this Framework Decision, accompanied, where necessary, by legislative proposals.

4. The Council shall in the second half of 2003 conduct a review, in particular of the practical application, of the provisions of this Framework Decision by the Member States as well as the functioning of the Schengen Information System.

Article 35

Entry into force

This Framework Decision shall enter into force on the twentieth day following that of its publication in the *Official journal of the European Communities.*

Done at Luxembourg, 13 June 2002.

For the Council
The President
M. RAJOY BREY

ANNEX

EUROPEAN ARREST WARRANT[1]

This warrant has been issued by a competent judicial authority. I request that the person mentioned below be arrested and surrendered for the purposes of conducting a criminal prosecution or executing a custodial sentence or detention order.

[1] This warrant must be written in, or translated into, one of the official languages of the executing Member State, when that State is known, or any other language accepted by that State.

(a) Information regarding the identity of the requested person: ....

Name: ....

Forename(s): ....

Maiden name, where applicable: ....

Aliases, where applicable: ....

Sex: ....

Nationality: ....

Date of birth: ....

Place of birth: ....

Residence and/or known address: ....

Language(s) which the requested person understands (if known): ....

....

Distinctive marks/description of the requested person: ....

....

Photo and fingerprints of the requested person, if they are available and can be transmitted, or contact details of the person to be contacted in order to obtain such information or a DNA profile (where this evidence can be supplied but has not been included)

(b) Decision on which the warrant is based:

1. Arrest warrant or judicial decision having the same effect: ....

Type: ....

2. Enforceable judgement: ....

....

Reference: ....

(c) Indications on the length of the sentence:

1. Maximum length of the custodial sentence or detention order which may be imposed for the offence(s):

   ....

   ....

2. Length of the custodial sentence or detention order imposed:

   ....

   Remaining sentence to be served: ....

   ....

   ....

d) Decision rendered in absentia and:

— the person concerned has been summoned in person or otherwise informed of the date and place of the hearing which led to the decision rendered in absentia,

or

— the person concerned has not been summoned in person or otherwise informed of the date and place of the hearing which led to the decision rendered in absentia but has the following legal guarantees after surrender (such guarantees can be given in advance)

Specify the legal guarantees

....

....

....

(e) Offences:

This warrant relates to in total: .... offences.

Description of the circumstances in which the offence(s) was (were) committed, including the time, place and degree of participation in the offence(s) by the requested person:

....

....

....

Nature and legal classification of the offence(s) and the applicable statutory provision/code:

....

....

....

....

....

I. If applicable, tick one or more of the following offences punishable in the issuing Member State by a custodial sentence or detention order of a maximum of at least 3 years as defined by the laws of the issuing Member State:

☐ participation in a criminal organisation;

☐ terrorism;

☐ trafficking in human beings;

☐ sexual exploitation of children and child pornography;

☐ illicit trafficking in narcotic drugs and psychotropic substances;

☐ illicit trafficking in weapons, munitions and explosives;

☐ corruption;

☐ fraud, including that affecting the financial interests of the European Communities within the meaning of the Convention of 26 July 1995 on the protection of European Communities' financial interests;

☐ laundering of the proceeds of crime;

☐ counterfeiting of currency, including the euro;

☐ computer-related crime;

☐ environmental crime, including illicit trafficking in endangered animal species and in endangered plant species and varieties;

☐ facilitation of unauthorised entry and residence;

☐ murder, grievous bodily injury;

☐ illicit trade in human organs and tissue;

☐ kidnapping, illegal restraint and hostage-taking;

☐ racism and xenophobia;

☐ organised or armed robbery;

☐ illicit trafficking in cultural goods, including antiques and works of art;

☐ swindling;

☐ racketeering and extortion;

☐ counterfeiting and piracy of products;

☐ forgery of administrative documents and trafficking therein;

☐ forgery of means of payment;

☐ illicit trafficking in hormonal substances and other growth promoters;

☐ illicit trafficking in nuclear or radioactive materials;

☐ trafficking in stolen vehicles;

☐ rape;

☐ arson;

☐ crimes within the jurisdiction of the International Criminal Court;

☐ unlawful seizure of aircraft/ships;

☐ sabotage.

II. Full descriptions of offence(s) not covered by section I above:

....

....

(f) Other circumstances relevant to the case (optional information):

(NB: This *could cover remarks on extraterritoriality, interruption of periods of time limitation and other consequences of the offence)*

....

....

(g) This warrant pertains also to the seizure and handing over of property which may be required as evidence:

This warrant pertains also to the seizure and handing over of property acquired by the requested person as a result of the offence:

Description of the property (and location) (if known):

....

....

....

(h) The offence(s) on the basis of which this warrant has been issued is(are) punishable by/has (have) led to a custodial life sentence or lifetime detention order:

— the legal system of the issuing Member State allows for a review of the penalty or measure imposed — on request or at least after 20 years — aiming at a non-execution of such penalty or measure,

and/or

— the legal system of the issuing Member State allows for the application of measures of clemency to which the person is entitled under the law or practice of the issuing Member State, aiming at non-execution of such penalty or measure.

(i) The judicial authority which issued the warrant:

Official name:

Name of its representative[1]: ....

....

Post held (title/grade): ....

....

File reference: ....

Address: ....

....

Tel: (country code) (area/city code) (...) ....

Fax: (country code) (area/city code) (...) ....

E-mail: ....

Contact details of the person to contact to make necessary practical arrangements for the surrender: ....

....

Where a central authority has been made responsible for the transmission and administrative reception of European arrest warrants:

Name of the central authority:

....

Contact person, if applicable (title/grade and name):

....

Address: ....

....

Tel: (country code) (area/city code) (...) ....

Fax: (country code) (area/city code) (...) ....

E-mail: ....

[1] In the different language versions a reference to the 'holder' of the judicial authority will be included.

Signature of the issuing judicial authority and/or its representative:

....

Name: ....

Post held (title/grade): ....

Date: ....

Official stamp (if available)

Extradition Treaty Between the Government of the United Kingdom of Great Britain and Northen Ireland and the Government of the United States of America C–007

The Government of the United Kingdom of Great Britain and Northern Ireland and the Government of the United States of America,

Recalling the Extradition Treaty between the Government of the United States of America and the Government of the United Kingdom of Great Britain and Northern Ireland signed at London, June 8, 1972[1], as amended by the Supplementary Treaty between the two States, signed at Washington, June 25, 1985[2]; and

Desiring to provide for more effective cooperation between the two States in the suppression of crime, and, for that purpose, to conclude a new treaty for the extradition of offenders;

Have agreed as follows:

Article 1

Obligation to Extradite

The Parties agree to extradite to each other, pursuant to the provisions of this Treaty, persons sought by the authorities in the Requesting State for trial or punishment for extraditable offences.

Article 2

Extraditable Offences

1. An offence shall be an extraditable offence if the conduct on which the offence is based is punishable under the laws in both States by deprivation of liberty for a period of one year or more or by a more severe penalty.

2. An offence shall also be an extraditable offence if it consists of an attempt or a conspiracy to commit, participation in the commission of, aiding or abetting, counseling or procuring the commission of, or being an accessory before or after the fact to any offence described in paragraph 1 of this Article.

3. For the purposes of this Article, an offence shall be an extraditable offence:

(a) whether or not the laws in the Requesting and Requested States place the offence within the same category of offences or describe the offence by the same terminology; or

(b) whether or not the offence is one for which United States federal law requires the showing of such matters as interstate transportation, or use of the mails or of other facilities affecting interstate or foreign commerce, such matters being jurisdictional only.

[1] Treaty Series No. 16 (1977) Cmnd 6723

[2] Treaty Series No. 6 (1988) Cm 294

4. If the offence has been committed outside the territory of the Requesting State, extradition shall be granted in accordance with the provisions of the Treaty if the laws in the Requested State provide for the punishment of such conduct committed outside its territory in similar circumstances. If the laws in the Requested State do not provide for the punishment of such conduct committed outside of its territory in similar circumstances, the executive authority of the Requested State, in its discretion, may grant extradition provided that all other requirements of this Treaty are met.

5. If extradition has been granted for an extraditable offence, it may also be granted for any other offence specified in the request if the latter offence is punishable by less than one year's deprivation of liberty, provided that all other requirements for extradition are met.

Article 3

Nationality

Extradition shall not be refused based on the nationality of the person sought.

Article 4

Political and Military Offences

1. Extradition shall not be granted if the offence for which extradition is requested is a political offence.

2. For the purposes of this Treaty, the following offences shall not be considered political offences:

(a) an offence for which both Parties have the obligation pursuant to a multilateral international agreement to extradite the person sought or to submit the case to their competent authorities for decision as to prosecution;
(b) a murder or other violent crime against the person of a Head of State of one of the Parties, or of a member of the Head of State's family;
(c) murder, manslaughter, malicious wounding, or inflicting grievous bodily harm;
(d) an offence involving kidnapping, abduction, or any form of unlawful detention, including the taking of a hostage;
(e) placing or using, or threatening the placement or use of, an explosive, incendiary, or destructive device or firearm capable of endangering life, of causing grievous bodily harm, or of causing substantial property damage;
(f) possession of an explosive, incendiary, or destructive device capable of endangering life, of causing grievous bodily harm, or of causing substantial property damage;
(g) an attempt or a conspiracy to commit, participation in the commission of, aiding or abetting, counseling or procuring the commission of, or being an accessory before or after the fact to any of the foregoing offences.

3. Notwithstanding the terms of paragraph 2 of this Article, extradition shall not be granted if the competent authority of the Requested State determines that the request was

politically motivated. In the United States, the executive branch is the competent authority for the purposes of this Article.

4. The competent authority of the Requested State may refuse extradition for offences under military law that are not offences under ordinary criminal law. In the United States, the executive branch is the competent authority for the purposes of this Article.

Article 5

Prior Prosecution

1. Extradition shall not be granted when the person sought has been convicted or acquitted in the Requested State for the offence for which extradition is requested.

2. The Requested State may refuse extradition when the person sought has been convicted or acquitted in a third state in respect of the conduct for which extradition is requested.

3. Extradition shall not be precluded by the fact that the competent authorities of the Requested State:

(a) have decided not to prosecute the person sought for the acts for which extradition is requested;
(b) have decided to discontinue any criminal proceedings which have been instituted against the person sought for those acts; or
(c) are still investigating the person sought for the same acts for which extradition is sought.

Article 6

Statute of Limitations

The decision by the Requested State whether to grant the request for extradition shall be made without regard to any statute of limitations in either State.

Article 7

Capital Punishment

When the offence for which extradition is sought is punishable by death under the laws in the Requesting State and is not punishable by death under the laws in the Requested State, the executive authority in the Requested State may refuse extradition unless the Requesting State provides an assurance that the death penalty will not be imposed or, if imposed, will not be carried out.

Article 8

Extradition Procedures and Required Documents

1. All requests for extradition shall be submitted through the diplomatic channel.

2. All requests for extradition shall be supported by:

(a) as accurate a description as possible of the person sought, together with any other information that would help to establish identity and probable location;
(b) a statement of the facts of the offence(s);
(c) the relevant text of the law(s) describing the essential elements of the offence for which extradition is requested;
(d) the relevant text of the law(s) prescribing punishment for the offence for which extradition is requested; and
(e) documents, statements, or other types of information specified in paragraphs 3 or 4 of this Article, as applicable.

3. In addition to the requirements in paragraph 2 of this Article, a request for extradition of a person who is sought for prosecution shall be supported by:

(a) a copy of the warrant or order of arrest issued by a judge or other competent authority;
(b) a copy of the charging document, if any; and
(c) for requests to the United States, such information as would provide a reasonable basis to believe that the person sought committed the offence for which extradition is requested.

4. In addition to the requirements in paragraph 2 of this Article, a request for extradition relating to a person who has been convicted of the offence for which extradition is sought shall be supported by:

(a) information that the person sought is the person to whom the finding of guilt refers;
(b) a copy of the judgment or memorandum of conviction or, if a copy is not available, a statement by a judicial authority that the person has been convicted;
(c) a copy of the sentence imposed, if the person sought has been sentenced, and a statement establishing to what extent the sentence has been carried out; and
(d) in the case of a person who has been convicted *in absentia*, information regarding the circumstances under which the person was voluntarily absent from the proceedings.

Article 9

Authentication of Documents

The documents that support an extradition request shall be deemed to be authentic and shall be received in evidence in extradition proceedings without further proof if:

(a) regarding a request from the United States

(i) they are authenticated by the oath of a witness, or

(ii) they purport to be signed by a judge, magistrate, or officer of the United States and they purport to be certified by being sealed with the official seal of the Secretary of State of the United States;

(b) regarding a request from the United Kingdom, they are certified by the principal diplomatic or principal consular officer of the United States resident in the United Kingdom, as provided by the extradition laws of the United States;
(c) regarding a request from a territory of the United Kingdom, they are certified either by the principal diplomatic or principal consular officer of the United States responsible for that territory; or
(d) regarding a request from either Party, they are certified or authenticated in any other manner acceptable under the law in the Requested State.

Article 10

Additional Information

If the Requested State requires additional information to enable a decision to be taken on the request for extradition, the Requesting State shall respond to the request within such time as the Requested State requires.

Article 11

Translation

All documents submitted under this Treaty by the Requesting State shall be in English or accompanied by a translation into English.

Article 12

Provisional Arrest

1. In an urgent situation, the Requesting State may request the provisional arrest of the person sought pending presentation of the request for extradition. A request for provisional arrest may be transmitted through the diplomatic channel or directly between the United States Department of Justice and such competent authority as the United Kingdom may designate for the purposes of this Article.

2. The application for provisional arrest shall contain:

(a) a description of the person sought;
(b) the location of the person sought, if known;
(c) a brief statement of the facts of the case including, if possible, the date and location of the offence(s);
(d) a description of the law(s) violated;

(e) a statement of the existence of a warrant or order of arrest or a finding of guilt or judgment of conviction against the person sought; and
(f) a statement that the supporting documents for the person sought will follow within the time specified in this Treaty.

3. The Requesting State shall be notified without delay of the disposition of its request for provisional arrest and the reasons for any inability to proceed with the request.

4. A person who is provisionally arrested may be discharged from custody upon the expiration of sixty (60) days from the date of provisional arrest pursuant to this Treaty if the executive authority of the Requested State has not received the formal request for extradition and the documents supporting the extradition request as required in Article 8. For this purpose, receipt of the formal request for extradition and supporting documents by the Embassy of the Requested State in the Requesting State shall constitute receipt by the executive authority of the Requested State.

5. The fact that the person sought has been discharged from custody pursuant to paragraph 4 of this Article shall not prejudice the subsequent re-arrest and extradition of that person if the extradition request and supporting documents are delivered at a later date.

Article 13

Decision and Surrender

1. The Requested State shall promptly notify the Requesting State of its decision on the request for extradition. Such notification should be transmitted directly to the competent authority designated by the Requesting State to receive such notification and through the diplomatic channel.

2. If the request is denied in whole or in part, the Requested State shall provide reasons for the denial. The Requested State shall provide copies of pertinent judicial decisions upon request.

3. If the request for extradition is granted, the authorities of the Requesting and Requested States shall agree on the time and place for the surrender of the person sought.

4. If the person sought is not removed from the territory of the Requested State within the time period prescribed by the law of that State, that person may be discharged from custody, and the Requested State, in its discretion, may subsequently refuse extradition for the same offence(s).

Article 14

Temporary and Deferred Surrender

1. If the extradition request is granted for a person who is being proceeded against or is serving a sentence in the Requested State, the Requested State may temporarily surrender the person sought to the Requesting State for the purpose of prosecution. If the Requested State requests, the Requesting State shall keep the person so surrendered in custody and shall return that person to the Requested State after the conclusion of the proceedings against that person, in accordance with conditions to be determined by mutual agreement of the States.

2. The Requested State may postpone the extradition proceedings against a person who is being prosecuted or who is serving a sentence in that State. The postponement may continue until the prosecution of the person sought has been concluded or until such person has served any sentence imposed.

Article 15

Requests for Extradition Made by Several States

If the Requested State receives requests from two or more States for the extradition of the same person, either for the same offence or for different offences, the executive authority of the Requested State shall determine to which State, if any, it will surrender the person. In making its decision, the Requested State shall consider all relevant factors, including but not limited to:

(a) whether the requests were made pursuant to a treaty;
(b) the place where each offence was committed;
(c) the gravity of the offences;
(d) the possibility of any subsequent extradition between the respective Requesting States; and
(e) the chronological order in which the requests were received from the respective Requesting States.

Article 16

Seizure and Surrender of Property

1. To the extent permitted under its law, the Requested State may seize and surrender to the Requesting State all items in whatever form, and assets, including proceeds, that are connected with the offence in respect of which extradition is granted. The items and assets mentioned in this Article may be surrendered even when the extradition cannot be effected due to the death, disappearance, or escape of the person sought.

2. The Requested State may condition the surrender of the items upon satisfactory assurances from the Requesting State that the property will be returned to the Requested State as soon as practicable. The Requested State may also defer the surrender of such items if they are needed as evidence in the Requested State.

Article 17

Waiver of Extradition

If the person sought waives extradition and agrees to be surrendered to the Requesting State, the Requested State may surrender the person as expeditiously as possible without further proceedings.

Article 18

Rule of Specialty

1. A person extradited under this Treaty may not be detained, tried, or punished in the Requesting State except for:

(a) any offence for which extradition was granted, or a differently denominated offence based on the same facts as the offence on which extradition was granted, provided such offence is extraditable, or is a lesser included offence;
(b) any offence committed after the extradition of the person; or
(c) any offence for which the executive authority of the Requested State waives the rule of specialty and thereby consents to the person's detention, trial, or punishment. For the purpose of this subparagraph:

(i) the executive authority of the Requested State may require the submission of the documentation called for in Article 8; and
(ii) the person extradited may be detained by the Requesting State for 90 days, or for such longer period of time as the Requested State may authorize, while the request for consent is being processed.

2. A person extradited under this Treaty may not be the subject of onward extradition or surrender for any offence committed prior to extradition to the Requesting State unless the Requested State consents.

3. Paragraphs 1 and 2 of this Article shall not prevent the detention, trial, or punishment of an extradited person, or the extradition of the person to a third State, if the person:

(a) leaves the territory of the Requesting State after extradition and voluntarily returns to it; or
(b) does not leave the territory of the Requesting State within 20 days of the day on which that person is free to leave.

4. If the person sought waives extradition pursuant to Article 17, the specialty provisions in this Article shall not apply.

Article 19

Transit

1. Either State may authorize transportation through its territory of a person surrendered to the other State by a third State or from the other State to a third State. A request for transit shall contain a description of the person being transported and a brief statement of the facts of the case. A person in transit shall be detained in custody during the period of transit.

2. Authorization is not required when air transportation is used by one State and no landing is scheduled on the territory of the other State. If an unscheduled landing does occur, the State in which the unscheduled landing occurs may require a request for transit pursuant to paragraph 1 of this Article, and it may detain the person until the request for transit is received and the transit is effected, as long as the request is received within 96 hours of the unscheduled landing.

Article 20

Representation and Expenses

1. The Requested State shall advise, assist, and appear on behalf of, the Requesting State in any proceedings in the courts of the Requested State arising out of a request for extradition or make all necessary arrangements for the same.

2. The Requesting State shall pay all the expenses related to the translation of extradition documents and the transportation of the person surrendered. The Requested State shall pay all other expenses incurred in that State in connection with the extradition proceedings.

3. Neither State shall make any pecuniary claim against the other State arising out of the arrest, detention, examination, or surrender of persons under this Treaty.

Article 21

Consultation

The Parties may consult with each other in connection with the processing of individual cases and in furtherance of efficient implementation of this Treaty.

Article 22

Application

1. This Treaty shall apply to offences committed before as well as after the date it enters into force.

2. This Treaty shall apply:

(a) in relation to the United Kingdom: to Great Britain and Northern Ireland, the Channel Islands, the Isle of Man; and to any territory for whose international relations the United Kingdom is responsible and to which this agreement has been extended by agreement of the Parties; and
(b) to the United States of America.

3. The application of this Treaty to any territory in respect of which extension has been made in accordance with paragraph 2 of this Article may be terminated by either State giving six months' written notice to the other through the diplomatic channel.

4. A request by the United States for the extradition of an offender who is found in any of the territories to which this Treaty applies in accordance with paragraph 2 of this Article may be made to the Governor or other competent authority of that territory, who may take the decision himself or refer the matter to the Government of the United Kingdom for its decision. A request on the part of any of the territories to which this Treaty applies in accordance with paragraph 2 of this Article for the extradition of an offender who is found in the United States of America may be made to the Government of the United States by the Governor or other competent authority of that territory.

Article 23

Ratification and Entry into Force

1. This Treaty shall be subject to ratification; the instruments of ratification shall be exchanged as soon as possible.

2. This Treaty shall enter into force upon the exchange of the instruments of ratification.

3. Upon the entry into force of this Treaty, the Extradition Treaty signed at London on June 8, 1972, and the Supplementary Treaty signed at Washington on June 25, 1985, (together, "the prior Treaty") shall cease to have any effect as between the United States and the United Kingdom, except as otherwise provided below. The prior Treaty shall apply to any extradition proceedings in which the extradition documents have already been submitted to the courts of the Requested State at the time this Treaty enters into force, except that Article 18 of this Treaty shall apply to persons found extraditable under the prior Treaty.

4. The prior Treaty shall also apply to any territory to which it has been extended in accordance with Article II of that Treaty, until such time as the provisions of this Treaty have been extended to such a territory under Article 22(2).

Article 24

Termination

Either State may terminate this Treaty at any time by giving written notice to the other State through the diplomatic channel, and the termination shall be effective six months after the date of receipt of such notice.

IN WITNESS WHEREOF, the undersigned, being duly authorized by their respective Governments, have signed this Treaty.

DONE at Washington, in duplicate, this 31st day of March, 2003.

FOR THE GOVERNMENT OF THE UNITED KINGDOM OF GREAT BRITAIN AND NORTHERN IRELAND:

DAVID BLUNKETT

FOR THE GOVERNMENT OF THE UNITED STATES OF AMERICA:
JOHN ASHCROFT

Agreement on Mutual Legal Assistance between the European Union and the United States of America

C–008

THE EUROPEAN UNION AND THE UNITED STATES OF AMERICA,

DESIRING further to facilitate cooperation between the European Union Member States and the United States of America,

DESIRING to combat crime in a more effective way as a means of protecting their respective democratic societies and common values,

HAVING DUE REGARD for rights of individuals and the rule of law,

MINDFUL of the guarantees under their respective legal systems which provide an accused person with the right to a fair trial, including the right to adjudication by an impartial tribunal established pursuant to law,

DESIRING to conclude an Agreement relating to mutual legal assistance in criminal matters,

HAVE AGREED AS FOLLOWS:

Article 1

Object and purpose

The Contracting Parties undertake, in accordance with the provisions of this Agreement, to provide for enhancements to cooperation and mutual legal assistance.

Article 2

Definitions

1. 'Contracting Parties' shall mean the European Union and the United States of America.
2. 'Member State' shall mean a Member State of the European Union.

Article 3

Scope of application of this Agreement in relation to bilateral mutual legal assistance treaties with Member States and in the absence thereof

1. The European Union, pursuant to the Treaty on European Union, and the United States of America shall ensure that the provisions of this Agreement are applied in relation to bilateral mutual legal assistance treaties between the Member States and the United States of America, in force at the time of the entry into force of this Agreement, under the following terms:

(a) Article 4 shall be applied to provide for identification of financial accounts and transactions in addition to any authority already provided under bilateral treaty provisions;

(b) Article 5 shall be applied to authorise the formation and activities of joint investigative teams in addition to any authority already provided under bilateral treaty provisions;

(c) Article 6 shall be applied to authorise the taking of testimony of a person located in the requested State by use of video transmission technology between the requesting and requested States in addition to any authority already provided under bilateral treaty provisions;

(d) Article 7 shall be applied to provide for the use of expedited means of communication in addition to any authority already provided under bilateral treaty provisions;

(e) Article 8 shall be applied to authorise the providing of mutual legal assistance to the administrative authorities concerned, in addition to any authority already provided under bilateral treaty provisions;

(f) subject to Article 9(4) and (5), Article 9 shall be applied in place of, or in the absence of bilateral treaty provisions governing limitations on use of information or evidence provided to the requesting State, and governing the conditioning or refusal of assistance on data protection grounds;

(g) Article 10 shall be applied in the absence of bilateral treaty provisions pertaining to the circumstances under which a requesting State may seek the confidentiality of its request.

2. (a) The European Union, pursuant to the Treaty on European Union, shall ensure that each Member State acknowledges, in a written instrument between such Member State and the United States of America, the application, in the manner set forth in this Article, of its bilateral mutual legal assistance treaty in force with the United States of America.

(b) The European Union, pursuant to the Treaty on European Union, shall ensure that new Member States acceding to the European Union after the entry into force of this Agreement, and having bilateral mutual legal assistance treaties with the United States of America, take the measures referred to in subparagraph (a).

(c) The Contracting Parties shall endeavour to complete the process described in subparagraph (b) prior to the scheduled accession of a new Member State, or as soon as possible thereafter. The European Union shall notify the United States of America of the date of accession of new Member States.

3. (a) The European Union, pursuant to the Treaty on European Union, and the United States of America shall also ensure that the provisions of this Agreement are applied in the absence of a bilateral mutual legal assistance treaty in force between a Member State and the United States of America.

(b) The European Union, pursuant to the Treaty on European Union, shall ensure that such Member State acknowledges, in a written instrument between such Member State and the United States of America, the application of the provisions of this Agreement.

(c) The European Union, pursuant to the Treaty on European Union, shall ensure that new Member States acceding to the European Union after the entry into force of this Agreement, which do not have bilateral mutual legal assistance treaties with the United States of America, take the measures referred to in subparagraph (b).

4. If the process described in paragraph 2(b) and 3(c) is not completed by the date of accession, the provisions of this Agreement shall apply in the relations between the United States of America and that new Member State as from the date on which they have notified each other and the European Union of the completion of thier internal procedures for that purpose.

5. The Contracting Parties agree that this Agreement is intended solely for mutual legal assistance between the States concerned. The provisions of this Agreement shall not give rise to a right on the part of any private person to obtain, suppress, or exclude any evidence, or to impede the execution of a request, nor expand or limit rights otherwise available under domestic law.

Article 4

Identification of bank information

1. (a) Upon request of the requesting State, the requested State shall, in accordance with the terms of this Article, promptly ascertain if the banks located in its territory possess information on whether an identified natural or legal person suspected of or charged with a criminal offence is the holder of a bank account or accounts. The requested State shall promptly communicate the results of its enquiries to the requesting State.
   (b) The actions described in subparagraph (a) may also be taken for the purpose of identifying:
      (i) information regarding natural or legal persons convicted of or otherwise involved in a criminal offence;
      (ii) information in the possession of non-bank financial institutions; or
      (iii) financial transactions unrelated to accounts.

2. A request for information described in paragraph 1 shall include:

   (a) the identity of the natural or legal person relevant to locating such accounts or transactions; and
   (b) sufficient information to enable the competent authority of the requested State to:
      (i) reasonably suspect that the natural or legal person concerned has engaged in a criminal offence and that banks or non-bank financial institutions in the territory of the requested State may have the information requested; and
      (ii) conclude that the information sought relates to the criminal investigation or proceeding;
   (c) to the extent possible, information concerning which bank or non-bank financial institution may be involved, and other information the availability of which may aid in reducing the breadth of the enquiry.

3. Requests for assistance under this Article shall be transmitted between:

   (a) central authorities responsible for mutual legal assistance in Member States, or national authorities of Member States responsible for investigation or prosecution of criminal offences as designated pursuant to Article 15(2); and
   (b) national authorities of the United States responsible for investigation or prosecution of criminal offences, as designated pursuant to Article 15(2).

The Contracting Parties may, following the entry into force of this Agreement, agree by Exchange of Diplomatic Note to modify the channels through which requests under this Article are made.

4. (a) Subject to subparagraph (b), a State may, pursuant to Article 15, limit its obligation to provide assistance under this Article to:

(i) offences punishable under the laws of both the requested and requesting States;
(ii) offences punishable by a penalty involving deprivation of liberty or a detention order of a maximum period of at least four years in the requesting State and at least two years in the requested State; or
(iii) designated serious offences punishable under the laws of both the requested and requesting States.

(b) A State which limits its obligation pursuant to subparagraph (a)(ii) or (iii) shall, at a minimum, enable identification of accounts associated with terrorist activity and the laundering of proceeds generated from a comprehensive range of serious criminal activities, punishable under the laws of both the requesting and requested States.

5. Assistance may not be refused under this Article on grounds of bank secrecy.

6. The requested State shall respond to a request for production of the records concerning the accounts or transactions identified pursuant to this Article, in accordance with the provisions of the applicable mutual legal assistance treaty in force between the States concerned, or in the absence thereof, in accordance with the requirements of its domestic law.

7. The Contracting Parties shall take measures to avoid the imposition of extraordinary burdens on requested States through application of this Article. Where extraordinary burdens on a requested State nonetheless result, including on banks or by operation of the channels of communications foreseen in this Article, the Contracting Parties shall immediately consult with a view to facilitating the application of this Article, including the taking of such measures as may be required to reduce pending and future burdens.

Article 5

Joint investigative teams

1. The Contracting Parties shall, to the extent they have not already done so, take such measures as may be necessary to enable joint investigative teams to be established and operated in the respective territories of each Member State and the United States of America for the purpose of facilitating criminal investigations or prosecutions involving one or more Member States and the United States of America where deemed appropriate by the Member State concerned and the United States of America.

2. The procedures under which the team is to operate, such as its composition, duration, location, organisation, functions, purpose, and terms of participation of team members of a State in investigative activities taking place in another State's territory shall be as agreed between the competent authorities responsible for the investigation or prosecution of criminal offences, as determined by the respective States concerned.

3. The competent authorities determined by the respective States concerned shall communicate directly for the purposes of the establishment and operation of such team except that where the exceptional complexity, broad scope, or other circumstances involved are deemed to require more central coordination as to some or all aspects, the States may agree upon other appropriate channels of communications to that end.

4. Where the joint investigative team needs investigative measures to be taken in one of the States setting up the team, a member of the team of that State may request its own compe-

tent authorities to take those measures without the other States having to submit a request for mutual legal assistance. The required legal standard for obtaining the measure in that State shall be the standard applicable to its domestic investigative activities.

Article 6

Video conferencing

1. The Contracting Parties shall take such measures as may be necessary to enable the use of video transmission technology between each Member State and the United States of America for taking testimony in a proceeding for which mutual legal assistance is available of a witness or expert located in a requested State, to the extent such assistance is not currently available. To the extent not specifically set forth in this Article, the modalities governing such procedure shall be as provided under the applicable mutual legal assistance treaty in force between the States concerned, or the law of the requested State, as applicable.

2. Unless otherwise agreed by the requesting and requested States, the requesting State shall bear the costs associated with establishing and servicing the video transmission. Other costs arising in the course of providing assistance (including costs associated with travel of participants in the requested State) shall be borne in accordance with the applicable provisions of the mutual legal assistance treaty in force between the States concerned, or where there is no such treaty, as agreed upon by the requesting and requested States.

3. The requesting and requested States may consult in order to facilitate resolution of legal, technical or logistical issues that may arise in the execution of the request.

4. Without prejudice to any jurisdiction under the law of the requesting State, making an intentionally false statement or other misconduct of the witness or expert during the course of the video conference shall be punishable in the requested State in the same manner as if it had been committed in the course of its domestic proceedings.

5. This Article is without prejudice to the use of other means for obtaining of testimony in the requested State available under applicable treaty or law.

6. This Article is without prejudice to application of provisions of bilateral mutual legal assistance agreements between Member States and the United States of America that require or permit the use of video conferencing technology for purposes other than those described in paragraph 1, including for purposes of identification of persons or objects, or taking of investigative statements. Where not already provided for under applicable treaty or law, a State may permit the use of video conferencing technology in such instances.

Article 7

Expedited transmission of requests

Requests for mutual legal assistance, and communications related thereto, may be made by expedited means of communications, including fax or e-mail, with formal confirmation to follow where required by the requested State. The requested State may respond to the request by any such expedited means of communication.

Article 8

Mutual legal assistance to administrative authorities

1. Mutual legal assistance shall also be afforded to a national administrative authority, investigating conduct with a view to a criminal prosecution of the conduct, or referral of the conduct to criminal investigation or prosecution authorities, pursuant to its specific administrative or regulatory authority to undertake such investigation. Mutual legal assistance may also be afforded to other administrative authorities under such circumstances. Assistance shall not be available for matters in which the administrative authority anticipates that no prosecution or referral, as applicable, will take place.

2. (a) Requests for assistance under this Article shall be transmitted between the central authorities designated pursuant to the bilateral mutual legal assistance treaty in force between the States concerned, or between such other authorities as may be agreed by the central authorities.
(b) In the absence of a treaty, requests shall be transmitted between the United States Department of Justice and the Ministry of Justice or, pursuant to Article 15(1), comparable Ministry of the Member State concerned responsible for transmission of mutual legal assistance requests, or between such other authorities as may be agreed by the Department of Justice and such Ministry.

3.The Contracting Parties shall take measures to avoid the imposition of extraordinary burdens on requested States through application of this Article. Where extraordinary burdens on a requested State nonetheless result, the Contracting Parties shall immediately consult with a view to facilitating the application of this Article, including the taking of such measures as may be required to reduce pending and future burdens.

Article 9

Limitations on use to protect personal and other data

1. The requesting State may use any evidence or information obtained from the requested State:

(a) for the purpose of its criminal investigations and proceedings:
(b) for preventing an immediate and serious threat to its public security;
(c) in its non-criminal judicial or administrative proceedings directly related to investigations or proceedings:

  (i) set forth in subparagraph (a); or
  (ii) for which mutual legal assistance was rendered under Article 8;

(d) for any other purpose, if the information or evidence has been made public within the framework of proceedings for which they were transmitted, or in any of the situations described in subparagraphs (a), (b) and (c); and
(e) for any other purpose, only with the prior consent of the requested State.

2. (a) This Article shall not prejudice the ability of the requested State to impose additional conditions in a particular case where the particular request for assistance could not be complied with in the absence of such conditions. Where additional conditions have been imposed in accordance with this subparagraph, the requested State may require the requesting State to give information on the use made of the evidence or information.

(b) Generic restrictions with respect to the legal standards of the requesting State for processing personal data may not be imposed by the requested State as a condition under subparagraph (a) to providing evidence or information.

3. Where, following disclosure to the requesting State, the requested State becomes aware of circumstances that may cause it to seek an additional condition in a particular case, the requested State may consult with the requesting State to determine the extent to which the evidence and information can be protected.

4. A requested State may apply the use limitation provision of the applicable bilateral mutual legal assistance treaty in lieu of this Article, where doing so will result in less restriction on the use of information and evidence than provided for in this Article.

5. Where a bilateral mutual legal assistance treaty in force between a Member State and the United States of America on the date of signature of this Agreement, permits limitation of the obligation to provide assistance with respect to certain tax offences, the Member State concerned may indicate, in its exchange of written instruments with the United States of America described in Article 3(2), that, with respect to such offences, it will continue to apply the use limitation provision of that treaty.

Article 10

Requesting State's request for confidentiality

The requested State shall use its best efforts to keep confidential a request and its contents if such confidentiality is requested by the requesting State. If the request cannot be executed without breaching the requested confidentiality, the central authority of the requested State shall so inform the requesting State, which shall then determine whether the request should nevertheless be executed.

Article 11

Consultations

The Contracting Parties shall, as appropriate, consult to enable the most effective use to be made of this Agreement, including to facilitate the resolution of any dispute regarding the interpretation or application of this Agreement.

Article 12

Temporal application

1. This Agreement shall apply to offences committed before as well as after it enters into force.

2. This Agreement shall apply to requests for mutual legal assistance made after its entry into force. Nevertheless, Articles 6 and 7 shall apply to requests pending in a requested State at the time this Agreement enters into force.

Article 13

Non-derogation

Subject to Article 4(5) and Article 9(2)(b), this Agreement is without prejudice to the invocation by the requested State of grounds for refusal of assistance available pursuant to a bilateral mutual legal assistance treaty, or, in the absence of a treaty, its applicable legal principles, including where execution of the request would prejudice its sovereignty, security, order public or other essential interests.

Article 14

Future bilateral mutual legal assistance treaties with Member States

This Agreement shall not preclude the conclusion, after its entry into force, of bilateral Agreements between a Member State and the United States of America consistent with this Agreement.

Article 15

Designations and notifications

1. Where a Ministry other than the Ministry of Justice has been designated under Article 8(2)(b), the European Union shall notify the United States of America of such designation prior to the exchange of written instruments described in Article 3(3) between the Member States and the United States of America.

2. The Contracting Parties, on the basis of consultations between them on which national authorities responsible for the investigation and prosecution of offences to designate pursuant to Article 4(3), shall notify each other of the national authorities so designated prior to the exchange of written instruments described in Article 3(2) and (3) between the Member States and the United States of America. The European Union shall, for Member States having no mutual legal assistance treaty with the United States of America, notify the United

States of America prior to such exchange of the identity of the central authorities under Article 4(3).

3. The Contracting Parties shall notify each other of any limitations invoked under Article 4(4) prior to the exchange of written instruments described in Article 3(2) and (3) between the Member States and the United States of America.

Article 16

Territorial application

1. This Agreement shall apply:

(a) to the United States of America:
(b) in relation to the European Union, to:

— Member States,
— territories for whose external relations a Member State has responsibility, or countries that are not Member States for whom a Member State has other duties with respect to external relations, where agreed upon by exchange of diplomatic note between the Contracting Parties, duly confirmed by the relevant Member State.

2. The application of this Agreement to any territory or country in respect of which extension has been made in accordance with subparagraph (b) of paragraph 1 may be terminated by either Contracting Party giving six months' written notice to the other Contracting Party through the diplomatic channel, where duly confirmed between the relevant Member State and the United States of America.

Article 17

Review

The Contracting Parties agree to carry out a common review of this Agreement no later than five years after its entry into force. The review shall address in particular the practical implementation of the Agreement and may also include issues such as the consequences of further development of the European Union relating to the subject matter of this Agreement.

Article 18

Entry into force and termination

1. This Agreement shall enter into force on the first day following the third month after the date on which the Contracting Parties have exchanged instruments indicating that they have completed their internal procedures for this purpose. These instruments shall also indicate that the steps specified in Article 3(2) and (3) have been completed.

2. Either Contracting Party may terminate this Agreement at any time by giving written notice to the other Party, and such termination shall be effective six months after the date of such notice.

In witness whereof the undersigned Plenipotentiaries have signed this Agreement.

Done at Washington D.C. on the twenty-fifth day of June in the year two thousand and three in duplicate in the Danish, Dutch, English, Finnish, French, German, Greek, Italian, Portuguese, Spanish and Swedish languages, each text being equally authentic.

EXPLANATORY NOTE ON THE AGREEMENT ON MUTUAL LEGAL ASSISTANCE BETWEEN THE EUROPEAN UNION AND THE UNITED STATES OF AMERICA

This note reflects understandings regarding the application of certain provisions of the Agreement on Mutual Legal Assistance between the European Union and the United States of America (hereinafter 'the Agreement') agreed between the Contracting Parties.

On Article 8

With respect to the mutual legal assistance to administrative authorities under Article 8(1), the first sentence of Article 8(1) imposes an obligation to afford mutual legal assistance to requesting United States of America federal administrative authorities and to requesting national administrative authorities of Member States. Under the second sentence of that paragraph mutual legal assistance may also be made available to other, that is non-federal or local, administrative authorities. This provision however, is available at the discretion of the requested State.

The Contracting Parties agree that under the first sentence of Article 8(1) mutual legal assistance will be made available to a requesting administrative authority that is, at the time of making the request, conducting investigations or proceedings in contemplation of criminal prosecution or referral of the investigated conduct to the competent prosecuting authorities, within the terms of its statutory mandate, as further described immediately below. The fact that, at the time of making the request referral for criminal prosecution is being contemplated does not exclude that, other sanctions than criminal ones may be pursued by that authority. Thus, mutual legal assistance obtained under Article 8(1) may lead the requesting administrative authority to the conclusion that pursuance of criminal proceedings or criminal referral would not be appropriate. These possible consequences do not affect the obligation upon the Contracting Parties to provide assistance under this Article.

However, the requesting administrative authority may not use Article 8(1) to request assistance where criminal prosecution or referral is not being contemplated, or for matters in which the conduct under investigation is not subject to criminal sanction or referral under the laws of the requesting State.

The European Union recalls that the subject matter of the Agreement for its part falls under the provisions on police and judicial cooperation in criminal matters set out in Title VI of the Treaty on European Union and that the Agreement has been concluded within the scope of these provisions.

On Article 9

Article 9(2)(b) is meant to ensure that refusal of assistance on data protection grounds may be invoked only in exceptional cases. Such a situation could arise if, upon balancing the important interests involved in the particular case (on the one hand, public interests, including the sound administration of justice and, on the other hand, privacy interests), furnishing the specific data sought by the requesting State would raise difficulties so fundamental as to be considered by the requested State to fall within the essential interests grounds for refusal. A broad, categorical, or systematic application of data protection principles by the requested State to refuse cooperation is therefore precluded. Thus, the fact the requesting and requested States have different systems of protecting the privacy of data (such as that the requesting State does not have the equivalent of a specialised data protection authority) or have different means of protecting personal data (such as that the requesting State uses means other than the process of deletion to protect the privacy or the accuracy of the personal data received by law enforcement authorities), may as such not be imposed as additional conditions under Article 9(2a).

On Article 14

Article 14 provides that the Agreement shall not preclude the conclusion, after its entry into force, of bilateral agreements on mutual legal assistance between a Member State and the United States of America consistent with the Agreement.

Should any measures set forth in the Agreement create an operational difficulty for the United States of America and one or more Member States, such difficulty should in the first place be resolved, if possible, through consultations between the Member State or Member States concerned and the United States of America, or, if appropriate, through the consultation procedures set out in the Agreement. Where it is not possible to address such operational difficulty through consultations alone, it would be consistent with the Agreement for future bilateral agreements between a Member State and the United States of America to provide an operationally feasible alternative mechanism that would satisfy the objectives of the specific provision with respect to which the difficulty has arisen.

C–009 # Agreement on Extradition between the European Union and the United States of America

THE EUROPEAN UNION AND THE UNITED STATES OF AMERICA,

DESIRING further to facilitate cooperation between the European Union Member States and the United States of America,

DESIRING to combat crime in a more effective way as a means of protecting their respective democratic societies and common values,

HAVING DUE REGARD for rights of individuals and the rule of law,

MINDFUL of the guarantees under their respective legal systems which provide for the right to a fair trial to an extradited person, including the right to adjudication by an impartial tribunal established pursuant to law,

DESIRING to conclude an Agreement relating to the extradition of offenders,

HAVE AGREED AS FOLLOWS:

Article 1

Object and Purpose

The Contracting Parties undertake, in accordance with the provisions of this Agreement, to provide for enhancements to cooperation in the context of applicable extradition relations between the Member States and the United States of America governing extradition of offenders.

Article 2

Definitions

1. 'Contracting Parties' shall mean the European Union and the United States of America.

2. 'Member State' shall mean a Member State of the European Union.

3. 'Ministry of Justice' shall, for the United States of America, mean the United States Department of Justice; and for a Member State, its Ministry of Justice, except that with respect to a Member State in which functions described in Articles 3, 5, 6, 8 or 12 are carried out by its Prosecutor General, that body may be designated to carry out such function in lieu of the Ministry of Justice in accordance with Article 19, unless the United States and the Member State concerned agree to designate another body.

Article 3

Scope of application of this Agreement in relation to bilateral extradition treaties with Member States

1. The European Union, pursuant to the Treaty on European Union, and the United States of America shall ensure that the provisions of this Agreement are applied in relation to

bilateral extradition treaties between the Member States and the United States of America, in force at the time of the entry into force of this Agreement, under the following terms:

(a) Article 4 shall be applied in place of bilateral treaty provisions that authorise extradition exclusively with respect to a list of specified criminal offences;
(b) Article 5 shall be applied in place of bilateral treaty provisions governing transmission, certification, authentication or legalisation of an extradition request and supporting documents transmitted by the requesting State;
(c) Article 6 shall be applied in the absence of bilateral treaty provisions authorising direct transmission of provisional arrest requests between the United States Department of Justice and the Ministry of Justice of the Member State concerned;
(d) Article 7 shall be applied in addition to bilateral treaty provisions governing transmission of extradition requests;
(e) Article 8 shall be applied in the absence of bilateral treaty provisions governing the submission of supplementary information; where bilateral treaty provisions do not specify the channel to be used, paragraph 2 of that Article shall also be applied;
(f) Article 9 shall be applied in the absence of bilateral treaty provisions authorising temporary surrender of persons being proceeded against or serving a sentence in the requested State;
(g) Article 10 shall be applied, except as otherwise specified therein, in place of, or in the absence of, bilateral treaty provisions pertaining to decision on several requests for extradition of the same person;
(h) Article 11 shall be applied in the absence of bilateral treaty provisions authorising waiver of extradition or simplified extradition procedures;
(i) Article 12 shall be applied in the absence of bilateral treaty provisions governing transit; where bilateral treaty provisions do not specify the procedure governing unscheduled landing of aircraft, paragraph 3 of that Article shall also be applied;
(j) Article 13 may be applied by the requested State in place of, or in the absence of, bilateral treaty provisions governing capital punishment;
(k) Article 14 shall be applied in the absence of bilateral treaty provisions governing treatment of sensitive information in a request.

2. (a) The European Union, pursuant to the Treaty on European Union, shall ensure that each Member State acknowledges, in a written instrument between such Member State and the United States of America, the application, in the manner set forth in this Article, of its bilateral extradition treaty in force with the United States of America.
(b) The European Union, pursuant to the Treaty on European Union, shall ensure that new Member States acceding to the European Union after the entry into force of this Agreement and having bilateral extradition treaties with the United States of America, take the measures referred to in subparagraph (a).
(c) The Contracting Parties shall endeavour to complete the process described in subparagraph (b) prior to the scheduled accession of a new Member State, or as soon as possible thereafter. The European Union shall notify the United States of America of the date of accession of new Member States.

3. If the process described in paragraph 2(b) is not completed by the date of accession, the provisions of this Agreement shall apply in the relations between that new Member State and the United States of America as from the date on which they have notified each other and the European Union of the completion of their internal procedures for that purpose.

Article 4

Extraditable offences

1. An offence shall be an extraditable offence if it is punishable under the laws of the requesting and requested States by deprivation of liberty for a maximum period of more than one year or by a more severe penalty. An offence shall also be an extraditable offence if it consists of an attempt or conspiracy to commit, or participation in the commission of, an extraditable offence. Where the request is for enforcement of the sentence of a person convicted of an extraditable offence, the deprivation of liberty remaining to be served must be at least four months.

2. If extradition is granted for an extraditable offence, it shall also be granted for any other offence specified in the request if the latter offence is punishable by one year's deprivation of liberty or less, provided that all other requirements for extradition are met.

3. For the purposes of this Article, an offence shall be considered an extraditable offence:

(a) regardless of whether the laws in the requesting and requested States place the offence within the same category of offences or describe the offence by the same terminology;
(b) regardless of whether the offence is one for which United States federal law requires the showing of such matters as interstate transportation, or use of the mails or of other facilities affecting interstate or foreign commerce, such matters being merely for the purpose of establishing jurisdiction in a United States federal court; and
(c) in criminal cases relating to taxes, customs duties, currency control and the import or export of commodities, regardless of whether the laws of the requesting and requested States provide for the same kinds of taxes, customs duties, or controls on currency or on the import or export of the same kinds of commodities.

4. If the offence has been committed outside the territory of the requesting State, extradition shall be granted, subject to the other applicable requirements for extradition, if the laws of the requested State provide for the punishment of an offence committed outside its territory in similar circumstances. If the laws of the requested State do not provide for the punishment of an offence committed outside its territory in similar circumstances, the executive authority of the requested State, at its discretion, may grant extradition provided that all other applicable requirements for extradition are met.

Article 5

Transmission and authentication of documents

1. Requests for extradition and supporting documents shall be transmitted through the diplomatic channel, which shall include transmission as provided for in Article 7.

2. Documents that bear the certificate or seal of the Ministry of Justice, or Ministry or Department responsible for foreign affairs, of the requesting State shall be admissible in extradition proceedings in the requested State without further certification, authentication, or other legalisation.

Article 6

Transmission of requests for provisional arrest

Requests for provisional arrest may be made directly between the Ministries of Justice of the requesting and requested States, as an alternative to the diplomatic channel. The facilities of the International Criminal Police Organisation (Interpol) may also be used to transmit such are quest.

Article 7

Transmission of documents following provisional arrest

1. If the person whose extradition is sought is held under provisional arrest by the requested State, the requesting State may satisfy its obligation to transmit its request for extradition and supporting documents through the diplomatic channel pursuant to Article 5(1), by submitting the request and documents to the Embassy of the requested State located in the requesting State. In that case, the date of receipt of such request by the Embassy shall be considered to be the date of receipt by the requested State for purposes of applying the time limit that must be met under the applicable extradition treaty to enable the person's continued detention.

2. Where a Member State on the date of signature of this Agreement, due to the established jurisprudence of its domestic legal system applicable at such date, cannot apply the measures referred to in paragraph 1, this Article shall not apply to it, until such time as that Member State and the United States of America, by exchange of diplomatic note, agree otherwise.

Article 8

Supplemental information

1. The requested State may require the requesting State to furnish additional information with in such reasonable length of time as it specifies, if it considers that the information furnished in support of the request for extradition is not sufficient to fulfil the requirements of the applicable extradition treaty.

2. Such supplementary information may be requested and furnished directly between the Ministries of Justice of the States concerned.

Article 9

Temporary surrender

1. If a request for extradition is granted in the case of a person who is being proceeded against or is serving a sentence in the requested State, the requested State may temporarily surrender the person sought to the requesting State for the purpose of prosecution.

2. The person so surrendered shall be kept in custody in the requesting State and shall be returned to the requested State at the conclusion of the proceedings against that person, in accordance with the conditions to be determined by mutual agreement of the requesting and requested States. The time spent in custody in the territory of the requesting State pending prosecution in that State may be deducted from the time remaining to be served in the requested State.

Article 10

Requests for extradition or surrender made by several States

1. If the requested State receives requests from the requesting State and from any other State or States for the extradition of the same person, either for the same offence or for different offences, the executive authority of the requested State shall determine to which State, if any, it will surrender the person.

2. If a requested Member State receives an extradition request from the United States of America and a request for surrender pursuant to the European arrest warrant for the same person, either for the same offence or for different offences, the competent authority of the requested Member State shall determine to which State, if any, it will surrender the person. For this purpose, the competent authority shall be the requested Member State's executive authority if, under the bilateral extradition treaty in force between the United States and the Member State, decisions on competing requests are made by that authority; if not so provided in the bilateral extradition treaty, the competent authority shall be designated by the Member State concerned pursuant to Article 19.

3. In making its decision under paragraphs 1 and 2, the requested State shall consider all of the relevant factors, including, but not limited to, factors already set forth in the applicable extradition treaty, and, where not already so set forth, the following:

(a) whether the requests were made pursuant to a treaty;
(b) the places where each of the offences was committed;
(c) the respective interests of the requesting States;
(d) the seriousness of the offences;
(e) the nationality of the victim;
(f) the possibility of any subsequent extradition between the requesting States; and
(g) the chronological order in which the requests were received from the requesting States.

Article 11

Simplified extradition procedures

If the person sought consents to be surrendered to the requesting State, the requested State may, in accordance with the principles and procedures provided for under its legal system, surrender the person as expeditiously as possible without further proceedings. The consent of the person sought may include agreement to waiver of protection of the rule of specialty.

Article 12

Transit

1. A Member State may authorise transportation through its territory of a person surrendered to the United States of America by a third State, or by the United States of America to a third State. The United States of America may authorise transportation through its territory of a person surrendered to a Member State by a third State, or by a Member State to a third State.

2. A request for transit shall be made through the diplomatic channel or directly between the United States Department of Justice and the Ministry of Justice of the Member State concerned. The facilities of Interpol may also be used to transmit such a request. The request shall contain a description of the person being transported and a brief statement of the facts of the case. A person in transit shall be detained in custody during the period of transit.

3. Authorisation is not required when air transportation is used and no landing is scheduled on the territory of the transit State. If an unscheduled landing does occur, the State in which the unscheduled landing occurs may require a request for transit pursuant to paragraph 2. All measures necessary to prevent the person from absconding shall be taken until transit is effected, as long as the request for transit is received with in 96 hours of the unscheduled landing.

Article 13

Capital punishment

Where the offence for which extradition is sought is punishable by death under the laws in the requesting State and not punishable by death under the laws in the requested State, the requested State may grant extradition on the condition that the death penalty shall not be imposed on the person sought, or if for procedural reasons such condition cannot be complied with by the requesting State, on condition that the death penalty if imposed shall not be carried out. If the requesting State accepts extradition subject to conditions pursuant to this Article, it shall comply with the conditions. If the requesting State does not accept the conditions, the request for extradition may be denied.

Article 14

Sensitive information in a request

Where the requesting State contemplates the submission of particularly sensitive information in support of its request for extradition, it may consult the requested State to determine the extent to which the information can be protected by the requested State. If the requested State cannot protect the information in the manner sought by the requesting State, the requesting State shall determine whether the information shall nonetheless be submitted.

Article 15

Consultations

The Contracting Parties shall, as appropriate, consult to enable the most effective use to be made of this Agreement, including to facilitate the resolution of any dispute regarding the interpretation or application of this Agreement.

Article 16

Temporal application

1. This Agreement shall apply to offences committed before as well as after it enters in to force.

2. This Agreement shall apply to requests for extradition made after its entry into force. Nevertheless, Articles 4 and 9 shall apply to requests pending in a requested State at the time this Agreement enters into force.

Article 17

Non-derogation

1. This Agreement is without prejudice to the invocation by the requested State of grounds for refusal relating to a matter not governed by this Agreement that is available pursuant to a bilateral extradition treaty in force between a Member State and the United States of America.

2. Where the constitutional principles of, or final judicial decisions binding upon, the requested State may pose an impediment to fulfilment of its obligation to extradite, and resolution of the matter is not provided for in this Agreement or the applicable bilateral treaty, consultations shall take place between the requested and requesting States.

Article 18

Future bilateral extradition treaties with Member States

This Agreement shall not preclude the conclusion, after its entry into force, of bilateral Agreements between a Member State and the United States of America consistent with this Agreement.

Article 19

Designation and notification

The European Union shall notify the United States of America of any designation pursuant to Article 2(3) and Article 10(2), prior to the exchange of written instruments described in Article 3(2) between the Member States and the United States of America.

Article 20

Territorial application

1. This Agreement shall apply:

(a) to the United States of America;
(b) in relation to the European Uniónto:

— Member States,
— territories for whose external relations a Member State has responsibility, or countries that are not Member States for whom a Member State has other duties with respect to external relations, where agreed upon by exchange of diplomatic note between the Contracting Parties, duly confirmed by the relevant Member State.

2. The application of this Agreement to any territory or country in respect of which extension has been made in accordance with subparagraph (b) of paragraph 1 may be terminated by either Contracting Party giving six months' written notice to the other Contracting Party through the diplomatic channel, where duly confirmed between the relevant Member State and the United States of America.

Article 21

Review

The Contracting Parties agree to carry out a common review of this Agreement as necessary, and in any event no later than five years after its entry into force. The review shall address in particular the practical implementation of the Agreement and may also include issues such as the consequences of further development of the European Union relating to the subject matter of this Agreement, including Article 10.

Article 22

Entry into force and termination

1. This Agreement shall enter into force on the first day following the third month after the date on which the Contracting Parties have exchanged instruments indicating that they have

completed their internal procedures for this purpose. These instruments shall also indicate that the steps specified in Article 3(2) have been completed.

2. Either Contracting Party may terminate this Agreement at any time by giving written notice to the other Party, and such termination shall be effective six months after the date of such notice.

In witness whereof the under signed Plenipotentiaries have signed this Agreement

Done at Washington DC on the twenty-fifth day of June in the year two thousand and three in duplicate in the Danish, Dutch, English, Finnish, French, German, Greek, Italian, Portuguese, Spanish and Swedish languages, each text being equally authentic.

EXPLANATORY NOTE ON THE AGREEMENT ON EXTRADITION BETWEEN THE EUROPEAN UNION AND THE UNITED STATES OF AMERICA

This Explanatory Note reflects understandings regarding the application of certain provisions of the Agreement on Extradition between the European Union and the United States of America (hereinafter 'the Agreement') agreed between the Contracting Parties.

On Article 10

Article 10 is not intended to affect the obligations of States Parties to the Rome Statute of the International Criminal Court, nor to affect the rights of the United States of America as a non-Party with regard to the International Criminal Court.

On Article 18

Article 18 provides that the Agreement shall not preclude the conclusion, after its entry into force, of bilateral agreements on extradition between a Member State and the United States of America consistent with the Agreement.

Should any measures set forth in the Agreement create an operational difficulty for either one or more Member States or the United States of America, such difficulty should in the first place be resolved, if possible, through consultations between the Member State or Member States concerned and the United States of America, or, if appropriate, through the consultation procedures set out in this Agreement. Where it is not possible to address such operational difficulty through consultations alone, it would be consistent with the Agreement for future bilateral agreements between the Member State or Member States and the United States of America to provide an operationally feasible alternative mechanism that would satisfy the objectives of the specific provision with respect to which the difficulty has arisen.

(ACTS ADOPTED PURSUANT TO TITLE VI OF THE TREATY ON EUROPEAN UNION)

Council Framework Decision 2003/577/JHA of 22 July 2003 on the execution in the European Union of orders freezing property or evidence C–010

THE COUNCIL OF THE EUROPEAN UNION,

Having regard to the Treaty on European Union, and in particular Article 31(a) and Article 34(2)(b) thereof,

Having regard to the initiative by the Republic of France, the Kingdom of Sweden and the Kingdom of Belgium[1],

Having regard to the opinion of the European Parliament[2],

Whereas:

(1) The European Council, meeting in Tampere on 15 and 16 October 1999, endorsed the principle of mutual recognition, which should become the cornerstone of judicial cooperation in both civil and criminal matters within the Union.

(2) The principle of mutual recognition should also apply to pre-trial orders, in particular to those which would enable competent judicial authorities quickly to secure evidence and to seize property which are easily movable.

(3) On 29 November 2000 the Council, in accordance with the Tampere conclusions, adopted a programme of measures to implement the principle of mutual recognition in criminal matters, giving first priority (measures 6 and 7) to the adoption of an instrument applying the principle of mutual recognition to the freezing of evidence and property.

(4) Cooperation between Member States, based on the principle of mutual recognition and immediate execution of judicial decisions, presupposes confidence that the decisions to be recognised and enforced will always be taken in compliance with the principles of legality, subsidiarity and proportionality.

(5) Rights granted to the parties or bona fide interested third parties should be preserved.

(6) This Framework Decision respects the fundamental rights and observes the principles recognised by Article 6 of the Treaty and reflected by the Charter of Fundamental Rights of the European Union, notably Chapter VI thereof. Nothing in this Framework Decision may be interpreted as prohibiting refusal to freeze property for which a freezing order has been issued when there are reasons to believe, on the basis of objective elements, that the freezing order is issued for the purpose of prosecuting or punishing a person on account of his or her sex, race, religion, ethnic origin, nationality, language, political opinions or sexual orientation, or that that person's position may be prejudiced for any of these reasons.

This Framework Decision does not prevent any Member State from applying its constitutional rules relating to due process, freedom of association, freedom of the press and freedom of expression in other media,

[1] OJ C 75, 7.3.2001, p. 3.

[2] Opinion delivered on 11 June 2002 (not yet published in the Official Journal).

HAS ADOPTED THIS FRAMEWORK DECISION:

TITLE 1

SCOPE

Article 1

Objective

The purpose of the Framework Decision is to establish the rules under which a Member State shall recognise and execute in its territory a freezing order issued by a judicial authority of another Member State in the framework of criminal proceedings. It shall not have the effect of amending the obligation to respect the fundamental rights and fundamental legal principles as enshrined in Article 6 of the Treaty.

Article 2

Definitions

For the purposes of this Framework Decision:

(a) 'issuing State' shall mean the Member State in which a judicial authority, as defined in the national law of the issuing State, has made, validated or in any way confirmed a freezing order in the framework of criminal proceedings;
(b) 'executing State' shall mean the Member State in whose territory the property or evidence is located;
(c) 'freezing order' property that could be subject to confiscation or evidence;
(d) 'property' includes property of any description, whether corporeal or incorporeal, movable or immovable, and legal documents and instruments evidencing title to or interest in such property, which the competent judicial authority in the issuing State considers:

— is the proceeds of an offence referred to in Article 3, or equivalent to either the full value or part of the value of such proceeds, or
— constitutes the instrumentalities or the objects of such an offence;

(e) 'evidence' shall mean objects, documents or data which could be produced as evidence in criminal proceedings concerning an offence referred to in Article 3.

Article 3

Offences

1. This Framework Decision applies to freezing orders issued for purposes of:

(a) securing evidence, or
(b) subsequent confiscation of property.

2. The following offences, as they are defined by the law of the issuing State, and if they are punishable in the issuing State by a custodial sentence of a maximum period of at least three years shall not be subject to verification of the double criminality of the act:

— participation in a criminal organisation,
— terrorism,
— trafficking in human beings,
— sexual exploitation of children and child pornography,
— illicit trafficking in narcotic drugs and psychotropic substances,
— illicit trafficking in weapons, munitions and explosives,
— corruption,
— fraud, including that affecting the financial interests of the European Communities within the meaning of the Convention of 26 July 1995 on the Protection of the European Communities' Financial Interests,
— laundering of the proceeds of crime,
— counterfeiting currency, including of the euro,
— computer-related crime,
— environmental crime, including illicit trafficking in endangered animal species and in endangered plant species and varieties,
— facilitation of unauthorised entry and residence,
— murder, grievous bodily injury,
— illicit trade in human organs and tissue,
— kidnapping, illegal restraint and hostage-taking,
— racism and xenophobia,
— organised or armed robbery,
— illicit trafficking in cultural goods, including antiques and works of art,
— swindling,
— racketeering and extortion,
— counterfeiting and piracy of products,
— forgery of administrative documents and trafficking therein,
— forgery of means of payment,
— illicit trafficking in hormonal substances and other growth promoters,
— illicit trafficking in nuclear or radioactive materials,
— trafficking in stolen vehicles,
— rape,
— arson,
— crimes within the jurisdiction of the International Criminal Tribunal,
— unlawful seizure of aircraft/ships,
— sabotage.

3. The Council may decide, at any time, acting unanimously after consultation of the European Parliament under the conditions laid down in Article 39(1) of the Treaty, to add

other categories of offence to the list contained in paragraph 2. The Council shall examine, in the light of the report submitted by the Commission pursuant to Article 14 of this Framework Decision, whether the list should be extended or amended.

4. For cases not covered by paragraph 2, the executing State may subject the recognition and enforcement of a freezing order made for purposes referred to in paragraph 1(a) to the condition that the acts for which the order was issued constitute an offence under the laws of that State, whatever the constituent elements or however described under the law of the issuing State.

For cases not covered by paragraph 2, the executing State may subject the recognition and enforcement of a freezing order made for purposes referred to in paragraph 1(b) to the condition that the acts for which the order was issued constitute an offence which, under the laws of that State, allows for such freezing, whatever the constituent elements or however described under the law of the issuing State.

TITLE II

PROCEDURE FOR EXECUTING FREEZING ORDERS

Article 4

Transmission of freezing orders

1. A freezing order within the meaning of this Framework Decision, together with the certificate provided for in Article 9, shall be transmitted by the judicial authority which issued it directly to the competent judicial authority for execution by any means capable of producing a written record under conditions allowing the executing State to establish authenticity.

2. The United Kingdom and Ireland, respectively, may, before the date referred to in Article 14(1), state in a declaration that the freezing order together with the certificate must be sent via a central authority or authorities specified by it in the declaration. Any such declaration may be modified by a further declaration or withdrawn any time. Any declaration or withdrawal shall be deposited with the General Secretariat of the Council and notified to the Commission. These Member States may at any time by a further declaration limit the scope of such a declaration for the purpose of giving greater effect to paragraph 1. They shall do so when the provisions on mutual assistance of the Convention implementing the Schengen Agreement are put into effect for them.

3. If the competent judicial authority for execution is unknown, the judicial authority in the issuing State shall make all necessary inquiries, including via the contact points of the European Judicial Network[1], in order to obtain the information from the executing State.

4. When the judicial authority in the executing State which receives a freezing order has no jurisdiction to recognise it and take the necessary measures for its execution, it shall, *ex officio*, transmit the freezing order to the competent judicial authority for execution and shall so inform the judicial authority in the issuing State which issued it.

[1] Council Joint Action 98/428/JHA of 29 June 1998 on the Creation of the European Judicial Network (OJ L 191, 7.7.1998, p. 4).

Article 5

Recognition and immediate execution

1. The competent judicial authorities of the executing State shall recognise a freezing order, transmitted in accordance with Article 4, without any further formality being required and shall forthwith take the necessary measures for its immediate execution in the same way as for a freezing order made by an authority of the executing State, unless that authority decides to invoke one of the grounds for non-recognition or non-execution provided for in Article 7 or one of the grounds for postponement provided for in Article 8.

Whenever it is necessary to ensure that the evidence taken is valid and provided that such formalities and procedures are not contrary to the fundamental principles of law in the executing State, the judicial authority of the executing State shall also observe the formalities and procedures expressly indicated by the competent judicial authority of the issuing State in the execution of the freezing order.

A report on the execution of the freezing order shall be made forthwith to the competent authority in the issuing State by any means capable of producing a written record.

2. Any additional coercive measures rendered necessary by the freezing order shall be taken in accordance with the applicable procedural rules of the executing State.

3. The competent judicial authorities of the executing State shall decide and communicate the decision on a freezing order as soon as possible and; whenever practicable, within 24 hours of receipt of the freezing order.

Article 6

Duration of the freezing

1. The property shall remain frozen in the executing State until that State has responded definitively to any request made under Article 10(1)(a) or (b).

2. However, after consulting the issuing State, the executing State may in accordance with its national law and practices lay down appropriate conditions in the light of the circumstances of the case in order to limit the period for which the property will be frozen. If, in accordance with those conditions, it envisages lifting the measure, it shall inform the issuing State, which shall be given the opportunity to submit its comments.

3. The judicial authorities of the issuing State shall forthwith notify the judicial authorities of the executing State that the freezing order has been lifted. In these circumstances it shall be the responsibility of the executing State to lift the measure as soon as possible.

Article 7

Grounds for non-recognition or non-execution

1. The competent judicial authorities of the executing State may refuse to recognise or execute the freezing order only if:

(a) the certificate provided for in Article 9 is not produced, is incomplete or manifestly does not correspond to the freezing order;
(b) there is an immunity or privilege under the law of the executing State which makes it impossible to execute the freezing order;
(c) it is instantly clear from the information provided in the certificate that rendering judicial assistance pursuant to Article 10 for the offence in respect of which the freezing order has been made, would infringe the *ne bis in idem* principle;
(d) if, in one of the cases referred to in Article 3(4), the act on which the freezing order is based does not constitute an offence under the law of the executing State; however, in relation to taxes or duties, customs and exchange, execution of the freezing order may not be refused on the ground that the law of the executing State does not impose the same kind of tax or duty or does not contain a tax, duty, customs and exchange regulation of the same kind as the law of the issuing State.

2. In case of paragraph 1(a), the competent judicial authority may:

(a) specify a deadline for its presentation, completion or correction; or
(b) accept an equivalent document; or
(c) exempt the issuing judicial authority from the requirement if it considers that the information provided is sufficient.

3. Any decision to refuse recognition or execution shall be taken and notified forthwith to the competent judicial authorities of the issuing State by any means capable of producing a written record.

4. In case it is in practice impossible to execute the freezing order for the reason that the property or evidence have disappeared, have been destroyed, cannot be found in the location indicated in the certificate or the location of the property or evidence has not been indicated in a sufficiently precise manner, even after consultation with the issuing State, the competent judicial authorities of the issuing State shall likewise be notified forthwith.

Article 8

Grounds for postponement of execution

1. The competent judicial authority of the executing State may postpone the execution of a freezing order transmitted in accordance with Article 4:

(a) where its execution might damage an ongoing criminal investigation, until such time as it deems reasonable;
(b) where the property or evidence concerned have already been subjected to a freezing order in criminal proceedings, and until that freezing order is lifted;
(c) where, in the case of an order freezing property in criminal proceedings with a view to its subsequent confiscation, that property is already subject to an order made in the course of other proceedings in the executing State and until that order is lifted. However, this point shall only apply where such an order would have priority over subsequent national freezing orders in criminal proceedings under national law.

2. A report on the postponement of the execution of the freezing order, including the grounds for the postponement and, if possible, the expected duration of the postponement, shall be made forthwith to the competent authority in the issuing State by any means capable of producing a written record.

3. As soon as the ground for postponement has ceased to exist, the competent judicial authority of the executing State shall forthwith take the necessary measures for the execution of the freezing order and inform the competent authority in the issuing State thereof by any means capable of producing a written record.

4. The competent judicial authority of the executing State shall inform the competent authority of the issuing State about any other restraint measure to which the property concerned may be subjected.

Article 9

Certificate

1. The certificate, the standard form for which is given in the Annex, shall be signed, and its contents certified as accurate, by the competent judicial authority in the issuing State that ordered the measure.

2. The certificate must be translated into the official language or one of the official languages of the executing State.

3. Any Member State may, either when this Framework Decision is adopted or at a later date, state in a declaration deposited with the General Secretariat of the Council that it will accept a translation in one or more other official languages of the institutions of the European Communities.

Article 10

Subsequent treatment of the frozen property

1. The transmission referred to in Article 4:

(a) shall be accompanied by a request for the evidence to be transferred to the issuing State;

or

(b) shall be accompanied by a request for confiscation requiring either enforcement of a confiscation order that has been issued in the issuing State or confiscation in the executing State and subsequent enforcement of any such order;

or

(c) shall contain an instruction in the certificate that the property shall remain in the executing State pending a request referred to in (a) or (b). The issuing State shall indicate in the certificate the (estimated) date for submission of this request. Article 6(2) shall apply.

2. Requests referred to in paragraph 1(a) and (b) shall be submitted by the issuing State and processed by the executing State in accordance with the rules applicable to mutual

assistance in criminal matters and the rules applicable to international cooperation relating to confiscation.

3. However, by way of derogation from the rules on mutual assistance referred to in paragraph 2, the executing State may not refuse requests referred to under paragraph 1(a) on grounds of absence of double criminality, where the requests concern the offences referred to in Article 3(2) and those offences are punishable in the issuing State by a prison sentence of at least three years.

Article 11

Legal remedies

1. Member States shall put in place the necessary arrangements to ensure that any interested party, including bona fide third parties, have legal remedies without suspensive effect against a freezing order executed pursuant to Article 5, in order to preserve their legitimate interests; the action shall be brought before a court in the issuing State or in the executing State in accordance with the national law of each.

2. The substantive reasons for issuing the freezing order can be challenged only in an action brought before a court in the issuing State.

3. If the action is brought in the executing State, the judicial authority of the issuing State shall be informed thereof and of the grounds of the action, so that it can submit the arguments that it deems necessary. It shall be informed of the outcome of the action.

4. The issuing and executing States shall take the necessary measures to facilitate the exercise of the right to bring an action mentioned in paragraph 1, in particular by providing adequate information to interested parties.

5. The issuing State shall ensure that any time limits for bringing an action mentioned in paragraph 1 are applied in a way that guarantees the possibility of an effective legal remedy for the interested parties.

Article 12

Reimbursement

1. Without prejudice to Article 11(2), where the executing State under its law is responsible for injury caused to one of the parties mentioned in Article 11 by the execution of a freezing order transmitted to it pursuant to Article 4, the issuing State shall reimburse to the executing State any sums paid in damages by virtue of that responsibility to the said party except if, and to the extent that, the injury or any part of it is exclusively due to the conduct of the executing State.

2. Paragraph 1 is without prejudice to the national law of the Member States on claims by natural or legal persons for compensation of damage.

Title III

Final Provisions

Article 13

Territorial application

This Framework Decision shall apply to Gibraltar.

Article 14

Implementation

1. Member States shall take the necessary measures to comply with the provisions of this Framework Decision before 2 August 2005.

2. By the same date Member States shall transmit to the General Secretariat of the Council and to the Commission the text of the provisions transposing into their national law the obligations imposed on them under this Framework Decision. On the basis of a report established using this information and a written report by the Commission, the Council shall, before 2 August 2006, assess the extent to which Member States have complied with the provisions of this Framework Decision.

3. The General Secretariat of the Council shall notify Member States and the Commission of the declarations made pursuant to Article 9(3).

Article 15

Entry into force

This Framework Decision shall enter into force on the day of its publication in the *Official Journal of the European Union.*

Done at Brussels, 22 July 2003.

For the Council
The President
G. ALEMANNO

ANNEX

CERTIFICATE PROVIDED FOR IN ARTICLE 9

(a) The judicial authority which issued the freezing order:

Official name: ....

....

Name of its representative: ....

Post held (title/grade): ....

File reference: ....

Address: ....

....

Tel: (country code) (area/city code) (...) ....

Fax: (country code) (area/city code) (...) ....

E-mail: ....

Languages in which it is possible to communicate with the issuing judicial authority

....

Contact details (including languages in which it is possible to communicate with the person(s)) of the person(s) to contact if additional information on the execution of the order is necessary or to make necessary practical arrangements for the transfer of evidence (if applicable): ....

....

(b) The authority competent for the enforcement of the freezing order in the issuing State

Official name: ....

....

Name of its representative: ....

Post held (title/grade): ....

File reference: ....

Address: ....

....

Tel: (country code) (area/city code) (...) ....

Fax: (country code) (area/city code) (...) ....

E-mail: ....

Languages in which it is possible to communicate with the authority competent for the enforcement..

Contact details (including languages in which it is possible to communicate with the person(s)) of the person(s) to contact if additional information on the execution of the order is necessary or to make necessary practical arrangements for the transfer of evidence (if applicable): ....

....

(c) In the case where points (a) and (b) have been filled, this point must be filled in order to indicate which/or both of these two authorities must be contacted: ....

☐ Authority mentioned under point (a)

☐ Authority mentioned under point (b)

(d) Where a central authority has been made responsible for the transmission and administrative reception of freezing orders (only applicable for Ireland and the United Kingdom):

Name of the central authority: ....

....

Contact person, if applicable (title/grade and name): ....

....

Address: ....

....

File reference: ....

Tel: (country code) (area/city code) ....

Fax: (country code) (area/city code) ....

E-mail: ....

(e) The freezing order:

1. Date and if applicable reference number
2. State the purpose of the order

2.1. Subsequent confiscation

2.2. Securing evidence

3. Description of formalities and procedures to be observed when executing a freezing order concerning evidence (if applicable)

(f) Information regarding the property or evidence in the executing State covered by the freezing order:

Description of the property or evidence and location:

1. (a) Precise description of the property and, where applicable, the maximum amount for which recovery is sought (if such maximum amount is indicated in the order concerning the value of proceeds)

   (b) Precise description of the evidence

2. Exact location of the property or evidence (if not known, the last known location)
3. Party having custody of the property or evidence or known beneficial owner of the property or evidence, if different from the person suspected of the offence or convicted (if applicable under the national law of the issuing State)

   ....

   ....

(g) Information regarding the identity of the (1) natural or (2) legal person(s), suspected of the offence or convicted (if applicable under the national law of the issuing State) or/and the person(s) to whom the freezing order relates (if available):

1. Natural persons

Name: ....

Forename(s): ....

Maiden name, where applicable: ....

Aliases, where applicable: ....

Sex: ....

Nationality: ....

Date of birth: ....

Place of birth: ....

Residence and/or known address; if not known state the last known address: ....

....

Language(s) which the person understands (if known): ....

....

2. Legal persons

Name: ....

Form of legal person: ....

Registration number: ....

Registered seat: ....

....

(h) Action to be taken by the executing State after executing the freezing order

Confiscation

1.1. The property is to be kept in the executing State for the purpose of subsequent confiscation of the property

1.1.1. Find enclosed request regarding enforcement of a confiscation order issued in the issuing State on .... (date)

1.1.2. Find enclosed request regarding confiscation in the executing State and subsequent enforcement of that order

1.1.3. Estimated date for submission of a request referred to in 1.1.1 or 1.1.2. ....

or

Securing of evidence

2.1. The property is to be transferred to the issuing State to serve as evidence

2.1.1. Find enclosed a request for the transfer

or

2.2. The property is to be kept in the executing State for the purpose of subsequent use as evidence in the issuing State

2.2.2. Estimated date for submission of a request referred to in 2.1.1. ....

(i) Offences:

Description of the relevant grounds for the freezing order and a summary of facts as known to the judicial authority issuing the freezing order and certificate:

....

....

....

Nature and legal classification of the offence(s) and the applicable statutory provision/code on basis of which the freezing order was made:

....

....

....

....

1. If applicable, tick one or more of the following offences to which the offence(s) identified above relate(s), if the offence(s) are punishable in the issuing State by a custodial sentence of a maximum of at least three years:

☐ participation in a criminal organisation;

☐ terrorism;

☐ trafficking in human beings;

☐ sexual exploitation of children and child pornography;

☐ illicit trafficking in narcotic drugs and psychotropic substances;

- ☐ illicit trafficking in weapons, munitions and explosives;
- ☐ corruption;
- ☐ fraud, including that affecting the financial interests of the European Communities within the meaning of the Convention of 26 July 1995 on the Protection of the European Communities' Financial Interests;
- ☐ laundering of the proceeds of crime;
- ☐ counterfeiting currency, including of the euro;
- ☐ computer-related crime;
- ☐ environmental crime, including illicit trafficking in endangered animal species and in endangered plant species and varieties;
- ☐ facilitation of unauthorised entry and residence;
- ☐ murder, grievous bodily injury;
- ☐ illicit trade in human organs and tissue;
- ☐ kidnapping, illegal restraint and hostage-taking;
- ☐ racism and xenophobia;
- ☐ organised or armed robbery;
- ☐ illicit trafficking in cultural goods, including antiques and works of art;
- ☐ swindling;
- ☐ racketeering and extortion;
- ☐ counterfeiting and piracy of products;
- ☐ forgery of administrative documents and trafficking therein;
- ☐ forgery of means of payment;
- ☐ illicit trafficking in hormonal substances and other growth promoters;
- ☐ illicit trafficking in nuclear or radioactive materials;
- ☐ trafficking in stolen vehicles;
- ☐ rape;
- ☐ arson;
- ☐ crimes within the jurisdiction of the International Criminal Court;
- ☐ unlawful seizure of aircraft/ships;
- ☐ sabotage.

2. Full descriptions of offence(s) not covered by section 1 above:

....

....

....

(j) Legal remedies against the freezing order for interested parties, including bona fide third parties, available in the issuing State:

Description of the legal remedies available including necessary steps to take

Court before which the action may be taken

Information as to those for whom the action is available

Time limit for submission of the action

Authority in the issuing State who can supply further information on procedures for submitting appeals in the issuing State and on whether legal assistance and translation is available:

Name: ....

Contact person (if applicable): ....

Address: ....

Tel: (country code) (area/city code) ....

Fax: (country code) (area/city code) ....

E-mail: ....

(k) Other circumstances relevant to the case (optional information): ....

....

....

(l) The text of the freezing order is attached to the certificate.

Signature of the issuing judicial authority and/or its representative certifying the content of the certificate as accurate:

....

Name: ....

Post held (title/grade): ....

Date: ....

Official stamp (if available)

Extradition Act 2003: Codes of Practice

C–011

INTRODUCTION

1.1 These Codes of Practice govern the exercise of police powers in Part 4 of the Extradition Act 2003 (the Act). They are issued by the Home Secretary under Section 173 of the Act. The Codes provide guidance on the operation of police powers in extradition cases in England, Wales and Northern Ireland and those of customs officers throughout the UK.

1.2 The Codes of Practice were first published in draft and issued for public consultation. The draft Codes were revised in the light of responses received to the consultation, in accordance with Section 173 (2) of the Act.

(a) Background

1.3 The extradition case, *Regina v Commissioner of Police for the Metropolis, Ex P Rottman [2002] 2 All ER 865*, cast doubt on whether the provisions contained in the 1984 Police and Criminal Evidence Act (PACE)[1] extend to police powers in cases where the offence was committed abroad. Part 4 of the Act puts the matter beyond doubt by setting down in statute the police powers which apply in extradition cases.

1.4 The Act makes changes to UK extradition arrangements. It includes provisions that could require any police officer to respond to an incoming extradition request where circumstances dictate.

(b) Status of the Codes of Practice

1.5 These Codes set out the police powers which may be relied upon in extradition cases, additional to the police's common law powers. The powers in the Act are modelled on those contained in PACE, but where necessary and appropriate, they supplement domestic provisions to enable officers to respond to extradition requests effectively.

1.6 Where these Codes are silent, officers should have regard to relevant domestic provisions set out in the revised edition of the PACE Codes of Practice (PACE Codes), effective from 1 April 2003. Where procedures in extradition cases are the same as those in domestic cases, these Codes refer officers to the relevant section in the PACE Codes.

1.7 Under Section 173(6) of the Act, failure by an officer to comply with any provision of the Codes does not in itself make him or her liable to criminal or civil proceedings. Under Section 173(7) of the Act, the Codes are admissible in evidence in proceedings under the Act and must be taken into account by a judge or court in determining any question to which they appear to the judge or court to be relevant. The provisions of these Codes do not include the Annexes.

(c) Application of the Codes in Northern Ireland

1.8 In Northern Ireland, references in these Codes of Practice to the Police and Criminal Evidence Act 1984 (PACE) should be read as references to the Police and Criminal Evidence Act (Northern Ireland) Order 1989 (S.I. 1989/1341 (N.I. 12)), and references to the PACE Codes of Practice or the revised PACE Codes of Practice should be read as references to the relevant parts of the PACE (Northern Ireland) Codes of Practice. Where there are no direct equivalents to the England and Wales PACE Codes of Practice, police officers in Northern

[1] Chapter 60.

Ireland should act having regard to the revised PACE Codes of Practice. In this regard, attention is also drawn to previous guidance issued by the Northern Ireland Office in circular POB 5/2003.

(d) Availability

1.9 These Codes of Practice must be readily available at all police stations for consultation by police officers, detained persons and members of the public.

1.10 Welsh translations of the Codes must be available for use in all police stations in Wales.

1.11 The Glossary to the Codes of Practice contains an explanation of terms used in the Codes.

(e) Persons covered by the Codes

1.12 These Codes of Practice apply to police officers operating in England, Wales and Northern Ireland and customs officers operating throughout the UK. The operation of powers under Part 4 of the Act by Service police will be governed by separate Codes of Practice.

1.13 In these Codes, 'designated person' has the same meaning as that given by PACE Code B 2.11. Designated persons must have regard to any relevant provisions of these Codes of Practice.

(f) Summary of police powers available under the Extradition Act

1.14 The police powers conferred by the Act and reflected in the Codes of Practice are:

- The power of arrest (Sections 3, 5, 71 and 73);
- The power to apply for and execute a warrant or a production order for material relating to the extradition offence (Sections 156 and 157);
- The power to apply for and execute a warrant to search premises for special procedure or excluded material relating to the extradition offence (Section 160);
- The power to seize and retain material relating to any offence committed abroad when searching premises for the purpose of arrest (Section 161), on arrest (Section 162) or after arrest (Section 164);
- The power to seize and retain material relating to the identity of the fugitive when searching premises or persons on arrest (Sections 162 and 163) or after arrest (section 164);
- The power, after arrest, to conduct an immediate search of premises without the prior authorisation of a senior police officer (Section 164);
- The power to search the person on arrest and to seize and retain material relating to the identity of the person and any offence committed abroad (Section 163);
- The power to take fingerprints and samples from a person arrested under an extradition arrest power (Section 166);
- The power to search and examine a person arrested under an extradition arrest power, for the purposes of ascertaining his or her identity (Section 167);
- The power to photograph a person arrested under an extradition arrest power (Section 168);
- The power to retain and deliver seized material to the requesting authority or territory (Section 172).

1.15 These Codes of Practice are modelled on the PACE Codes of Practice and follow the same format and structure. Under the Extradition Act 2003 there are no powers to stop and search or conduct interviews. Therefore these Codes do not contain equivalents to PACE Codes A and E.

CODE B

CODE OF PRACTICE FOR SEARCHES OF PREMISES BY POLICE OFFICERS AND THE SEIZURE, RETENTION, USE AND DELIVERY OF PROPERTY FOUND BY POLICE OFFICERS ON PERSONS OR PREMISES

1 Introduction

1.1 This Code of Practice deals with police powers in extradition cases to:

- search premises;
- seize and retain property found on premises and persons;
- deliver seized material to the authority or territory requesting extradition.

1.2 These powers may be used to find:

- persons requested for extradition;
- evidence of a requested person's identity;
- property and material relating to the extradition offence(s) for which a person is sought.

1.3 Searches conducted under powers in the Extradition Act 2003 (the Act) may only be undertaken for the purpose of obtaining evidence of the extradition offence for use in the prosecution of the person accused of the extradition offence. Officers may not investigate crimes on behalf of the requesting authority or territory, other than to speak to persons for the purpose of assisting establishing ownership or connection to the property. Items relating to a person's identity and offences other than the extradition offence may, if found, be seized in accordance with the provisions of the Act and this Code. Police powers in respect of offences committed in the UK are not limited by this paragraph.

1.4 The right to privacy and respect for personal property are key principles of the Human Rights Act 1998[2]. Powers of entry, search and seizure should be fully and clearly justified before use, because they may significantly interfere with an individual's privacy. Officers should consider whether the necessary objectives can be met by less intrusive means.

1.5 In all cases police officers should:

- exercise their powers courteously and with respect for persons and property;
- only use reasonable force when this is considered necessary and proportionate to the circumstances.

2 General

2.1 This Code must be readily available at all police stations for consultation by:

- police officers;
- detained persons;
- members of the public.

[2] Chapter 42.

2.2 Any police officer may apply to a justice of the peace or a circuit judge for a search warrant under the Act.

2.3 Nothing under the Act entitles police officers to seize and sift material which is subject to legal privilege. The principle of legal privilege applies equally to material that has originated or been sent from abroad.

2.4 For the purposes of this Code, 'premises', as defined in PACE Section 23, includes any place, vehicle, vessel, aircraft, hovercraft, tent or movable structure and any offshore installation as defined in the Mineral Workings (Offshore Installations) Act 1971[3], Section 1.

2.5 When this Code requires the prior authority or agreement of an officer of at least inspector or superintendent rank, that authority may be given by a sergeant or chief inspector authorised to perform the function of the higher rank under PACE Section 107. For customs officers the equivalent authorisations to police inspector or superintendent are customs Band 7 and Band 9.

2.6 This Code does not apply to the exercise of a statutory power to enter premises or to inspect goods, equipment or procedures if the exercise of that power is not dependent on the existence of grounds for suspecting that an offence may have been committed and the person exercising the power has no reasonable grounds for such suspicion.

2.7 Where written records of searches are required they shall be made in the search record, or if this is not practicable, in the recording officer's pocket book or on forms provided for this purpose.

2.8 For the purposes of this Code, the identity of officers (or anyone accompanying them during a search) need not be recorded or disclosed if officers reasonably believe recording or disclosing their names might put them in danger. In these cases, officers should use warrant or other identification numbers and the name of their police station.

2.9 Paragraphs 2.11–2.13 of PACE Code B apply in the operation of powers under this Code.

3 Search warrants and production orders

(a) Before making an application

Search and seizure warrants and production order

3.1 When information provided by the requesting authority or territory appears to justify an application, the officer must take reasonable steps to check the information is accurate, recent and not provided maliciously or irresponsibly.

3.2 The officer shall ascertain as specifically as possible the nature of the articles concerned and their location and make reasonable enquiries to establish any relevant information.

3.3 An application may be made by any officer to:

- a justice of the peace for a search warrant (Section 156);
- a circuit judge (in Northern Ireland a Crown Court judge) for a production order (Section 157);
- a circuit judge (in Northern Ireland a Crown Court judge) for a warrant to search for special procedure material or excluded material (Section 160).

3.4 Applications must be supported by a signed written authority from an officer of inspector rank or above. If the case is urgent and an inspector or above is not readily available, the next most senior officer on duty can give the written authority.

3.5 In all cases, before making an application under Sections 156, 157 or 160 of the Act, officers should refer to PACE Code B 3.2 and 3.3.

[3] Chapter 61.

3.6 Except in a case of urgency, if there is reason to believe a search might have an adverse effect on relations between the police executing the warrant and the local community, the officer shall consult the police/community liaison officer:

(a) before the search; or
(b) in urgent cases, as soon as practicable after the search.

In all cases consideration should be given to conducting a community impact assessment, where appropriate.

(b) Making an application

Search and seizure warrants

3.7 An application for a search warrant must be supported in writing, specifying:

(a) the section of the Act under which the application is made (Section 156);
(b) the premises to be searched;
(c) the material, or description of material sought, which must be:
    (i) material relating to the extradition offence; and
    (ii) believed to be located on the premises named in the application;
(d) the name of the person requested for extradition;
(e) the name and Category (e.g. 1 or 2) of the requesting territory;
(f) the extradition offence of which the person is accused; and
(g) if applicable, a request for the warrant to authorise a person or persons to accompany the officer who executes the warrant.

3.8 Before granting an application, the justice of the peace must be satisfied that:

(a) the offence specified in the application is an extradition offence and has been committed by the person requested for extradition;
(b) the person is in the UK or is on their way to the UK;
(c) the material would be likely to be admissible as evidence for the offence at a trial in the relevant part of the UK where the justice of the peace exercises jurisdiction;
(d) it is not practical or possible to enter the premises or gain access to the material without a warrant;
(e) the material sought does not consist of items subject to legal privilege, excluded material or special procedure material;
(f) the material cannot be obtained by any other or less intrusive means;
(g) it is not practicable to communicate with the person entitled to grant entry to the premises;
(h) it is not practicable to communicate with the person entitled to grant access to the material sought, even though access to the premises may be gained;
(i) that entry to the premises will not be granted unless a warrant is produced; and
(j) that the search may be frustrated or seriously prejudiced unless an officer arriving at the premises can secure immediate entry to them.

Production orders

3.9 An application for a production order to a circuit judge must be supported in writing and must specify:

(a) the section of the Act under which the application is made (Section 157);

(b) the material, or a description of material, sought;
(c) that the material is special procedure or excluded material;
(d) the premises where the material is located;
(e) the name of the person who appears to be in possession or control of the material;
(f) the name of the person requested for extradition;
(g) the name and Category (e.g. 1 or 2) of the requesting territory;
(h) the extradition offence of which the person is accused; and
(i) if applicable, a request for the order to authorise a person or persons to accompany the officer who executes the order.

3.10 Before granting an application, the circuit judge must be satisfied that:

(a) There are reasonable grounds for believing:

(i) the offence specified in the application is an extradition offence and has been committed by the person requested for extradition;
(ii) the person is in the UK or is on their way to the UK;
(iii) there is material which consists of or includes special procedure or excluded material on the premises specified in the application; and
(iv) the material would be likely to be admissible as evidence for the offence at a trial in the relevant part of the UK where the circuit judge exercises jurisdiction;

(b) it appears that other methods of obtaining the material have been tried without success, or have not been tried because they were bound to fail; and
(c) it is in the public interest that the material is obtained (and that this outweighs the disadvantages to the person or institution against whom the order is made).

Search warrants: special procedure and excluded material

3.11 Applications to a circuit judge for a search warrant for special procedure or excluded material must be supported in writing and should specify:

(a) the section of the Act under which the application is made (Section 160);
(b) the material, or a description of material, sought;
(c) that the material is special procedure or excluded material;
(d) the premises to be searched;
(e) the name of the person requested for extradition;
(f) the name and Category (e.g. 1 or 2) of the requesting territory;
(g) the extradition offence of which the person is accused; and
(h) if applicable, a request for the warrant to authorise a person or persons to accompany the officer who executes the warrant.

3.12 Before granting an application, the circuit judge must be satisfied that:

(a) the requirements for making a production order (in paragraph 3.10 (a)–(c) above) are fulfilled;

and additionally that:

(b) it is not practicable to communicate with the person entitled to grant entry to the premises;
(c) it is not practicable to communicate with the person entitled to grant access to the material sought, even though access to the premises may be gained;
(d) the material contains information which is subject to a restriction on disclosure or an obligation of secrecy contained in an enactment (including one passed after the

2003 Extradition Act) and is likely to be disclosed in breach of the restriction or obligation if a warrant is not issued.

3.13 The search warrant or production order may authorise any suitably qualified or skilled person, including representatives from the requesting authority or territory, to accompany the officer who executes the warrant, if their presence is needed to assist, for example, locating or identifying the material sought.

3.14 The accompanying person(s) does not have any right to force entry or to search for or seize property, but it gives them the right to be on the premises during the search without the occupier's permission.

3.15 If an application for a search and seizure warrant or a production order is refused, no further application may be made at the request of the requesting authority or territory in relation to the same premises or material, unless supported by additional grounds.

4 Entry without warrant — particular powers

(a) Making an arrest (etc)

Entry and search of premises for purposes of arrest

4.1 Under Section 161 of the Act, an officer may enter and search any premises for the purpose of exercising the power of arrest under Section 3, 5, 71 and 73, if the officer has reasonable grounds for believing that the person requested for extradition is on the premises.

(b) Search of premises where the arrest takes place or where the arrested person was immediately before arrest

Entry and search of premises on arrest

4.2 Under Section 162 of the Act, if a person has been arrested under any of the powers under the Act anywhere other than a police station, an officer may:

(a) enter and search premises which the person was:

- at the time of arrest; or
- immediately before arrest

if the officer has reasonable grounds for believing that there is evidence on the premises relating to:

- the extradition offence (if the person has not been convicted of the offence); or
- the identity of the person.

Search of person on arrest

4.3 Under Section 163 of the Act, if a person has been arrested under any of the powers under the Act, anywhere other than a police station, an officer may search the person if the officer has reasonable grounds for believing:

(a) the person may present a danger to himself/herself or others;
(b) the person may have concealed anything which might be:

- used to assist escape from lawful custody;
- evidence relating to an offence;
- evidence relating to the identity of the person.

4.4 For the purposes of this section, 'an offence' includes:

- the extradition offence(s);
- an offence(s) committed in the UK;
- an offence(s) committed abroad.

4.5 Before the search of the person takes place, the officer must take reasonable steps to give the person to be searched the following information:

(a) that they are to be the subject of a non-intimate search;
(b) the officer's name and the name of the police station to which the officer is attached;
(c) the legal search power which is being exercised (under Section 163 of the Act);
(d) a clear explanation of:

(i) the purpose of the search in terms of the article(s) for which there is a power to search; and
(ii) the grounds for the search.

4.6 If the person to be searched does not appear to understand what is being said, or there is any doubt about the person's ability to understand English, the officer must take reasonable steps to bring information regarding the person's rights and any relevant provisions of this Code to his or her attention. If the person is deaf or cannot understand English and is accompanied by someone, then the officer must try to establish whether that person can interpret or otherwise help the officer.

4.7 Police officers not in uniform must show their warrant cards. Customs officers not in uniform must show their identification cards.

4.8 Where practicable the search must be carried out at or near the place where the person was arrested.

4.9 Under Section 163(5)(a) an officer may not require a person to remove any clothing in public, other than an outer coat, jacket or gloves.

4.10 Under Section 163(5)(b) an officer is authorised to search a person's mouth.

4.11 Nothing in this Section affects the power conferred by Section 43 of the Terrorism Act 2000 (c 11).

(c) Search of premises occupied or controlled by the arrested person

Entry and search of premises after arrest

4.12 Under Section 164 of the Act, if a person has been arrested under any of the powers under the Act, an officer may enter and search any premises occupied or controlled by the person, if the officer has reasonable grounds for suspecting that there is on the premises evidence relating to:

(a) the extradition offence (if the person has not been convicted of the offence);
(b) the identity of the person.

4.13 Before entering and searching the premises, the officer must obtain written authorisation from an officer of inspector rank or above. If the case is urgent and an inspector or above is not readily available, the next most senior officer on duty can give the written authority.

4.14 The authority should only be given when the authorising officer is satisfied the necessary grounds (in paragraph 4.12 above) exist. If possible, the authorising officer should record the authority on the Notice of Powers and Rights and sign the Notice. The grounds for the search and the nature of the evidence sought should be made in:

- the custody record, if there is one; otherwise
- the officer's pocket book;
- the search record.

4.15 Authorisation is not required before the search if:

(a) the search is conducted before the arrested person is taken to a police station; and
(b) the presence of the arrested person at a place other than a police station is necessary for the effective exercise of the power to search.

4.16 If authorisation has not been obtained for the reasons in Section 4.14 above, an officer of the rank of inspector or above must be informed that a search has been made, as soon as practicable after it has been conducted.

5 *Search with consent*

5.1 Officers should follow PACE Code B5 and the corresponding Notes for Guidance.

6 *Searching premises — general considerations*

(a) Time of searches

6.1 Officers should follow the guidance in PACE Code B 6.1–6.3.

(b) Entry other than with consent

6.2 Officers should follow the guidance in PACE Code B 6.4.

(c) Notice of Powers and Rights

6.3 If an officer conducts a search of premises to which this Code applies, the officer shall, unless it is impracticable to do so, provide the occupier with a copy of a Notice:

(a) specifying that the search is made under warrant, with consent or in the exercise of powers described in paragraphs 4.1, 4.2, 4.12–4.15. Note: the Notice format shall provide for authority to be indicated, see paragraph 4.14;
(b) summarising the extent of the powers of search and seizure conferred by the Extradition Act 2003;
(c) explaining the rights of the occupier and the owner of the property seized;
(d) explaining that compensation may be payable in appropriate cases for damage caused by entering and searching premises, and giving the address to send a compensation application;
(e) stating that this Code is available at any police station.

(d) Conduct of searches

6.4 Premises may be searched only to the extent that is reasonably necessary to discover the material or person sought, in respect of which the power is available.

6.5 If the detained person's presence is required to facilitate a search after that person has been arrested and detained at a police station, the person or his or her legal representative may attend at the search.

6.6 Should the premises being searched contain two or more separate dwellings an officer may only enter and search dwellings in which, for example, the arrest took place or in which the person was immediately prior to arrest, or any communal area of the premises.

6.7 Officers may only question persons where it is necessary to establish identity or ownership of property, in furtherance of proper and effective conduct of a search, or to seek verification of a written record.

6.8 In all other respects, officers should follow the guidance in PACE Code B 6.9–6.12 in conducting a search.

(e) Leaving premises

6.9 Officers should follow the guidance in PACE Code B 6.13.

7 Seizure and retention

(a) Seizure

7.1 An officer searching a person or premises under the Act may seize and retain anything:

(a) covered by a warrant;
(b) that the officer has reasonable grounds for believing is evidence of an offence or has been obtained in consequence of the commission of a UK offence, but only if seizure is necessary to prevent the items being concealed, lost, damaged, altered or destroyed;
(c) covered by the powers in the Criminal Justice and Police Act 2001, as amended.

7.2 Officers searching persons or premises under Sections 161, 162, 163 and 164 may seize and retain anything which the officer has reasonable grounds for believing is evidence of or has been obtained in consequence of the commission of the extradition offence or an offence committed outside the UK, but only if seizure is necessary to prevent the items being concealed, lost, damaged, altered or destroyed.

7.3 Officers searching a person or premises on or after arrest under Sections 162, 163 or 164 may seize and retain material relating to the identity of the person, but only if seizure is necessary to prevent the items being concealed, lost, damaged, altered or destroyed.

7.4 Additionally, an officer searching a person on arrest may seize and retain any item, if there are reasonable grounds for believing that:

(a) the person might use it to cause physical injury to himself/herself or any other person;
(b) the person might use it to assist escape from lawful custody.

7.5 No item may be seized which an officer has reasonable grounds for believing to be subject to legal privilege as defined by in PACE Section 10, other than under the Criminal Justice and Police Act 2001, Part 2.

7.6 Officers may decide that it is not appropriate to seize property or may wish to photograph, image or copy any document or article they have the power to seize, in which case the provisions in PACE Code B 7.4–7.6 apply.

7.7 An officer must have regard to his or her statutory obligation to retain an original document or other article only when a photograph or copy would not be sufficient (PACE Section 22 (4)).

Computer information

7.8 Under Section 159 of the Act, if the material specified in a production order consists of information stored in any electronic form, the material must be produced either in a form:

(a) which can be taken away or to which access can be given, and which is visible and legible; or
(b) from which it can readily be produced in a visible and legible form (for example a computer printout or a removable computer disk).

(b) Criminal Justice and Police Act 2001: Specific procedures for seize and sift powers

7.9 Powers to seize property from premises or persons to be sifted or examined elsewhere extend to searches conducted under the Act. Officers should adhere to PACE Code B 7.7–7.13 when exercising or considering the exercise of these powers.

7.10 Any suitably qualified or skilled person, including appropriate representatives from the requesting authority or territory, may be present at the search and sift, providing that:

(a) (if the search is conducted under warrant) the warrant authorising entry to the premises also authorises that person to accompany the officer executing the warrant; and
(b) the presence of the person is needed to help in the accurate identification of the material sought or to advise where certain forms of evidence are most likely to be found.

7.11 The accompanying person(s) may not take part in conducting the sift, but they may be present when it takes place.

7.12 An appropriate representative may include the person's legal representative.

(c) Retention

7.13 Material seized or produced under Sections 156, 157, 160, 161, 162, 163 or 164 of the Act may be retained:

(a) to assist in establishing the identity of the person arrested;
(b) for use as evidence where the person's extradition is sought for the purposes of their trial and prosecution for the extradition offence;
(c) to facilitate the use in any proceedings of anything to which the material is inextricably linked;
(d) for forensic examination or other investigation in connection with an offence, committed in the United Kingdom or abroad (including the extradition offence);
(e) in order to establish its lawful owner when there are reasonable grounds for believing it has been stolen or obtained by the commission of an offence.

7.14 Perishable items seized should be photographed and a copy of the photograph retained as evidence.

7.15 Property shall not be retained under paragraph 7.13 (a), (b), (c) or (d) if a copy or image would be sufficient.

7.16 Material seized in relation to the extradition offence shall be retained only until:

(a) the person's extradition is ordered and the extradition proceedings are completed; or
(b) the person is discharged; or

(c) the extradition request is refused or withdrawn; or
(d) it is determined that the material is no longer required for the prosecution of the extradition offence.

7.17 If paragraph 7.16 (b), (c) or (d) apply, where possible the seized material must be returned to its lawful owner.

Evidence of a UK offence

7.18 The retention and use of property seized in relation to a UK offence is governed by the provisions in PACE Code B, 7.14–7.17.

(d) Rights of Owners

7.19 If property is retained under the Act, a list or description of the property must, on request, be provided to the person who had custody or control of it immediately before seizure, within a reasonable time.

7.20 PACE Code B 7.17 applies to all property seized under the Act.

8 *Delivery*

8.1 Under Section 172, an officer may deliver anything lawfully seized or produced under Part 4 of the Act to a person who is, or who is acting on behalf of, an authority of the requesting territory, which has functions making it appropriate for the material to be delivered to him or her.

8.2 It is the responsibility of the officer in charge of the search to ensure the secure storage and integrity of any material seized until such time as it is delivered to the requesting authority or territory or returned to its lawful owner.

8.3 Officers may not deliver:

(a) material, including copies or photographs of the material, seized in relation to the extradition offence; or
(b) anything that may be used as evidence in the prosecution of the person for the extradition offence,

to the requesting authority or territory until the order to extradite has been made and all legal proceedings relating to the extradition have been completed. The proceedings are not deemed to have been completed if the extradition case is adjourned.

8.4 Requests from appropriate representatives of the requesting authority or territory to view the property when visiting the UK are permitted.

Process of Delivery

8.5 After the order to extradite has been made, and the extradition proceedings have been completed, an officer must deliver seized material to representatives from the requesting authority or territory, as soon as is practicable:

(a) in person at the time and place the person is surrendered to representatives of the requesting authority or territory;
(b) in person by the officer who has assumed responsibility for retention of the property, at a location agreed with representatives of the requesting authority or territory; or
(c) by alternative means, with the consent of the requesting authority or territory.

8.6 Officers must be satisfied that the person to whom the material is being delivered is, or is acting on behalf of, an authority of the requesting territory, which has functions making it appropriate for the material to be delivered to him or her.

8.7 If it is not practical for material to be delivered in person at the time of surrender, the officer who has assumed responsibility for the material should arrange for the collection of the material by representatives from the requesting authority or territory.

8.8 Material may be delivered to the requesting authority or territory before the person has been handed over to the appropriate authorities from the requesting authority or territory, once extradition proceedings have been completed.

8.9 If material is delivered to the requesting authority or territory and it later transpires it is not needed, UK police are not required to assist in its return, but this does not preclude them providing assistance, where possible.

8.10 Material seized in response to a request from, for example, a Category 1 or Category 2 territory may be delivered to the requesting authority or territory if the person requested for extradition dies or escapes.

Material required in other prosecutions

8.11 Material seized under the Act which is also required for use in other proceedings abroad can only be delivered to the authority or territory requesting it, if a mutual legal assistance (MLA) request has been made and approved. Any such requests will be considered in accordance with the Criminal Justice (International Co-operation) Act 1990.

8.12 Where material is seized under the Act, which is:

- evidence relating to an offence(s) committed abroad, other than the extradition offence; or
- required for the prosecution abroad of persons in connection with an offence(s) other than the extradition offence; or
- required in the prosecution abroad of co-defendants of the person whose extradition is sought,

the material may only be delivered to the relevant territory if an MLA request for that material has been received and approved.

8.13 Delivery of the material for use in proceedings abroad (other than prosecution of the extradition offence) may take place before the extradition proceedings are completed, following approval of an MLA request.

8.14 Seized material also required for the prosecution of an offence committed in the UK, should be retained in the UK until proceedings on the UK offence have been completed.

9 *Action after searches and search registers*

9.1 If premises are searched under the powers contained in the Act, officers should follow the guidance in PACE Code B, Sections 8 and 9 regarding the action to be taken after a search and maintaining a search register.

9.2 Additionally, it is the responsibility of the officer in charge of the case to maintain a register of duplicate copies of the entries in the search register.

APPENDIX C

CODE C

CODE OF PRACTICE FOR THE ARREST, DETENTION AND TREATMENT OF PERSONS DETAINED UNDER THE EXTRADITION ACT 2003

1 General

1.1 This Code concerns the procedures for the arrest, detention and treatment of persons wanted for extradition. These supplement the guidance in PACE Code C.

1.2 The annexes are not provisions of this Code.

1.3 A custody officer must perform the functions in this Code as soon as practicable. A custody officer will not be in breach of this Code if delay is justifiable and reasonable steps are taken to prevent unnecessary delay. The custody record shall show when a delay has occurred and the reason.

1.4 This Code of Practice must be readily available at all police stations for consultation by:

- police officers;
- detained persons;
- members of the public.

1.5 In the operation of procedures under this Code, officers should have regard to the provisions of PACE Code C 1.4–1.7, 3.12–3.20, 10.12 and Annex E in respect of persons believed to be:

- mentally disordered or otherwise mentally vulnerable;
- under the age of 17;
- blind, seriously visually impaired, deaf, unable to read or speak, or has difficulty orally because of a speech impediment.

1.6 If this Code requires a person to be given certain information, they do not have to be given it if at the time they are incapable of understanding what is said, are violent or may become violent or are in urgent need of medical attention. But they must be given it as soon as practicable thereafter.

1.7 References to a custody officer include those performing the functions of custody officer.

1.8 When this Code requires the prior authority or agreement of an officer of at least inspector or superintendent rank, that authority may be given by a sergeant or chief inspector authorised to perform the functions of the higher rank under PACE, Section 107.

1.9 This Code applies to people in custody in police stations in England, Wales and Northern Ireland, who have been arrested under the Extradition Act 2003.

1.10 Paragraphs 1.13–1.17 in PACE Code C relating to designated persons and civilian support staff apply in the operation of this Code of Practice.

1.11 Nothing under this Code permits an officer to interview a person arrested under the Act.

2 Arrest

2.1 An officer arresting a person wanted for extradition under one of the following powers in the Act (see Annex A):

- Section 3: arrest under a certified Part 1 warrant;
- Section 5: provisional arrest under Part 1;
- Section 71: arrest warrant under Part 2, following certification of an extradition request;
- Section 73: provisional arrest warrant under Part 2;

shall:

(a) Caution the person in the following terms:

> **"You do not have to say anything, but anything you do say may be given in evidence."**

(b) Give the person a copy of the warrant as soon as practicable after arrest.

2.2 Minor deviations from the words of any caution given in accordance with this Code do not constitute a breach of this Code, provided the sense of the relevant caution is preserved.

2.3 The arresting officer need not be in possession of the Part 1 warrant or arrest warrant at the time of arrest.

2.4 A person arrested under Section 71 of the Act, must be served with copies of the following documentation:

- the papers containing the extradition request;
- the certificate issued by the Secretary of State;
- a copy of any relevant Order.

2.5 If it is not practicable (e.g. due to the large volume of papers contained in the request) to serve the request on the person on arrest, officers may give copies of the documentation to the person's legal adviser before or after arrest, as appropriate.

2.6 The officer must take all reasonable steps to ensure that the person understands that they are being arrested and why they are being arrested. The need for an interpreter will be fully assessed by the custody officer on arrival at the police station and if necessary, the process of arrest can be repeated to ensure the person understands that they have been arrested and why.

3 *Custody records*

3.1 A separate custody record must be opened as soon as practicable for each person brought to a police station arrested under the Act.

3.2 PACE Code C paragraphs 2.2–2.7 apply.

3.3 In addition to the specific provisions set out in PACE Code C, the custody officer shall record the following information on the custody record:

(a) the person's name and aliases, date of birth, gender and nationality;
(b) the person's address;
(c) a note of the person's self-defined ethnic background;
(d) the section of the Act the person was arrested under;
(e) the extradition offence(s) specified on the Part 1 warrant or a Part 2 extradition request (or, where known, the offence communicated by the requesting territory, if the person is arrested provisionally under Section 5);
(f) where possible, the date and location where the offence took place;
(g) the name of the country (e.g. Category 1 or 2) where the Part 1 warrant or extradition request issues from;

(h) the date, time and place that the person was arrested;
(i) whether the person has been given the rights and notices set out in Sections 4.3 and 4.4 of this Code;
(j) if the person required an interpreter and/or legal aid;
(k) if known, whether the person is claiming asylum in the UK.

3.4 All information recorded under this Code must be recorded as soon as practicable in the custody record unless otherwise specified.

4 *Custody Officers — responsibilities*

(a) Initial Action: detained persons

4.1 The person must be treated as continuing in legal custody from the point of arrest, until the person is either:

- first brought before the appropriate judge; or
- discharged (see paragraphs 4.9 (a)–(d) of this Code).

4.2 A checklist of the custody officer's duties under this Code is contained in Annex B.
4.3 When a person is brought to a police station under arrest, the custody officer must:

- assess the person's understanding of English and the need for an interpreter;
- give the person a copy of the arrest warrant (Part 1 warrant or domestic arrest warrant), if the person has not already been given a copy of the warrant by the arresting officer (see paragraph 2.1 (b));
- caution the person using the caution in the terms in paragraph 2.1(a) of this Code;
- inform the person that he or she will not be interviewed about the extradition offence;
- and make sure the person is told clearly about:

    (a) the stages of the extradition process including the right to consent to extradition (a form of words is set out in Annex C);
    (b) the following continuing rights which may be exercised at any stage during the period in custody:

        (i) the right to have someone informed of his or her arrest (under Section 171(3)(c) of the Act);
        (ii) the right to consult privately with a solicitor and that free independent legal advice is available (under Section 171 (3)(d) of the Act);
        (iii) the right to consult these Codes of Practice and the PACE Codes of Practice.

4.4 The custody officer must give the detainee:

(a) a written Extradition notice (Annex D) setting out:

    (i) the rights in paragraph 4.3(b);
    (ii) the arrangements for obtaining legal advice;
    (iii) the caution in the terms prescribed in 2.1(a) above;
    (iv) a fair processing notice, setting out the person's rights in respect of the use, retention and disclosure of personal data taken under the Act

(b) a copy of the form setting out the stages of the extradition process, including the right to consent to extradition (Annex C);
(c) a written notice briefly setting out their entitlements while in custody (see PACE Code C, Notes for Guidance 3A and 3B).

4.5 A citizen of an independent Commonwealth country or a national of a foreign country must be informed as soon as practicable about the right to communicate with their High Commission, Embassy or Consulate, as set out in PACE Code C Section 7. The list of countries to which this applies (as at 1st April 2003) is set out in Annex F of PACE Code C.

(b) Initial action: detained persons – special groups

4.6 PACE Code C paragraphs 3.12–3.20 apply in the operation of this Code.

(c) Documentation

4.7 The grounds for a person's detention shall be recorded in the person's presence, if practicable.

4.8 Action taken under paragraph 4.6 of this Code shall be recorded.

(d) Time limits for detention and discharge of person

4.9 Custody officers should note the specific obligations required under the Act in respect of persons arrested under an extradition arrest power.

(a) A copy of the arrest warrant (Part 1 warrant or domestic arrest warrant issued under Part 2) must be given to the person as soon as practicable after arrest (Sections 4(2), 6(5), 72(2) and 74(2));
Note: if this provision is not adhered to, the judge **may** order the person's discharge;
(b) A person arrested under Section 71 of the Act must be served copies of the extradition request, the certificate and any relevant Order before the extradition hearing (see paragraph 2.4 of this Code);
Note: if this provision is not adhered to, the judge **must** order the person's discharge;
(c) A person arrested under Section 3, 71 or 73 must be brought before the appropriate judge as soon as practicable (Sections 4(3), 72(3) and 74(3));
Note: if this provision is not adhered to and the person applies to an appropriate judge to be discharged, the judge **must** order the person's discharge;
(d) A person arrested provisionally under Section 5 of the Act must be brought before an appropriate judge **within 48 hours** of arrest;
Note: if this provision is not adhered to and the person applies to an appropriate judge to be discharged, the judge **must** order the person's discharge.

4.10 If a certified Part 1 warrant is issued subsequent to the person's discharge under Section 6(6), the person may be rearrested under Section 3 of the Act.

5 *Detainee's property*

(a) Action

5.1 The custody officer is responsible for:

(a) ascertaining what property a detainee:

(i) has with them when they come to the police station on arrest;
(ii) might have acquired for an unlawful or harmful purpose while in custody.

(b) the safekeeping of any property taken from a detainee which remains at the police station.

5.2 The custody officer may search the detainee or authorise their being searched to the extent they consider necessary. Intimate searches and strip searches are allowed under Section 171(3)(b) of the Act, provided they are carried out in accordance with PACE Code C, Annex A.

5.3 The custody officer may seize and retain any clothing or personal effects if there are reasonable grounds for believing that:

(a) the person might use it to cause physical injury to themselves or another person;
(b) the person might use it to assist escape from lawful custody;
(c) it is evidence relating to the extradition offence or an offence committed in the United Kingdom or abroad; or
(d) it is material relating to the identity of the person.

5.4 For the purposes of this section, 'an offence' includes:

- the extradition offence;
- an offence committed in the United Kingdom;
- an offence committed abroad.

5.5 An intimate or strip search under Section 171 may not be authorised for the purposes of ascertaining the person's identity.

5.6 PACE Code C, paragraphs 4.2 and 4.3 also apply in the operation of this Code.

(b) Documentation

5.7 PACE Code C paragraphs 4.4 and 4.5 apply.

6 *Person wanted for UK offence*

6.1 If, following arrest of a person under the Act, it becomes apparent that there is evidence or information connecting the person to a UK offence, it should be investigated in accordance with normal domestic procedures.

6.2 If the person is charged with the UK offence, the investigating police force must inform the appropriate judge of the UK charges as soon as practicable. Under Sections 22(2) and 88(2) the judge must adjourn the extradition proceedings.

7 *Right not to be held incommunicado*

7.1 PACE Code C, Section 5 and Annex B apply.

8 *Right to legal advice*

8.1 PACE Code C, paragraphs 6.1–6.5, 6.12–6.16 and Annex B apply.

9 Citizens of independent Commonwealth countries or foreign nationals

9.1 PACE Code C, Section 7 and paragraph 4.5 of this Code apply.

10 Conditions of detention

10.1 PACE Code C, Section 8 applies.

11 Care and treatment of detained persons

11.1 PACE Code C, Section 9 applies.

Annex A — Arrest Under The Extradition Act 2003

1.1 An officer may make an arrest under one of the following powers in the Act:

(a) Section 3: arrest under a certified Part 1 warrant

This applies where a Part 1 warrant has been received and certified by the UK designated authority, which contains the following information:

(i) Particulars of the person's identity;
(ii) That the person has been accused or convicted of an offence in a Category 1 territory and the warrant issued for the purposes of the person's arrest and extradition;
(iii) The circumstances of the offence, the time and place at which it is alleged to have been committed and the particulars of the law in the Category 1 territory which is alleged to have been broken;
(iv) The sentence which may be imposed by the Category 1 territory if the person is convicted of the offence;
(v) Details of any other warrant issued in a Category 1 territory for the person's arrest.

(b) Section 5: Provisional arrest under Part 1

This applies where the UK designated authority has reason to believe that a Part 1 warrant has been or will be issued by a designated judicial authority in a Category 1 territory in respect of a person. The UK designated authority will not have certified the Part 1 warrant.

Provisional arrest requests are usually made in urgent circumstances where the person is believed to be a flight risk or is expected to be in a particular location only fleetingly, and before there is time for a Part 1 warrant to be issued or received and certified.

(c) Section 71: arrest under Part 2, following certification of an extradition request

This applies when the Secretary of State has certified an extradition request from a Category 2 territory and a district judge has issued an arrest warrant in relation to the person whose extradition is sought.

(d) Section 73: Provisional arrest warrant under Part 2

This applies in urgent cases where a person is requested for extradition by a Category 2 territory, but full documentation has not yet been received. In this circumstance, an officer may apply to a justice of the peace for a provisional arrest warrant in respect of the person whose extradition is sought.

For a warrant to be issued, the officer must satisfy the justice of the peace in writing and on oath that:

i. Either:
   - The person is accused in a Category 2 territory of an offence; or
   - The person is alleged to be unlawfully at large following conviction or sentence by a court in a Category 2 territory;

ii. The offence is an extradition offence;
iii. The person is believed to be in the UK or on their way to the UK;
iv. There is written information or evidence that would justify the issue of a warrant for the arrest of a person accused of the offence or unlawfully at large, within the justice's jurisdiction.

1.2 The arresting officer need not be in possession of the warrant at the time of arrest.

Annex B—Checklist of Duties for Custody Officers in Extradition Cases

1.	Assess the need for an interpreter	☐
2.	Ensure the person understands that they have been arrested and why they have been arrested	☐
3.	Caution person in the following terms: "You do not have to say anything, but anything you do say may be given in evidence" and inform the person that he/she will not be interviewed or questioned about the extradition offence	☐
4.	Give person a copy of the arrest warrant. If person arrested under Part 2 of the Act, check the papers in Code C paragraph 2.4 have been served on the person	☐
5.	Inform the person of extradition process, including the right to consent to extradition (see form of words, Annex C to Extradition Code of Practice, Code C)	☐
6.	Inform person of their rights while in custody: (a) Right to have someone informed of the arrest and detention (b) Right to consult privately with a solicitor and that free, independent legal advice is available (c) Right to consult the Extradition Codes of Practice and the PACE Codes of Practice	☐

7.	Serve the person with the following forms: (a) The written extradition notice (Annex D to Extradition Code of Practice, Code C) setting out: ● The person's rights while in custody ● The arrangements for obtaining legal advice ● The extradition caution ● The fair processing notice regarding the use retention and disclosure of personal data taken (b) A written notice setting out the person's usual entitlements while in custody (c) A written copy of the form explaining the stages of the extradition process. and mark the custody record as appropriate	☐
8.	Inform person of the right to communicate with their High commission, Embassy or Consulate (the list of countries to which this applies, as at 1st April 2003, is set out in Annex F, PACE Code of Practice C) and mark the custody record as appropriate	☐
9.	Ask the detainee (a) whether they: ● Would like legal advice ● Want someone informed of their detention (b) to sign the custody record to confirm their decisions in respect of these	☐
10.	Conduct a risk assessment and determine whether the detainee: (a) is, or might be in need of medical treatment or attention (b) requires the presence of an appropriate adult (in accordance with paragraph 1.5 of this Code) or other special assistance and mark the custody record as appropriate	☐
11.	Search the person to ascertain what property the detained person has with them and document this. Record the reasons for retaining any items of property, and mark the custody record as appropriate	☐
12.	Ensure the following information is contained on the custody record and forward this information to the Fugitives Unit at NCIS (Part 1 cases) or the Judicial Co-operation Unit at the Home Office (Part 2 cases): (a) The person's name and aliases, date of birth, gender and nationality (b) The person's address (c) A note of the person's self-defined ethnic background (d) The Section of the Act the person was arrested under (e) The offence(s) specified on the Part 1 warrant or Part 2 extradition request (or, where known, the offence communicated by the requesting authority, if the person was arrested provisionally under Section 5) (f) Where possible, the date and location where the offence took place	☐

	(g) The name of the territory (Category 1 or 2) requesting extradition (h) The date, time and place that the person was arrested (i) That the person has been given the required rights and notices (j) If the person required an interpreter and/or legal aid (k) If known, whether the person has claimed asylum in the UK	

Annex C — Summary of the UK Extradition Process

Note: this form is not an exhaustive account of the extradition process, and is not a statement of the law, but is designed to help you to understand why you have been arrested and the main stages of the extradition process.

If you require a more detailed explanation of the process or have further questions, you should seek advice from your legal adviser.

PART 1: Persons Arrested under Section 3 of the Extradition Act 2003

1) You have been arrested under Section 3 of the Extradition Act 2003.

2) *Either (where person is accused of offences in the Requesting State):*

   Your extradition is sought by [Category 1 territory] in relation to an [offence(s)] which took place on [date/time] at [location]

   Or (Where person has been convicted for offences and is alleged to be unlawfully at large):

   Your extradition is sought by [Category 1 territory] for the purpose of [being sentenced] or [serving a sentence of imprisonment] in relation to [offence specified on the warrant].

3) You will be held in police custody until the initial extradition hearing.

4) There are two main stages to the extradition process.

5) The first is an initial hearing before a district judge. This will take place as soon as practicable.

6) At the initial hearing the judge will either remand you in custody or grant you bail.

7) The second hearing is the main extradition hearing. This will usually take place before a district judge within 21 days of your arrest.

8) At the extradition hearing, the judge will decide whether there are any reasons why you should not be extradited and then either order your extradition to [the Category 1 territory] or discharge you.

9) You may appeal against the judge's decision, within 7 days. If you do not appeal, you will be returned to [the Category 1 territory] within 10 days of the extradition hearing.

10) You have the right to consent to your extradition. If you wish to consent, you should consult your legal advisor on the implications. You may only give consent before the appropriate judge.

PART 1: Provisional Arrest under Section 5 of the Extradition Act 2003

Note: this form is not an exhaustive account of the extradition process, and is not a statement of the law, but is designed to help you to understand why you have been arrested and the main stages of the extradition process.

If you require a more detailed explanation of the process or have further questions, you should seek advice from your legal adviser.

1) You have been provisionally arrested under Section 5 of the Extradition Act 2003.
2) *Either (where person is accused of offences in the Requesting State):*

   Your extradition is sought by [Category 1 territory] in relation to an [offence(s)]

   Or (where person has been convicted in the Requesting State is alleged to be unlawfully at large):

   Your extradition is sought by [Category 1 territory] for the purpose of [being sentenced] or [serving a sentence of imprisonment].
3) If you are held in police custody for more than 48 hours after your arrest, pending receipt of a certified Part 1 warrant, you may apply to be discharged.
4) You have the right to be given a copy of the warrant as soon as is practicable.
5) There are two main stages to the extradition process.
6) The first is an initial hearing before a district judge. This will take place within 48 hours of your arrest.
7) At the initial hearing the judge will either remand you in custody or grant you bail.
8) The second hearing is the main extradition hearing. This will take place before a district judge within 21 days of your arrest.
9) At the extradition hearing the judge will decide whether there are any reasons why you should not be extradited and then either order your extradition to [the Category 1 territory] or discharge you.
10) You may appeal against the judge's decision, within 7 days. If you do not appeal, you will be returned to [the Category 1 territory] within 10 days of the extradition hearing.
11) You have the right to consent to your extradition. If you wish to consent you should consult your legal advisor on the implications. You may only give consent before the appropriate judge.

PART 2: Persons Arrested under Section 71 of the Extradition Act 2003

Note: this form is not an exhaustive account of the extradition process, and is not a statement of the law, but is designed to help you to understand why you have been arrested and the main stages of the extradition process.

If you require a more detailed explanation of the process or have further questions, you should seek advice from your legal adviser.

1) You have been arrested under Section 71 of the Extradition Act 2003.
2) *Either (where person is accused of offences in the Requesting State):*

   Your extradition is sought by [Category 2 territory] in relation to [offence(s)] which took place on [date/time] at [location].

Or (where person has been convicted by the Requesting State and is alleged to be unlawfully at large):

Your extradition is sought by [Category 2 territory] for the purpose of [being sentenced] or [serving a sentence of imprisonment] in relation to [offence(s) specified on the warrant]

3) You will be held in police custody until you are brought before a judge. You will be brought before a judge as soon as practicable.

4) There are three main stages to the extradition proceedings.

5) At the first stage, you will be brought before a judge as soon as practicable after your arrest. The judge will either remand you in custody or grant you bail.

6) The second stage is the main extradition hearing. This will take place within two months of you being brought before the judge for the first time.

7) At the extradition hearing, the judge will decide whether there are any reasons why you should not be extradited. The judge will then either discharge you or send your case to the Secretary of State for a decision as to whether you should be extradited.

8) If your case is sent to the Secretary of State for a decision, you will have the right of appeal, but the appeal will not be heard until after the Secretary of State has made his decision. If your case is sent to the Secretary of State, you will either be remanded in custody or granted bail.

9) If the Secretary of State orders your extradition to [the Category 2 territory], you have the right to appeal to the High Court against the decisions of the judge and the Secretary of State within 14 days.

10) If you do not appeal, you will be returned to [the Category 2 territory] within 28 days of the order to extradite.

11) You have the right to consent to your extradition. If you wish to consent you should consult your legal advisor on the implications. You may only consent before the appropriate judge.

PART 2: Provisional Arrest under Section 73 of the Extradition Act 2003

Note: this form is not an exhaustive account of the extradition process, and is not a statement of the law, but is designed to help you to understand why you have been arrested and the main stages of the extradition process.

If you require a more detailed explanation of the process or have further questions, you should seek advice from your legal adviser.

1) You have been provisionally arrested under Section 73 of the Extradition Act 2003.

Either (where person is accused of offences in the Requesting State):

Your extradition is sought by [Category 2 territory] in relation to [offence(s)] which took place on [date/time] at [location].

Or (where person has been convicted by the Requesting State and is alleged to be unlawfully at large):

Your extradition is sought by [Category 2 territory] for the purpose of [being sentenced] or [serving a sentence of imprisonment] in relation to [offence(s) specified on the warrant]

2) You will be held in police custody until you are brought before a judge. You will be brought before a judge as soon as practicable.
3) There are three main stages to the extradition proceedings
4) At the first stage, you will be brought before a judge as soon as practicable after your arrest. The judge will either remand you in custody or grant you bail.
5) Provided the judge has received all the necessary documentation relating to your case, within any applicable time limits, the judge will fix a date for the main extradition hearing. The main extradition hearing is the second stage of the proceedings.
6) The main extradition hearing will take place within 2 months of the judge receiving the necessary documentation.
7) At the extradition hearing the judge will decide whether there are any reasons why you should not be extradited. The judge will then either discharge you or send your case to the Secretary of State for a decision as to whether you will be extradited.
8) If your case is sent to the Secretary of State for a decision, you will have the right of appeal, but the appeal will not be heard until after the Secretary of State has made his decision. If your case is sent to the Secretary of State, you will either be remanded in custody or granted bail.
9) If the Secretary of State orders your extradition to [the Category 2 territory], you have the right to appeal to the High Court against the decisions of the judge and the Secretary of State within 14 days.
10) If you do not appeal, you will be returned to [the Category 2 territory] within 28 days of the order to extradite.
11) You have the right to consent to your extradition. If you wish to consent you should consult your legal advisor on the implications. You may only give consent before the appropriate judge.

Annex D — Extradition: Written Notice to Detained Person
Including Fair Processing Notice

The section in capital letters is to be read to the detained person by the Custody Officer before giving the notice to the detained person.

YOU HAVE THE RIGHT TO:

1. SPEAK TO AN INDEPENDENT SOLICITOR FREE OF CHARGE
2. HAVE SOMEONE TOLD THAT YOU HAVE BEEN ARRESTED
3. CONSULT THE CODES OF PRACTICE COVERING POLICE POWERS AND PROCEDURES
4. CONSULT THE CODES OF PRACTICE COVERING POLICE POWERS AND PROCEDURES FOR EXTRADITION

YOU MAY DO ANY OF THESE THINGS NOW, BUT IF YOU DO NOT, YOU MAY STILL DO SO AT ANY TIME WHILST DETAINED AT THE POLICE STATION

You do not have to say anything, but anything you do say may be given in evidence.
You will not be interviewed about the extradition offence.

More information is given below. The following 4 continuing rights may be exercised at any stage during the period in custody:

1. The right to consult privately with a solicitor. Free independent legal advice is available. (Section 172 (3)(d) of the Extradition Act 2003)

You can speak to a solicitor at the police station at any time, day or night. It will cost you nothing.

Access to legal advice can only be delayed in certain exceptional circumstances (see Annex B of PACE Code of Practice C)

If you do not know a solicitor, or you cannot contact your own solicitor, ask for the duty solicitor. He or she is nothing to do with the police. Or you can ask to see a list of local solicitors.

You can talk to a solicitor in private on the telephone and the solicitor can come to see you at the police station.

In extradition cases, the police will not interview you about the extradition offence

If you want to see a solicitor, tell the custody officer at once. You can ask for legal advice at any time during your detention. Even if you do tell the police that you do not want a solicitor, you may change your mind at any time.

Your right to legal advice does not entitle you to delay procedures under the Road Traffic Act 1988 which require the provision of breath, blood or urine specimens.

2. The right to have someone informed of your arrest and detention (under Section 172 (3)(c) of the Extradition Act 2003);

You may on request have one person known to you or who is likely to take an interest in your welfare, informed at public expense as soon as practicable of your whereabouts. If this person cannot be contacted, you may choose up to 2 alternatives. If they too cannot be contacted, the Custody Officer has discretion on the number of further attempts required made to make contact.

This right can only be delayed in exceptional circumstances (Annex B PACE Code of Practice C)

3. and 4. The right to consult the PACE Codes of Practice and the Extradition Codes of Practice.

Either or both of the Codes of Practice will be made available to you on request. These Codes govern police procedures.

The right does not entitle you to unreasonably delay any necessary action.

The right does not entitle you to delay procedures under the Road Traffic Act 1988 which require the provision of breath, blood or urine specimens.

Custody Record

The Custody Officer will keep a record of your detention. On request, when you leave police detention or are taken before a court, you or your legal representative or the appropriate adult shall be supplied with a copy of the Custody Record as soon as practicable. This entitlement lasts for 12 months after your release from police detention.

Fair Processing Notice

Fair processing in respect of the use, retention and disclosure of personal data taken under the Data Protection Act 1998.

On written request, you shall be told as soon as is practicable:

- of the identity of the data controller or have this made easily available to you (this may be an individual e.g. Chief Constable, or a registered body);
- the purpose(s) for which the data will be processed and to whom it may be passed. Under extradition proceedings, the purpose will include establishing identity, maintaining the Custody Record, statistics and monitoring - refer to Extradition Codes C 3.3 and D 1.2. The information may be passed between law enforcement agencies, both here and abroad, and within Her Majesty's Government.

Your rights under use, disclosure and retention of photographs, fingerprints and samples are explained in the Extradition Codes of Practice, Code D 3.13 to 3.18 and 4.17 to 4.19.

Individuals who make a subject access request are entitled to a copy of the information held about them, however, this right does not entitle you to this information where exemptions apply under section 29 (1) of the Data Protection Act or other exemptions apply under Part 4 of that Act. E.g. access would be likely to prejudice the prevention or detection of crime or the apprehension or prosecution of offenders

The rights do not entitle you to unreasonably delay any necessary action in connection with your case.

The police are not obliged to contact the Information Commissioner on your behalf.

Further information can be obtained from the Information Commissioner on **Enquiry Line** Telephone: 01625 545 745 or by Email: data@informationcommissioner.gov.uk

CODE D

CODE OF PRACTICE FOR THE IDENTIFICATION OF PERSONS DETAINED UNDER THE EXTRADITION ACT 2003

1 Introduction

1.1 This Code of Practice concerns the principal methods available to the police to identify people wanted for extradition and the keeping of accurate and reliable records of extradition cases.

1.2 Identification of persons wanted for extradition may be made using the following methods:

- taking of fingerprints;
- (non-intimate) body samples and impressions, including taking samples such as blood or hair to generate a DNA profile for comparison with material obtained from the requesting territory;

- taking of photographs;
- searching and examining detained persons to find, e.g. marks such as tattoos or scars which may help establish their identity.

1.3 Under this Code, intimate samples may not be taken for the purposes of ascertaining identity.

2 *General*

2.1 This Code must be readily available at all police stations for consultation by:

- police officers;
- detained persons;
- members of the public.

2.2 The provisions of PACE Code D paragraphs 2.3–2.6 and 2.12, 2.13 and 2.15 (and the corresponding Notes for Guidance) apply to this Code in respect of persons who are believed to be:

- mentally disordered or otherwise mentally vulnerable;
- under the age of 17;
- blind, seriously visually impaired, deaf, unable to read or speak or have difficulty orally because of a speech impediment.

2.3 References to custody officers include those performing the functions of a custody officer.

2.4 When a record of any action requiring the authority of an officer of a specified rank is made under this Code, subject to paragraph 2.9, the officer's name and rank must be recorded.

2.5 When this Code requires the prior authority or agreement of an officer of at least inspector or superintendent rank, that authority may be given by a sergeant or chief inspector who has been authorised to perform the functions of the higher rank under PACE, Section 107.

2.6 Subject to paragraph 2.10 all records must be timed and signed by the maker.

2.7 References to:

- 'taking a photograph', include the use of any process to produce a single, still, visual image;
- 'photographing a person', should be construed accordingly;
- 'photographs', 'films', 'negatives' and 'copies' include relevant visual images recorded, stored or reproduced through any medium;
- 'destruction' includes the deletion of computer data relating to such images or making access to that data impossible.

2.8 References to an 'intimate sample' mean a dental impression or sample of blood, semen or any other tissue fluid, urine or pubic hair, or a swab taken from a person's body orifice other than the mouth.

2.9 Nothing in this Code requires the identity of officers or civilian support staff to be recorded or disclosed if the officers or civilian support staff reasonably believe recording or disclosing their names might put them in danger. In these cases, they shall use warrant or other identification numbers and the name of their police station.

2.10 The provisions in PACE Code D 2.18–2.22 concerning the role of civilian support staff and designated persons apply to this Code.

3 Identification by fingerprints and samples

(a) General

3.1 References to 'fingerprints' means any record, produced by any method, of the skin pattern and other physical characteristics or features of a person's fingers or palms.

3.2 References to a 'non-intimate sample' mean a sample of hair, other than pubic, a sample taken from a nail or from under a nail, a swab taken from any part of a person's body including the mouth but not any other body orifice, saliva, or a skin impression (other than a fingerprint).

(b) Action

3.3 Under Section 166 of the Act fingerprints or a non-intimate sample may be taken from a person detained at a police station in connection with an extradition offence, in order to:

(a) assist in establishing the person's identity;
(b) assist in establishing the person's identity by cross-checking fingerprint data against records of current asylum claimants held by the Immigration Fingerprint Bureau;
(c) assist in the investigation of outstanding or unsolved UK offences;
(d) assist in the conduct of prosecutions by or on behalf of police or other law enforcement and prosecuting authorities inside and outside the United Kingdom;
(e) maintain a national police record of extradited persons.

3.4 A person's fingerprints or a non-intimate sample may only be taken:

(a) with the consent of the person in writing; or
(b) with the authorisation of a police officer of at least the rank of inspector, without that consent.

3.5 A person's fingerprints may be taken electronically.

3.6 Reasonable force may be used, if necessary, to take a person's fingerprints or a non-intimate sample, without their consent.

3.7 Intimate samples may not be taken under Section 166 of the Act.

3.8 Before any fingerprints or a non-intimate sample are taken, with or without consent, the person must be informed:

(a) of the reason for taking their fingerprints or the sample;
(b) of the grounds on which the relevant authority has been given;
(c) that their fingerprints and/or the information derived from the samples will be retained and may be the subject of a speculative search.

3.9 Officers should have regard to PACE Code D 6.9 and the corresponding Notes for Guidance in the procedures for taking non-intimate samples.

(c) Documentation

3.10 A record must made as soon as possible, of:

(a) the reason for taking a sample;
(b) the reason for taking a person's fingerprints without consent.

3.11 If force is used, a record shall be made of the circumstances and of those present.

3.12 A record shall be made of the fact that a person has been informed that fingerprints and samples (and the information derived from it) may be the subject of a speculative search.

(d) Use, disclosure and retention of fingerprints and samples

3.13 Fingerprints or samples (and the information derived from the samples) taken from a person under Section 166 of the Act may be used or disclosed only for purposes related to:

(a) establishing the person's identity;
(b) the prevention and detection of crime;
(c) the investigation of domestic offences;
(d) the conduct of prosecutions by or on behalf of police or other law enforcement and prosecuting authorities inside and outside the United Kingdom.

3.14 After being so used or disclosed the fingerprints and samples may be retained by the police and other law enforcement authorities in the United Kingdom, but the information must not be used or disclosed except for the purposes in paragraph 3.13 and being the subject of a speculative search.

3.15 A speculative search means the fingerprints or samples (and the information derived from the samples) may be checked against other fingerprints and DNA records held by, or on behalf of, the police and other law enforcement authorities in or outside the United Kingdom, or held in connection with, or as a result of, an offence committed inside or outside the United Kingdom.

3.16 Fingerprints and samples (and the information derived from the samples) or copies of this information, may be sent to the requesting authority or territory before completion of the extradition proceedings, to assist in establishing the person's identity.

(e) Destruction of fingerprints and samples

3.17 When fingerprints and samples are taken from a person wanted for extradition and the person is discharged from the extradition proceedings, they must be destroyed as soon as they have fulfilled the purpose for which they were taken, unless paragraph 3.18 applies.

3.18 If the person gives their written consent for their fingerprints or sample to be retained and used after they have fulfilled the purpose for which they were taken, the fingerprints or samples do not have to be destroyed.

3.19 When a person's fingerprints or samples are to be destroyed, officers shall follow the guidance in PACE Code D, Annex F, paragraph 3.

4 *Examinations to establish identity and taking of photographs*

(a) Searching or examination of detainees at police stations

4.1 Section 167 of the Act allows an officer or a designated person to search or examine a person wanted for extradition and detained at a police station in order to establish:

(a) whether they have any marks, features or injuries (e.g. tattoos or scars) that would tend to identify them as the person wanted in connection with the extradition offence, and to photograph any identifying marks (see paragraph below on the taking and use of photographs); or
(b) their identity.

4.2 Under Section 167 a search and/or examination to find marks may be carried out:

(a) with the person's consent; or
(b) without the person's consent, if it is not possible to obtain it and authorisation has been given in accordance with paragraph 4.4.

4.3 Identifying marks may be photographed with the person's consent or without their consent if it is withheld or it is not possible to obtain it. Authorisation by a senior officer is not required in the taking of photographs without consent, but proper documentation must be filed, according to paragraphs 4.15–4.16 below.

4.4 A search and/or examination without consent may only take place if authorised by an officer of the rank of inspector or above. Authorisation may be given orally or in writing. If given orally, the authorising officer must confirm it in writing as soon as practicable. A separate authority is required for each purpose which applies.

4.5 A detainee may only be searched, examined and photographed under Section 167 of the Act by a police officer of the same sex.

4.6 If it is established that a person is unwilling to co-operate to enable a search and/or examination to take place or a suitable photograph to be taken, an officer may use reasonable force to:

(a) search and/or examine a detainee without their consent; and
(b) photograph any identifying marks without their consent.

4.7 The thoroughness and extent of any search or examination carried out in accordance with the powers in Section 167 must be no more than the officer considers necessary to achieve the required purpose. Any search or examination which involves the removal of more than the person's outer clothing shall be conducted in accordance with PACE Code C, Annex A, paragraph 11.

4.8 An intimate search may not be carried out under Section 167 of the Act.

(b) Photographing

4.9 Section 168 of the Act allows an officer or a designated person to photograph a person wanted for extradition and detained at a police station:

(a) with their consent; or
(b) without their consent, if it is not possible to obtain consent.

4.10 The officer proposing to take a person's photograph may, for this purpose, require the person to remove any item or substance worn on, or over, all or any part of the head or face. If the person does not comply with such a requirement, the officer may remove the item or substance.

4.11 If it is established that a person is unwilling to co-operate sufficiently to enable a suitable photograph to be taken and it is not reasonably practicable to take the photograph covertly, an officer may use reasonable force:

(a) to take their photograph without their consent; and
(b) for the purpose of taking the photograph, remove any item or substance worn on, or over, all, or any part of the person's head or face which they have failed to remove when asked.

4.12 For the purposes of this Code, a photograph may be obtained without the person's consent by making a copy of an image of them taken at any time on a camera system installed anywhere in the police station.

(c) Information to be given

4.13 When a person is searched, examined or photographed, they must be informed of the:

(a) purpose of the search, examination or photograph;
(b) grounds on which the relevant authority, if applicable, has been given; and
(c) purposes for which a photograph may be used, disclosed or retained.

4.14 This information must be given before the photograph is taken, except if the photograph is:

(a) taken covertly;
(b) obtained as in paragraph 4.12 by making a copy of an image of the person taken at any time on a camera system installed anywhere in the police station.

(d) Documentation

4.15 A record must be made when the person is searched, examined or a photograph of the person or any identifying marks found on them is taken. The record must include the:

(a) identity of the officer carrying out the search, examination or taking the photograph;
(b) purpose of the search, examination or photograph and the outcome;
(c) person's consent to the search, examination or photograph, or the reason the person was searched, examined or photographed without consent;
(d) giving of any authority, the grounds for giving it and the authorising officer.

4.16 If, under paragraph 4.11, force is used when searching, examining or taking a photograph, a record shall be made of the circumstances and those present.

(e) Use, disclosure and retention of photographs of persons or identifying marks

4.17 Any photographs of persons or identifying marks taken under Sections 167 and 168 of the Act may be used or disclosed only for purposes related to:

(a) establishing the person's identity;
(b) the prevention and detection of crime;
(c) the investigation of domestic offences;
(d) the conduct of prosecutions by or on behalf of police or other law enforcement and prosecuting authorities inside and outside the United Kingdom.

4.18 After being so used or disclosed, the photographs may be retained by the police and other law enforcement authorities in the United Kingdom but they must not be used or disclosed except for the purposes in paragraph 4.17.

4.19 A photograph of the person or identifying marks (or a copy) taken under Section 167 or 168 of the Act may be sent to the requesting authority or territory in advance of the person's extradition to assist in establishing the identity of the person arrested.

GLOSSARY

Appropriate judge	Under Parts 1 and 2 of the Act, the appropriate judge is: ● District Judge (Magistrates' Courts) in England and Wales; ● County court judge or resident magistrate in Northern Ireland.
Category 1 territory	A country designated by an Order of the Secretary of State, with whom the UK operates extradition procedures in accordance with Part 1 of the Act (see the Home Office website: www.homeoffice.gov.uk for a full list of Category 1 territories).

Category 2 territory	Country designated by an Order of the Secretary of State, with whom the UK operates extradition procedures in accordance with Part 2 of the Act (see the Home Office website: www.homeoffice.gov.uk for a full list of Category 2 territories).
Certified warrant	A Part 1 warrant issued by a judicial authority of a Category 1 territory which is checked and certified as a valid warrant by the UK designated authority.
Certified request	An extradition request from a Category 2 territory which has been checked and certified as a valid request the Secretary of State.
Circuit judge	A judge who sits in the County Court and/or Crown Court (in Northern Ireland a Crown Court judge).
Designated Persons	A person, other than a police officer, designated by the chief officer of police for the area in which the police station in question is situated, or in Northern Ireland, the Chief Constable of the Police Service of Northern Ireland, who has specified powers and duties of police officers conferred and imposed on them.
Designated Central Authority	The organisation designated by Statutory Instrument with the function of certifying Part 1 warrants received from Category 1 territories prior to the person's arrest. The designated central authorities for the UK are: the National Criminal Intelligence Service (NCIS) and the Crown Agent of the Scottish Crown Office.
District judge	A judicial officer of the Court whose duties involve hearing applications made within proceedings and final hearings subject to any limit of jurisdiction.
Excluded material	Material, records or substances held in confidence (see PACE Section 11).
Extradition	The process whereby a person accused or convicted of a serious crime is, at the request of another country, returned by the UK to that jurisdiction, or vice versa.
Extradition hearing	The main part of the extradition process where a district judge considers the request for extradition of the person extradition against criteria laid out in the Act.
Extradition offence	An offence over which another country has jurisdiction, for which the person has been requested to stand trial, be sentenced or serve a sentence abroad and for which the UK will consider extradition. Alternatively, an offence for which the UK seeks a person's extradition from another country.
Extradition request	The documentation transmitted on a Government to Government basis from a Category 2 territory which requests a person's arrest and extradition. To be valid, the extradition request must meet the criteria in Section 70 of the Act.

Fingerprints	Any record, produced by any method, of the skin pattern and other physical characteristics or features of a person's fingers or palms (PACE Section 65).
Identifying Mark	A mark that assists in establishing a person's identity.
Inextricably linked material	Material it is not reasonably practicable to separate from other linked material without prejudicing the use of that other material in any investigation or proceedings (e.g. it may not be possible to separate items of data held on a computer disk without damaging their evidential integrity).
Initial hearing	A stage in the extradition process under Part 1 where the person is first brought before a district judge (Section 7).
Intimate Sample	A dental impression or sample of blood, semen or any other tissue fluid, urine or pubic hair, or a swab taken from a person's body orifice other than the mouth.
Intimate Search	A physical examination of a person's body orifices other than the mouth.
Items subject to legal privilege	Communications between a professional legal adviser and the client that is concerned with the proceedings. Anything held with the intention of furthering a criminal cause is not covered.
Judicial authority	The authority in a Category 1 territory which has the function of issuing a Part 1 warrant in that country.
Justice of the peace	A lay magistrate — person appointed to administer judicial business in a Magistrates Court.
Legal adviser	Barrister, solicitor or duty solicitor.
Legal privilege	See 'items subject to legal privilege'.
Mark	A feature or injury (e.g. body piercing, a tattoo, insignia or scar) which can assist in establishing their identity.
NCIS	National Criminal Intelligence Service (see 'designated central authority').
Non-intimate Sample	A sample of hair other than pubic, a sample taken from a nail or from under a nail, a swab taken from any part of a person's body including the mouth but not any other body orifice, saliva or a skin impression (other than a fingerprint).
Non-intimate search	Physical examination of a person's body, including the mouth, but no other body orifices.
Officer in charge	An officer, of any rank, designated in charge of a search with particular duties and responsibilities in carrying out the search.
Order to extradite	Requirement that the person requested for extradition by a Category 1 or 2 territory be returned to that country to stand trial, be sentenced or serve a sentence in respect of the extradition offence(s).
PACE	The Police and Criminal Evidence Act 1984.

Part 1	Part 1 of the Act, relating to the procedures and safeguards that govern an extradition request from a territory designated under Part 1 by an Order of the Secretary of State.
Part 1 warrant	Arrest warrant issued under Part 1 of the Extradition Act by a judicial authority in a Category 1 territory.
Part 2	Part 2 of the Act, relating to the procedures and safeguards that govern an extradition request from a territory designated under Part 2 by an Order of the Secretary of State.
Photograph	A process by means of which a visual image may be produced, including by making a copy of an image of the person taken at any time on a camera system installed anywhere in a police station.
Premises	Any place, vehicle, vessel, aircraft, hovercraft, tent or movable structure and any offshore installation as defined in the Mineral Workings (Offshore Installations) Act 1971, section 1 (see PACE Section 23).
Provisional Arrest	1) Arrest under Part 1 pending receipt of a certified Part 1 warrant or certified European Arrest Warrant; or 2) Arrest under Part 2 under a provisional arrest warrant issued by a UK magistrate, pending receipt of the necessary documents required under Section 70 of the Act.
Requesting authority	See 'judicial authority'.
Requesting territory	The Category 2 territory which has made an extradition request under Part 2 of the Act.
Special Procedure Material	Journalistic material or material held in confidence by someone in a professional or official capacity, other than excluded material or items subject to legal privilege (see PACE Section 14).
Speculative search	Checking of fingerprints, samples and the information derived from them against other fingerprint and DNA records held by, or on behalf of, the police and other law enforcement authorities in, as well as outside, the UK.
Surrender	The physical act of handing over a person, whose extradition has been ordered, to officials from the requesting authority or territory.
UK offence	An offence, as defined in PACE Schedule 1A committed in the United Kingdom.

C–012 # Mutual Legal Assistance Guidelines: Obtaining assistance in the UK and Overseas (First Edition)

UNITED KINGDOM CENTRAL AUTHORITY
JUDICIAL CO-OPERATION UNIT
HOME OFFICE
LONDON SW1H 9AT
APRIL 2004

Guidelines from the Serious Fraud Office (SFO) and HM Customs & Excise (HMCE) are also available. To view these please follow the links in Annex C and on the Home Office website[1]. Other website links are contained in Part II Chapter 4: Other Information.

References in this document to Central Authorities refer equally to the United Kingdom Central Authority at the Home Office (UKCA), the Crown Office and the Northern Ireland Office unless otherwise specified.

PART I — REQUESTS TO THE UK

Chapter 1: Introduction

The United Kingdom Government attaches great importance to assisting judicial and prosecuting authorities in other countries in combating national and international crime.

The UK is able to provide a full range of legal assistance in criminal matters to judicial and prosecuting authorities in other countries under Part I of the Crime (International Co-operation) Act 2003 (CICA 2003) and sections 5 & 6 of the Criminal Justice (International Co-operation) Act 1990 (CRIJICA). CICA 2003 is the UK's principal mutual legal assistance legislation.

These guidelines:

- give details of the assistance that can be provided under the Acts;
- give details regarding the procedures to follow when requesting assistance;
- explain the role of the Central Authorities in the execution of requests for legal assistance in criminal matters; and
- describe how the Central Authorities work in close co-operation with the UK National Central Bureau of Interpol, which is part of the UK's National Criminal Intelligence Service (NCIS) in dealing with international requests for assistance.

Staff of the central authorities working on requests for legal assistance are fully conversant with mutual legal assistance law and practice. They work to very high professional standards. These are reflected in the published Code of Practice, included in these guidelines.

[1] *http://www.homeoffice.gov.uk/crimpol/oic/mutuallegal/intex.html.*

Extradition matters and international co-operation between law enforcement agencies, tax administrations and regulatory authorities in the financial services industry are not included in these guidelines. Separate guidance on those matters can be obtained from the relevant contact shown in Annex C.

The UK's Central Authorities are *not* responsible for judicial co-operation with the Channel Islands, the Isle of Man or the UK Overseas Territories. Contact points for the competent authorities of the Islands and Territories are listed in Annex D.

Requests between Gibraltar and European Union/ Schengen Member States *must* be routed via the Foreign and Commonwealth Office "post-box," details of which are in Annex D).

Chapter 2: Range of assistance and channels of communication

Range of available assistance: What is possible?

The United Kingdom is able to provide a full range of legal assistance to judicial and prosecuting authorities in other countries and territories for the purposes of criminal investigations and criminal proceedings. The UK can also provide assistance in clemency proceedings and administrative investigations and prosecutions. The legal assistance that can be provided includes:

- service of summonses, judgements and other procedural documents;
- obtaining witness statements on oath and authenticated documentary evidence, including banking evidence;
- use of the investigation powers of the Serious Fraud Office in London and the Crown Office in Edinburgh in cases of serious or complex fraud;
- exercise of search and seizure powers;
- restraint and confiscation of proceeds of crime;
- evidence via video-conferencing;
- temporary transfer of prisoners, with their consent, to assist with criminal investigations and proceedings.

Which countries can the United Kingdom assist?

The UK can assist any country or territory in the world, whether or not that country is able to assist the UK.

Are international agreements required?

The UK can provide most forms of legal assistance without bilateral or international agreements - but assistance in the restraint and confiscation of proceeds of crime is dependent upon a bilateral agreement or other international agreement.
The UK has ratified:

- the 1959 European Convention on Mutual Assistance in Criminal Matters and its Additional Protocol;
- the 1990 European Convention on Laundering, Search, Seizure and Confiscation of the Proceeds from Crime, and
- the 1988 United Nations Convention against Illicit Traffic in Narcotic Drugs and Psychotropic Substances (the Vienna Convention).

The UK has also adopted the Commonwealth Scheme Relating to Mutual Assistance in Criminal Matters.

Does the UK require reciprocity?

No, but the UK would expect assistance from countries which are parties to relevant bilateral or international agreements with the UK.

Which authorities can make requests to the UK? What information should be included in requests?

Details of the authorities which may submit requests for legal assistance to the UK and what information should be included in letters of request (commission rogatoires) are given in Chapter 3.

What do the Central Authorities do?

The functions of the Central Authorities are described in Chapter 4.

Is it possible to submit requests to the Central Authorities through diplomatic channels?

Yes. Diplomatic channels, such as Embassies or High Commissions in London, may be used where required by the law and practice of the requesting country. But direct communication with the Central Authorities is preferred as this can help speed up the execution of requests.

At what stage of investigations or proceedings should requests be sent to the Central Authorities?

At any stage. In general, requests should be made as soon as the need for legal assistance is known and giving the UK authorities as much time as possible to execute the request. Delay in sending requests to the Central Authorities can result in an increase in the number of urgent cases, and delay the processing of other requests.

Requests for restraint (freezing) and confiscation of the proceeds of crime may only be considered where proceedings have been instituted or where it is certified that proceedings are to be instituted.

Will the Central Authorities take account of any requirements or procedures, which are specified in requests?

Yes. Testimony may be received or recorded and oaths or cautions administered in any specified form to the extent possible under the law of the part of the UK where the evidence is located.

May witnesses in the UK be approached directly without informing the Central Authorities?

Yes. Contact may be made directly by letter, fax or telephone. If the witness is willing to assist the enquiry voluntarily, an approach may be made through Interpol to record his or her statement or to the Central Authorities if testimony on oath is required.

How long does it take to execute a request?

This will depend on the circumstances of the request. Requesting authorities are kept informed of progress by the Central Authorities, in accordance with its Code of Practice, and provided with details of the officer(s) responsible for executing the request. These arrangements help ensure that timely assistance is provided. Any reasons for urgency such as statutory time limits, pre-trial court appearances or trial dates should be clearly stated in all requests.

May requests be sent to the Central Authorities via Interpol?

Yes, but direct communication with the Central Authorities is preferred as this helps speed up execution of requests. If requests for legal assistance intended for the Central Authorities are sent through Interpol channels, they must be marked clearly for the attention of the relevant Central Authority(ies).

What assistance do the Central Authorities provide which the NCIS, as UK National Central Bureau of Interpol, does not?

The respective competencies of the Central Authorities and the NCIS are set out in Annex A.

What requests may be sent to the UK National Central Bureau of Interpol at the NCIS?

Examples of requests that may be submitted directly to the UK National Central Bureau of Interpol without involving the Central Authorities include requests for:

- interviewing witnesses or suspects in criminal investigations where the person to be interviewed is willing to co-operate without appearing or needing to appear before a judicial authority in the UK;
- sharing of information and intelligence concerning investigations into offences which have been committed in the UK (provided that the information or intelligence is *not* being requested for use in proceedings);
- asset tracing enquiries;
- providing details of previous convictions;
- providing, for investigative purposes, details of UK telephone subscribers;
- providing details of keepers of motor vehicles registered in the UK and of driving licences issued in the UK;
- obtaining medical or dental statements or records where the patient has given written consent.

Such requests need not be sent to the Central Authorities unless it is a requirement of the judicial authority making the request. Requests for *both* legal assistance *and* for investigative assistance may be sent *both* to the Central Authorities *and* the UK National Central Bureau of Interpol. The will jointly co-ordinate the execution of the request. Any such requests should be clearly marked to show the request had been submitted to both authorities.

May requests for legal assistance be sent direct to courts or prosecuting authorities in the UK?

No. The courts in the UK have no investigative function and the prosecuting authorities, (with the exception of HMCE, the SFO and the prosecuting authorities in Scotland) do not, in general, have responsibilities for initiating enquiries on behalf of competent authorities abroad. The Central Authorities handle thousands of requests every year, and they are best placed to ensure that requests for legal assistance are dealt with speedily, efficiently and in accordance with the requirements of the requesting authorities.

Requests should be sent to the Central Authorities, HMCE in customs matters or to the UK National Central Bureau of Interpol at the NCIS.

May evidence be taken away by visiting judicial or investigating officers?

Yes. CICA 2003 allows for evidence to be transmitted directly to the requesting authority without sending the evidence via the Central Authorities. In cases where representatives of the requesting authority are present in the UK during the execution of the request and it is appropriate to do so, the evidence can be given directly to them.

Are requests kept confidential?

In line with established international practice, the Central Authorities do not disclose the existence or content of letters of request outside government departments or agencies or the courts or enforcement agencies in the UK. Requests are not disclosed more than is necessary to obtain the co-operation of the witness or other person concerned.

In general, requests are not shown or copied to any witness or other person, nor is any witness informed of the identity of any other witness. In the event that confidentiality requirements make execution of a request difficult or impossible, the Central Authorities will consult the requesting authorities.

Where public statements are made by authorities about the assistance they are requesting from the UK, the Central Authorities should be notified so that it may respond appropriately to any media or public enquiries.

Where should requests for the Crown Dependencies and the UK Overseas Territories be sent?

The Crown Dependencies, namely the Channel Islands (Guernsey and Jersey) and the Isle of Man, and the UK Overseas Territories[2] are not part of the United Kingdom. The Crown Dependencies and the Overseas Territories are themselves wholly responsible for executing requests within their own jurisdictions (although Interpol London is the Interpol office for the Crown Dependencies and certain of the Overseas Territories[3]). Requests should usually be sent to the Attorney General of the Crown Dependency or Overseas Territory from where the assistance is required. The contact details for these jurisdictions can be found at Annex D.

Chapter 3: Form and content of requests to the UK

Which authorities may make requests to the UK?

Requests for legal assistance in criminal matters may made by any competent court or tribunal, judicial or prosecuting authority. Requests may also be made by any other competent authority that the Central Authorities consider has the function of making requests for the purposes of criminal proceedings or criminal investigations. Such authorities include Attorneys General, investigating judges, examining magistrates, public prosecutors and Ministries or Departments of Justice having responsibilities for criminal matters. Requests can also be made in relation to administrative investigations, proceedings, appeals in relation to administrative proceedings[4] and clemency proceedings.

2 Anguilla, Bermuda, British Virgin Islands, Cayman Islands, Falklands, Gibraltar, Montserrat, St Helena and the Turks and Caicos Islands.

3 Falklands and St Helena: the other Overseas Territories host Interpol Sub-bureaux.

4 In some EU States offences such as driving infractions are classified as administrative offences and are dealt with in administrative courts and by way of administrative investigations and proceedings. The UK will assist with such requests where the proceeding may give rise to proceedings before a court with jurisdiction in criminal matters.

Should requests be made or confirmed in writing?

Yes, requests should always be made in writing, addressed to the relevant Central Authority or to the UK National Central Bureau of Interpol, depending on the nature of the assistance requested (see Annex A). They may be sent in advance by fax or e-mail but an undertaking should be given to send the original request by airmail or courier or other method of rapid delivery within a reasonable time, normally 7 days.

What language may requests to the Central Authorities be made in?

Requests **must** be made in writing in English or be submitted with an English translation. If no translation is provided the Central Authorities will ask for one and the request will remain unexecuted until the translation is received.

What information should be included in requests?

All relevant information must be included. This will vary according to the nature of the assistance required. Omission of any relevant information may delay execution of the request.

Wherever possible all requests should include:

- Any information which is likely to help the Central Authorities arrange for execution of the request in accordance with the requirements of the requesting authority.

Letters of request* must *include the following details:

- Details and the address of the judicial or prosecuting authority conducting the investigation or proceedings to which the request relates, and the name, telephone and fax and/or e-mail details of the responsible official(s) there.
- Full name(s) of the subject(s) of the investigation or proceedings if known[5].
- A summary of the facts of the offence(s) and details of the offence(s) committed or alleged. The request should make clear that there are reasonable grounds for suspecting that the offence has been committed and that proceedings have been instituted in relation to the offence or, if proceedings have not been instituted, that the offence is being investigated.
- A description of the evidence or material or other assistance required, clearly stating whether original evidence or certified copies are required.
- The purpose for which the evidence or material or other assistance is required and the relevance of the assistance to the investigation or proceedings.

Requests should also state, to the extent necessary and possible:

- The date of the trial or hearing and any other dates relevant for the purposes of executing the request; and any reasons why the request is urgent, for example because the accused person or suspect is in detention.
- The full name, date of birth and location of any person from whom evidence is required making clear whether they are a witness or an actual or potential accused.

[5] The UK can execute requests where the subject of the investigation is unknown at the time the request has been made e.g. a container being found to be carrying drugs, before final delivery. However, this is rare and the requesting authority must inform us of any people they later suspect of being involved in the commission of the offence.

- Details, including the telephone number, of any British law enforcement officer who is familiar with the investigation.
- The request should also say whether and why the presence of officers or officials of the requesting authorities is required during the execution of the request. The names of such persons should be provided (in general, such officers or officials may observe, but in certain circumstances may not participate in, the execution of requests).

Requests for service of summonses, judgements and other procedural documents should include:

- The original document(s) with a translation or, if the original documents cannot be provided, a translation *certified* as a true copy of the original.
- The identity, date of birth and location of any person on whom a summons or judgement is to be served; details of that person's connection with the proceedings and details of any particular way in which the summons or judgement should be served.
- Details of any allowances and expenses to which a person asked to appear in proceedings abroad is entitled; the address of the court where the proceedings are to take place; and the name and telephone number of an official of the court from whom the person asked to appear can seek further information if necessary.
- **Where such documents are being served directly upon a resident in the UK (as they do not need to be served via the Central Authorities) it is very important that information is given in English as to the nature of the document and contact details for that person to obtain further information.**

Requests for witness evidence (testimony), should include:

- Where evidence is required to be taken *on oath* before a court in the UK this should be expressly stated in the request. Expressions such as *"to hear"* or *"to examine"* witnesses or suspects should be avoided as they have no precise meaning in UK law. For the avoidance of doubt the requesting authority should set out as clearly as possible the conditions under which any interview or examination should be conducted, i.e. do they wish the evidence to be taken before a judge in court under oath, or via a police interview.
- A list of questions to be asked if possible.
- Details of the procedure to be followed in taking the evidence, including any rules on privilege which a witness or suspect may be entitled to claim.
- Any caution or formal notification of rights which should be given to the witness or suspect under the law of the requesting State.
- If **banking evidence** is required, the request **must** provide the name or number of the account and the address or number ("sort code") of the branch of the bank where the account is held. *This detail is required because there is no central record of bank accounts held in the UK*. Without this information it is very difficult for UK authorities to identify the relevant accounts. Furthermore the request should contain an indication of which transactions are relevant to the requests, an indication of the period of time for which information is sought and an explanation of how this information relates to the offence described.
- If **telecommunications data** is required the request should indicate clearly the type of telecoms data required, e.g. subscriber information, itemised billing etc; the telephone numbers that the data is required from; if you require itemised billing

then the time period this is required for, with explanations for any period that falls outside the time framework for the investigation and an explanation of how this information relates to the offence described.

Requests for search and seizure of evidence should include:

- The full address or a precise description of any place to be searched; full details of the specific material or type of material to be seized and a full description of the criminal conduct concerned. (Requests for search and seizure cannot be executed unless the criminal conduct would be an offence under UK law if it had occurred in the UK.)
- An explanation why the material requested is considered both relevant and important evidence to the investigation or proceedings; why the evidence is thought to be on the particular premises or in the possession of the particular person concerned and why the material would not be produced to a UK court if the natural or legal person holding the material were ordered to do so. (This is to help ensure that applications to the UK courts for search warrants are successful and less likely to fail or be subject to subsequent legal challenge.)
- Appropriate undertakings for the safekeeping and return of any seized evidence.

Please see Annex E for a pro-forma template that may assist overseas authorities in ensuring that they include all the relevant information needed to obtain search warrants under the law of England, Wales and Northern Ireland. The Crown Office in Scotland can give further information regarding obtaining search warrants in its jurisdiction.

Requests for the restraint (freezing) of property should include:

- The name, address, nationality, date and place of birth and present location of the defendant(s) or person(s) whose criminal conduct has given rise to civil confiscation proceedings.
- Details of the offence with which the defendant has been, or is about to be, charged (or the civil action brought or about to be brought).
- Details of the law applicable to the charges and the evidence against the defendant.
- Particulars of the property which it is intended to restrain in the United Kingdom, the persons holding it and details of the link between the defendant and the property (this is important if the property to be restrained is held in the name of a third party such as a company or another person).
- State clearly whether prior assistance in the case (including asset tracing assistance) has been provided and, if so, give particulars of the UK enforcement or other authority involved and details of the assistance already received.
- Where applicable, details of any court orders already made in the requesting State against the defendant in respect of his or her property. If any court order has been made a ***duly authenticated*** copy should be included with the request - that is a true copy of that order certified by a person in his or her capacity as a judge, magistrate or officer of the relevant court of the requesting State, or by an official of the Central Authority in the requesting State.
- Brief details of all known property held by the defendant *outside* the United Kingdom.
- A *certificate* issued by or on behalf of the requesting State's Central Authority stating:
    - that proceedings have been instituted in that country and have not been concluded, or that proceedings are to be instituted in the requesting State and, if so, when;

- that the confiscation order which it is expected the court of the requesting State will make will have the purpose of recovering property, or the value of property, received in connection with drug trafficking or other serious crime (or, in the case of a forfeiture order, has the purpose of ordering the forfeiture of instrumentalities of crime).

Requests for confiscation of property in the UK should include:

- Information as in requests for restraint.
- An original confiscation order or a ***duly authenticated*** copy of the confiscation order.
- A *certificate* issued by or on behalf of the requesting State's Central Authority stating:
    - that the confiscation order is in force and that neither the order nor any conviction to which it may relate is subject to appeal;
    - that all or a certain amount of the sum payable under the order remains unpaid in the territory of the requesting State or that other property recoverable under the order remains unrecovered there;
    - that the confiscation order has the purpose of recovering property, or the value of property obtained in connection with drug trafficking or other serious crime (or in the case of a forfeiture order has the purpose of ordering the forfeiture of instrumentalities of crime);
    - and where the person against whom the confiscation order was made did not appear in the proceedings, that he or she was notified of the proceedings in accordance with the requesting State's law in time to defend them.

Where the request is for the temporary transfer of a UK prisoner to give evidence or otherwise assist in criminal investigations or proceedings outside the UK, it should include:

- Dates on which the presence abroad of the prisoner is required, including the dates on which the court or other proceedings for which the prisoner is required will commence and are likely to be concluded;
- Information for the purpose of obtaining the prisoner's consent to the transfer and satisfying the UK authorities that arrangements will be made to keep the prisoner in secure custody such as:
    - whether the prisoner will have immunity from prosecution for previous offences;
    - details of proposed arrangements for collecting the prisoner from and returning the prisoner to the United Kingdom;
    - details of the type of secure accommodation in which the prisoner will be held in the requesting State;
    - details of the type of escort available abroad to and from the secure accommodation.

Where the request is for evidence to be given via television link (Video-conference)

- Sufficient information to enable the Central Authorities to identify and contact the witness(es)[6]

[6] The UK will not assist with requests to hear evidence from suspects via TV/video link.

- A list of questions to be asked if possible.
- Details of the procedure to be followed in taking the evidence, including any rules on privilege which a witness or suspect may be entitled to claim.
- Any caution or formal notification of rights which should be given to the witness or suspect under the law of the requesting State.
- Details (if known at the time) of the technical requirements for establishing the link to ensure compatibility.

The UK may require the requesting state to reimburse all or part of the costs associated with such requests.

The above lists are not exhaustive. The Central Authorities can provide further advice if necessary.

If the assistance requested is no longer required, the Central Authorities or the UK National Central Bureau of Interpol should be informed immediately so that enquiries are not made unnecessarily.

Chapter 4: Execution of requests in the UK

What is the role of the Central Authorities?

The Central Authorities' responsibilities include:

- Ensuring that requests for legal assistance conform with the requirements of law in the relevant part of the UK and the UK's international obligations (for example, requests for legal assistance must come from a competent authority and be for the purposes of criminal investigations or proceedings).
- Ensuring that execution of requests is not inappropriate on public policy grounds (for example, requests involving double jeopardy will not be executed).
- Deciding how requests might most appropriately be executed (for example, some requests asking for search and seizure of evidence may be executed effectively by a witness producing the evidence to a court).
- Maintaining confidentiality of requests where necessary.
- Ensuring, so far as possible, that assistance is provided within an appropriate time scale (for example, taking account of trial dates).
- Drawing to the attention of the courts, the police and other UK authorities and agencies requests that evidence be obtained in the presence of foreign law enforcement officers, prosecutors or defence lawyer
- Seeking requesting authorities' agreement to meet extra-ordinary costs of executing requests and for services such as interpreters or stenographers or for duplication of documents. (Ordinarily, the UK authorities, in accordance with established international practice will meet costs, with the exception of TV/Video link evidence).
- Transmitting evidence received to the requesting authorities when it is not returned directly (and checking whether any part of the request remains outstanding).

How are requests executed?

The information below explains the ways in which requests are executed in England and Wales. Where this differs from the practice in either Scotland or Northern Ireland, this is clearly indicated. Unless otherwise specified for the purposes of this Chapter the reference to the UKCA equally refers to the Crown Office and the Northern Ireland Office.

Save for service of summonses & judgements, referral to the SFO and Prisoner Transfer, the UKCA reference also applies to HMCE.

How are requests for service of summonses and judgements executed?

Summonses and judgements received by the UKCA from competent authorities abroad are normally served on the persons to whom they are addressed by recorded delivery post. Where personal service is requested, the UKCA arranges for the document to be served by the police. Under law in the UK, any person to whom a summons or judgement is addressed must be given a notice explaining, as appropriate, that:

- the document does not impose any obligation under law in the UK to comply with it;
- the person might wish to seek legal advice on the possible consequences under the law of the requesting country of failure to comply, and

If the evidence required does not *need to be taken on oath, the request may be sent to the UK National Central Bureau of Interpol which may then arrange for the evidence to be obtained directly by the police and the evidence would normally be returned to the requested authorities through Interpol channels or handed to visiting officers.*

How are requests for authenticated documentary evidence, including certified banking evidence, executed?

In England and Wales, the UKCA may nominate a court to receive such of the documentary evidence *as may appear to the court* to be appropriate. Normally, the custodian of the documents is required by the court to make a statement on oath. This may, for example, indicate whether the documents were created in the ordinary course of business or came into the custodian's possession from a third party and whether the documents are originals or genuine copies of the originals. Such a statement is for "chain of evidence" purposes. If banking evidence is required, an official of the bank concerned normally provides the statement.

The bank is under no obligation to inform the account holder that it has been ordered to disclose the information. In most cases, the nominated court will obtain the banking information without itself informing the account holder. This might not be appropriate if the account holder is a third party not complicit in the offence or if the account is administered by, for example, a firm of solicitors (professional legal advisers) or accountants. The decision whether to notify the account holder of the proceedings is entirely a matter for the court.

In Scotland, the normal procedure is for the Central Authority to obtain a warrant which will be served on the holder of the documentary evidence (such as a bank) and police officers will take possession of the documentary evidence as soon as practicable. They will also take statements from the appropriate witnesses. If evidence on oath is required by the requesting State, or there is no dual criminality, the procedure described above for England and Wales will be adopted.

Before an account holder is notified, the Central Authority will consult with the requesting authority to ensure that execution of the request would not breach the requesting authority confidentiality requirements.

The transmission requirements are the same as detailed in the section above "How are requests for evidence on oath executed?"

How can requests for evidence in serious or complex fraud cases be executed?

In England, Wales and Northern Ireland, the Central Authority can refer requests for assistance in serious or complex fraud cases, or any part of such a request, to the Director of the Serious Fraud Office to obtain such of the evidence *as may appear to the Director* to be appropriate. Under English law, the Director must be satisfied on reasonable grounds that the criminal conduct in the requesting country involves "serious or complex fraud". Frauds involving sums less than £1 million would not normally be regarded as "serious".

Before referring a request to the Director, the Central Authority will seek written assurance from the requesting authority that any statement which might be made by a person in response to a requirement imposed by virtue of the Director's investigation powers will not be used in evidence against that person, without consent. This assurance is required because witnesses do not in general have a right to refuse to answer questions where use is made of the Director's investigation powers. The assurance is therefore an important safeguard for the witness in the event of self-incrimination. The statement may, of course, be used against the accused person(s) *named in the request* if that is considered appropriate in the requesting country.

How are requests for restraint (freezing) of assets executed?

In the United Kingdom, a court order to freeze (restrain) assets may be obtained on behalf of a designated foreign jurisdiction when court proceedings which may lead to a confiscation order have been or are about to be instituted there; or if a confiscation order has already been made. It is vital therefore that any request for the restraint of assets in the United Kingdom should make clear whether a confiscation order has been made; and, if not, whether proceedings which may lead to confiscation have been instituted in the requesting state or, if not, when they expect to begin.

UK law enables a restraint or freezing order to be obtained on behalf of another country in our Courts only where that country has been designated by subsidiary legislation. Normally, a country will be designated for assistance in relation to drug assets when it ratifies the 1988 UN (Vienna) Drugs Convention; or for assistance in relation to the proceeds of all crimes when it ratifies the 1990 Council of Europe (Strasbourg) Convention or when a bilateral confiscation agreement with the UK is in place.

England and Wales

The UKCA will authorise a relevant prosecuting authority to represent the requesting Government in the High Court proceedings. Applications to the High Court in international restraint and confiscation cases are dealt with in England and Wales by two prosecuting authorities. They are the Central Confiscation Branch of the Crown Prosecution Service and the Asset Forfeiture Unit of HM Customs and Excise. As a general rule, the Central Confiscation Branch of the Crown Prosecution Service will deal with any restraint or confiscation request where a police officer has carried out the preliminary asset tracing enquiries in this country. The UKCA can advise which office might be appropriate in a particular case.

Scotland

The Scottish Central Authority will authorise the Criminal Confiscation Unit of Crown Office to represent the requesting Government in the Court proceedings (for both police and HMCE cases).

UK law requires that certain court orders, including restraint orders, should be served personally on the defendant and/or interested parties. Where the Court grants a restraint order on behalf of a foreign Government, the order will normally need to be channelled through the relevant Central Authority for service on the appropriate person(s) abroad.

Where a restraint order is granted on behalf of another government, the Central Authority will confirm this fact in writing, and request that such service be effected as specified in the order. The requesting country will be asked to complete and return to the Central Authority a memorandum of service. It is important that it receives the completed memorandum quickly since delays could affect the Court's willingness to continue the order. It is helpful if the completed memorandum is received within two weeks of its despatch and that in the event of unavoidable delay, an advance copy is sent to the Central Authority by fax.

How are requests for temporary transfer abroad of UK prisoners executed?

UK law allows for the temporary transfer abroad of UK prisoners, including remand prisoners, *who consent to assist* with criminal investigations and proceedings. Prisoners cannot be transferred from the UK without their consent. Requests for temporary transfer of prisoners must be sent to the appropriate Central Authority.

The relevant Central Authority must be satisfied before agreeing to the transfer that the presence of the prisoner is not already required in that part of the UK for the purposes of investigations or proceedings and that the transfer would not prolong the prisoner's period of detention.

Where the transfer is agreed with the requesting authority, the Central Authority arranges for:

- the taking of the prisoner in custody to a departure point in the UK and the delivery of the prisoner into the custody of a person representing the requesting authority;
- the escorting of the prisoner back to the UK by the requesting authority; and
- the subsequent transfer of the prisoner in custody from the arrival point in the UK to his or her place of detention.

THE COSTS OF ESCORTING AND ACCOMMODATING PRISONERS FROM THEIR POINT OF DEPARTURE FROM THE UK TO THEIR POINT OF RETURN TO THE UK ARE BORNE BY THE REQUESTING AUTHORITY.

Chapter 5: Code of Practice

The Central Authorities aim to ensure that requests for legal assistance are executed promptly, taking account of urgency, and that requesting authorities are kept informed of progress. All requests received by the Central Authorities are acknowledged and the requesting authorities are given the name and contact details of the person in the Authority responsible for co-ordinating its execution. As soon as possible, the Central Authorities will inform the requesting authority how the request is to be executed. In the relatively few instances where a request cannot be executed in whole or in part, the Central Authorities will provide an explanation and consult with the requesting authority about whether the assistance can be provided in a different way.

Where possible, the Central Authorities will give requesting authorities the contact details of the Police, Customs officer or court official or other person to whom the request, or part of the request, has been referred for the purposes of executing the request. **That person may then be contacted directly by the requesting authorities.**

Any enquiries about requests that have been sent to the Central Authorities are also acknowledged and dealt with as quickly as possible. When making enquiries, the reference number for the request should be quoted as this speeds up retrieval of information on the status of the request.

The sooner the Central Authorities are told about any difficulties which the requesting authorities may be having with any requests, the sooner they are able to reassure the requesting authorities that the matter is being dealt with.

A Code of Practice has been published. Although this refers to the Home Office, all the Central Authorities and HMCE agree to work to these standards in dealing with requests for legal assistance. The standards are closely monitored. The Code is set out at Annex B.

PART II — REQUESTS FROM THE UK

Chapter 1: Introduction

This section of the guidelines is designed primarily to provide Courts, non–designated prosecuting authorities, Solicitors and Counsel with information on how to obtain assistance from overseas authorities. Request templates are given at Annexes F & G and are a useful *starting point* for drafting, *although they do not need to be followed*. The Central Authorities will provide further information and guidance as required.

Chapter 2: Range of assistance and channels of communication

Range of assistance: What is possible?

The UK courts can request all the types of assistance detailed in Part 1 Chapter 2 of these guidelines e.g.

- request the service of summonses, judgements and other procedural documents
- obtain witness statements[7]
- obtain banking material, telecommunications data and other third party material
- request the exercise of search and seizure powers
- request restraint and confiscation of the proceeds of crime
- evidence via TV link/video-conferencing[8]
- temporary transfer of prisoners, with their consent, to assist with criminal investigations and proceedings

[7] You must bear in mind that for Civil Code States e.g. majority of EU, the concept of a witness statement may be alien to them, as many EU states do not have the same restrictions on hearsay as we do in the UK. Therefore, do not assume that overseas authorities will know how a witness statement should be drafted.

[8] Currently under s.29 CICA the list of offences to which TV link evidence from abroad can be used in UK criminal proceedings has not been extended beyond what is contained in s.32 (1A) of the Criminal Justice Act 1988. In Scotland, TV link evidence can be used in all cases which are being prosecuted on indictment.

Which countries may assist the United Kingdom?

This will depend upon whether a particular State needs a treaty base before it may be permitted to provide assistance. The UK has ratified the Council of Europe Convention on Mutual Assistance in Criminal Matters. As of the date of this guidance only 3 member states of the Council of Europe (Andorra, Bosnia & Herzegovina and San Marino) have not ratified this Convention.

We have bilateral treaties with states including the USA and Hong Kong. We are part of the Commonwealth Scheme on mutual legal assistance, which is not a legally binding agreement but a mutual understanding that the Commonwealth States should be able to provide similar forms of assistance. We are also signatories to a number of UN Conventions, which have MLA articles. The UK's Central Authorities can provide more assistance on this question if necessary.

Do they require reciprocity?

Again this will depend upon the Convention, Treaty or Agreement to which the UK and that State are parties or on their domestic law. However a general rule of reciprocity applies. Therefore, UK courts should not normally request any form of assistance that the UK itself could not provide if it received a like request. This question normally arises in relation to requesting interception of communications for evidential purposes. If such requests are made, the letter must make clear that the UK cannot currently reciprocate (although intercepts may be carried out for intelligence purposes). The UK's Central Authorities can provide more assistance on this question if necessary.

Do they require dual criminality?

Again this will depend on the nature of the assistance requested and the legal base of the request e.g. treaty. As a general rule all requests for search and seizure will require dual criminality.

Will they assist in fiscal offences?

As above this will depend upon the Convention, Treaty or Agreement to which the UK and that State are parties to or, their domestic law. The UK's Central Authorities can provide more assistance on this question if necessary.

Where should they be sent?

Annex H lists those States that will accept direct transmission of requests from UK courts. This means that requests can either be sent directly to their central authority or to the court or authority that is competent to execute the matter. Otherwise the request must be sent to one of the UK's Central Authorities. Your request should make clear however that an incoming request must be addressed to one of the UK's Central Authorities, not to the court.

At what stage should requests be sent?

As soon as possible, to avoid requests becoming urgent.

May overseas witnesses be contacted directly without first referring the matter to the overseas central authority?

This should not be undertaken without first consulting either the UK's Central Authorities or UK representation in that state e.g. Embassies, High Commissions. It is a criminal offence in some States for citizens to be contacted by foreign authorities before a request has been sent to central authority or other recognised body in that state.

May requests be sent via Interpol?

Yes in cases of urgency.

Are requests kept confidential?

Yes they should be kept confidential. However, you should only request confidentiality if this is strictly necessary as this can sometimes cause difficulties for some states, especially in relation to obtaining banking evidence without notifying the account holder.

Are requests ever declined?

Yes, if the request does not satisfy the requirements of any treaty etc. or the domestic law of the requested state. As with incoming requests, we would expect reasons to be given for the refusal to execute a request.

Chapter 3: Form and content of requests.

Which authorities may make requests?

- Designated Prosecuting Authority
- Courts on behalf of a defendant in criminal proceedings
- Courts on behalf of a non-designated prosecuting authority (England, Wales and Northern Ireland only).

Should requests be made in writing?

Yes. If a requested authority agrees to accept a request via email or fax this should always be followed up in writing within 7 days.

What language?

This will depend on where the request is being sent as some states have more than one official language, whereas others will accept requests in a language other than their official language. The UK's Central Authorities can provide assistance on this question if necessary.

What information should be included in requests?

This guidance cannot provide information in relation to all potential measure for all overseas states, however, please see the information in Part I Chapter 3 of this guidance as a starting point.

Drafting guidelines

The following information relates specifically to the templates given at Annex F & G or in Scotland to the templates contained in the Act of Adjournal (Criminal Procedure Rules) 1996, as amended.

Commission Rogatoire or Letter of Request?

The two documents are the same but it is important to use the correct title. Commission Rogatoires are used for Civil Code jurisdictions and Letters of Request are appropriate for Common law jurisdictions. It is important in relation to Commission Rogatoires that 'International' is left in the title as Magistrates within the same state send each other Commission Rogatoires for evidence. The Civil Code system is normally based on territorial jurisdiction e.g. a Magistrate in the 1st arrondissement in Paris has no jurisdiction to collect evidence in Lyon and would therefore have to transmit a commission rogatoire to his colleague there to request the collection of relevant evidence.

Letters of request are appropriate for Common law jurisdictions.

"Brief Statement of the Case"

There are some important legal principles here that should be taken into consideration by the draftsperson: Dual Criminality; Certainty; Nexus; Defamation.

Dual Criminality

The brief statement of the case should highlight enough admissible evidence to justify the alleged offence to a minimum standard of **reasonable suspicion**. It is not sufficient to simply re-iterate the allegation in the charge or indictment. The summary should be factual and precise. The foreign judicial authority must be satisfied that a substantial case has been established and if possible that this offence would constitute an offence in their jurisdiction especially if you are seeking the execution of search warrants.

Certainty

The statement should illustrate the existence of *evidence in the requested country* to a reasonable degree of certainty. There must be at least a reasonable probability that the evidence exists. When drafting a request a useful tip is to bear in mind that the foreign authority may need a coercive order. Imagine therefore what information would be necessary to obtain such an Order before a United Kingdom court: for example you would need to prove to the Court exactly why *this particular piece of evidence sought* is relevant to your prosecution. This would be the absolute minimum that you would need to include in the request to satisfy the foreign authority to execute that part of the request.

Nexus

This is establishing a direct link between the facts of the case as detailed in the request and the evidence that is held in the requested state, which you are requesting. This goes further than just stating that the material is relevant to your case as outlined above. In reading the case summary the executing authority should be able to anticipate what assistance you require. Why is the material relevant? How does it advance you case? What supporting evidence do you already possess or what facts are in existence that lends support to the necessity of obtaining the evidence you require?

Requests for assistance should be clear, unambiguous and time specific - not open ended. For example, any premises to be searched should be clearly stated together with the object of the search (e.g. for relevant documents). The connection between the premises and the suspect should be clearly stated in the brief statement of the case. A request for telephone records should place limits upon the period of the records sought commensurate with the alleged offence.

Defamation

No direct allegation or implication of criminality by a third party should be included in the request unless justified by available evidence. Inadvertent wording in a request could give rise to an action for defamation.

That being said, case summaries should be exactly that. A summary! Not a recital of all the evidence in the case, only that which relates to evidence being sought and gives a general background to the case. A rule of thumb: the more complex the case, the longer the summary will be and the clearer it will need to be. Please bear in mind that if the request has to be translated, the more confusing it appears in English the more likely it is to remain so in the translated language.

Annexes of law

These must always be included with the request and be translated if necessary. They help the requested authority to determine whether the issue of dual criminality has been satisfied.

Chapter 4: Other information

Defence requests to the USA

The UK-US Mutual Legal Assistance Treaty cannot be used by UK courts as a legal base to seek the execution of a request in the US on behalf of a defendant. The following information has been kindly provided by the US authorities to assist UK Courts, Solicitors and Counsel involved in seeking evidence from the US:

Initially, a defendant seeking assistance from within the United States should ascertain whether a U.S. person or entity in a position to assist will do so voluntarily. A defendant or his counsel may contact the U.S. person or entity (e.g., by letter, telephone) for this purpose. A U.S. person or entity may agree to provide assistance by, for example, travelling here to appear in proceedings, providing an affidavit for use in the proceeding, or appearing before an authorised consular officer to give an oral statement for use in the proceeding. However, a U.S. person or entity is under no obligation to provide voluntary assistance.

When a defendant is unable to secure assistance on a voluntary basis, he may formally request assistance pursuant to the U.S. international assistance statute, Title 28, section 1782, of the United States Code, which is available for use in connection with both civil and criminal proceedings in foreign jurisdictions. A defendant may transmit a formal request either indirectly through the U.S. Department of State or directly to a U.S. federal district court or the U.S. government agency or officer responsible for or having control over the information at issue. The request must be addressed to a court if court orders are required to secure assistance (e.g., for testimony from a witness who is unwilling to testify or give a statement voluntarily, for records from a bank or Internet service provider that cannot produce its records without a court order). The request should be addressed to a government agency or officer for the production of government records, statements of government employees, and the like.

Whether a defendant transmits a request directly or indirectly, he must identify the particular court, agency, or officer to receive the request and specify the location (mailing address) in the United States.

Transmitting a request directly to a court, agency, or officer is quicker than transmitting it indirectly through the Department of State. The most effective means of transmitting a request to a court is to retain private legal counsel licensed to practice before that court and have counsel present the request to the court,

A court receiving a request will determine whether to use its authority to execute it. When a court exercises its discretion in favor of execution, it will normally appoint a commissioner to collect the evidence (e.g., take testimony, procure documents). A defendant is strongly advised to obtain private legal counsel licensed to practice before the court not only to present the matter to the court, but also to serve as commissioner for the court if or to the extent that the court orders execution.

A British consular officer or other representative at the British Embassy may be able to aid the defendant in identifying (1) means for obtaining assistance on a voluntary basis, (2) the appropriate court, agency, or officer in the United States to whom a request for assistance should be addressed, and (3) private legal counsel (whether pro bono or paid legal counsel) to present the request to the court and/or serve as commissioner to the court in executing it.

Website links:

United Nations — *http://www.un.org*
Commonwealth — *http://www.thecommonwealth.org*
Council of Europe Treaty Office — *http://conventions.coe.int/*
European Union — *http://www.europa.eu.int*
Eurojust — *http://www.eurojust.eu.int/*

ANNEX A: CONDUCTING ENQUIRIES IN OR SEEKING ASSISTANCE FROM THE UNITED KINGDOM—COMPETENCIES OF CENTRAL AUTHORITIES AND NCIS (UK NATIONAL CENTRAL BUREAU OF INTERPOL)

The examples below are intended to indicate whether the Central Authorities, or the UK National Central Bureau of Interpol (Interpol London) at the UK National Criminal Intelligence Service, is more appropriate for conducting enquiries in or seeking assistance from the UK.

COMPETENCIES OF THE CENTRAL AUTHORITIES INCLUDE:	COMPETENCIES OF THE UK NATIONAL CENTRAL BUREAU OF INTERPOL INCLUDE:
Serving a summons or other judicial document requiring a person to appear before a judicial authority in the requesting country as a witness or defendant in criminal proceedings. Obtaining sworn evidence or other authenticated or certified evidence, including banking documentation, for use in criminal proceedings or investigations.	Interviewing witnesses and suspects in criminal investigations where the person is willing to co-operate without appearing before a judicial authority in the UK and where any statement made would be unsworn. Tracing assets in investigations preliminary to prosecution, particularly where the offence involves money laundering. Sharing information concerning investigations into offences, which have been committed in the UK. Obtaining medical or dental statements or records where the patient has given written consent.

COMPETENCIES OF THE CENTRAL AUTHORITIES INCLUDE:	COMPETENCIES OF THE UK NATIONAL CENTRAL BUREAU OF INTERPOL INCLUDE:
Authenticating or certifying evidence for use in the requesting country where that evidence has already been obtained by the UK police for their own purposes. Exercise of search and seizure powers where evidence is required for use in criminal proceedings or investigations. Temporarily transferring prisoners,with their consent, overseas to appear as witnesses in criminal proceedings or to assist in criminal investigations.	Providing details of previous convictions: ● for the purposes of police investigations, vetting applicants for employment in law enforcement or work with access to children or suitability for owning firearms and holding gambling licences — when provided with a copy of the person's fingerprints. ● for police intelligence purposes *only* — fingerprints. Providing telephone subscriber details (telephone companies can provide only the family name and initial of the subscriber and the address where the telephone is located). Seizing and securing in the UK property stolen abroad. Police in the UK can seize and retain property where the person in possession of it in the UK is suspected of knowing that the property is stolen. Providing passport details (all details held by the UK Passport Service can be provided including any photographs held). Providing medical samples (body orifice swabs and samples of blood, saliva, semen, hair, urine and other tissue fluids can be obtained with the consent of the person from whom the sample is required). Providing details of keepers of motor vehicles registered in UK and driving licences issued in UK.

ANNEX C: CONTACT DETAILS FOR THE CENTRAL AUTHORITIES AND OTHER RELEVANT UK AUTHORITIES

Requests for legal assistance

UK Central Authority
Judicial Co-operation Unit
Home Office
50 Queen Anne's Gate
London SW1H 9AT
Tel: +44 20 7273 2437
Fax: +44 20 7273 4400/4422
Mobile: +44 7879 668 694 (24HR)
Pager: +44 7623 523523 ask for no. 657782 (24HR)

Requests for execution in Scotland (including cases of serious fraud, restraint and confiscation of assets and extradition)

The International and Financial Crime Unit
Crown Office
25 Chambers Street
Edinburgh EH1 1LA
Tel: +44 131 226 2626
Fax: + 44 131 226 6861

Requests for execution in Northern Ireland

The Northern Ireland Office
11 Millbank
London
SW1P 4PN
Tel: +44 20 7210 6496
Fax: +44 20 7210 6565

Requests for investigative assistance

UK National Central Bureau of Interpol (Interpol London)
National Criminal Intelligence Service
PO Box 8000
London SE11 5EN

Contact with Interpol London should be made through the National Central Bureau of Interpol in the requesting country.

Tel (24 hours): +44 20 7238 8115
Fax: +44 20 7238 8112
Telex: 918734
Encrypted e-mail: Via X400

Requests in cases of serious or complex fraud — England, Wales and Northern Ireland Preliminary, informal enquiries may be sent to:

Serious Fraud Office
Elm House
10-16 Elm Street
London WC1X OBJ
Tel: +44 20 7239 7272
Fax: +44 20 7833 5430

Serious Fraud Office Guidelines: *http://www.sfo.gov.uk/international/evidence_uk.asp*

Advice on criminal law and procedure in England and Wales

Casework Directorate
Crown Prosecution Service
50 Ludgate Hill
London EC4M 7EX
Tel: + 44 20 7273 1382
Fax: + 44 20 7329 8171

Requests for assistance in Customs matters

HM Customs & Excise
Law Enforcement Legal Advisors
Solicitor's Office
New King's Beam House
22 Upper Ground
London SE1 9PJ
Tel: + 44 870 785 8074
Fax: + 44 870 785 8138

Advice on making requests for restraint and confiscation of assets

Central Confiscation Branch
Crown Prosecution Service
50 Ludgate Hill
London EC4M 7EX
Tel: + 44 20 7796 8283
Fax: + 44 20 7796 8270

Asset Forfeiture Unit
Solicitor's Office
HM Customs and Excise
New King's Beam House
22 Upper Ground
London SE1 9PJ
Tel: + 44 20 7865 5187
Fax: + 44 20 7865 5902

Requests for extradition of fugitives

Extradition Section
Judicial Co-operation Unit
Central Authorities
50 Queen Anne's Gate
London SW1H 9AT
Tel: + 44 20 7273 3991
Fax: + 44 20 7273 2496

Preliminary informal enquiries for assistance in revenue tax matters

Inland Revenue
Solicitor's Office
Somerset House
London WC2R 1LB
Tel: + 44 20 7438 7091
Fax: + 44 20 7438 6246

Requests for regulatory assistance in company matters

Department of Trade & Industry
Investigations & Enforcement Directorate
10 Victoria Street
London SW1 ONN
Tel: + 44 20 7215 3021
Fax: + 44 20 7215 3115

ANNEX D: CONTACT DETAILS FOR AUTHORITIES IN THE CHANNEL ISLANDS, THE ISLE OF MAN AND THE BRITISH OVERSEAS TERRITORIES

Requests for execution in the Channel Islands and the Isle of Man

Guernsey

HM Attorney General
Attorney General's Chambers
St James Chambers
St Peter Port
Guernsey
GY1 2PA
Tel: + 44 1481 723355
Fax: +44 1481 725439

Isle of Man

Attorney General's Chambers
2nd Floor New Wing
Victory House
Douglas
ISLE OF MAN
IM1 3PP
Tel: + 44 1624 685452
Fax: + 44 1624 629162

Jersey

HM Attorney General
Attorney General's Chambers
Morier House
St Helier
Jersey
JE1 1DD
Tel: + 44 1534 502280
Fax: + 44 1534 502299

Requests for execution in the British Overseas Territories (details of authorities not listed are obtainable from the Central Authorities)

Anguilla

The Attorney-General
The Attorney-General's Chambers
The Secretariat
The Valley
Anguilla
Tel: + 1 264 497 3044
Fax: + 1 264 497 3126

Bermuda

The Attorney-General's Chambers
Global House

43 Church Street
Hamilton HM12
Bermuda
Tel: + 1 441 292 2463
Fax: + 1 441 292 3608

British Virgin Islands

The Attorney-General
The Attorney-General's Chambers
Government of the British Virgin Islands
PO Box 242
Road Town
Tortola
Tel: + 1 284 494 3701
Fax: + 1 284 494 6760

Cayman Islands

The Attorney-General
The Attorney-General's Chambers
Government Administration Building
George Town, Grand Cayman
Cayman Islands
Tel: + 1 345 949 7900
Fax: + 1 345 949 6079

Gibraltar

Attorney-General
Attorney-General's Department
17 Town Range
Gibraltar
Tel: + 350 70723
Fax: + 350 79891

Requests from EU/Schengen Member States must be sent via:

"UKGLU"
UK Government/Gibraltar Liaison Unit
Foreign & Commonwealth Office
King Charles St
London
SW1H 2AH
Tel: +44 20 7008 2502

Montserrat

The Attorney-General
The Attorney-General's Chambers
PO Box 129
Olveston
Montserrat
Tel: + 1 664 491 4686
Fax: + 1 664 491 4687

Turks and Caicos Islands

The Governor
Government House
Grand Turk
Turks and Caicos Islands
Tel: + 1 649 946 2308
Fax: + 1 649 946 2903

Mutual Legal Assistance Part I of the Crime (International Co-operation) Act 2003 C–013

Dear Colleague,

This circular describes the legal assistance in criminal matters which judicial and prosecuting authorities in England, Wales, Scotland and Northern Ireland and overseas authorities may obtain through Part 1 of the Crime (International Co-operation) Act 2003 ("the Act") and sections 5 and 6 of the Criminal Justice (International Co-operation) Act 1990 ("the 1990 Act"). More detailed guidance is contained in the document "Mutual Legal Assistance Guidelines: Obtaining assistance in the UK and Overseas", available on the Home Office website[1], which also gives details of how to find relevant legislation and agreements.

THE 2003 ACT: OVERVIEW OF PART 1

1. Sections 1–9, 13–19, 26–31 and 47–51 of Part 1 of the Act came into force on 26th April 2004[2]. This circular covers those sections, plus sections 5 and 6 of the 1990 Act.

2. A revised circular will be issued once the Convention of 29th May 2000 on Mutual Assistance in Criminal Matters between the Member States of the European Union (EU) ("the 2000 Convention") comes into force for the United Kingdom. Sections 32–46 implement the Protocol to the Convention on Mutual Assistance in Criminal Matters ("the Protocol"). Sections 10–12 and 20–25 implement the Framework Decision on the recognition in the EU of orders freezing property and evidence and these sections will commence at later dates. Further circulars will be issued.

3. The Act repeals sections 1 to 4, 7, 8 and 11 of the Criminal Justice (International Co-operation) Act 1990.

What is covered?

4. Assistance under Part 1 of the Act includes:

- Service of process
- Obtaining evidence
- Search and seizure
- Television and telephone link court hearings
- Temporary transfer of prisoners to assist with criminal investigations and proceedings in another jurisdiction

5. The Act enables the UK to assist any country or territory in the world, irrespective of whether the country concerned would be able to assist the UK. Certain provisions implement specialised requirements of agreements to which the UK is or will be a party and are restricted to the states participating in those agreements. In particular, certain rules apply in relation to states that are parties to the Schengen Implementing Convention ("Schengen States") (see Annex A). These provisions are highlighted in the Circular.

[1] *http://www.homeoffice.gov.uk.*

[2] The Crime (International Co-operation) Act 2003 (Commencement No. 1) Order 2004 No. 786.

6. The Act does not in general require dual criminality; i.e. the overseas criminal conduct need not constitute an offence had it occurred in the UK. Exceptions are requests involving fiscal offences (in the absence of an agreement) or use of search and seizure powers.

7. Separate rules will apply to assistance under sections 10–12 (outgoing evidence freezing orders), 20–25 (incoming evidence freezing orders) and 32–46 (information about banking transactions), which have not yet commenced.

What is not covered?

8. The 2003 Act does not govern direct police to police and customs to customs co-operation or informal contacts between prosecutors and this circular does not give guidance on such matters. Examples of informal co-operation not covered by the Act include police requests to locate persons and take unsworn witness statements. Officers should seek advice if unsure about whether to use mutual legal assistance channels.

9. The UKCA (see below) is not involved in arranging or approving visits of UK police officers overseas or of overseas officers or officials to the UK. The National Central Bureau of Interpol at NCIS or, depending on the case, HM Customs and Excise or the Serious Fraud Office handle such arrangements and officers should *never* travel without such authorisation. Requests for officers or officials to travel from the UK in relation to the execution of a MLA request must however be routed via the appropriate territorial authority (see paragraph 11 below).

THE UK CENTRAL AUTHORITY AND THE TERRITORIAL AUTHORITIES

10. The UK Central Authority for Mutual Legal Assistance (UKCA) is located in the Home Office.

11. Under the 2003 Act, responsibility for dealing with mutual legal assistance requests is delegated to three jurisdictions, or **territorial authorities:**

- England and Wales — the Secretary of State, in practice this means the UKCA in the Home Office
- Northern Ireland — the Secretary of State, in practice this means the Northern Ireland Office
- Scotland — the Lord Advocate, in practice this means the Scottish Crown Office.

12. The Home Office acts both as the UCKA and the territorial authority for England and Wales. In its role as UKCA, it acts as first point of contact for general queries relating to mutual legal assistance and as the central authority for the whole United Kingdom where treaties and other arrangements require all requests to be routed through a single authority, or where a request involves execution in more than one jurisdiction.

13. References in this Circular to the UKCA mean the Home Office carrying out its function as the central authority for England, Wales, Scotland and Northern Ireland. See Annex B for contact details.

14. References to the Secretary of State in this Circular should be read as Lord Advocate in relation to Scotland, unless otherwise stated, or where the Lord Advocate is specifically mentioned for sake of clarity.

ASSISTANCE UNDER THE 2003 ACT

Chapter 1: Mutual Service of Process

Service of Overseas Process in the UK

15. Sections 1 and 2 of the 2003 Act deal with service of overseas process on persons who are located in the UK. They replace section 1 of the 1990 Act.

What is covered by the term "process"?

16. For England, Wales and Northern Ireland, "process" means any summons or order issued or made by a court; for Scotland, it means a citation by a court or prosecuting authority, or an order made by a court, and in both cases includes:

- any other document issued or made by a court for service on parties or witnesses;
- any document issued by a prosecuting authority outside the United Kingdom for the purpose of criminal proceedings, for administrative proceedings that have a right of appeal to a court with criminal jurisdiction and clemency proceedings.

Service of process in the UK

17. Schengen states (see Annex A) may send process directly by post to recipients located in the UK, rather than via a central authority. Process served directly should be accompanied by details of the issuing authority that can advise the recipient of their rights and obligations under the law of that country and should be translated into English.

18. Sections 1 and 2 of the Act regulate the service of overseas process when it is not sent directly to the recipient from the overseas authority.

19. Process received by the Secretary of State (or Lord Advocate) may either be served by post or by the police where personal service is requested. If it is served by post, a receipt is included for the recipient to sign and return. If served by the police, they must inform the Secretary of State whether and how the process was served and if possible return a receipt signed by the recipient. The Secretary of State will advise the overseas authority whether the process has been served.

20. When process is served by post from the Secretary of State a notice will be included to:

- inform recipients that overseas process requiring a person to appear as a party or attend as a witness does not impose any obligation under UK law to comply with it;
- advise that they might wish to seek legal advice on the consequences of non-compliance under the law of the issuing state;
- advise that they might not have the same rights and privileges in the overseas proceedings as in proceedings in the UK.

21. Process received by courts, prosecutors, police or customs officers should be forwarded to the Secretary of State for onward service.

UK Process for Service Overseas

22. Sections 3 and 4[3] of the 2003 Act deal with service overseas of process issued for the purpose of criminal proceedings in England, Wales and Northern Ireland. Sections 5 and 6 of the 2003 Act are the Scottish equivalents. References in Scotland to "service of process" should be read as "effecting citation". This group of sections replaces section 2 of the 1990 Act.

Requirements for service of process

23. The following requirements must be met:

- The process must not contain reference to penalties for non-compliance.
- Where the person requesting the court to issue the process has reason to believe that the recipient does not understand English, they must inform the court of this and provide a copy of the whole document, or the important parts of it, translated into an appropriate language. This may be the official language of the country of residence, or a third language, if the recipient is known only to understand another language.
- A notice containing details of the authority that can provide information about the recipient's rights and obligations under the applicable UK law must also accompany the process. The person on whose behalf the process is issued should be given as the contact point and is responsible for preparing and translating this notice.
- Rules of court[4] set out additional requirements for service of process overseas and should be referred to by the issuer.
- In Scotland, the same considerations apply as are outlined above. However, in Scotland, the prosecutor may effect citation, as well as the court.

Deciding on the correct method of service

24. Process may be served either directly by post or via the Secretary of State.

25. Where the recipient is located in a Schengen state, the process should be transmitted to them directly by post, unless one or more of the following conditions is met:

- the address of the person is unknown,
- it has not been possible to serve the process by post, or
- there are good reasons for thinking that service by post will not be effective or is inappropriate. This would include circumstances where there is a requirement under UK law to prove in subsequent proceedings that service was effected.

26. Where the recipient is not in a Schengen state, process may either be transmitted directly by post, or via the Secretary of State.

27. Where process is transmitted via the Secretary of State, he may:

- transmit the process directly by post to the recipient if it should have been sent directly to them by the issuing authority,
- transmit the process to the central or other competent authority in the country where the recipient is present, with a request for postal service, transmit the process to the central or other competent authority in the country where the recipient is present, with a request for personal service.

[3] This will be amended by Schedule 36 (paragraph 16) of the Criminal Justice Act 2003.

[4] England & Wales: Magistrates Courts Rules SI 2004 No. 1048; Crown Court Rules SI 2004 No. 1047.

28. Where the process is transmitted via the overseas competent authority, the Secretary of State may seek proof of service from that authority and will forward this to the issuing court upon request.

Chapter 2: Mutual Provision of Evidence

Assistance in obtaining evidence from abroad

29. Sections 7 and 8 enable certain authorities in the UK to request assistance in obtaining evidence from overseas authorities. They replace section 3 of the 1990 Act.

When can a request be made?

30. Assistance may be requested *where an offence has been committed or there are reasonable grounds for suspecting that one has been committed, and where* proceedings or an investigation into the offence are underway.

Who may request assistance?

31

- In England, Wales and Northern Ireland, prosecuting authorities may apply to a judicial authority (e.g. a judge) for a request to be issued.
- Designated Prosecuting Authorities may request assistance themselves without applying to a judicial authority (see Annex C).
- In Scotland, the Lord Advocate or Procurator Fiscal may apply to a judicial authority, or may request assistance themselves. The provisions with regard to designated prosecuting authorities referred to above do not apply in Scotland. Therefore, where, for example, customs officers in Scotland wish to request assistance, they must do so via the Lord Advocate or procurator fiscal, in effect the Crown Office.
- The person charged may make an application to a judicial authority, where proceedings have been instituted.

Format and content of requests

32. There is no prescribed format for letters of request (other than in Scotland), but the following details should be included:

- the name of the UK authority conducting the investigation or proceedings and contact details of the person dealing with it;
- the subject matter and nature of the investigation or proceedings;
- a summary of the facts giving rise to the request;
- a description of the evidence or material or other assistance required (if original evidence or a certified copy is required, the request should say so and include undertakings, as appropriate, for the safe-keeping and return of the evidence);
- the purpose for which the evidence or assistance is required and its relevance to the investigation or proceedings;
- the identity, date of birth and location of any person from whom evidence is required;
- a precise description of any place to be searched;

- a description of any particular procedures to be followed in executing the request and whether these are essential under domestic law, the manner in which any testimony or statement is to be taken and recorded, e.g. whether the person to be interviewed is to be regarded as a witness or a suspect; if appropriate, the questions to be asked and whether the presence of UK officials or officers is necessary;
- any other information which may facilitate execution of the request;
- requirements for confidentiality.

33. All requests should be accompanied by a translation where English is not an official language of the overseas country concerned (unless an English text is acceptable). The authority seeking assistance should arrange and pay for the translation.

Transmission of requests

34. Requests may be transmitted either directly to a court or other authority in the requested country, or via the Secretary of State for transmission to the overseas court or authority. The method of transmission depends on the category of request:

- Requests to Schengen states should be transmitted directly to the overseas competent judicial authority, with no involvement of the Secretary of State or the overseas central authority.
- Requests to other non-Schengen states should be transmitted directly to the overseas Central Authority, which will then forward or arrange for execution of the request as appropriate, unless transmission via the Secretary of State (the UKCA) is required by a treaty or other arrangement (see Annex D).
- Urgent requests may be transmitted via Interpol to the overseas court or authority.

Identifying the correct overseas authority

35. The UKCA or a contact point of the European Judicial Network (EJN) can assist with queries about the appropriate method of transmission and correct overseas authority. The Judicial Atlas, compiled by the EJN, may in particular be used (details of how to access this are available from the contact points, who can give a password to authorised persons). The UK's liaison magistrates posted overseas may also be contacted. If queries of difficulties arise which cannot be resolved by these sources, the UK team at Eurojust will assist. See Annex B for all contact details.

36. Where requests are sent directly, a copy must be emailed to the UKCA so that it can log it for statistical purposes.

Use of evidence obtained

37. Any evidence supplied may not be used for any purpose other than that specified in the request without the consent of the overseas authority.

Assisting overseas authorities to obtain evidence in the UK

38. Sections 13 to 15 provide for the execution of overseas requests for assistance in obtaining evidence and replace section 4 of the 1990 Act. Sections 16 and 17 provide for executing requests for searches and replace section 7 of the 1990 Act. Section 18 applies to searches in Scotland and replaces section 8 of the 1990 Act.

39. References to the territorial authority in this section of the Circular equally apply to HM Customs & Excise (except in Scotland) who will be exercising certain powers conferred on the Secretary of State by virtue of section 27.

40. Section 13 sets out the types of overseas authority that may request assistance, and gives the territorial authority the power to arrange for evidence to be obtained under section 15, 16, 17 or 18, depending on the type of assistance requested (section 18 applies only to Scotland). The territorial authority should send an acknowledgement to the requesting authority to confirm receipt of the request.

41. Section 14 sets out the conditions which need to be satisfied before a court may be nominated to receive evidence under section 15. These are that the request must be made in connection with:

- criminal investigations or proceedings
- administrative investigations or proceedings
- clemency proceedings or an appeal before the court against a decision made in administrative proceedings

42. These terms are further explained in section 51(1) of the Act. Administrative proceedings are those brought by administrative authorities where a decision in the proceedings may be the subject of an appeal before a court with criminal jurisdiction.

43. Where the request relates to criminal or administrative investigations or proceedings, assistance may be provided if the territorial authority is satisfied that an offence has been committed or that there are reasonable grounds for suspecting this, and that proceedings have been instituted or an investigation is being carried out.

Fiscal Offences

44. If the request is for evidence relating to a fiscal offence where proceedings have not commenced, if there is no relevant agreement between the UK and the requesting country, and it is not a member of the Commonwealth, dual criminality is required.

Obtaining authenticated evidence

Evidence received by the nominated court

45. Section 15 provides for a court to be nominated to receive the requested evidence.

46. The territorial authority will:

- Issue a notice nominating a court to receive the evidence (court proceedings are governed by Schedule I and rules of court made under section 49);
- Provide additional information to the court, such as names of officers with knowledge of the request, and requests for overseas officials wishing to be present;
- Point out any special procedures requested, which should be followed if essential to the requesting state, unless to do so would be contrary to domestic law.

47. The court will:

- Request attendance of witnesses and issue summonses if necessary;
- Arrange a hearing date;
- Notify parties with interests in the proceedings.

Evidence in serious or complex fraud cases

48. Where a request appears to relate to serious or complex fraud, the Secretary of State may refer it to the Director of the Serious Fraud Office. The power of referral to the Serious Fraud Office under section 15(2) is vested in the Secretary of State only. The equivalent arrangements in Scotland provide that the Lord Advocate may give a direction in respect of

investigation powers, the criteria he applies being identical to those applied by the Director of the SFO and the effect being the same.

49. If the Director has reasonable grounds to believe that the overseas offence involves serious or complex fraud, he will arrange to obtain such evidence as may appear to him to be appropriate.

50. The Secretary of State will obtain confirmation from the overseas authority that any statement made by a person in response to a requirement imposed by the Director's investigation powers will not be used in evidence against them.

Transmission of evidence obtained under section 15

51. Evidence obtained by the court or by the Serious Fraud Office may either be returned directly to the requesting authority or via the Secretary of State/territorial authority in accordance with Schedule I to the 2003 Act and (in the case of evidence obtained by the Serious Fraud Office) section 2 of the Criminal Justice Act 1987, as amended by the 2003 Act. The Act is not specific about when evidence should be transmitted directly. It is drafted to meet the various obligations imposed on the UK by different international agreements.

52. Evidence requested by a Schengen state should be returned directly to the requesting authority. It may either be given to a representative of that authority if they are present, or sent by post or other secure method.

53. Evidence requested by other non-Schengen countries may be returned directly, unless transmission via a central authority is required by a treaty or other arrangement between the UK and that country (see Annex D).

Search and Seizure

Requests for search and seizure in England, Wales and Northern Ireland

54. Under section 16 of the Act, search warrants and production orders may be applied for and obtained in England, Wales and Northern Ireland in response to an overseas request.

55. Execution of such requests must be consistent with domestic law, so warrants and orders may only be obtained in the same circumstances as would be possible in a domestic case. The conduct should equate to a serious arrestable offence, as defined in the Police and Criminal Evidence Act 1984 (in Northern Ireland, the Police and Criminal Evidence (Northern Ireland) Order 1989) and the relevant access conditions under the Act and Codes must be satisfied.

56. Under section 17 of the Act, warrants may be obtained in England, Wales and Northern Ireland where an investigation or proceeding is underway into an offence that would constitute an arrestable offence if it occurred here and there are reasonable grounds to suspect that there is evidence in premises occupied or controlled by the suspect.

57. It also provides that a search warrant or production order may be applied for and executed without an overseas request if the constable who makes the application is a member of an international joint investigation team[5].

[5] Section 16(5): "International joint investigation team" has the meaning given by section 88(7) of the Police Act 1996. This means "any investigation team formed in accordance with a) any framework decision on joint investigation teams adopted under Article 34 of the treaty on European Union; b) the Convention on Mutual Assistance in Criminal Matters between the Member States of the European Union, and the Protocol to that Convention, established in accordance with that Article of that Treaty; or c) any international agreement to which the UK is a party and which is specified for the purposes of this section in an order made by the Secretary of State".

58. Overseas police or customs officers or officials may observe the application for the warrant or order, with the agreement of the judge or magistrate concerned. If they are named on the warrant they may also observe its execution.

Requests for search and seizure in Scotland

59. Section 18 of the Act covers the issue of warrants in Scotland in response to an overseas request. It gives the sheriff the same power to issue a warrant as he does under section 134 of the Criminal Procedure (Scotland) Act 1995. He must be satisfied that an offence under the law of a country outside the UK has been committed and that the conduct would have constituted an offence punishable by imprisonment had it occurred in Scotland. Section 18(1) provides that, in Scotland, only a procurator fiscal may apply for a search warrant. Accordingly, where a Joint Investigation Team is operating in Scotland, a procurator fiscal will apply on behalf of the Team for any search warrant that is required. The statutory definition of a Joint Investigation Team is contained in section 39(6) of the Police (Scotland) Act 1967 and is identical to that for the rest of the UK (see footnote 5).

60. Overseas police or customs officers or officials may observe the application for the warrant or order, with the agreement of the judge or sheriff concerned. If they are named on the warrant they may also observe its execution.

Return of evidence

61. Evidence seized may either be returned directly to the requesting authority or to the territorial authority (see paragraph 11).

62. Evidence requested by a Schengen state should be returned directly to the requesting authority. It may either be given to a representative of that authority if they are present, or sent by post or other secure method.

63. Evidence requested by other countries may also be returned directly, unless transmission via a central authority is required by a treaty or other arrangement between the UK and that country (see Annex D).

Costs associated with obtaining evidence

64. Costs associated with executing requests are generally met by the requested state. However, where these costs are likely to be exceptionally high, the police/HMCE/SFO should inform the territorial authority, which will liaise with the requesting state over payment of certain costs or modification of the request. Such circumstances will be extremely rare.

Chapter 3: Hearing Evidence through Television Links or by Telephone

65. The 2000 Convention was the first binding international instrument to require the UK to be able to respond to requests for witnesses to be heard via television link. Other agreements will also require this, including the United Nations Convention against Transnational Organised Crime, the 2nd Additional Protocol to the European (Council of Europe) Convention on Mutual Assistance 2001 ("the 2nd Additional Protocol") and the Agreement between the EU and the US on Mutual Assistance in Criminal Matters.

66. Previously, while it was possible to request such assistance in relation to certain crimes under section 32 of the Criminal Justice Act 1988 ("the 1988 Act"), section 273 of the Criminal Procedure (Scotland) Act 1995 or Article 81 (A) of the Police and Criminal Evidence (Northern Ireland) Order 1989, it was not possible for England, Wales and

Northern Ireland to assist other countries with similar requests (there were no such restrictions in Scotland). Their provision of assistance was dependent on goodwill, but with no expectation of reciprocity.

67. In line with our international obligations, section 30 now enables all parts of the UK to assist **all countries** in the provision of evidence via television link.

Hearing witnesses abroad through television links

68. Section 32 of the 1988 Act provides that courts in England and Wales may hear witnesses via television link in relation to certain limited types of proceedings[6]. The 2003 Act contains a power to extend the scope of the 1988 Act to cover other types of criminal proceedings, or all criminal proceedings, but this has not yet been exercised, so at this stage requests from England and Wales may only be made in line with section 32. Article 81 (A) of the Police and Criminal Evidence (Northern Ireland) Order 1989 may similarly be extended to apply to further types of criminal proceedings. The Scottish equivalent, section 273(1) of the Criminal Procedure (Scotland) Act 1995, provides that courts in Scotland may hear witnesses through a live television link in proceedings on indictment and this scope may also be extended under the 2003 Act.

Requesting evidence via television link

69. When evidence is requested via television link, it should include the matters set out in the guidance on Chapter 2 (see paragraphs 32–33). In addition, requests to hear a witness via television link should also include the following information:

The reason why it is not desirable or possible for the witness or expert to be heard in person;

The name of the judicial authority and the persons who will be conducting the hearing.

70. The request should be transmitted in accordance with the arrangements described in paragraphs 34 to 36.

71. The practical arrangements for the hearing will be made between the requesting authority, the court, and the overseas authority. Direct contact with the overseas authority is strongly advised, prior to making the formal request, so that the practical arrangements can be made.

Hearing witnesses in the UK through television links

72. Section 30 enables the UK to assist with requests for a person in the UK to give evidence via a live television link in court proceedings outside the UK.

73. Provided the request relates to criminal proceedings that are being carried on in the requesting country, and includes the information covered in paragraph 69, the Secretary of State will issue a notice nominating a court where the witness will be heard. An occasional court can be arranged without notice, enabling facilities outside the court premises to be used if necessary. Proceedings in the court are governed by Part 1 of Schedule 2 to the Act and rules of court under section 49.

74. The UK will not agree to requests for accused persons to give evidence through television links.

75. If necessary, the court (in Scotland, the procurator fiscal) will summons witnesses to attend court to give evidence in the proceedings. Powers of sanction exist for witnesses who do not comply.

[6] See SI 1990/2084, which brought section 32 into force for proceedings for murder, manslaughter or any other offence consisting in the killing of any person; proceedings being conducted by the Director of the Serious Fraud Office under section 1(5) of the Criminal Justice Act 1987 and other proceedings in which a notice of transfer has been given under section 4 of the 1987 Act.

Hearing witnesses in the UK by telephone

76. Section 31 enables the UK to assist with requests for witnesses to give evidence by telephone link to proceedings in the requesting state. In all such cases, the witness must be willing to give the evidence via a telephone link.

77. If the request relates to criminal proceedings that are being carried on in the requesting country and includes the information covered in paragraph 69, the Secretary of State will nominate a court where the witness will be heard. Proceedings in the court are governed by Part 2 of Schedule 2 to the Act and rules of court made under section 49.

78. The court will notify the witness of the time and place of the hearing and ensure they are willing to attend and to give the evidence. It will not issue a summons as the provisions only apply to willing witnesses.

79. The 2003 Act does not enable UK authorities to request evidence via telephone link.

Costs of executing requests for evidence via television and telephone link

80. Under the terms of the 2000 Convention, as well as other agreements covering such hearings, the costs associated with these types of hearing, for example the payment of interpreters in the requested state, may be recouped from the requesting state, unless otherwise agreed between the parties. This contrasts with the general practice that the requested state meets the costs of execution of overseas requests. Allocation of costs should be agreed in principle prior to the hearing. The territorial authority can assist in negotiations over reimbursement of costs.

Chapter 5: Transfer of Prisoners

81. Where the prisoner is in Scotland or where the transfer request relates to Scottish criminal proceedings, references to the Secretary of State should be read as the Scottish Ministers. Equally, references to the Prison Service should be read as the Scottish Prison Service.

82. Sections 5 and 6 of the 1990 Act remain in force and provide for the transfer of prisoners from the requested to requesting state, to assist with an investigation or proceeding being conducted by authorities in the requesting state. These provisions apply to all countries.

83. Chapter 5 of the 2003 Act implements requirements in the 2000 Convention and the 2nd Additional Protocol to respond to requests for prisoners held by one state to be transferred (at its request) to the territory of another state to assist with the requesting state's investigation in the requested state.

84. In contrast to the provisions of the 1990 Act, these provisions are restricted to states participating in the reciprocal agreements detailed above.

Temporary transfer of prisoners from the UK

85. Section 5 of the 1990 Act provides for prisoners held in the UK to be transferred to another country at the request of the authorities of that country, to assist its criminal investigation.

86. Section 47 of the 2003 Act provides for prisoners held in the UK to be transferred to another country to assist with an UK criminal investigation.

87. Both sections allow the temporary transfer overseas of UK prisoners, including remand prisoners, **who consent to assist** with criminal investigations by travelling to the country concerned.

88. In such circumstances, the Secretary of State will arrange for a warrant to be issued to HM Prison Service. The warrant authorises:

- taking the prisoner in custody to a departure point in the UK and delivery there of the prisoner into the custody of a person representing the overseas authorities;
- bringing the prisoner back to the UK; and
- subsequent transfer of the prisoner in custody from the arrival point in the UK to the prisoner's place of detention.

89. The Prison Service makes arrangements for escorting the prisoner to and from the points of departure and arrival in the UK and delivering and receiving the prisoner to and from the overseas escorts. The precise details of these arrangements will depend on the particular circumstances of the individual case. For example, the Prison Service may contract out the escort duties or, for security reasons, may seek the assistance of the police.

90. Costs of escorting prisoners in the UK are borne by the Prison Service, unless the Prison Service has made other arrangements with the police or private security company.

91. Appropriate officials from the UK should accompany prisoners transferred under section 47 of the 2003 Act in order to conduct their investigations.

92. The Secretary of State will not normally agree to the temporary transfer of a prisoner if, as a consequence of the transfer:

- the prisoner would not then be able to participate in criminal investigations or proceedings in the UK (the Secretary of State will consult the UK prosecuting authorities and enforcement agencies before the warrant for transfer is issued);
- the period of detention would be prolonged (this could arise where the prisoner is nearing his or her earliest release date and cannot be given leave to remain in the overseas country after release under its immigration laws).

93. The Secretary of State will check to ensure that the prisoner is returned to the UK as soon as possible after completion of the investigation or proceedings and will ensure that the Prison Service is kept informed of the date and place of return of the prisoner to the UK.

Temporary transfer of overseas prisoners to the UK

94. Section 6 of the 1990 Act allows overseas prisoners to be transferred here at the UK's request to assist with a domestic investigation.

95. Section 48 of the 2003 Act provides for the transfer of a prisoner from another country to the UK in order to assist with that country's investigation, at its request.

96. The procedures for temporary transfer of prisoners to the UK largely mirror those for transfer from the UK, except that UK police or customs officers would travel to the overseas country both to receive and to return the prisoner.

97. The Secretary of State will ensure that the prisoner has consented to be transferred, that the period of detention in the UK would not extend beyond the earliest release date and that the prisoner's presence in the UK would not be contrary to the public interest.

98. The Secretary of State will consult with the Prison Service and the enforcement agencies about arrangements for escorting and holding the prisoner in custody while in the UK. In particular, the agencies involved should use British ships, aircraft or hovercraft where possible when escorting the prisoner to and from the UK, ensuring that the carrier is informed that the prisoner will remain in custody while on board. The Secretary of State will check to ensure that the prisoner is returned within the time agreed with the overseas authorities.

99. Appropriate officials from the requesting state should accompany prisoners transferred under section 48 of the 2003 Act in order to conduct their investigations.

ANNEX A: SCHENGEN STATES

Austria
Belgium
Denmark
France
Finland
Germany
Greece
Iceland
Italy
Luxembourg
Netherlands
Norway
Portugal
Spain
Sweden
United Kingdom

ANNEX B: CONTACT DETAILS

UKCA and Central authority for England and Wales

Stuart Blackley*
Judicial Co-operation Unit
Home Office
50 Queen Anne's Gate
London
SW1H 9AT
2 020 7273 4086
Fax 020 7273 4400
E-mail *stuart.blacklev2nahomeoffice.asi.gov.uk*

Central authority for Scotland

Elizabeth Munro*
International and Financial Crime Unit
Scottish Crown Office
25 Chambers Street
EDINBURGH
EH 11 LA
W 0131 247 2757
Fax 0131 226 6861
E-mail *elizabeth.munro(acorfsgsi.gov.uk*

Central authority for Northern Ireland

The Security and Extradition Unit
The Northern Ireland Office
11 Millbank
London

SW1 P 4PN
W 020 7210 6496
Fax 020 7210 6565
E-mail *seu@nio.x.gsi.gov.uk*

Direct transmission to HM Customs and Excise

Annabelle Bolt*
HM Customs and Excise
Solicitor's Office
New Kings Beam House
22 Upper Ground
London
SE1 9PJ
2 020 7865 5157
Fax 020 7865 5822
E-mail *annabelle.bolt@hmce.gsi.gov.uk*

United Kingdom National Central Bureau of Interpol

C/o National Criminal Intelligence Service
PO Box 8000
London
SE11 5EN
Tel 020 7238 8115
Fax 020 7238 8112
E-mail *London â ncis.x.asi.gov.uk*
(available 24 hours a day)

Liaison Magistrates

Claire Brown
Liaison Magistrate to France
Ministere de la Justice
13 Place Vendome
75042 Paris Cedex 01
France
Tel 0033 1 4486 1447
Fax 0033 1 4486 1441
E-mail *claire.brown@justice.gouv.fr*

Sally Cullen
Liaison Magistrate to *Italy*
Ministerio di Grazia e Giustizia
Direzione Generale degli Affari Penali
delle Grzie e del Casellario - Ufficio II
Via Arenula 70,
00186 ROMA
Italy
Tel 0039 0668852914
Fax 0039 0668853105
E-mail *sally.cullen@giustizia.it*

Aled Williams
Liaison Magistrate to Spain
Ministerio de Justicia
San Bernardo 62
(Despacho 109)
28071 Madrid
Spain
9 0034 91 390 4364
Fax 0034 91 522 1538/390 4462
E-mail *aled.williams@mju.es*

Gareth Julian
Liaison Magistrate to USA
Department of Justice
Organised Crime &
Racketeering Section
1301 Washington Avenue, N.W.
Suite 700
Washington, D.C. 20005
USA
Tel 001 202 514 4257
Fax 001 202 305 1148
E-mail *gareth.julian@usdoj.gov*

* European Judical Network contact points.

Eurojust

Mike Kennedy
President and National Member
Room B851
Eurojust
Maanweg 174
The Hague - 2516AB
The Netherlands
Tel 0031 70 412 5100
Fax 0031 70 412 5101
E-mail *mkennedy@eurojust.eu.int*

Rajka Vlahovic
Deputy National Member
Room B844
Eurojust
Maanweg 174
The Hague-216AB
The Netherlands
Tel 0031 70 412 5103
Fax 0031 70 412 5105
E-mail *rvlahovic@eurojust.eu.int*

ANNEX C: DESIGNATED PROSECUTING AUTHORITIES

The Attorney General for England and Wales
The Attorney General for Northern Ireland
The Commissioners of Customs and Excise
The Commissioners of Inland Revenue
The Financial Services Authority
The Director of Public Prosecutions and any Crown Prosecutor
The Director of Public Prosecutions for Northern Ireland
The Director of the Serious Fraud Office and any person designated under section 1(7) of the Criminal Justice Act 1987
The Secretary of State for Trade and Industry

ANNEX D: AGREEMENTS REQUIRING TRANSMISSION VIA UKCA

- Bilateral Treaties with:

  USA
  Hong Kong
  China
  Colombia
  Mexico
  Taiwan

- Commonwealth Scheme for Mutual Assistance in Criminal Matters

An updated list is available on the Home Office mutual legal assistance webpage.

INDEX